2025
ROAD ATLAS
BRITAIN

Scale 1:200,000
or 3.16 miles to 1 inch

38th edition June 2024 © AA Media Limited 2024
Original edition printed 1986.

All cartography in this atlas edited, designed and produced by the
Mapping Services Department of AA Media Limited (A05871).

This atlas contains Ordnance Survey data © Crown copyright and
database right 2024 and Royal Mail data © Royal Mail copyright and
database right 2024. Contains public sector information licensed
under the Open Government Licence v3.0.
Ireland mapping and distance chart contains data available from
openstreetmap.org © under the Open Database License found at
opendatacommons.org

Published by AA Media Limited, whose registered office is
Grove House, Lutyens Close, Basingstoke, Hampshire
RG24 8AG, UK. Registered number 06112600

ISBN: 978 0 7495 8400 9

A CIP catalogue record for this book is available from
The British Library.

The publishers would welcome information to correct any errors or
omissions and to keep this atlas up to date. Please write to the Atlas
Editor, AA Media Limited, Grove House, Lutyens Close, Basingstoke,
Hampshire RG24 8AG, UK.
E-mail: roadatlasfeedback@aamediagroup.co.uk

Acknowledgements: AA Media Limited would like to thank the
following for information used in the creation of this atlas:
Cadw, English Heritage, Forestry Commission, Historic Scotland,
National Trust and National Trust for Scotland, RSPB, The Wildlife
Trust, Scottish Natural Heritage, Natural England, The Countryside
Council for Wales. Award winning beaches from 'Blue Flag' and 'Keep
Scotland Beautiful' (summer 2023 data): for latest information visit
www.blueflag.org and www.keepscotlandbeautiful.org. Road signs are
© Crown Copyright 2024. Reproduced under the terms of the Open
Government Licence. Transport for London (Central London Map),
Nexus (Newcastle district map).
Ireland mapping: Republic of Ireland census 2016 © Central Statistics
Office and Northern Ireland census 2016 © NISRA (population
data); Irish Public Sector Data (CC BY 4.0) (Gaeltacht); Logainm.ie
(placenames); Roads Service and Transport Infrastructure Ireland
Printed by 1010 Printing International Ltd, China

* Nielsen BookScan Total Consumer Market (UK Standard scale
atlases) 1–39 weeks to 2 October 2023.

Contents

Map pages and distance chart	inside front cover
Route planning	**II–XVII**
Route planner	II–VII
Ferries and port plans	VIII–XI
Caravan and camping sites in Britain	XII–XV
Traffic signs	XVI–XVII
Motorways	**XVIII–XXV**
Restricted junctions	XVIII–XXI
M25 London Orbital motorway	XXII
M6 Toll motorway	XXIII
Smart motorways	XXIV–XXV
Map pages	**XXVI**
Road map symbols	**1**
Road maps	**2–173**
Britain 1:200,000 scale	2–169
Some islands are shown at slightly smaller scales	
Ireland 1:1,000,000 scale	170–173
District maps	**174–185**
Birmingham	174–175
Glasgow	176–177
London	178–181
Manchester	182–183
Tyne & Wear	184–185
Street map symbols	**186**
Towns, ports and airports	**187–237**
Town plans	188–234
Major airports	235–237
Port plans	VIII–XI
Channel Tunnel terminals	27
Central London street map and index	**238–253**
Index to place names	**254–302**
County, administrative area map	254
Place name index	255–302
Map pages and distance chart	inside back cover

Route planner

REPUBLIC
OF
IRELAND

66

68

70

54

56

44

46

42

40

28

30

32

16

18

20

8

10

4

6

2 Isles of Scilly inset

WALES

Anglesey
Holyhead
Bangor
Conwy
Llandudno
Colwyn Bay
Rhyl
Holywell
Abergele
Bethesda
Caernarfon
ERYRI (SNOWDONIA)
Betws-y-Coed
Pwllheli
Abersoch
Porthmadog
Barmouth
Dolgellau
Machynlleth
Cardigan Bay
Aberystwyth
New Quay
Aberaeron
Tregaron
Lampeter
Cardigan
Newcastle Emlyn
Carmarthen
Llandeilo
St Clears
Llanelli
Swansea
Port Talbot
Neath
Bridgend

St Davids
PEMBROKESHIRE COAST
Fishguard
Haverfordwest
Milford Haven
Pembroke Dock
Pembroke
Tenby

Rosslare
Rosslare

Llangurig
Llandovery
Brecon
BANNAU BRYCHEINIOG (BRECON BEACONS)
Merthyr Tydfil
Pontypridd
Cwmbran
CARDIFF
Cardiff

Birkenhead
Widnes
Runcorn
Knutsford
John Lennon
Ellesmere Port
Northwich
Queensferry
Chester
Middlewich
Denbigh
Mold
Ruthin
Crewe
Kidsgrove
Nantwich
Newcastle-under-Lyme
Wrexham
Whitchurch
Market Drayton
Oswestry
Newport
Shrewsbury
Welshpool
Telford
Newtown
WOLVERHAMPTON
Bridgnorth
Church Stretton
Dudley
Stourbridge
Halesowen
Kidderminster
Ludlow
Knighton
Bromsgrove
Rhayader
Leominster
Kington
Builth Wells
Llandrindod Wells
Worcester
Malvern
Hay-on-Wye
Hereford
Ledbury
Tewkesbury
Ross-on-Wye
Gloucester
Abergavenny
Monmouth
Stroud
Chepstow
Newport
Avonmouth
BRISTOL
Clevedon
Bath
Weston-super-Mare
Bristol
Cheddar
Wells
Frome
Trowbridge
Shepton Mallet
Warminster
Glastonbury
Wincanton
Bridgwater
Taunton
Yeovil
Shaftesbury
Ilminster
Sherborne
Chard
Crewkerne
Blandford Forum
Axminster
Honiton
Bridport
Lyme Regis
Dorchester
Weymouth
Fortuneswell

Bristol Channel
EXMOOR
Minehead
Lynton
Ilfracombe
Lundy
Barnstaple
Bideford
Great Torrington
South Molton
Tiverton
Crediton
Holsworthy
Hatherleigh
Okehampton
Exeter
Exmouth
Dawlish
Teignmouth
Newton Abbot
Torquay
Paignton
Dartmouth

Bude
Launceston
Tavistock
DARTMOOR
Buckfastleigh
Totnes
PLYMOUTH
Torpoint
Kingsbridge

Wadebridge
Bodmin
Cornwall Newquay
Newquay
Liskeard
Saltash
Lostwithiel
Fowey
St Austell
Redruth
Truro
Camborne
Falmouth
Penzance
Helston
Land's End
Lizard

Channel Islands inset

Guernsey
Jersey
St-Malo

Roscoff
Santander (Apr–Oct)

(Mar–Oct)

ENGLISH

Legend

═══	Motorway
═══	Toll motorway
═══	Primary route dual carriageway
───	Primary route single carriageway
───	Other A road
or ⊽	Vehicle ferry
	Fast vehicle ferry or catamaran
▢	National Park
▪	City with clean air or low/zero emission zone
16	Atlas page number

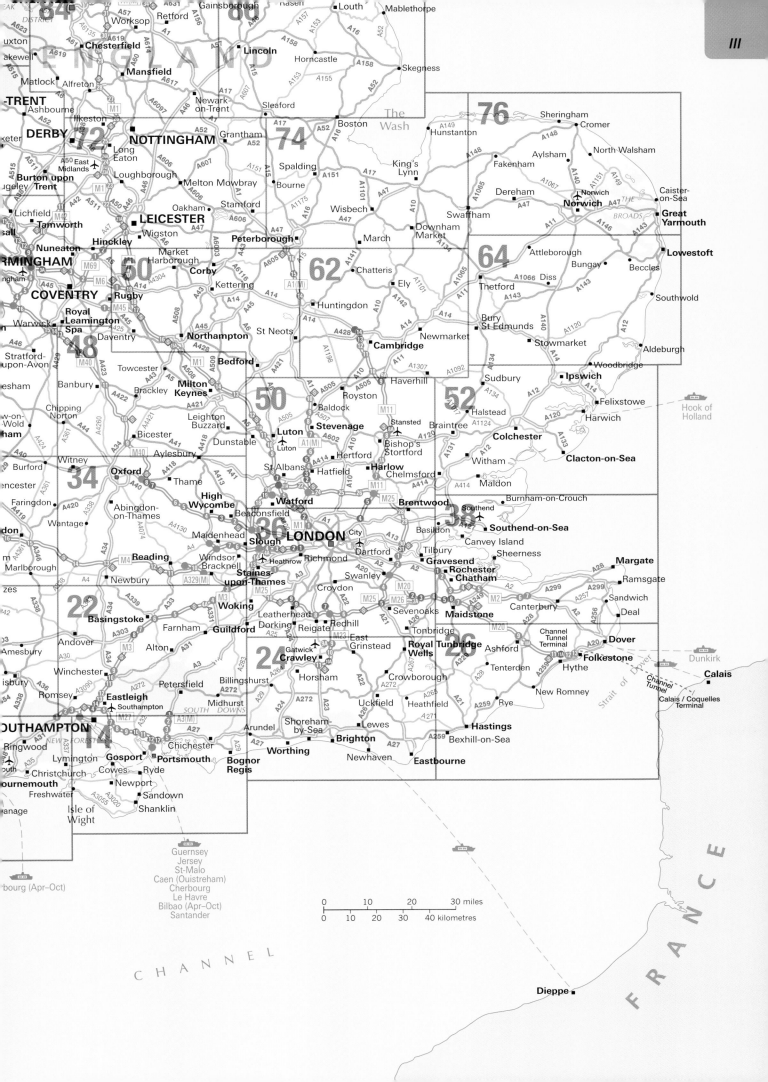

CHANNEL

FRANCE

0   10   20   30 miles
0 10 20 30 40 kilometres

Guernsey
Jersey
St-Malo
Caen (Ouistreham)
Cherbourg
Le Havre
Bilbao (Apr–Oct)
Santander

Calais / Coquelles
Terminal

Channel
Tunnel

Strait of Dover

Dunkirk

Calais

Dieppe

Hook of
Holland

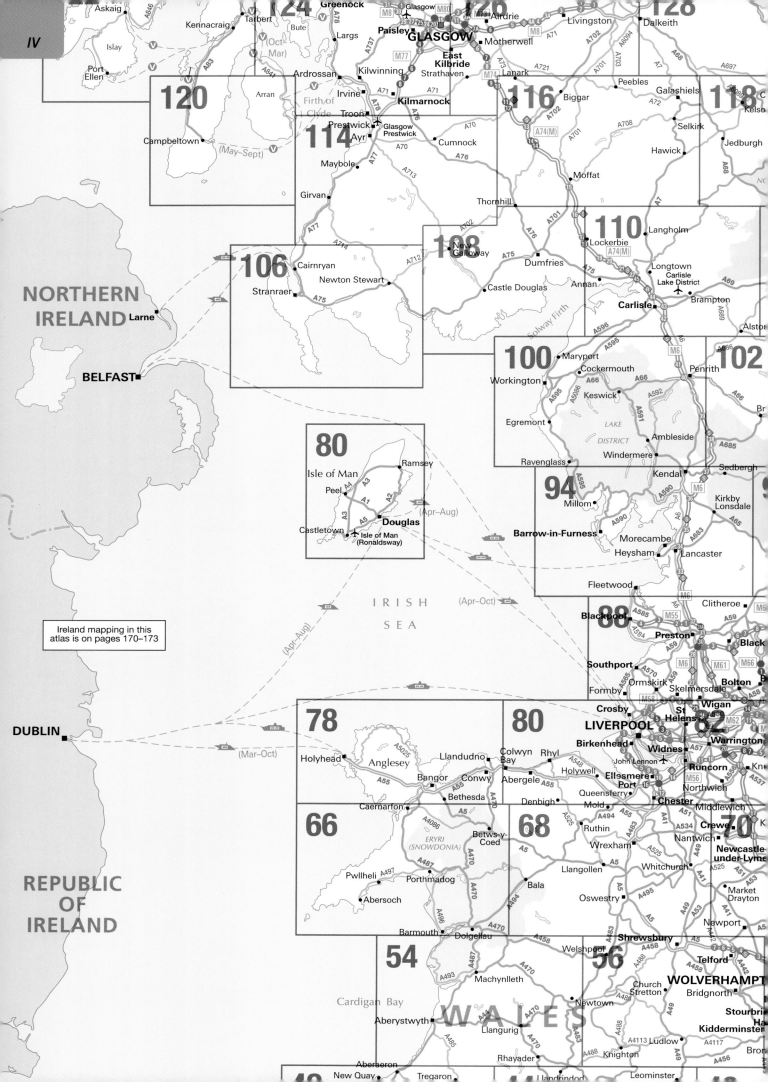

124
126
128

Askaig
Kennacraig
Tarbert
Greenock
M8 Glasgow M80
Airdrie
Livingston
Dalkeith

Islay
Bute
Largs
Paisley
GLASGOW
Motherwell

Port Ellen
Ardrossan
Kilwinning
Irvine
East Kilbride
Strathaven
Lanark
Peebles
Galashiels

120
Arran
Troon
Prestwick
116
Biggar
Selkirk

Campbeltown
(May–Sept)
114
Glasgow Prestwick
Ayr
Cumnock
Hawick
Jedburgh

Maybole
A76
Moffat

Girvan
Thornhill
110
Langholm

Lockerbie
Longtown
Carlisle
Lake District
Brampton

106
Cairnryan
New Galloway
Dumfries
Alston

Stranraer
Newton Stewart
Castle Douglas
Anran
Carlisle

NORTHERN IRELAND Larne
Solway Firth

BELFAST
100
Maryport
Cockermouth
Penrith
102

Workington
Keswick

Egremont
LAKE
DISTRICT
Ambleside

80
Ravenglass
Windermere

Isle of Man
Ramsey
Kendal
Sedbergh

Peel
94
Kirkby Lonsdale

Castletown
Douglas
Isle of Man (Ronaldsway)
Millom
(Apr–Aug)

Barrow-in-Furness
Morecambe
Lancaster

Heysham

Fleetwood

IRISH SEA
(Apr–Oct)
Clitheroe

Ireland mapping in this atlas is on pages 170–173
(Apr–Aug)
88
Blackpool
Preston
Black

Southport
Ormskirk
Skelmersdale
Bolton

Formby
Wigan

78
80
Crosby
St Helens
82
LIVERPOOL
Warrington

DUBLIN
(Mar–Oct)
Holyhead
Anglesey
Llandudno
Colwyn Bay
Rhyl
Birkenhead
Widnes
John Lennon
Runcorn
Kn

Bangor
Conwy
Abergele
Holywell
Ellesmere Port
Northwich

Bethesda
Denbigh
Queensferry
Chester
Middlewich

Caernarfon
Mold
Crewe
70

66
ERYRI
(SNOWDONIA)
Betws-y-Coed
68
Ruthin
Nantwich
Market Drayton

Wrexham
Newcastle-under-Lyme

REPUBLIC OF IRELAND
Pwllheli
Porthmadog
Llangollen
Whitchurch
Newport

Abersoch
Bala
Oswestry

Barmouth
Dolgellau
Shrewsbury
Telford

54
Welshpool
56
WOLVERHAMPT

Machynlleth
Church Stretton
Bridgnorth

Newtown
Stourbri
Ha

Cardigan Bay
Aberystwyth
W A L E S
Kidderminster

Llangurig
Ludlow

Aberaeron
Rhayader
Knighton
Leominster

New Quay
Tregaron
Llandrindod

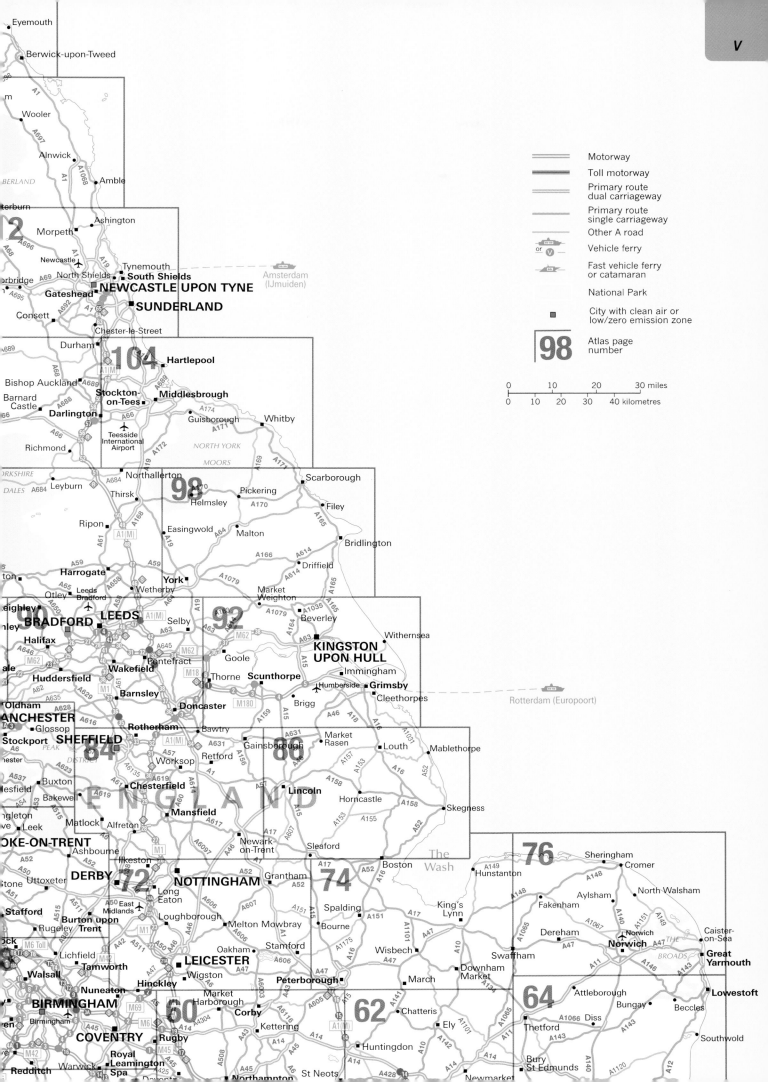

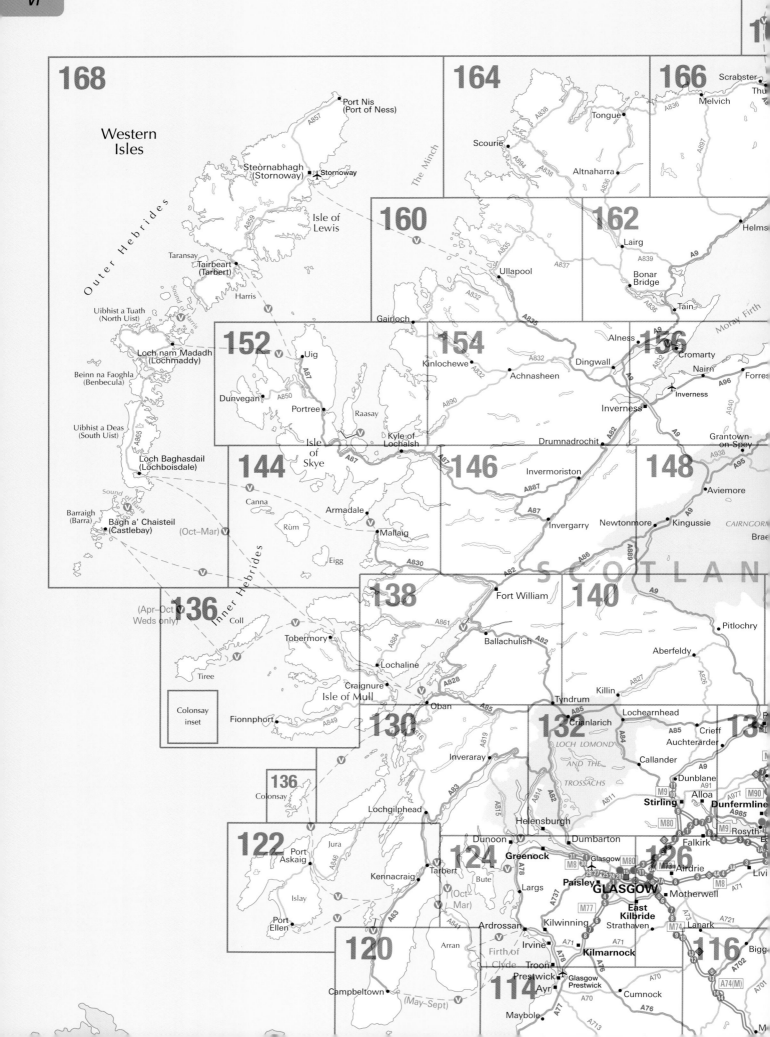

169
Orkney Islands

169
Shetland Islands

FERRY INFORMATION

Information on ferry routes and operators can be found on pages *VIII–XI*.

EMERGENCY DIVERSION ROUTES

In an emergency it may be necessary to close a section of motorway or other main road to traffic, so a temporary sign may advise drivers to follow a diversion route. To help drivers navigate the route, black symbols on yellow patches may be permanently displayed on existing direction signs, including motorway signs. Symbols may also be used on separate signs with yellow backgrounds.

NORTH SEA

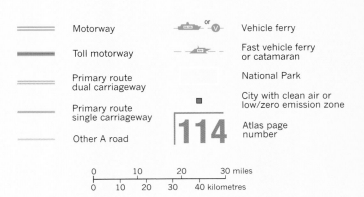

Motorway	Vehicle ferry
Toll motorway	Fast vehicle ferry or catamaran
Primary route dual carriageway	National Park
Primary route single carriageway	City with clean air or low/zero emission zone
Other A road	**114** Atlas page number

```
0        10        20        30 miles
0   10   20   30   40 kilometres
```

Channel hopping and the Isle of Wight

For business or pleasure, hopping on a ferry across to France, the Channel Islands or Isle of Wight has never been easier.

The vehicle ferry services listed in the table give you all the options, together with detailed port plans to help you navigate to and from the ferry terminals. Simply choose your preferred route, not forgetting the fast sailings (see 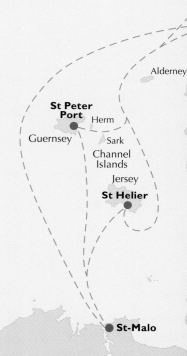). Bon voyage!

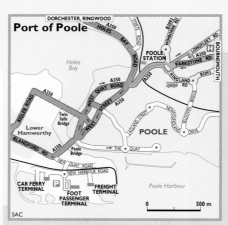

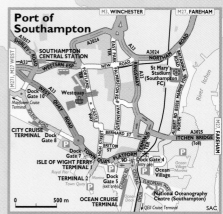

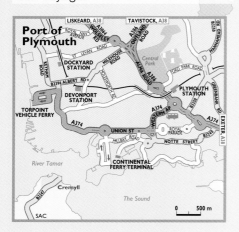

ENGLISH CHANNEL AND ISLE OF WIGHT FERRY CROSSINGS

From	To	Journey time	Operator website
Dover	Calais	1 hr 30 mins	dfdsseaways.co.uk
Dover	Calais	1 hr 30 mins	poferries.com
Dover	Dunkirk	2 hrs	dfdsseaways.co.uk
Folkestone	Calais (Coquelles)	35 mins	eurotunnel.com
Lymington	Yarmouth (IOW)	40 mins	wightlink.co.uk
Newhaven	Dieppe	4 hrs	dfdsseaways.co.uk
Plymouth	Roscoff	5 hrs 30 mins	brittany-ferries.co.uk
Poole	Cherbourg	4 hrs 30 mins (Apr–Oct)	brittany-ferries.co.uk
Poole	Guernsey	3 hrs	condorferries.co.uk
Poole	Jersey	4 hrs	condorferries.co.uk
Poole	St-Malo	6 hrs 20 mins–12 hrs (via Channel Is.)	condorferries.co.uk
Portsmouth	Caen (Ouistreham)	5 hrs 45 mins–7 hrs	brittany-ferries.co.uk
Portsmouth	Cherbourg	8 hrs	brittany-ferries.co.uk
Portsmouth	Fishbourne (IOW)	45 mins	wightlink.co.uk
Portsmouth	Guernsey	7 hrs	condorferries.co.uk
Portsmouth	Jersey	8–11 hrs	condorferries.co.uk
Portsmouth	Le Havre	5 hrs 30 mins–8 hrs	brittany-ferries.co.uk
Portsmouth	St-Malo	11 hrs	brittany-ferries.co.uk
Southampton	East Cowes (IOW)	1 hr	redfunnel.co.uk

The information listed is provided as a guide only, as services are liable to change at short notice and are weather dependent. Services shown are for vehicle ferries only, operated by conventional ferry unless indicated as a fast ferry service (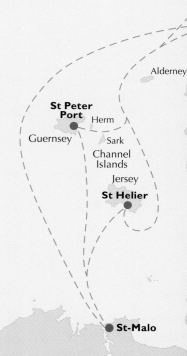). Please check sailings before planning your journey.

Travelling further afield? For ferry services to Northern Spain see brittany-ferries.co.uk.

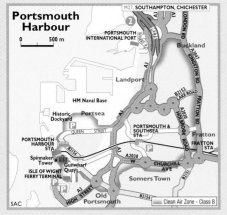

Portsmouth Harbour

Newhaven Harbour

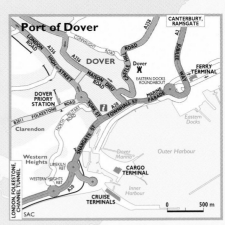

Port of Dover

Poole · Lymington · Southampton · Portsmouth · Yarmouth · East Cowes · Fishbourne · Isle of Wight · Newhaven · Folkestone · Dover · Calais · Dunkirk · Calais (Coquelles)

UK

CHANNEL

Cherbourg · Dieppe · Le Havre · Caen (Ouistreham)

F

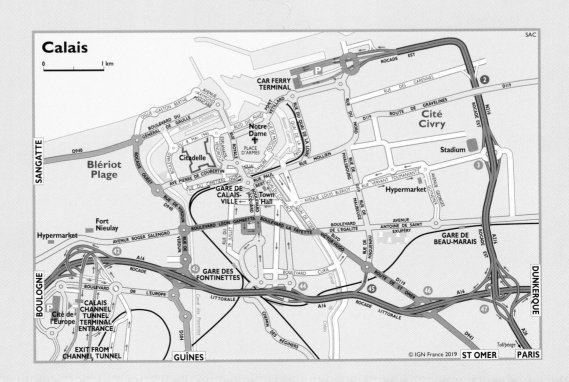

Calais

© IGN France 2019

With so many sea crossings to Ireland and the Isle of Man the information provided in the table to the right will help you make the right choice.

IRISH SEA FERRY CROSSINGS

From	To	Journey time	Operator website
Cairnryan	Belfast	2 hrs 15 mins 🚢	stenaline.co.uk
Cairnryan	Larne	2 hrs	poferries.com
Douglas (IOM)	Belfast	2 hrs 45 mins (April–Aug) 🚢	steam-packet.com
Douglas (IOM)	Dublin	2 hrs 55 mins (April–Aug) 🚢	steam-packet.com
Fishguard	Rosslare	3 hrs 15 mins	stenaline.co.uk
Heysham	Douglas (IOM)	3 hrs 45 mins	steam-packet.com
Holyhead	Dublin	2 hrs (Mar–Oct) 🚢	irishferries.com
Holyhead	Dublin	3 hrs 15 mins	irishferries.com
Holyhead	Dublin	3 hrs 15 mins	stenaline.co.uk
Liverpool	Douglas (IOM)	2 hrs 45 mins (Apr–Oct) 🚢	steam-packet.com
Liverpool	Dublin	8 hrs–8 hrs 30 mins	poferries.com
Liverpool (Birkenhead)	Belfast	8 hrs	stenaline.co.uk
Pembroke Dock	Rosslare	4 hrs	irishferries.com

The information listed is provided as a guide only, as services are liable to change at short notice and are weather dependent. Services shown are for vehicle ferries only, operated by conventional ferry unless indicated as a fast ferry service (🚢). Please check sailings before planning your journey.

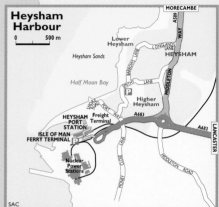
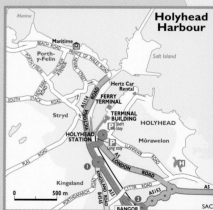

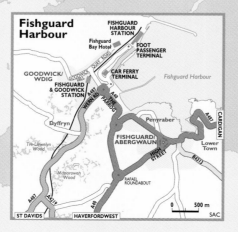
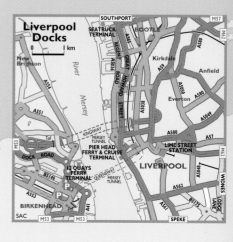

SCOTLAND FERRIES

From	To	Journey time	Operator website
Scottish Islands/west coast of Scotland			
Gourock	Dunoon	20 mins	*western-ferries.co.uk*
Glenelg	Skye	20 mins (Easter–Oct)	*skyeferry.co.uk*
Numerous and varied sailings from the west coast of Scotland to Scottish islands are provided by Caledonian MacBrayne. Please visit *calmac.co.uk* for all ferry information, including those of other operators.			
Orkney Islands			
Aberdeen	Kirkwall	6 hrs–7hrs 15mins	*northlinkferries.co.uk*
Gills	St Margaret's Hope	1 hr	*pentlandferries.co.uk*
Scrabster	Stromness	1 hr 30 mins	*northlinkferries.co.uk*
Lerwick	Kirkwall	5 hrs 30 mins	*northlinkferries.co.uk*
Inter-island services are operated by Orkney Ferries. Please see *orkneyferries.co.uk* for details.			
Shetland Islands			
Aberdeen	Lerwick	12 hrs	*northlinkferries.co.uk*
Kirkwall	Lerwick	7 hrs 45 mins	*northlinkferries.co.uk*
Inter-island services are operated by Shetland Island Council Ferries. Please see *shetland.gov.uk/ferries* for details.			

Please note that some smaller island services are day and weather dependent and reservations are required for some routes. Book and confirm sailing schedules by contacting the operator.

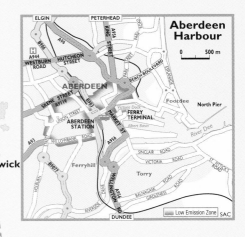

Aberdeen Harbour

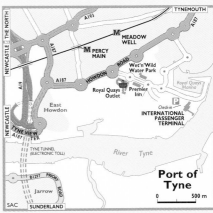

Port of Tyne

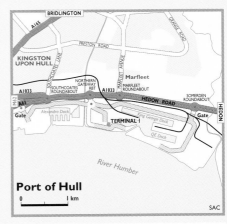

Port of Hull

For a port plan of Harwich see atlas page 53

NORTH SEA FERRY CROSSINGS

From	To	Journey time	Operator website
Harwich	Hook of Holland	6 hrs 30 mins	*stenaline.co.uk*
Kingston upon Hull	Rotterdam (Europoort)	11 hrs	*poferries.com*
Newcastle upon Tyne	Amsterdam (IJmuiden)	15 hrs 30 mins	*dfdsseaways.co.uk*

The information listed on this page is provided as a guide only, as services are liable to change at short notice. Services shown are for vehicle ferries only, operated by conventional ferry. Please check sailings before planning your journey as many are weather dependent.

Caravan and camping sites in Britain

These pages list the top 300 AA-inspected Caravan and Camping (C & C) sites in the Pennant rating scheme. Five Pennant Premier sites are shown in green, Four Pennant sites are shown in blue.

Listings include addresses, telephone numbers and websites together with page and grid references to locate the sites in the atlas. The total number of touring pitches is also included for each site.

To discover AA-rated caravan and camping sites not included on these pages please visit **RatedTrips.com**

ENGLAND

Alders Caravan Park
Home Farm, Alne,
York
YO61 1RY
Tel: 01347 838722   **97 R7**
alderscaravanpark.co.uk
Total Pitches: 87

Andrewshayes Holiday Park
Dalwood, Axminster
EX13 7DY
Tel: 01404 831225   **10 E5**
andrewshayes.co.uk
Total Pitches: 150

Atlantic Bays Holiday Park
Padstow, Cornwall
PL28 8PY
Tel: 01841 520855   **4 D7**
atlanticbaysholidaypark.co.uk
Total Pitches: 70

Ayr Holiday Park
St Ives, Cornwall
TR26 1EJ
Tel: 01736 795855   **2 E5**
ayrholidaypark.co.uk
Total Pitches: 100

Back of Beyond Touring Park
234 Ringwood Road,
St Leonards, Dorset
BH24 2SB
Tel: 01202 876968   **13 K4**
backofbeyondtouringpark.co.uk
Total Pitches: 80

Bagwell Farm Touring Park
Knights in the Bottom,
Chickerell, Weymouth
DT3 4EA
Tel: 01305 782575   **11 N8**
bagwellfarm.co.uk
Total Pitches: 320

Bardsea Leisure Park
Priory Road, Ulverston
LA12 9QE
Tel: 01229 584712   **94 F5**
bardsealeisure.co.uk
Total Pitches: 83

Bath Chew Valley Caravan Park
Ham Lane, Bishop Sutton
BS39 5TZ
Tel: 01275 332127   **19 Q3**
bathchewvalley.co.uk
Total Pitches: 45

Bay View Farm C & C Park
Croyde, Devon
EX33 1PN
Tel: 01271 890501   **16 G4**
bayviewfarm.co.uk
Total Pitches: 70

Bay View Holiday Park
Bolton-le-Sands,
Carnforth
LA5 9TN
Tel: 01524 732854   **95 K7**
holgates.co.uk
Total Pitches: 100

Beacon Cottage Farm Touring Park
Beacon Drive,
St Agnes
TR5 0NU
Tel: 01872 552347   **3 J3**
beaconcottagefarmholidays.co.uk
Total Pitches: 60

Beaconsfield Holiday Park
Battlefield, Shrewsbury
SY4 4AA
Tel: 01939 210370   **69 P11**
beaconsfieldholidaypark.co.uk
Total Pitches: 60

Beech Croft Farm C & C Park
Beech Croft,
Blackwell in the Peak,
Buxton
SK17 9TQ
Tel: 01298 85330   **83 P10**
beechcroftfarm.co.uk
Total Pitches: 30

Bellingham C & C Club Site
Brown Rigg, Bellingham
NE48 2JY
Tel: 01434 220175   **112 B4**
campingandcaravanning
club.co.uk/bellingham
Total Pitches: 64

Beverley Park C & C Park
Goodrington Road,
Paignton
TQ4 7JE
Tel: 01803 843887   **7 M7**
beverley-holidays.co.uk
Total Pitches: 125

Birchwood Tourist Park
Bere Road, Coldharbour,
Wareham
BH20 7PA
Tel: 01929 554763   **12 E6**
birchwoodtouristpark.co.uk
Total Pitches: 175

Blue Rose Caravan & Country Park
Star Carr Lane,
Brandesburton
YO25 8RU
Tel: 01964 543366   **99 N11**
bluerosepark.com
Total Pitches: 58

Briarfields Motel & Touring Park
Gloucester Road,
Cheltenham
GL51 0SX
Tel: 01242 235324   **46 H10**
briarfields.net
Total Pitches: 72

Bridge House Marina & Caravan Park
Nateby Crossing Lane,
Nateby, Garstang
PR3 0JJ
Tel: 01995 603207   **95 K11**
bridgehousemarina.co.uk
Total Pitches: 50

Broadhembury C & C Park
Steeds Lane, Kingsnorth,
Ashford
TN26 1NQ
Tel: 01233 620859   **26 H4**
broadhembury.co.uk
Total Pitches: 100

Brook Lodge Farm C & C Park
Cowslip Green, Redhill, Bristol,
Somerset
BS40 5RB
Tel: 01934 862311   **19 N2**
brooklodgefarm.com
Total Pitches: 29

Burns Farm Caravan, Camping & Glamping
St Johns in the Vale,
Keswick
CA12 4RR
Tel: 017687 79225   **101 K6**
burns-farm.co.uk
Total Pitches: 32

Burrowhayes Farm C & C Site & Riding Stables
West Luccombe, Porlock,
Minehead
TA24 8HT
Tel: 01643 862463   **18 A5**
burrowhayes.co.uk
Total Pitches: 120

Burton Constable Holiday Park & Arboretum
Old Lodges, Sproatley,
Kingston upon Hull
HU11 4LJ
Tel: 01964 562508   **93 L3**
burtonconstableholidaypark.co.uk
Total Pitches: 105

Caistor Lakes
99a Brigg Road,
Caistor
LN7 6RX
Tel: 01472 859626   **93 K10**
caistorlakes.co.uk
Total Pitches: 28

Cakes & Ale
Abbey Lane, Theberton,
Leiston
IP16 4TE
Tel: 01728 831655   **65 N9**
cakesandale.co.uk
Total Pitches: 55

Camping Caradon Touring Park
Trelawne, Looe
PL13 2NA
Tel: 01503 272388   **5 L11**
campingcaradon.co.uk
Total Pitches: 75

Capesthorne Hall
Congleton Road, Siddington,
Macclesfield
SK11 9JY
Tel: 01625 861221   **82 H10**
capesthorne.com/caravan-park
Total Pitches: 50

Carlyon Bay C & C Park
Bethesda, Cypress Avenue,
Carlyon Bay
PL25 3RE
Tel: 01726 812735   **3 R3**
carlyonbay.net
Total Pitches: 180

Carnevas Holiday Park
Carnevas Farm, St Merryn,
Cornwall
PL28 8PN
Tel: 01841 520230   **4 D7**
carnevasholidaypark.com
Total Pitches: 195

Cartref C & C
Cartref, Ford Heath,
Shrewsbury, Shropshire
SY5 9GD
Tel: 01743 821688   **56 G2**
cartrefcaravansite.co.uk
Total Pitches: 44

Carvynick Holiday Park
Summercourt, Newquay
TR8 5AF
Tel: 01872 510716   **4 D10**
carvynick.co.uk
Total Pitches: 47

Castlerigg Hall C & C Park
Castlerigg Hall, Keswick
CA12 4TE
Tel: 017687 74499   **101 J6**
castlerigg.co.uk
Total Pitches: 68

Cheddar Mendip Heights C & C Club Site
Townsend, Priddy,
Wells
BA5 3BP
Tel: 01749 870241   **19 P4**
campingandcaravanning
club.co.uk/cheddar
Total Pitches: 90

Clippesby Hall
Hall Lane, Clippesby,
Great Yarmouth
NR29 3BL
Tel: 01493 367800   **77 N9**
clippesbyhall.com
Total Pitches: 120

Cofton Holidays
Starcross, Dawlish
EX6 8RP
Tel: 01626 890111   **9 N8**
coftonholidays.co.uk
Total Pitches: 450

Concierge Camping
Ratham Estate, Ratham Lane,
West Ashling, Chichester
PO18 8DL
Tel: 01243 573118   **15 M5**
conciergecamping.co.uk
Total Pitches: 27

Coombe Touring Park
Race Plain, Netherhampton,
Salisbury
SP2 8PN
Tel: 01722 328451   **21 L9**
coombecaravanpark.co.uk
Total Pitches: 50

Cornish Farm Touring Park
Shoreditch,
Taunton
TA3 7BS
Tel: 01823 327746   **18 H10**
cornishfarm.com
Total Pitches: 48

Cosawes Park
Perranarworthal, Truro
TR3 7QS
Tel: 01872 863724   **3 K6**
cosawes.co.uk
Total Pitches: 59

Cote Ghyll C & C Park
Osmotherley,
Northallerton
DL6 3AH
Tel: 01609 883425   **104 E11**
coteghyll.com
Total Pitches: 77

Country View Holiday Park
Sand Road, Sand Bay,
Weston-super-Mare
BS22 9UJ
Tel: 01934 627595   **19 K2**
cvhp.co.uk
Total Pitches: 190

Crealy Theme Park & Resort
Sidmouth Road, Clyst St Mary,
Exeter
EX5 1DR
Tel: 01395 234888   **9 P6**
crealy.co.uk
Total Pitches: 120

Crows Nest Caravan Park
Gristhorpe, Filey
YO14 9PS
Tel: 01723 582206   **99 M4**
crowsnestcaravanpark.com
Total Pitches: 43

Deepdale Camping & Rooms
Deepdale Farm, Burnham
Deepdale
PE31 8DD
Tel: 01485 210256   **75 R2**
deepdalecamping.co.uk
Total Pitches: 80

Dibles Park
Dibles Road, Warsash,
Southampton, Hampshire
SO31 9SA
Tel: 01489 575232   **14 F5**
diblespark.co.uk
Total Pitches: 11

Easewell Farm Holiday Village
Mortehoe Station Road,
Mortehoe, Woolacombe
EX34 7EH
Tel: 01271 872302   **16 H2**
woolacombe.co.uk
Total Pitches: 328

East Fleet Farm Touring Park
Chickerell, Weymouth
DT3 4DW
Tel: 01305 785768   **11 N9**
eastfleet.co.uk
Total Pitches: 400

Eastham Hall Holiday Park
Saltcotes Road,
Lytham St Annes, Lancashire
FY8 4LS
Tel: 01253 737907   **88 D5**
easthamhall.co.uk
Total Pitches: 113

Eden Valley Holiday Park
Lanlivery,
Nr Lostwithiel
PL30 5BU
Tel: 01208 872277   **4 H10**
edenvalleyholidaypark.co.uk
Total Pitches: 56

Exe Valley Caravan Site
Mill House, Bridgetown,
Dulverton
TA22 9JR
Tel: 01643 851432   **18 B8**
exevalleycamping.co.uk
Total Pitches: 48

Eye Kettleby Lakes
Eye Kettleby,
Melton Mowbray
LE14 2TN
Tel: 01664 565900   **73 J7**
eyekettlebylakes.com
Total Pitches: 130

Fernwood Caravan Park
Lyneal, Ellesmere,
Shropshire
SY12 0QF
Tel: 01948 710221   **69 N8**
fernwoodpark.co.uk
Total Pitches: 60

Fields End Water Caravan Park & Fishery
Benwick Road, Doddington,
March
PE15 0TY
Tel: 01354 740199   **62 E2**
fieldsendwater.co.uk
Total Pitches: 80

Flaxton Meadows
York Lane, Flaxton, York
YO60 7QZ
Tel: 01904 393943   **98 D8**
flaxtonmeadows.co.uk
Total Pitches: 35

Flower of May Holiday Park
Lebberston Cliff, Filey,
Scarborough
YO11 3NU
Tel: 01723 584311   **99 M4**
flowerofmay.com
Total Pitches: 300

Forest Glade Holiday Park
Near Kentisbeare,
Cullompton, Devon
EX15 2DT
Tel: 01404 841381   **10 C3**
forest-glade.co.uk
Total Pitches: 80

Freshwater Beach Holiday Park
Burton Bradstock, Bridport
DT6 4PT
Tel: 01308 897317   **11 K6**
freshwaterbeach.co.uk
Total Pitches: 500

Globe Vale Holiday Park
Radnor, Redruth
TR16 4BH
Tel: 01209 891183   **3 J5**
globevale.co.uk
Total Pitches: 138

Glororum Caravan Park
Glororum Farm,
Bamburgh
NE69 7AW
Tel: 01670 860256   **119 N4**
northumbrianleisure.co.uk
Total Pitches: 43

Golden Cap Holiday Park
Seatown, Chideock, Bridport
DT6 6JX
Tel: 01308 422139   **11 J6**
wdlh.co.uk
Total Pitches: 108

Golden Coast Holiday Park
Station Road,
Woolacombe
EX34 7HW
Tel: 01271 872302   **16 H3**
woolacombe.com
Total Pitches: 89

Golden Sands Holiday Park
Quebec Road,
Mablethorpe
LN12 1QJ
Tel: 01507 477871   **87 N3**
haven.com/goldensands
Total Pitches: 172

Golden Square C & C Park
Oswaldkirk, Helmsley
YO62 5YQ
Tel: 01439 788269   **98 C5**
goldensquarecaravanpark.com
Total Pitches: 129

Golden Valley C & C Park
Coach Road, Ripley,
Derbyshire
DE55 4ES
Tel: 01773 513881   **84 F10**
goldenvalleycaravanpark.co.uk
Total Pitches: 45

Goosewood Holiday Park
Sutton-on-the-Forest,
York
YO61 1ET
Tel: 01347 810829   **98 B8**
flowerofmay.com
Total Pitches: 100

Greenacre Place Touring Caravan Park
Bristol Road, Edithmead,
Highbridge
TA9 4HA
Tel: 01278 785227   **19 K5**
greenacreplace.com
Total Pitches: 10

Green Acres Caravan Park
High Knells, Houghton,
Carlisle
CA6 4JW
Tel: 01228 675418   **110 H8**
caravanpark-cumbria.com
Total Pitches: 35

Greenhill Farm C & C Park
Greenhill Farm, New Road,
Landford, Salisbury
SP5 2AZ
Tel: 01794 324117   **21 Q11**
greenhillfarm.co.uk
Total Pitches: 160

Greenhills Holiday Park
Crowhill Lane, Bakewell,
Derbyshire
DE45 1PX
Tel: 01629 813052 **84 B7**
greenhillsholidaypark.co.uk
Total Pitches: 172

Grouse Hill Caravan Park
Flask Bungalow Farm,
Fylingdales,
Robin Hood's Bay
YO22 4QH
Tel: 01947 880543 **105 P10**
grousehill.co.uk
Total Pitches: 175

Gunvenna Holiday Park
St Minver, Wadebridge
PL27 6QN
Tel: 01208 862405 **4 F6**
gunvenna.com
Total Pitches: 75

Haggerston Castle Holiday Park
Beal,
Berwick-upon-Tweed
TD15 2PA
Tel: 01289 381333 **119 K2**
haven.com/haggerstoncastle
Total Pitches: 140

Hallsdown Farm Touring Park
Arlington, Barnstaple
EX31 4SW
Tel: 01271 850847 **17 L3**
hallsdownfarm.co.uk
Total Pitches: 30

Harbury Fields
Harbury Fields Farm, Harbury,
Nr Leamington Spa
CV33 9JN
Tel: 01926 612457 **48 C2**
harburyfields.co.uk
Total Pitches: 59

Harford Bridge Holiday Park
Peter Tavy,
Tavistock
PL19 9LS
Tel: 01822 810349 **8 D9**
harfordbridge.co.uk
Total Pitches: 125

Haw Wood Farm Caravan Park
Hinton, Saxmundham
IP17 3QT
Tel: 01502 359550 **65 N7**
hawwoodfarm.co.uk
Total Pitches: 72

Heathfield Farm Camping
Heathfield Road, Freshwater,
Isle of Wight
PO40 9SH
Tel: 01983 407822 **13 P7**
heathfieldcamping.co.uk
Total Pitches: 81

Heathland Beach Holiday Park
London Road,
Kessingland
NR33 7PJ
Tel: 01502 740337 **65 Q4**
heathlandbeach.co.uk
Total Pitches: 63

Heligan C & C Park
Pentewan,
St Austell
PL26 6BT
Tel: 01726 842714 **3 P4**
heligancampsite.com
Total Pitches: 89

Hendra Holiday Park
Newquay
TR8 4NY
Tel: 01637 875778 **4 C10**
hendra-holidays.com
Total Pitches: 548

Herding Hill Farm Touring & Camping Site
Shield Hill, Haltwhistle,
Northumberland
NE49 9NW
Tel: 01434 320175 **111 P7**
herdinghillfarm.co.uk
Total Pitches: 22

Hidden Valley Park
West Down, Braunton,
Ilfracombe, Devon
EX34 8NU
Tel: 01271 813837 **17 J3**
hiddenvalleypark.com
Total Pitches: 114

Highfield Farm Touring Park
Long Road, Comberton,
Cambridge
CB23 7DG
Tel: 01223 262308 **62 E9**
highfieldfarmtouringpark.co.uk
Total Pitches: 120

Highlands End Holiday Park
Eype, Bridport, Dorset
DT6 6AR
Tel: 01308 422139 **11 K6**
wdlh.co.uk
Total Pitches: 195

Hillside Caravan Park
Canvas Farm, Moor Road,
Knayton, Thirsk
YO7 4BR
Tel: 01845 537349 **97 P3**
hillsidecaravanpark.co.uk
Total Pitches: 60

Holiday Resort Unity
Coast Road, Brean Sands,
Brean
TA8 2RB
Tel: 01278 751235 **19 J4**
hru.co.uk
Total Pitches: 453

Hollins Farm Holiday Park
Far Arnside, Carnforth
LA5 0SL
Tel: 01524 701767 **95 J5**
holgates.co.uk
Total Pitches: 12

Homing Park
Church Lane, Seasalter,
Whitstable
CT5 4BU
Tel: 01227 771777 **39 J9**
homingpark.co.uk
Total Pitches: 43

Hutton-le-Hole Caravan Park
Westfield Lodge,
Hutton-le-Hole
YO62 6UG
Tel: 01751 417261 **98 E3**
huttonleholecaravanpark.co.uk
Total Pitches: 42

Hylton Caravan Park
Eden Street,
Silloth
CA7 4AY
Tel: 016973 32666 **109 P10**
stanwix.com
Total Pitches: 90

Island Lodge C & C Site
Stumpy Post Cross,
Kingsbridge
TQ7 4BL
Tel: 01548 852956 **7 J9**
islandlodgesite.co.uk
Total Pitches: 30

Isle of Avalon Touring Caravan Park
Godney Road,
Glastonbury
BA6 9AF
Tel: 01458 833618 **19 N7**
avaloncaravanpark.co.uk
Total Pitches: 120

Jasmine Caravan Park
Cross Lane, Snainton,
Scarborough
YO13 9BE
Tel: 01723 859240 **99 J4**
jasminepark.co.uk
Total Pitches: 68

Kennford International Holiday Park
Kennford, Exeter
EX6 7YN
Tel: 01392 833046 **9 M7**
kennfordinternational.co.uk
Total Pitches: 22

Killiwerris Touring Park
Penstraze, Chacewater,
Truro, Cornwall
TR4 8PF
Tel: 01872 561356 **3 K4**
killiwerris.co.uk
Total Pitches: 17

King's Lynn C & C Park
New Road, North Runcton,
King's Lynn
PE33 0RA
Tel: 01553 840004 **75 M7**
kl-cc.co.uk
Total Pitches: 150

Knight Stainforth Hall Caravan & Campsite
Stainforth, Settle
BD24 0DP
Tel: 01729 822200 **96 B7**
knightstainforth.co.uk
Total Pitches: 100

Ladycross Plantation Caravan Park
Egton, Whitby
YO21 1UA
Tel: 01947 895502 **105 M9**
ladycrossplantation.co.uk
Total Pitches: 130

Lady Heyes Holiday Park
Kingsley Road, Frodsham
WA6 6SU
Tel: 01928 788557 **82 B9**
ladyheyespark.com
Total Pitches: 65

Lady's Mile Holiday Park
Dawlish, Devon
EX7 0LX
Tel: 01626 863411 **9 N9**
ladysmile.co.uk
Total Pitches: 570

Lakeland Leisure Park
Moor Lane, Flookburgh
LA11 7LT
Tel: 01539 558556 **94 H6**
haven.com/lakeland
Total Pitches: 177

Lamb Cottage Caravan Park
Dalefords Lane, Whitegate,
Northwich
CW8 2BN
Tel: 01606 882302 **82 D11**
lambcottage.co.uk
Total Pitches: 45

Langstone Manor C & C Park
Moortown, Tavistock
PL19 9JZ
Tel: 01822 613371 **6 E4**
langstonemanor.co.uk
Total Pitches: 40

Lanyon Holiday Park
Loscombe Lane, Four Lanes,
Redruth
TR16 6LP
Tel: 01209 313474 **2 H6**
lanyonholidaypark.co.uk
Total Pitches: 25

Lickpenny Caravan Site
Lickpenny Lane, Tansley,
Matlock
DE4 5GF
Tel: 01629 583040 **84 D9**
lickpennycaravanpark.co.uk
Total Pitches: 80

Lime Tree Park
Dukes Drive, Buxton
SK17 9RP
Tel: 01298 22988 **83 N10**
limetreeparkbuxton.com
Total Pitches: 106

Lincoln Farm Park Oxfordshire
High Street, Standlake
OX29 7RH
Tel: 01865 300239 **34 C4**
lincolnfarmpark.co.uk
Total Pitches: 90

Littlesea Holiday Park
Lynch Lane, Weymouth
DT4 9DT
Tel: 01305 774414 **11 P9**
haven.com/littlesea
Total Pitches: 141

Long Acres Touring Park
Station Road, Old Leake,
Boston
PE22 9RF
Tel: 01205 871555 **87 L10**
long-acres.co.uk
Total Pitches: 40

Long Hazel Park
High Street, Sparkford, Yeovil,
Somerset
BA22 7JH
Tel: 01963 440002 **20 B9**
longhazelpark.co.uk
Total Pitches: 46

Longnor Wood Holiday Park
Newtown, Longnor,
Nr Buxton
SK17 0NG
Tel: 01298 83648 **71 K2**
longnorwood.co.uk
Total Pitches: 47

Lynmouth Holiday Retreat
Lynton, Devon
EX35 6LD
Tel: 01598 753349 **17 N2**
channel-view.co.uk
Total Pitches: 76

Manor Farm Holiday Centre
Charmouth, Bridport
DT6 6QL
Tel: 01297 560226 **10 H6**
manorfarmholidaycentre.co.uk
Total Pitches: 400

Manor Wood Country Caravan Park
Manor Wood, Coddington,
Chester
CH3 9EN
Tel: 01829 782990 **69 M4**
cheshire-caravan-sites.co.uk
Total Pitches: 45

Marsh House Holiday Park
Marsh House Farm, Carnforth,
Lancashire
LA5 9JA
Tel: 01524 732854 **95 K6**
holgates.co.uk/our-parks/
marsh-house
Total Pitches: 74

Marton Mere Holiday Village
Mythop Road, Blackpool
FY4 4XN
Tel: 01253 767544 **88 C4**
haven.com/martonmere
Total Pitches: 82

Mayfield Park
Cheltenham Road,
Cirencester
GL7 7BH
Tel: 01285 831301 **33 K3**
mayfieldpark.co.uk
Total Pitches: 105

Meadowbank Holidays
Stour Way,
Christchurch
BH23 2PQ
Tel: 01202 483597 **13 K6**
meadowbank-holidays.co.uk
Total Pitches: 41

Mena Farm: Touring, Camping, Glamping
Bodmin, Lanivet
PL30 5HW
Tel: 01208 831845 **4 G9**
menafarm.co.uk
Total Pitches: 25

Mill Farm C & C Park
Fiddington, Bridgwater,
Somerset
TA5 1JQ
Tel: 01278 732286 **18 H6**
millfarm.biz
Total Pitches: 275

Mill Park Touring C & C Park
Mill Lane, Berrynarbor,
Ilfracombe, Devon
EX34 9SH
Tel: 01271 882647 **17 K2**
millpark.com
Total Pitches: 125

Minnows Touring Park
Holbrook Lane, Sampford
Peverell
EX16 7EN
Tel: 01884 821770 **18 D11**
minnowstouringpark.co.uk
Total Pitches: 59

Monkey Tree Holiday Park
Hendra Croft, Scotland Road,
Newquay
TR8 5QR
Tel: 01872 572032 **3 K3**
monkeytreeholidaypark.co.uk
Total Pitches: 511

Monkton Wyld Holiday Park
Scott's Lane, Charmouth,
Dorset
DT6 6DB
Tel: 01297 631131 **10 G5**
monktonwyld.co.uk
Total Pitches: 155

Moon & Sixpence
Newbourn Road, Waldringfield,
Woodbridge
IP12 4PP
Tel: 01473 736650 **53 N2**
moonandsixpence.co.uk
Total Pitches: 50

Moss Wood Caravan Park
Crimbles Lane, Cockerham
LA2 0ES
Tel: 01524 791041 **95 K11**
mosswood.co.uk
Total Pitches: 25

Naburn Lock Caravan Park
Naburn
YO19 4RU
Tel: 01904 728697 **98 C11**
naburnlock.co.uk
Total Pitches: 115

New Lodge Farm C & C Site
New Lodge Farm, Bulwick,
Corby
NN17 3DU
Tel: 01780 450493 **73 P11**
newlodgefarm.com
Total Pitches: 72

Newberry Valley Park
Woodlands, Combe Martin
EX34 0AT
Tel: 01271 882334 **17 K2**
newberryvalleypark.co.uk
Total Pitches: 110

Newlands Holidays
Charmouth, Bridport
DT6 6RB
Tel: 01297 560259 **10 H6**
newlandsholidays.co.uk
Total Pitches: 240

Ninham Country Holidays
Ninham, Shanklin, Isle of Wight
PO37 7PL
Tel: 01983 864243 **14 G10**
ninham-holidays.co.uk
Total Pitches: 140

Northam Farm Caravan & Touring Park
Brean, Burnham-on-Sea
TA8 2SE
Tel: 01278 751244 **19 K3**
northamfarm.co.uk
Total Pitches: 350

North Morte Farm C & C Park
North Morte Road, Mortehoe,
Woolacombe
EX34 7EG
Tel: 01271 870381 **16 H2**
northmortefarm.co.uk
Total Pitches: 180

Oakdown Holiday Park
Gatedown Lane, Weston,
Sidmouth
EX10 0PT
Tel: 01297 680387 **10 D6**
oakdown.co.uk
Total Pitches: 150

Old Hall Caravan Park
Capernwray, Carnforth
LA6 1AD
Tel: 01524 733276 **95 L6**
oldhallcaravanpark.co.uk
Total Pitches: 38

Old Oaks Touring & Glamping
Wick Farm, Wick, Glastonbury
BA6 8JS
Tel: 01458 831437 **19 P7**
theoldoaks.co.uk
Total Pitches: 88

Orchard Farm Holiday Village
Stonegate, Hunmanby, Filey,
North Yorkshire
YO14 0PU
Tel: 01723 891582 **99 N5**
orchardfarmholidayvillage.co.uk
Total Pitches: 91

Ord House Country Park
East Ord, Berwick-upon-Tweed
TD15 2NS
Tel: 01289 305288 **129 P9**
maguirescountryparks.co.uk
Total Pitches: 79

Otterington Park
Station Farm, South Otterington,
Northallerton, North Yorkshire
DL7 9JB
Tel: 01609 780656 **97 N3**
otteringtonpark.com
Total Pitches: 62

Oxon Hall Touring Park
Welshpool Road, Shrewsbury
SY3 5FB
Tel: 01743 340868 **56 H2**
morris-leisure.co.uk
Total Pitches: 105

Park Cliffe C & C Estate
Birks Road, Tower Wood,
Windermere
LA23 3PG
Tel: 015395 31344 **94 H2**
parkcliffe.co.uk
Total Pitches: 60

Park Foot Holiday Park
Howtown Road, Pooley Bridge
CA10 2NA
Tel: 017684 86309 **101 N6**
parkfootullswater.co.uk
Total Pitches: 323

Parkers Farm Holiday Park
Higher Mead Farm, Ashburton,
Devon
TQ13 7LJ
Tel: 01364 654869 **7 K4**
parkersfarmholidays.com
Total Pitches: 100

Parkland C & C Site
Sorley Green Cross, Kingsbridge
TQ7 4AF
Tel: 01548 852723 **7 J9**
parklandsite.co.uk
Total Pitches: 50

Pebble Bank Caravan Park
Camp Road, Wyke Regis,
Weymouth
DT4 9HF
Tel: 01305 774844 **11 P9**
pebblebank.co.uk
Total Pitches: 40

Perran Sands Holiday Park
Perranporth, Truro
TR6 0AQ
Tel: 01872 573551 **4 B10**
haven.com/perransands
Total Pitches: 341

Petwood Caravan Park
Off Stixwould Road,
Woodhall Spa
LN10 6QH
Tel: 01526 354799 **86 G8**
petwoodcaravanpark.com
Total Pitches: 98

Piccadilly Caravan Park
Folly Lane West, Lacock
SN15 2LP
Tel: 01249 263164 **32 H11**
piccadillylacock.co.uk
Total Pitches: 41

**Plough Lane Touring
Caravan Site**
Plough Lane, Chippenham,
Wiltshire
SN15 5PS
Tel: 01249 750146 **32 H9**
ploughlane.co.uk
Total Pitches: 52

Polladras Holiday Park
Carleen, Breage, Helston
TR13 9NX
Tel: 01736 762220 **2 G7**
polladrasholidaypark.co.uk
Total Pitches: 39

Polmanter Touring Park
Halsetown, St Ives
TR26 3LX
Tel: 01736 795640 **2 E6**
polmanter.com
Total Pitches: 294

Porthtowan Tourist Park
Mile Hill, Porthtowan, Truro
TR4 8TY
Tel: 01209 890256 **2 H4**
porthtowantouristpark.co.uk
Total Pitches: 80

Presingoll Farm C & C Park
St Agnes
TR5 0PB
Tel: 01872 552333 **3 J4**
presingollfarm.co.uk
Total Pitches: 90

Primrose Valley Holiday Park
Filey
YO14 9RF
Tel: 01723 513771 **99 N5**
haven.com/primrosevalley
Total Pitches: 35

Ranch Caravan Park
Station Road, Honeybourne,
Evesham
WR11 7PR
Tel: 01386 830744 **47 M6**
ranch.co.uk
Total Pitches: 120

Ripley Caravan Park
Knaresborough Road, Ripley,
Harrogate
HG3 3AU
Tel: 01423 770050 **97 L8**
ripleycaravanpark.com
Total Pitches: 60

River Dart Country Park
Holne Park, Ashburton
TQ13 7NP
Tel: 01364 652511 **7 J5**
riverdart.co.uk
Total Pitches: 170

River Valley Holiday Park
London Apprentice, St Austell
PL26 7AP
Tel: 01726 73533 **3 Q3**
rivervalleyholidaypark.co.uk
Total Pitches: 45

Riverside C & C Park
Marsh Lane, North Molton Road,
South Molton
EX36 3HQ
Tel: 01769 579269 **17 N6**
exmoorriverside.co.uk
Total Pitches: 58

Riverside Caravan Park
Leigham Manor Drive, Plymouth
PL6 8LL
Tel: 01752 344122 **6 E7**
riversidecaravanpark.com
Total Pitches: 259

Riverside Caravan Park
High Bentham, Lancaster
LA2 7FJ
Tel: 015242 61272 **95 P7**
riversidecaravanpark.co.uk
Total Pitches: 61

Robin Hood C & C Park
Green Dyke Lane, Slingsby
YO62 4AP
Tel: 01653 628391 **98 E6**
robinhoodcaravanpark.co.uk
Total Pitches: 46

**Rose Farm Touring
& Camping Park**
Stepshort, Belton,
Nr Great Yarmouth
NR31 9JS
Tel: 01493 738292 **77 P11**
rosefarmtouringpark.com
Total Pitches: 145

Rosedale Abbey Caravan Park
Rosedale Abbey, Pickering
YO18 8SA
Tel: 01751 417272 **105 K11**
rosedaleabbeycaravanpark.co.uk
Total Pitches: 100

Rudding Holiday Park
Follifoot, Harrogate
HG3 1JH
Tel: 01423 870439 **97 M10**
ruddingholidaypark.co.uk
Total Pitches: 86

Run Cottage Touring Park
Alderton Road, Hollesley,
Woodbridge
IP12 3RQ
Tel: 01394 411309 **53 Q3**
runcottage.co.uk
Total Pitches: 45

Rutland C & C
Park Lane, Greetham,
Oakham
LE15 7FN
Tel: 01572 813520 **73 N8**
rutlandcaravanandcamping.co.uk
Total Pitches: 130

St Helens in the Park
Wykeham, Scarborough
YO13 9QD
Tel: 01723 862771 **99 K4**
sthelenscaravanpark.co.uk
Total Pitches: 250

St Ives Bay Beach Resort
73 Loggans Road, Upton
Towans, Hayle
TR27 5BH
Tel: 01736 752274 **2 F6**
stivesbay.co.uk
Total Pitches: 240

Salcombe Regis C & C Park
Salcombe Regis, Sidmouth
EX10 0JH
Tel: 01395 514303 **10 D7**
salcombe-regis.co.uk
Total Pitches: 100

Sand le Mere Holiday Village
Southfield Lane, Tunstall
HU12 0JF
Tel: 01964 670403 **93 P4**
sand-le-mere.co.uk
Total Pitches: 72

Scratby Hall Caravan Park
Scratby, Great Yarmouth
NR29 3SR
Tel: 01493 730283 **77 P8**
scratbyhall.co.uk
Total Pitches: 85

Searles Leisure Resort
South Beach Road,
Hunstanton
PE36 5BB
Tel: 01485 534211 **75 N3**
searles.co.uk
Total Pitches: 255

Seaview Holiday Park
Preston, Weymouth
DT3 6DZ
Tel: 01305 832271 **11 Q8**
haven.com/parks/dorset/seaview
Total Pitches: 82

Severn Gorge Park
Bridgnorth Road, Tweedale,
Telford
TF7 4JB
Tel: 01952 684789 **57 N3**
severngorgepark.co.uk
Total Pitches: 12

Shrubbery Touring Park
Rousdon, Lyme Regis
DT7 3XW
Tel: 01297 442227 **10 F6**
shrubberypark.co.uk
Total Pitches: 120

Silverdale Caravan Park
Middlebarrow Plain, Cove Road,
Silverdale, Nr Carnforth
LA5 0SH
Tel: 01524 701508 **95 K5**
holgates.co.uk
Total Pitches: 80

Skegness Holiday Park
Richmond Drive,
Skegness
PE25 3TQ
Tel: 01754 762097 **87 Q8**
haven.com/parks/lincolnshire/
skegness-holiday-park
Total Pitches: 49

Skelwith Fold Caravan Park
Ambleside, Cumbria
LA22 0HX
Tel: 015394 32277 **101 L10**
skelwith.com
Total Pitches: 150

Skirlington Leisure Park
Driffield, Skipsea
YO25 8SY
Tel: 01262 468213 **99 P10**
skirlington.com
Total Pitches: 280

**Sleningford Watermill
Caravan Camping Park**
North Stainley, Ripon
HG4 3HQ
Tel: 01765 635201 **97 L5**
sleningfordwatermill.co.uk
Total Pitches: 150

Southfork Caravan Park
Parrett Works, Martock,
Somerset
TA12 6AE
Tel: 01935 825661 **19 M11**
southforkcaravans.co.uk
Total Pitches: 27

**South Lytchett Manor
C & C Park**
Dorchester Road, Lytchett
Minster, Poole
BH16 6JB
Tel: 01202 622577 **12 G6**
southlytchettmanor.co.uk
Total Pitches: 150

South Meadows Caravan Park
South Road, Belford
NE70 7DP
Tel: 01668 213326 **119 M4**
southmeadows.co.uk
Total Pitches: 169

Stanmore Hall Touring Park
Stourbridge Road,
Bridgnorth
WV15 6DT
Tel: 01746 761761 **57 N6**
morris-leisure.co.uk
Total Pitches: 129

Stanwix Park Holiday Centre
Greenrow, Silloth
CA7 4HH
Tel: 016973 32666 **109 P10**
stanwix.com
Total Pitches: 121

Summer Valley Touring Park
Shortlanesend, Truro,
Cornwall
TR4 9DW
Tel: 07933 212643 **3 L4**
summervalley.co.uk
Total Pitches: 55

**Sumners Ponds
Fishery & Campsite**
Chapel Road, Barns Green,
Horsham
RH13 0PR
Tel: 01403 732539 **24 D5**
sumnersponds.co.uk
Total Pitches: 86

Swiss Farm Touring & Camping
Marlow Road,
Henley-on-Thames
RG9 2HY
Tel: 01491 573419 **35 L8**
swissfarmhenley.co.uk
Total Pitches: 140

**Tanner Farm Touring
C & C Park**
Tanner Farm, Goudhurst Road,
Marden
TN12 9ND
Tel: 01622 832399 **26 B3**
tannerfarmpark.co.uk
Total Pitches: 120

Tehidy Holiday Park
Harris Mill, Illogan, Portreath
TR16 4JQ
Tel: 01209 216489 **2 H5**
tehidy.co.uk
Total Pitches: 18

Tencreek Holiday Park
Polperro Road, Looe
PL13 2JR
Tel: 01503 262447 **5 L11**
dolphinholidays.co.uk
Total Pitches: 254

The Inside Park
Down House Estate,
Blandford Forum, Dorset
DT11 9AD
Tel: 01258 453719 **12 E4**
theinsidepark.co.uk
Total Pitches: 125

The Laurels Holiday Park
Padstow Road, Whitecross,
Wadebridge
PL27 7JQ
Tel: 01208 813341 **4 F7**
thelaurelsholidaypark.co.uk
Total Pitches: 30

The Old Brick Kilns
Little Barney Lane, Barney,
Fakenham
NR21 0NL
Tel: 01328 878305 **76 E5**
old-brick-kilns.co.uk
Total Pitches: 65

**The Orchards Holiday
Caravan Park**
Main Road, Newbridge,
Yarmouth,
Isle of Wight
PO41 0TS
Tel: 01983 531331 **14 D9**
orchards-holiday-park.co.uk
Total Pitches: 120

The Quiet Site
Ullswater,
Watermillock
CA11 0LS
Tel: 07768 727016 **101 M6**
thequietsite.co.uk
Total Pitches: 100

Thornwick Bay Holiday Village
North Marine Road,
Flamborough
YO15 1AU
Tel: 01262 850569 **99 Q6**
haven.com/parks/yorkshire/
thornwick-bay
Total Pitches: 67

Thorpe Park Holiday Centre
Cleethorpes
DN35 0PW
Tel: 01472 813395 **93 P9**
haven.com/thorpepark
Total Pitches: 134

Tollgate Farm C & C Park
Budnick Hill,
Perranporth
TR6 0AD
Tel: 01872 572130 **3 K3**
tollgatefarm.co.uk
Total Pitches: 102

Treago Farm Caravan Site
Crantock,
Newquay
TR8 5QS
Tel: 01637 830277 **4 B9**
treagofarm.co.uk
Total Pitches: 90

Treloy Touring Park
Newquay
TR8 4JN
Tel: 01637 872063 **4 D9**
treloy.co.uk
Total Pitches: 223

Trencreek Holiday Park
Hillcrest, Higher Trencreek,
Newquay
TR8 4NS
Tel: 01637 874210 **4 C9**
trencreekholidaypark.co.uk
Total Pitches: 194

Trethem Mill Touring Park
St Just-in-Roseland,
Nr St Mawes, Truro
TR2 5JF
Tel: 01872 580504 **3 M6**
trethem.com
Total Pitches: 84

Trevalgan Touring Park
Trevalgan, St Ives
TR26 3BJ
Tel: 01736 791892 **2 D6**
trevalgantouringpark.co.uk
Total Pitches: 135

Trevarrian Holiday Park
Mawgan Porth, Newquay,
Cornwall
TR8 4AQ
Tel: 01637 860381 **4 D8**
trevarrian.co.uk
Total Pitches: 185

Trevarth Holiday Park
Blackwater, Truro
TR4 8HR
Tel: 01872 560266 **3 J4**
trevarth.co.uk
Total Pitches: 30

Trevedra Farm C & C Site
Sennen, Penzance
TR19 7BE
Tel: 01736 871818 **2 B8**
trevedrafarm.co.uk
Total Pitches: 100

Trevornick
Holywell Bay, Newquay
TR8 5PW
Tel: 01637 830531 **4 B10**
trevornick.co.uk
Total Pitches: 575

Trewan Hall
St Columb Major, Cornwall
TR9 6DB
Tel: 01637 880261 **4 E9**
trewan-hall.co.uk
Total Pitches: 200

Tudor C & C
Shepherds Patch, Slimbridge,
Gloucester
GL2 7BP
Tel: 01453 890483 **32 D4**
tudorcaravanpark.com
Total Pitches: 75

Twitchen House Holiday Village
Mortehoe Station Road,
Mortehoe, Woolacombe
EX34 7ES
Tel: 01271 872302 **16 H3**
woolacombe.co.uk
Total Pitches: 252

Two Mills Touring Park
Yarmouth Road,
North Walsham
NR28 9NA
Tel: 01692 405829 **77 K6**
twomills.co.uk
Total Pitches: 81

Ulwell Cottage Caravan Park
Ulwell Cottage, Ulwell, Swanage
BH19 3DG
Tel: 01929 422823 **12 H8**
ulwellcottagepark.co.uk
Total Pitches: 77

Upper Lynstone Caravan Park
Lynstone, Bude
EX23 0LP
Tel: 01288 352017 **16 C10**
upperlynstone.co.uk
Total Pitches: 65

Vale of Pickering Caravan Park
Carr House Farm, Allerston,
Pickering
YO18 7PQ
Tel: 01723 859280 **98 H4**
valeofpickering.co.uk
Total Pitches: 120

Waldegraves Holiday Park
Mersea Island, Colchester
CO5 8SE
Tel: 01206 382898 **52 H9**
waldegraves.co.uk
Total Pitches: 126

Waleswood C & C Park
Delves Lane, Waleswood, Wales
Bar, Wales, South Yorkshire
S26 5RN
Tel: 07825 125328 **84 G4**
waleswood.co.uk
Total Pitches: 163

Wareham Forest Tourist Park
North Trigon, Wareham
BH20 7NZ
Tel: 01929 551393 **12 E6**
warehamforest.co.uk
Total Pitches: 200

Waren C & C Park
Waren Mill, Bamburgh
NE70 7EE
Tel: 01668 214366 **119 N4**
meadowhead.co.uk/parks/waren
Total Pitches: 150

Warren Farm Holiday Centre
Brean Sands, Brean,
Burnham-on-Sea
TA8 2RP
Tel: 01278 751227 **19 J3**
warrenfarm.co.uk
Total Pitches: 575

Waterfoot Caravan Park
Pooley Bridge, Penrith,
Cumbria
CA11 0JF
Tel: 017684 86302 **101 N6**
waterfootpark.co.uk
Total Pitches: 34

Watergate Bay Touring Park
Watergate Bay, Tregurrian
TR8 4AD
Tel: 01637 860387   **4 D8**
watergatebaytouringpark.co.uk
Total Pitches: 171

Waterrow Touring Park
Wiveliscombe, Taunton
TA4 2AZ
Tel: 01984 623464   **18 E9**
waterrowpark.co.uk
Total Pitches: 42

Waters Edge Country Park
River Road, Stanah,
Thornton-Cleveleys, Blackpool
FY5 5LR
Tel: 01253 823632   **88 D2**
knepsfarm.co.uk
Total Pitches: 40

Wayfarers C & C Park
Relubbus Lane, St Hilary,
Penzance
TR20 9EF
Tel: 01736 763326   **2 F7**
wayfarerspark.co.uk
Total Pitches: 32

Wells Touring Park
Haybridge, Wells
BA5 1AJ
Tel: 01749 676869   **19 P5**
wellstouringpark.co.uk
Total Pitches: 56

Westbrook Park
Little Hereford, Herefordshire
SY8 4AU
Tel: 01584 711280   **57 J11**
westbrookpark.co.uk
Total Pitches: 53

Whitefield Forest Touring Park
Brading Road, Ryde,
Isle of Wight
PO33 1QL
Tel: 01983 617069   **14 H9**
whitefieldforest.co.uk
Total Pitches: 90

Whitehill Country Park
Stoke Road, Paignton, Devon
TQ4 7PF
Tel: 01803 782338   **7 M7**
whitehill-park.co.uk
Total Pitches: 260

Whitemead Caravan Park
East Burton Road, Wool
BH20 6HG
Tel: 01929 462241   **12 D7**
whitemeadcaravanpark.co.uk
Total Pitches: 105

Widdicombe Farm Touring Park
Marldon, Paignton, Devon
TQ3 1ST
Tel: 01803 558325   **7 M6**
widdicombefarm.co.uk
Total Pitches: 180

Willow Valley Holiday Park
Bush, Bude, Cornwall
EX23 9LB
Tel: 01288 353104   **16 C10**
willowvalley.co.uk
Total Pitches: 41

Willowbank Holiday Home & Touring Park
Coastal Road, Ainsdale,
Southport
PR8 3ST
Tel: 01704 571566   **88 C8**
willowbankcp.co.uk
Total Pitches: 87

Wolds View Country Park
115 Brigg Road, Caistor
LN7 6RX
Tel: 01472 851099   **93 K10**
woldsviewtouringpark.co.uk
Total Pitches: 60

Wooda Farm Holiday Park
Poughill, Bude
EX23 9HJ
Tel: 01288 352069   **16 C10**
wooda.co.uk
Total Pitches: 200

Woodclose Caravan Park
High Casterton,
Kirkby Lonsdale
LA6 2SE
Tel: 01524 271597   **95 N5**
woodclosepark.com
Total Pitches: 22

Woodhall Country Park
Stixwold Road, Woodhall Spa
LN10 6UJ
Tel: 01526 353710   **86 G8**
woodhallcountrypark.co.uk
Total Pitches: 141

Woodlands Grove C & C Park
Blackawton,
Dartmouth
TQ9 7DQ
Tel: 01803 712598   **7 L8**
woodlandsgrove.com
Total Pitches: 350

Woodland Springs Adult Touring Park
Venton,
Drewsteignton
EX6 6PG
Tel: 01647 231648   **8 G6**
woodlandsprings.co.uk
Total Pitches: 93

Woodovis Park
Gulworthy,
Tavistock
PL19 8NY
Tel: 01822 832968   **6 C4**
woodovis.com
Total Pitches: 50

Woolsbridge Manor Farm Caravan Park
Three Legged Cross,
Wimborne
BH21 6RA
Tel: 01202 826369   **13 K4**
woolsbridgemanorcaravanpark.co.uk
Total Pitches: 60

Yeatheridge Farm Caravan Park
East Worlington, Crediton,
Devon
EX17 4TN
Tel: 01884 860330   **9 J2**
yeatheridge.co.uk
Total Pitches: 103

York Caravan Park
Stockton Lane, York,
North Yorkshire
YO32 9UB
Tel: 01904 424222   **98 C10**
yorkcaravanpark.com
Total Pitches: 55

York Meadows Caravan Park
York Road, Sheriff Hutton,
York, North Yorkshire
YO60 6QP
Tel: 01347 878508   **98 C7**
yorkmeadowscaravanpark.com
Total Pitches: 45

SCOTLAND

Auchenlarie Holiday Park
Gatehouse of Fleet
DG7 2EX
Tel: 01556 506200   **107 P7**
swalwellholidaygroup.co.uk
Total Pitches: 49

Barrhill Holiday Park
Barrhill, Girvan
KA26 0PZ
Tel: 01465 821355   **114 D11**
barrhillholidaypark.com
Total Pitches: 20

Beecraigs C & C Site
Beecraigs Country Park,
The Visitor Centre,
Linlithgow
EH49 6PL
Tel: 01506 284516   **127 J3**
westlothian.gov.uk/stay-at-beecraigs
Total Pitches: 36

Belhaven Bay C & C Park
Belhaven Bay, Dunbar,
East Lothian
EH42 1TS
Tel: 01368 865956   **128 H4**
meadowhead.co.uk
Total Pitches: 52

Blair Castle Caravan Park
Blair Atholl,
Pitlochry
PH18 5SR
Tel: 01796 481263   **141 L4**
blaircastlecaravanpark.co.uk
Total Pitches: 184

Brighouse Bay Holiday Park
Brighouse Bay, Borgue,
Kirkcudbright
DG6 4TS
Tel: 01557 870267   **108 D11**
gillespie-leisure.co.uk
Total Pitches: 190

Cairnsmill Holiday Park
Largo Road,
St Andrews
KY16 8NN
Tel: 01334 473604   **135 M5**
cairnsmill.co.uk
Total Pitches: 62

Craigtoun Meadows Holiday Park
Mount Melville, St Andrews
KY16 8PQ
Tel: 01334 475959   **135 M4**
craigtounmeadows.co.uk
Total Pitches: 56

Faskally Caravan Park
Pitlochry
PH16 5LA
Tel: 01796 472007   **141 M6**
faskally.co.uk
Total Pitches: 300

Glenearly Caravan Park
Dalbeattie, Dumfries & Galloway
DG5 4NE
Tel: 01556 611393   **108 H8**
glenearlycaravanpark.co.uk
Total Pitches: 39

Glen Nevis C & C Park
Glen Nevis, Fort William
PH33 6SX
Tel: 01397 702191   **139 L3**
glen-nevis.co.uk
Total Pitches: 380

Hoddom Castle Caravan Park
Hoddom, Lockerbie
DG11 1AS
Tel: 01576 300251   **110 C6**
hoddomcastle.co.uk
Total Pitches: 200

Huntly Castle Caravan Park
The Meadow, Huntly
AB54 4UJ
Tel: 01466 794999   **158 D9**
huntlycastle.co.uk
Total Pitches: 90

Invercoe C & C Park
Ballachulish, Glencoe
PH49 4HP
Tel: 01855 811210   **139 K6**
invercoe.co.uk
Total Pitches: 60

Linwater Caravan Park
West Clifton, East Calder
EH53 0HT
Tel: 0131 333 3326   **127 L4**
linwater.co.uk
Total Pitches: 60

Milton of Fonab Caravan Park
Bridge Road, Pitlochry
PH16 5NA
Tel: 01796 472882   **141 M6**
fonab.co.uk
Total Pitches: 154

Sands of Luce Holiday Park
Sands of Luce, Sandhead,
Stranraer
DG9 9JN
Tel: 01776 830456   **106 F7**
sandsofluce.com
Total Pitches: 80

Seal Shore Camping and Touring Site
Kildonan, Isle of Arran,
North Ayrshire
KA27 8SE
Tel: 01770 820320   **121 K7**
campingarran.com
Total Pitches: 43

Seaward Holiday Park
Dhoon Bay, Kirkcudbright
DG6 4TJ
Tel: 01557 870267   **108 E11**
gillespie-leisure.co.uk
Total Pitches: 25

Seton Sands Holiday Village
Longniddry
EH32 0QF
Tel: 01875 813333   **128 C4**
haven.com/setonsands
Total Pitches: 40

Shieling Holidays Mull
Craignure, Isle of Mull,
Argyll & Bute
PA65 6AY
Tel: 01680 812496   **138 C10**
shielingholidays.co.uk
Total Pitches: 90

The Paddocks Motorhome Site
Ingliston Estate & Country Club,
Old Greenock Road, Bishopton,
Renfrewshire
PA7 5PA
Tel: 01505 864333   **125 L3**
ingliston.com
Total Pitches: 30

Thurston Manor Leisure Park
Innerwick, Dunbar
EH42 1SA
Tel: 01368 840643   **129 J5**
thurstonmanor.co.uk
Total Pitches: 120

Witches Craig C & C Park
Blairlogie, Stirling
FK9 5PX
Tel: 01786 474947   **133 N8**
witchescraig.co.uk
Total Pitches: 60

WALES

Beach View Caravan Park
Bwlchtocyn, Abersoch
LL53 7BT
Tel: 01758 712956   **66 E9**
beachviewabersoch.co.uk
Total Pitches: 47

Bron Derw Touring Caravan Park
Llanrwst
LL26 0YT
Tel: 01492 640494   **67 Q2**
bronderw-wales.co.uk
Total Pitches: 48

Caerfai Bay Caravan & Tent Park
Caerfai Bay, St Davids,
Haverfordwest
SA62 6QT
Tel: 01437 720274   **40 E6**
caerfaibay.co.uk
Total Pitches: 106

Cenarth Falls Resort Limited
Cenarth,
Newcastle Emlyn
SA38 9JS
Tel: 01239 710345   **41 Q2**
cenarth-holipark.co.uk
Total Pitches: 30

Daisy Bank Caravan Park
Snead, Montgomery
SY15 6EB
Tel: 01588 620471   **56 E6**
daisy-bank.co.uk
Total Pitches: 64

Deucoch Touring & Camping Park
Sarn Bach, Abersoch
LL53 7LD
Tel: 01758 713293   **66 E9**
deucoch.com
Total Pitches: 70

Dinlle Caravan Park
Dinas Dinlle,
Caernarfon
LL54 5TW
Tel: 01286 830324   **66 G3**
thornleyleisure.co.uk
Total Pitches: 175

Eisteddfa
Eisteddfa Lodge, Pentrefelin,
Criccieth
LL52 0PT
Tel: 01766 522696   **67 J7**
eisteddfapark.co.uk
Total Pitches: 100

Fforest Fields C & C Park
Hundred House,
Builth Wells
LD1 5RT
Tel: 01982 570406   **44 G4**
fforestfields.co.uk
Total Pitches: 120

Fishguard Bay Resort
Garn Gelli, Fishguard
SA65 9ET
Tel: 01348 811415   **41 J3**
fishguardbay.com
Total Pitches: 50

Greenacres Holiday Park
Black Rock Sands, Morfa
Bychan, Porthmadog
LL49 9YF
Tel: 01766 512781   **67 J7**
haven.com/greenacres
Total Pitches: 39

Hafan y Môr Holiday Park
Pwllheli
LL53 6HJ
Tel: 01758 612112   **66 G7**
haven.com/hafanymor
Total Pitches: 75

Hendre Mynach Touring C & C Park
Llanaber Road, Barmouth
LL42 1YR
Tel: 01341 280262   **67 L11**
hendremynach.co.uk
Total Pitches: 240

Home Farm Caravan Park
Marian-glas,
Isle of Anglesey
LL73 8PH
Tel: 01248 410614   **78 H8**
homefarm-anglesey.co.uk
Total Pitches: 102

Islawrffordd Caravan Park
Talybont, Barmouth
LL43 2AQ
Tel: 01341 247269   **67 K10**
islawrffordd.co.uk
Total Pitches: 105

Kiln Park Holiday Centre
Marsh Road, Tenby
SA70 8RB
Tel: 01834 844121   **41 M10**
haven.com/kilnpark
Total Pitches: 146

Lakeside Caravan Park
Llangors, Brecon
LD3 7TR
Tel: 01874 658226   **44 G9**
llangorselake.co.uk
Total Pitches: 40

Pencelli Castle C & C Park
Pencelli, Brecon
LD3 7LX
Tel: 01874 665451   **44 F10**
pencelli-castle.com
Total Pitches: 80

Penisar Mynydd Caravan Park
Caerwys Road, Rhuallt,
St Asaph
LL17 0TY
Tel: 01745 582227   **80 F9**
penisarmynydd.co.uk
Total Pitches: 71

Plassey Holiday Park
The Plassey, Eyton,
Wrexham
LL13 0SP
Tel: 01978 780277   **69 L5**
plassey.com
Total Pitches: 90

Pont Kemys C & C Park
Chainbridge,
Abergavenny
NP7 9DS
Tel: 01873 880688   **31 L3**
pontkemys.com
Total Pitches: 65

Presthaven Beach Holiday Park
Gronant, Prestatyn
LL19 9TT
Tel: 01745 856471   **80 F8**
haven.com/presthaven
Total Pitches: 50

Red Kite Touring and Lodge Park
Van Road, Llanidloes
SY18 6NG
Tel: 01686 412122   **55 L7**
redkitetouringpark.co.uk
Total Pitches: 66

Riverside Camping
Seiont Nurseries, Pont Rug,
Caernarfon
LL55 2BB
Tel: 01286 678781   **67 J2**
riversidecamping.co.uk
Total Pitches: 73

The Trotting Mare Caravan Park
Overton, Wrexham
LL13 0LE
Tel: 01978 711963   **69 L7**
thetrottingmare.co.uk
Total Pitches: 54

Trawsdir Touring C & C Park
Llanaber,
Barmouth
LL42 1RR
Tel: 01341 280999   **67 K11**
barmouthholidays.co.uk
Total Pitches: 70

Tyddyn Isaf Caravan Park
Lligwy Bay, Dulas,
Isle of Anglesey
LL70 9PQ
Tel: 01248 410203   **78 H7**
tyddynisaf.co.uk
Total Pitches: 80

White Tower Holiday Park
Llandwrog,
Caernarfon
LL54 5UH
Tel: 01286 830649   **66 H3**
whitetowerpark.co.uk
Total Pitches: 52

CHANNEL ISLANDS

La Bailloterie Camping
Bailloterie Lane, Vale,
Guernsey
GY3 5HA
Tel: 01481 243636   **10 c1**
campinginguernsey.com
Total Pitches: 100

Signs giving orders

Signs with red circles are mostly prohibitive. Plates below signs qualify their message

Entry to 20mph zone

End of 20mph zone

Maximum speed

National speed limit applies

School crossing patrol

Stop and give way

Give way to traffic on major road

Manually operated temporary STOP and GO signs

No entry for vehicular traffic

No vehicles except bicycles being pushed

No cycling

No motor vehicles

No buses (over 8 passenger seats)

No overtaking

No towed caravans

No vehicles carrying explosives

No vehicle or combination of vehicles over length shown

No vehicles over height shown

No vehicles over width shown

Give priority to vehicles from opposite direction

No right turn

No left turn

No U-turns

No goods vehicles over maximum gross weight shown (in tonnes) except for loading and unloading

No vehicles over maximum gross weight shown (in tonnes)

Parking restricted to permit holders

No stopping during period indicated except for buses

No stopping during times shown except for as long as necessary to set down or pick up passengers

No waiting

No stopping (Clearway)

Signs with blue circles but no red border mostly give positive instruction.

Ahead only

Turn left ahead (right if symbol reversed)

Turn left (right if symbol reversed)

Keep left (right if symbol reversed)

Vehicles may pass either side to reach same destination

Mini-roundabout (roundabout circulation - give way to vehicles from the immediate right)

Route to be used by pedal cycles only

Segregated pedal cycle and pedestrian route

Minimum speed

End of minimum speed

Buses and cycles only

Trams only

Pedestrian crossing point over tramway

One-way traffic (note: compare circular 'Ahead only' sign)

With-flow bus and cycle lane

Contraflow bus lane

With-flow pedal cycle lane

Warning signs

Mostly triangular

Distance to 'STOP' line ahead

Dual carriageway ends

Road narrows on right (left if symbol reversed)

Road narrows on both sides

Distance to 'Give Way' line ahead

Crossroads

Junction on bend ahead

T-junction with priority over vehicles from the right

Staggered junction

Traffic merging from left ahead

The priority through route is indicated by the broader line.

Double bend first to left (symbol may be reversed)

Bend to the right (or left if symbol reversed)

Roundabout

Uneven road

Plate below some signs

Two-way traffic crosses one-way road

Two-way traffic straight ahead

Opening or swing bridge ahead

Low-flying aircraft or sudden aircraft noise

Falling or fallen rocks

Traffic signals not in use

Traffic signals

Slippery road

Steep hill downwards

Steep hill upwards

Gradients may be shown as a ratio i.e. 20% = 1:5

Tunnel ahead

Trams crossing ahead

Level crossing with barrier or gate ahead

Level crossing without barrier or gate ahead

Level crossing without barrier

School crossing patrol ahead (some signs have amber lights which flash when crossings are in use)

Frail (or blind or disabled if shown) pedestrians likely to cross road ahead

No footway for 400 yds
Pedestrians in road ahead

Zebra crossing

Safe height 16'-6" (5.0 m)
Overhead electric cable; plate indicates maximum height of vehicles which can pass safely

Available width of headroom indicated

Sharp deviation of route to left (or right if chevrons reversed)

STOP when lights show
Light signals ahead at level crossing, airfield or bridge

Red — STOP
Green — Clear
IF NO LIGHT - PHONE CROSSING OPERATOR
Minature warning lights at level crossings

Cattle

Wild animals

Wild horses or ponies

Accompanied horses or ponies

Cycle route ahead

Ice
Risk of ice

Queues likely
Traffic queues likely ahead

Humps for ½ mile
Distance over which road humps extend

Hidden dip
Other danger; plate indicates nature of danger

Soft verges for 2 miles
Soft verges

Side winds

Hump bridge

Ford
Worded warning sign

Quayside or river bank

Risk of grounding

Direction signs

Mostly rectangular
Signs on motorways - blue backgrounds

At a junction leading directly into a motorway (junction number may be shown on a black background)

On approaches to junctions (junction number on black background)

M1
The NORTH
Sheffield 32
Leeds 59
Route confirmatory sign after junction

Downward pointing arrows mean 'Get in lane'
The left-hand lane leads to a different destination from the other lanes.

The panel with the inclined arrow indicates the destinations which can be reached by leaving the motorway at the next junction.

Signs on primary routes - green backgrounds

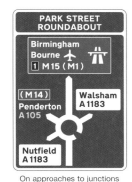
On approaches to junctions

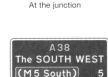
At the junction

A38
The SOUTH WEST
(M5 South) 5
Gloucester 11
Route confirmatory sign after the junction

On approaches to junctions

Swansea Abertawe A483
On approaches to junction in Wales (bilingual)

Blue panels indicate that the motorway starts at the junction ahead.
Motorways shown in brackets can also be reached along the route indicated.
White panels indicate local or non-primary routes leading from the junction ahead.
Brown panels show the route to tourist attractions.
The name of the junction may be shown at the top of the sign.
The aircraft symbol indicates the route to an airport.
A symbol may be included to warn of a hazard or restriction along that route.

Signs on non-primary and local routes - black borders

On approaches to junctions

Market Walborough B486
At the junction

WC
Direction to toilets with access for the disabled

Green panels indicate that the primary route starts at the junction ahead.
Route numbers on a blue background show the direction to a motorway.
Route numbers on a green background show the direction to a primary route.

Emergency diversion routes

In an emergency it may be necessary to close a section of motorway or other main road to traffic, so a temporary sign may advise drivers to follow a diversion route. To help drivers navigate the route, black symbols on yellow patches may be permanently displayed on existing direction signs, including motorway signs. Symbols may also be used on separate signs with yellow backgrounds.

Note: The signs shown in this road atlas are those most commonly in use and are not all drawn to the same scale. In Scotland and Wales bilingual versions of some signs are used, showing both English and Gaelic or Welsh spellings. Some older designs of signs may still be seen on the roads. A comprehensive explanation of the signing system illustrating the vast majority of road signs can be found in the AA's handbook *Know Your Road Signs*. Where there is a reference to a rule number, this refers to *The Highway Code*.

Restricted junctions

Motorway and primary route junctions which have access or exit restrictions are shown on the map pages thus:

M1 London - Leeds

Northbound
Access only from A1 (northbound)

Southbound
Exit only to A1 (southbound)

Northbound
Access only from A41 (northbound)

Southbound
Exit only to A41 (southbound)

Northbound
Access only from M25 (no link from A405)

Southbound
Exit only to M25 (no link from A405)

Northbound
Access only from A414

Southbound
Exit only to A414

Northbound
Exit only to M45

Southbound
Access only from M45

Northbound
Exit only to M6 (northbound)

Southbound
Exit only to A14 (southbound)

Northbound
Exit only, no access

Southbound
Access only, no exit

Northbound
No exit, access only

Southbound
Access only from A50 (eastbound)

Northbound
Exit only, no access

Southbound
Access only, no exit

Northbound
Exit only to M621

Southbound
Access only from M621

Northbound
Exit only to A1(M) (northbound)

Southbound
Access only from A1(M) (southbound)

M2 Rochester - Faversham

Westbound
No exit to A2 (eastbound)

Eastbound
No access from A2 (westbound)

M3 Sunbury - Southampton

Northeastbound
Access only from A303, no exit

Southwestbound
Exit only to A303, no access

Northbound
Exit only, no access

Southbound
Access only, no exit

Northeastbound
Access from M27 only, no exit

Southwestbound
No access to M27 (westbound)

M4 London - South Wales

For junctions 1 & 2 see London district map on pages 178–181

Westbound
Exit only to M48

Eastbound
Access only from M48

Westbound
Access only from M48

Eastbound
Exit only to M48

Westbound
Exit only, no access

Eastbound
Access only, no exit

Westbound
Exit only, no access

Eastbound
Access only, no exit

Westbound
Exit only to A48(M)

Eastbound
Access only from A48(M)

Westbound
Exit only, no access

Eastbound
No restriction

Westbound
Access only, no exit

Eastbound
No access or exit

Westbound
Exit only to A483

Eastbound
Access only from A483

M5 Birmingham - Exeter

Northeastbound
Access only, no exit

Southwestbound
Exit only, no access

Northeastbound
Access only from A417 (westbound)

Southwestbound
Exit only to A417 (eastbound)

Northeastbound
Exit only to M49

Southwestbound
Access only from M49

Northeastbound
No access, exit only

Southwestbound
No exit, access only

M6 Toll Motorway

See M6 Toll motorway map on page *XXIII*

M6 Rugby - Carlisle

Northbound
Exit only to M6 Toll

Southbound
Access only from M6 Toll

Northbound
Exit only to M42 (southbound) and A446

Southbound
Exit only to A446

Northbound
Access only from M42 (southbound)

Southbound
Exit only to M42

Northbound
Exit only, no access

Southbound
Access only, no exit

Northbound
Exit only to M54

Southbound
Access only from M54

Northbound
Access only from M6 Toll

Southbound
Exit only to M6 Toll

Northbound
No restriction

Southbound
Access only from M56 (eastbound)

Northbound
Exit only to M56 (westbound)

Southbound
Access only from M56 (eastbound)

Northbound
Access only, no exit

Southbound
Exit only, no access

Northbound
Exit only, no access

Southbound
Access only, no exit

Northbound
Access only from M61

Southbound
Exit only to M61

Northbound
Exit only, no access

Southbound
Access only, no exit

Northbound
Exit only, no access

Southbound
Access only, no exit

M8 Edinburgh - Bishopton

For junctions 7A to 29A see Glasgow district map on pages 176–177

Westbound
Exit only, no access

Eastbound
Access only, no exit

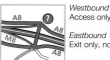
Westbound
Access only, no exit

Eastbound
Exit only, no access

Westbound
Access only, no exit

Eastbound
Exit only, no access

M9 Edinburgh - Dunblane

Northwestbound
Access only, no exit

Southeastbound
Exit only, no access

Northwestbound
Exit only, no access

Southeastbound
Access only, no exit

Northwestbound
Access only, no exit

Southeastbound
Exit only to A905

Northwestbound
Exit only to M876
(southwestbound)

Southeastbound
Access only from M876
(northeastbound)

M11 London - Cambridge

Northbound
Access only from A406
(eastbound)

Southbound
Exit only to A406

Northbound
Exit only, no access

Southbound
Access only, no exit

Northbound
Exit only, no access

Southbound
No direct access,
use jct 8

Northbound
Exit only to A11

Southbound
Access only from A11

Northbound
Exit only, no access

Southbound
Access only, no exit

Northbound
Exit only, no access

Southbound
Access only, no exit

M20 Swanley - Folkestone

Northwestbound
Staggered junction; follow
signs - access only

Southeastbound
Staggered junction; follow
signs - exit only

Northwestbound
Exit only to M26
(westbound)

Southeastbound
Access only from M26
(eastbound)

Northwestbound
Access only from A20

Southeastbound
For access follow signs -
exit only to A20

Northwestbound
No restriction

Southeastbound
For exit follow signs

Westbound
Access only, no exit

Eastbound
Exit only, no access

Northwestbound
Access only, no exit

Southeastbound
Exit only, no access

M23 Hooley - Crawley

Northbound
Exit only to A23
(northbound)

Southbound
Access only from A23
(southbound)

Northbound
Access only, no exit

Southbound
Exit only, no access

M25 London Orbital

See M25 London Orbital motorway map on
page *XXII*

M26 Sevenoaks - Wrotham

Westbound
Exit only to clockwise
M25 (westbound)

Eastbound
Access only from
anticlockwise M25
(eastbound)

Westbound
Access only from M20
(northwestbound)

Eastbound
Exit only to M20
(southeastbound)

M27 Cadnam - Portsmouth

Westbound
Staggered junction; follow
signs - access only from
M3 (southbound). Exit
only to M3 (northbound)

Eastbound
Staggered junction; follow
signs - access only from
M3 (southbound). Exit
only to M3 (northbound)

Westbound
Exit only, no access

Eastbound
Access only, no exit

Westbound
Staggered junction; follow
signs - exit only to M275
(southbound)

Eastbound
Staggered junction; follow
signs - access only from
M275 (northbound)

M40 London - Birmingham

Northwestbound
Exit only, no access

Southeastbound
Access only, no exit

Northwestbound
Exit only, no access

Southeastbound
Access only, no exit

Northwestbound
Exit only to M40/A40

Southeastbound
Access only from
M40/A40

Northwestbound
Exit only, no access

Southeastbound
Access only, no exit

Northwestbound
Access only, no exit

Southeastbound
Exit only, no access

Northwestbound
Access only, no exit

Southeastbound
Exit only, no access

M42 Bromsgrove - Measham

See Birmingham district map on pages
174–175

M45 Coventry - M1

Westbound
Access only from A45
(northbound)

Eastbound
Exit only, no access

Westbound
Access only from M1
(northbound)

Eastbound
Exit only to M1
(southbound)

M48 Chepstow

Westbound
Access only from M4
(westbound)

Eastbound
Exit only to M4
(eastbound)

Westbound
No exit to M4 (eastbound)

Eastbound
No access from M4
(westbound)

M53 Mersey Tunnel - Chester

Northbound
Access only from M56
(westbound). Exit only to
M56 (eastbound)

Southbound
Access only from M56
(westbound). Exit only to
M56 (eastbound)

M54 Telford - Birmingham

Westbound
Access only from M6
(northbound)

Eastbound
Exit only to M6
(southbound)

M56 Chester - Manchester

For junctions 1,2,3,4 & 7 see Manchester
district map on pages 182–183

Westbound
Access only, no exit

Eastbound
No access or exit

Westbound
No exit to M6
(southbound)

Eastbound
No access from M6
(northbound)

Westbound
Exit only to M53

Eastbound
Access only from M53

Westbound
No access or exit

Eastbound
No restriction

M57 Liverpool Outer Ring Road

Northwestbound
Access only, no exit

Southeastbound
Exit only, no access

Northwestbound
Access only from A580
(westbound)

Southeastbound
Exit only, no access

M60 Manchester Orbital

See Manchester district map on pages
182–183

M61 Manchester - Preston

Northwestbound
No access or exit

Southeastbound
Exit only, no access

Northwestbound
Exit only to M6
(northbound)

Southeastbound
Access only from M6
(southbound)

M62 Liverpool - Kingston upon Hull

Westbound
Access only, no exit

Eastbound
Exit only, no access

Westbound
No access to A1(M)
(southbound)

Eastbound
No restriction

M65 Preston - Colne

Northeastbound
Exit only, no access

Southwestbound
Access only, no exit

Northeastbound
Access only, no exit

Southwestbound
Exit only, no access

M66 Bury

Northbound
Exit only to A56
(northbound)

Southbound
Access only from A56
(southbound)

Northbound
Exit only, no access

Southbound
Access only, no exit

M67 Hyde Bypass

Westbound
Access only, no exit

Eastbound
Exit only, no access

Westbound
Exit only, no access

Eastbound
Access only, no exit

M69 Coventry - Leicester

Northbound
Access only, no exit

Southbound
Exit only, no access

M73 East of Glasgow

Northbound
No exit to A74 and A721

Southbound
No exit to A74 and A721

Northbound
No access from or exit to
A89. No access from M8
(eastbound)

Southbound
No access from or exit to
A89. No exit to M8
(westbound)

M74 Glasgow - Abington

Northbound
Exit only, no access

Southbound
Access only, no exit

Northbound
Access only, no exit

Southbound
Exit only, no access

Northbound
No access from A74 and
A721

Southbound
Access only, no exit to
A74 and A721

Northbound
Access only, no exit

Southbound
Exit only, no access

Northbound
No access or exit

Southbound
Exit only, no access

Northbound
No restriction

Southbound
Access only, no exit

Northbound
Access only, no exit

Southbound
Exit only, no access

Northbound
Exit only, no access

Southbound
Access only, no exit

M77 Glasgow - Kilmarnock

Northbound
No exit to M8
(westbound)

Southbound
No access from M8
(eastbound)

Northbound
Access only, no exit

Southbound
Exit only, no access

Northbound
Access only, no exit

Southbound
Exit only, no access

Northbound
Access only, no exit

Southbound
No restriction

Northbound
Exit only, no access

Southbound
Exit only, no access

M80 Glasgow - Stirling

For junctions 1 & 4 see Glasgow district map
on pages 176–177

Northbound
Exit only, no access

Southbound
Access only, no exit

Northbound
Access only, no exit

Southbound
Exit only, no access

Northbound
Exit only to M876
(northeastbound)

Southbound
Access only from M876
(southwestbound)

M90 Edinburgh - Perth

Northbound
No exit, access only

Southbound
Exit only to A90
(eastbound)

Northbound
Exit only to A92
(eastbound)

Southbound
Access only from A92
(westbound)

Northbound
Access only, no exit

Southbound
Exit only, no access

Northbound
Exit only, no access

Southbound
Access only, no exit

Northbound
No access from A912
No exit to A912
(southbound)

Southbound
Access only from A912
(northbound).
No exit to A912

M180 Doncaster - Grimsby

Westbound
Access only, no exit

Eastbound
Exit only, no access

M606 Bradford Spur

Northbound
Exit only, no access

Southbound
No restriction

M621 Leeds - M1

Clockwise
Access only, no exit

Anticlockwise
Exit only, no access

Clockwise
No exit or access

Anticlockwise
No restriction

Clockwise
Access only, no exit

Anticlockwise
Exit only, no access

Clockwise
Exit only, no access

Anticlockwise
Access only, no exit

Clockwise
Exit only to M1
(southbound)

Anticlockwise
Access only from M1
(northbound)

M876 Bonnybridge - Kincardine Bridge

Northeastbound
Access only from M80
(northbound)

Southwestbound
Exit only to M80
(southbound)

Northeastbound
Exit only to M9
(eastbound)

Southwestbound
Access only from M9
(westbound)

A1(M) South Mimms - Baldock

Northbound
Exit only, no access

Southbound
Access only, no exit

Northbound
No restriction

Southbound
Exit only, no access

Northbound
Access only, no exit

Southbound
No access or exit

A1(M) Pontefract - Bedale

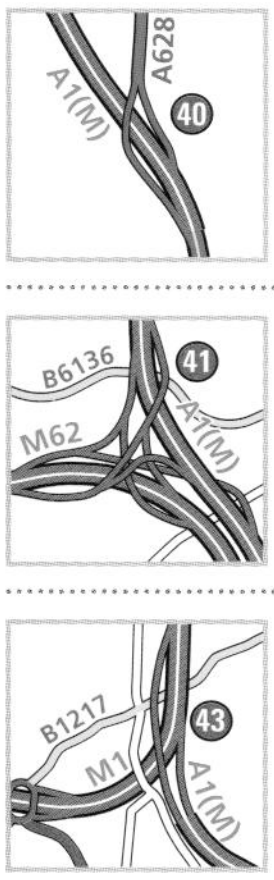

Northbound
Exit only to A162 (M62),
No access

Southbound
Access only, no exit

Northbound
No access to M62
(eastbound)

Southbound
No restriction

Northbound
Access only from M1
(northbound)

Southbound
Exit only to M1
(southbound)

A1(M) Scotch Corner - Newcastle upon Tyne

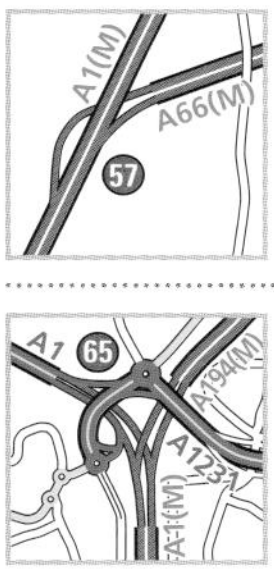

Northbound
Exit only to A66(M)
(eastbound)

Southbound
Access only from A66(M)
(westbound)

Northbound
No access. Exit only to
A194(M) & A1
(northbound)

Southbound
No exit. Access only from
A194(M) & A1
(southbound)

A3(M) Horndean - Havant

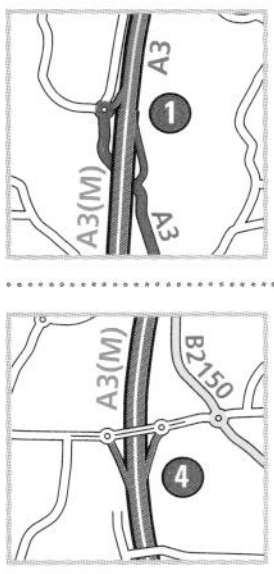

Northbound
Access only from A3

Southbound
Exit only to A3

Northbound
Exit only, no access

Southbound
Access only, no exit

A38(M) Birmingham Victoria Road (Park Circus)

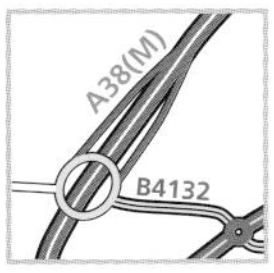

Northbound
No exit

Southbound
No access

A48(M) Cardiff Spur

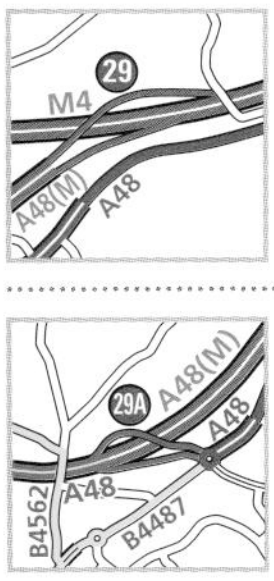

Westbound
Access only from M4
(westbound)

Eastbound
Exit only to M4
(eastbound)

Westbound
Exit only to A48
(westbound)

Eastbound
Access only from A48
(eastbound)

A57(M) Manchester Brook Street (A34)

Westbound
No exit

Eastbound
No access

A58(M) Leeds Park Lane and Westgate

Northbound
No restriction

Southbound
No access

A64(M) Leeds Clay Pit Lane (A58)

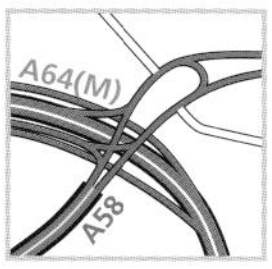

Westbound
No exit (to Clay Pit Lane)

Eastbound
No access (from Clay Pit Lane)

A66(M) Darlington Spur

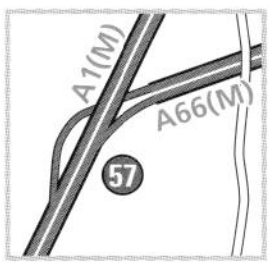

Westbound
Exit only to A1(M)
(southbound)

Eastbound
Access only from A1(M)
(northbound)

A74(M) Gretna - Abington

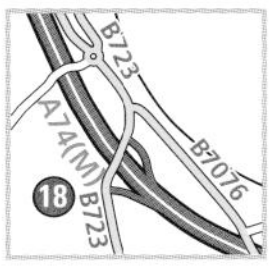

Northbound
Exit only, no access

Southbound
Access only, no exit

A194(M) Gateshead

Northbound
Access only from A1(M)
(northbound)

Southbound
Exit only to A1(M)
(southbound)

A12 M25 - Ipswich

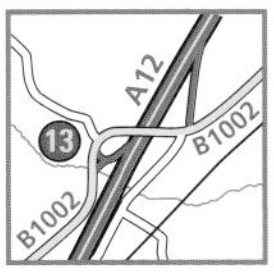

Northeastbound
Access only, no exit

Southwestbound
No restriction

Northeastbound
Exit only, no access

Southwestbound
Access only, no exit

Northeastbound
Exit only, no access

Southwestbound
Access only, no exit

Northeastbound
Access only, no exit

Southwestbound
Exit only, no access

Northeastbound
No restriction

Southwestbound
Access only, no exit

Northeastbound
Exit only, no access

Southwestbound
Access only, no exit

Northeastbound
Access only, no exit

Southwestbound
Exit only, no access

Northeastbound
Exit only, no access

Southwestbound
Access only, no exit

Northeastbound
Exit only (for Stratford
St Mary and Dedham)

Southwestbound
Access only

A14 M1 - Felixstowe

Westbound
Exit only to M6 & M1
(northbound)

Eastbound
Access only from M6 &
M1 (southbound)

Westbound
Exit only, no access

Eastbound
Access only, no exit

Westbound
Access only, no exit

Eastbound
Exit only, no access

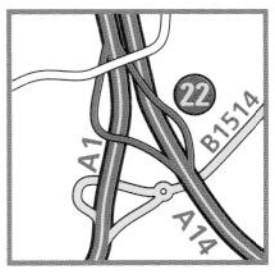

Westbound
Exit only, no access

Eastbound
Access only from A1
(southbound)

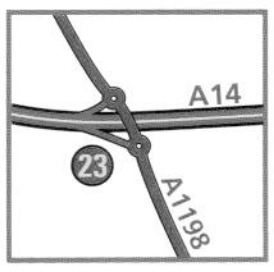

Westbound
Access only, no exit

Eastbound
Exit only, no access

Westbound
No restriction

Eastbound
Exit only, no access

Westbound
Access only, no exit

Eastbound
Exit only, no access

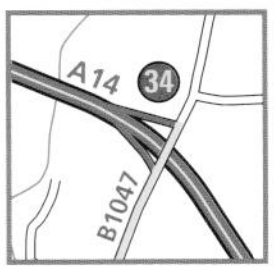

A55 Holyhead - Chester

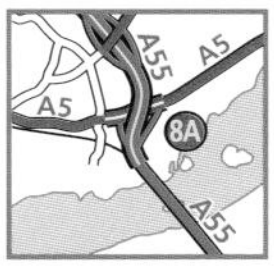

Westbound
Exit only, no access

Eastbound
Access only, no exit

Westbound
Access only, no exit

Eastbound
Exit only, no access

Westbound
Exit only, no access

Eastbound
No access or exit.

Westbound
No restriction

Eastbound
No access or exit

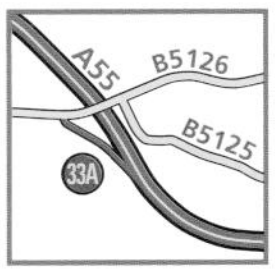

Westbound
Exit only, no access

Eastbound
No access or exit

Westbound
Exit only, no access

Eastbound
Access only, no exit

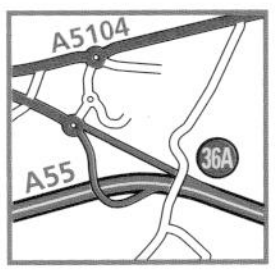

Westbound
Exit only to A5104

Eastbound
Access only from A5104

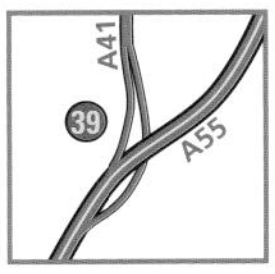

Westbound
Access only, no exit

Eastbound
Exit only, no access

(Right column duplicate set - A11/A14 junctions)

Westbound
Exit only to A11
Access only from A1303

Eastbound
Access only from A11

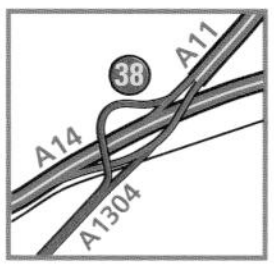

Westbound
Access only from A11

Eastbound
Exit only to A11

Westbound
Exit only, no access

Eastbound
Access only, no exit

Westbound
Access only, no access

Eastbound
Exit only, no access

Refer also to atlas pages 36–37 and 50–51

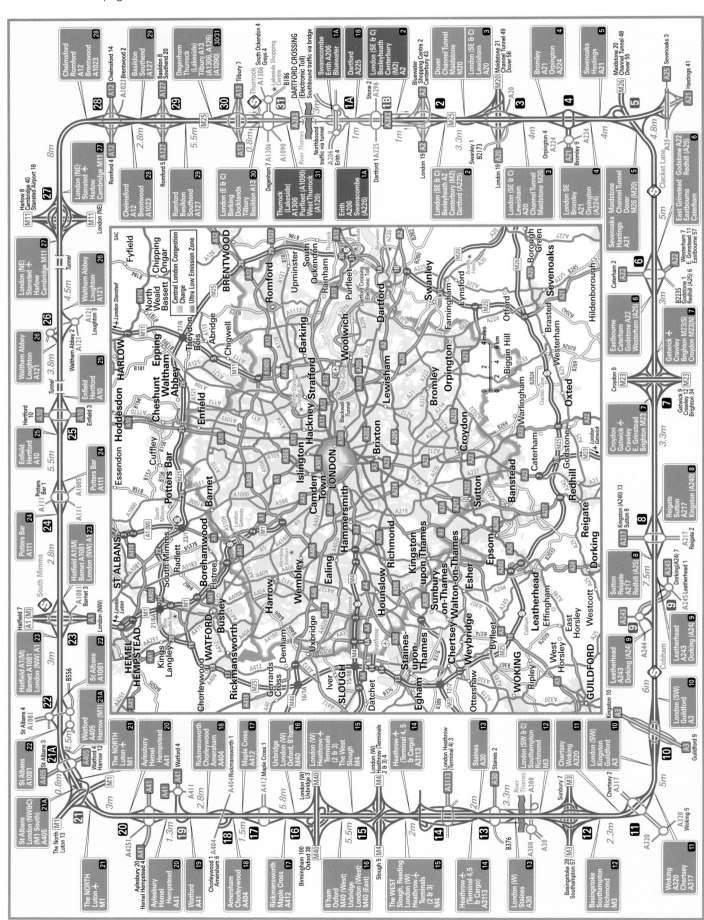

Refer also to atlas pages 58–59

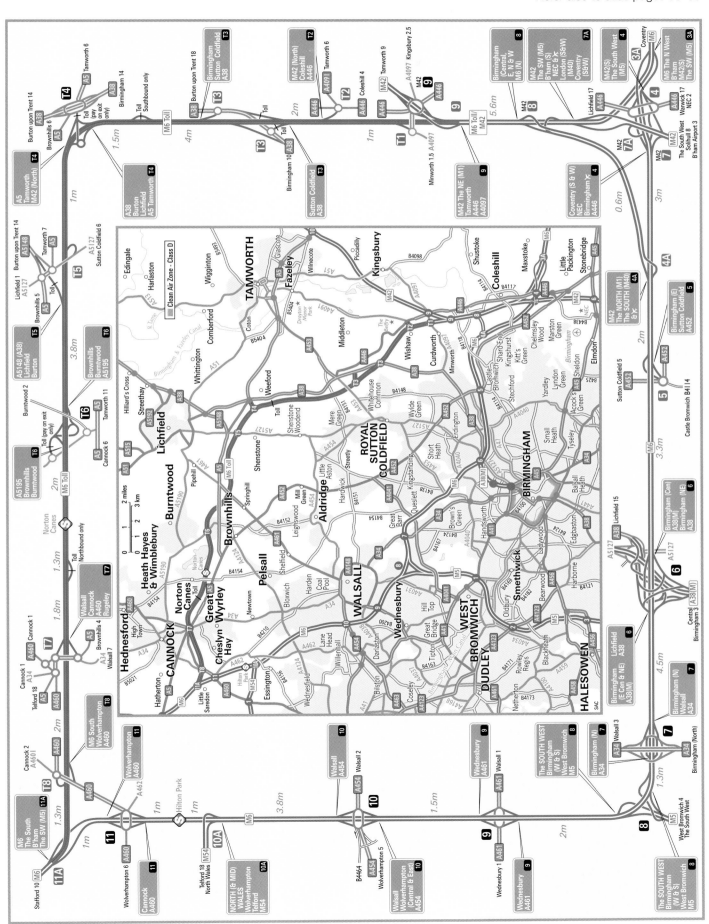

Smart motorways

Since Britain's first motorway (the Preston Bypass) opened in 1958, motorways have changed significantly. A vast increase in car journeys over the last 65 years has meant that motorways quickly filled to capacity. To combat this, the recent development of **smart motorways** uses technology to monitor and actively manage traffic flow and congestion.

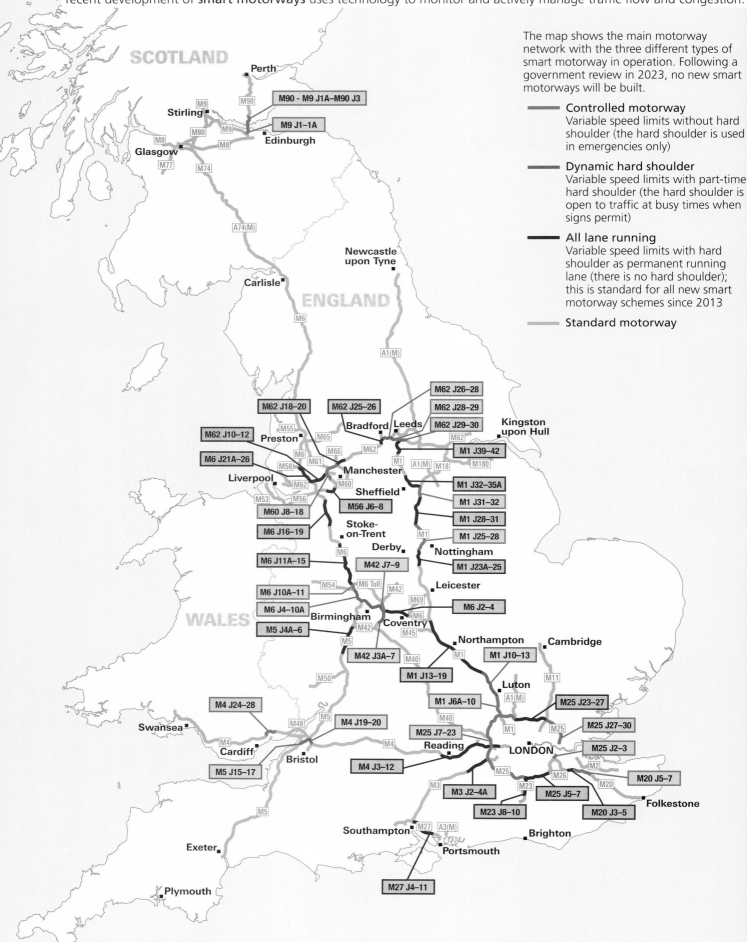

The map shows the main motorway network with the three different types of smart motorway in operation. Following a government review in 2023, no new smart motorways will be built.

Controlled motorway
Variable speed limits without hard shoulder (the hard shoulder is used in emergencies only)

Dynamic hard shoulder
Variable speed limits with part-time hard shoulder (the hard shoulder is open to traffic at busy times when signs permit)

All lane running
Variable speed limits with hard shoulder as permanent running lane (there is no hard shoulder); this is standard for all new smart motorway schemes since 2013

Standard motorway

Smart motorways (*Intelligent Transport Systems* in Scotland) are the responsibility of National Highways, Transport Scotland and Transport for Wales

How they work

Smart motorways utilise various active traffic management methods, monitored through a regional traffic control centre:

- Traffic flow is monitored using CCTV
- Speed limits are changed to smooth traffic flow and reduce stop-start driving
- Capacity of the motorway can be increased by either temporarily or permanently opening the hard shoulder to traffic

- Warning signs and messages alert drivers to hazards and traffic jams ahead
- Lanes can be closed in the case of an accident or emergency by displaying a red X sign
- Emergency refuge areas are located regularly along the motorway where there is no hard shoulder available

In an emergency

On a smart motorway there is often no hard shoulder so in an emergency you will need to make your way to the nearest **emergency refuge area** or motorway service area.

Sign indicating presence of emergency refuge areas ahead

Emergency refuge areas are lay-bys marked with blue signs featuring an orange SOS telephone symbol. The telephone connects to the regional control centre and pinpoints your location. The control centre will advise you on what to do, send help and assist you in returning to the motorway.

If you are unable to reach an emergency refuge area or hard shoulder (if there is one) move as close to the nearside (left hand) boundary or verge as you can.

This sign is located at each emergency refuge area

If it is not possible to get out of your vehicle safely, or there is no other place of relative safety to wait, stay in your vehicle with your seat-belt on and dial 999 if you have a mobile phone. If you don't have a phone, sit tight and wait to be rescued. Once the regional traffic control centre is aware of your situation, via the police or CCTV, they will use the smart motorway technology to set overhead signs and close the lane to keep traffic away from you. They will also send a traffic officer or the police to help you.

Signs

Motorway signals and messages advise of abnormal traffic conditions ahead and may indicate speed limits. They may apply to individual lanes when mounted overhead or, when located on the central reservation or at the side of the motorway, to the whole carriageway.

Where traffic is allowed to use the hard shoulder as a traffic lane, each lane will have overhead signals and signs. A red cross (with no signals) displayed above the hard shoulder indicates when it is closed. When the hard shoulder is in use as a traffic lane the red cross will change to a speed limit. Should it be necessary to close any lane, a red cross with red lamps flashing in vertical pairs will be shown above that lane. Prior to this, the signal will show an arrow directing traffic into the adjacent lane.

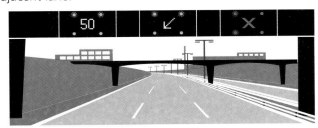

These signals are mounted above the carriageway with a signal for each traffic lane; each signal has two pairs of lamps that flash. You should obey the signal for your lane

Move to adjacent lane (arrow may point downwards to the right)

Leave motorway at next exit

Red lamps flashing from side to side in pairs, together with a red cross, mean 'do not proceed in the traffic lane directly below'. More than one lane may be closed to traffic

Where variable speed limit signs are mounted over individual lanes and the speed limit is shown in a red ring, the limit is mandatory. You will be at risk of a driving offence if you do not keep to the speed limit. Speed limits that do not include the red ring are the maximum speeds advised for the prevailing conditions.

Speed limits of 60, 50 and 40mph are used on all types of smart motorways. When no speed limit is shown the national speed limit of 70mph is in place (this is reduced to 60mph for particular vehicles such as heavy or articulated goods vehicles and vehicles towing caravans or trailers).

Quick tips

- Never drive in a lane closed by a red X
- Keep to the speed limit shown on the gantries
- A solid white line indicates the hard shoulder – do not drive in it unless directed or in the case of an emergency
- A broken white line indicates a normal running lane

- Exit the smart motorway where possible if your vehicle is in difficulty. In an emergency, move onto the hard shoulder where there is one, or the nearest emergency refuge area
- Put on your hazard lights if you break down

Orkney Islands

169
Kirkwall

Shetland Islands

169
Lerwick

Western Isles

Steòrnabhagh (Stornoway)

168

Thurso
164 165 166 167
Wick

160 161 162 163
Ullapool
Gairloch Tain

Uig
152 153 154 155 156 157 158 159
Portree Dingwall Elgin Banff
Kyle of Lochalsh Inverness Peterhead
Isle of Skye
144 145 146 147 148 149 150 151
Mallaig Aviemore Aberdeen

Fort William
136 137 138 139 140 141 142 143
Pitlochry Montrose
Isle of Mull
Oban Dundee
130 131 132 133 134 135
Crianlarich Perth
Stirling

122 123 176 177
Glasgow Edinburgh 128 129
Islay 124 125 126 127 Berwick-upon-Tweed

120 121
Campbeltown Kilmarnock Galashiels
Ayr 116 117 118 119
114 115 Alnwick
Moffat

Londonderry
Derry Dumfries Newcastle upon Tyne
Larne 108 109 110 111 112 113
Belfast Carlisle 184 185
172 173 Stranraer
106 107 Penrith Durham
Sligo 100 101 102 103 104 105
Brough Middlesbrough
Westport Cavan Newry
Kendal Thirsk Scarborough
Galway Athlone DUBLIN 94 95 96 97 98 99
Lancaster Skipton York
80
Douglas Blackpool Burnley Leeds Kingston upon Hull
Isle of Man 88 89 90 91 92 93
182 Grimsby
Limerick 78 79 Liverpool 81 183 Manchester
170 171 Holyhead Colwyn 80 82 83 Sheffield
Bay Chester 84 85 86 87
Tralee Caernarfon Newark-on-Trent Lincoln
Killarney Waterford Wrexham Stoke-on-Trent Nottingham
66 67 68 69 70 71 72 73 74 75 76 77
Cork Rosslare Dolgellau Stafford King's Lynn Norwich
Shrewsbury Leicester Peterborough Great Yarmouth
Newtown Birmingham 58 59 60 61 62 63 64 65
54 55 56 57 174 175 Bury
Aberystwyth Ludlow Coventry Northampton Cambridge St Edmunds
Cardigan Stratford-upon-Avon Ipswich
42 43 Hereford 45 46 47 48 49 52 53
Fishguard Carmarthen 44 Brecon Milton Luton Chelmsford
40 41 Worcester Keynes 50 51
Pembroke Gloucester Oxford Watford 36 37
Swansea 30 31 32 33 34 35 LONDON 38 39
28 29 Cardiff Swindon Reading 178–181 Maidstone
Bristol Bath Guildford Dover
Barnstaple 18 19 20 21 22 23 24 25 Folkestone
16 17 Yeovil Salisbury Basingstoke Brighton 26 27
Bude Taunton Lyme Southampton Newhaven Hastings
8 9 Regis 12 13 14 15
4 Exeter 10 11
5 Bodmin Weymouth Bournemouth
6 7
2 Truro Torquay
3 Plymouth

Isles of Scilly
2

Channel Islands
10–11

Motoring information

M4 — Motorway with number	S — Primary route service area	City with clean air zone, low/zero emission zone	Airport (major/minor), heliport
Toll / T4 — Toll motorway with toll station	BATH — Primary route destination	Toll — Road toll, steep gradient (arrows point downhill)	F — International freight terminal
6 — Motorway junction with and without number	A1123 — Other A road single/dual carriageway	5 — Distance in miles between symbols	H — 24-hour Accident & Emergency hospital
5 — Restricted motorway junctions	B2070 — B road single/dual carriageway	Vehicle ferry (all year, seasonal)	C — Crematorium
Fleet / Todhills — Motorway service area, rest area	Minor road more than 4 metres wide, less than 4 metres wide	Fast vehicle ferry or catamaran	P+R — Park and Ride (at least 6 days per week)
Motorway and junction under construction	Roundabout	Passenger ferry (all year, seasonal)	City, town, village or other built-up area
A3 — Primary route single/dual carriageway	Interchange/junction	Railway line, in tunnel	628 / 637 Lecht Summit — Height in metres, mountain pass
11 — Primary route junction with and without number	Narrow primary/other A/B road with passing places (Scotland)	Railway station, tram stop, level crossing	Snow gates (on main routes)
3 — Restricted primary route junctions	Road under construction, road tunnel	Preserved or tourist railway	National boundary, county or administrative boundary

Touring information   To avoid disappointment, check opening times before visiting

Scenic route	Garden	Waterfall	Motor-racing circuit
Tourist Information Centre	Arboretum	Hill-fort	Air show venue
Tourist Information Centre (seasonal)	Country park	Roman antiquity	Ski slope (natural, artificial)
Visitor or heritage centre	Showground	Prehistoric monument	National Trust site
Picnic site	Theme park	Battle site with year 1066	National Trust for Scotland site
Caravan site (AA inspected)	Farm or animal centre	Preserved or tourist railway	English Heritage site
Camping site (AA inspected)	Zoological or wildlife collection	Cave or cavern	Historic Scotland site
Caravan & camping site (AA inspected)	Bird collection	Windmill, monument or memorial	Cadw (Welsh heritage) site
Abbey, cathedral or priory	Aquarium	Beach (award winning)	Other place of interest
Ruined abbey, cathedral or priory	RSPB site	Lighthouse	Boxed symbols indicate attractions within urban area
Castle	National Nature Reserve (England, Scotland, Wales)	Golf course	World Heritage Site (UNESCO)
Historic house or building	Local nature reserve	Football stadium	National Park and National Scenic Area (Scotland)
Museum or art gallery	Wildlife Trust reserve	County cricket ground	Forest Park
Industrial interest	Forest drive	Rugby Union national stadium	Sandy beach
Aqueduct, viaduct	National trail	International athletics stadium	Heritage coast
Vineyard, brewery or distillery	Viewpoint	Horse racing, show jumping	Major shopping centre

Isles of Scilly

White Island

St Helen's
King Charles's Castle
Lower Town
ST-MARTIN'S
Cromwell's Castle
Old Grimsby
38
St Martin's Head
BRYHER 42
Old Blockhouse
Higher Town
The Town
New Grimsby
Isles of Scilly Heritage Coast
Eastern Isles
Great Ganilly
Crow Bar
North West Passage
Tresca Abbey
TRESCO
Innisidgen Tombs
Crow Sound
Samson
Bant's Carn Burial
ST MARY'S
SV
Harry's Walls
A3111
Higher & Lower Moors
Deep Point
Hugh Town
Porth Hellick Down Tomb
Garrison Walls
Isles of Scilly (St Mary's)
Old Town
Middle Town
Peninnis Head
Broad Sound
Annet
Gugh
St Mary's Sound
Penzance (Mar-Oct)
ST AGNES
Horse Point
Smith Sound

0   1   2   3 miles
0 1 2 3 4 5 kilometres

a   Western Rocks   b   c   d

St Agnes Heritage Coast
ST AGNES HEA
Wheal Coat
Go

SW

Porthtow

Portreath
B3300
Illogan
Tehidy
Park Bottom
Paynter's Lane End
South Tehidy
Coombe
B3301
Reskadinnick
Treswithian
C
Tuckingmill
Pool
Carn Brea
Camborne
A304
Penponds
B3303
Godrevy-Portreath Heritage Coast
Navax Point
Godrevy Island
Godrevy Point
Gwealavellan
Gwithian
Kehelland
Roseworthy
Connor Downs
Angarrack
Barripper
Troon
Bolenowe
Carnhell Green
Rosewarne
Praze-an-Beeble
Croft Mitchell
Blackrock
Burras
Farm Common
Porke
Lezerea

Carn Naun Point
The Island or St Ives Head
St Ives Bay
Porthmeor
Hellesveor
St Ives
Treveal
The Towans
Carbis Bay
Phillack
Hayle
Copperhouse
High Lanes
St Gwinear
Reawla
Zennor Head
Trendrine
Halsetown
Gurnards Head
Zennor
B3306
Lelant
Brunnion
P·R
St Erth Praze
Townshend
Kerthen Wood
Fraddam
St Erth
Leedstown
Horsedown
Crowan
B3280
Nancegollan
Trenear
Treen
Towednack
Georgia
Whitecross
Castle Gate
A30
Cockwells
Godolphin House
Godolphin Cross
Trenwheal
Releath
Porthmeor
Cripplesease
Nancledra
Canonstown
Crowlas
B3302
Ludgvan
Relubbus
St Hilary
Tregonning & Gwinear Mining District
Trescowe
Crowntown
Wendron
Prospidnick
Pendeen Watch
Pendeen
Carn Galver Mine
Mulfra Quoit
Chysauster Ancient Village
Bakers Pit
New Mill
Badger's Cross
Tremenheere
Penwith Heritage Coast
Morvah
Men-An-Tol
Boskednan
Mulfra
Madron
Trevarrack
Gulval
Marazion
Goldsithney
Balwest
Germoe
Carleen
Helston Heritage Railway
Coverack Bridges
Lower Boscaswell
Bojewyan
Great Bosullow
Lanyon Quoit
Boswarthan
Longrock
Millpool
Newtown
Ashton
Trew
Sithney
Levant Mine & Beam Engine
Geevor Tin Mine
Trengwainton Garden
Heamoor Poltsoon
Chyandour
St Michael's Mount
Rosudgeon
Kenneggy
Breage
Sithney Green
Country Life M
Helston
Trewavas Mining District
Trewellard
Pendeen
Carnyorth
St Just Mining District
A3071
Newbridge
Tremethick Cross
A30
Penlee House
Penzance
Perranuthnoe
Prussia Cove
Praa Sands
Rinsey
Rinsey Head
Trewavas Head
A394
Sithney Common
Mellangoose
Botallack
St Just
Tregeseal
7
Sellan
Chyandour
St Michael's Mount
Newlyn
Cudden Point
Rinsey Croft
Trewavas
Flambards
A3083
Cape Cornwall
Ballowall Barrow
Bosavern
Grumbla
Carn Euny Ancient Village
Brane
Sancreed
Drift
Tredavoe
Kerris
Paul
Mousehole
MOUNT'S BAY
Penrose
Porthleven
Kelynack
Nanquidno
Catchall
Sheffield
Raginnis
Higher Pentire
Whitesand Bay
Land's End
A30
Crows-an-Wra
St Buryan
Trevorgans
Castallack
Lamorna
Chyvarloe
Gunwalloe
Berepper
Gar
Sennen Cove
Escalls
Sennen
Bottoms
The Merry Maidens
Boskenna
Lamorna Cove
Chyanvounder
White Cross
LAND'S END
Land's End
Trethewey
Treen
B3315
Merthen Point
Isles of Scilly (Mar-Oct)
Cury
Trevescan
B3315
Polgigga
Boskenna
B3283
Angrouse
Poldhu Point
Marconi Memorial
Trev
B3296
Porthcurno
Roskestal
PK Porthcurno
Minack Open Air Theatre
Cribba Head
Mullion Cove
Mullion Island
Mullion
Porthgwarra
Gwennap Head
St Levan
Predannack Head
Predannack Wollas
Mount Hermo
South West Coast Path
Vellan Head
The Lizard Heritage Coast
The Lizard
Lizard Head
Kynance Cove
Liza
LIZARD POINT

0   1   2   3   4   5 miles
0 1 2 3 4 5 6 7 8 kilometres

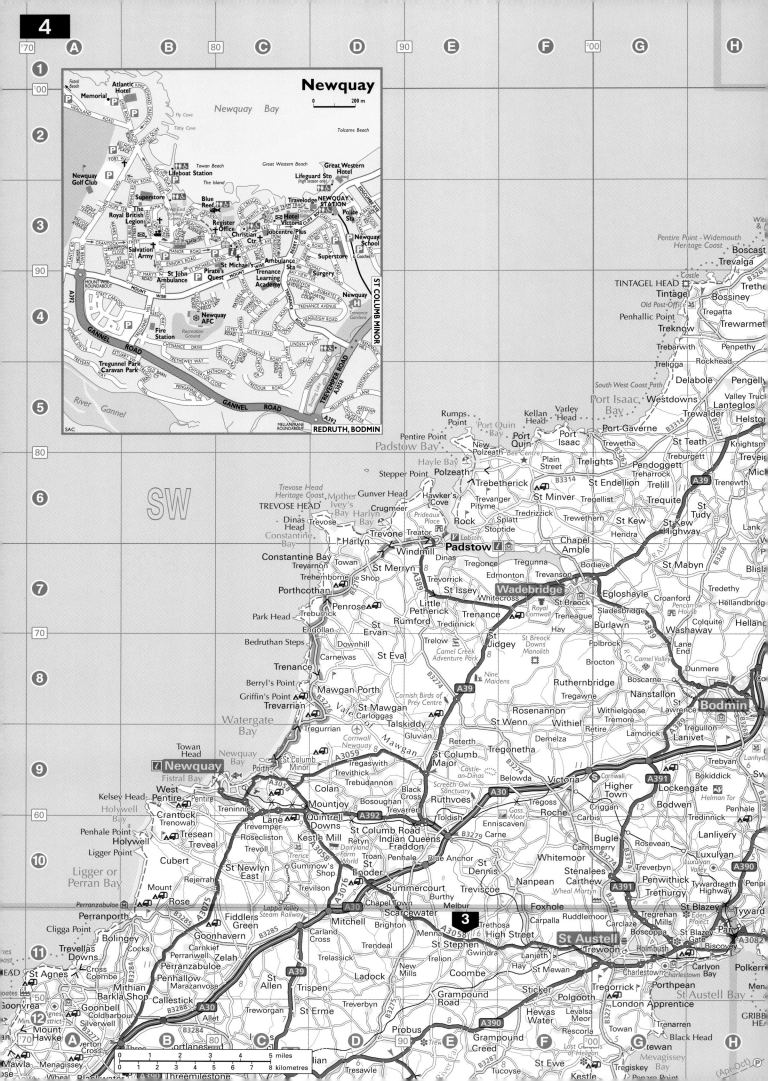

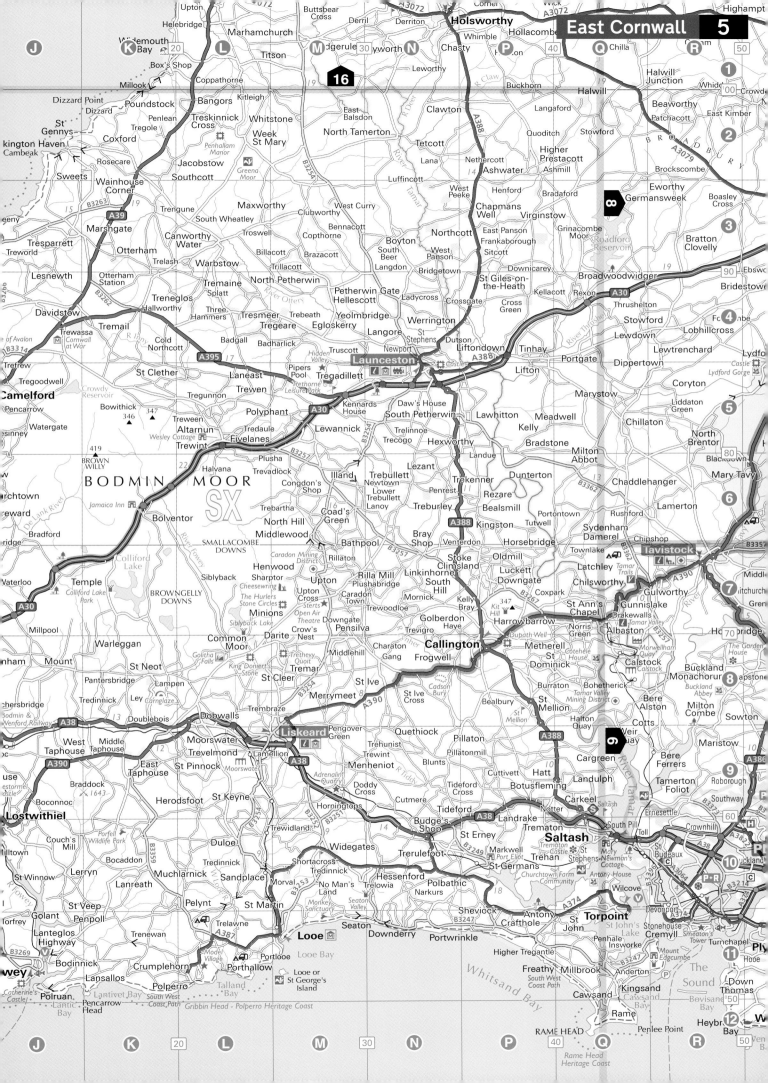

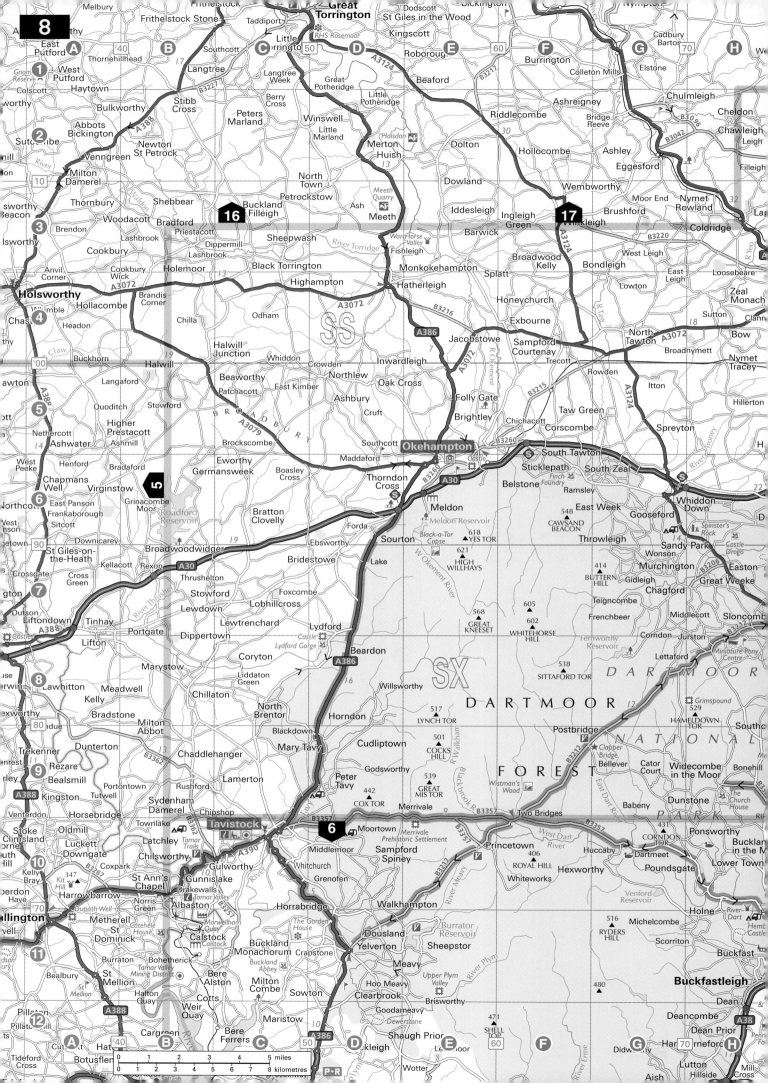

Jersey

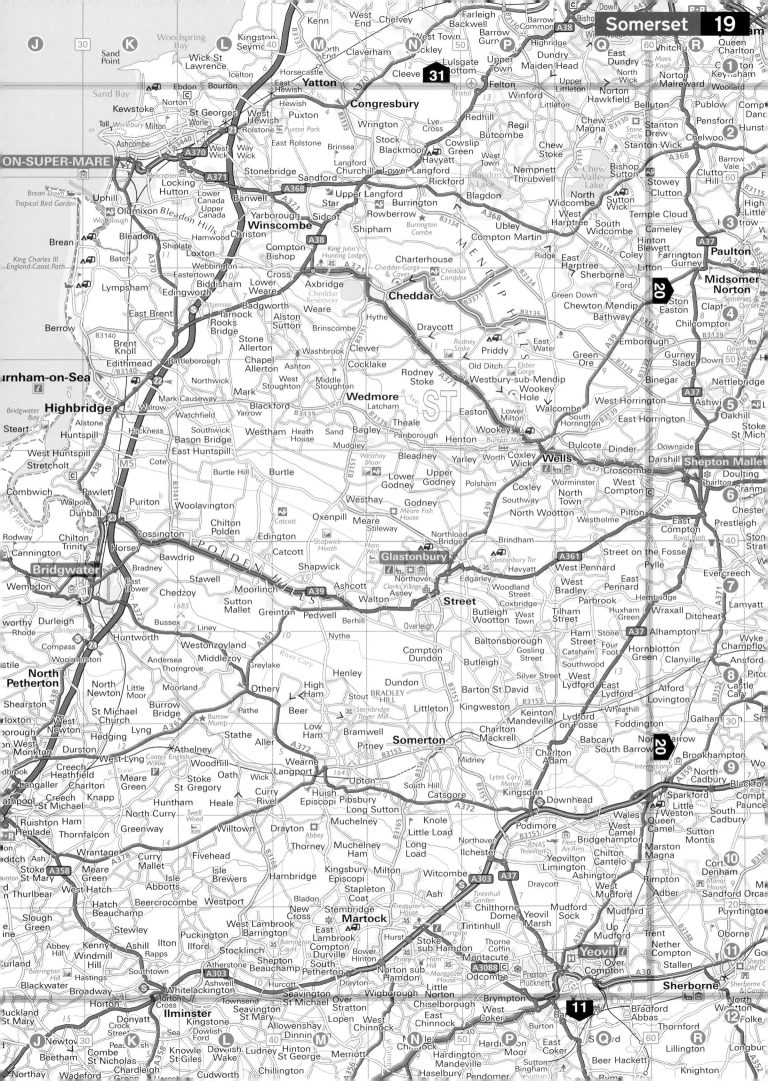

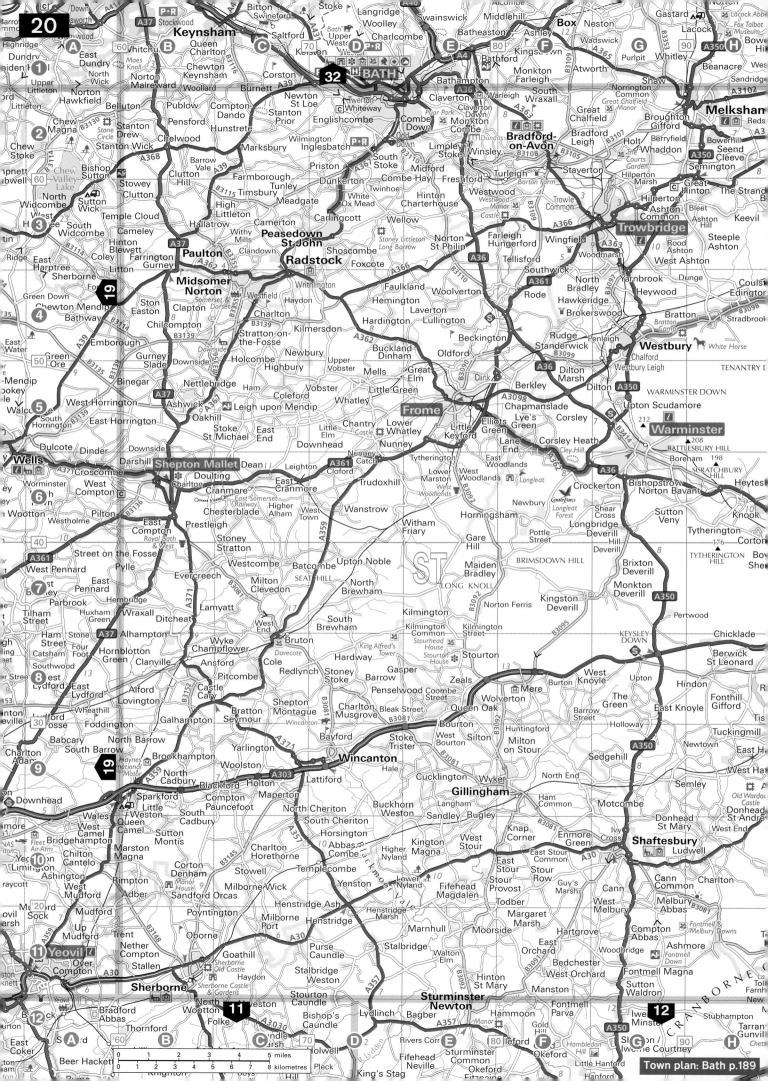

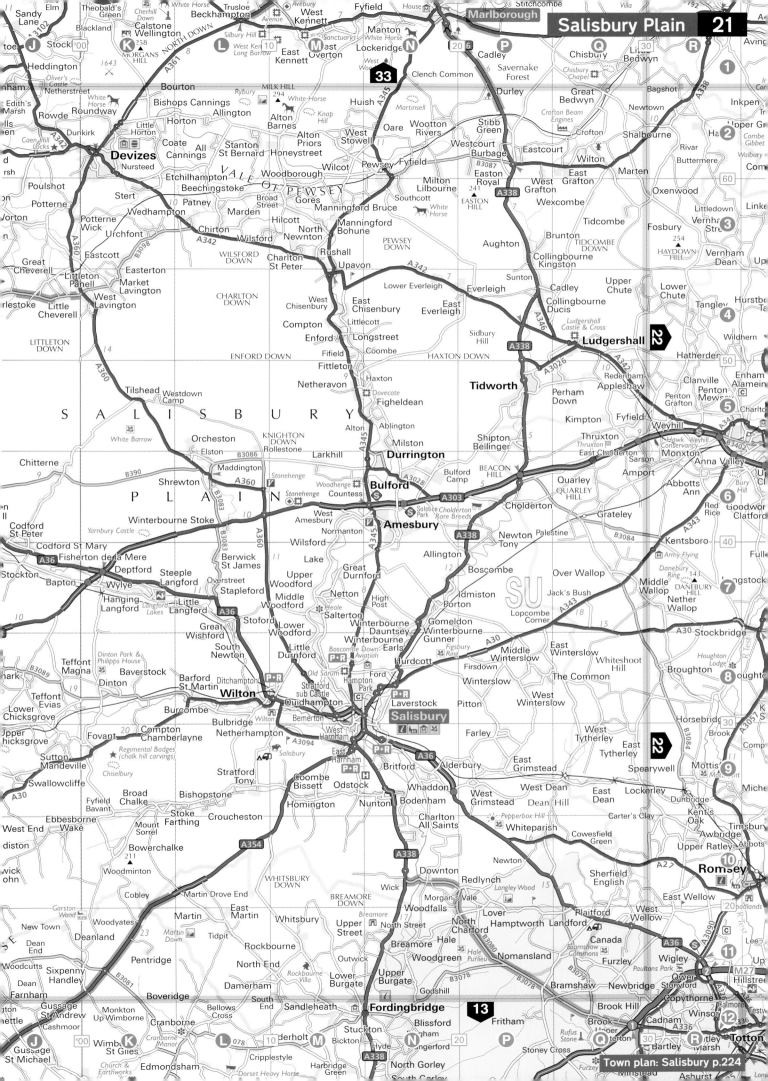

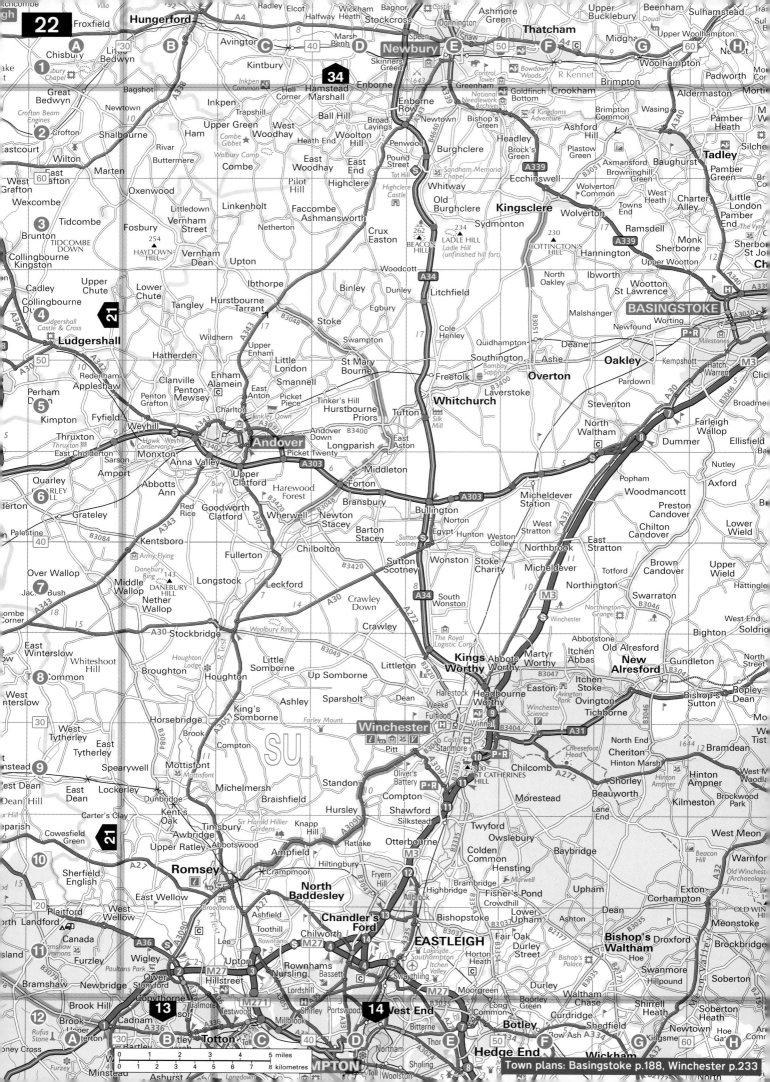

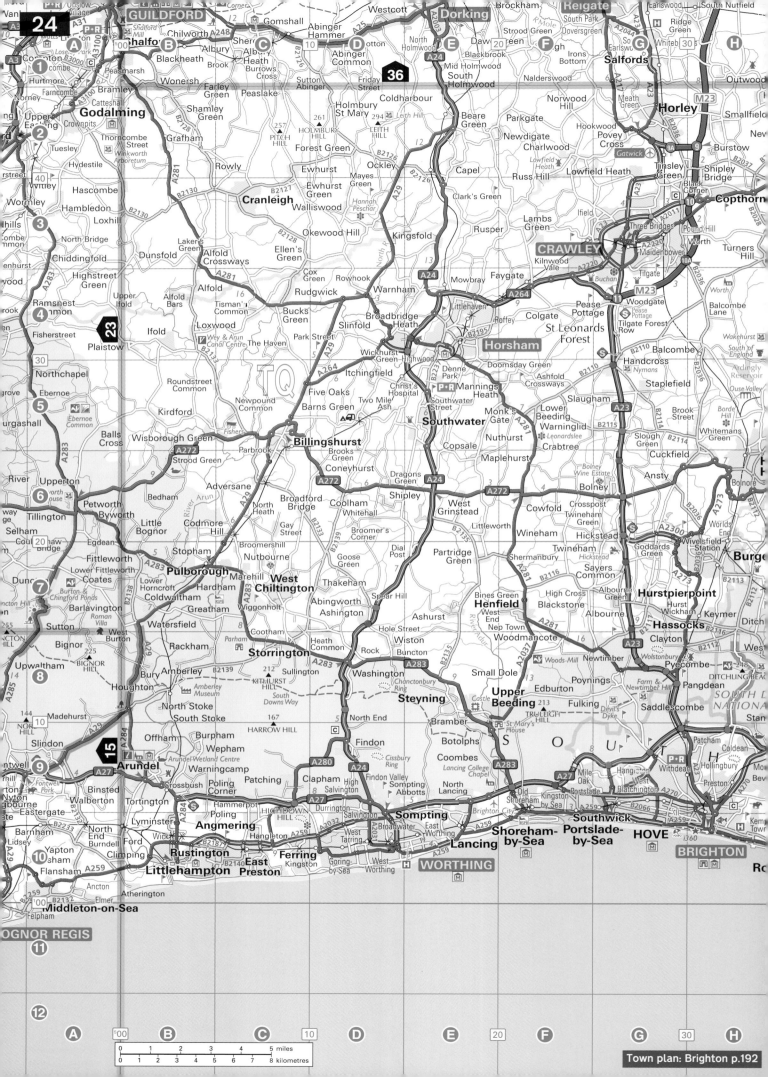

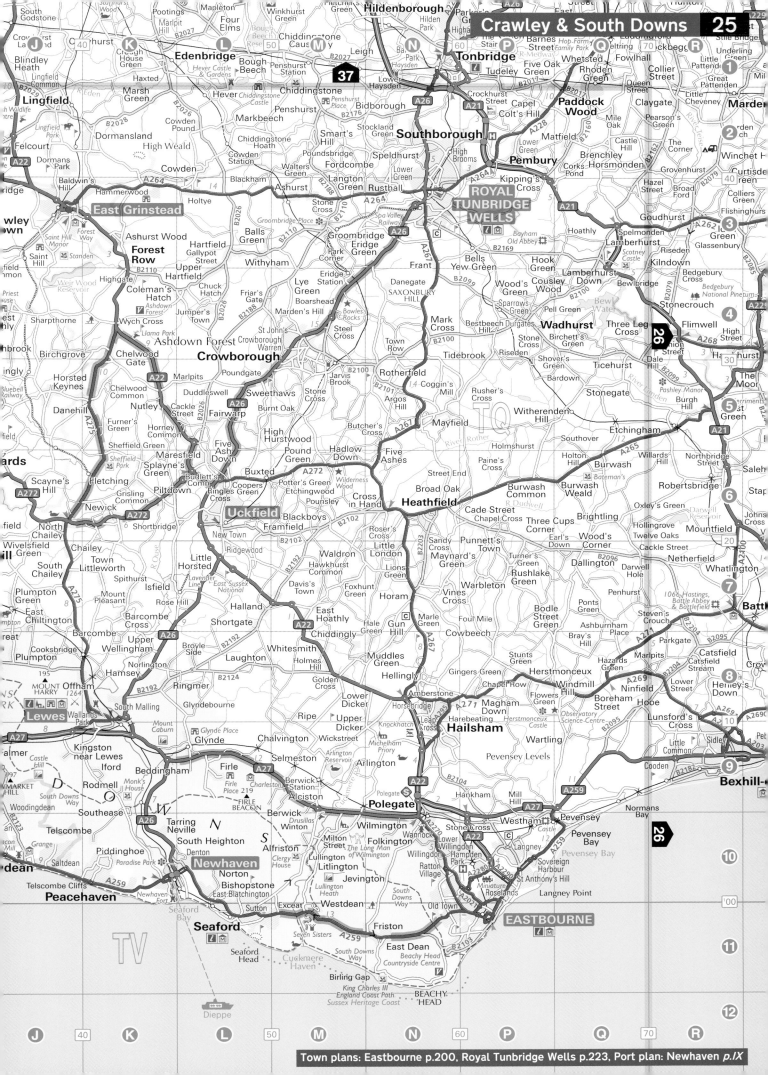

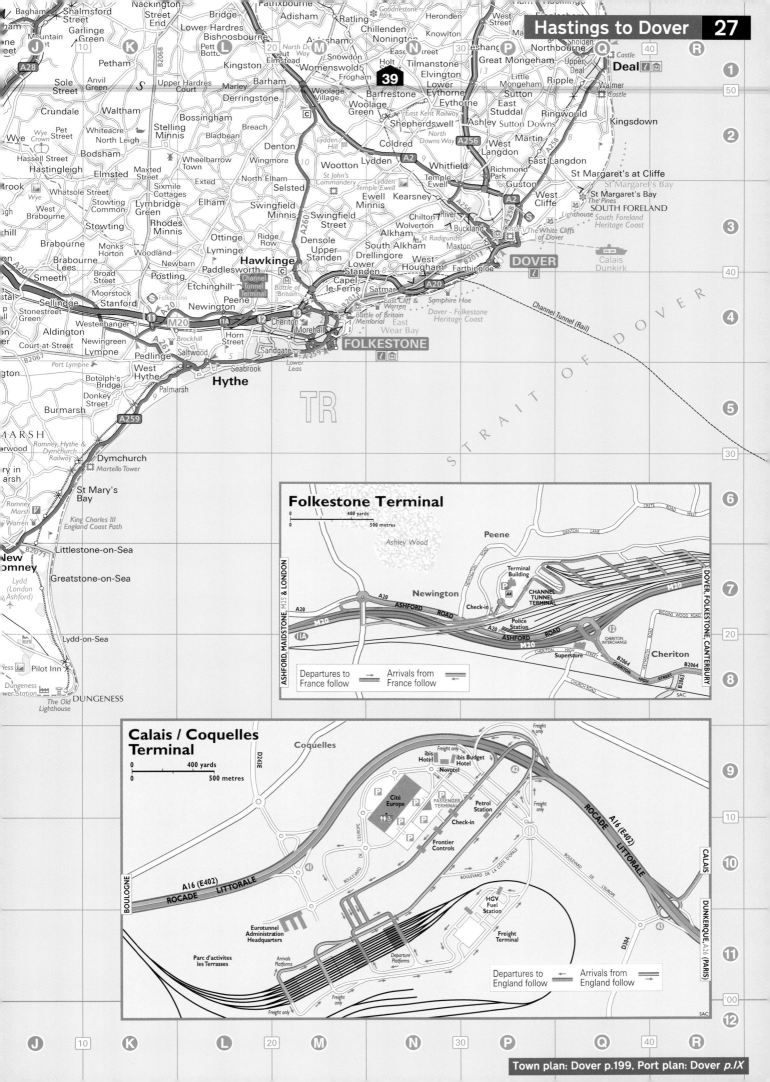

Folkestone Terminal

Departures to France follow →
Arrivals from France follow ←

Calais / Coquelles Terminal

Departures to England follow ←
Arrivals from England follow →

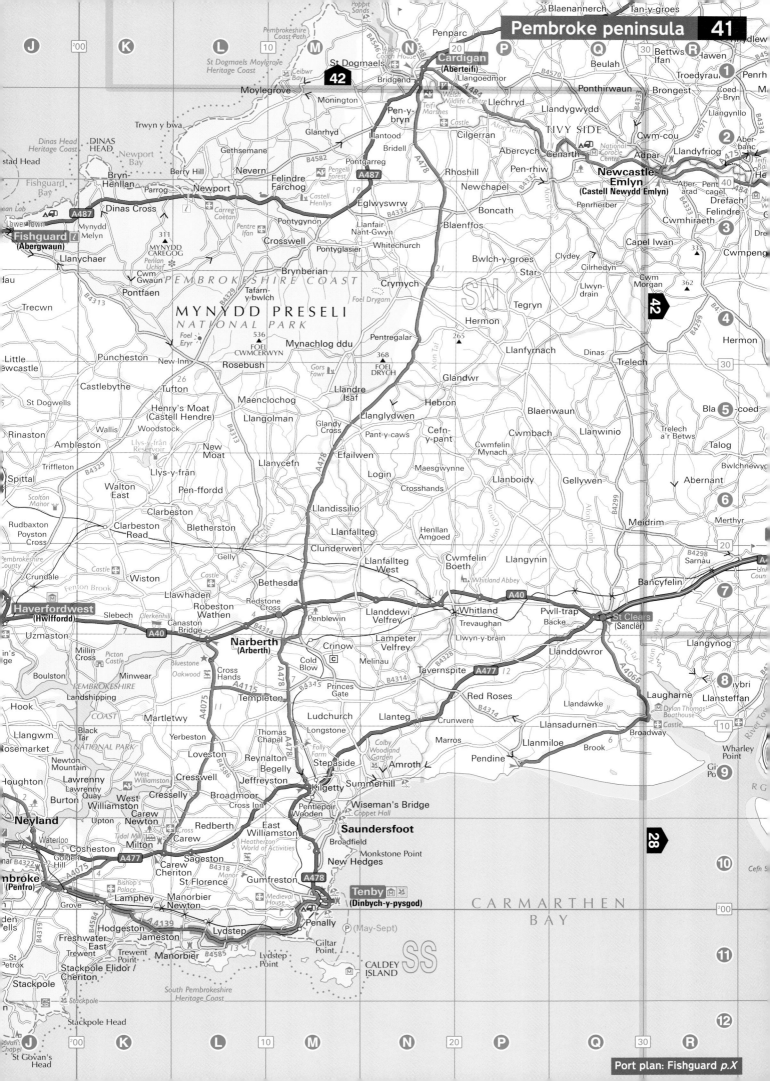

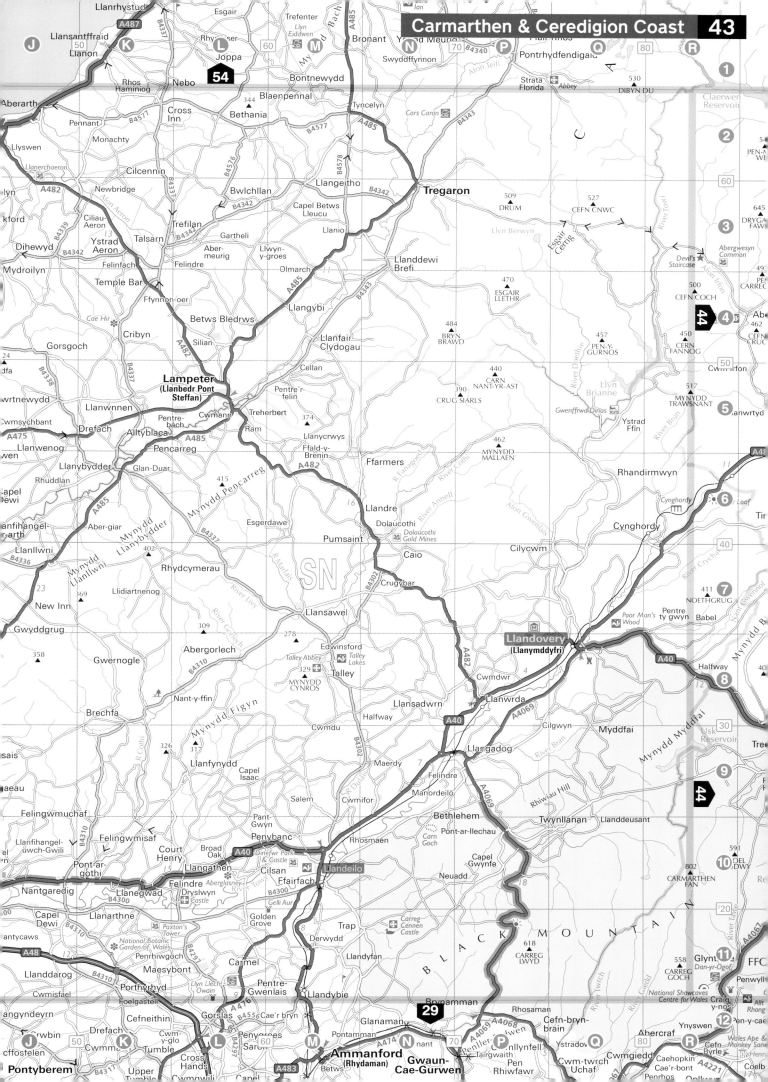

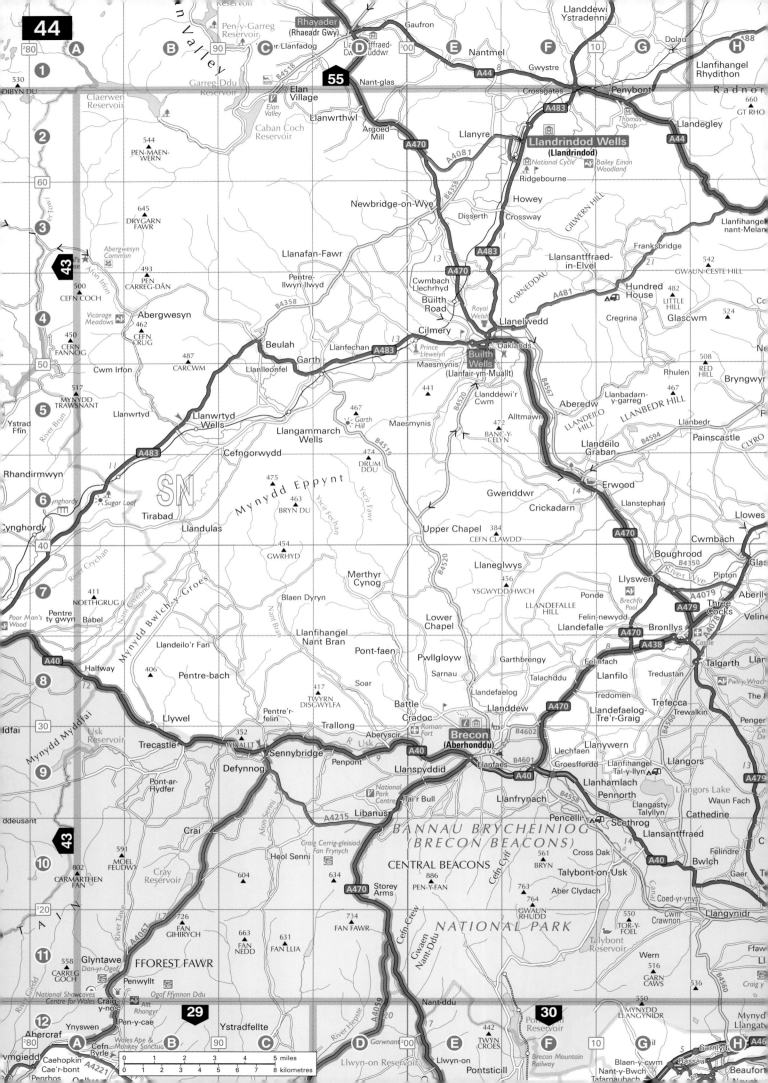

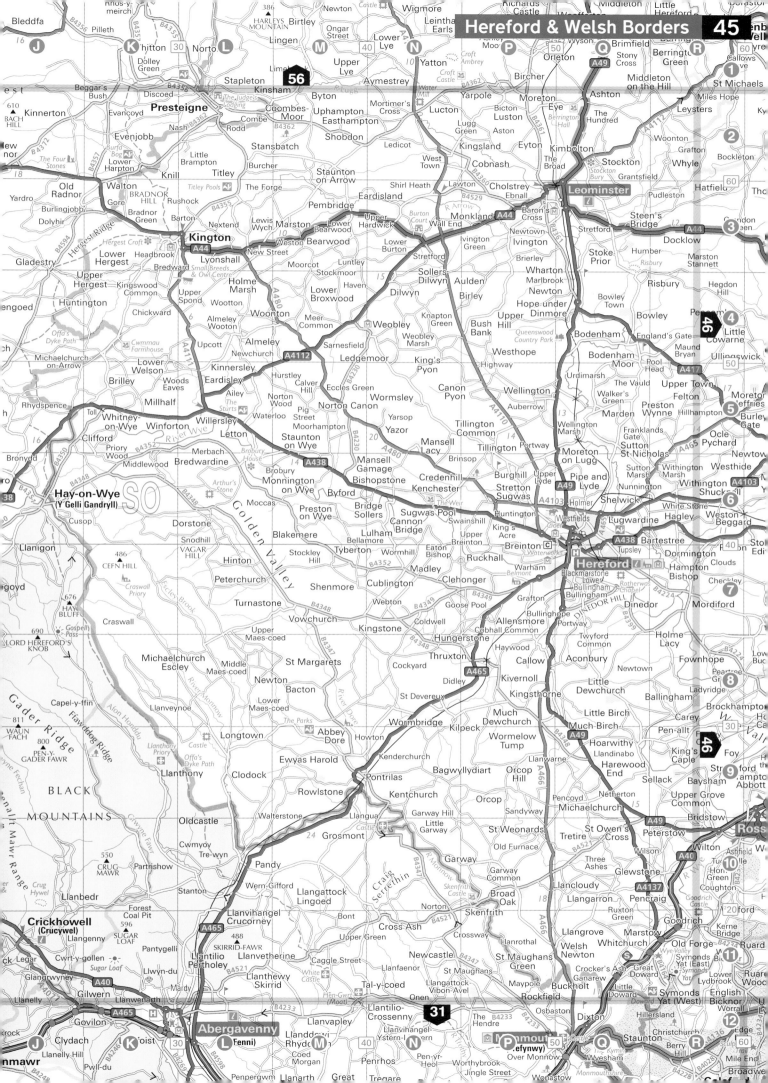

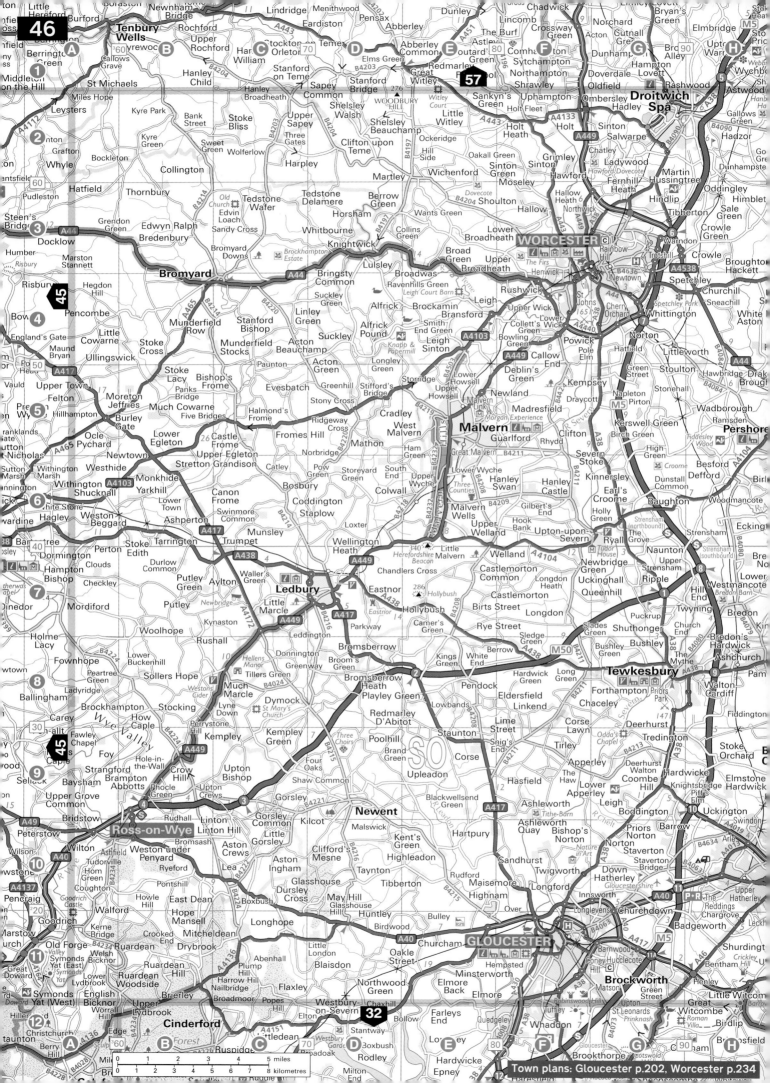

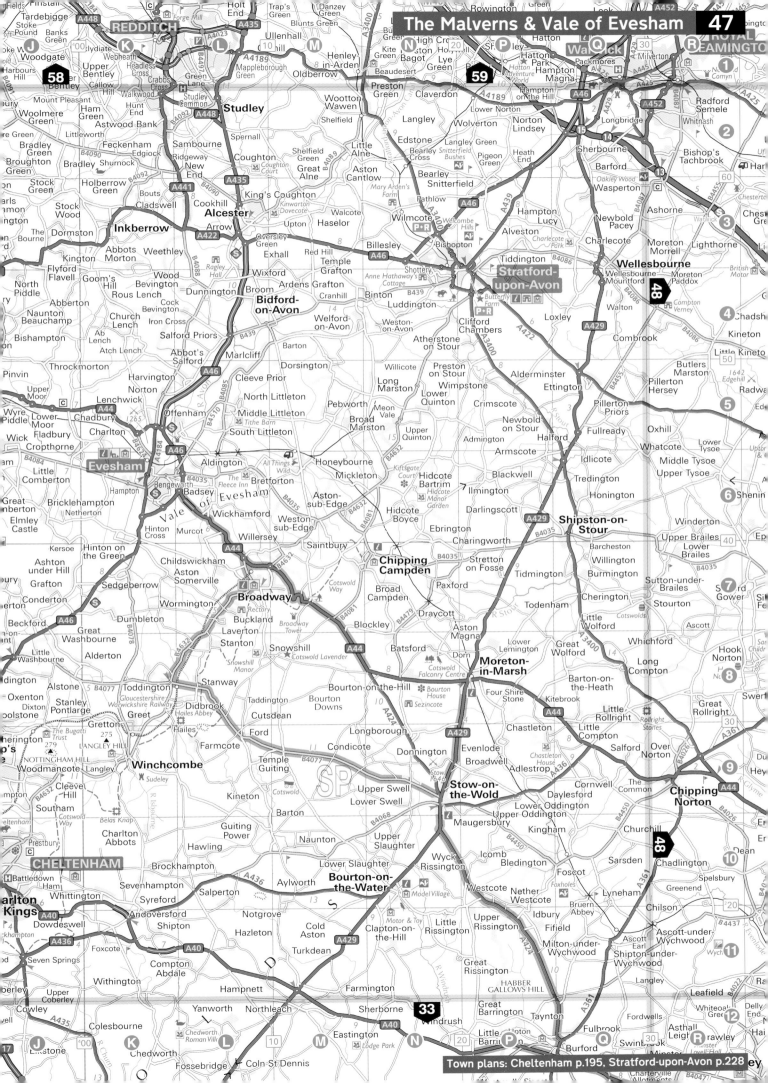

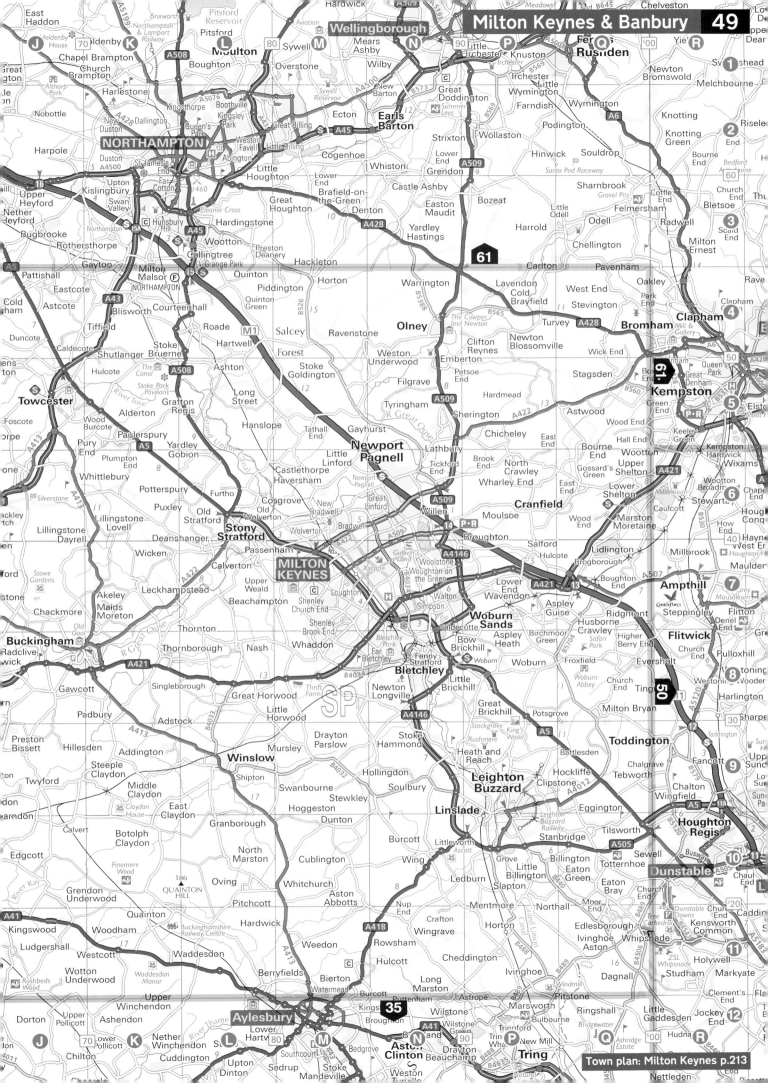

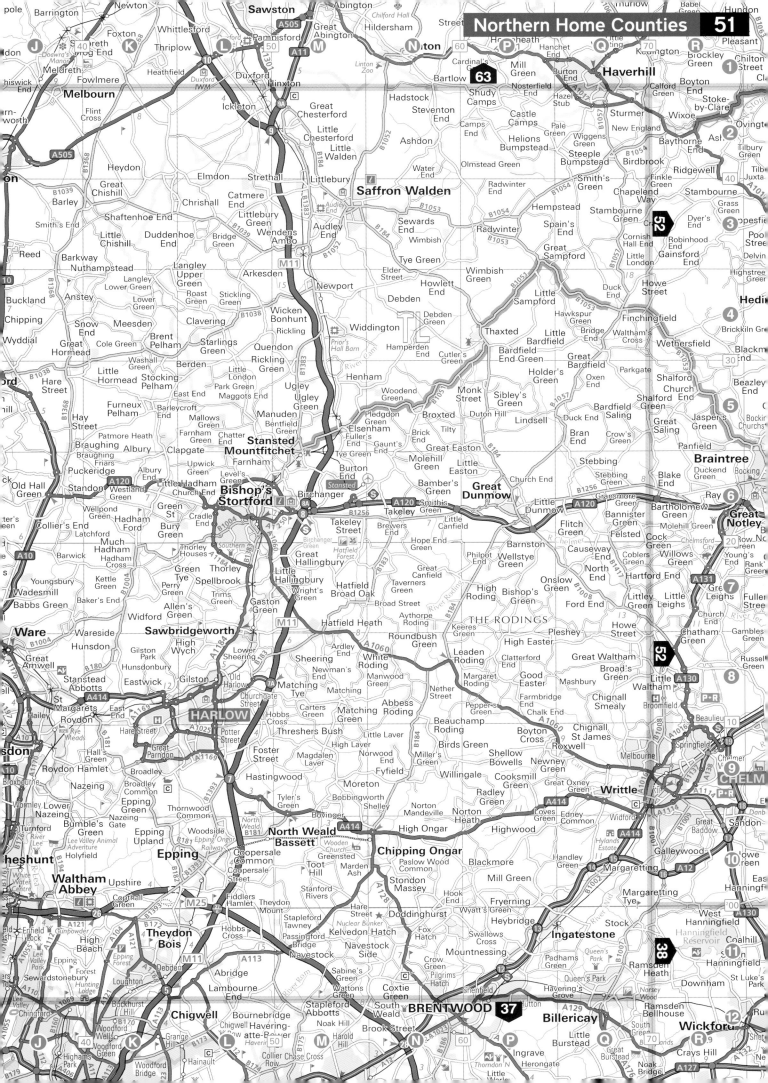

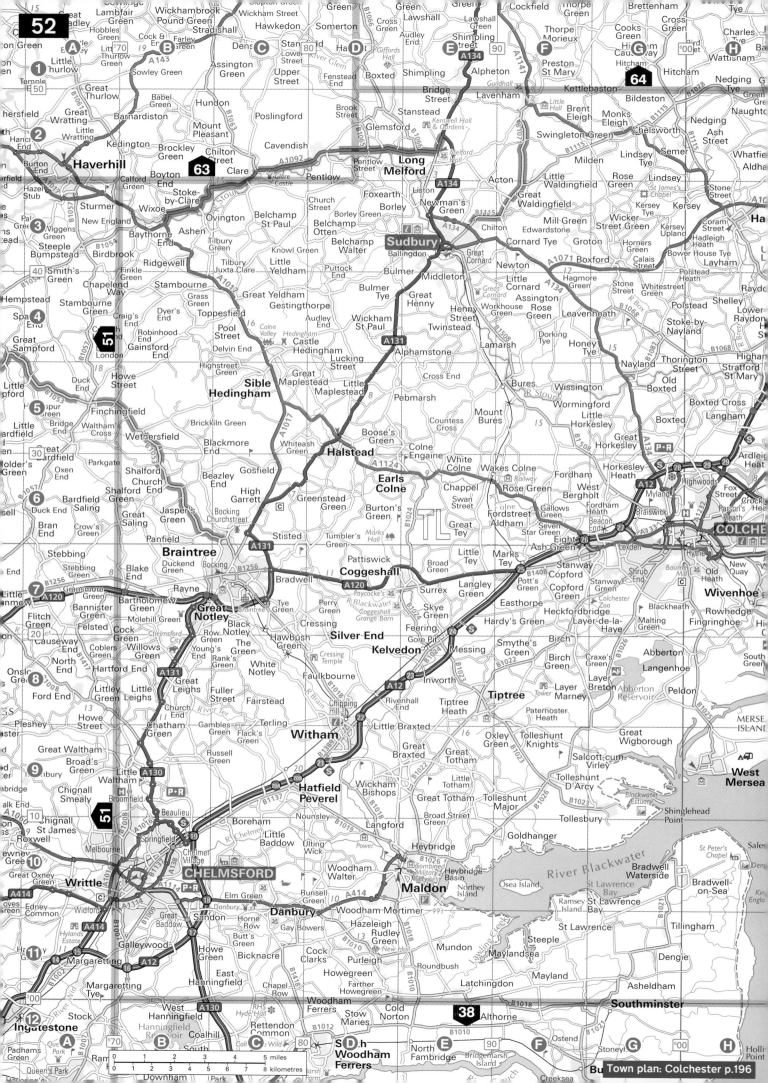

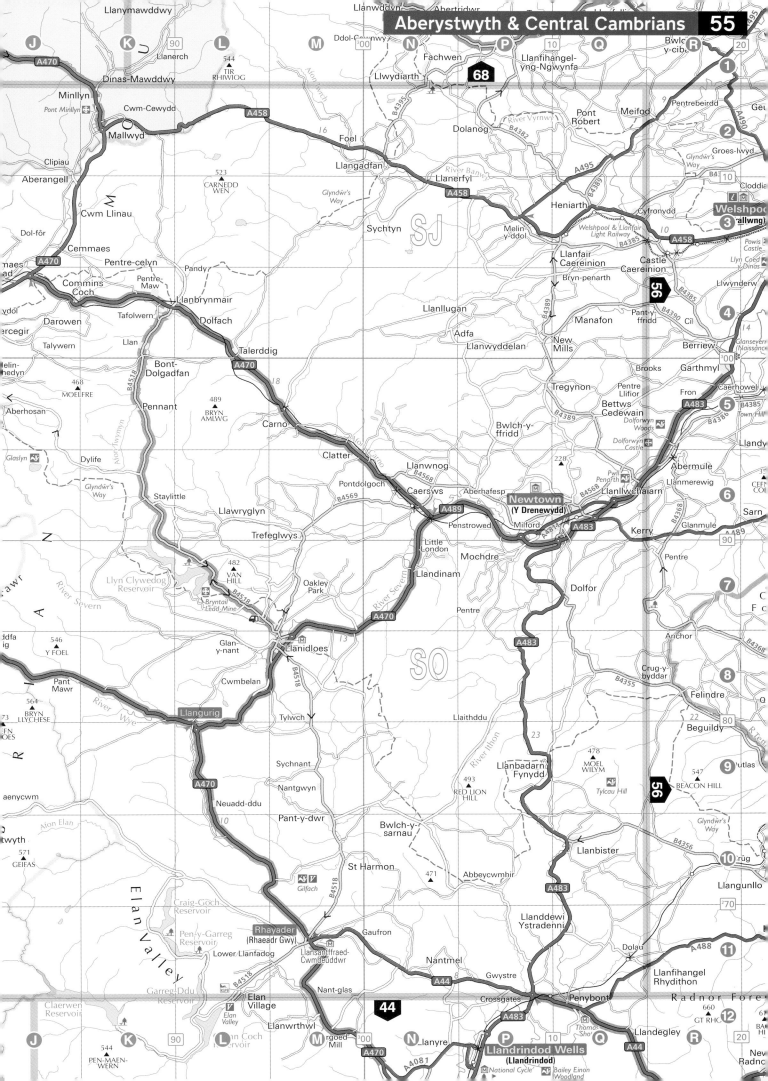

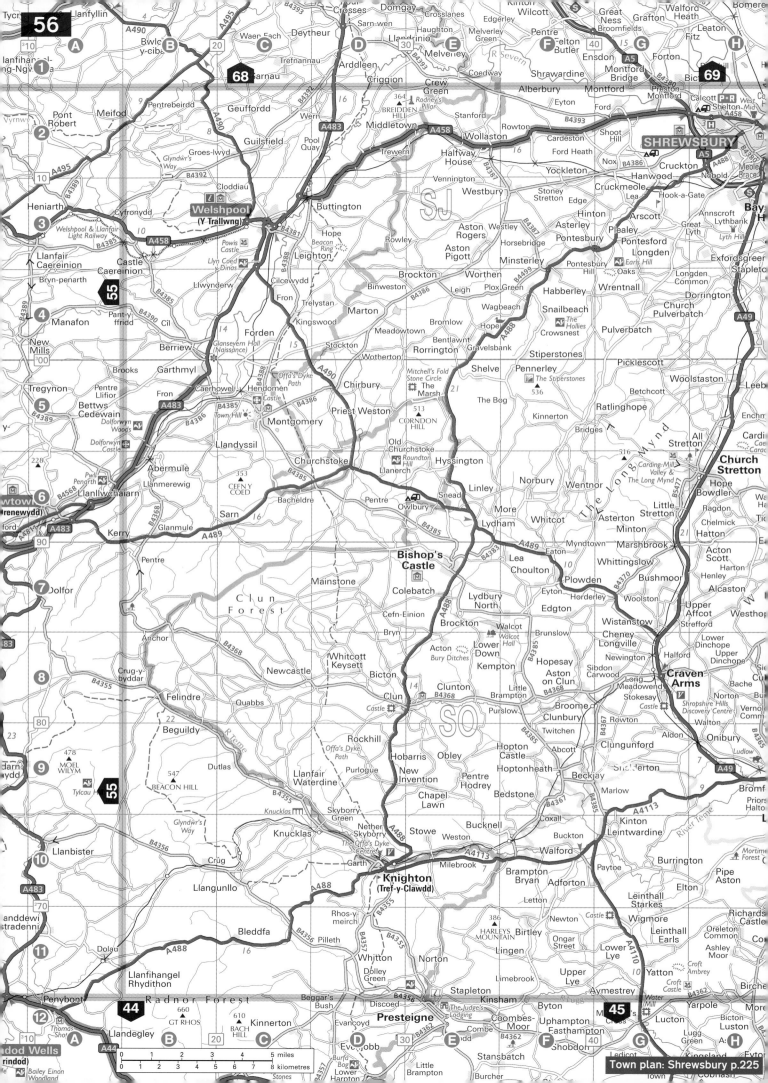

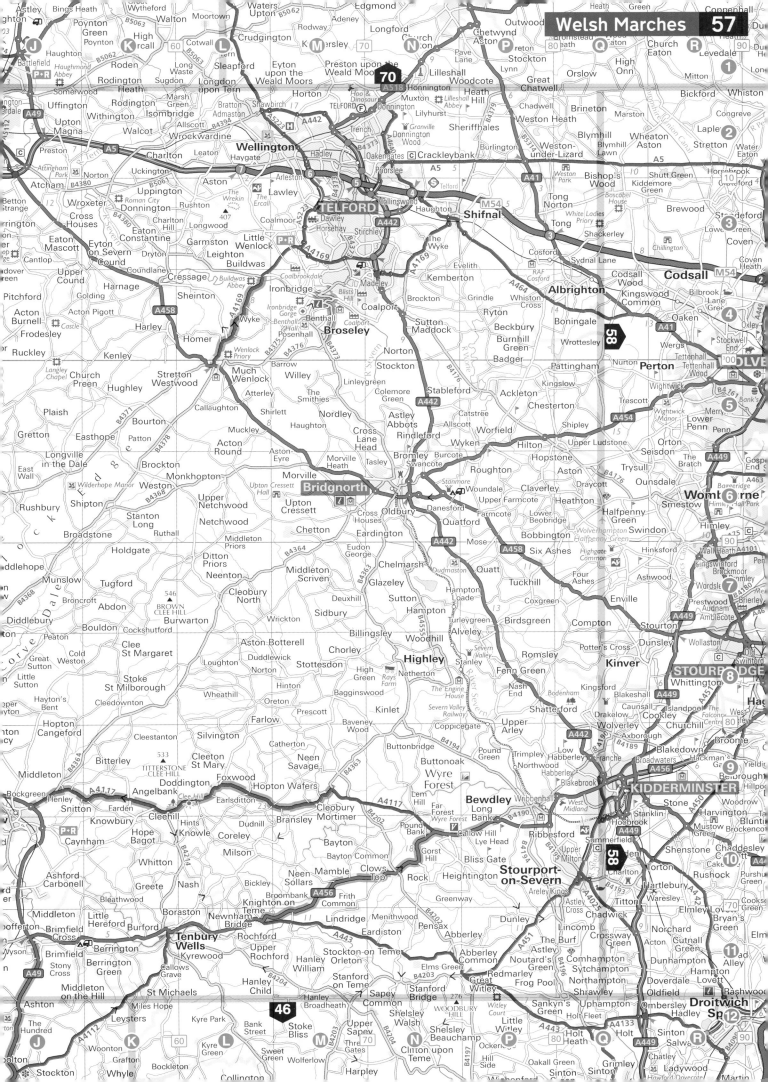

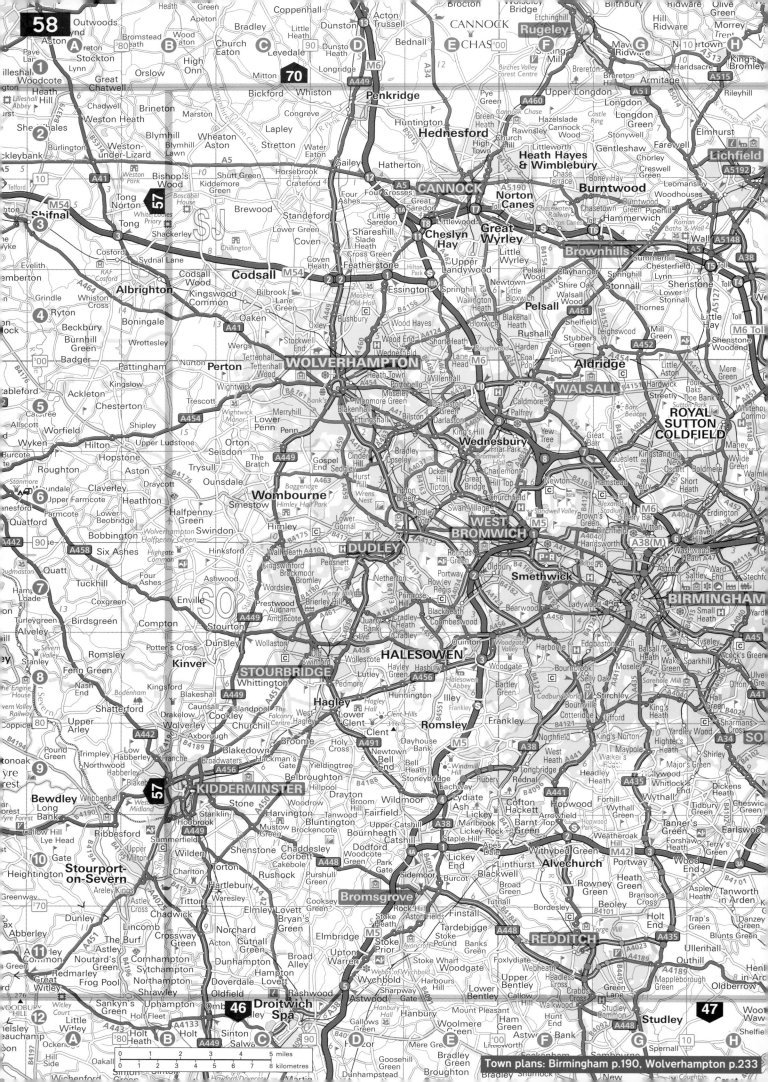

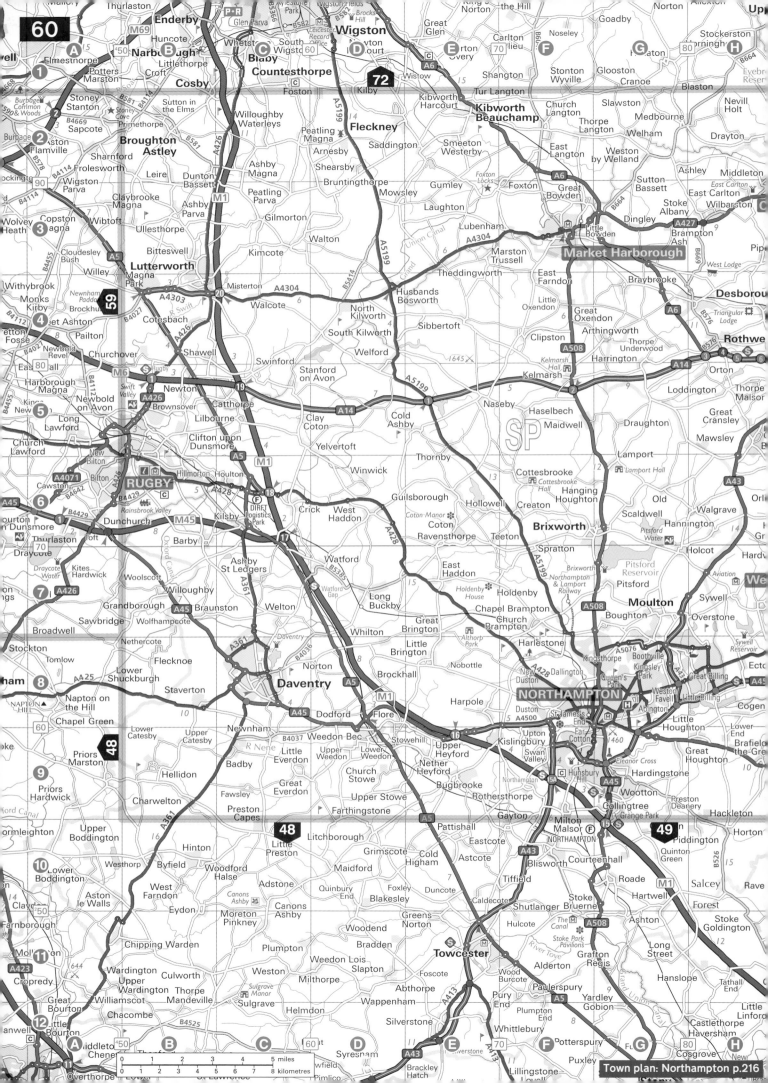

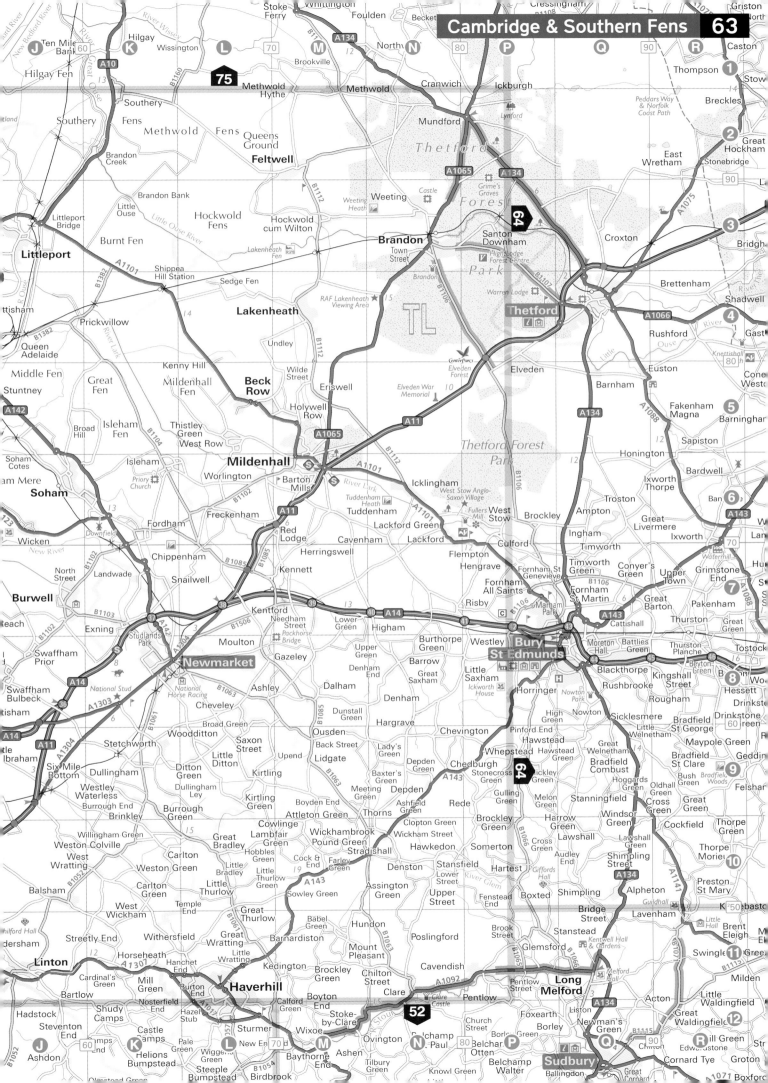

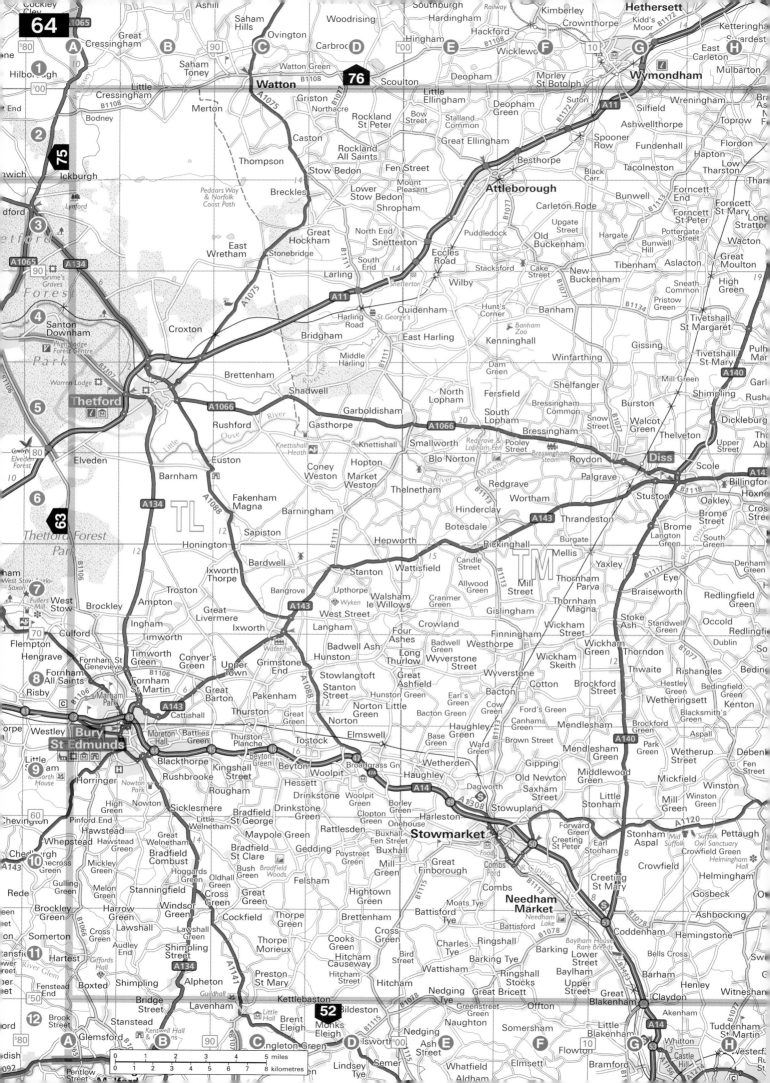

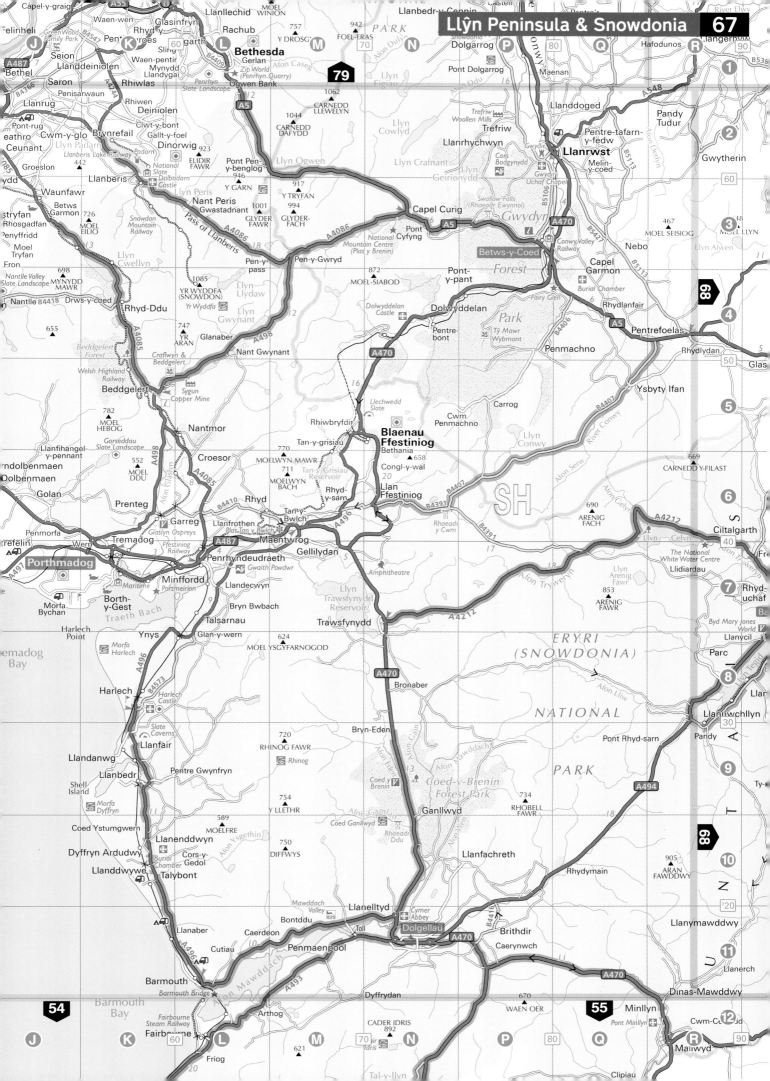

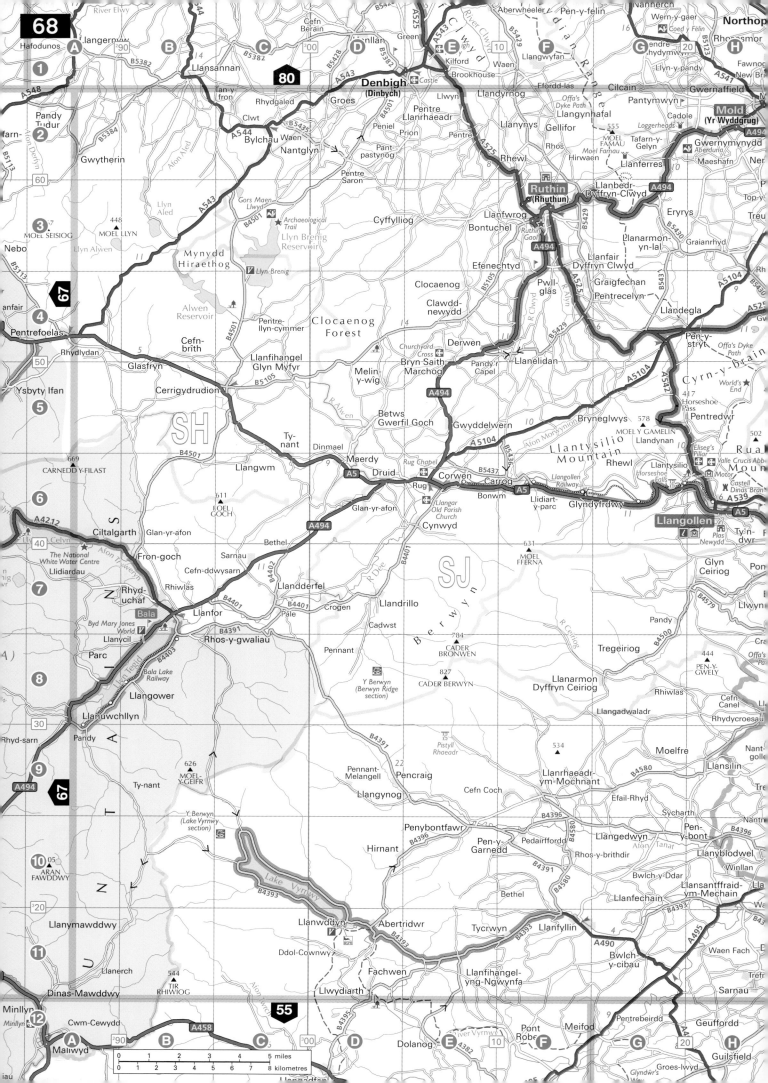

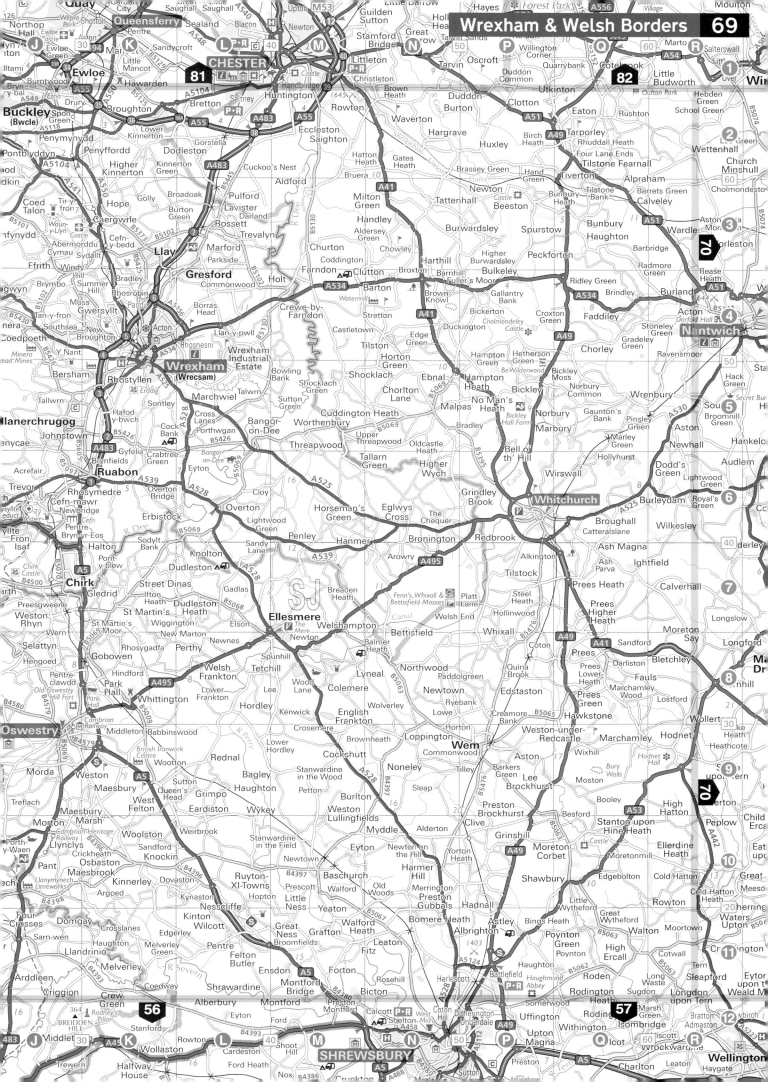

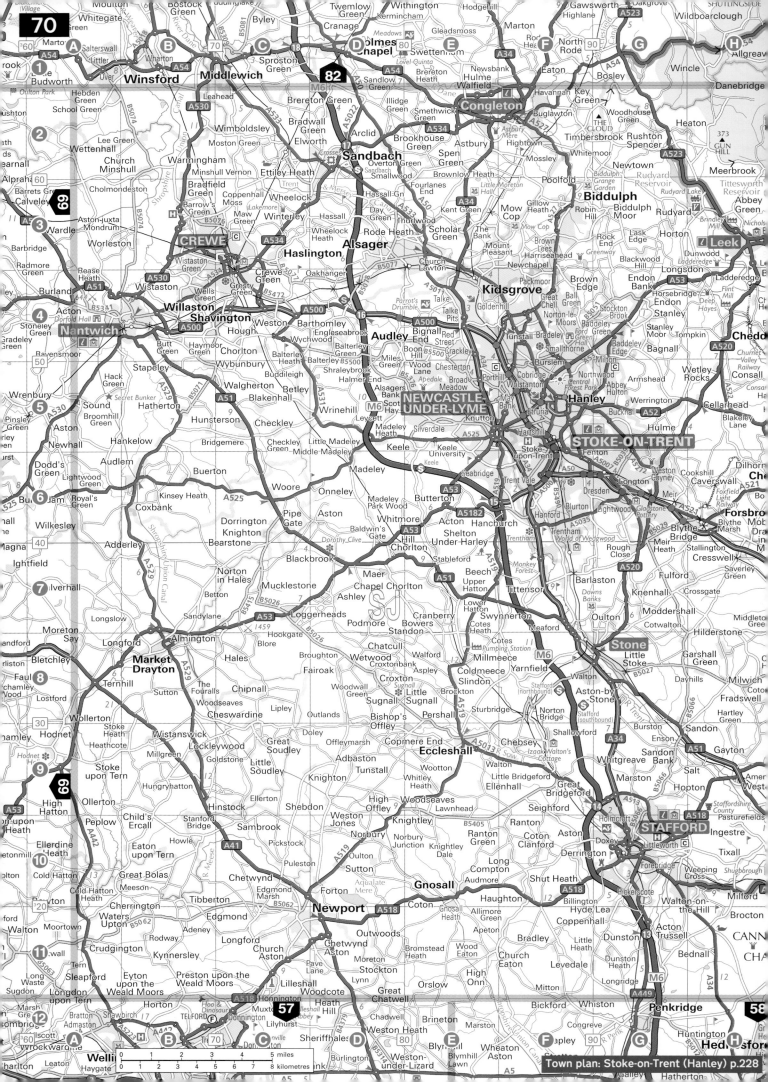

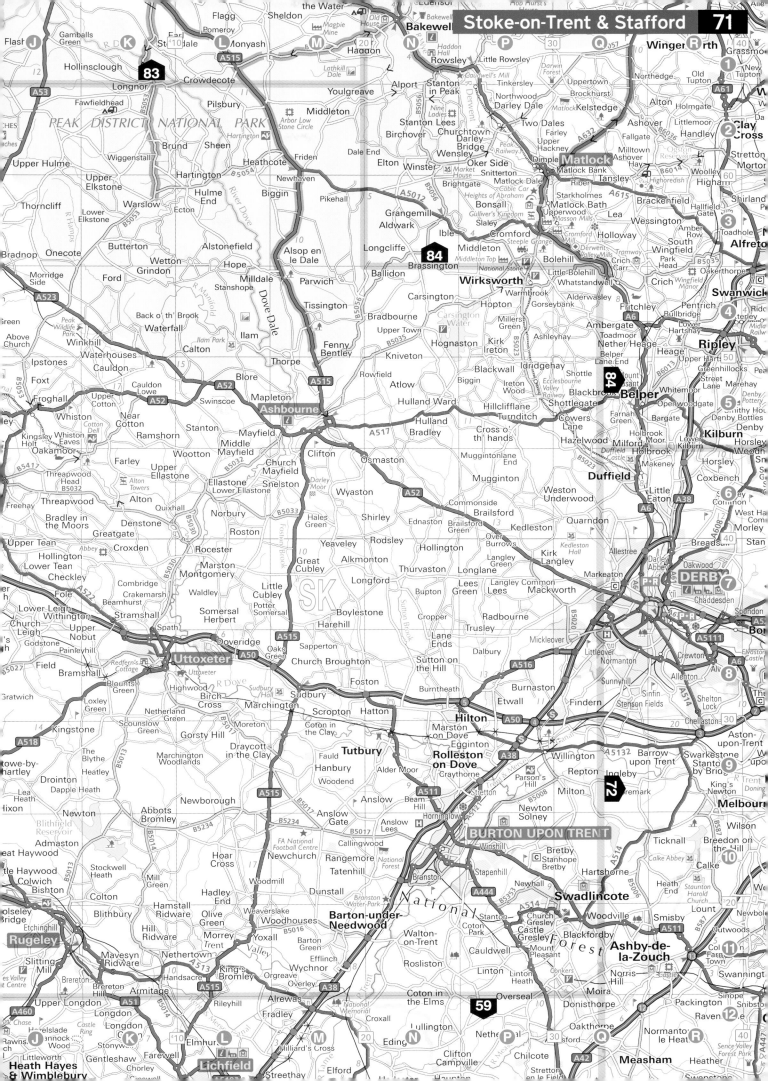

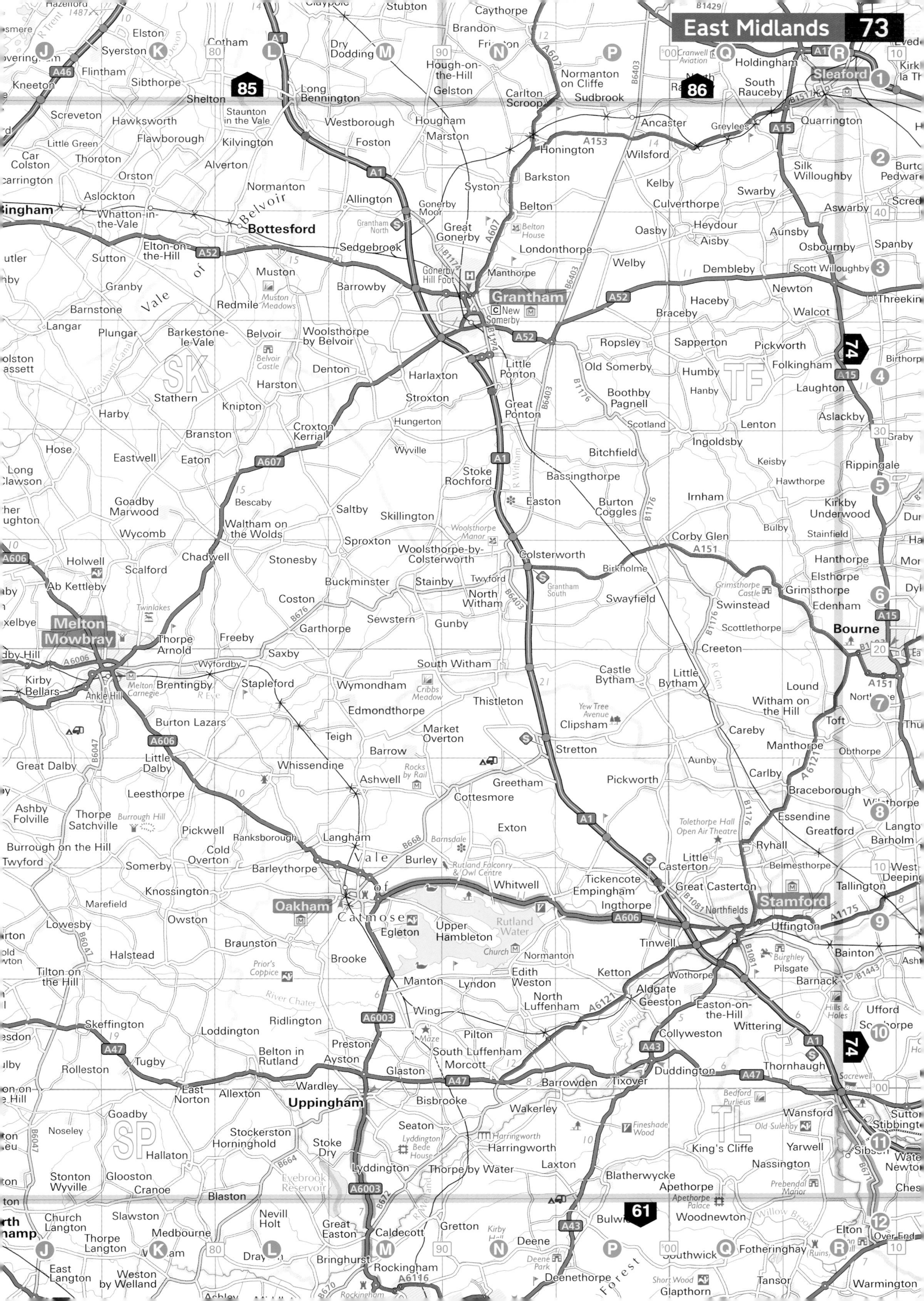

85   86   74

Sleaford 1

Holdingham
Cranwell Aviation
Quarrington
Greylees
Ancaster
South Rauceby
Normanton on Cliffe
Carlton Scroop
Sudbrook
Honington
Wilsford
Swarby 2
Silk Willoughby
Aswarby
Kelby
Culverthorpe
Oasby
Heydour
Aisby
Aunsby
Osbournby
Spanby
Scott Willoughby 3
Dembleby
Newton
Welby
Haceby
Braceby
Threekin
Ropsley
Sapperton
Pickworth
Folkingham 74
Old Somerby
Humby
Hanby
Laughton 4
Boothby Pagnell
Scotland
Ingoldsby
Keisby
Aslackby
Bitchfield
Irnham
Hawthorpe
Rippingale 5
Bassingthorpe
Burton Coggles
Bulby
Stainfield
Kirkby Underwood
Corby Glen
Hanthorpe
Elsthorpe
Grimsthorpe Castle
Grimsthorpe
Edenham 6
Birkholme
Swinstead
Swayfield
Scottlethorpe
Bourne
Creeton
Castle Bytham
Little Bytham
Lound
Witham on the Hill
Northorpe 7
Toft
Manthorpe
Careby
Obthorpe
Braceborough 8
Aunby
Carlby
Essendine
Greatford
Langto
Barholm
Toletethorpe Hall Open Air Theatre
Ryhall
West Deeping 10
Pickworth
Little Casterton
Belmesthorpe
Great Casterton
Northfields
Stamford
Tallington 8
Uffington
Tinwell
Bainton 9
Burghley House
Pilsgate
Wothorpe
Barnack
Aldgate Geeston
Easton-on-the-Hill
Ufford
Scothorpe 10
Collyweston
Wittering
Duddington
Thornhaugh
Sacrewell
Wansford
Yarwell
Nassington
Stibbingt
Sutto
Water Newto
King's Cliffe
Blatherwycke
Apethorpe
Apethorpe Palace
Woodnewton
Elton 12
Over End
Prebendal Manor
Deene
Deene Park
Southwick
Fotheringhay
Tansor
Warmington
Glapthorn

Sleaford, Grantham, Bottesford, Melton Mowbray, Oakham, Stamford, Bourne, Uppingham areas

(Map of East Midlands – place names and roads)

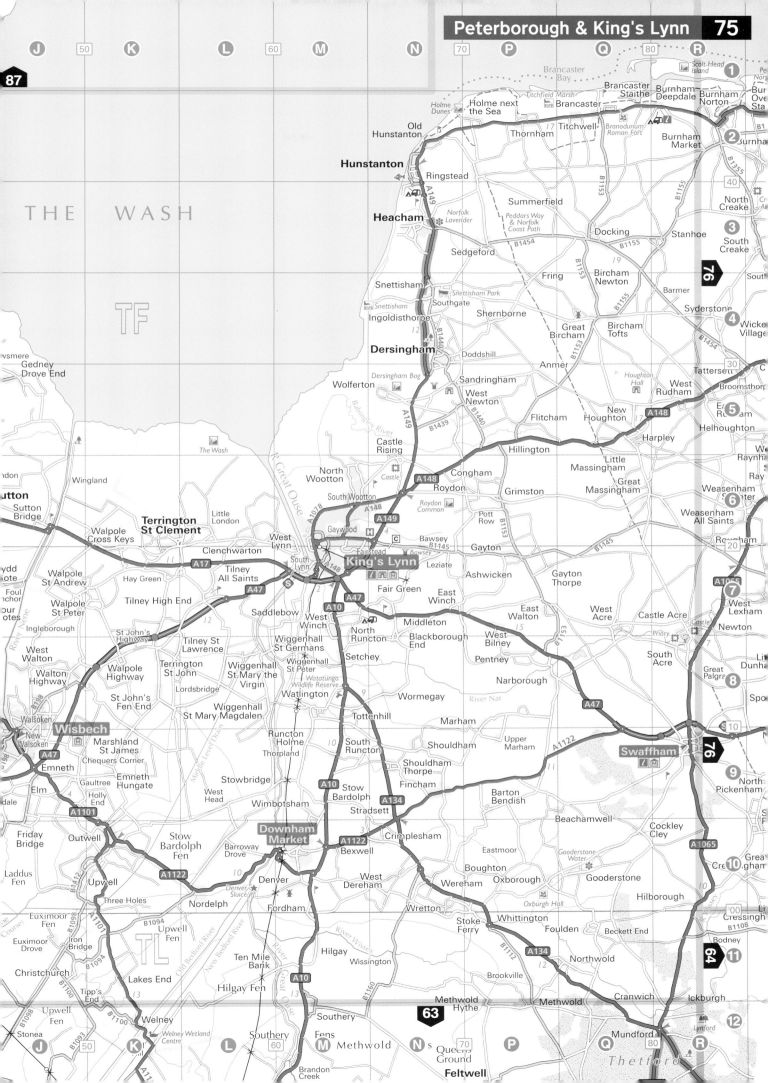

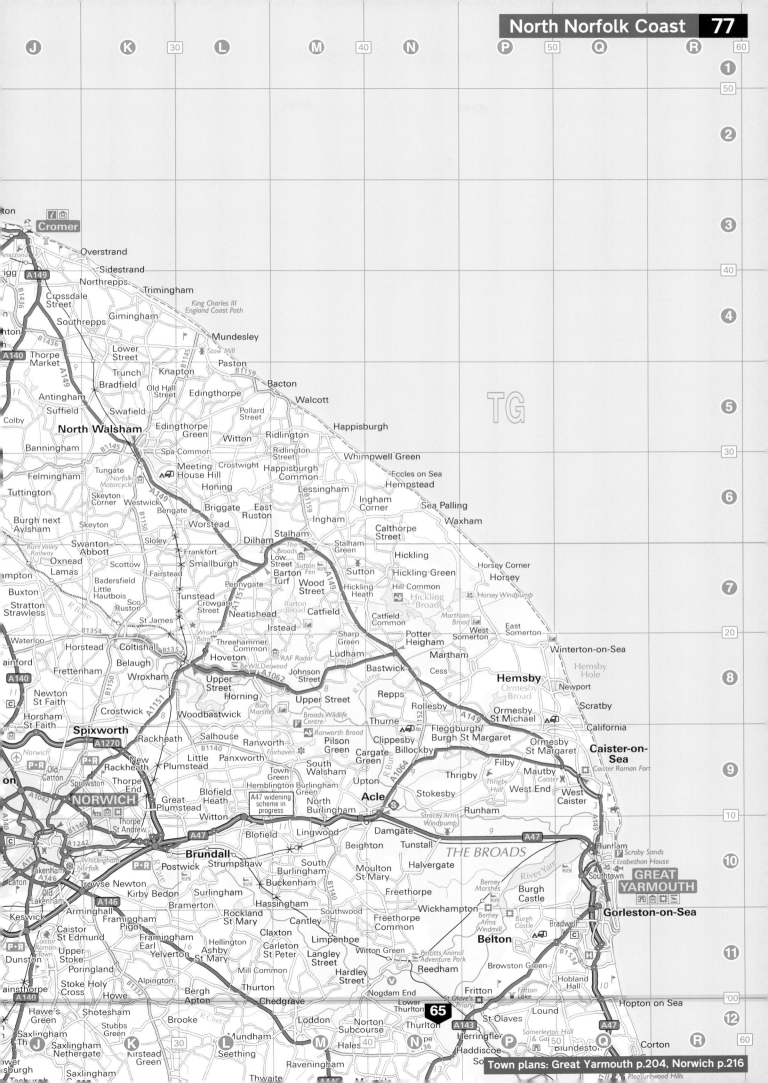

Town plans: Great Yarmouth p.204, Norwich p.216

Llandudno

Llandudno (inset map)

TABOR HILL
Great Orme Tramway
PLAS ROAD
HILL TERRACE
Llandudno Pier
OLD ROAD
Great Orme
Victoria Station
TY-COCH ROAD
MOCOURT ST
NORTH PARADE
The Grand Hotel
CWLACH ROAD
CWLACH WALKS
CLEMENT AVE
LLEWELYN AVENUE
NORTH
North Shore Beach
RECTORY LANE
ABBEY ROAD
WHITON PASSAGE
CHURCH WALKS
Tabernacle Welsh Baptist Chapel
War Memorial
SOUTH PARADE
Travelodge
ST STREET
TY-ISA ROAD
GEORGE ST
Llandudno Bay
GLODDAETH
A546
DEGANWY
New Street
Town Hall
Mostyn Street
Somerset St
The Promenade
CLIFTON ROAD
DEGANWY AVENUE
MADOC STREET
Our Lady Star of the Sea
St John's
LLOYD STREET
ST ANDREW'S PL
St David's Pl
CAROLINE ROAD
BROOKES STREET
Trinity Square
Holy Trinity
Victoria
CHARLTON STREET
BODAFON STREET
Medical Centre
THE PARADE
A546
MELGWYN ROAD
ST DAVID'S ROAD
CLAREMONT ROAD
ABBEY STREET
ST MARY'S ROAD
VAUGHAN STREET
Mostyn Gallery
AUGUSTA STREET
ADELPHI ST
Coach
MOSTYN BROADWAY
Swimming Pool
Venue Cymru
St Paul's
B5115
Parc Llandudno Retail Park
GARAGE STREET
CONWAY ROAD
CLARENCE ROAD
MOSTYN AVE
LLANDUDNO STATION
OXFORD RD
Police Station
Magistrates' Court
CYLCH Y TUDUR
Mostyn Champneys Retail Park
CLARENCE CRESCENT
CAE CLYD
JUBILEE ROAD
ST SEIRIOL'S RD
Ysgol Tudno
ARGYLL ROAD
NORMAN ROAD
BUILDER STREET
Fire & Ambulance Station
CLARENCE DRIVE
Ysgol Craig Y Don
AVENUE
ERYL AVENUE
TRINITY
Superstore
FFORDD PENRHYN
A470
CONWAY ROAD
MAES CLYD
DINAS ROAD
KING'S AVENUE
WEST COUNCIL STREET WEST
HOWARD RD
WERN WYLAN
CWM
FFORDD TUDNO
KINGWAY
Ysgol Ffordd Dyffryn
Coach
Ysgol Morfa Rhianedd
FFORDD GWYNEDD
FFORDD DEWI
FFORDD DWYFOR
CYTOR ROAD
LIDDELL PARK
MOXBRAY ROAD
FFORDD DERWN
Llandudno FC
Ysgol John Bright
CWM PLACE
MAEDU ROAD
A470
SAC
A55, BETWS-Y-COED

0   200 m

Main map

SH

RNLI Moelfre Seawatch Centre
Moelfre
lanallgo
Marian-glas
Benllech
Red Wharf Bay
Goch
Red Wharf Bay
Llanddona
Pentraeth
Puffin Island
Penmon Priory
Caim
Toll
Penmon
Black Point
GREAT ORME'S HEAD
Great Orme Heritage Coast
GREAT ORME'S HEAD
Great Orme Tramway
Toll
Little Ormes Head
Penrhyn Bay
Llandudno
Deganwy
Llanrhos
Penrhynside
Llandrillo-yn-Rhos
Bryn Pydew
Rhôs-on-Sea
Colwyn Bay (Bae Colwyn)
A55
llandd
Glan-yr-afon
B5109
Conwy Bay
Tywyn
Esgyryn
Old Colwyn
Llysfaen
Rh
Ta
Glanyr-afon
Hafoty Medieval House
Gaol
Llangoed
Llanfaes
Beaumaris Castle
B5109
Dwygyfylchi
Conwy
Conwy Castle
Llandudno Junction
Mochdre
Llanelian-yn-Rhôs
B5383
Bryn-y-Maen
Welsh
A470
B5113
Dolwen
Beaumaris
Llansadwrn
Courthouse
Penmaenan
Penmaenmawr
Capelulo
Llansanffraid Glan Conwy
B538
Llandegfan
Llanfairfechan
A55
Henryd
80
Plas Cadnant
Menai Bridge (Porthaethwy)
Bangor
Penrhyn Castle
Nant-y-pandy
Gorddinog
Rowen
Ty'n-y-Groes
Bodnant
Dawn
Betws n-Rho
Pili Palas
Anglesey Column
Spinnies Abergowen
Abergwyngregyn
610 TAL-Y-FAN
Graig
Tal-y-Cafn
Pentre'r Felin
L
irpwllgwyngyll
Llandygai
Coedydd Aber
Aber-Falls
ERYRI (SNOWDONIA)
Caerhun
Castell
A5106
Adventure Parc Snowdonia
Trofarth
Newydd
Britannia Bridge
Penrhos garnedd
Tal-y-bont
580 MOEL WNION
Afon Anafon
NATIONAL
Llanbedr-y-Cennin
Tal-y-Bont
A470
Eglwysbach
Hafodunos
Capel-y-graig
Waen-wen
Glasinfryn
Llanllechid
Rachub
757 Y DROSGL
PARK
942 FOEL-FRAS
Afon Dulyn
Dolgarrog
Pont Dolgarrog
Vale of Conwy
Llanddoged
Llang yw
Seion
Llanddeiniolen
Waen-pentir
Mynydd Llandygai
Bethesda
Gerlan
Zip World (Penrhyn Quarry)
Ogwen Bank
Penrhyn Slate Landscape
Afon Caseg
Llyn Figiau
A548
Maenan
B5113
GreenWood Family Park
B4547
Pentir
Rhyd-y-groes
Tregarth
Sling
A487
Llanrug
Penisarwaun
Rhiwen
Deiniolen
1062 CARNEDD LLEWELYN
67
1044 CARNEDD DAFYDD
Afon Llugwy
N
Llanrhychwyn
Trefriw Woollen Mills
Tref
80
Pen e-tafarn-y-fedw
B5113
Pandy Tudur
B538
Bethel
Saron
J
Cwm-y-glo
Brynrefail
eathro
Ceunant
Llyn Padarn
K
Clwt-y-b 60
Gallt-y-foel
Dinorwig
Llanberis Lake Railway
923 ELIDIR
L
Pont Pen-
M
CARNEDD DAFYDD
Llyn Ogwen
70
N
Llyn Cowly
Llyn Crafnant
Gwydir
Cors Bodgynydd
Llanrwst
P
Melin-
Q
Gwytherin
R
B538 90

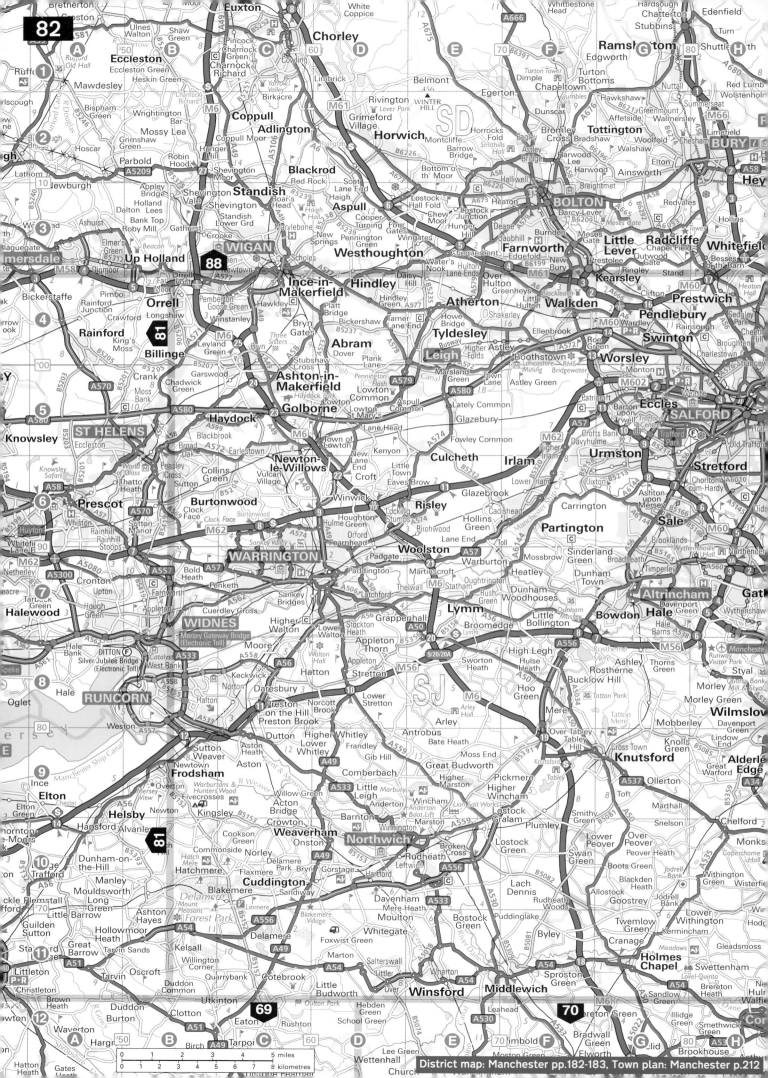

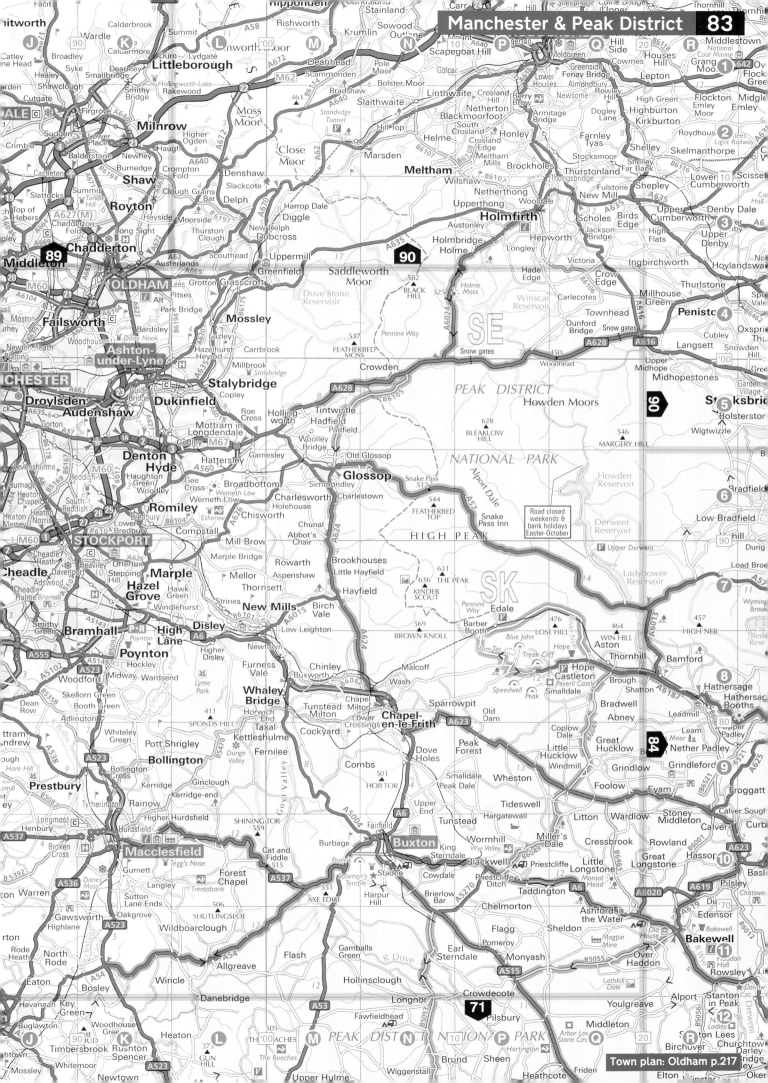

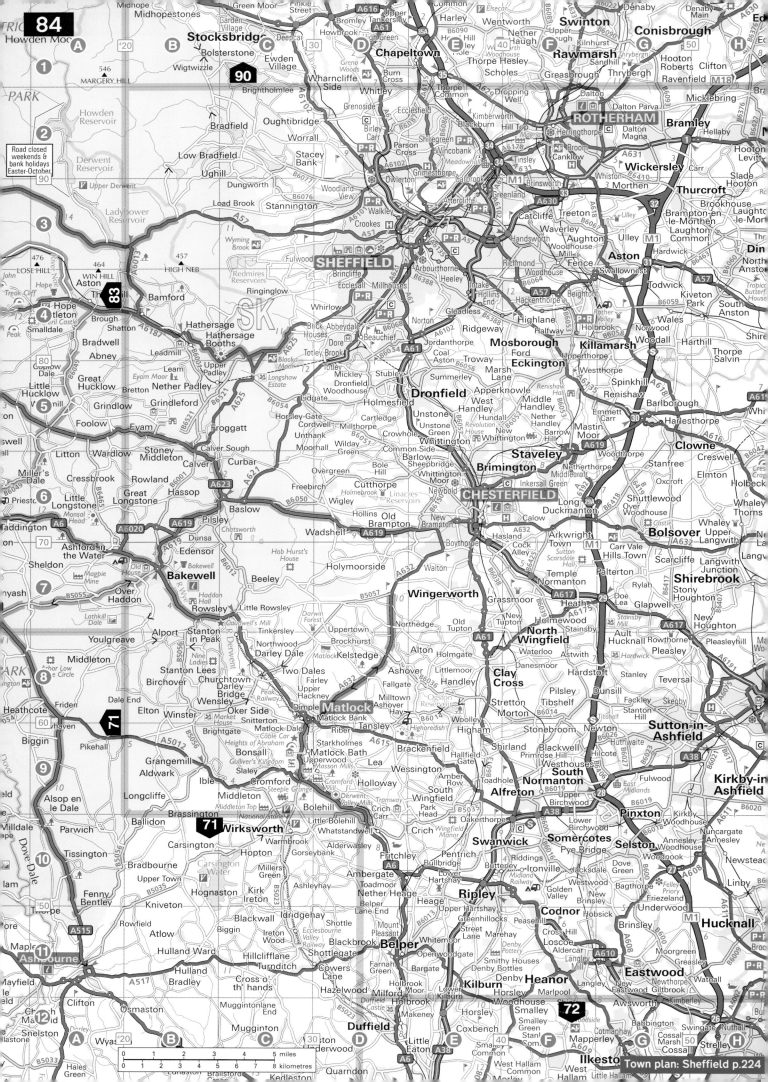

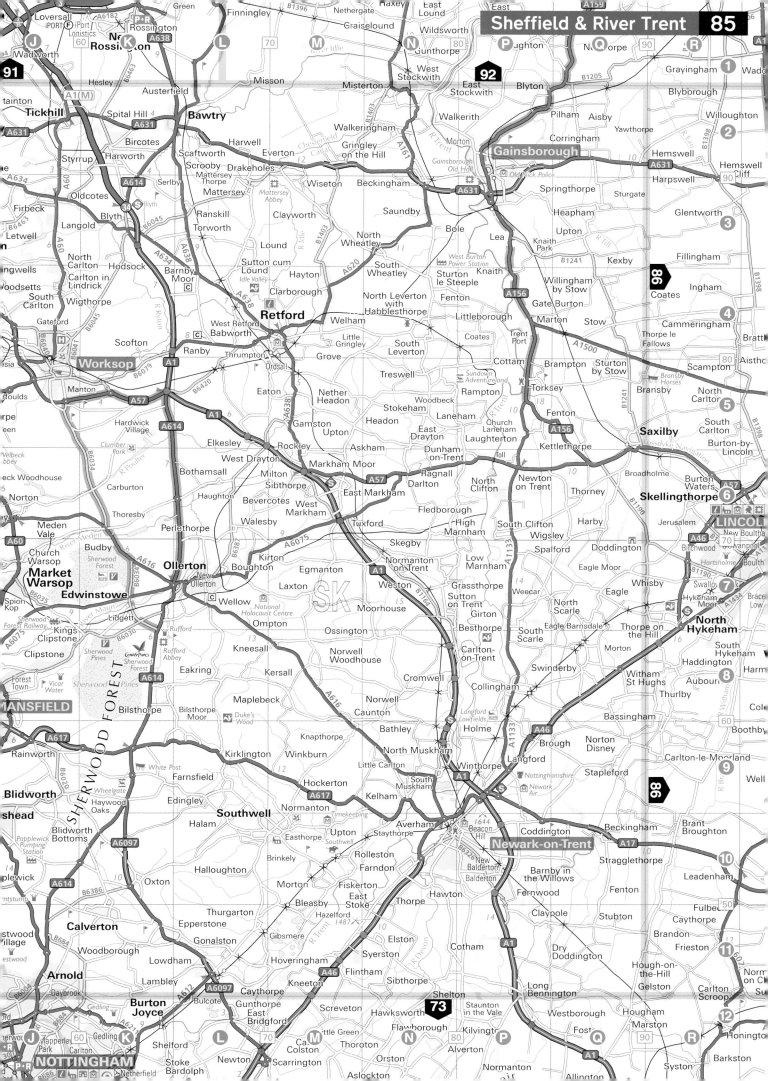

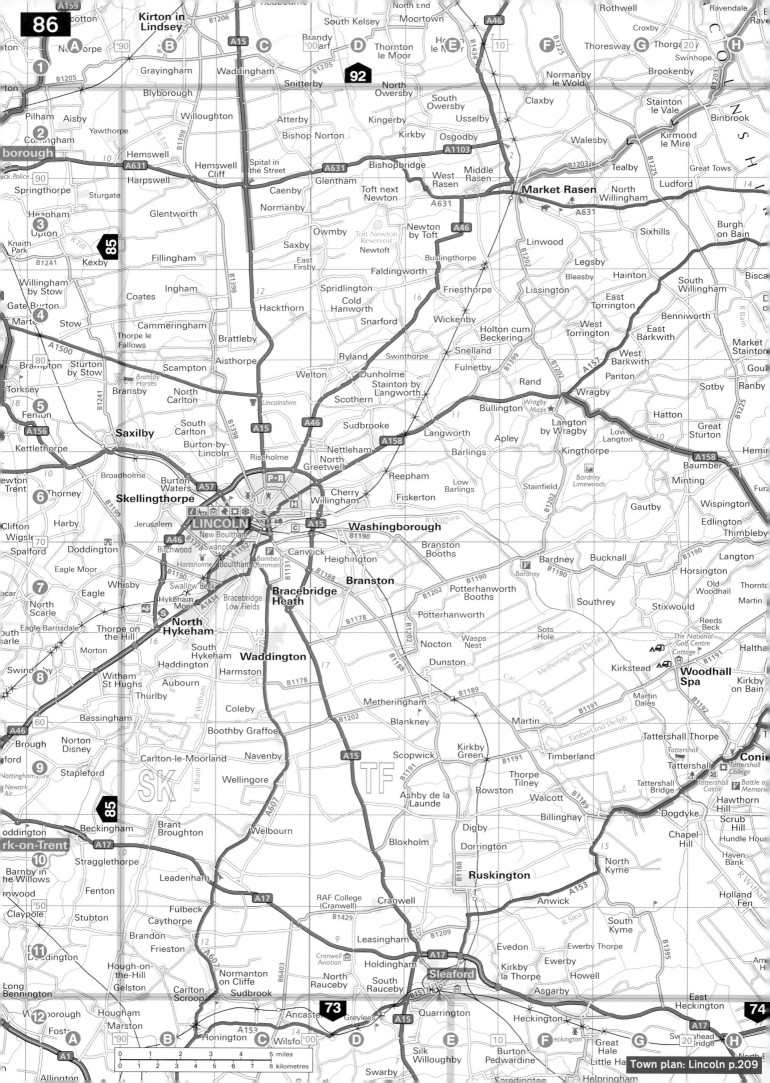

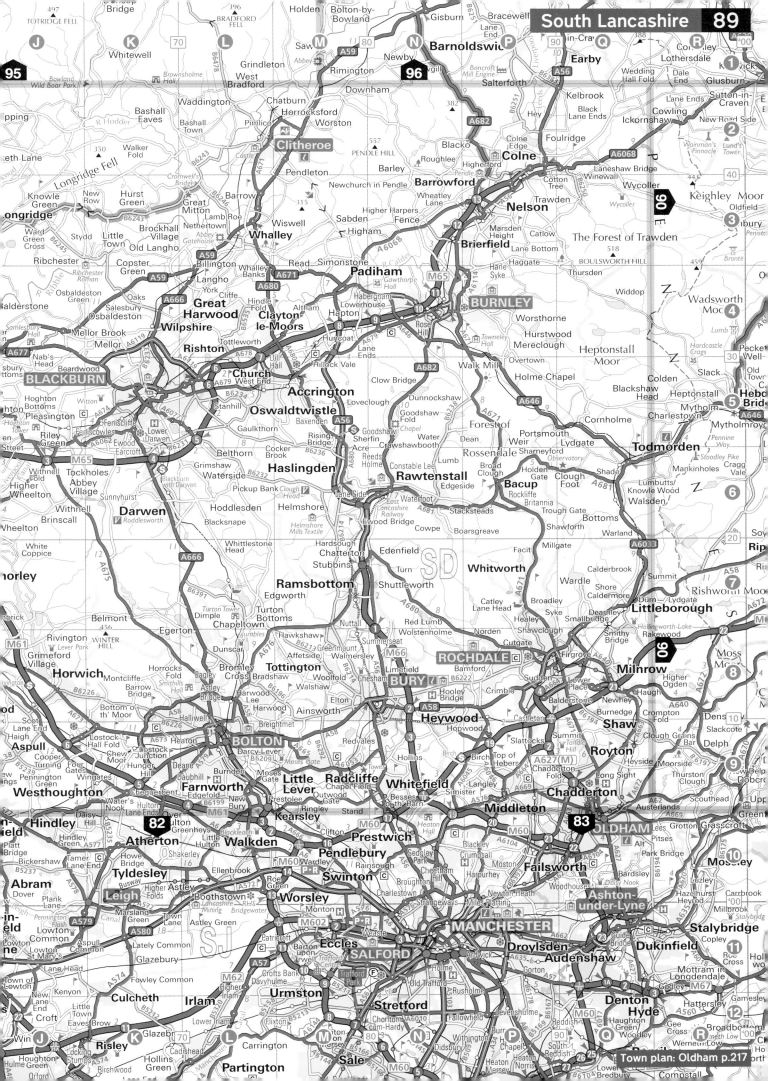

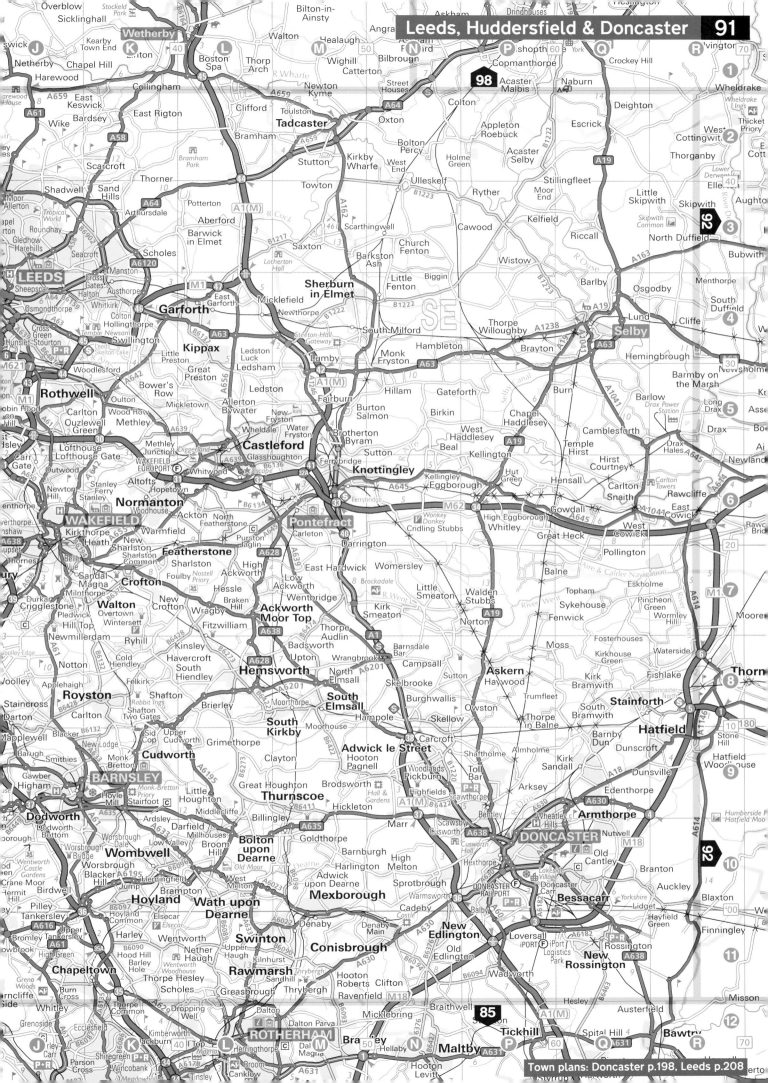

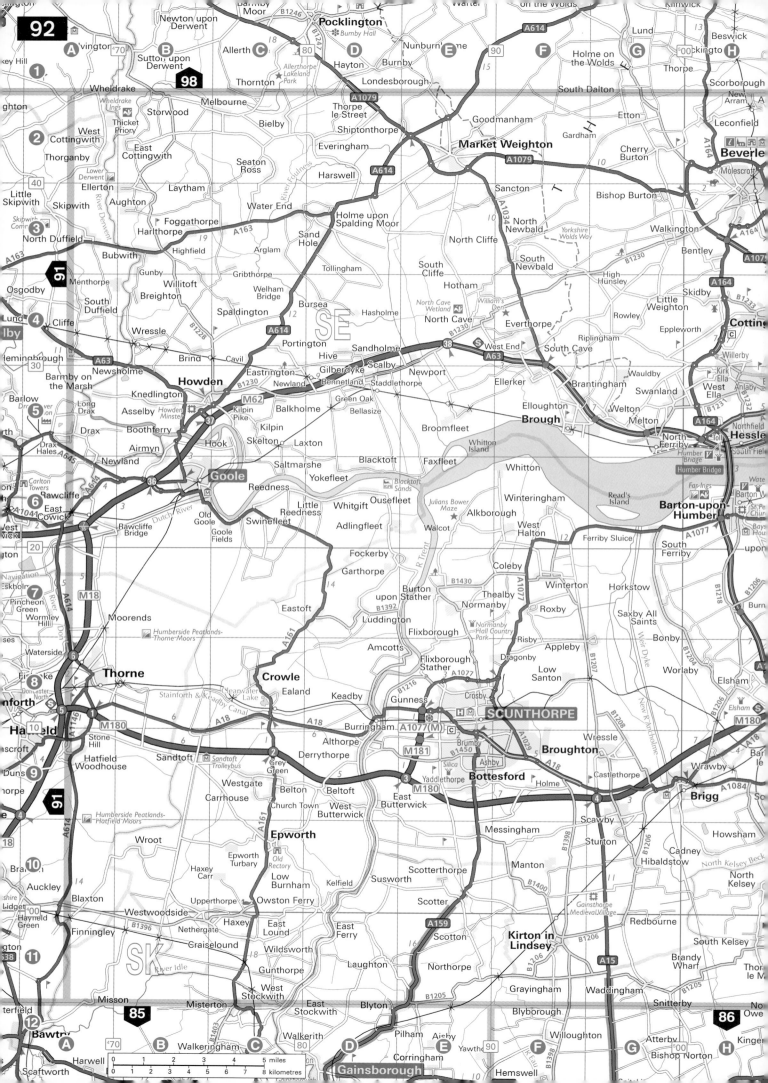

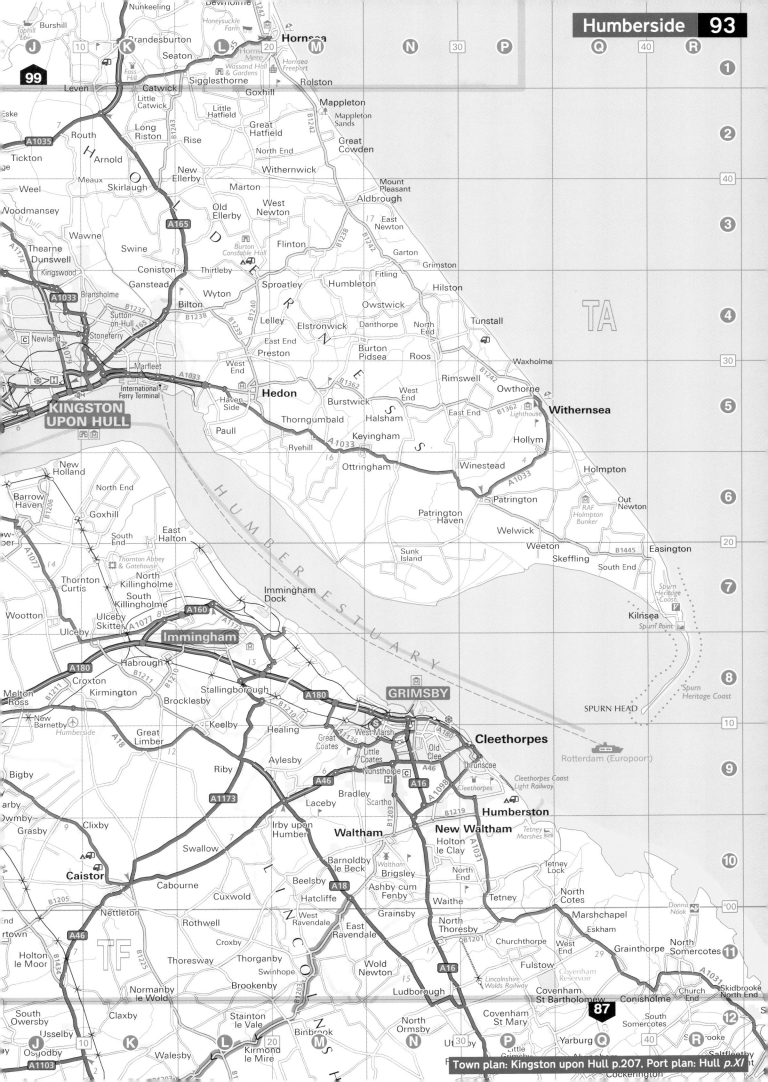

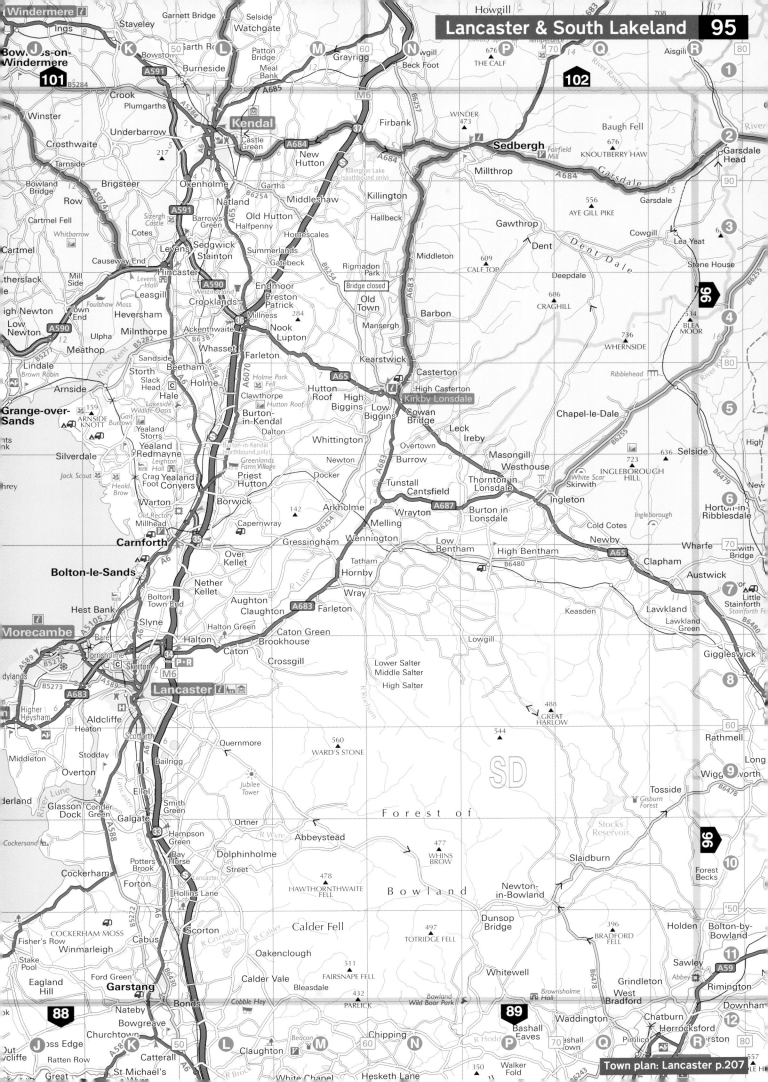

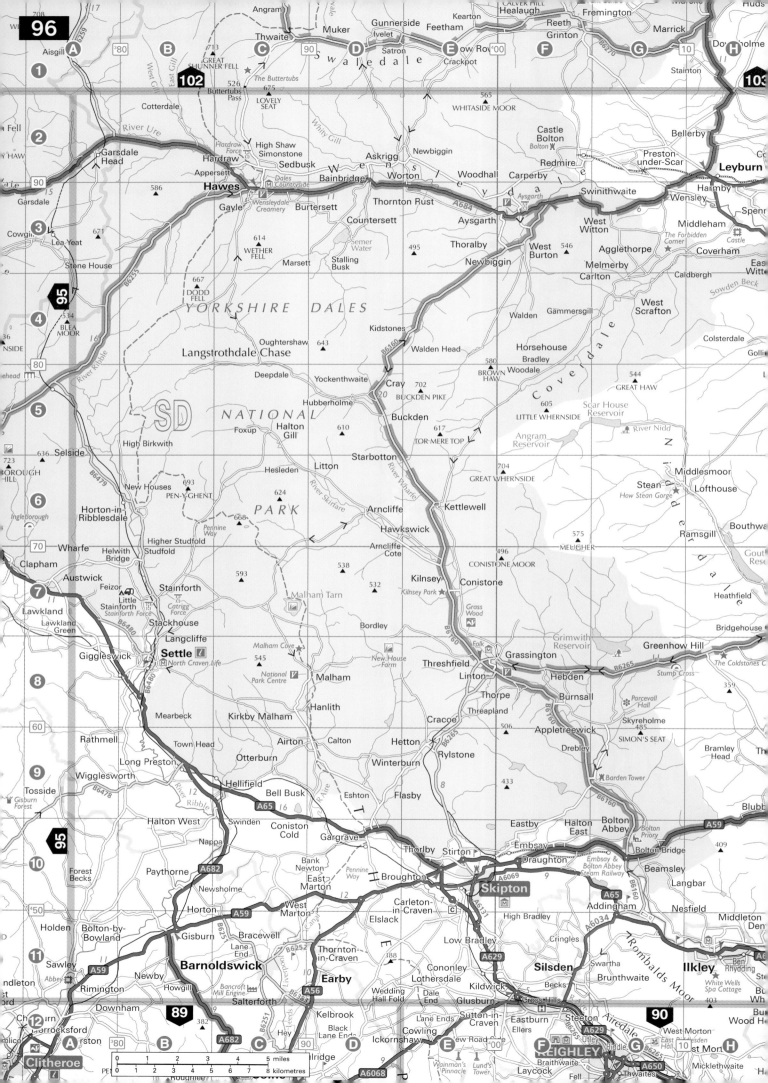

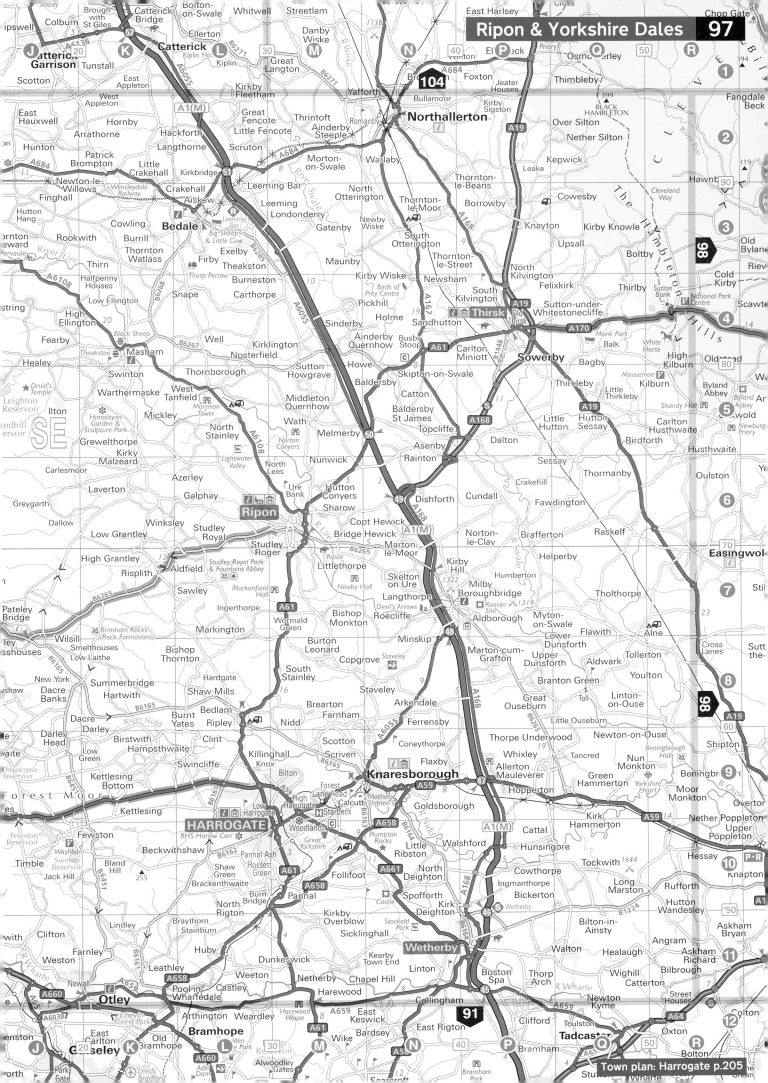

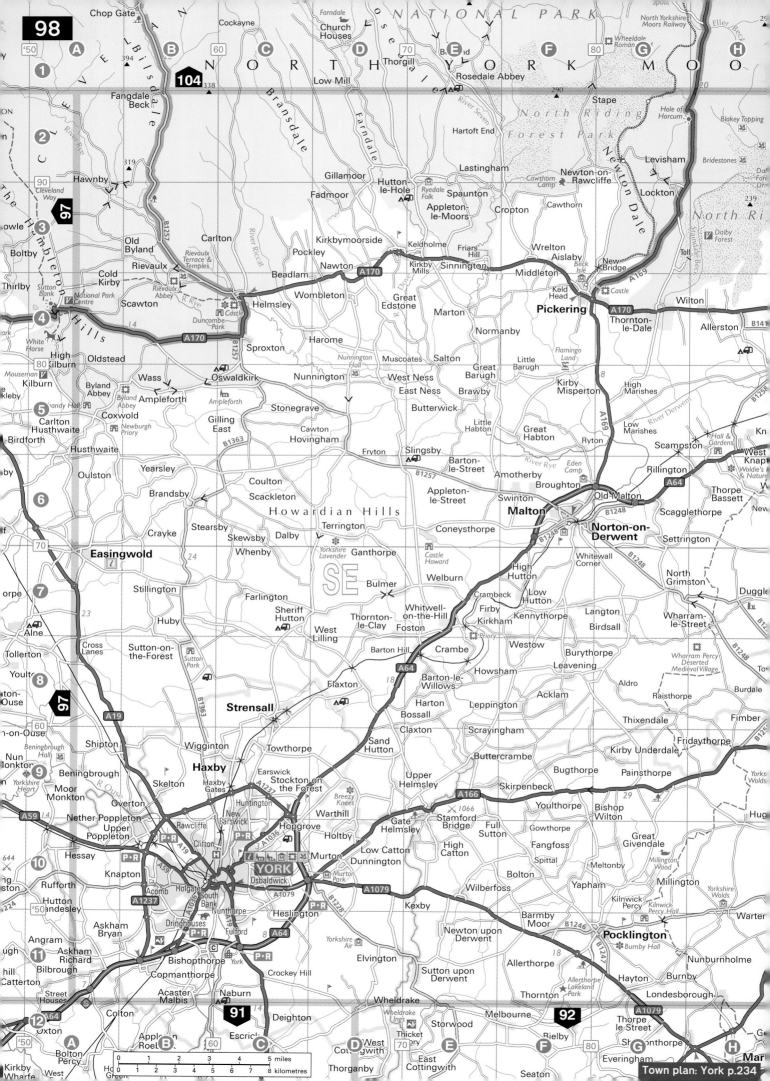

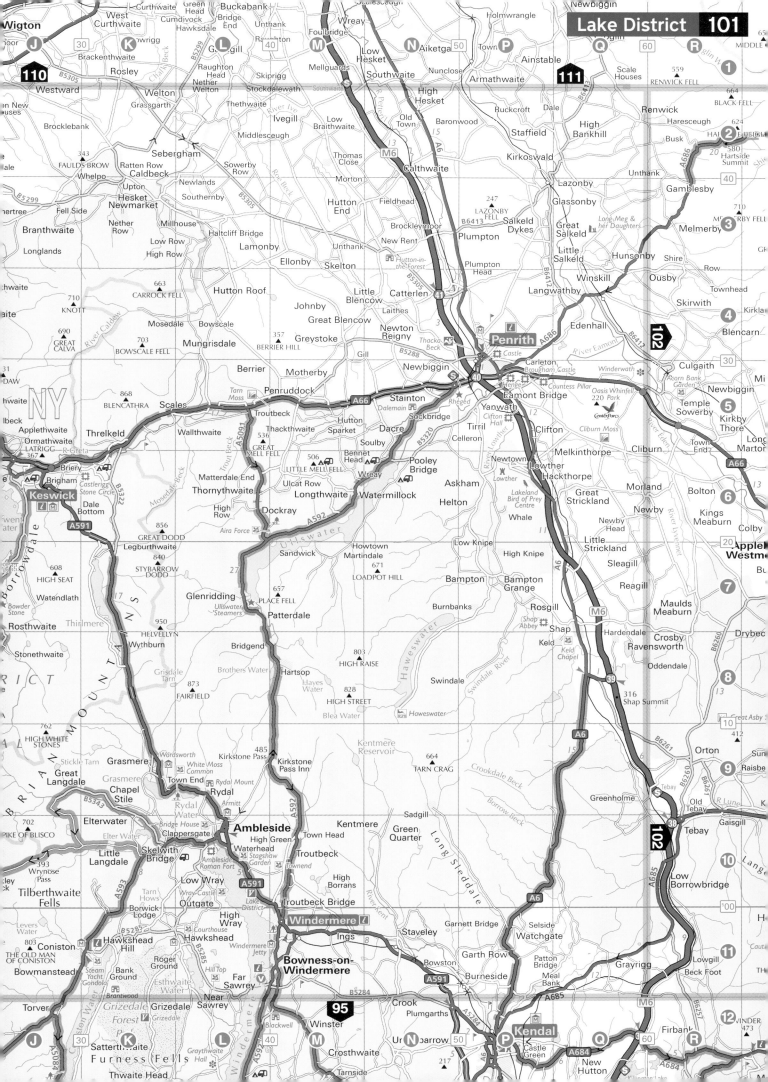

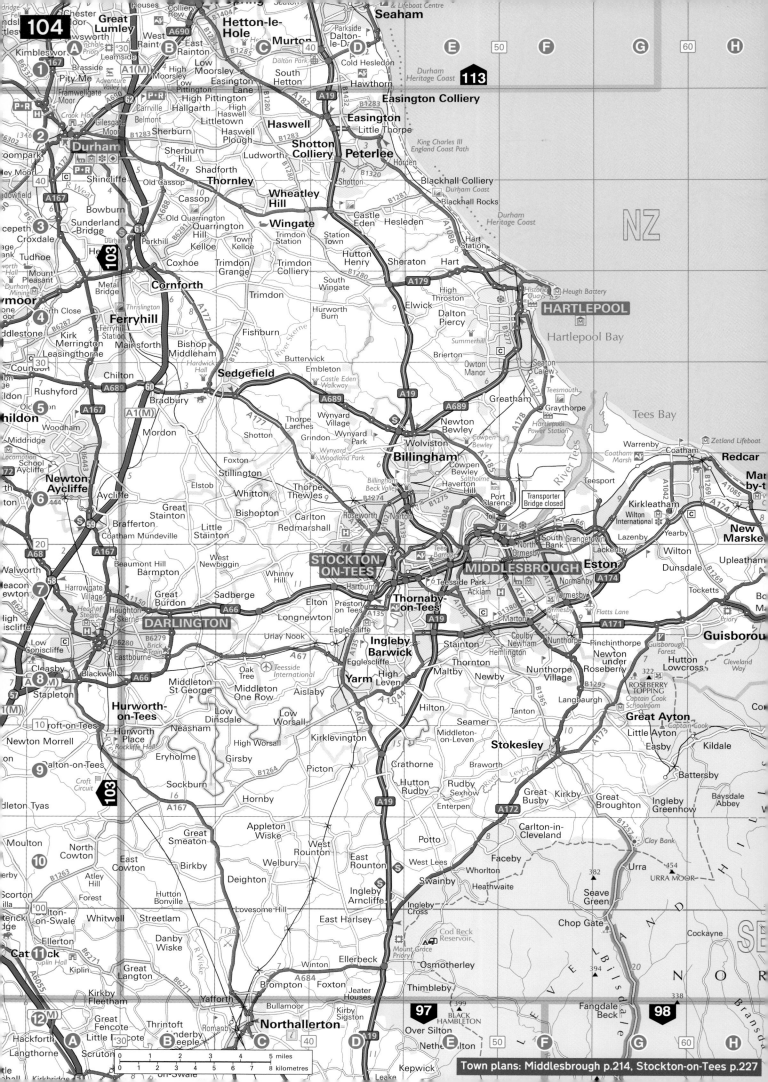

J 70 K L 80 M N 90 P Q 00 R

Saltburn-by-the-Sea

Brotton

Skelton

New Skelton
North Skelton
Lingdale
Kilton Thorpe
Carlin How
Loftus

Skinningrove
Ironstone Mining
Upton
Boulby
Staithes
Captain Cook & Staithes
Port Mulgrave

Daléhouse
Easington
Hinderwell
Roxby
Newton Mulgrave
Runswick
Kettleness
Goldsborough

Woodhill
Stanghow
Liverton Mines
Handale
Borrowby
Ellerby
Runswick Bay
North Yorkshire and Cleveland Heritage Coast

A171
Moorsholm
Scaling
B1266
Mickleby
West Barnby
East Barnby
Lythe
Sandsend
Overdale Wyke
NZ

Gerrick
Scaling Dam
22
A174
Dunsley
Raithwaite
Newholm
Sandsend Wyke
Whitby

The Moors National Park Centre
301
Stonegate
Ugthorpe
Hutton Mulgrave
A171
Aislaby
Briggswath
B1410
Ruswarp
Stainsacre
Abbey
Saltwick Bay
King Charles III England Coast Path

Danby
Castleton Ainthorpe
Lealholm Side
Lealholm
Egton
River Esk
Sleights
Iburndale
Sneaton
Ugglebarnby
High Hawsker
Low Hawsker
Ness Point or North Cheek

The Green
Glaisdale
Egton Bridge
Key Green
Grosmont
Esk Dale
Blue Bank
Littlebeck
Sneatonthorpe
Raw
Old Coastguard
Fylingthorpe
Robin Hood's Bay

Danby Bottom
Street
Beck Hole
Falling Foss
B1416
A171
Old Peak or South Cheek

N O R T H   Y O R K   M O O R S
326
PIKE HILL
Goathland
Mallyan Spout
Ravenscar

369
N A T I O N A L   P A R K
North Yorkshire Moors Railway
Eller Beck
292
20
Staintondale

Rose dale
Low Bell End
Thorgill
Wheeldale Roman Road
Hayburn Wyke

Rosedale Abbey
290
Stape
Harwood Dale
Cloughton Newlands
Cloughton Wyke

T H   Y O R K   M O O R S
River Seven
N o r t h   R i d i n g
Hole of Horcum
`99`
Cloughton

Faddale
70
K rtoft End
F o r st P r k
L t 80
M
Levisham
Blakey Topping
Bridestones
Crosscliff
Toll
N 90
Bickley
P
Broxa
Silpho
Suffield
Q
Bur ton
Scalby
R 00
Cromer Point
Cleveland Way

Lastingham
Newton-on-
Dalby
Langdale
Hackness

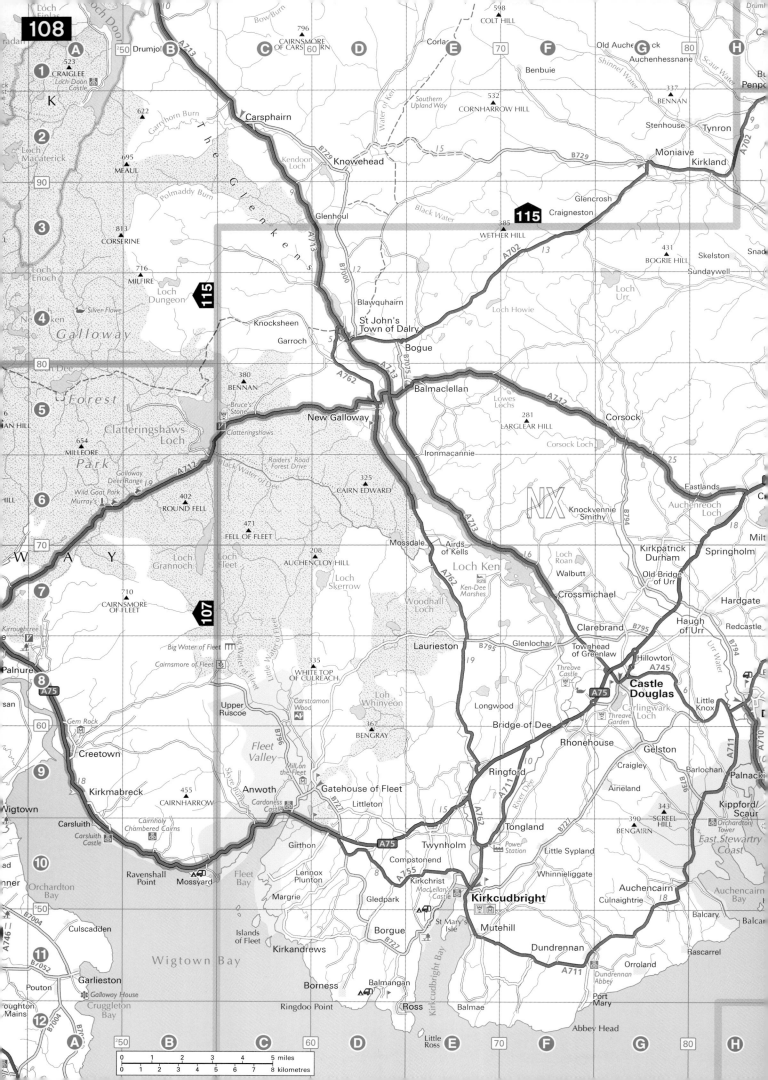

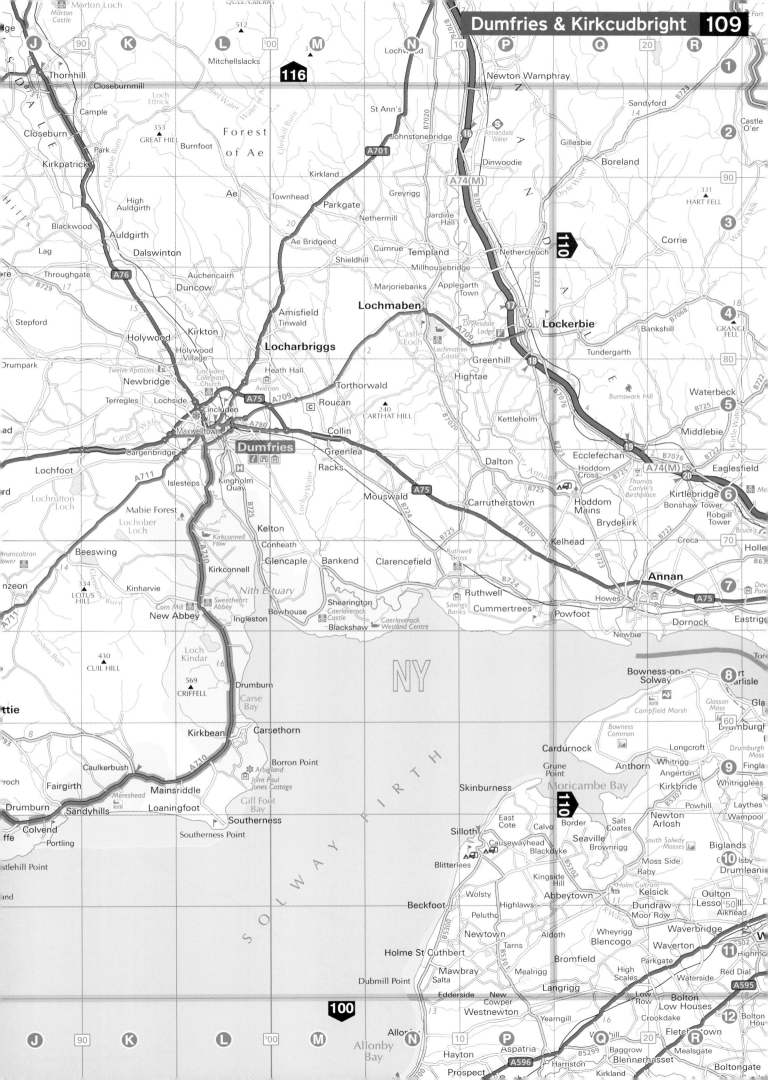

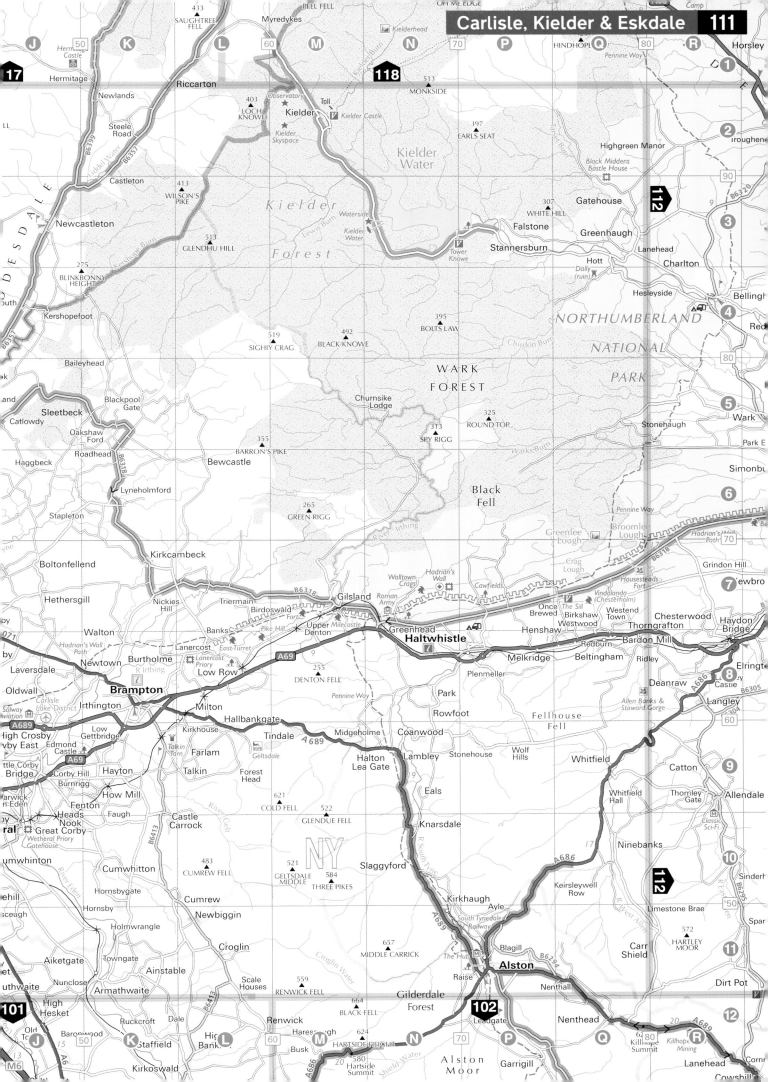

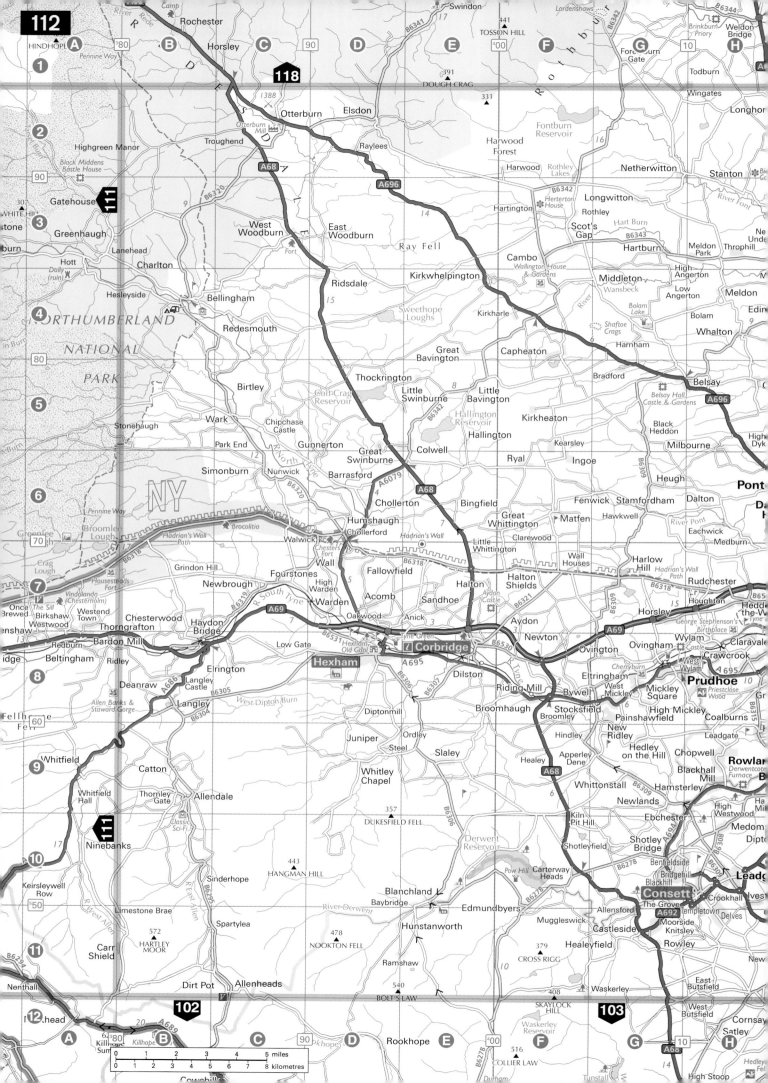

Port of Tyne

TYNEMOUTH

MEADOW WELL
M PERCY MAIN

Wet'n'Wild Water Park

NEWCASTLE THE NORTH

Royal Quays Outlet
Premier Inn

East Howdon

Royal Quays Marina

INTERNATIONAL PASSENGER TERMINAL
Check-in

NEWCASTLE
TYNE VIEW TER

TYNE TUNNEL (ELECTRONIC TOLL)

River Tyne

Jarrow

SUNDERLAND

SAC

0   500 m

West Thirston
Eshott
Broomhill
Red Row
Druridge Bay
Druridge

19
Causey Park
Helm
West Chevington
Widdrington
North Northumberland Heritage Coast

Causey Park Bridge
Earsdon
Stobswood
Widdrington Station
Cresswell

Tritlington
Ulgham
Linton
Ellington
Lynemouth

Fenrother
Hebron
Longhirst
Woodhorn
Beacon Point
Woodhorn Demesne

Ashington
Hirst
North Seaton
Newbiggin-by-the-Sea

Pegswood
Bothal
Sheepwash
Wansbeck Riverside
North Seaton Colliery

Morpeth
Hepscott
Choppington
Scotland Gate
Guide Post
Bomarsund
West Sleekburn
Stakeford

Chantry Bagpipe
Clifton
Nedderton
East Sleekburn
Cambois
North Blyth

Tranwell
Bedlington
Cowpen
Blyth

Saltwick
Stannington Station
Bebside
Newsham

Stannington
East Hartford
New Delaval
South Newsham

Plessey Woods
Shotton
Shankhouse
New Hartley
Seaton
Seaton Sluice

Cramlington
East Cramlington
Seaton
Hartley

Berwick Hill
Brenkley
Big Waters
Seghill
St Mary's

Dinnington
Seaton Burn
Annitsford
Seaton Delaval
Holywell

Brunswick Village
Dudley
Wideopen
Burradon
Backworth
Earsdon

Prestwick
Hazlerigg
Camperdown
Killingworth
Monkseaton

High Callerton
Newcastle Great Park
Woolsington
Forest Hall
Shiremoor
Murton
Whitley Bay
Cullercoats

Black Callerton
Kenton Bankfoot
New York
NZ

North Walbottle
Fawdon
Rising Sun
North Shields
Tynemouth
Tynemouth Priory & Castle
Amsterdam (IJmuiden)

Callerton
Gosforth
South Gosforth
Longbenton
Willington
Int. Ferry Terminal
SOUTH SHIELDS

Westerhope
Kenton
Jesmond
Heaton
Wallsend
Tyne Tunnel (Electronic Toll)
Westoe

Walbottle
Newburn
NEWCASTLE UPON TYNE
Walker
Byker
Jarrow
Harton
Marsden Bay

Stella
Scotswood
Elswick
Sage Gateshead
Hebburn
Monkton
Marsden
Souter Lighthouse & The Leas

Blaydon
Dunston
Felling
Wardley
Monkton
Cleadon Park
Cleadon
Souter Point

Metro Centre
Shipley
GATESHEAD
Boldon Colliery
West Boldon
Whitburn
Whitburn Coastal Park

Winlaton
Whickham
Low Wrekenton
East Boldon
Whitburn Bay

Winlaton Mill
Derwent Walk
Team Valley
Bowes Railway
North East Land Sea & Air
Hylton Castle
Seaburn

Barlow
A692
Street Gate
Springwell
Wetland Centre
Fulwell
Southwick
Roker

Sunniside
Lamesley
Usworth
Castletown
Monkwearmouth

Gibside
Marley Hill
Angel of the North
South Hylton
Pennywell
SUNDERLAND

Sheep Hill
Byermoor
Kibblesworth
Portobello
WASHINGTON
Offerton
Hendon

Hobson
Tanfield Railway
Birtley
Washington
Penshaw Monument
New Silksworth
Tunstall

Tanfield
Causey Arch
Fatfield
Mount Pleasant
Herrington
High Newport
Durham Heritage Coast

White-le-Head
Tanfield Lea
High Urpeth
Urpeth
Ouston
Penshaw
New Herrington
High Silksworth
Grangetown

Catchgate
Beamish
Perkinsville
A195
Philadelphia
Ryhope

Stanley
West Pelton
Shiney Row
Bournmoor
Newbottle
Seaton

Pelton
Grange
Houghton Gate
High Dubmire
Houghton-le-Spring

Quaking Houses
The Middles
Pelton Fell
Newfield
Fence Houses
Colliery Row
Seaham
East Durham Heritage & Lifeboat Centre

South Moor
Villa Real
Chester-le-Street
Great Lumley
West Rainton
Hetton-le-Hole
Seaham

Lanchester
Craghead
Waldridge
Chester Moor
Fence Houses
East Rainton
Hetton Lyons
Murton
Dalton-le-Dale

Maiden Law
Burnhope
Waldridge Fell
Plawsworth
Finchale Priory
Leamside
Low Moorsley
Dalton Park
Parkside

Ornsby Hill
Holmside
Edmondsley
Nettlesworth
Kimblesworth
Brasside
High Moorsley
High Pittington
South Hetton
Cold Hesledon

Quebec
Sacriston
Witton Gilbert
Pity Me
Low Pittington
Hawthorn
Durham Heritage Coast

Esh
Langley Park
Framwellgate Moor
Carrville
Hallgarth
High Pittington
Easington
Easington Colliery

Esh Winning
Bearpark
Crook Hall
Gilesgate
Belmont
Littletown
Haswell Plough
Easington
Little Thorpe

Waterhouses
Durham
Broompark
DURHAM
St Giles Burn
Haswell
Shotton
King Charles III

New Brancepeth
Shadforth

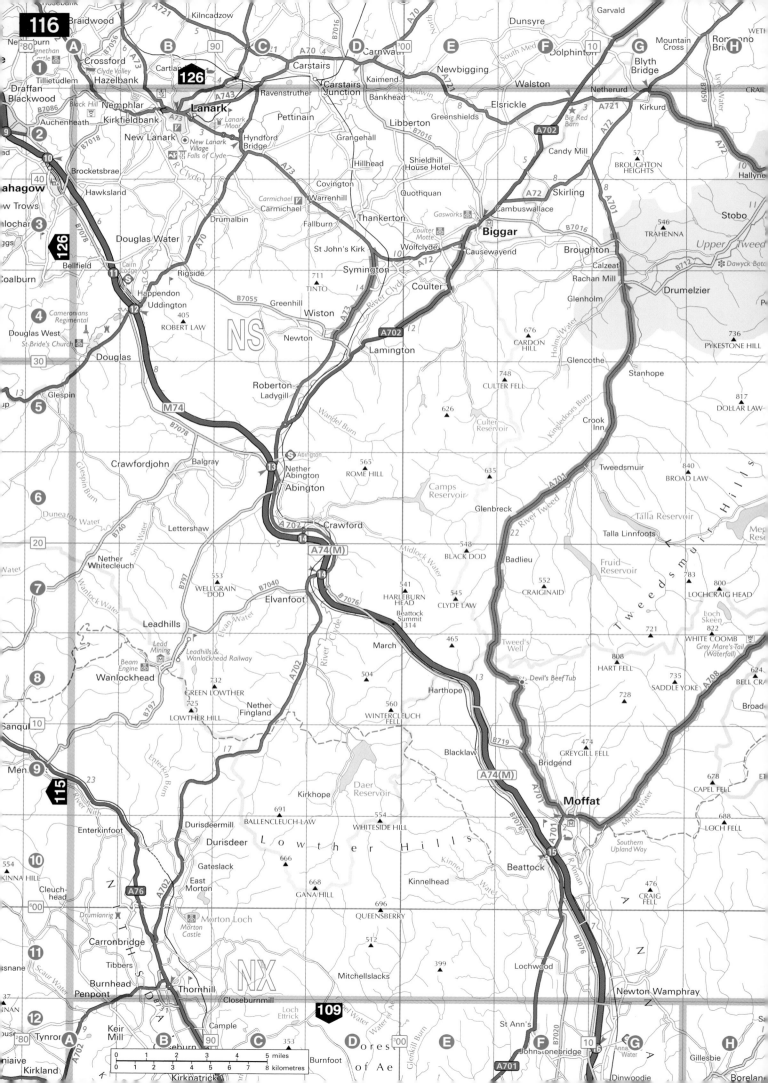

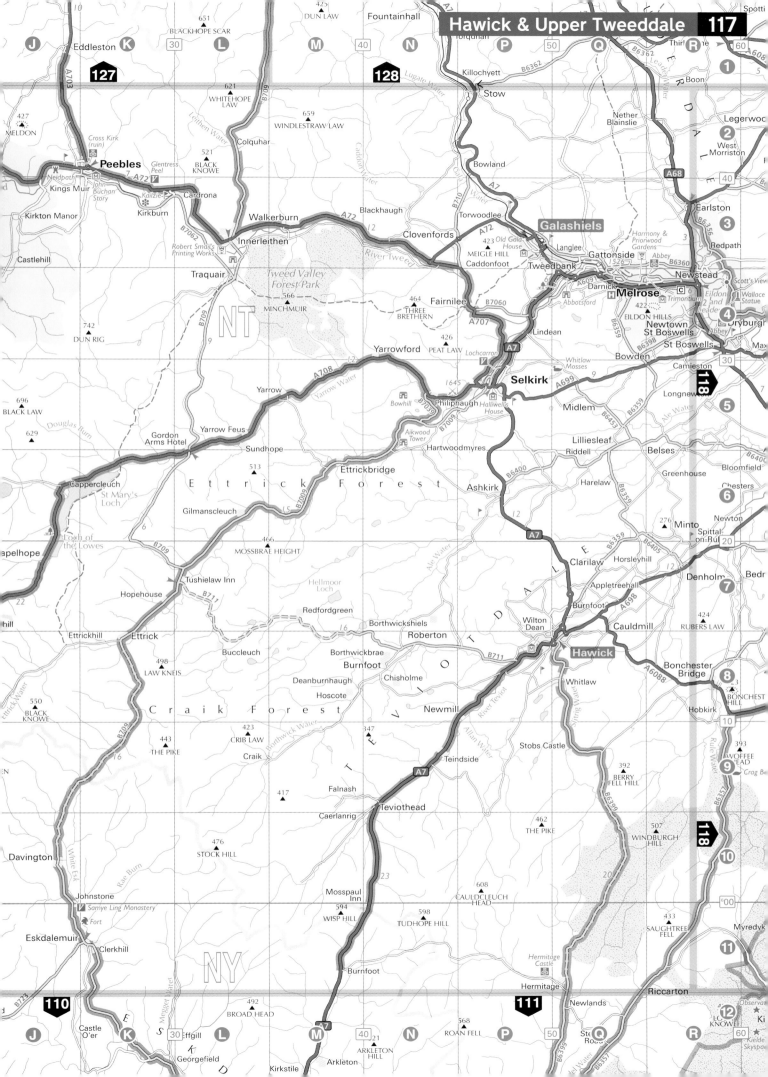

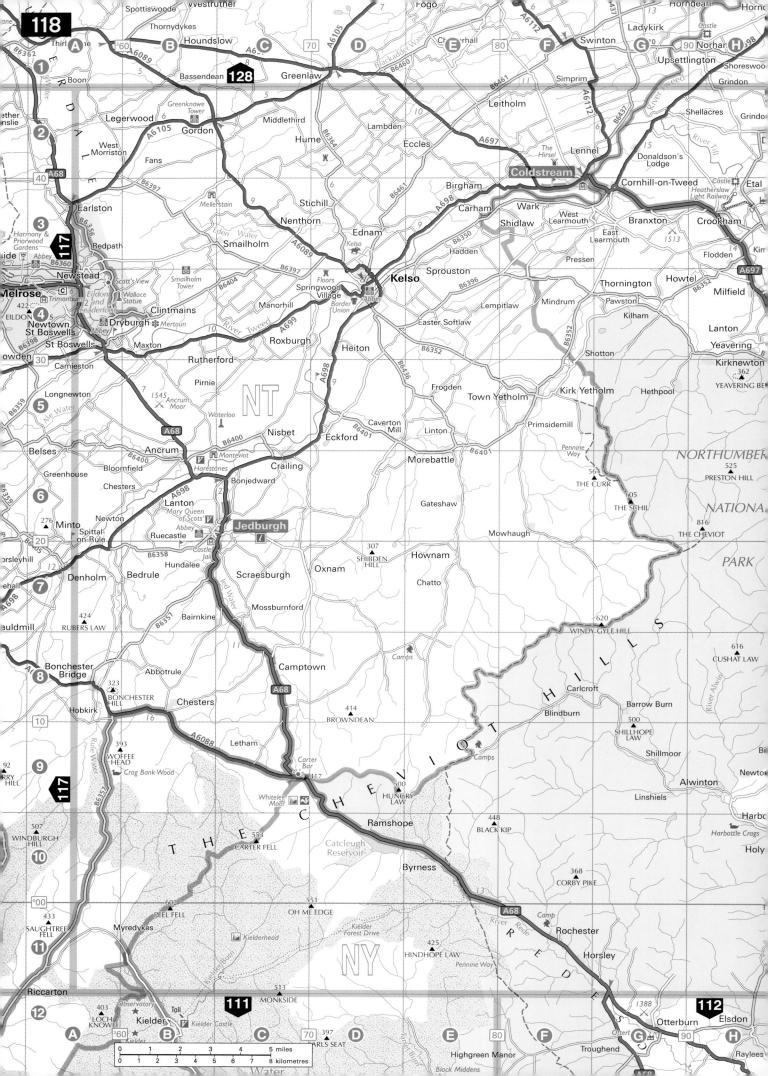

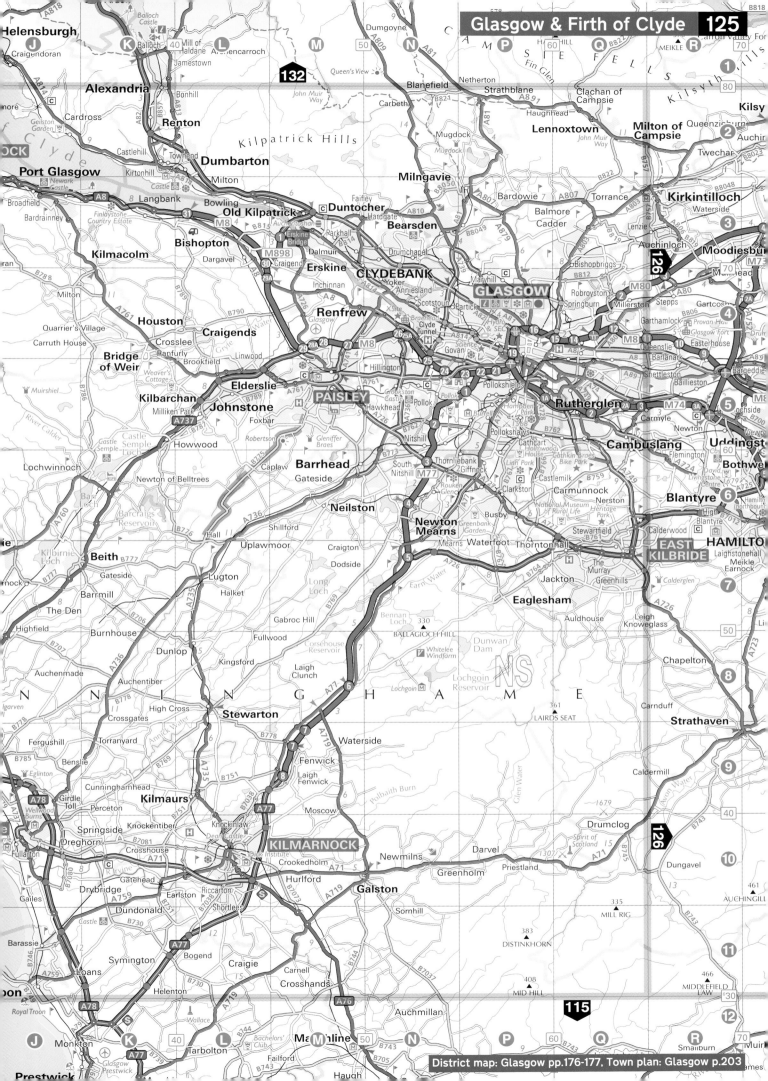

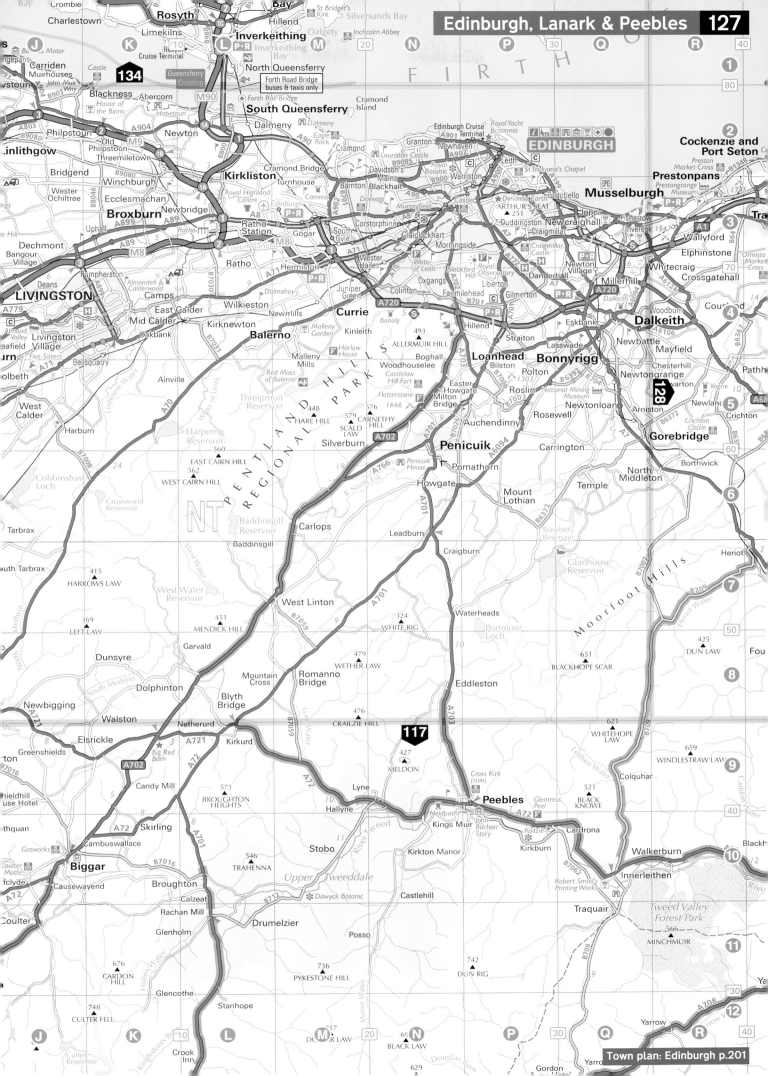

FIRTH

1

Charlestown
Crombie
Rosyth
Bay
St Bridget's Kirk
Silversands Bay
80

Limekilns
Inverkeithing
Hillend
Dalgety
Inchcolm Abbey
N
P
30
Q
R
40

J
K
L P·R
Inverkeithing Bay
M
Cruise Terminal
North Queensferry

Carriden
Muirhouses
Castle
134
Queensferry Crossing
Forth Road Bridge buses & taxis only
Royal Yacht Britannia
Cockenzie and Port Seton
2

Blackness
Abercorn
M90
South Queensferry
Forth Rail Bridge
Cramond Island
Edinburgh Cruise Terminal
EDINBURGH
Preston Market Cross
Prestonpans

Philpstoun
A904
Newton
Dalmeny
Dalmeny
A90
Cramond
Eagle Rock
Granton
Newhaven
Leith
A901
Royal Botanic
St Triduana's Chapel
Prestongrange Museum
Musselburgh
3

linlithgow
M9
Old Philpstoun
Threemiletown
Kirkliston
B800
Cramond Bridge
Turnhouse
Royal Highland Centre
Davidson's Mains
Barnton
Blackhall
Warriston
Portobello
Joppa
P·R
Fisherrow
Inveresk
A1
Wallyford
Tranent

Bridgend
Winchburgh
Newbridge
A89
Ratho Station
Gogar
South Gyle
Corstorphine
Craiglockhart
Murrayfield
Castle
Dynamic Earth
Arthur's Seat
Duddingston
Newcraighall
Craigmillar
Elphinstone
Crossgatehall
70

Broxburn
A899
Uphall
Ratho
Union Canal
Hermiston
A71
Wester Hailes
Water of Leith
Morningside
Blackford Hill
Royal Observatory
Craigmillar Castle
Liberton
Danderhall
Newton Village
Millerhill
Whitecraig
4

Dechmont
Bangour Village
Deans
Pumpherston
Camps
Wilkieston
Newmills
Juniper Green
Colinton
Oxgangs
Fairmilehead
Gilmerton
A720
Dalkeith
Eskbank
Newbattle
Mayfield
Woodburn
Dalkeith

LIVINGSTON
Livingston Village
Mid Calder
East Calder
Kirknewton
Balerno
Currie
Kinleith
Bonaly
Hillend
Straiton
Lasswade
Loanhead
Bonnyrigg
Newtongrange
Chesterhill
128
5

West Calder
Harburn
Ainville
Malleny Mills
Red Moss of Balerno
PENTLAND HILLS
Harlaw House
Malleny Garden
Boghall
Woodhouselee
Castlelaw Hill Fort
448
HARE HILL
576
1666
Flotterstone
Easter Howgate
Milton Bridge
Bilston
Polton
Roslin
National Mining Museum
Rosewell
Newtonloan
Arniston
Gorebridge
Newlanc
Crichton
A6

Cobbinshaw Loch
Harperrig Reservoir
579
SCALD LAW
CARNETHY HILL
Silverburn
A702
Penicuik
Penicuik House
Pomathorn
Carrington
Borthwick
6

Tarbrax
560
EAST CAIRN HILL
562
WEST CAIRN HILL
REGIONAL PARK
Baddinsgill Reservoir
A766
Howgate
Mount Lothian
Temple
North Middleton
60

South Tarbrax
Crosswood Reservoir
NT
Baddinsgill
Carlops
Leadburn
Craigburn
Rosebery Reservoir
Gladhouse Reservoir
Moorfoot Hills
Heriot
7

415
HARROWS LAW
West Water Reservoir
West Linton
B7059
Waterheads
Portmore Loch
Dun Law
50

Newbigging
369
LEFT-LAW
451
MENDICK HILL
324
WHITE RIG
479
WETHER LAW
651
BLACKHOPE SCAR
425
DUN LAW
Fou
8

Dunsyre
Garvald
Mountain Cross
Romanno Bridge
Eddleston
621
WHITEHOPE LAW
659
WINDLESTRAW LAW
9

Walston
Netherurd
Blyth Bridge
Kirkurd
476
CRAILZIE HILL
117
A703
521
BLACK KNOWE
Colquhar
40

Elsrickle
Greenshields
Big Red Barn
A721
A72
Candy Mill
571
BROUGHTON HEIGHTS
427
MELDON
Lyne
Cross Kirk (ruin)
Peebles
Glentress Peel
A72
Cardrona
Walkerburn
10

Biggar
Cambuswallace
Skirling
A702
A701
Stobo
546
TRAHENNA
Hallyne
River Tweed
Neidpath
Kings Muir
John Buchan Story
Kirkton Manor
Kirkburn
Kailzie
Kirkburn
Robert Small's Printing Works
Innerleithen

Causewayend
Broughton
Calzeat
B712
Dawyck Botanic
Castlehill
Upper Tweeddale
Traquair
Tweed Valley Forest Park
566
MINCHMUIR
11

Coulter
Rachan Mill
Glenholm
Drumelzier
Posso
748
CULTER FELL
676
CARDON HILL
Glencothe
Stanhope
736
PYKESTONE HILL
742
DUN RIG
629
12

J
K
L
M
20
N
BLACK LAW
P
30
Q
R
40
A708

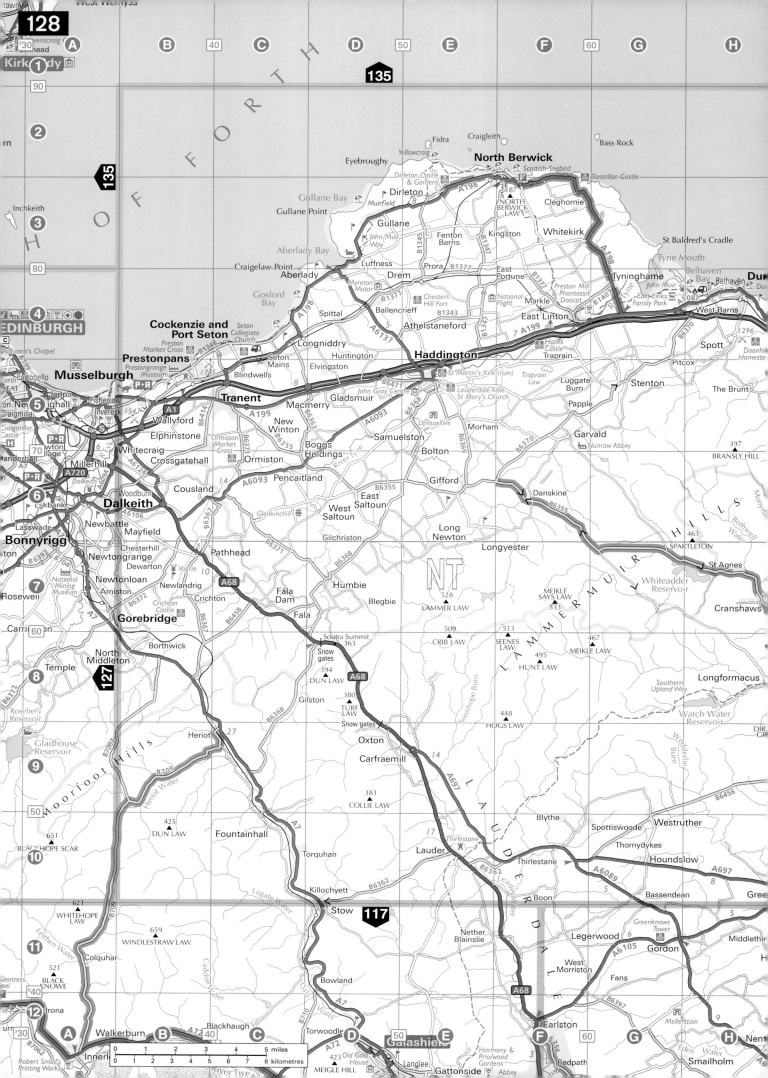

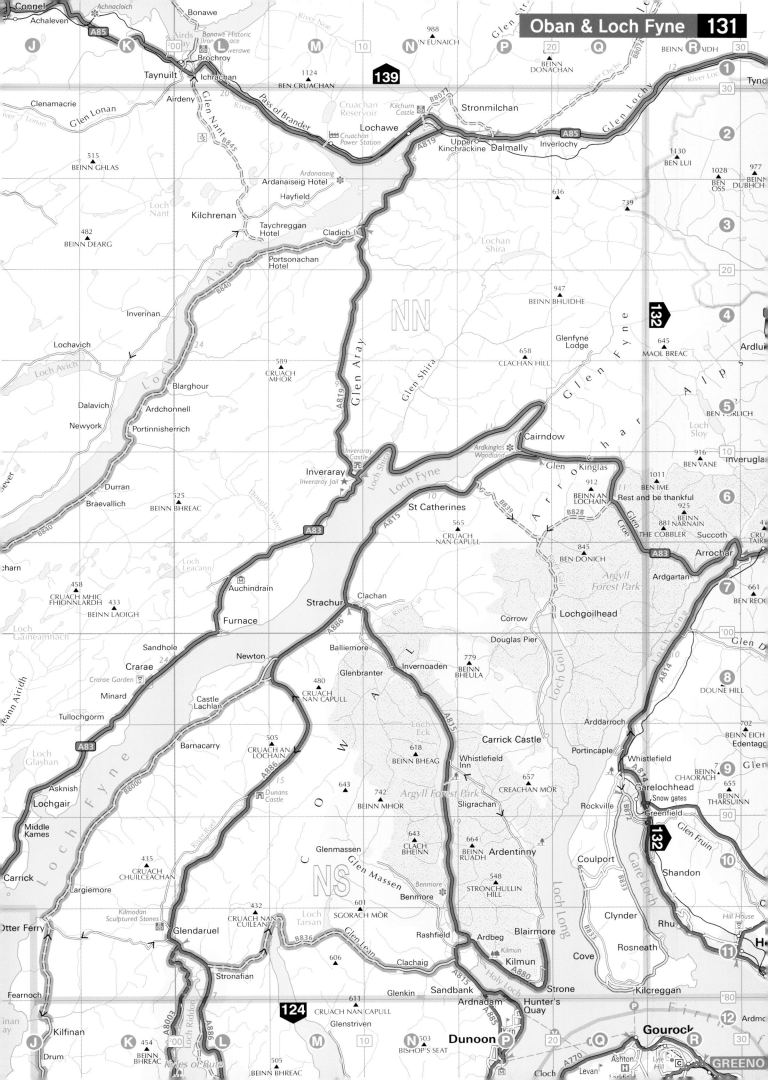

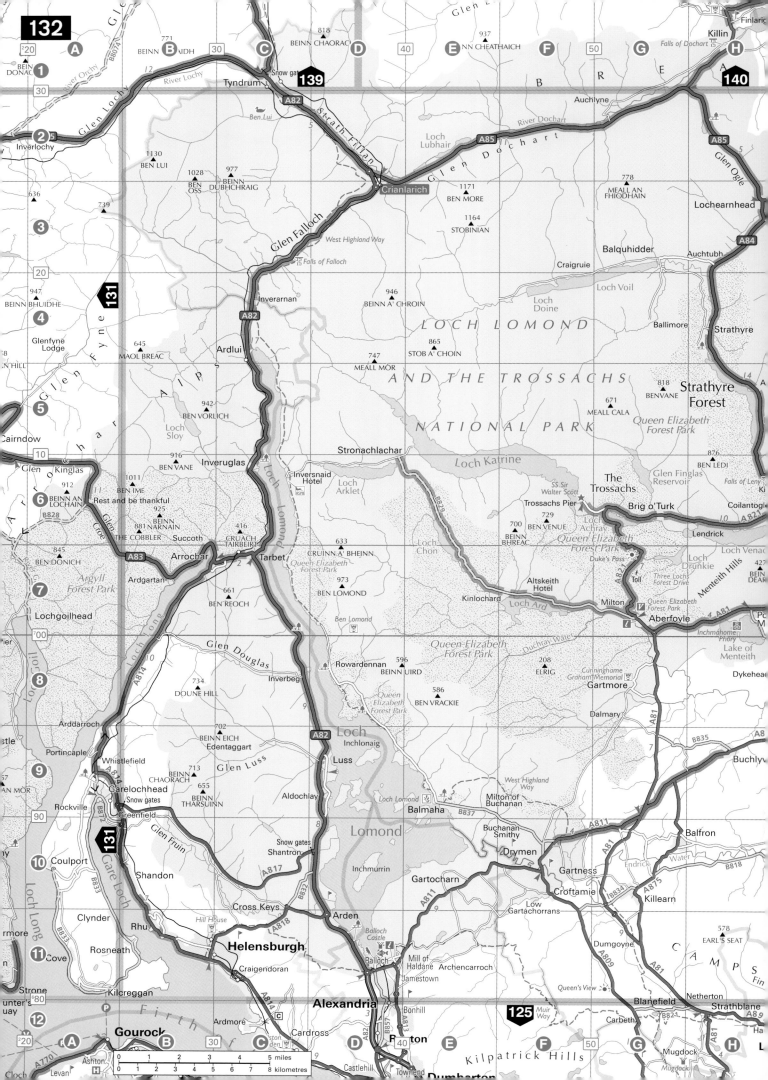

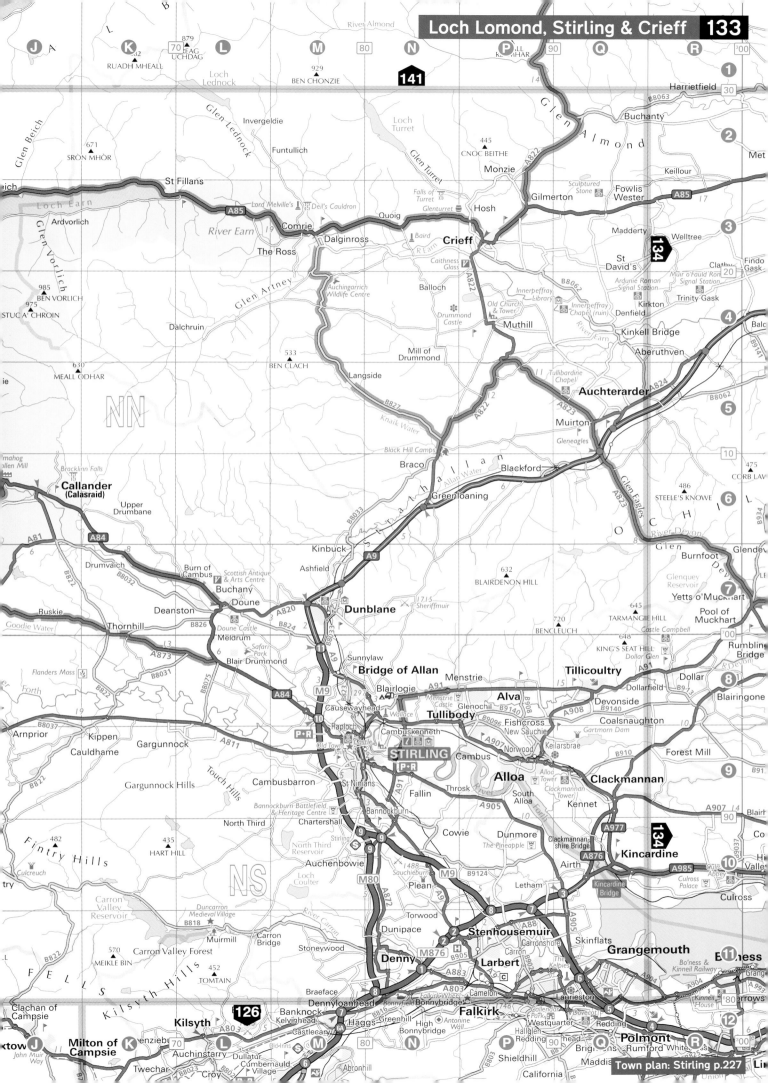

141

134

J A L B
K
L
M 80
N
P KILLIHAR 90
Q
R 300

1 Harrietfield 30
B8063

Glen Almond

Buchanty 2

River Almond

Glen Lednock
Loch Lednock

879 70
BEAG UCHDAG
RUADH MHEALL
32

929
BEN CHONZIE

Loch Turret

Invergeldie
Funtullich

445
CNOC BEITHE

Monzie

A822

Keillour

Sculptured Stone

Fowlis Wester

A85 17

671
SRÒN MHÒR

St Fillans

Glen Turret

Gilmerton

Falls of Turret

Lord Melville's Deil's Cauldron

A85

Comrie 19
Quoig

Glenturret

Hosh

Crieff

Maddety 3
St David's

Welltree

134

Ardvorlich

River Earn

Dalginross

Glen Beich

Balloch

Caithness Glass

Ardunie Roman Signal Station 20

Muir o' Fauld Roman Signal Station

Findo Gask

The Ross

985 BEN VORLICH
975 STUC A' CHROIN

Glen Artney

Dalchruin

Auchingarrich Wildlife Centre

Drummond Castle

Muthill

Mill of Drummond

B8062

Innerpeffray Library
Innerpeffray Chapel (ruin)

Old Church & Tower

River Earn

Kirkton
Denfield

Trinity Gask

Kinkell Bridge

Balc

B9141

630 MEALL ODHAR

533 BEN CLACH

Langside

B827

A822

Tullibardine Chapel

Auchterarder

A824

B8062

NN

Knaik Water

2

Muirton

Gleneagles

A823

5

10

Black Hill Camps

Braco

Strathallan

Blackford

Glen Eagles

475
CORB LAW

B934

Bracklinn Falls

Callander (Calasraid)

Upper Drumbane

Greenloaning

Allan Water

6

486 STEELE'S KNOWE

O C H I L

6

A84

A81

B822

B8033

B8032

Kinbuck

A9

Ashfield

632

BLAIRDENON HILL

Glenquey Reservoir

Glen Devon

Burnfoot

Glendevon

7

Drumvaich

Burn of Cambus

Scottish Antique & Arts Centre

645

Yetts o'Muckhart

Drumvaich
Doune
Buchany

B826

Deanston

A820

Dunblane

1715 Sheriffmuir

TARMANGIE HILL

720

BENCLEUCH

Castle Campbell

Pool of Muckhart

Rumbling Bridge

8

Ruskie
Thornhill

Goodie Water

B824

Doune Castle

2

11

A9

Meldrum

Safari Park

Blair Drummond

Sunnylaw

Bridge of Allan

Blairlogie

648 KING'S SEAT HILL

Dollar Glen

Tillicoultry

Dollar

B9

Blairingone

A84

M9

Menstrie

Castle Campbell

A91

Devonside

Dollarfield

9

Flanders Moss

B822

B8031

B8075

Causewayhead

Raploch

Wallace

Menstrie Castle

Alva

Blairlogie

Tullibody

B9140

B9096

Fishcross New Sauchie

Coalsnaughton

A908

B9140

Gartmorn Dam

B910

Forest Mill

Kippen
Cauldhame

Arnprior

A811

Gargunnock

Touch Hills

Cambusbarron

P+R

Old Town

Castle

STIRLING

P+R

Cambuskenneth

A91

Cambus

Norwood

A907

Keilarsbrae

Alloa Tower

Alloa

Clackmannan Tower

Clackmannan

9

B9

Gargunnock Hills

St Ninians

Fallin

Throsk

River Forth

South Alloa

Kennet

A907 4

90

Blairh

NS

Bannockburn Battlefield & Heritage Centre

Chartershall

Bannockburn

Cowie

A905

Dunmore
The Pineapple

Clackmannan shire Bridge

A876

Kincardine

A985

Culross Abbey

10

Valle

Fintry Hills

482

HART HILL 435

North Third Reservoir

9

Stirling

9

S

9

Auchenbowie

1488 Sauchieburn

Plean

A9

Letham

A977

Kincardine Bridge

Culross Palace

Culross

Culcreuch

North Third

Loch Coulter

M80

Airth

3

Kincardine Bridge

F

570 MEIKLE BIN

Duncarron Medieval Village

Muirmill

B818

Carron Valley Reservoir

Carron Valley Forest

452 TOMTAIN

Braeface

Carron Bridge

Stoneywood

A872

Torwood

Dunipace

B9124

8

7

Stenhousemuir

2

A88

Carronshore

Skinflats

A905

Grangemouth

E 11

A904

Bo'ness & Kinneil Railway

Kinneil House

80

Clachan of Campsie

Kilsyth Hills

126

Kilsyth

Banknock
Kelvinhead

Dennyloanhead

Denny

M876

A883

B905

Larbert

Carron

H C

Camelon

Falkirk

748

Laurieston

A803

Antonine Wall

A9

Bannock

The Kelpies

1

Callendar Park

Westquarter

Redding

90

12

Milton of Campsie

John Muir Way

J

K

70

Auchinstarry

L

Castlecary

Croy

M

80

Kelvinhead

Haggs-Greenhill
Bonnybridge

Bonnyfield

High Bonnybridge

N

B816

Shieldhill

P

Brigh ens
Maddis

R

Polmont
Rumford

Li

Dullatur
Cumbernauld Village

6

Abronhill

B8023

California

Union

NL

COLL

Eilean Mòr
Rubha Mòr
Rubha Sgor-inr
Sorisdale
Bousd
Cliad Bay
Arnabost
Grishipoll
Clabhach
Loch Cliad
Hogh Bay
Ballyhaugh
Arinagour
Totronald
Coll
Acha
Arileod
Uig
Eilean Ornsay
Feall Bay
Bàgh a' Chaisteil (Castlebay)
(Apr–Oct, Weds only)
Calgary Point
Crossapol Bay
Rubha Fàsachd
Loch Breachacha
Gunna
Rubha Dubh

Rubha Port Bhiosd
Clachan Mor
Balephetrish Bay
Caoles
Ruaig
Loch Bhasapoll
B8069
Hough Bay
Ballevullin
Cornoigmore
Kenovay
B8068
Gott Bay
Kilkenneth
Tiree
B8068
Scarinish
Moss
Heylipoll
B8065
Middleton
Crossapol
TIREE
Barrapoll
B8065
Hynish Bay
Loch a Phuill
B8067
Balemartine
Rinn Thorbhais
Mannal
Skerryvore Lighthouse
Balephuil Bay
Hynish

TRESHNISH ISLES
Flac
Lunga
Bac Mòr or Dutchman's
Bac Beag

Colonsay

NM

NR

① 700
Eilean Dubh
Kiloran Bay
Rubh' a' Geodha
143 CARNAN EOIN
Oban
② **COLONSAY**
Kiloran
Kilchattan
B8087
Scalasaig
③ Machrins
B8086
B8085
Colonsay
Garvard
'90
Oronsay
Rubha Bàn
Dubh Eilean
Eilean Ghaoideamal
Port Askaig
④ **ORONSAY**
Oronsay

ⓐ   ⓑ   '40   ⓒ   ⓓ

0 1 2 3 miles
0 1 2 3 4 5 kilometres

IONA
Iona Abbey & Nunnery
Baile Mòr
MacLean's Cross
Sound of Iona
Soa Island
Erraid

0 1 2 3 4 5 miles
0 1 2 3 4 5 6 7 8 kilometres

J   K   40   L   M   50   N   P   60   Q   R

Filean

Rubha Àird
Druimnich

Seven Men
of Moid
239 Ardmolich
1
BEINN BHR

*Morar, Moidart and
Ardnamurchan*

Ockle
Point
Ockle
Ardtoe   Shielfoot   70
Kilmory   Ardtoe
Branault   356   Ardtoe   B8044   Mingarry
BEINN   Kentra   Blain   Dalna
BHREAC   Arevegaig   Acharacle   **2**
Sanna Point
A861
Sanna
Portuairk   Achaha   436
Achosnich   MEALL NAN CON   ARDNAMURCHAN
Ardnamurchan
Point   B8007   437   Salen
Bàgh a' Chaisteil
(Castlebay)
Loch Baghasdail
(Lochboisdale)
(Oct–Mar)   342   527   512   B8007   **3**
BEINN NA SEILG   Kilchoan   BEN HIANT   19   Natural   BEN LAGA   60   GEÀRR CI
Ormsaigmore   Mingary   History   Glenbeg
Glenborrodale   Laga
Ardslignish   RSPB   Carna   138
Oronsay   **4**
Auliston   571
Ardmore   Point   BEINN
Point   Rubha   LADAIN
V   nan Gall
Sorne   437
Point   Drimnin   BEINN   Loch   **5**
Quinish Point   Glengorm Castle   **Tobermory**   BHUIDHE   550   Loch   Ach
Caliach Point   Mull   M   SÌTHEAN NA RAPLAICH   Arienas   G
292   Calve   50   Clagg
NM   'S AIRDE   Mull   Island   Larachbeg
BEINN   A884   **6**
Dervaig   Achnadrish   Ach
Calgary   B8073   5   A848   Loch
Art in   6   Sound   Aline
Nature   Old Byre   444   Fuinary   Lochaline
Calgary Bay   V   SPEINNE MÒR   Aros   V
Treshnish Point   Ensay   342   Loch Frisa   Glen Aros   Áros   **7**
CÀRN MÒR   of   Salen   Fishnish   Fishnish Pier
Rubh' a' Chaoil   Burg   Glenaros House   A849   Point   11
390   Killiechronan   Mull   40
Fanmore   CNOC AN   B8035   408   Scanastle Bay
DÀ CHINN   333   2   BEINN   Altcreich
Ballygown   BEINN   Gruline   NAN LUS   **8**
Eas Fors   NAN CÀRN   Macquarie   ISLE   636   766
Loch   19   Oskamull   B8073   Mausoleum   BEINN MHEADHON   DUN DA   Craig
Gometra   Tuath   ULVA   P   Eorsa   591   OF   GHAOITHE
Little Colonsay   BEINN A' GHRÀIG   Loch   MULL   **9**
Staffa   B8035   17   Bà   Strathcoil
Inch Kenneth   966   704   A849   30
Fingal's   Inchkenneth Chapel   Balnahard   BEN MORE   CRUACHAN DEARG   Glen   Loch
(ruin)   More   698   Lo
Loch na Keal   519   BEN CREACH   **10**
Isle of Mull   BEIN NA   Tiroran   717   Cro
SRÈINE   Aird of   BEN BUIE
491   Kinloch   A849   Loch
CREACH BHEINN   Pennycross   Loch   Fuaran   Lochbuie   **11**
Fossil Tree   Burg   Pennyghael   Fuaran   503   130   337
Rubha nan Cearc   BEINN NA   Loch   MAOL
Kintra   Loch Scridain   CROISE   Uisg   BÀN
nphort   14   Leidle Water
Aridhglas   Loch na   A849   Loch Buie   377   **12**
Columba   Lathaich   DRUIM FADA
hibition   376   Carsaig   Rubha
Centre   Bunessan   CRUACHAN MIN   376   Dubh
ROSS OF MULL   Loch Assapol   BEINN   20   70
Ardchiavaig   Uisken   CHREAGACH
Rubh'   Malcolm's
Ardalanish   Rubha nam   Point
Bràithrean

J   K   40   L   M   50   N   P   60   Q   R

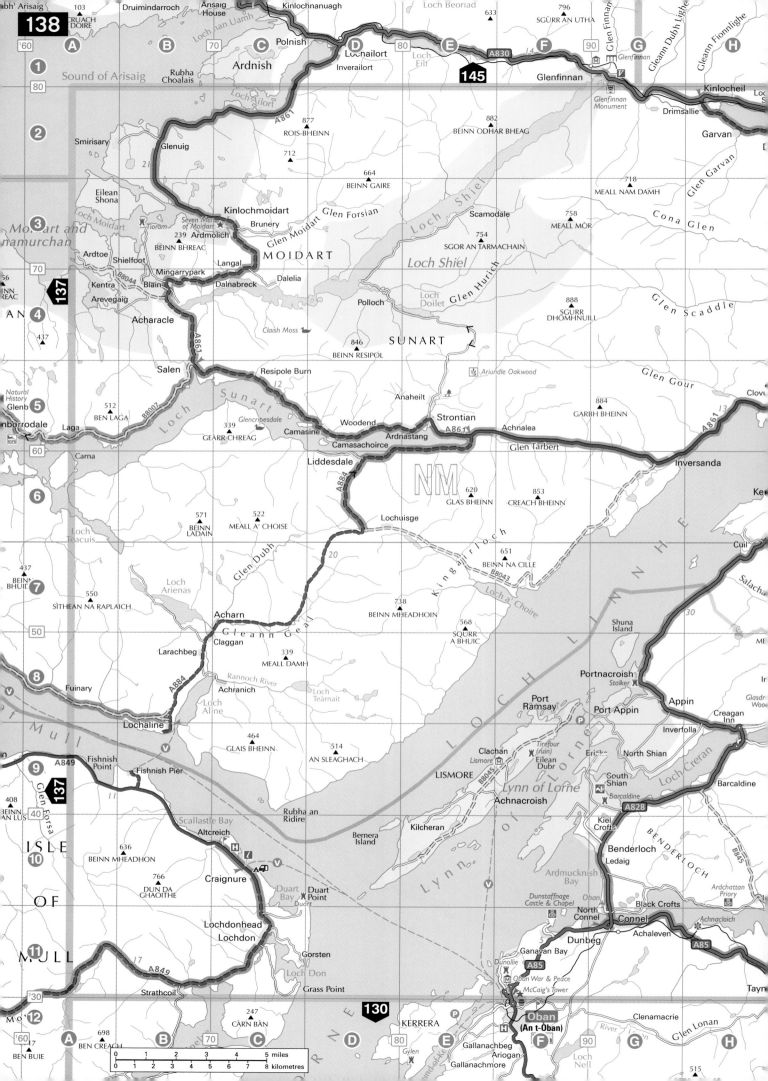

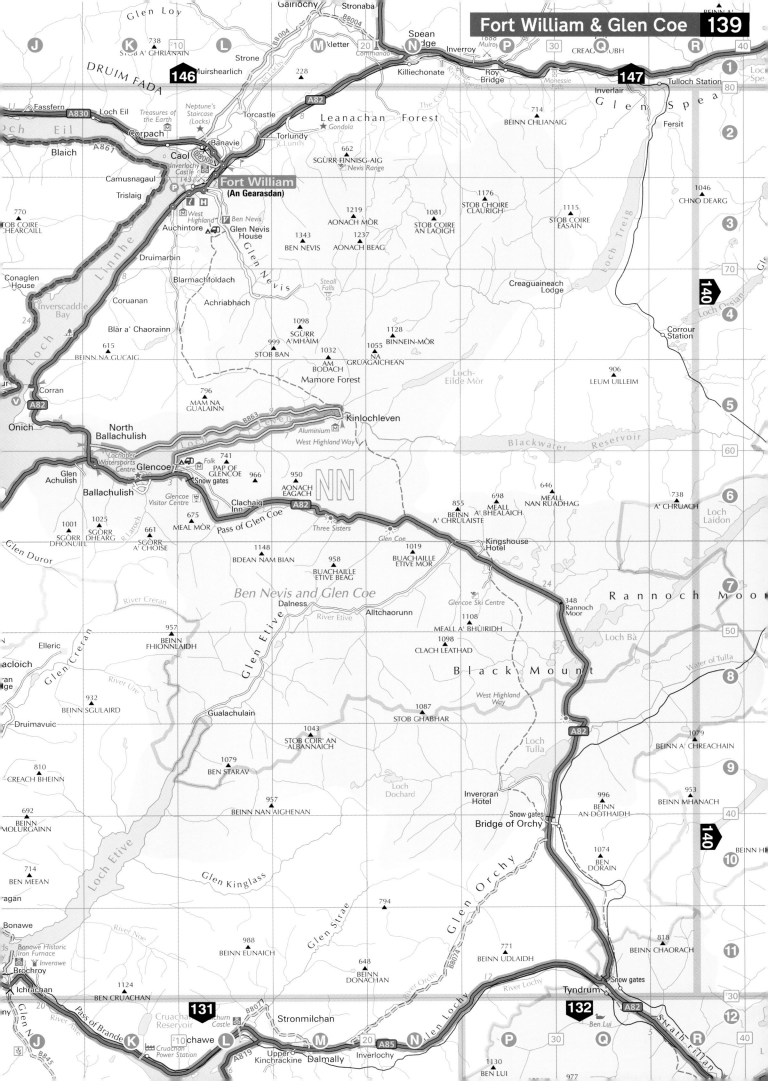

Glen Loy

Gairlochy Stronaba

Spean
dge Inverroy

1688
Mulroy

CREAG
UBH

BEINN A

1

J K 738 L M kletter N P Q R

STOB A' GHRIANAIN

210

146 Muirshearlich B8004 20 Commando 30 1431m 147 Tulloch Station 80

DRUIM FADA Strone B8004 Killiechonate Roy Monessie Inverlair 147 80

228 Bridge Falls Fersit Glen Spea

Fassfern A830 Loch Eil Treasures of Neptune's 8 Leanachan Forest 714 1046 40

the Earth Staircase (Locks) Gondola BEINN CHLIANAIG CHNO DEARG 2

Corpach Torcastle R Lundy Nevis Range 1

Blaich A867 Banavie 662 1176 1115 3

Caol SGÙRR FINNISG-AIG STOB CHOIRE STOB COIRE

Camusnagaul B8006 Inverlochy 1219 1081 CLAURIGH EASAIN

Castle Fort William AONACH MÒR STOB COIRE Loch Treig 70

A82 1431 (An Gearasdan) AN LAOIGH

Trislaig P H 1343 1237 Creaguaineach 140 4

West Highland Ben Nevis BEN NEVIS AONACH BEAG Lodge Corrour

Auchintore Glen Nevis Station

Druimarbin House 1098 1128

Conaglen SGÙRR BINNEIN-MÒR 5

House Blarmachfoldach Steall 999 A'MHÀIM 1055

Falls STOB BAN 1032 NA 906

Coruanan AM GRUAGAICHEAN LEUM UILLEIM

Inverscaddle 615 Achriabhach BODACH

Bay BEINN NA GUCAIG Mamore Forest Loch-

24 Blàr a' Chaorainn Eilde Mòr

770 796 60

OB COIRE MAM NA B863

HEARCAILL GUALAINN Kinlochleven

V A82 Aluminium Blackwater Reservoir

Corran Onich North Leven West Highland Way

Ballachulish 741 NN

Lochaber Folk PAP OF 950 646 738 6

Glencoe Watersports GLENCOE AONACH 855 MEALL A' CHRUACH Loch

Centre 966 EAGACH 698 NAN RUADHAG Laidon

Glen Snow gates BEINN MEALL

Achulish Glencoe A82 675 A' CHRÙLAISTE A' BHEALAICH

Ballachulish Visitor Centre R Laroch MEAL MÒR Pass of Glen Coe Three Sisters Glen Coe Kingshouse 7

1001 1025 661 1148 Hotel

SGÒRR SGÒRR SGÒRR BDEAN NAM BIAN 958 1019 348 Rannoch Moor

DHONUILL DHEARG A' CHOISE BUACHAILLE BUACHAILLE Rannoch

Glen Duror ETIVE BEAG ETIVE MÒR Moor 50

Ben Nevis and Glen Coe Glencoe Ski Centre

Elleric Dalness 1108 Black Mount 8

River Creran Alltchaorunn MEALL A' BHÙIRIDH

acloich 957 1098

ran BEINN River Etive CLACH LEATHAD West Highland

dge FHIONNLAIDH Way A82

932 Gualachulain 1087 Loch Loch

Druimavuic BEINN SGULAIRD STOB GHABHAR Tulla 9

810 1043 1079

CREACH BHEINN STOB COIR' AN Inveroran BEINN BEINN MHANACH

ALBANNAICH Hotel 953

1079 Snow gates 996 AN DÒTHAIDH 40

692 BEN STARAV AN DOTHAIDH

BEINN 957 Bridge of Orchy

MOLURGAINN BEINN NAN AIGHENAN 1074 140

BEINN BEINN H

714 BEN 10

BEN MEEAN DORAIN

ragan Glen Kinglass Loch Etive 1

Bonawe 794 818 11

Bonawe Historic River Noe Glen Strae BEINN CHAORACH

Iron Furnace 988 771

Inverawe BEINN EUNAICH BEINN UDLAIDH Snow gates 12

Brochroy 648 Tyndrum

Ichrachan 1124 BEINN Ben Lui

BEN CRUACHAN DONACHAN 132 A82

131 B8077 Glen Lochy River Lochy J

ny Cruachan Churn Stronmilchan 132

Glen N Reservoir Castle 1130 977

B845 Cruachan A819 BEN LUI

Power Station A85

chawe J K L M N P Q

210 Upper 20

Kincirackine Dalmally Inverlochy

30 40

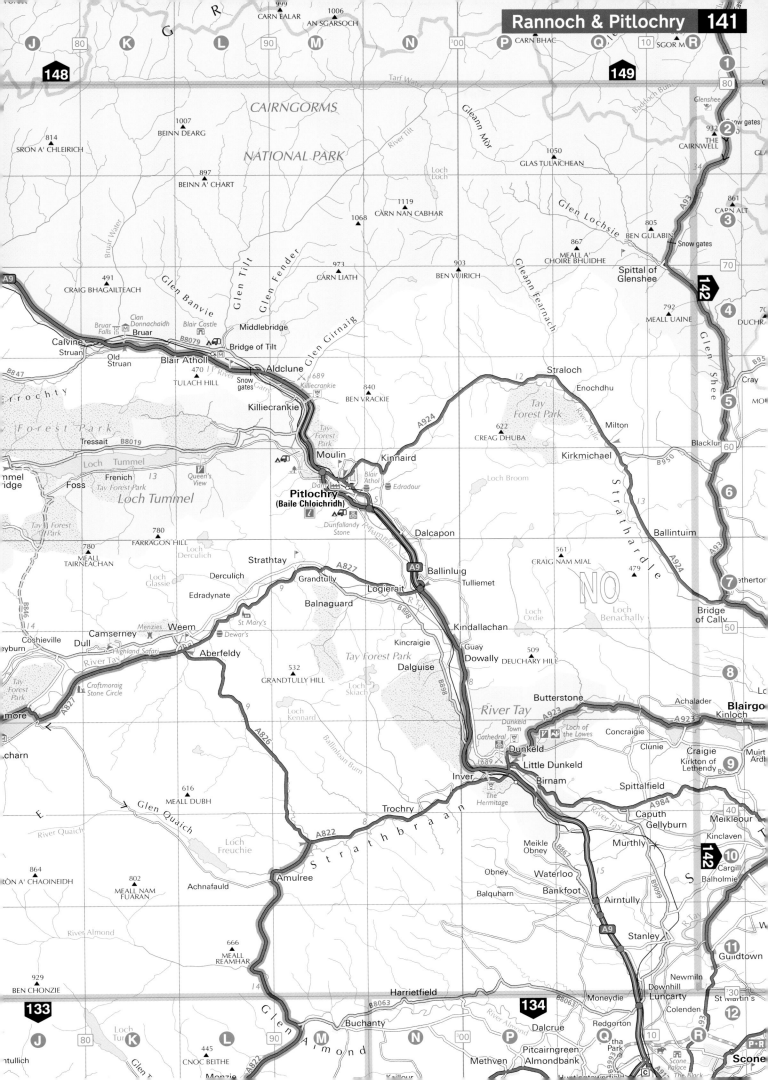

MOUNT BATTOCK

Water of Dye

J
150

475
HILL OF FINGRAY

K

60

L

B974

M 465
GOYLE HILL

70

Cairn O'Mount

N

Glen of Drumtochty

P

80

Temple Fiddes

Q
151

R

90

1
Fowlsneugh
Crawton

454
Cairn O'Mount

Drumlithie

Glenbervie

Mondynes

Crawton

Catterline

2
Todhead Point

Tennet

Glenesk Folk

Snow gates

Auchenblae
FINELLA HILL

Fordoun

Pittarrow

B966

Redmyre

Arbuthnott

B967

Grassic Gibbon Centre

Kinneff

3
Bervie Bay

Maritime

70

544
STURDY HILL

Mains of Balnakettle

B9120

B974

Fettercairn

Mains of Haulkerton

Laurencekirk

B9120

Redford

Inverbervie

Gourdon

605
BULG

River North Esk

Bogmuir

Sauchieburn

Dykelands

Benholm

4

677
HILL OF WIRREN

Bridgend

Balfield

Dunlappie

Gannachy

Edzell Castle & Garden

Edzell

Edzell Woods

Luthermuir

A90

B974

A937

Marykirk

13

Johnshaven

West Water

Kirkton of Menmuir

Tigerton

White Caterthun

Inchbare

Newtonmill

Logie Pert

Graigo

Logie

Lochside

Morphie

Bush

St Cyrus

Milton Ness

5

Glen Esk

Brown Caterthun

Keithock

Hillside

A92

60

Mains of Balhall

Lochty

Little Brechin

Maison Dieu Chapel (ruin)

Trinity

Careston

Dun

House of Dun

Montrose Air Station

Montrose

6
NO

Ford

Brechin

A935

9

Bridge of Dun

Caledonian Railway

Montrose Basin

Scurdie Ness

R. South Esk

Netherton

Haughs of Kinnaird

Barnhead

Ferryden

of osston

Sculptured Stones

Aberlemno

A933

Farnell

Maryton

A934

Craig

Usan

B9134

Mains of Melgunds

Kemp's Castle

B9113

Westerton of Rossie

Braehead

Boddin Point

7

allie

9

A932

Guthrie

132
WUDDY LAW

Bolshan

Glasterlaw

Kinnell

Lunan

Lunan Bay

50

Burnside

Pitmuies

Friockheim

C
B965

Boysack

Lunan Water

Inverkeilor

8

chen

Letham

Glasterlaw

13

uld

Leysmill

Chapelton

raichie

A933

Cauldcots

Red Head

Redford

Colliston

Letham Grange

A92

Greystone

Carmyllie

St Vigeans

Marywell

9

yhillock

B9127

B9127

Auchmithie

Carlingheugh Bay

Crombie

B961

Bonnington

Arbirlot

Arbroath Abbey

The Deil's Head

Craigton

Kirkton of Monikie

A92

Arbroath

Signal Tower

40

Muirdrum

17

Upper Victoria

East Haven

10

Barry Mill

Panbride

7

961

Barry

West Haven

Carnoustie

11

A930

Carnoustie

A92

30

nifieth

BUDDON NESS

135

12

Tentsmu Point
Tentsmui

J

K

60

L

M

70

N

P

80

Q

R

90

A '20 B C 30 D E 40 F G 50 H

SKYE

Rubha nan Clach

Fernilea
Carbost
152 Talisker Bay
Talisker
Merkadale
Drynoch
B8009
B8009
Glen Drynoch
A863
Sligachan

444 BEN LEE
Peinch
conser
773 GLAMAIG
A87
Sligachan

369 ARNAVAL

Minginish

Glen Eynort

Glen Brittle Forest

447 BEINN BHREAC

Grula

369 BEINN BHREAC

Loch Eynort

Fairy Pools

965 SGURR NAN GILLEAN

The Cuillin Hills

434 AN CRUACHIN

974 SGURR A' GHEADAIDH

Cuillin Hills

927 BLAVEN

Glenbrittle
Bualintur

1009 SGURR ALASDAIR

Loch Coruisk

Loch na Crèitheach

Loch Brittle

894 GARS BHEINN

Kirkib

225 CEANN NA BEINNE

Rubha an Dùnain

Soay Sound

139 BEINN BHREAC

Loch Scavaig

344 BEN MEABOS

Mol-chlach

Elgol

SOAY

Rubh' Aonghais

Stratha Point

Loch Baghasdail (Lochboisdale)

CUILLIN SOUND

NG

CANNA

210 CÀRN A' GHAILL

Kilmory Bay

Rubha Shamhnan Insir

Garrisdale Point

A'Chill

Canna Harbour

Sanday

Sound of Canna

302 MULLACH MÒR

Rubha na Roinne

A' Brìdeanach

570 ORVAL

Kinloch

Loch-Scresort

Oigh-sgeir

RÙM

810 ASKIVAL

Harris Bay

All vehicles must have the relevant island permit prior to travel to The Small Isles. Services are seasonal, day & weather dependent.

763 SGURR NAN GILLEAN

The Small Isles

Rubha nam Meirleach

Sound of Rùm

NM

Bay of Laig

Cleadale

Rubha an Fhasaidh

Laig

299 AN CRUACHAN

EIGG

Kildonnan

393 AN SGÙRR

Galmisdale

Sound of Eigg

Eilean nan Each

Eilean Chathastail

MUCK

Port Mòr

A '20 B 30 C 30 D E 40 F G 50 H

0 1 2 3 4 5 miles
0 1 2 3 4 5 6 7 8 kilometres

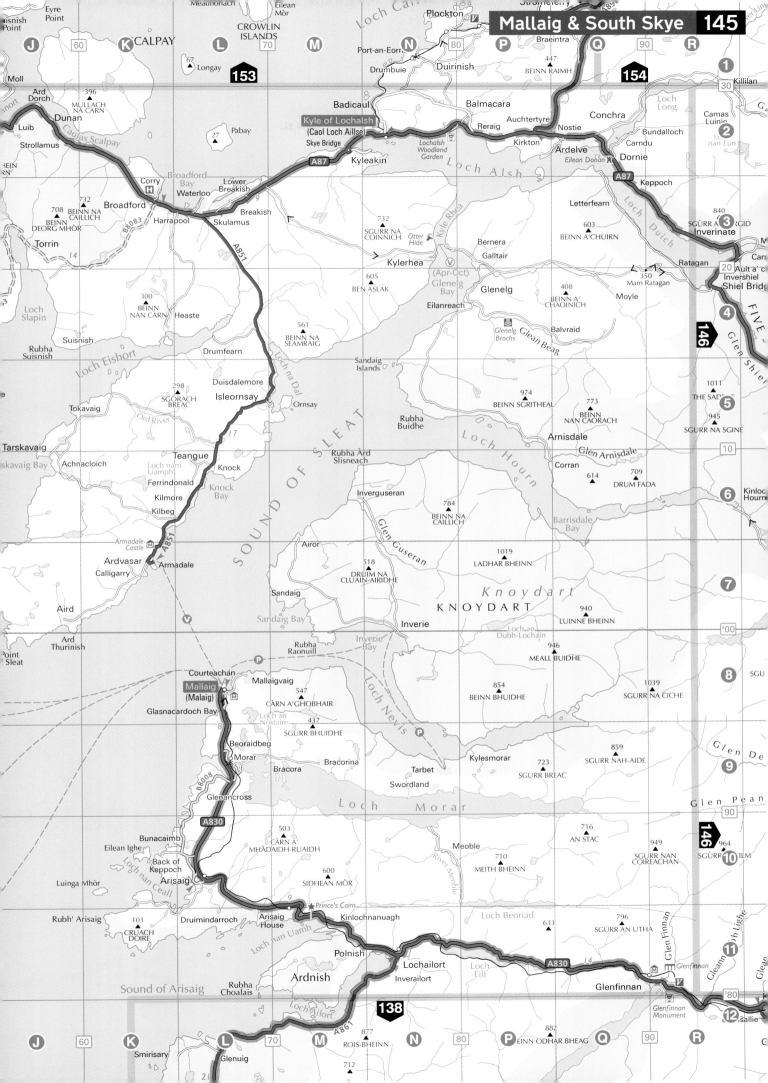

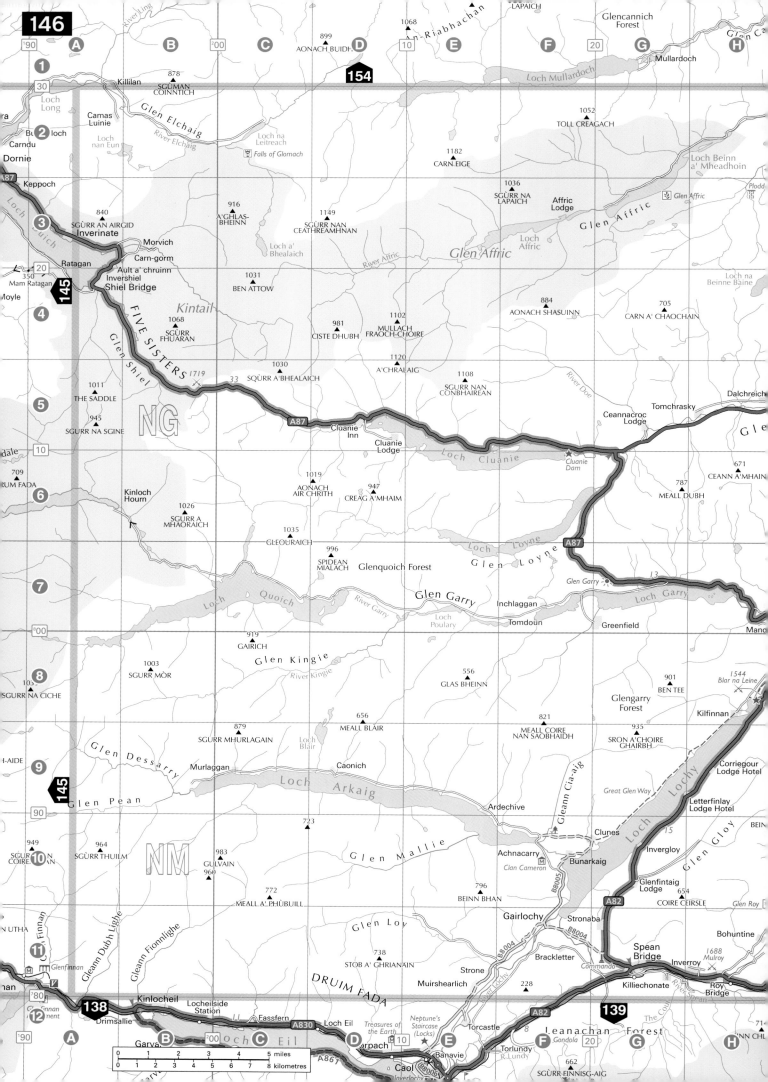

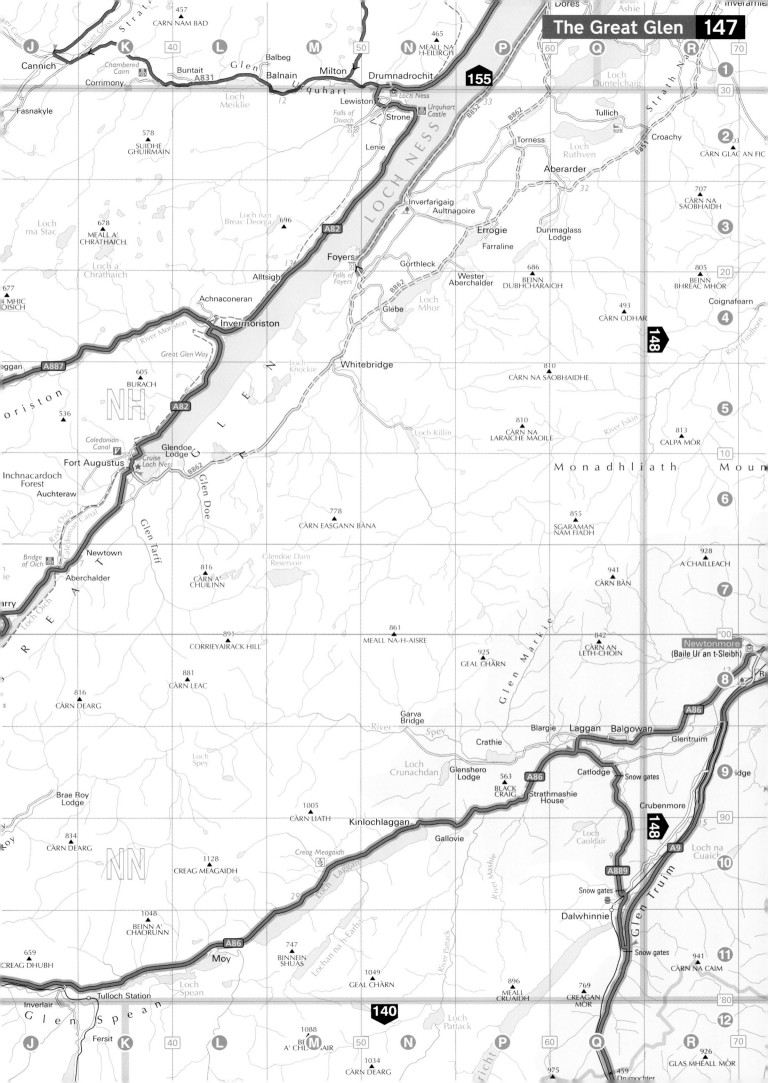

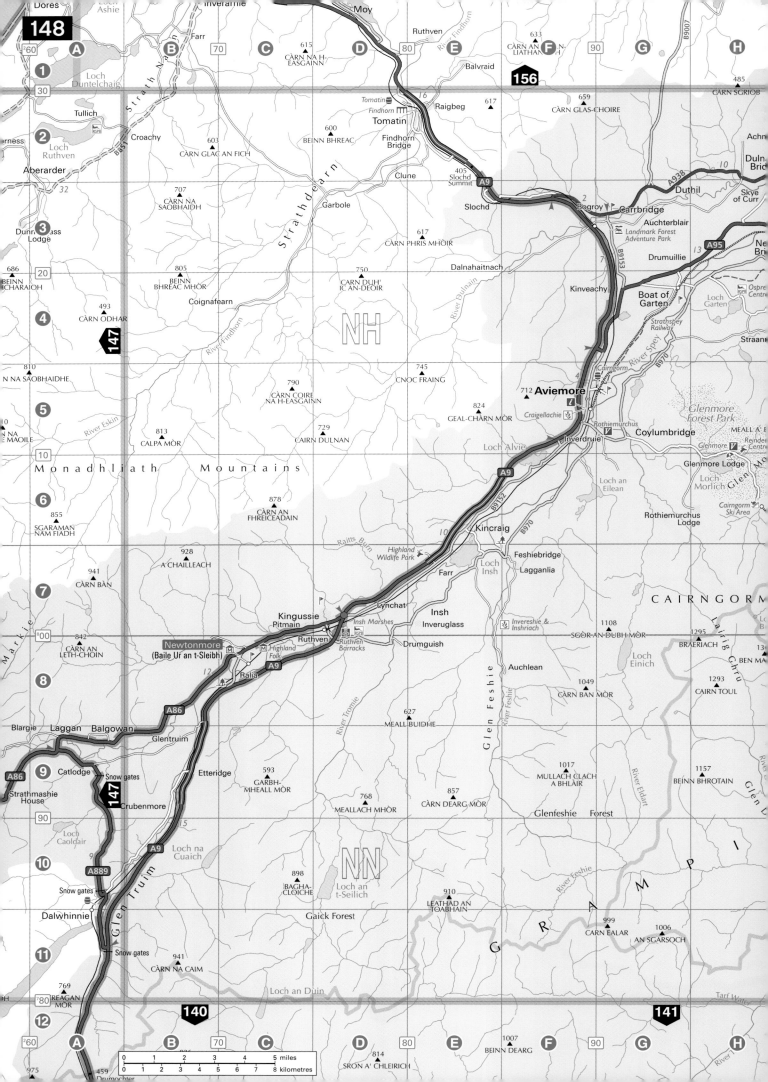

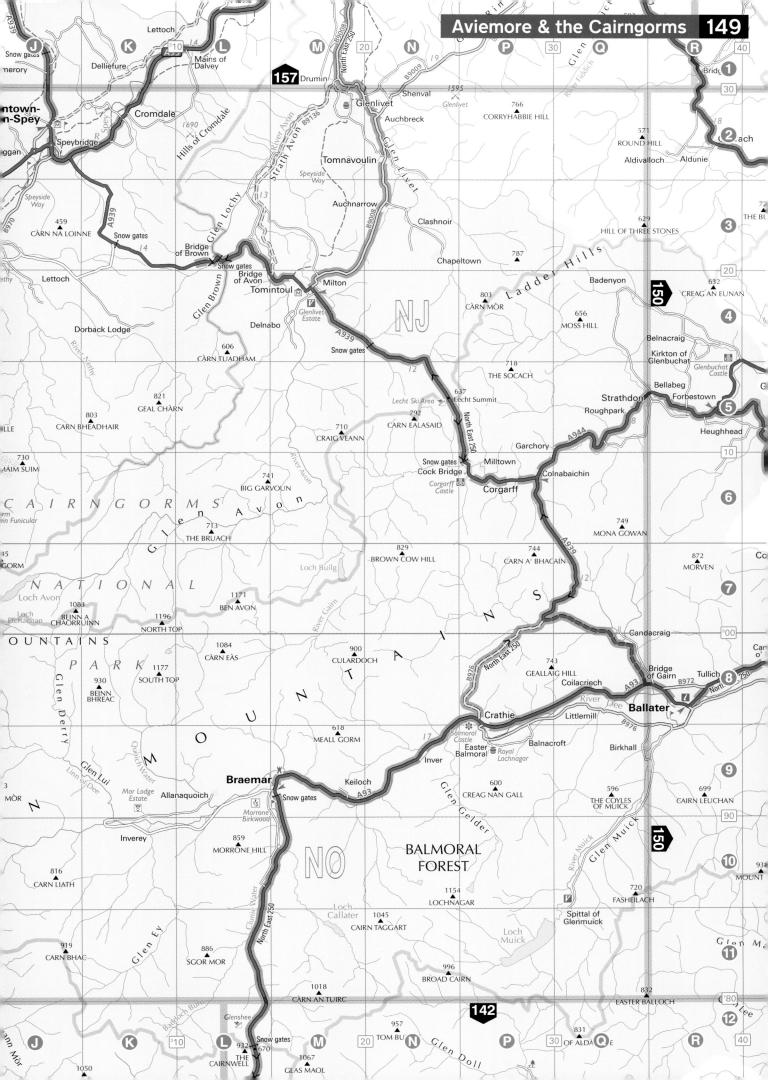

J K L M N P Q R

157 Drumin
Lettoch
Delliefure
Mains of Dalvey
Snow gates
Cromdale
Shenval
Glenlivet
1595 Glenlivet
Auchbreck
766
CORRYHABBIE HILL
571
ROUND HILL
Aldivalloch
Aldunie
Speybridge
Hills of Cromdale
1690
Tomnavoulin
629
HILL OF THREE STONES
THE BU
Càrn na Loinne 459
Snow gates
Bridge of Brown
Auchnarrow
Clashnoir
Chapeltown
787
Badenyon
632
CREAG AN EUNAN
150
Lettoch
Bridge of Avon
Milton
Tomintoul
803
CÀRN MÒR
656
MOSS HILL
Belnacraig
Kirkton of Glenbuchat
Glenbuchat Castle
Dorback Lodge
Delnabo
Glenlivet Estate
NJ
718
THE SOCACH
Bellabeg
Forbestown
Càrn Tuadham 606
Snow gates
637
Strathdon
Roughpark
Heughhead
Geal Chàrn 821
Lecht Ski Area
Lecht Summit
Garchory
A944
Carn Bheadhair 803
792
CARN EALASAID
Milltown
Colnabaichin
730
MÀIM SUIM
Craig Veann 710
Snow gates
Cock Bridge
Corgarff Castle
Corgarff
749
MONA GOWAN
CAIRNGORMS
741
BIG GARVOUN
829
BROWN COW HILL
744
CÀRN A' BHACAIN
872
MORVEN
713
THE BRUACH
Loch Builg
A939
NATIONAL
Loch Avon
1083
BEINN A CHAORRUINN
1171
BEN AVON
Loch Etchachan
1196
NORTH TOP
OUNTAINS
1084
CÀRN EÀS
900
CULARDOCH
743
GEALLAIG HILL
Candacraig
PARK
1177
SOUTH TOP
Coilacriech
Bridge of Gairn
Tullich
930
BEINN BHREAC
Glen Derry
618
MEALL GORM
Crathie
Littlemill
River Dee
Ballater
Glen Lui
Linn of Dee
Braemar
Keiloch
A93
Inver
Balmoral Castle
Easter Balmoral
Royal Lochnagar
Balnacroft
Birkhall
Mar Lodge Estate
Allanaquoich
Snow gates
600
CREAG NAN GALL
596
THE COYLES OF MUICK
699
CAIRN LEUCHAN
Inverey
Morrone Birkwood
NO
BALMORAL FOREST
1154
LOCHNAGAR
720
FASHEILACH
150
816
CARN LIATH
859
MORRONE HILL
1045
CAIRN TAGGART
996
BROAD CAIRN
Spittal of Glenmuick
Loch Muick
919
CARN BHAC
886
SGOR MOR
Loch Callater
832
EASTER BALLOCH
1018
CÀRN AN TUIRC
957
TOM BU
831
OF ALDA
142
1050
Glenshee
Snow gates
932
670
THE CAIRNWELL
1067
GLAS MAOL
Glen Doll

J K L M N P Q R

NK

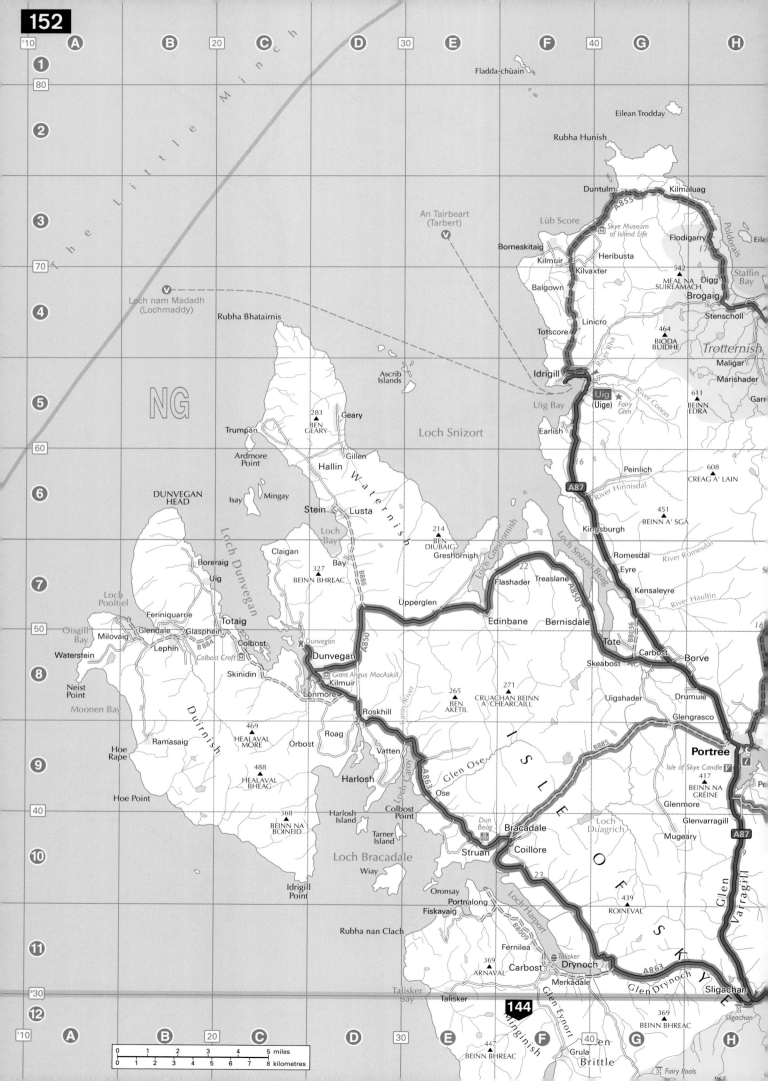

J   K   60   L   M   70   N   B8021   P   80   Q   R   13   90

CNOC
BREAC

Garden

1 ALL NA

North Erradale

Poolewe   Londubh

80

Big Sand   Strath   A832   **2**

160   Smithstown   Heritage
Lonemore   Auchtercairn

Longa   Loch   Gairloch   Gairloch
Island   Gairloch   & Loch Ewe

421   Loch

Port   Eilean   Charlestown   MEALL AN   **3**
Henderson   B8056   Horrisdale   DOIREIN

Badachro   River Kerry   Loch Bad
Opinan   an Sgalaig

South Erradale   70   Talla   **4**

Red Point   Loch Ghaireamhach   **154**

Loch a'   875   Loch na
Ghodhainn   BAOSBHEINN   h-Oidh   855

Red   NG   619   BEINN   **5**
Point   BEINN BHREAC   Loch a'   AN EÒI

Loch   Bhealaich

Kilt Rock   Rubha   Torridon   985   914
Ellishader   na Fearn   Lower   BEINN   BEINN DEARG
Diabaig   ALLIGIN   60

Valtos   Fearnmore   Loch
Rubha nam Brathairean   Fearnbeg   Diabaig   **6**

Culnaknock   Arrina   Alligin Shuas   Inveralligin
Ob   Kenmore   Torridon
Tote   Chuaig   House   Torr

A855   Cuaig   Ardheslaig   Upper Loch Torridon   Deer   **7**
RONA   Loch   West Ros

Callakille   Shieldaig   Shieldaig   Annat

Eilean   Lonbain   492   A896   902
Tigh   AN GARBH-   Loch   B
MHEALL   493   Damph   DAMPH   50

Loch   Eilean   CRÒIC-   Glenshieldaig Forest   **8**
eathan   Fladday   BHEINN

Manish   Eilean   North Coast 500   Loch Lundie   Loch
Point   Loch   Torran   River Applecross   Coultrie
Arnish   895   730
Arnish   Applecross   M   BEINN BHAN   SGURR A GHARAIDH   **9**

Brochel   Applecross   Rassal
312   Applecross Bay   Milltown   Ashwood

RAASAY   Applecross   626   Kishorn
Camusteel   Pass of the Cattle   774   Kirkton   40

BEN   444   Bealach na Bà   774   Kishorn   Lochcarron
ANAVAIG   DÙN CAAN   Camusterrach   SGURR A'CHAORACHAIN   **154**
412   Rubha na' Leac   Aird Dhubh   A896
Camastianavaig   Culduie   Kishorn   Slumbay
Tianavaig   Ardarroch   **10**
Bay   Oskaig   310   Toscaig   Achintraid
Ollach   BEINN NA LEAC   Kishorn   394
Clachan   Island   BAD A
Inverarish   Eyre   CHREAMHA   Strome
Braes   Peinchorran   Point   Ardaneaskan   Ardnarff
Suisnish   Stromeferry   A890
conser   Point   Eilean   Achmore
SCALPAY   Meadhonach   Eilean   Plockton   Braeintra   **11**
Mòr
CROWLIN   Port-an-Eorna   447
773   Moll   ISLANDS   BEINN RAIMH
GLAMAIG   Ard   396   Duirinish   30
Dorch   MULLACH   Drumbuie   Balmacara   **12**
A87   Dunan   NA CARN   **145**   Badicaul   Auchtertyre   Conchra
J   K   L   M   Pabay   70   Badicaul   Rera   Nostie   R
Strollamus   Kyle of Lochalsh   Kirkton   90
564   N   Loch Ailise   Lochalsh   P   Q   Ardelve   Carndu
GLAS BHEIN   A87   Kyleakin   Woodland   Eilean Donan   Dornie
Garden

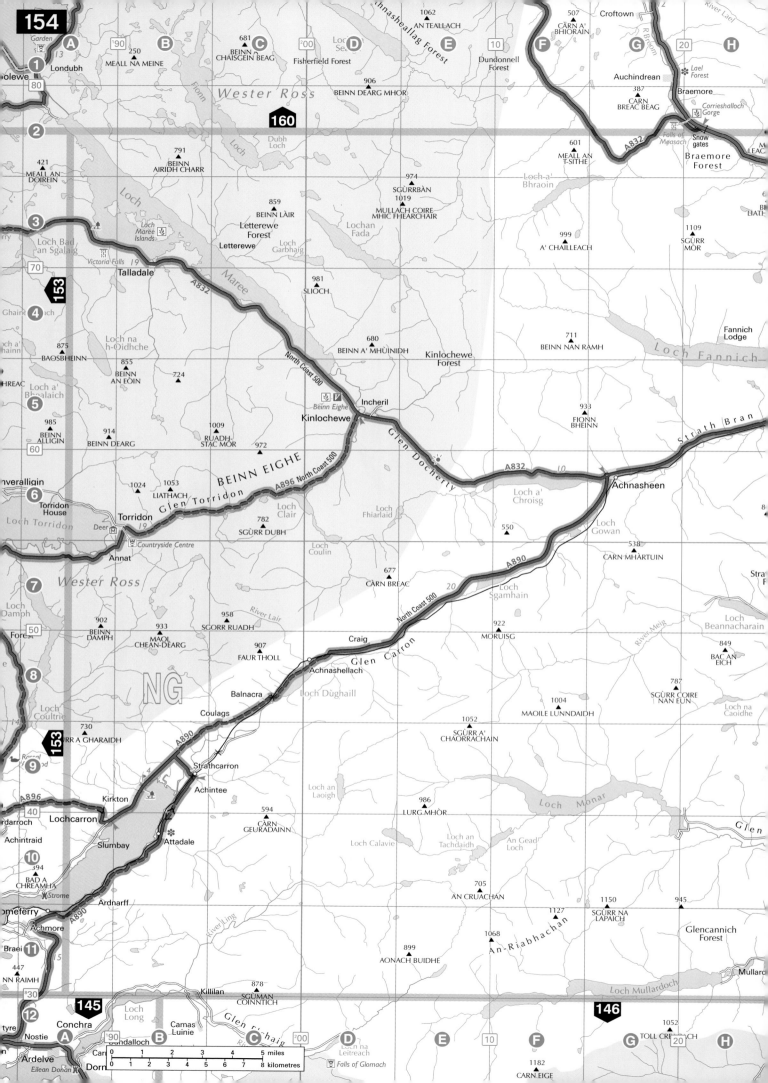

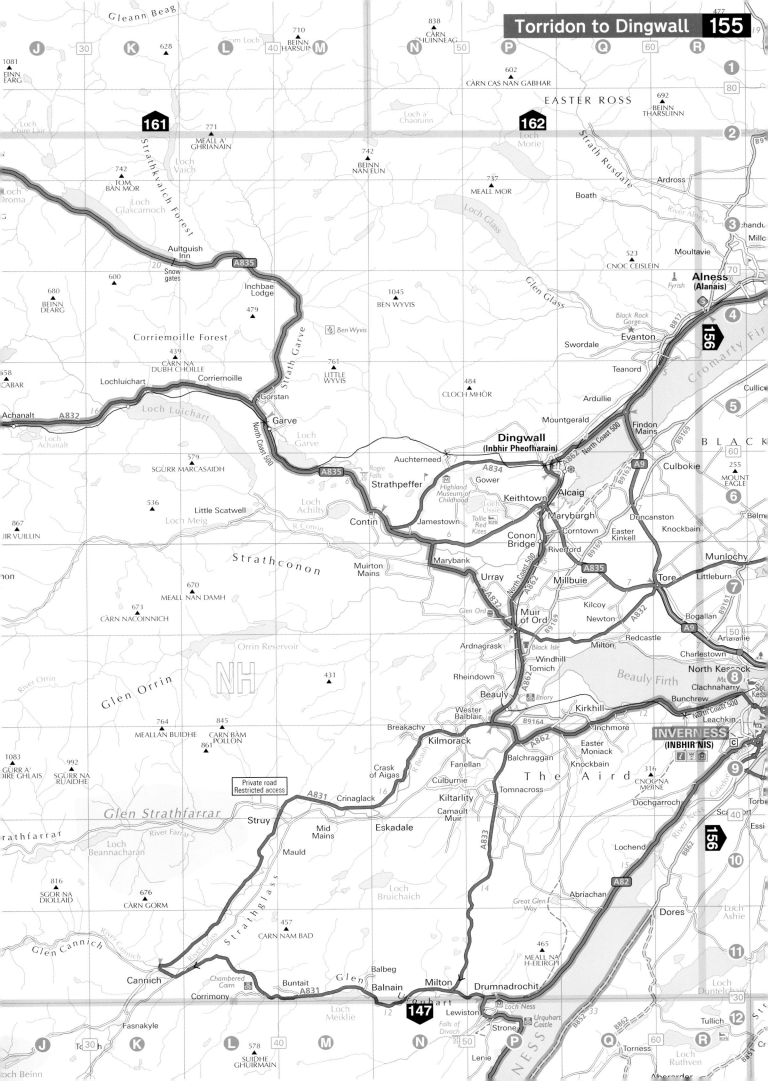

J   K   ³10   L   M   20   N   P   30   Q   R   40

1
80
2
3
70
158
4

Fisheries &
Community
B9040   Branderburgh
Stotfield   **Lossiemouth**
Burghead   Burnside   St Peter's Kirk   Seatown
Well   Hopeman   B9012   & Parish Cross
Burghead   Duffus
Cummingston   B9013   Spey Bay
Roseisle   Duffus   Loch   Scottish
Burghead Bay   B9012   Castle   Spynie   Stonewells   Kingston   Dolphin   **Bud**
College of   6   Lochill   on Spey   Centre   Spey Bay
Roseisle   Spynie   Nether
Findhorn   Hempriggs   Quarrywood   Palace   Viewfield   Garmouth   Dallachy   Upper   Portgor
Kinloss   B9089   Innesmill   Bogmoor   Dallachy
Newton   Bishopmill   Calcots   The   Newton   Broadle
Findhorn   Coltfield   **Elgin**   Urquhart   Lochs   Stynie   Auchenhalrig   Bridge   Cloc
Bay   Kincorth   Alves   H   Glen Moray   Lhanbryde   9   Gordon   of Tynet   5
House   12   New Elgin   Linkwood   B9015   Castle   Rochabers   60
Grange Hall   Kilbuiack   Mosstodloch   Crofts   Braes o
hiterow   Sueno's Stone   Muir of   Clackmarras   of Dipple   Folk   264   6
Forres   Califer   Miltonduff   Longmorn   Orbliston   Dipple   WHITEASH HILL   MIL
Dallas Dhu   Pluscarden   Barnhill   Fogwatt   Millbuies   Inchberry   Ordiequish   A96
Distillery   Rafford   Thomshill   North East 250   250   Forgie
B9010   Kellas   Shougle   13   Glen of Rothes   262   THIEF'S HILL   8
Branchill   Dallas   River Lossie   FINDLAY'S SEAT   Cairnty   Sound   Rumbe   7
NJ   355   A941   Garbity   Muir   Upper Mulben
Logie   Mill Buie   365   PIKEY HILL   Newlands of   Auchroisk   B9103   50
371   CAIRN UISH   Glen Grant   Dundurcas   Mulben   Rosan
Dunphail   MILL BUIE   400   Crofts   Deanshaugh   338
Glenerney   400   369   Rothes   471   12   Tauchers   HILL OF TOWIE   8
CARN NA   HUNT HILL   North East 250   BEN AIGAN   A95   372   B9014
CAILLEICHE   Arndilly House   KNOCKAN   Keith &
Archiestown   Dandaleith   Maggieknockater   Dufftown
River Divie   522   Upper   B9102   Ringorm   Craigellachie   Railway
Dava   CARN KITTY   Knockando   Cardhu   Cooperage   4   B9115
Way   Charlestown   Glenfiddich   Drummuir
Knockando   Carron   Speyview   of Aberlour   B9014   9
515   ROY'S HILL   Glenallachie   A941   **158**
543   LARIG HILL   Daugh of   Milltown of   Dufftown   Milltown of
Dava   Maypark   Kinermony   Edinvillie   Balvenie   Auchindoun
Snow gates   Blacksboat   A95   Castle   40
Dava   Pitchroy   Glenfarclas   Kirktown   10
Moor   548   Craigganmore   Ballindalloch   of Mortlach   Auchindoun
CARN NA LOINE   Ballindalloch   Bridge   840   Castle
Advie   of Avon   BEN RINNES   503
A95   B9102   B9008   Achnastank   CARN CHROM   11
A939   Lettoch   North East 250   Glen Rinnes   Glen Fiddich   River Fiddich   Bridgend
Snow gates   A95   Mains of   1595   30
amerory   Delliefure   Dalvey   Glenlivet   **149**   766   12
Drumin   B9009   Shenval   CORRYHABBIE HILL   571
ntown-   Cromdale   B9136   River Avon   Glenlivet   ROUND HILL   R   Cabrach
on-Spey   Speybridge   Hills of Cromdale   Auchbreck   P   Q   Aldunie   40
aggan   ³10   690   Tomnavoulin

NK

Troup Head
Cullykhan Bay
Gamrie Bay
Gardenstown
Crovie
Pennan
Dubford
Protstonhill
Gamrie
Clenerty
Minnonie
Netherbrae
Crudie
Fintry
B9105
B9031
B9031
North East 250
Aberdour Bay
New Aberdour
Boyndlie
Tyrie
A98
Craigiefold
Coburby
Percyhorner
Peathill
Pitsligo
Rosehearty
Pittulie
Sandhaven
Castle, Lighthouse & Museum
Kinnaird Head
Fraserburgh
Fraserburgh Bay
Maggie's Hoosie
Cairnbulg
Inverallochy
Whitelinks Bay
St Combs
Kirkton
Pitblae
Mid Ardlaw
Memsie
A90
B9032
B9033
Rattray Head
Glasslaw
221
BRACKLAMORE HILL
New Pitsligo
New Byth
Bonnykelly
Garmond
Cuminestown
Balthangie
B9027
B9093
B9093
A981
Newburgh
234
WAUGHTON HILL
Strichen
New Leeds
Denhead
Fetterangus
A952
A950
Memsie Cairn
Rathen
Lonmay
Crofts of Savoch
Loch of Strathbeg
Crimond
Blackhill
North East 250
Leys
Backfolds
Rora
Kirktown
St Fergus
Scotstown Head
A90
Howe of Teuchar
B9170
B9170
New Deer
Maud
Old Deer
Deer Abbey
Dunshillock
Aden
Mintlaw
Longside
Inverugie
Peterhead
Buchanhaven
Arbuthnot
Peterhead Bay
Prison
Invernettie
Railway
B9106
B9029
B9029
Blackhill of Clackriach
Bulwark
Stuartfield
A950
Inverquhomery
Nether Kinmundy
Hillhead of Cocklaw
Slacks of Cairnbanno
Drymuir
Nethermuir
B9028
A948
Knaven
Kinnadie
B9030
Auchnagatt
Clola
Millbreck
Blackhill
Stirling
Lendrum Terrace
Boddam
Buchan Ness
North Millbrex
Cairnorrie
Brownhill
Inkhorn
Kinknockie
Longhaven
Gourdas
Lethenty
Cottown of Gight
Crofts of Haddo
Coldwells
Ardallie
Hatton
Auchiries
Bullers of Buchan
North Haven
Slains
Fyvie Castle
Woodhead
Fyvie
Methlick
R. Ythan
B9005
Arthrath
Muirtack
A952
Bogbrae
Chapel Hill
North East 250
A975
Cruden Bay
Bay of Cruden
St Katherines
Bartholl Chapel
Earlsford
Haddo House
Ythanbank
Toll of Birness
Birness
Artrochie
Whinnyfold
The Skares
ss of Jackston
Tulloch
Wedderlairs
Auchedly
B9005
Kinharrachie
Altar Tomb of William Forbes
Tarves
Ythsie
Ellon
P+R
Kirkton of Logie Buchan
Colliesion
Kirktown of Slains
`151`
A920
aviot
Glen Garioch
Oldmeldrum
Craigdam
Tolquhon Castle
Pitmedden
Esslemont
A920
Udny
edden
B9170
Logierieve
B9000
Forvie
Carnbrogie
Housieside

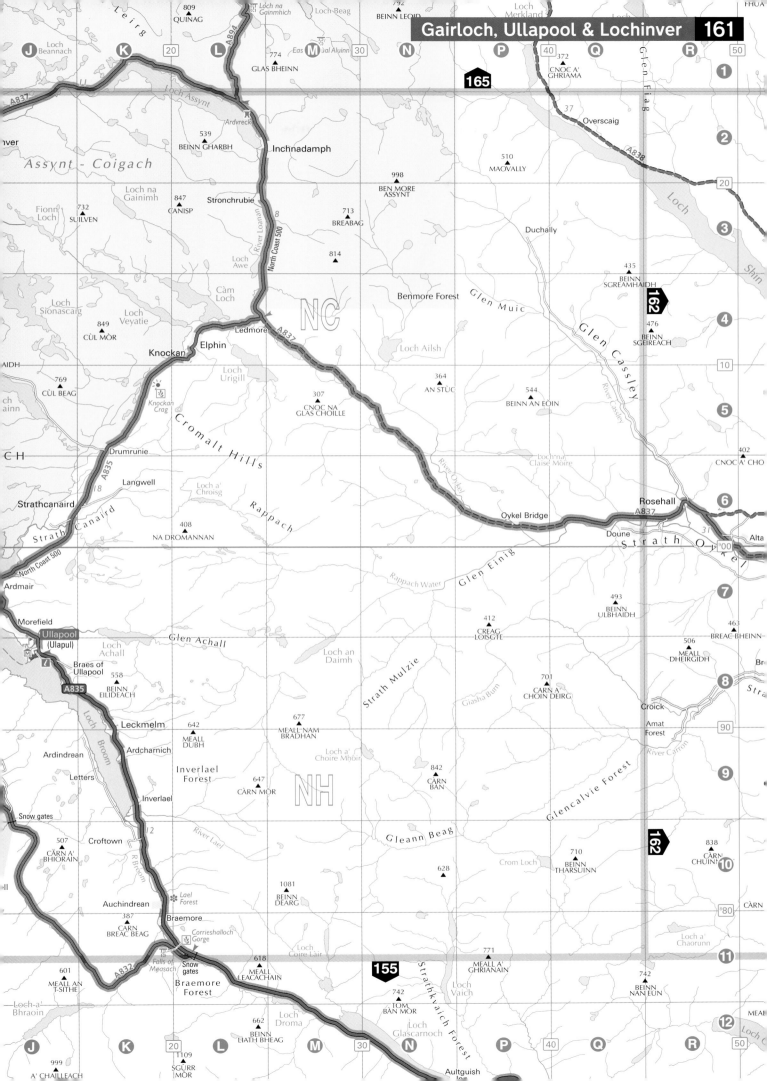

165

162

162

155

J   K   L   M   N   P   Q   R

1
2
3
4
5
6
7
8
9
10
11
12

20   40   50
37
20
10
00
31
90
80
50

A894
A838
A837
A835
A832
A837

QUINAG 809
Loch na Gainmhich
Loch-Beag
792 BEINN LEOID
Loch Merkland
FHUA

Leirg
Loch Beannach

Loch Assynt
774 GLAS BHEINN
Eas Mual Aluinn 30
CNOC A' GHRIAMA 372

Glas Bheinn

Ardvreck
539 BEINN GHARBH
Inchnadamph
510 MAOVALLY
Overscaig

Assynt - Coigach
847 CANISP
Stronchrubie
998 BEN MORE ASSYNT
Duchally

River Loanan
713 BREABAG
435 BEINN SGREAMHAIDH

732 SUILVEN
Fionn Loch
Loch na Gainimh
Loch Awe
814
Benmore Forest
Glen Muic
476 BEINN SGEIREACH

North Coast 500
Càm Loch
Loch Urigill
Glen Cassley

Loch Sìonascaig
849 CÙL MÒR
Loch Veyatie
Ledmore
A837
307 CNOC NA GLAS CHOILLE
Loch Ailsh
364 AN STÙC
River Cassley
402 CNOC A' CHO

Knockan
Elphin
544 BEINN AN EÒIN
Loch na Claise Mòire

CÙL BEAG 769
Knockan Crag
Cromalt Hills

Drumrunie
Loch a' Chroisg
Rappach
River Oykel
Oykel Bridge
Rosehall
A837

Strath Canaird
Langwell
408 NA DROMANNAN
Doune
Strath Oykel
Alta

Strathcanaird
North Coast 500
Rappach Water
Glen Einig
493 BEINN ULBHAIDH
463 BREAC-BHEINN

Ardmair
412 CREAG LOISGTE
506 MEALL DHEIRGIDH
Br

Morefield
Glen Achall
Loch an Daimh
701 CARN A' CHOIN DEIRG
Croick

Ullapool (Ulapul)
Loch Achall
Strath Mulzie
Glasha Burn
Amat Forest

Braes of Ullapool
558 BEINN EILIDEACH
Leckmelm
642 MEALL DUBH
677 MEALL-NAM BRADHAN
Loch a' Choire Mhòir
River Carron

Ardindrean
Ardcharnich
Loch a' Choire Mhòir
842 CARN BÀN
Glencalvie Forest

Letters
Inverlael Forest
647 CÀRN MÒR
NH

Inverlael
Snow gates
Gleann Beag
838 CÀRN CHUINN

Croftown
507 CÀRN A' BHIORAIN
River Lael
628
710 BEINN THARSUINN
Crom Loch
CÀRN

Auchindrean
Lael Forest
1081 BEINN DEARG
Braemore
387 CARN BREAC BEAG
Corrieshalloch Gorge
771 MEALL A' GHRIANAIN
Loch a' Chaorunn

601 MEALL AN T-SITHE
Falls of Measach
Snow gates
Braemore Forest
618 MEALL LEACACHAIN
742

Loch-a' Bhraoin
662 BEINN LIATH BHEAG
742 TOM BÀN MOR
Strathvaich Forest
742 BEINN NAN EUN

999 A' CHAILLEACH
1109 SGURR MÒR
Loch Droma
Loch Vaich
Loch Glascarnoch
Loch

Aultguish

J   K   L   M   N   P   Q   R

20   30   40   50

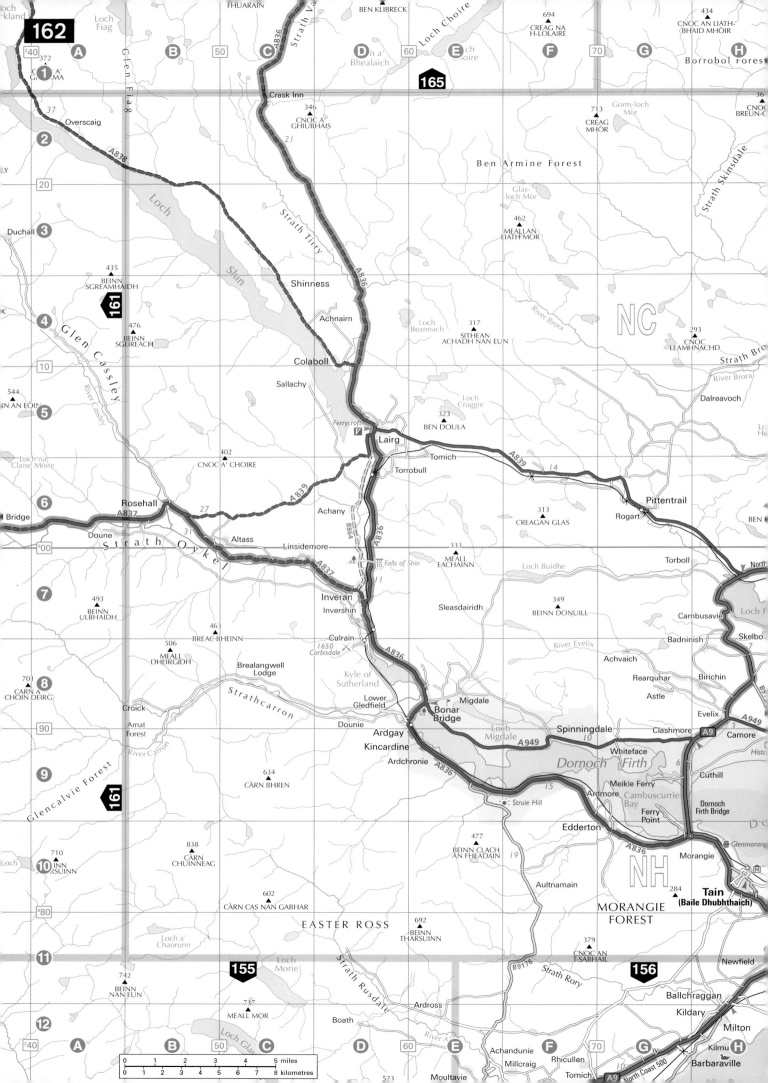

A | B | C | D | E | F | G | H

1

2

70

3

CAPE WRATH

Kearvaig
Bay

Cléit
Dhubh

371
SGRIBHIS-
BHEINN

297
CNOC A'
GHIUBHAIS

300
MAOVALLY

THE PARPH

457
FASHVEN

Loch
na E

Sandwood
Bay

Sandwood
Loch

4

Rubh' an Fhir Lèithe

485
CREAG
467 RIABHACH
AN GRIANAN

464
MEALL
NA MÒINE

331
GHLAS
BHEINN

60

Sheigra

Strath Shinary

Balchrick

Blairmore

521
FARRMHEALL

19

5

Oldshoremore

355
AN SOCACH

Kinlochbervie
Loch Clash

Badcall

Achriesgill

North Coast 500

Strath Di

Loch Inchard

B801

Achlyness

6

Rubha Ruadh

Rhiconich

Loch na
Claise Càrnaich

908
FOINAVEN

50

Skerricha

Fanagmore

Loch Laxford

A838

Tarbet

Foindle

North-west Sutherland

Loch na Tua

7

NC

HANDA
ISLAND

7

Laxford
Bridge

River Laxford

786
ARKLE

Scourie Bay

Scourie

A894

Loch
Stack

8

Scourie More

Upper
Badcall

Lower
Badcall

721
BEN STACK

40

Badcall Bay

Loch a'
Mhuilinn

386
BEN
AUSKAIRD

Strath Stack

333
BEN
SCREAVIE

Achfary

9

Rubh' a'
Mhucard

North Coast 500

17

419
BEN STROME

Loch an
Leathaid Bhuain

A838

Loch Mòr

Point of Stoer

OLDANY
ISLAND

Eddrachillis
Bay

Locha Chàirn Bhàin

Kylestrome

Glendhu Forest

Old Man
of Stoer

Culkein
Drumbeg

Kylesku

Loch Glendhu

10

Culkein

Clashnessie
Bay

Oldany

Drumbeg

B869

Unapool

The Rock Stop

525
BEINN AIRD
DA LOCH

Achnacarnin

Nedd

Loch Glencoul

Clashmore

Loch
Poll

Glen Leirg

Loch an
Leothaid

776
SAIL GHORM

Loch na
Gàinmhich

Loch Beag

792
BEINN LEOID

930

Clashnessie

809
QUINAG

A894

Stoer

11

Clachtoll

B869

North Coast 500

Loch
Beannach

774
GLAS BHEINN

Eas-a' Chùal Aluinn

Bay of Clachtoll

Rhicarn

Achmelvich
Bay

A837

Loch Assynt

12

160

Achmelvich

Baddidarach

Lochinver

Ardvreck

161

539
BEINN GHARBH

Inchnadamph

A | B | C | D | E | F | G | H

0   1   2   3   4   5 miles
0 1 2 3 4 5 6 7 8 kilometres

Assynt - Coigach

Strathan

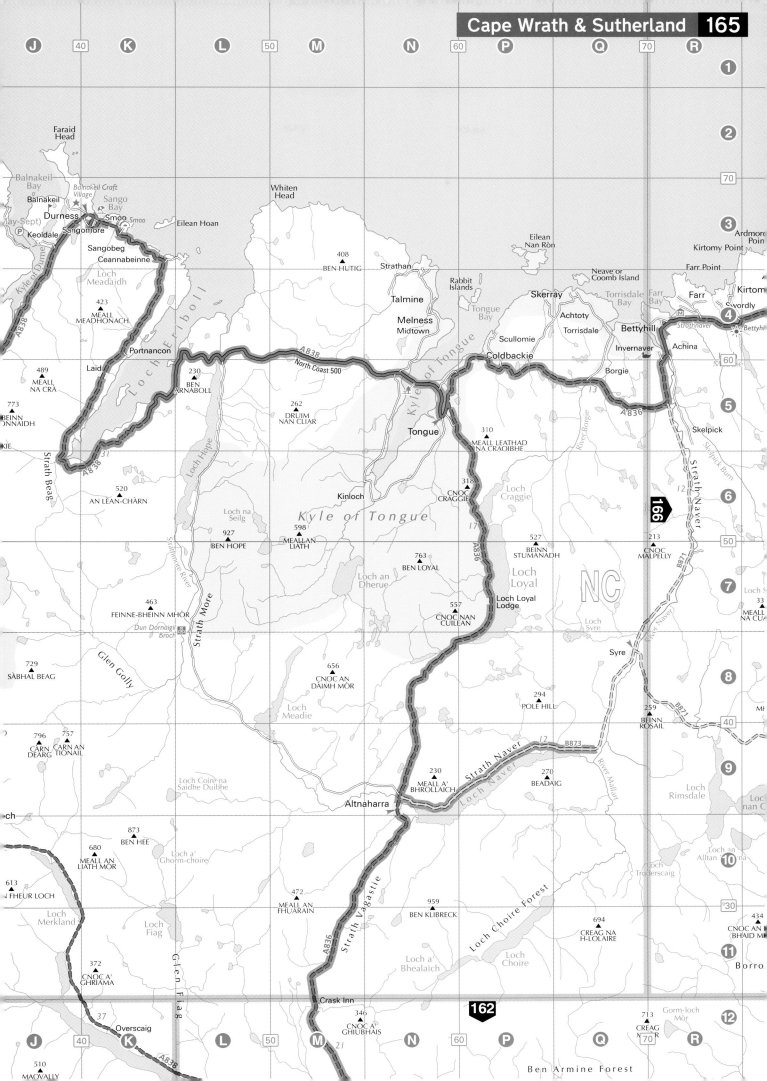

J 40 K L 50 M N 60 P Q 70 R

Faraid
Head

Balnakeil
Bay
Balnakeil Craft
Village
Balnakeil
Durness
(May–Sept)
Keoldale
P
Sangomore
Smoo Smoo
Sango
Bay
Eilean Hoan

Sangobeg
Ceannabeinne

Whiten
Head

Loch
Meadaidh

423
MEALL
MEADHONACH

Loch Eriboll

Portnancon

Laid

489
MEALL
NA CRÀ

A838

Strath Beag

773
BEINN
ONNAIDH

KIE

230
BEN
ARNABOLL

A838 31

262
DRUIM
NAN CLIAR

A838

North Coast 500

408
BEN-HUTIG

Strathan

Talmine

Melness
Midtown

Rabbit
Islands

Tongue
Bay

Kyle of Tongue

Coldbackie

Eilean
Nan Ròn

Skerray

Achtoty

Scullomie

Torrisdale

Invernaver

Neave or
Coomb Island

Torrisdale
Bay

Bettyhill

Borgie

Farr
Bay

Ardmore
Poin

Kirtomy Point

Farr Point

Farr

Achina

Swordly

Kirtom

Bettyhi

M

Strathnaver

A836 13

520
AN LEAN-CHÀRN

Loch na
Seilg

927
BEN HOPE

Strathmore River

463
FEINNE-BHEINN MHÒR

Dun Dornaigil
Broch

Strath More

Glen Golly

598
MEALLAN
LIATH

Kinloch

Tongue

310
MEALL LEATHAD
NA CRAOIBHE

318
CNOC
CRAGGIE

17

Loch an
Dherue

763
BEN LOYAL

557
CNOC NAN
CUILEAN

A836

Loch
Craggie

527
BEINN
STUMANADH

Loch Loyal
Lodge

Loch
Loyal

NC

213
CNOC
MALPELLY

166

B871

River Borgie

Skelpick

River Naver

Skelpick Burn

Strath Naver

12

Loch S

33
MEALL
NA CUA

Loch
Syre

Syre

River Naver

B871

40

Mi

729
SÀBHAL BEAG

656
CNOC AN
DÀIMH MÒR

Loch
Meadie

Loch Coire na
Saidhe Duibhe

796
CÀRN
DEARG

757
CARN AN
TIONAIL

230
MEALL A'
BHROLLAICH

Altnaharra

Strath Naver

12

Loch Naver

B873

270
BEADAIG

294
POLE HILL

259
BEINN
ROSAIL

Loch
Rimsdale

Loc
nan C

Loch an
Alltan

873
BEN HEE

680
MEALL AN
LIATH MÒR

613
N FHEUR LOCH

Loch
Merkland

Loch a'
Ghorm-choire

Loch
Fiag

472
MEALL AN
FHUARAIN

A836

Strath Vagastie

Glen Fiag

959
BEN KLIBRECK

Loch a'
Bhealaich

Loch Choire Forest

Loch
Choire

694
CREAG NA
H-LOLAIRE

Loch
Truderscaig

30

434
CNOC AN
BHAID M

Borro

372
CNOC A'
GHRIAMA

37
Overscaig

A838

Crask Inn

346
CNOC A'
GHIUBHAIS

162

21

713
CREAG
N R

Gorm-loch
Mòr

510
MAOVALLY

Ben Armine Forest

J 40 K 50 L 50 M 60 N P 60 Q R 70

1 2 3 4 5 6 7 8 9 10 11 12

70

70

60

50

40

30

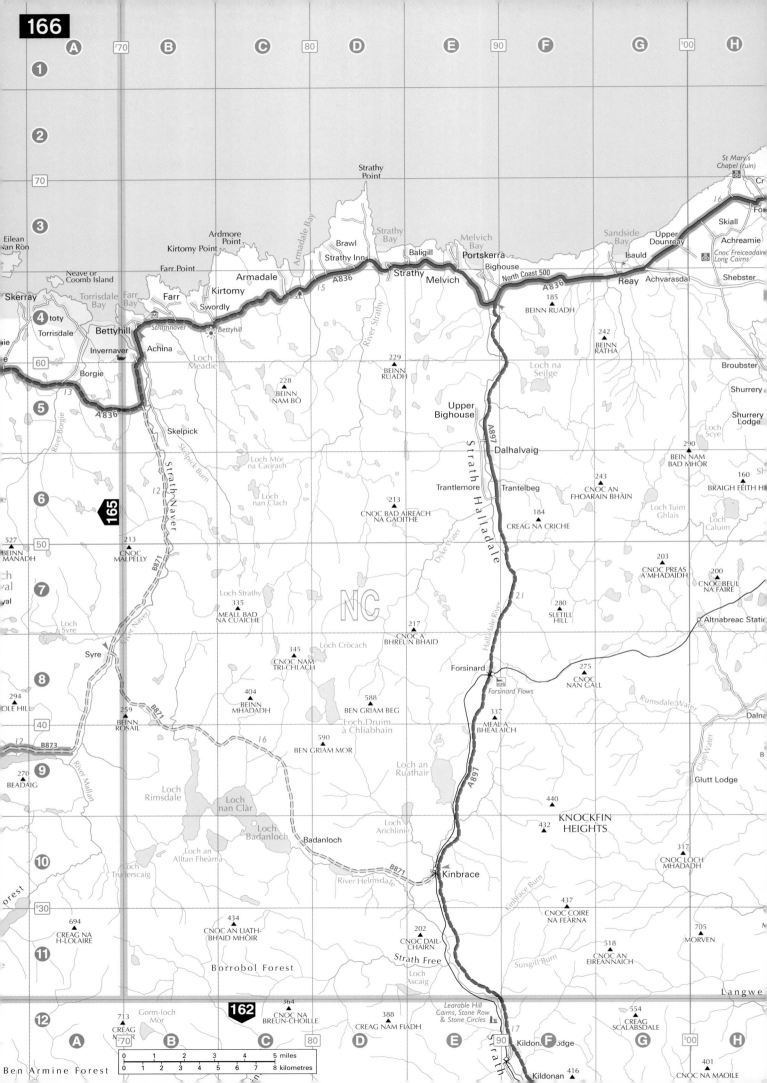

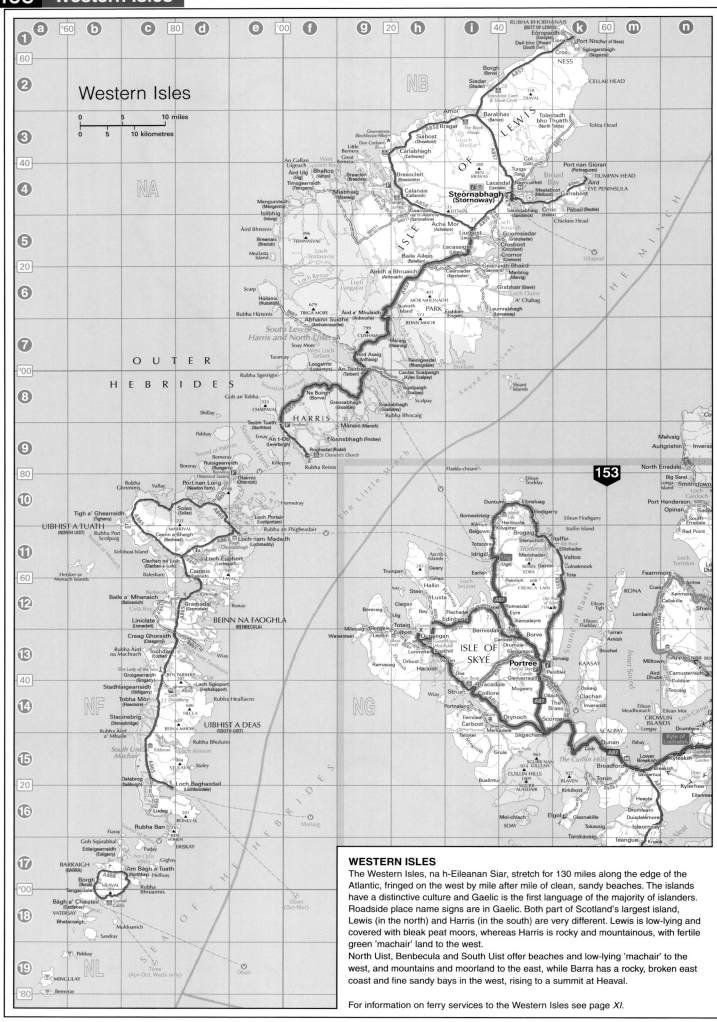

Western Isles

WESTERN ISLES

The Western Isles, na h-Eileanan Siar, stretch for 130 miles along the edge of the Atlantic, fringed on the west by mile after mile of clean, sandy beaches. The islands have a distinctive culture and Gaelic is the first language of the majority of islanders. Roadside place name signs are in Gaelic. Both part of Scotland's largest island, Lewis (in the north) and Harris (in the south) are very different. Lewis is low-lying and covered with bleak peat moors, whereas Harris is rocky and mountainous, with fertile green 'machair' land to the west.

North Uist, Benbecula and South Uist offer beaches and low-lying 'machair' to the west, and mountains and moorland to the east, while Barra has a rocky, broken east coast and fine sandy bays in the west, rising to a summit at Heaval.

For information on ferry services to the Western Isles see page XI.

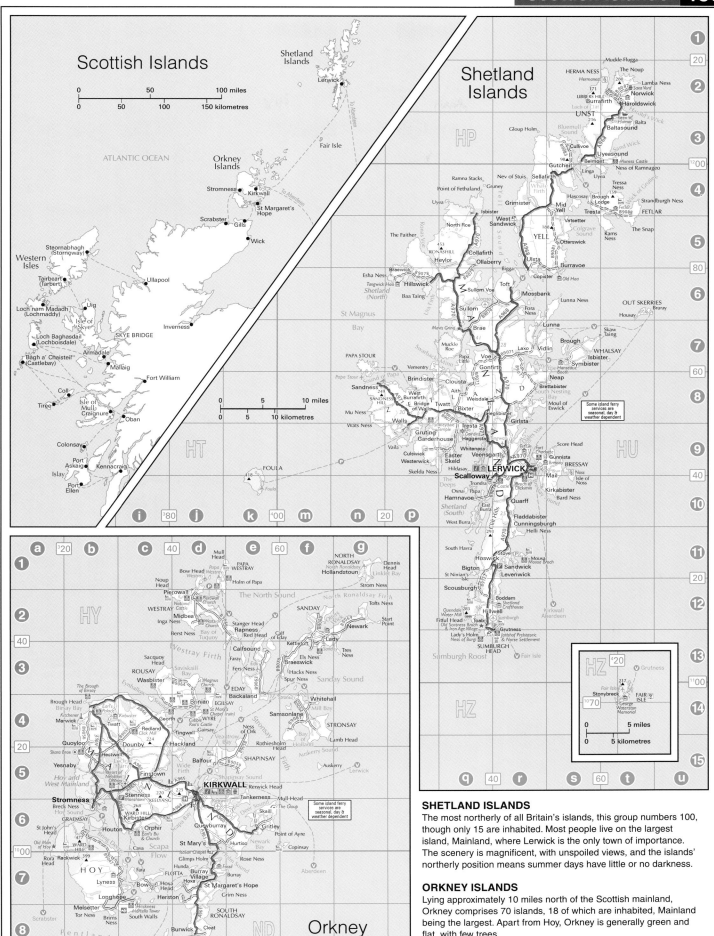

Scottish Islands

ATLANTIC OCEAN

Orkney Islands

Shetland Islands

Western Isles

Shetland Islands

Orkney Islands

SHETLAND ISLANDS

The most northerly of all Britain's islands, this group numbers 100, though only 15 are inhabited. Most people live on the largest island, Mainland, where Lerwick is the only town of importance. The scenery is magnificent, with unspoiled views, and the islands' northerly position means summer days have little or no darkness.

ORKNEY ISLANDS

Lying approximately 10 miles north of the Scottish mainland, Orkney comprises 70 islands, 18 of which are inhabited, Mainland being the largest. Apart from Hoy, Orkney is generally green and flat, with few trees.

The islands abound with prehistoric antiquities and rare birds. The climate is one of even temperatures and 'twilight' summer nights, but with violent winds at times.

For information on ferry services to the Shetland and Orkney Islands see page XI.

Legend

- M1 — Toll-free motorway
- M1 Toll — Toll motorway and plaza
- Motorway junctions with and without number
- Restricted motorway junctions
- Motorway service area
- N17 — National primary route (Republic of Ireland)
- N81 — National secondary route (Republic of Ireland)
- R116 — Regional route (Republic of Ireland)
- Distance in kilometres between symbols (Republic of Ireland)
- A4 — Primary route (Northern Ireland)
- A42 — A road (Northern Ireland)
- B176 — B road (Northern Ireland)
- Distance in miles between symbols (Northern Ireland)
- Minor road
- Road tunnel, with toll
- Road under construction
- Airport
- International boundary
- Vehicle ferry
- Fast vehicle ferry or catamaran
- Gaeltacht (Irish language area)
- National Park

To reflect the distances shown on road signs, distances are shown in miles in Northern Ireland and kilometres in the Republic of Ireland.

16 kilometres = 10 miles

For key to touring information see page 1

Ireland index

Abbeydorney....C12
Abbeyfeale....D12
Abbeyleix....G11
Adamstown....H12
Adare....D12
Adrigole....C14
Aghalee....J5
Ahascragh....E9
Ahoghill....J4
Allenwood....H9
Allihies....B15
An Bun Beag....E4
An Charraig....E5
An Cheathrú Rua....C9
An Clochán Liath....E4
An Coireán....B14
An Fál Carrach....F3
An Fhairche....C9
Annahilt....J6
Annascaul....B13
Annestown....G13
An Rinn....G13
An Spidéal....D9
Antrim....J5
Ardagh....D12
Ardara....E5
Ardee....H8
Ardfert....C12
Ardfinnan....F12
Ardglass....K6
Ardgroom....B14
Ardmore....F14
Ardnacrusha....E11
Arklow....J11
Armagh....H6
Armoy....J3
Arvagh....G7
Ashbourne....J9
Ashford....J10
Askeaton....D12
Athboy....H8
Athea....D12
Athenry....E9
Athleague....E8
Athlone....F9
Athy....H10
Augher....G6
Aughnacloy....H6
Aughrim....E9
Aughrim....J11
Avoca....J11

Bagenalstown....H11
Baile an Fheirtéaraigh....B13
Baile Chláir....D9
Baile Mhic Íre....D14
Baile na Finne....F4
Bailieborough....H7
Balbriggan....J8
Balla....D8
Ballacolla....G11
Ballaghaderreen....E7
Ballina....D7
Ballina....E11
Ballinafad....E7
Ballinagar....G9
Ballinagh....G7
Ballinamallard....G6
Ballinamore....F7
Ballinascarty....D14
Ballinasloe....E9
Ballincollig....E14
Ballindaggan....H12
Ballineen....D14
Ballingarry....D12
Ballingarry....G12
Ballingeary....D14
Ballinlough....E8
Ballinrobe....D8
Ballinspittle....E14
Ballintra....F5
Ballivor....H9
Ballon....H11
Ballybay....H7
Ballybofey....F5
Ballybunion....C12
Ballycanew....J11
Ballycarry....K5
Ballycastle....J3

Ballycastle....C6
Ballyclare....J5
Ballyclerahan....F12
Ballyconneely....B9
Ballyconnell....G7
Ballycotton....F14
Ballycumber....F9
Ballydehob....C15
Ballydesmond....D13
Ballyduff....C12
Ballyduff....F13
Ballyfarnon....E7
Ballyferriter....B13
Ballygally....J4
Ballygar....E9
Ballygawley....H6
Ballygawley....E6
Ballygowan....K5
Ballyhack....H13
Ballyhaise....G7
Ballyhalbert....K5
Ballyhaunis....E8
Ballyhean....D8
Ballyheige....C12
Ballyjamesduff....G8
Ballylanders....E12
Ballylickey....C14
Ballyliffin....G3
Ballylongford....C12
Ballylynan....H10
Ballymacarbry....F13
Ballymahon....F8
Ballymakeery....D14
Ballymena....J4
Ballymoe....E8
Ballymoney....H4
Ballymore....F9
Ballymore Eustace....H10
Ballymote....E7
Ballynacarrigy....G8
Ballynahinch....J6
Ballynure....J5
Ballyporeen....F13
Ballyragget....G11
Ballyroan....G10
Ballysadare....E6
Ballyshannon....F5
Ballyvaughan....D10
Ballywalter....K5
Balrothery....J8
Baltimore....C15
Baltinglass....H10
Banagher....F10
Banbridge....J6
Bandon....E14
Bangor....K5
Bangor Erris....C7
Bansha....F12
Banteer....D13
Bantry....C14
Barna....D9
Béal an Mhuirthead....B6
Béal Átha an Ghaorthaidh....D14
Bearna....D9
Belcoo....F6
Belfast....J5
Belgooly....E14
Bellaghy....H4
Belleek....F6
Belmullet....B6
Belturbet....G7
Benburb....H6
Bennettsbridge....G12
Beragh....G5
Bessbrook....J6
Bettystown....J8
Birr....F10
Blacklion....F6
Blackwater....J12
Blarney....E14
Blessington....H10
Boherbue....D13
Borris....H12
Borris-in-Ossory....F10
Borrisokane....F10
Borrisoleigh....F11
Boyle....E7
Bray....J10
Bridgetown....H13
Brittas....J9

Broadford....E11
Broadford....D12
Brookeborough....G6
Broughshane....J4
Bruff....E12
Bunbeg....E4
Bunclody....H11
Buncrana....G3
Bundoran....E6
Bunmahon....G13
Bunnyconnellan....D7
Bushmills....H3
Buttevant....E13
Bweeng....E13

Cadamstown....F10
Caherconlish....E12
Caherdaniel....B14
Cahersiveen....B14
Cahir....F12
Caledon....H6
Callan....G12
Caltra....E9
Camp....B13
Carndonagh....G3
Cappawhite....F12
Cappoquin....F13
Carlanstown....H8
Carlingford....J7
Carlow....H11
Carna....C9
Carnew....J11
Carnlough....J4
Carragh....H9
Carraig Áirt....F3
Carraroe....C9
Carrick....E5
Carrickfergus....K5
Carrickmacross....H7
Carrickmore....G5
Carrick-on-Shannon....F7
Carrick-on-Suir....G12
Carrigaline....E14
Carrigallen....F7
Carriganimmy....D13
Carrigart....F3
Carrigtwohill....E14
Carryduff....J5
Cashel....F12
Castlebar....D8
Castlebellingham....J7
Castleblakeney....E9
Castleblayney....H7
Castlebridge....J12
Castlecomer....G11
Castleconnell....E11
Castlederg....G5
Castledermot....H11
Castlegregory....B13
Castleisland....C13
Castlemaine....C13
Castlemartyr....F14
Castleplunket....E8
Castlepollard....G8
Castlerea....E8
Castlerock....H3
Castletownbere....B15
Castletownroche....E13
Castletownshend....D15
Castlewellan....J6
Cathair Dónall....B14
Causeway....C12
Cavan....G7
Celbridge....H9
Charlestown....D7
Charleville....E12
Cill Charthaigh....E5
Cill Chiaráin....C9
Clady....G5
Clane....H9
Clara....G9
Claregalway....D9
Claremorris....D8
Clashmore....F13
Cleggan....B8
Clifden....B9
Cliffoney....E6
Cloghan....F10
Clogheen....F13
Clogher....G6

Clogherhead....J8
Clogh Mills....J4
Clonakilty....D15
Clonaslee....G10
Clonbur....D9
Clondalkin....J9
Clonea....G13
Clonmany....G3
Clonmel....F12
Clonmellon....H8
Clonroche....H12
Clough....K6
Cloughjordan....F10
Cloyne....F14
Coachford....D14
Coagh....H5
Coalisland....H5
Cobh....E14
Coleraine....H3
Collinstown....G8
Collon....H8
Collooney....E7
Comber....K5
Cong....D9
Convoy....F4
Cookstown....H5
Coole....G8
Cooraclare....C11
Cootehill....G7
Cork....E14
Cornamona....D9
Corofin....D10
Corr na Móna....C9
Courtmacsherry....E15
Courtown....J11
Craighwell....E10
Craughwell....E10
Creeslough....F4
Croithlí....E4
Crolly....E4
Crookhaven....C15
Crookstown....D14
Croom....E12
Crossakeel....H8
Crosshaven....E14
Crossmaglen....H7
Crossmolina....D7
Crumlin....J5
Crusheen....D10
Culdaff....G3
Cullybackey....J4
Culmore....G4
Curracloe....J12
Curry....E7
Cushendall....J4
Cushendun....J3

Daingean....G9
Daingean Uí Chúis....B13
Delvin....G8
Derrinturn....H9
Derry....G4
Derrygonnelly....F6
Derrylin....G6
Dervock....H3
Dingle....B13
Doagh....J5
Donabate....J9
Donaghadee....K5
Donaghmore....H5
Donaghmore....H6
Donegal....F5
Donemana....G4
Doolin....C10
Doon....E12
Doonbeg....C11
Downings....F3
Downpatrick....K6
Dowra....F6
Draperstown....H5
Drimoleague....D14
Drogheda....J8
Droichead Nua....H10
Dromahair....E6
Dromara....J6
Dromcolloher....D12
Dromiskin....J7
Drommahane....E13
Dromod....F8
Dromore....J6

Dromore....G5
Dromore West....D6
Drumaness....K6
Drumfries....G3
Drumkeeran....F7
Drumlish....F8
Drumquin....G5
Drumshanbo....F7
Drumsna....F7
Duagh....C12
Dublin....J9
Duleek....J8
Dunboyne....J9
Dún Chaoin....A13
Dundalk....J7
Dundonald....K5
Dundrum....F12
Dunfanaghy....F3
Dungannon....H5
Dungarvan....G13
Dungiven....H4
Dunglow....E4
Dungourney....F14
Dunkineely....E5
Dún Laoghaire....J9
Dunlavin....H10
Dunleer....J8
Dunloy....J4
Dunmanway....D14
Dunmore....E8
Dunmore East....H13
Dunquin....A13
Dunshaughlin....H9
Durrow....G11
Durrus....G9
Durrus....C15
Dysart....E9

Easky....D6
Edenderry....H9
Edgeworthstown....G8
Eglinton....G4
Elphin....F8
Emyvale....H6
Enfield....H9
Ennis....D11
Enniscorthy....H12
Enniscrone....D6
Enniskean....D14
Enniskillen....F6
Ennistymon....D10
Eyrecourt....F10

Fahan....G4
Falcarragh....F3
Fanore....D10
Farranfore....C13
Feakle....E11
Fenagh....F7
Fenit....B13
Ferbane....F9
Fermoy....E13
Ferns....J12
Fethard....F12
Fethard....H13
Fivemiletown....G6
Foxford....D7
Foynes....D12
Freemount....D13
Frenchpark....E7
Freshford....G11

Galbally....E12
Galway....D9
Garrison....F6
Garvagh....H4
Gilford....J6
Glandore....D15
Glanworth....E13
Glaslough....H6
Glassan....F9
Gleann Cholm Cille....E5
Glenamaddy....E8
Glenarm....J4
Glenavy....J5
Glenbeigh....B13
Glencolumbkille....E5
Glenealy....J10
Glengarriff....C14
Glenties....E5

Glin....D12
Golden....F12
Goleen....C15
Goresbridge....H11
Gorey....J11
Gort....D10
Gorteen....E7
Gortin....G5
Gowran....H11
Graiguenamanagh....H12
Granard....G8
Grange....E6
Greencastle....H3
Greencastle....G5
Greenore....J7
Greyabbey....K5
Greystones....J10
Gulladuff....H4

Hackettstown....H11
Headford....D9
Hillsborough....J6
Hilltown....J6
Holycross....F11
Holywood....K5
Hospital....E12
Howth....J9

Inagh....D11
Inch....B13
Inchigeelagh....D14
Inishcrone....D6
Innishannon....E14
Irvinestown....F6

Johnstown....G11

Kanturk....D13
Keadue....F7
Keady....H6
Kealkill....C14
Keel....B7
Kells....J4
Kells....H8
Kenmare....C14
Kesh....F6
Kilbeggan....G9
Kilcar....E5
Kilcock....H9
Kilcolgan....D10
Kilconnell....E9
Kilcoole....J10
Kilcormac....F10
Kilcullen....H10
Kildare....H10
Kildorrery....E13
Kilfenora....D10
Kilfinane....E12
Kilgarvan....C14
Kilkee....C11
Kilkeel....J7
Kilkenny....G11
Kilkieran....C9
Kill....H9
Kill....G13
Killadysert....D11
Killala....D6
Killaloe....E11
Killarney....C13
Killashandra....G7
Killeagh....F14
Killenaule....F12
Killimer....C11
Killiney....J9
Killinick....J13
Killorglin....C13
Killough....K6
Killucan....G9
Killurin....G10
Killybegs....E5
Killyleagh....K6
Kilmacanogue....J10
Kilmacrenan....F4
Kilmacthomas....G13
Kilmaganny....G12
Kilmaine....D8
Kilmallock....E12
Kilmanagh....G11
Kilmeedy....D12
Kilmichael....D14
Kilmihil....C11
Kilmore Quay....H13

Kilmuckridge....J12
Kilpedder....J10
Kilrea....H4
Kilrush....C11
Kilsheelan....G12
Kiltegan....H11
Kiltimagh....D8
Kilworth....E13
Kingscourt....H7
Kinlough....E6
Kinnegad....G9
Kinnitty....F10
Kinsale....E14
Kinvarra....D10
Kircubbin....K5
Knock....D8
Knockcroghery....F8

Lahinch....C10
Lanesborough....F8
Laragh....J10
Larne....K4
Lauragh....C14
Laurencetown....F10
Leap....D15
Leenaun....C8
Leighlinbridge....H11
Leitrim....F7
Leixlip....H9
Letterfrack....B8
Letterkenny....F4

Lifford....G4
Limavady....H4
Limerick....E11
Lisbellaw....G6
Lisburn....J5
Liscarroll....D13
Lisdoonvarna....D10
Lismore....E13
Lisnaskea....G6
Listowel....C12
Loghill....D12
Londonderry....G4
Longford....F8
Longwood....H9
Loughbrickland....J6
Loughglinn....E8
Loughrea....E10
Louisburgh....C8
Lucan....J9
Lurgan....J6
Lusk....J9

Macroom....D14
Maghera....H4
Magherafelt....H5
Maguiresbridge....G6
Maigh Cuilinn....D9
Malahide....J9
Málainn Mhóir....E5
Malin....G3
Malin More....E5

170

0 10 20 miles
0 10 20 30 kilometres

Mallow....E13
Manorhamilton....F6
Markethill....H6
Martinstown....J4
Maynooth....H9
Mayobridge....J6
Midleton....F14
Milford....F4
Millstreet....D13
Milltown....C13
Milltown Malbay....C11
Mitchelstown....E13
Moate....F9
Mohill....F7
Monaghan....H6
Monasterevin....G10
Moneymore....H5
Monivea....E9
Mooncoin....G13
Mountbellew....E9
Mountcharles....F5
Mountmellick....G10
Mountrath....G10
Mountshannon....E10
Moville....G3
Moy....H6
Moycullen....D9
Moynalty....H8
Mucklagh....G9
Muff....G4
Muine Bheag....H11

Mullagh....H8
Mullaghmore....E6
Mullinahone....G12
Mullinavat....G12
Mullingar....G9
Mulranny....C7
Murrisk....C8
Murroe....E11

Naas....H10
Na Dúnaibh....F3
Naul....J8
Navan....H8
Nenagh....E11
Newbawn....H12
Newbliss....G7
Newbridge....H10
Newcastle....J6
Newcastle....J10
Newcastle West....D12
New Inn....F12
Newmarket....D13
Newmarket-on-
Fergus....D11
Newport....C7
Newport....E11
New Ross....H12
Newry....J6
Newtownabbey....J5
Newtownards....K5
Newtownbutler....G7

Newtown
Cunningham....G4
Newtownforbes....F8
Newtownhamilton....H6
Newtownmount-
kennedy....J10
Newtownstewart....G5
Nobber....H8

Ogonnelloe....E11
Oilgate....H12
Oldcastle....G8
Omagh....G5
Omeath....J6
Oola....E12
Oranmore....D9
Oughterard....D9

Pallasgreen....E12
Partry....D8
Passage East....H13
Passage West....E14
Patrickswell....E12
Pettigo....F5
Piltown....G12
Plumbridge....G5
Pomeroy....H5
Portadown....H6
Portaferry....K6
Portarlington....G10
Portavogie....K6

Portballintrae....H3
Portglenone....H4
Port Laoise....G10
Portlaw....G13
Portmagee....B14
Portmarnock....J9
Portnablagh....F3
Portnoo....E4
Portroe....E11
Portrush....H3
Portstewart....H3
Portumna....E10
Poyntzpass....J6
Prosperous....H9

Quin....D11

Raharney....G9
Ramelton....F4
Randalstown....J5
Raphoe....G4
Rasharkin....H4
Rathangan....H10
Rathcoole....J9
Rathcormac....E13
Rathdowney....G11
Rathdrum....J10
Rathfriland....J6
Rathkeale....D12
Ráth Luirc....E12
Rathmore....D13

Rathmullan....G4
Rathnew....J10
Rathvilly....H11
Ratoath....J9
Recess....C9
Rhode....G9
Ring....G13
Ringaskiddy....E14
Riverchapel....J11
Riverstick....E14
Rochfortbridge....G9
Rockcorry....H7
Roosky....F8
Rosbercon....H12
Roscommon....F8
Roscrea....F10
Rosscarbery....D15
Rosses Point....E6
Rosslare....J13
Rosslare Harbour....J13
Rosslea....G6
Rossnowlagh....E5
Rostrevor....J7
Roundstone....B9
Roundwood....J10
Rush....J9

Saintfield....K6
St Johnston....G4
Sallins....H9
Salthill....D9

Scarriff....E11
Scartaglin....C13
Schull....C15
Seskinore....G5
Shanagarry....F14
Shannon....D11
Shannonbridge....F9
Shercock....H7
Shillelagh....H11
Shinrone....F10
Shrule....F13
Silvermines....E11
Sion Mills....G5
Sixmilebridge....D11
Skerries....J8
Skibbereen....D15
Slane....H8
Sligo....E6
Smithborough....G6
Sneem....B14
Spanish Point....C11
Spiddal....D9
Sraith Salach....C9
Stewartstown....H5
Stoneyford....G12
Strabane....G4
Stradbally....G10
Stradone....G7
Strandhill....E6
Strangford....K6
Stranorlar....F5

Strokestown....F8
Summerhill....H9
Swan....G11
Swanlinbar....F6
Swinford....D7
Swords....J9

Taghmon....H12
Tagoat....J13
Tallaght....J9
Tallow....F13
Tandragee....J6
Tarbert....C12
Templemore....F11
Termonfeckin....J8
Thomastown....G12
Thurles....F11
Timahoe....G10
Timoleague....D15
Tinahely....J11
Tipperary....F12
Tobercurry....E7
Tobermore....H4
Toome....H5
Toomevara....F11
Toomore....C15
Tower....E14
Tralee....C13
Tramore....G13
Trim....H8
Tuam....D9

Tubbercurry....E7
Tulla....D11
Tullamore....G9
Tullow....H11
Tulsk....E8
Turlough....D7

Urlingford....G11

Virginia....G8

Warrenpoint....J7
Waterford....G13
Watergrasshill....E13
Waterville....B14
Wellingtonbridge....H13
Westport....C8
Wexford....J12
Whitegate....E14
Whitehead....K5
Wicklow....J10
Woodenbridge....J11
Woodford....E10

Youghal....F14

171

Town plan : Central London p.238–247

For Central London see pages 238–247

NORTH

SEA

WHITLEY BAY

TYNEMOUTH

NORTH SHIELDS

SOUTH SHIELDS

JARROW

HEBBURN

SUNDERLAND

Amsterdam (IJmuiden)

River Tyne

River Wear

Town, port and airport plans

Motorway and junction	One-way, gated/ closed road	Railway station	Toilet, with facilities for the less able
Primary road single/ dual carriageway and numbered junction	Restricted access road	Preserved or tourist railway	Car park, with electric charging point
A road single/ dual carriageway and numbered junction	Pedestrian area	Light rapid transit system station	Park and Ride (at least 6 days per week)
B road single/ dual carriageway	Footpath	Level crossing	Bus/coach station
Local road single/ dual carriageway	Road under construction	Tramway	Hospital, 24-hour Accident & Emergency hospital
Other road single/ dual carriageway, minor road	Road tunnel	Airport, heliport	Beach (award winning)
Building of interest	Lighthouse	Railair terminal	City wall
Ruined building	Castle	Theatre or performing arts centre	Escarpment
Tourist Information Centre	Castle mound	Cinema	Cliff lift
Visitor or heritage centre	Monument, memorial, statue	Abbey, chapel, church	River/canal, lake
World Heritage Site (UNESCO)	Post Office	Synagogue	Lock, weir
Museum	Public library	Mosque	Viewpoint
English Heritage site	Shopping centre	Golf course	Park/sports ground
Historic Scotland site	Shopmobility	Racecourse	Cemetery
Cadw (Welsh heritage) site	Football stadium	Nature reserve	Woodland
National Trust site	Rugby stadium	Aquarium, zoological or wildlife collection	Built-up area
National Trust for Scotland site	County cricket ground	Showground	Beach

Central London street map (see pages 238–247)

London Underground station	London Overground station
Docklands Light Railway (DLR) station	Central London Congestion Charge boundary

Royal Parks

Green Park	Park open 5am–midnight. Constitution Hill and The Mall closed to traffic Sundays and public holidays 8am–dusk.
Hyde Park	Park open 5am–midnight. Park roads closed to traffic midnight–5am.
Kensington Gardens	Park open 6am–dusk.
Regent's Park	Park open 5am–dusk. Park roads closed to traffic midnight–7am, except for residents.
St James's Park	Park open 5am–midnight. The Mall closed to traffic Sundays and public holidays 8am–dusk.
Victoria Tower Gardens	Park open dawn–dusk.

Traffic regulations in the City of London include security checkpoints and restrict the number of entry and exit points.

Note: Oxford Street is closed to through-traffic (except buses & taxis) 7am–7pm Monday–Saturday.

Bishopsgate Streetspace Scheme: Temporary traffic restrictions are in operation between Shoreditch and London Bridge, 7am–7pm Monday–Friday. Follow local road signs for changes to permitted routes.

Central London Congestion Charge Zone (CCZ)
You need to pay a £15 daily charge for driving a vehicle on public roads in this central London area. Payment permits entry, travel within and exit from the CCZ by the vehicle as often as required on that day.

The daily charge applies 07:00–18:00 Mon–Fri, 12:00–18:00 Sat–Sun and bank holidays. There is no charge between Christmas Day and New Year's Day bank holiday (inclusive).

For up to date information on the CCZ, exemptions, discounts or ways to pay, visit **www.tfl.gov.uk/modes/driving/congestion-charge**

Ultra Low Emission Zone (ULEZ)
Most vehicles in Central London, including cars and vans, need to meet minimum exhaust emission standards or drivers must pay a daily charge to drive within the zone. From 29 August 2023 the ULEZ was expanded from central and inner London, to include all London boroughs. The ULEZ operates 24 hours a day, every day of the year, except Christmas Day (25 December). The charge is £12.50 for motorcycles, cars and vans and is in addition to the Congestion Charge.

For further information visit **www.tfl.gov.uk/modes/driving/ultra-low-emission-zone**

In addition the Low Emission Zone (LEZ) operates across Greater London, 24 hours every day of the year, and is aimed at the most heavy-polluting vehicles. It does not apply to cars or motorcycles.

For details visit **www.tfl.gov.uk/modes/driving/low-emission-zone**

Town Plans

Central London

Ferry Ports

Channel Tunnel

Airports

PADDINGTON 238 239 240 241 FINSBURY STEPNEY
SOHO CITY
246 247
KENSINGTON 242 243 244 245 SOUTHWARK BERMONDSEY
WESTMINSTER
CHELSEA KENNINGTON

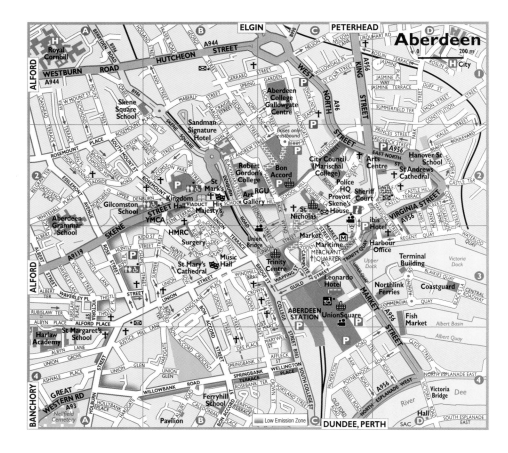

Aberdeen

Aberdeen is found on atlas page **151 N6**

Street	Grid	Street	Grid
Affleck Street	C4	Maberly Street	B1
Albert Street	A3	Marischal Street	D2
Albury Road	B4	Market Street	C3
Alford Place	A3	Nelson Street	C1
Ann Street	B1	Palmerston Road	C4
Beach Boulevard	D2	Park Street	D2
Belgrave Terrace	A2	Portland Street	C4
Berryden Road	A1	Poynernook Road	C4
Blackfriars Street	B2	Regent Quay	D3
Blaikies Quay	D3	Richmond Street	A2
Bon Accord Crescent	B4	Rose Place	A3
Bon Accord Street	B3	Rose Street	A3
Bridge Street	C3	Rosemount Place	A2
Caledonian Place	B4	Rosemount Viaduct	A2
Carmelite Street	C3	St Andrew Street	B2
Chapel Street	A3	St Clair Street	C1
Charlotte Street	B1	School Hill	C2
College Street	C3	Skene Square	B2
Constitution Street	D1	Skene Street	A3
Crimon Place	B3	Skene Terrace	B2
Crown Street	B3	South College Street	C4
Dee Street	B3	South Esplanade East	D4
Denburn Road	B2	South Mount Street	A2
Diamond Street	B3	Spa Street	B2
East North Street	D2	Springbank Street	B4
Esslemont Avenue	A2	Springbank Terrace	B4
Gallowgate	C1	Summer Street	B3
George Street	B1	Summerfield Terrace	D1
Gilcomston Park	B2	Thistle Lane	A3
Golden Square	B3	Thistle Place	A3
Gordon Street	B3	Thistle Street	A3
Great Western Road	A4	Trinity Quay	C3
Guild Street	C3	Union Bridge	B3
Hadden Street	C3	Union Grove	A4
Hanover Street	D2	Union Street	B3
Hardgate	B4	Union Terrace	B2
Harriet Street	C2	Upper Denburn	A2
Holburn Street	A4	Victoria Road	D4
Huntly Street	A3	Victoria Street	B3
Hutcheon Street	B1	View Terrace	A1
Jasmine Terrace	D1	Virginia Street	D2
John Street	B2	Wapping Street	C3
Justice Mill Lane	A4	Waverley Place	A3
King Street	C1	Wellington Place	C4
Langstane Place	B3	West North Street	C1
Leadside Road	A2	Westburn Road	A1
Loanhead Terrace	A1	Whitehall Place	A2
Loch Street	C1	Willowbank Road	A4

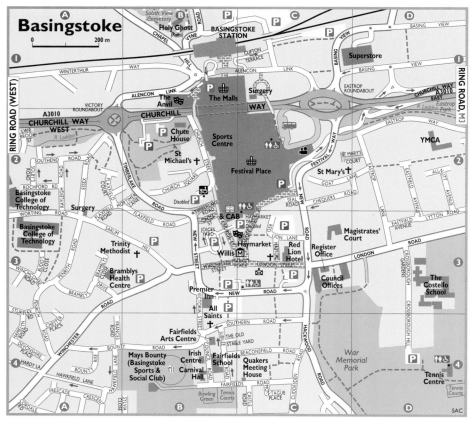

Basingstoke

Basingstoke is found on atlas page **22 H4**

Street	Grid	Street	Grid
Alencon Link	C1	London Street	C3
Allnutt Avenue	D2	Lower Brook Street	A2
Basing View	C1	Lytton Road	D3
Beaconsfield Road	C4	Market Place	B3
Bounty Rise	A4	May Place	C3
Bounty Road	A4	Montague Place	C4
Bramblys Close	A3	Mortimer Lane	A2
Bramblys Drive	A3	New Road	B3
Budd's Close	A3	New Road	C2
Castle Road	C4	New Street	B3
Chapel Hill	B1	Penrith Road	A3
Chequers Road	C2	Rayleigh Road	A2
Chester Place	A4	Red Lion Lane	C3
Churchill Way	B2	Rochford Road	A2
Churchill Way East	D1	St Mary's Court	C2
Churchill Way West	A2	Sarum Hill	A3
Church Square	B2	Seal Road	C2
Church Street	B2	Solby's Road	A2
Church Street	B3	Southend Road	A2
Cliddesden Road	C3	Southern Road	B4
Clifton Terrace	C1	Stukeley Road	A3
Cordale Road	A4	Sylvia Close	B4
Council Road	B4	Timberlake Road	B2
Crossborough Gardens	D3	Victoria Street	B3
Crossborough Hill	D3	Victory Roundabout	A2
Cross Street	B3	Vyne Road	B1
Devonshire Place	A4	Winchcombe Road	A3
Eastfield Avenue	D2	Winchester Road	A4
Eastrop Lane	D2	Winchester Street	B3
Eastrop Roundabout	C1	Winterthur Way	A1
Eastrop Way	D2	Worting Road	A3
Essex Road	A2	Wote Street	C3
Fairfields Road	B4		
Festival Way	C2		
Flaxfield Court	A2		
Flaxfield Road	A3		
Flaxfield Road	B3		
Frances Road	A4		
Frescade Crescent	A4		
Goat Lane	C2		
Hackwood Road	C4		
Hamelyn Road	A4		
Hardy Lane	A4		
Hawkfield Lane	A4		
Haymarket Yard	C3		
Joices Yard	B3		
Jubilee Road	B4		
London Road	D3		

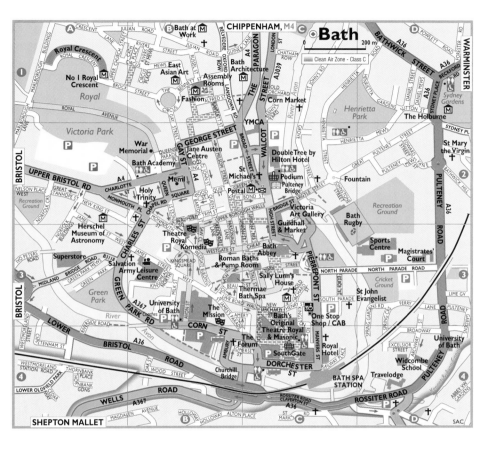

Bath

Bath is found on atlas page **20 D2**

Archway Street D4	Lower Borough Walls B3
Argyle Street C2	Lower Bristol Road A3
Avon Street B3	Lower Oldfield Park..................A4
Bartlett Street B1	Manvers Street C3
Barton Street B2	Midland Bridge Road A3
Bathwick Street D1	Milk Street B3
Beauford Square B2	Milsom Street B2
Beau Street B3	Monmouth Place A2
Beckford Road........................D1	Monmouth Street B2
Bennett Street B1	New Bond Street B2
Bridge Street C2	New King Street A2
Broad Street C2	New Orchard Street C3
Broadway D4	Norfolk Buildings A3
Brock Street A1	North Parade...........................C3
Chapel Road............................B2	North Parade Road D3
Charles Street A3	Old King Street B2
Charlotte Street A2	Oxford Row B1
Cheap Street C3	Pierrepont Street C3
Cheltenham Street..................A4	Princes Street B2
Circus Mews B1	Pulteney Road D2
Claverton Street C4	Queen Square B2
Corn Street B4	Queen Street...........................B2
Daniel Street D1	Railway Place C4
Dorchester Street C4	Rivers Street B1
Edward Street D2	Rossiter Road C4
Ferry Lane D3	Royal Avenue A1
Gay Street B1	Royal Crescent A1
George Street B2	St James's Parade B3
Great Pulteney Street C2	St John's Road........................C4
Great Stanhope Street............A2	Saw Close B3
Green Park Road.....................A3	Southgate Street C4
Green Street B2	South Parade C3
Grove Street C2	Stall Street C3
Guinea Lane B1	Sutton Street D1
Henrietta Gardens...................D1	Sydney Place D1
Henrietta Mews C2	The Circus B1
Henrietta Road C1	The Paragon C1
Henrietta Street C2	Thornbank Place A4
Henry Street C3	Union Street B2
High Street C2	Upper Borough Walls...............B2
Hot Bath Street B3	Upper Bristol Road A2
James Street West B3	Upper Church Street A1
John Street B2	Walcot Street C1
Julian Road B1	Wells Road A4
Kingsmead North B3	Westgate Buildings B3
Kingston Road C3	Westgate Street B2
Lansdown Road.......................B1	Westmoreland Station Road ...A4
London Street C1	York Street C3

Blackpool

Blackpool is found on atlas page **88 C3**

Abingdon Street......................B1	Havelock Street C4
Adelaide Street B3	High Street C1
Albert Road.............................B3	Hornby Road B3
Albert Road.............................C3	Hornby Road D3
Alfred Street C2	Hull Road B3
Ashton Road D4	Kay Street C4
Bank Hey Street B2	Kent Road C4
Banks Street B1	King Street C2
Belmont Avenue C4	Leamington Road D2
Bennett Avenue D3	Leicester Road D2
Bethesda Road C4	Leopold Grove.........................C2
Birley Street B2	Lincoln Road D2
Blenheim Avenue D4	Livingstone Road D2
Bonny Street B4	Lord Street..............................B1
Buchanan Street C1	Louise Street C4
Butler Street C1	Milbourne Street C1
Caunce Street D1	Montreal Avenue D3
Cedar Square C2	New Bonny Street B3
Central Drive...........................C4	New Larkhill Street C1
Chapel Street B4	Palatine Road C4
Charles Street C1	Palatine Road D3
Charnley Road C3	Park Road D2
Cheapside...............................B2	Park Road D4
Church Street B2	Peter Street B2
Church Street C2	Pier Street B4
Church Street D2	Princess Parade B1
Clifton Street B2	Promenade B1
Clinton Avenue D4	Queen Street...........................B1
Cookson Street C2	Raikes Parade D2
Coop Street B4	Reads Avenue C3
Coronation Street C3	Reads Avenue D3
Corporation Street B2	Regent Road C2
Dale Street B4	Ribble Road C4
Deansgate...............................B2	Ripon Road D3
Dickson Road B1	Seasiders Way.........................B4
Edward Street D2	Selbourne Road D1
Elizabeth Street D1	South King Street C2
Fairhurst Street D1	Springfield Road B1
Fisher Street C1	Stanley Road C3
Fleet Street C3	Talbot Road B2
Foxhall Road B4	Talbot Road C1
Freckleton Street D4	Topping Street C2
General Street B1	Vance Road B3
George Street C1	Victoria Street B2
Gorton Street D1	Victory Road D1
Granville Road D2	West Street B2
Grosvenor Street.....................C1	Woolman Road D4
Harrison Street D4	York Street B4

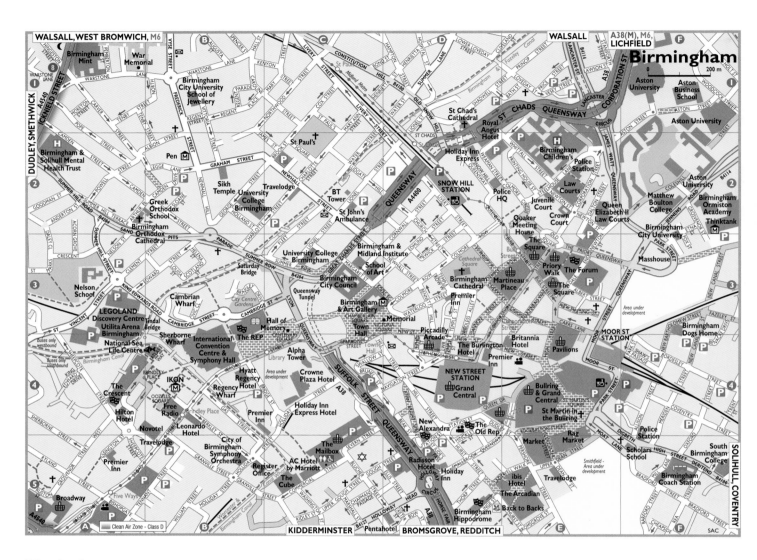

Birmingham

Birmingham is found on atlas page **58 G7**

Acorn Grove	A2
Albert Street	E3
Albert Street	F3
Albion Street	B2
Allison Street	F4
Anderton Street	A2
Arthur Place	A2
Aston Street	F1
Atlas Way	B4
Banbury Street	F3
Barford Street	F5
Bartholomew Street	F3
Barwick Street	D3
Bath Street	E1
Beak Street	D4
Benacre Drive	F4
Bennetts Hill	D3
Berkley Street	B4
Bishopgate Street	A5
Blucher Street	C5
Bond Street	C1
Bordesley Street	F4
Bow Street	D5
Bradford Street	F5
Bridge Street	B4
Brindley Drive	B3
Brindley Place	B4
Broad Street	A5
Bromsgrove Street	E5
Brook Street	C2
Brunel Street	C4
Bull Street	E3
Cambridge Street	B3
Camden Drive	B2
Camden Street	A2
Cannon Street	D3

Caroline Street	B1
Carrs Lane	E3
Carver Street	A1
Chamberlain Square	C3
Chapmans Passage	C5
Charlotte Street	B3
Cheapside	F5
Cherry Street	D3
Church Street	D2
Civic Close	B3
Clement Street	A3
Cleveland Street	D1
Coleshill Street	F2
Colmore Circus Queensway	E2
Colmore Row	D3
Commercial Street	C5
Constitution Hill	C1
Cornwall Street	D3
Corporation Street	E1
Corporation Street	E3
Coventry Street	F4
Cox Street	C1
Dale End	E3
Daley Close	A3
Dalton Street	E2
Dean Street	E5
Digbeth	E4
Dudley Street	D4
Eden Place	C3
Edgbaston Street	E4
Edmund Street	D3
Edward Street	B3
Ellis Street	D5
Essington Street	A5
Ethel Street	D4
Etna Street	F2

Exeter Street	D5
Fazeley Street	F3
Fleet Street	C3
Fox Street	F3
Frederick Street	B1
Gas Street	B4
George Street	B2
Gloucester Street	E5
Goodman Street	A2
Gough Street	C5
Graham Street	B2
Granville Street	B5
Great Charles Street Queensway	C3
Grosvenor Street	F2
Grosvenor Street West	A5
Hall Street	B1
Hampton Street	D1
Helena Street	B3
Henrietta Street	C1
High Street	E4
High Street Deritend	F5
Hill Street	C4
Hinckley Street	D4
Hingeston Street	A1
Holland Street	B2
Holliday Street	B5
Holloway Circus	D5
Holloway Head	C5
Holt Street	F1
Horse Fair	D5
Hospital Street	D1
Hurst Street	D5
Icknield Street	A1
Inge Street	D5
James Street	B2
James Watt Queensway	E2
Jennens Road	F2
John Bright Street	D4
Kenyon Street	B1
King Edward's Drive	A4

King Edwards Road	A3
Ladywell Walk	D5
Lancaster Circus	E1
Lancaster Street	E1
Lawson Street	E1
Legge Lane	B2
Lighthouse Avenue	A3
Lionel Street	C3
Livery Street	C1
Louisa Street	B3
Loveday Street	E1
Lower Loveday Street	D1
Lower Temple Street	D4
Ludgate Hill	C2
Lyon Queensway	C3
Margaret Street	C3
Marshall Street	C5
Martineau Way	E3
Mary Ann Street	C1
Mary Street	C1
Meriden Street	F4
Mill Lane	F5
Moat Lane	E4
Moor Street	E4
Moor Street Queensway	E4
Moreton Street	A1
Navigation Street	C4
Needless Alley	D3
Nelson Street	A3
New Bartholomew Street	F4
New Canal Street	F4
Newhall Hill	B2
Newhall Street	C2
New Meeting Street	E3
Newton Street	E3
Newton Street	E2
Northwood Street	C1
Old Snow Hill	D1
Old Square	E3
Oozells Square	B4
Oxford Street	F5

Parade	B3
Paradise Street	C4
Park Street	E4
Pemberton Street	A1
Pershore Street	E5
Pope Street	A1
Powell Street	A2
Price Street	E1
Princip Street	E1
Printing House Street	E2
Queens Drive	D4
Queensway Tunnel	C3
Rea Street	E5
Regent Parade	B1
Regent Place	B1
Regent Street	B1
Ridley Street	C5
Ruston Street	A5
Ryland Street	A5
St Chads Queensway	E1
St Jude's Pass	D5
St Marks Crescent	A3
St Martin's Square	E4
St Paul's Square	C1
St Philip's Place	D3
St Vincent Street	A4
Sand Pitts	A2
Saturday Bridge	B3
Scotland Street	B3
Severn Street	C5
Shadwell Street	D1
Shaw's Passage	F4
Sheepcote Street	A4
Sherborne Street	A4
Sloane Street	B2
Smallbrook Queensway	D5
Snow Hill Queensway	D2
Spencer Street	B1
Staniforth Street	E1
Station Street	D5
Steelhouse Lane	E2

Stephenson Street	D4
Suffolk Street Queensway	C4
Summer Hill Road	A2
Summer Hill Street	A2
Summer Hill Terrace	A2
Summer Lane	D1
Summer Row	B3
Swallow Street	C4
Temple Row	D3
Temple Row West	D3
Temple Street	D3
Tenby Street	A1
Tenby Street North	A1
Tennant Street	A5
The Priory Queensway	E3
Thorp Street	D5
Tindal Bridge	B3
Trent Street	F4
Union Street	E3
Upper Dean Street	E5
Upper Gough Street	C5
Vesey Street	E1
Victoria Square	C3
Vittoria Street	B1
Vyse Street	B1
Warstone Lane	A1
Washington Street	C5
Waterloo Street	D3
Water Street	C2
Weaman Street	D2
Whittall Street	E2
William Street	B5
Woodcock Street	F1

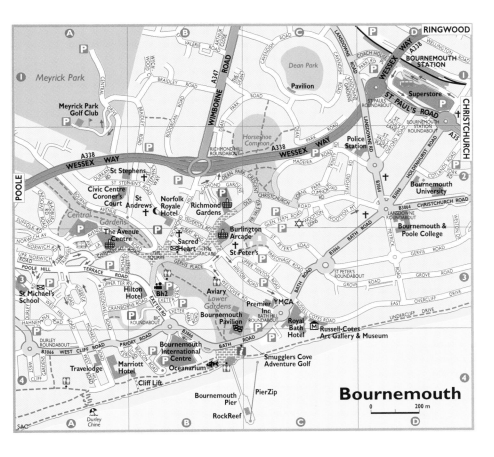

Bournemouth

Bournemouth is found on atlas page **13 J6**

Albert Road	B3	Old Christchurch Road	C2
Avenue Lane	A3	Orchard Street	A3
Avenue Road	A3	Oxford Road	D2
Bath Hill Roundabout	C3	Park Road	D1
Bath Road	B4	Parsonage Road	C3
Beacon Road	B4	Poole Hill	A3
BIC Roundabout	B3	Priory Road	A4
Bodorgan Road	B2	Purbeck Road	A3
Bourne Avenue	A2	Richmond Gardens	B2
Bournemouth Street		Richmond Hill	B3
Roundabout	D1	Richmond Hill Roundabout	B2
Bradburne Road	A2	Russell Cotes Road	C3
Braidley Road	B1	St Michael's Road	A3
Cavendish Road	C1	St Paul's Lane	D1
Central Drive	A1	St Paul's Place	D2
Christchurch Road	D2	St Paul's Road	D1
Coach House Place	D1	St Pauls Roundabout	D1
Commercial Road	A3	St Peter's Road	C3
Cotlands Road	D2	St Peter's Roundabout	C3
Cranborne Road	A3	St Stephen's Road	A2
Crescent Road	A2	St Stephen's Way	B2
Cumnor Road	C2	St Valerie Road	B1
Dean Park Crescent	B2	Stafford Road	C2
Dean Park Road	B2	Suffolk Road	A2
Durley Road	A3	Terrace Road	A3
Durley Roundabout	A4	The Arcade	B3
Durrant Road	A2	The Deans	B1
East Overcliff Drive	D3	The Square	B3
Exeter Crescent	B3	The Triangle	A3
Exeter Park Road	B3	Tregonwell Road	A3
Exeter Road	B3	Trinity Road	C2
Fir Vale Road	C2	Undercliff Drive	D3
Gervis Place	B3	Upper Hinton Road	C3
Gervis Road	D3	Upper Norwich Road	A3
Glen Fern Road	C2	Upper Terrace Road	A3
Grove Road	C3	Wellington Road	D1
Hahnemann Road	A3	Wessex Way	A2
Hinton Road	B3	West Cliff Gardens	A4
Holdenhurst Road	D2	West Cliff Road	A4
Kerley Road	A4	West Hill Road	A3
Lansdowne Gardens	C1	Weston Drive	D2
Lansdowne Road	C1	Westover Road	B3
Lansdowne Roundabout	D2	Wimborne Road	B1
Lorne Park Road	C2	Wootton Gardens	C2
Madeira Road	C2	Wootton Mount	C2
Meyrick Road	D3	Wychwood Close	B1
Norwich Avenue	A3	Yelverton Road	B2
Norwich Road	A3	York Road	D2

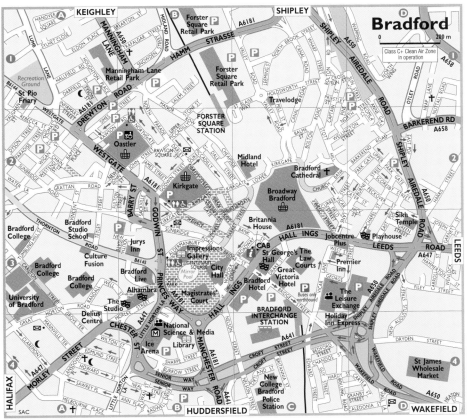

Bradford

Bradford is found on atlas page **90 F4**

Aldermanbury	B3	Lower Kirkgate	C2
Bank Street	B2	Lumb Lane	A1
Barkerend Road	D2	Manchester Road	B4
Barry Street	B2	Manningham Lane	A1
Bolling Road	C4	Manor Row	B1
Bolton Road	C2	Market Street	B3
Bridge Street	C3	Midland Road	B1
Broadway	C3	Morley Street	A4
Burnett Street	D2	Neal Street	B4
Canal Road	C1	Nelson Street	B4
Carlton Street	A3	North Brook Street	C1
Centenary Square	B3	Northgate	B2
Chandos Street	C4	North Parade	B1
Chapel Street	D3	North Street	C2
Cheapside	B2	North Wing	D1
Chester Street	A4	Otley Road	D1
Church Bank	C2	Paradise Street	A2
Claremont	A4	Peckover Street	D2
Croft Street	C4	Piccadilly	B2
Darfield Street	A1	Pine Street	C2
Darley Street	B2	Princes Way	B3
Drewton Road	A2	Randall Well Street	A3
Dryden Street	D4	Rawson Road	A2
Duke Street	B2	Rawson Square	B2
East Parade	D3	Rebecca Street	A2
Edmund Street	A4	St Blaise Way	C1
Edward Street	C4	St Thomas's Road	A2
Eldon Place	A1	Sawrey Place	A4
Filey Street	D3	Senior Way	B4
George Street	C3	Shipley Airedale Road	C1
Godwin Street	B2	Stott Hill	C2
Grattan Road	A2	Sunbridge Road	A2
Great Horton Road	A4	Tetley Street	A3
Grove Terrace	A4	Thornton Road	A3
Hallfield Road	A1	Trafalgar Street	B1
Hall Ings	B4	Tyrrel Street	B3
Hammerton Street	D3	Upper Park Gate	D2
Hamm Strasse	B1	Upper Piccadilly	B2
Holdsworth Street	C1	Valley Road	C1
Houghton Place	A1	Vicar Lane	C3
Howard Street	A4	Wakefield Road	D4
Hustlergate	B3	Wapping Road	D1
Infirmary Street	A1	Water Lane	A2
John Street	B2	Wellington Street	C2
Lansdowne Place	A4	Westgate	A2
Leeds Road	D3	Wharf Street	C1
Little Horton	A4	Wigan Street	A2
Little Horton Lane	B4	Wilton Street	A4

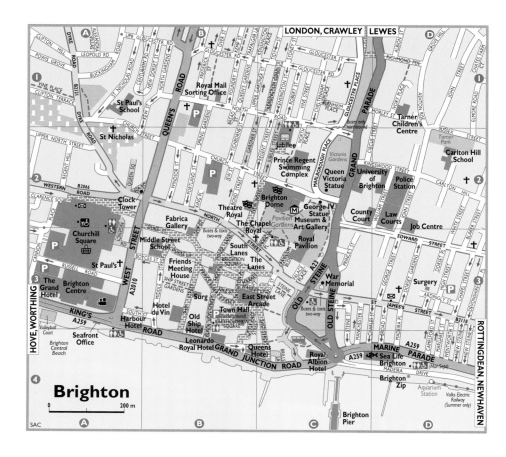

Brighton

Brighton is found on atlas page **24 H10**

Ardingly Street	D3	Madeira Place	D4
Ashton Rise	D1	Manchester Street	C4
Bartholomew Square	B3	Margaret Street	D4
Black Lion Street	B3	Marine Parade	D4
Blaker Street	D3	Market Street	B3
Bond Street	B2	Marlborough Place	C2
Boyces Street	A3	Meeting House Lane	B3
Brighton Place	B3	Middle Street	B3
Broad Street	D4	Morley Street	D1
Buckingham Road	A1	New Dorset Street	B1
Camelford Street	D4	New Road	B2
Cannon Place	A3	New Steine	D4
Carlton Hill	D2	Nile Street	B3
Centurion Road	A1	North Gardens	B1
Chapel Street	D3	North Place	C2
Charles Street	C4	North Road	B1
Cheltenham Place	C1	North Street	B2
Church Street	A1	Old Steine	C3
Church Street	B2	Portland Street	B2
Circus Street	C2	Powis Grove	A1
Clifton Hill	A1	Prince Albert Street	B3
Clifton Terrace	A1	Prince's Street	C3
Devonshire Place	D3	Queen's Gardens	B1
Dukes Lane	B3	Queen Square	A2
Duke Street	B2	Queen's Road	B2
East Street	C3	Regency Road	A2
Edward Street	D3	Regent Hill	A2
Elmore Road	D1	Regent Street	C2
Foundry Street	B1	Robert Street	C1
Frederick Street	B1	St James's Street	D3
Gardner Street	B2	St Nicholas Road	A1
George Street	D3	Ship Street	B3
Gloucester Place	B2	Spring Gardens	B1
Gloucester Road	B1	Steine Street	C4
Gloucester Street	C1	Sussex Street	D2
Grand Junction Road	B4	Sydney Street	C1
Grand Parade	C2	Tichborne Street	B2
High Street	D3	Tidy Street	C1
Ivory Place	D1	Upper Gardner Street	B1
John Street	D2	Upper Gloucester Road	A1
Jubilee Street	C2	Upper North Street	A2
Kensington Gardens	C1	Vine Street	C1
Kensington Street	C1	Wentworth Street	D4
Kew Street	B1	Western Road	A2
King's Road	A3	West Street	A3
Kingswood Street	C2	White Street	D3
Leopold Road	A1	William Street	D2
Little East Street	B4	Windsor Street	B2

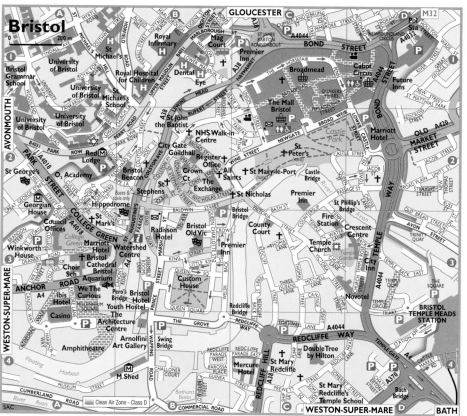

Bristol

Bristol is found on atlas page **31 Q10**

Anchor Road	A3	Passage Street	C2
Avon Street	D3	Pembroke Street	C1
Baldwin Street	B2	Penn Street	C1
Bath Bridge	D4	Pero's Bridge	B3
Bond Street	C1	Perry Road	A2
Bond Street	D2	Philadelphia Street	C2
Broadmead	C1	Portwall Lane	C4
Broad Plain	D2	Prewett Street	C4
Broad Quay	B3	Prince Street	B3
Broad Street	B2	Queen Charlotte Street	B3
Broad Weir	C2	Queen Square	B3
Canons Way	A3	Redcliffe Parade West	B4
Canynge Street	C3	Redcliffe Way	C4
Castle Street	C2	Redcliff Hill	C4
College Green	A3	Redcliff Mead Lane	C4
Colston Avenue	B2	Redcliff Street	C3
Colston Street	B2	Royal Fort Road	A1
Commercial Road	B4	Rupert Street	B2
Corn Street	B2	St Augustine's Parade	B3
Counterslip	C3	St George's Road	A3
Cumberland Road	A4	St Matthias Park	D1
Deanery Road	A3	St Michael's Hill	A1
Denmark Street	A3	St Stephen's Street	B2
Explore Lane	A3	St Thomas Street	C3
Fairfax Street	C2	Small Street	B2
Ferry Street	C3	Somerset Street	C4
Friary	D3	Southwell Street	A1
Frogmore Street	A2	Tankards Close	A1
Great George Street	A3	Telephone Avenue	B3
Great George Street	D1	Temple Back	C3
Guinea Street	B4	Temple Back East	D3
Haymarket	C1	Temple Gate	D4
Hill Street	A2	Temple Street	C3
Horfield Road	B1	Temple Way	D3
Jacob Street	D2	The Grove	B4
King Street	B3	The Horsefair	C1
Lewins Mead	B2	The Pithay	C2
Lodge Street	A2	Tower Hill	D2
Lower Castle Street	D2	Trenchard Street	A2
Lower Church Lane	A2	Tyndall Avenue	A1
Lower Maudlin Street	B1	Union Street	C2
Marlborough Hill	B1	Upper Maudlin Street	B1
Marlborough Street	B1	Victoria Street	C3
Marsh Street	B3	Wapping Road	B4
Museum Avenue	A4	Welsh Back	B3
Newgate	C2	Whitson Street	B1
Old Market Street	D2	Wine Street	C2
Park Street	A2	Woodland Road	A1

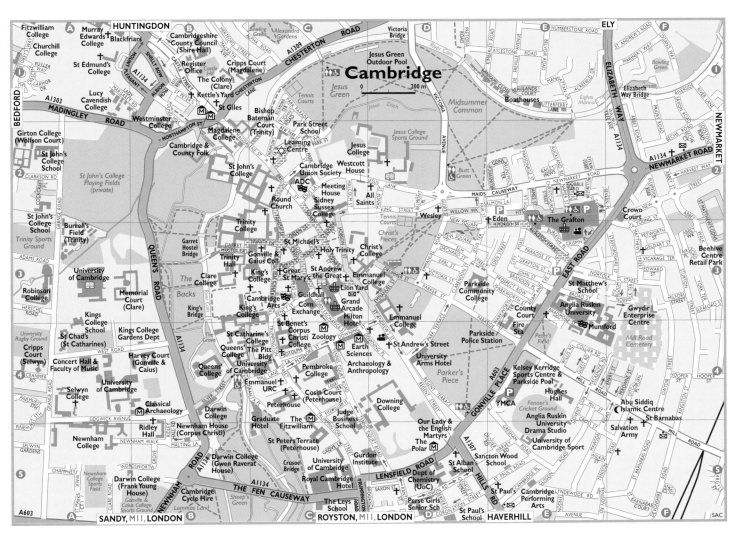

Cambridge

Cambridge is found on atlas page **62 G9**

Abbey Road	F1
Abbey Street	F2
Abbey Walk	F3
Acrefield Drive	E1
Adam and Eve Street	E3
Albion Row	B1
Alpha Road	C1
Auckland Road	E2
Aylestone Road	E1
Bailey Mews	E2
Banhams Close	D1
Beaulands Court	E1
Beche Road	F2
Belmont Place	D2
Belvoir Road	E1
Bene't Street	C3
Bloom Street	F3
Bradmore Street	E3
Brandon Place	E3
Bridge Street	C2
Broad Street	E3
Brookside	D5
Brunswick Gardens	E2
Brunswick Terrace	E2
Burleigh Place	E3
Burleigh Street	E3
Cambridge Place	E5
Castle Row	B1
Castle Street	B1
Champneys Walk	A5
Chesterton Lane	B1
Chesterton Road	C1
Christchurch Street	E2
City Road	E3
Clarendon Street	D3
Cobble Yard	E2

Collier Road	E4
Corn Exchange Street	C3
Coronation Street	D5
Covent Garden	E4
Crispin Place	E3
Cross Street	E4
Crusoe Bridge	B5
Cutler Ferry Close	E1
Cutterferry Lane	E1
De Freville Avenue	E1
Devonshire Road	F5
Ditchburn Place	F4
Downing Place	C4
Downing Street	C4
Drosier Road	D5
Drummer Street	D3
Earl Street	D3
East Road	E3
Eden Street	E3
Eden Street Back	E3
Edward Street	F3
Elizabeth Way	F1
Elm Street	D3
Emery Street	F4
Emmanuel Road	D3
Emmanuel Street	D3
Evening Court	E2
Fairsford Place	F3
Fair Street	D2
Fitzroy Lane	E2
Fitzroy Street	E3
Fitzwilliam Street	C4
Garret Hostel Bridge	B3
Garret Hostel Lane	B3
Geldart Street	F3
George IV Street	D5

Glisson Road	E5
Godstone Road	F2
Gonville Place	D4
Grange Road	A3
Grange Road	A4
Granta Place	B4
Green Street	C3
Gresham Road	E5
Gwydir Street	F4
Harvest Way	F2
Harvey Road	E5
Hertford Street	B1
Hills Road	D5
Hobson Street	C3
Humberstone Road	E1
James Street	E2
Jesus Lane	C2
Jesus Terrace	D3
John Street	E3
Kimberley Road	E1
King's Bridge	B3
King's Parade	C3
Kingston Street	F4
King Street	D2
Lady Margaret Road	A1
Lensfield Road	D5
Logan's Way	F1
Lwr Park Street	C2
Lyndewode Road	E5
Mackenzie Road	E4
Madingley Road	A1
Magdalene Street	B2
Magrath Avenue	B1
Maids Causeway	D2
Malcolm Street	C2
Malting Lane	B5
Manhattan Drive	E1
Manor Street	D2
Mariner's Way	F1
Market Street	C3
Mawson Road	E5

Milford Street	F3
Mill Lane	C4
Mill Road	E4
Mill Street	E4
Mortimer Road	E4
Mount Pleasant	B1
Napier Street	E2
Newmarket Road	E2
Newnham Road	B5
Newnham Walk	A5
New Park Street	C2
New Square	D3
New Street	F2
Norfolk Street	E3
Norfolk Terrace	F3
Northampton Street	B2
Occupation Road	F2
Orchard Street	D3
Panton Street	D5
Paradise Street	E3
Parker Street	D3
Park Parade	C1
Parkside	D3
Park Street	C2
Park Terrace	D4
Parsonage Street	E2
Peas Hill	C3
Pembroke Street	C4
Perowne Street	F4
Petworth Street	F3
Pound Hill	B1
Priory Road	F1
Prospect Row	E3
Queen's Road	B3
Regent Street	D4
Regent Terrace	D4
River Lane	F1
Riverside	F1
St Andrew's Road	F1
St Andrew's Street	D3
St Barnabas Road	F5

St Mary's Street	C3
St Matthew's Gardens	F2
St Matthew's Street	F3
St Paul's Road	E5
St Peter's Street	B1
Salmon Lane	E2
Saxon Road	F1
Saxon Street	D5
Severn Place	F2
Shelly Row	B1
Short Street	D2
Sidgwick Avenue	A4
Sidney Street	C2
Silver Street	B4
Staffordshire Street	F3
Sturton Street	F3
Sussex Street	C3
Tenison Avenue	E5
Tenison Road	E5
Tennis Court Road	C4
Tennis Court Terrace	C4
The Fen Causeway	B5
Thompson's Lane	C2
Trinity Lane	C3
Trinity Street	C2
Trumpington Road	C5
Trumpington Street	C4
Union Road	D5
Vicarage Terrace	F3
Victoria Avenue	D1
Victoria Bridge	D1
Victoria Street	D3
Warkworth Street	E3
Warkworth Terrace	E4
Wellington Street	E2
West Road	A4
Wilkin Street	E5
Willis Road	E4
Willow Walk	D2
Wordsworth Grove	A5
Young Street	F3

University Colleges

Christ's College	C3
Clare College	A3
Clare College	B1
Clare College	B3
Corpus Christi College	C4
Darwin College	B4
Downing College	D4
Emmanuel College	C3
Emmanuel College	D3
Fitzwilliam College	A1
Girton College (Wolfson Court)	A2
Gonville & Caius College	C3
Gonville & Caius College	B4
Jesus College	C2
King's College	B3
Lucy Cavendish College	A1
Magdalene College	B2
Murray Edwards College	A1
Newnham College	A5
Pembroke College	C4
Peterhouse	C4
Queens' College	B4
Robinson College	A3
St Catharine's College	C4
St Edmund's College	A1
St John's College	B2
Selwyn College	C2
Sidney Sussex College	C2
Trinity College	B3
Westminster College	B1

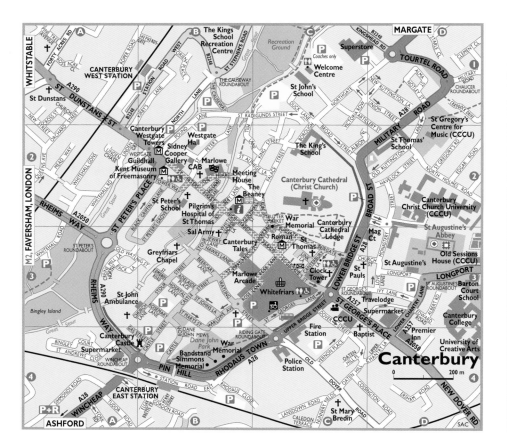

Canterbury

Canterbury is found on atlas page **39 K10**

Adelaide Place	B3	Nunnery Fields	C4
Albion Place	C2	Oaten Hill	C4
Alma Street	D1	Old Dover Road	C4
Artillery Street	C1	Old Ruttington Lane	D2
Beercart Lane	B3	Orchard Street	A2
Best Lane	B2	Palace Street	C2
Black Griffin Lane	A3	Parade	C3
Borough	C2	Pin Hill	B4
Broad Street	D2	Pound Lane	B2
Burgate	C3	Queens Avenue	A2
Butter Market	C2	Rheims Way	A3
Canterbury Lane	C3	Rhodaus Town	B4
Castle Row	B4	Rose Lane	B3
Castle Street	B3	Rosemary Lane	C4
Cossington Road	C4	St Alphege Lane	B2
Dover Street	C3	St Dunstans Street	A1
Duck Lane	C1	St Edmunds Road	B3
Edgar Road	D2	St George's Lane	C3
Edward Road	D3	St George's Place	C3
Ersham Road	D4	St George's Street	C3
Gas Street	A4	St Gregory's Road	D2
Gordon Road	B4	St Johns Lane	B3
Guildhall Street	B2	St Margaret's Street	B3
Havelock Street	D2	St Marys Street	B3
Hawks Lane	B3	St Peter's Grove	B3
High Street	B2	St Peter's Lane	B2
Hospital Lane	B3	St Peter's Place	A3
Ivy Lane	C3	St Peters Street	B2
Jewry Lane	B3	St Radigunds Street	B1
King Street	C2	Station Road East	B4
Kirby's Lane	B1	Station Road West	A1
Lansdown Road	C4	Stour Street	B3
Linden Grove	A2	Sturry Road	D1
Longport	D3	Sun Street	C2
Love Lane	D3	The Causeway	B1
Lower Bridge Street	C3	The Friars	B2
Lower Chantry Lane	D4	Tourtel Road	D1
Marlowe Avenue	B3	Tower Way	B2
Mead Way	A2	Tudor Road	A4
Mercery Lane	C3	Union Street	D1
Military Road	D2	Upper Bridge Street	C4
Mill Lane	B1	Vernon Place	C4
Monastery Street	D3	Victoria Row	C1
New Dover Road	D4	Watling Street	B3
New Ruttington Lane	D1	Whitehall Gardens	A2
North Lane	B1	Whitehall Road	A2
Northgate	C1	Wincheap	A4
Notley Street	D1	York Road	A4

Cardiff

Cardiff is found on atlas page **30 G9**

Adam Street	C3	Museum Avenue	B1
Adams Court	D2	Museum Place	B1
Adamscroft Place	D3	Newport Road	D1
Atlantic Wharf	D4	Newport Road Lane	D2
Boulevard de Nantes	B1	North Luton Place	D2
Bridge Street	C3	North Road	A1
Brigantine Place	D4	Oxford Lane	D1
Bute Street	C4	Oxford Street	D1
Bute Terrace	C3	Park Grove	B1
Callaghan Square	B4	Park Lane	B1
Caroline Street	B3	Park Place	B1
Castle Lane	D1	Park Street	A3
Castle Street	A2	Pellett Street	C3
Central Link	D3	Pendyris Street	A4
Charles Street	B2	Quay Street	A3
Churchill Way	C2	Queen Street	B2
City Hall Road	A1	Richmond Crescent	C1
City Road	D1	Richmond Road	C1
Crockherbtown Lane	B2	St Andrew's Crescent	B1
Custom House Street	B4	St Andrew's Lane	C1
David Street	C3	St Andrew's Place	B1
Davis Street	D3	St John Street	B3
Duke Street	A2	St Mary Street	B3
Dumfries Place	C2	St Peter's Street	C1
East Bay Close	D3	Salisbury Road	C1
East Grove	D1	Sandon Street	C3
Fford Churchill	C2	Saunders Road	B4
Fitzalan Place	D2	Schooner Way	D4
Fitzalan Road	D2	Stuttgarter Strasse	B1
Fitzhamon Embankment	A4	The Friary	B2
Glossop Road	D1	The Hayes	B3
Greyfriars Road	B2	The Parade	D1
Guildford Street	C3	The Walk	C1
Guildhall Place	A3	Trinity Street	B3
Havelock Street	B3	Tudor Street	A4
Hayes Bridge Road	B3	Tyndall Street	D4
Heol Siarl	B2	Vere Street	D1
Herbert Street	C4	Wesley Lane	C2
High Street	B3	West Canal Wharf	B4
High Street Arcade	B2	West Grove	C1
Hills Street	B3	Westgate Street	A3
King Edward VII Avenue	A1	Wharton Street	B3
Knox Road	D2	Windsor Lane	C2
Lloyd George Avenue	C4	Windsor Place	C1
Mary Ann Street	C3	Windsor Road	D3
Mill Lane	B4	Womanby Street	A3
Moira Place	D2	Wood Street	A4
Moira Terrace	D2	Working Street	B3

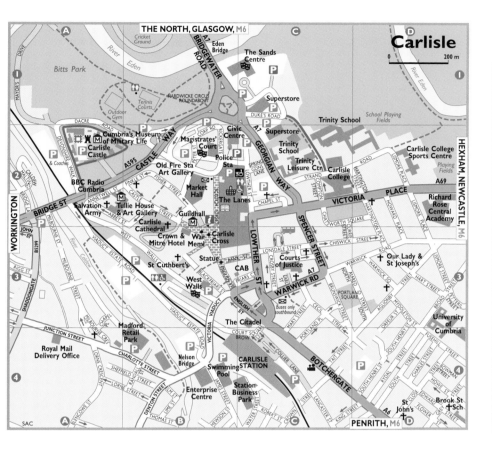

Carlisle

Carlisle is found on atlas page **110 G9**

Abbey Street	A2	Howard Place	D2
Aglionby Street	D3	Howe Street	D4
Annetwell Street	A2	James Street	B4
Bank Street	B3	John Street	A3
Blackfriars Street	B3	Junction Street	A4
Blencowe Street	A4	King Street	C4
Botchergate	C4	Lancaster Street	C4
Bridge Lane	A2	Lime Street	B4
Bridge Street	A2	Lismore Place	D2
Bridgewater Road	B1	Lismore Street	D3
Broad Street	D3	Lonsdale Street	C3
Brunswick Street	C3	Lorne Crescent	A4
Caldew Maltings	A2	Lorne Street	A4
Castle Street	B2	Lowther Street	C3
Castle Way	B2	Mary Street	C3
Cecil Street	C3	Mayor's Drive	A1
Chapel Place	A3	Milbourne Crescent	A3
Chapel Street	C2	Milbourne Street	A3
Charles Street	D4	Myddleton Street	D3
Charlotte Street	B4	North Alfred Street	D3
Chatsworth Square	C2	Orfeur Street	D3
Chiswick Street	C2	Peter Street	B2
Close Street	D4	Petteril Street	D3
Collier Lane	C4	Portland Place	C4
Compton Street	C2	Portland Square	C3
Corp Road	B2	Randall Street	B4
Court Square Brow	C4	Rickergate	B2
Crosby Street	C3	Rigg Street	A3
Crown Street	C4	Robert Street	C4
Currie Street	C3	Rydal Street	D4
Dacre Road	A1	Scotch Street	B2
Denton Street	B4	Shaddongate	A3
Devonshire Walk	A2	Sheffield Street	A4
Duke's Road	C1	South Alfred Street	D3
Edward Street	D4	South Henry Street	D4
Elm Street	B4	Spencer Street	C2
English Street	B3	Spring Gardens Lane	C2
Finkle Street	B2	Strand Road	C2
Fisher Street	B2	Tait Street	C4
Flower Street	D4	Thomas Street	B4
Friars Court	C3	Viaduct Estate Road	A3
Fusehill Street	D4	Victoria Place	C2
Georgian Way	C2	Victoria Viaduct	B4
Grey Street	D4	Warwick Road	C3
Hartington Place	D2	Warwick Square	D3
Hartington Street	D2	Water Street	C4
Hart Street	D3	West Tower Street	B2
Hewson Street	B4	West Walls	B3

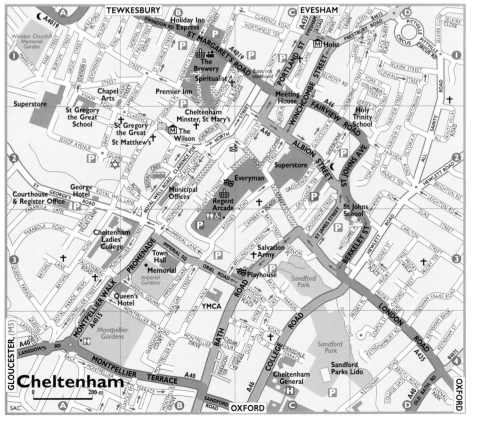

Cheltenham

Cheltenham is found on atlas page **46 H10**

Albion Street	C2	Montpellier Parade	B4
All Saints' Road	D2	Montpellier Spa Road	B4
Ambrose Street	B1	Montpellier Street	A4
Argyll Road	D4	Montpellier Terrace	A4
Back Montpellier Terrace	A4	Montpellier Walk	A4
Bath Road	B4	New Street	A1
Bath Street	C3	North Street	B2
Bayshill Road	A3	Old Bath Road	D4
Bayshill Villas Lane	A3	Oriel Road	B3
Bennington Street	B1	Parabola Lane	A3
Berkeley Street	C3	Parabola Road	A3
Burton Street	A1	Park Street	A1
Carlton Street	D3	Pittville Circus	D1
Church Street	B2	Pittville Circus Road	D1
Clarence Parade	B2	Pittville Street	C2
Clarence Road	C1	Portland Street	C1
Clarence Street	B2	Prestbury Road	C1
College Road	C4	Priory Street	D3
Crescent Terrace	B2	Promenade	B3
Devonshire Street	A1	Queens Parade	A3
Duke Street	D3	Regent Street	B2
Dunalley Street	B1	Rodney Road	B3
Evesham Road	C1	Royal Well Lane	A2
Fairview Road	C2	Royal Well Road	B2
Fairview Street	D2	St Anne's Road	D2
Fauconberg Road	A3	St Anne's Terrace	D2
Glenfall Street	D1	St George's Place	B2
Grosvenor Street	C3	St George's Road	A2
Grove Street	A1	St George's Street	B1
Henrietta Street	B1	St James' Square	A2
Hewlett Road	D2	St James Street	C3
High Street	A1	St Johns Avenue	C2
High Street	C2	St Margaret's Road	B1
Imperial Lane	B3	St Paul's Street South	B1
Imperial Square	B3	Sandford Street	C3
Jersey Street	D1	Selkirk Street	D1
Jessop Avenue	A2	Sherborne Street	C2
Keynsham Road	D4	Station Street	A1
King Street	A1	Suffolk Parade	B4
Knapp Road	A1	Swindon Road	B1
Lansdown Road	A4	Sydenham Villas Road	D3
Leighton Road	D2	Trafalgar Street	B4
London Road	D3	Union Street	D2
Malden Road	D1	Wellington Street	C3
Market Street	A1	Winchcombe Street	C2
Milsom Street	A1	Winstonian Road	D2
Monson Avenue	B1	Witcombe Place	C3
Montpellier Grove	B4	York Street	D1

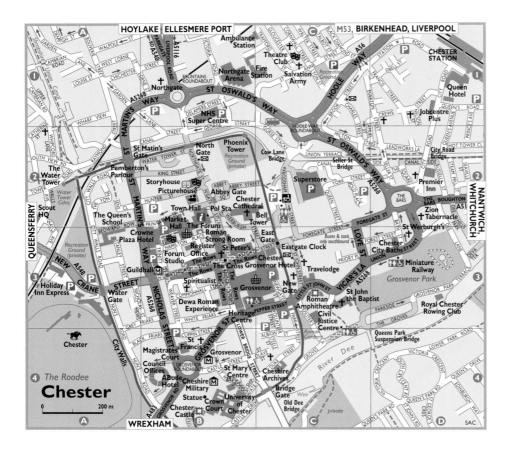

Chester

Chester is found on atlas page **81 N11**

Albion Street	C4	Nicholas Street	B3
Bath Street	D2	Northgate Street	B2
Black Diamond Street	C1	Nun's Road	A3
Boughton	D2	Parkgate Road	B1
Bouverie Street	A1	Park Street	C3
Bridge Street	B3	Pepper Street	C3
Brook Street	C1	Princess Street	B2
Canal Side	C2	Priory Place	C3
Castle Street	B4	Queen's Park Road	C4
Charles Street	C1	Queen's Road	D1
Chichester Street	A1	Queen Street	C2
City Road	D2	Raymond Street	A2
City Walls Road	A2	Russell Street	D2
Commonhall Street	B3	St Anne Street	C1
Cornwall Street	C1	St John's Road	D4
Crewe Street	D1	St John Street	C3
Cuppin Street	B4	St Martin's Way	A2
Dee Hills Park	D2	St Mary's Hill	B4
Dee Lane	D2	St Olave Street	C4
Delamere Street	B1	St Oswald's Way	B1
Duke Street	C4	St Werburgh Street	B2
Eastgate Street	B3	Samuel Street	C2
Egerton Street	C1	Seller Street	D2
Foregate Street	C2	Shipgate Street	B4
Forest Street	C3	Souter's Lane	C3
Francis Street	D1	South View Road	A2
Frodsham Street	C2	Stanley Street	A3
Garden Lane	A1	Station Road	D1
George Street	B2	Steam Mill Street	D2
Gloucester Street	C1	Steele Street	C1
Gorse Stacks	C2	Talbot Street	C1
Grosvenor Park Terrace	D3	Tower Road	A2
Grosvenor Road	B4	Trafford Street	C1
Grosvenor Street	B4	Trinity Street	B3
Hamilton Place	B3	Union Street	D3
Hoole Way	C1	Union Terrace	C1
Hunter Street	B2	Upper Cambrian Road	A1
King Street	B2	Vicar's Lane	C3
Leadworks Lane	D2	Victoria Crescent	D4
Little St John Street	C3	Victoria Road	B1
Liverpool Road	B1	Volunteer Street	C2
Lorne Street	A1	Walpole Street	A1
Love Street	C3	Walter Street	C1
Lower Bridge Street	B4	Watergate Street	B3
Lower Park Road	D4	Water Tower Street	B2
Milton Street	C2	Weaver Street	B3
New Crane Street	A3	White Friars	B3
Newgate Street	C3	York Street	C2

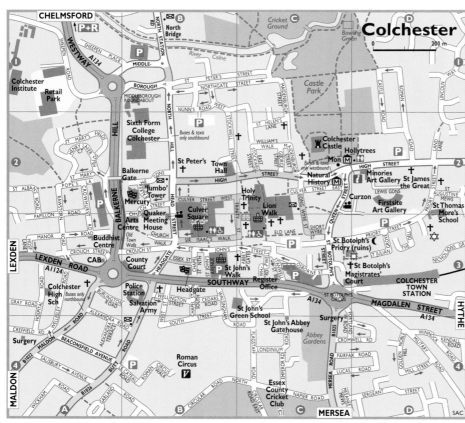

Colchester

Colchester is found on atlas page **52 G6**

Abbey Gates	C3	Middleborough Roundabout	A1
Alexandra Road	A3	Military Road	D4
Balkerne Hill	A3	Mill Street	D4
Beaconsfield Avenue	A4	Napier Road	C4
Burlington Road	A3	Nicholsons Green	D3
Butt Road	A4	North Bridge	B1
Castle Road	D1	Northgate Street	B1
Cedars Road	B3	North Hill	B1
Chapel Street North	B3	North Station Road	B1
Chapel Street South	B3	Nunn's Road	B1
Church Street	B3	Osborne Street	C3
Church Walk	B3	Papillon Road	A3
Circular Road East	C4	Pope's Lane	A2
Circular Road North	B4	Portland Road	C4
Creffield Road	A4	Priory Street	C3
Cromwell Road	C4	Queen Street	C3
Crouch Street	A3	Rawstorn Road	A2
Crouch Street	B3	Roman Circus Walk	B4
Crowhurst Road	A2	Roman Road	D1
Culver Street East	C2	St Alban's Road	A2
Culver Street West	B2	St Augustine Mews	D2
East Hill	D2	St Botolph's Circus	C3
East Stockwell Street	C2	St Botolph's Street	C3
Essex Street	B3	St Helen's Lane	C2
Fairfax Road	C4	St John's Avenue	B3
Flagstaff Road	C4	St John's Street	B3
Garland Road	A4	St Julian Grove	D3
George Street	C2	St Mary's Fields	A2
Golden Noble Hill	D4	St Peter's Street	B1
Gray Road	A3	Salisbury Avenue	A4
Headgate	B3	Sheepen Place	A1
Head Street	B2	Sheepen Road	A1
Henry Laver Court	A2	Short Wyre Street	C3
High Street	B2	Sir Isaac's Walk	B3
Hospital Road	A4	South Street	B3
Hospital Lane	A3	Southway	B3
Land Lane	D2	Stanwell Street	C3
Le Cateau Road	B4	Trinity Street	B2
Lewis Gardens	D2	Walsingham Road	A4
Lexden Road	A3	Wellesley Road	A3
Long Wyre Street	C2	Wellington Street	B3
Lucas Road	C4	West Stockwell Street	B1
Magdalen Street	D3	West Street	B4
Maidenburgh Street	C1	Westway	A1
Maldon Road	A4	Whitewell Road	C3
Manor Road	A3	Wickham Road	A4
Mersea Road	C4	William's Walk	C2
Middleborough	B1	Winnock Road	D4

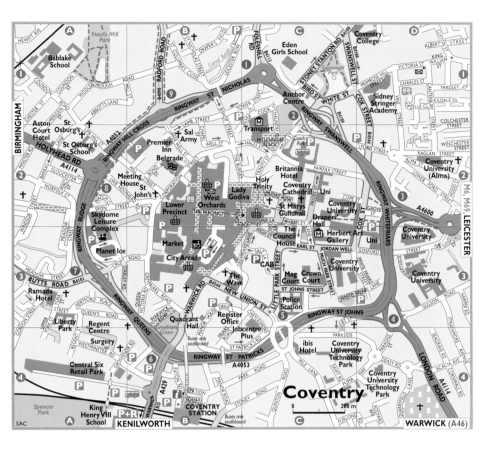

Coventry

Coventry is found on atlas page **59 M9**

Abbotts Lane	A1	Much Park Street	C3
Acacia Avenue	D4	New Union Street	B3
Alma Street	D2	Norfolk Street	A2
Barras Lane	A2	Park Road	B4
Bayley Lane	C2	Parkside	C4
Bird Street	C1	Primrose Hill Street	D1
Bishop Street	B1	Priory Row	C2
Broadgate	B2	Priory Street	C2
Butts Road	A3	Puma Way	C4
Butts Street	A3	Quarryfield Lane	D4
Canterbury Street	D1	Queen's Road	A3
Chester Street	A2	Queen Victoria Road	B3
Cheylesmore	C3	Quinton Road	C4
Cornwall Road	D4	Radford Road	B1
Corporation Street	B2	Raglan Street	D2
Coundon Road	A1	Regent Street	A4
Cox Street	D1	Ringway Hill Cross	A2
Cox Street	D2	Ringway Queens	A3
Croft Road	A3	Ringway Rudge	A2
Earl Street	C3	Ringway St Johns	C3
Eaton Road	B4	Ringway St Nicholas	B1
Fairfax Street	C2	Ringway St Patricks	B4
Foleshill Road	C1	Ringway Swanswell	C1
Gloucester Street	A2	Ringway Whitefriars	D2
Gosford Street	D3	St Johns Street	C3
Greyfriars Lane	B3	St Nicholas Street	B1
Greyfriars Road	B3	Salt Lane	C3
Grosvenor Road	A4	Seagrave Road	D4
Gulson Road	D3	Spon Street	A2
Hales Street	C2	Starley Road	A3
Hertford Place	A3	Stoney Road	B4
High Street	C3	Stoney Stanton Road	C1
Hill Street	B2	Strathmore Avenue	D3
Holyhead Road	A2	Swanswell Street	C1
Jordan Well	C3	The Burges	B2
Lamb Street	B2	Tower Street	B1
Leicester Row	B1	Trinity Street	C2
Little Park Street	C3	Upper Hill Street	A2
London Road	D4	Upper Well Street	B2
Lower Ford Street	D2	Victoria Street	D1
Lower Holyhead Road	A2	Vine Street	D1
Manor House Drive	B4	Warwick Road	B3
Manor Road	B4	Warwick Road	B4
Meadow Street	A3	Westminster Road	A4
Meriden Street	A1	White Friars Street	D1
Middleborough Road	A1	White Street	C1
Mile Lane	C4	Windsor Street	A3
Mill Street	A1	Yardley Street	D1

Darlington

Darlington is found on atlas page **103 Q8**

Abbey Road	A3	Maude Street	A2
Albert Street	D4	Melland Street	D3
Appleby Close	D4	Neasham Road	D4
Barningham Street	B1	Northgate	C2
Bartlett Street	B1	North Lodge Terrace	B2
Beaumont Street	B3	Northumberland Street	B4
Bedford Street	C4	Oakdene Avenue	A4
Beechwood Avenue	A4	Outram Street	A2
Blackwellgate	B3	Parkgate	D3
Bondgate	B2	Park Lane	D4
Borough Road	D3	Park Place	C4
Brunswick Street	C3	Pendower Street	B1
Brunton Street	D4	Pensbury Street	D4
Chestnut Street	C1	Polam Lane	B4
Cleveland Terrace	A4	Portland Place	A3
Clifton Road	C4	Powlett Street	B3
Commercial Street	B2	Priestgate	C3
Coniscliffe Road	A4	Raby Terrace	B3
Corporation Road	B1	Russell Street	C2
Crown Street	C2	St Augustine's Way	B2
Dodds Street	B1	St Cuthbert's Way	C2
Duke Street	A3	St Cuthbert's Way	C4
Easson Road	B1	St James Place	D4
East Mount Road	D1	Salisbury Terrace	A1
East Raby Street	B3	Salt Yard	B3
East Street	C3	Scarth Street	A4
Elms Road	A2	Skinnergate	B3
Elwin Lane	B4	Southend Avenue	A4
Feethams	C4	Stanhope Road North	A2
Fife Road	A3	Stanhope Road South	A3
Four Riggs	B2	Stonebridge	C3
Freeman's Place	C2	Sun Street	B2
Gladstone Street	B2	Swan Street	C2
Grange Road	B4	Swinburne Road	A3
Greenbank Road	A1	Trinity Road	A2
Greenbank Road	B2	Tubwell Row	B3
Hargreave Terrace	C4	Uplands Road	A3
Haughton Road	D2	Valley Street North	C2
High Northgate	C1	Vane Terrace	A2
High Row	B3	Victoria Embankment	C4
Hollyhurst Road	A1	Victoria Road	B4
Houndgate	B3	Victoria Road	C4
John Street	C1	West Crescent	A2
John Williams Boulevard	D3	West Powlett Street	A3
Kendrew Street	B2	West Row	B3
Kingston Street	B1	West Street	B4
Langholm Crescent	A4	Woodland Road	A2
Larchfield Street	A3	Yarm Road	D3

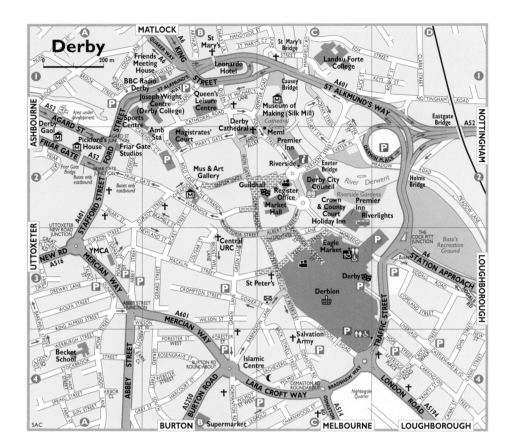

Derby

Derby is found on atlas page **72 B3**

Abbey Street	A4	King Alfred Street	A3
Agard Street	A1	King Street	B1
Albert Street	C3	Lara Croft Way	B4
Babington Lane	B4	Leopold Street	B4
Back Sitwell Street	C4	Liversage Road	D4
Becket Street	B3	Liversage Street	D3
Bold Lane	B2	Lodge Lane	A1
Bradshaw Way	C4	London Road	C3
Bramble Street	B2	Macklin Street	B3
Bridge Street	A1	Mansfield Road	C1
Brook Street	A1	Meadow Lane	D2
Burton Road	B4	Meadow Road	D2
Canal Street	D4	Mercian Way	B3
Carrington Street	D4	Morledge	C3
Cathedral Road	B1	Newland Street	A3
Cavendish Court	A2	New Road	A3
Chapel Street	B1	New Street	D4
Clarke Street	D1	Nottingham Road	D1
Copeland Street	D3	Osmaston Road	C4
Corn Market	B2	Phoenix Street	C1
Crompton Street	B3	Queen Street	B1
Curzon Street	A2	Robert Street	D1
Curzon Street	A3	Rosengrave Street	B4
Darwin Place	C2	Sacheverel Street	C4
Derwent Street	C2	Sadler Gate	B2
Drewry Lane	A3	St Alkmund's Way	C1
Duke Street	C1	St Helen's Street	B1
Dunkirk	A3	St Mary's Gate	B2
East Street	C3	St Peter's Street	C3
Exchange Street	C3	Siddals Road	D3
Exeter Place	C2	Sowter Road	C1
Exeter Street	C2	Spring Street	A4
Ford Street	A2	Stafford Street	A3
Forester Street West	B4	Station Approach	D3
Forman Street	A3	Stockbrook Street	A4
Fox Street	C1	Stuart Street	C1
Friary Street	A2	Sun Street	A4
Full Street	B1	The Cock Pitt	D3
Gerard Street	B3	The Strand	B2
Gower Street	B3	Thorntree Lane	C3
Green Lane	B3	Traffic Street	D4
Grey Street	A4	Trinity Street	D4
Handyside Street	B1	Victoria Street	B2
Harcourt Street	B4	Wardwick	B2
Iron Gate	B2	Werburgh Street	A4
John Street	D4	Wilmot Street	C4
Jury Street	B2	Wolfa Street	A3
Keys Street	D1	Woods Lane	A4

Doncaster

Doncaster is found on atlas page **91 P10**

Alderson Drive	D3	Nelson Street	B4
Apley Road	B3	Nether Hall Road	B1
Balby Road Bridge	A4	North Bridge Road	A1
Beechfield Road	B3	North Street	C4
Broxholme Lane	C1	Osborne Road	D1
Carr House Road	C4	Palmer Street	C4
Carr Lane	B4	Park Road	B2
Chamber Road	B3	Park Terrace	B2
Chequer Avenue	C4	Prince's Street	B2
Chequer Road	C3	Priory Place	A2
Childers Street	C4	Prospect Place	B4
Christ Church Road	B1	Queen's Road	C1
Church View	A1	Rainton Road	C4
Church Way	B1	Ravensworth Road	C3
Clark Avenue	C4	Rectory Gardens	C1
Cleveland Street	A4	Regent Square	C2
College Road	B3	Roman Road	D3
Cooper Street	C4	Royal Avenue	C1
Coopers Terrace	B2	St Georges Gate	B2
Copley Road	B1	St James Street	B4
Cunningham Road	B3	St Mary's Road	C1
Danum Road	D3	St Sepulchre Gate	A2
Dockin Hill Road	B1	St Sepulchre Gate West	A3
Duke Street	A2	St Vincent Avenue	C1
East Laith Gate	B2	St Vincent Road	C1
Elmfield Road	C3	Scot Lane	B2
Firbeck Road	D3	Silver Street	B2
Frances Street	B2	Somerset Road	C4
Glyn Avenue	C1	South Parade	C2
Green Dyke Lane	A4	South Street	C4
Grey Friars' Road	A1	Spring Gardens	A2
Hall Cross Hill	C2	Stirling Street	A4
Hall Gate	B2	Stockil Road	C4
Hamilton Road	D4	Theobald Avenue	D4
Harrington Street	B1	Thorne Road	C1
High Street	A2	Town Fields	C2
Highfield Road	C1	Town Moor Avenue	C1
Jarratt Street	B4	Trafford Way	A2
King's Road	C1	Vaughan Avenue	C1
Lawn Avenue	C2	Waterdale	B3
Lawn Road	C2	Welbeck Road	D3
Lime Tree Avenue	D4	Welcome Way	A4
Manor Drive	D3	West Laith Gate	A2
Market Place	A2	West Street	A3
Market Road	B1	Whitburn Road	C3
Milbanke Street	B1	White Rose Way	B4
Milton Walk	B4	Windsor Road	D1
Montague Street	B1	Wood Street	B2

Dover

Dover is found on atlas page **27 P3**

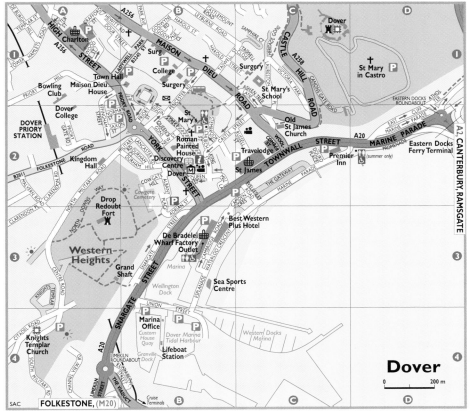

Dover

0 _____ 200 m

Adrian Street B3	Marine Parade..........................C2
Albany Place B2	Marine Parade..........................D2
Ashen Tree Lane.......................C1	Military Road B2
Athol Terrace D1	Mill Lane B2
Biggin Street............................B2	New Street B2
Cambridge Road B3	Norman Street A2
Camden Crescent C2	North Downs Way A3
Canons Gate Road C1	North Military Road A3
Castle Hill Road C1	Park Avenue B1
Castlemount Road B1	Park Street B1
Castle Street B2	Pencester Road B2
Centre Road A3	Peter Street A1
Channel View Road A4	Priory Gate Road.......................A2
Church Street B2	Priory Hill A1
Citadel Road A4	Priory Road A1
Clarendon Place A3	Priory Street B2
Clarendon Road A2	Promenade D2
Cowgate Hill B2	Queen's Gardens......................B2
Crafford Street A1	Queen Street.............................B2
De Burgh Hill A1	Russell Street B2
Douro Place C2	Samphire Court C1
Dour Street A1	Saxon Street A2
Durham Close B2	Snargate Street A4
Durham Hill B2	South Military Road A4
East Cliff D2	Stembrook B2
Eastern Docks	Taswell Close C1
Roundabout D2	Taswell Street B1
Effingham Street A2	Templar Street A1
Elizabeth Street A4	The Viaduct A4
Esplanade B3	Tower Hamlets Road A1
Folkestone Road A2	Townwall Street C2
Godwyne Close B1	Union Street B3
Godwyne Road B1	Victoria Park C1
Harold Street B1	Waterloo Crescent B3
Harold Street B1	Wellesley Road C2
Heritage Gardens......................C1	Wood Street..............................A1
Hewitt Road A1	Woolcomber Street.....................C2
High Street A1	York Street................................B2
King Street...............................B2	
Knights Templar A3	
Ladywell...................................A1	
Lancaster Road B2	
Laureston Place C1	
Leyburne Road B1	
Limekiln Roundabout.................A4	
Limekiln Street A4	
Maison Dieu Road.....................B1	
Malvern Road............................A2	

Dundee

Dundee is found on atlas page **142 G11**

Dundee

0 _____ 200 m

Albert Square..........................B2	Laurel Bank B1
Bank Street.............................B2	Lochee Road A1
Barrack Road...........................A1	McDonald Street D2
Barrack Road...........................B2	Meadowside..............................B2
Bell Street...............................B2	Miln Street A2
Blackscroft D1	Murraygate...............................C2
Blinshall Street.........................A1	Nethergate...............................A4
Blinshall Street.........................A2	North Lindsay Street..................B2
Bonnybank Road.......................C1	North Marketgait.......................B1
Brown Street A2	North Victoria Road C1
Candle Lane C2	Old Hawkhill.............................A3
Castle Street C2	Panmure Street.........................B2
Chapel Street C2	Perth Road A4
City Square C3	Princes Street D1
Commercial Street.....................C2	Prospect Place B1
Constable Street D1	Queen Street.............................C1
Constitution Crescent A1	Reform Street B2
Constitution Road A1	Riverside Drive...........................B4
Constitution Road B2	Riverside Esplanade C3
Court House Square A2	Roseangle A4
Cowgate...................................C1	St Andrews Street......................C1
Cowgate...................................D1	Scrimgeour Place.......................A1
Crichton Street C3	Seabraes Lane..........................A4
Dock Street C3	Seagate C2
Douglas Street A2	Session Street...........................A2
Dudhope Street B1	South Castle Street.....................C3
East Dock Street D2	South Commercial Street.............D3
East Marketgait.........................C1	South Crichton Street..................C3
East Whale Lane D1	South Marketgait.......................B3
Euclid Crescent B2	South Tay Street........................B3
Euclid Street B2	South Union Street.....................C3
Exchange Street C3	South Victoria Dock Road D3
Forebank Road..........................C1	South Ward Road.......................B2
Foundry Lane D1	Sugarhouse Wynd.....................C1
Gellatly Street C2	Tay Road Bridge D3
Greenmarket............................B4	Tay Square B3
Guthrie Street A2	Thomson Avenue.......................C3
Hawkhill..................................A3	Trades Lane C2
High Street C3	Union Street B3
Hilltown B1	Union Terrace A1
Hilltown Terrace B1	Ward Road B2
Hunter Street............................A3	Weavers Yard D1
Infirmary Brae A1	West Marketgait.........................A2
Johnston Street B2	West Port A3
King Street...............................C1	West Victoria Dock Road D2
Kirk Lane C1	Whitehall Crescent C3
Laburn Street A1	Whitehall Street.........................C3
Ladywell Avenue.......................C1	Yeaman Shore...........................B3

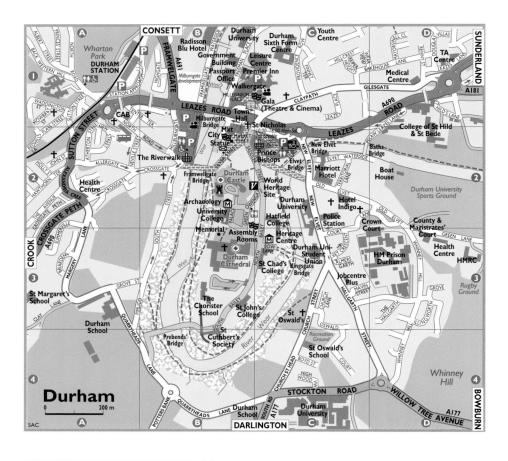

Durham

Durham is found on atlas page **103 Q2**

Albert Street A1
Alexandria Crescent..............A2
Allergate A2
Atherton Street.....................A2
Back Western Hill..................A1
Bakehouse Lane C1
Baths Bridge.........................C2
Bow Lane C3
Boyd Street C4
Briardene A3
Church Lane C3
Church Street C4
Church Street Head C4
Clay Lane A3
Claypath...............................C1
Court Lane C3
Crossgate A2
Crossgate Peth A3
Douglas Villas D1
Elvet Bridge.........................C2
Elvet Crescent C3
Elvet Waterside.....................C2
Finney Terrace C1
Flass Street A2
Framwelgate B1
Framwelgate Waterside B1
Framwellgate Bridge B2
Freeman Place B1
Gilesgate..............................C1
Green Lane D3
Grove Street A3
Hallgarth Street....................C3
Hawthorn Terrace..................A2
Highgate B1
High Street C2
High Wood View....................C4
Hillcrest...............................C1
Holly Street A2
Illingworth Grove..................D3
John Street A2
Keiper Heights C1
Kingsgate Bridge C3
Leazes Lane D1
Leazes Place C1
Leazes Road B1
Margery Lane A3
Market Place B2
Mavin Street C3

Mayorswell Close D1
Milburngate Bridge B1
Millburngate..........................B2
Millennium Place B1
Mowbray Street A1
Neville Street A2
New Elvet..............................C2
New Elvet Bridge...................C2
New Street A2
North Bailey C3
North Road A1
Old Elvet C2
Oswald Court C3
Owengate..............................B2
Palace Green B2
Palmers Garth C3
Pelaw Leazes Lane D2
Pimlico.................................A3
Potters Bank.........................B4
Prebends' Bridge...................B4
Princes' Street A1
Providence Row C1
Quarryheads Lane A3
Redhills Lane A2
Renny Street D1
Saddler Street B2
St Hild's Lane D1
Silver Street B2
South Bailey B3
South Road C4
South Street B3
Station Approach...................A1
Stockton Road C4
Summerville..........................A3
Sutton Street A2
Tenter Terrace A1
Territorial Lane......................C2
The Avenue...........................A2
The Hallgarth D3
Waddington Street A1
Wear View C1
Whinney Hill D3
Willow Tree Avenue D4

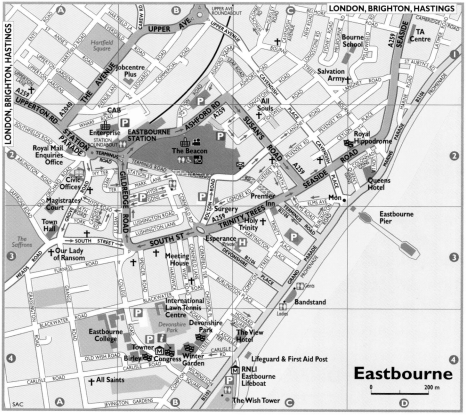

Eastbourne

Eastbourne is found on atlas page **25 P11**

Arlington Road.......................A2
Ashford Road B2
Ashford Road C1
Ashford Square B1
Avenue Lane A1
Belmore Road C1
Blackwater Road A4
Bolton Road B3
Bourne Street C1
Burlington Place.....................B3
Burlington Road C3
Camden Road A3
Carew Road B1
Carlisle Road A4
Carlisle Road B4
Cavendish Avenue C1
Cavendish Place C1
Ceylon Place C2
Chiswick Place B3
College Road.........................B3
Colonnade Gardens................D2
Commercial Road B1
Compton Street B4
Compton Street C3
Cornfield Lane B3
Cornfield Road B2
Cornfield Terrace B3
Devonshire Place B3
Dursley Road C1
Elms Road C3
Enys Road A1
Eversfield Road A1
Furness Road A3
Gildredge Road B2
Grand Parade C3
Grange Road A3
Grassington Road A3
Grove Road A2
Hardwick Road B3
Hartfield Lane A1
Hartfield Road A1
Hartington Place....................C3
Howard Square C4
Hyde Gardens B2
Hyde Road A2
Ivy Terrace A2
Jevington Gardens..................A4
Junction Road B2

Langney Road D1
Langney Road C2
Lascelles Terrace B4
Latimer Road D1
Leaf Road B1
Lismore Road B2
Longstone Road C1
Lushington Road B3
Marine Parade D2
Marine Road D1
Mark Lane B2
Meads Road A3
Melbourne Road C1
Old Orchard Road A2
Old Wish Road.......................A4
Pevensey Road C2
Promenade C3
Queen's Gardens D2
Saffrons Road A2
St Anne's Road A1
St Aubyn's Road D1
St Leonard's Road..................B1
Seaside D1
Seaside Road C2
Southfields Road...................A2
South Street A2
South Street B3
Spencer Road........................B3
Station Parade A2
Station Street B2
Susan's Road C2
Sutton Road B2
Sydney Road C1
Terminus Road A2
Terminus Road C3
The Avenue...........................A1
Tideswell Road.......................C2
Trinity Place C3
Trinity Trees..........................B3
Upper Avenue........................B1
Upperton Gardens..................A1
Upperton Road.......................A1
West Street A3
West Terrace A2
Willowfield Road....................D1
Wilmington Square.................B4
Wish Road B3
York Road A3

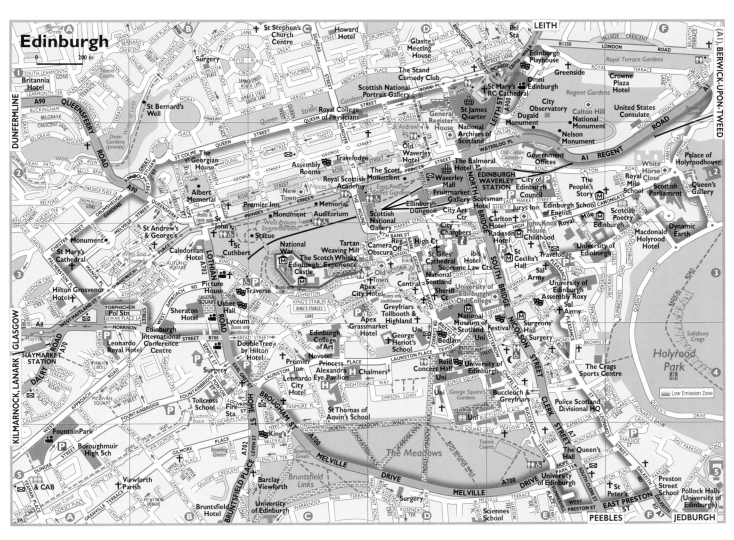

Edinburgh

Edinburgh is found on atlas page **127 P3**

Abbeyhill	F2	Chapel Street	E4	Gardener's Crescent	B4
Abercromby Place	C1	Charlotte Square	B2	George IV Bridge	D3
Adam Street	E3	Chester Street Gardens	A3	George Square	D4
Albany Street	D1	Circus Lane	B1	George Square Lane	D5
Ann Street	A1	Circus Place	B1	George Street	B2
Argyle Place	D5	Clarendon Crescent	A1	George Street	C2
Atholl Crescent Lane	A3	Clerk Street	E4	Gifford Park	E5
Bank Street	D3	Cockburn Street	D2	Gillespie Crescent	B5
Barclay Terrace	C5	Coronation Walk	C5	Gilmore Park	A5
Belford Road	A2	Cowan's Close	E4	Gilmore Place	B5
Belgrave Crescent	A2	Cowgate	D3	Gilmour Street	E4
Bernard Terrace	E5	Dalkeith Road	F5	Glenfinlas Street	B2
Boys Brigade Walk	D5	Dalry Road	A4	Gloucester Lane	B1
Brandfield Street	A4	Danube Street	B1	Granville Terrace	A5
Bread Street	B4	Davie Street	E4	Great King Street	C1
Bristo Place	D4	Dean Park Crescent	A1	Great Stuart Street	B2
Brougham Street	C4	Dean Street	A1	Greenmarket	C3
Broughton Street	D1	Dewar Place Lane	A3	Greenside Row	E1
Broughton Street Lane	E1	Douglas Gardens	A3	Grindlay Street	B3
Brunton Terrace	F1	Doune Terrace	B1	Grosvenor Street	A3
Bruntsfield Place	B5	Drummond Street	E3	Grove Street	A4
Buccleuch Place	D4	Dublin Street	D1	Haddon's Court	E4
Buccleuch Street	E4	Dumbiedykes Road	F3	Hanover Street	C2
Caledonian Place	A4	Dunbar Street	B4	Haymarket Terrace	A4
Caledonian Road	A4	Dundas Street	C1	Heriot Row	C1
Caledonian Street	A5	Dundee Street	A5	Hermits Croft	F5
Calton Road	E2	Earl Grey Street	B4	High Street	D3
Candlemaker Row	D3	Easter Road	F1	High Street	E3
Canning Street	B3	East Market Street	E2	Hillside Crescent	E1
Canongate	E2	East Parkside	F5	Hill Street	C2
Carlton Terrace	F1	East Preston Street	F5	Holyrood Park Road	F5
Castle Hill	C3	Elder Street	D1	Holyrood Road	E3
Castle Street	C2	Forrest Road	D4	Home Street	C4
Castle Terrace	B3	Forth Street	D1	Hope Street	B2
Chalmers Street	D4	Fountainbridge	A4	Horse Wynd	F2
Chambers Street	D3	Frederick Street	C2	Howden Street	E4
				Howe Street	C1
				India Place	B1
				India Street	B1
				Jamaica Street South Lane	B1
				Jawbone Walk	D5

Jeffrey Street	E2	New Street	E2	St Patrick Street	E4
Johnston Terrace	C3	Nicolson Square	E4	St Stephen Street	B1
Keir Street	C4	Nicolson Street	E4	St Vincent Street	C1
Kerr Street	B1	Nightingale Way	C4	Saunders Street	B1
King's Stables Road	B3	North Bridge	D2	Sciennes	E5
Lady Lawson Street	C3	North Castle Street	C2	Semple Street	B4
Lansdowne Crescent	A3	North Meadow Walk	C5	Shandwick Place	A3
Lauriston Gardens	C4	North St Andrew Street	D1	Simpson Loan	D4
Lauriston Place	C4	North St David Street	D1	South Bridge	E3
Lauriston Street	C4	Northumberland Street	C1	South Charlotte Street	B2
Lawnmarket	D3	Oxford Street	F5	South Clerk Street	E5
Leamington Terrace	B5	Palmerston Place	A3	South Learmonth Gardens	A1
Leith Street	E1	Panmure Place	C4	South St Andrew Street	D2
Leith Walk	E1	Pleasance	E3	South St David Street	D2
Lennox Street	A1	Ponton Street	B4	Spittal Street	C4
Leven Place	C5	Potterrow	E4	Stafford Street	B3
Lochrin Place	B4	Princes Street	C2	Tarvit Street	C5
Lochrin Street	B4	Queens Drive	F3	The Mound	C2
London Road	E1	Queensferry Road	A1	Thistle Street	C2
Lothian Road	B3	Queensferry Street	B2	Torphichen Street	A3
Lower Gilmore Place	B5	Queen Street	B2	Union Street	E1
Lutton Place	E5	Radical Road	F3	Upper Gilmore Place	B5
Lynedoch Place Lane	A2	Ramsay Lane	C3	Victoria Street	D3
Manor Place	A3	Randolph Crescent	B2	Viewcraig Gardens	E4
Marchmont Crescent	D5	Randolph Lane	B2	Viewcraig Street	F3
Marchmont Road	D5	Rankeillor Street	E5	Viewforth	A5
Market Street	D2	Regent Road	E2	Walker Street	A3
Meadow Lane	E5	Richmond Place	E3	Warrender Park Terrace	C5
Melville Drive	C5	Rose Street	B2	Waterloo Place	D2
Melville Street	A3	Roseneath Place	D5	Waverley Bridge	D2
Melville Terrace	D5	Rothesay Place	A3	West Approach Road	A5
Middle Meadow Walk	D5	Royal Circus	B1	West Maitland Street	A3
Millerfield Place	D5	Royal Terrace	E1	West Nicolson Street	E4
Miller Row	A2	St Andrew Square	D1	West Port	C4
Moncrieff Terrace	E5	St Bernard's Crescent	A1	West Richmond Street	E4
Montague Street	E5	St Colme Street	B2	West Toll Cross	B4
Moray Place	B1	St James Place	D1	William Street	A3
Morrison Link	A4	St Leonard's Bank	F4	Yeaman Place	A5
Morrison Street	A4	St Leonard's Hill	E4	York Lane	D1
Mound Place	D3	St Leonard's Lane	F4	York Place	D1
Nelson Street	C1	St Leonard's Street	E4	Young Street	B2

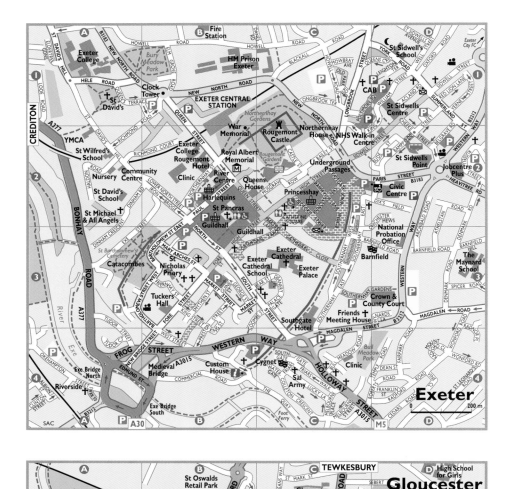

Exeter

Exeter is found on atlas page **9 M6**

Acland Road	D1	King Street	B3
Archibald Road	D3	King William Street	D1
Athelstan Road	D3	Longbrook Street	C1
Bailey Street	C2	Lower North Street	B2
Bampfylde Lane	C2	Magdalen Road	D3
Bampfylde Street	D2	Magdalen Street	C4
Barnfield Road	D3	Market Street	B3
Bartholomew Street East	B3	Martins Lane	C2
Bartholomew Street West	B3	Mary Arches Street	B3
Bear Street	C3	Musgrave Row	C2
Bedford Street	C2	New Bridge Street	A4
Belgrave Road	D2	New North Road	A1
Blackall Road	C1	Northernhay Street	B2
Bonhay Road	A2	North Street	B3
Bude Street	D2	Old Park Road	C1
Bull Meadow Road	C4	Oxford Road	D1
Castle Street	C2	Palace Gate	C3
Cathedral Close	C3	Paris Street	D2
Cathedral Yard	B3	Paul Street	B2
Cedars Road	D4	Preston Street	B4
Cheeke Street	D1	Princesshay	C2
Chichester Mews	C3	Queens Crescent	C1
Commercial Road	B4	Queen's Terrace	A1
Coombe Street	B3	Queen Street	B1
Deanery Place	C3	Radford Road	D4
Dean Street	D4	Richmond Court	B2
Denmark Road	D3	Richmond Road	A2
Dinham Crescent	A3	Roberts Road	C4
Dinham Road	A2	Roman Walk	C2
Dix's Field	D2	St David's Hill	A1
Eastgate	C2	Sidwell Street	C2
Edmund Street	A4	Sidwell Street	D1
Elm Grove Road	B1	Smythen Street	B3
Exe Street	A3	Southernhay East	C3
Fairpark Road	D4	Southernhay Gardens	C3
Fore Street	B3	Southernhay West	C3
Franklin Street	D4	South Street	B3
Friernhay Street	B3	Spicer Road	D3
Frog Street	A4	Summerland Street	D1
George Street	B3	Temple Road	D4
Guinea Street	B3	Tudor Court	A4
Haldon Road	A2	Tudor Street	A3
Heavitree Road	D2	Verney Street	D1
Hele Road	A1	Well Street	D1
High Street	C2	Western Way	B4
Holloway Street	C4	West Street	B4
Howell Road	B1	Wonford Road	D4
Iron Bridge	B2	York Road	D1

Gloucester

Gloucester is found on atlas page **46 F11**

Albert Street	D4	Millbrook Street	D4
Albion Street	B4	Montpellier	B4
All Saints' Road	D4	Napier Street	D4
Alvin Street	C2	Nettleton Road	C3
Archdeacon Street	B2	New Inn Lane	C3
Arthur Street	C4	Norfolk Street	B4
Barbican Road	B3	Northgate Street	C3
Barrack Square	B3	Old Tram Road	B4
Barton Street	D4	Over Causeway	A1
Bedford Street	C3	Oxford Road	D1
Belgrave Road	C4	Oxford Street	D2
Berkeley Street	B3	Park Road	C4
Black Dog Way	C2	Park Street	C2
Blenheim Road	D4	Parliament Street	B3
Brunswick Road	B4	Pembroke Street	C4
Brunswick Square	B4	Pitt Street	B2
Bruton Way	D3	Priory Road	B1
Bull Lane	B3	Quay Street	B2
Castle Meads Way	A2	Royal Oak Road	A2
Clarence Street	C3	Russell Street	C3
Clare Street	B2	St Aldate Street	C2
College Court	B2	St Catherine Street	C1
Commercial Road	C4	St John's Lane	B3
Cromwell Street	C4	St Mark Street	C1
Cross Keys Lane	B3	St Mary's Square	B2
Deans Walk	C1	St Mary's Street	B2
Eastgate Street	C3	St Michael's Square	C4
Gouda Way	B1	St Oswald's Road	B1
Great Western Road	D2	Sebert Street	C1
Greyfriars	B3	Severn Road	A3
Hampden Way	C3	Sherborne Street	D2
Hare Lane	C2	Sinope Street	D4
Heathville Road	D2	Southgate Street	B4
Henry Road	D1	Spa Road	B4
Henry Street	D2	Station Road	C3
High Orchard Street	A4	Swan Road	C1
Honyatt Road	D1	Sweetbriar Street	C1
Kings Barton Street	C4	The Cross	B3
Kingsholm Road	C1	The Oxebode	C3
King's Square	C3	The Quay	A2
Ladybellegate Street	B3	Union Street	C1
Llanthony Road	A4	Upper Quay Street	B2
London Road	D2	Vauxhall Road	D4
Longsmith Street	B3	Wellington Street	C4
Market Parade	C3	Westgate Street	A2
Merchants' Road	A4	Widden Street	D4
Mercia Road	B1	Worcester Parade	C2
Metz Way	D3	Worcester Street	C2

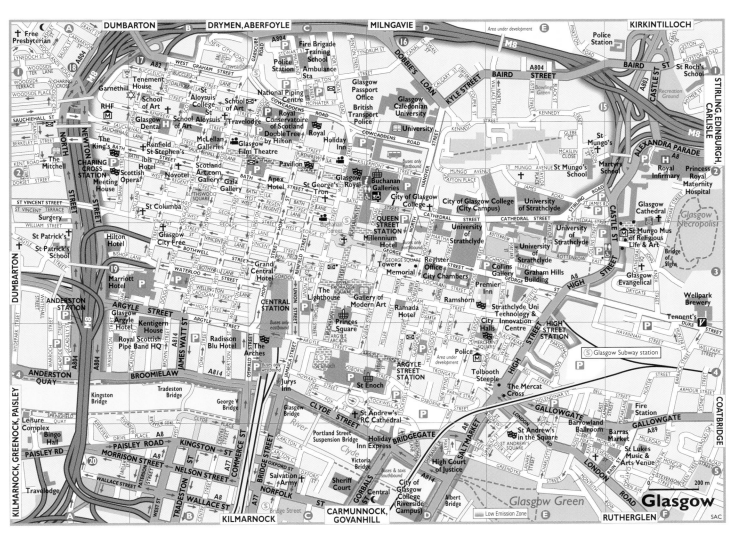

Glasgow

Glasgow is found on atlas page **125 P4**

Albert Bridge	D5
Albion Street	D4
Albion Street	E3
Alexandra Parade	F2
Anderston Quay	A4
Argyle Arcade	C4
Argyle Street	A3
Armour Street	F4
Ashley Street	A1
Bain Street	F5
Baird Street	E1
Baliol Street	A1
Barrack Street	F4
Bath Lane	B2
Bath Street	A2
Bell Street	E4
Berkeley Street	A2
Blackfriars Street	D4
Black Street	E1
Blythswood Square	B2
Blythswood Street	B3
Bothwell Lane	B3
Bothwell Street	B3
Bridgegate	D5
Bridge of Sighs	F3
Bridge Street	C5
Broomielaw	B4
Brown Street	B4
Brunswick Street	D4
Buccleuch Lane	B1
Buccleuch Street	B1
Buchanan Street	C4
Cadogan Street	B3
Calgary Street	D1
Cambridge Street	C1
Canal Street	D1
Candleriggs	D4
Carlton Place	C5
Carnarvon Street	A1
Castle Street	F1
Castle Street	F2
Cathedral Square	F3
Cathedral Street	D2
Centre Street	B5
Chalmer Street	F5
Charing Cross	A1
Charles Street	F1
Charlotte Street	E5
Cheapside Street	A4
Claythorn Avenue	F5
Claythorn Park	F5
Clyde Place	B4
Clyde Street	C4
Cochrane Street	D3
Collins Street	E3
Commerce Street	B5
Couper Street	D1
Cowcaddens Road	C1
Dalhousie Lane	B1
Dixon Street	C4
Dobbie's Loan	D1
Dorset Street	A2
Douglas Street	B3
Drury Street	C3
Drygate	F3
Duke Street	F4
Dundas Street	D3
Dunlop Street	D4
Dyer's Lane	E5
East Campbell Street	E4
Elmbank Street	A2
Fox Street	C4
Gallowgate	E4
Garnethill Street	B1
Garnet Street	B2
Garscube Road	C1
Garth Street	D3
George Square	D3
George Street	E3
George V Bridge	B4
Glasgow Bridge	C5
Glassford Street	D4
Glebe Court	E2
Gorbals Street	C5
Gordon Street	C3
Grafton Place	D2
Granville Street	A2
Greendyke Street	E5
Green Street	F5
Hanover Street	D3
High Street	E4
Hill Street	B1
Holland Street	B2
Holm Street	B3
Hope Street	C3
Howard Street	C4
Hunter Street	F4
Hutcheson Street	D4
Hydepark Street	A4
Ingram Street	D3
Jamaica Street	C4
James Watt Street	B4
John Knox Street	F3
John Street	D3
Kennedy Street	D2
Kennedy Street	E1
Kent Road	A2
Kent Street	E5
Killermont Street	C2
Kingston Bridge	A5
Kingston Street	B5
King Street	D4
Kyle Street	D1
Lanark Street	E5
Larbert Street	C1
Lister Street	E1
London Road	E4
Maitland Street	C1
Martha Street	D3
Mart Street	D5
Maxwell Street	C4
McAlpine Street	B4
McAslin Close	E2
McFarlane Street	F4
McPhater Street	C1
Merchant Lane	D5
Miller Street	D4
Millroad Drive	F5
Millroad Street	F5
Milton Street	C1
Mitchell Street	C4
Moir Street	E5
Molendinar Street	E4
Moncur Street	E5
Monteith Row	E5
Montrose Street	D3
Morrison Street	A5
Nelson Street	B5
New City Road	B1
Newton Street	A2
New Wynd	D4
Norfolk Street	C5
North Frederick Street	D3
North Hanover Street	D3
North Portland Street	E3
North Street	A2
North Wallace Street	E1
Osborne Street	C4
Oswald Street	C4
Oxford Street	C5
Paisley Road	A5
Parnie Street	D4
Parsonage Square	E4
Parson Street	E2
Paterson Street	B5
Pinkston Road	E1
Pitt Street	B2
Port Dundas Road	C1
Portland Street Suspension Bridge	C5
Queen Street	C4
Renfield Lane	C3
Renfield Street	C3
Renfrew Lane	C2
Renfrew Street	B1
Renton Street	C1
Rhymer Street	F1
Richmond Street	E3
Riverview Drive	A4
Robertson Street	B4
Rose Street	B2
Ross Street	E5
Rottenrow	E3
Rottenrow East	E3
Royal Exchange Square	C3
Royston Road	F1
Royston Square	F1
St Andrew's Square	E5
St Andrew's Street	E4
St James Road	E2
St Mungo Avenue	D2
St Vincent Lane	B3
St Vincent Place	C3
St Vincent Street	A2
St Vincent Terrace	A2
Saltmarket	D5
Sauchiehall Lane	A2
Sauchiehall Street	B2
Scott Street	B1
Shipbank Lane	D5
Shuttle Street	E3
South Frederick Street	D3
Springfield Quay	A4
Stafford Street	D1
Steel Street	D5
Stevenson Street	F5
Stewart Street	C1
Stirling Road	E2
Stockwell Place	D4
Stockwell Street	D4
Suffolk Street	E5
Sydney Street	F4
Taylor Place	E2
Taylor Street	E2
Tradeston Bridge	B4
Tradeston Street	B5
Trongate	D4
Turnbull Street	D5
Tyndrum Street	C1
Union Street	C3
Virginia Street	D4
Wallace Street	A5
Walls Street	E4
Warroch Street	A4
Washington Street	A4
Waterloo Street	B3
Wellington Lane	B3
Wellington Street	B3
Wellpark Street	F4
West Campbell Street	B3
West George Lane	B2
West George Street	B2
West Graham Street	B1
West Nile Street	C3
West Regent Lane	C2
West Regent Street	B2
West Street	B5
William Street	A3
Wilson Street	D4
Wishart Street	F3
Woodlands Road	A1
Woodside Crescent	A1
Woodside Terrace	A1
Woodside Terrace Lane	A1
York Street	B4

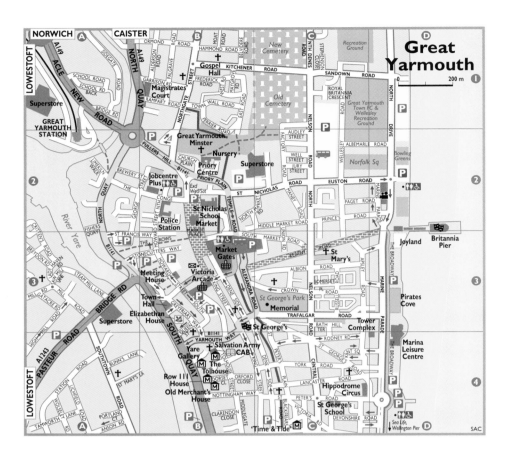

Great Yarmouth

Great Yarmouth is found on atlas page **77 Q10**

Acle New Road	A1	North Drive	D1
Albemarle Road	C2	North Market Road	C2
Albion Road	C3	North Quay	A2
Alderson Road	B1	Northgate Street	B1
Alexandra Road	B3	Nottingham Way	B4
Apsley Road	C3	Ormond Road	B1
Belvidere Road	B1	Paget Road	C2
Blackfriars Road	C4	Palgrave Road	B1
Brewery Street	A2	Pasteur Road	A4
Breydon Road	A3	Prince's Road	C2
Bridge Road	A1	Priory Plain	B2
Bridge Road	A3	Queen Street	B4
Bunn's Lane	A4	Rampart Road	B1
Church Plain	B2	Regent Road	C3
Critten's Road	A3	Rodney Road	C4
Crown Road	C3	Russell Road	C4
Dene Side	B3	St Francis Way	A3
Devonshire Road	C4	St George's Road	C4
East Road	B1	St Nicholas Road	B2
Euston Road	C2	St Peter's Plain	C4
Factory Road	C2	St Peter's Road	C4
Ferrier Road	B1	Sandown Road	C1
Fishers Quay	A2	Saw Mill Lane	A3
Frederick Road	B1	School Road	A1
Fullers Hill	B2	School Road Back	A1
Garrison Road	B1	Sidegate Road	A1
Gatacre Road	A3	South Market Road	C3
George Street	A2	South Quay	B3
Greyfriars Way	B3	Southtown Road	A4
Hammond Road	B1	Station Road	A4
High Mill Road	A3	Steam Mill Lane	A3
Howard Street North	B2	Stephenson Close	C1
Howard Street South	B3	Stonecutters Way	B3
King Street	B3	Tamworth Lane	A4
Kitchener Road	B1	Temple Road	B2
Lady Haven Road	A3	The Broadway	D3
Lancaster Road	C4	The Conge	A2
Lichfield Road	A4	The Rows	B3
Limekiln Walk	A2	Tolhouse Street	B4
Manby Road	C2	Town Wall Road	B1
Marine Parade	D3	Trafalgar Road	C3
Maygrove Road	B1	Union Road	C3
Middle Market Road	C2	Victoria Road	C4
Middlegate	B4	Wellesley Road	C2
Moat Road	B1	West Road	B1
Nelson Road Central	C3	Wolseley Road	A4
Nelson Road North	C1	Yarmouth Way	B4
North Denes Road	C1	York Road	C4

Guildford

Guildford is found on atlas page **23 Q5**

Abbot Road	C4	Millmead	B3
Angel Gate	B3	Millmead Terrace	B4
Artillery Road	B1	Mount Pleasant	A4
Artillery Terrace	C1	Nightingale Road	D1
Bedford Road	A2	North Street	B3
Bridge Street	A3	Onslow Road	C1
Bright Hill	C3	Onslow Street	B2
Brodie Road	D3	Oxford Road	C3
Bury Fields	B4	Pannells Court	C2
Bury Street	B4	Park Street	B3
Castle Hill	C4	Pewley Bank	D3
Castle Street	C3	Pewley Fort Inner Court	D4
Chapel Street	B3	Pewley Hill	C3
Chertsey Street	C2	Pewley Way	D3
Cheselden Road	D2	Phoenix Court	B3
Church Road	B1	Porridge Pot Alley	B4
College Road	B2	Portsmouth Road	A4
Commercial Road	B2	Poyle Road	D4
Dene Road	D2	Quarry Street	B3
Drummond Road	B1	Sandfield Terrace	C2
Eagle Road	C1	Semaphore Road	D3
Eastgate Gardens	D2	South Hill	C3
Epsom Road	D2	Springfield Road	C1
Falcon Road	C1	Station Approach	D1
Farnham Road	A3	Station View	A2
Fort Road	C4	Stoke Fields	C1
Foxenden Road	D1	Stoke Grove	C1
Friary Bridge	A3	Stoke Road	B1
Friary Street	B3	Swan Lane	B3
George Road	B1	Sydenham Road	C3
Guildford Park Road	A2	Testard Road	A3
Harvey Road	D3	The Bars	C2
Haydon Place	C2	The Mount	A4
High Pewley	D4	The Shambles	B3
High Street	C3	Tunsgate	C3
Jeffries Passage	C2	Upperton Road	A3
Jenner Road	D2	Victoria Road	D1
Laundry Road	B2	Walnut Tree Close	A1
Leapale Lane	B2	Ward Street	C2
Leapale Road	B2	Warwicks Bench	A3
Leas Road	B1	Wherwell Road	A3
London Road	D2	William Road	B1
Mareschal Road	A4	Wodeland Avenue	A3
Market Street	C3	Woodbridge Road	B1
Martyr Road	C2	York Road	C2
Mary Road	A1		
Millbrook	B3		
Mill Lane	B3		

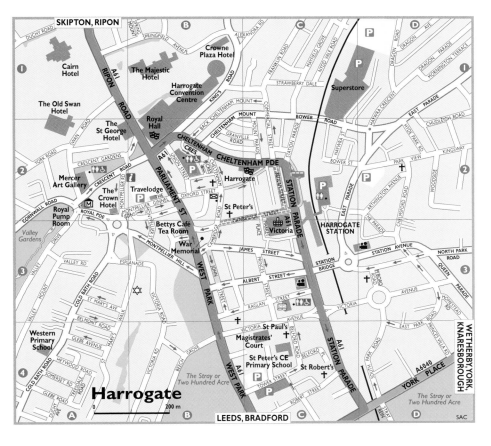

Harrogate

Harrogate is found on atlas page **97 M9**

Albert Street...................C3	Montpellier Hill....................B3
Alexandra Road................B1	Montpellier Road A2
Arthington Avenue D2	Montpellier Street...............B2
Back Cheltenham Mount.........B2	Mornington Terrace..............D1
Beech Grove.....................B4	Mount Parade C2
Belford Place....................C4	North Park Road D3
Belford Road C4	Nydd Vale Road C1
Belmont Road A3	Oxford Street B2
Beulah Street C2	Park View D2
Bower Road......................C1	Parliament Street................B2
Bower Street C2	Princes Street C3
Cambridge Road B3	Princes Villa Road D4
Cambridge Street C2	Queen Parade D3
Chelmsford Road D3	Raglan Street C3
Cheltenham Crescent B2	Ripon Road A1
Cheltenham Mount B2	Robert Street C4
Cheltenham Parade B2	Royal Parade A2
Chudleigh Road D2	St Mary's Avenue...............A3
Cold Bath Road A3	St Mary's Walk..................A4
Commercial Street.............C1	Somerset Road A4
Cornwall Road A2	South Park Road D4
Crescent Gardens A2	Springfield Avenue B1
Crescent Road A2	Spring Mount B1
Dragon Avenue D1	Station Avenue D3
Dragon Parade D1	Station Bridge C3
Dragon Road D1	Station Parade C2
Duchy Avenue A4	Strawberry Dale C1
Duchy Road A1	Stray Rein D4
East Parade C2	Swan Road A2
East Park Road D4	The Ginnel B2
Esplanade A3	The Parade D2
Franklin Road C1	Tower Street C4
Glebe Avenue A4	Treesdale Road A4
Glebe Road A4	Union Street B2
Granville Road B2	Valley Drive A3
Haywra Street C2	Valley Mount......................A3
Heywood Road A4	Valley Road A3
Homestead Road D3	Victoria Avenue B4
Hyde Park Road D2	Victoria Road B3
Haywra Crescent...............D2	West Park..........................B3
James Street B3	West Park Street B4
John Street B3	Woodside D2
King's Road B1	York Place D4
Kingsway D2	York Road A2
Market Place C3	
Marlborough Road D3	
Mayfield Grove C1	
Montpellier Gardens B2	

Huddersfield

Huddersfield is found on atlas page **90 E7**

Albion Street....................B4	New North Road A2
Alfred Street.....................C4	New Street.........................B4
Back Union Street..............C1	Northgate..........................C1
Bankfield Road A4	Northumberland Street.........C2
Bath Street.......................B1	Old Leeds Road D2
Belmont Street..................A1	Old South Street................B3
Brook Street......................C2	Outcote Bank B4
Byram Street.....................C2	Oxford Street C1
Cambridge Road B1	Page Street C4
Carforth Street..................D4	Park Avenue......................A2
Castlegate........................B1	Park Drive South A2
Chancery Lane B3	Peel Street.........................C4
Chapel Hill.......................B4	Portland Street A2
Chapel Street....................B4	Princess Street..................B4
Church Street C2	Prospect Street..................A4
Clare Hill..........................B1	Quay Street D2
Claremont Street...............B1	Queen Street......................C3
Cloth Hall Street...............B3	Queen Street South C4
Cross Church Street...........C3	Queensgate.......................C4
Dundas Street B3	Railway Street....................B2
Elizabeth Queen Gardens........A2	Ramsden Street B3
Elmwood Avenue...............A1	Rook Street........................B1
Firth Street.......................D4	St Andrew's Road D2
Fitzwilliam Street...............A2	St George's Square.............B2
Fitzwilliam Street...............B2	St John's Road B1
Gasworks Street.................D1	St Peter's Street.................C2
Great Northern Street..........C1	Southgate..........................C2
Greenhead Road A3	Spring Grove Street A4
Half Moon Street B3	Spring Street A3
High Street B3	Springwood Avenue A3
Highfields Road A1	Stadium Way D1
John William Street............B2	Station Street B2
King Street.........................C3	Trinity Street......................A2
King's Mill Lane.................D4	Turnbridge Road D2
Kirkgate............................C3	Union Street C1
Leeds Road.......................C2	Upper George Street............A3
Lincoln Street D3	Upperhead Row B3
Lord Street........................C2	Viaduct Street....................B3
Lower Fitzwilliam Street.......C1	Victoria Lane......................C3
Lynton Avenue A4	Wakefield Road D4
Manchester Road...............A4	Water Street A3
Market Place A1	Watergate..........................D2
Market Street B3	Waverley Road A2
Merton Street A3	Wentworth Street A2
Milford Street....................B4	Westgate............................B3
Mountjoy Road..................A1	William Street.....................C1
New North Parade..............B2	Wood Street.......................C2
New North Road A1	Zetland Street....................C3

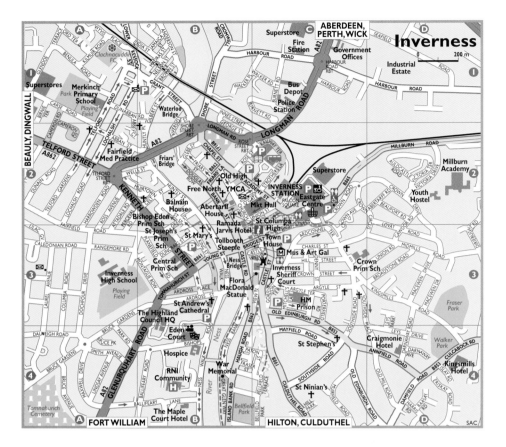

Inverness

Inverness is found on atlas page **156 B8**

Abertaff Road	D2	Glenurquhart Road	A4
Academy Street	B2	Gordon Terrace	C3
Anderson Street	B1	Grant Street	B1
Annfield Road	D4	Great Glen Way	B4
Ardconnel Terrace	C3	Harbour Road	C1
Ardross Street	B3	Harris Road	D4
Argyle Street	C3	Harrowden Road	A2
Argyle Terrace	C3	Haugh Road	B4
Ballifeary Lane	A4	High Street	C3
Ballifeary Road	B4	Hill Park	C4
Bank Street	B2	Hill Street	C3
Bellfield Terrace	C4	Huntly Street	B2
Benula Road	A1	Innes Street	B1
Birnie Terrace	A1	Kenneth Street	A2
Bishops Road	B4	King Street	B3
Bridge Street	B3	Kingsmills Road	D3
Broadstone Road	D3	Laurel Avenue	A3
Bruce Gardens	A4	Lindsay Avenue	A4
Bruce Park	A4	Lochalsh Road	A2
Burnett Road	C1	Longman Road	D2
Caledonian Road	A3	Lovat Road	D3
Cameron Road	A2	Lower Kessock Street	A1
Cameron Square	A2	Maxwell Drive	A4
Carse Road	A1	Mayfield Road	C4
Castle Road	B3	Midmills Road	D3
Castle Street	C3	Millburn Road	D2
Chapel Street	B2	Mitchell's Lane	C3
Charles Street	C3	Muirfield Road	C4
Columba Road	A3	Ness Bank	B4
Crown Circus	C2	Old Edinburgh Road	C3
Crown Drive	D2	Park Road	A4
Crown Road	C2	Planefield Road	B3
Crown Street	C3	Porterfield Road	C3
Culcabock Road	D4	Raasay Road	D4
Culduthel Road	C4	Rangemore Road	A3
Dalneigh Road	A4	Ross Avenue	A2
Damfield Road	D4	Seafield Road	D1
Darnaway Road	D4	Shore Street	B1
Denny Street	C3	Smith Avenue	A4
Dochfour Drive	A3	Southside Place	C3
Dunabban Road	A1	Southside Road	C4
Dunain Road	A2	Telford Gardens	A2
Duncraig Street	B3	Telford Road	A2
Eriskay Road	D4	Telford Street	A2
Fairfield Road	A3	Tomnahurich Street	B3
Falcon Square	C2	Union Road	D3
Friars' Lane	B2	Walker Road	C1
Glendoe Terrace	A1	Young Street	A3

Ipswich

Ipswich is found on atlas page **53 L3**

Alderman Road	A3	Key Street	C3
Anglesea Road	B1	King Street	B2
Argyle Street	D2	London Road	A2
Austin Street	C4	Lower Brook Street	C3
Barrack Lane	A1	Lower Orwell Street	C3
Belstead Road	B4	Museum Street	B2
Berners Street	B1	Neale Street	C1
Black Horse Lane	B2	Neptune Quay	D3
Blanche Street	D2	New Cardinal Street	B3
Bolton Lane	C1	Newson Street	A1
Bond Street	D3	Northgate Street	C2
Bramford Road	A1	Norwich Road	A1
Bridge Street	C4	Old Foundry Road	C2
Burlington Road	A2	Orchard Street	D2
Burrell Road	B4	Orford Street	A1
Cardigan Street	A1	Orwell Place	C3
Carr Street	C2	Orwell Quay	D4
Cecil Road	B1	Portman Road	A3
Cemetery Road	D1	Princes Street	A3
Chancery Road	A4	Quadling Street	B3
Charles Street	B1	Queen Street	B3
Christchurch Street	D1	Ranelagh Road	A4
Civic Drive	B2	Russell Road	A3
Clarkson Street	A1	St George's Street	B1
Cobbold Street	C1	St Helen's Street	D2
College Street	C4	St Margaret's Street	C2
Commercial Road	A3	St Matthews Street	B2
Constantine Road	A3	St Nicholas Street	B3
Crown Street	B2	St Peter's Street	B3
Cumberland Street	A1	Silent Street	B3
Dalton Road	A2	Sir Alf Ramsey Way	A3
Dock Street	C4	Soane Street	C2
Duke Street	C4	South Street	A1
Eagle Street	C3	Star Lane	C3
Elm Street	B2	Stoke Quay	C4
Falcon Street	B3	Suffolk Road	D1
Fonnereau Road	B1	Tacket Street	C3
Foundation Street	C3	Tavern Street	B3
Franciscan Way	B3	Tower Ramparts	B2
Geneva Road	A1	Tuddenham Avenue	D1
Grafton Way	B3	Turret Lane	C3
Great Gipping Street	A2	Upper Orwell Street	C3
Great Whip Street	C4	Vernon Street	C4
Grey Friars Road	B3	West End Road	A3
Grimwade Street	D3	Westgate Street	B2
Handford Road	A2	Willoughby Road	B4
Hervey Street	D1	Wolsey Street	B3
High Street	B1	Woodbridge Road	D2

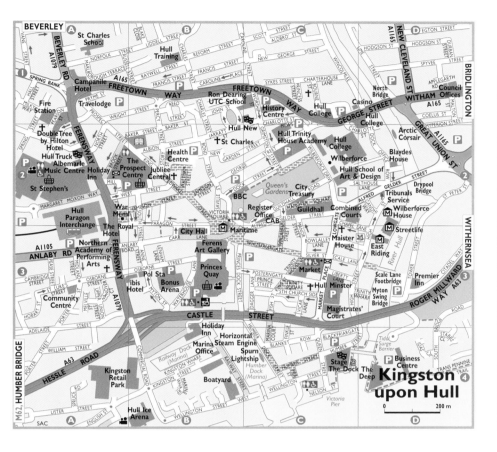

Kingston upon Hull

Kingston upon Hull is found on atlas page **93 J5**

Adelaide Street	A4	Market Place	C3
Albion Street	B2	Mill Street	A2
Alfred Gelder Street	C2	Myton Street	B3
Anlaby Road	A3	New Cleveland Street	D1
Baker Street	B2	New Garden Street	B2
Beverley Road	A1	New George Street	C1
Blackfriargate	C4	Norfolk Street	A1
Blanket Row	C4	Osborne Street	B3
Bond Street	B2	Osborne Street	A3
Brook Street	A2	Paragon Street	B2
Caroline Street	B1	Percy Street	B1
Carr Lane	B3	Porter Street	A3
Castle Street	B3	Portland Place	A2
Chapel Lane	C2	Portland Street	A2
Charles Street	B1	Posterngate	C3
Charterhouse Lane	C1	Princes Dock Street	B3
Citadel Way	D3	Prospect Street	A1
Commercial Road	B4	Queen Street	C4
Dagger Lane	C3	Railway Street	B4
Dock Office Row	D2	Raywell Street	B1
Dock Street	B2	Reform Street	B1
Durban Street	D1	Russell Street	A1
Egginton Street	B1	St Luke's Street	A3
Ferensway	A2	St Peter Street	D2
Freetown Way	A1	Saville Street	B2
Gandhi Way	D2	Scale Lane	C3
Garrison Road	D3	Scott Street	C1
George Street	B2	Silver Street	C3
George Street	D1	South Bridge Road	D4
Great Union Street	D1	South Church Side	C3
Grimston Street	C2	South Street	B2
Guildhall Road	C2	Spring Bank	A1
Hanover Square	C2	Spyvee Street	D1
Hessle Road	A4	Sykes Street	C1
High Street	C3	Tower Street	D3
Hodgson Street	D1	Upper Union Street	A3
Humber Dock Street	C4	Victoria Square	B2
Humber Street	C4	Waterhouse Lane	B3
Hyperion Street	D1	Wellington Street	C4
Jameson Street	B2	Wellington Street West	A3
Jarratt Street	B2	West Street	A2
King Edward Street	B2	Whitefriargate	C3
Kingston Street	B4	Wilberforce Drive	C2
Liddell Street	B1	William Street	A4
Lime Street	C1	Wincolmlee	D1
Lister Street	A4	Witham	D1
Lowgate	C3	Worship Street	C1
Margaret Moxon Way	A2	Wright Street	A1

Lancaster

Lancaster is found on atlas page **95 K8**

Aberdeen Road	D4	Lincoln Road	A3
Aldcliffe Road	B4	Lindow Street	B4
Alfred Street	C2	Lodge Street	C2
Ambleside Road	D1	Long Marsh Lane	A2
Balmoral Road	D4	Lune Street	B1
Bath Street	D3	Market Street	B3
Blades Street	A3	Meeting House Lane	A3
Bond Street	D3	Middle Street	B3
Borrowdale Road	D2	Moor Gate	D3
Brewery Lane	C3	Moor Lane	C3
Bridge Lane	B2	Morecambe Road	B1
Brock Street	C3	Nelson Street	C3
Bulk Road	D2	North Road	C2
Bulk Street	C3	Owen Road	C1
Cable Street	B2	Park Road	D3
Castle Hill	B3	Parliament Street	C2
Castle Park	A3	Patterdale Road	D2
Caton Road	C2	Penny Street	B4
Cheapside	C3	Portland Street	B4
China Street	B3	Primrose Street	D4
Church Street	B2	Prospect Street	D4
Common Garden Street	B3	Quarry Road	C4
Dale Street	D4	Queen Street	B4
Dallas Road	B3	Regent Street	B4
Dalton Road	D2	Ridge Lane	D1
Dalton Square	C3	Ridge Street	D1
Damside Street	B2	Robert Street	C3
Derby Road	C1	Rosemary Lane	C2
De Vitre Street	C2	St George's Quay	A1
Dumbarton Road	D4	St Leonard's Gate	C2
East Road	D3	St Peter's Road	C3
Edward Street	C3	Sibsey Street	A3
Fairfield Road	A3	South Road	C4
Fenton Street	B3	Station Road	A3
Gage Street	C3	Stirling Road	D4
Garnet Street	D2	Sulyard Street	C3
George Street	C3	Sun Street	B3
Grasmere Road	D3	Thurnham Street	C4
Great John Street	C3	Troutbeck Road	D2
Gregson Road	D4	Ulleswater Road	D3
Greyhound Bridge Road	B1	West Road	A3
High Street	B4	Westbourne Road	A3
Kelsey Street	A3	Wheatfield Street	A3
Kentmere Road	D2	Williamson Road	D3
King Street	B3	Wingate-Saul Road	A3
Kingsway	C1	Wolseley Street	D2
Kirkes Road	D4	Woodville Street	D3
Langdale Road	D1	Wyresdale Road	D3

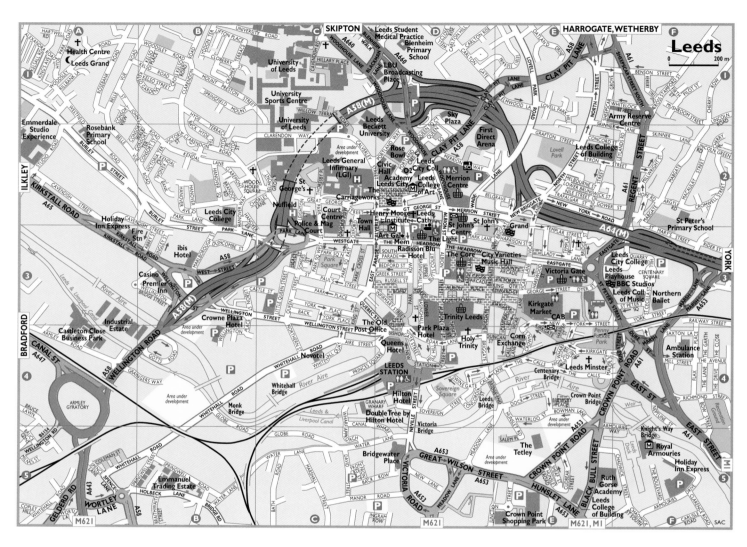

Leeds

Leeds is found on atlas page **90 H4**

Abbey Street	B3	Call Lane	E4	Duke Street	F4	King's Avenue	A1	Northern Street	C4	Springfield Mount	B1
Aire Street	C4	Calverley Street	C2	Duke Street	F4	King Street	C3	North Street	E2	Springwell Road	B5
Albion Place	D3	Canal Street	A4	Duncan Street	D4	Kirkgate	E3	Oxford Place	C3	Springwell Street	B5
Albion Street	D2	Canal Wharf	C4	Duncombe Street	B3	Kirkstall Road	A2	Oxford Row	C3	Studio Road	A2
Alexandra Road	A1	Carlton Hill	D1	Dyer Street	E3	Lady Lane	E3	Park Cross Street	C3	Swinegate	D4
Argyle Road	F2	Carlton Rise	D1	Eastgate	E3	Lands Lane	D3	Park Lane	B2	Templar Street	E3
Armley Gyratory	A4	Castle Street	B3	East Parade	C3	Leighton Street	C2	Park Place	C3	The Avenue	F4
Armley Road	A4	Cavendish Road	C1	East Street	F4	Leylands Road	F2	Park Row	D3	The Boulevard	F5
Armouries Drive	F5	Cavendish Street	A2	Elmwood Lane	E1	Lifton Place	B1	Park Square East	C3	The Calls	E4
Armouries Way	E4	Centenary Square	F3	Flax Place	F4	Lincoln Green Road	F2	Park Square North	C3	The Headrow	D3
Back Hyde Terrace	B2	Central Road	E3	Front Street	C5	Lisbon Street	B3	Park Square West	C3	Thoresby Place	C2
Back Row	C5	Chadwick Street	F5	Geldard Road	A5	Little Queen Street	C3	Park Street	C3	Trafalgar Street	E2
Bath Road	C5	Cherry Row	F1	George Street	E3	Lovell Park Hill	E1	Pilot Street	F1	Upper Basinghall Street	D3
Bedford Street	D3	City Square	D3	Globe Road	B4	Lovell Park Road	E1	Portland Crescent	D2	Vicar Lane	E3
Belgrave Street	D2	Claremont	B2	Gotts Road	B4	Lower Basinghall Street	D3	Portland Way	D2	Victoria Road	D5
Belle Vue Road	A1	Clarence Road	F5	Gower Street	E2	Lower Brunswick Street	E2	Princes Square	C4	Victoria Street	B2
Belmont Grove	C2	Clarendon Road	B1	Grace Street	C3	Lyddon Terrace	B1	Quarry Hill	F3	Victoria Terrace	B2
Benson Street	F1	Clarendon Way	C2	Grafton Street	E2	Mabgate	F2	Quebec Street	C3	Wade Lane	D2
Bingley Street	B3	Clay Pit Lane	D2	Graingers Way	A4	Macaulay Street	F2	Queen Square	D2	Water Lane	B5
Bishopgate Street	D4	Cloberry Street	B1	Great George Street	C2	Manor Road	C5	Queen Square Court	D2	Waterloo Street	E4
Black Bull Street	E5	Commercial Street	D3	Great Wilson Street	D5	Mark Lane	D3	Queen Street	C3	Wellington Bridge Street	B3
Blackman Lane	C1	Concordia Street	D4	Greek Street	D3	Marlborough Street	B3	Railway Street	F3	Wellington Road	A4
Blenheim Walk	C1	Concord Street	E2	Hanover Avenue	B2	Marshall Street	C5	Regent Street	F2	Wellington Road	A5
Boar Lane	D4	Consort Street	B2	Hanover Lane	B2	Marsh Lane	F4	Richmond Street	F4	Wellington Road	B3
Bond Street	D3	Consort View	A1	Hanover Square	B2	Maude Street	E4	Rider Street	F3	Westfield Road	A1
Bowman Lane	E4	County Arcade	E3	Harewood Street	E3	Meadow Lane	D5	Rillbank Lane	A1	Westgate	C3
Bow Street	F4	Cromer Terrace	B1	Harper Street	E4	Melbourne Street	E2	Rosebank Road	A1	West Street	B3
Brandon Road	B2	Cromwell Street	F2	Harrison Street	E3	Merrion Street	D2	St Cecilia Street	F3	Wharf Approach	C4
Bridge End	D4	Cross Arcade	D3	Hartwell Road	A1	Merrion Way	D2	St John's Road	A1	Wharf Street	E4
Bridge Road	B5	Cross Kelso Road	B1	High Court	E4	Millennium Square	D2	St Mary's Street	F3	Whitehall Quay	C4
Bridge Street	E2	Cross Stamford Street	F1	Holbeck Lane	B5	Mill Street	F4	St Paul's Street	C3	Whitehall Road	A5
Bridge Street	E3	Crown Point Road	E5	Hope Road	F2	Millwright Street	F2	St Peter's Square	F3	Whitehall Road	B4
Briggate	D4	Crown Street	E4	Hunslet Lane	E4	Mount Preston Street	B1	St Peter's Street	E3	Whitelock Street	F1
Burley Street	A2	Cudbear Street	E5	Hunslet Road	E5	Mushroom Street	F1	Salem Place	E5	Willow Terrace Road	C1
Butts Court	D3	David Street	C5	Hyde Park Road	A1	Neptune Street	F4	Saxton Lane	F4	Woodhouse Lane	C1
Byron Street	E2	Dock Street	E4	Hyde Terrace	B1	Neville Street	D4	Sheepscar Grove	E1	Woodhouse Square	B2
				Infirmary Street	D3	New Briggate	E3	Sheepscar Street South	F1	Woodsley Road	A1
				Junction Street	D5	New Lane	D5	Skinner Lane	E1	Wortley Lane	A5
				Kelso Road	B1	New Station Street	D4	South Parade	D3	Wortley Lane	A5
				Kendal Lane	B1	New York Road	E2	Sovereign Street	D4	York Place	C3
				King Edward Street	E3	New York Street	E3	Spence Lane	A5	York Street	F3

Leicester

Leicester is found on atlas page **72 F10**

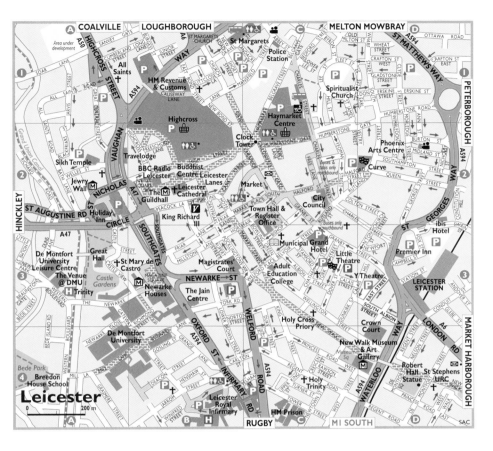

Albion Street	C3	Infirmary Road	B4
All Saints Road	A1	Jarrom Street	B4
Bath Lane	A2	Jarvis Street	A1
Bedford Street	C1	King Street	C3
Belgrave Gate	C1	Lee Street	C1
Belvoir Street	C3	London Road	D3
Bishop Street	C3	Lower Brown Street	B3
Bonners Lane	B4	Magazine Square	B3
Bowling Green Street	C3	Mansfield Street	B1
Burgess Street	B1	Market Place South	B2
Burton Street	D2	Market Street	C3
Calais Hill	C3	Mill Lane	B4
Campbell Street	D3	Morledge Street	D1
Cank Street	B2	Newarke Street	B3
Castle Street	A3	New Walk	C3
Charles Street	C1	Oxford Street	B3
Chatham Street	C3	Peacock Lane	B2
Cheapside	C2	Pocklingtons Walk	B3
Church Gate	B1	Princess Road East	D4
Clyde Street	D1	Princess Road West	C4
Colton Street	C2	Queen Street	D2
Conduit Street	D3	Regent Road	C4
Crafton Street West	D1	Regent Street	D4
Deacon Street	B4	Richard III Road	A2
De Montfort Street	D4	Rutland Street	C2
Dover Street	C3	St Augustine Road	A2
Duke Street	C3	St George Street	D2
Duns Lane	A3	St Georges Way	D2
East Bond Street Lane	B1	St James Street	C1
Erskine Street	D1	St Matthews Way	D1
Fleet Street	C1	St Nicholas Circle	A2
Friar Lane	B3	Sanvey Gate	A1
Gallowtree Gate	C2	Soar Lane	A1
Gateway Street	A3	South Albion Street	D3
Granby Street	C2	Southampton Street	D2
Grasmere Street	A4	Southgates	B3
Gravel Street	B1	Station Street	D3
Great Central Street	A1	The Newarke	A3
Greyfriars	B2	Tower Street	C4
Halford Street	C2	Vaughan Way	A2
Haymarket	C2	Waterloo Way	D4
Highcross Street	A1	Welford Road	C3
Highcross Street	B2	Welles Street	A2
High Street	B2	Wellington Street	C3
Hill Street	C1	Western Boulevard	A4
Horsefair Street	B3	West Street	C4
Humberstone Gate	C2	Wharf Street South	D1
Humberstone Road	D1	Yeoman Street	C2

Lincoln

Lincoln is found on atlas page **86 C6**

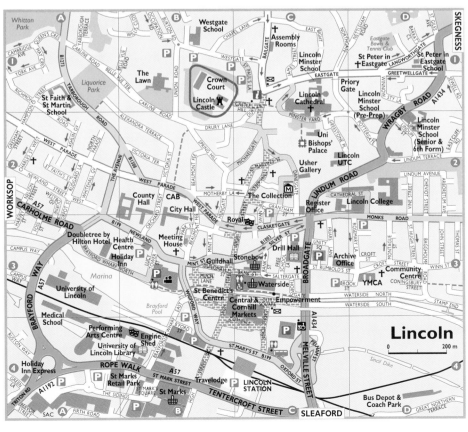

Alexandra Terrace	B2	Montague Street	D3
Arboretum Avenue	D2	Motherby Lane	B2
Baggholme Road	D3	Nelson Street	A2
Bailgate	C1	Newland	B3
Bank Street	C3	Newland Street West	A2
Beaumont Fee	B3	Northgate	C1
Belle Vue Terrace	A1	Orchard Street	B3
Brayford Way	A4	Oxford Street	C4
Brayford Wharf East	B4	Park Street	B3
Brayford Wharf North	A3	Pelham Street	C4
Broadgate	C3	Pottergate	D2
Burton Road	B1	Queen's Crescent	A1
Carholme Road	A2	Richmond Road	A1
Carline Road	A1	Rope Walk	A4
Cathedral Street	C2	Rosemary Lane	D3
Chapel Lane	B1	Rudgard Lane	A2
Charles Street West	A2	St Hugh Street	D3
Cheviot Street	D2	St Mark Street	B4
City Square	C3	St Martin's Street	C2
Clasketgate	C3	St Mary's Street	B4
Cornhill	B4	St Rumbold's Street	C3
Croft Street	D3	Saltergate	C3
Danesgate	C2	Silver Street	C3
Depot Street	A3	Sincil Street	C4
Drury Lane	B2	Spring Hill	B2
East Bight	C1	Steep Hill	C2
Eastgate	C1	Swan Street	C3
Free School Lane	C3	Tentercroft Street	B4
Friars Lane	C3	The Avenue	A2
Grantham Street	C2	The Sidings	A4
Greetwellgate	D1	Thorngate	C3
Gresham Street	A2	Triton Road	A4
Guildhall Street	B3	Union Road	B1
Hampton Street	A1	Unity Square	C3
High Street	B3	Victoria Street	B2
Hungate	B3	Victoria Terrace	B2
John Street	D3	Vine Street	D2
Langworthgate	D1	Waterside North	C3
Lindum Road	C2	Waterside South	C3
Lindum Terrace	D2	Westgate	B1
Lucy Tower Street	B3	West Parade	A2
May Crescent	A1	Whitehall Grove	A2
Melville Street	C4	Wigford Way	B3
Michaelgate	C2	Winnow Sty Lane	D1
Minster Yard	C2	Winn Street	D3
Mint Lane	B3	Wragby Road	D2
Mint Street	B3	Yarborough Terrace	A1
Monks Road	D3	York Avenue	A1

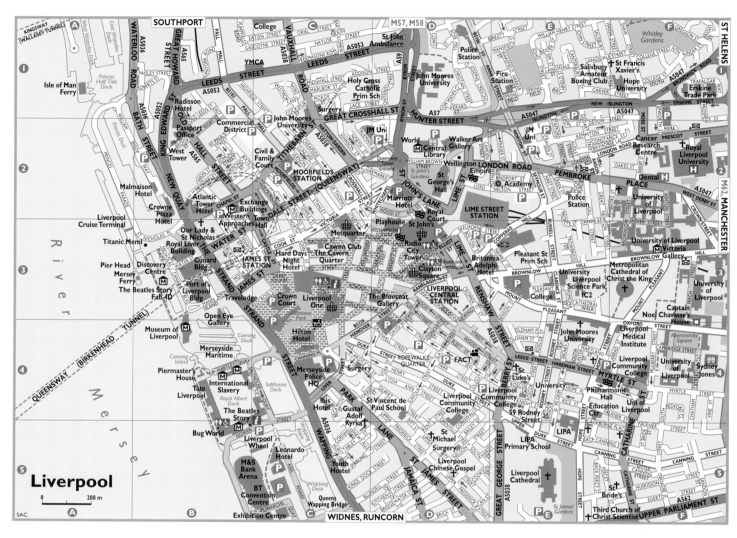

Liverpool

Liverpool is found on atlas page **81 L6**

Addison Street	C1	
Anson Street	E2	
Argyle Street	C4	
Arrad Street	F4	
Ashton Street	F2	
Audley Street	E2	
Back Canning Street	E5	
Baltimore Street	E4	
Bath Street	B2	
Beckwith Street	C4	
Bedford Street South	F5	
Benson Street	E3	
Berry Street	E4	
Bidder Street	E1	
Birkett Street	D1	
Bixteth Street	B2	
Blackburne Place	E5	
Blundell Street	C5	
Bold Street	D3	
Bosnett Street	D3	
Bridgewater Street	D5	
Bridport Street	E2	
Brook Street	B2	
Brownlow Hill	E3	
Brownlow Street	F3	
Brunswick Road	F1	
Brunswick Street	B3	
Byrom Street	D1	
Cambridge Street	F4	
Camden Street	D2	
Canada Boulevard	B3	
Canning Place	C4	
Canning Street	E5	
Canterbury Street	E1	
Carver Street	E1	
Castle Street	C3	

Catharine Street	F5	
Cathedral Walk	E3	
Chapel Street	B2	
Chatham Street	F4	
Cheapside	C2	
Christian Street	D1	
Churchill Way	D2	
Church Street	C3	
Clarence Street	E3	
Cockspur Street	C2	
College Lane	C3	
College Street North	E1	
College Street South	F1	
Colquitt Street	D4	
Constance Street	E2	
Cook Street	C3	
Copperas Hill	D3	
Cornhill	C5	
Cornwallis Street	D5	
Craven Street	E2	
Cropper Street	D3	
Crosshall Street	C2	
Crown Street	F2	
Dale Street (Queensway)	C2	
Dansie Street	E2	
Daulby Street	F2	
Derby Square	C3	
Devon Street	E2	
Dover Street	F3	
Drury Lane	B3	
Duke Street	D4	
East Street	B1	
Eaton Street	B1	
Edmund Street	B2	
Egerton Street	F5	
Elliot Street	D3	

Epworth Street	F1	
Erskine Street	F1	
Falkner Street	E4	
Fazakerley Street	B2	
Fenwick Street	B3	
Fleet Street	D3	
Fontenoy Street	D1	
Fraser Street	E2	
Gascoyne Street	B1	
Gilbert Street	D4	
Gildart Street	E2	
Gill Street	E2	
Gower Street	B5	
Gradwell Street	D4	
Great Crosshall Street	C1	
Great George Street	E5	
Great Howard Street	B1	
Great Newton Street	E2	
Greek Street	E2	
Gregson Street	F1	
Grenville Street South	D5	
Hackins Hey	C2	
Hanover Street	C4	
Hardman Street	E4	
Harker Street	E1	
Hartley Quay	B4	
Hart Street	E2	
Hatton Garden	C2	
Hawke Street	E3	
Henry Street	D4	
Highfield Street	B1	
Hood Street	D2	
Hope Place	E4	
Hope Street	E5	
Hotham Street	E2	
Hunter Street	D1	
Huskisson Street	F5	
Islington	E2	
Jamaica Street	D5	
James Street	B3	
Johnson Street	C2	

Keel Wharf	C5	
Kempston Street	E2	
Kent Street	D5	
Kinder Street	F1	
King Edward Street	B2	
Kingsway (Wallasey Tunnel)	A1	
Knight Street	E4	
Lace Street	C1	
Langsdale Street	E1	
Leece Street	E4	
Leeds Street	B1	
Lime Street	D2	
Liver Street	C4	
London Road	D2	
London Road	E2	
Lord Nelson Street	D2	
Lord Street	C3	
Lydia Ann Street	D4	
Mann Island	B3	
Mansfield Street	E1	
Marybone	C1	
Maryland Street	E4	
Midghall Street	C1	
Moorfields	B2	
Moor Street	B3	
Moss Street	F1	
Mount Pleasant	E3	
Mount Street	E4	
Mulberry Street	F4	
Myrtle Street	E4	
Naylor Street	C1	
Nelson Street	D5	
Newington	D4	
New Islington	E1	
New Quay	B2	
North John Street	C3	
Norton Street	E2	
Old Hall Street	B2	
Oldham Street	E4	
Old Haymarket	C2	
Old Leeds Street	B1	

Ormond Street	B2	
Oxford Street	F4	
Paisley Street	B1	
Pall Mall	B1	
Paradise Street	C3	
Parker Street	D3	
Park Lane	C4	
Parr Street	D4	
Peech Street	F3	
Pembroke Place	E2	
Pembroke Street	F2	
Percey Street	E5	
Pilgrim Street	E4	
Pleasant Street	E3	
Pomona Street	E3	
Prescot Street	F2	
Princes Parade	A2	
Prospect Street	F1	
Queensway (Birkenhead Tunnel)	A4	
Ranelagh Street	D3	
Redcross Street	C3	
Renshaw Street	D3	
Richmond Lane	C3	
Rigby Street	B2	
Rodney Street	E4	
Roscoe Street	E4	
Rose Hill	D1	
Russell Street	E3	
St Anne Street	D1	
St James Street	D5	
St John's Lane	D2	
St Josephs Crescent	D1	
St Nicholas Place	B3	
St Paul's Street	B2	
Salisbury Street	E1	
Salthouse Quay	C4	
Sandon Street	F5	
School Lane	C3	
Seel Street	D4	
Seymour Street	E2	

Shaw Street	F1	
Sir Thomas Street	C2	
Skelhorne Street	D3	
Slater Street	D4	
Soho Street	E1	
Sparling Street	C5	
Springfield	E1	
Stafford Street	E2	
Stanley Street	C2	
Strand Street	B3	
Suffolk Street	D4	
Tabley Street	C5	
Tarleton Street	D3	
Temple Street	C2	
The Strand	B3	
Tithe Barn Street	C2	
Trafalgar Way	F1	
Trowbridge Street	E3	
Trueman Street	C2	
Upper Duke Street	E5	
Upper Frederick Street	D4	
Upper Parliament Street	F5	
Upper Pitt Street	D5	
Vauxhall Road	C1	
Vernon Street	C2	
Victoria Street	C3	
Wakefield Street	E1	
Wall Street	C3	
Wapping	C5	
Waterloo Road	A1	
Water Street	B3	
West Derby Street	F2	
Westmorland Drive	C1	
Whitechapel	D2	
William Brown Street	D2	
William Henry Street	E1	
William Jessop Way	A2	
Williamson Square	C3	
Williamson Street	C3	
Wood Street	D3	
York Street	C4	

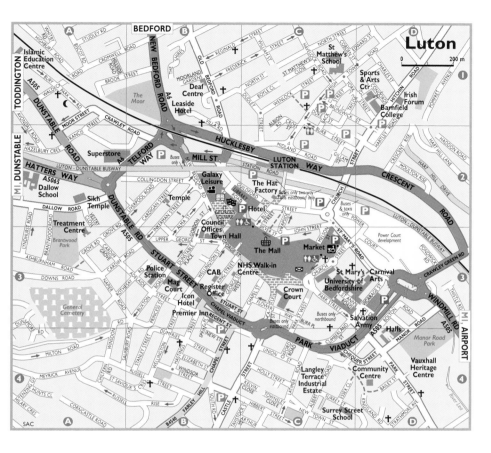

Luton

Luton is found on atlas page **50 C6**

Adelaide Street B3	Hibbert Street.......................C4
Albert Road C4	Highbury Road A1
Alma Street..........................B2	High Town Road C1
Arthur Street........................C4	Hitchin Road D1
Ashburnham Road A3	Holly Street..........................C4
Biscot Road A1	Hucklesby Way......................B2
Brantwood Road A3	Inkerman Street B3
Brunswick Street...................C1	John Street...........................C3
Burr Street...........................C2	King Street...........................B3
Bury Park Road A1	Latimer Road C4
Bute Street...........................C2	Liverpool Road B2
Buxton Road B3	Manor Road D4
Cardiff Road A3	Meyrick Avenue.....................A4
Cardigan Street.....................B2	Midland Road C2
Castle Street B4	Mill Street............................B2
Chapel Street B4	Milton Road A4
Chapel Viaduct B3	Moor Street A1
Charles Street D1	Napier Road A3
Chequer Street C4	New Bedford Road B1
Church Street........................C2	New Town Street....................C4
Church Street........................C3	Old Bedford Road B1
Cobden Street C1	Park Street C3
Collingdon Street...................B2	Park Street West C3
Concorde Street D1	Park Viaduct C4
Crawley Green Road D3	Princess Street B3
Crawley Road A1	Regent Street B3
Crescent Road D2	Reginald Street B1
Cromwell Road A1	Rothesay Road A3
Cumberland Street C4	Russell Rise..........................A4
Dallow Road A2	Russell Street........................B4
Dudley Street........................C1	St Mary's Road......................C3
Dumfries Street.....................B4	St Saviour's Crescent A4
Dunstable Road A1	Salisbury Road A4
Farley Hill.............................B4	Stanley Street........................B4
Flowers Way..........................C3	Station Road C2
Frederick Street.....................B1	Strathmore Avenue D4
George Street B3	Stuart Street B3
George Street West B3	Surrey Street.........................C4
Gordon Street B3	Tavistock Street B4
Grove Road A3	Telford Way..........................B2
Guildford Street B2	Upper George Street...............B3
Hart Hill Drive......................D2	Vicarage Street......................D3
Hart Hill Lane.......................D2	Waldeck Road A1
Hartley Road D2	Wellington Street...................B4
Hastings Street B4	Wenlock Street......................C1
Hatters Way A2	Windmill Road D3
Havelock Road C1	Windsor Street.......................B4
Hazelbury Crescent A2	Winsdon Road.......................A4

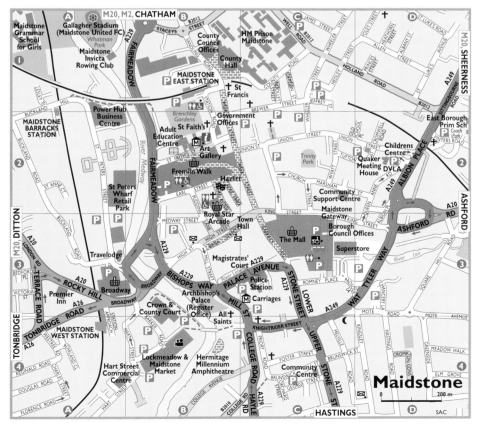

Maidstone

Maidstone is found on atlas page **38 C10**

Albany Street........................ D1	Market Buildings B2
Albion Place......................... D2	Marsham Street C2
Allen Street.......................... D1	Meadow Walk D4
Ashford Road D3	Medway Street.......................B3
Bank Street B3	Melville Road C4
Barker Road B4	Mill Street............................B3
Bedford Place....................... A3	Mote Avenue.........................D3
Bishops Way......................... B3	Mote Road D3
Brewer Street C2	Old School Place D2
Broadway A3	Orchard Street.......................C4
Broadway B3	Padsole Lane.........................C3
Brunswick Street................... C4	Palace Avenue.......................B3
Buckland Hill A2	Princes Street D1
Buckland Road A2	Priory Road C4
Camden Street...................... C1	Pudding Lane........................B2
Chancery Lane...................... D3	Queen Anne Road D2
Charles Street....................... A4	Reginald Road.......................A4
Church Street C2	Rocky Hill.............................A3
College Avenue..................... B4	Romney Place........................C3
College Road........................ C4	Rose Yard B2
County Road C1	Rowland Close.......................A4
Crompton Gardens D4	St Anne Court........................A2
Cromwell Road D2	St Faith's Street B2
Douglas Road....................... A4	St Luke's Avenue D1
Earl Street B2	St Luke's Road D1
Elm Grove D4	St Peters Street A2
Fairmeadow B1	Sandling Road B1
Florence Road....................... A4	Sittingbourne Road D1
Foley Street D1	Square Hill Road D3
Foster Street......................... C4	Staceys Street........................B1
Gabriel's Hill C3	Station Approach....................A4
George Street C4	Station Road B1
Greenside D4	Terrace Road A3
Hart Street A4	Tonbridge Road A4
Hastings Road D4	Tufton Street.........................C2
Hayle Road D4	Union Street..........................C2
Heathorn Street D1	Upper Stone Street.................C4
Hedley Street D2	Victoria Street.......................A3
High Street B3	Vinters Road D2
Holland Road D1	Wat Tyler Way.......................C3
James Street C1	Week Street B1
Jeffrey Street........................ C1	Well Road C1
King Street C2	Westree Road A4
Kingsley Road D4	Wheeler Street.......................C1
Knightrider Street................. C4	Woollett Street C1
Lesley Place A1	Wyatt Street..........................C2
London Road A3	
Lower Stone Street................ C3	

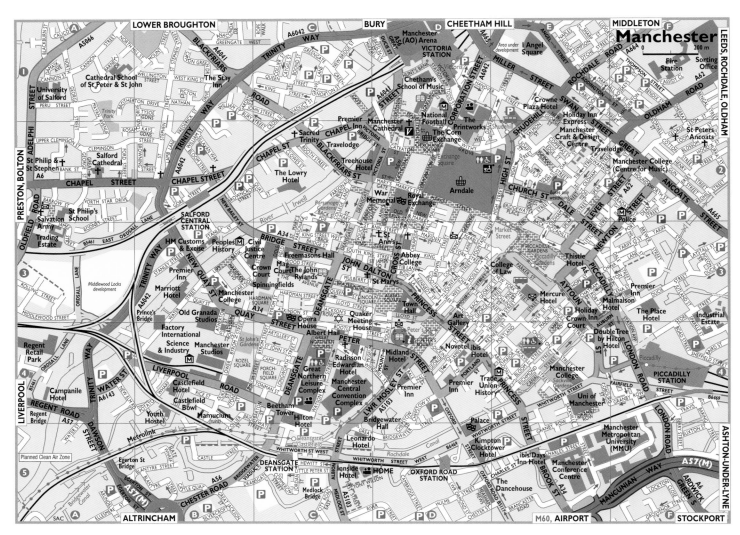

Manchester

Manchester is found on atlas page **82 H5**

Abingdon Street	E4
Addington Street	E1
Adelphi Street	A2
Albion Street	C5
Angel Street	E1
Ardwick Green South	F5
Artillery Street	C4
Atherton Street	B4
Atkinson Street	C3
Auburn Street	E4
Aytoun Street	E3
Back Piccadilly	E3
Bank Street	A2
Baring Street	F4
Barton Street	C4
Berry Street	F4
Blackfriars Road	B1
Blackfriars Street	C2
Blantyre Street	B5
Bloom Street	B2
Bloom Street	E4
Blossom Street	F2
Boad Street	F4
Boond Street	C1
Booth Street	D3
Bootle Street	C4
Brancaster Road	E5
Brazennose Street	C3
Brewer Street	F3
Bridge Street	C2
Bridgewater Place	E2
Bridgewater Street	B4
Bridgewater Viaduct	B5
Brook Street	E5
Brotherton Drive	A1
Browncross Street	B2

Browning Street	B2
Brown Street	D3
Bury Street	B1
Byrom Street	B4
Cable Street	E1
Cambridge Street	D5
Camp Street	C4
Canal Street	E4
Cannon Street	A1
Canon Green Drive	B1
Castle Street	B5
Cathedral Street	D2
Chadderton Street	F1
Chapel Street	A2
Charles Street	E5
Charlotte Street	D3
Chatham Street	E3
Cheapside	D3
Chester Road	B5
China Lane	E3
Chorlton Street	E4
Church Street	E2
City Road East	C5
Cleminson Street	A2
College Land	C2
Collier Street	C1
Commercial Street	C5
Copperas Street	E2
Cornell Street	F2
Corporation Street	D2
Cotton Street	F2
Crosskeys Street	F1
Cross Street	C2
Cross Street	D3
Dale Street	E2
Dantzic Street	D2

Dawson Street	A5
Deansgate	C4
Dickinson Street	D4
Duke Street	B4
Dulcie Street	F3
East Ordsall Lane	A3
Egerton Street	A5
Exchange Square	D2
Fairfield Street	F4
Faulkner Street	D4
Fennel Street	D1
Ford Street	A2
Fountain Street	D3
Frederick Street	B2
Garden Lane	B1
Gartside Street	B3
George Leigh Street	E1
George Street	D4
Gore Street	B2
Granby Row	E5
Gravel Lane	C1
Great Ancoats Street	F2
Great Bridgewater Street	C5
Great Ducie Street	C1
Great George Street	A2
Great Jackson Street	B5
Great John Street	B4
Greengate	C1
Greengate West	B1
Gun Street	E2
Hanover Street	D1
Hardman Street	C3
Hewitt Street	C5
High Street	E2
Hood Street	F2
Hope Street	E3
Houndsworth Street	D4
Hulme Street	D5
James Street	A3
Jersey Street	F2
John Dalton Street	C3

John Street	D1
John Street	E2
Joiner Street	E2
Jutland Street	F3
Kennedy Street	D3
King Street	C1
King Street	C3
King Street West	C3
Lamb Lane	B2
Laystall Street	F3
Left Bank	B3
Lena Street	F3
Lever Street	E2
Little Lever Street	E3
Little Peter Street	C5
Liverpool Road	B4
Lloyd Street	C3
London Road	F4
Long Millgate	D1
Longworth Street	C4
Lower Byrom Street	B4
Lower Mosley Street	C4
Lower Ormond Street	D5
Ludgate Street	E1
Major Street	E4
Mancunian Way	E5
Marble Street	D3
Market Street	D2
Marsden Street	D3
Marshall Street	E1
Mason Street	E1
Mayan Avenue	A1
Medlock Street	C5
Middlewood Street	A3
Miller Street	E1
Minshull Street	E3
Mirabel Street	C1
Mosley Street	D3
Mount Street	B1
Mount Street	D4
Museum Street	C4

Nathan Drive	B1
New Bailey Street	B2
New Bridge Street	C1
New Cathedral Street	D2
New Elm Road	A4
New George Street	E2
New Quay Street	B3
Newton Street	E3
New York Street	E3
Nicholas Street	D3
North George Street	A1
North Hill Street	A1
North Star Drive	A2
Norton Street	C1
Oldfield Road	A3
Oldham Road	F1
Oldham Street	E2
Ordsall Lane	A4
Oxford Road	D5
Oxford Street	D4
Pall Mall	D3
Parker Street	E3
Peru Street	A1
Peter Street	C4
Piccadilly	E3
Piccadilly Gardens	E3
Portland Street	D4
Port Street	F3
Potato Wharf	A5
Princess Street	D3
Quay Street	B3
Queen Street	C1
Queen Street	D3
Redhill Street	F2
Regent Road	A4
Reyner Street	D4
Rice Street	B4
Richmond Street	E4
Rochdale Road	E1
Rodney Street	A3
Rosamond Drive	A2

Sackville Street	E4
St Anns Square	C2
St Ann Street	C3
St James Square	C3
St James Street	D4
St Mary's Parsonage	C3
St Stephen Street	B2
Store Street	F3
Sharp Street	E1
Shudehill	E2
Silk Street	A1
Simpson Street	E1
South King Street	C3
Spear Street	E3
Spring Gardens	D3
Station Approach	F3
Swan Street	E1
Tariff Street	F3
Thomas Street	E2
Thompson Street	F1
Tib Lane	D3
Tib Street	E2
Todd Street	D1
Tonman Street	C4
Travis Street	F4
Trinity Way	A4
Turner Street	E2
Victoria Bridge Street	C2
Victoria Station Approach	D1
Victoria Street	C2
Warwick Street	C4
Watson Street	C4
Well Street	D2
West King Street	B1
West Mosley Street	D3
Whitworth Street	D5
Whitworth Street West	C5
Windmill Street	C4
Withy Grove	D2
Wood Street	C3
York Street	D3

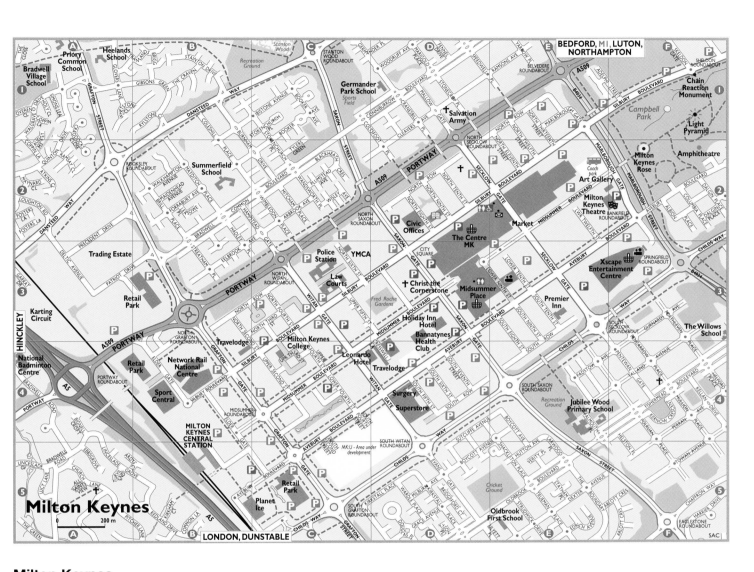

Milton Keynes

Milton Keynes is found on atlas page **49 N7**

Adelphi Street	E1	
Albion Place	F2	
All Saints View	A5	
Arbrook Avenue	C2	
Ardys Court	A5	
Arlott Crescent	F5	
Atkins Close	A2	
Audley Mews	A2	
Avebury Boulevard	C5	
Bankfield Roundabout	E2	
Belvedere Roundabout	E1	
Bignell Croft	A4	
Blackheath Crescent	C2	
Booker Avenue	C1	
Boycott Avenue	D5	
Boycott Avenue	E4	
Bradwell Common Boulevard	B2	
Bradwell Road	A4	
Bradwell Road	A5	
Bridgeford Court	D5	
Brill Place	B2	
Burnham Drive	B1	
Chaffron Way	F5	
Childs Way	C5	
Childs Way	F3	
Church Lane	A5	
City Square	D3	
Cleavers Avenue	D1	
Coleshill Place	B1	
Coltsfoot Place	C1	
Columbia Place	F2	
Common Lane	B5	
Conniburrow Boulevard	C1	
Coppin Lane	A2	
Craddocks Close	A1	
Cranesbill Place	D1	
Cresswell Lane	D3	
Dalgin Place	F2	
Dansteed Way	A2	
Dansteed Way	B1	
Deltic Avenue	A3	
Dexter Avenue	E5	
Douglas Place	D5	
Eaglestone Roundabout	F5	
Ebbsgrove	A5	
Edrich Avenue	E5	
Eelbrook Avenue	B3	
Elder Gate	B4	
Evans Gate	D5	
Falmouth Place	E4	
Fennel Drive	D1	
Fishermead Boulevard	F4	
Forrabury Avenue	B2	
Fosters Lane	A2	
Garrat Drive	A3	
Germander Place	C1	
Gibsons Green	B1	
Glovers Lane	A1	
Grace Avenue	D5	
Grafton Gate	B4	
Grafton Street	A1	
Grafton Street	C5	
Gurnards Avenue	F3	
Hadley Place	B2	
Hampstead Gate	B2	
Harrier Drive	F5	
Helford Place	F4	
Helston Place	F4	
Holy Close	A1	
Hutton Avenue	E5	
Ibistone Avenue	C1	
Kellan Drive	F4	
Kernow Crescent	F4	
Kirkham Court	B5	
Kirkstall Place	C5	
Larwood Place	E5	
Leasowe Place	B2	
Linceslade Grove	A5	
Loughton Road	A2	
Lower Fourth Street	C4	
Lower Ninth Street	E3	
Lower Tenth Street	E3	
Lower Twelfth Street	E2	
Lucy Lane	A5	
Maidenhead Avenue	B2	
Mallow Gate	D1	
Marigold Place	D1	
Marlborough Gate	E1	
Marlborough Gate	E2	
Marlborough Street	F2	
Mayditch Place	B2	
Maynard Close	A2	
Midsummer Boulevard	C4	
Midsummer Boulevard	E2	
Midsummer Roundabout	B4	
Milburn Avenue	D5	
Mitcham Place	C2	
Mullion Place	F4	
North Eighth Street	D2	
North Eleventh Street	E1	
North Fourth Street	C3	
North Grafton Roundabout	B3	
North Ninth Street	D2	
North Row	B3	
North Row	D2	
North Saxon Roundabout	C2	
North Secklow Roundabout	D1	
North Second Street	B3	
North Sixth Street	C3	
North Tenth Street	D2	
North Third Street	C3	
North Thirteenth Street	E1	
North Twelfth Street	E1	
North Witan Roundabout	C3	
Oldbrook Boulevard	C5	
Overend Close	A1	
Padstow Avenue	E4	
Patriot Drive	A3	
Pencarrow Place	F3	
Pentewan Gate	F4	
Perran Avenue	F4	
Pitcher Lane	A5	
Plumstead Avenue	C2	
Polruan Place	F4	
Porthleven Place	F3	
Portway	A4	
Portway Roundabout	A4	
Precedent Drive	A3	
Quinton Drive	A2	
Ramsay Close	A2	
Ramsons Avenue	E1	
Redland Drive	B5	
Rooksley Roundabout	A2	
Rylstone Close	B1	
Saxon Gate	D2	
Saxon Street	C1	
Secklow Gate	D2	
Shackleton Place	E5	
Sheldon Roundabout	F1	
Silbury Boulevard	B4	
Silbury Roundabout	B4	
Simons Lea	A1	
Skeldon Gate	F1	
South Eighth Street	E3	
South Fifth Street	D4	
South Fourth Street	C4	
South Grafton Roundabout	C5	
South Ninth Street	E3	
South Row	D4	
South Saxon Roundabout	E4	
South Secklow Roundabout	E3	
South Second Street	C5	
South Seventh Street	D4	
South Sixth Street	D4	
South Tenth Street	E3	
South Witan Roundabout	D5	
Speedwell Place	D1	
Springfield Roundabout	F3	
Stainton Drive	B1	
Stanton Wood Roundabout	C1	
Statham Place	E5	
Stokenchurch Place	C1	
Stonecrop Place	D1	
Streatham Place	B3	
Strudwick Drive	E5	
Sutcliffe Avenue	D4	
Talland Avenue	F4	
The Boundary	E5	
The Close	A1	
The Craven	B1	
The Green	A5	
Towan Avenue	F5	
Tranlands Brigg	B1	
Trueman Place	E5	
Turvil End	A5	
Tylers Green	C2	
Tyson Place	D5	
Ulyett Place	D5	
Upper Fifth Street	C3	
Upper Fourth Street	C4	
Upper Second Street	C4	
Upper Third Street	C4	
Verity Place	E5	
Walgrave Drive	A1	
Walkhampton Avenue	B2	
Wandsworth Place	C2	
Wardle Place	D5	
Whetstone Close	A1	
Wimbledon Place	C2	
Wisely Avenue	C2	
Witan Gate	C3	
Woodruff Avenue	D1	
Yarrow Place	E1	

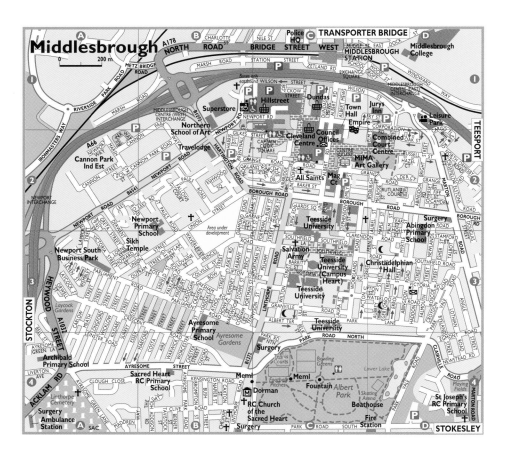

Middlesbrough

Middlesbrough is found on atlas page **104 E7**

Acklam Road	A4	Ironmasters Way	A2
Acton Street	C3	Kensington Road	B4
Aire Street	B4	Kildare Street	A4
Albert Road	C2	Laurel Street	D3
Amber Street	C2	Lees Road	A2
Athol Street	B3	Linthorpe Road	B4
Aubrey Street	D3	Longford Street	A4
Ayresome Park Road	B4	Lorne Street	A3
Ayresome Street	A4	Lothian Road	D3
Borough Road	C2	Marsh Street	A2
Brentnall Street	B2	Marton Road	D2
Bridge Street East	C1	Melrose Street	D2
Bridge Street West	C1	Metz Bridge Road	A1
Bush Street	B4	Myrtle Street	D3
Cadogen Street	B3	Newlands Road	D3
Camden Street	D2	Newport Road	A2
Cannon Park Road	A2	Palm Street	D3
Cannon Park Way	A2	Park Lane	C3
Cannon Street	A2	Park Road North	C4
Carlow Street	A3	Park Vale Road	D4
Centre Square	C2	Parliament Road	A3
Clairville Road	D4	Pearl Street	C2
Clarendon Road	C3	Pelham Street	C3
Clifton Street	B3	Portman Street	B3
Corporation Road	D1	Princes Road	B3
Costa Street	B4	Riverside Park Road	A1
Craven Street	B3	Ruby Street	C2
Crescent Road	A3	Russell Street	D2
Croydon Road	D3	St Pauls Road	B2
Derwent Street	A2	Southfield Road	C3
Diamond Road	B3	Station Street	C1
Egmont Road	D4	Stowe Street	B3
Emily Street	C2	Tavistock Street	B4
Errol Street	D3	Tennyson Street	B3
Essex Street	A4	Union Street	A3
Fairbridge Street	C2	Victoria Road	C3
Falmouth Street	D3	Victoria Street	A3
Finsbury Street	B3	Waterloo Road	D3
Garnet Street	B2	Waverley Street	B3
Glebe Road	B3	Wembley Street	A3
Grange Road	B2	Wilson Street	B2
Grange Road	D2	Wilton Street	C3
Granville Road	C3	Woodlands Road	C3
Gresham Road	B3	Worcester Street	B4
Harewood Street	B3	Zetland Road	C1
Harford Street	B4		
Hartington Road	B2		
Heywood Street	A3		

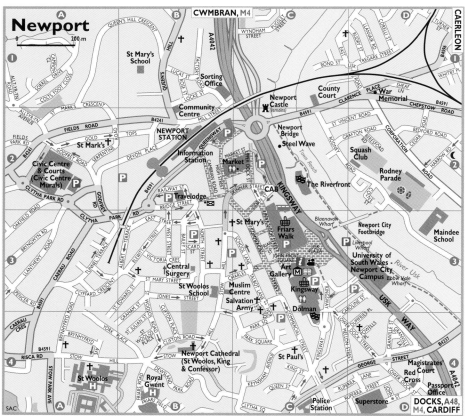

Newport

Newport is found on atlas page **31 K7**

Albert Terrace	B3	Jones Street	B3
Allt-Yr-Yn Avenue	A2	Keynsham Avenue	C4
Bailey Street	B3	King Street	C4
Bedford Road	D2	Kingsway	C2
Blewitt Street	B3	Kingsway	C4
Bond Street	C1	Llanthewy Road	A3
Bridge Street	B2	Locke Street	B1
Bryngwyn Road	A3	Lower Dock Street	C4
Brynhyfryd Avenue	A4	Lucas Street	B1
Brynhyfryd Road	A4	Market Street	B2
Caerau Crescent	A4	Mellon Street	C4
Caerau Road	A3	Mill Street	B2
Cambrian Road	B2	North Street	B3
Caroline Street	D3	Oakfield Road	A3
Cedar Road	D2	Park Square	C4
Charles Street	C3	Queen's Hill	B1
Chepstow Road	D1	Queen's Hill Crescent	A1
Clarence Place	C1	Queen Street	C4
Clifton Place	B4	Queensway	B2
Clifton Road	B4	Risca Road	A4
Clyffard Crescent	A3	Rodney Road	C2
Clytha Park Road	A2	Rudry Street	D1
Clytha Square	C4	Ruperra Lane	C4
Colts Foot Close	A1	Ruperra Street	D4
Commercial Street	C3	St Edward Street	B3
Corelli Street	D1	St Julian Street	B4
Corn Street	C2	St Mark's Crescent	A2
Corporation Road	D2	St Mary Street	B3
Devon Place	A2	St Vincent Road	C2
Dewsland Park Road	B4	St Woolos Road	B3
Dumfries Place	D4	School Lane	C3
East Street	B3	Serpentine Road	A2
East Usk Road	C1	Skinner Street	C2
Factory Road	B1	Sorrel Drive	A1
Fields Road	A2	Spencer Road	A3
Friars Field	B4	Stow Hill	B3
Friars Road	B4	Stow Hill	B4
Friar Street	C3	Stow Park Avenue	A4
George Street	D4	Talbot Lane	C3
Godfrey Road	A2	Tregare Street	D1
Gold Tops	A2	Tunnel Terrace	A3
Grafton Road	C2	Upper Dock Street	C2
Granville Lane	D4	Upper Dock Street	C3
Granville Street	D4	Usk Way	D3
High Street	B2	Victoria Crescent	B3
Hill Street	C3	West Street	B3
John Frost Square	C3	Wyndham Stret	C1
John Street	D4	York Place	A4

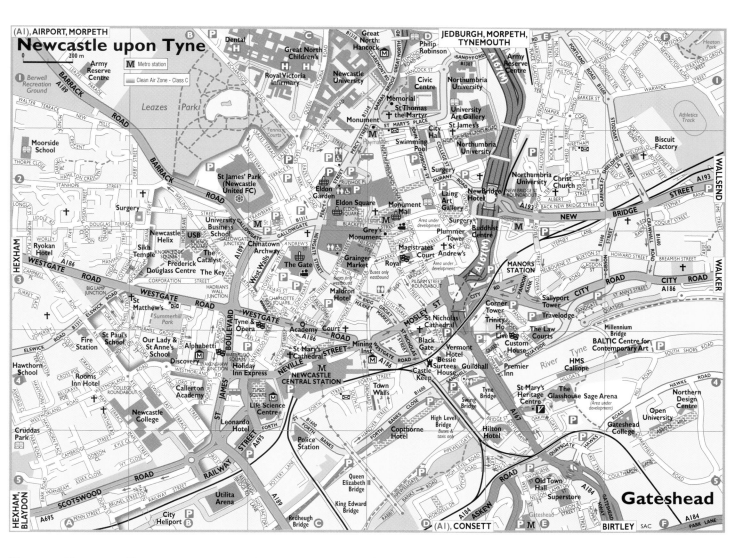

Newcastle upon Tyne

Newcastle upon Tyne is found on atlas page **113 K8**

Abbots Hill	F4	Clayton Street West	C4
Albert Street	E2	Cloth Market	D3
Argyle Street	E2	Colby Court	A4
Askew Road	D5	College Roundabout	A4
Avision Street	A2	College Street	D2
Back New Bridge Street	E2	Cookson Close	A3
Barker Street	E1	Copland Terrace	E2
Barrack Road	A1	Coppice Way	E1
Barras Bridge	D1	Coquet Street	F2
Bath Lane	B3	Corporation Street	B3
Belgrave Parade	A4	Cottenham Street	A3
Big Lamp Junction	A3	Coulthards Lane	F5
Blackett Street	C2	Crawhall Road	F2
Blagdon Street	E3	Cross Parade	A4
Blandford Square	B4	Cross Street	C3
Blandford Street	B4	Darnell Place	A2
Bottle Bank	E4	Dean Street	D3
Boyd Street	F2	Derby Street	B2
Breamish Street	F3	Diana Street	B3
Bridge Street	E4	Dinsdale Place	F1
Broad Chare	E3	Dinsdale Road	F1
Brunel Street	A5	Dobson Close	A5
Buckingham Street	B3	Douglas Terrace	A2
Buxton Street	E3	Duke Street	B4
Byron Street	E1	Dunn Street	A5
Cambridge Street	A5	Durant Road	D2
Camden Street	E2	East Street	E5
Campbell Place	A3	Edward Place	A3
Carliol Square	D3	Eldon Square	C2
Charlotte Square	C3	Ellison Street	E5
Chelmsford Grove	F1	Elswick East Terrace	B4
Chester Street	E1	Elswick Road	A3
City Road	E3	Elswick Row	A3
Claremont Road	D1	Essex Close	A5
Clarence Street	E2	Falconar's Court	C3
Clayton Street	C3	Falconer Street	E2

Fenkle Street	C3	King Edward Bridge	C5
Field Close	F2	King Street	E4
Fletcher Road	D5	Kirkdale Green	A4
Forth Banks	C4	Kyle Close	A5
Forth Banks Close	D5	Lambton Street	E5
Forth Street	C4	Leazes Crescent	C2
Friars Street	C3	Leazes Lane	C2
Gallowgate	B2	Leazes Park Road	C2
Gallowgate Junction	B3	Leazes Terrace	C2
Gateshead Highway	E5	Liddle Road	A2
George Street	B4	Lime Street	F2
Gibson Street	F3	Lombard Street	E4
Gladstone Terrace	E1	Longley Street	A2
Gloucester Terrace	A4	Lord Street	B4
Grainger Street	C3	Low Friar Street	C3
Grantham Road	E1	Maiden Street	B5
Great North Road	D1	Mansfield Street	A3
Grey Street	D3	Maple Street	B5
Groat Market	C3	Maple Terrace	A4
Hamilton Crescent	A2	Market Street	D3
Hanover Street	C5	Mather Road	A4
Harrison Place	E1	Melbourne Street	E3
Hawks Road	E5	Mill Road	F4
Hawthorn Place	A4	Milton Close	E1
Hawthorn Terrace	A4	Milton Place	E1
Helmsley Road	E1	Monday Crescent	A1
Henry Square	E2	Mosley Street	D3
High Bridge	D3	Napier Street	E1
High Level Road	D5	Nelson Street	C3
High Street	E5	Nelson Street	E5
Hillgate	E4	Neville Street	C4
Hood Street	D3	New Bridge Street	E2
Hopper Street	A5	Newgate Street	C3
Hornbeam Place	A5	Newington Road	F1
Houston Street	A5	New Mills	A1
Howard Street	F3	Northumberland Road	D2
Hudson Street	E5	Northumberland Street	D2
Ivy Close	A5	Nun Street	C3
Jesmond Road West	D1	Oakwellgate	E4
John Dobson Street	D2	Orchard Street	C4
Jubilee Road	E3	Ord Street	B5

Oxford Street	D2	Scotswood Road	A5
Pandon	E3	Shieldfield Lane	F2
Pandon Bank	E3	Shield Street	E2
Park Lane	F5	Shot Factory Lane	C5
Park Road	A5	Simpson Terrace	E2
Peel Lane	B4	Somerset Place	A4
Penn Street	A5	South Shore Road	F4
Percy Street	C2	South Street	C4
Pilgrim Street	D2	Stanhope Street	A2
Pink Lane	C4	Stepney Bank	F2
Pipewellgate	D5	Stepney Lane	E3
Pitt Street	B2	Stepney Road	F2
Portland Road	E1	Stoddart Street	F1
Portland Road	F1	Stowell Street	C3
Pottery Lane	A5	Stratford Grove West	F1
Prospect Place	A2	Strawberry Place	C2
Prudhoe Street	C2	Summerhill Grove	B3
Quarryfield Road	F5	Summerhill Street	A3
Quayside	F3	Summerhill Terrace	B4
Quayside	E4	Swinburne Street	E5
Queen Street	E4	Tarset Road	F3
Queen Victoria Road	C1	Terrace Place	C2
Rabbit Banks Road	D5	Tindal Street	A3
Railway Street	B5	Tower Street	E3
Red Barnes	F2	Tyne Bridge	E4
Redheugh Bridge Road	B5	Union Street	F2
Richardson Road	B1	Vallum Way	A3
Rock Terrace	E1	Victoria Street	B4
Rosedale Terrace	E1	Walter Terrace	A1
Rye Hill	A4	Warwick Street	F1
St Andrew's Street	C3	Waterloo Square	B4
St Ann's Street	F3	Waterloo Street	C4
St James' Boulevard	B4	Wellington Street	B2
St Mary's Place	D1	Westgate Road	A3
St Nicholas Street	D4	Westmorland Road	A4
St Thomas' Crescent	C2	West Street	E5
St Thomas' Street	C1	West Walls	C3
Sandgate	E3	Worley Close	A5
Sandhill	D4	Worsdell Drive	D5
Sandyford Road	D1	Wretham Place	E2
		York Street	A3

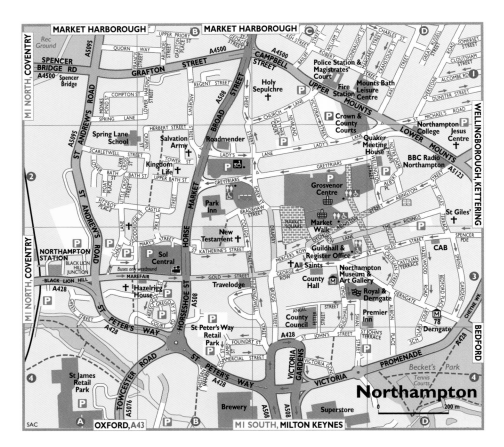

Northampton

Northampton is found on atlas page **60 G8**

Abington Street C2	Little Cross Street A2
Albert Place D2	Lower Bath Street A2
Albion Place D3	Lower Cross Street A2
Angel Street C3	Lower Harding Street............ B1
Arundel Street B1	Lower Mounts D2
Ash Street C1	Marefair A3
Bailiff Street C1	Margaret Street C1
Black Lion Hill A3	Market Square C2
Bradshaw Street.................... B2	Mercers Row C3
Bridge Street C3	Moat Place A2
Broad Street B1	Monkspond Street A1
Campbell Street C1	Newland C1
Castilian Street D3	Notredame Mews D2
Castle Street B2	Overstone Road D1
Chalk Lane A3	Pike Lane B3
Cheyne Walk D3	Quorn Way A1
Church Lane C1	Regent Street B1
College Street B2	Robert Street C1
Commercial Street B4	St Andrew's Road A2
Connaught Street C1	St Andrew's Street B1
Court Road B3	St Giles' Street D3
Cranstoun Street D1	St Giles' Terrace D2
Crispin Street B2	St John's Street C4
Derngate D3	St Katherine's Street B3
Doddridge Street A3	St Mary's Street A3
Drapery C3	St Michael's Road D1
Dunster Street D1	St Peter's Way B4
Dychurch Lane C3	Scarletwell Street A2
Earl Street D1	Scholars Court D4
Fetter Street C3	Sheep Street B1
Fitzroy Place A2	Sheep Street C2
Foundry Street B4	Spencer Bridge Road A1
Francis Street A1	Spencer Parade D3
Freeschool Street B3	Spring Gardens D3
George Row C3	Spring Lane A1
Gold Street B3	Swan Street C3
Grafton Street A1	Tanner Street A4
Great Russell Street.............. D1	The Ridings D2
Green Street A3	Towcester Road A4
Gregory Street B3	Tower Street B2
Greyfriars B2	Upper Bath Street B2
Guildhall Road C3	Upper Mounts C1
Hazelwood Road D3	Upper Priory Street............... B1
Herbert Street B2	Victoria Gardens C4
Horse Market B3	Victoria Promenade C4
Horseshoe Street B3	Victoria Street C1
Kingswell Street C3	Wellington Street.................. D2
Lady's Lane B2	Western Wharf...................... B4

Norwich

Norwich is found on atlas page **77 J10**

All Saints Green B4	Pottergate A2
Bank Plain C2	Prince of Wales Road............ C2
Barn Road A1	Princes Street C2
Bedding Lane C1	Quay Side............................. C1
Bedford Street B2	Queens Road B4
Ber Street............................. C4	Queen Street C2
Bethel Street A3	Rampant Horse Street B3
Bishopgate D1	Recorder Road D2
Brigg Street B3	Red Lion Street B3
Calvert Street B1	Riverside Road D3
Castle Meadow C3	Riverside Walk D1
Cathedral Street D2	Rose Lane C3
Cattle Market Street C3	Rouen Road C3
Chantry Road B3	Rupert Street A4
Chapelfield East A3	St Andrews Street B2
Chapelfield North A3	St Benedicts Street A2
Chapelfield Road A3	St Faiths Lane D2
Cleveland Road A3	St Georges Street B1
Colegate B1	St Giles Street A2
Convent Road A3	St Julians Alley C4
Coslany Street B2	St Marys Plain B1
Cow Hill A2	St Peters Street B3
Davey Place B3	St Stephens Road B4
Dove Street B2	St Stephens Square A4
Duke Street B1	St Stephens Street B4
Elm Hill C2	St Swithins Road A2
Exchange Street B2	St Verdast Street D2
Farmers Avenue.................... C3	Surrey Street B4
Ferry Lane D2	Ten Bell Lane........................ A2
Fishergate C1	Theatre Street B3
Friars Quay B1	Thorn Lane............................ C4
Gaol Hill B3	Tombland C2
Gentlemans Walk B3	Unicorn Yard A1
Golden Ball Street C3	Union Street A4
Grapes Hill A2	Unthank Road A3
Haymarket B3	Upper Goat Lane................... B2
Heigham Street A1	Upper King Street C2
King Street C2	Upper St Giles Street............ A3
London Street B2	Vauxhall Street A3
Lower Goat Lane B2	Walpole Street A3
Magdalen Street C1	Wensum Street C1
Market Avenue...................... C3	Wessex Street A4
Mountergate D3	Westlegate............................ B3
Music House Lane.................. D4	Westwick Street.................... A1
Muspole Street B1	Wherry Road D4
New Mills Yard...................... A1	Whitefriars C1
Oak Street A1	White Lion Street.................. B3
Palace Street......................... C1	Willow Lane A2

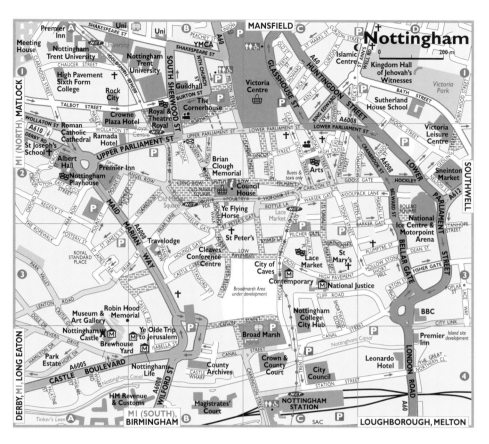

Nottingham

Nottingham is found on atlas page **72 F3**

Albert Street	B3	King Street	B2
Angel Row	B2	Lenton Road	A3
Barker Gate	D2	Lincoln Street	C2
Bath Street	D1	Lister Gate	B3
Bellar Gate	D3	London Road	D4
Belward Street	D2	Long Row	B2
Broad Street	C2	Lower Parliament Street	C2
Broadway	C3	Low Pavement	B3
Bromley Place	A2	Maid Marian Way	A2
Brook Street	D1	Market Street	B2
Burton Street	B1	Middle Hill	C3
Canal Street	C4	Milton Street	B1
Carlton Street	C2	Mount Street	A3
Carrington Street	C4	Norfolk Place	B2
Castle Boulevard	A4	North Circus Street	A2
Castle Gate	B3	Park Row	A3
Castle Road	B3	Pelham Street	C2
Chaucer Street	A1	Peveril Drive	A4
City Link	D3	Pilcher Gate	C3
Clarendon Street	A1	Popham Street	C3
Cliff Road	C3	Poultry	B2
Collin Street	B4	Queen Street	B2
Cranbrook Street	D2	Regent Street	A2
Cumber Street	C2	St Ann's Well Road	D1
Curzon Place	C1	St James's Street	A3
Derby Road	A2	St Marks Gate	C3
Exchange Walk	B2	St Marks Street	C1
Fisher Gate	D3	St Mary's Gate	C3
Fletcher Gate	C3	St Peter's Gate	B3
Forman Street	B1	Shakespeare Street	A1
Friar Lane	A3	Smithy Row	B2
Gedling Street	D2	South Parade	B2
George Street	C2	South Sherwood Street	B1
Glasshouse Street	C1	Spaniel Row	B3
Goldsmith Street	A1	Station Street	C4
Goose Gate	C2	Stoney Street	C2
Halifax Place	C3	Talbot Street	A1
Heathcote Street	C2	Thurland Street	C2
High Cross Street	C2	Trent Street	C4
High Pavement	C3	Upper Parliament Street	A2
Hockley	D2	Victoria Street	C2
Hollow Stone	D3	Warser Gate	C3
Hope Drive	A4	Weekday Cross	C3
Hounds Gate	B3	Wellington Circus	A2
Howard Street	C1	Wheeler Gate	B2
Huntingdon Street	C1	Wilford Street	B4
Kent Street	C1	Wollaton Street	A1
King Edward Street	C1	Woolpack Lane	C2

Oldham

Oldham is found on atlas page **83 K4**

Ascroft Street	B3	Napier Street East	A4
Bar Gap Road	B1	New Radcliffe Street	A2
Barlow Street	D4	Oldham Way	A3
Barn Street	B3	Park Road	B4
Beever Street	D2	Park Street	A4
Bell Street	D2	Peter Street	B3
Belmont Street	B1	Prince Street	D3
Booth Street	A3	Queen Street	C3
Bow Street	C3	Radcliffe Street	B1
Brook Street	D2	Ramsden Street	A1
Brunswick Street	B3	Regent Street	D2
Cardinal Street	C2	Rhodes Bank	C3
Chadderton Way	A1	Rhodes Street	C2
Chaucer Street	B3	Rifle Street	B1
Clegg Street	C3	Rochdale Road	A1
Coldhurst Road	B1	Rock Street	B2
Crossbank Street	B4	Roscoe Street	C3
Curzon Street	B2	Ruskin Street	A1
Dunbar Street	A1	St Hilda's Drive	A1
Eden Street	B2	St Marys Street	B1
Egerton Street	C2	St Mary's Way	B2
Emmott Way	C4	Shaw Road	D1
Firth Street	C3	Shaw Street	C1
Fountain Street	B2	Shore Street	D1
Franklin Street	B1	Siddall Street	C1
Gower Street	D2	Silver Street	B3
Grange Street	A2	Southgate Street	C3
Greaves Street	C3	South Hill Street	D4
Greengate Street	D4	Spencer Street	D2
Hardy Street	D4	Sunfield Road	B1
Harmony Street	C4	Thames Street	D1
Henshaw Street	B2	Trafalgar Street	A1
Higginshaw Road	C1	Trinity Street	B1
Highfield Street	A2	Tulbury Street	A1
High Street	B3	Union Street	B3
Hobson Street	B3	Union Street West	A4
Horsedge Street	C1	Union Street West	B3
John Street	A3	University Way	B4
King Street	B3	Wallshaw Street	D2
Lemnos Street	D2	Wall Street	B4
Malby Street	C1	Ward Street	A1
Malton Street	A4	Waterloo Street	C3
Manchester Street	A3	Wellington Street	B4
Market Place	B3	West End Street	A2
Marlborough Street	C4	West Street	B3
Middleton Road	A3	Willow Street	D2
Mortimer Street	D1	Woodstock Street	C4
Mumps	D2	Yorkshire Street	C3

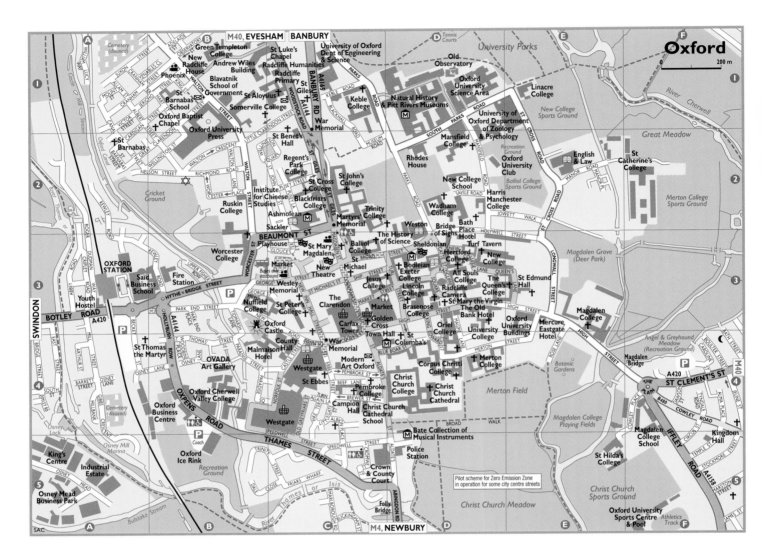

Oxford

Oxford is found on atlas page **34 F3**

Abbey Road	A3
Abingdon Road	D5
Adelaide Street	B1
Albert Street	A1
Albion Place	C4
Allam Street	A1
Alma Place	F4
Arthur Street	A4
Banbury Road	C1
Barrett Street	A4
Bath Street	F4
Beaumont Street	C3
Becket Street	A3
Beef Lane	C4
Blackhall Road	C1
Blue Boar Street	C4
Bonn Square	C4
Botley Road	A3
Boulter Street	F4
Brewer Street	C4
Bridge Street	A4
Broad Street	C3
Broad Walk	D4
Buckingham Street	C5
Canal Street	A1
Cardigan Street	A2
Caroline Street	F4
Castle Street	C4
Catte Street	D3
Circus Street	F5
Cornmarket Street	C3
Cowley Place	F4
Cowley Road	F4
Cranham Street	A1
Cranham Terrace	A1
Cripley Road	A3

Cromwell Street	C5
Dale Close	B5
Dawson Street	F4
East Street	A4
Folly Bridge	C5
Friars Wharf	C5
George Street	B3
George Street Mews	B3
Gibbs Crescent	A4
Gloucester Street	C3
Great Clarendon Street	A2
Hart Street	B1
High Street	D3
High Street	E4
Hollybush Row	B3
Holywell Street	D2
Hythe Bridge Street	B3
Iffley Road	F4
James Street	F5
Jericho Street	A1
Jowett Walk	D2
Juxon Street	A1
Keble Road	C1
King Edward Street	D3
King Street	B1
Little Clarendon Street	B2
Littlegate Street	C4
Longwall Street	E3
Magdalen Bridge	E4
Magdalen Street	C3
Magpie Lane	D3
Manor Place	E2
Manor Road	E2
Mansfield Road	D2
Market Street	C3
Marlborough Road	C5

Marston Street	F5
Merton Street	D4
Millbank	A4
Mill Street	A4
Mount Street	A1
Museum Road	C2
Nelson Street	A2
New College Lane	D3
New Inn Hall Street	C3
New Road	B3
Norfolk Street	C4
Observatory Street	B1
Old Greyfriars Street	C4
Osney Lane	A4
Osney Lane	B4
Osney Mead	A5
Oxpens Road	B4
Paradise Square	B4
Paradise Street	B4
Park End Street	B3
Parks Road	C1
Parks Road	D2
Pembroke Street	C4
Pike Terrace	C4
Pusey Lane	C2
Pusey Street	C2
Queen's Lane	D3
Queen Street	C3
Radcliffe Square	D3
Rewley Road	A2
Rewley Road	B3
Richmond Road	B2
Roger Dudman Way	A3
Rose Lane	E4
St Aldate's	C4
St Aldate's	D5

St Barnabas Street	A2
St Clement's Street	F4
St Cross Road	E1
St Cross Road	E2
St Ebbes Street	C4
St Giles	C2
St John Street	C2
St Michael's Street	C3
St Thomas' Street	B4
Savile Road	D2
Ship Street	C3
South Parks Road	D2
South Street	A4
Speedwell Street	C5
Stockmore Street	F5
Temple Street	F5
Thames Street	C5
The Plain	F4
Tidmarsh Lane	B3
Trinity Street	B5
Turl Street	D3
Turn Again Lane	C4
Tyndale Road	F4
Upper Fisher Row	B3
Venables Close	A1
Victor Street	A1
Walton Crescent	B2
Walton Lane	B2
Walton Street	B1
Wellington Square	B2
Wellington Street	B2
William Lucy Way	A1
Woodbine Place	B4
Woodstock Road	C1
Worcester Place	B2
Worcester Street	B3

University Colleges

All Souls College	D3
Balliol College	C3
Brasenose College	D3
Christ Church College	D4
Corpus Christi College	D4
Exeter College	D3
Harris Manchester College	D2
Hertford College	D3
Jesus College	C3
Keble College	C1
Linacre College	E1
Lincoln College	D3
Magdalen College	E3
Mansfield College	D2
Merton College	D4
New College	D3
Nuffield College	B3
Oriel College	D3
Pembroke College	C4
Ruskin College	B2
St Catherine's College	F2
St Cross College	C2
St Hilda's College	E5
St John's College	C2
St Peter's College	C3
Somerville College	B1
The Queen's College	D3
Trinity College	C2
University College	D3
Wadham College	D2
Worcester College	B3

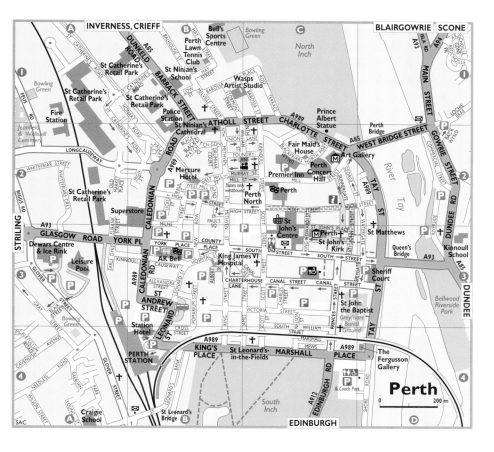

Perth

Perth is found on atlas page **134 E3**

Albert Place...........................B3	Melville Street.......................B1
Alexandra Street....................B3	Mill Street.............................C2
Atholl Street..........................B1	Milne Street...........................B2
Back Wynd............................D2	Monart Road.........................A1
Balhousie Street.....................B1	Murray Street.........................B2
Barossa Place.........................B1	Needless Road.......................A4
Barrack Street........................B1	New Row...............................B3
Blackfriars Wynd...................C2	North Methven Street.............B2
Black Watch Gardens.............B2	North Port.............................C2
Caledonian Road...................B2	North William Street..............B2
Caledonian Road...................B3	Old Market Place...................A2
Canal Street...........................C3	Paul Street.............................B2
Cavendish Avenue A4	Perth Bridge..........................D2
Charles Street........................C3	Pickletullum Road..................A4
Charlotte Street......................C2	Pomarium Street.....................B3
Charterhouse Lane.................B3	Princes Street.........................C3
Commercial Street..................D2	Queen's Bridge.......................D3
County Place.........................B3	Raeburn Park.........................A4
Cross Street...........................B4	Riggs Road............................A2
Dundee Road........................D3	Riverside...............................D3
Dunkeld Road........................B1	Rose Terrace..........................C1
Earls Dykes...........................A3	St Andrew Street....................B3
Edinburgh Road.....................C4	St Catherine's Road................A1
Elibank Street........................A3	St John's Place.......................C3
Feus Road..............................A1	St John Street.........................C3
Foundry Lane.........................B2	St Leonard's Bank..................B4
George Street.........................C2	St Paul's Square.....................B2
Glasgow Road........................A3	Scott Street............................C3
Glover Street..........................A3	Shore Road............................D4
Glover Street..........................A4	Skinnergate...........................C2
Gowrie Street.........................D2	South Methven Street.............B2
Gray Street............................A3	South Street...........................C3
Hay Street.............................B1	South William Street..............C4
High Street............................B2	Speygate...............................D3
High Street............................C2	Stormont Street......................B1
Hospital Street.......................B3	Tay Street..............................D2
Isla Road...............................D1	Tay Street..............................D4
James Street..........................C3	Union Lane............................B2
King Edward Street................C3	Victoria Street........................C3
King's Place...........................B4	Watergate..............................D2
King Street.............................B3	West Bridge Street..................D2
Kinnoull Causeway................A3	West Mill Street......................B2
Kinnoull Street.......................C2	West Mill Wynd......................B2
Leonard Street.......................B3	Whitefriars Crescent..............A2
Lochie Brae...........................D1	Whitefriar Street.....................A2
Longcauseway........................A2	Wilson Street.........................A4
Main Street............................D1	York Place.............................A3
Marshall Place........................C4	York Place.............................B3

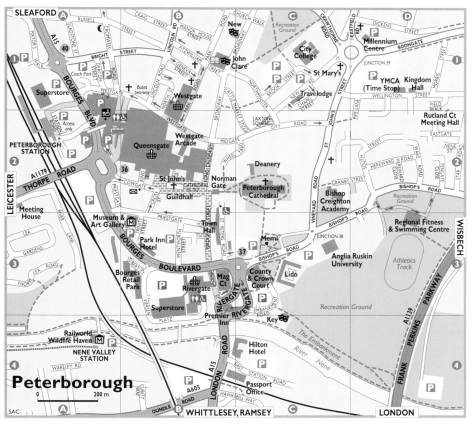

Peterborough

Peterborough is found on atlas page **74 C11**

Albert Place...........................B3	New Road..............................C1
Bishop's Road.......................C3	Northminster.........................C1
Boongate...............................D1	North Street...........................B1
Bourges Boulevard.................A1	Oundle Road.........................B4
Bridge Street.........................B3	Park Road..............................B1
Bright Street..........................A1	Pipe Lane..............................D2
Broadway..............................B2	Priestgate.............................A2
Brook Street...........................C1	Rivergate...............................B3
Cathedral Square....................B2	River Lane.............................A2
Cattle Market Street...............B1	Russell Street.........................A1
Chapel Street.........................C1	St John's Street......................C2
Church Street.........................B2	St Peters Road........................B3
Church Walk..........................C1	South Street...........................D2
City Road..............................C2	Star Road..............................D2
Cowgate................................B2	Station Road..........................A2
Craig Street...........................B1	Thorpe Lea Road....................A3
Crawthorne Road...................C1	Thorpe Road..........................A2
Cromwell Road......................A1	Trinity Street..........................B3
Cross Street...........................B2	Viersen Platz.........................B3
Cubitt Way............................B4	Vineyard Road.......................C3
Deacon Street........................A1	Wake Road............................D2
Dickens Street........................D1	Wareley Road........................A4
Eastfield Road........................D1	Wellington Street....................D1
Eastgate................................D2	Wentworth Street....................B3
East Station Road...................C4	Westgate................................A1
Embankment Road..................C3	
Exchange Street.....................B2	
Fengate Close........................D2	
Field Walk.............................D1	
Fitzwilliam Street...................B1	
Frank Perkins Parkway...........D4	
Geneva Street........................B1	
Gladstone Street....................A1	
Granby Street.........................C2	
Hawksbill Way.......................B4	
Hereward Close......................D2	
Hereward Road......................D2	
King Street.............................B2	
Laxton Square........................C2	
Lea Gardens..........................A3	
Lincoln Road.........................B1	
London Road.........................B4	
Long Causeway......................B2	
Manor House Street................B1	
Mayor's Walk........................A1	
Midgate................................B2	
Morris Street..........................D1	
Nene Street............................D2	

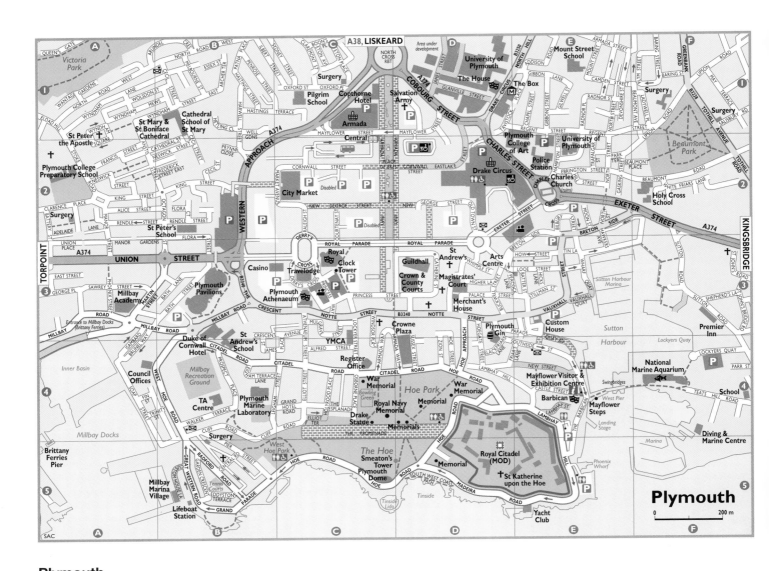

Plymouth

Plymouth is found on atlas page **6 D8**

Addison Road	E1
Adelaide Lane	A2
Alfred Street	C4
Alice Street	A2
Anstis Street	A2
Archer Terrace	B1
Armada Street	E1
Armada Way	C2
Armada Way	C4
Arundel Crescent	A1
Athenaeum Street	C3
Baring Street	F1
Bath Lane	B3
Bath Street	B3
Batter Street	E3
Battery Street	A2
Beaumont Avenue	F1
Beaumont Place	E2
Beaumont Road	F2
Bilbury Street	E2
Blackfriars Lane	D4
Boon's Place	C1
Breton Side	D3
Brunel Way	A4
Buckwell Street	D3
Camden Street	E1
Castle Street	E4
Cathedral Street	A2
Catherine Street	D3
Cecil Street	B1
Central Road	B5
Chapel Street	E1
Charles Cross	E2
Charles Street	D2
Citadel Road	B4
Citadel Road	C4

Claremont Street	C1
Clarence Place	A2
Cliff Road	B4
Cobourg Street	D1
Cornwall Street	C2
Courtenay Street	C3
Crescent Avenue	B3
Custom House Lane	B5
Derry's Cross	C3
Devonshire Street	E1
Drake Circus	D1
Eastlake Street	D2
East Street	A3
Ebrington Street	E2
Eddystone Terrace	B5
Eldad Hill	A1
Elliot Street	C4
Elliot Terrace	C4
Essex Street	B1
Eton Avenue	C1
Eton Place	C1
Exeter Street	D2
Exeter Street	E2
Fin Street	A4
Flora Court	B2
Flora Street	B2
Francis Street	A2
Frederick Street East	B2
Friar's Lane	D4
Garden Crescent	B5
Gasking Street	E2
George Place	A3
Gibbon Lane	E1
Gibbons Street	E1
Gilwell Street	E1
Glanville Street	D1

Grand Hotel Road	C4
Grand Parade	B5
Great Western Road	B5
Greenbank Road	F1
Hampton Street	E2
Harwell Street	B1
Hastings Street	B1
Hastings Terrace	B1
Hawkers Avenue	E2
Hetling Close	B1
Hicks Lane	E3
Higher Lane	D3
Hill Street	E2
Hoe Approach	D4
Hoegate Street	D3
Hoe Road	C5
Hoe Street	D3
Holyrood Place	C4
How Street	E3
Ilbert Street	B1
Isambard Brunel Way	A4
James Street	D1
King Street	A2
Ladywell Place	F1
Lambhay Hill	D4
Lambhay Street	E4
Leigham Street	B4
Leigham Terrace Lane	B4
Lipson Road	F1
Lockyers Quay	F4
Lockyer Street	C3
Looe Street	E3
Madeira Road	D5
Manor Gardens	A3
Manor Street	A2
Market Avenue	C2

Martin Street	A3
Mayflower Street	C1
Mayflower Street	D1
May Terrace	F1
Melbourne Street	B1
Millbay Road	A3
Moon Street	E2
Mount Street	E1
Mulgrave Street	C3
Neswick Street	A2
New George Street	C2
New Street	E4
North Cross Roundabout	C1
North Hill	E1
North Road West	A1
North Street	E2
Notte Street	C3
Octagon Street	B2
Old Town Street	D2
Osborne Place	C4
Oxford Street	C1
Palace Street	D3
Park Terrace	E2
Parr Street	F4
Peacock Lane	D3
Penrose Street	B1
Phoenix Street	A3
Pier Street	B5
Place de Brest	C2
Plym Street	F1
Princess Street	C3
Princess Way	C3
Prospect Place	B4
Prynne Close	B2
Quay Road	E4

Queen's Gate	A1
Radford Road	B5
Radnor Place	E1
Radnor Street	E1
Raleigh Street	C2
Regent Street	E1
Rendle Street	A2
Royal Parade	C3
St James Place	B4
St John's Bridge Road	F3
St John's Road	F3
Salisbury Road	F1
Sawrey Street	A3
Shepherd's Lane	F3
Soap Street	A4
Southside Street	D4
South West Coast Path	D5
Stillman Street	E3
Stoke Road	A2
Sussex Street	D3
Sutton Road	F3
Sydney Street	B1
Tavistock Place	D1
Teats Hill Road	F4
The Barbican	E4
The Crescent	B3
The Esplanade	C4
The Promenade	C4
Tin Lane	E3
Tothill Avenue	F1
Tothill Road	F2
Trafalgar Street	E2
Trinity Street	A4
Union Place	A3
Union Street	A3
Vauxhall Quay	E3

Vauxhall Street	E3
Walker Terrace	B4
Wantage Gardens	A1
Well Gardens	B1
Western Approach	B2
West Hoe Road	A4
Wharf Quay	E3
Whimple Street	D3
White Friars Lane	F2
Windsor Place	C3
Wolsdon Street	A1
Wyndham Lane	A1
Wyndham Mews	A1
Wyndham Square	A1
Wyndham Street East	A1
Zion Street	D4

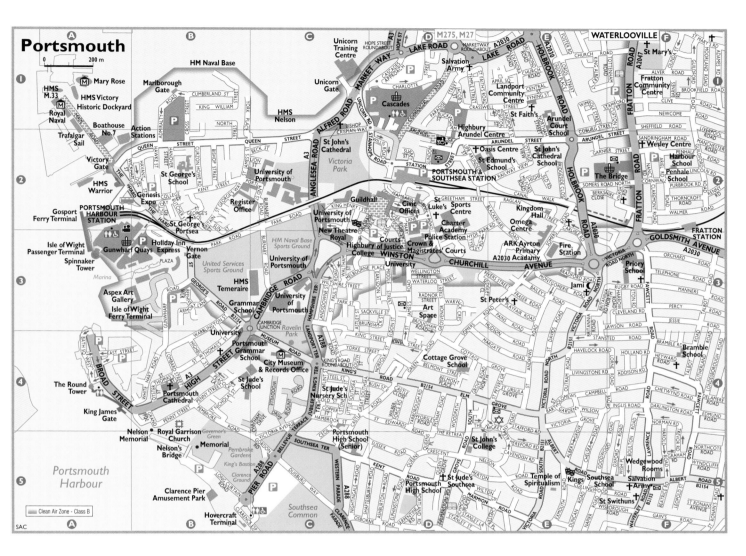

Portsmouth

Portsmouth is found on atlas page **14 H7**

Admiralty Road B2	Cavendish Road E5	Foster Road E1	Lake Road D1	Paradise Street D1	Stanhope Road D2
Albany Road E5	Central Street E1	Fratton Road F2	Landport Street E1	Park Road B3	Stansted Road E4
Albert Grove E5	Charlotte Street D1	Gain's Road F5	Landport Terrace C3	Pelham Road D4	Station Street D2
Albert Road E5	Chelsea Road E5	Garnier Street E2	Landsdowne Street C3	Pembroke Road B4	Steel Street C4
Alec Rose Lane D3	Chester Place E5	Goldsmith Avenue F3	Lawrence Road F5	Penhale Road F2	Stone Street C4
Alexandra Road E1	Chetwynd Road F4	Gold Street C4	Lawson Road F3	Penny Street B4	Sussex Road D5
Alfred Road C1	Churchill Avenue D3	Goodwood Road E5	Leopold Street F5	Percy Road F3	Sutherland Road F4
Alver Road F1	Church Road E1	Gordon Road C5	Lincoln Road F2	Pier Road C5	Talbot Road F4
Anglesea Road C2	Claremont Road F2	Great Southsea Street C4	Little Southsea Street C4	Playfair Road E3	Telephone Road F3
Ariel Road F2	Clarence Parade C5	Green Road D4	Livingstone Road E4	Portland Road D5	Temple Street D1
Armory Lane B3	Cleveland Road F3	Greetham Street D2	Lombard Street B4	Purbrook Road F2	The Hard A2
Arundel Street D2	Clive Road F1	Grosvenor Street D3	Londesborough Road F4	Queens Crescent D5	The Retreat D5
Arundel Street E2	Clock Street B2	Grove Road North D4	Lords Street E1	Queen Street B2	The Thicket D4
Ashburton Road D5	College Street B2	Grove Road South D5	Lorne Road F4	Raglan Street E2	Thorncroft Road F2
Bailey's Road E3	Collingwood Road E5	Guildford Road F1	Main Road A1	Railway View E2	Tottenham Road F1
Bath Square A4	Commercial Road D1	Guildhall Walk C2	Manners Road F3	Richmond Place D5	Trevor Road F4
Bellevue Terrace C5	Cornwall Road F2	Gunwharf Road B3	Margate Road D4	Rivers Street D3	Unicorn Road C1
Belmont Place D4	Cottage Grove D4	Hambrook Street C4	Market Way C1	Rugby Road F3	Upper Arundel Street D2
Bishop Crispian Way C2	Cottage View E2	Hampshire Terrace C3	Marmion Road D5	Sackville Street C3	Victoria Avenue C5
Bishop Street B2	Crasswell Street D1	Harold Road F5	Mary Rose Street D2	St Andrews Road E4	Victoria Grove E4
Blackfriars Road E2	Cross Street B2	Havant Street B2	Melbourne Place C3	St Bartholomews Gardens E4	Victoria Road North E4
Blount Road C4	Cumberland Street B1	Havelock Road E4	Merton Road D5	St Davids Road D4	Victoria Road North F3
Boulton Road F5	Curzon Howe Road B2	Hawke Street B2	Middle Street D3	St Edwards Road D4	Victoria Road South E5
Bramble Road F4	Darlington Road F4	Hereford Road E5	Milford Road E2	St Faith's Road D1	Vivash Road F2
Bridgeside Close E2	Drummond Road E1	Highbury Street B4	Montgomerie Road E3	St George's Road B3	Walmer Road F2
Britain Street B2	Duisburg Way C5	High Street B4	Moorland Road F1	St George's Square B2	Warblington Street B4
Broad Street A4	Duncan Road E5	Holbrook Road E1	Museum Road C4	St George's Way B2	Warwick Crescent D3
Brookfield Road F1	Earlsdon Street D3	Holland Road F4	Napier Road E5	St James's Road D3	Waterloo Street D3
Brunswick Street C3	East Street A4	Hudson Road E3	Nelson Road D5	St James's Street B2	Waverley Road F5
Buckingham Street D1	Eldon Street D4	Hyde Park Road D3	Newcome Road F1	St Nicholas Street B4	Western Parade C5
Cambridge Road C3	Elm Grove D4	Inglis Road F4	Nightingale Road C5	St Paul's Road C3	West Street A4
Campbell Road E4	Elphinstone Road D5	Jessie Road F3	Norfolk Street D4	St Peters Grove E4	White Hart Road B4
Canal Walk E2	Exmouth Road E5	Jubilee Terrace C4	Norman Road F4	St Thomas's Street B4	Wilson Grove E4
Carlisle Road E2	Fawcett Road F3	Kent Road D5	Olinda Street F1	Sandringham Road F2	Wiltshire Street C3
Cascades Approach D1	Fawcett Road F4	Kent Street B2	Orchard Road E4	Shaftesbury Road C5	Winston Churchill Avenue D3
Castle Road C4	Flint Street C4	King Albert Street E1	Osborne Road C5	Somers Road D4	Wisborough Road E5
		King Henry I Street C2	Outram Road E4	Somers Road E3	Woodpath D4
		King's Road C4	Oxford Road F5	Somers Road North E2	Woodville Drive C4
		King's Terrace C4	Oyster Street B4	Southsea Terrace C5	Yarborough Road D4
		King Street C4	Pains Road E3	Stafford Road E4	Yorke Street C4
		King William Street B1	Palmerston Road D5	Stamford Street E1	

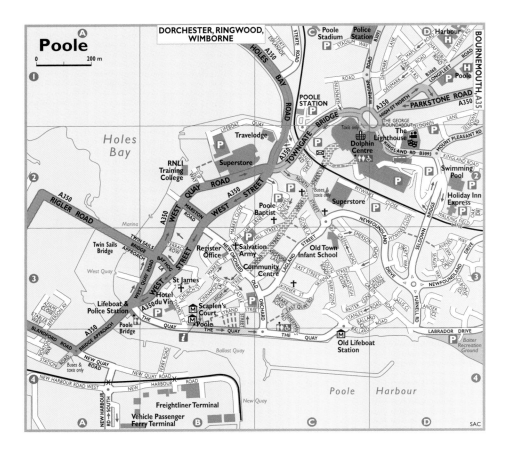

Poole

Poole is found on atlas page **12 H6**

Adams Close	A3	New Harbour Road West	A4
Avenel Way	D3	New Orchard	B3
Baiter Gardens	C3	New Quay Road	A4
Ballard Close	C3	New Street	B3
Ballard Road	C4	North Street	C2
Bay Hog Lane	B3	Norton Way	A4
Blandford Road	A3	Oak Drive	D2
Bridge Approach	A4	Old Orchard	B3
Castle Street	B3	Parkstone Road	D1
Chapel Lane	C2	Perry Gardens	C3
Church Street	B3	Pitwines Close	C2
Cinnamon Lane	B3	Poole Bridge	A3
Colborne Close	D3	Rigler Road	A2
Dear Hay Lane	B3	St Mary's Road	D1
Denmark Lane	D1	Seager Way	D3
Denmark Road	D1	Seldown Bridge	D3
Drake Road	C3	Seldown Lane	D2
Durrell Way	D3	Seldown Road	D2
East Quay Road	C3	Serpentine Road	C1
East Street	C3	Shaftesbury Road	D1
Elizabeth Road	D1	Skinner Street	C3
Emerson Road	C3	Slip Way	B2
Ferry Road	B4	South Road	C3
Fisherman's Road	C3	Stabler Way	A3
Furnell Road	D3	Stadium Way	C1
Globe Lane	C2	Stanley Road	C3
Green Close	D3	Sterte Esplanade	C1
Green Road	C3	Sterte Road	C1
High Street	B3	Strand Street	B3
High Street North	D1	Terrace Row	B3
Hill Street	C3	Thames Street	B3
Holes Bay Road	C1	The Quay	B3
Jefferson Avenue	A3	Towngate Bridge	C2
Kingland Road	D2	Twin Sails Bridge Approach	A3
Labrador Drive	D4	Twin Sails Bridge	A3
Lagland Street	C3	Vallis Close	D3
Lander Close	D3	Vanguard Road	C2
Liberty Way	D3	Walking Field Lane	D2
Lifeboat Quay	B2	Westons Lane	C3
Longfleet Road	D1	West Quay Road	B2
Maple Road	D1	West Street	B3
Market Close	B2	Whatleigh Close	C3
Market Street	B3	Wimborne Road	D1
Marston Road	B2		
Mount Pleasant Road	D2		
Newfoundland Drive	C2		
New Harbour Road	A4		
New Harbour Road South	A4		

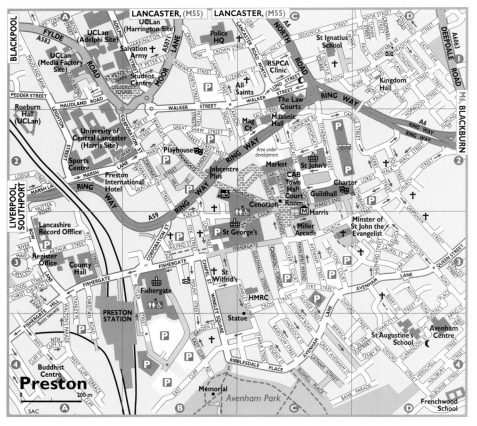

Preston

Preston is found on atlas page **88 G5**

Adelphi Street	A1	Holstein Street	D1
Arthur Street	A3	Hopwood Street	D2
Avenham Lane	C4	Jutland Street	D1
Avenham Road	C3	Lancaster Road	C2
Avenham Street	C3	Lancaster Road North	C1
Berwick Road	C4	Latham Street	C4
Birley Street	C2	Lawson Street	B1
Boltons Court	C3	Leighton Street	A2
Bow Lane	A3	Lund Street	C1
Butler Street	B3	Lune Street	B3
Cannon Street	C3	Main Sprit Weind	C3
Carlisle Street	C2	Manchester Road	D3
Chaddock Street	C4	Market Street	C2
Chapel Street	B3	Market Street West	B2
Charlotte Street	D4	Marsh Lane	A2
Cheapside	C3	Maudland Road	A1
Christ Church Street	A3	Meadow Street	C1
Church Street	C3	Moor Lane	B1
Clarendon Street	D4	Mount Street	B3
Corporation Street	B2	North Road	C1
Corporation Street	B3	Oak Street	D3
Craggs Row	B1	Ormskirk Road	C2
Cross Street	B1	Oxford Street	C3
Crown Street	B1	Pedder Street	A1
Deepdale Road	D1	Percy Street	D2
Derby Street	D2	Pitt Street	A3
Earl Street	C2	Pole Street	D2
East Cliff	B4	Pump Street	D1
East Street	D1	Queen Street	D3
Edmund Street	D2	Ribblesdale Place	B4
Edward Street	A2	Ring Way	B2
Elizabeth Street	B1	Rose Street	D3
Fishergate	B3	St Austin's Road	D3
Fishergate Hill	A4	St Paul's Road	D1
Fleet Street	B3	St Paul's Square	D1
Fox Street	B3	St Peter's Street	B1
Friargate	B2	Sedgwick Street	C1
Friargate	C2	Selborne Street	D4
Fylde Road	A1	Shepherd Street	D3
Glover's Court	C3	Snow Hill	B2
Glover Street	C3	Syke Street	D3
Great Avenham Street	C4	Tithebarn Street	C2
Great Shaw Street	B2	Walker Street	B1
Grimshaw Street	D2	Walton's Parade	A3
Guildhall Street	C3	Ward's End	C2
Harrington Street	B1	Warwick Street	B1
Heatley Street	B2	West Cliff	A4
Herschell Street	D4	Winkley Square	B3

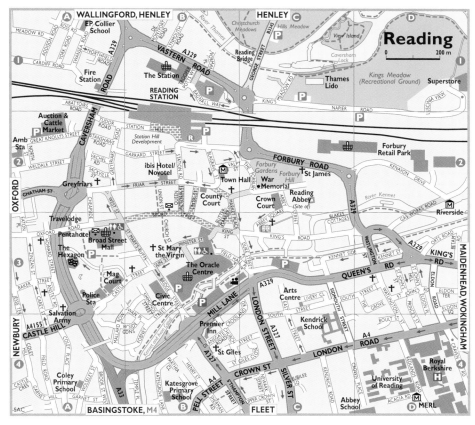

Reading

Reading is found on atlas page **35 K10**

Abbey Square	C3	King's Meadow Road	C1
Abbey Street	C2	King's Road	D3
Addison Road	A1	King Street	B3
Anstey Road	A3	Livery Close	C3
Baker Street	A3	London Road	C4
Blagrave Street	B2	London Street	C3
Blakes Cottages	C3	Mallard Row	A4
Boult Street	D4	Market Place	B2
Bridge Street	B3	Mill Lane	B4
Broad Street	B3	Minster Street	B3
Brook Street West	A4	Napier Road	C1
Buttermarket	B3	Newark Street	C4
Cardiff Road	A1	Northfield Road	A1
Carey Street	A3	Oxford Road	A3
Castle Hill	A4	Parthia Close	B4
Castle Street	A3	Pell Street	B4
Caversham Road	A2	Prince's Street	D3
Chatham Street	A2	Queen's Road	C3
Cheapside	A2	Queen Victoria Street	B2
Church Street	B3	Redlands Road	D4
Church Street	B4	Ross Road	A1
Coley Place	A4	Sackville Street	A2
Craven Road	D4	St Giles Close	B4
Crossland Road	B4	St John's Road	D3
Cross Street	B2	St Mary's Butts	B3
Crown Street	C4	Sidmouth Street	C3
Deansgate Road	B4	Silver Street	C4
Duke Street	C3	Simmonds Street	B3
East Street	C3	Southampton Street	B4
Eldon Road	D3	South Street	C3
Field Road	A4	Station Hill	B2
Fobney Street	B4	Station Road	B2
Forbury Road	C2	Swan Place	B3
Friar Street	B2	Swansea Road	A1
Garnet Street	A4	The Forbury	C2
Garrard Street	B2	Tudor Road	A2
Gas Works Road	D3	Union Street	B2
George Street	C1	Upper Crown Street	C4
Great Knollys Street	A2	Vachel Road	A2
Greyfriars Road	A2	Valpy Street	B2
Gun Street	B3	Vastern Road	B1
Henry Street	B4	Watlington Street	D3
Howard Street	A3	Weldale Street	A2
Katesgrove Lane	B4	West Street	A2
Kenavon Drive	D2	Wolseley Street	A4
Kendrick Road	C4	Yield Hall Place	B3
Kennet Side	C3	York Road	A1
Kennet Street	D3	Zinzan Street	A3

Royal Tunbridge Wells

Royal Tunbridge Wells is found on atlas page **25 N3**

Albert Street	C1	Lansdowne Road	C2
Arundel Road	C4	Lime Hill Road	B1
Bayhall Road	D2	Linden Park Road	A4
Belgrave Road	C1	Little Mount Sion	B4
Berkeley Road	B4	London Road	A2
Boyne Park	A1	Lonsdale Gardens	B2
Buckingham Road	C4	Madeira Park	B4
Calverley Park	C2	Major York's Road	A4
Calverley Park Gardens	D2	Meadow Road	B1
Calverley Road	C2	Molyneux Park Road	A1
Calverley Street	C2	Monson Road	C2
Cambridge Gardens	D4	Monson Way	B2
Cambridge Street	D3	Mount Edgcumbe Road	A3
Camden Hill	D3	Mount Ephraim	A2
Camden Park	D3	Mount Ephraim Road	B1
Camden Road	C1	Mountfield Gardens	C3
Carlton Road	D2	Mountfield Road	C3
Castle Road	A2	Mount Pleasant Avenue	B2
Castle Street	B3	Mount Pleasant Road	B2
Chapel Place	B4	Mount Sion	B4
Christchurch Avenue	B3	Nevill Street	B4
Church Road	A2	Newton Road	B1
Civic Way	B2	Norfolk Road	C4
Claremont Gardens	C4	North Street	D2
Claremont Road	C4	Oakfield Court Road	D3
Clarence Road	B2	Park Street	D3
Crescent Road	C2	Pembury Road	D2
Culverden Street	B1	Poona Road	C4
Dale Street	C1	Prince's Street	D3
Dudley Road	B1	Prospect Road	D3
Eden Road	B4	Rock Villa Road	B1
Eridge Road	A4	Royal Chase	A1
Farmcombe Lane	C4	St James' Road	D1
Farmcombe Road	C4	Sandrock Road	D1
Ferndale	D1	Somerville Gardens	A1
Frant Road	A4	South Green	B3
Frog Lane	B4	Station Approach	D1
Garden Road	C1	Stone Street	D1
Garden Street	C1	Sussex Mews	A4
George Street	D3	Sutherland Road	C3
Goods Station Road	B1	Tunnel Road	C1
Grecian Road	C4	Upper Grosvenor Road	B1
Grosvenor Road	B1	Vale Avenue	B3
Grove Hill Gardens	C3	Vale Road	B3
Grove Hill Road	C3	Victoria Road	C1
Guildford Road	C3	Warwick Park	B4
Hanover Road	B1	Wood Street	C1
High Street	B4	York Road	B2

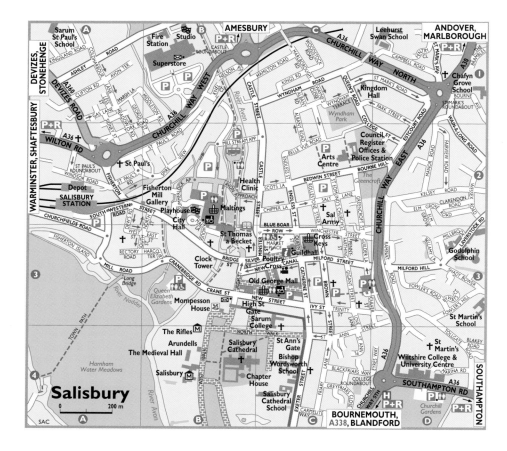

Salisbury

Salisbury is found on atlas page **21 M9**

Albany Road	C1	Kingsland Road	A1
Ashley Road	A1	Kings Road	C1
Avon Approach	B2	Laverstock Road	D3
Bedwin Street	C2	Malthouse Lane	B3
Belle Vue Road	C2	Manor Road	D2
Blackfriars Way	C4	Marlborough Road	C1
Blue Boar Row	C3	Meadow Road	A1
Bourne Avenue	D1	Middleton Road	A1
Bourne Hill	C2	Milford Hill	D3
Bridge Street	B3	Milford Street	C3
Brown Street	C3	Mill Road	A3
Campbell Road	D1	Minster Street	C3
Castle Street	B1	Nelson Road	B1
Catherine Street	C3	New Canal	B3
Chipper Lane	C2	New Street	B3
Churchfields Road	A2	North Street	B3
Churchill Way East	D3	Park Street	D1
Churchill Way North	C1	Pennyfarthing Street	C3
Churchill Way South	C4	Queen's Road	C1
Churchill Way West	B2	Queen Street	C3
Clarendon Road	D2	Rampart Road	D3
Clifton Road	A1	Rectory Road	A3
Coldharbour Lane	A1	Rollestone Street	C2
College Street	C1	St Ann Street	C4
Cranebridge Road	B3	St Edmund's Church Street	C2
Crane Street	B3	St Mark's Avenue	D1
Devizes Road	A1	St Mark's Road	D1
Dew's Road	A3	St Paul's Road	B2
East Street	B3	Salt Lane	C2
Elm Grove	D2	Scots Lane	C2
Elm Grove Road	D2	Sidney Street	A1
Endless Street	C2	Silver Street	B3
Estcourt Road	D2	Southampton Road	D4
Exeter Street	C4	South Street	A3
Eyres Way	D4	South Western Road	A2
Fairview Road	D2	Spire View	B2
Fisherton Street	A2	Summerlock Approach	B2
Fowler's Road	D3	Tollgate Road	D4
Friary Lane	C4	Trinity Street	C3
Gas Lane	A1	Wain-A-Long Road	D1
George Street	A1	Wessex Road	D2
Gigant Street	C3	West Street	A3
Greencroft Street	C2	Wilton Road	A2
Guilder Lane	C3	Winchester Street	C3
Hamilton Road	C1	Windsor Road	A2
High Street	B3	Woodstock Road	C1
Ivy Street	C3	Wyndham Road	C1
Kelsey Road	D2	York Road	A2

Sheffield

Sheffield is found on atlas page **84 E3**

Angel Street	C2	Hoyle Street	A1
Arundel Gate	C3	King Street	C2
Arundel Street	C4	Lambert Street	B1
Backfields	B3	Leopold Street	B3
Bailey Street	A2	Mappin Street	A3
Balm Green	B3	Meetinghouse Lane	C2
Bank Street	C2	Mulberry Street	C3
Barkers Pool	B3	Newcastle Street	A2
Broad Lane	A2	New Street	C3
Broad Street	D2	Norfolk Street	C3
Brown Street	C4	North Church Street	B2
Cambridge Street	B3	Orchard Street	B2
Campo Lane	B2	Paradise Street	B2
Carver Street	B3	Pinstone Street	B3
Castlegate	C1	Pond Hill	C3
Castle Street	C2	Pond Street	C3
Charles Street	B4	Portobello Street	A3
Charter Row	B4	Queen Street	B2
Church Street	B2	Rockingham Street	A2
Commercial Street	C2	St James Street	B2
Corporation Street	B1	Scargill Croft	C2
Cross Burgess Street	B3	Scotland Street	A1
Cutlers Gate	D1	Shalesmoor	B1
Derek Dooley Way	D1	Sheaf Street	D4
Devonshire Street	A3	Shoreham Street	C4
Division Street	A3	Shrewsbury Road	D4
Dixon Lane	C2	Silver Street	B2
Duke Street	D2	Smithfield	A1
Exchange Street	D2	Snig Hill	C2
Eyre Street	B4	Solly Street	A2
Fig Tree Lane	C2	South Street Park	D3
Fitzwilliam Street	A4	Suffolk Road	C4
Flat Street	C3	Surrey Street	C3
Furnace Hill	B1	Talbot Street	D4
Furnival Gate	B4	Tenter Street	B2
Furnival Road	D1	Townhead Street	B2
Furnival Street	C4	Trafalgar Street	A2
Garden Street	A2	Trippet Lane	B3
George Street	C2	Union Street	B3
Harmer Lane	C3	Vicar Lane	B2
Harts Head	C2	Victoria Station Road	D1
Hawley Street	B2	Waingate	C2
Haymarket	C2	Wellington Street	A4
High Street	C2	West Bar	B2
Holland Street	A3	West Bar Green	B2
Hollis Croft	A2	West Street	A3
Holly Street	B3	White Croft	A2
Howard Street	C4	York Street	C2

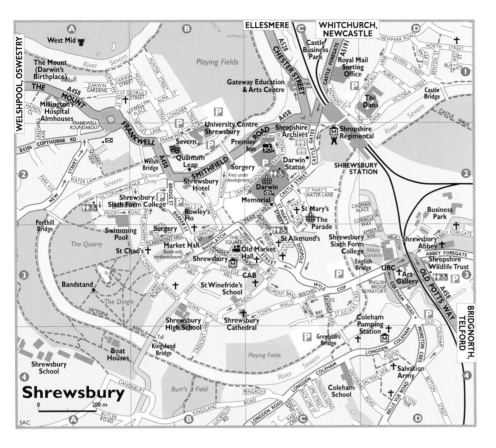

Shrewsbury

Shrewsbury is found on atlas page **56 H2**

Abbey Foregate	D3	Longner Street	B1
Albert Street	D1	Mardol	B2
Alma Street	B1	Market Street	B3
Amber Rise	D3	Milk Street	C3
Barker Street	B2	Moreton Crescent	D4
Beacall's Lane	D1	Mount Street	B1
Beeches Lane	C3	Murivance	B3
Belle Vue Gardens	C4	Nettles Lane	B1
Belle Vue Road	D4	Newpark Road	D1
Belmont	B3	New Street	A2
Belmont Bank	C3	North Street	D1
Benyon Street	D1	Old Coleham	D3
Betton Street	D4	Old Potts Way	D3
Bridge Street	B2	Park Avenue	A2
Burton Street	D1	Pengrove	C4
Butcher Row	C2	Pound Close	D4
Cadnam Place	C2	Pride Hill	C2
Canonbury	A4	Princess Street	B3
Castle Foregate	C1	Priory Road	A2
Castle Gates	C2	Quarry Place	B3
Castle Street	C2	Quarry View	A2
Chester Street	C1	Raven Meadows	B2
Claremont Bank	B3	Roushill	B2
Claremont Hill	B3	St Chad's Terrace	B3
Claremont Street	B3	St George's Street	A1
Coleham Head	D3	St Johns Hill	B3
College Hill	B3	St Julians Crescent	C3
Copthorne Road	A2	St Julians Friars	C3
Coracle Way	D2	St Mary's Place	C2
Crescent Lane	B4	St Mary's Street	C2
Cross Hill	B3	St Mary's Water Lane	C2
Darwin Gardens	A1	Salters Lane	D4
Darwin Street	A1	Severn Street	D1
Dogpole	C3	Shoplatch	B3
Drinkwater Street	A1	Smithfield Road	B2
Fish Street	C3	Swan Hill	B3
Frankwell	A2	The Dana	D1
Frankwell Quay	B2	The Mount	A1
Greenhill Avenue	A2	The Old Meadow	D3
Greyfriars Road	C4	The Square	B3
High Street	C3	Town Walls	B3
Hill's Lane	B2	Victoria Avenue	A2
Howard Street	C1	Victoria Street	D1
Hunter Street	B1	Water Lane	A2
Kingsland Road	B4	Water Street	D1
Lime Street	C4	West Street	D1
Longden Coleham	C4	Williams Way	C3
Longden Road	C4	Wyle Cop	C3

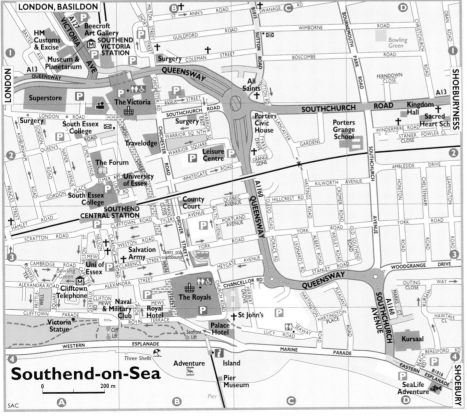

Southend-on-Sea

Southend-on-Sea is found on atlas page **38 E4**

Albert Road	C3	Lancaster Gardens	C2
Alexandra Road	A3	Leamington Road	D2
Alexandra Street	A3	London Road	A2
Ambleside Drive	D2	Lucy Road	C4
Ashburnham Road	A2	Luker Road	A2
Baltic Avenue	B3	Marine Parade	C4
Baxter Avenue	A1	Milton Street	B1
Beach Road	D4	Napier Avenue	A2
Boscombe Road	C1	Nelson Street	A3
Bournemouth Park Road	D1	Oban Road	D1
Cambridge Road	A3	Old Southend Road	D3
Capel Terrace	A3	Outing Close	D3
Chancellor Road	B3	Pitmans Close	B2
Cheltenham Road	D2	Pleasant Road	C3
Chichester Road	B1	Portland Avenue	B3
Christchurch Road	D1	Princes Street	A2
Church Road	B3	Prittlewell Square	A3
Clarence Road	A3	Quebec Avenue	B2
Clarence Street	B3	Queen's Road	A2
Clifftown Parade	A4	Queensway	A1
Clifftown Road	B3	Queensway	C3
Coleman Street	B1	Royal Terrace	B4
Cromer Road	C2	Runwell Terrace	A3
Devereux Road	A4	St Ann's Road	B1
Eastern Esplanade	D4	St Leonard's Road	C3
Elmer Approach	A2	Scratton Road	A3
Elmer Avenue	A2	Short Street	B1
Essex Street	B1	Southchurch Avenue	D2
Ferndown Close	D1	Southchurch Road	C2
Fowler Close	D2	Stanier Close	D2
Gordon Place	A2	Stanley Road	C3
Gordon Road	A2	Sutton Road	C1
Grange Gardens	C2	Swanage Road	C1
Grover Street	B3	Toledo Road	C2
Guildford Road	B1	Tylers Avenue	B3
Hamlet Road	A3	Tyrrel Drive	C2
Hartington Place	C4	Victoria Avenue	A1
Hartington Road	C3	Warrior Square East	B2
Hastings Road	C2	Warrior Square North	B2
Hawtree Close	D4	Warrior Square	B2
Herbert Grove	C4	Wesley Road	C3
Heygate Avenue	B3	Western Esplanade	A4
High Street	B2	Weston Road	B3
Hillcrest Road	C2	Whitegate Road	B2
Honiton Road	D2	Wimborne Road	C1
Horace Road	C3	Windermere Road	D2
Kilworth Avenue	C2	Woodgrange Drive	D3
Kursaal Way	D4	York Road	B3

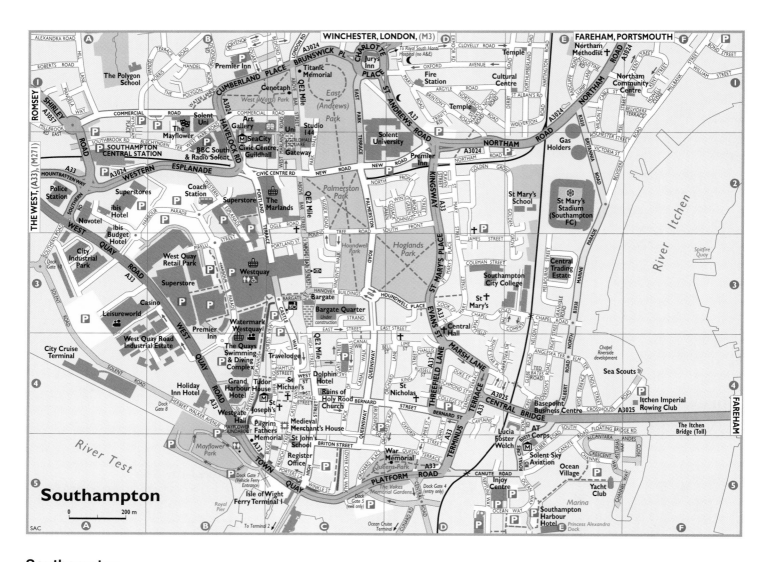

Southampton

Southampton is found on atlas page **14 D4**

Above Bar Street...................C1
Albert Road North.................E4
Albert Road South................E5
Alcantara Crescent...............E5
Alexandra Road.....................A1
Anderson's Road....................E4
Andes Close...........................F5
Anglesea Terrace...................E4
Argyle Road D1
Asturias Way..........................E5
Augustine Road......................E1
Back Of The Walls C4
Bargate Street........................C3
Bedford Place.........................C1
Bell Street D4
Belvidere Road.......................E2
Belvidere Terrace...................F1
Bernard Street........................C4
Blechynden Terrace...............B2
Bond Street.............................F1
Brinton's Road........................D1
Britannia Road E1
Briton Street...........................C5
Broad Green...........................D2
Brunswick Place.....................C1
Brunswick Square...................C4
Bugle Street C5
Cable Street...........................E1
Canal Walk.............................C4
Canute Road D5
Captains Place D4
Carpathia Drive D4
Castle Way..............................C3
Central Bridge........................D4
Central Road D5
Challis Court D4

Channel Way E5
Chapel Road D3
Charlotte Place C1
Civic Centre Road B2
Clovelly Road D1
Coleman Street D3
College Street.........................D4
Commercial Road...................A1
Cook Street D3
Cossack Green D2
Craven Street D2
Crosshouse Road E4
Cumberland Place..................B1
Cunard Road D5
Derby Road.............................E1
Devonshire Road....................B1
Duke Street.............................D4
Eastgate Street C4
East Park Terrace...................C1
East Street..............................C3
Elm Terrace............................E4
Endle Street............................E4
Evans Street...........................D3
Exmoor Road..........................D1
Floating Bridge Road E4
Forest View C4
French Street..........................C5
Glebe Road E4
Golden Grove D2
Granville Street E3
Grosvenor Square B1
Hamtun Street C4
Handel Road B1
Handel Terrace.......................B1
Hanover Buildings..................C3
Harbour Parade......................B2

Hartington Road E1
Havelock Road B1
Herbert Walker Avenue B4
High Street C4
Hill Lane.................................A1
Houndwell Place.....................D3
Howell Close...........................F1
Itchen Bridge..........................F4
James Street...........................D3
Johnson Street.......................D2
John Street D5
Kent Street..............................F1
King Street..............................D4
Kingsway.................................D2
Latimer Street........................D5
Lime Street.............................D4
London Road...........................C1
Lower Canal Walk..................C5
Lumpy Lane............................E1
Mandela Way..........................A1
Marine Parade........................E3
Marsh Lane.............................D4
Maryfield................................E5
Mayflower Roundabout..........B4
Melbourne Street....................E3
Millbank Street.......................F1
Millbrook Road East...............A1
Morris Road............................B1
Mountbatten Way A2
Nelson Street..........................E4
Neptune Way D5
New Road.................................C2
Nichols Road...........................D1
Northam Road.........................D2
Northbrook Road.....................D1
North Front C2

Northumberland Road E1
Ocean Way..............................D5
Ogle Road C2
Orchard Place.........................C5
Oxford Avenue D1
Oxford Street..........................D4
Paget Street............................E4
Palmerston Road....................C2
Park Walk C2
Peel Street..............................E1
Pirelli Street...........................B3
Platform Road.........................C5
Porters Lane...........................C5
Portland Street C3
Portland Terrace.....................B2
Pound Tree Road....................C3
Queens Terrace D5
Queensway..............................C3
Radcliffe Road........................E1
Richmond Street.....................D4
Roberts Road..........................A1
Rochester Street.....................E2
Royal Crescent Road..............E5
Russell Street.........................D4
Ryde Terrace E4
St Alban's Road......................E1
St Andrews Road D1
St Marks Road D1
St Mary's Place D3
St Mary's Road.......................D1
St Mary Street D2
St Michael Street....................C4
Shirley Road...........................A1
Solent Road A3
Southbrook Road....................A2
Southern Road.......................A2

South Front.............................C2
Strand C3
Sussex Road............................C2
Ted Bates Road E4
Terminus Terrace D5
The Compass D3
The Polygon............................B1
Threefield Lane D4
Town Quay B5
Trinity Road D1
Upper Bugle Street C4
Victoria Street E2
Vincent's Walk C3
Water Lane B1
Western Esplanade A2
Western Esplanade B4
West Marlands Road...............C2
West Park Road B2
West Quay Road A2
West Street C4
White Star Place D4
William Street F1
Wilson Street E1
Winkle Street C5
Winton Street D2
Wolverton Road.......................E1
Wyndham Place A1

Stirling

Stirling is found on atlas page **133 M9**

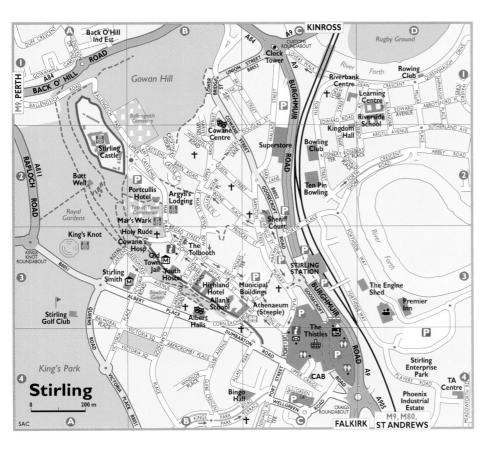

Abbey Road D2	James Street C2
Abbotsford Place D1	Kings Knot Roundabout A3
Abercromby Place B4	Kings Park Road B4
Academy Road B3	King Street C3
Albert Place A3	Lovers Walk C1
Alexandra Place D1	Lower Bridge Street B1
Allan Park B4	Lower Castlehill B2
Argyll Avenue D2	Mar Place B2
Back O' Hill Road A1	Maxwell Place C3
Baker Street B3	Meadowforth Road D4
Ballengeich Road A1	Millar Place D1
Ballengeich Pass A1	Morris Terrace B3
Balmoral Place A3	Murray Place C3
Bank Street B3	Ninians Road C4
Barn Road B2	Park Lane C2
Barnton Street C2	Park Terrace B4
Bayne Street B1	Players Road D4
Bow Street B3	Port Street C4
Broad Street B3	Princes Street B3
Bruce Street B1	Queenshaugh Drive D1
Burghmuir Road C1	Queens Road A3
Castle Court B2	Queen Street B2
Clarendon Place B4	Raploch Road A2
Clarendon Road B3	Ronald Place C2
Corn Exchange Road B3	Rosebery Place C2
Cowane Street B1	Rosebery Terrace C2
Craigs Roundabout C4	Royal Gardens A3
Crofthead Court B2	St John Street B3
Customs Roundabout C1	St Mary's Wynd B2
Dean Crescent D1	Shiphaugh Place D1
Douglas Street C2	Shore Road C2
Dumbarton Road B4	Spittal Street B3
Edward Avenue D1	Sutherland Avenue D2
Edward Road C1	Tannery Lane B2
Forrest Road D2	Union Street B1
Forth Crescent C2	Upper Bridge Street B2
Forthside Way C3	Upper Castlehill A2
Forth Street C1	Upper Craigs C4
Forth Place C3	Victoria Place A4
Forth View C1	Victoria Road B3
Glebe Avenue B4	Victoria Square A4
Glebe Crescent B4	Viewfield Street C2
Glendevon Drive A1	Wallace Street C2
Goosecroft Road C2	Waverley Crescent D1
Gowanhill Gardens A1	Wellgreen Lane C4
Greenwood Avenue A3	Wellgreen Road C4
Harvey Wynd B1	Whinwell Road B2
Irvine Place B2	Windsor Place B4

Stockton-on-Tees

Stockton-on-Tees is found on atlas page **104 D7**

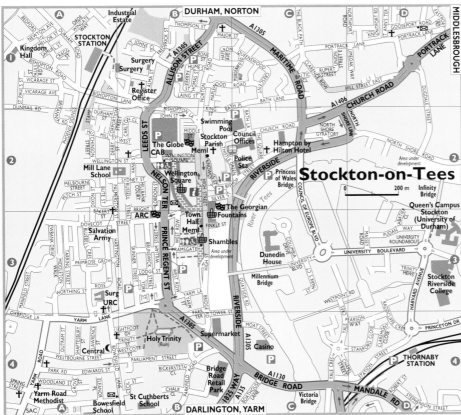

1825 Way B4	Massey Road D3
Allison Street B1	Melbourne Street A2
Alma Street B1	Middle Street B2
Bath Lane C1	Mill Street West A2
Bedford Street A1	Nelson Terrace B2
Bishop Street B2	North Shore Road D2
Bishopton Lane A1	Northport Road D1
Bishopton Road A1	North Shore Link.................. C2
Bowesfield Lane A4	Norton Road B1
Bridge Road B3	Palmerston Street A2
Bridge Road C4	Park Road A4
Bright Street B2	Park Terrace C3
Britannia Road A1	Parkfield Road B4
Brunswick Street B3	Parliament Street B4
Bute Street A2	Portrack Lane D1
Church Road D1	Prince Regent Street B3
Clarence Row C1	Princeton Drive D4
Corporation Street A2	Quayside Road C3
Council of Europe	Queenswood Crescent C1
Boulevard C2	Raddcliffe Crescent D3
Dixon Street A2	Ramsgate B3
Dovecot Street A3	Riverside C3
Dugdale Street D1	Russell Street B2
Durham Road A1	St Paul's Street A1
Durham Street A2	Silver Street B2
Edwards Street A4	Skinner Street B3
Farrer Street B1	Station Street D4
Finkle Street B3	Sydney Street B2
Frederick Street B1	The Square D2
Fudan Way D3	Thistle Green C2
Gooseport Road D1	Thomas Street B1
Hartington Road A3	Thompson Street B1
Harvard Avenue D3	Tower Street B4
High Street B2	Union Street East C1
Hill Street East D1	University Boulevard C3
Hume Street B1	Vane Street B2
Hutchinson Street A2	Vicarage Street A1
John Street B2	Wellington Street A2
King Street B2	West Row B3
Knightport Road D1	Westbourne Street A4
Knowles Street C2	Westpoint Road C3
Laing Street B1	William Street B3
Leeds Street B2	Woodland Street A4
Lobdon Street B2	Worthing Street A3
Lodge Street B3	Yale Crescent C4
Mandale Road D4	Yarm Lane A4
Maritime Road C1	Yarm Road A4
Maplewood Road B1	Yarm Street B3

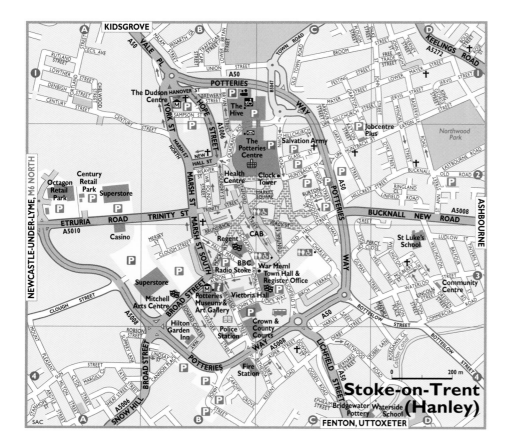

Stoke-on-Trent (Hanley)

Stoke-on-Trent (Hanley) is found on atlas page **70 F5**

Albion Street	B3	Linfield Road	D2
Bagnall Street	B3	Lower Mayer Street	D1
Balfour Street	D3	Lowther Street	A1
Baskerville Road	D1	Ludlow Street	D3
Bathesda Street	B4	Malam Street	B1
Bernard Street	C4	Marsh Street	B2
Bethesda Street	B3	Marsh Street North	B2
Birch Terrace	C3	Marsh Street South	B3
Botteslow Street	C3	Mayer Street	C1
Broad Street	B4	Mersey Street	B3
Broom Street	C1	Milton Street	A4
Brunswick Street	B3	Mount Pleasant	A4
Bryan Street	B1	Mynors Street	D1
Bucknall New Road	C2	New Hall Street	B2
Bucknall Old Road	D2	Ogden Road	C4
Cardiff Grove	B4	Old Hall Street	C3
Century Street	A1	Old Town Road	C1
Charles Street	C3	Pall Mall	B3
Cheapside	B3	Percy Street	C2
Chelwood Street	A1	Piccadilly	B3
Clough Street	A3	Portland Street	A1
Clyde Street	A4	Potteries Way	B1
Commercial Road	D3	Potteries Way	B4
Denbigh Street	A1	Quadrant Road	B2
Derby Street	C4	Regent Road	C4
Dyke Street	D2	Rutland Street	A1
Eastwood Road	C4	St John Street	D1
Eaton Street	D2	St Luke Street	D3
Etruria Road	A2	Sampson Street	B1
Foundry Street	B2	Sheaf Street	A4
Garth Street	C2	Slippery Lane	A4
Gilman Street	C3	Snow Hill	A4
Goodson Street	C2	Stafford Street	B2
Grafton Street	C1	Sun Street	A4
Hanover Street	B1	Tontine Street	C3
Harley Street	C4	Town Road	C2
Hillchurch	C2	Trafalgar Street	B1
Hillcrest Street	C2	Trinity Street	B2
Hinde Street	B4	Union Street	B1
Hope Street	B1	Upper Hillchurch Street	C2
Hordley Street	C3	Upper Huntbach Street	C2
Huntbach Street	C2	Warner Street	B3
Jasper Street	A4	Waterloo Street	D3
Jervis Street	D1	Well Street	D3
John Street	B3	Wellington Road	D3
Keelings Road	D1	Wellington Street	D3
Lichfield Street	C3	Yates Street	A4
Lidice Way	C3	York Street	B1

Stratford-upon-Avon

Stratford-upon-Avon is found on atlas page **47 P3**

Albany Road	A3	Narrow Lane	B4
Alcester Road	A2	New Broad Street	B4
Arden Street	B2	New Street	B4
Avenue Road	C1	Old Red Lion Court	C2
Bancroft Place	C2	Old Town	C4
Bell Court	B2	Orchard Way	A4
Birmingham Road	B1	Payton Street	C2
Brewery Street	B1	Percy Street	C1
Bridge Foot	D2	Rother Street	B3
Bridge Street	C2	Rowley Crescent	D1
Bridgeway	D2	Ryland Street	B4
Broad Street	B4	St Andrew's Crescent	A3
Brookvale Road	A4	St Gregory's Road	C1
Brunel Way	A2	St Martin's Close	A3
Bull Street	B4	Sanctus Drive	B4
Cedar Close	D1	Sanctus Road	A4
Chapel Lane	C3	Sanctus Street	B4
Chapel Street	C3	Sandfield Road	A4
Cherry Orchard	A4	Scholars Lane	B3
Cherry Street	B4	Seven Meadows Road	A4
Chestnut Walk	B3	Shakespeare Street	B1
Church Street	B3	Sheep Street	C3
Clopton Bridge	D3	Shipston Road	D4
Clopton Road	C1	Shottery Road	A3
College Lane	B4	Shrieves Walk	C3
College Mews	B4	Southern Lane	C3
College Street	B4	Swan's Nest	D3
Ely Gardens	B3	The Willows	A3
Ely Street	B3	Tiddington Road	D3
Evesham Place	B3	Tramway Bridge	D3
Evesham Road	A4	Tyler Street	C2
Garrick Way	A4	Union Street	C2
Great William Street	C1	Warwick Court	C1
Greenhill Street	B2	Warwick Crescent	D1
Grove Road	B3	Warwick Road	C2
Guild Street	C2	Waterside	D3
Henley Street	C2	Welcombe Road	D1
High Street	C3	Wellesbourne Grove	A3
Holtom Street	B4	Western Road	B1
John Street	C2	West Street	B4
Kendall Avenue	B1	Willows Drive North	A2
Lock Close	C2	Windsor Street	B2
Maidenhead Road	C1	Wood Street	B2
Mansell Street	B2		
Mayfield Avenue	C1		
Meer Street	B2		
Mill Lane	C4		
Mulberry Street	C1		

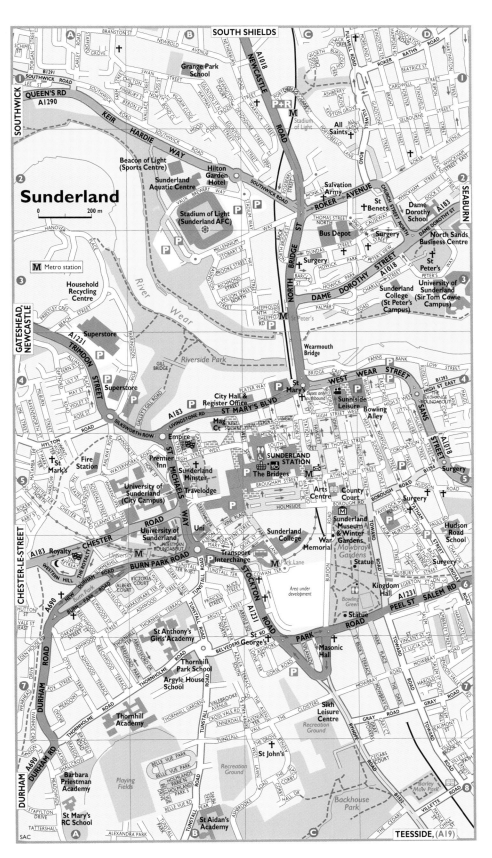

Sunderland

Sunderland is found on atlas page **113 N9**

Abbotsford Green	B7	Milburn Street	A4
Abbs Street	C2	Millennium Way	B3
Albion Place	B6	Monk Street	C2
Alice Street	B6	Moreland Street	D1
Alliance Place	A4	Morgan Street	A1
Amberley Street	D6	Mowbray Road	D7
Argyle Square	B6	Netherburn Road	B1
Argyle Street	B6	Newbold Avenue	B1
Ashbrooke Road	B8	Newcastle Road	C1
Ashmore Street	C7	New Durham Road	A6
Ashwood Street	A7	Nile Street	D4
Ashwood Terrace	A7	Norfolk Street	D5
Association Road	D1	North Bridge Street	C3
Athenaeum Street	C5	Northcote Avenue	D6
Azalea Terrace North	B6	North Street	B1
Azalea Terrace South	B7	Oakwood Street	A6
Back North Bridge Street	C3	Olive Street	B6
Beach Street	A3	Otto Terrace	A7
Bedford Street	C4	Palmer's Hill Road	C3
Beechwood Street	A6	Panns Bank	D4
Beechwood Terrace	A7	Park Lane	C5
Belvedere Road	B7	Park Place	D6
Beresford Park	A7	Park Road	C6
Birchfield Road	A7	Pauls Road	D5
Borough Road	D5	Peel Street	D6
Bridge Crescent	C4	Portobello Lane	C1
Bridge Street	C4	Queen's Road	A1
Briery Vale Road	C7	Railway Row	A5
Bright Street	D1	Ravensworth Street	A4
Brooke Street	B3	Richmond Street	B3
Brougham Street	C5	Ripon Street	D1
Burdon Road	C5	Roker Avenue	C2
Burn Park Road	B6	Roker Baths Road	D1
Cardwell Street	D1	Rosedale Street	A5
Carley Road	A1	Ross Street	B1
Charles Street	D3	Russell Street	D4
Chester Road	A6	Ryhope Road	C7
Churchill Street	D6	St Bede's Terrace	D7
Church Street North	D2	St Mary's Boulevard	B4
Clanny Street	A5	St Michaels Way	B5
Cork Street	D4	St Peter's View	D3
Coronation Street	D5	St Thomas' Street	C5
Cowan Terrace	C6	St Vincent Street	D7
Cross Vale Road	B7	Salem Road	D6
Crozier Street	B1	Salem Street	D6
Dame Dorothy Street	C3	Salem Street South	D7
Deptford Road	A4	Salisbury Street	D6
Derby Street	B6	Sans Street	D4
Derwent Street	B6	Selbourne Street	D1
Devonshire Street	B1	Shakespeare Terrace	A6
Dock Street	D2	Shallcross	A8
Dundas Street	C3	Sheepfolds Road	C3
Durham Road	A7	Silksworth Row	A4
Easington Street	B3	South Street	C5
East Cross Street	D4	Southwick Road	A1
Eden House Road	A7	Southwick Road	C2
Egerton Street	D6	Stadium Way	C2
Eglinton Street	B1	Stansfield Street	D1
Eglinton Street North	B1	Station Street	C4
Elmwood Street	A6	Stobart Street	B3
Ennerdale	B7	Stockton Road	C6
Farm Street	A1	Swan Street	B1
Farringdon Row	B4	Tatham Street	D5
Fawcett Street	C4	Tatham Street Back	D5
Forster Street	D1	The Avenue	C7
Fox Street	A7	The Cloisters	C7
Foyle Street	D5	The Royalty	A6
Frederick Street	D5	Thomas Street North	C2
Fulwell Road	C1	Thornhill Terrace	B6
Galley's Gill Road	B4	Thornholme Road	A7
Gladstone Street	D1	Toward Road	D5
Gorse Road	C7	Trimdon Street	A4
Gray Road	D7	Tunstall Road	B7
Green Terrace	B5	Tunstall Terrace	B6
Hampden Road	D1	Tunstall Terrace West	B6
Hanover Place	A2	Tunstall Vale	B8
Harlow Road	A5	Union Street	C4
Harrogate Street	D6	Valebrooke Avenue	B7
Hartington Street	D1	Villette Road	D8
Havelock Terrace	A6	Villiers Street	D4
Hay Street	C3	Vine Place	B5
Hendon Valley Road	D7	Wallace Street	B1
High Street East	D4	Warwick Street	C1
High Street West	B5	Waterloo Place	C5
Holmeside	C5	Waterworks Road	A5
Hope Street	B5	Wayman Street	B1
Howick Park	C3	Wearhead Drive	A7
Hudson Road	D5	Westbourne Road	A5
Hylton Road	A5	Western Hill	A6
Johnson Street	A5	West Lawn	C8
John Street	C4	West Street	C5
Keir Hardie Way	A1	West Sunniside	D4
Laura Street	D5	West Wear Street	C4
Lindsay Road	D6	Wharncliffe Street	A5
Little Villiers Street	D4	Whickham Street	D2
Livingstone Road	B4	Whickham Street East	D2
Low Street	D4	Whitburn Street	D3
Mary Street	B6	William Street	D4
Mauds Lane	D4	Wilson Street North	B3
Meadowside	A8	York Street	C4
Middle Street	C5	Zetland Street	D2

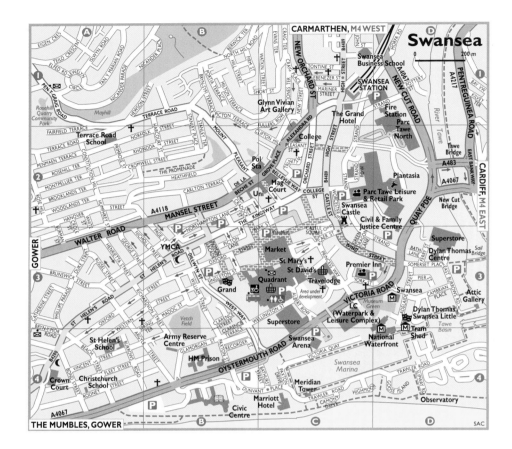

Swansea

Swansea is found on atlas page **29 J6**

Adelaide Street	D3	Mount Pleasant	B2
Alexandra Road	C2	New Cut Road	D1
Argyle Street	A4	New Orchard Street	C1
Bath Lane	D3	New Street	C1
Beach Street	A4	Nicander Parade	A1
Bellevue Way	C2	Nicholl Street	A3
Bond Street	A4	Norfolk Street	A2
Brunswick Street	A3	North Hill Road	B1
Burrows Road	A4	Northampton Lane	B2
Caer Street	C3	Orchard Street	C2
Carlton Terrace	B2	Oxford Street	A3
Castle Street	C2	Oystermouth Road	B4
Catherine Street	A3	Page Street	B3
Clarence Street	B3	Park Street	B3
Clifton Hill	C2	Paxton Street	B4
College Street	C2	Pentreguinea Road	D1
Constituion Hill	A2	Pen-Y-Graig Road	A1
Cradock Street	B2	Picton Lane	B3
Craig Place	C1	Pier Street	D3
Cromwell Street	A2	Primrose Street	A2
De La Beche Street	B2	Princess Way	C3
Dillwyn Street	B3	Quay Parade	D2
Duke Street	A3	Recorder Street	B4
Dunvant Place	B4	Rhondda Street	A2
East Bank Way	D2	Richardson Street	A3
East Burrows Road	D3	Rodney Street	A4
Ebenezer Street	C1	Russel Street	A3
Elfed Road	A1	St Helen's Road	A3
Ferry Street	D3	Short Street	B1
Firm Street	B1	Singleton Street	B3
Fleet Street	A4	Somerset Place	D3
George Street	A3	Strand	C1
Glamorgan Street	B4	Tan Y Marian Road	A1
Green Dragon Lane	C3	Terrace Road	A2
Grove Place	C2	The Kingsway	B2
Hanover Street	A2	Tontine Street	C1
Harcourt Street	B2	Trawler Road	C4
Heathfield	B2	Victoria Quay	C4
Henrietta Street	A3	Victoria Road	C3
Hewson Street	A1	Vincent Street	A4
High Street	C2	Walter Road	A3
Hill Street	B1	Watkin Street	C1
Humphrey Street	A2	Wellington Street	C3
Islwyn Road	A1	West Way	B3
Llewelyn Circle	A1	Western Street	A4
Madoc Street	B3	William Street	B3
Mansel Street	B2	Wind Street	C3
Mariner Street	C1	York Street	C3

Swindon

Swindon is found on atlas page **33 M8**

Albion Street	A4	Islington Street	C3
Alfred Street	C2	John Street	B3
Ashford Road	B4	King Street	B3
Aylesbury Street	B2	London Street	A3
Bathurst Road	C2	Manchester Road	C2
Beckhampton Street	C3	Market Street	B3
Bridge Street	B2	Maxwell Street	A3
Bristol Street	A3	Medgbury Road	C2
Broad Street	C2	Milford Street	B2
Cambria Bridge Road	A4	Milton Road	B3
Canal Walk	B3	Morley Street	B3
Carr Street	B3	Morse Street	B4
Chester Street	A3	Newcastle Street	D3
Church Place	A3	Newcombe Drive	A1
Cirencester Way	D1	Newhall Street	B4
Clarence Street	C3	Northampton Street	D3
College Street	B3	North Star Avenue	B1
Commercial Road	B3	Ocotal Way	D1
Corporation Street	C2	Park Lane	A3
County Road	D2	Plymouth Street	D3
Crombey Street	B4	Polaris Way	B1
Curtis Street	A4	Ponting Street	C2
Deacon Street	B4	Portsmouth Street	D3
Dixon Street	B4	Princes Street	C3
Dover Street	C4	Prospect Hill	C4
Dowling Street	B4	Queen Street	B3
Drove Road	D4	Radnor Street	A4
Dryden Street	A3	Regent Place	C3
Eastcott Hill	C4	Regent Street	B3
East Street	B2	Rosebery Street	C2
Edgeware Road	B3	Salisbury Street	C2
Elmina Road	C1	Sanford Street	B3
Emlyn Square	A3	Sheppard Street	B2
Euclid Street	C3	Southampton Street	D3
Faringdon Road	A3	Stafford Street	B4
Farnsby Street	B3	Stanier Street	B4
Fire Fly Avenue	A2	Station Road	B2
Fleet Street	B2	Swindon Road	C4
Fleming Way	C3	Tennyson Street	A3
Gladstone Street	C2	Theobald Street	B3
Gooch Street	C2	Victoria Road	C4
Graham Street	C2	Villett Street	B3
Great Western Way	A1	Westcott Place	A4
Groundwell Road	C3	Western Street	C4
Havelock Street	B3	Whitehead Street	B4
Hawksworth Way	A1	Whitney Street	B4
Haydon Street	C2	William Street	A4
Holbrook Way	B2	York Road	D3

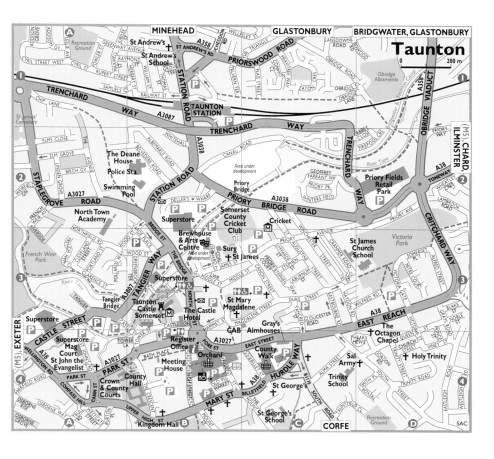

Taunton

Taunton is found on atlas page **18 H10**

Abbey Close	D2	Middle Street	B3
Albemarle Road	B2	Northfield Road	A3
Alfred Street	D3	North Street	B3
Alma Street	C4	Obridge Road	C1
Belvedere Road	B2	Obridge Viaduct	D2
Billetfield	C4	Old Pig Market	B4
Billet Street	C4	Parkfield Road	A4
Bridge Street	B2	Park Street	A4
Canal Road	B2	Paul Street	B4
Cann Street	A4	Plais Street	C1
Canon Street	C3	Portland Street	A3
Castle Street	A4	Priorswood Road	B1
Cheddon Road	B1	Priory Avenue	C3
Chip Lane	A1	Priory Bridge Road	B2
Church Street	D4	Queen Street	D4
Clarence Street	A3	Railway Street	B1
Cleveland Street	A3	Raymond Street	A1
Compass Hill	A4	Rupert Street	A1
Cranmer Road	C3	St Andrew's Road	B1
Critchard Way	D2	St Augustine Street	C3
Cyril Street	A1	St James Street	B3
Deller's Wharf	B2	St John's Road	A4
Duke Street	C3	Samuels Court	A1
Eastbourne Road	C3	South Road	C4
Eastleigh Road	D4	South Street	D4
East Reach	D3	Staplegrove Road	A2
East Street	C4	Station Road	B2
Fore Street	B4	Stephen Street	C3
Fowler Street	A1	Stephen Way	C3
French Weir Avenue	A2	Tancred Street	C3
Gloucester Road	C3	The Avenue	A2
Grays Road	D3	The Bridge	B3
Greenway Avenue	A1	The Crescent	B4
Gyffarde Street	C3	The Triangle	C1
Hammet Street	B4	Thomas Street	B1
Haydon Road	C3	Toneway	D2
Herbert Street	B1	Tower Street	B4
High Street	B4	Trenchard Way	B1
Hugo Street	C3	Trinity Street	D4
Hurdle Way	C4	Upper High Street	B4
Laburnum Street	C3	Victoria Gate	D3
Lansdowne Road	C1	Victoria Street	D3
Leslie Avenue	A1	Viney Street	D4
Linden Grove	A2	Wellington Road	A4
Lower Middle Street	B3	Wilfred Road	C3
Magdalene Street	B3	William Street	B1
Mary Street	B4	Winchester Street	C2
Maxwell Street	A1	Wood Street	B3

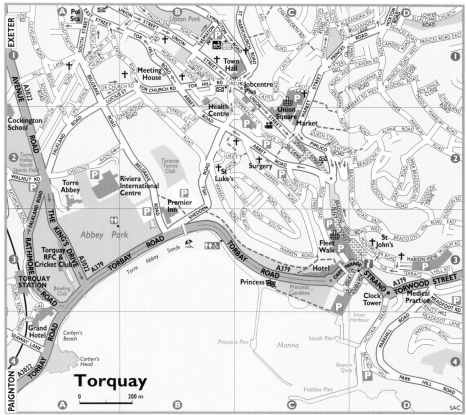

Torquay

Torquay is found on atlas page **7 N6**

Abbey Road	B1	Middle Warbury Road	D1
Alexandra Road	C1	Mill Lane	A1
Alpine Road	C2	Montpellier Road	D3
Ash Hill Road	C1	Morgan Avenue	B1
Avenue Road	A1	Palm Road	B1
Bampfylde Road	A2	Parkhill Road	D4
Beacon Hill	D4	Pembroke Road	C1
Belgrave Road	A1	Pennsylvania Road	D1
Braddons Hill Road East	D3	Pimlico	C2
Braddons Hill Road West	C2	Potters Hill	C1
Braddons Street	D2	Princes Road	C1
Bridge Road	A1	Queen Street	C2
Camden Road	D1	Rathmore Road	A2
Cary Parade	C3	Rock Road	C2
Cary Road	C3	Rosehill Road	D1
Castle Lane	C1	St Efride's Road	A1
Castle Road	C1	St Luke's Road	B2
Cavern Road	D1	St Marychurch Road	C1
Chestnut Avenue	A2	Scarborough Road	B2
Church Lane	A1	Seaway Lane	A4
Church Street	A1	Shedden Hill Road	B3
Cleveland Road	A1	Solbro Road	A3
Croft Hill	B2	South Hill Road	D3
Croft Road	B2	South Street	A1
East Street	A1	Stentiford Hill Road	C2
Ellacombe Road	C1	Strand	D3
Falkland Road	A2	Sutherland Road	D1
Fleet Street	C2	Temperance Street	C2
Grafton Road	D2	The King's Drive	A3
Hennapyn Road	A4	The Terrace	D3
Higher Union Lane	B1	Torbay Road	A4
Hillesdon Road	D2	Tor Church Road	A1
Hoxton Road	D1	Tor Hill Road	B1
Hunsdon Road	D3	Torwood Street	D3
Laburnum Street	A1	Trematon Ave	B1
Lime Avenue	A2	Trinity Hill	D3
Lower Ellacombe		Union Street	B1
Church Road	D1	Upper Braddons Hill	D2
Lower Union Lane	C2	Vanehill Road	D4
Lower Warbury Road	D2	Vansittart Road	A1
Lucius Street	A1	Vaughan Parade	C3
Lymington Road	B1	Victoria Parade	D4
Magdalene Road	B1	Victoria Road	C1
Market Street	C2	Vine Road	A1
Marion View	D3	Walnut Road	A2
Meadfoot Lane	D4	Warberry Road West	C1
Melville Lane	C2	Warren Road	B2
Melville Street	C2	Wellington Road	C1

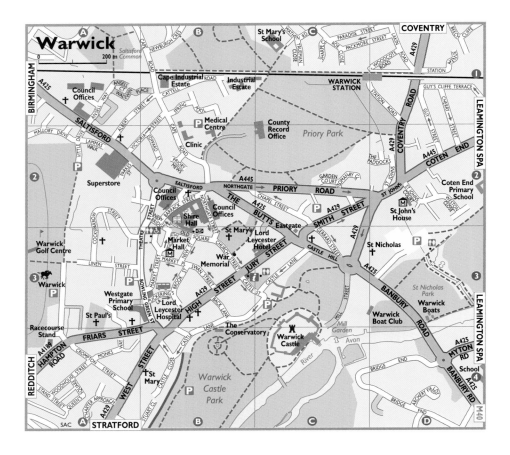

Warwick

Warwick is found on atlas page **59 L11**

Albert Street	A2	Old Square	B3
Ansell Court	A1	Packmore Street	C1
Ansell Way	A1	Paradise Street	C1
Archery Fields	D4	Parkes Street	A2
Back Lane	B3	Priory Mews	B2
Banbury Road	D3	Priory Road	C2
Barrack Street	B2	Puckering's Lane	B3
Beech Cliffe	D1	Queen's Square	A4
Bowling Green Street	B3	Roe Close	C1
Bridge End	D4	St Johns	D2
Brook Street	B3	St Johns Court	D2
Cape Road	B1	Saltisford	A1
Castle Close	B4	Sharpe Close	C1
Castle Hill	C3	Smith Street	C2
Castle Lane	B4	Spring Pool	B1
Castle Street	B3	Stand Street	A4
Cattell Road	B1	Station Avenue	D1
Chapel Street	C2	Station Road	D1
Charter Approach	A4	Stuart Close	B4
Cherry Street	D1	Swan Street	B3
Church Street	B3	Theatre Street	B3
Cocksparrow Street	A3	The Butts	B2
Coten End	D2	The Paddocks	D2
Coventry Road	D2	Trueman Close	C1
Crompton Street	A4	Victoria Street	A2
Edward Street	B2	Vittle Drive	A2
Friars Street	A4	Wallwin Place	A1
Garden Court	C2	Wathen Road	C1
Gerrard Street	C3	Weston Close	D2
Guy's Cliffe Terrace	D1	West Street	A4
Guy Street	D1	Woodcote Road	D1
Hampton Road	A4	Woodhouse Street	A4
High Street	B3	Yeomanry Close	C2
Jury Street	B3		
Lakin Road	D1		
Lammas Walk	A2		
Linen Street	A3		
Mallory Drive	A2		
Market Place	B3		
Market Street	B3		
Mill Street	C3		
Monks Way	A4		
Myton Road	D4		
New Bridge	B2		
Newburgh Crescent	B1		
New Street	B3		
Northgate	B2		
Northgate Street	B2		

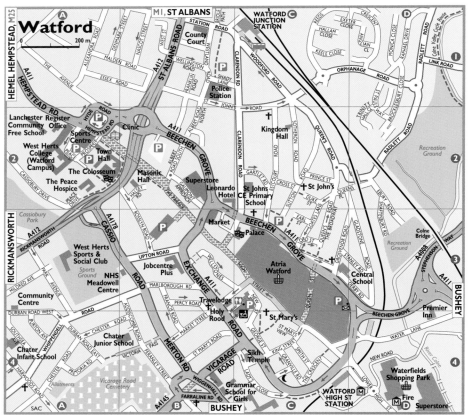

Watford

Watford is found on atlas page **50 D11**

Addiscombe Road	B3	Merton Road	B4
Albert Road North	B2	Mildred Avenue	A3
Albert Road South	B2	Monica Close	D1
Alexandra Road	A1	Nascot Street	B1
Anglian Close	D1	New Road	D4
Beechen Grove	C3	New Street	C3
Brocklesbury Close	D2	Orphanage Road	C1
Burton Avenue	A4	Park Avenue	A3
Cassiobury Drive	A2	Peace Drive	A2
Cassio Road	A3	Peace Prospect	A2
Chester Road	A4	Percy Road	B3
Clarendon Road	C1	Pretoria Road	A4
Cross Street	C2	Prince Street	C2
Denmark Street	A1	Queen's Road	C2
Derby Road	C3	Queen Street	C3
Duke Street	C2	Radlett Road	D2
Durban Road East	A4	Raphael Drive	D1
Durban Road West	A4	Reeds Crescent	C1
Earl Street	C3	Rickmansworth Road	A3
Ebury Road	D2	Rosslyn Road	B3
Essex Road	A1	St Albans Road	B1
Estcourt Road	C2	St John's Road	B1
Exchange Road	B3	St Mary's Road	B4
Farraline Road	B4	St Pauls Way	D1
Feranley Street	B4	Shady Lane	B1
Francis Road	B3	Shaftesbury Road	D2
Franklin Road	B1	Smith Street	C4
Gartlet Road	C2	Sotheron Road	C2
Gaumont Approach	B2	Southsea Avenue	A4
George Street	C4	Stanley Road	C3
Gladstone Road	D3	Station Road	B1
Granville Road	C4	Stephenson Way	D3
Grosvenor Road	C3	Sutton Road	C2
Halsey Road	B2	The Avenue	A1
Harwoods Road	A4	The Broadway	C3
Hempstead Road	A1	The Crescent	C4
High Street	C3	The Parade	B2
Hyde Road	A2	Upton Road	B2
Keele Close	C1	Vicarage Road	B4
King Street	C4	Victoria Passage	B4
Lady's Close	C4	Water Lane	D4
Link Road	D1	Wellington Road	B1
Loates Lane	C3	Wellstones	B3
Lord Street	C3	Westland Road	B1
Lower High Street	D4	West Street	B1
Malden Road	A1	Whippendell Road	A4
Market Street	B4	Wiggenhall Road	B4
Marlborough Road	B3	Woodford Road	C1

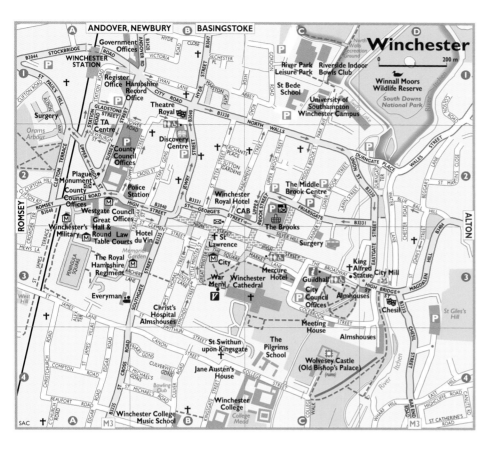

Winchester

Winchester is found on atlas page **22 E9**

Alex Terrace	A3	Market Lane	C3
Alison Way	A1	Marston Gate	B1
Andover Road	B1	Merchants Place	B2
Archery Lane	A3	Mews Lane	A3
Bar End Road	D4	Middle Brook Street	C2
Beaufort Road	A4	Minster Lane	B3
Beggar's Lane	D2	Newburgh Street	A2
Blue Ball Hill	D2	North Walls	C1
Bridge Street	D3	Parchment Street	B2
Canon Street	B4	Park Avenue	C2
Canute Road	D4	Romsey Road	A2
Chesil Street	D3	St Clement Street	B2
Chester Road	D2	St Cross Road	A4
Christchurch Road	A4	St George's Street	B2
City Road	B1	St James' Lane	A3
Clifton Hill	A2	St James Terrace	A3
Clifton Road	A1	St James' Villas	A4
Clifton Terrace	A2	St John's Street	D3
Colebrook Street	C3	St Martin's Close	D2
College Street	B4	St Michael's Gardens	B4
College Walk	C4	St Michael's Road	B4
Colson Road	D1	St Paul's Hill	A1
Compton Road	A4	St Peter Street	B2
Cross Street	B2	St Swithun Street	B3
Crowder Terrace	A3	St Thomas Street	B3
Culver Road	B4	Silchester Place	B1
Culverwell Gardens	B4	Silver Hill	C3
Durngate Place	D2	Southgate Street	B3
Durngate Terrace	D2	Staple Gardens	B2
Eastgate Street	D3	Station Road	A1
East Hill	D4	Stockbridge Road	A1
Edgar Road	A4	Sussex Street	A2
Friarsgate	C2	Sutton Gardens	B2
Friary Gardens	B4	Swan Lane	B1
Gladstone Street	A1	Symonds Street	B3
Gordon Road	C1	Tanner Street	C3
Great Minster Street	B3	The Broadway	C3
Highcliffe Road	D4	The Square	B3
High Street	B2	Tower Road	A1
Hyde Abbey Road	B1	Tower Street	A2
Hyde Close	B1	Trafalgar Street	B3
Hyde Street	B1	Union Street	C2
Jewry Street	B2	Upper Brook Street	C2
Kingsgate Street	B4	Upper High Street	A2
Lawn Street	C2	Victoria Road	B1
Little Minster Street	B3	Wales Street	D2
Lower Brook Street	C2	Water Lane	D3
Magdalen Hill	D3	Wharf Hill	D4

Wolverhampton

Wolverhampton is found on atlas page **58 D5**

Bath Avenue	A1	Peel Street	B3
Bath Road	A2	Penn Road	B4
Bell Street	B3	Piper's Row	D2
Berry Street	C2	Pitt Street	B3
Bilston Road	D3	Powlett Street	D4
Bilston Street	C3	Princess Street	C2
Birch Street	B2	Queen Square	B2
Broad Street	C2	Queen Street	C2
Castle Street	C3	Raby Street	D4
Chapel Ash	A3	Raglan Street	A3
Church Lane	B4	Red Lion Street	B2
Church Street	B4	Retreat Street	A4
Clarence Road	B2	Ring Road St Andrews	A2
Clarence Street	B2	Ring Road St Davids	D2
Cleveland Road	D4	Ring Road St Georges	C4
Cleveland Street	B3	Ring Road St Johns	B4
Corn Hill	D2	Ring Road St Marks	B3
Culwell Street	D1	Ring Road St Patricks	C1
Dale Street	A4	Ring Road St Peters	B2
Darlington Street	B3	Russell Street	A4
Dudley Road	C4	St George's Parade	C3
Dudley Street	C2	St John's Square	C4
Fold Street	B3	St Mark's Road	A3
Fryer Street	C2	St Mark's Street	A3
Garrick Street	C3	Salop Street	B3
Graiseley Street	A4	School Street	B3
Great Brickkiln Street	A4	Skinner Street	B3
Great Western Street	C1	Snow Hill	C3
Grimstone Street	D1	Stafford Street	C1
Horseley Fields	D2	Stephenson Street	A3
Hospital Street	D4	Stewart Street	B4
Lansdowne Road	A1	Summer Row	B3
Lever Street	C4	Tempest Street	C3
Lichfield Street	C2	Temple Street	B3
Little's Lane	C1	Thomas Street	B4
Long Street	C2	Tower Street	C3
Lord Street	A3	Vicarage Road	D4
Mander Street	A4	Victoria Street	B3
Market Street	C3	Walsall Street	D3
Merridale Street	A4	Warwick Street	D3
Middle Cross	D3	Waterloo Road	B1
Mitre Fold	B2	Wednesfield Road	D1
Molineux Street	B1	Westbury Street	C2
Newhampton Road East	A1	Whitemore Hill	B1
North Street	B2	Whitmore Street	C2
Park Avenue	A1	Worcester Street	B4
Park Road East	B1	Wulfruna Street	C2
Park Road West	A2	Zoar Street	A4

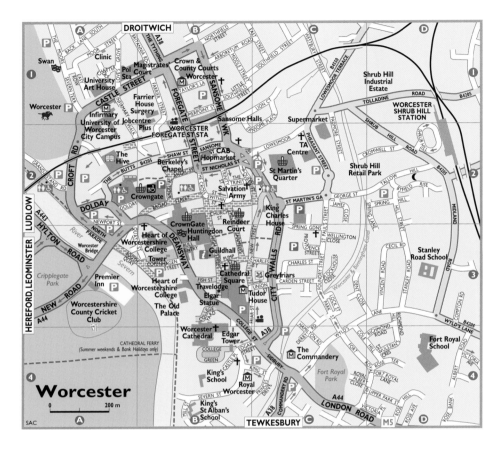

Worcester

Worcester is found on atlas page **46 G4**

Albert Road	D4	Middle Street	B1
Angel Street	B2	Midland Road	D2
Arboretum Road	B1	Mill Street	B4
Back Lane South	A1	Moor Street	A1
Blockhouse Close	C3	Newport Street	A2
Britannia Road	A1	New Road	A3
Broad Street	B2	New Street	C3
Byfield Rise	D2	Northfield Street	B1
Carden Street	C3	North Parade	A3
Castle Street	A1	Padmore Street	C1
Cathedral Ferry	A4	Park Street	C3
Cecil Road	D3	Pheasant Street	C2
Charles Street	C3	Pierpoint Street	B1
Charter Place	A1	Providence Street	C3
Church Street	B2	Pump Street	B3
City Walls Road	C3	Quay Street	A3
Cole Hill	C4	Queen Street	B2
College Street	B3	Richmond Road	D4
Commandery Road	C4	Rose Hill	D4
Compton Road	D3	Rose Terrace	D4
Copenhagen Street	B3	St Martin's Gate	C2
Croft Road	A2	St Nicholas Street	B2
Cromwell Street	D2	St Paul's Street	C3
Deansway	B3	St Swithin Street	B2
Dent Close	C3	Sansome Walk	B1
Derby Road	C4	Severn Street	B4
Dolday	A2	Severn Terrace	A1
East Street	B1	Shaw Street	B2
Edgar Street	B4	Shrub Hill Road	D2
Farrier Street	B1	Sidbury	C4
Fish Street	B3	Southfield Street	C1
Foregate Street	B1	Spring Hill	D2
Fort Royal Hill	C4	Stanley Road	D3
Foundry Street	C3	Tallow Hill	D2
Friar Street	C3	Taylor's Lane	B1
George Street	C2	The Butts	A2
Grandstand Road	A2	The Cross	B2
Hamilton Road	C3	The Moors	A1
High Street	B3	The Shambles	B2
Hill Street	D2	The Tything	B1
Hylton Road	A3	Tolladine Road	C1
King Street	B4	Trinity Street	B2
Little Southfield Street	C3	Union Street	C3
Lock Street	C3	Upper Park Street	D4
London Road	C4	Vincent Road	D3
Love's Grove	A1	Wellington Close	C3
Lowesmoor	C2	Westbury Street	C1
Lowesmoor Terrace	C1	Wyld's Lane	C4

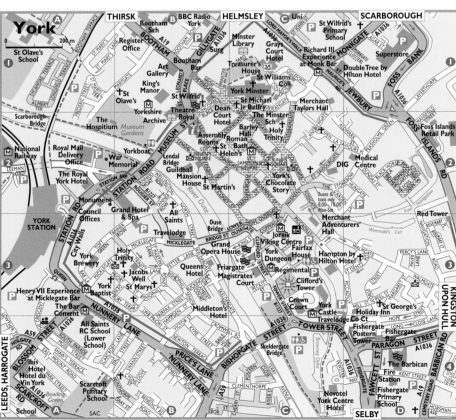

York

York is found on atlas page **98 C10**

Aldwark	C2	Lord Mayor's Walk	C1
Barbican Road	D4	Lower Ousegate	C3
Bishopgate Street	B4	Lower Priory Street	B3
Bishophill Senior	B3	Low Petergate	C2
Black Horse Lane	D2	Margaret Street	D3
Blake Street	B2	Market Street	C2
Blossom Street	A4	Micklegate	A3
Bootham	B1	Minster Yard	B1
Bridge Street	B3	Monkgate	C1
Buckingham Street	B3	Museum Street	B2
Cemetery Road	D4	Navigation Road	D3
Church Street	C2	New Street	B2
Clifford Street	C3	North Street	B2
College Street	C1	Nunnery Lane	A3
Colliergate	C2	Ogleforth	C1
Coney Street	B2	Palmer Street	D2
Coppergate	C3	Paragon Street	D4
Cromwell Road	B4	Parliament Street	C2
Davygate	B2	Pavement	C2
Deangate	C1	Peasholme Green	D2
Dove Street	B4	Percy's Lane	D3
Duncombe Place	B2	Piccadilly	C3
Dundas Street	D2	Price's Lane	B4
Fairfax Street	B3	Priory Street	C3
Fawcett Street	D4	Queen Street	A3
Feasegate	C2	Rougier Street	B2
Fetter Lane	B3	St Andrewgate	C2
Finkle Street	C2	St Denys' Road	D3
Fishergate	D4	St Leonard's Place	B1
Foss Bank	D1	St Martins Lane	B3
Fossgate	C2	St Maurice's Road	C1
Foss Islands Road	D2	St Saviourgate	C2
George Street	D3	St Saviours Place	C2
Gillygate	B1	Scarcroft Road	A4
Goodramgate	C2	Shambles	C2
Hampden Street	B4	Skeldergate	B3
High Ousegate	C3	Spen Lane	C2
High Petergate	B1	Station Road	A3
Holgate Road	A4	Stonegate	B2
Hope Street	D4	Swinegate	C2
Hungate	D2	The Stonebow	C2
Jewbury	D1	Toft Green	A3
Kent Street	D4	Tower Street	C4
King Street	C3	Trinity Lane	B3
Kings Pool Walk	D2	Victor Street	B4
Kyme Street	B4	Walmgate	D3
Lendal	B2	Wellington Row	B2
Long Close Lane	D4		

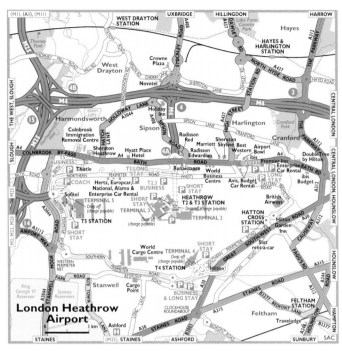

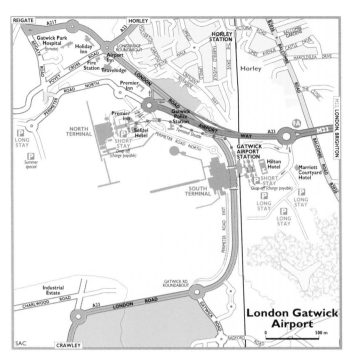

London Heathrow Airport – 17 miles west of central London, M25 junction 14 and M4 junction 4A

Satnav Location: TW6 1EW (Terminal 2), TW6 1QG (T3), TW6 3XA (T4), TW6 2GA (T5)
Information: visit www.heathrow.com
Parking: short-stay, long-stay and business parking is available.
Public Transport: coach, bus, rail and London Underground.
There are several 4-star and 3-star hotels within easy reach of the airport.
Car hire facilities are available.

London Gatwick Airport – 29 miles south of central London, M23 junction 9A

Satnav Location: RH6 0NP (South terminal), RH6 0PJ (North terminal)
Information: visit www.gatwickairport.com
Parking: short and long-stay parking is available at both the North and South terminals.
Public Transport: coach, bus and rail.
There are several 4-star and 3-star hotels within easy reach of the airport.
Car hire facilities are available.

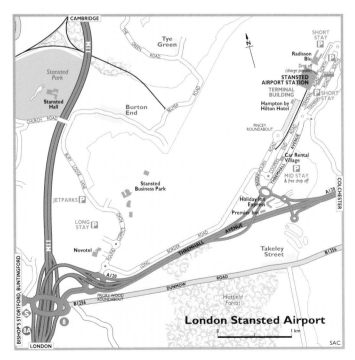

London Stansted Airport – 36 miles north-east of central London, M11 junction 8/8A

Satnav Location: CM24 1RW
Information: visit www.stanstedairport.com
Parking: short, mid and long-stay open-air parking is available.
Public Transport: coach, bus and direct rail link to London (Liverpool Street Station) on the Stansted Express.
There are several hotels within easy reach of the airport.
Car hire facilities are available.

London Luton Airport – 34 miles north of central London

Satnav Location: LU2 9QT
Information: visit www.london-luton.co.uk
Parking: short-term, mid-term and long-stay parking is available.
Public Transport: coach, bus, rail and Luton DART.
There are several 3-star hotels within easy reach of the airport.
Car hire facilities are available.

London City Airport – 8 miles east of central London

Satnav Location: E16 2PX
Information: visit *www.londoncityairport.com*
Parking: short and long-stay open-air parking is available.
Public Transport: easy access to the rail network, Docklands Light Railway and the London Underground.
There are 5-star, 4-star and 3-star hotels within easy reach of the airport.
Car hire facilities are available.

Birmingham Airport – 10 miles east of Birmingham, M42 junction 6

Satnav Location: B26 3QJ
Information: visit *www.birminghamairport.co.uk*
Parking: short and long-stay parking is available.
Public Transport: Monorail service (Air-Rail Link) operates to and from Birmingham International Railway Station.
There are several 4-star and 3-star hotels within easy reach of the airport.
Car hire facilities are available.

East Midlands Airport – 14 miles south-west
of Nottingham, M1 junction 23A/24

Satnav Location: DE74 2SA
Information: visit *www.eastmidlandsairport.com*
Parking: short-term, mid-term and long-stay parking is available.
Public Transport: bus and coach services to major towns and cities in the East Midlands.
There are several 4-star and 3-star hotels within easy reach of the airport.
Car hire facilities are available.

Manchester Airport – 10 miles south of Manchester,
M56 junction 5

Satnav Location: M90 1QX
Information visit *www.manchesterairport.co.uk*
Parking: short-term, mid-term and long-stay parking is available.
Public Transport: coach, bus, rail and tram (Metrolink).
There are several 4-star and 3-star hotels within easy reach of the airport.
Car hire facilities are available.

Leeds Bradford Airport – 8 miles north-east of
Bradford and 8 miles north-west of Leeds

Satnav Location: LS19 7TU
Information: visit *www.leedsbradfordairport.co.uk*
Parking: short, mid-term and long-stay parking is available.
Public Transport: regular bus services to Bradford, Leeds and Harrogate.
There are several 4-star and 3-star hotels within easy reach of the airport.
Car hire facilities are available.

Aberdeen Airport – 7 miles north-west of Aberdeen

Satnav Location: AB21 7DU
Information: visit *www.aberdeenairport.com*
Parking: short and long-stay parking is available.
Public Transport: regular bus services to central Aberdeen.
There are several 4-star and 3-star hotels within easy reach of the airport.
Car hire facilities are available.

Edinburgh Airport – 9 miles west of Edinburgh

Satnav Location: EH12 9DN
Information: visit *www.edinburghairport.com*
Parking: short and long-stay parking is available.
Public Transport: regular bus services to Scottish cities including central Edinburgh,
Glasgow, Dundee and Fife and a tram service to central Edinburgh.
There are several 4-star and 3-star hotels within easy reach of the airport.
Car hire and valet parking facilities are available.

Glasgow Airport – 10 miles west of Glasgow, M8 junction 28/29

Satnav Location: PA3 2SW
Information: visit *www.glasgowairport.com*
Parking: short and long-stay parking is available.
Public Transport: regular direct bus services to central Glasgow.
There are several 3-star hotels within easy reach of the airport.
Car hire facilities are available.

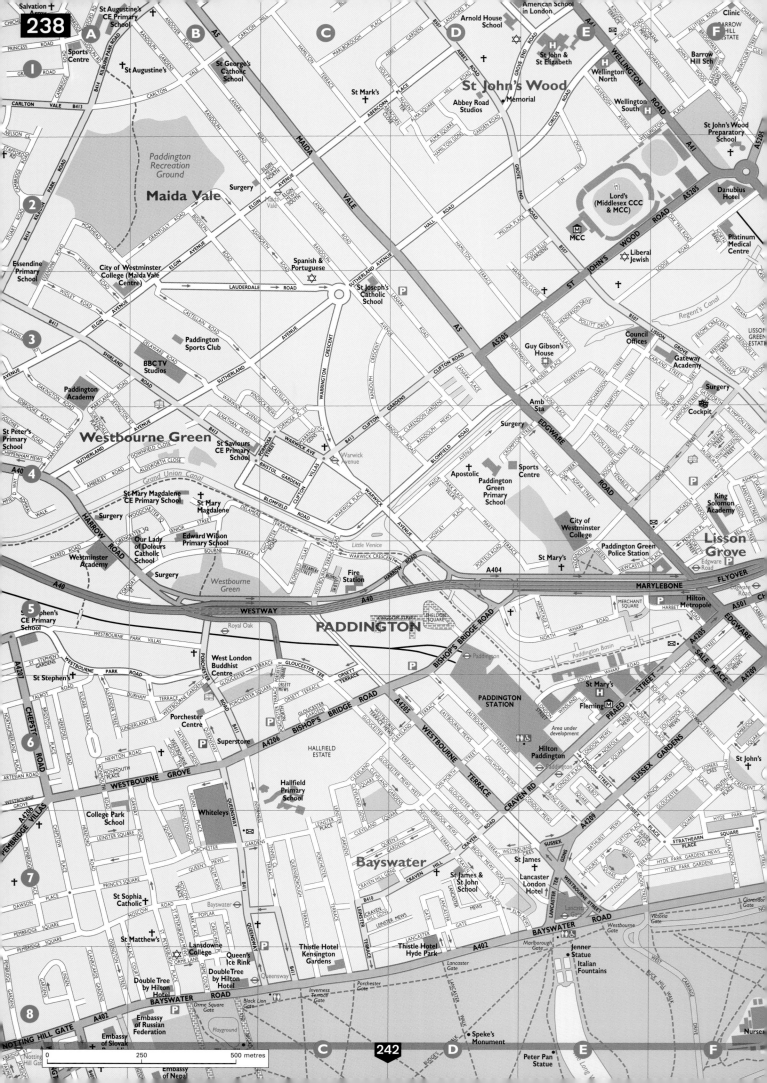

A B C D E F

Salvation Army †
St Augustine's CE Primary School
Sports Centre
PRINCESS ROAD
KILBURN PARK ROAD
† St Augustine's
St George's Catholic School
CARLTON
A5
VIOLET HILL
Arnold House School
American School in London
H
St John & St Elizabeth
BARROW HILL ESTATE
Clinic

I

CARLTON VALE B413
ANDOVER PLACE
YALE
ABERCORN PLACE
St Mark's †
ABBEY ROAD
St John's Wood
Wellington North
WELLINGTON ROAD
St John's Wood Preparatory School

Paddington Recreation Ground
Surgery
Maida Vale
RANDOLPH AVENUE
ELGIN
MAIDA
VALE
Abbey Road Studios
Memorial
Wellington South
H
Lord's (Middlesex CCC & MCC)
Danubius Hotel

2

MORSHEAD ROAD
WIDLEY ROAD
ELGIN AVENUE
ELGIN MEWS NORTH
MAIDA VALE
LAUDERDALE ROAD
HALL ROAD
GROVE END ROAD
MELINA PLACE
MCC
Liberal Jewish
Platinum Medical Centre

Essendine Primary School
City of Westminster College (Maida Vale Centre)
Spanish & Portuguese
St Joseph's Catholic School
P
HAMILTON TERRACE
A5
A5205
ST JOHN'S WOOD ROAD
Regent's Canal

3

LANHILL ROAD
ELGIN AVENUE
SHIRLAND ROAD
DELAWARE ROAD
CASTELLAIN ROAD
WARRINGTON CRESCENT
AVENUE
RANDOLPH CRESCENT
LANARK ROAD
CLIFTON ROAD
Guy Gibson's House
Council Offices
Gateway Academy
Surgery

Paddington Sports Club
BBC TV Studios
Paddington Academy
SUTHERLAND ROAD
WARWICK AVENUE
Amb Sta
EDGWARE
ROAD
Surgery
Cockpit

St Peter's Primary School
Westbourne Green
St Saviours CE Primary School
Warwick Avenue †
BLOMFIELD
CLARENDON GARDENS
Apostolic †
Paddington Green Primary School
Sports Centre
King Solomon Academy

4

A40
HARROW ROAD
St Mary Magdalene CE Primary School
St Mary Magdalene †
Grand Union Canal
WARWICK AVE
BRISTOL GARDENS
BLOMFIELD ROAD
CLIFTON VILLAS
WARWICK
AVENUE
Little Venice
WARWICK CRESCENT
St Mary's †
City of Westminster College
Paddington Green Police Station
Lisson Grove
Edgware Road

Surgery
Westminster Academy
Our Lady of Dolours Catholic School
Edward Wilson Primary School
Surgery
BOURNE TERRACE
DELAMERE TERRACE
Westbourne Green
HARROW ROAD
A404
MARYLEBONE FLYOVER
A501
Hilton Metropole

5

St Stephen's CE Primary School
A40
WESTWAY
WESTBOURNE PARK VILLAS
Royal Oak
PADDINGTON
Kingdom Street
SHELDON SQUARE
BISHOP'S BRIDGE ROAD
Merchant Square
Hilton Metropole
A4205
EDGWARE ROAD

A4207
WESTBOURNE PARK ROAD
West London Buddhist Centre
PORCHESTER
Paddington
SALE PLACE
A4209

6

CHEPSTOW ROAD
St Stephen's †
Porchester Centre
GLOUCESTER TERRACE
PADDINGTON STATION
St Mary's H
Fleming
PRAED STREET
St John's †

Superstore
WESTBOURNE GROVE
HALLFIELD ESTATE
BISHOP'S BRIDGE ROAD
A4206
WESTBOURNE TERRACE
CRAVEN RD
A4209
Hilton Paddington
SUSSEX GARDENS

College Park School
Hallfield Primary School
Whiteleys
QUEENSWAY
Bayswater
St James & St John School
St James †
Lancaster London Hotel
STRATHEARN PLACE
HYDE PARK GARDENS MEWS
HYDE PARK GARDENS

7

PEMBRIDGE VILLAS
St Sophia Catholic †
Lansdowne College
Queen's Ice Rink
CRAVEN HILL
LANCASTER GATE
Lancaster Gate
Clarendon Gate
Victoria Gate

St Matthew's †
Double Tree by Hilton Hotel
Thistle Hotel Kensington Gardens
Thistle Hotel Hyde Park
A402
BAYSWATER ROAD
Marlborough Gate
Jenner Statue
Italian Fountains

8

NOTTING HILL GATE
A402
BAYSWATER ROAD
Embassy of Russian Federation
Embassy of Slovak Republic
Playground
Orme Square Gate
Black Lion Gate
Inverness Terrace Gate
Porchester Gate
Lancaster Gate
Speke's Monument
Peter Pan Statue

Embassy of Nepal

0   250   500 metres

This index lists street and station names, and top places of tourist interest shown in red. Names are listed in alphabetical order and written in full, but may be abbreviated on the map. Each entry is followed by its Postcode District and then the page number and grid reference to the square in which the name is found. Names are asterisked (*) in the index where there is insufficient space to show them on the map.

Cavendish Avenue NW8 ...238 E1
Cavendish Place W1G ...239 L6
Cavendish Square W1G ...239 L6
Cavendish Street N1 ...241 L1
Caversham Street SW3 ...243 G8
Caxton Street SW1H ...244 B4
Cayton Street EC1V ...241 K2
Centaur Street SE1 ...244 F4
Central Street EC1V ...241 J2
Chadwell Street EC1R ...241 G1
Chadwick Street SW1P ...244 B4
Chagford Street NW1 ...239 H4
Chalton Street NW1 ...240 B1
Chambers Street SE16 ...246 D7
Chamber Street E1 ...246 C3
Chambers Wharf SE16 ...246 D6
Chancel Street SE1 ...245 H1
Chancery Lane WC2A ...240 F5
Chancery Lane ⊖ WC1V ...240 F5
Chandos Place WC2N ...240 C8
Chandos Street W1G ...239 L5
Chantry Square W8 ...242 B4
Chapel Market N1 ...240 F1
Chapel Street NW1 ...238 F5
Chapel Street SW1X ...243 K3
Chaplin Close SE1 ...245 G3
Chapman Street E1 ...246 E3
Chapter Road SE17 ...245 H7
Chapter Street SW1P ...244 B6
Chargrove Close SE16 ...247 H6
Charing Cross ⇌ ⊖ WC2N ...244 D1
Charing Cross Road WC2H ...240 B6
Charing Cross Road WC2N ...240 C7
Charlbert Street NW8 ...238 F1
Charles II Street SW1Y ...240 B8
Charles Square N1 ...241 M2
Charles Street W1J ...243 K1
Charleston Street SE17 ...245 K6
Charlotte Road EC2A ...241 M3
Charlotte Street W1T ...240 A4
Charlwood Place SW1V ...244 A6
Charlwood Street SW1V ...243 M7
Charlwood Street SW1V ...244 A6
Charrington Street NW1 ...240 B1
Charterhouse Square EC1M ...241 H4
Charterhouse Street EC1M ...241 G5
Chart Street N1 ...241 L2
Chaseley Street E14 ...247 J2
Chatham Street SE17 ...245 L5
Cheapside EC2V ...241 K6
Chelsea Bridge SW1W ...243 K8
Chelsea Bridge Road SW1W ...243 J7
Chelsea Embankment SW3 ...243 G8
Chelsea Manor Gardens SW3 ...242 F7
Chelsea Manor Street SW3 ...243 G7
Chelsea Park Gardens SW3 ...242 E8
Chelsea Physic Garden SW3 ...243 H8
Chelsea Square SW3 ...242 E7
Cheltenham Terrace SW3 ...243 H6
Chenies Mews WC1E ...240 B4
Chenies Street WC1E ...240 B4
Cheniston Gardens W8 ...242 A4
Chepstow Place W2 ...238 A7
Chepstow Road W2 ...238 A6
Chequer Street EC1Y ...241 K3
Cherbury Street N1 ...241 L1
Cherry Garden Street SE16 ...246 E7
Chesham Close SW1X ...243 J4
Chesham Place SW1X ...243 J4
Chesham Street SW1X ...243 J4
Chester Close SW1X ...243 K3
Chester Close North NW1 ...239 L2
Chester Close South NW1 ...239 L2
Chesterfield Gardens W1J ...243 K1
Chesterfield Hill W1J ...239 K8
Chesterfield Street W1J ...243 K1
Chester Gate NW1 ...239 L2
Chester Mews SW1X ...243 K3
Chester Place NW1 ...239 L1
Chester Road NW1 ...239 K2
Chester Row SW1W ...243 K5
Chester Square SW1W ...243 K5
Chester Square Mews SW1W ...243 K4
Chester Street SW1X ...243 K4
Chester Terrace NW1 ...239 L2
Chester Way SE11 ...245 G6
Cheval Place SW7 ...243 G4
Cheval Street E14 ...247 M7
Cheyne Gardens SW3 ...243 G8
Cheyne Row SW3 ...242 F8
Cheyne Walk SW3 ...242 F8
Chicheley Street SE1 ...244 E2
Chichester Road NW6 ...238 A1
Chichester Road W2 ...238 C5
Chichester Street SW1V ...244 A7
Chicksand Street E1 ...246 C1
Chigwell Hill E1 ...246 E4
Child's Place SW5 ...242 A5
Child's Street SW5 ...242 A5
Chiltern Street W1U ...239 J4
Chilworth Mews W2 ...238 D6
Chilworth Street W2 ...238 D6
China Hall Mews SE16 ...247 G8
Chinatown W1D ...240 B7
Chippenham Mews W9 ...238 A4
Chiswell Street EC1Y ...241 K4
Chitty Street W1T ...240 A4
Christchurch Street SW3 ...243 G8
Christian Street E1 ...246 D3
Christina Street EC2A ...241 M3
Christopher Close SE16 ...247 H6
Christopher Street EC2A ...241 L4
Chudleigh Street E1 ...247 H2
Chumleigh Street SE5 ...245 M8
Churchill Gardens Road SW1V ...243 L7
Churchill War Rooms SW1A ...244 C3
Church Street E2 ...238 F4
Church Way NW1 ...240 B2
Churchyard Row SE11 ...245 H5
Churton Place SW1V ...244 A6
Churton Street SW1V ...244 A6
Circus Road NW8 ...238 E1
Cirencester Square W2 ...238 A5
City Garden Row N1 ...241 J1
City Road EC1V ...241 J1
City Road EC1Y ...241 L3
City Thameslink ⇌ EC4M ...241 H6
Clabon Mews SW1X ...243 H5
Clack Street SE16 ...247 G7
Clanricarde Gardens W2 ...238 A8
Claremont Square N1 ...240 F1
Clarence Gardens NW1 ...239 L2
Clarence Mews SE16 ...247 G6
Clarendon Gardens W9 ...238 D4
Clarendon Gate W2 ...238 F7

Clarendon Place W2 ...238 F7
Clarendon Street SW1V ...243 L6
Clareville Grove SW7 ...242 D6
Clareville Street SW7 ...242 D6
Clarges Mews W1J ...243 L1
Clarges Street W1J ...243 L1
Clark Street E1 ...246 F2
Carkson Row NW1 ...239 M1
Claverton Street SW1V ...244 A7
Clave Street E1W ...246 F5
Clay Street W1U ...239 H5
Clayton Street SE11 ...244 F8
Cleaver Square SE11 ...245 G7
Cleaver Street SE11 ...245 G7
Clegg Street E1W ...246 F5
Clemence Street E14 ...247 L2
Clements Lane EC4N ...241 L7
Clement's Road SE16 ...246 E8
Clenston Mews W1H ...239 H6
Clere Street EC2A ...241 L3
Clerkenwell Close EC1R ...241 G3
Clerkenwell Green EC1R ...241 G4
Clerkenwell Road EC1M ...241 G4
Cleveland Gardens W2 ...238 C6
Cleveland Mews W1T ...239 M4
Cleveland Place SW1Y ...244 A1
Cleveland Row SW1A ...244 A2
Cleveland Square W2 ...238 C6
Cleveland Street W1T ...239 M4
Cleveland Terrace W2 ...238 D6
Clifford Street W1S ...239 M7
Clifton Gardens W9 ...238 C4
Clifton Place SE16 ...247 G6
Clifton Place W2 ...238 E7
Clifton Road W9 ...238 D3
Clifton Street EC2A ...241 M3
Clifton Villas W9 ...238 C4
Clink Street SE1 ...245 K1
Clipper Close SE16 ...247 H6
Clipstone Mews W1W ...239 M4
Clipstone Street W1W ...239 L4
Cliveden Place SW1W ...243 J5
Cloak Lane EC4R ...241 K7
Cloth Fair EC1A ...241 J5
Cloth Street EC1A ...241 J5
Cluny Place SE1 ...246 A8
Cobb Street E1 ...246 B2
Cobourg Street NW1 ...240 A2
Coburg Close SW1P ...244 A5
Cochrane Mews NW8 ...238 E1
Cochrane Street NW8 ...238 E1
Cock Lane EC1A ...241 H5
Cockspur Street SW1Y ...244 C1
Codling Close * E1W ...246 D5
Coin Street SE1 ...245 G1
Coke Street E1 ...246 D2
Colbeck Mews SW7 ...242 C6
Colebrook Row N1 ...241 H1
Coleherne Road SW10 ...242 B7
Coleman Street EC2R ...241 L6
Cole Street SE1 ...245 K3
Coley Street WC1X ...240 F3
College Hill EC4R ...241 K7
College Street EC4R ...241 K7
Collett Road SE16 ...246 D8
Collier Street N1 ...240 E1
Collingham Gardens SW5 ...242 B6
Collingham Place SW5 ...242 B5
Collingham Road SW5 ...242 B5
Colnbrook Street SE1 ...245 H4
Colombo Street SE1 ...245 H1
Colonnade WC1N ...240 D4
Coltman Street E14 ...247 K2
Commercial Road E1 ...246 D2
Commercial Road E14 ...247 K3
Commercial Street E1 ...246 B1
Compton Street EC1V ...241 H3
Concert Hall Approach SE1 ...244 E2
Conder Street E14 ...247 K2
Conduit Place W2 ...238 E6
Conduit Place W2 ...238 E6
Conduit Street W1S ...239 L7
Congreve Street SE17 ...245 M5
Connaught Close W2 ...238 F7
Connaught Place W2 ...239 G7
Connaught Square W2 ...239 G6
Connaught Street W2 ...239 G6
Cons Street SE1 ...245 G2
Constitution Hill SW1A ...243 L3
Content Street SE17 ...245 K5
Conway Street W1T ...239 M4
Cookham Crescent SE16 ...247 H6
Cook's Road SE17 ...245 H8
Coombs Street N1 ...241 J1
Cooper's Lane Estate NW1 ...240 B1
Cooper's Row EC3N ...246 B3
Copenhagen Place E14 ...247 L2
Cope Place W8 ...242 A4
Copley Court SE17 ...245 J8
Copley Street E1 ...247 H2
Copperfield Road E3 ...247 K1
Copperfield Street SE1 ...245 J2
Copthall Avenue EC2R ...241 L6
Coptic Street WC1A ...240 C5
Coral Street SE1 ...245 G3
Coram Street WC1H ...240 C3
Cork Gate E1W ...246 E5
Cork Street W1S ...239 M8
Corlett Street NW1 ...238 F5
Cornhill EC3V ...241 L6
Cornwall Gardens SW7 ...242 C4
Cornwall Mews South SW7 ...242 C5
Cornwall Road SE1 ...244 F1
Cornwall Road SE1 ...245 G2
Cornwall Street E1 ...246 E3
Cornwall Terrace Mews NW1 ...239 H4
Cornwood Drive E1 ...247 G2
Coronet Street N1 ...241 M2
Corporation Row EC1R ...241 G3
Corsham Street N1 ...241 L2
Cosser Street SE1 ...244 F4
Cosway Street NW1 ...239 G4
Cottage Place SW3 ...242 F4
Cottesmore Gardens W8 ...242 B4
Cottons Lane SE1 ...245 M1
Coulson Street SW3 ...243 H6
Counter Street SE1 ...245 M1
County Street SE1 ...245 K5
Courtenay Square SE11 ...244 F7
Courtenay Street SE11 ...244 F6
Courtfield Gardens SW5 ...242 B5
Courtfield Mews * SW5 ...242 C5
Courtfield Road SW7 ...242 C5
Court Street E1 ...246 E1
Cousin Lane EC4R ...241 K8
Covent Garden ⊖ WC2E ...240 D7

Covent Garden WC2E ...240 D7
Coventry Street W1D ...240 B8
Cowcross Street EC1M ...241 H4
Cowper Street EC2A ...241 L3
Crail Row SE17 ...245 L5
Cramer Street W1U ...239 J5
Crampton Street SE17 ...245 J6
Cranbourn Street WC2H ...240 C7
Cranleigh Street NW1 ...240 A1
Cranley Gardens SW7 ...242 D6
Cranley Mews SW7 ...242 D6
Cranley Place SW7 ...242 E6
Cranston Estate N1 ...241 L1
Cranwood Street EC1V ...241 L2
Craven Hill W2 ...238 D7
Craven Hill Gardens W2 ...238 C7
Craven Road W2 ...238 D7
Craven Street WC2N ...244 D1
Craven Terrace W2 ...238 D7
Crawford Passage EC1R ...241 G3
Crawford Place W1H ...239 G5
Crawford Street W1H ...239 G5
Creechurch Lane EC3A ...246 A3
Creed Lane EC4V ...241 H7
Cresswell Place SW10 ...242 D6
Cressy Place E1 ...247 G1
Crestfield Street WC1H ...240 D2
Crimscott Street SE1 ...246 A8
Crispin Street E1 ...246 B1
Cromer Street WC1H ...240 D2
Crompton Street W2 ...238 D4
Cromwell Mews * SW7 ...242 E5
Cromwell Place SW7 ...242 E5
Cromwell Road SW5 ...242 B5
Cromwell Road SW7 ...242 E5
Crondall Court N1 ...241 M1
Crondall Street N1 ...241 L1
Cropley Street N1 ...241 K1
Crosby Row SE1 ...245 L3
Cross Lane EC3R ...246 A4
Crosswall EC3N ...246 B3
Crowder Street E1 ...246 E3
Crucifix Lane SE1 ...246 A6
Cruikshank Street WC1X ...240 F1
Crutched Friars EC3N ...246 A3
Cuba Street E14 ...247 M6
Cubitt Street WC1X ...240 E2
Culford Gardens SW3 ...243 H6
Culling Road SE16 ...246 F7
Cullum Street EC3M ...241 M7
Culross Street W1K ...239 J8
Culworth Street NW8 ...238 F1
Cumberland Gardens WC1X ...240 F2
Cumberland Gate W2 ...239 H7
Cumberland Market NW1 ...239 L2
Cumberland Street SW1V ...243 L6
Cumberland Terrace NW1 ...239 K1
Cumberland Terrace Mews NW1 ...239 L1
Cumberland Wharf SE16 ...247 G6
Cumming Street N1 ...240 E1
Cundy Street SW1W ...243 K6
Cunningham Place NW8 ...238 E3
Cureton Street SW1P ...244 C6
Curlew Street SE1 ...246 B6
Cursitor Street EC4A ...240 F6
Curtain Road EC2A ...241 M3
Curtain Road EC2A ...241 M4
Curzon Gate W2 ...243 K2
Curzon Street W1J ...243 K1
Cuthbert Street W2 ...238 E4
Cutler Street EC3A ...246 A2
Cynthia Street N1 ...240 F1
Cypress Place W1T ...240 A4
Cyrus Street EC1V ...241 H3

D
Dacre Street SW1H ...244 B3
Dakin Place E1 ...247 J1
Dallington Street EC1V ...241 H3
Damien Street E1 ...246 F2
Dane Street WC1R ...240 E5
Dansey Place W1D ...240 B7
Dante Road SE11 ...245 H5
Danvers Street SW3 ...242 F8
D'Arblay Street W1F ...240 A6
Dartford Street SE17 ...245 K8
Dartmouth Street SW1H ...244 B3
Darwin Street SE17 ...245 L5
Date Street SE17 ...245 K7
Davenant Street E1 ...246 D1
Daventry Street NW1 ...238 F4
Davidge Street SE1 ...245 H3
Davies Mews W1K ...239 K7
Davies Street W1K ...239 K7
Dawes Street SE17 ...245 L6
Dawson Place W2 ...238 A7
Deacon Street SE17 ...245 J5
Deal Porters Way SE16 ...247 G8
Deal Street E1 ...246 D1
Dean Bradley Street SW1P ...244 C5
Dean Close SE16 ...247 H6
Deancross Street E1 ...246 F3
Deanery Street W1K ...243 K1
Dean Farrar Street SW1H ...244 B3
Dean Ryle Street SW1P ...244 C5
Dean's Buildings SE17 ...245 L6
Dean Stanley Street SW1P ...244 C4
Dean Street W1D ...240 B6
Dean's Yard SW1P ...244 C4
Decima Street SE1 ...245 M4
Deck Close SE16 ...247 J6
Defoe Close SE16 ...247 K7
Delamere Street W2 ...238 C5
Delamere Terrace W2 ...238 B4
De Laune Street SE17 ...245 H7
Delaware Road W9 ...238 B3
Dellow Street E1 ...246 F3
Delverton Road SE17 ...245 H7
Denbigh Place SW1V ...243 M6
Denbigh Street SW1V ...243 M6
Denbigh Street SW1V ...244 A6
Denman Street W1D ...240 B7
Denmark Street WC2H ...240 C6
Denny Close SE11 ...245 G6
Denny Street SE11 ...245 G6
Denyer Street SW3 ...243 G5
Derby Gate SW1A ...244 D3
Derby Street W1J ...243 K1
Dering Street W1S ...239 L6
Derry Street W8 ...242 B3
De Vere Gardens W8 ...242 C3
Deverell Street SE1 ...245 L4
Devonport Street E1 ...247 G3

Devonshire Close W1G ...239 K4
Devonshire Mews South W1G ...239 K4
Devonshire Mews West W1G ...239 K4
Devonshire Place W1G ...239 K4
Devonshire Place Mews W1G ...239 K4
Devonshire Row EC2M ...246 A2
Devonshire Square EC2M ...246 A2
Devonshire Street W1G ...239 K4
Devonshire Terrace W2 ...238 D7
De Walden Street W1G ...239 K5
Dickens Estate SE16 ...246 D7
Dickens Square SE1 ...245 K4
Dilke Street SW3 ...243 H8
Dingley Place EC1V ...241 K2
Dingley Road EC1V ...241 J2
Disney Place SE1 ...245 K2
Distaff Lane EC4V ...241 J7
Distin Street SE11 ...244 F6
Dockhead SE1 ...246 C7
Dock Hill Avenue SE16 ...247 J6
Dockley Road SE16 ...246 D8
Dock Street E1 ...246 D4
Doddington Grove SE17 ...245 H7
Doddington Place SE17 ...245 H8
Dodson Street SE1 ...245 G3
Dod Street E14 ...247 M2
Dolben Street SE1 ...245 H2
Dolland Street SE11 ...244 E7
Dolphin Square SW1V ...244 A7
Dolphin Square SW1V ...244 B7
Dombey Street WC1N ...240 E4
Dominion Drive SE16 ...247 H7
Dominion Street EC2A ...241 L5
Donegal Street N1 ...240 F1
Dongola Road E1 ...247 J1
Donne Place SW3 ...243 G5
Doon Street SE1 ...244 F1
Dora Street E14 ...247 L2
Doric Way NW1 ...240 B2
Dorset Rise EC4Y ...241 G7
Dorset Square NW1 ...239 H4
Dorset Street W1U ...239 H5
Doughty Mews WC1N ...240 E3
Doughty Street WC1N ...240 E3
Douglas Street SW1P ...244 B6
Douro Place W8 ...242 C3
Douthwaite Square * E1W ...246 D5
Dovehouse Street SW3 ...242 E6
Dover Street W1J ...243 L1
Dover Street W1S ...239 L8
Dowgate Hill EC4R ...241 K7
Downfield Close W9 ...238 B4
Downing Street SW1A ...244 C2
Down Street W1J ...243 K2
Downtown Road SE16 ...247 K6
D'Oyley Street SW1X ...243 J5
Draco Street SE17 ...245 J8
Drake Close SE16 ...247 H6
Draycott Avenue SW3 ...243 G5
Draycott Place SW3 ...243 H6
Draycott Terrace SW3 ...243 H5
Drayson Mews W8 ...242 A3
Drayton Gardens SW10 ...242 D6
Druid Street SE1 ...246 A6
Druid Street SE1 ...246 B6
Drummond Crescent NW1 ...240 B2
Drummond Gate * SW1V ...244 B6
Drummond Road SE16 ...246 E8
Drummond Street NW1 ...240 A3
Drury Lane WC2B ...240 D6
Dryden Court SE11 ...245 G5
Dryden Street WC2B ...240 D6
Duchess Mews W1G ...239 L5
Duchess Street W1B ...239 L5
Duchy Street SE1 ...245 G1
Duckett Street E1 ...247 J1
Duck Lane W1F ...240 B6
Dufferin Street EC1Y ...241 K4
Duke of Wellington Place SW1W ...243 K3
Duke of York Square SW3 ...243 H6
Duke of York Street SW1Y ...244 A1
Duke Shore Wharf E14 ...247 K4
Duke's Lane W8 ...242 A3
Duke's Place EC3A ...246 B2
Duke's Road WC1H ...240 C2
Duke Street W1K ...239 K7
Duke Street W1U ...239 J6
Duke Street Hill SE1 ...245 L1
Duke Street St James's SW1Y ...244 A1
Dunbar Wharf E14 ...247 L4
Duncannon Street WC2N ...240 C8
Duncan Terrace N1 ...241 H1
Dundee Street E1W ...246 E5
Dundee Wharf E14 ...247 L4
Dunelm Street E1 ...247 H2
Dunlop Place SE16 ...246 C8
Dunraven Street W1K ...239 H7
Dunster Court EC3R ...246 A3
Duplex Ride SW1X ...243 H3
Durand's Wharf SE16 ...247 H6
Durham Row E1 ...247 J1
Durham Street SE11 ...244 E7
Durham Terrace W2 ...238 A6
Dyott Street WC1A ...240 C6
Dysart Street EC2A ...241 M4

E
Eagle Court EC1M ...241 H4
Eagle Street WC1R ...240 E5
Eamont Street NW8 ...239 G1
Eardley Crescent SW5 ...242 A7
Earlham Street WC2H ...240 C6
Earl's Court ⊖ SW5 ...242 A6
Earl's Court Gardens SW5 ...242 B6
Earl's Court Road SW5 ...242 A5
Earl's Court Square SW5 ...242 A6
Earlstoke Street EC1V ...241 H2
Earl Street EC2A ...241 M4
Earnshaw Street WC2H ...240 C6
East Arbour Street E1 ...247 H2
Eastbourne Mews W2 ...238 D6
Eastbourne Terrace W2 ...238 D6
Eastcastle Street W1W ...240 A6
Eastcheap EC3M ...241 M7
Eastfield Street E14 ...247 K1
East India Dock Road E14 ...247 M3
East Lane SE16 ...246 D6
East Poultry Avenue EC1A ...241 H5
East Road N1 ...241 L2
East Smithfield E1W ...246 C4
East Street SE17 ...245 L6
East Tenter Street E1 ...246 C3

Eaton Close SW1W ...243 J5
Eaton Gate SW1W ...243 J5
Eaton Lane SW1W ...243 L4
Eaton Mews North SW1W ...243 K5
Eaton Mews South SW1W ...243 K5
Eaton Mews West SW1W ...243 K5
Eaton Place SW1X ...243 J4
Eaton Row SW1W ...243 K4
Eaton Square SW1W ...243 K5
Eaton Terrace SW1W ...243 J5
Ebbisham Drive SW8 ...244 E8
Ebury Bridge SW1W ...243 K6
Ebury Bridge Road SW1W ...243 K7
Ebury Mews SW1W ...243 K5
Ebury Square SW1W ...243 K6
Ebury Street SW1W ...243 K5
Eccleston Bridge SW1W ...243 L5
Eccleston Mews SW1X ...243 K4
Eccleston Place SW1W ...243 L5
Eccleston Square SW1V ...243 L6
Eccleston Street SW1X ...243 K4
Edbrooke Road W9 ...238 A3
Edge Street W8 ...242 A1
Edgware Road W2 ...238 F5
Edgware Road ⊖ NW1 ...238 F5
Edinburgh Gate SW1X ...243 H3
Edith Grove SW10 ...242 C8
Edwards Mews W1H ...239 J6
Egerton Crescent SW3 ...242 F5
Egerton Gardens SW3 ...242 F5
Egerton Terrace SW3 ...243 G4
Eglington Court SE17 ...245 J7
Elba Place SE17 ...245 K5
Eldon Road W8 ...242 B4
Eldon Street EC2M ...241 L5
Eleanor Close SE16 ...247 H6
Elephant & Castle SE1 ...245 J4
Elephant & Castle ⇌ ⊖ SE1 ...245 J5
Elephant Lane SE16 ...246 F6
Elephant Road SE17 ...245 J5
Elf Row E1W ...247 G3
Elgar Street SE16 ...247 K7
Elgin Avenue W9 ...238 B2
Elgin Mews North W9 ...238 C2
Elgin Mews South W9 ...238 C2
Elia Mews N1 ...241 H1
Elia Street N1 ...241 H1
Elim Estate SE1 ...245 M3
Elim Street SE1 ...245 M3
Elizabeth Bridge SW1V ...243 L6
Elizabeth Street SW1W ...243 K5
Ellen Street E1 ...246 D3
Elliott's Row SE11 ...245 H5
Ellis Street SW1X ...243 J5
Elmfield Way W9 ...238 A4
Elm Park Gardens SW10 ...242 E7
Elm Park Lane SW3 ...242 E7
Elm Park Road SW3 ...242 E8
Elm Place SW7 ...242 E7
Elms Mews W2 ...238 D7
Elm Street WC1X ...240 F4
Elm Tree Road NW8 ...238 E2
Elnathan Mews W9 ...238 B4
Elsa Street E1 ...247 J1
Elsted Street SE17 ...245 L6
Elvaston Mews SW7 ...242 D4
Elvaston Place SW7 ...242 D4
Elverton Street SW1P ...244 B5
Ely Place EC1N ...241 G5
Elystan Place SW3 ...243 G6
Elystan Street SW3 ...242 F6
Embankment ⊖ WC2N ...244 D1
Embankment Gardens SW3 ...243 H8
Embankment Place WC2N ...244 D1
Emba Street SE16 ...246 D7
Emerald Street WC1N ...240 E4
Emerson Street SE1 ...245 J1
Emery Hill Street SW1P ...244 A5
Emery Street SE1 ...245 G3
Emperor's Gate SW7 ...242 C5
Empire Square SE1 ...245 L3
Empress Place SW6 ...242 A7
Endell Street WC2H ...240 C6
Endsleigh Gardens WC1H ...240 B3
Endsleigh Place WC1H ...240 B3
Endsleigh Street WC1H ...240 B3
Enford Street W1H ...239 G5
English Grounds SE1 ...245 M1
Enid Street SE16 ...246 C8
Ennismore Gardens SW7 ...242 F3
Ennismore Gardens Mews SW7 ...242 F3
Ennismore Mews SW7 ...242 F3
Ennismore Street SW7 ...242 F4
Ensign Street E1 ...246 D4
Epworth Street EC2A ...241 L3
Erasmus Street SW1P ...244 C6
Errol Street EC1Y ...241 K4
Essendine Road W9 ...238 A3
Essex Street WC2R ...240 F7
Essex Villas W8 ...242 A3
Europa Place EC1V ...241 J2
Euston ⇌ ⊖ NW1 ...240 B2
Euston Road NW1 ...240 B3
Euston Square NW1 ...240 B2
Euston Square ⊖ NW1 ...240 A3
Euston Street NW1 ...240 A3
Evelyn Gardens SW7 ...242 D7
Evelyn Walk N1 ...241 L1
Eversholt Street NW1 ...240 A1
Everton Mews NW1 ...239 M2
Ewer Street SE1 ...245 J2
Ewhurst Close E1 ...247 G1
Exchange Square EC2A ...241 M4
Exeter Street WC2E ...240 D7
Exhibition Road SW7 ...242 E3
Exmouth Market EC1R ...241 G3
Exon Street SE17 ...245 M6
Exton Street SE1 ...244 F2
Eyre Street Hill EC1R ...240 F4

F
Fairclough Street E1 ...246 D3
Fair Street SE1 ...246 B6
Falmouth Road SE1 ...245 K4
Fann Street EC1M ...241 J4
Fanshaw Street N1 ...241 M1
Farm Street W8 ...242 A1
Farm Lane SW6 ...242 A8
Farm Street W1K ...239 K8
Farnham Place SE1 ...245 J1
Farrance Street E14 ...247 M3
Farringdon ⇌ ⊖ EC1M ...241 G4
Farringdon Lane EC1R ...241 G4

Farringdon Road EC1R	240	F3
Farringdon Road EC1M	241	H5
Farrins Rents SE16	247	J5
Farrow Place SE16	247	K7
Farthing Fields * E1W	246	F5
Fashion Street E1	246	B1
Faunce Street SE17	245	H7
Fawcett Street SW10	242	C8
Featherstone Street EC1Y	241	L3
Fenchurch Avenue EC3M	246	A3
Fenchurch Buildings EC3M	246	A3
Fenchurch Place EC3M	246	A3
Fenchurch Street EC3M	246	A3
Fenchurch Street ⇌ EC3M	246	A3
Fendall Street SE1	246	B8
Fenning Street SE1	245	M2
Fentiman Road SW8	244	D8
Fernsbury Street WC1X	240	F2
Fetter Lane EC4A	241	G6
Fieldgate Street E1	246	D2
Fielding Street SE17	245	J7
Field Street WC1X	240	E1
Finborough Road SW10	242	B8
Finch Lane EC3V	241	L6
Finland Street SE16	247	K8
Finsbury Circus EC2M	241	L5
Finsbury Estate EC1R	241	G3
Finsbury Market EC2A	241	M4
Finsbury Square EC2A	241	L4
Finsbury Street EC2Y	241	L4
First Street SW3	243	G5
Fishermans Drive SE16	247	J6
Fisher Street WC1R	240	D5
Fisherton Street NW8	238	E3
Fish Street Hill EC3R	241	L7
Fitzalan Street SE11	244	F5
Fitzhardinge Street W1H	239	J6
Fitzroy Square W1T	239	M4
Fitzroy Street W1T	239	M4
Flamborough Street E14	247	J3
Flank Street E1	246	C4
Flaxman Terrace WC1H	240	C3
Fleet Street EC4A	241	G6
Fleming Road SE17	245	H8
Fletcher Street E1	246	D3
Flint Street SE17	245	L6
Flitcroft Street WC2H	240	C6
Flockton Street SE16	246	D7
Flood Street SW3	243	G7
Flood Walk SW3	243	G7
Floral Street WC2E	240	D7
Foley Street W1W	239	M5
Forbes Street E1	246	D3
Fordham Street E1	246	D2
Ford Square E1	246	F2
Fore Street EC2Y	241	K5
Formosa Street W9	238	C4
Forset Street W1H	239	G6
Forsyth Gardens SE17	245	H8
Fort Street E1	246	B1
Fortune Street EC1Y	241	K4
Forum Magnum Square SE1	244	E3
Foster Lane EC2V	241	J6
Foulis Terrace SW7	242	E6
Foundry Close SE16	247	J5
Fournier Street E1	246	B1
Fowey Close E1W	246	E5
Frampton Street NW8	238	E4
Francis Street SW1P	244	A5
Franklin's Row SW3	243	H6
Frazier Street SE1	245	G3
Frean Street SE16	246	C8
Frederick Close W2	239	G7
Frederick Street WC1X	240	E2
Frederic Mews * SW1X	243	J3
Freemantle Street SE17	245	M6
Friday Street EC4V	241	J7
Friend Street EC1V	241	H2
Frith Street W1D	240	B6
Fulbourne Street E1	246	E1
Fulford Street SE16	246	F7
Fulham Road SW10	242	D8
Fulham Road SW3	242	F6
Furnival Street EC4A	240	F5
Fynes Street SW1P	244	B5

G

Gabriel's Wharf SE1	245	G1
Gainsford Street SE1	246	B6
Galleon Close SE16	247	G6
Galsworthy Avenue E14	247	K2
Galway Street EC1V	241	K2
Gambia Street SE1	245	H2
Garden Road NW8	238	D1
Garden Row SE1	245	H4
Garden Street E1	247	H1
Garden Terrace * SW1V	244	B6
Garden Walk EC2A	241	M3
Gard Street EC1V	241	J2
Garford Street E14	247	M4
Garlick Hill EC4R	241	K7
Garnault Place EC1R	241	G3
Garnet Street E1W	246	F4
Garrett Street EC1Y	241	K3
Garrick Street WC2E	240	C7
Garterway SE16	247	H7
Garway Road W2	238	B6
Gaspar Mews SW7	242	C5
Gataker Street * SE16	246	E8
Gate Mews SW7	242	F3
Gateforth Street NW8	238	F3
Gate Mews NW1	239	L3
Gatesborough Street * EC2A	241	M3
Gate Street WC2A	240	E5
Gatliff Road SW1W	243	K7
Gaunt Street SE1	245	J4
Gayfere Street SW1P	244	C4
Gaywood Street SE1	245	H4
Gaza Street SE17	245	H7
Gedling Place SE1	246	C7
Gee Street EC1V	241	J3
George Mathers Road SE11	245	H5
George Row SE16	246	C7
George Street W1H	239	H6
George Yard W1K	239	K7
Geraldine Street SE11	245	H4
Gerald Road SW1W	243	K5
Gerrard Street W1D	240	B7
Gerridge Street SE1	245	G3
Gertrude Street SW10	242	D8
Gibson Road SE11	244	E5
Gilbert Place WC1A	240	C5
Gilbert Street SE11	245	L6

Gilbert Street W1K	239	K7
Gildea Street W1W	239	L5
Gillingham Street SW1V	243	M5
Gill Street E14	247	L3
Gilston Road SW10	242	D7
Giltspur Street EC1A	241	H6
Gladstone Street SE1	245	H4
Glamis Place E1W	247	G4
Glamis Road E1W	247	G4
Glasgow Terrace SW1V	243	M7
Glasshill Street SE1	245	J3
Glasshouse Street W1B	240	A8
Glasshouse Walk SE11	244	D7
Glasshouse Yard EC1	241	J4
Glebe Place SW3	242	F7
Gledhow Road SW5	242	C6
Glentworth Street NW1	239	H4
Globe Pond Road SE16	247	J5
Globe Street SE1	245	K3
Gloucester Court * EC3R	246	A4
Gloucester Gardens W2	238	C6
Gloucester Mews W2	238	D6
Gloucester Mews West W2	238	C6
Gloucester Place NW1	239	H3
Gloucester Place W1U	239	H5
Gloucester Place Mews W1U	239	H5
Gloucester Road SW7	242	C4
Gloucester Road SW7	242	D6
Gloucester Road ⊖ SW7	242	C5
Gloucester Square W2	238	F6
Gloucester Street SW1V	243	M7
Gloucester Terrace W2	238	B5
Gloucester Terrace W2	238	D6
Gloucester Walk W8	242	A2
Gloucester Way EC1R	241	G2
Glyn Street SE11	244	E7
Godfrey Street SW3	243	G6
Goding Street SE11	244	D7
Godliman Street EC4V	241	J7
Godwin Close N1	241	K1
Golden Hinde II SE1	245	L1
Golden Jubilee Bridge WC2N	244	D1
Golden Lane EC1Y	241	J4
Golden Square W1F	240	A7
Golding Street E1	246	E3
Goldney Road W9	238	A4
Goldsmith Street EC2V	241	K6
Gomm Road SE16	247	G8
Goodge Place W1T	240	A5
Goodge Street W1T	240	A5
Goodge Street ⊖ W1T	240	B5
Goodwin Close SE16	246	C8
Gordon Place W8	242	A2
Gordon Square WC1H	240	B3
Gordon Street WC1H	240	B3
Gore Street SW7	242	D4
Goring Street * EC3A	246	A2
Gosfield Street W1W	239	L5
Goslett Yard WC2H	240	B6
Goswell Road EC1V	241	H1
Gough Street WC1X	240	F3
Goulston Street E1	246	B2
Gower Mews WC1E	240	B5
Gower Place NW1	240	A3
Gower Street WC1E	240	B3
Gower's Walk E1	246	D2
Gracechurch Street EC3V	241	M7
Grafton Mews W1T	239	M4
Grafton Place NW1	240	B2
Grafton Street W1S	239	L8
Grafton Way W1T	240	A4
Graham Street N1	241	J1
Graham Terrace SW1W	243	J6
Granby Terrace NW1	239	M1
Grand Avenue EC1A	241	H5
Grange Road SE1	246	B8
Grange Walk SE1	246	A8
Grange Yard SE1	246	B8
Grantully Road W9	238	B2
Granville Place W1H	239	J6
Granville Road NW6	238	A1
Granville Square WC1X	240	F2
Grape Street WC2H	240	C6
Gravel Lane E1	246	B2
Gray's Inn Road WC1X	240	D2
Gray's Inn Square WC1R	240	F5
Gray Street SE1	245	G3
Great Castle Street W1G	239	L6
Great Central Street NW1	239	G4
Great Chapel Street W1D	240	B6
Great College Street SW1P	244	C4
Great Cumberland Place W1H	239	H6
Great Dover Street SE1	245	K3
Great Eastern Street EC2A	241	M3
Great George Street SW1P	244	C3
Great Guildford Street SE1	245	J1
Great James Street WC1N	240	E4
Great Marlborough Street W1F	239	M7
Great Maze Pond SE1	245	L2
Great Newport Street WC2H	240	C7
Greatorex Street E1	246	D1
Great Ormond Street WC1N	240	D4
Great Percy Street WC1X	240	F2
Great Peter Street SW1P	244	B4
Great Portland Street W1W	239	L4
Great Portland Street ⊖ W1W	239	L4
Great Pulteney Street W1F	240	A7
Great Queen Street WC2B	240	D6
Great Russell Street WC1B	240	C5
Great St Helen's EC3A	241	M6
Great Scotland Yard SW1A	244	C1
Great Smith Street SW1P	244	C4
Great Suffolk Street SE1	245	H2
Great Sutton Street EC1V	241	H4
Great Swan Alley EC2R	241	L6
Great Titchfield Street W1W	239	M4
Great Tower Street EC3M	241	M7
Great Tower Street EC3R	246	A4
Great Winchester Street EC2N	241	L6
Great Windmill Street W1D	240	B7
Greek Street W1D	240	B6
Greenacre Square SE16	247	J6
Green Bank E1W	246	E5
Greenberry Street NW8	238	F1
Greencoat Place SW1P	244	A5
Green Coat Row SW1P	244	A4
Greenfield Road E1	246	D2
Greenham Close SE1	244	F3
Green Park ⊖ W1J	243	M1
Green Street W1K	239	J7
Greenwell Street W1W	239	L4
Greet Street SE1	245	G2
Grenade Street E14	247	L4
Grendon Street NW8	238	F3
Grenville Place SW7	242	C5
Gresham Street EC2V	241	J6

Gresse Street W1T	240	B5
Greville Street EC1N	241	G5
Greycoat Place SW1P	244	B4
Greycoat Street SW1P	244	B4
Grigg's Place SE1	246	A8
Grosvenor Bridge SW8	243	L8
Grosvenor Crescent SW1X	243	J3
Grosvenor Crescent Mews SW1X	243	J3
Grosvenor Gardens SW1W	243	L4
Grosvenor Gardens Mews East SW1W	243	L4
Grosvenor Gardens Mews North SW1W	243	L4
Grosvenor Gardens Mews South * SW1W	243	L4
Grosvenor Gate W2	239	H8
Grosvenor Hill W1K	239	L7
Grosvenor Place SW1X	243	K3
Grosvenor Road SW1V	243	L8
Grosvenor Square W1K	239	J7
Grosvenor Street W1K	239	K7
Grosvenor Terrace SE5	245	J8
Grove End Road NW8	238	D2
Guildhouse Street SW1V	243	M5
Guilford Street WC1N	240	D4
Guinness Square SE1	245	M5
Gulliver Street SE16	247	K8
Gunpowder Square EC4A	241	G6
Gun Street E1	246	B1
Gunthorpe Street E1	246	C2
Gutter Lane EC2V	241	J6
Guy Street SE1	245	L3

H

Haberdasher Street N1	241	L2
Haddonhall Estate SE1	245	M4
Hainton Close E1	246	F3
Halcrow Street * E1	246	F2
Half Moon Street W1J	243	L1
Halford Road W6	242	A8
Halkin Place SW1X	243	J4
Halkin Street SW1X	243	K3
Hallam Street W1W	239	L5
Halley Street E14	247	K1
Hallfield Estate W2	238	C6
Hall Place W2	238	E4
Hall Road NW8	238	D2
Hall Street EC1V	241	H2
Halpin Place SE17	245	M6
Halsey Street SW3	243	G5
Hamilton Close NW8	238	D2
Hamilton Close SE16	247	K7
Hamilton Gardens NW8	238	D2
Hamilton Place W1J	243	K2
Hamilton Terrace NW8	238	C1
Hamlet Way SE1	245	L3
Hammett Street EC3N	246	B4
Hampden Close NW1	240	B1
Hampden Gurney Street W2	239	H6
Hampstead Road NW1	239	M2
Hampton Street SE17	245	J6
Hanbury Street E1	246	C1
Hand Court WC1V	240	E5
Handel Street WC1N	240	D3
Hankey Place SE1	245	L3
Hannibal Road E1	247	G1
Hanover Square W1S	239	L6
Hanover Street W1S	239	L7
Hans Crescent SW3	243	H3
Hanson Street W1W	239	M4
Hans Place SW1X	243	H4
Hans Road SW3	243	G3
Hans Street SW1X	243	H4
Hanway Place W1T	240	B6
Hanway Street W1T	240	B6
Harbet Road W2	238	F5
Harcourt Street W1H	239	G5
Harcourt Terrace SW10	242	C7
Hardinge Street E1W	247	G3
Hardwick Street EC1R	241	G2
Hardwidge Street SE1	245	M2
Hardy Close SE16	247	H6
Harewood Place W1G	239	L6
Harewood Row NW1	239	G4
Harewoood Avenue NW1	239	G4
Harford Street E1	247	J1
Harleyford Road SE11	244	E8
Harley Gardens SW10	242	D7
Harley Place W1G	239	L5
Harley Street W1G	239	K4
Harmsworth Street SE17	245	G7
Harold Estate SE1	246	A8
Harper Road SE1	245	K4
Harpour Street WC1N	240	E4
Harriet Street SW1X	243	H3
Harriet Walk SW1X	243	H3
Harrington Gardens SW7	242	C6
Harrington Road SW7	242	E5
Harrington Square NW1	239	M1
Harrington Street NW1	239	M2
Harrison Street WC1H	240	D2
Harrods SW1X	243	G4
Harrowby Street W1H	239	G6
Harrow Place E1	246	B2
Harrow Road W2	238	A3
Hart Street EC3R	246	A3
Hasker Street SW3	243	G5
Hastings Street WC1H	240	C2
Hatfields SE1	245	G1
Hatherley Grove W2	238	B6
Hatteraick Road SE16	247	G6
Hatton Garden EC1N	241	G4
Hatton Street W2	238	E4
Hatton Wall EC1N	241	G4
Havering Street E1	247	H3
Haverstock Street N1	241	J1
Hawke Place * SE16	247	H6
Haydon Street EC3N	246	B3
Hayes Place NW1	239	G4
Hay Hill W1J	239	L8
Hayles Street SE11	245	H5
Haymarket SW1Y	240	B8
Hay's Lane SE1	245	M1
Hay's Mews W1J	239	L8
Haywood Place EC1V	241	H4
Headfort Place SW1X	243	K3
Head Street E1	247	H2
Hearnshaw Street E14	247	K2
Hearn Street EC2A	241	M4
Heathcote Street WC1N	240	E3
Heddon Street W1B	239	M7
Heddon Street W1S	240	A7

Hedger Street SE11	245	H5
Heiron Street SE17	245	J8
Hellings Street E1W	246	D5
Helmet Row EC1V	241	K3
Helsinki Square SE16	247	L8
Henderson Drive NW8	238	E3
Heneage Lane EC3A	246	A3
Heneage Street E1	246	C1
Henrietta Place W1G	239	L6
Henrietta Street WC2E	240	D7
Henriques Street E1	246	D2
Henshaw Street SE17	245	L5
Herbal Hill EC1R	241	G4
Herbert Crescent SW1X	243	H4
Herbrand Street WC1H	240	C3
Hercules Road SE1	244	F4
Hereford Road W2	238	A6
Hereford Square SW7	242	D6
Hermitage Street W2	238	E5
Hermitage Wall E1W	246	D5
Hermit Street EC1V	241	H2
Heron Place SE16	247	K5
Heron Quays E14	247	M5
Herrick Street SW1P	244	C6
Hertford Street W1J	243	K2
Hertsmere Road E14	247	M4
Hesper Mews SW5	242	B6
Hessel Street E1	246	E3
Hewett Street EC2A	241	M3
Heygate Street SE17	245	J5
Hide Place SW1P	244	B6
High Holborn WC1V	240	E5
High Holborn WC1V	240	E5
High Street Kensington ⊖ W8	242	A3
Hildyard Road SW6	242	A8
Hilliards Court E1W	246	F5
Hillingdon Street SE17	245	J8
Hill Road NW8	238	D1
Hills Place W1F	239	M6
Hill Street W1J	239	K8
Hinde Street W1U	239	K6
Hind Grove E14	247	M3
Hindgrove Area E14	247	M3
Hithe Grove SE16	247	H8
HMS Belfast SE1	246	A5
Hobart Place SW1W	243	K4
Hobury Street SW10	242	D8
Hogarth Road SW5	242	B6
Holbein Mews SW1W	243	J6
Holbein Place SW1W	243	J6
Holborn EC1N	241	G5
Holborn ⊖ WC2B	240	E5
Holborn Circus EC1N	241	G5
Holborn Viaduct EC1A	241	G5
Holford Street WC1X	241	H1
Holland Street SE1	245	H1
Holland Street W8	242	A3
Hollen Street W1F	240	A6
Holles Street W1C	239	L6
Hollywood Road SW10	242	C8
Holyoak Road SE11	245	H5
Holyrood Street SE1	245	M2
Holyrood Street SE1	246	A6
Holywell Row EC2A	241	M4
Homefield Street * N1	241	M1
Homer Row W1H	239	G5
Homer Street W1H	239	G5
Hooper Street E1	246	D3
Hopetown Street E1	246	C1
Hopkins Street W1F	240	A7
Hopton Street SE1	245	H1
Hopwood Road SE17	245	L8
Hornton Place W8	242	A3
Hornton Street W8	242	A2
Horse & Dolphin Yard W1D	240	B7
Horseferry Road E14	247	J3
Horseferry Road SW1P	244	B4
Horse Guards Avenue SW1A	244	C2
Horse Guards Parade SW1A	244	C2
Horse Guards Road SW1A	244	C2
Horselydown Lane SE1	246	B6
Horsley Street SE17	245	K8
Hosier Lane EC1A	241	H5
Hothfield Place SE16	247	G8
Hotspur Street SE11	244	F6
Houghton Street WC2A	240	E6
Houndsditch EC3A	246	A2
Houses of Parliament SW1A	244	D3
Howick Place SW1E	244	A4
Howland Street W1T	240	A4
Howland Way SE16	247	K7
Howley Place W2	238	D4
Hoxton Square N1	241	M2
Hoxton Street N1	241	M1
Hudson's Place SW1V	243	M5
Hugh Mews SW1V	243	L6
Hugh Street SW1V	243	L6
Hugh Street SW1V	243	L6
Hull Close SE16	247	J6
Hull Street EC1V	241	J2
Hungerford Bridge SE1	244	E1
Hunter Close SE1	245	M4
Hunter Street WC1N	240	D3
Huntley Street WC1E	240	A4
Huntsman Street SE17	245	M6
Huntsworth Mews NW1	239	H3
Hurley Crescent SE16	247	H6
Hutching's Street E14	247	M7
Hutton Street EC4Y	241	G7
Hyde Park W2	243	G1
Hyde Park Corner W1J	243	K2
Hyde Park Corner ⊖ W1J	243	K2
Hyde Park Court SW7	242	D3
Hyde Park Crescent W2	238	F6
Hyde Park Gardens W2	238	F7
Hyde Park Gardens Mews W2	238	F7
Hyde Park Gardens W2	238	F7
Hyde Park Gate SW7	242	C3
Hyde Park Gate SW7	242	D3
Hyde Park Square W2	238	F7
Hyde Park Street W2	238	F7

I

Idol Lane EC3R	241	M7
Ifield Road SW10	242	B8
Iliffe Street SE17	245	J6
Iliffe Yard SE17	245	J6
Imperial College Road SW7	242	D4
Imperial War Museum SE1	245	G4
India Street EC3N	246	B3
Ingestre Place W1F	240	A7
Inglebert Street EC1R	241	F2
Ingram Close SE11	244	F5
Inner Circle NW1	239	J2
Inverness Terrace W2	238	B5

Inverness Terrace Gate W2	238	C8
Inville Road SE17	245	L7
Ironmonger Lane EC2V	241	K6
Ironmonger Row EC1V	241	K2
Irving Street WC2N	240	C8
Isambard Place SE16	247	G6
Island Row E14	247	K3
Iverna Court W8	242	A4
Iverna Gardens W8	242	A4
Ives Street SW3	243	G5
Ivor Place NW1	239	H3
Ixworth Place SW3	242	F6

J

Jacob Street SE1	246	C6
Jamaica Gate SE16	246	F8
Jamaica Road SE1	246	C7
Jamaica Road SE16	246	E7
Jamaica Street E1	247	G2
Jamaica Wharf SE1	246	C6
James Street W1U	239	K6
James Street WC2E	240	D7
Jameson Street W8	242	A1
Jamuna Close E14	247	K1
Janeway Street SE16	246	D7
Jardine Road E1W	247	J4
Java Wharf SE1	246	C6
Jay Mews SW7	242	D3
Jermyn Street SW1Y	240	A8
Jerome Crescent NW8	238	F3
Jewery Street EC3N	246	B3
Joan Street SE1	245	G2
Jockey's Fields WC1R	240	E4
Johanna Street SE1	244	F3
John Adam Street WC2N	240	D8
John Carpenter Street EC4Y	241	G7
John Fisher Street E1	246	C4
John Islip Street SW1P	244	C5
John Prince's Street W1G	239	L6
John Roll Way SE16	246	D7
John Ruskin Street SE5	245	J8
John's Mews WC1N	240	E4
Johnson's Place SW1V	244	A7
Johnson Street E1	247	G3
John Street WC1N	240	E4
Joiner Street SE1	245	L1
Jonathan Street SE11	244	E6
Jubilee Place SW3	243	G6
Jubilee Street E1	247	G2
Jubilee Walk W8	242	B1
Judd Street WC1H	240	C2
Junction Mews W2	238	F5
Juxon Street SE11	244	E5

K

Katherine Close SE16	247	H5
Kean Street WC2B	240	E6
Keel Close SE16	247	J6
Keeley Street WC2B	240	E6
Keeton's Road SE16	246	E7
Kell Street SE1	245	H3
Kelso Place W8	242	B4
Kemble Street WC2B	240	E6
Kempsford Gardens SW5	242	A7
Kempsford Road SE11	245	G6
Kendall Place W1U	239	J5
Kendal Street W2	239	G6
Kennet Street E1W	246	D5
Kenning Street SE16	247	G6
Kennings Way SE11	245	G7
Kennington ⊖ SE11	245	H7
Kennington Lane SE11	244	F7
Kennington Oval SE11	244	E8
Kennington Park Gardens SE11	245	G8
Kennington Park Place SE11	245	G8
Kennington Park Road SE11	245	G7
Kennington Road SE1	244	F4
Kennington Road SE11	245	G5
Kennnington Oval SE11	244	F8
Kenrick Place W1U	239	J5
Kensington Church Street W8	242	A1
Kensington Court W8	242	B3
Kensington Gardens W2	242	C1
Kensington Gardens Square W2	238	B6
Kensington Gate W8	242	C4
Kensington Gore SW7	242	D3
Kensington High Street W8	242	A4
Kensington Palace W8	242	B2
Kensington Palace Gardens W8	242	B1
Kensington Palace Gardens W8	242	B2
Kensington Place W8	242	A1
Kensington Road SW7	242	G3
Kensington Road W8	242	B3
Kensington Square W8	242	B3
Kenton Street WC1H	240	C3
Kenway Road SW5	242	A6
Keystone Close N1	240	D1
Keyworth Street SE1	245	H4
Kia Oval (Surrey County Cricket Ground) SE11	244	F8
Kilburn Park Road NW6	238	A2
Kildare Terrace W2	238	A6
Killick Street N1	240	E1
Kinburn Street SE16	247	H6
Kinder Street E1	246	E2
King & Queen Wharf SE16	247	H5
King and Queen Street SE17	245	K6
King Charles Street SW1A	244	C2
King David Lane E1W	247	G3
Kingdom Street W2	238	C5
King Edward Street EC1A	241	J6
King Edward Walk SE1	245	G4
King James Street SE1	245	H3
Kingly Street W1F	239	M7
King's Arms Yard EC2R	241	L6
King's Bench Street SE1	245	H2
Kingscote Street EC4V	241	H7
King's Cross ⇌ N1C	240	D1
King's Cross Road WC1X	240	E2
King's Cross Square N1C	240	D1
King's Cross St Pancras ⊖ N1C	240	D1
Kingsgate Walk * SW1E	244	A4
King's Head Yard SE1	245	L1
King's Mews WC1N	240	F4
Kingsmill Terrace NW8	238	E1
King Square EC1V	241	J2
King's Road SW3	243	G5
King's Scholars Passage SW1P	243	M5
King's Stairs Close SE16	246	F6
King Street WC2E	240	D7

Name		Page	Grid
King Street	SW1Y	244	A1
King Street	EC2V	241	K6
Kingsway	WC2B	240	E6
King William Street	EC4N	241	L7
Kinnerton Place North *	SW1X	243	J3
Kinnerton Place South *	SW1X	243	J3
Kinnerton Street	SW1X	243	J3
Kinnerton Yard *	SW1X	243	J3
Kipling Estate	SE1	245	L3
Kipling Street	SE1	245	L3
Kirby Estate	SE16	246	D7
Kirby Grove	SE1	245	M3
Kirby Street	EC1N	241	G4
Knaresborough Place	SW5	242	B5
Knightrider Street	EC4V	241	H7
Knightsbridge	SW1X	243	H3
Knightsbridge ⊖	SW3	243	H3
Knox Street	W1H	239	H4
Kynance Mews	SW7	242	C4
Kynance Place	SW7	242	C4
L			
Lackington Street	EC2A	241	L4
Lafone Street	SE1	246	B6
Lagado Mews	SE16	247	H5
Lambeth Bridge	SW1P	244	D5
Lambeth High Street	SE1	244	E5
Lambeth Hill	EC4V	241	J7
Lambeth North ⊖	SE1	244	F3
Lambeth Palace Road	SE1	244	E4
Lambeth Road	SE1	244	F4
Lambeth Walk	SE11	244	F5
Lamb's Conduit Street	WC1N	240	E4
Lamb's Passage	EC1Y	241	K4
Lamb Street	E1	246	B1
Lamb Way	SE1	246	A7
Lamlash Street	SE11	245	H5
Lanark Place	W9	238	D3
Lanark Road	W9	238	B1
Lancaster Gate	W2	238	D7
Lancaster Gate	W2	238	D8
Lancaster Gate ⊖	W2	238	E7
Lancaster Mews	W2	238	D7
Lancaster Place	WC2E	240	E7
Lancaster Street	SE1	245	H3
Lancaster Terrace	W2	238	E7
Lancaster Walk	W2	238	D8
Lancelot Place	SW7	243	G3
Lancing Street	NW1	240	B2
Lanesborough Place *	SW1X	243	J3
Langdale Street	E1	246	E3
Langford Place	NW8	238	D1
Langham Place	W1B	239	L5
Langham Street	W1W	239	L5
Langham Street	W1W	239	M5
Langley Lane	SW8	244	D8
Langley Street	WC2E	240	C7
Langton Close	WC1X	240	E3
Lanhill Road	W9	238	A3
Lansdowne Place	SE1	245	L4
Lant Street	SE1	245	J3
Larcom Street	SE17	245	K6
Lauderdale Road	W9	238	B3
Laud Street	SE11	244	E7
Launcelot Street	SE1	244	F3
Launceston Place	W8	242	C4
Laurence Pountney Lane	EC4V	241	L7
Lavender Close	SE16	247	K5
Lavender Wharf	SE16	247	K4
Lavington Street	SE1	245	J1
Lawn Lane	SW8	244	D8
Lawrence Street	SW3	243	F8
Lawrence Wharf	SE16	247	L4
Law Street	SE1	245	L4
Laxton Place	NW1	239	L3
Laystall Street	EC1R	240	F4
Leadenhall Street	EC3A	246	A3
Leadenhall Street	EC3V	241	M6
Leake Street	SE1	244	E2
Leather Lane	EC1N	241	G4
Leathermarket Street	SE1	245	M3
Leeke Street	WC1X	240	E2
Lees Place	W1K	239	J7
Leicester Square ⊖	WC2H	240	C7
Leicester Square	WC2H	240	C7
Leicester Street	WC2H	240	B7
Leigh Street	WC1H	240	C3
Leinster Gardens	W2	238	C7
Leinster Mews	W2	238	C7
Leinster Place	W2	238	C7
Leinster Square	W2	238	A7
Leinster Terrace	W2	238	C7
Leman Street	E1	246	C3
Lennox Gardens	SW1X	243	G4
Lennox Gardens Mews	SW1X	243	G5
Leonard Street	EC2A	241	L3
Leopold Estate	E3	247	M1
Leopold Estate	E3	247	L1
Leroy Street	SE1	245	M5
Lever Street	EC1V	241	J2
Lewisham Street	SW1H	244	A3
Lexham Gardens	W8	242	A5
Lexham Mews	W8	242	A5
Lexington Street	W1F	240	A7
Leyden Street	E1	246	B2
Leydon Close	SE16	247	H5
Library Street	SE1	245	H3
Lidlington Place	NW1	240	A1
Lilestone Street	NW8	238	F3
Lilley Close	E1W	246	D5
Lillie Road	W6	242	A7
Lillie Yard	SW6	242	A7
Limeburner Lane	EC4M	241	H6
Lime Close	E1W	246	D5
Limehouse Causeway	E14	247	L4
Limehouse Link	E14	247	L3
Limehouse ⊖	E14	247	J3
Limerston Street	SW10	242	D8
Lime Street	EC3M	241	M7
Lincoln's Inn Fields	WC2A	240	E6
Linden Gardens	W2	238	A8
Lindley Street	E1	246	F1
Lindsay Square	SW1V	244	B7
Lindsey Street	EC1A	241	H4
Linhope Street	NW1	239	G3
Linsey Street	SE16	246	D8
Lisle Street	WC2H	240	B7
Lisson Green Estate	NW8	238	F3
Lisson Grove	NW1	239	G4
Lisson Grove	NW8	238	F3
Lisson Street	NW1	238	F4
Litchfield Street	WC2H	240	C7
Little Argyll Street	W1F	239	M6
Little Britain	EC1A	241	J5
Little Chester Street	SW1X	243	K4
Little George Street	SW1P	244	C3
Little Marlborough Street	W1F	240	A7
Little New Street	EC4A	241	G6
Little Portland Street	W1G	239	L6
Little Russell Street	WC1A	240	C5
Little St James's Street	SW1A	243	M2
Little Sanctuary	SW1A	244	C3
Little Somerset Street	E1	246	B3
Little Titchfield Street	W1W	239	M5
Little Trinity Lane	EC4R	241	K7
Liverpool Grove	SE17	245	K7
Liverpool Street	EC2M	241	M5
Liverpool Street ⊇⊖	EC2M	241	M5
Lizard Street	EC1V	241	K3
Llewellyn Street	SE16	246	D7
Lloyd Baker Street	WC1X	240	F2
Lloyd's Avenue	EC3N	246	B3
Lloyd Square	WC1X	240	F2
Lloyds Row	EC1R	241	G2
Lloyd Street	WC1X	240	F2
Locksley Estate	E14	247	L2
Locksley Street	E14	247	L1
Lockyer Street	SE1	245	L3
Lodge Road	NW8	238	F3
Loftie Street	SE16	246	D7
Logan Place	W8	242	A5
Lolesworth Close	E1	246	B1
Lollard Street	SE11	244	F5
Lollard Street	SE11	244	F6
Loman Street	SE1	245	J2
Lomas Street	E1	246	D1
Lombard Lane	EC4Y	241	G6
Lombard Street	EC3V	241	L7
London Bridge	EC4R	241	L8
London Bridge ⊇⊖	SE1	245	L1
London Bridge Street	SE1	245	L1
London Dungeon	SE1	244	E2
London Eye	SE1	244	E2
London Mews	W2	238	E6
London Road	SE1	245	H4
London Street	EC3R	246	A3
London Street	W2	238	E6
London Transport Museum	WC2E	240	D7
London Wall	EC2M	241	K5
London Zoo ZSL	NW1	239	J1
Long Acre	WC2E	240	D7
Long Lane	EC1A	241	J5
Long Lane	SE1	245	L3
Longmoore Street	SW1V	243	M5
Longridge Road	SW5	242	A5
Longville Road	SE11	245	H5
Long Walk	SE1	246	A8
Long Yard	WC1N	240	E4
Lord North Street	SW1P	244	C4
Lord's Cricket Ground	NW8	238	E2
Lorenzo Street	WC1X	240	E1
Lorrimore Road	SE17	245	J8
Lorrimore Square	SE17	245	H8
Lothbury	EC2R	241	L6
Loughborough Street	SE11	244	F7
Lovat Lane	EC3R	241	M7
Love Lane	EC2V	241	K6
Lovell Place	SE16	247	K7
Lowell Street	E14	247	K2
Lower Belgrave Street	SW1W	243	K4
Lower Grosvenor Place	SW1W	243	L4
Lower James Street	W1F	240	A7
Lower John Street	W1F	240	A7
Lower Marsh	SE1	244	F3
Lower Road	SE16	247	G7
Lower Sloane Street	SW1W	243	J6
Lower Thames Street	SE1	246	A4
Lower Thames Street	EC3R	241	M8
Lowndes Close *	SW1X	243	J4
Lowndes Place	SW1X	243	J4
Lowndes Square	SW1X	243	H3
Lowndes Street	SW1X	243	J4
Lucan Place	SW3	242	F5
Lucey Road	SE16	246	C8
Ludgate Circus	EC4M	241	H6
Ludgate Hill	EC4M	241	H6
Luke Street	EC2A	241	M3
Lukin Street	E1	247	G3
Lumley Street	W1K	239	K7
Lupus Street	SW1V	243	L7
Lupus Street	SW1V	244	B7
Luton Street	NW8	238	E4
Luxborough Street	W1U	239	J4
Lyall Mews	SW1X	243	J4
Lyall Street	SW1X	243	J4
Lyons Place	NW8	238	E3
Lytham Street	SE17	245	K7
M			
Macclesfield Road	EC1V	241	J2
Macclesfield Street *	W1D	240	B7
Mace Close	E1W	246	E5
Macklin Street	WC2B	240	D6
Mackworth Street	NW1	239	M2
Macleod Street	SE17	245	K7
Madame Tussauds	NW1	239	J4
Maddox Street	W1S	239	M7
Magdalen Street	SE1	245	M2
Magee Street	SE11	244	F8
Maguire Street	SE1	246	C6
Maida Avenue	W9	238	D4
Maida Vale	W9	238	C2
Maida Vale ⊖	W9	238	C2
Maiden Lane	SE1	245	K1
Maiden Lane	WC2E	240	D7
Major Road	SE16	246	D7
Makins Street	SW3	243	G6
Malet Street	WC1E	240	B4
Mallord Street	SW3	242	E8
Mallory Street	NW8	238	F3
Mallow Street	EC1Y	241	L3
Malta Street	EC1V	241	H3
Maltby Street	SE1	246	B7
Manchester Square	W1U	239	J6
Manchester Street	W1U	239	J5
Manciple Street	SE1	245	L3
Mandeville Place	W1U	239	K6
Manette Street	W1D	240	B6
Manilla Street	E14	247	M6
Manningford Close	EC1V	241	H2
Manor Place	SE17	245	J7
Manresa Road	SW3	242	F7
Mansell Street	E1	246	C3
Mansfield Mews	W1G	239	L5
Mansfield Street	W1G	239	L5
Mansion House ⊖	EC4V	241	K7
Manson Mews	SW7	242	D5
Manson Place	SW7	242	D6
Mapleleaf Square	SE16	247	J6
Maples Place	E1	246	F1
Maple Street	W1T	239	M4
Marble Arch ⊖	W1C	239	H7
Marchmont Street	WC1H	240	C3
Margaret Street	W1G	239	L6
Margaretta Terrace	SW3	242	F7
Margery Street	WC1X	240	F3
Marigold Street	SE16	246	D7
Marine Street	SE16	246	C7
Market Mews	W1J	243	K1
Market Place	W1W	239	M6
Markham Square	SW3	243	G6
Markham Street	SW3	243	G6
Mark Lane	EC3R	246	A4
Marlborough Gate	W2	238	E7
Marlborough Place	NW8	238	C1
Marlborough Road	SW1A	244	A2
Marlborough Street	SW3	242	F6
Marloes Road	W8	242	B4
Marlow Way	SE16	247	H6
Maroon Street	E14	247	K2
Marshall Street	W1F	240	A7
Marshalsea Road	SE1	245	K2
Marsham Street	SW1P	244	C4
Marsh Wall	E14	247	M5
Martha's Buildings	EC1V	241	L3
Martha Street	E1	246	F3
Martin Lane	EC4V	241	L7
Maryland Road	W9	238	A4
Marylands Road	W9	238	A4
Marylebone ⊇⊖	NW1	239	G4
Marylebone Flyover	W2	238	E5
Marylebone High Street	W1U	239	K5
Marylebone Lane	W1U	239	K6
Marylebone Road	NW1	239	G4
Marylebone Street	W1G	239	K5
Marylee Way	SE11	244	F6
Masjid Lane	E14	247	M2
Mason Street	SE17	245	M5
Massinger Street	SE17	245	M6
Masters Street	E1	247	J1
Matlock Street	E14	247	K2
Matthew Parker Street	SW1H	244	C3
Maunsel Street	SW1P	244	B4
Mayfair Place	W1J	243	L1
Mayflower Street	SE16	247	F7
Mayford Estate	NW1	240	A1
Maynards Quay	E1W	246	F4
May's Court	WC2N	240	C8
McAuley Close	SE1	244	F4
McLeod's Mews	SW7	242	C5
Meadcroft Road	SE11	245	G8
Meadcroft Road	SE11	245	H8
Meadow Road	SW8	244	E8
Meadow Row	SE1	245	J5
Mead Row	SE1	244	F4
Meakin Estate	SE1	245	M4
Mecklenburgh Square	WC1N	240	E3
Medway Street	SW1P	244	B5
Meeting House Alley	E1W	246	E5
Melcombe Place	NW1	239	G4
Melcombe Street	W1U	239	H4
Melina Place	NW8	238	D2
Melior Street	SE1	245	M2
Melton Street	NW1	240	A2
Memorial Gates	SW1W	243	K3
Mepham Street	SE1	244	F2
Mercer Street	WC2H	240	C7
Merchant Square	W2	238	E5
Merlin Street	EC1R	240	F2
Mermaid Court	SE1	245	K2
Merrick Square	SE1	245	K4
Merrington Road	SW6	242	A8
Merrow Street	SE17	245	L7
Methley Street	SE11	245	G7
Meymott Street	SE1	245	G2
Micawber Street	N1	241	K1
Micklethwaite Road	SW6	242	A8
Middlesex Street	E1	246	A1
Middlesex Street	E1	246	B2
Middle Street	EC1A	241	J5
Middle Temple	WC2R	240	F7
Middle Temple Lane	EC4Y	240	F7
Middleton Drive	SE16	247	H6
Midland Road	NW1	240	C1
Midship Close	SE16	247	H6
Milborne Grove	SW10	242	D7
Milcote Street	SE1	245	H3
Miles Street	SW8	244	D8
Milford Lane	WC2R	240	F7
Milk Street	EC2V	241	K6
Milk Yard	E1W	247	G4
Millbank	SW1P	244	D4
Millennium Bridge	SE1	241	J8
Millennium Harbour	E14	247	M6
Milligan Street	E14	247	L4
Millman Mews	WC1N	240	E4
Millman Street	WC1N	240	E4
Mill Place	E14	247	K3
Millstream Road	SE1	246	B7
Mill Street	SE1	246	C6
Mill Street	W1S	239	L7
Milner Street	SW3	243	G5
Milton Street	EC2Y	241	K4
Milverton Street	SE11	245	G7
Mincing Lane	EC3M	246	A4
Minera Mews	SW1W	243	J5
Minories	EC3N	246	B3
Mitchell Street	EC1V	241	J3
Mitre Road	SE1	245	G2
Mitre Street	EC3A	246	A3
Molyneux Street	W1H	239	G6
Monck Street	SW1P	244	C4
Monkton Street	SE11	245	G5
Monkwell Square	EC2Y	241	K5
Monmouth Place	W2	238	A6
Monmouth Road	W2	238	A6
Monmouth Street	WC2H	240	C6
Montague Close	SE1	245	L1
Montague Place	WC1E	240	C5
Montague Street	WC1B	240	C5
Montagu Mansions	W1U	239	H5
Montagu Mews North	W1H	239	H6
Montagu Mews West	W1H	239	H6
Montagu Place	W1H	239	H5
Montagu Row	W1U	239	H5
Montagu Square	W1H	239	H5
Montagu Street	W1H	239	H6
Montford Place	SE11	244	F7
Monthorpe Road	E1	246	C2
Montpelier Square	SW7	243	G3
Montpelier Street	SW7	243	G3
Montpelier Walk	SW7	242	G3
Montrose Place	SW1X	243	K3
Monument ⊖	EC4R	241	L7
Monument Street	EC3R	241	L7
Monument Street	EC3R	241	M7
Monza Street	E1W	247	G4
Moodkee Street	SE16	247	G7
Moore Street	SW3	243	H5
Moorfields	EC2Y	241	L5
Moorgate	EC2R	241	L6
Moorgate ⊇⊖	EC2Y	241	L5
Moor Lane	EC2Y	241	K5
Moor Street	W1D	240	C7
Mora Street	EC1V	241	K2
Morecambe Street	SE17	245	K6
Moreland Street	EC1V	241	H2
More London	SE1	246	A5
Moreton Place	SW1V	244	A6
Moreton Street	SW1V	244	B6
Moreton Terrace	SW1V	244	A6
Morgan's Lane	SE1	245	M2
Morgan's Lane	SE1	246	A5
Morley Street	SE1	245	G3
Mornington Crescent	NW1	239	M1
Mornington Place	NW1	239	L1
Mornington Terrace	NW1	239	L1
Morocco Street	SE1	246	A7
Morpeth Terrace	SW1P	244	A5
Morris Street	E1	246	F3
Morshead Road	W9	238	A2
Mortimer Market	WC1E	240	A4
Mortimer Street	W1T	240	A5
Mortimer Street	W1W	239	M5
Morton Place	SE1	244	F4
Morwell Street	WC1B	240	B5
Moscow Place	W2	238	B7
Moscow Road	W2	238	B7
Mossop Street	SW3	243	G5
Motcomb Street	SW1X	243	J4
Mount Gate	W2	242	E2
Mount Mills	EC1V	241	J3
Mount Pleasant	WC1X	240	F4
Mount Row	W1K	239	K8
Mount Street	W1K	239	K8
Mount Street Mews	W1K	239	K8
Mount Terrace	E1	246	E1
Moxon Street	W1U	239	J5
Mulberry Street	E1	246	D2
Mulberry Walk	SW3	242	E8
Mulready Street	NW8	238	F4
Mundy Street	N1	241	M2
Munster Square	NW1	239	L3
Munton Road	SE17	245	K5
Murphy Street	SE1	244	F3
Murray Grove	N1	241	K1
Musbury Street	E1	247	G2
Muscovy Street	EC3N	246	A4
Museum Street	WC1A	240	C5
Myddelton Passage	EC1R	241	G2
Myddelton Square	EC1R	241	G1
Myddelton Street	EC1R	241	G2
Myrdle Street	E1	246	D2
N			
Naoroji Street	WC1X	240	F2
Napier Grove	N1	241	K1
Narrow Street	E14	247	K4
Nash Street	NW1	239	L2
Nassau Street	W1W	239	M5
Nathaniel Close *	E1	246	C2
National Portrait Gallery	WC2H	240	C8
Natural History Museum	SW7	242	E4
Neal Street	WC2H	240	C6
Neathouse Place *	SW1V	243	M5
Neckinger	SE1	246	C8
Needleman Street	SE16	247	H7
Nelson Close	NW6	238	A1
Nelson Place	N1	241	H1
Nelson's Column	WC2N	240	C8
Nelson Square	SE1	245	H2
Nelson Street	E1	246	E2
Nelson Terrace	N1	241	H1
Neptune Street	SE16	247	G7
Nesham Street	E1W	246	D4
Netherton Grove	SW10	242	D8
Netley Street	NW1	239	M2
Nevern Place	SW5	242	A6
Nevern Square	SW5	242	A6
Neville Street	SW7	242	E6
Newark Street	E1	246	E2
New Atlas Wharf	E14	247	M8
New Bond Street	W1S	239	L7
New Bond Street	W1S	239	M7
New Bridge Street	EC4V	241	H6
New Broad Street	EC2M	241	M5
New Burlington Street	W1S	239	M7
Newburn Street	SE11	244	F7
Newbury Street	EC1A	241	J5
Newcastle Place	W2	238	E5
New Cavendish Street	W1G	239	L5
New Change	EC4M	241	J6
New Church Road	SE5	245	L8
Newcomen Street	SE1	245	K2
New Compton Street	WC2H	240	C6
Newcourt Street	NW8	238	F1
Newell Street	E14	247	L3
New Fetter Lane	EC4A	241	G6
Newgate Street	EC1A	241	H6
New Globe Walk	SE1	241	J8
New Goulston Street	E1	246	B2
Newham's Row	SE1	246	A7
Newington Butts	SE1	245	H5
Newington Causeway	SE1	245	J4
New Kent Road	SE1	245	K5
Newlands Quay	E1W	246	F4
Newman Street	W1T	240	A5
New North Place	EC2A	241	M3
New North Road	N1	241	L1
New North Street	WC1N	240	D4
New Oxford Street	WC1A	240	C6
Newport Street	SE11	244	E5
New Quebec Street	W1H	239	H6
New Ride	SW7	242	E3
New Road	E1	246	E2
New Row	WC2N	240	C7
New Spring Gardens Walk	SE1	244	D7
New Square	WC2A	240	F6
New Street	EC2M	246	A2
New Street Square	EC4A	241	G6
Newton Road	W2	238	A6
Newton Street	WC2B	240	D5
New Union Street	EC2Y	241	K5
Nicholas Lane	EC3V	241	L7
Nicholson Street	SE1	245	H1
Nightingale Place	SW10	242	D8
Nile Street	N1	241	K2
Nine Elms Lane	SW8	244	C8
Noble Street	EC2V	241	J6
Noel Road	N1	241	J1
Noel Street	W1F	240	A6
Norbiton Road	E14	247	L2
Norfolk Crescent	W2	239	G6
Norfolk Place	W2	238	E6
Norfolk Square	W2	238	E6
Norman Street	EC1V	241	J3
Norris Street	SW1Y	240	B8
Northampton Road	EC1R	241	G3
Northampton Square	EC1V	241	H2
North Audley Street	W1K	239	J7
North Bank	NW8	238	F2
Northburgh Street	EC1V	241	H3
North Carriage Drive	W2	238	F7
Northdown Street	N1	240	D1
Northey Street	E14	247	K4
North Gower Street	NW1	240	A2
Northington Street	WC1N	240	E4
North Mews	WC1N	240	E4
North Ride	W2	239	G7
North Row	W1K	239	J7
North Terrace	SW3	242	F5
Northumberland Alley	EC3N	246	B3
Northumberland Avenue	WC2N	244	C1
Northumberland Place	W2	238	A6
Northumberland Street	WC2N	244	C1
North Wharf Road	W2	238	E5
Northwick Terrace	NW8	238	D3
Norway Gate	SE16	247	K7
Norway Place	E14	247	L3
Norwich Street	EC4A	240	F5
Nottingham Place	W1U	239	J4
Nottingham Street	W1U	239	J4
Notting Hill Gate	W11	238	A8
Notting Hill Gate ⊖	W11	242	A1
Nugent Terrace	NW8	238	D1
Nutford Place	W1H	239	G6
O			
Oakden Street	SE11	245	G5
Oakington Road	W9	238	A3
Oak Lane	E14	247	L3
Oakley Close	EC1V	241	H1
Oakley Gardens	SW3	243	G8
Oakley Square	NW1	240	A1
Oakley Street	SW3	242	F8
Oak Tree Road	NW8	238	F2
Oat Lane	EC2V	241	J5
Occupation Road	SE17	245	J6
Ocean Square	E1	247	J1
Ocean Street	E1	247	J1
Odessa Street	SE16	247	L7
Ogle Street	W1W	239	M5
Old Bailey	EC4M	241	H6
Old Barrack Yard	SW1X	243	J3
Old Bond Street	W1S	239	M8
Old Broad Street	EC2N	241	M6
Old Brompton Road	SW5	242	B6
Old Brompton Road	SW7	242	D6
Old Burlington Street	W1S	239	M7
Oldbury Place	W1U	239	J4
Old Castle Street	E1	246	B2
Old Cavendish Street	W1G	239	L6
Old Church Road	E1	247	H2
Old Church Street	SW3	242	E7
Old Compton Street	W1D	240	B7
Old Court Place	W8	242	B3
Old Gloucester Street	WC1N	240	D4
Old Jamaica Road	SE16	246	C7
Old Jewry	EC2R	241	K6
Old Kent Road	SE1	245	M5
Old Marylebone Road	NW1	239	G5
Old Montague Street	E1	246	C1
Old North Street	WC1X	240	E5
Old Paradise Street	SE11	244	E5
Old Park Lane	W1J	243	K2
Old Pye Street	SW1P	244	B4
Old Queen Street	SW1H	244	B3
Old Square	WC2A	240	F6
Old Street	EC1V	241	K3
Old Street ⊇⊖	EC1Y	241	L3
Old Street Junction	EC1Y	241	L3
Oliver's Yard	EC1Y	241	L3
Olney Road	SE17	245	J8
O'Meara Street	SE1	245	K2
Omega Place	N1	240	D1
Onega Gate	SE16	247	K8
Ongar Road	SW6	242	A8
Onslow Gardens	SW7	242	D6
Onslow Square	SW7	242	E5
Onslow Square	SW7	242	E6
Ontario Street	SE1	245	J4
Ontario Way	E14	247	M4
Opal Street	SE1	245	H6
Orange Place	SE16	247	G8
Orange Square	SW1W	243	K6
Orange Street	WC2H	240	B8
Orb Street	SE17	245	L6
Orchardson Street	NW8	238	E4
Orchard Street	W1H	239	J6
Orde Hall Street	WC1N	240	E4
Orient Street	SE11	245	H5
Orme Court	W2	238	B8
Orme Lane	W2	238	B8
Orme Square Gate	W2	238	B8
Ormond Close	WC1N	240	D4
Ormonde Gate	SW3	243	H7
Ormond Yard	SW1Y	240	A8
Orsett Mews	W2	238	C6
Orsett Street	SE11	244	E6
Orsett Terrace	W2	238	C5
Orton Street	E1W	246	D5
Osbert Street	SW1V	244	B6
Osborn Street	E1	246	C2
Oslo Square	SE16	247	K7
Osnaburgh Street	NW1	239	L3
Osnaburgh Terrace	NW1	239	L3
Ossington Buildings	W1U	239	J5
Ossington Street	W2	238	A7
Ossulston Street	NW1	240	B1
Osten Mews	SW7	242	C4
Oswin Street	SE11	245	H5
Othello Close	SE1	245	H6
Otto Street	SE17	245	H8

Entry	Page	Grid
Outer Circle NW1	239	H3
Outer Circle NW1	239	K1
Oval ⊖ SE11	244	F8
Oval Way SE11	244	E7
Ovington Square SW3	243	G4
Ovington Street SW3	243	G5
Owen Street EC1V	241	G1
Oxendon Street SW1Y	240	B8
Oxford Circus ⊖ W1B	239	M6
Oxford Road NW6	238	A1
Oxford Square W2	238	F6
Oxford Street W1C	239	L6
Oxford Street WC1A	240	A6

P

Entry	Page	Grid
Pace Place E1	246	E3
Pacific Wharf SE16	247	H5
Paddington ≥⊖ W2	238	D6
Paddington Green W2	238	E5
Paddington Street W1U	239	J5
Pageant Crescent SE16	247	K5
Page Street SW1P	244	B5
Paget Street EC1V	241	H2
Pakenham Street WC1X	240	E3
Palace Avenue W8	242	B2
Palace Court W2	238	A7
Palace Gardens Terrace W8	242	A1
Palace Gate W8	242	D3
Palace Green W8	242	B2
Palace of Westminster SW1A	244	D3
Palace Place SW1E	243	M4
Palace Street SW1E	243	M4
Pall Mall SW1Y	244	A1
Pall Mall East SW1Y	244	B1
Palmer Street SW1H	244	B3
Pancras Lane EC4N	241	K6
Pancras Road N1C	240	C1
Panton Street SW1Y	240	B8
Paradise Street SE16	246	E7
Paradise Walk SW3	243	H8
Pardoner Street SE1	245	L4
Pardon Street EC1V	241	H3
Parfett Street E1	246	D2
Paris Garden SE1	245	G1
Park Crescent W1B	239	K4
Park Crescent Mews West W1G	239	K4
Parker's Row SE1	246	C7
Parker Street WC2B	240	D6
Park Lane W1K	239	H7
Park Lane W2	243	J1
Park Place SW1A	243	M1
Park Place Villas W2	238	D4
Park Road NW1	239	H3
Park Square East NW1	239	K3
Park Square Mews NW1	239	K3
Park Square West NW1	239	K3
Park Street SE1	245	K1
Park Street W1K	239	J7
Park Village East NW1	239	L1
Park Walk SW10	242	D8
Park West Place W2	239	G6
Parliament Street SW1A	244	C2
Parry Street SW8	244	D8
Passmore Street SW1W	243	J6
Paternoster Square	241	J6
Pater Street W8	242	A4
Pattina Walk SE16	247	K5
Paul Street EC2A	241	M3
Paultons Square SW3	242	E8
Paveley Street NW1	239	G3
Pavilion Road SW1X	243	H3
Pavilion Street SW1X	243	H4
Paxton Terrace SW1V	243	L7
Peabody Avenue SW1V	243	L7
Peabody Estate SE1	245	J1
Peacock Street SE17	245	J6
Pearl Street E1W	246	F5
Pearman Street SE1	245	G3
Pear Tree Court EC1R	241	G3
Peartree Lane E1W	247	G4
Pear Tree Street EC1V	241	J3
Peel Street W8	242	A1
Peerless Street EC1V	241	K2
Pelham Crescent SW7	242	F6
Pelham Place SW7	242	F5
Pelham Street SW7	242	F5
Pelier Street SE17	245	K8
Pemberton Row EC4A	241	G6
Pembridge Gardens W2	238	A8
Pembridge Place W2	238	A7
Pembridge Square W2	238	A7
Pembridge Villas W11	238	A7
Pembroke Close SW1X	243	J3
Penang Street E1W	246	F5
Penfold Place NW8	238	F5
Penfold Street NW8	238	E4
Pennant Mews W8	242	B5
Pennington Street E1W	246	D4
Pennyfields E14	247	M4
Penrose Grove SE17	245	J7
Penrose Street SE17	245	J7
Penton Place SE17	245	H6
Penton Rise WC1X	240	E2
Penton Street N1	240	F1
Pentonville Road N1	240	E1
Penywern Road SW5	242	A6
Pepper Street SE1	245	J2
Pepys Street EC3N	246	A4
Percival Street EC1V	241	H3
Percy Circus WC1X	240	F2
Percy Street W1T	240	B5
Perkin's Rents SW1P	244	B4
Perryn Road SE16	246	E7
Petersham Mews SW7	242	D4
Petersham Place SW7	242	C4
Peter Street W1F	240	B7
Peto Place NW1	239	L3
Petticoat Lane E1	246	B2
Petty France SW1H	244	A3
Petty Wales EC3R	246	A4
Petyward SW3	243	G6
Phelp Street SE17	245	L7
Phene Street SW3	243	G8
Phillimore Walk W8	242	A3
Philpot Lane EC3M	241	M7
Philpot Street E1	246	E2
Phipp's Mews SW1W	243	L5
Phipp Street EC2A	241	M3
Phoenix Place WC1X	240	F3
Phoenix Road NW1	240	B1
Phoenix Street WC2H	240	C6
Piccadilly W1J	243	L2
Piccadilly Arcade SW1Y	243	M1
Piccadilly Circus W1B	240	A8
Piccadilly Circus ⊖ W1J	240	B8
Pickard Street EC1V	241	J2
Picton Place W1U	239	K6
Pier Head E1W	246	E6
Pigott Street E14	247	M3
Pilgrimage Street SE1	245	L3
Pimlico ⊖ SW1V	244	B6
Pimlico Road SW1W	243	J6
Pinchin Street E1	246	D3
Pindar Street EC2A	241	M4
Pindock Mews W9	238	B3
Pine Street EC1R	240	F3
Pitfield Street N1	241	M1
Pitsea Street E1	247	H3
Pitt's Head Mews W1J	243	K2
Pitt Street W8	242	A2
Pixley Street E14	247	L2
Platina Street * EC2A	241	L3
Plover Way SE16	247	K8
Plumbers Row E1	246	D2
Plumtree Court EC4A	241	G5
Plympton Street NW8	238	F4
Pocock Street SE1	245	H2
Poland Street W1F	240	A6
Pollen Street W1S	239	L7
Pollitt Drive NW8	238	E3
Polperro Mews SE11	245	G5
Polygon Road NW1	240	B1
Pond Place SW3	242	F6
Ponler Street E1	246	E3
Ponsonby Place SW1P	244	C6
Ponsonby Terrace SW1P	244	C6
Ponton Road SW1V	244	B8
Pont Street SW1X	243	H4
Poolmans Street SE16	247	H6
Pope Street SE1	246	B7
Poplar Place W2	238	B7
Poppin's Court EC4A	241	H6
Porchester Gardens W2	238	B7
Porchester Gate W2	238	C8
Porchester Place W2	239	G6
Porchester Road W2	238	B5
Porchester Square W2	238	B6
Porchester Terrace W2	238	C7
Porchester Terrace North W2	238	C6
Porlock Street SE1	245	L3
Porter Street NW1	239	H4
Porteus Road W2	238	D5
Portland Place W1B	239	L4
Portland Place W1B	239	L5
Portland Square E1W	246	E5
Portland Street SE17	245	L7
Portman Close W1H	239	J6
Portman Mews South W1H	239	J6
Portman Square W1H	239	J6
Portman Street W1H	239	J6
Portpool Lane EC1N	240	F4
Portsea Place W2	239	G6
Portsmouth Street WC2A	240	E6
Portsoken Street E1	246	B3
Portugal Street WC2A	240	E6
Potier Street SE1	245	L4
Potters Fields SE1	246	B6
Pottery Street SE16	246	E7
Poultry EC2V	241	K6
Powis Place WC1N	240	D4
Praed Mews W2	238	E6
Praed Street W2	238	E6
Pratt Walk SE1	244	E5
Premier Place E14	247	M4
Prescot Street E1	246	C3
Preston Close SE1	245	M5
Price's Street SE1	245	H1
Prideaux Place WC1X	240	F2
Primrose Street EC2A	246	A1
Prince Albert Road NW8	238	F1
Prince Consort Road SW7	242	D3
Princelet Street E1	246	C1
Prince of Wales Gate SW7	242	F3
Princes Arcade SW1Y	240	A8
Prince's Gardens SW7	242	E4
Prince's Gate Mews SW7	242	E4
Princes Riverside Road SE16	247	H5
Prince's Square W2	238	A7
Princess Road NW6	238	A1
Princess Street SE1	245	H4
Princes Street W1B	239	L6
Prince's Street EC2R	241	L6
Princeton Street WC1R	240	E5
Prioress Street SE1	245	L4
Priory Green Estate N1	240	E1
Priory Walk SW10	242	D7
Proctor Street WC1V	240	E5
Prospect Place E1W	247	G5
Prospect Street SE16	246	E7
Provident Court W1K	239	J7
Provost Street N1	241	L1
Prusom Street E1W	246	F5
Pudding Lane EC3R	241	M7
Pumphouse Mews E1	246	D3
Purbrook Street SE1	246	A7
Purcell Street N1	241	M1
Purchese Street NW1	240	B1

Q

Entry	Page	Grid
Quebec Way SE16	247	J7
Queen Anne's Gate SW1H	244	B3
Queen Anne Street W1G	239	K5
Queen Elizabeth Street SE1	246	B6
Queen Mother Gate W2	243	J2
Queensborough Terrace W2	238	C7
Queensbury Place SW7	242	E5
Queen's Gardens SW7	238	C7
Queen's Gate SW7	242	D3
Queen's Gate SW7	242	D4
Queen's Gate Gardens SW7	242	D5
Queen's Gate Mews SW7	242	D4
Queen's Gate Place SW7	242	D4
Queen's Gate Place Mews SW7	242	D4
Queen's Gate Terrace SW7	242	C4
Queen's Mews W2	238	B7
Queen Square WC1N	240	D4
Queen's Row SE17	245	K7
Queen Street EC4N	241	K7
Queen Street W1J	243	L1
Queen Street Place EC4R	241	K7
Queen's Walk SE1	246	A5
Queen's Walk SW1A	243	M2
Queensway W2	238	B6
Queensway ⊖ W2	238	B8
Queen Victoria Street EC4V	241	J7
Quick Street N1	241	H1

R

Entry	Page	Grid
Raby Street E14	247	K2
Radcliffe Road SE1	246	B8
Radcot Street SE11	245	G7
Radnor Mews W2	238	E6
Radnor Place W2	238	F6
Radnor Street EC1V	241	K3
Radnor Walk SW3	243	G7
Railway Approach SE1	245	L1
Railway Avenue SE16	247	G6
Railway Street N1	240	D1
Raine Street E1W	246	F5
Ralston Street SW3	243	H7
Ramillies Place W1F	239	M6
Ramillies Street W1F	239	M6
Rampart Street E1	246	E2
Rampayne Street SW1V	244	B6
Randall Road SE11	244	D6
Randall Row SE11	244	E6
Randolph Avenue W9	238	B1
Randolph Crescent W9	238	C3
Randolph Gardens NW6	238	B1
Randolph Mews W9	238	D4
Randolph Road W9	238	C4
Ranelagh Grove SW1W	243	K6
Ranelagh Road SW1V	244	A7
Rangoon Street * EC3N	246	B3
Ranston Street NW8	238	F4
Raphael Street SW7	243	G3
Ratcliffe Cross Street E1W	247	J3
Ratcliffe Lane E14	247	J3
Rathbone Place W1T	240	B5
Rathbone Street W1T	240	A5
Raven Row E1	246	F1
Ravensdon Street SE11	245	G7
Ravey Street EC2A	241	M3
Rawlings Street SW3	243	G5
Rawstorne Street EC1V	241	H2
Ray Street EC1R	241	G4
Reardon Place E1W	246	E5
Reardon Street E1W	246	E5
Rectory Square E1	247	H1
Redan Place W2	238	B6
Redburn Street SW3	243	G7
Redcastle Close E1W	247	G4
Redcliffe Gardens SW10	242	B7
Redcliffe Mews SW10	242	C7
Redcliffe Place SW10	242	C8
Redcliffe Road SW10	242	D7
Redcliffe Square SW10	242	B7
Redcliffe Street SW10	242	B8
Redcross Way SE1	245	K2
Redesdale Street SW3	243	G7
Redfield Lane SW5	242	A5
Redhill Street NW1	239	L1
Red Lion Row SE5	245	K8
Red Lion Square WC1R	240	E5
Red Lion Street WC2B	240	E5
Redman's Road E1	247	G1
Red Place W1K	239	J7
Redriff Road SE16	247	J8
Reedworth Street SE11	245	G6
Reeves Mews W1K	239	J8
Regal Close E1	246	D1
Regan Way N1	241	M1
Regency Street SW1P	244	B5
Regent Place W1B	240	A7
Regent's Park ⊖ W1B	239	L4
Regent's Park NW1	239	J1
Regent's Park Estate NW1	239	L2
Regent Square WC1H	240	D2
Regent Street SW1Y	240	B8
Regent Street W1S	239	M7
Relton Mews SW7	243	G4
Remington Street N1	241	H1
Remnant Street WC2A	240	E6
Renforth Street SE16	247	G7
Renfrew Road SE11	245	H5
Rennie Street SE1	245	H1
Rephidim Street SE1	245	M4
Repton Street E14	247	K2
Reveley Square SE16	247	K7
Rex Place W1K	239	J8
Rhodeswell Road E14	247	L2
Rich Street E14	247	M3
Rickett Street SW6	242	A8
Ridgemount Street WC1E	240	B4
Ridgemount Gardens WC1E	240	B4
Riding House Street W1W	239	M5
Riley Road SE1	246	B7
Risborough Street SE1	245	J2
Risdon Street SE16	247	G7
Rissinghill Street N1	240	F1
River Street EC1R	240	F2
Rivington Street EC2A	241	M3
Robert Adam Street W1U	239	J6
Roberts Close SE16	247	J7
Robert Street NW1	239	L2
Rochester Row SW1P	244	A5
Rochester Street SW1P	244	B5
Rockingham Street SE1	245	J4
Rocliffe Street N1	241	H1
Roding Mews E1W	246	D5
Rodmarton Street W1U	239	H5
Rodney Place SE17	245	K5
Rodney Road SE17	245	K5
Rodney Street N1	240	E1
Roger Street WC1N	240	E4
Roland Gardens SW7	242	D6
Roland Way SE17	245	L7
Romford Street E1	246	E2
Romilly Street W1D	240	B7
Romney Street SW1P	244	C5
Rood Lane EC3M	241	M7
Ropemaker Road SE16	247	K7
Ropemaker Street EC2Y	241	L4
Roper Lane SE1	246	B7
Rope Street SE16	247	K8
Rope Walk Gardens E1	246	E2
Rosary Gardens SW7	242	D6
Roscoe Street EC1Y	241	K3
Rose Alley SE1	241	K8
Rosebery Avenue EC1R	240	F3
Rosemoor Street SW3	243	G6
Rose Street WC2E	240	C7
Rossmore Road NW1	239	G3
Rotary Street SE1	245	H3
Rotherhithe ⊖ SE16	247	G6
Rotherhithe Street SE16	247	G6
Rotherhithe Street SE16	247	J4
Rotherhithe Tunnel SE16	247	H5
Rothsay Street SE1	245	M4
Rotten Row W2	242	F2
Rouel Road SE16	246	C8
Roupell Street SE1	245	G2
Royal Albert Hall SW7	242	E3
Royal Avenue SW3	243	H6
Royal Hospital Road SW3	243	H7
Royal Mint Street E1	246	C4
Royal Oak ⊖ W2	238	B5
Royal Oak Yard SE1	246	A7
Royal Opera House WC2E	240	D7
Royal Road SE17	245	H8
Royal Street SE1	244	E3
Rudolph Road NW6	238	A1
Rugby Street WC1N	240	E4
Rum Close E1W	246	F4
Rupack Street SE16	247	G7
Rupert Street W1D	240	B7
Rushworth Street SE1	245	H2
Russell Court SW1A	244	A2
Russell Square WC1B	240	C4
Russell Square ⊖ WC1B	240	D4
Russell Street WC2B	240	D7
Russia Dock Road SE16	247	K6
Rutherford Street SW1P	244	B5
Rutland Gardens SW7	243	G3
Rutland Gate SW7	242	F3
Rutland Mews SW7	242	F4
Rutland Street SW7	242	F4
Ryder Street SW1Y	244	A1

S

Entry	Page	Grid
Sackville Street W1S	240	A8
Saffron Hill EC1N	241	G4
Saffron Street EC1N	241	G4
Sail Street SE11	244	F5
St Agnes Place SE11	245	G8
St Alban's Grove W8	242	C4
St Alban's Street SW1Y	240	B8
St Alphage Garden EC2Y	241	K5
St Andrews Hill EC4V	241	H7
St Andrew's Place NW1	239	L3
St Andrew Street EC4A	241	G5
St Anne's Court W1F	240	B6
St Ann's Street SW1P	244	C4
St Anselm's Place W1K	239	K7
St Barnabas Street SW1W	243	K6
St Botolph Street EC3N	246	B2
St Bride Street EC4A	241	G6
St Chad's Street WC1H	240	D2
St Clare Street EC3N	246	B3
St Clements Lane WC2A	240	E6
St Cross Street EC1N	241	G4
St Dunstan's Hill EC3R	241	M8
St Dunstan's Lane EC3R	241	M7
St Elmos Road SE16	247	J7
St Ermin's Hill SW1H	244	B3
St George's Circus SE1	245	H3
St George's Drive SW1V	243	M6
St George's Estate E1	246	D3
St George's Lane * EC3R	241	M7
St George's Road SE1	245	G4
St George's Square SW1V	244	B7
St George Street W1S	239	L7
St Giles High Street WC2H	240	C6
St Helen's Place EC3A	241	M6
St James Market * SW1Y	240	B8
St James's Park ⊖ SW1H	244	B3
St James's Park SW1A	244	B3
St James's Place SW1A	243	M2
St James's Road SE16	246	D8
St James's Square SW1Y	244	A1
St James's Street SW1A	243	M1
St James Walk EC1R	241	G3
St John's Lane EC1M	241	H4
St John's Place EC1M	241	H4
St John's Square EC1V	241	H4
St John's Wood High Street NW8	238	F1
St John's Wood Road NW8	238	E3
St Katharine's Way E1W	246	C5
St Leonard's Terrace SW3	243	H7
St Loo Avenue SW3	243	G8
St Luke's Close EC1V	241	K3
St Luke's Street SW3	242	F6
St Manningtree E1	246	C2
St Mark Street E1	246	C3
St Martin's Lane WC2N	240	C7
St Martin's le Grand EC1A	241	J6
St Martin's Place WC2N	240	C8
St Mary at Hill EC3R	241	M8
St Mary Axe EC3A	246	A3
St Marychurch Street SE16	246	F7
St Mary's Gardens SE11	245	G5
St Mary's Terrace W2	238	D4
St Mary's Walk SE11	245	G5
St Matthew Street SW1P	244	B4
St Michael's Street W2	238	F6
St Olav's Square SE16	246	F7
St Oswald's Place SE11	244	E7
St Oswulf Street * SW1P	244	C5
St Pancras International ≥ N1C	240	C1
St Paul's ⊖ EC1A	241	J6
St Paul's Avenue SE16	247	J5
St Paul's Cathedral EC4M	241	J6
St Paul's Churchyard EC4M	241	J6
St Paul's Way E3	247	L1
St Petersburgh Mews W2	238	B7
St Petersburgh Place W2	238	B7
St Stephen's Gardens W2	238	A5
St Swithin's Lane EC4N	241	L7
St Thomas Street SE1	245	L2
St Vincent Street W1U	239	J5
Salamanca Street SE11	244	D6
Sale Place W2	238	F5
Salisbury Court EC4Y	241	H6
Salisbury Place W1H	239	H4
Salisbury Street NW8	238	F4
Salmon Lane E14	247	J2
Salter Road SE16	247	J5
Salter Street E14	247	M3
Samford Street NW8	238	F4
Sampson Street E1W	246	D5
Sancroft Street SE11	244	F6
Sandland Street WC1R	240	E5
Sandpiper Close SE16	247	L6
Sandwich Street WC1H	240	C2
Sandy's Row E1	246	B1
Sans Walk EC1R	241	G3
Sardinia Street WC2A	240	E6
Savage Gardens EC3N	246	B3
Savile Row W1S	239	M7
Savoy Hill WC2R	240	E8
Savoy Place WC2R	240	D8
Savoy Street WC2E	240	E7
Sawyer Street SE1	245	J2
Sayer Street SE17	245	J6
Scala Street W1T	240	A5
Scandrett Street E1W	246	E5
Scarborough Street E1	246	C3
Scarsdale Villas W8	242	A4
Schooner Close * SE16	247	H6
Science Museum SW7	242	E4
Scoresby Street SE1	245	H2
Scotch House Junction SW1X	243	G3
Scotland Place SW1A	244	C1
Scott Ellis Gardens NW8	238	E2
Scott Lidgett Crescent SE16	246	D7
Scrutton Street EC2A	241	M3
Seaford Street WC1H	240	D2
Seagrave Road SW6	242	A8
Sea Life London Aquarium SE1	244	E3
Searles Road SE1	245	L5
Sebastian Street EC1V	241	H2
Secker Street SE1	244	F2
Sedan Way SE17	245	M6
Sedding Street SW1X	243	J5
Seddon Street WC1X	240	E3
Seething Lane EC3N	246	A4
Sekforde Street EC1R	241	H3
Selfridges W1A	239	J6
Selsey Street E14	247	M1
Selwood Place SW7	242	E6
Semley Place SW1W	243	K6
Senior Street W2	238	B4
Senrab Street E1	247	H2
Serle Street WC2A	240	F6
Serpentine Bridge W2	242	F1
Serpentine Road W2	242	F2
Seth Street SE16	247	G7
Settles Street E1	246	D2
Seven Dials WC2H	240	C6
Seville Street SW1X	243	H3
Sevington Street W9	238	A3
Seward Street EC1V	241	J3
Seymour Mews W1H	239	J6
Seymour Place W1H	239	G5
Seymour Street W1H	239	H6
Seymour Street W2	239	G7
Seymour Walk SW10	242	C7
Shad Thames SE1	246	B6
Shad Thames SE1	246	C6
Shadwell ⊖ E1	246	F3
Shadwell Gardens E1	246	F3
Shaftesbury Avenue WC2H	240	B7
Shaftesbury Avenue WC2H	240	C6
Shaftesbury Street N1	241	L1
Shakespeare's Globe SE1	241	J8
Shand Street SE1	246	A6
Sharsted Street SE17	245	H7
Shaw Crescent E14	247	K2
Shawfield Street SW3	243	G7
Sheffield Terrace W8	242	A2
Sheldon Square W2	238	D5
Shelmerdine Close E3	247	M1
Shelton Street WC2H	240	D6
Shepherdess Walk N1	241	K1
Shepherd Street W1J	243	K1
Sheraton Street W1F	240	B6
Sherborne Lane EC4N	241	L7
Sherwood Street W1D	240	A7
Ship and Mermaid Row SE1	245	M2
Shipwright Road SE16	247	K7
Shirland Road W9	238	A3
Shoe Lane EC4A	241	G5
Shorter Street EC3N	246	B4
Shorts Gardens WC2H	240	C6
Short Street SE1	245	G2
Shoulder of Mutton Alley E14	247	K4
Shouldham Street W1H	239	G5
Shroton Street NW1	238	F4
Siddons Lane W1H	239	H4
Sidmouth Street WC1N	240	D3
Sidney Square E1	246	F2
Sidney Street E1	246	F1
Silex Street SE1	245	H3
Silk Street EC2Y	241	K4
Silver Walk SE16	247	K5
Silvester Street SE1	245	K3
Singer Street EC2A	241	L3
Sir John Soane's Museum WC2A	240	E5
Sir Simon Milton Square SW1V	243	L4
Skinner Place * SW1W	243	J6
Skinners Lane EC4V	241	K7
Skinner Street EC1R	241	G3
Slippers Place SE16	246	F8
Sloane Avenue SW3	243	G6
Sloane Court East SW3	243	J6
Sloane Court West SW3	243	J6
Sloane Gardens SW1W	243	J6
Sloane Square SW1W	243	J6
Sloane Square ⊖ SW1W	243	J6
Sloane Street SW1X	243	H3
Sloane Terrace SW1X	243	J5
Smeaton Street E1W	246	E5
Smithfield Street EC1A	241	H5
Smith Square SW1P	244	C4
Smith Street SW3	243	G7
Smith Terrace SW3	243	G7
Smithy Street E1	247	G1
Snowden Street EC2A	241	M4
Snow Hill EC1A	241	H5
Snowsfields SE1	245	L2
Soho Square W1D	240	B6
Soho Street W1D	240	B6
Somerford Way SE16	247	K6
Somers Crescent W2	238	F6
Somerset House WC2R	240	E7
Somerstown Estate NW1	240	A1
Sondes Street SE17	245	L7
South & West Africa Gate SW1A	244	C3
Southall Place SE1	245	L3
Southampton Buildings WC2A	240	F5
Southampton Place WC1A	240	D5
Southampton Row WC1B	240	D4
Southampton Street WC2E	240	D7
South Audley Street W1K	239	K8
South Carriage Drive SW1X	243	H3
South Carriage Drive W2	242	F3
South Eaton Place SW1W	243	J5
Southern Street N1	240	E1
South Kensington ⊖ SW7	242	E4
South Kensington ⊖ SW7	242	E5
South Lambeth Road SW8	244	D8

South Molton Lane W1K......239 K7
South Molton Street W1K......239 K7
South Parade SW3......242 E7
South Place EC2M......241 L5
South Sea Street SE16......247 L8
South Square WC1R......240 F5
South Street W1K......243 J1
South Tenter Street E1......246 C3
South Terrace SW7......242 F5
Southwark ⊖ SE1......245 H2
Southwark Bridge SE1......241 K8
Southwark Bridge Road SE1......245 J3
Southwark Park Road SE16......246 E8
Southwark Street SE1......245 H1
Southwell Gardens SW7......242 C5
South Wharf Road W2......238 E6
Southwick Mews W2......238 F6
Southwick Place W2......238 F6
Southwick Street W2......238 F6
Sovereign Close E1W......246 F4
Sovereign Crescent SE16......247 J4
Spanish Place W1U......239 J5
Spa Road SE16......246 C8
Spear Mews SW5......242 A6
Spelman Street E1......246 C1
Spence Close SE16......247 K7
Spencer Street EC1V......241 H2
Spenser Street SW1E......244 A4
Spert Street E14......247 J4
Spital Square E1......246 A1
Spring Gardens SW1A......244 C1
Spring Street W2......238 E6
Spurgeon Street SE1......245 L4
Spur Road SE1......244 F3
Stables Way SE11......244 F7
Stable Yard Road SW1A......244 A2
Stacey Street WC2H......240 C6
Stafford Place SW1E......243 M3
Stafford Road NW6......238 A2
Stafford Street W1S......239 M8
Stafford Terrace W8......242 A3
Stainer Street SE1......245 L2
Staining Lane EC2V......241 K6
Stainsby Road E14......247 M2
Stalham Street SE16......246 F8
Stamford Street SE1......245 G1
Stanford Place SE1......245 M6
Stanford Road W8......242 B4
Stanford Street * SW1V......244 B6
Stanhope Close * SE16......247 H6
Stanhope Gardens SW7......242 D5
Stanhope Gate W1K......243 K1
Stanhope Mews SW7......242 D5
Stanhope Mews East SW7......242 D5
Stanhope Mews West SW7......242 D5
Stanhope Place W2......239 G7
Stanhope Place Gate W2......239 G7
Stanhope Row W1J......243 K1
Stanhope Street NW1......239 M1
Stanhope Terrace W2......238 E7
Stannary Street SE11......245 G2
Staples Close SE16......247 J5
Staple Street SE1......245 L3
Starcross Street NW1......240 A2
Star Street W2......238 F6
Station Approach SE1......244 F3
Stave Yard Road SE16......247 J5
Stead Street SE17......245 K6
Steedman Street SE17......245 J6
Steel's Lane E1......247 G3
Steeres Way SE16......247 K7
Stephenson Way NW1......240 A3
Stephen Street W1T......240 B5
Stepney Green E1......247 H1
Stepney High Street E1......247 J1
Stepney Way E1......246 E1
Sterling Street SW7......243 G3
Stevedore Street E1W......246 E5
Stevens Street SE1......246 A7
Steward Street * E1......246 B1
Stewart's Grove SW3......242 F6
Stew Lane EC4V......241 J7
Stillington Street SW1P......244 A5
Stockholm Way E1W......246 D5
Stocks Place E14......247 M3
Stone Buildings WC2A......240 F5
Stonecutter Street EC4A......241 G6
Stoney Lane E1......246 B2
Stoney Street SE1......245 K1
Stopford Road SE17......245 J7
Store Street WC1E......240 B5
Storey's Gate SW1H......244 C3
Storks Road SE16......246 D8
Stoughton Close SE11......244 E6
Stourcliffe Street W1H......239 G6
Strafford Street E14......247 M6
Strand WC2R......240 D8
Stratford Place W1C......239 K6
Stratford Road W8......242 A5
Strathearn Place W2......238 F7
Stratton Street W1J......243 L1
Strutton Ground SW1P......244 B4
Strype Street E1......246 B2
Stuart Road NW6......238 A2
Stukeley Street WC2B......240 D6
Sturgeon Road SE17......245 J7
Sturge Street SE1......245 J3
Sturt Street N1......241 K1
Stutfield Street E1......246 D3
Sudley Street N1......241 H1
Sudrey Street SE1......245 J3
Suffolk Lane EC4V......241 L7
Suffolk Street SW1Y......240 B8
Sugar Lane SE16......246 D7
Sugar Quay Walk EC3R......246 A4
Sullivan Road SE11......245 G5
Summercourt Road E1......247 G2
Summers Street EC1R......240 F4
Sumner Place SW7......242 E6
Sumner Street SE1......245 J1
Sunderland Terrace W2......238 A6
Sun Passage SE16......246 D8
Sun Street EC2M......241 M4
Sun Street Passage EC2M......241 M5
Surrendale Place W9......238 A4
Surrey Quays Road SE16......247 H7
Surrey Row SE1......245 H2
Surrey Square SE17......245 M6
Surrey Street WC2E......240 E7
Surrey Water Road SE16......247 H6
Sussex Gardens W2......238 E6
Sussex Mews East W2......238 E7
Sussex Place NW1......239 H3
Sussex Place W2......238 E6
Sussex Square W2......238 E7
Sussex Street SW1V......243 L7

Sutherland Avenue W9......238 A4
Sutherland Row SW1V......243 L6
Sutherland Square SE17......245 J7
Sutherland Street SW1V......243 L7
Sutton Row W1D......240 B6
Sutton Street E1......247 G3
Suttons Way EC1Y......241 K4
Swain Street NW8......238 F3
Swallow Place W1B......239 L6
Swallow Street W1B......240 A8
Swan Lane EC4R......241 L8
Swan Mead SE1......245 M4
Swan Road SE16......247 G6
Swan Street SE1......245 K3
Swan Walk SW3......243 H8
Swedenborg Gardens E1......246 E4
Sweeney Crescent SE1......246 C7
Swinton Street WC1X......240 E2
Sydney Place SW7......242 F6
Sydney Street SW3......242 F6
Symons Street SW3......243 H6

T

Tabard Gardens Estate SE1......245 L3
Tabard Street SE1......245 L3
Tabernacle Street EC2A......241 L3
Tachbrook Street SW1V......244 A6
Talbot Road W2......238 A6
Talbot Square W2......238 E6
Talbot Yard SE1......245 L2
Tallis Street EC4Y......241 G7
Tamworth Street SW6......242 A8
Tanner Street SE1......246 A7
Taplow Street N1......241 K1
Tarling Street E1......246 F3
Tarver Road SE17......245 H7
Tatum Street SE17......245 M6
Taunton Place NW1......239 G3
Tavistock Place WC1H......240 C3
Tavistock Square WC1H......240 C3
Tavistock Street WC2E......240 D7
Taviton Street WC1H......240 B3
Teak Close SE16......247 K6
Tedworth Square SW3......243 G7
Telford Terrace SW1V......243 M7
Temeraire Street SE16......247 G6
Temple ⊖ WC2R......240 F7
Temple Avenue EC4Y......241 G7
Temple Lane EC4Y......241 G7
Temple Place WC2R......240 F7
Templeton Place SW5......242 A5
Tench Street E1W......246 E5
Tenniel Close W2......238 C7
Tennis Street SE1......245 L2
Tenterden Street W1S......239 L6
Tenterground E1......246 B1
Teredo Street SE16......247 J8
Terminus Place SW1V......243 L4
Thame Road SE16......247 H6
Thanet Street WC1H......240 C2
Thavies Inn EC4A......241 G6
Thayer Street W1U......239 K5
The Arches WC2N......240 D8
The Boltons SW10......242 C7
The British Library NW1......240 C2
The British Museum WC1B......240 C5
The Broad Walk W2......238 B8
The Broad Walk W8......242 C2
The Cut SE1......245 G2
Theed Street SE1......245 G2
The Flower Walk W2......242 D3
The Grange SE1......246 B8
The Highway E1W......246 E4
The Little Boltons SW10......242 C7
The Mall SW1A......244 B2
The Mitre E14......247 L3
The Monument EC3R......241 L7
The National Gallery WC2N......240 C8
Theobald's Road WC1X......240 E4
Theobald Street SE1......245 L5
The Oval (Surrey County
Cricket Ground) SE11......244 F8
The Shard SE1......245 L2
The Vale SW3......242 E8
Thirleby Road SW1P......244 A4
Thomas More Street E1W......246 D4
Thomas Road E14......247 M2
Thoresby Street N1......241 K1
Thorney Street SW1P......244 C5
Thornton Place W1H......239 H4
Thrale Street SE1......245 K1
Thrawl Street E1......246 C1
Threadneedle Street EC2R......241 L6
Three Colt Street E14......247 L3
Three Oak Lane SE1......246 B6
Throgmorton Avenue EC2N......241 L6
Throgmorton Street EC2N......241 L6
Thurland Road SE16......246 D8
Thurloe Place SW7......242 F5
Thurloe Square SW7......242 F5
Thurloe Street SW7......242 E5
Thurlow Street SE17......245 M7
Tichbourne Row W2......238 F6
Tiller Road E14......247 M8
Tillman Street E1......246 E3
Tilney Street W1J......243 K1
Timber Pond Road SE16......247 J6
Tinsley Road E1......247 G1
Tinworth Street SE11......244 D6
Tisdall Place SE17......245 L6
Tite Street SW3......243 H8
Tiverton Street SE1......245 J4
Token House Yard EC2R......241 L6
Tolmer's Square NW1......240 A3
Tomlin's Terrace E14......247 K2
Tonbridge Street WC1H......240 D2
Tooley Street SE1......245 L1
Tooley Street SE1......246 B6
Tor Gardens W8......242 A2
Torquay Street W2......238 A5
Torrens Street EC1V......241 G1
Torrington Place E1W......246 D5
Torrington Place WC1E......240 B4
Torrington Square WC1E......240 B4
Tothill Street SW1H......244 B3
Tottenham Court Road W1T......240 A4
Tottenham Court Road ⊖ W1D......240 B6
Tottenham Street W1T......240 A4
Toulmin Street SE1......245 J3
Tower Bridge SE1......246 B5
Tower Bridge Approach EC3N......246 B5

Tower Bridge Road SE1......246 A7
Tower Bridge Wharf E1W......246 C5
Tower Gateway ⊖ EC3N......246 B4
Tower Hill EC3N......246 B4
Tower Hill ⊖ EC3N......246 B4
Tower of London EC3N......246 B4
Tower Place EC3R......246 A4
Tower Street WC2H......240 C7
Townsend Street SE17......245 M5
Toynbee Street E1......246 B1
Trafalgar Gardens E1......247 H1
Trafalgar Square WC2N......240 C8
Trafalgar Street SE17......245 L7
Transept Street NW1......238 F5
Trebeck Street W1J......243 L1
Trebovir Road SW5......242 A6
Tregunter Road SW10......242 C7
Trenton Road SE16......246 E8
Tresham Crescent NW8......238 F3
Trevor Place SW7......243 G3
Trevor Square SW7......243 G3
Trevor Street SW7......243 J5
Trinidad Street E14......247 M4
Trinity Church Square SE1......245 K3
Trinity Square EC3N......246 B4
Trinity Street SE1......245 K3
Trump Street EC2V......241 K6
Tudor Street EC4Y......241 G7
Tufton Street SW1P......244 C4
Tunnel Road SE16......247 G6
Turks Row SW3......243 J6
Turner's Road E3......247 L2
Turner Street E1......246 E2
Turnmill Street EC1N......241 G4
Turpentine Lane SW1V......243 L7
Turquand Street SE17......245 K6
Tyers Gate SE1......245 M3
Tyers Street SE11......244 E7
Tyers Terrace SE11......244 E7
Tyron Street SW3......243 H6
Tysoe Street EC1R......241 G3

U

Udall Street SW1P......244 A5
Ufford Street SE1......245 G2
Ulster Place NW1......239 K4
Umberston Street E1......246 E2
Undershaft EC3A......246 A2
Underwood Road N1......241 K2
Underwood Street N1......241 K1
Union Street SE1......245 H2
University Street WC1E......240 A4
Upbrook Mews W2......238 D6
Upper Belgrave Street SW1X......243 K4
Upper Berkeley Street W1H......239 H6
Upper Brook Street W1K......239 J7
Upper Cheyne Row SW3......242 F8
Upper Grosvenor Street W1K......239 J8
Upper Ground SE1......244 F1
Upper Harley Street NW1......239 K3
Upper James Street W1F......240 A7
Upper John Street W1F......240 A7
Upper Marsh SE1......244 E3
Upper Montagu Street W1H......239 H5
Upper St Martin's WC2N......240 C7
Upper Tachbrook Street SW1V......244 A5
Upper Thames Street EC4V......241 J7
Upper Wimpole Street W1G......239 K4
Upper Woburn Place WC1H......240 B2
Urlwin Street SE5......245 J8
Uxbridge Street W8......242 A1

V

Valentine Place SE1......245 G3
Vandon Passage SW1H......244 A3
Vandon Street SW1H......244 A4
Varden Street E1......246 E2
Varndell Street NW1......239 M2
Vauban Street SE16......246 C8
Vaughan Street SE16......247 L7
Vaughan Way E1W......246 D5
Vauxhall ≋ ⊖ SW8......244 D7
Vauxhall Bridge SW1V......244 C7
Vauxhall Bridgefoot SE1......244 D7
Vauxhall Bridge Road SW1V......243 M5
Vauxhall Cross SE1......244 D7
Vauxhall Grove SW8......244 D8
Vauxhall Street SE11......244 E6
Vauxhall Walk SE11......244 E6
Venables Street W2......238 E4
Vere Street W1G......239 K6
Vernon Place WC1A......240 D5
Vernon Rise WC1X......240 E2
Verulam Street WC1X......240 F4
Vestry Street N1......241 L2
Victoria ≋ ⊖ SW1V......243 L5
Victoria & Albert Museum SW7......242 E4
Victoria Embankment SW1A......244 D2
Victoria Embankment WC2R......240 F7
Victoria Gate W2......238 E7
Victoria Road W8......242 C4
Victoria Square SW1W......243 L4
Victoria Street SW1E......243 L4
Victory Place SE17......245 K5
Victory Way SE16......247 K7
Vigo Street W1S......239 M8
Villa Street SE17......245 L7
Villiers Street WC2N......240 D8
Vincent Close SE16......247 K7
Vincent Square SW1P......244 B5
Vincent Street SW1P......244 B5
Vincent Terrace N1......241 H1
Vince Street EC1V......241 L2
Vine Court E1......246 D1
Vinegar Street E1W......246 E5
Vine Hill EC1R......240 F4
Vine Lane SE1......246 A6
Vine Street EC3N......246 B3
Violet Hill NW8......238 C1
Virgil Street SE1......244 F4
Virginia Street E1W......246 D4
Viscount Street EC2Y......241 J4

W

Wadding Street SE17......245 K6
Wakefield Street WC1H......240 D3
Wakeling Street E14......247 J3

Wakley Street EC1V......241 H2
Walbrook EC4N......241 L7
Walcorde Avenue SE17......245 K6
Walcot Square SE11......245 G5
Walden Street E1......246 E2
Waley Street E1......247 J1
Wallwood Street E14......247 M1
Walnut Tree Walk SE11......244 F5
Walpole Street SW3......243 H6
Walter Terrace E1......247 J2
Walton Place SW3......243 H4
Walton Street SW3......243 G4
Walworth Place SE17......245 K7
Walworth Road SE17......245 J5
Wandsworth Road SW8......244 C8
Wansey Street SE17......245 K5
Wapping ⊖ E1W......246 F5
Wapping High Street E1W......246 E6
Wapping Lane E1W......246 F4
Wapping Wall E1W......247 G5
Warden's Grove SE1......245 J2
Wardour Street W1F......240 B6
Warner Street EC1R......240 F4
Warren Street W1T......239 M4
Warren Street ⊖ NW1......239 M3
Warrington Crescent W9......238 C3
Warrington Gardens W9......238 C4
Warwick Avenue W9......238 B3
Warwick Avenue ⊖ W9......238 C4
Warwick Crescent W2......238 C5
Warwick House Street
SW1Y......244 B1
Warwick Lane EC4M......241 H6
Warwick Place W9......238 C4
Warwick Road SW5......242 A6
Warwick Row SW1E......243 L4
Warwick Square SW1V......243 M6
Warwick Street W1B......240 A7
Warwick Way SW1V......243 L6
Waterhouse Square EC1N......241 G5
Waterloo ⊖ ≋ SE1......244 F2
Waterloo Bridge SE1......244 E1
Waterloo Bridge WC2R......240 E8
Waterloo East ≋ SE1......245 G2
Waterloo Place SW1Y......244 B1
Waterloo Road SE1......244 F1
Waterloo Street SE1......245 G2
Waterman Way E1W......246 E5
Waterside Close SE16......246 D7
Watling Street EC4N......241 K7
Watney Street E1......246 F3
Watts Street E1W......246 E5
Waveney Close E1W......246 D5
Waverton Street W1J......239 K8
Weavers Lane SE1......246 A6
Webber Row SE1......245 G3
Webber Street SE1......245 H3
Webb Street SE1......246 A8
Webster Road SE16......246 D8
Weighhouse Street W1K......239 K7
Welbeck Street W1G......239 K5
Welbeck Way W1G......239 K6
Welland Mews E1W......246 E5
Wellclose Square E1......246 D4
Wellesley Street E1......247 H2
Wellesley Terrace N1......241 K2
Wellington Arch W1J......243 K2
Wellington Square SW3......243 H6
Wellington Place NW8......238 E2
Wellington Road NW8......238 E1
Wellington Street WC2E......240 D7
Wells Mews W1T......240 A5
Wells Street W1T......240 A5
Wells Way SE5......245 M8
Wenlock Road N1......241 K1
Wenlock Street N1......241 K1
Wentworth Street E1......246 B2
Werrington Street NW1......240 A1
Wesley Street W1G......239 K5
West Arbour Street E1......247 G2
Westbourne Crescent W2......238 D7
Westbourne Gardens W2......238 B6
Westbourne Gate W2......238 E7
Westbourne Grove W2......238 A6
Westbourne Grove Terrace W2......238 B6
Westbourne Park Road W2......238 A5
Westbourne Park Villas W2......238 A5
Westbourne Street W2......238 E7
Westbourne Terrace W2......238 D6
Westbourne Terrace Mews W2......238 C6
Westbourne Terrace Road W2......238 C5
West Brompton ≋ ⊖ SW5......242 A7
West Carriage Drive W2......242 E2
Westcott Road SE17......245 H8
West Cromwell Road SW5......242 A5
Western Place SE16......247 G6
Westferry ⊖ E14......247 M4
Westferry Circus E14......247 M5
Westferry Road E14......247 M5
West Gardens E1W......246 F4
Westgate Terrace SW10......242 B7
West Halkin Street SW1X......243 J4
West Harding Street EC4A......241 G6
West India Avenue E14......247 M5
West India Dock Road E14......247 M3
Westland Place N1......241 K2
West Lane SE16......246 E7
Westminster ⊖ SW1A......244 D3
Westminster Abbey SW1P......244 C3
Westminster Bridge SE1......244 D3
Westminster Bridge Road SE1......244 F3
Westmoreland Place SW1V......243 L7
Westmoreland Road SE17......245 K8
Westmoreland Street W1G......239 K5
Westmoreland Terrace SW1V......243 L7
Weston Rise WC1X......240 E2
Weston Street SE1......245 M2
Weston Street SE1......245 M3
Westport Street E1......247 H2
West Poultry Avenue EC1A......241 H5
West Road SW3......243 H7
West Smithfield EC1A......241 H5
West Square SE11......245 H4
West Tenter Street E1......246 C3
West Warwick Place SW1V......243 M6
Westway W2......238 B5
Wetherby Gardens SW5......242 C6
Weyhill Road E1......246 D2
Weymouth Mews W1G......239 L5
Weymouth Street W1G......239 K5
Wharfdale Road N1......240 D1
Wharfedale Street SW10......242 B7
Wharf Road N1......241 J1
Wharton Street WC1X......240 F2
Wheatley Street W1G......239 K5

Whetstone Park WC2A......240 E5
Whidborne Street WC1H......240 D2
Whiskin Street EC1R......241 G2
Whitcomb Street WC2H......240 B8
Whitechapel ≋ ⊖ E1......246 E1
Whitechapel Estate E1......246 C4
Whitechapel High Street E1......246 C2
Whitechapel Road E1......246 D1
Whitecross Street EC1Y......241 K3
Whitefriars Street EC4Y......241 G6
Whitehall SW1A......244 C2
Whitehall Court SW1A......244 D2
Whitehall Place SW1A......244 D1
White Hart Street SE11......245 G6
White Hart Yard SE1......245 L2
Whitehaven Street NW8......238 F4
Whitehead's Grove SW3......243 G6
White Horse Lane E1......247 H1
White Horse Road E1......247 J1
White Horse Road E1......247 J3
White Horse Street W1J......243 L1
White Kennett Street E1......246 B2
White Lion Hill EC4V......241 H7
White Lion Street N1......240 F1
White's Grounds SE1......246 A7
White's Row E1......246 B1
White Tower Way E1......247 J1
Whitfield Place W1T......240 A4
Whitfield Street W1T......240 A4
Whitgift Street SE11......244 E5
Whittaker Street SW1W......243 J6
Whittlesey Street SE1......245 G2
Wicker Street E1......246 E3
Wickham Close E1......247 G1
Wickham Street SE11......244 E7
Wicklow Street WC1X......240 E2
Widegate Street E1......246 A1
Widley Road W9......238 A3
Wigmore Place W1G......239 K5
Wigmore Street W1U......239 K6
Wigton Place SE11......245 G7
Wilbraham Place SW1X......243 J5
Wilcox Place * SW1E......244 A4
Wild Court WC2B......240 E6
Wild's Rents SE1......245 M4
Wild Street WC2B......240 D6
Wilfred Street SW1E......243 M4
Wilkes Street E1......246 B1
William IV Street WC2N......240 C8
William Mews SW1X......243 H3
William Road NW1......239 M3
Willow Place SW1P......244 A5
Willow Street EC2A......241 M3
Wilmington Square WC1X......240 F3
Wilmington Street WC1X......240 F2
Wilson Grove SE16......246 E7
Wilson Street EC2A......241 L4
Wilton Crescent SW1X......243 J3
Wilton Mews SW1X......243 K4
Wilton Place SW1X......243 J3
Wilton Road SW1V......243 M5
Wilton Row SW1X......243 J3
Wilton Street SW1X......243 K4
Wimpole Mews W1G......239 K5
Wimpole Street W1G......239 K5
Winchester Street SW1V......243 L6
Winchester Walk SE1......245 K1
Wincott Street SE11......245 G5
Windmill Road SE11......244 F7
Windmill Street W1T......240 B5
Windrose Close SE16......247 H6
Windsor Terrace N1......241 K1
Wine Close E1W......246 F5
Winnett Street W1D......240 B7
Winsland Street W2......238 E6
Winsley Street W1W......240 A6
Winthrop Street E1......246 E1
Woburn Place WC1H......240 C3
Woburn Square WC1H......240 C4
Wodeham Gardens E1......246 E1
Wolfe Crescent SE16......247 H7
Wolseley Street SE1......246 C6
Woodbridge Street EC1R......241 G3
Woodchester Square W9......238 A4
Woodfall Street SW3......243 H7
Woodland Crescent SE16......247 H7
Woodseer Street E1......246 C1
Woods Mews W1K......239 J7
Woods Place SE1......246 A8
Woodstock Street W1C......239 K6
Wood Street EC2V......241 K6
Woolaston Close SE1......245 J3
Wooler Street SE17......245 L7
Wootton Street SE1......245 G2
Worgan Street SE11......244 E6
Worgan Street SE16......247 H8
Wormwood Street EC2M......241 M5
Worship Street EC2A......241 M4
Wren Street WC1X......240 E3
Wright's Lane W8......242 A3
Wyatt Close SE16......247 L7
Wyclif Street EC1V......241 H2
Wymering Road W9......238 A2
Wynard Terrace SE11......244 F7
Wyndham Place W1H......239 H5
Wyndham Street W1H......239 G4
Wynnstay Gardens W8......242 A4
Wynyatt Street EC1V......241 H2
Wythburn Place W1H......239 H6

Y

Yalding Road * SE16......246 C8
Yardley Street WC1X......240 F2
Yeoman's Row SW3......243 G4
York Boulevard WC2N......240 D8
York Bridge NW1......239 J3
York Gate NW1......239 J4
York Road SE1......244 E2
Yorkshire Road E14......247 K3
York Square E14......247 J2
York Street W1H......239 G5
York Street W1U......239 H5
York Terrace East NW1......239 J4
York Terrace West NW1......239 J4
York Way N1......240 D1
Young Street W8......242 B3

Z

Zoar Street SE1......245 J1
ZSL London Zoo NW1......239 J1

This index lists places appearing in the main map section of the atlas in alphabetical order. The reference following each name gives the atlas page number and grid reference of the square in which the place appears. The map shows counties, unitary authorities and administrative areas, together with a list of the abbreviated name forms used in the index. The top 100 places of tourist interest are indexed in **red**, World Heritage sites in **green**, motorway service areas in **blue**, airports in **blue** *italic* and National Parks in **green** *italic*.

Scotland

Abers	Aberdeenshire
Ag & B	Argyll and Bute
Angus	Angus
Border	Scottish Borders
C Aber	City of Aberdeen
C Dund	City of Dundee
C Edin	City of Edinburgh
C Glas	City of Glasgow
Clacks	Clackmannanshire (1)
D & G	Dumfries & Galloway
E Ayrs	East Ayrshire
E Duns	East Dunbartonshire (2)
E Loth	East Lothian
E Rens	East Renfrewshire (3)
Falk	Falkirk
Fife	Fife
Highld	Highland
Inver	Inverclyde (4)
Mdloth	Midlothian (5)
Moray	Moray
N Ayrs	North Ayrshire
N Lans	North Lanarkshire (6)
Ork	Orkney Islands
P & K	Perth & Kinross
Rens	Renfrewshire (7)
S Ayrs	South Ayrshire
S Lans	South Lanarkshire
Shet	Shetland Islands
Stirlg	Stirling
W Duns	West Dunbartonshire (8)
W Isls	Western Isles (Na h-Eileanan an Iar)
W Loth	West Lothian

Wales

Blae G	Blaenau Gwent (9)
Brdgnd	Bridgend (10)
Caerph	Caerphilly (11)
Cardif	Cardiff
Carmth	Carmarthenshire
Cerdgn	Ceredigion
Conwy	Conwy
Denbgs	Denbighshire
Flints	Flintshire
Gwynd	Gwynedd
IoA	Isle of Anglesey
Mons	Monmouthshire
Myr Td	Merthyr Tydfil (12)
Neath	Neath Port Talbot (13)
Newpt	Newport (14)
Pembks	Pembrokeshire
Powys	Powys
Rhondd	Rhondda Cynon Taf (15)
Swans	Swansea
Torfn	Torfaen (16)
V Glam	Vale of Glamorgan (17)
Wrexhm	Wrexham

Channel Islands & Isle of Man

Guern	Guernsey
Jersey	Jersey
IoM	Isle of Man

England

BaNES	Bath & N E Somerset (18)
Barns	Barnsley (19)
BCP	Bournemouth, Christchurch and Poole (20)
Bed	Bedford
Birm	Birmingham
Bl w D	Blackburn with Darwen (21)
Bolton	Bolton (22)
Bpool	Blackpool
Br & H	Brighton & Hove (23)
Br For	Bracknell Forest (24)
Bristl	City of Bristol
Bucks	Buckinghamshire
Bury	Bury (25)
C Beds	Central Bedfordshire
C Brad	City of Bradford
C Derb	City of Derby
C KuH	City of Kingston upon Hull
C Leic	City of Leicester
C Nott	City of Nottingham

C Pete	City of Peterborough
C Plym	City of Plymouth
C Port	City of Portsmouth
C Sotn	City of Southampton
C Stke	City of Stoke-on-Trent
C York	City of York
Calder	Calderdale (26)
Cambs	Cambridgeshire
Ches E	Cheshire East
Ches W	Cheshire West and Chester
Cnwll	Cornwall
Covtry	Coventry
Cumb	Cumberland
Darltn	Darlington (27)
Derbys	Derbyshire
Devon	Devon
Donc	Doncaster (28)
Dorset	Dorset
Dudley	Dudley (29)
Dur	Durham
E R Yk	East Riding of Yorkshire
E Susx	East Sussex
Essex	Essex
Gatesd	Gateshead (30)
Gloucs	Gloucestershire
Gt Lon	Greater London
Halton	Halton (31)
Hants	Hampshire
Hartpl	Hartlepool (32)
Herefs	Herefordshire
Herts	Hertfordshire
IoS	Isles of Scilly
IoW	Isle of Wight
Kent	Kent
Kirk	Kirklees (33)
Knows	Knowsley (34)
Lancs	Lancashire
Leeds	Leeds
Leics	Leicestershire
Lincs	Lincolnshire
Lpool	Liverpool
Luton	Luton
M Keyn	Milton Keynes
Manch	Manchester

Medway	Medway
Middsb	Middlesbrough
N Linc	North Lincolnshire
N Nthn	North Northamptonshire
N Som	North Somerset
N Tyne	North Tyneside (35)
N u Ty	Newcastle upon Tyne
N York	North Yorkshire
NE Lin	North East Lincolnshire
Norfk	Norfolk
Notts	Nottinghamshire
Nthumb	Northumberland
Oldham	Oldham (36)
Oxon	Oxfordshire
R & Cl	Redcar & Cleveland
Readg	Reading
Rochdl	Rochdale (37)
Rothm	Rotherham (38)
Rutlnd	Rutland
S Glos	South Gloucestershire (39)
S on T	Stockton-on-Tees (40)
S Tyne	South Tyneside (41)
Salfd	Salford (42)
Sandw	Sandwell (43)
Sefton	Sefton (44)
Sheff	Sheffield
Shrops	Shropshire
Slough	Slough (45)
Solhll	Solihull (46)
Somset	Somerset
St Hel	St Helens (47)
Staffs	Staffordshire
Sthend	Southend-on-Sea
Stockp	Stockport (48)
Suffk	Suffolk
Sundld	Sunderland
Surrey	Surrey
Swindn	Swindon
Tamesd	Tameside (49)
Thurr	Thurrock (50)
Torbay	Torbay
Traffd	Trafford (51)
W & F	Westmorland & Furness
W & M	Windsor & Maidenhead (52)
W Berk	West Berkshire
W Nthn	West Northamptonshire
W Susx	West Sussex
Wakefd	Wakefield (53)
Warrtn	Warrington (54)
Warwks	Warwickshire
Wigan	Wigan (55)
Wilts	Wiltshire
Wirral	Wirral (56)
Wokham	Wokingham (57)
Wolves	Wolverhampton (58)
Worcs	Worcestershire
Wrekin	Telford & Wrekin (59)
Wsall	Walsall (60)

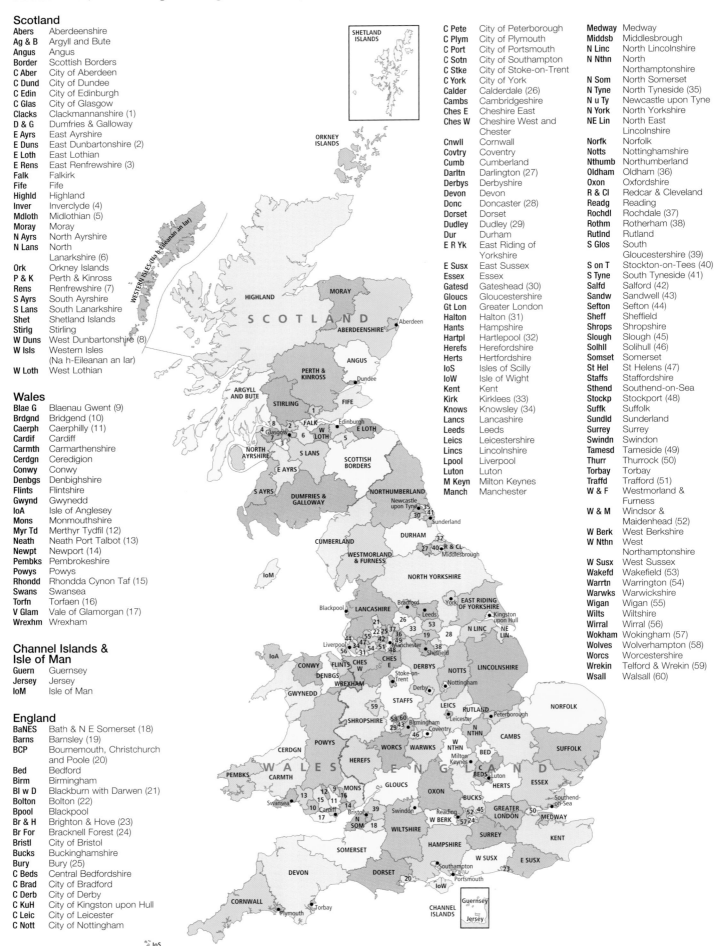

A

Abbas Combe Somset......20 D10
Abberley Worcs......57 P11
Abberley Common Worcs......57 N11
Abberton Essex......52 H8
Abberton Worcs......47 J4
Abberwick Nthumb......119 M8
Abbess Roding Essex......51 N8
Abbey Devon......10 C2
Abbeycwmhir Powys......55 P10
Abbeydale Sheff......84 D4
Abbey Dore Herefs......45 M8
Abbey Green Staffs......70 H3
Abbey Hill Somset......19 J11
Abbey Hulton C Stke......70 G5
Abbey St Bathans Border......129 K7
Abbeystead Lancs......95 M10
Abbeytown Cumb......110 C10
Abbey Village Lancs......89 J6
Abbey Wood Gt Lon......37 L5
Abbotrule Border......118 B8
Abbots Bickington Devon......16 F9
Abbots Bromley Staffs......71 K10
Abbotsbury Dorset......11 M7
Abbot's Chair Derbys......83 M6
Abbots Deuglie P & K......134 E5
Abbotsham Devon......16 G6
Abbotskerswell Devon......7 M5
Abbots Langley Herts......50 C10
Abbotsleigh Devon......7 L9
Abbots Leigh N Som......31 P10
Abbotsley Cambs......62 B9
Abbots Morton Worcs......47 K3
Abbots Ripton Cambs......62 B5
Abbot's Salford Warwks......47 L4
Abbotstone Hants......22 G8
Abbotswood Hants......22 C10
Abbots Worthy Hants......22 E8
Abbotts Ann Hants......22 B6
Abbott Street Dorset......12 G4
Abcott Shrops......56 F9
Abdon Shrops......57 K7
Abenhall Gloucs......46 C11
Aberaeron Cerdgn......43 J2
Aberaman Rhondd......30 D4
Aberangell Gwynd......55 J2
Aber-arad Carmth......42 F6
Aberarder Highld......147 Q2
Aberargie P & K......134 F4
Aberarth Cerdgn......43 J2
Aberavon Neath......29 K7
Aber-banc Cerdgn......42 G6
Aberbargoed Caerph......30 G4
Aberbeeg Blae G......30 H4
Abercanaid Myr Td......30 E4
Abercarn Caerph......30 H6
Abercastle Pembks......40 G4
Abercegir Powys......55 J4
Aberchalder Highld......147 J7
Aberchirder Abers......158 F7
Aber Clydach Powys......44 G10
Abercorn W Loth......127 K2
Abercraf Powys......29 M2
Abercregan Neath......29 M5
Abercwmboi Rhondd......30 D5
Abercych Pembks......41 P2
Abercynon Rhondd......30 E6
Aberdalgie P & K......134 D3
Aberdare Rhondd......30 D4
Aberdaron Gwynd......66 B9
Aberdeen C Aber......151 N6
Aberdeen Airport C Aber......151 M5
Aberdesach Gwynd......66 G4
Aberdour Fife......134 F10
Aberdulais Neath......29 L5
Aberdyfi Gwynd......54 E5
Aberedw Powys......44 F5
Abereiddy Pembks......40 E4
Abererch Gwynd......66 F7
Aberfan Myr Td......30 E4
Aberfeldy P & K......141 L8
Aberffraw IoA......78 F11
Aberffrwd Cerdgn......54 F9
Aberford Leeds......91 L3
Aberfoyle Stirlg......132 G7
Abergarw Brdgnd......29 P8
Abergarwed Neath......29 M4
Abergavenny Mons......31 J2
Abergele Conwy......80 C9
Aber-giar Carmth......43 K6
Abergorlech Carmth......43 L8
Abergwesyn Powys......44 B4
Abergwili Carmth......42 H10
Abergwydol Powys......54 H4
Abergwynfi Neath......29 N5
Abergwyngregyn Gwynd......79 M10
Abergynolwyn Gwynd......54 F3
Aberhafesp Powys......55 P6
Aberhosan Powys......55 J5
Aberkenfig Brdgnd......29 N8
Aberlady E Loth......128 D4
Aberlemno Angus......143 J6
Aberllefenni Gwynd......54 H3
Aberllynfi Powys......44 H7
Aberlour, Charlestown of
Moray......157 P9
Abermagwr Cerdgn......54 F10
Aber-meurig Cerdgn......43 L3
Abermorddu Flints......69 K3
Abermule Powys......56 B6
Abernant Carmth......42 F10
Abernant Rhondd......30 D4
Abernethy P & K......134 F4
Abernyte P & K......142 D11
Aberporth Cerdgn......42 E4
Abersoch Gwynd......66 E9
Abersychan Torfn......31 J4
Aberthin V Glam......30 D10
Abertillery Blae G......30 H4
Abertridwr Caerph......30 F7
Abertridwr Powys......68 D11
Abertysswg Caerph......30 F3
Aberuthven P & K......134 B4
Aberwheeler Denbgs......80 F11
Aberyscir Powys......44 D9
Aberystwyth Cerdgn......54 D8
Abingdon-on-Thames Oxon......34 E5
Abinger Common Surrey......36 D11
Abinger Hammer Surrey......36 C11
Abington S Lans......116 C6
Abington W Nthn......60 G8
Abington Pigotts Cambs......62 H2
Abington Services S Lans......116 C6
Abingworth W Susx......24 D7

Ab Kettleby Leics......73 J6
Ab Lench Worcs......47 K4
Ablington Gloucs......33 M3
Ablington Wilts......21 N5
Abney Derbys......83 Q8
Above Church Staffs......71 J4
Aboyne Abers......150 E8
Abhainn Suidhe W Isls......168 f7
Abram Wigan......82 D4
Abriachan Highld......155 Q10
Abronhill N Lans......126 D2
Abson S Glos......32 D10
Abthorpe W Nthn......48 H5
Aby Lincs......87 M5
Acaster Malbis C York......98 B11
Acaster Selby N York......91 P2
Accrington Lancs......89 M5
Acha Ag & B......136 F5
Achahoish Ag & B......123 N4
Achalader P & K......141 R8
Achaleven Ag & B......138 G11
Achanalt Highld......154 D6
Achandunie Highld......156 A3
Achany Highld......162 D6
Acharacle Highld......138 B4
Acharn Highld......138 C7
Acharn P & K......141 J9
Achavanich Highld......167 L8
Achduart Highld......160 G6
Achfary Highld......164 G9
Achgarve Highld......160 D8
A'Chill Highld......144 C6
Achiltibuie Highld......160 G5
Achina Highld......166 B4
Achinhoan Ag & B......120 E8
Achintee Highld......154 B9
Achintraid Highld......153 Q10
Achlyness Highld......164 F6
Achmelvich Highld......160 H2
Achmore Highld......153 R11
Achmore W Isls......168 i5
Achnacarnin Highld......164 B10
Achnacarry Highld......146 F10
Achnacloich Highld......145 J6
Achnaconeran Highld......147 L4
Achnacroish Ag & B......138 F9
Achnadrish Ag & B......137 M5
Achnafauld P & K......141 L10
Achnagarron Highld......156 B3
Achnaha Highld......137 M2
Achnahaird Highld......160 G4
Achnahannet Highld......148 H2
Achnairn Highld......162 D4
Achnalea Highld......138 F5
Achnamara Ag & B......130 F10
Achnasheen Highld......154 G6
Achnashellach Highld......154 D8
Achosnich Highld......137 L2
Achranich Highld......138 C8
Achreamie Highld......166 H3
Achriabhach Highld......139 L4
Achriesgill Highld......164 G6
Achtoty Highld......165 Q4
Achurch N Nthn......61 M4
Achvaich Highld......162 G8
Achvarasdal Highld......166 G4
Ackenthwaite W & F......95 L4
Ackergill Highld......167 Q6
Acklam Middsb......104 E7
Acklam N York......98 F8
Ackleton Shrops......57 P5
Acklington Nthumb......119 Q10
Ackton Wakefd......91 L6
Ackworth Moor Top Wakefd......91 L7
Acle Norfk......77 N9
Acock's Green Birm......58 H8
Acol Kent......39 P8
Acomb C York......98 B10
Acomb Nthumb......112 D7
Acombe Somset......10 D2
Aconbury Herefs......45 Q8
Acre Lancs......89 M6
Acrefair Wrexhm......69 J6
Acresford Derbys......59 L2
Acton Ches E......70 A4
Acton Dorset......12 G9
Acton Gt Lon......36 F4
Acton Shrops......56 E8
Acton Staffs......70 E6
Acton Suffk......52 E2
Acton Worcs......58 B11
Acton Wrexhm......69 K4
Acton Beauchamp Herefs......46 C4
Acton Bridge Ches W......82 C9
Acton Burnell Shrops......57 J4
Acton Green Herefs......46 C4
Acton Pigott Shrops......57 J4
Acton Round Shrops......57 L5
Acton Scott Shrops......56 H7
Acton Trussell Staffs......70 G11
Acton Turville S Glos......32 F8
Adbaston Staffs......70 D9
Adber Dorset......19 Q10
Adbolton Notts......72 F3
Adderbury Oxon......48 E7
Adderley Shrops......70 B7
Adderstone Nthumb......119 M4
Addiewell W Loth......126 H5
Addingham C Brad......96 G11
Addington Bucks......49 K9
Addington Gt Lon......37 J8
Addington Kent......37 Q9
Addiscombe Gt Lon......36 H7
Addlestone Surrey......36 C7
Addlestonemoor Surrey......36 C7
Addlethorpe Lincs......87 P7
Adeney Wrekin......70 B11
Adeyfield Herts......50 C9
Adfa Powys......55 P4
Adforton Herefs......56 G10
Adisham Kent......39 M11
Adlestrop Gloucs......47 P9
Adlingfleet E R Yk......92 D6
Adlington Ches E......83 J8
Adlington Lancs......89 J8
Admaston Staffs......71 J10
Admaston Wrekin......57 L2
Admington Warwks......47 P5
Adpar Cerdgn......42 F6
Adsborough Somset......19 J9
Adscombe Somset......18 G7
Adstock Bucks......49 K8
Adstone W Nthn......48 G4

Adswood Stockp......83 J7
Adversane W Susx......24 C6
Advie Highld......157 L11
Adwalton Leeds......90 G5
Adwell Oxon......35 J5
Adwick le Street Donc......91 N9
Adwick upon Dearne Donc......91 M10
Ae D & G......109 L3
Ae Bridgend D & G......109 M3
Afan Forest Park Neath......29 N5
Affetside Bury......89 M8
Affleck Abers......158 E9
Affpuddle Dorset......12 D6
Affric Lodge Highld......146 F3
Afon-wen Flints......80 G10
Afton Devon......7 L6
Afton IoW......13 P7
Agglethorpe N York......96 G3
Aigburth Lpool......81 M7
Aike E R Yk......99 L11
Aiketgate W & F......111 J11
Aikhead Cumb......110 D11
Aikton Cumb......110 E10
Ailby Lincs......87 M5
Ailey Herefs......45 L5
Ailsworth C Pete......74 B11
Ainderby Quernhow N York......97 M4
Ainderby Steeple N York......97 M2
Aingers Green Essex......53 L7
Ainsdale Sefton......88 C8
Ainsdale-on-Sea Sefton......88 B8
Ainstable W & F......111 K11
Ainsworth Bury......89 M8
Ainthorpe N York......105 K9
Aintree Sefton......81 M5
Ainville W Loth......127 L5
Aird Ag & B......130 F7
Aird D & G......106 E5
Aird Highld......145 J7
Aird W Isls......168 k4
Àird a' Mhulaidh W Isls......168 g6
Aird Asaig W Isls......168 g7
Aird Dhubh Highld......153 N9
Airdeny Ag & B......131 K2
Airdrie N Lans......126 D4
Airdriehill N Lans......126 D4
Airds of Kells D & G......108 G6
Àird Uig W Isls......168 f4
Airidh a bhruaich W Isls......168 h6
Airieland D & G......108 G9
Airlie Angus......142 F7
Airmyn E R Yk......92 B6
Airntully P & K......141 Q10
Airor Highld......145 M6
Airth Falk......133 Q10
Airton N York......96 D9
Aisby Lincs......73 Q3
Aisby Lincs......85 Q2
Aisgill W & F......102 E11
Aish Devon......6 H6
Aish Devon......7 L7
Aisholt Somset......18 G7
Aiskew N York......97 L3
Aislaby N York......98 F3
Aislaby N York......105 N9
Aislaby S on T......104 D8
Aisthorpe Lincs......86 B4
Aith Shet......169 q8
Akeld Nthumb......119 J5
Akeley Bucks......49 K7
Akenham Suffk......53 L2
Albaston Cnwll......5 Q7
Alberbury Shrops......56 F2
Albourne W Susx......24 G7
Albourne Green W Susx......24 G7
Albrighton Shrops......57 Q4
Albrighton Shrops......69 N11
Alburgh Norfk......65 K4
Albury Herts......51 K6
Albury Oxon......35 J3
Albury Surrey......36 B11
Albury End Herts......51 K6
Albury Heath Surrey......36 C11
Alby Hill Norfk......76 H5
Alcaig Highld......155 Q6
Alcaston Shrops......56 H7
Alcester Warwks......47 L3
Alciston E Susx......25 M9
Alcombe Somset......18 C5
Alcombe Wilts......32 F11
Alconbury Cambs......61 Q5
Alconbury Weald Cambs......62 B5
Alconbury Weston Cambs......61 Q5
Aldborough N York......97 P7
Aldborough Norfk......76 H5
Aldbourne Wilts......33 Q9
Aldbrough E R Yk......93 M3
Aldbrough St John N York......103 P8
Aldbury Herts......35 Q2
Aldcliffe Lancs......95 K8
Aldclune P & K......141 L5
Aldeburgh Suffk......65 P10
Aldeby Norfk......65 N3
Aldenham Herts......50 D11
Alderbury Wilts......21 N9
Aldercar Derbys......84 F11
Alderford Norfk......76 G8
Alderholt Dorset......13 K2
Alderley Gloucs......32 E6
Alderley Edge Ches E......82 H9
Aldermans Green Covtry......59 N8
Aldermaston W Berk......34 G11
Alderminster Warwks......47 P5
Alder Moor Staffs......71 N9
Aldersey Green Ches W......69 N3
Aldershot Hants......23 N4
Alderton Gloucs......47 K8
Alderton Shrops......69 N10
Alderton Suffk......53 P3
Alderton W Nthn......49 K5
Alderton Wilts......32 F8
Alderwasley Derbys......71 Q4
Aldfield N York......97 L7
Aldford Ches W......69 M3
Aldgate Rutlnd......73 P10
Aldham Essex......52 F6
Aldham Suffk......52 H2
Aldingbourne W Susx......15 P5
Aldingham W & F......94 F6
Aldington Kent......27 J4
Aldington Worcs......47 L6
Aldington Corner Kent......27 J4
Aldivalloch Moray......150 B5
Aldochlay Ag & B......132 D9
Aldon Shrops......56 G9

Aldoth Cumb......109 P11
Aldreth Cambs......62 F5
Aldridge Wsall......58 G4
Aldringham Suffk......65 N9
Aldro N York......98 G8
Aldsworth Gloucs......33 N3
Aldsworth W Susx......15 L5
Aldunie Moray......150 B2
Aldwark Derbys......84 B9
Aldwark N York......97 Q8
Aldwick W Susx......15 N7
Aldwincle N Nthn......61 M4
Aldworth W Berk......34 F9
Alexandria W Duns......125 K2
Aley Somset......18 G7
Alfardisworthy Devon......16 D9
Alfington Devon......10 C5
Alfold Surrey......24 B4
Alfold Bars W Susx......24 B4
Alfold Crossways Surrey......24 B3
Alford Abers......150 F4
Alford Lincs......87 N5
Alford Somset......20 B8
Alfreton Derbys......84 F9
Alfrick Worcs......46 D4
Alfrick Pound Worcs......46 D4
Alfriston E Susx......25 M10
Algarkirk Lincs......74 E4
Alhampton Somset......20 B8
Alkborough N Linc......92 E6
Alkerton Gloucs......32 E3
Alkerton Oxon......48 C6
Alkham Kent......27 N3
Alkington Shrops......69 P7
Alkmonton Derbys......71 M7
Alladale Lodge Highld......149 L9
Allanbank N Lans......126 E6
Allanton Border......129 M9
Allanton N Lans......126 E6
Allanton S Lans......126 C7
Allaston Gloucs......32 B4
Allbrook Hants......22 E10
All Cannings Wilts......21 L2
Allendale Nthumb......112 B9
Allen End Warwks......59 J5
Allenheads Nthumb......112 C11
Allensford Dur......112 G10
Allen's Green Herts......51 L7
Allensmore Herefs......45 P7
Allenton C Derb......72 B4
Aller Devon......17 P6
Aller Somset......19 M9
Allerby Cumb......100 E3
Allercombe Devon......9 P6
Aller Cross Devon......17 N6
Allerford Somset......18 B5
Allerston N York......98 H4
Allerthorpe E R Yk......98 E11
Allerton C Brad......90 E4
Allerton Highld......156 D6
Allerton Lpool......81 M7
Allerton Bywater Leeds......91 L5
Allerton Mauleverer N York......97 P9
Allesley Covtry......59 M8
Allestree C Derb......72 A3
Allet Cnwll......3 K4
Allexton Leics......73 L10
Allgreave Ches E......83 L11
Allhallows Medway......38 D6
Allhallows-on-Sea Medway......38 D6
Alligin Shuas Highld......153 Q6
Allimore Green Staffs......70 F11
Allington Dorset......11 K6
Allington Kent......38 C10
Allington Lincs......73 M2
Allington Wilts......21 L2
Allington Wilts......21 P7
Allington Wilts......33 G9
Allithwaite W & F......94 H5
Alloa Clacks......133 P9
Allonby Cumb......100 E2
Allostock Ches W......82 F10
Alloway S Ayrs......114 F4
Allowenshay Somset......10 H2
All Saints South Elmham
Suffk......65 L5
Allscott Shrops......57 N5
Allscott Wrekin......57 L2
All Stretton Shrops......56 H5
Alltami Flints......81 K11
Alltchaorunn Highld......139 M7
Alltmawr Powys......44 F5
Alltsigh Highld......147 M4
Alltwalis Carmth......42 H8
Alltwen Neath......29 K4
Alltyblaca Cerdgn......43 K5
Allwood Green Suffk......64 E7
Almeley Herefs......45 L4
Almeley Wooton Herefs......45 L4
Almer Dorset......12 F5
Almholme Donc......91 P9
Almington Staffs......70 C8
Almodington W Susx......15 M7
Almondbank P & K......134 D2
Almondbury Kirk......90 F8
Almondsbury S Glos......32 B8
Alne N York......97 Q7
Alness Highld......156 B4
Alnham Nthumb......119 J8
Alnmouth Nthumb......119 P8
Alnwick Nthumb......119 N8
Alperton Gt Lon......36 E4
Alphamstone Essex......52 E4
Alpheton Suffk......64 B11
Alphington Devon......9 M6
Alpington Norfk......77 K11
Alport Derbys......84 B8
Alpraham Ches E......69 Q3
Alresford Essex......53 J7
Alrewas Staffs......59 J2
Alsager Ches E......70 D3
Alsagers Bank Staffs......70 D5
Alsop en le Dale Derbys......71 M4
Alston Cumb......111 P11
Alston Devon......10 G4
Alstone Gloucs......47 K5
Alstone Somset......19 K5
Alstonefield Staffs......71 L3
Alston Sutton Somset......19 M4
Alswear Devon......17 N7
Alt Oldham......83 K4
Altandhu Highld......160 F4
Altarnun Cnwll......5 L5
Altass Highld......162 C6
Altcreich Ag & B......138 B10

Altgaltraig Ag & B......124 C3
Altham Lancs......89 M4
Althorne Essex......38 F2
Althorpe N Linc......92 D9
Altnabreac Station Highld......166 H7
Altnaharra Highld......165 N9
Altofts Wakefd......91 K6
Alton Derbys......84 E8
Alton Hants......23 K7
Alton Staffs......71 K6
Alton Wilts......21 N5
Alton Barnes Wilts......21 M2
Alton Pancras Dorset......11 Q4
Alton Priors Wilts......21 M2
Alton Towers Staffs......71 K6
Altrincham Traffd......82 G7
Altskeith Hotel Stirlg......132 F7
Alva Clacks......133 P8
Alvanley Ches W......81 P10
Alvaston C Derb......72 B4
Alvechurch Worcs......58 F10
Alvecote Warwks......59 K4
Alvediston Wilts......21 J10
Alveley Shrops......57 P8
Alverdiscott Devon......17 J6
Alverstoke Hants......14 H7
Alverstone IoW......14 G9
Alverthorpe Wakefd......91 J6
Alverton Notts......73 K2
Alves Moray......157 L5
Alvescot Oxon......33 Q4
Alveston S Glos......32 B7
Alveston Warwks......47 P3
Alvingham Lincs......87 L2
Alvington Gloucs......32 B4
Alwalton C Pete......74 B11
Alweston Dorset......11 P2
Alwinton Nthumb......118 H9
Alwoodley Leeds......90 H2
Alwoodley Gates Leeds......91 J2
Alyth P & K......142 C8
Am Bàgh a Tuath W Isls......168 c17
Ambergate Derbys......84 D10
Amber Hill Lincs......86 H11
Amberley Gloucs......32 G4
Amberley W Susx......24 B8
Amber Row Derbys......84 E9
Amberstone E Susx......25 N8
Amble Nthumb......119 Q10
Amblecote Dudley......58 C7
Ambler Thorn C Brad......90 D5
Ambleside W & F......101 L10
Ambleston Pembks......41 K5
Ambrosden Oxon......48 H11
Amcotts N Linc......92 E8
America Cambs......62 F5
Amersham Bucks......35 Q5
Amersham Common Bucks......35 Q5
Amersham Old Town Bucks......35 Q5
Amersham on the Hill
Bucks......35 Q5
Amerton Staffs......70 H9
Amesbury Wilts......21 N6
Amhuinnsuidhe W Isls......168 f7
Amington Staffs......59 K4
Amisfield D & G......109 M4
Amlwch IoA......78 G6
Ammanford Carmth......28 H2
Amotherby N York......98 E6
Ampfield Hants......22 D10
Ampleforth N York......98 B5
Ampney Crucis Gloucs......33 L4
Ampney St Mary Gloucs......33 L4
Ampney St Peter Gloucs......33 L4
Amport Hants......22 B6
Ampthill C Beds......50 B3
Ampton Suffk......64 B7
Amroth Pembks......41 N9
Amulree P & K......141 L10
Amwell Herts......50 E8
Anaheilt Highld......138 E5
Ancaster Lincs......73 P2
Ancells Farm Hants......23 M3
Anchor Shrops......56 B7
Ancroft Nthumb......129 P11
Ancrum Border......118 B6
Ancton W Susx......15 Q6
Anderby Lincs......87 P5
Anderby Creek Lincs......87 Q5
Andersea Somset......19 K8
Andersfield Somset......18 H8
Anderson Dorset......12 E5
Anderton Ches W......82 D9
Anderton Cnwll......6 C8
Andover Hants......22 C5
Andover Down Hants......22 C5
Andoversford Gloucs......47 K11
Andreas IoM......80 f2
Anelog Gwynd......66 B9
Anerley Gt Lon......36 H7
Anfield Lpool......81 M6
Angarrack Cnwll......2 F7
Angarrick Cnwll......3 K6
Angelbank Shrops......57 K9
Angersleigh Somset......18 G11
Angerton Cumb......110 D9
Angle Pembks......40 G10
Anglesey IoA......78 G8
Anglesey Abbey Cambs......62 H8
Angmering W Susx......24 C9
Angram N York......97 R11
Angram N York......102 H3
Angrouse Cnwll......2 H10
Anick Nthumb......112 D7
Ankerville Highld......156 E3
Ankle Hill Leics......73 K7
Anlaby E R Yk......92 H5
Anmer Norfk......75 P5
Anmore Hants......14 H4
Annan D & G......110 C7
Annandale Water Services
D & G......109 P2
Annaside Cumb......94 B3
Annat Highld......154 A7
Annathill N Lans......126 C3
Anna Valley Hants......22 C6
Annbank S Ayrs......114 H3
Anne Hathaway's Cottage
Warwks......47 N4
Annesley Notts......84 H10
Annesley Woodhouse Notts......84 G10
Annfield Plain Dur......113 J10
Anniesland C Glas......125 N4
Annitsford N Tyne......113 L6
Annscroft Shrops......56 H3
Ansdell Lancs......88 C5

Ansford Somset — 20 B8
Ansley Warwks — 59 M6
Anslow Staffs — 71 N9
Anslow Gate Staffs — 71 M10
Anslow Lees Staffs — 71 N10
Ansteadbrook Surrey — 23 P8
Anstey Hants — 23 K6
Anstey Herts — 51 K4
Anstey Leics — 72 F9
Anstruther Fife — 135 P7
Ansty W Susx — 24 G6
Ansty Warwks — 59 P8
Ansty Wilts — 21 J9
Ansty Cross Dorset — 12 C4
An Tairbeart W Isls — 168 g7
Anthill Common Hants — 14 H4
Anthonys Surrey — 36 B8
Anthorn Cumb — 110 C9
Antingham Norfk — 77 K5
An t-Ob W Isls — 168 f9
Antonine Wall — 126 E2
Anton's Gowt Lincs — 87 K11
Antony Cnwll — 5 Q11
Antrobus Ches W — 82 D9
Anvil Corner Devon — 16 F11
Anvil Green Kent — 27 K2
Anwick Lincs — 86 F10
Anwoth D & G — 108 C9
Aperfield Gt Lon — 37 K9
Apes Dale Worcs — 58 E10
Apethorpe N Nthn — 73 Q11
Apeton Staffs — 70 F11
Apley Lincs — 86 F5
Apperknowle Derbys — 84 E5
Apperley Gloucs — 46 G9
Apperley Bridge C Brad — 90 F3
Apperley Dene Nthumb — 112 G9
Appersett N York — 96 C2
Appin Ag & B — 138 G8
Appleby N Linc — 92 G8
Appleby-in-Westmorland W & F — 102 C6
Appleby Magna Leics — 59 M3
Appleby Parva Leics — 59 M3
Appleby Street Herts — 50 H10
Applecross Highld — 153 N9
Appledore Devon — 9 Q2
Appledore Devon — 16 H5
Appledore Kent — 26 G6
Appledore Heath Kent — 26 G5
Appleford Oxon — 34 F6
Applegarth Town D & G — 109 P4
Applehaigh Wakefd — 91 K8
Applemore Hants — 14 C5
Appleshaw Hants — 22 B5
Applethwaite Cumb — 101 J5
Appleton Halton — 81 Q7
Appleton Oxon — 34 D4
Appleton Wartn — 82 D8
Appleton-le-Moors N York — 98 E3
Appleton-le-Street N York — 98 E6
Appleton Roebuck N York — 91 P2
Appleton Thorn Wartn — 82 D8
Appleton Wiske N York — 104 C10
Appletreehall Border — 117 Q7
Appletreewick N York — 96 G8
Appley Somset — 18 E10
Appley Bridge Lancs — 88 G9
Apse Heath IoW — 14 G10
Apsley End C Beds — 50 D4
Apuldram W Susx — 15 M6
Arabella Highld — 156 E2
Arbirlot Angus — 143 L9
Arborfield Wokham — 35 L11
Arborfield Cross Wokham — 35 L11
Arborfield Green Wokham — 35 L11
Arbourthorne Sheff — 84 E3
Arbroath Angus — 143 L9
Arbuthnott Abers — 143 P2
Arcadia Kent — 26 E4
Archddu Carmth — 28 D4
Archdeacon Newton Darltn — 103 Q7
Archencarroch W Duns — 132 E11
Archiestown Moray — 157 N9
Archirondel Jersey — 11 c1
Arclid Ches E — 70 D2
Ardallie Abers — 159 P10
Ardanaiseig Hotel Ag & B — 131 M3
Ardaneaskan Highld — 153 Q10
Ardarroch Highld — 153 Q10
Ardbeg Ag & B — 122 F10
Ardbeg Ag & B — 124 D4
Ardbeg Ag & B — 131 P11
Ardcharnich Highld — 161 K9
Ardchiavaig Ag & B — 137 K12
Ardchonnell Ag & B — 131 K5
Ardchronie Highld — 162 E9
Ardchullarie More Stirlg — 132 H5
Arddarroch Ag & B — 131 Q9
Arddleen Powys — 69 J11
Ard Dorch Highld — 145 J2
Ardechive Highld — 146 E9
Ardeer N Ayrs — 124 H9
Ardeley Herts — 50 H5
Ardelve Highld — 145 Q2
Arden Ag & B — 132 D11
Ardens Grafton Warwks — 47 M4
Ardentallen Ag & B — 130 G3
Ardentinny Ag & B — 131 P10
Ardentraive Ag & B — 124 C3
Ardeonaig Stirlg — 140 G10
Ardersier Highld — 156 D7
Ardessie Highld — 160 H9
Ardfern Ag & B — 130 G7
Ardfernal Ag & B — 123 J5
Ardgartan Ag & B — 132 B7
Ardgay Highld — 162 D8
Ardgour Highld — 139 J5
Ardgowan Inver — 124 G3
Ardhallow Ag & B — 124 F3
Ardhasig W Isls — 168 g7
Ardheslaig Highld — 153 P6
Ardindrean Highld — 161 K9
Ardingly W Susx — 24 H5
Ardington Oxon — 34 D7
Ardington Wick Oxon — 34 D7
Ardlamont Ag & B — 124 B4
Ardleigh Essex — 53 J6
Ardleigh Heath Essex — 52 H5
Ardler P & K — 142 D9
Ardley Oxon — 48 F9
Ardley End Essex — 51 M8
Ardlui Ag & B — 132 C4
Ardlussa Ag & B — 130 C10
Ardmair Highld — 161 J7
Ardmaleish Ag & B — 124 D4

Ardminish Ag & B — 123 K10
Ardmolich Highld — 138 C3
Ardmore Ag & B — 125 J2
Ardmore Highld — 162 G9
Ardnadam Ag & B — 131 P11
Ardnagrask Highld — 155 P8
Ardnamurchan Highld — 137 P2
Ardnarff Highld — 154 A10
Ardnastang Highld — 138 E5
Ardpatrick Ag & B — 123 N8
Ardrishaig Ag & B — 130 H10
Ardross Highld — 155 R3
Ardrossan N Ayrs — 124 G9
Ardsley Barns — 91 K9
Ardslignish Highld — 137 P3
Ardtalla Ag & B — 122 G9
Ardtoe Highld — 138 A3
Arduaine Ag & B — 130 F5
Ardullie Highld — 155 Q5
Ardvasar Highld — 145 K7
Ardvorlich P & K — 133 J3
Ardvourlie W Isls — 168 g6
Ardwell D & G — 106 F8
Ardwick Manch — 83 J5
Areley Kings Worcs — 57 P10
Arevegaig Highld — 138 B4
Arford Hants — 23 M7
Argam E R Yk — 92 C3
Argoed Caerph — 30 G5
Argoed Shrops — 69 K10
Argoed Mill Powys — 44 D2
Argos Hill E Susx — 25 N5
Argyll Forest Park Ag & B — 131 Q7
Aribruach W Isls — 168 h6
Aridhglas Ag & B — 137 J11
Arileod Ag & B — 136 F5
Arinagour Ag & B — 136 G4
Ariogan Ag & B — 130 H2
Arisaig Highld — 145 L10
Arisaig House Highld — 145 L11
Arkendale N York — 97 N8
Arkesden Essex — 51 L4
Arkholme Lancs — 95 M6
Arkleby Cumb — 100 F3
Arkleton D & G — 110 G2
Arkle Town N York — 103 K10
Arkley Gt Lon — 50 F11
Arksey Donc — 91 P9
Arkwright Town Derbys — 84 F6
Arle Gloucs — 46 H10
Arlecdon Cumb — 100 D7
Arlescote Warwks — 48 C5
Arlesey C Beds — 50 E3
Arleston Wrekin — 57 M2
Arley Ches E — 82 E8
Arlingham Gloucs — 32 D2
Arlington Devon — 17 L3
Arlington E Susx — 25 M9
Arlington Gloucs — 33 M3
Arlington Beccott Devon — 17 L3
Armadale Highld — 145 K7
Armadale Highld — 166 C4
Armadale W Loth — 126 G4
Armaside Cumb — 100 G5
Armathwaite W & F — 111 K11
Arminghall Norfk — 77 K11
Armitage Staffs — 71 K11
Armitage Bridge Kirk — 90 E8
Armley Leeds — 90 H4
Armscote Warwks — 47 P6
Armshead Staffs — 70 G5
Armston N Nthn — 61 N3
Armthorpe Donc — 91 Q10
Arnabost Ag & B — 136 G3
Arnaby Cumb — 94 D4
Arncliffe N York — 96 D6
Arncliffe Cote N York — 96 D6
Arncroach Fife — 135 N6
Arndilly House Moray — 157 P8
Arne Dorset — 12 G7
Arnesby Leics — 60 D2
Arngask P & K — 134 E5
Arnisdale Highld — 145 P5
Arnish Highld — 153 K8
Arniston Mdloth — 127 Q5
Arnol W Isls — 168 i3
Arnold E R Yk — 93 K2
Arnold Notts — 85 J11
Arnprior Stirlg — 133 J7
Arnside W & F — 95 K5
Aros Ag & B — 137 P6
Arowry Wrexhm — 69 N7
Arrad Foot W & F — 94 G4
Arram E R Yk — 92 H2
Arran N Ayrs — 120 H4
Arrathorne N York — 97 K2
Arreton IoW — 14 F9
Arrina Highld — 153 N6
Arrington Cambs — 62 D10
Arrochar Ag & B — 132 B7
Arrow Warwks — 47 L3
Arrowfield Top Worcs — 58 F10
Arscott Shrops — 56 G3
Artafallie Highld — 156 A8
Arthington Leeds — 90 H2
Arthingworth W Nthn — 60 G4
Arthog Gwynd — 54 E2
Arthrath Abers — 159 N10
Arthursdale Leeds — 91 K3
Artrochie Abers — 159 P11
Arundel W Susx — 24 B9
Asby Cumb — 100 E6
Ascog Ag & B — 124 E5
Ascot W & M — 35 P11
Ascott Warwks — 48 B8
Ascott Earl Oxon — 48 B11
Ascott-under-Wychwood Oxon — 48 B11
Asenby N York — 97 N5
Asfordby Leics — 73 J7
Asfordby Hill Leics — 73 J7
Asgarby Lincs — 86 F11
Asgarby Lincs — 87 K7
Ash Devon — 7 L9
Ash Devon — 7 J10
Ash Dorset — 12 E2
Ash Kent — 27 P8
Ash Kent — 39 N10
Ash Somset — 19 J10
Ash Somset — 19 N10
Ash Surrey — 23 P4
Ashampstead W Berk — 34 G9
Ashampstead Green W Berk — 34 G9
Ashbocking Suffk — 64 H11
Ashbourne Derbys — 71 M5
Ashbrittle Somset — 18 E10

Ashburnham Place E Susx — 25 Q8
Ashburton Devon — 7 J4
Ashbury Devon — 8 D5
Ashbury Oxon — 33 Q7
Ashby N Linc — 92 H9
Ashby by Partney Lincs — 87 M7
Ashby cum Fenby NE Lin — 93 N10
Ashby de la Launde Lincs — 86 E9
Ashby-de-la-Zouch Leics — 72 B7
Ashby Folville Leics — 73 J8
Ashby Magna Leics — 60 C2
Ashby Parva Leics — 60 B3
Ashby Puerorum Lincs — 87 K6
Ashby St Ledgers W Nthn — 60 C7
Ashby St Mary Norfk — 77 L11
Ashchurch Gloucs — 46 H8
Ashcombe Devon — 9 M7
Ashcombe N Som — 19 K2
Ashcott Somset — 19 M7
Ashdon Essex — 51 N2
Ashdown Forest E Susx — 25 L4
Ashe Hants — 22 H4
Asheldham Essex — 52 G11
Ashen Essex — 52 B3
Ashendon Bucks — 35 K2
Asheridge Bucks — 35 P4
Ashfield Hants — 22 C11
Ashfield Herefs — 46 A10
Ashfield Stirlg — 133 M7
Ashfield cum Thorpe Suffk — 65 J9
Ashfield Green Suffk — 63 N9
Ashfield Green Suffk — 65 K7
Ashfold Crossways W Susx — 24 F5
Ashford Devon — 6 H9
Ashford Devon — 17 J4
Ashford Kent — 26 H3
Ashford Surrey — 36 C6
Ashford Bowdler Shrops — 57 J10
Ashford Carbonell Shrops — 57 J10
Ashford Hill Hants — 22 G2
Ashford in the Water Derbys — 83 Q11
Ashgill S Lans — 126 D7
Ash Green Surrey — 23 P5
Ash Green Warwks — 59 M8
Ashill Devon — 10 B2
Ashill Norfk — 76 B11
Ashill Somset — 19 K11
Ashingdon Essex — 38 E3
Ashington BCP — 12 H5
Ashington Nthumb — 113 L3
Ashington Somset — 19 Q10
Ashington W Susx — 24 D7
Ashkirk Border — 117 P6
Ashlett Hants — 14 E6
Ashleworth Gloucs — 46 F9
Ashleworth Quay Gloucs — 46 F9
Ashley Cambs — 63 L8
Ashley Ches E — 82 G8
Ashley Devon — 17 M9
Ashley Dorset — 13 K4
Ashley Gloucs — 32 H6
Ashley Hants — 13 N5
Ashley Hants — 22 C8
Ashley Kent — 27 P2
Ashley N Nthn — 60 G2
Ashley Staffs — 70 D7
Ashley Wilts — 32 F11
Ashley Green Bucks — 35 Q3
Ashleyhay Derbys — 71 P4
Ashley Heath Dorset — 13 K4
Ashley Moor Herefs — 56 H11
Ash Magna Shrops — 69 Q7
Ashmansworth Hants — 22 D3
Ashmansworthy Devon — 16 E8
Ashmead Green Gloucs — 32 E5
Ashmill Devon — 5 P2
Ash Mill Devon — 17 P7
Ashmore Dorset — 20 H11
Ashmore Green W Berk — 34 F11
Ashorne Warwks — 48 B3
Ashover Derbys — 84 D8
Ashover Hay Derbys — 84 D8
Ashow Warwks — 59 M10
Ash Parva Shrops — 69 Q7
Ashperton Herefs — 46 B6
Ashprington Devon — 7 L7
Ash Priors Somset — 18 F9
Ashreigney Devon — 17 L9
Ash Street Suffk — 52 H2
Ashtead Surrey — 36 E9
Ash Thomas Devon — 9 P2
Ashton C Pete — 74 B9
Ashton Cnwll — 2 G8
Ashton Devon — 9 L8
Ashton Hants — 22 F11
Ashton Herefs — 45 Q2
Ashton Inver — 124 G2
Ashton N Nthn — 61 N3
Ashton Somset — 19 M5
Ashton W Nthn — 49 L5
Ashton Common Wilts — 20 G3
Ashton Hayes Ches W — 81 Q11
Ashton Hill Wilts — 20 H3
Ashton-in-Makerfield Wigan — 82 C5
Ashton Keynes Wilts — 33 K6
Ashton-on-Ribble Lancs — 88 G4
Ashton under Hill Worcs — 47 J7
Ashton-under-Lyne Tamesd — 83 K5
Ashton upon Mersey Traffd — 82 G6
Ashton Vale Bristl — 31 Q10
Ashurst Hants — 13 P2
Ashurst Kent — 25 M3
Ashurst Lancs — 88 F9
Ashurst W Susx — 24 E7
Ashurst Wood W Susx — 25 K3
Ash Vale Surrey — 23 N4
Ashwater Devon — 5 P2
Ashwell Herts — 50 G3
Ashwell Rutlnd — 73 M8
Ashwell End Herts — 50 G2
Ashwellthorpe Norfk — 64 G2
Ashwick Somset — 20 B5
Ashwicken Norfk — 75 P7
Ashwood Staffs — 58 C7
Askam in Furness W & F — 94 E5
Askern Donc — 91 P8
Askerswell Dorset — 11 L6
Askett Bucks — 35 M3
Askham Notts — 85 M6
Askham W & F — 101 P6
Askham Bryan C York — 98 B11
Askham Richard C York — 98 A11
Asknish Ag & B — 131 J9
Askrigg N York — 96 D2

Askwith N York — 97 J11
Aslackby Lincs — 74 A4
Aslacton Norfk — 64 H3
Aslockton Notts — 73 J3
Asney Somset — 19 N7
Aspall Suffk — 64 H9
Aspatria Cumb — 100 F2
Aspenden Herts — 51 J5
Aspenshaw Derbys — 83 M7
Asperton Lincs — 74 E3
Aspley Staffs — 70 E8
Aspley Guise C Beds — 49 P7
Aspley Heath C Beds — 49 P8
Aspley Heath Warwks — 58 G10
Aspull Wigan — 89 J9
Aspull Common Wigan — 82 D5
Asselby E R Yk — 92 B5
Asserby Lincs — 87 N5
Asserby Turn Lincs — 87 N5
Assington Suffk — 52 F4
Assington Green Suffk — 63 N10
Astbury Ches E — 70 E2
Astcote W Nthn — 49 J4
Asterby Lincs — 87 J5
Asterley Shrops — 56 F3
Asterton Shrops — 56 F6
Asthall Oxon — 33 Q2
Asthall Leigh Oxon — 34 B2
Astle Highld — 162 G8
Astley Shrops — 69 P11
Astley Warwks — 59 M7
Astley Wigan — 82 F4
Astley Worcs — 57 P11
Astley Abbots Shrops — 57 N5
Astley Bridge Bolton — 89 L8
Astley Cross Worcs — 57 Q11
Astley Green Wigan — 82 F5
Aston Birm — 58 G7
Aston Ches E — 69 R5
Aston Ches W — 82 C9
Aston Derbys — 83 Q8
Aston Flints — 81 L11
Aston Herefs — 45 P2
Aston Herts — 50 G6
Aston Oxon — 34 B4
Aston Rothm — 84 G3
Aston Shrops — 57 Q6
Aston Shrops — 57 P9
Aston Staffs — 70 D6
Aston Staffs — 70 F10
Aston Wokham — 35 L8
Aston Wrekin — 57 L3
Aston Abbotts Bucks — 49 M10
Aston Botterell Shrops — 57 L8
Aston-by-Stone Staffs — 70 G8
Aston Cantlow Warwks — 47 M2
Aston Clinton Bucks — 35 N2
Aston Crews Herefs — 46 C10
Aston Cross Gloucs — 46 H8
Aston End Herts — 50 G6
Aston-Eyre Shrops — 57 M6
Aston Fields Worcs — 58 E11
Aston Flamville Leics — 59 Q6
Aston Heath Ches W — 82 C9
Aston Ingham Herefs — 46 C10
Aston juxta Mondrum Ches E — 70 A3
Aston le Walls W Nthn — 48 E4
Aston Magna Gloucs — 47 N7
Aston Munslow Shrops — 57 J7
Aston-on-Carrant Gloucs — 46 H8
Aston on Clun Shrops — 56 F8
Aston Pigott Shrops — 56 E3
Aston Rogers Shrops — 56 E3
Aston Rowant Oxon — 35 K5
Aston Sandford Bucks — 35 L3
Aston Somerville Worcs — 47 K7
Aston-sub-Edge Gloucs — 47 M6
Aston Tirrold Oxon — 34 G7
Aston-upon-Trent Derbys — 72 C5
Aston Upthorpe Oxon — 34 G7
Astrop W Nthn — 48 F7
Astrope Herts — 35 N2
Astwick C Beds — 50 F3
Astwith Derbys — 84 F8
Astwood M Keyn — 49 Q5
Astwood Worcs — 58 D11
Astwood Bank Worcs — 47 K2
Aswarby Lincs — 73 R3
Aswardby Lincs — 87 L6
Atcham Shrops — 57 J3
Atch Lench Worcs — 47 K4
Athelhampton Dorset — 12 C6
Athelington Suffk — 65 J9
Athelney Somset — 19 K9
Athelstaneford E Loth — 128 E4
Atherfield Green IoW — 14 E11
Atherington Devon — 17 J4
Atherington W Susx — 24 B10
Atherstone Somset — 19 L5
Atherstone Warwks — 59 M5
Atherstone on Stour Warwks — 47 P4
Atherton Wigan — 82 E4
Atley Hill N York — 103 Q10
Atlow Derbys — 71 N5
Attadale Highld — 154 B10
Attenborough Notts — 72 E4
Atterby Lincs — 86 C2
Attercliffe Sheff — 84 E3
Atterley Shrops — 57 L5
Atterton Leics — 72 B11
Attingham Park Shrops — 57 J2
Attleborough Norfk — 64 E2
Attleborough Warwks — 59 N6
Attlebridge Norfk — 76 H8
Attleton Green Suffk — 63 N10
Atwick E R Yk — 99 P10
Atworth Wilts — 32 G11
Auberrow Herefs — 45 P5
Aubourn Lincs — 86 B8
Auchbreck Moray — 149 N2
Auchedly Abers — 159 L11
Auchenblae Abers — 143 N4
Auchenbowie Stirlg — 133 M10
Auchencairn D & G — 108 G10
Auchencairn D & G — 109 L4
Auchencairn N Ayrs — 121 K6
Auchencrow Border — 129 M7
Auchendinny Mdloth — 127 P5
Auchengray S Lans — 126 H6
Auchenhalrig Moray — 157 R5
Auchenheath S Lans — 126 E6
Auchenhessnane D & G — 115 R3
Auchenlochan Ag & B — 124 B3
Auchenmade N Ayrs — 125 K8

Auchenmalg D & G — 106 H7
Auchentiber N Ayrs — 125 K8
Auchindrain Ag & B — 131 L7
Auchindrean Highld — 161 K10
Auchininna Abers — 158 G8
Auchinleck E Ayrs — 115 L3
Auchinloch N Lans — 126 B3
Auchinstarry N Lans — 126 C2
Auchintore Highld — 139 K3
Auchiries Abers — 159 Q10
Auchlean Highld — 148 F8
Auchlee Abers — 151 M8
Auchleven Abers — 150 G3
Auchlochan S Lans — 126 E10
Auchlossan Abers — 150 F7
Auchlyne Stirlg — 132 G2
Auchmillan E Ayrs — 115 K2
Auchmithie Angus — 143 M9
Auchmuirbridge Fife — 134 G7
Auchnacree Angus — 142 H5
Auchnagatt Abers — 159 M9
Auchnarrow Moray — 149 N3
Auchnotteroch D & G — 106 C5
Auchroisk Moray — 157 Q7
Auchterarder P & K — 133 Q5
Auchteraw Highld — 147 K6
Auchterblair Highld — 148 G3
Auchtercairn Highld — 153 Q2
Auchterderran Fife — 134 G8
Auchterhouse Angus — 142 E10
Auchterless Abers — 158 H9
Auchtermuchty Fife — 134 G5
Auchterneed Highld — 155 N6
Auchtertool Fife — 134 G9
Auchtertyre Highld — 145 P2
Auchtubh Stirlg — 132 H3
Auckengill Highld — 167 Q4
Auckley Donc — 91 Q10
Audenshaw Tamesd — 83 K5
Audlem Ches E — 70 B6
Audley Staffs — 70 D4
Audley End Essex — 51 M3
Audley End Essex — 52 D4
Audley End Essex — 64 B11
Audley End House & Gardens Essex — 51 M3
Audmore Staffs — 70 E10
Audnam Dudley — 58 C7
Aughertree Cumb — 101 J3
Aughton E R Yk — 92 B3
Aughton Lancs — 88 D9
Aughton Lancs — 95 M7
Aughton Rothm — 84 G3
Aughton Wilts — 21 P3
Aughton Park Lancs — 88 E9
Auldearn Highld — 156 G6
Aulden Herefs — 45 P4
Auldgirth D & G — 109 K3
Auldhouse S Lans — 125 Q7
Ault a' chruinn Highld — 146 A3
Aultbea Highld — 160 D9
Aultgrishin Highld — 160 A9
Aultguish Inn Highld — 155 L3
Ault Hucknall Derbys — 84 G7
Aultmore Moray — 158 B7
Aultnagoire Highld — 147 N3
Aultnamain Highld — 162 F10
Aunby Lincs — 73 Q8
Aunk Devon — 9 P4
Aunsby Lincs — 73 Q3
Aust S Glos — 31 Q7
Austendike Lincs — 74 E9
Austerfield Donc — 85 L2
Austerlands Oldham — 90 B9
Austhorpe Leeds — 91 K4
Austonley Kirk — 90 F9
Austrey Warwks — 59 L3
Austwick N York — 95 N8
Authorpe Lincs — 87 L4
Authorpe Row Lincs — 87 P6
Avebury Wilts — 33 M11
Avebury Trusloe Wilts — 33 L11
Aveley Thurr — 37 N4
Avening Gloucs — 32 G5
Averham Notts — 85 N10
Aveton Gifford Devon — 6 H9
Aviemore Highld — 148 F5
Avington W Berk — 34 C11
Avoch Highld — 156 C6
Avon Hants — 13 K5
Avonbridge Falk — 126 G3
Avon Dassett Warwks — 48 C4
Avonmouth Bristl — 31 P9
Avonwick Devon — 7 J7
Awbridge Hants — 22 B10
Awkley S Glos — 31 Q7
Awliscombe Devon — 10 C4
Awre Gloucs — 32 D3
Awsworth Notts — 72 D2
Axborough Worcs — 58 C9
Axbridge Somset — 19 M4
Axford Hants — 22 H6
Axford Wilts — 33 P10
Axmansford Hants — 22 G2
Axminster Devon — 10 F5
Axmouth Devon — 10 E6
Axton Flints — 80 G8
Aycliffe Dur — 103 P4
Aydon Nthumb — 112 F7
Ayle Nthumb — 111 P11
Aylburton Gloucs — 32 C4
Aylesbeare Devon — 9 P6
Aylesbury Bucks — 35 M2
Aylesby NE Lin — 93 M9
Aylesford Kent — 38 B10
Aylesham Kent — 39 M11
Aylestone C Leic — 72 F10
Aylestone Park C Leic — 72 F10
Aylmerton Norfk — 76 H4
Aylsham Norfk — 76 H6
Aylton Herefs — 46 C7
Aylworth Gloucs — 47 M10
Aymestrey Herefs — 56 G11
Aynho W Nthn — 48 F8
Ayot Green Herts — 50 E7
Ayot St Lawrence Herts — 50 E7
Ayot St Peter Herts — 50 E7
Ayr S Ayrs — 114 F3
Aysgarth N York — 96 F3
Ayshford Devon — 18 D11
Ayside W & F — 94 H3
Ayston Rutlnd — 73 M10
Aythorpe Roding Essex — 51 N7
Ayton Border — 129 N7
Azerley N York — 97 L6

B

Babbacombe Torbay ...7 N5
Babbington Notts ...72 D2
Babbinswood Shrops ...69 K9
Babbs Green Herts ...51 J7
Babcary Somset ...19 Q9
Babel Carmth ...44 A7
Babel Green Suffk ...63 M11
Babell Flints ...80 H10
Babeny Devon ...8 G9
Bablock Hythe Oxon ...34 D4
Babraham Cambs ...62 H10
Babworth Notts ...85 L4
Bachau IoA ...78 G8
Bache Shrops ...56 H8
Bacheldre Powys ...56 C6
Bachelor's Bump E Susx ...26 D9
Backaland Ork ...169 e3
Backbarrow W & F ...94 H4
Backe Carmth ...41 Q7
Backfolds Abers ...159 P7
Backford Ches W ...81 M10
Backford Cross Ches W ...81 M10
Backies Highld ...163 J6
Back of Keppoch Highld ...145 L10
Back o' th' Brook Staffs ...71 K4
Back Street Suffk ...63 M9
Backwell N Som ...31 N11
Backworth N Tyne ...113 M6
Bacon's End Solhll ...59 J7
Baconsthorpe Norfk ...76 G4
Bacton Herefs ...45 M8
Bacton Norfk ...77 L5
Bacton Suffk ...64 F8
Bacton Green Suffk ...64 F8
Bacup Lancs ...89 P6
Badachro Highld ...153 P3
Badanloch Highld ...166 C10
Badbury Swindn ...33 N8
Badby W Nthn ...60 C9
Badcall Highld ...164 F5
Badcaul Highld ...160 G8
Baddeley Edge C Stke ...70 G4
Baddeley Green C Stke ...70 G4
Baddesley Clinton Warwks ...59 K10
Baddesley Ensor Warwks ...59 L5
Baddidarroch Highld ...160 H2
Baddinsgill Border ...127 L7
Badenscoth Abers ...158 G10
Badentarbet Highld ...160 G5
Badenyon Abers ...149 Q4
Badersfield Norfk ...77 K7
Badgall Cnwll ...5 L4
Badgeney Cambs ...74 H11
Badger Shrops ...57 P5
Badger's Cross Cnwll ...2 D7
Badgers Mount Kent ...37 L8
Badgeworth Gloucs ...46 H11
Badgworth Somset ...19 L4
Badharlick Cnwll ...5 M4
Badicaul Highld ...145 N2
Badingham Suffk ...65 L8
Badlesmere Kent ...38 H11
Badlieu Border ...116 F7
Badlipster Highld ...167 M7
Badluarach Highld ...160 F8
Badninish Highld ...162 H8
Badrallach Highld ...160 H8
Badsey Worcs ...47 L6
Badshot Lea Surrey ...23 N5
Badsworth Wakefd ...91 M8
Badwell Ash Suffk ...64 D8
Badwell Green Suffk ...64 E8
Bagber Dorset ...12 C2
Bagby N York ...97 Q4
Bag Enderby Lincs ...87 L6
Bagendon Gloucs ...33 K3
Bagginswood Shrops ...57 M8
Baggrow Cumb ...100 G2
Bàgh a' Chaisteil W Isls ...168 b18
Bagham Kent ...39 J11
Bagillt Flints ...81 J9
Baginton Warwks ...59 M10
Baglan Neath ...29 K6
Bagley Leeds ...90 G3
Bagley Shrops ...69 M9
Bagley Somset ...19 N5
Bagmore Hants ...23 J6
Bagnall Staffs ...70 G4
Bagnor W Berk ...34 E11
Bagshot Surrey ...23 P2
Bagshot Wilts ...34 B11
Bagstone S Glos ...32 C7
Bagthorpe Notts ...84 G10
Bagworth Leics ...72 C9
Bagwyllydiart Herefs ...45 N9
Baildon C Brad ...90 F3
Baildon Green C Brad ...90 E3
Baile Ailein W Isls ...168 h5
Baile a' Mhanaich W Isls ...168 c12
Baile Mòr Ag & B ...136 H11
Bailey Green Hants ...23 J9
Baileyhead Cumb ...111 K5
Bailiff Bridge Calder ...90 E5
Baillieston C Glas ...126 B5
Bailrigg Lancs ...95 K9
Bainbridge N York ...96 D2
Bainshole Abers ...158 F10
Bainton C Pete ...74 A9
Bainton E R Yk ...99 K10
Bainton Oxon ...48 G9
Baintown Fife ...135 K7
Bairnkine Border ...118 C7
Baker's End Herts ...51 J7
Baker Street Thurr ...37 P4
Bakewell Derbys ...84 B7
Bala Gwynd ...68 B7
Balallan W Isls ...168 h5
Balbeg Highld ...155 M11
Balbeggie P & K ...134 F2
Balblair Highld ...156 C4
Balby Donc ...91 P10
Balcary D & G ...108 H11
Balchraggan Highld ...155 P9
Balchrick Highld ...164 E4
Balcombe W Susx ...24 H4
Balcombe Lane W Susx ...24 H4
Balcomie Links Fife ...135 Q6
Baldersby N York ...97 N5
Baldersby St James N York ...97 N5
Balderstone Lancs ...89 J4
Balderstone Rochdl ...89 P8
Balderton Notts ...85 P10
Baldhu Cnwll ...3 K5

Baldinnie Fife ...135 L5
Baldinnies P & K ...134 C4
Baldock Herts ...50 F4
Baldock Services Herts ...50 F3
Baldovie C Dund ...142 H11
Baldrine IoM ...80 f5
Baldslow E Susx ...26 D9
Baldwin IoM ...80 e5
Baldwinholme Cumb ...110 F10
Baldwin's Gate Staffs ...70 D7
Baldwin's Hill W Susx ...25 J3
Bale Norfk ...76 E4
Baledgarno P & K ...142 D11
Balemartine Ag & B ...136 B7
Balerno C Edin ...127 M4
Balfarg Fife ...134 H7
Balfield Angus ...143 J4
Balfour Ork ...169 d5
Balfron Stirlg ...132 G10
Balgaveny Abers ...158 G9
Balgonar Fife ...134 C9
Balgowan D & G ...106 F9
Balgowan Highld ...147 Q9
Balgown Highld ...152 F4
Balgracie D & G ...106 C5
Balgray S Lans ...116 B6
Balham Gt Lon ...36 G6
Balhary P & K ...142 D8
Baligill Highld ...166 E3
Balintore Angus ...142 D6
Balintore Highld ...156 F2
Balintraid Highld ...156 C3
Balivanich W Isls ...168 c12
Balk N York ...97 Q4
Balkeerie Angus ...142 E9
Balkholme E R Yk ...92 C5
Ballabeg IoM ...80 c7
Ballachulish Highld ...139 K6
Ballafesson IoM ...80 b7
Ballajora IoM ...80 g3
Ballakilpheric IoM ...80 b7
Ballamodha IoM ...80 c7
Ballantrae S Ayrs ...114 A11
Ballards Gore Essex ...38 F3
Ballards Green Warwks ...59 L6
Ballasalla IoM ...80 c7
Ballater Abers ...150 B8
Ballaugh IoM ...80 d3
Ballchraggan Highld ...156 D2
Ballencrieff E Loth ...128 D4
Ballevullin Ag & B ...136 B6
Ball Green C Stke ...70 F4
Ball Haye Green Staffs ...70 H3
Ball Hill Hants ...22 D2
Ballianlay Ag & B ...124 C5
Balliekine N Ayrs ...120 G4
Balliemore Ag & B ...131 N8
Balligmorrie S Ayrs ...114 D9
Ballimore Stirlg ...132 G4
Ballindalloch Moray ...157 M10
Ballindean P & K ...134 H2
Ballingdon Suffk ...52 E3
Ballinger Common Bucks ...35 P4
Ballingham Herefs ...46 A8
Ballingry Fife ...134 F8
Ballinluig P & K ...141 N7
Ballinshoe Angus ...142 G7
Ballintuim P & K ...141 R6
Balloch Highld ...156 C8
Balloch N Lans ...126 C3
Balloch S Ayrs ...133 N4
Balloch S Ayrs ...114 F8
Balloch W Duns ...132 D11
Balls Cross W Susx ...23 Q9
Balls Green E Susx ...25 L3
Ball's Green Gloucs ...32 G5
Ballygown Ag & B ...137 L7
Ballygrant Ag & B ...122 E6
Ballyhaugh Ag & B ...136 F4
Balmacara Highld ...145 P2
Balmaclellan D & G ...108 E5
Balmae D & G ...108 E12
Balmaha Stirlg ...132 E9
Balmalcolm Fife ...135 J6
Balmangan D & G ...108 D11
Balmedie Abers ...151 P4
Balmer Heath Shrops ...69 M8
Balmerino Fife ...135 K3
Balmerlawn Hants ...13 P4
Balmichael N Ayrs ...120 H5
Balmore E Duns ...125 P3
Balmuchy Highld ...163 K11
Balmule Fife ...134 G10
Balmullo Fife ...135 L3
Balnacoil Highld ...163 J4
Balnacra Highld ...154 C8
Balnacroft Abers ...149 P9
Balnafoich Highld ...156 B10
Balnaguard P & K ...141 M7
Balnahard Ag & B ...137 M9
Balnain Highld ...155 M11
Balnakeil Highld ...165 J3
Balne N York ...91 P7
Balquharn P & K ...141 P10
Balquhidder Stirlg ...132 G3
Balsall Common Solhll ...59 K9
Balsall Heath Birm ...58 G8
Balsall Street Solhll ...59 K9
Balscote Oxon ...48 C6
Balsham Cambs ...63 J10
Baltasound Shet ...169 t3
Balterley Staffs ...70 D4
Balterley Green Staffs ...70 D4
Balterley Heath Staffs ...70 C4
Baltersan D & G ...107 M5
Balthangie Abers ...159 K7
Baltonsborough Somset ...19 P8
Balvicar Ag & B ...130 F4
Balvraid Highld ...145 P4
Balvraid Highld ...156 E11
Balwest Cnwll ...2 F7
Bamber Bridge Lancs ...88 H5
Bamber's Green Essex ...51 N6
Bamburgh Nthumb ...119 N3
Bamburgh Castle Nthumb ...119 N3
Bamford Derbys ...84 B4
Bamford Rochdl ...89 P8
Bampton Cumb ...101 P7
Bampton Devon ...18 C10
Bampton Oxon ...34 B4
Bampton Grange W & F ...101 P7
Banavie Highld ...139 L2
Banbury Oxon ...48 E6
Bancffosfelen Carmth ...28 E2

Banchory Abers ...150 H8
Banchory-Devenick Abers ...151 N7
Bancycapel Carmth ...28 D2
Bancyfelin Carmth ...42 F11
Banc-y-ffordd Carmth ...42 H7
Bandirran P & K ...142 C11
Bandrake Head W & F ...94 G3
Banff Abers ...158 G5
Bangor Gwynd ...79 K10
Bangor-on-Dee Wrexhm ...69 L5
Bangors Cnwll ...5 L2
Bangor's Green Lancs ...88 D9
Bangour Village W Loth ...127 J3
Bangrove Suffk ...64 C7
Banham Norfk ...64 F4
Bank Hants ...13 N3
Bankend D & G ...109 M7
Bankfoot P & K ...141 Q10
Bankglen E Ayrs ...115 L5
Bank Ground W & F ...101 K11
Bankhead C Aber ...151 M5
Bankhead S Lans ...116 D2
Bank Newton N York ...96 D10
Banknock Falk ...126 D2
Banks Cumb ...111 L8
Banks Lancs ...88 D6
Banks Green Worcs ...58 E11
Bankshill D & G ...110 C4
Bank Street Worcs ...46 B2
Bank Top Calder ...90 E6
Bank Top Lancs ...88 G9
Bannau Brycheiniog National Park ...44 E10
Banningham Norfk ...77 J6
Bannister Green Essex ...51 Q6
Bannockburn Stirlg ...133 N9
Banstead Surrey ...36 G9
Bantham Devon ...6 H10
Banton N Lans ...126 C2
Banwell N Som ...19 L3
Bapchild Kent ...38 F9
Bapton Wilts ...21 J7
Barabhas W Isls ...168 i3
Barassie S Ayrs ...125 J11
Barbaraville Highld ...156 C3
Barber Booth Derbys ...83 P8
Barber Green W & F ...94 H4
Barbieston S Ayrs ...114 H4
Barbon W & F ...95 N4
Barbridge Ches E ...69 R3
Barbrook Devon ...17 N2
Barby W Nthn ...60 B6
Barcaldine Ag & B ...138 H9
Barcheston Warwks ...47 Q7
Barclose Cumb ...110 H8
Barcombe E Susx ...25 K8
Barcombe Cross E Susx ...25 K7
Barcroft C Brad ...90 C3
Barden N York ...96 H2
Barden Park Kent ...37 N11
Bardfield End Green Essex ...51 P4
Bardfield Saling Essex ...51 Q5
Bardney Lincs ...86 F7
Bardon Leics ...72 C8
Bardon Mill Nthumb ...111 Q8
Bardowie E Duns ...125 P3
Bardown E Susx ...25 Q5
Bardrainney Inver ...125 J3
Bardsea W & F ...94 G6
Bardsey Leeds ...91 K2
Bardsey Island Gwynd ...66 B10
Bardsley Oldham ...83 K4
Bardwell Suffk ...64 C7
Bare Lancs ...95 K8
Bareppa Cnwll ...3 K8
Barfad D & G ...107 K4
Barford Norfk ...76 G10
Barford Warwks ...47 Q2
Barford St John Oxon ...48 D8
Barford St Martin Wilts ...21 L8
Barford St Michael Oxon ...48 D8
Barfrestone Kent ...39 N11
Bargate Derbys ...84 E11
Bargeddie N Lans ...126 B5
Bargoed Caerph ...30 G5
Bargrennan D & G ...107 L2
Barham Cambs ...61 P5
Barham Kent ...39 M11
Barham Suffk ...64 G11
Bar Hill Cambs ...62 E8
Barholm Lincs ...74 A8
Barkby Leics ...72 G9
Barkby Thorpe Leics ...72 G9
Barkers Green Shrops ...69 P9
Barkestone-le-Vale Leics ...73 K4
Barkham Wokham ...35 L11
Barking Gt Lon ...37 K4
Barking Suffk ...64 F11
Barking Riverside Gt Lon ...37 L4
Barkingside Gt Lon ...37 K3
Barking Tye Suffk ...64 F11
Barkisland Calder ...90 D6
Barkla Shop Cnwll ...3 J3
Barkston Lincs ...73 N2
Barkston Ash N York ...91 M3
Barkway Cambs ...51 J3
Barlanark C Glas ...126 B5
Barlaston Staffs ...70 F7
Barlavington W Susx ...23 Q11
Barlborough Derbys ...84 G5
Barlby N York ...91 Q4
Barlestone Leics ...72 C9
Barley Herts ...51 K3
Barley Lancs ...89 N2
Barleycroft End Herts ...51 K5
Barley Hole Rothm ...91 K11
Barleythorpe RutInd ...73 L9
Barling Essex ...38 F4
Barlings Lincs ...86 E6
Barlochan D & G ...108 H9
Barlow Derbys ...84 D6
Barlow Gatesd ...113 J8
Barlow N York ...91 Q5
Barmby Moor E R Yk ...98 F11
Barmby on the Marsh E R Yk ...92 A5
Barmer Norfk ...75 P4
Barming Heath Kent ...38 B10
Barmollack Ag & B ...120 F3
Barmouth Gwynd ...67 L11
Barmpton Darltn ...104 B7
Barmston E R Yk ...99 P9
Barnaby Green Suffk ...65 P5
Barnacarry Ag & B ...131 L4
Barnack C Pete ...74 A9
Barnacle Warwks ...59 N8

Barnard Castle Dur ...103 L7
Barnard Gate Oxon ...34 D2
Barnardiston Suffk ...63 M11
Barnbarroch D & G ...108 H9
Barnburgh Donc ...91 M10
Barnby Suffk ...65 P4
Barnby Dun Donc ...91 Q9
Barnby in the Willows Notts ...85 Q10
Barnby Moor Notts ...85 L4
Barncorkrie D & G ...106 E10
Barnehurst Gt Lon ...37 L5
Barnes Gt Lon ...36 F5
Barnes Street Kent ...37 P11
Barnet Gt Lon ...50 F11
Barnetby le Wold N Linc ...93 J9
Barnet Gate Gt Lon ...50 F11
Barney Norfk ...76 D5
Barnham Suffk ...64 B6
Barnham W Susx ...15 Q6
Barnham Broom Norfk ...76 F10
Barnhead Angus ...143 M6
Barnhill C Dund ...142 H11
Barnhill Ches W ...69 N4
Barnhill Moray ...157 L6
Barnhills D & G ...106 C3
Barningham Dur ...103 L8
Barningham Suffk ...64 D6
Barnoldby le Beck NE Lin ...93 M10
Barnoldswick Lancs ...96 C11
Barns Green W Susx ...24 D5
Barnsley Barns ...91 J9
Barnsley Gloucs ...33 L4
Barnsole Kent ...39 N10
Barnstaple Devon ...17 K5
Barnston Essex ...51 P7
Barnston Wirral ...81 K8
Barnstone Notts ...73 J3
Barnt Green Worcs ...58 F10
Barnton C Edin ...127 M3
Barnton Ches W ...82 D10
Barnwell All Saints N Nthn ...61 M4
Barnwell St Andrew N Nthn ...61 M4
Barnwood Gloucs ...46 G11
Baron's Cross Herefs ...45 P3
Baronwood W & F ...101 P2
Barr S Ayrs ...114 E9
Barra W Isls ...168 b17
Barra Airport W Isls ...168 c17
Barrachan D & G ...107 L8
Barraigh W Isls ...168 b17
Barrananaoil Ag & B ...130 G6
Barrapoll Ag & B ...136 A7
Barras W & F ...102 F8
Barrasford Nthumb ...112 D6
Barregarrow IoM ...80 d4
Barrets Green Ches E ...69 Q3
Barrhead E Rens ...125 M6
Barrhill S Ayrs ...114 D11
Barrington Cambs ...62 E11
Barrington Somset ...19 L11
Barripper Cnwll ...2 G6
Barrmill N Ayrs ...125 K7
Barrock Highld ...167 N2
Barrow Gloucs ...46 G10
Barrow Lancs ...89 L3
Barrow RutInd ...73 M7
Barrow Shrops ...57 M4
Barrow Somset ...20 D8
Barrow Somset ...20 D8
Barrow Suffk ...63 N8
Barroway Drove Norfk ...75 L10
Barrow Bridge Bolton ...89 K8
Barrow Burn Nthumb ...118 G8
Barrowby Lincs ...73 M3
Barrow Common N Som ...31 P11
Barrowden RutInd ...73 N10
Barrowford Lancs ...89 P3
Barrow Gurney N Som ...31 P11
Barrow Haven N Linc ...93 J6
Barrow Hill Derbys ...84 F5
Barrow-in-Furness W & F ...94 E7
Barrow Island W & F ...94 D7
Barrow Nook Lancs ...81 N4
Barrow's Green Ches E ...70 B3
Barrows Green W & F ...95 L3
Barrow Street Wilts ...20 F8
Barrow-upon-Humber N Linc ...93 J6
Barrow upon Soar Leics ...72 F7
Barrow upon Trent Derbys ...72 B5
Barrow Vale BaNES ...20 B2
Barry Angus ...143 J11
Barry V Glam ...30 F11
Barry Island V Glam ...30 F11
Barsby Leics ...72 H8
Barsham Suffk ...65 M4
Barston Solhll ...59 K9
Bartestree Herefs ...45 R5
Barthol Chapel Abers ...159 K11
Bartholomew Green Essex ...52 B7
Barthomley Ches E ...70 D4
Bartley Hants ...13 P4
Bartley Green Birm ...58 F8
Bartlow Cambs ...63 J11
Barton Cambs ...62 F9
Barton Ches W ...69 M4
Barton Gloucs ...47 L9
Barton Herefs ...45 K3
Barton Lancs ...88 D9
Barton Lancs ...88 G3
Barton N York ...103 P9
Barton Oxon ...34 G3
Barton Torbay ...7 N5
Barton Warwks ...47 M4
Barton Bendish Norfk ...75 P9
Barton End Gloucs ...32 F5
Barton Green Staffs ...71 M11
Barton Hartshorn Bucks ...48 H8
Barton Hill N York ...98 E8
Barton in Fabis Notts ...72 E4
Barton in the Beans Leics ...72 B9
Barton-le-Clay C Beds ...50 C4
Barton-le-Street N York ...98 E6
Barton-le-Willows N York ...98 E8
Barton Mills Suffk ...63 M6
Barton-on-Sea Hants ...13 M6
Barton-on-the-Heath Warwks ...47 Q8
Barton St David Somset ...19 P8
Barton Seagrave N Nthn ...61 J5
Barton Stacey Hants ...22 D6
Barton Town Devon ...17 M3
Barton Turf Norfk ...77 M7
Barton-under-Needwood Staffs ...71 M11

Barton-upon-Humber N Linc ...92 H6
Barton upon Irwell Salfd ...82 G5
Barton Waterside N Linc ...92 H6
Barugh Barns ...91 J9
Barugh Green Barns ...91 J9
Barvas W Isls ...168 i3
Barway Cambs ...63 J5
Barwell Leics ...72 C11
Barwick Devon ...17 K10
Barwick Herts ...51 J7
Barwick Somset ...11 M2
Barwick in Elmet Leeds ...91 L3
Baschurch Shrops ...69 M10
Bascote Warwks ...48 D2
Bascote Heath Warwks ...48 C2
Base Green Suffk ...64 E9
Basford Green Staffs ...70 H4
Bashall Eaves Lancs ...89 K2
Bashall Town Lancs ...89 L2
Bashley Hants ...13 M5
Basildon Essex ...38 B4
Basingstoke Hants ...22 H4
Baslow Derbys ...84 C6
Bason Bridge Somset ...19 K5
Bassaleg Newpt ...31 J7
Bassendean Border ...128 G10
Bassenthwaite Cumb ...100 H4
Bassett C Sotn ...22 D11
Bassingbourn-cum-Kneesworth Cambs ...50 H2
Bassingfield Notts ...72 G3
Bassingham Lincs ...86 B8
Bassingthorpe Lincs ...73 P5
Bassus Green Herts ...50 H5
Basted Kent ...37 P9
Baston Lincs ...74 B8
Bastwick Norfk ...77 N8
Batch Somset ...19 K3
Batchworth Herts ...36 C2
Batchworth Heath Herts ...36 C2
Batcombe Dorset ...11 N4
Batcombe Somset ...20 C7
Bate Heath Ches E ...82 E9
Batford Herts ...50 D7
Bath BaNES ...20 D2
Bath BaNES ...20 E2
Bathampton BaNES ...32 E11
Bathealton Somset ...18 E10
Batheaston BaNES ...32 E11
Bathford BaNES ...32 E11
Bathgate W Loth ...126 H4
Bathley Notts ...85 N9
Bathpool Cnwll ...5 M7
Bathpool Somset ...19 J9
Bath Side Essex ...53 N5
Bathville W Loth ...126 G4
Bathway Somset ...19 Q4
Batley Kirk ...90 H5
Batsford Gloucs ...47 N8
Batson Devon ...7 J11
Battersby N York ...104 G9
Battersea Gt Lon ...36 G5
Battisborough Cross Devon ...6 F9
Battisford Suffk ...64 F11
Battisford Tye Suffk ...64 E11
Battle E Susx ...26 C8
Battle Powys ...44 E8
Battleborough Somset ...19 K4
Battledown Gloucs ...47 J10
Battledykes Angus ...142 H6
Battlefield Shrops ...69 P11
Battlesbridge Essex ...38 C3
Battlesden C Beds ...49 Q9
Battleton Somset ...18 B9
Battlies Green Suffk ...64 C9
Battramsley Cross Hants ...13 P5
Batt's Corner Hants ...23 M6
Baughton Worcs ...46 G6
Baughurst Hants ...22 G2
Baulds Abers ...150 G9
Baulking Oxon ...34 B6
Baumber Lincs ...86 H6
Baunton Gloucs ...33 K4
Baveney Wood Shrops ...57 M9
Baverstock Wilts ...21 K8
Bawburgh Norfk ...76 H10
Bawdeswell Norfk ...76 E7
Bawdrip Somset ...19 K7
Bawdsey Suffk ...53 P3
Bawsey Norfk ...75 N6
Bawtry Donc ...85 K2
Baxenden Lancs ...89 M5
Baxterley Warwks ...59 L5
Baxter's Green Suffk ...63 N9
Bay Highld ...152 D7
Bayble W Isls ...168 k4
Baybridge Hants ...22 F10
Baybridge Nthumb ...112 E10
Baycliff W & F ...94 F6
Baydon Wilts ...33 Q9
Bayford Herts ...50 H9
Bayford Somset ...20 D9
Bayhead W Isls ...168 c11
Bay Horse Lancs ...95 K10
Bayley's Hill Kent ...37 M10
Baylham Suffk ...64 G11
Baynard's Green Oxon ...48 F9
Baysdale Abbey N York ...104 H9
Baysham Herefs ...45 R9
Bayston Hill Shrops ...56 H3
Baythorne End Essex ...52 B3
Bayton Worcs ...57 M10
Bayton Common Worcs ...57 N10
Bayworth Oxon ...34 E4
Beach S Glos ...32 D10
Beachampton Bucks ...49 L7
Beachamwell Norfk ...75 P9
Beachley Gloucs ...31 Q6
Beachy Head E Susx ...25 N11
Beacon Devon ...10 D3
Beacon End Essex ...52 G6
Beacon Hill Kent ...26 D5
Beacon Hill Notts ...85 P10
Beacon Hill Surrey ...23 N7
Beacon's Bottom Bucks ...35 K5
Beaconsfield Bucks ...35 P6
Beaconsfield Services Bucks ...35 Q7
Beadlam N York ...98 D4
Beadlow C Beds ...50 D3
Beadnell Nthumb ...119 P5
Beaford Devon ...17 K8
Beal N York ...91 N5
Beal Nthumb ...119 L2

258 Bealbury – Bishopsworth

Bealbury Cnwll 5 P8
Bealsmill Cnwll 5 P6
Beam Hill Staffs 71 N9
Beamhurst Staffs 71 K7
Beaminster Dorset 11 K4
Beamish Dur 113 K10
Beamish - The Living Museum of the North Dur 113 K10
Beamsley N York 96 G10
Bean Kent 37 N6
Beanacre Wilts 32 H11
Beanley Nthumb 119 L7
Beardon Devon 8 D8
Beardwood Bl w D 89 K5
Beare Devon 9 N4
Beare Green Surrey 24 E2
Bearley Warwks 47 N2
Bearley Cross Warwks 47 N2
Bearpark Dur 103 P2
Bearsden E Duns 125 N3
Bearsted Kent 38 D10
Bearstone Shrops 70 C7
Bearwood BCP 12 H5
Bearwood Birm 58 F7
Bearwood Herefs 45 M3
Beattock D & G 116 F10
Beauchamp Roding Essex 51 N9
Beauchief Sheff 84 D4
Beaudesert Warwks 59 J11
Beaufort Blae G 30 G2
Beaulieu Essex 52 B10
Beaulieu Hants 14 C6
Beaulieu (National Motor Museum/Palace House) Hants 14 C6
Beaulieu Road Station Hants 13 P3
Beauly Highld 155 P8
Beaumaris IoA 79 L9
Beaumaris Castle IoA 79 L9
Beaumont Cumb 110 F9
Beaumont Essex 53 L7
Beaumont Jersey 11 b2
Beaumont Hill Darltn 103 Q7
Beaumont Leys C Leic 72 F9
Beausale Warwks 59 K10
Beauworth Hants 22 G9
Beaworthy Devon 8 C5
Beazley End Essex 52 B6
Bebington Wirral 81 L8
Bebside Nthumb 113 L4
Beccles Suffk 65 N4
Becconsall Lancs 88 F6
Beckbury Shrops 57 P4
Beckenham Gt Lon 37 J7
Beckermet Cumb 100 D9
Beckett End Norfk 75 Q11
Beckfoot Cumb 94 D3
Beckfoot Cumb 100 G10
Beckfoot Cumb 109 N11
Beck Foot W & F 102 B11
Beckford Worcs 47 J7
Beckhampton Wilts 33 L11
Beck Hole N York 105 M10
Beckingham Lincs 85 Q10
Beckingham Notts 85 N3
Beckington Somset 20 F4
Beckjay Shrops 56 F9
Beckley E Susx 26 E7
Beckley Hants 13 M5
Beckley Oxon 34 G2
Beck Row Suffk 63 L5
Becks C Brad 96 F11
Beck Side W & F 94 E4
Beck Side W & F 94 H4
Beckton Gt Lon 37 K4
Beckwithshaw N York 97 L10
Becontree Gt Lon 37 L3
Becquet Vincent Jersey 11 b1
Bedale N York 97 L3
Bedburn Dur 103 L4
Bedchester Dorset 20 G11
Beddau Rhondd 30 E7
Beddgelert Gwynd 67 K5
Beddingham E Susx 25 K9
Beddington Gt Lon 36 H7
Beddington Corner Gt Lon 36 G7
Bedfield Suffk 65 J8
Bedfield Little Green Suffk 65 J8
Bedford Bed 61 M11
Bedgebury Cross Kent 26 B5
Bedgrove Bucks 35 M2
Bedham W Susx 24 B6
Bedhampton Hants 15 K5
Bedingfield Suffk 64 H8
Bedingfield Green Suffk 64 H8
Bedlam N York 97 L8
Bedlington Nthumb 113 L4
Bedlinog Myr Td 30 E4
Bedminster Bristl 31 Q10
Bedminster Down Bristl 31 Q10
Bedmond Herts 50 C10
Bednall Staffs 70 H11
Bedrule Border 118 B7
Bedstone Shrops 56 F9
Bedwas Caerph 30 G7
Bedwellty Caerph 30 G4
Bedworth Warwks 59 N7
Bedworth Woodlands Warwks 59 M7
Beeby Leics 72 H9
Beech Hants 23 J7
Beech Staffs 70 F7
Beech Hill W Berk 23 J2
Beechingstoke Wilts 21 L3
Beedon W Berk 34 E9
Beedon Hill W Berk 34 E9
Beeford E R Yk 99 N10
Beeley Derbys 84 C7
Beelsby NE Lin 93 M10
Beenham W Berk 34 G11
Beenham's Heath W & M 35 M9
Beeny Cnwll 5 J3
Beer Devon 10 E7
Beer Somset 19 M8
Beercrocombe Somset 19 K10
Beer Hackett Dorset 11 N2
Beesands Devon 7 L10
Beesby Lincs 87 N4
Beeson Devon 7 L10
Beeston C Beds 61 Q11
Beeston Ches W 69 P3
Beeston Leeds 90 H4
Beeston Norfk 76 C8
Beeston Notts 72 E3
Beeston Regis Norfk 76 H3
Beeswing D & G 109 J7
Beetham Somset 10 F2
Beetham W & F 95 K5
Beetley Norfk 76 D8
Began Cardif 30 H8
Begbroke Oxon 34 E2
Begdale Cambs 75 J9
Begelly Pembks 41 M9
Beggarington Hill Leeds 90 H6
Beggar's Bush Powys 45 K2
Beguildy Powys 56 B9
Beighton Norfk 77 M10
Beighton Sheff 84 F4
Beinn Na Faoghla W Isls 168 d12
Beith N Ayrs 125 K7
Bekesbourne Kent 39 L10
Bekesbourne Hill Kent 39 L10
Belaugh Norfk 77 K8
Belbroughton Worcs 58 D9
Belchalwell Dorset 12 C3
Belchalwell Street Dorset 12 C3
Belchamp Otten Essex 52 D3
Belchamp St Paul Essex 52 C3
Belchamp Walter Essex 52 D3
Belchford Lincs 87 J5
Belford Nthumb 119 M4
Belgrave C Leic 72 F9
Belhaven E Loth 128 H4
Belhelvie Abers 151 N4
Belhinnie Abers 150 D2
Bellabeg Abers 150 B5
Bellamore Herefs 45 M6
Bellanoch Ag & B 130 F9
Bellasize E R Yk 92 D5
Bellaty Angus 142 C6
Bell Bar Herts 50 G9
Bell Busk N York 96 D9
Belleau Lincs 87 M5
Bell End Worcs 58 D9
Bellerby N York 96 H2
Bellever Devon 8 G9
Belle Vue Cumb 110 G9
Belle Vue Wakefd 91 J7
Bellfield S Lans 126 E11
Bellfields Surrey 23 Q4
Bell Heath Worcs 58 D9
Bell Hill Hants 23 K10
Bellingdon Bucks 35 P3
Bellingham Nthumb 112 B4
Belloch Ag & B 120 C4
Bellochantuy Ag & B 120 C5
Bell o' th' Hill Ches W 69 P5
Bellows Cross Dorset 13 J2
Bells Cross Suffk 64 H11
Bellshill N Lans 126 C5
Bellshill Nthumb 119 M4
Bellside N Lans 126 E6
Bellsquarry W Loth 127 K4
Bells Yew Green E Susx 25 P3
Belluton BaNES 20 B2
Belmaduthy Highld 156 A6
Belmesthorpe Rutlnd 73 Q8
Belmont Bl w D 89 K7
Belmont Dur 104 B2
Belmont Gt Lon 36 G8
Belmont S Ayrs 114 F4
Belmont Shet 169 s3
Belnacraig Abers 150 B4
Belowda Cnwll 4 F9
Belper Derbys 84 D11
Belper Lane End Derbys 84 D11
Belph Derbys 84 H5
Belsay Nthumb 112 G5
Belses Border 117 R5
Belsford Devon 7 K7
Belsize Herts 50 B10
Belstead Suffk 53 K3
Belstone Devon 8 F6
Belthorn Bl w D 89 L6
Beltinge Kent 39 L8
Beltingham Nthumb 111 Q8
Beltoft N Linc 92 D9
Belton Leics 72 C6
Belton Lincs 73 N3
Belton N Linc 92 C9
Belton Norfk 77 P11
Belton House Lincs 73 N3
Belton in Rutland Rutlnd 73 L10
Beltring Kent 37 Q11
Belvedere Gt Lon 37 L5
Belvoir Leics 73 L4
Bembridge IoW 14 H9
Bemerton Wilts 21 M8
Bempton E R Yk 99 P6
Benacre Suffk 65 Q5
Benbecula W Isls 168 d12
Benbecula Airport W Isls 168 c12
Benbuie D & G 115 P8
Benderloch Ag & B 138 G10
Benenden Kent 26 D5
Benfieldside Dur 112 G10
Benfleet Essex 38 C4
Bengate Norfk 77 L6
Bengeo Herts 50 H8
Bengeworth Worcs 47 K6
Benhall Green Suffk 65 M9
Benhall Street Suffk 65 M9
Benholm Abers 143 Q4
Beningbrough N York 98 A9
Benington Herts 50 G6
Benington Lincs 87 L11
Benington Sea End Lincs 87 M11
Benllech IoA 79 J8
Benmore Ag & B 131 N10
Bennacott Cnwll 5 M3
Bennan N Ayrs 121 J7
Bennet Head W & F 101 M6
Bennetland E R Yk 92 D5
Bennett End Bucks 35 L5
Ben Nevis Highld 139 M3
Benniworth Lincs 86 H4
Benover Kent 26 B2
Ben Rhydding C Brad 96 H11
Benslie N Ayrs 125 J9
Benson Oxon 34 H6
Bentfield Green Essex 51 M5
Benthall Shrops 57 M4
Bentham Gloucs 46 H11
Benthoul C Aber 151 L7
Bentlawnt Shrops 56 E4
Bentley Donc 91 P9
Bentley E R Yk 92 H3
Bentley Hants 23 L6
Bentley Suffk 53 K4
Bentley Warwks 59 L5
Bentley Heath Herts 50 G11
Bentley Heath Solhll 59 J9
Benton Devon 17 M4
Bentpath D & G 110 F2
Bentwichen Devon 17 N5
Bentworth Hants 23 J6
Benvie Angus 142 E11
Benville Dorset 11 L4
Benwick Cambs 62 D2
Beoley Worcs 58 G11
Beoraidbeg Highld 145 L9
Bepton W Susx 23 N11
Berden Essex 51 L5
Berea Pembks 40 E4
Bere Alston Devon 6 C5
Bere Ferrers Devon 6 D6
Berepper Cnwll 2 H9
Bere Regis Dorset 12 D6
Bergh Apton Norfk 77 L11
Berhill Somset 19 M7
Berinsfield Oxon 34 G5
Berkeley Gloucs 32 C5
Berkeley Heath Gloucs 32 C5
Berkeley Road Gloucs 32 D4
Berkhamsted Herts 35 Q3
Berkley Somset 20 F5
Berkswell Solhll 59 K9
Bermondsey Gt Lon 36 H5
Bermuda Warwks 59 N7
Bernera Highld 145 P3
Bernisdale Highld 152 G7
Berrick Prior Oxon 34 H6
Berrick Salome Oxon 34 H6
Berriedale Highld 163 Q2
Berrier W & F 101 L5
Berriew Powys 56 B4
Berrington Nthumb 119 K2
Berrington Shrops 57 J3
Berrington Worcs 57 K11
Berrington Green Worcs 57 K11
Berrow Somset 19 J4
Berrow Worcs 46 E8
Berrow Green Worcs 46 D3
Berry Brow Kirk 90 E8
Berry Cross Devon 16 H9
Berry Down Cross Devon 17 K3
Berryfield Wilts 20 H2
Berryfields Bucks 49 L11
Berry Hill Gloucs 31 Q2
Berry Hill Pembks 41 L2
Berryhillock Moray 158 D5
Berryhillock Moray 158 D7
Berrynarbor Devon 17 K2
Berry Pomeroy Devon 7 L6
Berry's Green Gt Lon 37 K9
Bersham Wrexhm 69 K5
Bersted W Susx 15 P6
Bertha Park P & K 134 D2
Berthengam Flints 80 G9
Berwick E Susx 25 M9
Berwick Bassett Wilts 33 L10
Berwick Hill Nthumb 113 J5
Berwick St James Wilts 21 L7
Berwick St John Wilts 20 H10
Berwick St Leonard Wilts 20 H8
Berwick Station E Susx 25 M9
Berwick-upon-Tweed Nthumb 129 P9
Bescaby Leics 73 L5
Bescar Lancs 88 D8
Besford Shrops 69 Q9
Besford Worcs 46 H6
Bessacarr Donc 91 Q10
Bessels Leigh Oxon 34 E4
Besses o' th' Barn Bury 89 N9
Bessingby E R Yk 99 P7
Bessingham Norfk 76 H4
Bestbeech Hill E Susx 25 P4
Besthorpe Norfk 64 F2
Besthorpe Notts 85 P8
Bestwood Village Notts 85 J11
Beswick E R Yk 99 L11
Betchcott Shrops 56 G5
Betchworth Surrey 36 F10
Bethania Cerdgn 43 L2
Bethania Gwynd 67 N6
Bethel Gwynd 68 C7
Bethel Gwynd 79 J11
Bethel IoA 78 F10
Bethel Powys 68 F10
Bethersden Kent 26 F3
Bethesda Gwynd 79 L11
Bethesda Gwynd 79 L11
Bethesda Pembks 41 L7
Bethlehem Carmth 43 N9
Bethnal Green Gt Lon 36 H4
Betley Staffs 70 D5
Betsham Kent 37 P6
Betteshanger Kent 39 P11
Bettiscombe Dorset 10 H4
Bettisfield Wrexhm 69 N7
Betton Shrops 70 B7
Betton Strange Shrops 57 J3
Bettws Brdgnd 29 P7
Bettws Newpt 31 J6
Bettws Cedewain Powys 55 Q5
Bettws Ifan Cerdgn 42 F5
Bettws-Newydd Mons 31 L3
Bettyhill Highld 166 B4
Betws Carmth 28 H2
Betws Bledrws Cerdgn 43 L4
Betws Garmon Gwynd 67 J3
Betws Gwerfil Goch Denbgs 68 D5
Betws-y-Coed Conwy 67 P3
Betws-yn-Rhos Conwy 80 C10
Beulah Cerdgn 42 E5
Beulah Powys 44 C4
Bevendean Br & H 24 H9
Bevercotes Notts 85 L6
Beverley E R Yk 92 H3
Beverston Gloucs 32 G6
Bevington Gloucs 32 C5
Bewaldeth Cumb 100 H4
Bewcastle Cumb 111 L6
Bewdley Worcs 57 P9
Bewerley N York 97 J7
Bewholme E R Yk 99 P11
Bewlbridge Kent 25 Q4
Bexhill-on-Sea E Susx 26 B10
Bexley Gt Lon 37 L6
Bexleyheath Gt Lon 37 L5
Bexleyhill W Susx 23 P9
Bexon Kent 38 E10
Bexwell Norfk 75 M10
Beyton Suffk 64 C9
Beyton Green Suffk 64 C9
Bhaltos W Isls 168 f4
Bhatarsaigh W Isls 168 b18
Bibstone S Glos 32 C6
Bibury Gloucs 33 M3
Bicester Oxon 48 G10
Bickenhill Solhll 59 J8
Bicker Lincs 74 D3
Bicker Bar Lincs 74 D3
Bicker Gauntlet Lincs 74 D3
Bickershaw Wigan 82 D4
Bickerstaffe Lancs 81 N4
Bickerton Ches E 69 P4
Bickerton Devon 7 L11
Bickerton N York 97 Q10
Bickerton Nthumb 119 J10
Bickford Staffs 58 C2
Bickington Devon 7 L4
Bickington Devon 17 J5
Bickleigh Devon 6 E6
Bickleigh Devon 9 M3
Bickleton Devon 17 J5
Bickley Ches W 69 P5
Bickley Gt Lon 37 K7
Bickley N York 99 J2
Bickley Worcs 57 L10
Bickley Moss Ches W 69 P5
Bicknacre Essex 52 C11
Bicknoller Somset 18 F7
Bicknor Kent 38 E10
Bickton Hants 13 K2
Bicton Herefs 45 P2
Bicton Shrops 56 D8
Bicton Shrops 69 M11
Bidborough Kent 25 N2
Bidden Hants 23 K5
Biddenden Kent 26 E4
Biddenden Green Kent 26 E3
Biddenham Bed 61 M10
Biddestone Wilts 32 G10
Biddisham Somset 19 L4
Biddlesden Bucks 48 H7
Biddlestone Nthumb 119 J9
Biddulph Staffs 70 F3
Biddulph Moor Staffs 70 G3
Bideford Devon 16 H6
Bidford-on-Avon Warwks 47 M4
Bidston Wirral 81 K6
Bielby E R Yk 92 C2
Bieldside C Aber 151 M7
Bierley IoW 14 F11
Bierton Bucks 49 M11
Big Balcraig D & G 107 L9
Bigbury Devon 6 H9
Bigbury-on-Sea Devon 6 H10
Bigby Lincs 93 J9
Biggar S Lans 116 E3
Biggar W & F 94 D7
Biggin Derbys 71 M3
Biggin Derbys 71 P5
Biggin N York 91 N4
Biggin Hill Gt Lon 37 K9
Biggleswade C Beds 50 E2
Bigholms D & G 110 F4
Bighouse Highld 166 E4
Bighton Hants 22 H8
Biglands Cumb 110 E10
Bignall End Staffs 70 E4
Bignor W Susx 15 Q4
Bigrigg Cumb 100 D8
Big Sand Highld 160 B11
Bigton Shet 169 q11
Bilborough C Nott 72 E2
Bilbrook Somset 18 D6
Bilbrook Staffs 58 C4
Bilbrough N York 98 A11
Bilbster Highld 167 N6
Bildershaw Dur 103 P6
Bildeston Suffk 52 G2
Billacott Cnwll 5 M3
Billericay Essex 37 Q2
Billesdon Leics 73 J10
Billesley Warwks 47 M3
Billingborough Lincs 74 B4
Billinge St Hel 82 B4
Billingford Norfk 64 H6
Billingford Norfk 76 E7
Billingham S on T 104 E6
Billinghay Lincs 86 G10
Billingley Barns 91 L10
Billingshurst W Susx 24 C5
Billingsley Shrops 57 N8
Billington C Beds 49 P10
Billington Lancs 89 L3
Billington Staffs 70 F10
Billockby Norfk 77 N9
Billy Row Dur 103 N3
Bilsborrow Lancs 88 G3
Bilsby Lincs 87 N5
Bilsham W Susx 15 Q6
Bilsington Kent 26 H5
Bilsthorpe Notts 85 K8
Bilsthorpe Moor Notts 85 L8
Bilston Mdloth 127 P5
Bilston Wolves 58 E5
Bilstone Leics 72 B9
Bilting Kent 27 J2
Bilton E R Yk 93 L4
Bilton N York 97 M9
Bilton Nthumb 119 P8
Bilton Warwks 59 Q10
Bilton Banks Nthumb 119 P8
Bilton-in-Ainsty N York 97 Q11
Binbrook Lincs 86 H2
Binchester Blocks Dur 103 P4
Bincombe Dorset 11 P8
Binegar Somset 20 B5
Bines Green W Susx 24 E7
Binfield Br For 35 M10
Binfield Heath Oxon 35 K9
Bingfield Nthumb 112 E6
Bingham Notts 73 J3
Bingham's Melcombe Dorset 12 C4
Bingley C Brad 90 E3
Bings Heath Shrops 69 P11
Binham Norfk 76 D4
Binley Covtry 59 N9
Binley Hants 22 D4
Binley Woods Warwks 59 N9
Binnegar Dorset 12 E7
Binniehill Falk 126 F3
Binscombe Surrey 23 Q5
Binsey Oxon 34 E3
Binstead IoW 14 G8
Binsted Hants 23 L6
Binsted W Susx 15 Q5
Binton Warwks 47 M4
Bintree Norfk 76 E7
Binweston Shrops 56 E4
Birch Essex 52 F8
Birch Rochdl 89 P9
Birchall Staffs 70 H4
Bircham Newton Norfk 75 Q4
Bircham Tofts Norfk 75 Q4
Birchanger Essex 51 M6
Birchanger Green Services Essex 51 M6
Birch Cross Staffs 71 L8
Birchencliffe Kirk 90 E7
Bircher Herefs 56 H11
Birchett's Green E Susx 25 Q4
Birchfield Birm 58 G6
Birch Green Essex 52 F8
Birch Green Herts 50 G8
Birch Green Worcs 46 G5
Birchgrove Cardif 30 G9
Birchgrove Swans 29 K5
Birchgrove W Susx 25 K5
Birch Heath Ches W 69 P2
Birch Hill Ches W 81 Q10
Birchington Kent 39 P8
Birchington-on-Sea Kent 39 N8
Birchley Heath Warwks 59 L6
Birchmoor Warwks 59 L4
Birchmoor Green C Beds 49 Q8
Birchover Derbys 84 B8
Birch Services Rochdl 89 N9
Birch Vale Derbys 83 M7
Birchwood Lincs 86 B7
Birch Wood Somset 10 E2
Birchwood Warrtn 82 E6
Bircotes Notts 85 K2
Birdbrook Essex 52 B3
Birdforth N York 97 Q5
Birdham W Susx 15 M6
Birdingbury Warwks 59 P11
Birdlip Gloucs 32 H2
Birdoswald Cumb 111 M7
Birdsall N York 98 G7
Birds Edge Kirk 90 G9
Birds Green Essex 51 N9
Birdsgreen Shrops 57 P7
Birdsmoorgate Dorset 10 H4
Bird Street Suffk 64 E11
Birdwell Barns 91 J10
Birdwood Gloucs 46 D11
Birgham Border 118 E3
Birichin Highld 162 H8
Birkacre Lancs 88 H8
Birkby N York 104 B10
Birkdale Sefton 88 C8
Birkenbog Abers 158 D4
Birkenhead Wirral 81 L7
Birkenhead (Queensway) Tunnel Lpool 81 L7
Birkenhills Abers 158 H8
Birkenshaw Kirk 90 G5
Birkhall Abers 149 Q9
Birkhill Angus 142 F11
Birkhill D & G 117 J7
Birkholme Lincs 73 P6
Birkin N York 91 N5
Birks Leeds 90 H5
Birkshaw Nthumb 111 Q7
Birley Herefs 45 P4
Birley Carr Sheff 84 D2
Birling Kent 37 Q8
Birling Nthumb 119 P9
Birling Gap E Susx 25 N11
Birlingham Worcs 46 H6
Birmingham Birm 58 G7
Birmingham Airport Solhll 59 J8
Birnam P & K 141 P9
Birness Abers 159 N11
Birse Abers 150 F8
Birsemore Abers 150 E8
Birstall Kirk 90 G5
Birstall Leics 72 F9
Birstwith N York 97 K9
Birthorpe Lincs 74 B4
Birtley Gatesd 113 L9
Birtley Herefs 56 F11
Birtley Nthumb 112 C5
Birts Street Worcs 46 E7
Bisbrooke Rutlnd 73 M11
Biscathorpe Lincs 86 H4
Biscovey Cnwll 3 R3
Bisham W & M 35 M7
Bishampton Worcs 47 J4
Bish Mill Devon 17 N6
Bishop Auckland Dur 103 P5
Bishopbridge Lincs 86 D2
Bishopbriggs E Duns 125 Q3
Bishop Burton E R Yk 92 G3
Bishop Middleham Dur 104 B4
Bishopmill Moray 157 N5
Bishop Monkton N York 97 M7
Bishop Norton Lincs 86 C2
Bishopsbourne Kent 39 L11
Bishops Cannings Wilts 21 K2
Bishop's Castle Shrops 56 E7
Bishop's Caundle Dorset 11 P2
Bishop's Cleeve Gloucs 47 J9
Bishop's Frome Herefs 46 C5
Bishops Gate Surrey 35 Q10
Bishop's Green Essex 51 P7
Bishop's Green Hants 22 F2
Bishop's Hull Somset 18 H10
Bishop's Itchington Warwks 48 C3
Bishops Lydeard Somset 18 G9
Bishop's Norton Gloucs 46 F10
Bishop's Nympton Devon 17 P7
Bishop's Offley Staffs 70 D9
Bishop's Stortford Herts 51 L6
Bishop's Sutton Hants 22 H8
Bishop's Tachbrook Warwks 48 B2
Bishop's Tawton Devon 17 K6
Bishopsteignton Devon 7 N4
Bishopstoke Hants 22 E11
Bishopston Swans 28 G7
Bishopstone Bucks 35 M2
Bishopstone E Susx 25 L10
Bishopstone Herefs 45 N6
Bishopstone Kent 39 M8
Bishopstone Swindn 33 P8
Bishopstone Wilts 21 L9
Bishopstrow Wilts 20 G6
Bishop Sutton BaNES 19 Q3
Bishop's Waltham Hants 22 G11
Bishopswood Somset 10 F2
Bishop's Wood Staffs 58 B3
Bishopsworth Bristl 31 Q11

Bishop Thornton N York ...97 L8
Bishopthorpe C York ...98 B11
Bishopton Darltn ...104 C6
Bishopton Rens ...125 L3
Bishopton Warwks ...47 N3
Bishop Wilton E R Yk ...98 F9
Bishton Newpt ...31 L7
Bishton Staffs ...71 J10
Bisley Gloucs ...32 H3
Bisley Surrey ...23 Q3
Bisley Camp Surrey ...23 P3
Bispham Bpool ...88 C2
Bispham Green Lancs ...88 F8
Bissoe Cnwll ...3 K5
Bisterne Hants ...13 K4
Bitchet Green Kent ...37 N10
Bitchfield Lincs ...73 P5
Bittadon Devon ...17 J3
Bittaford Devon ...6 H7
Bittering Norfk ...76 C8
Bitterley Shrops ...57 K9
Bitterne C Sotn ...14 E4
Bitteswell Leics ...60 B3
Bitton S Glos ...32 C11
Bix Oxon ...35 K8
Bixter Shet ...169 q8
Blaby Leics ...72 F11
Blackadder Border ...129 L3
Blackawton Devon ...7 L8
Blackbeck Cumb ...100 D9
Blackborough Devon ...10 B3
Blackborough End Norfk ...75 N7
Black Bourton Oxon ...33 Q4
Blackboys E Susx ...25 M6
Blackbrook Derbys ...84 D11
Blackbrook St Hel ...82 B5
Blackbrook Staffs ...70 D7
Blackbrook Surrey ...36 E11
Blackburn Abers ...151 L5
Blackburn Bl w D ...89 K5
Blackburn W Loth ...126 H4
Blackburn with Darwen
    Services Bl w D ...89 K6
Black Callerton N u Ty ...113 J7
Black Carr Norfk ...64 F2
Black Corner W Susx ...24 G3
Blackcraig E Ayrs ...115 M6
Black Crofts Ag & B ...138 G11
Black Cross Cnwll ...4 E9
Blackden Heath Ches E ...82 G10
Blackdog Abers ...151 P5
Black Dog Devon ...9 K3
Blackdown Devon ...8 D9
Blackdown Dorset ...10 H4
Blackdyke Cumb ...109 P10
Blacker Barns ...91 J9
Blacker Hill Barns ...91 K10
Blackfen Gt Lon ...37 L6
Blackfield Hants ...14 D6
Blackford Cumb ...110 G8
Blackford P & K ...133 P6
Blackford Somset ...19 M5
Blackford Somset ...20 C9
Blackfordby Leics ...72 A7
Blackgang IoW ...14 E11
Blackhall C Edin ...127 N3
Blackhall Colliery Dur ...104 E3
Blackhall Mill Gatesd ...112 H9
Blackhall Rocks Dur ...104 E3
Blackham E Susx ...25 L2
Blackhaugh Border ...117 N3
Blackheath Essex ...52 H7
Blackheath Gt Lon ...37 J5
Blackheath Sandw ...58 E7
Blackheath Suffk ...65 N7
Blackheath Surrey ...36 B11
Black Heddon Nthumb ...112 G5
Blackhill Abers ...159 Q6
Blackhill Abers ...159 Q9
Blackhill Dur ...112 G10
Blackhill of Clackriach
    Abers ...159 M8
Blackjack Lincs ...74 E3
Blackland Wilts ...33 K11
Black Lane Ends Lancs ...89 Q2
Blacklaw D & G ...116 E9
Blackley Manch ...83 J4
Blacklunans P & K ...142 A5
Blackmarstone Herefs ...45 Q7
Blackmill Brdgnd ...29 P7
Blackmoor Hants ...23 L8
Black Moor Leeds ...90 H3
Blackmoor N Som ...19 N2
Blackmoorfoot Kirk ...90 D8
Blackmoor Gate Devon ...17 L3
Blackmore Essex ...51 P10
Blackmore End Essex ...52 B5
Blackmore End Herts ...50 E7
Black Mountains ...45 K9
Blackness Falk ...127 K2
Blacknest Hants ...23 L6
Blacknest W & M ...35 Q11
Black Notley Essex ...52 C7
Blacko Lancs ...89 P2
Black Pill Swans ...28 H6
Blackpool Bpool ...88 C3
Blackpool Devon ...7 L4
Blackpool Devon ...7 M9
Blackpool Gate Cumb ...111 K5
Blackpool Zoo Bpool ...88 C3
Blackridge W Loth ...126 F4
Blackrock Cnwll ...2 H7
Blackrock Mons ...30 H2
Blackrod Bolton ...89 J8
Blacksboat Moray ...157 M10
Blackshaw D & G ...109 M7
Blackshaw Head Calder ...90 B5
Blacksmith's Green Suffk ...64 G8
Blacksnape Bl w D ...89 L6
Blackstone W Susx ...24 F7
Black Street Suffk ...65 Q4
Black Tar Pembks ...41 J9
Blackthorn Oxon ...48 H11
Blackthorpe Suffk ...64 C9
Blacktoft E R Yk ...92 D6
Blacktop C Aber ...151 M7
Black Torrington Devon ...8 C3
Blackwall Derbys ...71 P5
Blackwall Tunnel Gt Lon ...37 J4
Blackwater Cnwll ...3 J4
Blackwater Hants ...23 M3
Blackwater IoW ...14 F9
Blackwater Somset ...19 J11
Blackwaterfoot N Ayrs ...120 H6
Blackwell Cumb ...110 H10

Blackwell Darltn ...103 Q8
Blackwell Derbys ...83 P10
Blackwell Derbys ...84 F9
Blackwell Warwks ...47 P6
Blackwell Worcs ...58 E10
Blackwellsend Green Gloucs ...46 E9
Blackwood Caerph ...30 G5
Blackwood D & G ...109 K3
Blackwood S Lans ...126 D9
Blackwood Hill Staffs ...70 G3
Blacon Ches W ...81 M11
Bladbean Kent ...27 L2
Bladnoch D & G ...107 M7
Bladon Oxon ...34 E2
Bladon Somset ...19 M10
Blaenannerch Cerdgn ...42 D5
Blaenau Ffestiniog Gwynd ...67 N5
Blaenau Ffestiniog Gwynd ...67 N5
Blaenavon Torfn ...31 J3
Blaenavon Industrial
    Landscape Torfn ...30 H3
Blaencwm Rhondd ...29 P5
Blaen Dyryn Powys ...44 C7
Blaenffos Pembks ...41 N3
Blaengarw Brdgnd ...29 P6
Blaengeuffordd Cerdgn ...54 E8
Blaengwrach Neath ...29 N3
Blaengwynfi Neath ...29 N5
Blaenllechau Rhondd ...30 D5
Blaenpennal Cerdgn ...43 M2
Blaenplwyf Cerdgn ...54 D9
Blaenporth Cerdgn ...42 E5
Blaenrhondda Rhondd ...29 P5
Blaenwaun Carmth ...41 P5
Blaen-y-coed Carmth ...42 F9
Blaen-y-cwm Blae G ...30 F2
Blaenycwm Cerdgn ...55 J9
Blagdon N Som ...19 P3
Blagdon Somset ...18 H11
Blagdon Torbay ...7 M6
Blagdon Hill Somset ...18 H11
Blagill W & F ...111 P11
Blaguegate Lancs ...88 F9
Blaich Highld ...139 J2
Blaina Blae G ...30 H3
Blair Atholl P & K ...141 L4
Blair Drummond Stirlg ...133 L8
Blairgowrie P & K ...142 B8
Blairhall Fife ...134 C10
Blairingone P & K ...134 B8
Blairlogie Stirlg ...133 N8
Blairmore Ag & B ...131 P11
Blairmore Highld ...164 E5
Blair's Ferry Ag & B ...124 B4
Blaisdon Gloucs ...46 D11
Blakebrook Worcs ...57 Q9
Blakedown Worcs ...58 C9
Blake End Essex ...52 B7
Blakeley Lane Staffs ...70 H5
Blakemere Ches W ...82 C10
Blakemere Herefs ...45 M6
Blakemore Devon ...7 K6
Blakenall Heath Wsall ...58 F4
Blakeney Gloucs ...32 C3
Blakeney Norfk ...76 E3
Blakenhall Ches E ...70 C5
Blakenhall Wolves ...58 D5
Blakesley W Nthn ...48 H4
Blanchland Nthumb ...112 E10
Blandford Camp Dorset ...12 F3
Blandford Forum Dorset ...12 E3
Blandford St Mary Dorset ...12 E3
Bland Hill N York ...97 K10
Blanefield Stirlg ...125 N2
Blankney Lincs ...86 E8
Blantyre S Lans ...126 B6
Blàr a' Chaorainn Highld ...139 L4
Blarghour Ag & B ...131 K5
Blarmachfoldach Highld ...139 K4
Blashford Hants ...13 L3
Blaston Leics ...73 L11
Blatherwycke N Nthn ...73 P11
Blawith W & F ...94 F3
Blawquhairn D & G ...108 D4
Blaxhall Suffk ...65 M10
Blaxton Donc ...91 R10
Blaydon Gatesd ...113 J8
Bleadney Somset ...19 N5
Bleadon N Som ...19 K3
Bleak Street Somset ...20 E8
Blean Kent ...39 K9
Bleasby Lincs ...86 F4
Bleasby Notts ...85 M11
Bleasdale Lancs ...95 M11
Bleatarn W & F ...102 D8
Bleathwood Herefs ...57 K10
Blebocraigs Fife ...135 L4
Bleddfa Powys ...56 C11
Bledington Gloucs ...47 P10
Bledlow Bucks ...35 L4
Bledlow Ridge Bucks ...35 L5
Bleet Wilts ...20 G3
Blegbie E Loth ...128 D7
Blencarn W & F ...102 B4
Blencogo Cumb ...110 C11
Blendworth Hants ...15 K4
Blenheim Palace Oxon ...48 D11
Blennerhasset Cumb ...100 G2
Bletchingdon Oxon ...48 F11
Bletchingley Surrey ...36 H10
Bletchley M Keyn ...49 N8
Bletchley Shrops ...69 R8
Bletchley Park Museum
    M Keyn ...49 N8
Bletherston Pembks ...41 L6
Bletsoe Bed ...61 M9
Blewbury Oxon ...34 F7
Blickling Norfk ...76 H6
Blidworth Notts ...85 J9
Blidworth Bottoms Notts ...85 J10
Blindburn Nthumb ...118 F8
Blindcrake Cumb ...100 F4
Blindley Heath Surrey ...37 J11
Blindwells E Loth ...128 C5
Blisland Cnwll ...5 J7
Blissford Hants ...13 L2
Bliss Gate Worcs ...57 N10
Blisworth W Nthn ...49 K4
Blithbury Staffs ...71 K11
Blitterlees Cumb ...109 P10
Blockley Gloucs ...47 N7
Blofield Norfk ...77 L10
Blofield Heath Norfk ...77 L9

Blo Norton Norfk ...64 E6
Bloomfield Border ...118 A6
Blore Staffs ...70 C8
Blore Staffs ...71 L5
Blounce Hants ...23 K5
Blounts Green Staffs ...71 K8
Blowick Sefton ...88 D7
Bloxham Oxon ...48 D7
Bloxholm Lincs ...86 E10
Bloxwich Wsall ...58 E4
Bloxworth Dorset ...12 E6
Blubberhouses N York ...97 J9
Blue Anchor Cnwll ...4 E10
Blue Anchor Somset ...18 D6
Blue Bell Hill Kent ...38 B9
Blue John Cavern Derbys ...83 P8
Blundellsands Sefton ...81 L5
Blundeston Suffk ...65 Q2
Blunham C Beds ...61 Q10
Blunsdon St Andrew Swindn ...33 M7
Bluntington Worcs ...58 D10
Bluntisham Cambs ...62 E6
Blunts Cnwll ...5 N9
Blunts Green Warwks ...58 H11
Blurton C Stke ...70 F6
Blyborough Lincs ...86 B2
Blyford Suffk ...65 N6
Blymhill Staffs ...57 Q2
Blymhill Lawn Staffs ...57 Q2
Blyth Nthumb ...113 M4
Blyth Border ...127 L8
Blyth Bridge Border ...127 L8
Blythburgh Suffk ...65 N6
Blythe Border ...128 F10
Blythe Bridge Staffs ...70 H6
Blythe End Warwks ...59 K6
Blythe Marsh Staffs ...70 H6
Blyth Services Notts ...85 K3
Blyton Lincs ...85 Q2
Boarhills Fife ...135 N5
Boarhunt Hants ...14 H5
Boarley Kent ...38 C10
Boarsgreave Lancs ...89 N6
Boarshead E Susx ...25 M4
Boar's Head Wigan ...88 H9
Boars Hill Oxon ...34 E4
Boarstall Bucks ...34 H2
Boasley Cross Devon ...8 D6
Boath Highld ...155 Q3
Boat of Garten Highld ...148 G4
Bobbing Kent ...38 E8
Bobbington Staffs ...57 Q6
Bobbingworth Essex ...51 M9
Bocaddon Cnwll ...5 K10
Bocking Essex ...52 C7
Bocking Churchstreet Essex ...52 C6
Bockleton Worcs ...46 A3
Boconnoc Cnwll ...5 J9
Boddam Abers ...159 R9
Boddam Shet ...169 q12
Boddington Gloucs ...46 G9
Bodedern IoA ...78 E8
Bodelwyddan Denbgs ...80 E9
Bodenham Herefs ...45 Q4
Bodenham Wilts ...21 N9
Bodenham Moor Herefs ...45 Q4
Bodewryd IoA ...78 G6
Bodfari Denbgs ...80 F10
Bodffordd IoA ...78 G9
Bodham Norfk ...76 G3
Bodiam E Susx ...26 C6
Bodicote Oxon ...48 E7
Bodieve Cnwll ...4 F7
Bodinnick Cnwll ...5 J11
Bodle Street Green E Susx ...25 P8
Bodmin Cnwll ...4 H8
Bodmin Moor Cnwll ...5 K6
Bodney Norfk ...64 A2
Bodorgan IoA ...78 F11
Bodsham Kent ...27 K2
Boduan Gwynd ...66 E7
Bodwen Cnwll ...4 G8
Bodymoor Heath Warwks ...59 J5
Bogallan Highld ...156 A7
Bogbrae Abers ...159 P10
Bogend S Ayrs ...125 L11
Boggs Holdings E Loth ...128 C5
Boghall Mdloth ...127 N4
Boghall W Loth ...126 H4
Boghead S Lans ...126 D9
Bogmoor Moray ...157 R5
Bogmuir Abers ...143 L3
Bogniebrae Abers ...158 E8
Bognor Regis W Susx ...15 P7
Bogroy Highld ...148 G3
Bogue D & G ...108 D4
Bohetherick Cnwll ...5 Q8
Bohortha Cnwll ...3 M7
Bohuntine Highld ...146 H11
Bojewyan Cnwll ...2 B7
Bokiddick Cnwll ...4 H9
Bolam Dur ...103 N6
Bolam Nthumb ...112 H4
Bolberry Devon ...6 H11
Bold Heath St Hel ...82 B7
Boldmere Birm ...58 H6
Boldon Colliery S Tyne ...113 M8
Boldre Hants ...13 P5
Boldron Dur ...103 K8
Bole Notts ...85 N3
Bolehill Derbys ...84 C9
Bole Hill Derbys ...84 D6
Bolenowe Cnwll ...2 H6
Bolham Devon ...18 C11
Bolham Water Devon ...10 D2
Bolingey Cnwll ...3 K3
Bollington Ches E ...83 K9
Bollington Cross Ches E ...83 K9
Bollow Gloucs ...32 D2
Bolney W Susx ...24 G6
Bolnhurst Bed ...61 N9
Bolnore W Susx ...24 H6
Bolshan Angus ...143 L6
Bolsover Derbys ...84 G6
Bolster Moor Kirk ...90 D7
Bolsterstone Sheff ...90 H11
Boltby N York ...97 Q3
Bolter End Bucks ...35 L6
Bolton Bolton ...89 L9
Bolton E Loth ...128 C6
Bolton E R Yk ...98 F10
Bolton Nthumb ...119 M8
Bolton W & F ...102 B6
Bolton Abbey N York ...96 G10
Bolton Bridge N York ...96 G10
Bolton-by-Bowland Lancs ...96 A11

Boltonfellend Cumb ...111 J7
Boltongate Cumb ...100 H2
Bolton-le-Sands Lancs ...95 K7
Bolton Low Houses Cumb ...100 H2
Bolton New Houses Cumb ...100 H2
Bolton-on-Swale N York ...103 Q11
Bolton Percy N York ...91 N2
Bolton Town End Lancs ...95 K7
Bolton upon Dearne Barns ...91 M10
Bolventor Cnwll ...5 K6
Bomarsund Nthumb ...113 L4
Bomere Heath Shrops ...69 N11
Bonar Bridge Highld ...162 E8
Bonawe Ag & B ...139 J11
Bonby N Linc ...92 H7
Boncath Pembks ...41 P3
Bonchester Bridge Border ...118 A8
Bonchurch IoW ...14 G11
Bondleigh Devon ...8 G4
Bonds Lancs ...88 F2
Bonehill Devon ...8 H9
Bonehill Staffs ...59 J4
Bo'ness Falk ...134 C11
Boney Hay Staffs ...58 F2
Bonhill W Duns ...125 K2
Boningale Shrops ...57 Q4
Bonjedward Border ...118 C6
Bonkle N Lans ...126 E6
Bonnington Angus ...143 K10
Bonnington Kent ...27 J4
Bonnybank Fife ...135 K7
Bonnybridge Falk ...126 E2
Bonnykelly Abers ...159 L7
Bonnyrigg Mdloth ...127 Q4
Bonnyton Angus ...142 E10
Bonsall Derbys ...84 C9
Bonshaw Tower D & G ...110 D6
Bont Mons ...45 M11
Bontddu Gwynd ...67 M11
Bont-Dolgadfan Powys ...55 K4
Bont-goch Cerdgn ...54 F7
Bonthorpe Lincs ...87 N6
Bontnewydd Cerdgn ...54 E11
Bontnewydd Gwynd ...66 H3
Bontuchel Denbgs ...68 E3
Bonvilston V Glam ...30 E10
Bonwm Denbgs ...68 F5
Bon-y-maen Swans ...29 J5
Boode Devon ...17 J4
Booker Bucks ...35 M6
Booley Shrops ...69 Q9
Boon Border ...128 F10
Boon Hill Staffs ...70 E4
Boorley Green Hants ...14 F4
Boosbeck R & Cl ...105 J7
Boose's Green Essex ...52 D5
Boot Cumb ...100 G10
Boothby Graffoe Lincs ...86 C9
Boothby Pagnell Lincs ...73 P4
Boothferry E R Yk ...92 B5
Booth Green Ches E ...83 K8
Boothstown Salfd ...82 F4
Boothtown Calder ...90 D5
Boothville W Nthn ...60 G8
Bootle Cumb ...94 C3
Bootle Sefton ...81 L5
Boots Green Ches W ...82 G10
Boot Street Suffk ...53 M2
Booze N York ...103 K10
Boraston Shrops ...57 L11
Bordeaux Guern ...10 c1
Borden Kent ...38 E9
Borden W Susx ...23 M10
Border Cumb ...110 C10
Bordesley Worcs ...58 F11
Bordley N York ...96 E7
Bordon Hants ...23 L7
Boreham Essex ...52 C10
Boreham Wilts ...20 G6
Boreham Street E Susx ...25 Q8
Borehamwood Herts ...50 E11
Boreland D & G ...110 C2
Boreraig Highld ...152 B7
Boreton Shrops ...57 J3
Borgh W Isls ...168 b17
Borgh W Isls ...168 j2
Borgie Highld ...165 Q5
Borgue D & G ...108 D11
Borgue Highld ...167 K11
Borley Essex ...52 D3
Borley Green Essex ...52 D3
Borley Green Suffk ...64 D9
Borneskitaig Highld ...152 F3
Borness D & G ...108 D11
Boroughbridge N York ...97 N7
Borough Green Kent ...37 P9
Borras Head Wrexhm ...69 L4
Borrowash Derbys ...72 C4
Borrowby N York ...97 P3
Borrowby N York ...105 J7
Borrowdale Cumb ...101 J7
Borrowstoun Falk ...134 B11
Borstal Medway ...38 B8
Borth Cerdgn ...54 E6
Borthwick Mdloth ...128 B8
Borthwickbrae Border ...117 M8
Borthwickshiels Border ...117 N7
Borth-y-Gest Gwynd ...67 K7
Borve Highld ...152 G8
Borve W Isls ...168 b17
Borve W Isls ...168 j2
Borve W Isls ...168 j2
Borwick Lancs ...95 L6
Borwick Lodge W & F ...101 K11
Borwick Rails Cumb ...94 D5
Bosavern Cnwll ...2 B7
Bosbury Herefs ...46 C6
Boscarne Cnwll ...4 H8
Boscastle Cnwll ...4 H3
Boscombe BCP ...13 K6
Boscombe Wilts ...21 P7
Boscoppa Cnwll ...3 Q3
Bosham W Susx ...15 M6
Bosham Hoe W Susx ...15 M6
Bosherston Pembks ...41 J12
Boskednan Cnwll ...2 C7
Boskenna Cnwll ...2 C9
Bosley Ches E ...83 K11
Bosoughan Cnwll ...4 E9
Bossall N York ...98 E8
Bossiney Cnwll ...4 H4
Bossingham Kent ...27 L2
Bossington Somset ...18 A4
Bostock Green Ches W ...82 E11
Boston Lincs ...74 F2

Boston Spa Leeds ...97 P11
Boswarthan Cnwll ...2 C7
Boswinger Cnwll ...3 P5
Botallack Cnwll ...2 B7
Botany Bay Gt Lon ...50 G11
Botcheston Leics ...72 D10
Botesdale Suffk ...64 E6
Bothal Nthumb ...113 K3
Bothampstead W Berk ...34 F9
Bothamsall Notts ...85 L6
Bothel Cumb ...100 G3
Bothenhampton Dorset ...11 K6
Bothwell S Lans ...126 C6
Bothwell Services
    (southbound) S Lans ...126 C6
Botley Bucks ...35 Q4
Botley Hants ...14 F4
Botley Oxon ...34 E3
Botolph Claydon Bucks ...49 K10
Botolphs W Susx ...24 E9
Botolph's Bridge Kent ...27 K5
Bottesford Leics ...73 L3
Bottesford N Linc ...92 E9
Bottisham Cambs ...62 H8
Bottomcraig Fife ...135 K3
Bottom of Hutton Lancs ...88 F5
Bottom o' th' Moor Bolton ...89 K8
Bottoms Calder ...89 Q6
Bottoms Cnwll ...2 B9
Botts Green Warwks ...59 K6
Botusfleming Cnwll ...5 Q9
Botwnnog Gwynd ...66 D8
Bough Beech Kent ...37 L11
Boughrood Powys ...44 G7
Boughspring Gloucs ...31 Q5
Boughton Norfk ...75 P10
Boughton Notts ...85 L7
Boughton W Nthn ...60 G7
Boughton Aluph Kent ...26 H2
Boughton End C Beds ...49 Q7
Boughton Green Kent ...38 C11
Boughton Lees Kent ...26 H2
Boughton Malherbe Kent ...26 E2
Boughton Monchelsea Kent ...38 C11
Boughton Street Kent ...39 J10
Boulby R & Cl ...105 L7
Boulder Clough Calder ...90 C6
Bouldnor IoW ...14 C9
Bouldon Shrops ...57 J7
Boulmer Nthumb ...119 Q8
Boulston Pembks ...41 J8
Boultenstone Abers ...150 C5
Boultham Lincs ...86 C7
Boundary Staffs ...70 H6
Bourn Cambs ...62 D9
Bournbrook Birm ...58 F8
Bourne Lincs ...74 A6
Bournebridge Essex ...37 M2
Bourne End Bed ...61 M8
Bourne End Bucks ...35 N7
Bourne End C Beds ...49 Q6
Bourne End Herts ...50 B9
Bournemouth BCP ...13 J6
Bournemouth Airport BCP ...13 K5
Bournes Green Gloucs ...32 H4
Bournes Green Sthend ...38 F4
Bournheath Worcs ...58 E10
Bournmoor Dur ...113 M10
Bournstream Gloucs ...32 D6
Bournville Birm ...58 F8
Bourton Dorset ...20 E8
Bourton N Som ...19 L2
Bourton Oxon ...33 P7
Bourton Shrops ...57 K5
Bourton Wilts ...21 K2
Bourton on Dunsmore
    Warwks ...59 P10
Bourton-on-the-Hill
    Gloucs ...47 N8
Bourton-on-the-Water
    Gloucs ...47 N10
Bousd Ag & B ...136 H3
Boustead Hill Cumb ...110 E9
Bouth W & F ...94 G3
Bouthwaite N York ...96 H6
Bouts Worcs ...47 K3
Boveney Bucks ...35 P9
Boveridge Dorset ...13 J2
Bovey Tracey Devon ...9 J7
Bovingdon Herts ...50 B10
Bovingdon Green Bucks ...35 M7
Bovinger Essex ...51 M9
Bovington Dorset ...12 D7
Bovington Camp Dorset ...12 D7
Bow Cumb ...110 G9
Bow Devon ...7 L7
Bow Devon ...8 H4
Bow Gt Lon ...37 J4
Bow Ork ...169 c7
Bowbank Dur ...102 H6
Bow Brickhill M Keyn ...49 P8
Bowbridge Gloucs ...32 G3
Bowburn Dur ...104 B3
Bowcombe IoW ...14 E9
Bowd Devon ...10 C6
Bowden Border ...117 R4
Bowden Devon ...7 L9
Bowden Hill Wilts ...32 H11
Bowdon Traffd ...82 G7
Bower Highld ...167 M4
Bowerchalke Wilts ...21 K10
Bowerhill Wilts ...20 H2
Bower Hinton Somset ...19 N11
Bower House Tye Suffk ...52 G3
Bowermadden Highld ...167 M4
Bowers Staffs ...70 E7
Bowers Gifford Essex ...38 C4
Bowershall Fife ...134 D9
Bower's Row Leeds ...91 L5
Bowes Dur ...103 J8
Bowgreave Lancs ...88 F2
Bowhouse D & G ...109 M7
Bowithick Cnwll ...5 K5
Bowker's Green Lancs ...81 N4
Bowland Border ...117 P2
Bowland Bridge W & F ...95 J3
Bowley Herefs ...45 Q4
Bowley Town Herefs ...45 Q4
Bowlhead Green Surrey ...23 P7
Bowling C Brad ...90 F4
Bowling W Duns ...125 L3
Bowling Bank Wrexhm ...69 L5
Bowling Green Worcs ...46 F4
Bowmanstead W & F ...101 K11
Bowmore Ag & B ...122 D8
Bowness-on-Solway Cumb ...110 D8

Bowness-on-Windermere W & F 101 M11
Bow of Fife Fife 135 J5
Bowriefauld Angus 143 J8
Bowscale W & F 101 L4
Bowston Nthumb 119 J2
Bowston W & F 101 N11
Bow Street Cerdgn 54 E7
Bow Street Norfk 64 E2
Bowthorpe Norfk 76 H10
Box Gloucs 32 G4
Box Wilts 32 F11
Boxbush Gloucs 32 D2
Boxbush Gloucs 28 C10
Box End Bed 61 M11
Boxford Suffk 52 G3
Boxford W Berk 34 D10
Boxgrove W Susx 15 P5
Box Hill Surrey 36 E10
Boxley Kent 38 C10
Boxmoor Herts 50 B9
Box's Shop Cnwll 16 C11
Boxted Essex 52 H5
Boxted Suffk 64 A11
Boxted Cross Essex 52 H5
Boxwell Gloucs 32 F6
Boxworth Cambs 62 D8
Boyden End Suffk 63 M9
Boyden Gate Kent 39 M8
Boylestone Derbys 71 M7
Boyndie Abers 158 F5
Boyndlie Abers 159 M5
Boynton E R Yk 99 N7
Boysack Angus 143 L8
Boys Hill Dorset 11 P2
Boythorpe Derbys 84 E7
Boyton Cnwll 5 N3
Boyton Suffk 53 Q2
Boyton Wilts 21 J7
Boyton Cross Essex 51 P9
Boyton End Suffk 52 B3
Bozeat N Nthn 61 K9
Braaid IoM 80 d6
Brabling Green Suffk 65 K9
Brabourne Kent 27 K3
Brabourne Lees Kent 27 J3
Brabstermire Highld 167 P3
Bracadale Highld 152 F10
Braceborough Lincs 74 A8
Bracebridge Heath Lincs 86 C7
Bracebridge Low Fields Lincs 86 C7
Braceby Lincs 73 Q3
Bracewell Lancs 96 C11
Brackenfield Derbys 84 E9
Brackenhirst N Lans 126 C4
Brackenthwaite Cumb 110 E11
Brackenthwaite N York 97 L10
Brackla Brdgnd 29 P9
Bracklesham W Susx 15 M7
Brackletter Highld 146 F11
Brackley W Nthn 48 G7
Brackley Hatch W Nthn 48 H6
Bracknell Br For 35 N11
Braco P & K 133 N6
Bracobrae Moray 158 D7
Bracon Ash Norfk 64 H2
Bracora Highld 145 M9
Bracorina Highld 145 M9
Bradaford Devon 5 P3
Bradbourne Derbys 71 N4
Bradbury Dur 104 B5
Bradden W Nthn 48 H5
Braddock Cnwll 5 K9
Bradeley C Stke 70 F4
Bradenham Bucks 35 M5
Bradenstoke Wilts 33 K9
Bradfield Devon 9 Q3
Bradfield Essex 53 K5
Bradfield Norfk 77 K5
Bradfield Sheff 84 C2
Bradfield W Berk 34 H10
Bradfield Combust Suffk 64 B10
Bradfield Green Ches E 70 B3
Bradfield Heath Essex 53 K5
Bradfield St Clare Suffk 64 C10
Bradfield St George Suffk 64 C10
Bradfield Southend W Berk 34 G10
Bradford C Brad 90 F4
Bradford Cnwll 5 J6
Bradford Devon 16 G10
Bradford Nthumb 112 G5
Bradford Nthumb 119 N4
Bradford Abbas Dorset 11 M2
Bradford Leigh Wilts 20 F2
Bradford-on-Avon Wilts 20 F2
Bradford-on-Tone Somset 18 G10
Bradford Peverell Dorset 11 P6
Bradiford Devon 17 K5
Brading IoW 14 H9
Bradley Ches W 69 P5
Bradley Derbys 71 N5
Bradley Hants 22 H6
Bradley Kirk 90 F6
Bradley N York 96 F4
Bradley NE Lin 93 M9
Bradley Staffs 70 F11
Bradley Wolves 58 E5
Bradley Worcs 47 J2
Bradley Wrexhm 69 K4
Bradley Green Somset 19 J7
Bradley Green Warwks 59 L4
Bradley Green Worcs 47 J2
Bradley in the Moors Staffs 71 K6
Bradley Stoke S Glos 32 B8
Bradmore Notts 72 F4
Bradney Somset 19 K7
Bradninch Devon 9 N4
Bradninch Devon 17 L5
Bradnop Staffs 71 J3
Bradnor Green Herefs 45 K3
Bradpole Dorset 11 K6
Bradshaw Bolton 89 L8
Bradshaw Calder 90 D5
Bradshaw Kirk 90 D8
Bradstone Devon 5 P5
Bradwall Green Ches E 70 D2
Bradwell Derbys 83 Q8
Bradwell Devon 17 J3
Bradwell Essex 52 D7
Bradwell M Keyn 49 M6
Bradwell Norfk 77 Q11
Bradwell-on-Sea Essex 52 H10
Bradwell Waterside Essex 52 G10
Bradworthy Devon 16 E9
Brae Highld 156 B5

Brae Shet 169 q7
Braeface Falk 133 M11
Braehead Angus 143 M7
Braehead D & G 107 M7
Braehead S Lans 126 H7
Braeintra Highld 153 R11
Braemar Abers 149 M9
Braemore Highld 161 K11
Braemore Highld 167 J11
Brae Roy Lodge Highld 147 J9
Braeside Inver 124 G3
Braes of Coul Angus 142 D6
Braes of Enzie Moray 158 A6
Braes of Ullapool Highld 161 J8
Braeswick Ork 169 f3
Braevallich Ag & B 131 K6
Braewick Shet 169 p6
Brafferton Darltn 103 Q6
Brafferton N York 97 P6
Brafield-on-the-Green N Nthn 60 H9
Bragar W Isls 168 h3
Bragbury End Herts 50 G6
Braidwood S Lans 126 F7
Brailsford Derbys 71 P6
Brailsford Green Derbys 71 P6
Brain's Green Gloucs 32 C3
Braintree Essex 52 C7
Braiseworth Suffk 64 G7
Braishfield Hants 22 C9
Braiswick Essex 52 G6
Braithwaite C Brad 90 C2
Braithwaite Cumb 100 H6
Braithwell Donc 84 H2
Braken Hill Wakefd 91 L7
Bramber W Susx 24 E8
Brambridge Hants 22 E10
Bramcote Notts 72 E3
Bramcote Warwks 59 P7
Bramdean Hants 22 H9
Bramerton Norfk 77 K11
Bramfield Herts 50 G7
Bramfield Suffk 65 M7
Bramford Suffk 53 K2
Bramhall Stockp 83 J8
Bramhope Leeds 91 L2
Bramley Hants 23 J3
Bramley Leeds 90 G3
Bramley Rothm 84 G2
Bramley Surrey 24 B2
Bramley Corner Hants 22 H3
Bramley Green Hants 23 J3
Bramley Head N York 96 H9
Bramling Kent 39 M10
Brampford Speke Devon 9 M5
Brampton Cambs 62 B6
Brampton Cumb 111 K8
Brampton Lincs 85 P5
Brampton Norfk 77 J7
Brampton Rothm 91 L10
Brampton Suffk 65 N5
Brampton W & F 102 C6
Brampton Abbotts Herefs 46 B9
Brampton Ash N Nthn 60 G3
Brampton Bryan Herefs 56 F10
Brampton-en-le-Morthen Rothm 84 G3
Bramshall Staffs 71 K8
Bramshaw Hants 21 Q11
Bramshill Hants 23 K2
Bramshott Hants 23 M8
Bramwell Somset 19 M9
Branault Highld 137 N2
Brancaster Norfk 75 Q2
Brancaster Staithe Norfk 75 Q2
Brancepeth Dur 103 P3
Branchill Moray 157 K7
Brand End Lincs 87 L11
Branderburgh Moray 157 N3
Brandesburton E R Yk 99 N11
Brandeston Suffk 65 J9
Brand Green Gloucs 46 D9
Brandis Corner Devon 16 G11
Brandiston Norfk 76 G7
Brandon Dur 103 P2
Brandon Lincs 86 B11
Brandon Nthumb 119 K7
Brandon Suffk 63 N3
Brandon Warwks 59 P9
Brandon Bank Norfk 63 K3
Brandon Creek Norfk 63 K2
Brandon Parva Norfk 76 F10
Brandsby N York 98 B6
Brandy Wharf Lincs 92 H11
Brane Cnwll 2 C8
Bran End Essex 51 Q5
Branksome BCP 12 H6
Branksome Park BCP 13 J6
Bransbury Hants 22 D6
Bransby Lincs 85 Q5
Branscombe Devon 10 D7
Bransford Worcs 46 E4
Bransgore Hants 13 L5
Bransholme C KuH 93 K4
Bransley Shrops 57 M9
Branson's Cross Worcs 58 G10
Branston Leics 73 L5
Branston Lincs 86 D7
Branston Staffs 71 N10
Branston Booths Lincs 86 E7
Branstone IoW 14 G10
Brant Broughton Lincs 86 B10
Brantham Suffk 53 K5
Branthwaite Cumb 100 E6
Branthwaite Cumb 101 J3
Brantingham E R Yk 92 F5
Branton Donc 91 Q10
Branton Nthumb 119 K7
Branton Green N York 97 P8
Branxton Nthumb 118 G3
Brassey Green Ches W 69 P2
Brasside Dur 113 L11
Brassington Derbys 71 N4
Brasted Kent 37 L9
Brasted Chart Kent 37 L10
Brathens Abers 150 H8
Bratoft Lincs 87 N8
Brattleby Lincs 86 B4
Bratton Somset 18 B5
Bratton Wilts 20 H4
Bratton Wrekin 57 L2
Bratton Clovelly Devon 8 C6
Bratton Fleming Devon 17 M4
Bratton Seymour Somset 20 C9
Braughing Herts 51 J5

Braughing Friars Herts 51 K6
Braunston Rutlnd 73 L9
Braunston N Nthn 60 B7
Braunstone Town Leics 72 F10
Braunton Devon 16 H4
Brawby N York 98 E5
Brawl Highld 166 D3
Braworth N York 104 F9
Bray W & M 35 P9
Braybrooke N Nthn 60 G4
Braydon Wilts 33 L7
Braydon Brook Wilts 33 J6
Braydon Side Wilts 33 K7
Brayford Devon 17 M5
Bray's Hill E Susx 25 Q8
Bray Shop Cnwll 5 N7
Braystones Cumb 100 D9
Braythorn N York 97 K11
Brayton N York 91 Q4
Braywick W & M 35 N9
Braywoodside W & M 35 N9
Brazacott Cnwll 5 M3
Breach Kent 27 L2
Breach Kent 38 D8
Breachwood Green Herts 50 E6
Breacleit W Isls 168 g4
Breaclete W Isls 168 g4
Breaden Heath Shrops 69 M7
Breadsall Derbys 72 B3
Breadstone Gloucs 32 D4
Breage Cnwll 2 G8
Breakachy Highld 155 N9
Breakish Highld 145 L3
Brealangwell Lodge Highld 162 C8
Bream Gloucs 32 B3
Breamore Hants 21 N11
Brean Somset 19 J3
Breanais W Isls 168 e5
Brearley Calder 90 C5
Brearton N York 97 M8
Breascleit W Isls 168 h4
Breasclete W Isls 168 h4
Breaston Derbys 72 D4
Brechfa Carmth 43 K8
Brechin Angus 143 L5
Breckles Norfk 64 D3
Brecon Powys 44 E9
Brecon Beacons National Park 44 E10
Bredbury Stockp 83 K6
Brede E Susx 26 D8
Bredenbury Herefs 46 B3
Bredfield Suffk 65 K11
Bredgar Kent 38 D9
Bredhurst Kent 38 C9
Bredon Worcs 46 H7
Bredon's Hardwick Worcs 46 H7
Bredon's Norton Worcs 46 H7
Bredward Herefs 45 K4
Bredwardine Herefs 45 L6
Breedon on the Hill Leics 72 C6
Breich W Loth 126 H5
Breightmet Bolton 89 L9
Breighton E R Yk 92 B4
Breinton Herefs 45 P7
Bremhill Wilts 33 J10
Bremridge Devon 17 M6
Brenchley Kent 25 Q2
Brendon Devon 16 F10
Brendon Devon 17 P2
Brendon Hill Somset 18 D8
Brenfield Ag & B 123 P3
Brenish W Isls 168 e5
Brenkley N u Ty 113 K5
Brent Cross Gt Lon 36 F3
Brent Eleigh Suffk 52 F2
Brentford Gt Lon 36 E5
Brentingby Leics 73 K7
Brent Knoll Somset 19 K4
Brent Mill Devon 6 H7
Brent Pelham Herts 51 K4
Brentwood Essex 37 N2
Brenzett Kent 26 H6
Brenzett Green Kent 26 H6
Brereton Staffs 71 K11
Brereton Green Ches E 70 D2
Brereton Heath Ches E 82 H11
Brereton Hill Staffs 71 K11
Bressay Shet 169 s9
Bressingham Norfk 64 F5
Bressingham Common Norfk 64 F5
Bretby Derbys 71 P10
Bretford Warwks 59 P9
Bretforton Worcs 47 L6
Bretherton Lancs 88 F6
Brettabister Shet 169 r8
Brettenham Norfk 64 C5
Brettenham Suffk 64 D11
Bretton C Pete 74 C10
Bretton Derbys 84 B5
Bretton Flints 69 L2
Brewers End Essex 51 N6
Brewer Street Surrey 36 H10
Brewood Staffs 58 C3
Briantspuddle Dorset 12 D6
Brick End Essex 51 N5
Brickendon Herts 50 H9
Bricket Wood Herts 50 D9
Brick Houses Sheff 84 D4
Brickkiln Green Essex 52 B5
Bricklehampton Worcs 47 J6
Bride IoM 80 f1
Bridekirk Cumb 100 F4
Bridell Pembks 41 M2
Bridestowe Devon 8 D7
Brideswell Abers 158 F10
Bridford Devon 9 K7
Bridge Kent 39 L11
Bridge End Cumb 94 D4
Bridge End Cumb 110 D11
Bridge End Devon 6 H9
Bridge End Dur 103 K3
Bridge End Essex 51 Q4
Bridge End Lincs 74 B3
Bridgefoot Angus 142 F11
Bridgefoot Cumb 100 E5
Bridge Green Essex 51 L3
Bridgehampton Somset 19 Q10
Bridge Hewick N York 97 M6
Bridgehill Dur 112 G10
Bridgehouse Gate N York 97 J7
Bridgemary Hants 14 G6
Bridgemere Ches E 70 C4
Bridgend Abers 158 D10
Bridgend Ag & B 120 E4

Bridgend Ag & B 122 D7
Bridgend Ag & B 130 H9
Bridgend Angus 143 J4
Bridgend Brdgnd 29 P9
Bridgend Cerdgn 42 C5
Bridgend Devon 6 F9
Bridgend Devon 6 F9
Bridgend Fife 135 K5
Bridgend Moray 158 A11
Bridgend P & K 134 E3
Bridgend W & F 101 M8
Bridgend W Loth 127 J2
Bridgend of Lintrathen Angus 142 D7
Bridge of Alford Abers 150 F4
Bridge of Allan Stirlg 133 M8
Bridge of Avon Moray 149 M4
Bridge of Avon Moray 157 M10
Bridge of Balgie P & K 140 E8
Bridge of Brewlands Angus 142 B5
Bridge of Brown Highld 149 L3
Bridge of Cally P & K 142 A7
Bridge of Canny Abers 150 H8
Bridge of Craigisla Angus 142 D7
Bridge of Dee D & G 108 F9
Bridge of Don C Aber 151 N6
Bridge of Dun Angus 143 M6
Bridge of Dye Abers 150 H10
Bridge of Earn P & K 134 E4
Bridge of Ericht P & K 140 D6
Bridge of Feugh Abers 151 J8
Bridge of Gairn Abers 150 B8
Bridge of Gaur P & K 140 D6
Bridge of Marnoch Abers 158 E7
Bridge of Orchy Ag & B 139 P10
Bridge of Tilt P & K 141 L4
Bridge of Tynet Moray 158 A5
Bridge of Walls Shet 169 p8
Bridge of Weir Rens 125 K4
Bridge Reeve Devon 17 M9
Bridgerule Devon 16 D11
Bridges Shrops 56 F5
Bridge Sollers Herefs 45 N6
Bridge Street Suffk 52 E2
Bridgetown Cnwll 5 N4
Bridgetown Somset 18 B8
Bridge Trafford Ches W 81 P10
Bridge Yate S Glos 32 C10
Bridgham Norfk 64 D4
Bridgnorth Shrops 57 N6
Bridgwater Somset 19 J7
Bridgwater Services Somset 19 K8
Bridlington E R Yk 99 P7
Bridport Dorset 11 K6
Bridstow Herefs 46 A10
Brierfield Lancs 89 N3
Brierley Barns 91 L8
Brierley Gloucs 46 B11
Brierley Herefs 45 P3
Brierley Hill Dudley 58 D7
Brierlow Bar Derbys 83 N11
Brierton Hartpl 104 E4
Briery Cumb 101 J6
Brigg N Linc 92 H9
Briggate Norfk 77 L6
Briggswath N York 105 N9
Brigham Cumb 100 E4
Brigham Cumb 101 J6
Brigham E R Yk 99 M10
Brighouse Calder 90 E6
Brighstone IoW 14 D10
Brightgate Derbys 84 C9
Brighthampton Oxon 34 C4
Brightholmlee Sheff 90 H11
Brightley Devon 8 F5
Brightling E Susx 25 Q6
Brightlingsea Essex 53 J8
Brighton Br & H 24 H10
Brighton Cnwll 3 N3
Brighton City Airport W Susx 24 E9
Brighton le Sands Sefton 81 L5
Brightons Falk 126 G2
Brightwalton W Berk 34 D9
Brightwalton Green W Berk 34 D9
Brightwalton Holt W Berk 34 D9
Brightwell Suffk 53 N3
Brightwell Baldwin Oxon 35 J5
Brightwell-cum-Sotwell Oxon 34 G6
Brightwell Upperton Oxon 35 J6
Brignall Dur 103 L8
Brig o'Turk Stirlg 132 G6
Brigsley NE Lin 93 N10
Brigsteer W & F 95 K3
Brigstock N Nthn 61 K3
Brill Bucks 35 J2
Brill Cnwll 3 J8
Brilley Herefs 45 K5
Brimfield Herefs 57 J11
Brimfield Cross Herefs 57 J11
Brimington Derbys 84 F6
Brimley Devon 9 K9
Brimpsfield Gloucs 32 H2
Brimpton W Berk 22 G2
Brimpton Common W Berk 22 G2
Brimscombe Gloucs 32 G4
Brimstage Wirral 81 L8
Brincliffe Sheff 84 D4
Brind E R Yk 92 B4
Brindham Somset 19 P7
Brindister Shet 169 p8
Brindle Lancs 88 H6
Brindley Ches E 69 Q4
Brineton Staffs 57 Q2
Bringhurst Leics 60 H2
Bringsty Common Herefs 46 D3
Brington Cambs 61 N5
Brinian Ork 169 d4
Briningham Norfk 76 E5
Brinkely Notts 85 M10
Brinkhill Lincs 87 L6
Brinkley Cambs 63 K10
Brinklow Warwks 59 P9
Brinkworth Wilts 33 K8
Brinscall Lancs 89 J6
Brinsea N Som 19 M2
Brinsley Notts 84 G11
Brinsop Herefs 45 N6
Brinsworth Rothm 84 F3
Brinton Norfk 76 E4
Brisco Cumb 110 H10
Brisley Norfk 76 C7
Brislington Bristl 32 B10

Brissenden Green Kent 26 F4
Bristol Bristl 31 Q10
Bristol Airport N Som 31 P11
Briston Norfk 76 F5
Brisworthy Devon 6 F5
Britannia Lancs 89 P6
Britford Wilts 21 N9
Brithdir Caerph 30 F4
Brithdir Gwynd 67 P11
British Legion Village Kent 38 B10
Briton Ferry Neath 29 K6
Britwell Salome Oxon 35 J6
Brixham Torbay 7 N6
Brixton Devon 6 F8
Brixton Gt Lon 36 H5
Brixton Deverill Wilts 20 G7
Brixworth N Nthn 60 F6
Brize Norton Oxon 33 Q3
Brize Norton Airport Oxon 33 Q3
Broad Alley Worcs 58 C11
Broad Blunsdon Swindn 33 M6
Broadbottom Tamesd 83 L6
Broadbridge W Susx 15 M5
Broadbridge Heath W Susx 24 D4
Broad Campden Gloucs 47 N7
Broad Carr Calder 90 D7
Broad Chalke Wilts 21 K9
Broad Clough Lancs 89 P6
Broadclyst Devon 9 N5
Broadfield Inver 125 J3
Broadfield Pembks 41 M10
Broadford Highld 145 K3
Broad Ford Kent 26 B4
Broadford Bridge W Susx 24 C6
Broadgairhill Border 117 J8
Broadgrass Green Suffk 64 D9
Broad Green Cambs 63 L8
Broad Green Essex 52 E7
Broad Green Worcs 46 E3
Broad Green Worcs 58 E10
Broadhaugh Border 129 M9
Broad Haven Pembks 40 G8
Broadheath Traffd 82 G7
Broadhembury Devon 10 C4
Broadhempston Devon 7 L5
Broad Hill Cambs 63 J5
Broad Hinton Wilts 33 M9
Broadholme Lincs 85 Q6
Broadland Row E Susx 26 D8
Broadlay Carmth 28 C3
Broad Layings Hants 22 D2
Broadley Essex 51 K9
Broadley Lancs 89 P7
Broadley Moray 158 A5
Broadley Common Essex 51 K9
Broad Marston Worcs 47 M5
Broadmayne Dorset 12 B7
Broad Meadow Staffs 70 E5
Broadmere Hants 22 H5
Broadmoor Gloucs 46 B11
Broadmoor Pembks 41 L9
Broadnymett Devon 8 H4
Broad Oak Carmth 43 L10
Broad Oak Cumb 94 C2
Broadoak Dorset 11 J5
Broad Oak E Susx 25 P6
Broad Oak E Susx 26 D8
Broadoak Gloucs 32 C2
Broad Oak Hants 23 L4
Broad Oak Herefs 45 P10
Broad Oak Kent 39 L9
Broad Oak St Hel 82 B5
Broadoak Wrexhm 69 L3
Broad Road Suffk 65 K6
Broadsands Torbay 7 M7
Broad's Green Essex 51 Q8
Broadstairs Kent 39 Q8
Broadstone BCP 12 H5
Broadstone Mons 31 P4
Broadstone Shrops 57 J7
Broad Street E Susx 26 E8
Broad Street Essex 51 N7
Broad Street Kent 27 K3
Broad Street Kent 38 D10
Broad Street Medway 38 C7
Broad Street Wilts 21 M3
Broad Street Green Essex 52 E10
Broad Town Wilts 33 L9
Broadwas Worcs 46 E3
Broadwater Herts 50 F6
Broadwater W Susx 24 D9
Broadwaters Worcs 58 B9
Broadway Carmth 28 C3
Broadway Carmth 41 Q8
Broadway Pembks 40 G8
Broadway Somset 19 K11
Broadway Suffk 65 M6
Broadway Worcs 47 L7
Broadwell Gloucs 31 Q2
Broadwell Gloucs 47 P9
Broadwell Oxon 33 Q4
Broadwell Warwks 59 Q11
Broadwey Dorset 11 P8
Broadwindsor Dorset 11 J4
Broadwood Kelly Devon 8 F3
Broadwoodwidger Devon 5 Q4
Brobury Herefs 45 L6
Brochel Highld 153 K8
Brochroy Ag & B 139 J11
Brock Lancs 88 G2
Brockamin Worcs 46 E4
Brockbridge Hants 22 H11
Brockdish Norfk 65 J6
Brockencote Worcs 58 C10
Brockenhurst Hants 13 P4
Brocketsbrae S Lans 126 E10
Brockford Green Suffk 64 G8
Brockford Street Suffk 64 G8
Brockhall N Nthn 60 D8
Brockhall Village Lancs 89 L3
Brockham Surrey 36 E11
Brockhampton Gloucs 46 H9
Brockhampton Gloucs 47 K10
Brockhampton Hants 15 K5
Brockhampton Herefs 46 A8
Brockhampton Green Dorset 11 Q3
Brockholes Kirk 90 F8
Brockhurst Derbys 84 D8
Brockhurst Warwks 59 Q8
Brocklebank Cumb 101 K2
Brocklesby Lincs 93 K8
Brockley N Som 31 N11
Brockley Suffk 64 A7
Brockley Green Suffk 63 M11
Brockley Green Suffk 64 A11

Brockleymoor – Bush Hill Park 261

Brockleymoor W & F 101 N3
Brockmoor Dudley 58 D7
Brockscombe Devon 8 C5
Brock's Green Hants 22 F2
Brockton Shrops 56 E4
Brockton Shrops 56 E7
Brockton Shrops 57 K6
Brockton Shrops 57 N4
Brockton Staffs 70 E8
Brockweir Gloucs 31 P4
Brockwood Park Hants 22 H9
Brockworth Gloucs 46 G11
Brocton Cnwll 4 G8
Brocton Staffs 70 H11
Brodick N Ayrs 121 K4
Brodie Moray 156 H6
Brodsworth Donc 91 N9
Brogaig Highld 152 H4
Brogborough C Beds 49 Q7
Brokenborough Wilts 32 H7
Broken Cross Ches E 83 J10
Broken Cross Ches W 82 E10
Brokerswood Wilts 20 F4
Bromborough Wirral 81 M8
Brome Suffk 64 G6
Brome Street Suffk 64 H6
Bromeswell Suffk 65 L11
Bromfield Cumb 110 C11
Bromfield Shrops 56 H9
Bromham Bed 61 M10
Bromham Wilts 33 J11
Bromley Barns 91 J11
Bromley Dudley 58 D7
Bromley Gt Lon 37 K7
Bromley Shrops 57 N5
Bromley Common Gt Lon 37 K7
Bromley Cross Bolton 89 L8
Bromley Cross Essex 53 J6
Bromley Green Kent 26 G4
Bromlow Shrops 56 E4
Brompton Medway 38 C8
Brompton N York 104 C11
Brompton-by-Sawdon N York 99 J4
Brompton-on-Swale N York 103 P11
Brompton Ralph Somset 18 E8
Brompton Regis Somset 18 C8
Bromsash Herefs 46 C10
Bromsberrow Gloucs 46 D8
Bromsberrow Heath Gloucs 46 D8
Bromsgrove Worcs 58 E10
Bromstead Heath Staffs 70 D11
Bromyard Herefs 46 C4
Bromyard Downs Herefs 46 C3
Bronaber Gwynd 67 N8
Bronant Cerdgn 54 E11
Broncroft Shrops 57 J7
Brongest Cerdgn 42 F5
Bronington Wrexhm 69 N7
Bronllys Powys 44 G8
Bronwydd Carmth 42 H10
Bronydd Powys 45 J5
Bronygarth Shrops 69 J7
Brook Carmth 41 Q9
Brook Hants 13 N2
Brook Hants 22 B9
Brook IoW 14 C10
Brook Kent 27 J3
Brook Surrey 23 P7
Brook Surrey 36 C11
Brooke Norfk 65 K2
Brooke Rutlnd 73 L9
Brookenby Lincs 93 M11
Brook End Bed 61 N8
Brook End C Beds 61 Q11
Brook End Cambs 61 N6
Brook End M Keyn 49 P6
Brookfield Rens 125 L5
Brookhampton Oxon 34 H5
Brookhampton Somset 20 B9
Brook Hill Hants 13 N2
Brookhouse Denbgs 80 F11
Brookhouse Lancs 95 L8
Brookhouse Rothm 84 H3
Brookhouse Green Ches E 70 E2
Brookhouses Derbys 83 M7
Brookland Kent 26 G6
Brooklands Traffd 82 G6
Brookmans Park Herts 50 F10
Brooks Powys 55 Q5
Brooksby Leics 72 H7
Brooks End Kent 39 N8
Brooks Green W Susx 24 D6
Brook Street Essex 37 N2
Brook Street Kent 26 F5
Brook Street Suffk 52 D2
Brook Street W Susx 24 H5
Brookthorpe Gloucs 32 F2
Brookville Norfk 75 P11
Brookwood Surrey 23 Q3
Broom C Beds 50 E2
Broom Rothm 84 F2
Broom Warwks 47 L4
Broombank Worcs 57 M10
Broome Norfk 65 M3
Broome Shrops 56 G8
Broome Worcs 58 D9
Broomedge Warrtn 82 F7
Broome Park Nthumb 119 M8
Broomer's Corner W Susx 24 D6
Broomershill W Susx 24 C7
Broomfield Essex 52 B9
Broomfield Kent 38 D11
Broomfield Kent 39 L8
Broomfield Somset 18 H8
Broomfields Shrops 69 M11
Broomfleet E R Yk 92 E5
Broom Green Norfk 76 D7
Broomhall W & M 35 Q11
Broomhaugh Nthumb 112 F8
Broom Hill Barns 91 L10
Broom Hill Dorset 12 H4
Broom Hill Notts 84 H11
Broomhill Nthumb 119 P10
Broom Hill Worcs 58 D9
Broomhill Green Ches E 70 A5
Broomley Nthumb 112 F8
Broompark Dur 103 P2
Broom's Green Gloucs 46 D8
Broomsthorpe Norfk 76 A6
Broom Street Kent 38 H9
Brora Highld 163 L6
Broseley Shrops 57 M4
Brotherhouse Bar Lincs 74 E8
Brotherlee Dur 102 H3
Brothertoft Lincs 87 J11
Brotherton N York 91 M5
Brotton R & Cl 105 J7
Broubster Highld 166 H5
Brough Derbys 83 Q8
Brough E R Yk 92 F5
Brough Highld 167 M2
Brough Notts 85 P9
Brough Shet 169 s7
Brough W & F 102 E8
Broughall Shrops 69 Q6
Brough Lodge Shet 169 s4
Brough Sowerby W & F 102 E8
Broughton Border 116 G3
Broughton Bucks 35 M2
Broughton Cambs 62 C5
Broughton Flints 69 K2
Broughton Hants 22 B8
Broughton Lancs 88 G4
Broughton M Keyn 49 N7
Broughton N Linc 92 G9
Broughton N Nthn 60 H5
Broughton N York 96 D10
Broughton N York 98 F6
Broughton Oxon 48 D7
Broughton Salfd 82 H4
Broughton Staffs 70 D8
Broughton V Glam 29 P10
Broughton Astley Leics 60 B2
Broughton Beck W & F 94 F4
Broughton Gifford Wilts 20 G2
Broughton Green Worcs 47 J2
Broughton Hackett Worcs 46 H4
Broughton-in-Furness W & F 94 E3
Broughton Mains D & G 107 N8
Broughton Mills W & F 94 E2
Broughton Moor Cumb 100 E4
Broughton Poggs Oxon 33 P4
Broughton Tower W & F 94 E3
Broughty Ferry C Dund 142 H11
Brough with St Giles N York 103 P11
Brow End W & F 94 F6
Brownber W & F 102 D9
Brown Candover Hants 22 G7
Brown Edge Lancs 88 D8
Brown Edge Staffs 70 G4
Brown Heath Ches W 69 N2
Brownheath Shrops 69 N9
Brownhill Abers 159 L9
Brownhills Fife 135 N4
Brownhills Wsall 58 F3
Brownieside Nthumb 119 N6
Browninghill Green Hants 22 G2
Brown Knowl Ches W 69 N4
Brown Lees Staffs 70 F3
Brownlow Heath Ches E 70 E2
Brownrigg Cumb 100 D6
Brownrigg Cumb 110 C10
Brownsea Island Dorset 12 H7
Brown's Green Birm 58 G6
Brownsham Devon 16 D6
Browns Hill Gloucs 32 G4
Brownsover Warwks 60 B5
Brownston Devon 6 H8
Brown Street Suffk 64 F9
Browston Green Norfk 77 P11
Broxa N York 99 J2
Broxbourne Herts 51 J9
Broxburn E Loth 128 H4
Broxburn W Loth 127 K3
Broxfield Nthumb 119 P7
Broxted Essex 51 N5
Broxton Ches W 69 N4
Broyle Side E Susx 25 L8
Bruan Highld 167 P9
Bruar P & K 141 K4
Bruchag Ag & B 124 E6
Bruera Ches W 69 M2
Bruern Abbey Oxon 47 Q10
Bruichladdich Ag & B 122 C7
Bruisyard Suffk 65 L8
Bruisyard Street Suffk 65 L8
Brumby N Linc 92 E9
Brund Staffs 71 L2
Brundall Norfk 77 L10
Brundish Suffk 65 K8
Brundish Street Suffk 65 K7
Brunery Highld 138 C3
Brunnion Cnwll 2 E6
Brunslow Shrops 56 F8
Brunswick Village N u Ty 113 K6
Bruntcliffe Leeds 90 H5
Brunthwaite C Brad 96 G11
Bruntingthorpe Leics 60 D3
Brunton Fife 135 J3
Brunton Nthumb 119 P6
Brunton Wilts 21 P3
Brushford Devon 17 M10
Brushford Somset 18 B9
Bruton Somset 20 C7
Bryan's Green Worcs 58 C11
Bryanston Dorset 12 E3
Bryant's Bottom Bucks 35 N5
Brydekirk D & G 110 C6
Bryher IoS 2 b2
Brymbo Wrexhm 69 J4
Brympton Somset 19 P11
Bryn Carmth 28 F4
Bryn Ches W 82 D10
Bryn Neath 29 M6
Bryn Shrops 56 D7
Bryn Wigan 82 C4
Brynamman Carmth 29 K2
Brynberian Pembks 41 M3
Brynbryddan Neath 29 L6
Bryn Bwbach Gwynd 67 L7
Bryncae Rhondd 30 C8
Bryncethin Brdgnd 29 P8
Bryncir Gwynd 66 H6
Bryn-côch Neath 29 K5
Bryncrach Farm Caravan Park Powys 44 G4
Bryncroes Gwynd 66 C8
Bryncrug Gwynd 54 E4
Bryn Du IoA 78 E10
Bryn-Eden Gwynd 67 N9
Bryneglwys Denbgs 68 F5
Bryneglwys & Abergynolwyn Slate Landscape Gwynd 54 F3
Brynfields Wrexhm 69 K6
Brynford Flints 80 H10
Bryn Gates Wigan 82 C4
Bryn Golau Rhondd 30 D7
Bryngwran IoA 78 F9
Bryngwyn Mons 31 L3
Bryngwyn Powys 44 H5
Bryn-Henllan Pembks 41 K3
Brynhoffnant Cerdgn 42 F4
Bryning Lancs 88 E5
Brynithel Blae G 30 H4
Brynmawr Blae G 30 G2
Bryn-mawr Gwynd 66 C8
Brynmenyn Brdgnd 29 P8
Brynmill Swans 28 H6
Brynna Rhondd 30 C8
Brynnau Gwynion Rhondd 30 C8
Bryn-penarth Powys 55 Q4
Bryn Pydew Conwy 79 Q9
Brynrefail Gwynd 67 K2
Brynrefail IoA 78 H7
Brynsadler Rhondd 30 D8
Bryn Saith Marchog Denbgs 68 E4
Brynsiencyn IoA 78 H11
Brynteg IoA 78 H8
Bryn-y-bal Flints 69 J2
Bryn-y-Maen Conwy 79 Q9
Bryn-yr-Eos Wrexhm 69 J6
Bualintur Highld 144 F3
Buarth-draw Flints 80 H9
Bubbenhall Warwks 59 N10
Bubwith E R Yk 92 B3
Buccleuch Border 117 L8
Buchanan Smithy Stirlg 132 F10
Buchanhaven Abers 159 R8
Buchanty P & K 133 Q2
Buchany Stirlg 133 L7
Buchlyvie Stirlg 132 H9
Buckabank Cumb 110 G11
Buckden Cambs 61 Q7
Buckden N York 96 D5
Buckenham Norfk 77 M10
Buckerell Devon 10 C4
Buckfast Devon 7 J5
Buckfastleigh Devon 7 J5
Buckhaven Fife 135 K8
Buckholt Mons 45 Q11
Buckhorn Devon 5 P2
Buckhorn Weston Dorset 20 E10
Buckhurst Hill Essex 37 K2
Buckie Moray 158 B4
Buckingham Bucks 49 J8
Buckland Bucks 35 N2
Buckland Devon 6 H10
Buckland Gloucs 47 L7
Buckland Hants 13 P5
Buckland Herts 51 J4
Buckland Kent 27 P3
Buckland Oxon 34 B5
Buckland Surrey 36 F10
Buckland Brewer Devon 16 G7
Buckland Common Bucks 35 P3
Buckland Dinham Somset 20 E4
Buckland Filleigh Devon 16 H10
Buckland in the Moor Devon 7 J4
Buckland Monachorum Devon 6 D5
Buckland Newton Dorset 11 P3
Buckland Ripers Dorset 11 P8
Buckland St Mary Somset 10 F2
Buckland-Tout-Saints Devon 7 K9
Bucklebury W Berk 34 G10
Bucklers Hard Hants 14 D6
Bucklesham Suffk 53 M3
Buckley Flints 69 J2
Buckley Green Warwks 59 J11
Bucklow Hill Ches E 82 F8
Buckminster Leics 73 M6
Bucknall C Stke 70 G5
Bucknall Lincs 86 G7
Bucknell Oxon 48 G9
Bucknell Shrops 56 F10
Buckpool Moray 158 B4
Bucksburn C Aber 151 M6
Buck's Cross Devon 16 F7
Bucks Green W Susx 24 C4
Buckshaw Village Lancs 88 H6
Bucks Hill Herts 50 C10
Bucks Horn Oak Hants 23 M6
Buck's Mills Devon 16 F7
Buckton E R Yk 99 P6
Buckton Herefs 56 F10
Buckton Nthumb 119 L3
Buckworth Cambs 61 P5
Budby Notts 85 K7
Buddileigh Staffs 70 C5
Bude Cnwll 16 C10
Budge's Shop Cnwll 5 N10
Budlake Devon 9 N4
Budle Nthumb 119 N3
Budleigh Salterton Devon 9 Q8
Budlett's Common E Susx 25 L6
Budock Water Cnwll 3 K7
Buerton Ches E 70 B6
Bugbrooke W Nthn 60 E9
Bugford Devon 7 L8
Buglawton Ches E 70 F2
Bugle Cnwll 4 G10
Bugley Dorset 20 E10
Bugthorpe E R Yk 98 F9
Buildwas Shrops 57 L4
Builth Road Powys 44 E4
Builth Wells Powys 44 E4
Bulbourne Herts 35 P2
Bulbridge Wilts 21 L8
Bulby Lincs 73 R5
Bulcote Notts 72 H2
Bulford Wilts 21 N6
Bulford Camp Wilts 21 N6
Bulkeley Ches E 69 P4
Bulkington Warwks 59 N7
Bulkington Wilts 20 H3
Bulkworthy Devon 16 F9
Bullamoor N York 97 N2
Bull Bay IoA 78 G6
Bullbridge Derbys 84 E10
Bullbrook Br For 35 N11
Bullen's Green Herts 50 F9
Bulley Gloucs 46 E11
Bullgill Cumb 100 E3
Bullingham Herefs 45 Q7
Bullinghope Herefs 45 Q7
Bullington Hants 22 E6
Bullington Lincs 86 E5
Bullockstone Kent 39 L8
Bull's Green Herts 50 G7
Bull's Green Norfk 65 N3
Bulmer Essex 52 D3
Bulmer N York 98 D7
Bulmer Tye Essex 52 D4
Bulphan Thurr 37 P3
Bulstone Devon 10 D7
Bulstrode Herts 50 B10
Bulverhythe E Susx 26 C10
Bulwark Abers 159 M8
Bulwell C Nott 72 E2
Bulwick N Nthn 61 L2
Bumble's Green Essex 51 K9
Bunacaimb Highld 145 L10
Bunarkaig Highld 146 F10
Bunbury Ches E 69 Q3
Bunbury Heath Ches E 69 Q3
Bunchrew Highld 155 R8
Buncton W Susx 24 D8
Bundalloch Highld 145 Q2
Bunessan Ag & B 137 K11
Bungay Suffk 65 L4
Bunker's Hill Lincs 87 J10
Bunnahabhain Ag & B 122 F5
Bunny Notts 72 F5
Buntait Highld 155 M11
Buntingford Herts 51 J5
Bunwell Norfk 64 G3
Bunwell Hill Norfk 64 G3
Bupton Derbys 71 N7
Burbage Derbys 83 M10
Burbage Leics 59 P6
Burbage Wilts 21 P2
Burcher Herefs 45 L2
Burchett's Green W & M 35 M8
Burcombe Wilts 21 L8
Burcot Oxon 34 G5
Burcot Worcs 58 E10
Burcote Shrops 57 N5
Burcott Bucks 49 M11
Burcott Bucks 49 N10
Burdale N York 98 H8
Bures Essex 52 F5
Burford Oxon 33 Q2
Burford Shrops 57 K11
Burg Ag & B 137 K6
Burgate Suffk 64 F6
Burgates Hants 23 L9
Burge End Herts 50 D4
Burgess Hill W Susx 24 H7
Burgh Suffk 65 J11
Burgh by Sands Cumb 110 F9
Burgh Castle Norfk 77 P10
Burghclere Hants 22 E2
Burghead Moray 157 L4
Burghfield W Berk 35 J11
Burghfield Common W Berk 35 J11
Burgh Heath Surrey 36 F9
Burgh Hill E Susx 26 B6
Burghill Herefs 45 P6
Burgh Island Devon 6 G10
Burgh le Marsh Lincs 87 P7
Burgh next Aylsham Norfk 77 J6
Burgh on Bain Lincs 86 H3
Burgh St Margaret Norfk 77 N9
Burgh St Peter Norfk 65 P3
Burghwallis Donc 91 N8
Burham Kent 38 B9
Buriton Hants 23 K11
Burland Ches E 69 R4
Burlawn Cnwll 4 F7
Burleigh Gloucs 32 G4
Burlescombe Devon 18 E11
Burleston Dorset 12 C6
Burlestone Devon 7 L9
Burley Hants 13 M4
Burley Rutlnd 73 M8
Burley Shrops 56 H8
Burleydam Ches E 69 R6
Burley Gate Herefs 46 A5
Burley in Wharfedale C Brad 97 J11
Burley Lawn Hants 13 M4
Burley Street Hants 13 M4
Burley Wood Head C Brad 90 F2
Burlingham Green Norfk 77 M9
Burlingjobb Powys 45 K3
Burlington Shrops 57 P2
Burlton Shrops 69 N9
Burmarsh Kent 27 K5
Burmington Warwks 47 Q7
Burn N York 91 P5
Burnage Manch 83 J6
Burnaston Derbys 71 P8
Burnbanks W & F 101 P7
Burnbrae N Lans 126 F6
Burn Bridge N York 97 L10
Burnby E R Yk 98 G11
Burn Cross Sheff 91 J11
Burndell W Susx 15 Q6
Burnden Bolton 89 L9
Burnedge Rochdl 89 Q8
Burneside W & F 101 P11
Burneston N York 97 M4
Burnett BaNES 32 C11
Burnfoot Border 117 N8
Burnfoot Border 117 Q7
Burnfoot D & G 109 L2
Burnfoot D & G 110 F3
Burnfoot D & G 117 M11
Burnfoot P & K 134 B7
Burnham Bucks 35 P8
Burnham N Linc 93 J7
Burnham Deepdale Norfk 75 R2
Burnham Green Herts 50 G7
Burnham Market Norfk 76 A3
Burnham Norton Norfk 76 A3
Burnham-on-Crouch Essex 38 F2
Burnham-on-Sea Somset 19 K5
Burnham Overy Norfk 76 A3
Burnham Overy Staithe Norfk 76 A3
Burnham Thorpe Norfk 76 B3
Burnhead D & G 116 B11
Burnhervie Abers 151 J4
Burnhill Green Staffs 57 P4
Burnhope Dur 113 J11
Burnhouse N Ayrs 125 K7
Burniston N York 99 L2
Burnley Lancs 89 N4
Burnmouth Border 129 P7
Burn Naze Lancs 88 C2
Burn of Cambus Stirlg 133 L7
Burnopfield Dur 113 J9
Burnrigg Cumb 111 J9
Burnsall N York 96 F8
Burnside Angus 142 G6
Burnside Angus 143 J7
Burnside Fife 134 F6
Burnside Moray 157 M4
Burnside of Duntrune Angus 142 G11
Burntcommon Surrey 36 B10
Burntheath Derbys 71 N8
Burnt Heath Essex 53 J6
Burnt Hill W Berk 34 G10
Burnthouse Cnwll 3 K6
Burnt Houses Dur 103 M6
Burntisland Fife 134 G10
Burnt Oak E Susx 25 M5
Burnton E Ayrs 115 J6
Burntwood Flints 69 J2
Burntwood Staffs 58 G3
Burntwood Green Staffs 58 G3
Burnt Yates N York 97 L8
Burnworthy Somset 18 G11
Burpham Surrey 36 B10
Burpham W Susx 24 B9
Burradon N Tyne 113 L6
Burradon Nthumb 119 J9
Burrafirth Shet 169 t2
Burras Cnwll 2 H7
Burraton Cnwll 5 Q8
Burravoe Shet 169 s5
Burray Village Ork 169 d7
Burrells W & F 102 C7
Burrelton P & K 142 C10
Burridge Devon 10 G3
Burridge Devon 17 K4
Burridge Hants 14 F4
Burrill N York 97 K3
Burringham N Linc 92 D9
Burrington Devon 17 L8
Burrington Herefs 56 G10
Burrington N Som 19 N3
Burrough End Cambs 63 K9
Burrough Green Cambs 63 K9
Burrough on the Hill Leics 73 K8
Burrow Lancs 95 N6
Burrow Somset 18 B6
Burrow Bridge Somset 19 L8
Burrowhill Surrey 23 Q2
Burrows Cross Surrey 36 C11
Burry Swans 28 E6
Burry Green Swans 28 E6
Burry Port Carmth 28 D4
Burscough Lancs 88 E8
Burscough Bridge Lancs 88 E8
Bursea E R Yk 92 D4
Burshill E R Yk 99 M11
Bursledon Hants 14 E5
Burslem C Stke 70 F5
Burstall Suffk 53 J3
Burstock Dorset 11 J4
Burston Norfk 64 G5
Burston Staffs 70 G8
Burstow Surrey 24 H2
Burstwick E R Yk 93 M5
Burtersett N York 96 C3
Burtholme Cumb 111 K8
Burthorpe Green Suffk 63 N8
Burthwaite Cumb 110 H11
Burthy Cnwll 4 E10
Burtle Somset 19 L6
Burtle Hill Somset 19 L6
Burtoft Lincs 74 E3
Burton BCP 13 L6
Burton Ches W 69 P2
Burton Ches W 81 L10
Burton Dorset 11 P6
Burton Nthumb 119 N4
Burton Pembks 41 J9
Burton Somset 11 L2
Burton Somset 18 G6
Burton Wilts 20 F8
Burton Wilts 32 F9
Burton Agnes E R Yk 99 N8
Burton Bradstock Dorset 11 K7
Burton-by-Lincoln Lincs 86 C6
Burton Coggles Lincs 73 P5
Burton Dassett Warwks 48 C4
Burton End Essex 51 M6
Burton End Suffk 63 L11
Burton Fleming E R Yk 99 M6
Burton Green Warwks 59 L9
Burton Green Wrexhm 69 K3
Burton Hastings Warwks 59 P7
Burton Hill Wilts 32 H7
Burton-in-Kendal W & F 95 L5
Burton-in-Kendal Services W & F 95 L5
Burton in Lonsdale N York 95 P6
Burton Joyce Notts 72 G2
Burton Latimer N Nthn 61 K6
Burton Lazars Leics 73 K7
Burton Leonard N York 97 M8
Burton on the Wolds Leics 72 F6
Burton Overy Leics 72 H11
Burton Pedwardine Lincs 74 B2
Burton Pidsea E R Yk 93 M4
Burton Salmon N York 91 M5
Burton's Green Essex 52 D6
Burton upon Stather N Linc 92 E7
Burton upon Trent Staffs 71 N10
Burton Waters Lincs 86 B6
Burtonwood Warrtn 82 C6
Burtonwood Services Warrtn 82 C6
Burwardsley Ches W 69 P3
Burwarton Shrops 57 L7
Burwash E Susx 25 Q6
Burwash Common E Susx 25 P6
Burwash Weald E Susx 25 Q6
Burwell Cambs 63 J7
Burwell Lincs 87 L5
Burwen IoA 78 G6
Burwick Ork 169 d8
Bury Bury 89 N8
Bury Cambs 62 C4
Bury Somset 18 B9
Bury W Susx 24 B8
Bury End C Beds 50 D3
Bury Green Herts 51 L6
Bury St Edmunds Suffk 64 B9
Burythorpe N York 98 F8
Busby E Rens 125 P6
Busby Stoop N York 97 N4
Buscot Oxon 33 P5
Bush Abers 143 P4
Bush Cnwll 16 C10
Bush Bank Herefs 45 P4
Bushbury Wolves 58 D4
Bushby Leics 72 H10
Bushey Herts 50 D11
Bushey Heath Herts 36 D2
Bush Green Norfk 65 J4
Bush Green Suffk 64 C10
Bush Hill Park Gt Lon 50 H11

262 Bushley – Catfield Common

Bushley Worcs 46 G8
Bushley Green Worcs 46 G8
Bushmead Bed 61 P8
Bushmoor Shrops 56 G7
Bushton Wilts 33 L9
Busk W & F 102 B2
Buslingthorpe Lincs 86 E3
Bussage Gloucs 32 G4
Bussex Somset 19 L7
Butcher's Cross E Susx 25 N5
Butcombe N Som 19 P2
Bute Ag & B 124 C4
Butleigh Somset 19 P8
Butleigh Wootton Somset 19 P7
Butler's Cross Bucks 35 M3
Butler's Hill Notts 84 H11
Butlers Marston Warwks 48 B4
Butley Suffk 65 M11
Butley High Corner Suffk 53 Q2
Buttercrambe N York 98 E9
Butterdean Border 129 K7
Butterknowle Dur 103 M5
Butterleigh Devon 9 N3
Butterley Derbys 84 F10
Buttermere Cumb 100 G7
Buttermere Wilts 22 B2
Buttershaw C Brad 90 E5
Butterstone P & K 141 Q8
Butterton Staffs 70 E6
Butterton Staffs 71 K3
Butterwick Dur 104 C4
Butterwick Lincs 87 L11
Butterwick N York 98 E5
Butterwick N York 99 K6
Butt Green Ches E 70 B4
Buttington Powys 56 C3
Buttonbridge Shrops 57 N9
Buttonoak Shrops 57 P9
Buttsash Hants 14 D5
Buttsbear Cross Cnwll 16 D11
Butt's Green Essex 52 C11
Buxhall Suffk 64 E10
Buxhall Fen Street Suffk 64 E10
Buxted E Susx 25 L6
Buxton Derbys 83 N10
Buxton Norfk 77 J7
Buxton Heath Norfk 76 H7
Buxworth Derbys 83 M8
Bwlch Powys 44 H10
Bwlchgwyn Wrexhm 69 J4
Bwlchllan Cerdgn 43 L3
Bwlchnewydd Carmth 42 G10
Bwlchtocyn Gwynd 66 E9
Bwlch-y-cibau Powys 68 G11
Bwlch-y-Ddar Powys 68 G10
Bwlchyfadfa Cerdgn 42 H5
Bwlch-y-ffridd Powys 55 P5
Bwlch-y-groes Pembks 41 P3
Bwlchymyrdd Swans 28 G5
Bwlch-y-sarnau Powys 55 N10
Byermoor Gatesd 113 J9
Byers Green Dur 103 P4
Byfield W Nthn 48 F4
Byfleet Surrey 36 C8
Byford Herefs 45 M6
Bygrave Herts 50 G3
Byker N u Ty 113 L8
Byland Abbey N York 98 A5
Bylaugh Norfk 76 E8
Bylchau Conwy 68 C2
Byley Ches W 82 F11
Bynea Carmth 28 F5
Byram N York 91 M5
Byrness Nthumb 118 E10
Bystock Devon 9 P8
Bythorn Cambs 61 N5
Byton Herefs 45 M2
Bywell Nthumb 112 F8
Byworth W Susx 23 Q10

C

Cabbacott Devon 16 G7
Cabourne Lincs 93 K10
Cabrach Ag & B 122 G7
Cabrach Moray 150 B2
Cabus Lancs 95 K11
Cackle Street E Susx 25 L5
Cackle Street E Susx 25 Q7
Cackle Street E Susx 26 D8
Cadbury Devon 9 M3
Cadbury Barton Devon 17 M8
Cadbury World Birm 58 F8
Cadder E Duns 125 Q3
Caddington C Beds 50 C7
Caddonfoot Border 117 P3
Cadeby Donc 91 N10
Cadeby Leics 72 C10
Cadeleigh Devon 9 M3
Cade Street E Susx 25 P6
Cadgwith Cnwll 3 J11
Cadham Fife 134 H7
Cadishead Salfd 82 F6
Cadle Swans 28 H5
Cadley Lancs 88 G4
Cadley Wilts 21 P4
Cadley Wilts 33 P11
Cadmore End Bucks 35 L6
Cadnam Hants 13 P2
Cadney N Linc 92 H10
Cadole Flints 68 H2
Cadoxton V Glam 30 F11
Cadoxton Juxta-Neath Neath 29 L5
Cadwst Denbgs 68 D7
Caeathro Gwynd 67 J2
Caehopkin Powys 29 M2
Caenby Lincs 86 C3
Caerau Brdgnd 29 N6
Caerau Cardif 30 F9
Cae'r-bont Powys 29 M2
Cae'r bryn Carmth 28 G2
Caerdeon Gwynd 67 M11
Caer Farchell Pembks 40 E5
Caergeiliog IoA 78 E9
Caergwrle Flints 69 K3
Caerhowel Powys 56 C5
Caerhun Conwy 79 P10
Caerlanrig Border 117 M10
Caerleon Newpt 31 K6
Caernarfon Gwynd 66 H2
Caernarfon Castle Gwynd 66 H2
Caerphilly Caerph 30 G7
Caersws Powys 55 N6
Caerwedros Cerdgn 42 G3
Caerwent Mons 31 N6
Caerwys Flints 80 G10
Caerynwch Gwynd 67 P11
Caggle Street Mons 45 M11
Caim IoA 79 L8
Caio Carmth 43 N7
Cairinis W Isls 168 d11
Cairnbaan Ag & B 130 G9
Cairnbulg Abers 159 P4
Cairncross Border 129 M7
Cairncurran Inver 125 J3
Cairndow Ag & B 131 P5
Cairneyhill Fife 134 C10
Cairngarroch D & G 106 E8
Cairngorms National Park 149 K7
Cairnie Abers 158 C9
Cairn Lodge Services S Lans 116 B4
Cairnorrie Abers 159 L9
Cairnryan D & G 106 E4
Cairnty Moray 157 Q7
Caister-on-Sea Norfk 77 Q9
Caistor Lincs 93 K10
Caistor St Edmund Norfk 77 J11
Cakebole Worcs 58 C10
Cake Street Norfk 64 F3
Calais Street Suffk 52 G4
Calanais W Isls 168 h4
Calbourne IoW 14 D9
Calceby Lincs 87 L5
Calcoed Flints 80 H10
Calcot Gloucs 33 L2
Calcot W Berk 35 J10
Calcot Row W Berk 35 J10
Calcots Moray 157 P5
Calcott Kent 39 L9
Calcott Shrops 56 G2
Calcutt N York 97 M9
Calcutt Wilts 33 M6
Caldbeck Cumb 101 K2
Caldbergh N York 96 G3
Caldecote Cambs 61 P3
Caldecote Cambs 62 D9
Caldecote Herts 50 F3
Caldecote W Nthn 49 J4
Caldecott N Nthn 61 L7
Caldecott Oxon 34 E5
Caldecott Rutlnd 61 J2
Caldecotte M Keyn 49 N7
Calder Cumb 100 D10
Calderbank N Lans 126 D5
Calder Bridge Cumb 100 D9
Calderbrook Rochdl 89 Q7
Caldercruix N Lans 126 E4
Calder Grove Wakefd 91 J7
Caldermill S Lans 126 B9
Caldermore Rochdl 89 Q7
Calder Vale Lancs 95 L11
Calderwood S Lans 126 B6
Caldey Island Pembks 41 M11
Caldicot Mons 31 N7
Caldmore Wsall 58 F5
Caldwell N York 103 N8
Caldy Wirral 81 J7
Calenick Cnwll 3 L5
Calf of Man IoM 80 a8
Calford Green Suffk 63 M11
Calfsound Ork 169 e3
Calgary Ag & B 137 K5
Califer Moray 157 K6
California Falk 126 G2
California Norfk 77 Q8
California Cross Devon 7 J8
Calke Derbys 72 B6
Calke Abbey Derbys 72 B6
Callakille Highld 153 M6
Callander Stirlg 133 J6
Callanish W Isls 168 h4
Callaughton Shrops 57 L5
Callerton N u Ty 113 J7
Callestick Cnwll 3 K3
Calligarry Highld 145 K7
Callington Cnwll 5 P8
Callingwood Staffs 71 M10
Callow Herefs 45 P8
Callow End Worcs 46 F4
Callow Hill Wilts 33 K8
Callow Hill Worcs 47 K2
Callow Hill Worcs 57 N10
Callows Grave Worcs 57 K11
Calmore Hants 13 P2
Calmsden Gloucs 33 K3
Calne Wilts 33 J10
Calow Derbys 84 F6
Calshot Hants 14 E6
Calstock Cnwll 6 C5
Calstone Wellington Wilts 33 K11
Calthorpe Norfk 76 H5
Calthorpe Street Norfk 77 N6
Calthwaite W & F 101 N2
Calton N York 96 D9
Calton Staffs 71 L5
Calveley Ches E 69 Q3
Calver Derbys 84 B6
Calverhall Shrops 69 R7
Calver Hill Herefs 45 M5
Calverleigh Devon 9 M2
Calverley Leeds 90 G3
Calver Sough Derbys 84 B6
Calvert Bucks 49 J10
Calverton M Keyn 49 L7
Calverton Notts 85 K11
Calvine P & K 141 K4
Calvo Cumb 109 P10
Calzeat Border 116 G3
Cam Gloucs 32 E5
Camasachoirce Highld 138 D5
Camasine Highld 138 D5
Camas Luinie Highld 146 A2
Camastianavaig Highld 153 J10
Camault Muir Highld 155 P9
Camber E Susx 26 G8
Camberley Surrey 23 N2
Camberwell Gt Lon 36 H5
Camblesforth N York 91 Q5
Cambo Nthumb 112 F3
Cambois Nthumb 113 M4
Camborne Cnwll 2 G5
Camborne & Redruth Mining District Cnwll 2 G5
Cambourne Cambs 62 D9
Cambridge Cambs 62 G9
Cambridge Gloucs 32 D4
Cambridge Airport Cambs 62 G9
Cambrose Cnwll 2 H4
Cambus Clacks 133 P9
Cambusavie Highld 162 H7
Cambusbarron Stirlg 133 M9
Cambuskenneth Stirlg 133 N9
Cambuslang S Lans 125 Q5
Cambus o' May Abers 150 C8
Cambuswallace S Lans 116 E3
Camden Town Gt Lon 36 G4
Cameley BaNES 20 B3
Camelford Cnwll 5 J5
Camelon Falk 133 P11
Camerory Highld 157 J11
Camer's Green Worcs 46 E7
Camerton BaNES 20 C3
Camerton Cumb 100 D4
Camghouran P & K 140 E6
Camieston Border 117 R4
Cammachmore Abers 151 N8
Cammeringham Lincs 86 B4
Camore Highld 162 H9
Campbeltown Ag & B 120 D7
Campbeltown Airport Ag & B 120 C7
Camperdown N Tyne 113 L6
Cample D & G 109 J2
Campmuir P & K 142 C10
Camps W Loth 127 K4
Campsall Donc 91 N8
Campsea Ash Suffk 65 L10
Camps End Cambs 51 P2
Campton C Beds 50 D3
Camptown Border 118 C8
Camrose Pembks 40 H6
Camserney P & K 141 K8
Camusnagaul Highld 139 K3
Camusnagaul Highld 160 H9
Camusteel Highld 153 N9
Camusterrach Highld 153 N9
Canada Hants 21 Q11
Canal Foot W & F 94 G5
Canaston Bridge Pembks 41 L7
Candacraig Abers 149 Q8
Candlesby Lincs 87 N7
Candle Street Suffk 64 E7
Candover Green Shrops 57 J3
Candy Mill Border 116 F2
Cane End Oxon 35 J9
Canewdon Essex 38 F3
Canford Bottom Dorset 12 H4
Canford Cliffs BCP 13 J7
Canford Heath BCP 12 H6
Canford Magna BCP 12 H5
Canhams Green Suffk 64 F8
Canisbay Highld 167 P2
Canklow Rothm 84 F2
Canley Covtry 59 M9
Cann Dorset 20 G10
Canna Highld 144 B6
Cann Common Dorset 20 G10
Cannich Highld 155 K11
Cannington Somset 19 J7
Canning Town Gt Lon 37 K4
Cannock Staffs 58 E2
Cannock Chase Staffs 70 H11
Cannock Wood Staffs 58 F2
Cannon Bridge Herefs 45 N6
Canonbie D & G 110 G5
Canon Frome Herefs 46 B6
Canon Pyon Herefs 45 P5
Canons Ashby W Nthn 48 G4
Canonstown Cnwll 2 E6
Canterbury Kent 39 K10
Canterbury Cathedral Kent 39 L10
Cantley Norfk 77 M11
Cantlop Shrops 57 J3
Canton Cardif 30 G9
Cantraywood Highld 156 D8
Cantsfield Lancs 95 N6
Canvey Island Essex 38 C5
Canwick Lincs 86 C7
Canworthy Water Cnwll 5 L3
Caol Highld 139 L2
Caolas Scalpaigh W Isls 168 h8
Caoles Ag & B 136 D6
Caonich Highld 146 D9
Capel Kent 25 P2
Capel Surrey 24 E2
Capel Bangor Cerdgn 54 F8
Capel Betws Lleucu Cerdgn 43 M3
Capel Coch IoA 78 H8
Capel Curig Conwy 67 N3
Capel Cynon Cerdgn 42 G5
Capel Dewi Carmth 43 J10
Capel Dewi Cerdgn 43 J6
Capel-Dewi Cerdgn 54 E8
Capel Garmon Conwy 67 Q3
Capel Green Suffk 53 Q2
Capel Gwyn Carmth 43 J10
Capel Gwyn IoA 78 E9
Capel Gwynfe Carmth 43 P10
Capel Hendre Carmth 28 G2
Capel Isaac Carmth 43 L9
Capel Iwan Carmth 41 Q3
Capel-le-Ferne Kent 27 N4
Capelles Guern 10 c1
Capel Llanilltern Cardif 30 E9
Capel Mawr IoA 78 G10
Capel Parc IoA 78 G7
Capel St Andrew Suffk 53 Q2
Capel St Mary Suffk 53 J4
Capel Seion Cerdgn 54 E9
Capel Trisant Cerdgn 54 G9
Capeluchaf Gwynd 66 G5
Capelulo Conwy 79 N9
Capel-y-ffin Powys 45 K8
Capel-y-graig Gwynd 79 J11
Capenhurst Ches W 81 M10
Capernwray Lancs 95 L6
Cape Wrath Highld 164 G1
Capheaton Nthumb 112 F4
Caplaw E Rens 125 L6
Capon's Green Suffk 65 K8
Cappercleuch Border 117 J6
Capstone Medway 38 C8
Capton Devon 7 L8
Capton Somset 18 E7
Caputh P & K 141 Q9
Caradon Mining District Cnwll 5 M7
Caradon Town Cnwll 5 M7
Carbeth Stirlg 125 N2
Carbis Cnwll 4 G10
Carbis Bay Cnwll 2 E6
Carbost Highld 152 F11
Carbost Highld 152 G8
Carbrook Sheff 84 E3
Carbrooke Norfk 76 C11
Carburton Notts 85 K6
Carclaze Cnwll 3 Q3
Car Colston Notts 73 J2
Carcroft Donc 91 N9
Cardenden Fife 134 G8
Cardeston Shrops 56 F2
Cardewlees Cumb 110 G10
Cardhu Moray 157 M9
Cardiff Cardif 30 G9
Cardiff Airport V Glam 30 E11
Cardiff Gate Services Cardif 30 H8
Cardiff West Services Cardif 30 E9
Cardigan Cerdgn 42 C5
Cardinal's Green Cambs 63 K11
Cardington Bed 61 N11
Cardington Shrops 57 J5
Cardinham Cnwll 5 J8
Cardrain D & G 106 F11
Cardrona Border 117 L3
Cardross Ag & B 125 J2
Cardryne D & G 106 F11
Cardurnock Cumb 110 C9
Careby Lincs 73 Q7
Careston Angus 143 J5
Carew Pembks 41 K10
Carew Cheriton Pembks 41 K10
Carew Newton Pembks 41 K10
Carey Herefs 45 R8
Carfin N Lans 126 D6
Carfraemill Border 128 E9
Cargate Green Norfk 77 M9
Cargenbridge D & G 109 L6
Cargill P & K 142 B10
Cargo Cumb 110 G9
Cargreen Cnwll 6 C6
Cargurrel Cnwll 3 M6
Carham Nthumb 118 E3
Carhampton Somset 18 D6
Carharrack Cnwll 3 J5
Carie P & K 140 F6
Carinish W Isls 168 d11
Carisbrooke IoW 14 E9
Cark W & F 94 H5
Carkeel Cnwll 5 Q9
Càrlabhagh W Isls 168 h3
Carland Cross Cnwll 3 L3
Carlbury Darltn 103 P7
Carlby Lincs 73 Q8
Carlcroft Nthumb 118 F8
Carlecotes Barns 83 Q4
Carleen Cnwll 2 G7
Carlesmoor N York 97 K6
Carleton Cumb 100 D9
Carleton Cumb 110 H10
Carleton Lancs 88 C2
Carleton W & F 101 P5
Carleton Wakefd 91 M6
Carleton Forehoe Norfk 76 F10
Carleton-in-Craven N York 96 E11
Carleton Rode Norfk 64 G3
Carleton St Peter Norfk 77 L11
Carlidnack Cnwll 3 K8
Carlincraig Abers 158 G9
Carlingcott BaNES 20 C3
Carlin How R & Cl 105 K7
Carlisle Cumb 110 H9
Carlisle Lake District Airport Cumb 111 J8
Carloggas Cnwll 4 D8
Carlops Border 127 M6
Carloway W Isls 168 h3
Carlton Barns 91 K8
Carlton Bed 61 L9
Carlton Cambs 63 K10
Carlton Leeds 91 J5
Carlton Leics 72 B10
Carlton N York 91 Q6
Carlton N York 96 G4
Carlton N York 98 C3
Carlton Notts 72 G2
Carlton S on T 104 C6
Carlton Suffk 65 M9
Carlton Colville Suffk 65 Q4
Carlton Curlieu Leics 72 H11
Carlton Green Cambs 63 K10
Carlton Husthwaite N York 97 Q5
Carlton-in-Cleveland N York 104 F10
Carlton in Lindrick Notts 85 J4
Carlton-le-Moorland Lincs 86 B9
Carlton Miniott N York 97 N4
Carlton-on-Trent Notts 85 N8
Carlton Scroop Lincs 86 B11
Carluke S Lans 126 E7
Carlyon Bay Cnwll 3 R3
Carmacoup S Lans 115 Q2
Carmarthen Carmth 42 H10
Carmel Carmth 43 L11
Carmel Flints 80 H9
Carmel Gwynd 66 H4
Carmichael S Lans 116 C3
Carmunnock C Glas 125 P6
Carmyle C Glas 125 Q5
Carmyllie Angus 143 J9
Carnaby E R Yk 99 N7
Carnbee Fife 135 N6
Carnbo P & K 134 D7
Carn Brea Cnwll 2 H5
Carnbrogie Abers 151 M2
Carndu Highld 145 Q2
Carnduff S Lans 126 B8
Carne Cnwll 3 K9
Carne Cnwll 3 N6
Carne Cnwll 4 F10
Carnell E Ayrs 125 M11
Carnewas Cnwll 4 D8
Carnforth Lancs 95 K6
Carn-gorm Highld 146 B3
Carnhedryn Pembks 40 F5
Carnhell Green Cnwll 2 G6
Carnie Abers 151 L6
Carnkie Cnwll 2 H5
Carnkie Cnwll 3 J7
Carnkief Cnwll 3 K3
Carno Powys 55 M5
Carnock Fife 134 C10
Carnon Downs Cnwll 3 K5
Carnousie Abers 158 G7
Carnoustie Angus 143 K11
Carnsmerry Cnwll 4 G10
Carnwath S Lans 126 H8
Carnyorth Cnwll 2 B7
Carol Green Solhll 59 L9
Carpalla Cnwll 3 P3
Carperby N York 96 F3
Carr Rothm 84 H2
Carradale Ag & B 120 F4
Carradale Village Ag & B 120 E4
Carrbridge Highld 148 G3
Carrbrook Tamesd 83 L4
Carrefour Jersey 11 b1
Carreglefn IoA 78 F7
Carr Gate Wakefd 91 J6
Carrhouse N Linc 92 C9
Carrick Ag & B 131 J10
Carrick Castle Ag & B 131 P9
Carriden Falk 134 C11
Carrington Lincs 87 K9
Carrington Mdloth 127 Q5
Carrington Traffd 82 F6
Carrog Conwy 67 P5
Carrog Denbgs 68 F6
Carron Falk 133 P11
Carron Moray 157 N9
Carronbridge D & G 116 B11
Carron Bridge Stirlg 133 L11
Carronshore Falk 133 P11
Carrow Hill Mons 31 M6
Carr Shield Nthumb 112 B11
Carrutherstown D & G 109 P6
Carruth House Inver 125 K4
Carr Vale Derbys 84 G7
Carrville Dur 104 B2
Carsaig Ag & B 137 N11
Carseriggan D & G 107 K4
Carsethorn D & G 109 L9
Carshalton Gt Lon 36 G8
Carsington Derbys 71 P4
Carskey Ag & B 120 C10
Carsluith D & G 107 N7
Carsphairn D & G 115 L9
Carstairs S Lans 126 G8
Carstairs Junction S Lans 126 H8
Carswell Marsh Oxon 34 B5
Carter's Clay Hants 22 B10
Carters Green Essex 51 M8
Carterton Oxon 33 Q3
Carterway Heads Nthumb 112 F10
Carthew Cnwll 4 G10
Carthorpe N York 97 M4
Cartington Nthumb 119 K10
Cartland S Lans 126 F8
Cartledge Derbys 84 D5
Cartmel W & F 94 H5
Cartmel Fell W & F 95 J3
Carway Carmth 28 E3
Carwinley Cumb 110 H6
Cashe's Green Gloucs 32 F3
Cashmoor Dorset 12 G2
Cassington Oxon 34 E2
Cassop Dur 104 B3
Castallack Cnwll 2 D8
Castel Guern 10 b2
Castell Conwy 79 P11
Castell-y-bwch Torfn 31 J6
Casterton W & F 95 N5
Castle Cnwll 4 H10
Castle Acre Norfk 75 R7
Castle Ashby W Nthn 61 J9
Castlebay W Isls 168 b18
Castle Bolton N York 96 F2
Castle Bromwich Solhll 58 H7
Castle Bytham Lincs 73 P7
Castlebythe Pembks 41 K5
Castle Caereinion Powys 56 B3
Castle Camps Cambs 51 P2
Castle Carrock Cumb 111 K9
Castlecary N Lans 126 D2
Castle Cary Somset 20 B8
Castle Combe Wilts 32 F9
Castlecraig Highld 156 E4
Castle Donington Leics 72 C5
Castle Douglas D & G 108 G8
Castle Eaton Swindn 33 M5
Castle Eden Dur 104 D3
Castle End C Pete 74 B9
Castleford Wakefd 91 L5
Castle Frome Herefs 46 C5
Castle Gate Cnwll 2 D7
Castle Green Surrey 23 Q2
Castle Green W & F 95 L2
Castle Gresley Derbys 71 P11
Castle Hedingham Essex 52 C4
Castlehill Border 117 J3
Castlehill Highld 167 L3
Castle Hill Kent 25 Q2
Castle Hill Suffk 53 K2
Castlehill W Duns 125 K2
Castle Howard N York 98 E6
Castle Kennedy D & G 106 F6
Castle Lachlan Ag & B 131 L8
Castlemartin Pembks 40 H11
Castlemilk C Glas 125 P6
Castle Morris Pembks 40 H4
Castlemorton Worcs 46 E7
Castlemorton Common Worcs 46 E7
Castle O'er D & G 110 D2
Castle Rising Norfk 75 N6
Castleside Dur 112 G11
Castle Stuart Highld 156 C8
Castlethorpe M Keyn 49 M6
Castlethorpe N Linc 92 G9
Castleton Ag & B 130 H11
Castleton Border 111 K3
Castleton Derbys 83 Q8
Castleton N York 105 J9
Castleton Newpt 31 J8
Castleton Rochdl 89 P8
Castletown Ches W 69 M4
Castletown Dorset 11 P10
Castletown Highld 167 L3
Castletown IoM 80 c8
Castletown Sundld 113 N9
Castley N York 97 L11
Caston Norfk 64 D2
Castor C Pete 74 B11
Caswell Bay Swans 28 G7
Catacol N Ayrs 123 R10
Cat and Fiddle Derbys 83 M10
Catbrain S Glos 31 Q8
Catbrook Mons 31 P4
Catch Flints 81 J10
Catchall Cnwll 2 C8
Catchem's Corner Solhll 59 L9
Catchgate Dur 113 J10
Catcliffe Rothm 84 F3
Catcomb Wilts 33 K9
Catcott Somset 19 L7
Caterham Surrey 36 H9
Catfield Norfk 77 M7
Catfield Common Norfk 77 N7

Catford – Church End 263

Catford Gt Lon 37 J6
Catforth Lancs 88 F3
Cathcart C Glas 125 P5
Cathedine Powys 44 G9
Catherine-de-Barnes Solhll 59 J8
Catherine Slack C Brad 90 D5
Catherington Hants 15 J4
Catherston Leweston Dorset 10 H6
Catherton Shrops 57 M9
Catisfield Hants 14 G5
Catley Herefs 46 C6
Catley Lane Head Rochdl 89 P7
Catlodge Highld 147 Q9
Catlow Lancs 89 P3
Catlowdy Cumb 111 J5
Catmere End Essex 51 L3
Catmore W Berk 34 E8
Caton Devon 7 K4
Caton Lancs 95 L8
Caton Green Lancs 95 M7
Cator Court Devon 8 G9
Catrine E Ayrs 115 K2
Cat's Ash Newpt 31 L6
Catsfield E Susx 26 B9
Catsfield Stream E Susx 26 B9
Catsgore Somset 19 P9
Catsham Somset 19 Q8
Catshill Worcs 58 E10
Catstree Shrops 57 N5
Cattadale Ag & B 120 C9
Cattal N York 97 P10
Cattawade Suffk 53 K5
Catterall Lancs 88 F2
Catteralslane Shrops 69 Q6
Catterick N York 103 P11
Catterick Bridge N York 103 P11
Catterick Garrison N York 103 N11
Catterlen W & F 101 N4
Catterline Abers 143 R2
Catterton N York 97 R11
Catteshall Surrey 23 Q6
Catthorpe Leics 60 C5
Cattishall Suffk 64 B8
Cattistock Dorset 11 M5
Catton N York 97 N5
Catton Nthumb 112 B9
Catwick E R Yk 99 N11
Catworth Cambs 61 N6
Caudle Green Gloucs 32 H2
Caulcott C Beds 50 B2
Caulcott Oxon 48 F10
Cauldcots Angus 143 M8
Cauldhame Stirlg 133 J9
Cauldmill Border 117 Q7
Cauldon Staffs 71 K5
Cauldon Lowe Staffs 71 K5
Cauldwell Derbys 71 P11
Caulkerbush D & G 109 K9
Caulside D & G 110 H4
Caundle Marsh Dorset 11 P2
Caunsall Worcs 58 C8
Caunton Notts 85 M8
Causeway Hants 23 K10
Causeway End D & G 107 M6
Causeway End Essex 51 Q7
Causewayend S Lans 116 E3
Causeway End W & F 95 K3
Causewayhead Cumb 109 P10
Causewayhead Stirlg 133 N8
Causeyend Abers 151 N4
Causey Park Nthumb 113 J2
Causey Park Bridge Nthumb 113 J2
Cavendish Suffk 63 P11
Cavenham Suffk 63 N6
Caversfield Oxon 48 G9
Caversham Readg 35 K10
Caverswall Staffs 70 H6
Caverton Mill Border 118 D5
Cavil E R Yk 92 C4
Cawdor Highld 156 E7
Cawkwell Lincs 87 J5
Cawood N York 91 P3
Cawsand Cnwll 6 C8
Cawston Norfk 76 G7
Cawston Warwks 59 Q10
Cawthorn N York 98 F3
Cawthorne Barns 90 H9
Cawton N York 98 C5
Caxton Cambs 62 D9
Caxton End Cambs 62 D9
Caxton Gibbet Cambs 62 C8
Caynham Shrops 57 K10
Caythorpe Lincs 86 B11
Caythorpe Notts 85 L11
Cayton N York 99 M4
Ceannabeinne Highld 165 K3
Ceann a Bhaigh W Isls 168 c11
Ceannacroc Lodge Highld 146 G5
Cearsiadar W Isls 168 i6
Ceciliford Mons 31 P4
Cefn Newpt 31 J7
Cefn Berain Conwy 80 D11
Cefn-brîth Conwy 68 B4
Cefn-bryn-brain Carmth 29 K2
Cefn Byrle Powys 29 M2
Cefn Canel Powys 68 H8
Cefn Coch Powys 68 F9
Cefn-coed-y-cymmer Myr Td 30 D3
Cefn Cribwr Brdgnd 29 N8
Cefn Cross Brdgnd 29 N8
Cefn-ddwysarn Gwynd 68 C7
Cefn-Einion Shrops 56 D7
Cefneithin Carmth 28 G2
Cefngorwydd Powys 44 C5
Cefn-mawr Wrexhm 69 J6
Cefnpennar Rhondd 30 D4
Cefn-y-bedd Flints 69 K3
Cefn-y-pant Carmth 41 N5
Ceint IoA 78 H9
Cellan Cerdgn 43 M5
Cellardyke Fife 135 P7
Cellarhead Staffs 70 H5
Celleron W & F 101 N5
Celynen Caerph 30 H5
Cemaes IoA 78 F6
Cemmaes Powys 55 J3
Cemmaes Road Powys 55 J4
Cenarth Cerdgn 41 Q2
Cerbyd Pembks 40 F5
Ceres Fife 135 L5
Cerne Abbas Dorset 11 P4
Cerney Wick Gloucs 33 L5
Cerrigceinwen IoA 78 G10
Cerrigydrudion Conwy 68 C5
Cess Norfk 77 N8
Ceunant Gwynd 67 J2
Chaceley Gloucs 46 G8
Chacewater Cnwll 3 K5
Chackmore Bucks 49 J7
Chacombe W Nthn 48 E6
Chadbury Worcs 47 K5
Chadderton Oldham 89 Q9
Chadderton Fold Oldham 89 Q9
Chaddesden C Derb 72 B3
Chaddesley Corbett Worcs 58 C10
Chaddlehanger Devon 8 C9
Chaddleworth W Berk 34 D9
Chadlington Oxon 48 B10
Chadshunt Warwks 48 B4
Chadwell Leics 73 K6
Chadwell Shrops 57 P2
Chadwell End Bed 61 N7
Chadwell Heath Gt Lon 37 L3
Chadwell St Mary Thurr 37 P5
Chadwick Worcs 58 B11
Chadwick End Solhll 59 K10
Chadwick Green St Hel 82 B5
Chaffcombe Somset 10 H2
Chafford Hundred Thurr 37 P5
Chagford Devon 8 H7
Chailey E Susx 25 J7
Chainbridge Cambs 74 H10
Chainhurst Kent 26 B2
Chalbury Dorset 12 H3
Chalbury Common Dorset 12 H3
Chaldon Surrey 36 H9
Chaldon Herring Dorset 12 C8
Chale IoW 14 E11
Chale Green IoW 14 E11
Chalfont Common Bucks 36 B2
Chalfont St Giles Bucks 35 Q6
Chalfont St Peter Bucks 36 B2
Chalford Gloucs 32 G4
Chalford Oxon 35 K4
Chalford Wilts 20 G4
Chalgrave C Beds 50 B5
Chalgrove Oxon 34 H5
Chalk Kent 37 Q6
Chalk End Essex 51 P8
Chalkhouse Green Oxon 35 K9
Chalkway Somset 10 H3
Chalkwell Kent 38 E9
Challaborough Devon 6 H10
Challacombe Devon 17 M3
Challoch D & G 107 L4
Challock Kent 38 H11
Chalmington Dorset 11 M4
Chalton C Beds 50 B5
Chalton C Beds 61 P10
Chalton Hants 23 K11
Chalvey Slough 35 Q9
Chalvington E Susx 25 M9
Chambers Green Kent 26 F3
Chandler's Cross Herts 50 C11
Chandlers Cross Worcs 46 E7
Chandler's Ford Hants 22 D11
Channel's End Bed 61 P9
Channel Tunnel Terminal Kent 27 L4
Chantry Somset 20 D5
Chantry Suffk 53 K3
Chapel Cumb 100 H4
Chapel Fife 134 H9
Chapel Allerton Leeds 91 J3
Chapel Allerton Somset 19 M4
Chapel Amble Cnwll 4 F6
Chapel Brampton W Nthn 60 F7
Chapelbridge Cambs 62 C2
Chapel Chorlton Staffs 70 E7
Chapel Cross E Susx 25 P6
Chapel End Bed 61 P9
Chapel End C Beds 50 C2
Chapel End Cambs 61 P4
Chapel End Warwks 59 M6
Chapelend Way Essex 52 B4
Chapel-en-le-Frith Derbys 83 N8
Chapel Field Bury 89 M9
Chapelgate Lincs 74 H6
Chapel Green Warwks 48 E2
Chapel Green Warwks 59 L7
Chapel Haddlesey N York 91 P5
Chapelhall N Lans 126 D5
Chapel Hill Abers 159 Q10
Chapel Hill Lincs 86 H10
Chapel Hill Mons 31 P5
Chapel Hill N York 97 M11
Chapelhope Border 117 J7
Chapelknowe D & G 110 F6
Chapel Lawn Shrops 56 E9
Chapel-le-Dale N York 95 Q5
Chapel Leigh Somset 18 F9
Chapel Milton Derbys 83 N8
Chapel of Garioch Abers 151 J3
Chapel Rossan D & G 106 F9
Chapel Row E Susx 25 P8
Chapel Row Essex 52 C11
Chapel Row W Berk 34 G11
Chapels W & F 94 E4
Chapel St Leonards Lincs 87 Q6
Chapel Stile W & F 101 K9
Chapelton Abers 151 M9
Chapelton Angus 143 L8
Chapelton Devon 17 K6
Chapelton S Lans 126 B8
Chapeltown Bl w D 89 L7
Chapel Town Cnwll 4 D10
Chapeltown Moray 149 N3
Chapeltown Sheff 91 K11
Chapmanslade Wilts 20 F5
Chapmans Well Devon 5 P3
Chapmore End Herts 50 H7
Chappel Essex 52 E6
Charaton Cnwll 5 N8
Chard Somset 10 G3
Chard Junction Somset 10 G4
Chardleigh Green Somset 10 G2
Chardstock Devon 10 G4
Charfield S Glos 32 D6
Chargrove Gloucs 46 H11
Charing Kent 26 G2
Charing Heath Kent 26 F2
Charing Hill Kent 38 G11
Charingworth Gloucs 47 N7
Charlbury Oxon 48 C11
Charlcombe BaNES 32 D11
Charlcutt Wilts 33 J9
Charlecote Warwks 47 Q3
Charlemont Sandw 58 F6
Charles Devon 17 M5
Charleshill Surrey 23 N6
Charleston Angus 142 F8
Charlestown C Aber 151 N7
Charlestown C Brad 90 F3
Charlestown Calder 90 B5
Charlestown Cnwll 3 Q3
Charlestown Cnwll 3 Q3
Charlestown Derbys 83 M6
Charlestown Dorset 11 P9
Charlestown Fife 134 D11
Charlestown Highld 153 Q3
Charlestown Highld 156 A8
Charlestown Salfd 82 H4
Charlestown of Aberlour Moray 157 P9
Charles Tye Suffk 64 E11
Charlesworth Derbys 83 M6
Charlinch Somset 18 H7
Charlottetown Fife 134 H5
Charlton Gt Lon 37 K5
Charlton Hants 22 C5
Charlton Herts 50 E5
Charlton Nthumb 112 B4
Charlton Somset 19 J9
Charlton Somset 20 B6
Charlton Somset 20 C4
Charlton Surrey 36 C7
Charlton W Nthn 48 F7
Charlton W Susx 15 N4
Charlton Wilts 20 H10
Charlton Wilts 33 J7
Charlton Worcs 47 K5
Charlton Worcs 58 B10
Charlton Wrekin 57 K2
Charlton Abbots Gloucs 47 K10
Charlton Adam Somset 19 P9
Charlton All Saints Wilts 21 N10
Charlton Down Dorset 11 P5
Charlton Hill Shrops 57 K3
Charlton Horethorne Somset 20 C10
Charlton Kings Gloucs 47 J10
Charlton Mackrell Somset 19 P9
Charlton Marshall Dorset 12 F4
Charlton Musgrove Somset 20 D9
Charlton-on-Otmoor Oxon 48 G11
Charlton on the Hill Dorset 12 E4
Charlton St Peter Wilts 21 M3
Charlwood Hants 23 J8
Charlwood Surrey 24 F2
Charminster Dorset 11 P6
Charmouth Dorset 10 H6
Charndon Bucks 49 J10
Charney Bassett Oxon 34 C6
Charnock Green Lancs 88 H7
Charnock Richard Lancs 88 H7
Charnock Richard Services Lancs 88 G7
Charsfield Suffk 65 K10
Chart Corner Kent 38 C11
Charter Alley Hants 22 G3
Charterhall Border 129 K10
Charterhouse Somset 19 N3
Chartershall Stirlg 133 M9
Charterville Allotments Oxon 34 B2
Chartham Kent 39 K11
Chartham Hatch Kent 39 K10
Chart Hill Kent 26 C2
Chartridge Bucks 35 P4
Chart Sutton Kent 26 D2
Chartway Street Kent 38 D11
Charvil Wokham 35 L9
Charwelton W Nthn 60 B9
Chase Cross Gt Lon 37 M2
Chase Terrace Staffs 58 F3
Chasetown Staffs 58 F3
Chastleton Oxon 47 P9
Chasty Devon 16 E11
Chatburn Lancs 89 M2
Chatcull Staffs 70 D8
Chatham Caerph 30 H7
Chatham Medway 38 C8
Chatham Green Essex 52 B8
Chathill Nthumb 119 N5
Chatley Worcs 46 G2
Chatsworth Derbys 84 C6
Chattenden Medway 38 C7
Chatter End Essex 51 L5
Chatteris Cambs 62 E3
Chatterton Lancs 89 M7
Chattisham Suffk 53 J3
Chatto Border 118 E7
Chatton Nthumb 119 L5
Chaul End C Beds 50 C6
Chawleigh Devon 17 N9
Chawley Oxon 34 E4
Chawston Bed 61 Q9
Chawton Hants 23 K7
Chaxhill Gloucs 32 D2
Chazey Heath Oxon 35 J9
Cheadle Staffs 71 J6
Cheadle Stockp 83 J7
Cheadle Heath Stockp 83 J7
Cheadle Hulme Stockp 83 J7
Cheam Gt Lon 36 F8
Cheapside W & M 35 P11
Chearsley Bucks 35 K2
Chebsey Staffs 70 F9
Checkendon Oxon 35 J8
Checkley Ches E 70 C5
Checkley Herefs 46 A7
Checkley Staffs 71 J7
Checkley Green Ches E 70 C5
Chedburgh Suffk 63 N9
Cheddar Somset 19 N4
Cheddington Bucks 49 P11
Cheddleton Staffs 70 H4
Cheddleton Heath Staffs 70 H4
Cheddon Fitzpaine Somset 18 H9
Chedglow Wilts 32 H6
Chedgrave Norfk 65 M2
Chedington Dorset 11 K3
Chediston Suffk 65 M6
Chediston Green Suffk 65 M6
Chedworth Gloucs 33 L2
Chedzoy Somset 19 K7
Cheeseman's Green Kent 26 H4
Cheetham Hill Manch 82 H4
Cheldon Devon 8 H2
Chelford Ches E 82 H10
Chellaston C Derb 72 B4
Chellington Bed 61 L9
Chelmarsh Shrops 57 N7
Chelmer Village Essex 52 B10
Chelmick Shrops 56 H6
Chelmondiston Suffk 53 M4
Chelmorton Derbys 83 P11
Chelmsford Essex 52 B10
Chelmsley Wood Solhll 59 J7
Chelsea Gt Lon 36 G5
Chelsfield Gt Lon 37 L8
Chelsham Surrey 37 J9
Chelston Somset 18 G10
Chelsworth Suffk 52 G2
Cheltenham Gloucs 46 H10
Chelveston N Nthn 61 L7
Chelvey N Som 31 N11
Chelwood BaNES 20 B2
Chelwood Common E Susx 25 K5
Chelwood Gate E Susx 25 K4
Chelworth Wilts 33 J6
Chelworth Lower Green Wilts 33 L6
Chelworth Upper Green Wilts 33 L6
Cheney Longville Shrops 56 G8
Chenies Bucks 50 B11
Chepstow Mons 31 P6
Chequerbent Bolton 89 K9
Chequers Corner Norfk 75 J9
Cherhill Wilts 33 K10
Cherington Gloucs 32 H5
Cherington Warwks 47 Q7
Cheriton Devon 17 N2
Cheriton Hants 22 G9
Cheriton Kent 27 M4
Cheriton Pembks 41 J11
Cheriton Swans 28 E6
Cheriton Bishop Devon 9 J6
Cheriton Fitzpaine Devon 9 L3
Cherrington Wrekin 70 B11
Cherry Burton E R Yk 92 G2
Cherry Hinton Cambs 62 G9
Cherry Orchard Worcs 46 G4
Cherry Willingham Lincs 86 D6
Chertsey Surrey 36 B7
Cherwell Valley Services Oxon 48 F9
Cheselbourne Dorset 12 C5
Chesham Bucks 35 Q4
Chesham Bury 89 N8
Chesham Bois Bucks 35 Q5
Cheshunt Herts 51 J10
Chesil Beach Dorset 11 N9
Chesley Kent 38 E9
Cheslyn Hay Staffs 58 E3
Chessetts Wood Warwks 59 J10
Chessington Gt Lon 36 E8
Chessington World of Adventures Gt Lon 36 E8
Chester Ches W 81 N11
Chesterblade Somset 20 C6
Chesterfield Derbys 84 E6
Chesterfield Staffs 58 G3
Chesterhill Mdloth 128 B7
Chester-le-Street Dur 113 L10
Chester Moor Dur 113 L11
Chesters Border 118 B6
Chesters Border 118 B8
Chester Services Ches W 81 P9
Chesterton Cambs 62 G8
Chesterton Cambs 74 B11
Chesterton Gloucs 33 K4
Chesterton Oxon 48 G10
Chesterton Shrops 57 P5
Chesterton Staffs 70 E5
Chesterton Green Warwks 48 C3
Chesterwood Nthumb 112 B7
Chester Zoo Ches W 81 N10
Chestfield Kent 39 K8
Chestnut Street Kent 38 E9
Cheston Devon 6 H7
Cheswardine Shrops 70 C8
Cheswick Nthumb 129 Q10
Cheswick Green Solhll 58 H9
Chetnole Dorset 11 N3
Chettiscombe Devon 9 N2
Chettisham Cambs 62 H4
Chettle Dorset 12 G2
Chetton Shrops 57 M6
Chetwode Bucks 48 H9
Chetwynd Wrekin 70 C10
Chetwynd Aston Wrekin 70 D11
Cheveley Cambs 63 L8
Chevening Kent 37 L9
Cheverton IoW 14 E10
Chevington Suffk 63 N9
Cheviot Hills 118 E9
Chevithorne Devon 18 C11
Chew Magna BaNES 19 Q2
Chew Moor Bolton 89 K9
Chew Stoke BaNES 19 Q2
Chewton Keynsham BaNES 32 C11
Chewton Mendip Somset 19 Q4
Chichacott Devon 8 F5
Chicheley M Keyn 49 P5
Chichester W Susx 15 N6
Chickerell Dorset 11 N8
Chickering Suffk 65 J6
Chicklade Wilts 20 H8
Chicksands C Beds 50 D3
Chickward Herefs 45 K4
Chidden Hants 23 J11
Chiddingfold Surrey 23 Q7
Chiddingly E Susx 25 M8
Chiddingstone Kent 25 M2
Chiddingstone Causeway Kent 37 M11
Chiddingstone Hoath Kent 25 L2
Chideock Dorset 11 J6
Chidham W Susx 15 L6
Chidswell Kirk 90 H6
Chieveley W Berk 34 E10
Chieveley Services W Berk 34 E10
Chignall St James Essex 51 Q8
Chignall Smealy Essex 51 Q8
Chigwell Essex 37 K2
Chigwell Row Essex 37 L2
Chilbolton Hants 22 C6
Chilcomb Hants 22 F9
Chilcombe Dorset 11 L6
Chilcompton Somset 20 B4
Chilcote Leics 59 L2
Childer Thornton Ches W 81 M9
Child Okeford Dorset 12 D2
Childrey Oxon 34 C7
Child's Ercall Shrops 70 B9
Childswickham Worcs 47 L7
Childwall Lpool 81 N7
Childwick Bury Herts 50 D8
Childwick Green Herts 50 D8
Chilfrome Dorset 11 M5
Chilgrove W Susx 15 M4
Chilham Kent 39 J11
Chilla Devon 8 B4
Chillaton Devon 8 B8
Chillenden Kent 39 N11
Chillerton IoW 14 E10
Chillesford Suffk 65 M11
Chillingham Nthumb 119 L5
Chillington Devon 7 K10
Chillington Somset 10 H2
Chilmark Wilts 21 J8
Chilmington Green Kent 26 G3
Chilson Oxon 48 B11
Chilsworthy Cnwll 5 Q7
Chilsworthy Devon 16 E10
Chiltern Green C Beds 50 D7
Chiltern Hills 35 L5
Chilthorne Domer Somset 19 P11
Chilton Bucks 35 J2
Chilton Devon 9 L4
Chilton Dur 103 Q5
Chilton Kent 27 N3
Chilton Oxon 34 E7
Chilton Suffk 52 E3
Chilton Candover Hants 22 G6
Chilton Cantelo Somset 19 Q10
Chilton Foliat Wilts 34 B10
Chilton Polden Somset 19 L6
Chilton Street Suffk 63 N11
Chilton Trinity Somset 19 J7
Chilwell Notts 72 E3
Chilworth Hants 22 D11
Chilworth Surrey 36 B11
Chimney Oxon 34 C4
Chineham Hants 23 J3
Chingford Gt Lon 37 J2
Chinley Derbys 83 M8
Chinnor Oxon 35 L4
Chipchase Castle Nthumb 112 C5
Chipnall Shrops 70 C8
Chippenham Cambs 63 L7
Chippenham Wilts 32 H10
Chipperfield Herts 50 B10
Chipping Herts 51 J4
Chipping Lancs 89 J2
Chipping Campden Gloucs 47 N7
Chipping Hill Essex 52 D8
Chipping Norton Oxon 48 B9
Chipping Ongar Essex 51 N10
Chipping Sodbury S Glos 32 D8
Chipping Warden W Nthn 48 E5
Chipshop Devon 8 B9
Chipstable Somset 18 D9
Chipstead Kent 37 M9
Chipstead Surrey 36 G9
Chirbury Shrops 56 D5
Chirk Wrexhm 69 J7
Chirnside Border 129 M8
Chirnsidebridge Border 129 M8
Chirton Wilts 21 L3
Chisbury Wilts 33 Q11
Chiselborough Somset 11 K2
Chiseldon Swindn 33 N8
Chiselhampton Oxon 34 G5
Chiserley Calder 90 C5
Chisholme Border 117 N8
Chislehurst Gt Lon 37 K6
Chislet Kent 39 M9
Chiswell Green Herts 50 D10
Chiswick Gt Lon 36 F5
Chiswick End Cambs 62 E11
Chisworth Derbys 83 L6
Chitcombe E Susx 26 D7
Chithurst W Susx 23 M10
Chittering Cambs 62 G7
Chitterne Wilts 21 J6
Chittlehamholt Devon 17 M7
Chittlehampton Devon 17 L6
Chittoe Wilts 33 J11
Chivelstone Devon 7 K11
Chivenor Devon 17 J5
Chiverton Cross Cnwll 3 J4
Chlenry D & G 106 F5
Chobham Surrey 23 Q2
Cholderton Wilts 21 P6
Cholesbury Bucks 35 P3
Chollerford Nthumb 112 D6
Chollerton Nthumb 112 D6
Cholmondeston Ches E 70 A3
Cholsey Oxon 34 G7
Cholstrey Herefs 45 P3
Chop Gate N York 104 G11
Choppington Nthumb 113 L4
Chopwell Gatesd 112 H9
Chorley Ches E 69 Q4
Chorley Lancs 88 H7
Chorley Shrops 57 M8
Chorley Staffs 58 G2
Chorleywood Herts 50 B11
Chorleywood West Herts 50 B11
Chorlton Ches E 70 C4
Chorlton-cum-Hardy Manch 82 H6
Chorlton Lane Ches W 69 N5
Choulton Shrops 56 F7
Chowley Ches W 69 N3
Chrishall Essex 51 K3
Chrisswell Inver 124 G3
Christchurch BCP 13 L6
Christchurch Cambs 75 J11
Christchurch Gloucs 31 Q2
Christchurch Newpt 31 K7
Christian Malford Wilts 33 J9
Christleton Ches W 81 N11
Christmas Common Oxon 35 K6
Christmas Pie Surrey 23 P5
Christon N Som 19 L3
Christon Bank Nthumb 119 P6
Christow Devon 9 K7
Christ's Hospital W Susx 24 D5
Chuck Hatch E Susx 25 L4
Chudleigh Devon 9 L9
Chudleigh Knighton Devon 9 K9
Chulmleigh Devon 17 M9
Chunal Derbys 83 M6
Church Lancs 89 L5
Churcham Gloucs 46 E11
Church Aston Wrekin 70 C11
Church Brampton W Nthn 60 F7
Church Brough W & F 102 E8
Church Broughton Derbys 71 N8
Church Cove Cnwll 3 J11
Church Crookham Hants 23 M4
Churchdown Gloucs 46 G11
Church Eaton Staffs 70 E11
Church End Bed 61 N9
Church End Bed 61 P9

Church End Bucks...35 K3
Church End C Beds...49 Q10
Church End C Beds...49 Q8
Church End C Beds...50 B4
Church End C Beds...50 B7
Church End C Beds...50 E3
Church End C Beds...61 Q10
Church End Cambs...61 N6
Church End Cambs...62 B4
Church End Cambs...62 D5
Churchend Essex...38 H3
Church End Essex...51 P6
Church End Essex...52 B6
Church End Essex...52 B8
Church End Gloucs...46 G7
Church End Gt Lon...36 F2
Church End Herts...50 D8
Church End Herts...50 G4
Church End Herts...51 K6
Church End Lincs...74 D4
Church End Lincs...93 R11
Church End Suffk...53 M4
Church End Warwks...59 K6
Church End Warwks...59 L6
Church Enstone Oxon...48 C9
Church Fenton N York...91 N3
Churchfield Sandw...58 F6
Churchgate Herts...50 H10
Churchgate Street Essex...51 L8
Church Green Devon...10 D5
Church Gresley Derbys...71 P11
Church Hanborough Oxon...34 D2
Church Hill Staffs...58 F2
Church Houses N York...105 J11
Churchill Devon...10 F4
Churchill Devon...17 K3
Churchill N Som...19 M3
Churchill Oxon...47 Q10
Churchill Worcs...46 H4
Churchill Worcs...58 C9
Churchinford Somset...10 E2
Church Knowle Dorset...12 F8
Church Laneham Notts...85 P5
Church Langton Leics...60 F2
Church Lawford Warwks...59 Q9
Church Lawton Ches E...70 E3
Church Leigh Staffs...71 J7
Church Lench Worcs...47 K4
Church Mayfield Staffs...71 M6
Church Minshull Ches E...70 B2
Church Norton W Susx...15 N7
Churchover Warwks...60 B4
Church Preen Shrops...57 J5
Church Pulverbatch Shrops...56 G4
Churchstanton Somset...10 D2
Churchstoke Powys...56 D6
Churchstow Devon...7 J9
Church Stowe W Nthn...60 D9
Church Street Essex...52 C3
Church Street Kent...38 B7
Church Street Suffk...65 P5
Church Stretton Shrops...56 H6
Churchthorpe Lincs...93 P11
Churchtown Bpool...88 C2
Churchtown Cnwll...4 H6
Churchtown Derbys...84 C8
Churchtown Devon...17 M3
Churchtown IoM...80 f3
Churchtown Lancs...88 F2
Church Town N Linc...92 C9
Churchtown Sefton...88 D7
Church Village Rhondd...30 E7
Church Warsop Notts...85 J7
Church Wilne Derbys...72 C4
Churnsike Lodge Nthumb...111 N5
Churston Ferrers Torbay...7 N7
Churt Surrey...23 N7
Churton Ches W...69 M3
Churwell Leeds...90 H5
Chwilog Gwynd...66 G7
Chyandour Cnwll...2 D7
Chyanvounder Cnwll...2 H9
Chyeowling Cnwll...3 K5
Chyvarloe Cnwll...2 H9
Cil Powys...56 B4
Cilcain Flints...80 H11
Cilcennin Cerdgn...43 K2
Cilcewydd Powys...56 C4
Cilfrew Neath...29 L4
Cilfynydd Rhondd...30 E6
Cilgerran Pembks...41 N2
Cilgwyn Carmth...43 P9
Cilgwyn Gwynd...66 H4
Ciliau-Aeron Cerdgn...43 K3
Cilmaengwyn Neath...29 K3
Cilmery Powys...44 E4
Cilrhedyn Pembks...41 Q4
Cilsan Carmth...43 L10
Ciltalgarth Gwynd...68 A6
Cilycwm Carmth...43 Q7
Cimla Neath...29 L5
Cinderford Gloucs...32 C2
Cinder Hill Wolves...58 D6
Cippenham Slough...35 Q8
Cirencester Gloucs...33 K4
Citadilla N York...103 P11
City Gt Lon...36 H4
City V Glam...30 C9
City Airport Gt Lon...37 K4
City Dulas IoA...78 H7
Clabhach Ag & B...136 F4
Clachaig Ag & B...131 N11
Clachaig Inn Highld...139 L6
Clachan Ag & B...123 N8
Clachan Ag & B...130 F4
Clachan Ag & B...131 M7
Clachan Ag & B...138 F9
Clachan Highld...153 J10
Clachan-a-Luib W Isls...168 d11
Clachan Mor Ag & B...136 B6
Clachan na Luib W Isls...168 d11
Clachan of Campsie E Duns...125 Q2
Clachan-Seil Ag & B...130 F4
Clachnaharry Highld...156 A8
Clachtoll Highld...164 B11
Clacket Lane Services Surrey...37 K10
Clackmannan Clacks...133 Q9
Clackmannanshire Bridge Fife...133 Q10
Clackmarras Moray...157 N6
Clacton-on-Sea Essex...53 L8
Cladich Ag & B...131 K4
Cladswell Worcs...47 L3
Claggan Highld...138 C8
Claigan Highld...152 C7

Clandown BaNES...20 C3
Clanfield Hants...23 J11
Clanfield Oxon...33 Q4
Clannaborough Devon...8 H4
Clanville Hants...22 B5
Clanville Somset...20 B4
Claonaig Ag & B...123 Q8
Clapgate Dorset...12 H4
Clapgate Herts...51 K6
Clapham Bed...61 M10
Clapham Devon...9 L7
Clapham Gt Lon...36 G5
Clapham N York...95 Q7
Clapham W Susx...24 C9
Clapham Green Bed...61 M10
Clap Hill Kent...27 J4
Clappersgate W & F...101 L10
Clapton Somset...11 J3
Clapton Somset...20 B4
Clapton-in-Gordano N Som...31 N10
Clapton-on-the-Hill Gloucs...47 N11
Clapworthy Devon...17 M7
Clarach Cerdgn...54 E8
Claravale Gatesd...112 H8
Clarbeston Pembks...41 L6
Clarbeston Road Pembks...41 L6
Clarborough Notts...85 M4
Clare Suffk...63 N11
Clarebrand D & G...108 G7
Clarencefield D & G...109 N7
Clarewood Nthumb...112 F7
Clarilaw Border...117 Q7
Clark's Green Surrey...24 E3
Clarkston E Rens...125 P6
Clashmore Highld...162 G9
Clashmore Highld...164 B10
Clashnessie Highld...164 C10
Clashnoir Moray...149 N3
Clathy P & K...134 B3
Clathymore P & K...134 C3
Clatt Abers...150 E2
Clatter Powys...55 M6
Clatterford End Essex...51 P8
Clatworthy Somset...18 E8
Claughton Lancs...88 G2
Claughton Lancs...95 M7
Claughton Wirral...81 L7
Clavelshay Somset...19 J8
Claverdon Warwks...59 J11
Claverham N Som...31 N11
Clavering Essex...51 L4
Claverley Shrops...57 P6
Claverton BaNES...20 E2
Claverton Down BaNES...20 E2
Clawdd-coch V Glam...30 E9
Clawdd-newydd Denbgs...68 E4
Clawthorpe W & F...95 L5
Clawton Devon...5 P2
Claxby Lincs...86 F2
Claxby Lincs...87 N6
Claxton N York...98 D9
Claxton Norfk...77 L11
Claybrooke Magna Leics...59 Q7
Clay Common Suffk...65 P5
Clay Coton W Nthn...60 C5
Clay Cross Derbys...84 E8
Claydon Oxon...48 E5
Claydon Suffk...53 K2
Clay End Herts...50 H6
Claygate D & G...110 G5
Claygate Kent...26 B3
Claygate Surrey...36 E8
Claygate Cross Kent...37 P9
Clayhall Gt Lon...37 K2
Clayhanger Devon...18 D10
Clayhanger Wsall...58 F4
Clayhidon Devon...18 G11
Clayhill E Susx...26 D7
Clayhill Hants...13 P3
Clayhithe Cambs...62 H8
Clayock Highld...167 L5
Claypit Hill Cambs...62 E10
Claypits Gloucs...32 E3
Claypole Lincs...85 P11
Claythorpe Lincs...87 M5
Clayton C Brad...90 E4
Clayton Donc...91 M9
Clayton W Susx...24 G8
Clayton Green Lancs...88 H6
Clayton-le-Moors Lancs...89 M4
Clayton-le-Woods Lancs...88 H6
Clayton West Kirk...90 H8
Clayworth Notts...85 M3
Cleadale Highld...144 G10
Cleadon S Tyne...113 N8
Cleadon Park S Tyne...113 N8
Clearbrook Devon...6 E5
Clearwell Gloucs...31 Q3
Cleasby N York...103 Q8
Cleat Ork...169 d8
Cleatlam Dur...103 M7
Cleator Cumb...100 D8
Cleator Moor Cumb...100 D7
Cleckheaton Kirk...90 F5
Cleedownton Shrops...57 K8
Cleehill Shrops...57 K9
Cleekhimin N Lans...126 D6
Clee St Margaret Shrops...57 K8
Cleestanton Shrops...57 K9
Cleethorpes NE Lin...93 P9
Cleeton St Mary Shrops...57 L9
Cleeve N Som...31 N11
Cleeve Oxon...34 H8
Cleeve Hill Gloucs...47 J9
Cleeve Prior Worcs...47 L5
Cleghornie E Loth...128 F3
Clehonger Herefs...45 N7
Cleish P & K...134 D8
Cleland N Lans...126 D6
Clement's End C Beds...50 B8
Clement Street Kent...37 M6
Clenamacrie Ag & B...131 J2
Clench Common Wilts...33 N11
Clenchwarton Norfk...75 L6
Clenerty Abers...159 J5
Clent Worcs...58 D9
Cleobury Mortimer Shrops...57 M9
Cleobury North Shrops...57 L7
Cleongart Ag & B...120 C5
Clephanton Highld...156 E7
Clerkhill D & G...117 K11
Cleuch-head D & G...115 R7
Clevancy Wilts...33 L9
Clevedon N Som...31 M10
Cleveley Oxon...48 C10
Cleveleys Lancs...88 C2

Cleverton Wilts...33 J7
Clewer Somset...19 M4
Cley next the Sea Norfk...76 E3
Cliddesden Hants...22 H5
Cliff Warwks...59 K5
Cliffe Lancs...89 L4
Cliffe Medway...38 B6
Cliffe N York...91 R4
Cliffe N York...103 P7
Cliff End E Susx...26 E9
Cliffe Woods Medway...38 B7
Clifford Herefs...45 J5
Clifford Leeds...91 L2
Clifford Chambers Warwks...47 N4
Clifford's Mesne Gloucs...46 D10
Cliffsend Kent...39 P9
Clifton Bristl...31 Q10
Clifton C Beds...50 E3
Clifton C Nott...72 E4
Clifton C York...98 B10
Clifton Calder...90 F6
Clifton Derbys...71 M6
Clifton Devon...17 L3
Clifton Donc...91 N11
Clifton Lancs...88 F4
Clifton N York...97 J11
Clifton Nthumb...113 K4
Clifton Oxon...48 D8
Clifton Salfd...82 G4
Clifton W & F...101 P5
Clifton Worcs...46 F5
Clifton Campville Staffs...59 L2
Clifton Hampden Oxon...34 F5
Clifton Reynes M Keyn...49 P4
Clifton upon Dunsmore Warwks...60 B5
Clifton upon Teme Worcs...46 D2
Cliftonville Kent...39 Q7
Climping W Susx...15 Q6
Clink Somset...20 E5
Clint N York...97 L9
Clinterty C Aber...151 L5
Clint Green Norfk...76 E9
Clintmains Border...118 B4
Clipiau Gwynd...55 J2
Clippesby Norfk...77 N9
Clipsham Rutlnd...73 P7
Clipston N Nthn...60 F4
Clipstone C Beds...49 P9
Clipstone Notts...85 J8
Clitheroe Lancs...89 L2
Clive Shrops...69 P10
Clixby Lincs...93 J10
Cloatley Wilts...33 J6
Clocaenog Denbgs...68 E4
Clochan Moray...158 B5
Clock Face St Hel...82 B6
Cloddiau Powys...56 C3
Clodock Herefs...45 L9
Cloford Somset...20 D6
Clola Abers...159 P9
Clophill C Beds...50 C3
Clopton N Nthn...61 N4
Clopton Suffk...65 J11
Clopton Corner Suffk...65 J11
Clopton Green Suffk...63 N10
Clopton Green Suffk...64 D10
Clos du Valle Guern...10 c1
Closeburn D & G...109 J2
Closeburnmill D & G...109 K2
Closeclark IoM...80 c6
Closworth Somset...11 M2
Clothall Herts...50 G4
Clothall Common Herts...50 G4
Clotton Ches W...69 P2
Cloudesley Bush Warwks...59 Q7
Clouds Herefs...46 A7
Clough Oldham...89 Q9
Clough Foot Calder...89 Q6
Clough Head Calder...90 D7
Cloughton N York...99 L2
Cloughton Newlands N York...105 R11
Clousta Shet...169 q8
Clova Angus...142 E3
Clovelly Devon...16 E7
Clovenfords Border...117 P3
Clovulin Highld...139 J5
Clow Bridge Lancs...89 N5
Clowne Derbys...84 G5
Clows Top Worcs...57 N10
Cloy Wrexhm...69 L6
Cluanie Inn Highld...146 D5
Cluanie Lodge Highld...146 D5
Clubworthy Cnwll...5 M3
Clugston D & G...107 L6
Clun Shrops...56 E8
Clunas Highld...156 E7
Clunbury Shrops...56 F8
Clunderwen Carmth...41 M7
Clune Highld...148 D2
Clunes Highld...146 F10
Clungunford Shrops...56 F9
Clunie P & K...141 R9
Clunton Shrops...56 E8
Cluny Fife...134 G8
Clutton BaNES...20 B3
Clutton Ches W...69 N4
Clutton Hill BaNES...20 B3
Clwt Conwy...79 R2
Clwt-y-bont Gwynd...67 K2
Clydach Mons...30 H2
Clydach Swans...29 J4
Clydach Vale Rhondd...30 C6
Clydebank W Duns...125 M3
Clydey Pembks...41 Q3
Clyffe Pypard Wilts...33 L9
Clynder Ag & B...131 Q11
Clyne Neath...29 M4
Clynnog Fawr Gwynd...66 G5
Clyro Powys...45 J6
Clyst Honiton Devon...9 N6
Clyst Hydon Devon...9 P4
Clyst St George Devon...9 N7
Clyst St Lawrence Devon...9 P4
Clyst St Mary Devon...9 N6
Cnoc W Isls...168 j4
Cnwch Coch Cerdgn...54 F10
Coad's Green Cnwll...5 M6
Coal Aston Derbys...84 E5
Coalbrookvale Blae G...30 G3
Coalburn S Lans...126 E11
Coalburns Gatesd...112 H8
Coaley Gloucs...32 E4

Coalhill Essex...38 C2
Coalmoor Wrekin...57 M3
Coalpit Heath S Glos...32 C8
Coal Pool Wsall...58 F5
Coalport Wrekin...57 M4
Coalsnaughton Clacks...133 Q8
Coal Street Suffk...65 J7
Coaltown of Balgonie Fife...134 H8
Coaltown of Wemyss Fife...135 J8
Coalville Leics...72 C8
Coanwood Nthumb...111 N9
Coat Somset...19 N10
Coatbridge N Lans...126 C4
Coatdyke N Lans...126 C4
Coate Swindn...33 N8
Coate Wilts...21 K2
Coates Cambs...74 F11
Coates Gloucs...33 J4
Coates Lincs...86 B4
Coates W Susx...23 Q11
Coatham R & Cl...104 G5
Coatham Mundeville Darltn...103 Q6
Cobbaton Devon...17 M6
Coberley Gloucs...47 J11
Cobhall Common Herefs...45 P7
Cobham Kent...37 Q7
Cobham Surrey...36 D8
Cobham Services Surrey...36 D9
Coblers Green Essex...51 Q7
Cobley Dorset...21 K10
Cobnash Herefs...45 P2
Cobo Guern...10 b1
Cobridge C Stke...70 F5
Coburby Abers...159 M5
Cockayne N York...104 H11
Cockayne Hatley C Beds...62 C11
Cock Bank Wrexhm...69 L5
Cock Bevington Warwks...47 L4
Cock Bridge Abers...149 P6
Cockburnspath Border...129 K5
Cock Clarks Essex...52 D11
Cock & End Suffk...63 M10
Cockenzie and Port Seton E Loth...128 C4
Cocker Bar Lancs...88 G6
Cocker Brook Lancs...89 L5
Cockerham Lancs...95 K10
Cockermouth Cumb...100 F4
Cockernhoe Herts...50 D6
Cockersdale Leeds...90 G5
Cockett Swans...28 H6
Cockfield Dur...103 M6
Cockfield Suffk...64 C11
Cockfosters Gt Lon...50 G11
Cock Green Essex...51 Q7
Cocking W Susx...23 N11
Cocking Causeway W Susx...23 N11
Cockington Torbay...7 M6
Cocklake Somset...19 M5
Cockley Beck W & F...100 H11
Cockley Cley Norfk...75 Q10
Cock Marling E Susx...26 E8
Cockpole Green Wokham...35 L8
Cocks Cnwll...3 K3
Cockshutford Shrops...57 K7
Cockshutt Shrops...69 M9
Cock Street Kent...38 C11
Cockthorpe Norfk...76 D3
Cockwells Cnwll...2 E7
Cockwood Devon...9 N8
Cockwood Somset...18 H6
Cockyard Derbys...83 M9
Cockyard Herefs...45 N8
Coddenham Suffk...64 G11
Coddington Ches W...69 N3
Coddington Herefs...46 D6
Coddington Notts...85 P10
Codford St Mary Wilts...21 J7
Codford St Peter Wilts...21 J7
Codicote Herts...50 F7
Codmore Hill W Susx...24 C6
Codnor Derbys...84 F11
Codrington S Glos...32 D9
Codsall Staffs...58 C4
Codsall Wood Staffs...58 B4
Coed Darcy Neath...29 K5
Coedely Rhondd...30 D7
Coed Hirwaun Neath...29 M8
Coedkernew Newpt...31 J8
Coed Morgan Mons...31 L2
Coedpoeth Wrexhm...69 J3
Coed Talon Flints...69 J3
Coedway Powys...69 K11
Coed-y-Bryn Cerdgn...42 G5
Coed-y-caerau Newpt...31 L6
Coed-y-Cwm Rhondd...30 E6
Coed-y-paen Mons...31 K5
Coed-yr-ynys Powys...44 H10
Coed Ystumgwern Gwynd...67 K10
Coelbren Powys...29 N2
Coffinswell Devon...7 M5
Coffle End Bed...61 M9
Cofton Devon...9 N8
Cofton Hackett Worcs...58 F9
Cogan V Glam...30 G10
Cogenhoe W Nthn...60 H8
Cogges Oxon...34 C3
Coggeshall Essex...52 E7
Coggin's Mill E Susx...25 N5
Coignafearn Highld...148 C3
Coilacriech Abers...149 Q8
Coilantogle Stirlg...132 H6
Coillore Highld...152 F10
Coity Brdgnd...29 P9
Col W Isls...168 j4
Colaboll Highld...162 D4
Colan Cnwll...4 D9
Colaton Raleigh Devon...10 B7
Colbost Highld...152 C8
Colburn N York...103 N10
Colby IoM...80 b7
Colby Norfk...77 J5
Colby W & F...102 C6
Colchester Zoo Essex...52 G7
Cold Ash W Berk...34 F11
Cold Ashby N Nthn...60 E5
Cold Ashton S Glos...32 D10
Cold Aston Gloucs...47 M11
Coldbackie Highld...165 P4
Coldbeck W & F...102 D10
Cold Blow Pembks...41 M8
Cold Brayfield M Keyn...49 P4
Cold Cotes N York...95 Q6

Coldean Br & H...24 H9
Coldeast Devon...7 L4
Colden Calder...90 B5
Colden Common Hants...22 E10
Coldfair Green Suffk...65 N9
Coldham Lincs...74 H10
Cold Hanworth Lincs...86 D4
Coldharbour Cnwll...3 K6
Coldharbour Devon...9 Q2
Coldharbour Gloucs...31 Q4
Cold Harbour Herts...50 D11
Cold Harbour Oxon...34 H9
Coldharbour Surrey...24 D2
Cold Hatton Wrekin...70 A10
Cold Hatton Heath Wrekin...70 A10
Cold Hesledon Dur...113 P11
Cold Hiendley Wakefd...91 K8
Cold Higham W Nthn...49 J4
Coldingham Border...129 N6
Cold Kirby N York...98 A4
Coldmeece Staffs...70 F8
Cold Newton Leics...73 J9
Cold Northcott Cnwll...5 L4
Cold Norton Essex...52 E11
Cold Overton Leics...73 L8
Coldred Kent...27 N2
Coldridge Devon...17 M10
Coldstream Border...118 F3
Coldwaltham W Susx...24 B7
Coldwell Herefs...45 N7
Coldwells Abers...159 N10
Cold Weston Shrops...57 K8
Cole Somset...20 C8
Colebatch Shrops...56 E7
Colebrook C Plym...6 E7
Colebrook Devon...9 P3
Colebrooke Devon...9 J5
Coleby Lincs...86 C8
Coleby N Linc...92 E7
Cole End Warwks...59 K7
Coleford Devon...9 J4
Coleford Gloucs...31 Q2
Coleford Somset...20 C5
Coleford Water Somset...18 F8
Colegate End Norfk...64 H4
Cole Green Herts...50 G8
Cole Green Herts...51 K4
Cole Henley Hants...22 E4
Colehill Dorset...12 H4
Coleman Green Herts...50 E8
Coleman's Hatch E Susx...25 K4
Colemere Shrops...69 M8
Colemore Hants...23 K8
Colemore Green Shrops...57 N5
Colenden P & K...134 E2
Coleorton Leics...72 C7
Colerne Wilts...32 F10
Colesbourne Gloucs...33 K2
Cole's Cross Devon...7 J4
Coles Cross Dorset...10 H4
Coles Green Suffk...53 K3
Coleshill Bucks...35 P5
Coleshill Oxon...33 P6
Coleshill Warwks...59 K7
Colestocks Devon...10 B4
Coley BaNES...19 Q3
Colgate W Susx...24 F4
Colinsburgh Fife...135 M7
Colinton C Edin...127 N4
Colintraive Ag & B...124 C3
Colkirk Norfk...76 C6
Coll Ag & B...136 G4
Coll W Isls...168 j4
Collace P & K...142 C11
Collafirth Shet...169 q5
Coll Airport Ag & B...136 F4
Collaton Devon...7 J11
Collaton St Mary Torbay...7 M6
College of Roseisle Moray...157 L4
College Town Br For...23 N3
Collessie Fife...134 H5
Colleton Mills Devon...17 M8
Collett's Green Worcs...46 F4
Collier Row Gt Lon...37 M2
Collier's End Herts...51 J6
Collier's Green E Susx...26 C4
Colliers Green Kent...26 B2
Colliery Row Sundld...113 M11
Collieston Abers...151 Q2
Collin D & G...109 M5
Collingbourne Ducis Wilts...21 P4
Collingbourne Kingston Wilts...21 P3
Collingham Leeds...97 N11
Collingham Notts...85 P8
Collington Herefs...46 B2
Collingtree W Nthn...60 G9
Collins Green Warrtn...82 C5
Collins Green Worcs...46 D3
Colliston Angus...143 L9
Colliton Devon...10 B4
Collyweston N Nthn...73 P10
Colmonell S Ayrs...114 B10
Colmworth Bed...61 N9
Colnabaichin Abers...149 P6
Colnbrook Slough...36 B5
Colne Cambs...62 E5
Colne Lancs...89 P3
Colne Bridge Kirk...90 F6
Colne Edge Lancs...89 P2
Colne Engaine Essex...52 D5
Colney Norfk...76 H10
Colney Heath Herts...50 F9
Colney Street Herts...50 E10
Coln Rogers Gloucs...33 M3
Coln St Aldwyns Gloucs...33 M3
Coln St Dennis Gloucs...33 L2
Colonsay Ag & B...136 b2
Colonsay Airport Ag & B...136 b3
Colpy Abers...158 F11
Colquhar Border...117 J2
Colquite Cnwll...4 H7
Colscott Devon...16 H9
Colsterdale N York...96 H4
Colsterworth Lincs...73 N6
Colston Bassett Notts...73 J4
Coltfield Moray...157 L5
Colt Hill Hants...23 L4
Coltishall Norfk...77 K8
Colton Leeds...91 K4
Colton N York...91 N2
Colton Norfk...76 G10
Colton Staffs...71 J10
Colton W & F...94 G3

Colt's Hill – Crewe 265

Colt's Hill Kent 25 P2
Columbjohn Devon 9 N5
Colva Powys 44 H4
Colvend D & G 109 J10
Colwall Herefs 46 E6
Colwell Nthumb 112 E5
Colwich Staffs 71 J10
Colwick Notts 72 G2
Colwinston V Glam 29 P9
Colworth W Susx 15 P6
Colwyn Bay Conwy 80 B9
Colyford Devon 10 F6
Colyton Devon 10 E6
Combe Devon 7 J11
Combe Herefs 45 L2
Combe Oxon 48 D11
Combe W Berk 22 C2
Combe Almer Dorset 12 G5
Combe Common Surrey 23 P7
Combe Down BaNES 20 E2
Combe Fishacre Devon 7 L5
Combe Florey Somset 18 G8
Combe Hay BaNES 20 D3
Combeinteignhead Devon 7 N4
Combe Martin Devon 17 K2
Combe Raleigh Devon 10 D4
Comberbach Ches W 82 D9
Comberford Staffs 59 J3
Comberton Cambs 62 E9
Comberton Herefs 56 H11
Combe St Nicholas Somset 10 G2
Combpyne Devon 10 F6
Combridge Staffs 71 K7
Combrook Warwks 48 B4
Combs Derbys 83 M9
Combs Suffk 64 E10
Combs Ford Suffk 64 E10
Combwich Somset 19 J6
Comers Abers 150 H6
Comeytrowe Somset 18 H10
Comhampton Worcs 58 B11
Commercial End Cambs 63 J8
Commins Coch Powys 55 J4
Commondale N York 105 J8
Common Edge Bpool 88 C4
Common End Cumb 100 D6
Common Moor Cnwll 5 L8
Common Platt Wilts 33 M7
Commonside Ches W 82 B10
Commonside Derbys 71 N6
Common Side Derbys 84 D5
Commonwood Shrops 69 N9
Commonwood Wrexhm 69 L4
Compass Somset 19 J8
Compstall Stockp 83 L6
Compstonend D & G 108 E10
Compton Devon 7 M6
Compton Hants 22 C9
Compton Hants 22 E9
Compton Staffs 57 Q8
Compton Surrey 23 Q5
Compton W Berk 34 F8
Compton W Susx 15 L4
Compton Wilts 21 M4
Compton Abbas Dorset 20 G11
Compton Abdale Gloucs 47 L11
Compton Bassett Wilts 33 K10
Compton Beauchamp Oxon 33 Q7
Compton Bishop Somset 19 L3
Compton Chamberlayne Wilts 21 K9
Compton Dando BaNES 20 B2
Compton Dundon Somset 19 N8
Compton Durville Somset 19 M11
Compton Greenfield S Glos 31 Q8
Compton Martin BaNES 19 P3
Compton Pauncefoot Somset 20 B9
Compton Valence Dorset 11 M6
Comrie Fife 134 C10
Comrie P & K 133 M3
Conaglen House Highld 139 J4
Conchra Highld 145 Q2
Concraigie P & K 141 Q9
Conder Green Lancs 95 K9
Conderton Worcs 47 J7
Condicote Gloucs 47 N9
Condorrat N Lans 126 C3
Condover Shrops 56 H3
Coney Hill Gloucs 46 G11
Coneyhurst W Susx 24 D6
Coneysthorpe N York 98 E6
Coneythorpe N York 97 N9
Coney Weston Suffk 64 D6
Conford Hants 23 M8
Congdon's Shop Cnwll 5 M6
Congerstone Leics 72 B9
Congham Norfk 75 P6
Congleton Ches E 70 F2
Congl-y-wal Gwynd 67 N6
Congresbury N Som 19 M2
Congreve Staffs 58 D2
Conheath D & G 109 L7
Conicavel Moray 156 H7
Coningsby Lincs 86 H9
Conington Cambs 61 Q3
Conington Cambs 62 D7
Conisbrough Donc 91 N11
Conisholme Lincs 93 R11
Coniston E R Yk 93 L3
Coniston W & F 101 K11
Coniston Cold N York 96 D10
Conistone N York 96 E7
Connah's Quay Flints 81 K11
Connel Ag & B 138 G11
Connel Park E Ayrs 115 M5
Connor Downs Cnwll 2 F6
Conon Bridge Highld 155 P6
Cononley N York 96 E11
Consall Staffs 70 H5
Consett Dur 112 H10
Constable Burton N York 97 J2
Constable Lee Lancs 89 N6
Constantine Cnwll 3 J8
Constantine Bay Cnwll 4 D7
Contin Highld 155 N6
Conwy Conwy 79 P9
Conwy Castle Conwy 79 P9
Conyer Kent 38 G9
Conyer's Green Suffk 64 B8
Cooden E Susx 26 B10
Cookbury Devon 16 G10
Cookbury Wick Devon 16 F10
Cookham W & M 35 N7
Cookham Dean W & M 35 N7
Cookham Rise W & M 35 N7
Cookhill Worcs 47 L3
Cookley Suffk 65 L6
Cookley Worcs 58 B8
Cookley Green Oxon 35 J6
Cookney Abers 151 M9
Cooksbridge E Susx 25 K8
Cooksey Green Worcs 58 D11
Cook's Green Essex 53 L8
Cooks Green Suffk 64 D11
Cookshill Staffs 70 G6
Cooksland Cnwll 4 H8
Cooksmill Green Essex 51 P9
Cookson Green Ches W 82 C10
Coolham W Susx 24 D6
Cooling Medway 38 C6
Cooling Street Medway 38 B7
Coombe Cnwll 2 G5
Coombe Cnwll 3 L5
Coombe Cnwll 3 N3
Coombe Devon 7 N4
Coombe Devon 9 K8
Coombe Devon 10 C6
Coombe Gloucs 32 E6
Coombe Hants 23 J10
Coombe Wilts 21 M4
Coombe Bissett Wilts 21 M9
Coombe Cellars Devon 7 N4
Coombe Cross Hants 23 J10
Coombe Hill Gloucs 46 G9
Coombe Keynes Dorset 12 D8
Coombe Pafford Torbay 7 N5
Coombes W Susx 24 E9
Coombes-Moor Herefs 45 M2
Coombe Street Somset 20 E8
Coombeswood Dudley 58 E7
Coopersale Common Essex 51 L10
Coopersale Street Essex 51 L10
Cooper's Corner Kent 37 L11
Coopers Green E Susx 25 L6
Coopers Green Herts 50 E9
Cooper Street Kent 39 P9
Cooper Turning Bolton 89 J9
Cootham W Susx 24 C8
Copdock Suffk 53 K3
Copford Essex 52 F7
Copford Green Essex 52 F7
Copgrove N York 97 M8
Copister Shet 169 r6
Cople Bed 61 P11
Copley Calder 90 D6
Copley Dur 103 L5
Copley Tamesd 83 L5
Coplow Dale Derbys 83 Q9
Copmanthorpe C York 98 B11
Copmere End Staffs 70 E9
Copp Lancs 88 E3
Coppathorne Cnwll 16 C11
Coppenhall Staffs 70 G11
Coppenhall Moss Ches E 70 C3
Copperhouse Cnwll 2 F6
Coppicegate Shrops 57 N8
Coppingford Cambs 61 Q5
Coppins Corner Kent 26 F2
Copplestone Devon 9 J4
Coppull Lancs 88 H8
Coppull Moor Lancs 88 H8
Copsale W Susx 24 E6
Copster Green Lancs 89 K4
Copston Magna Warwks 59 Q7
Cop Street Kent 39 N9
Copthall Green Essex 51 K10
Copt Heath Solhll 59 J9
Copt Hewick N York 97 M6
Copthorne Cnwll 5 M3
Copthorne W Susx 24 H3
Copt Oak Leics 72 D8
Copy's Green Norfk 76 C4
Copythorne Hants 13 P2
Coram Street Suffk 52 H3
Corbets Tey Gt Lon 37 N3
Corbière Jersey 11 a2
Corbridge Nthumb 112 E8
Corby N Nthn 61 J3
Corby Glen Lincs 73 Q6
Corby Hill Cumb 111 J9
Cordon N Ayrs 121 K5
Cordwell Derbys 84 D5
Coreley Shrops 57 L10
Cores End Bucks 35 P7
Corfe Somset 18 H11
Corfe Castle Dorset 12 G8
Corfe Mullen Dorset 12 G5
Corfton Shrops 56 H7
Corgarff Abers 149 P6
Corhampton Hants 22 H10
Corks Pond Kent 25 Q2
Corlae D & G 115 N8
Corley Warwks 59 M7
Corley Ash Warwks 59 L7
Corley Moor Warwks 59 L8
Corley Services Warwks 59 M7
Cormuir Angus 142 E4
Cornard Tye Suffk 52 F3
Corndon Devon 8 G7
Corner Row Lancs 88 E4
Corney Cumb 94 C2
Cornforth Dur 104 B4
Cornhill Abers 158 E6
Cornhill-on-Tweed Nthumb 118 G3
Cornholme Calder 89 Q5
Cornish Hall End Essex 51 Q3
Cornoigmore Ag & B 136 B6
Cornriggs Dur 102 F2
Cornsay Dur 103 M2
Cornsay Colliery Dur 103 N2
Corntown Highld 155 Q6
Corntown V Glam 29 P9
Cornwall Airport Newquay Cnwll 4 D9
Cornwell Oxon 47 Q9
Cornwood Devon 6 G7
Cornworthy Devon 7 L7
Corpach Highld 139 K2
Corpusty Norfk 76 G6
Corrachree Abers 150 D7
Corran Highld 139 J5
Corran Highld 145 P6
Corrany IoM 80 g4
Corrie D & G 110 D3
Corrie N Ayrs 121 K3
Corriecravie N Ayrs 120 H7
Corriegills N Ayrs 121 K4
Corriegour Lodge Hotel Highld 146 H9
Corriemoille Highld 155 L5
Corrimony Highld 155 L11
Corringham Lincs 85 Q2
Corringham Thurr 38 B5
Corris Gwynd 54 H3
Corris Uchaf Gwynd 54 G3
Corrow Ag & B 131 P7
Corry Highld 145 K3
Corscombe Devon 8 F5
Corscombe Dorset 11 L3
Corse Gloucs 46 E9
Corse Lawn Gloucs 46 F8
Corsham Wilts 32 G10
Corsindae Abers 150 H6
Corsley Wilts 20 F5
Corsley Heath Wilts 20 F5
Corsock D & G 108 G5
Corston BaNES 32 C11
Corston Wilts 32 H8
Corstorphine C Edin 127 M3
Cors-y-Gedol Gwynd 67 L10
Cortachy Angus 142 F6
Corton Suffk 65 Q2
Corton Wilts 20 H6
Corton Denham Somset 20 B10
Coruanan Highld 139 K4
Corwen Denbgs 68 E6
Coryates Dorset 11 N7
Coryton Devon 8 C8
Coryton Thurr 38 B5
Cosby Leics 72 E11
Coseley Dudley 58 D6
Cosford Shrops 57 Q3
Cosgrove W Nthn 49 L6
Cosham C Port 15 J5
Cosheston Pembks 41 K10
Coshieville P & K 141 J8
Cossall Notts 72 D2
Cossall Marsh Notts 72 D2
Cossington Leics 72 G8
Cossington Somset 19 L6
Costessey Norfk 76 H9
Costock Notts 72 F5
Coston Leics 73 L6
Coston Norfk 76 F10
Cote Oxon 34 C4
Cote Somset 19 K6
Cotebrook Ches W 82 C11
Cotehill Cumb 111 J10
Cotes Leics 72 F6
Cotes Staffs 70 E8
Cotes W & F 95 K3
Cotesbach Leics 60 B4
Cotes Heath Staffs 70 E8
Cotford St Luke Somset 18 G9
Cotgrave Notts 72 G3
Cothal Abers 151 M4
Cotham Notts 85 N11
Cothelstone Somset 18 G8
Cotherstone Dur 103 K7
Cothill Oxon 34 E5
Cotleigh Devon 10 E4
Cotmanhay Derbys 72 D2
Coton Cambs 62 F9
Coton Shrops 69 P8
Coton Staffs 59 J4
Coton Staffs 70 E10
Coton Staffs 70 H8
Coton W Nthn 60 E6
Coton Clanford Staffs 70 F10
Coton Hayes Staffs 70 H8
Coton Hill Shrops 56 H2
Coton in the Clay Staffs 71 M9
Coton in the Elms Derbys 71 N11
Coton Park Derbys 71 P11
Cotswold Airport Wilts 33 J5
Cotswolds 33 J3
Cotswold Wildlife Park & Gardens Oxon 33 P3
Cott Devon 7 K6
Cottam E R Yk 99 K7
Cottam Lancs 88 G4
Cottam Notts 85 P5
Cottenham Cambs 62 F7
Cotterdale N York 96 B2
Cottered Herts 50 H5
Cotteridge Birm 58 F8
Cotterstock N Nthn 61 M2
Cottesbrooke W Nthn 60 F6
Cottesmore Rutlnd 73 N8
Cottingham E R Yk 92 H4
Cottingham N Nthn 60 H2
Cottingley C Brad 90 E3
Cottisford Oxon 48 G8
Cotton Suffk 64 F8
Cotton End Bed 61 N11
Cotton Tree Lancs 89 Q3
Cottown Abers 150 E2
Cottown Abers 151 K4
Cottown of Gight Abers 159 K9
Cotts Devon 6 C5
Cotwall Wrekin 69 R11
Cotwalton Staffs 70 G8
Couch's Mill Cnwll 5 J10
Coughton Herefs 46 A10
Coughton Warwks 47 L2
Coulaghailtro Ag & B 123 M6
Coulags Highld 154 C9
Coulby Newham Middsb 104 F8
Coulderton Cumb 100 C9
Coull Abers 150 E7
Coulport Ag & B 131 Q10
Coulsdon Gt Lon 36 G9
Coulston Wilts 21 J4
Coulter S Lans 116 E4
Coultershaw Bridge W Susx 23 Q11
Coultings Somset 18 H6
Coulton N York 98 C6
Coultra Fife 135 K3
Cound Shrops 57 K3
Coundlane Shrops 57 K4
Coundon Dur 103 P5
Coundon Grange Dur 103 P5
Countersett N York 96 D3
Countess Wilts 21 N6
Countess Cross Essex 52 E5
Countess Wear Devon 9 M7
Countesswells C Aber 151 M7
Countesthorpe Leics 72 F11
Countisbury Devon 17 N2
Coupar Angus P & K 142 C10
Coupe Green Lancs 88 H5
Coupland Nthumb 118 H4
Coupland W & F 102 D7
Cour Ag & B 123 P10
Court-at-Street Kent 27 J4
Courteachan Highld 145 L8
Courteenhall W Nthn 49 L4
Court Henry Carmth 43 L10
Courtsend Essex 38 H3
Courtway Somset 18 H8
Cousland Mdloth 128 B6
Cousley Wood E Susx 25 Q4
Cove Ag & B 131 Q11
Cove Border 129 K5
Cove Devon 18 C11
Cove Hants 23 N3
Cove Highld 160 C8
Cove Bay C Aber 151 P7
Cove Bottom Suffk 65 P6
Covehithe Suffk 65 Q5
Coven Staffs 58 D3
Coveney Cambs 62 G4
Covenham St Bartholomew Lincs 87 K2
Covenham St Mary Lincs 87 K2
Coven Heath Staffs 58 D3
Coventry Covtry 59 M9
Coverack Cnwll 3 K10
Coverack Bridges Cnwll 2 H7
Coverham N York 96 H3
Covington Cambs 61 N6
Covington S Lans 116 D3
Cowan Bridge Lancs 95 N5
Cowbeech E Susx 25 P8
Cowbit Lincs 74 E7
Cowbridge V Glam 30 C10
Cowdale Derbys 83 N10
Cowden Kent 25 L2
Cowdenbeath Fife 134 F9
Cowden Pound Kent 25 L2
Cowden Station Kent 25 L2
Cowers Lane Derbys 71 Q5
Cowes IoW 14 E7
Cowesby N York 97 Q3
Cowesfield Green Wilts 21 Q10
Cowfold W Susx 24 F6
Cowgill W & F 95 R3
Cow Green Suffk 64 F8
Cowhill S Glos 32 B6
Cowie Stirlg 133 N10
Cowlam E R Yk 99 K7
Cowley Devon 9 M5
Cowley Gloucs 33 J2
Cowley Gt Lon 36 C4
Cowley Oxon 34 F4
Cowling Lancs 88 H7
Cowling N York 90 B2
Cowling N York 97 K3
Cowlinge Suffk 63 M10
Cowmes Kirk 90 F7
Cowpe Lancs 89 N6
Cowpen Nthumb 113 L4
Cowpen Bewley S on T 104 E6
Cowplain Hants 15 J4
Cowshill Dur 102 G2
Cowslip Green N Som 19 N2
Cowthorpe N York 97 P10
Coxall Herefs 56 F10
Coxbank Ches E 70 B6
Coxbench Derbys 72 B2
Coxbridge Somset 19 P7
Cox Common Suffk 65 N5
Coxford Cnwll 5 K2
Coxford Norfk 76 B6
Coxgreen Staffs 57 Q7
Cox Green Surrey 24 C4
Coxheath Kent 38 B11
Coxhoe Dur 104 B3
Coxley Somset 19 P6
Coxley Wakefd 90 H7
Coxley Wick Somset 19 P6
Coxpark Cnwll 5 Q7
Coxtie Green Essex 51 N11
Coxwold N York 98 A5
Coychurch Brdgnd 29 P9
Coylton S Ayrs 114 H4
Coylumbridge Highld 148 G5
Coytrahen Brdgnd 29 N7
Crabbs Cross Worcs 58 F11
Crab Orchard Dorset 13 J3
Crabtree W Susx 24 F5
Crabtree Green Wrexhm 69 K6
Crackenthorpe W & F 102 C6
Crackington Haven Cnwll 5 J2
Crackley Staffs 70 E4
Crackley Warwks 59 L10
Crackleybank Shrops 57 P2
Crackpot N York 103 J11
Cracoe N York 96 E8
Craddock Devon 10 B2
Cradle End Herts 51 L6
Cradley Dudley 58 D7
Cradley Herefs 46 D5
Cradley Heath Sandw 58 D7
Cradoc Powys 44 E8
Crafthole Cnwll 5 P11
Crafton Bucks 49 N11
Crag Foot Lancs 95 K6
Craggan Highld 149 J2
Cragganmore Moray 157 M10
Cragg Hill Leeds 90 G3
Cragg Vale Calder 90 C6
Craghead Dur 113 K10
Cragside Nthumb 119 L10
Crai Powys 44 B10
Craibstone Moray 158 C6
Craichie Angus 143 J8
Craig Angus 143 M6
Craig Highld 154 D8
Craigbank E Ayrs 115 L5
Craigburn Border 127 N7
Craig-cefn-parc Swans 29 J4
Craigcleuch D & G 110 F3
Craigdam Abers 159 K11
Craigdhu Ag & B 130 G6
Craigearn Abers 151 J5
Craigellachie Moray 157 P9
Craigend P & K 134 E3
Craigend Rens 125 M3
Craigendoran Ag & B 132 C11
Craigends Rens 125 L4
Craighlaw D & G 107 K5
Craighouse Ag & B 122 H6
Craigie P & K 141 R9
Craigie S Ayrs 125 L11
Craigiefold Abers 159 M4
Craigley D & G 108 G9
Craig Llangiwg Neath 29 K4
Craiglockhart C Edin 127 N3
Craigmillar C Edin 127 Q3
Craignant Shrops 69 J7
Craigneston D & G 115 Q10
Craigneuk N Lans 126 D4
Craigneuk N Lans 126 D6
Craignure Ag & B 138 C10
Craigo Angus 143 M5
Craig Penllyn V Glam 30 C9
Craigrothie Fife 135 K5
Craigruie Stirlg 132 F3
Craig's End Essex 52 B4
Craigton Angus 143 J10
Craigton C Aber 151 L7
Craigton E Rens 125 M7
Craigton of Airlie Angus 142 E7
Craig-y-Duke Neath 29 K4
Craig-y-nos Powys 44 A11
Craik Border 117 L9
Crail Fife 135 Q6
Crailing Border 118 C6
Craiselound N Linc 92 C11
Crakehall N York 97 K3
Crakehill N York 97 P6
Crakemarsh Staffs 71 K7
Crambe N York 98 E8
Crambeck N York 98 E7
Cramlington Nthumb 113 L5
Cramond C Edin 127 M2
Cramond Bridge C Edin 127 M2
Crampmoor Hants 22 C10
Cranage Ches E 82 G11
Cranberry Staffs 70 E7
Cranborne Dorset 13 J2
Cranbourne Br For 35 P10
Cranbrook Devon 9 N6
Cranbrook Kent 26 C4
Cranbrook Common Kent 26 C4
Crane Moor Barns 91 J10
Crane's Corner Norfk 76 C9
Cranfield C Beds 49 Q6
Cranford Devon 16 E7
Cranford Gt Lon 36 D5
Cranford St Andrew N Nthn 61 K5
Cranford St John N Nthn 61 K5
Cranham Gloucs 32 G2
Cranham Gt Lon 37 N3
Cranhill Warwks 47 M4
Crank St Hel 81 Q5
Cranleigh Surrey 24 C3
Cranmer Green Suffk 64 E7
Cranmore IoW 14 C8
Cranmore Somset 20 C6
Cranoe Leics 73 K11
Cransford Suffk 65 L9
Cranshaws Border 128 H7
Cranstal IoM 80 g1
Cranswick E R Yk 99 L10
Crantock Cnwll 4 B9
Cranwell Lincs 86 D11
Cranwich Norfk 63 N2
Cranworth Norfk 76 D11
Craobh Haven Ag & B 130 F6
Crapstone Devon 6 E5
Crarae Ag & B 131 K8
Crask Inn Highld 162 C2
Crask of Aigas Highld 155 N9
Craster Nthumb 119 Q7
Craswall Herefs 45 K7
Crateford Staffs 58 D3
Cratfield Suffk 65 L6
Crathes Abers 151 K8
Crathie Abers 149 P8
Crathie Highld 147 P9
Crathorne N York 104 D9
Craven Arms Shrops 56 G8
Crawcrook Gatesd 112 H8
Crawford Lancs 81 P4
Crawford S Lans 116 D6
Crawfordjohn S Lans 116 B6
Crawley Hants 22 D8
Crawley Oxon 34 B2
Crawley W Susx 24 G3
Crawley Down W Susx 24 H3
Crawleyside Dur 103 J2
Crawshawbooth Lancs 89 N5
Crawton Abers 143 R2
Craxe's Green Essex 52 F8
Cray N York 96 D5
Cray P & K 142 A5
Crayford Gt Lon 37 M5
Crayke N York 98 B6
Craymere Beck Norfk 76 F5
Crays Hill Essex 38 B3
Cray's Pond Oxon 34 H8
Craythorne Staffs 71 N9
Craze Lowman Devon 9 N2
Crazies Hill Wokham 35 L8
Creacombe Devon 17 Q8
Creagan Inn Ag & B 138 H9
Creag Ghoraidh W Isls 168 c13
Creagorry W Isls 168 c13
Creaguaineach Lodge Highld 139 Q4
Creamore Bank Shrops 69 P8
Creaton W Nthn 60 F6
Creca D & G 110 D6
Credenhill Herefs 45 P6
Crediton Devon 9 K4
Creebank D & G 107 K2
Creebridge D & G 107 M4
Creech Dorset 12 F8
Creech Heathfield Somset 19 J9
Creech St Michael Somset 19 J9
Creed Cnwll 3 N4
Creekmoor BCP 12 H6
Creekmouth Gt Lon 37 L4
Creeksea Essex 38 F2
Creeting St Mary Suffk 64 F10
Creeting St Peter Suffk 64 F10
Creeton Lincs 73 Q6
Creetown D & G 107 N6
Cregneash IoM 80 a8
Creg ny Baa IoM 80 e5
Cregrina Powys 44 G4
Creich Fife 135 J3
Creigiau Cardif 30 E8
Cremyll Cnwll 6 D8
Cressage Shrops 57 K4
Cressbrook Derbys 83 Q10
Cresselly Pembks 41 L9
Cressex Bucks 35 M6
Cressing Essex 52 C7
Cresswell Nthumb 113 L2
Cresswell Pembks 41 L9
Cresswell Staffs 70 H7
Creswell Derbys 84 H6
Creswell Green Staffs 58 G2
Cretingham Suffk 65 J9
Cretshengan Ag & B 123 M6
Crewe Ches E 70 C3

Crewe-by-Farndon Ches W 69 M4
Crewe Green Ches E 70 C3
Crew Green Powys 69 K11
Crewkerne Somset 11 J3
Crews Hill Gt Lon 50 H11
Crewton C Derb 72 B4
Crianlarich Stirlg 132 D2
Cribyn Cerdgn 43 K4
Criccieth Gwynd 66 H7
Crich Derbys 84 D10
Crich Carr Derbys 84 D10
Crichton Mdloth 128 B7
Crick Mons 31 N6
Crick W Nthn 60 C6
Crickadarn Powys 44 F6
Cricket St Thomas Somset 10 H3
Crickheath Shrops 69 J10
Crickhowell Powys 45 J11
Cricklade Wilts 33 L6
Cricklewood Gt Lon 36 F3
Cridling Stubbs N York 91 N6
Crieff P & K 133 P3
Criggan Cnwll 4 G9
Criggion Powys 69 J11
Crigglestone Wakefd 91 J7
Crimble Rochdl 89 P8
Crimond Abers 159 Q6
Crimplesham Norfk 75 N10
Crimscote Warwks 47 P5
Crinaglack Highld 155 M9
Crinan Ag & B 130 F9
Crindledyke N Lans 126 E6
Cringleford Norfk 76 H10
Cringles C Brad 96 F11
Crinow Pembks 41 M8
Cripplesease Cnwll 2 E6
Cripplestyle Dorset 13 J2
Cripp's Corner E Susx 26 C7
Croachy Highld 148 B2
Croanford Cnwll 4 G7
Crockenhill Kent 37 M7
Crocker End Oxon 35 K7
Crockerhill W Susx 15 P5
Crockernwell Devon 9 J6
Crocker's Ash Herefs 45 Q11
Crockerton Wilts 20 G6
Crocketford D & G 108 H6
Crockey Hill C York 98 C11
Crockham Hill Kent 37 K10
Crockhurst Street Kent 37 P11
Crockleford Heath Essex 52 H6
Crock Street Somset 10 G2
Croeserw Neath 29 N5
Croes-goch Pembks 40 F4
Croes-lan Cerdgn 42 G6
Croesor Gwynd 67 L6
Croesyceiliog Carmth 42 H11
Croesyceiliog Torfn 31 K5
Croes-y-mwyalch Torfn 31 K6
Croes-y-pant Mons 31 K4
Croft Leics 72 E11
Croft Lincs 87 P8
Croft Warrtn 82 D6
Croftamie Stirlg 132 F10
Crofton Cumb 110 F10
Crofton Wakefd 91 K7
Crofton Wilts 21 Q2
Croft-on-Tees N York 103 Q9
Croftown Highld 161 K10
Crofts Moray 157 P7
Crofts Bank Traffd 82 G5
Crofts of Dipple Moray 157 Q6
Crofts of Haddo Abers 159 K10
Crofts of Savoch Abers 159 P5
Crofty Swans 28 F6
Crogen Gwynd 68 D7
Croggan Ag & B 130 E2
Croglin W & F 111 L11
Croick Highld 162 B8
Cromarty Highld 156 D4
Crombie Fife 134 D11
Cromdale Highld 149 K2
Cromer Herts 50 G5
Cromer Norfk 77 J3
Cromford Derbys 84 C9
Cromhall S Glos 32 C6
Cromhall Common S Glos 32 C7
Cromor W Isls 168 j5
Cromore W Isls 168 j5
Crompton Fold Oldham 89 Q9
Cromwell Notts 85 N8
Cronberry E Ayrs 115 M3
Crondall Hants 23 L5
Cronkbourne IoM 80 e6
Cronk-y-Voddy IoM 80 d4
Cronton Knows 81 P7
Crook Dur 103 N3
Crook W & F 101 N11
Crookdake Cumb 100 G2
Crooke Wigan 88 H9
Crooked End Gloucs 46 B11
Crookedholm E Ayrs 125 M10
Crooked Soley Wilts 34 B10
Crookes Sheff 84 D3
Crookhall Dur 112 H10
Crookham Nthumb 118 H3
Crookham W Berk 22 F2
Crookham Village Hants 23 L4
Crook Inn Border 116 G5
Crooklands W & F 95 L4
Crook of Devon P & K 134 C7
Cropper Derbys 71 N7
Cropredy Oxon 48 E5
Cropston Leics 72 F8
Cropthorne Worcs 47 J5
Cropton N York 98 F3
Cropwell Bishop Notts 72 H3
Cropwell Butler Notts 72 H3
Cros W Isls 168 k1
Crosbost W Isls 168 i5
Crosby Cumb 100 E3
Crosby IoM 80 d6
Crosby N Linc 92 E8
Crosby Sefton 81 L5
Crosby Garret W & F 102 D9
Crosby Ravensworth W & F 102 B8
Crosby Villa Cumb 100 E3
Croscombe Somset 19 Q6
Crosemere Shrops 69 M9
Crosland Edge Kirk 90 E8
Crosland Hill Kirk 90 E8
Cross Somset 19 M4
Crossaig Ag & B 123 P9
Crossapol Ag & B 136 B7
Cross Ash Mons 45 N11

Cross-at-Hand Kent 26 C2
Crossbost W Isls 168 i5
Crossbush W Susx 24 B9
Crosscanonby Cumb 100 E3
Cross Coombe Cnwll 3 J3
Crossdale Street Norfk 77 J4
Cross End Bed 61 N9
Cross End Essex 52 E5
Crossens Sefton 88 D6
Cross Flatts C Brad 90 E2
Crossford Fife 134 D10
Crossford S Lans 126 E8
Crossgate Cnwll 5 N4
Crossgate Lincs 74 D5
Crossgate Staffs 70 G7
Crossgatehall E Loth 128 B6
Crossgates E Ayrs 125 K9
Crossgates Fife 134 E10
Cross Gates Leeds 91 K4
Crossgates N York 99 L4
Crossgates Powys 44 F2
Crossgill Lancs 95 M8
Cross Green Devon 5 P4
Cross Green Leeds 91 J4
Cross Green Staffs 58 D3
Cross Green Suffk 64 A11
Cross Green Suffk 64 B10
Cross Green Suffk 64 D11
Cross Hands Carmth 28 G2
Crosshands Carmth 41 N6
Crosshands E Ayrs 125 M11
Cross Hands Pembks 41 L8
Cross Hill Derbys 84 F11
Crosshill Fife 134 F8
Crosshill S Ayrs 114 F6
Cross Hills N York 96 F11
Crosshouse E Ayrs 125 K10
Cross Houses Shrops 57 J3
Cross Houses Shrops 57 M6
Cross in Hand E Susx 25 N6
Cross Inn Cerdgn 42 G3
Cross Inn Cerdgn 43 K2
Cross Inn Pembks 41 M9
Cross Inn Rhondd 30 E8
Cross Keys Ag & B 132 C10
Crosskeys Caerph 30 H6
Cross Keys Wilts 32 G10
Crosskirk Highld 166 H3
Crosslands W & F 94 G3
Cross Lane IoW 14 F9
Cross Lane Head Shrops 57 N5
Cross Lanes Cnwll 2 H9
Cross Lanes Cnwll 3 K5
Cross Lanes N York 98 A8
Crosslanes Shrops 69 K11
Cross Lanes Wrexhm 69 L5
Crosslee Rens 125 L4
Crossmichael D & G 108 F7
Cross Oak Powys 44 G10
Cross of Jackston Abers 158 H11
Cross o' th' hands Derbys 71 P5
Crossroads Abers 150 F6
Crossroads Abers 151 K9
Cross Roads C Brad 90 D3
Cross Street Suffk 64 H6
Crosston Angus 143 J6
Cross Town Ches E 82 G9
Crossway Mons 45 N11
Crossway Powys 44 F3
Crossway Green Mons 31 P6
Crossway Green Worcs 58 B11
Crossways Dorset 12 C7
Crosswell Pembks 41 M3
Crosthwaite W & F 95 J2
Croston Lancs 88 F7
Crostwick Norfk 77 K8
Crostwight Norfk 77 L6
Crouch Kent 37 P9
Crouch Kent 39 J10
Crouch End Gt Lon 36 H3
Croucheston Wilts 21 L9
Crouch Hill Dorset 11 Q2
Crough House Green Kent 37 K11
Croughton W Nthn 48 F8
Crovie Abers 159 K4
Crow Hants 13 L4
Crowan Cnwll 2 G7
Crowborough E Susx 25 M4
Crowborough Warren E Susx 25 M4
Crowcombe Somset 18 F7
Crowdecote Derbys 83 P11
Crowden Derbys 83 N5
Crowden Devon 8 C5
Crowdhill Hants 22 E10
Crowdleham Kent 37 N9
Crow Edge Barns 83 Q4
Crowell Oxon 35 K5
Crow End Cambs 62 D9
Crowfield Suffk 64 G10
Crowfield W Nthn 48 H6
Crowfield Green Suffk 64 G10
Crowgate Street Norfk 77 L7
Crow Green Essex 51 N11
Crowhill E Loth 129 J5
Crow Hill Herefs 46 B9
Crowhole Derbys 84 D5
Crowhurst E Susx 26 C9
Crowhurst Surrey 37 J11
Crowhurst Lane End Surrey 37 J11
Crowland Lincs 74 D8
Crowland Suffk 64 E7
Crowlas Cnwll 2 E7
Crowle N Linc 92 C8
Crowle Worcs 46 H3
Crowle Green Worcs 46 H3
Crowmarsh Gifford Oxon 34 H7
Crown Corner Suffk 65 K7
Crownhill C Plym 6 D7
Crownpits Surrey 23 Q6
Crownthorpe Norfk 76 F11
Crowntown Cnwll 2 G7
Crows-an-Wra Cnwll 2 B8
Crow's Green Essex 51 Q5
Crowshill Norfk 76 D10
Crow's Nest Cnwll 5 M8
Crowsnest Shrops 56 F4
Crowthorne Wokham 23 M2
Crowton Ches W 82 C10
Croxall Staffs 59 J2
Croxby Lincs 93 L11
Croxdale Dur 103 Q3
Croxden Staffs 71 K7
Croxley Green Herts 50 C11

Croxteth Lpool 81 N5
Croxton Cambs 62 B8
Croxton N Linc 93 J8
Croxton Norfk 64 B4
Croxton Norfk 76 D5
Croxton Staffs 70 D8
Croxtonbank Staffs 70 D8
Croxton Green Ches E 69 Q4
Croxton Kerrial Leics 73 L5
Croy Highld 156 D8
Croy N Lans 126 C2
Croyde Devon 16 G4
Croyde Bay Devon 16 G4
Croydon Cambs 62 D11
Croydon Gt Lon 36 H7
Crubenmore Highld 148 B9
Cruckmeole Shrops 56 G3
Cruckton Shrops 56 G2
Cruden Bay Abers 159 Q10
Crudgington Wrekin 70 A11
Crudie Abers 159 J6
Crudwell Wilts 33 J4
Cruft Devon 8 D5
Crûg Powys 56 B10
Crugmeer Cnwll 4 E6
Crugybar Carmth 43 N7
Crug-y-byddar Powys 56 B8
Crumlin Caerph 30 H5
Crumplehorn Cnwll 5 L11
Crumpsall Manch 82 H4
Crundale Kent 27 J2
Crundale Pembks 41 J7
Crunwere Pembks 41 N8
Cruwys Morchard Devon 9 L2
Crux Easton Hants 22 D3
Cruxton Dorset 11 N5
Crwbin Carmth 28 E2
Cryers Hill Bucks 35 N5
Crymych Pembks 41 N4
Crynant Neath 29 L4
Crystal Palace Gt Lon 36 H6
Cuaig Highld 153 N6
Cuan Ag & B 130 F5
Cubbington Warwks 59 M11
Cubert Cnwll 4 B10
Cubley Barns 90 G10
Cublington Bucks 49 N10
Cublington Herefs 45 N7
Cuckfield W Susx 24 H5
Cucklington Somset 20 E9
Cuckney Notts 85 J6
Cuckoo Bridge Lincs 74 D6
Cuckoo's Corner Hants 23 K6
Cuckoo's Nest Ches W 69 L2
Cuddesdon Oxon 34 G4
Cuddington Bucks 35 K2
Cuddington Ches W 82 C10
Cuddington Heath Ches W 69 N5
Cuddy Hill Lancs 88 F3
Cudham Gt Lon 37 K9
Cudliptown Devon 8 D8
Cudnell BCP 13 J5
Cudworth Barns 91 K9
Cudworth Somset 10 H2
Cuerdley Cross Warrtn 82 B7
Cufaude Hants 23 J3
Cuffley Herts 50 H10
Cuil Highld 138 H6
Culbokie Highld 155 R6
Culbone Somset 17 Q2
Culburnie Highld 155 N9
Culcabock Highld 156 B9
Culcharry Highld 156 F7
Culcheth Warrtn 82 E6
Culdrain Abers 158 D11
Culduie Highld 153 N9
Culford Suffk 64 A7
Culgaith W & F 102 B5
Culham Oxon 34 F5
Culkein Highld 164 B10
Culkein Drumbeg Highld 164 D10
Culkerton Gloucs 32 H5
Cullen Moray 158 D4
Cullercoats N Tyne 113 N6
Cullerlie Abers 151 K7
Cullicudden Highld 156 A5
Cullingworth C Brad 90 D3
Cuillin Hills Highld 144 G3
Cullipool Ag & B 130 E5
Cullivoe Shet 169 s3
Culloden Highld 156 C8
Cullompton Devon 9 P3
Cullompton Services Devon 9 P3
Culm Davy Devon 18 F11
Culmington Shrops 56 H8
Culmstock Devon 10 C2
Culnacraig Highld 160 H6
Culnaightrie D & G 108 G10
Culnaknock Highld 153 J5
Culpho Suffk 53 M2
Culrain Highld 162 D8
Culross Fife 134 B10
Culroy S Ayrs 114 F5
Culsalmond Abers 158 G11
Culscadden D & G 107 N8
Culshabbin D & G 107 K7
Culswick Shet 169 p9
Cultercullen Abers 151 N3
Cults C Aber 151 M7
Culverstone Green Kent 37 P8
Culverthorpe Lincs 73 Q2
Culworth W Nthn 48 F5
Culzean Castle & Country Park S Ayrs 114 D5
Cumbernauld N Lans 126 D3
Cumbernauld Village N Lans 126 D2
Cumberworth Lincs 87 P6
Cumdivock Cumb 110 F11
Cuminestown Abers 159 K7
Cumledge Border 129 K8
Cummersdale Cumb 110 G10
Cummertrees D & G 109 P7
Cummingston Moray 157 L4
Cumnock E Ayrs 115 L3
Cumnor Oxon 34 E4
Cumrew Cumb 111 L10
Cumrue D & G 109 N3
Cumwhinton Cumb 111 J10
Cumwhitton Cumb 111 K10
Cundall N York 97 Q6
Cunninghamhead N Ayrs 125 K9
Cunningsburgh Shet 169 r10
Cupar Fife 135 K5
Cupar Muir Fife 135 K5
Curbar Derbys 84 C6
Curbridge Hants 14 F4

Curbridge Oxon 34 B3
Curdridge Hants 14 F4
Curdworth Warwks 59 J6
Curland Somset 19 J11
Curridge W Berk 34 E10
Currie C Edin 127 M4
Curry Mallet Somset 19 K10
Curry Rivel Somset 19 L9
Curteis Corner Kent 26 E4
Curtisden Green Kent 26 B3
Curtisknowle Devon 7 J8
Cury Cnwll 2 H9
Cushnie Abers 150 E5
Cushuish Somset 18 G8
Cusop Herefs 45 J6
Cusworth Donc 91 N10
Cutcloy D & G 107 N11
Cutcombe Somset 18 B7
Cutgate Rochdl 89 P8
Cuthill Highld 162 H9
Cutiau Gwynd 67 L11
Cutler's Green Essex 51 N4
Cutmadoc Cnwll 4 H9
Cutmere Cnwll 5 N9
Cutnall Green Worcs 58 C11
Cutsdean Gloucs 47 L8
Cutthorpe Derbys 84 D6
Cuttivett Cnwll 5 P9
Cuxham Oxon 35 J5
Cuxton Medway 38 B8
Cuxwold Lincs 93 L10
Cwm Blae G 30 G3
Cwm Denbgs 80 F9
Cwmafan Neath 29 L6
Cwmaman Rhondd 30 D5
Cwmann Carmth 43 L5
Cwmavon Torfn 31 J3
Cwmbach Carmth 28 E4
Cwmbach Carmth 41 Q5
Cwmbâch Powys 44 H7
Cwmbach Rhondd 30 D4
Cwmbach Llechrhyd Powys 44 E4
Cwmbelan Powys 55 L8
Cwmbran Torfn 31 J6
Cwm Capel Carmth 28 E4
Cwmcarn Caerph 30 H6
Cwmcarvan Mons 31 N3
Cwm-celyn Blae G 30 H3
Cwm-Cewydd Gwynd 55 K2
Cwm-cou Cerdgn 41 Q2
Cwm Crawnon Powys 44 G11
Cwmdare Rhondd 30 C4
Cwmdu Carmth 43 M8
Cwmdu Powys 44 H10
Cwmdu Swans 28 H6
Cwmduad Carmth 42 G8
Cwm Dulais Swans 28 H4
Cwmdwr Carmth 43 P8
Cwmfelin Brdgnd 29 N7
Cwmfelin Myr Td 30 E4
Cwmfelin Boeth Carmth 41 N7
Cwmfelinfach Caerph 30 G6
Cwmfelin Mynach Carmth 41 P6
Cwmffrwd Carmth 42 H11
Cwmgiedd Powys 29 L2
Cwmgorse Carmth 29 K2
Cwm Gwaun Pembks 41 K4
Cwmgwili Carmth 28 G2
Cwmgwrach Neath 29 N4
Cwmhiraeth Carmth 42 F7
Cwmifor Carmth 43 N9
Cwm Irfon Powys 44 B5
Cwmisfael Carmth 43 J11
Cwm Llinau Powys 55 J3
Cwmllynfell Neath 29 K2
Cwmmawr Carmth 28 F2
Cwm Morgan Carmth 41 Q4
Cwmparc Rhondd 29 Q4
Cwmpengraig Carmth 42 G7
Cwm Penmachno Conwy 67 P5
Cwmpennar Rhondd 30 D4
Cwmrhos Powys 44 H10
Cwmrhydyceirw Swans 29 J5
Cwmsychbant Cerdgn 43 J5
Cwmtillery Blae G 30 H3
Cwm-twrch Isaf Powys 29 L2
Cwm-twrch Uchaf Powys 29 L2
Cwm-y-glo Carmth 28 G2
Cwm-y-glo Gwynd 67 K2
Cwmyoy Mons 45 K10
Cwmystwyth Cerdgn 54 H10
Cwrt Gwynd 54 F5
Cwrtnewydd Cerdgn 43 J5
Cwrt-y-gollen Powys 45 J11
Cyfarthfa Castle Museum Myr Td 30 D3
Cyffylliog Denbgs 68 E3
Cyfronydd Powys 55 Q3
Cylibebyll Neath 29 K4
Cymau Flints 69 J3
Cymmer Neath 29 N5
Cymmer Rhondd 30 D6
Cyncoed Cardif 30 G8
Cynghordy Carmth 43 R6
Cynheidre Carmth 28 E3
Cynonville Neath 29 M5
Cynwyd Denbgs 68 E6
Cynwyl Elfed Carmth 42 G9

D

Daccombe Devon 7 N5
Dacre N York 97 J8
Dacre W & F 101 N5
Dacre Banks N York 97 J8
Daddry Shield Dur 102 G3
Dadford Bucks 49 J7
Dadlington Leics 72 C11
Dafen Carmth 28 F4
Daffy Green Norfk 76 D10
Dagenham Gt Lon 37 M4
Daglingworth Gloucs 33 J3
Dagnall Bucks 49 Q11
Dagworth Suffk 64 E9
Dail bho Dheas W Isls 168 j1
Dailly S Ayrs 114 E7
Dainton Devon 7 M5
Dairsie Fife 135 L4
Daisy Hill Bolton 82 E4
Daisy Hill Leeds 90 H5
Dalabrog W Isls 168 c15
Dalavich Ag & B 131 K5
Dalbeattie D & G 108 H8
Dalbury Derbys 71 P8
Dalby IoM 80 b6
Dalby Lincs 87 M7
Dalby N York 98 C6
Dalcapon P & K 141 N7
Dalchalm Highld 163 L5
Dalchreichart Highld 146 H5
Dalchruin P & K 133 L4
Dalcrue P & K 134 C2
Dalderby Lincs 87 J7
Dalditch Devon 9 P8
Dale Pembks 40 F9
Dale W & F 101 P2
Dale Abbey Derbys 72 C3
Dale Bottom Cumb 101 J4
Dale End Derbys 84 B8
Dale End N York 96 E11
Dale Hill E Susx 26 B5
Dalehouse N York 105 L7
Dalelia Highld 138 C4
Dalgarven N Ayrs 124 H8
Dalgety Bay Fife 134 F11
Dalgig E Ayrs 115 L5
Dalginross P & K 133 M3
Dalguise P & K 141 N8
Dalhalvaig Highld 166 E6
Dalham Suffk 63 M8
Daliburgh W Isls 168 c15
Dalkeith Mdloth 127 Q4
Dallas Moray 157 L7
Dallinghoo Suffk 65 K10
Dallington E Susx 25 Q7
Dallington W Nthn 60 F8
Dallow N York 97 J6
Dalmally Ag & B 131 P2
Dalmary Stirlg 132 G8
Dalmellington E Ayrs 115 J6
Dalmeny C Edin 127 L2
Dalmore Highld 156 B4
Dalmuir W Duns 125 M3
Dalnabreck Highld 138 C4
Dalnacardoch P & K 140 H3
Dalnahaitnach Highld 148 F4
Dalnaspidal P & K 140 F3
Dalnawillan Lodge Highld 166 H8
Dalness Highld 139 M7
Dalqueich P & K 134 D7
Dalquhairn S Ayrs 114 F8
Dalreavoch Highld 162 H5
Dalry N Ayrs 124 H8
Dalrymple E Ayrs 114 G5
Dalserf S Lans 126 D7
Dalsmeran Ag & B 120 B9
Dalston Cumb 110 G10
Dalston Gt Lon 36 H4
Dalswinton D & G 109 K3
Dalton D & G 109 P6
Dalton Lancs 88 G8
Dalton N York 97 P5
Dalton N York 103 N9
Dalton Nthumb 112 H6
Dalton Nthumb 113 K6
Dalton Rothm 84 G3
Dalton W & F 101 L5
Dalton-in-Furness W & F 94 E6
Dalton-le-Dale Dur 113 P11
Dalton Magna Rothm 84 G2
Dalton-on-Tees N York 103 Q9
Dalton Parva Rothm 84 G2
Dalton Piercy Hartpl 104 E4
Dalveich Stirlg 133 J3
Dalwhinnie Highld 147 Q11
Dalwood Devon 10 E4
Damask Green Herts 50 G5
Damerham Hants 21 M11
Damgate Norfk 77 N10
Dam Green Norfk 64 E4
Damnaglaur D & G 106 F10
Danaway Kent 38 E9
Danbury Essex 52 C10
Danby N York 105 K9
Danby Bottom N York 105 J9
Danby Wiske N York 104 B11
Dandaleith Moray 157 P8
Danderhall Mdloth 127 Q4
Danebridge Ches E 83 L11
Dane End Herts 50 H6
Danegate E Susx 25 M4
Danehill E Susx 25 K5
Dane Hills C Leic 72 F10
Danemoor Green Norfk 76 F10
Danesford Shrops 57 N5
Danesmoor Derbys 84 F8
Dane Street Kent 39 J11
Daniel's Water Kent 26 G3
Danshillock Abers 158 H6
Danskine E Loth 128 E5
Danthorpe E R Yk 93 M4
Danzey Green Warwks 58 H11
Dapple Heath Staffs 71 J9
Darby Green Hants 23 M2
Darcy Lever Bolton 89 L9
Dardy Powys 45 J11
Darenth Kent 37 N6
Daresbury Halton 82 C8
Darfield Barns 91 L10
Darfoulds Notts 85 K6
Dargate Kent 39 J9
Dargavel Rens 125 L3
Darite Cnwll 5 M8
Darland Medway 38 C8
Darland Wrexhm 69 L3
Darlaston Wsall 58 E5
Darlaston Green Wsall 58 E5
Darley N York 97 K9
Darley Abbey C Derb 72 B3
Darley Bridge Derbys 84 C8
Darley Dale Derbys 84 C8
Darley Green Solhll 59 J10
Darleyhall Herts 50 D6
Darley Head N York 97 J9
Darlingscott Warwks 47 N5
Darlington Darltn 103 Q8
Darliston Shrops 69 Q8
Darlton Notts 85 N6
Darnford Staffs 58 H3
Darnick Border 117 Q3
Darowen Powys 55 J4
Darra Abers 158 H8
Darracott Devon 16 C3
Darracott Devon 16 H4
Darras Hall Nthumb 113 J6
Darrington Wakefd 91 M7
Darsham Suffk 65 N8
Darshill Somset 20 B6
Dartford Kent 37 N6
Dartford Crossing Kent 37 N5

Dartington *Devon*	7	K6
Dartmeet *Devon*	6	H4
Dartmoor National Park		
Devon	8	G9
Dartmouth *Devon*	7	M8
Darton *Barns*	91	J8
Darvel *E Ayrs*	125	P10
Darwell Hole *E Susx*	25	Q7
Darwen *Bl w D*	89	K6
Datchet *W & M*	35	Q9
Datchworth *Herts*	50	G7
Datchworth Green *Herts*	50	G7
Daubhill *Bolton*	89	L9
Daugh of Kinermony *Moray*	157	N9
Dauntsey *Wilts*	33	J8
Dava *Highld*	157	J10
Davenham *Ches W*	82	E10
Davenport *Stockp*	83	K7
Davenport Green *Ches E*	82	H9
Davenport Green *Traffd*	82	H7
Daventry *W Nthn*	60	C8
Davidson's Mains *C Edin*	127	N2
Davidstow *Cnwll*	5	K4
David Street *Kent*	37	P8
Davington *D & G*	117	J10
Davington *Kent*	38	H9
Daviot *Abers*	151	J2
Daviot *Highld*	156	C10
Daviot House *Highld*	156	C9
Davis's Town *E Susx*	25	M7
Davoch of Grange *Moray*	158	C7
Davyhulme *Traffd*	82	G5
Daw End *Wsall*	58	F4
Dawesgreen *Surrey*	36	F11
Dawley *Wrekin*	57	M3
Dawlish *Devon*	9	N9
Dawlish Warren *Devon*	9	N9
Dawn *Conwy*	80	B10
Daws Green *Somset*	18	G10
Daws Heath *Essex*	38	D4
Daw's House *Cnwll*	5	N5
Dawsmere *Lincs*	74	H4
Daybrook *Notts*	85	J11
Day Green *Ches E*	70	D3
Dayhills *Staffs*	70	H8
Dayhouse Bank *Worcs*	58	E9
Daylesford *Gloucs*	47	P9
Ddol *Flints*	80	G10
Ddol-Cownwy *Powys*	68	D11
Deal *Kent*	39	Q11
Dean *Cumb*	100	E5
Dean *Devon*	7	J6
Dean *Devon*	17	L2
Dean *Devon*	17	N2
Dean *Dorset*	21	J11
Dean *Hants*	22	D8
Dean *Hants*	22	G11
Dean *Lancs*	89	P5
Dean *Oxon*	48	B10
Dean *Somset*	20	C6
Dean Bottom *Kent*	37	N7
Deanburnhaugh *Border*	117	M8
Deancombe *Devon*	7	J6
Dean Court *Oxon*	34	E3
Deane *Bolton*	89	K9
Deane *Hants*	22	F4
Dean End *Dorset*	21	J11
Dean Head *Barns*	90	H10
Deanland *Dorset*	21	J11
Deanlane End *W Susx*	15	K4
Dean Prior *Devon*	7	J6
Deanraw *Nthumb*	112	B8
Dean Row *Ches E*	83	J8
Deans *W Loth*	127	J4
Deanscales *Cumb*	100	E5
Deanshanger *W Nthn*	49	L7
Deanshaugh *Moray*	157	R7
Deanston *Stirlg*	133	L7
Dean Street *Kent*	38	B11
Dearham *Cumb*	100	E3
Dearnley *Rochdl*	89	Q7
Debach *Suffk*	65	J11
Debden *Essex*	51	K11
Debden *Essex*	51	N4
Debden Green *Essex*	51	N4
Debenham *Suffk*	64	H9
Deblin's Green *Worcs*	46	F5
Dechmont *W Loth*	127	J3
Deddington *Oxon*	48	E8
Dedham *Essex*	53	J5
Dedham Heath *Essex*	53	J5
Dedworth *W & M*	35	P9
Deene *N Nthn*	61	K2
Deenethorpe *N Nthn*	61	L2
Deepcar *Sheff*	90	H11
Deepcut *Surrey*	23	P3
Deepdale *N York*	96	C5
Deepdale *W & F*	95	Q4
Deeping Gate *C Pete*	74	B9
Deeping St James *Lincs*	74	C9
Deeping St Nicholas *Lincs*	74	D7
Deerhurst *Gloucs*	46	G8
Deerhurst Walton *Gloucs*	46	G9
Deerton Street *Kent*	38	G9
Deeside Industrial Park		
Flints	81	L10
Defford *Worcs*	46	H6
Defynnog *Powys*	44	C9
Deganwy *Conwy*	79	P9
Degnish *Ag & B*	130	F5
Deighton *C York*	91	Q2
Deighton *N York*	104	C10
Deiniolen *Gwynd*	67	K2
Delabole *Cnwll*	4	H5
Delamere *Ches W*	82	C11
Delamere Park *Ches W*	82	C10
Delfrigs *Abers*	151	P3
Delley *Devon*	17	J7
Delliefure *Highld*	157	K11
Dell Quay *W Susx*	15	M6
Delly End *Oxon*	34	C2
Delnabo *Moray*	149	M4
Delny *Highld*	156	C3
Delph *Oldham*	90	B9
Delves *Dur*	112	H11
Delvin End *Essex*	52	C4
Dembleby *Lincs*	73	Q3
Demelza *Cnwll*	4	F9
Denaby *Donc*	91	M11
Denaby Main *Donc*	91	M11
Denbies *Surrey*	36	D10
Denbigh *Denbgs*	80	F11
Denbrae *Fife*	135	K4
Denbury *Devon*	7	L5
Denby *Derbys*	84	E11

Denby Bottles *Derbys*	84	E11
Denby Dale *Kirk*	90	G9
Denchworth *Oxon*	34	C6
Dendron *W & F*	94	E6
Denel End *C Beds*	50	B3
Denfield *P & K*	134	B4
Denford *N Nthn*	61	L5
Dengie *Essex*	52	G11
Denham *Bucks*	36	B3
Denham *Suffk*	63	N8
Denham *Suffk*	64	H7
Denham End *Suffk*	63	N8
Denham Green *Bucks*	36	B3
Denham Green *Suffk*	64	H7
Denhead *Abers*	159	N7
Denhead *Fife*	135	M5
Denhead of Gray *C Dund*	142	E11
Denholm *Border*	117	R7
Denholme *C Brad*	90	D4
Denholme Clough *C Brad*	90	D4
Denio *Gwynd*	66	F7
Denmead *Hants*	15	J4
Denmore *C Aber*	151	N5
Denne Park *W Susx*	24	E5
Dennington *Suffk*	65	K8
Denny *Falk*	133	N11
Dennyloanhead *Falk*	133	N11
Den of Lindores *Fife*	134	H4
Denshaw *Oldham*	90	B8
Denside of Durris *Abers*	151	L8
Densole *Kent*	27	M3
Denston *Suffk*	63	N10
Denstone *Staffs*	71	K6
Denstroude *Kent*	39	K9
Dent *W & F*	95	Q3
Denton *Cambs*	61	Q3
Denton *Darltn*	103	P7
Denton *E Susx*	25	L10
Denton *Kent*	27	M2
Denton *Kent*	37	Q6
Denton *Lincs*	73	M4
Denton *N York*	96	H11
Denton *Norfk*	65	K4
Denton *Oxon*	34	G4
Denton *Tamesd*	83	K5
Denton *W Nthn*	60	H9
Denver *Norfk*	75	M10
Denwick *Nthumb*	119	P8
Deopham *Norfk*	76	E11
Deopham Green *Norfk*	64	E2
Depden *Suffk*	63	N9
Depden Green *Suffk*	63	N9
Deptford *Gt Lon*	37	J5
Deptford *Wilts*	21	K7
Derby *C Derb*	72	B3
Derby *Devon*	17	K5
Derbyhaven *IoM*	80	c8
Derculich *P & K*	141	L7
Dereham *Norfk*	76	D9
Deri *Caerph*	30	F4
Derril *Devon*	16	E11
Derringstone *Kent*	27	M2
Derrington *Staffs*	70	F10
Derriton *Devon*	16	E11
Derry Hill *Wilts*	33	J10
Derrythorpe *N Linc*	92	D9
Dersingham *Norfk*	75	N4
Dervaig *Ag & B*	137	L5
Derwen *Denbgs*	68	E4
Derwenlas *Powys*	54	G5
Derwent Valley Mills *Derbys*	84	D9
Derwent Water *Cumb*	101	J6
Derwydd *Carmth*	43	M11
Desborough *N Nthn*	60	H4
Desford *Leics*	72	D10
Detchant *Nthumb*	119	L3
Detling *Kent*	38	C10
Deuxhill *Shrops*	57	M7
Devauden *Mons*	31	N5
Devil's Bridge *Cerdgn*	54	G9
Devitts Green *Warwks*	59	L6
Devizes *Wilts*	21	K2
Devonport *C Plym*	6	D8
Devonside *Clacks*	133	Q8
Devoran *Cnwll*	3	K6
Devoran & Perran *Cnwll*	3	K6
Dewarton *Mdloth*	128	B7
Dewlish *Dorset*	12	C5
Dewsbury *Kirk*	90	G6
Dewsbury Moor *Kirk*	90	G6
Deytheur *Powys*	68	H11
Dial *N Som*	31	P11
Dial Green *W Susx*	23	P9
Dial Post *W Susx*	24	E7
Dibberford *Dorset*	11	K4
Dibden *Hants*	14	D5
Dibden Purlieu *Hants*	14	D5
Dickens Heath *Solhll*	58	H9
Dickleburgh *Norfk*	64	H5
Didbrook *Gloucs*	47	L8
Didcot *Oxon*	34	F6
Diddington *Cambs*	61	Q7
Diddlebury *Shrops*	57	J7
Didley *Herefs*	45	P8
Didling *W Susx*	23	M11
Didmarton *Gloucs*	32	F7
Didsbury *Manch*	82	H6
Didworthy *Devon*	6	H6
Digby *Lincs*	86	E10
Digg *Highld*	152	H4
Diggle *Oldham*	90	C9
Digmoor *Lancs*	88	F9
Digswell *Herts*	50	F7
Digswell Water *Herts*	50	G8
Dihewyd *Cerdgn*	43	J3
Dilham *Norfk*	77	L6
Dilhorne *Staffs*	70	H6
Dill Hall *Lancs*	89	M5
Dillington *Cambs*	61	P7
Dilston *Nthumb*	112	E8
Dilton *Wilts*	20	G5
Dilton Marsh *Wilts*	20	F5
Dilwyn *Herefs*	45	N4
Dimple *Bolton*	89	L7
Dimple *Derbys*	84	C8
Dinas *Carmth*	41	Q4
Dinas *Cnwll*	4	E7
Dinas *Gwynd*	66	D7
Dinas *Gwynd*	66	H3
Dinas *Rhondd*	30	D6
Dinas Cross *Pembks*	41	K3
Dinas Dinlle *Gwynd*	66	G3
Dinas-Mawddwy *Gwynd*	67	R11
Dinas Powys *V Glam*	30	G10
Dinder *Somset*	19	Q6
Dinedor *Herefs*	45	Q7

Dingestow *Mons*	31	N2
Dingle *Lpool*	81	M7
Dingleden *Kent*	26	D5
Dingley *N Nthn*	60	G3
Dingwall *Highld*	155	P6
Dinmael *Conwy*	68	D6
Dinnet *Abers*	150	D8
Dinnington *N u Ty*	113	K4
Dinnington *Rothm*	84	H3
Dinnington *Somset*	11	J2
Dinorwig *Gwynd*	67	K2
Dinorwig Slate Landscape		
Gwynd	67	K2
Dinton *Bucks*	35	L2
Dinton *Wilts*	21	K8
Dinwoodie *D & G*	109	P2
Dinworthy *Devon*	16	E8
Dipford *Somset*	18	H10
Dipley *Hants*	23	K3
Dippen *Ag & B*	120	F4
Dippenhall *Surrey*	23	M5
Dippermill *Devon*	8	D7
Dippertown *Devon*	8	B8
Dippin *N Ayrs*	121	K7
Dipple *Moray*	157	Q6
Dipple *S Ayrs*	114	D7
Diptford *Devon*	7	J7
Dipton *Dur*	113	J10
Diptonmill *Nthumb*	112	D8
Dirleton *E Loth*	128	E3
Dirt Pot *Nthumb*	112	C11
Discoed *Powys*	45	K2
Diseworth *Leics*	72	D6
Dishforth *N York*	97	N6
Disley *Ches E*	83	L8
Diss *Norfk*	64	G5
Disserth *Powys*	44	E3
Distington *Cumb*	100	D6
Ditchampton *Wilts*	21	L8
Ditcheat *Somset*	20	B7
Ditchingham *Norfk*	65	L3
Ditchling *E Susx*	24	H7
Ditherington *Shrops*	57	J2
Ditteridge *Wilts*	32	F11
Dittisham *Devon*	7	M7
Ditton *Kent*	38	B10
Ditton Green *Cambs*	63	L9
Ditton Priors *Shrops*	57	L7
Dixton *Gloucs*	47	J8
Dixton *Mons*	31	P2
Dizzard *Cnwll*	5	K2
Dobcross *Oldham*	90	B9
Dobwalls *Cnwll*	5	L8
Doccombe *Devon*	9	J7
Dochgarroch *Highld*	155	R9
Dockenfield *Surrey*	23	M6
Docker *Lancs*	95	M6
Docking *Norfk*	75	Q3
Docklow *Herefs*	45	R3
Dockray *Cumb*	110	E11
Dockray *W & F*	101	L6
Dodbrooke *Devon*	7	J10
Doddinghurst *Essex*	51	N11
Doddington *Cambs*	62	F2
Doddington *Kent*	38	F10
Doddington *Lincs*	86	B6
Doddington *Nthumb*	119	J4
Doddington *Shrops*	57	L9
Doddiscombsleigh *Devon*	9	L7
Dodd's Green *Ches E*	69	R6
Doddshill *Norfk*	75	N4
Doddy Cross *Cnwll*	5	N9
Dodford *W Nthn*	60	D8
Dodford *Worcs*	58	D10
Dodington *S Glos*	32	E8
Dodington *Somset*	18	G6
Dodleston *Ches W*	69	L2
Dodscott *Devon*	17	J8
Dodside *E Rens*	125	N7
Dod's Leigh *Staffs*	71	J8
Dodworth *Barns*	91	J9
Dodworth Bottom *Barns*	91	J10
Dodworth Green *Barns*	91	J10
Doe Bank *Birm*	58	H5
Doe Lea *Derbys*	84	G7
Dogdyke *Lincs*	86	H9
Dogley Lane *Kirk*	90	F8
Dogmersfield *Hants*	23	L4
Dogridge *Wilts*	33	L7
Dogsthorpe *C Pete*	74	C10
Dog Village *Devon*	9	N5
Dolanog *Powys*	55	P2
Dolau *Powys*	55	Q11
Dolaucothi *Carmth*	43	N6
Dolbenmaen *Gwynd*	66	J6
Doley *Staffs*	70	C9
Dolfach *Powys*	55	L4
Dol-för *Powys*	55	J3
Dolfor *Powys*	55	Q7
Dolgarrog *Conwy*	79	P11
Dolgellau *Gwynd*	67	N11
Dolgoch *Gwynd*	54	F4
Dol-gran *Carmth*	42	H8
Doll *Highld*	163	K6
Dollar *Clacks*	134	B8
Dollarfield *Clacks*	134	B8
Dolley Green *Powys*	56	D11
Dollwen *Cerdgn*	54	F8
Dolphin *Flints*	80	H10
Dolphinholme *Lancs*	95	L10
Dolphinton *S Lans*	127	L8
Dolton *Devon*	17	K9
Dolwen *Conwy*	80	B10
Dolwyddelan *Conwy*	67	N4
Dolybont *Cerdgn*	54	E7
Dolyhir *Powys*	45	J3
Domgay *Powys*	69	J11
Donaldson's Lodge *Nthumb*	118	G2
Doncaster *Donc*	91	P10
Doncaster Carr *Donc*	91	P10
Doncaster North Services		
Donc	91	R8
Donhead St Andrew *Wilts*	20	H10
Donhead St Mary *Wilts*	20	H10
Donibristle *Fife*	134	F10
Doniford *Somset*	18	E6
Donington *Lincs*	74	D3
Donington on Bain *Lincs*	86	H4
Donington Park Services		
Leics	72	D5
Donington Southing *Lincs*	74	D4
Donisthorpe *Leics*	59	M2
Donkey Street *Kent*	27	K5
Donkey Town *Surrey*	23	P2
Donnington *Gloucs*	47	N9
Donnington *Herefs*	46	D8

Donnington *Shrops*	57	K3
Donnington *W Berk*	34	E11
Donnington *W Susx*	15	N6
Donnington *Wrekin*	57	N2
Donnington Wood *Wrekin*	57	N2
Donyatt *Somset*	10	G2
Doomsday Green *W Susx*	24	E5
Doonfoot *S Ayrs*	114	F4
Dora's Green *Hants*	23	M5
Dorback Lodge *Highld*	149	K4
Dorchester *Dorset*	11	P6
Dorchester-on-Thames		
Oxon	34	G6
Dordon *Warwks*	59	L4
Dore *Sheff*	84	D4
Dores *Highld*	155	Q11
Dorking *Surrey*	36	E11
Dorking Tye *Suffk*	52	F4
Dormansland *Surrey*	25	K2
Dormans Park *Surrey*	25	J2
Dormington *Herefs*	46	A6
Dormston *Worcs*	47	J3
Dorn *Gloucs*	47	P8
Dorney *Bucks*	35	P9
Dorney Reach *Bucks*	35	P9
Dornie *Highld*	145	Q2
Dornoch *Highld*	162	H9
Dornock *D & G*	110	D7
Dorrery *Highld*	167	J6
Dorridge *Solhll*	59	J10
Dorrington *Lincs*	86	E10
Dorrington *Shrops*	56	H4
Dorrington *Shrops*	70	C6
Dorsington *Warwks*	47	M5
Dorstone *Herefs*	45	L6
Dorton *Bucks*	35	J2
Dosthill *Staffs*	59	K5
Dothan *IoA*	78	F10
Dottery *Dorset*	11	K5
Doublebois *Cnwll*	5	K9
Doughton *Gloucs*	32	G6
Douglas *IoM*	80	e6
Douglas *S Lans*	116	A4
Douglas and Angus *C Dund*	142	G11
Douglas Pier *Ag & B*	131	P8
Douglastown *Angus*	142	G8
Douglas Water *S Lans*	116	B3
Douglas West *S Lans*	126	E11
Doulting *Somset*	20	B6
Dounby *Ork*	169	b4
Doune *Highld*	161	Q6
Doune *Stirlg*	133	L7
Dounepark *S Ayrs*	114	C8
Dounie *Highld*	162	D8
Dousland *Devon*	6	E5
Dovaston *Shrops*	69	L10
Dove Dale *Derbys*	71	L4
Dove Green *Notts*	84	G10
Dove Holes *Derbys*	83	N9
Dovenby *Cumb*	100	E4
Dover *Kent*	27	P3
Dover *Wigan*	82	D4
Dover Castle *Kent*	27	P3
Dovercourt *Essex*	53	M5
Doverdale *Worcs*	58	C11
Doveridge *Derbys*	71	L8
Doversgreen *Surrey*	36	G11
Dowally *P & K*	141	P8
Dowbridge *Lancs*	88	E4
Dowdeswell *Gloucs*	47	K11
Dowlais *Myr Td*	30	E3
Dowland *Devon*	17	K9
Dowlish Ford *Somset*	10	H2
Dowlish Wake *Somset*	10	H2
Down Ampney *Gloucs*	33	L5
Downderry *Cnwll*	5	N11
Downe *Gt Lon*	37	K8
Downend *Gloucs*	32	F5
Downend *IoW*	14	F9
Downend *S Glos*	32	C9
Downend *W Berk*	34	E9
Downfield *C Dund*	142	F11
Downgate *Cnwll*	5	M7
Downgate *Cnwll*	5	P7
Downham *Essex*	38	B2
Downham *Gt Lon*	37	J6
Downham *Lancs*	89	M2
Downham Market *Norfk*	75	M10
Down Hatherley *Gloucs*	46	G10
Downhead *Somset*	19	Q9
Downhead *Somset*	20	C5
Downhill *Cnwll*	4	D8
Downhill *P & K*	134	C2
Downholland Cross *Lancs*	88	D9
Downholme *N York*	103	M11
Downicarey *Devon*	5	P3
Downies *Abers*	151	N9
Downing *Flints*	80	H9
Downley *Bucks*	35	M5
Down St Mary *Devon*	8	H4
Downside *Somset*	20	B4
Downside *Somset*	20	B6
Downside *Surrey*	36	D9
Down Thomas *Devon*	6	E8
Downton *Hants*	13	N6
Downton *Wilts*	21	N10
Dowsby *Lincs*	74	B5
Dowsdale *Lincs*	74	E8
Doxey *Staffs*	70	F10
Doxford *Nthumb*	119	N6
Doynton *S Glos*	32	D10
Draethen *Caerph*	30	H7
Draffan *S Lans*	126	D3
Dragonby *N Linc*	92	G7
Dragons Green *W Susx*	24	D6
Drakeholes *Notts*	85	M3
Drakelow *Worcs*	57	Q8
Drakemyre *N Ayrs*	124	H7
Drakes Broughton *Worcs*	46	H5
Drakewalls *Cnwll*	6	C4
Draughton *N York*	96	F10
Draughton *W Nthn*	60	G5
Drax *N York*	92	A5
Drax Hales *N York*	91	R5
Draycote *Warwks*	59	P10
Draycot Foliat *Swindn*	33	N9
Draycott *Gloucs*	72	C4
Draycott *Gloucs*	47	Q6
Draycott *Shrops*	57	Q6
Draycott *Somset*	19	M4
Draycott *Somset*	19	Q10
Draycott *Worcs*	46	G5
Draycott in the Clay *Staffs*	71	M9
Draycott in the Moors		
Staffs	70	H6
Drayford *Devon*	9	J2

Drayton *C Port*	15	J5
Drayton *Leics*	60	H2
Drayton *Lincs*	74	D3
Drayton *Norfk*	76	H9
Drayton *Oxon*	34	E6
Drayton *Oxon*	48	D8
Drayton *Somset*	19	M10
Drayton *Somset*	19	N11
Drayton *Worcs*	58	D9
Drayton Bassett *Staffs*	59	J4
Drayton Beauchamp *Bucks*	35	P2
Drayton Manor Resort		
Staffs	59	J4
Drayton Parslow *Bucks*	49	M9
Drayton St Leonard *Oxon*	34	G5
Drebley *N York*	96	G9
Dreemskerry *IoM*	80	g3
Dreen Hill *Pembks*	40	H8
Drefach *Carmth*	28	F2
Drefach *Carmth*	42	G7
Drefach *Cerdgn*	43	J5
Drefelin *Carmth*	42	G7
Dreghorn *N Ayrs*	125	K10
Drellingore *Kent*	27	M3
Drem *E Loth*	128	E4
Dresden *C Stke*	70	G6
Drewsteignton *Devon*	8	H6
Driby *Lincs*	87	L6
Driffield *E R Yk*	99	L9
Driffield *Gloucs*	33	L5
Driffield Cross Roads		
Gloucs	33	L5
Drift *Cnwll*	2	C8
Drigg *Cumb*	100	E11
Drighlington *Leeds*	90	G5
Drimnin *Highld*	137	P5
Drimpton *Dorset*	11	J4
Drimsallie *Highld*	138	H2
Dringhouses *C York*	98	B11
Drinkstone *Suffk*	64	D9
Drinkstone Green *Suffk*	64	D9
Drive End *Dorset*	11	M3
Driver's End *Herts*	50	F6
Drointon *Staffs*	71	J9
Droitwich Spa *Worcs*	46	G2
Dron *P & K*	134	E4
Dronfield *Derbys*	84	E5
Dronfield Woodhouse		
Derbys	84	D5
Drongan *E Ayrs*	114	H4
Dronley *Angus*	142	E10
Droop *Dorset*	12	C3
Dropping Well *Rothm*	84	E2
Droxford *Hants*	22	H11
Droylsden *Tamesd*	83	K5
Druid *Denbgs*	68	D6
Druidston *Pembks*	40	G7
Druimarbin *Highld*	139	K3
Druimavuic *Ag & B*	139	J8
Druimdrishaig *Ag & B*	123	M5
Druimindarroch *Highld*	145	L11
Drum *Ag & B*	124	A2
Drum *P & K*	134	C7
Drumalbin *S Lans*	116	C3
Drumbeg *Highld*	164	D10
Drumblade *Abers*	158	E9
Drumbreddon *D & G*	106	C9
Drumbuie *Highld*	153	P11
Drumburgh *Cumb*	110	E9
Drumburn *D & G*	109	J10
Drumburn *D & G*	109	L8
Drumchapel *C Glas*	125	N3
Drumchastle *P & K*	140	G6
Drumclog *S Lans*	125	Q10
Drumeldrie *Fife*	135	L7
Drumelzier *Border*	116	G4
Drumfearn *Highld*	145	L4
Drumfrennie *Abers*	151	J8
Drumgley *Angus*	142	G7
Drumguish *Highld*	148	B8
Drumin *Moray*	157	M11
Drumjohn *D & G*	115	K8
Drumlamford *S Ayrs*	107	J2
Drumlasie *Abers*	150	G6
Drumleaning *Cumb*	110	E10
Drumlemble *Ag & B*	120	C8
Drumlithie *Abers*	151	K11
Drummoddie *D & G*	107	L8
Drummore *D & G*	106	F10
Drummuir *Moray*	158	A9
Drumnadrochit *Highld*	155	P11
Drumnagorrach *Moray*	158	D7
Drumoak *Abers*	151	K8
Drumpark *D & G*	109	J5
Drumrunie *Highld*	161	K5
Drumshang *S Ayrs*	114	E5
Drumuie *Highld*	152	H8
Drumuillie *Highld*	148	G3
Drumvaich *Stirlg*	133	K7
Drunzie *P & K*	134	E6
Druridge *Nthumb*	119	Q11
Drury *Flints*	69	J2
Drws-y-coed *Gwynd*	67	J4
Drybeck *W & F*	102	C7
Drybridge *Moray*	158	B5
Drybridge *N Ayrs*	125	K10
Drybrook *Gloucs*	46	B11
Dryburgh *Border*	118	A4
Dry Doddington *Lincs*	85	Q11
Dry Drayton *Cambs*	62	E8
Dryhill *Kent*	37	L10
Drymen *Stirlg*	132	F10
Drymuir *Abers*	159	M8
Drynoch *Highld*	152	G11
Dry Sandford *Oxon*	34	E4
Dryslwyn *Carmth*	43	L10
Dry Street *Essex*	37	Q3
Dryton *Shrops*	57	K3
Dubford *Abers*	159	J5
Dublin *Suffk*	64	H8
Duchally *Highld*	161	P3
Duck End *Bed*	50	C2
Duck End *Cambs*	62	B8
Duck End *Essex*	51	Q4
Duck End *Essex*	51	R4
Duckend Green *Essex*	52	B7
Duckington *Ches W*	69	N4
Ducklington *Oxon*	34	C3
Duck's Cross *Bed*	61	P9
Duddenhoe End *Essex*	51	L3
Duddingston *C Edin*	127	P3
Duddington *N Nthn*	73	P10
Duddlestone *Somset*	18	H10
Duddleswell *E Susx*	25	L5
Duddlewick *Shrops*	57	M8
Duddo *Nthumb*	118	H2

Duddon Ches W....69 P2
Duddon Bridge Cumb....94 D3
Duddon Common Ches W....81 Q11
Dudleston Shrops....69 K7
Dudleston Heath Shrops....69 L7
Dudley Dudley....58 D6
Dudley N Tyne....113 L6
Dudley Hill C Brad....90 F4
Dudley Port Sandw....58 E6
Dudnill Shrops....57 L10
Dudsbury Dorset....13 J5
Dudswell Herts....35 Q3
Duffield Derbys....72 A2
Duffryn Neath....29 M5
Dufftown Moray....157 Q9
Duffus Moray....157 M4
Dufton W & F....102 C5
Duggleby N York....98 H7
Duirinish Highld....153 P11
Duisdalemore Highld....145 M5
Duisky Highld....139 J2
Dukestown Blae G....30 F2
Duke Street Suffk....53 J3
Dukinfield Tamesd....83 K5
Dulas IoA....78 H7
Dulcote Somset....19 Q6
Dulford Devon....9 Q3
Dull P & K....141 K8
Dullatur N Lans....126 C2
Dullingham Cambs....63 K9
Dullingham Ley Cambs....63 K9
Dulnain Bridge Highld....148 H3
Duloe Bed....61 Q8
Duloe Cnwll....5 L10
Dulsie Bridge Highld....156 G9
Dulverton Somset....18 B9
Dulwich Gt Lon....36 H6
Dumbarton W Duns....125 L2
Dumbleton Gloucs....47 K7
Dumfries D & G....109 L5
Dumgoyne Stirlg....132 G11
Dummer Hants....22 G5
Dumpton Kent....39 Q8
Dun Angus....143 M6
Dunalastair P & K....140 H6
Dunan Highld....145 J2
Dunan P & K....140 C6
Dunaverty Ag & B....120 C10
Dunball Somset....19 K6
Dunbar E Loth....128 H4
Dunbeath Highld....167 L11
Dunbeg Ag & B....138 F11
Dunblane Stirlg....133 M7
Dunbog Fife....134 H4
Dunbridge Hants....22 B9
Duncanston Highld....155 Q6
Duncanstone Abers....150 F2
Dunchideock Devon....9 L7
Dunchurch Warwks....59 Q10
Duncote W Nthn....49 J4
Duncow D & G....109 L4
Duncrievie P & K....134 E6
Duncton W Susx....23 Q11
Dundee C Dund....142 G11
Dundee Airport C Dund....135 K2
Dundon Somset....19 N8
Dundonald S Ayrs....125 K11
Dundonnell Highld....160 H9
Dundraw Cumb....110 D11
Dundreggan Highld....147 J5
Dundrennan D & G....108 F11
Dundry N Som....31 Q11
Dunecht Abers....151 K6
Dunfermline Fife....134 D10
Dunfield Gloucs....33 M5
Dunford Bridge Barns....83 Q4
Dungate Kent....38 F10
Dungavel S Lans....126 B10
Dunge Wilts....20 G4
Dungeness Kent....27 J8
Dungworth Sheff....84 C3
Dunham Massey Traffd....82 F7
Dunham-on-the-Hill
   Ches W....81 P10
Dunham-on-Trent Notts....85 P6
Dunhampstead Worcs....46 H2
Dunhampton Worcs....58 B11
Dunham Town Traffd....82 F7
Dunham Woodhouses Traffd....82 F7
Dunholme Lincs....86 D5
Dunino Fife....135 N5
Dunipace Falk....133 N11
Dunkeld P & K....141 P9
Dunkerton BaNES....20 D3
Dunkeswell Devon....10 C3
Dunkeswick N York....97 M11
Dunkirk Ches W....81 M10
Dunkirk Kent....39 J10
Dunkirk S Glos....32 E7
Dunkirk Wilts....21 J2
Dunk's Green Kent....37 P10
Dunlappie Angus....143 K4
Dunley Hants....22 E4
Dunley Worcs....57 P11
Dunlop E Ayrs....125 L8
Dunmaglass Highld....147 P3
Dunmere Cnwll....4 G9
Dunmore Falk....133 P10
Dunnet Highld....167 M2
Dunnichen Angus....143 J8
Dunning P & K....134 C5
Dunnington C York....98 D10
Dunnington E R Yk....99 P10
Dunnington Warwks....47 L4
Dunnockshaw Lancs....89 N5
Dunn Street Kent....38 C9
Dunoon Ag & B....124 F2
Dunphail Moray....157 J8
Dunragit D & G....106 G6
Duns Border....129 K9
Dunsa Derbys....84 B6
Dunsby Lincs....74 B5
Dunscar Bolton....89 L8
Dunscore D & G....109 J4
Dunscroft Donc....91 Q9
Dunsdale R & Cl....104 H7
Dunsden Green Oxon....35 K9
Dunsdon Devon....16 E10
Dunsfold Surrey....24 B3
Dunsford Devon....9 K7
Dunshalt Fife....134 G5
Dunshillock Abers....159 N8
Dunsill Notts....84 G8
Dunsley N York....105 N8
Dunsley Staffs....58 C8
Dunsmore Bucks....35 N3

Dunsop Bridge Lancs....95 P11
Dunstable C Beds....50 B6
Dunstall Staffs....71 M10
Dunstall Common Worcs....46 G6
Dunstall Green Suffk....63 M8
Dunstan Nthumb....119 P7
Dunstan Steads Nthumb....119 P6
Dunster Somset....18 C6
Duns Tew Oxon....48 E9
Dunston Gatesd....113 K8
Dunston Lincs....86 E8
Dunston Norfk....77 J11
Dunston Staffs....70 G11
Dunstone Devon....6 F8
Dunstone Devon....8 H9
Dunston Heath Staffs....70 G11
Dunsville Donc....91 Q9
Dunswell E R Yk....93 J3
Dunsyre S Lans....127 K8
Dunterton Devon....5 P6
Dunthrop Oxon....48 C9
Duntisbourne Abbots
   Gloucs....33 J3
Duntisbourne Leer Gloucs....33 J3
Duntisbourne Rouse Gloucs....33 J3
Duntish Dorset....11 P3
Duntocher W Duns....125 M3
Dunton Bucks....49 M10
Dunton C Beds....50 F2
Dunton Norfk....76 B5
Dunton Bassett Leics....60 B2
Dunton Green Kent....37 M9
Dunton Wayletts Essex....37 Q2
Duntulm Highld....152 G3
Dunure S Ayrs....114 E4
Dunvant Swans....28 G6
Dunvegan Highld....152 D8
Dunwich Suffk....65 P7
Dunwood Staffs....70 G3
Durdar Cumb....110 H10
Durgan Cnwll....3 K6
Durgates E Susx....25 P4
Durham Dur....103 Q2
Durham Cathedral Dur....103 Q2
Durham Services Dur....104 B3
Durisdeer D & G....116 B10
Durisdeermill D & G....116 B10
Durkar Wakefd....91 J7
Durleigh Somset....19 J7
Durley Hants....22 F11
Durley Wilts....21 P2
Durley Street Hants....22 F11
Durlock Kent....39 N10
Durlock Kent....39 P9
Durlow Common Herefs....46 B7
Durn Rochdl....89 Q7
Durness Highld....165 K3
Durno Abers....151 J2
Duror Highld....138 H6
Durran Ag & B....131 K6
Durrington W Susx....24 D9
Durrington Wilts....21 N6
Dursley Gloucs....32 E5
Dursley Cross Gloucs....46 C10
Durston Somset....19 J9
Durweston Dorset....12 E3
Duston W Nthn....60 F8
Duthil Highld....148 G3
Dutlas Powys....56 C9
Duton Hill Essex....51 P5
Dutson Cnwll....5 N4
Dutton Ches W....82 C9
Duxford Cambs....62 G11
Duxford Oxon....34 C5
Duxford IWM Cambs....62 G11
Dwygyfylchi Conwy....79 N9
Dwyran IoA....78 G11
Dyce C Aber....151 M5
Dyer's End Essex....52 B4
Dyfatty Carmth....28 E4
Dyffrydan Gwynd....54 F2
Dyffryn Brdgnd....29 N6
Dyffryn Myr Td....30 E4
Dyffryn V Glam....30 E10
Dyffryn Ardudwy Gwynd....67 K10
Dyffryn Castell Cerdgn....54 H8
Dyffryn Cellwen Neath....29 N2
Dyke Lincs....74 B6
Dyke Moray....156 H6
Dykehead Angus....142 C7
Dykehead Angus....142 F6
Dykehead N Lans....126 F6
Dykehead Stirlg....132 H8
Dykelands Abers....143 N4
Dykends Angus....142 D6
Dykeside Abers....158 H9
Dykes of Gray C Dund....142 E11
Dylife Powys....55 K6
Dymchurch Kent....27 K6
Dymock Gloucs....46 D8
Dynamic Earth C Edin....127 P3
Dyrham S Glos....32 D9
Dysart Fife....135 J9
Dyserth Denbgs....80 F9

E

Eachway Worcs....58 E9
Eachwick Nthumb....112 H6
Eagland Hill Lancs....95 J11
Eagle Lincs....85 Q7
Eagle Barnsdale Lincs....85 Q7
Eagle Moor Lincs....85 Q7
Eaglescliffe S on T....104 D7
Eaglesfield Cumb....100 E5
Eaglesfield D & G....110 D6
Eaglesham E Rens....125 P7
Eagley Bolton....89 L8
Eairy IoM....80 c6
Eakring Notts....85 L8
Ealand N Linc....92 C8
Ealing Gt Lon....36 E4
Eamont Bridge W & F....101 P5
Earby Lancs....96 D11
Earcroft Bl w D....89 K6
Eardington Shrops....57 N6
Eardisland Herefs....45 N3
Eardisley Herefs....45 L5
Eardiston Shrops....69 L9
Eardiston Worcs....57 M11
Earith Cambs....62 E5
Earle Nthumb....119 J5
Earlestown St Hel....82 C5

Earley Wokham....35 K10
Earlham Norfk....76 H10
Earlish Highld....152 F5
Earls Barton N Nthn....61 J8
Earls Colne Essex....52 E6
Earls Common Worcs....47 J3
Earl's Croome Worcs....46 G6
Earlsditton Shrops....57 L9
Earlsdon Covtry....59 M9
Earl's Down E Susx....25 P7
Earlsferry Fife....135 M7
Earlsfield Gt Lon....36 G6
Earlsford Abers....159 K11
Earl's Green Suffk....64 E8
Earlsheaton Kirk....90 H6
Earl Shilton Leics....72 D11
Earl Soham Suffk....65 J9
Earl Sterndale Derbys....83 N11
Earlston Border....117 R3
Earlston E Ayrs....125 L10
Earl Stonham Suffk....64 G10
Earlswood Surrey....36 G11
Earlswood Warwks....58 H10
Earlswood Common Mons....31 N6
Earnley W Susx....15 M7
Earnshaw Bridge Lancs....88 G5
Earsdon N Tyne....113 M6
Earsdon Nthumb....113 J2
Earsham Norfk....65 L4
Earswick C York....98 C9
Eartham W Susx....15 P5
Earthcott S Glos....32 C7
Easby N York....104 F9
Easdale Ag & B....130 E4
Easebourne W Susx....23 N4
Easenhall Warwks....59 Q9
Eashing Surrey....23 P6
Easington Bucks....35 J2
Easington Dur....104 D2
Easington E R Yk....93 Q7
Easington Nthumb....119 M4
Easington Oxon....35 J5
Easington R & Cl....105 K7
Easington Colliery Dur....104 D2
Easington Lane Sundld....113 N10
Easingwold N York....98 A7
Easole Street Kent....39 N11
Eassie and Nevay Angus....142 E9
East Aberthaw V Glam....30 D11
East Allington Devon....7 K9
East Anstey Devon....17 R6
East Anton Hants....22 C5
East Appleton N York....103 P11
East Ardsley Leeds....91 J5
East Ashey IoW....14 G9
East Ashling W Susx....15 M5
East Aston Hants....22 D5
East Ayton N York....99 K3
East Balsdon Cnwll....5 M2
East Bank Blae G....30 H3
East Barkwith Lincs....86 G4
East Barming Kent....38 B11
East Barnby N York....105 M8
East Barnet Gt Lon....50 G11
East Barns E Loth....129 J4
East Barsham Norfk....76 C5
East Beckham Norfk....76 H4
East Bedfont Gt Lon....36 C6
East Bergholt Suffk....53 J5
East Bierley Kirk....90 F5
East Bilney Norfk....76 D8
East Blatchington E Susx....25 L11
East Bloxworth Dorset....12 E6
East Boldon S Tyne....113 N8
East Boldre Hants....14 C6
East Bolton Nthumb....119 M7
Eastbourne Darltn....104 B8
Eastbourne E Susx....25 P11
East Bower Somset....19 K7
East Bradenham Norfk....76 C10
East Brent Somset....19 K4
Eastbridge Suffk....65 P8
East Bridgford Notts....72 H2
East Briscoe Dur....103 J7
Eastbrook V Glam....30 G10
East Buckland Devon....17 M5
East Budleigh Devon....9 Q8
Eastburn C Brad....90 C2
Eastburn E R Yk....99 K9
East Burnham Bucks....35 Q8
East Burton Dorset....12 D7
Eastbury W Berk....34 B9
East Butsfield Dur....112 H11
East Butterwick N Linc....92 D9
Eastby N York....96 F10
East Calder W Loth....127 K4
East Carleton Norfk....76 H11
East Carlton Leeds....90 G2
East Carlton N Nthn....60 H3
East Chaldon Dorset....12 C8
East Challow Oxon....34 C7
East Charleton Devon....7 K10
East Chelborough Dorset....11 M3
East Chiltington E Susx....25 J7
East Chinnock Somset....11 L2
East Chisenbury Wilts....21 M4
Eastchurch Kent....38 G7
East Clandon Surrey....36 C10
East Claydon Bucks....49 K9
East Clevedon N Som....31 M10
East Coker Somset....11 L2
Eastcombe Gloucs....32 G4
Eastcombe Somset....18 G8
East Compton Somset....20 B6
East Cornworthy Devon....7 L7
East Cote Cumb....109 P9
Eastcote Gt Lon....36 D3
Eastcote Solhll....59 J9
Eastcote W Nthn....49 J4
Eastcott Cnwll....16 D8
Eastcott Wilts....21 K3
East Cottingwith E R Yk....92 B2
Eastcourt Wilts....21 P2
Eastcourt Wilts....21 J6
East Cowes IoW....14 F7
East Cowick E R Yk....91 R6
East Cowton N York....104 B10
East Cramlington Nthumb....113 L5
East Cranmore Somset....20 C6
East Creech Dorset....12 F8
East Curthwaite Cumb....110 F11
East Dean E Susx....25 N11
East Dean Gloucs....46 C10
East Dean Hants....21 Q9
East Dean W Susx....15 P4

Eastdown Devon....7 L9
East Down Devon....17 L3
East Drayton Notts....85 N5
East Dulwich Gt Lon....36 H5
East Dundry N Som....31 Q11
East Ella C KuH....93 J5
East End Bed....61 P9
East End C Beds....49 Q6
East End E R Yk....93 L4
East End E R Yk....93 N5
East End Essex....38 F3
East End Essex....51 K8
East End Hants....14 C7
East End Hants....22 D2
East End Herts....51 L5
East End Kent....26 D4
East End Kent....38 G7
East End M Keyn....49 P6
East End Oxon....48 C11
East End Somset....20 C5
East End Suffk....53 K4
Easter Balmoral Abers....149 P9
Easter Compton S Glos....31 Q8
Easter Dalziel Highld....156 D7
Eastergate W Susx....15 P5
Easterhouse C Glas....126 B4
Easter Howgate Mdloth....127 N5
Easter Kinkell Highld....155 Q6
Easter Moniack Highld....155 Q9
Eastern Green Covtry....59 L9
Easter Ord Abers....151 L7
Easter Pitkierie Fife....135 P6
Easter Skeld Shet....169 q9
Easter Softlaw Border....118 E4
Easterton Wilts....21 K4
Eastertown Somset....19 K4
East Everleigh Wilts....21 P4
East Farleigh Kent....38 B11
East Farndon N Nthn....60 F4
East Ferry Lincs....92 D11
Eastfield N Lans....126 F5
Eastfield N York....99 L4
East Firsby Lincs....86 D3
East Fortune E Loth....128 E4
East Garforth Leeds....91 L4
East Garston W Berk....34 C9
Eastgate Dur....103 J3
Eastgate Lincs....74 B7
Eastgate Norfk....76 G7
East Ginge Oxon....34 D7
East Goscote Leics....72 G8
East Grafton Wilts....21 Q2
East Green Suffk....65 N8
East Grimstead Wilts....21 P9
East Grinstead W Susx....25 J3
East Guldeford E Susx....26 F7
East Haddon N Nthn....60 E7
East Hagbourne Oxon....34 F7
East Halton N Linc....93 K7
East Ham Gt Lon....37 K4
Eastham Wirral....81 M8
Eastham Ferry Wirral....81 M8
Easthampton Herefs....45 N2
East Hanney Oxon....34 D6
East Hanningfield Essex....52 C11
East Hardwick Wakefd....91 M7
East Harling Norfk....64 D4
East Harlsey N York....104 D11
East Harnham Wilts....21 M9
East Harptree BaNES....19 Q3
East Hartford Nthumb....113 L5
East Harting W Susx....23 L11
East Hatch Wilts....20 H9
East Hatley Cambs....62 C10
East Hauxwell N York....97 J2
East Haven Angus....143 K10
Eastheath Wokham....35 L11
East Heckington Lincs....74 C2
East Hedleyhope Dur....103 N2
East Helmsdale Highld....163 N3
East Hendred Oxon....34 E7
East Heslerton N York....99 J5
East Hewish N Som....19 L2
East Hoathly E Susx....25 M7
East Holme Dorset....12 E7
East Hope Dur....103 K9
Easthope Shrops....57 K5
Easthorpe Essex....52 F7
Easthorpe Notts....85 M10
East Horrington Somset....19 Q5
East Horsley Surrey....36 C10
East Horton Nthumb....119 K4
East Howe BCP....13 J5
East Huntspill Somset....19 K5
East Hyde C Beds....50 D7
East Ilkerton Devon....17 N2
East Ilsley W Berk....34 E8
Eastington Devon....8 H3
Eastington Gloucs....32 E3
Eastington Gloucs....33 M2
East Keal Lincs....87 L8
East Kennett Wilts....33 M11
East Keswick Leeds....91 K2
East Kilbride S Lans....125 Q7
East Kimber Devon....8 D5
East Kirkby Lincs....87 K8
East Knighton Dorset....12 D7
East Knowstone Devon....17 Q7
East Knoyle Wilts....20 G8
East Lambrook Somset....19 M11
Eastlands D & G....108 H4
East Langdon Kent....27 P2
East Langton Leics....60 F2
East Lavant W Susx....15 M5
East Lavington W Susx....23 P11
East Layton N York....103 N9
Eastleach Martin Gloucs....33 P4
Eastleach Turville Gloucs....33 N3
East Leake Notts....72 F5
East Learmouth Nthumb....118 G3
East Leigh Devon....6 H8
East Leigh Devon....7 K7
East Leigh Devon....8 G3
Eastleigh Devon....16 H6
Eastleigh Hants....22 E11
East Lexham Norfk....76 B8
East Linton E Loth....128 F4
East Liss Hants....23 L9
East Lockinge Oxon....34 D7
East Lound N Linc....92 C11
East Lulworth Dorset....12 E8
East Lutton N York....99 J7
East Lydeard Somset....18 G9
East Lydford Somset....19 Q9
East Lyng Somset....19 K9
East Malling Kent....38 B10

East Malling Heath Kent....37 Q9
East Marden W Susx....15 M4
East Markham Notts....85 M6
East Martin Hants....21 L11
East Marton N York....96 D10
East Meon Hants....23 J10
East Mere Devon....18 C11
East Mersea Essex....52 H7
East Midlands Airport Leics....72 D5
East Molesey Surrey....36 D7
Eastmoor Norfk....75 P10
East Morden Dorset....12 F6
East Morton C Brad....90 D2
East Morton D & G....116 B10
East Ness N York....98 D5
East Newton E R Yk....93 N3
Eastney C Port....15 J7
Eastnor Herefs....46 D7
East Norton Leics....73 K10
Eastoft N Linc....92 D7
East Ogwell Devon....7 L4
Easton Cambs....61 P6
Easton Cumb....110 E9
Easton Cumb....110 H7
Easton Dorset....11 P10
Easton Hants....22 F8
Easton Lincs....73 N5
Easton Norfk....76 G9
Easton Somset....19 P5
Easton Suffk....65 K10
Easton W Berk....34 D10
Easton Wilts....32 G10
Easton Grey Wilts....32 G7
Easton-in-Gordano N Som....31 P9
Easton Maudit N Nthn....61 J9
Easton-on-the-Hill N Nthn....73 Q10
Easton Royal Wilts....21 P2
East Orchard Dorset....20 F11
East Ord Nthumb....129 P9
East Panson Devon....5 P3
East Parley BCP....13 J5
East Peckham Kent....37 Q11
East Pennard Somset....19 Q7
East Portlemouth Devon....7 K11
East Prawle Devon....7 K11
East Preston W Susx....24 C10
East Pulham Dorset....11 Q3
East Putford Devon....16 F8
East Quantoxhead Somset....18 F6
East Rainham Medway....38 D8
East Rainton Sundld....113 M11
East Ravendale NE Lin....93 M11
East Raynham Norfk....76 B6
Eastrea Cambs....74 E11
Eastriggs D & G....110 D7
East Rigton Leeds....91 K2
Eastrington E R Yk....92 C5
East Rolstone N Som....19 L2
Eastrop Swindn....33 P6
East Rounton N York....104 D10
East Rudham Norfk....76 A6
East Runton Norfk....76 H3
East Ruston Norfk....77 L6
Eastry Kent....39 P11
East Saltoun E Loth....128 D6
Eastshaw W Susx....23 N10
East Sheen Gt Lon....36 F6
East Shefford W Berk....34 C10
East Sleekburn Nthumb....113 L4
East Somerton Norfk....77 P8
East Stockwith Lincs....85 P3
East Stoke Dorset....12 E7
East Stoke Notts....85 N11
East Stour Dorset....20 F10
East Stour Common Dorset....20 F10
East Stourmouth Kent....39 N9
East Stowford Devon....17 L7
East Stratton Hants....22 F6
East Studdal Kent....27 P2
East Sutton Kent....26 D2
East Taphouse Cnwll....5 K9
East-the-Water Devon....16 H6
East Thirston Nthumb....119 N10
East Tilbury Thurr....37 Q5
East Tilbury Village Thurr....37 Q5
East Tisted Hants....23 K8
East Torrington Lincs....86 F4
East Tuddenham Norfk....76 F9
East Tytherley Hants....21 Q9
East Tytherton Wilts....33 J10
East Village Devon....9 K3
Eastville Bristl....32 B10
Eastville Lincs....87 M9
East Wall Shrops....57 J6
East Walton Norfk....75 P7
East Water Somset....19 P4
East Week Devon....8 G6
Eastwell Leics....73 K5
East Wellow Hants....22 B10
East Wemyss Fife....135 K9
East Whitburn W Loth....126 H4
Eastwick Herts....51 K8
East Wickham Gt Lon....37 L5
East Williamston Pembks....41 L10
East Winch Norfk....75 N7
East Winterslow Wilts....21 P8
East Wittering W Susx....15 L7
East Witton N York....96 H3
Eastwood Notts....84 G11
East Woodburn Nthumb....112 D3
Eastwood End Cambs....62 D2
East Woodhay Hants....22 D2
East Woodlands Somset....20 E6
East Worldham Hants....23 L7
East Worthing W Susx....24 E10
East Wretham Norfk....64 C3
East Youlstone Devon....16 D9
Eathorpe Warwks....59 N11
Eaton Ches E....83 J11
Eaton Ches W....69 Q3
Eaton Leics....73 K5
Eaton Norfk....77 J10
Eaton Notts....85 M5
Eaton Oxon....34 C4
Eaton Shrops....56 F7
Eaton Shrops....57 J7
Eaton Bishop Herefs....45 N7
Eaton Bray C Beds....49 Q10
Eaton Constantine Shrops....57 K3
Eaton Ford Cambs....61 Q9
Eaton Green C Beds....49 Q10
Eaton Hastings Oxon....33 Q5
Eaton Mascott Shrops....57 J3
Eaton Socon Cambs....61 Q9
Eaton upon Tern Shrops....70 B10

Eaves Brow – Farleton 269

Eaves Brow Warrtn 82 D6
Eaves Green Solhll 59 L8
Ebberston N York 98 H4
Ebbesborne Wake Wilts 21 J10
Ebbsfleet Kent 37 P6
Ebbw Vale Blae G 30 G3
Ebchester Dur 112 H9
Ebdon N Som 19 L2
Ebernoe W Susx 23 Q9
Ebford Devon 9 N7
Ebley Gloucs 32 F3
Ebnal Ches W 69 N5
Ebnall Herefs 45 P3
Ebrington Gloucs 47 N6
Ebsworthy Devon 8 D6
Ecchinswell Hants 22 E3
Ecclaw Border 129 K6
Ecclefechan D & G 110 C6
Eccles Border 118 E2
Eccles Kent 38 B9
Eccles Salfd 82 G5
Ecclesall Sheff 84 D4
Ecclesfield Sheff 84 E2
Eccles Green Herefs 45 M5
Eccleshall Staffs 70 E9
Eccleshill C Brad 90 F3
Ecclesmachan W Loth 127 K3
Eccles on Sea Norfk 77 N6
Eccles Road Norfk 64 E4
Eccleston Ches W 69 M2
Eccleston Lancs 88 G7
Eccleston St Hel 81 P5
Eccleston Green Lancs 88 G7
Echt Abers 151 J6
Eckford Border 118 D5
Eckington Derbys 84 F5
Eckington Worcs 46 H6
Ecton N Nthn 60 H8
Ecton Staffs 71 K3
Edale Derbys 83 P7
Eday Ork 169 e3
Eday Airport Ork 169 e3
Edburton W Susx 24 F8
Edderside Cumb 109 P11
Edderton Highld 162 G10
Eddington Cambs 62 F9
Eddington Kent 39 L8
Eddleston Border 127 N8
Eddlewood S Lans 126 C7
Edenbridge Kent 37 K11
Edenfield Lancs 89 N7
Edenhall W & F 101 Q4
Edenham Lincs 73 R6
Eden Mount W & F 95 J5
Eden Park Gt Lon 37 J7
Eden Project Cnwll 3 Q3
Edensor Derbys 84 B7
Edentaggart Ag & B 132 C9
Edenthorpe Donc 91 Q9
Edern Gwynd 66 D7
Edgarley Somset 19 P7
Edgbaston Birm 58 G8
Edgcott Bucks 49 J10
Edgcott Somset 17 Q4
Edgcumbe Cnwll 3 J7
Edge Gloucs 32 F3
Edge Shrops 56 F3
Edgebolton Shrops 69 Q10
Edge End Gloucs 31 Q2
Edgefield Norfk 76 F5
Edgefield Green Norfk 76 F5
Edgefold Bolton 89 L9
Edge Green Ches W 69 N4
Edgehill Warwks 48 C5
Edgerley Shrops 69 L11
Edgerton Kirk 90 E7
Edgeside Lancs 89 N6
Edgeworth Gloucs 32 H3
Edgeworthy Devon 9 K2
Edginswell Torbay 7 M5
Edgiock Worcs 47 K2
Edgmond Wrekin 70 C11
Edgmond Marsh Wrekin 70 C10
Edgton Shrops 56 F7
Edgware Gt Lon 36 E2
Edgworth Bl w D 89 L7
Edinbane Highld 152 E7
Edinburgh C Edin 127 P3
Edinburgh Airport C Edin 127 L3
Edinburgh Castle C Edin 127 P3
Edinburgh Old & New Town C Edin 127 P3
Edinburgh Zoo RZSS C Edin 127 N3
Edingale Staffs 59 K2
Edingham D & G 108 H8
Edingley Notts 85 L9
Edingthorpe Norfk 77 L5
Edingthorpe Green Norfk 77 L5
Edington Border 129 M9
Edington Nthumb 113 J4
Edington Somset 19 L7
Edington Wilts 20 H4
Edingworth Somset 19 L4
Edistone Devon 16 D7
Edithmead Somset 19 K5
Edith Weston Rutlnd 73 N9
Edlesborough Bucks 49 Q11
Edlingham Nthumb 119 M9
Edlington Lincs 86 H6
Edmond Castle Cumb 111 J9
Edmondsham Dorset 13 J2
Edmondsley Dur 113 K11
Edmondstown Rhondd 30 D6
Edmondthorpe Leics 73 M7
Edmonton Cnwll 4 F7
Edmonton Gt Lon 36 H2
Edmundbyers Dur 112 F10
Ednam Border 118 D3
Ednaston Derbys 71 N6
Edney Common Essex 51 Q10
Edradynate P & K 141 L7
Edrom Border 129 L8
Edstaston Shrops 69 P8
Edstone Warwks 47 N2
Edvin Loach Herefs 46 C3
Edwalton Notts 72 F3
Edwardstone Suffk 52 F3
Edwardsville Myr Td 30 E5
Edwinsford Carmth 43 M8
Edwinstowe Notts 85 K7
Edworth C Beds 50 F2
Edwyn Ralph Herefs 46 B3
Edzell Angus 143 L4
Edzell Woods Abers 143 L4
Efail-fach Neath 29 L5
Efail Isaf Rhondd 30 E8
Efailnewydd Gwynd 66 F7
Efail-Rhyd Powys 68 G9
Efailwen Carmth 41 M5
Efenechtyd Denbgs 68 F3
Effgill D & G 110 F2
Effingham Surrey 36 D10
Effingham Junction Surrey 36 D9
Efflinch Staffs 71 M11
Efford Devon 9 L4
Egbury Hants 22 D4
Egdean W Susx 23 Q10
Egerton Bolton 89 L8
Egerton Kent 26 F2
Egerton Forstal Kent 26 E2
Eggborough N York 91 P6
Eggbuckland C Plym 6 E7
Eggesford Devon 17 M9
Eggington C Beds 49 Q9
Egginton Derbys 71 P9
Egglescliffe S on T 104 D8
Eggleston Dur 103 J6
Egham Surrey 36 B6
Egham Wick Surrey 35 Q10
Egleton Rutlnd 73 M9
Eglingham Nthumb 119 M7
Egloshayle Cnwll 4 G7
Egloskerry Cnwll 5 M4
Eglwysbach Conwy 79 Q10
Eglwys-Brewis V Glam 30 D11
Eglwys Cross Wrexhm 69 N6
Eglwys Fach Cerdgn 54 F5
Eglwyswrw Pembks 41 M3
Egmanton Notts 85 M7
Egremont Cumb 100 D8
Egremont Wirral 81 L6
Egton N York 105 M9
Egton Bridge N York 105 M10
Egypt Bucks 35 Q7
Egypt Hants 22 E6
Eigg Highld 144 G10
Eight Ash Green Essex 52 F6
Eilanreach Highld 145 P4
Eilean Donan Castle Highld 145 Q2
Eisgein W Isls 168 i6
Eishken W Isls 168 i6
Eisteddfa Gurig Cerdgn 54 H8
Elan Valley Powys 55 K11
Elan Village Powys 44 C2
Elberton S Glos 32 B7
Elbridge W Susx 15 P6
Elburton C Plym 6 E8
Elcombe Swindn 33 M8
Elcot W Berk 34 C11
Eldernell Cambs 74 F11
Eldersfield Worcs 46 E8
Elderslie Rens 125 L5
Elder Street Essex 51 N4
Eldon Dur 103 P5
Eldwick C Brad 90 E2
Elerch Cerdgn 54 F7
Elfhill Abers 151 L10
Elford Nthumb 119 N4
Elford Staffs 59 J2
Elgin Moray 157 N5
Elgol Highld 144 H5
Elham Kent 27 L3
Elie Fife 135 M7
Elilaw Nthumb 119 J9
Elim IoA 78 F8
Eling Hants 14 C4
Elkesley Notts 85 L5
Elkstone Gloucs 33 J2
Ella Abers 158 F6
Ellacombe Torbay 7 N6
Elland Calder 90 E6
Elland Lower Edge Calder 90 E6
Ellary Ag & B 123 M4
Ellastone Staffs 71 L6
Ellel Lancs 95 K9
Ellemford Border 129 J7
Ellenabeich Ag & B 130 E4
Ellenborough Cumb 100 D3
Ellenbrook Salfd 82 F4
Ellenhall Staffs 70 E9
Ellen's Green Surrey 24 C3
Ellerbeck N York 104 D11
Ellerby N York 105 L8
Ellerdine Heath Wrekin 69 R10
Ellerhayes Devon 9 N4
Elleric Ag & B 139 J8
Ellerker E R Yk 92 F5
Ellers N York 90 C2
Ellerton E R Yk 92 B3
Ellerton N York 103 Q11
Ellerton Shrops 70 C9
Ellesborough Bucks 35 M3
Ellesmere Shrops 69 L8
Ellesmere Port Ches W 81 N9
Ellicombe Somset 18 C6
Ellingham Hants 13 K3
Ellingham Norfk 65 M3
Ellingham Nthumb 119 N5
Ellingstring N York 97 J4
Ellington Cambs 61 Q6
Ellington Nthumb 113 L2
Ellington Thorpe Cambs 61 Q6
Elliots Green Somset 20 E5
Ellisfield Hants 22 H5
Ellishader Highld 153 J4
Ellistown Leics 72 C8
Ellon Abers 159 N11
Ellonby W & F 101 M3
Ellough Suffk 65 N4
Elloughton E R Yk 92 F5
Ellwood Gloucs 31 Q3
Elm Cambs 75 J9
Elmbridge Worcs 58 D11
Elmdon Essex 51 L3
Elmdon Solhll 59 J8
Elmdon Heath Solhll 59 J8
Elmer W Susx 15 Q6
Elmers End Gt Lon 37 J7
Elmer's Green Lancs 88 G9
Elmesthorpe Leics 72 D11
Elm Green Essex 52 C10
Elmhurst Staffs 58 H2
Elmington N Nthn 61 N3
Elmley Castle Worcs 47 J6
Elmley Lovett Worcs 58 C11
Elmore Gloucs 46 E11
Elmore Back Gloucs 46 E11
Elm Park Gt Lon 37 M3
Elmscott Devon 16 C7
Elmsett Suffk 53 J2
Elms Green Worcs 57 N11
Elmstead Heath Essex 53 J7
Elmstead Market Essex 53 J7
Elmstead Row Essex 53 J7
Elmsted Kent 27 K3
Elmstone Kent 39 N9
Elmstone Hardwicke Gloucs 46 H9
Elmswell E R Yk 99 K9
Elmswell Suffk 64 D9
Elmton Derbys 84 H6
Elphin Highld 161 L4
Elphinstone E Loth 128 B6
Elrick Abers 151 L6
Elrig D & G 107 K8
Elrington Nthumb 112 C8
Elsdon Nthumb 112 D2
Elsecar Barns 91 K11
Elsenham Essex 51 M5
Elsfield Oxon 34 F2
Elsham N Linc 92 H8
Elsing Norfk 76 F8
Elslack N York 96 D11
Elson Hants 14 H6
Elson Shrops 69 L7
Elsrickle S Lans 116 F2
Elstead Surrey 23 P6
Elsted W Susx 23 M11
Elsted Marsh W Susx 23 M10
Elsthorpe Lincs 73 R6
Elstob Dur 104 B6
Elston Lancs 88 H4
Elston Notts 85 N11
Elston Wilts 21 L6
Elstone Devon 17 M8
Elstow Bed 61 N11
Elstree Herts 50 E11
Elstronwick E R Yk 93 M4
Elswick Lancs 88 E3
Elswick N u Ty 113 K8
Elsworth Cambs 62 D8
Elterwater W & F 101 K10
Eltham Gt Lon 37 K6
Eltisley Cambs 62 C9
Elton Bury 89 M8
Elton Cambs 61 N2
Elton Ches W 81 P9
Elton Derbys 84 B8
Elton Gloucs 32 D2
Elton Herefs 56 H10
Elton S on T 104 D7
Elton Green Ches W 81 P10
Elton-on-the-Hill Notts 73 K3
Eltringham Nthumb 112 G8
Elvanfoot S Lans 116 D7
Elvaston Derbys 72 C4
Elveden Suffk 63 P4
Elvetham Heath Hants 23 M3
Elvingston E Loth 128 D5
Elvington C York 98 E11
Elvington Kent 39 N11
Elwell Devon 17 M5
Elwick Hartpl 104 E4
Elwick Nthumb 119 M3
Elworth Ches E 70 C2
Elworthy Somset 18 E8
Ely Cambs 62 H4
Ely Cardif 30 F9
Emberton M Keyn 49 N5
Embleton Cumb 100 G4
Embleton Dur 104 D5
Embleton Nthumb 119 P6
Embo Highld 163 J8
Emborough Somset 20 B4
Embo Street Highld 163 J8
Embsay N York 96 F10
Emery Down Hants 13 N3
Emley Kirk 90 G8
Emley Moor Kirk 90 G8
Emmbrook Wokham 35 M11
Emmer Green Readg 35 K9
Emmett Carr Derbys 84 G5
Emmington Oxon 35 K4
Emneth Norfk 75 J9
Emneth Hungate Norfk 75 K9
Empingham Rutlnd 73 N9
Empshott Hants 23 L8
Empshott Green Hants 23 K8
Emsworth Hants 15 K5
Enborne W Berk 34 D11
Enborne Row W Berk 22 D2
Enchmarsh Shrops 57 J5
Enderby Leics 72 E11
Endmoor W & F 95 L4
Endon Staffs 70 G4
Endon Bank Staffs 70 G4
Enfield Gt Lon 51 J11
Enfield Lock Gt Lon 51 J11
Enfield Wash Gt Lon 51 J11
Enford Wilts 21 M4
Engine Common S Glos 32 C8
England's Gate Herefs 45 Q4
Englefield W Berk 34 H10
Englefield Green Surrey 35 Q10
Engleseabrook Ches E 70 D4
English Bicknor Gloucs 46 A11
Englishcombe BaNES 20 D2
English Frankton Shrops 69 N9
Engollan Cnwll 4 D7
Enham Alamein Hants 22 C5
Enmore Somset 18 H7
Enmore Green Dorset 20 G10
Ennerdale Bridge Cumb 100 E7
Enniscaven Cnwll 4 F10
Enochdhu P & K 141 Q5
Ensay Ag & B 137 K6
Ensbury BCP 13 J5
Ensdon Shrops 69 M11
Ensis Devon 17 K6
Enson Staffs 70 G9
Enstone Oxon 48 C10
Enterkinfoot D & G 116 B10
Enterpen N York 104 E9
Enville Staffs 58 B7
Eochar W Isls 168 c13
Eòlaigearraidh W Isls 168 c17
Eoligarry W Isls 168 c17
Eòropaidh W Isls 168 k1
Eoropie W Isls 168 k1
Epney Gloucs 32 E2
Epperstone Notts 85 L11
Epping Essex 51 L10
Epping Green Essex 51 K9
Epping Green Herts 50 G9
Epping Upland Essex 51 K10
Eppleby N York 103 N8
Eppleworth E R Yk 92 H4
Epsom Surrey 36 F8
Epwell Oxon 48 C6
Epworth N Linc 92 C10
Epworth Turbary N Linc 92 C10
Erbistock Wrexhm 69 L6
Erdington Birm 58 H6
Eridge Green E Susx 25 N3
Eridge Station E Susx 25 M4
Erines Ag & B 123 Q4
Eriska Ag & B 138 G9
Eriskay W Isls 168 c17
Eriswell Suffk 63 M5
Erith Gt Lon 37 M5
Erlestoke Wilts 21 J4
Ermington Devon 6 G8
Ernesettle C Plym 6 D6
Erpingham Norfk 76 H5
Erriottwood Kent 38 F10
Errogie Highld 147 P3
Errol P & K 134 G3
Erskine Rens 125 M3
Erskine Bridge Rens 125 M3
Ervie D & G 106 D4
Erwarton Suffk 53 M5
Erwood Powys 44 F6
Eryholme N York 104 B9
Eryri National Park Gwynd 67 Q9
Eryrys Denbgs 68 H3
Escalls Cnwll 2 B8
Escomb Dur 103 N4
Escott Somset 18 E7
Escrick N York 91 Q2
Esgair Carmth 42 G9
Esgair Cerdgn 54 D11
Esgairgeiliog Powys 54 H3
Esgerdawe Carmth 43 M6
Esgyryn Conwy 79 Q9
Esh Dur 103 N2
Esher Surrey 36 D8
Esholt C Brad 90 F2
Eshott Nthumb 119 P11
Eshton N York 96 D9
Esh Winning Dur 103 N2
Eskadale Highld 155 N9
Eskbank Mdloth 127 Q4
Eskdale Green Cumb 100 F10
Eskdalemuir D & G 117 K11
Eske E R Yk 93 J2
Eskham Lincs 93 Q11
Eskholme Donc 91 Q7
Esperley Lane Ends Dur 103 M6
Esprick Lancs 88 E3
Essendine Rutlnd 73 Q8
Essendon Herts 50 G9
Essich Highld 156 A10
Essington Staffs 58 E4
Esslemont Abers 151 N2
Eston R & Cl 104 F7
Etal Nthumb 118 H3
Etchilhampton Wilts 21 K2
Etchingham E Susx 26 B6
Etchinghill Kent 27 L4
Etchinghill Staffs 71 J11
Etchingwood E Susx 25 M6
Etling Green Norfk 76 E9
Etloe Gloucs 32 C3
Eton W & M 35 Q9
Eton Wick W & M 35 P9
Etruria C Stke 70 F5
Etteridge Highld 148 B9
Ettersgill Dur 102 G5
Ettiley Heath Ches E 70 C2
Ettingshall Wolves 58 D5
Ettington Warwks 47 Q5
Etton C Pete 74 B9
Etton E R Yk 92 G2
Ettrick Border 117 K8
Ettrickbridge Border 117 M6
Ettrickhill Border 117 K8
Etwall Derbys 71 P8
Eudon George Shrops 57 M7
Euston Suffk 64 B6
Euximoor Drove Cambs 75 J11
Euxton Lancs 88 H7
Evancoyd Powys 45 K2
Evanton Highld 155 R4
Evedon Lincs 86 E11
Evelith Shrops 57 N3
Evelix Highld 162 H8
Evenjobb Powys 45 K2
Evenley W Nthn 48 G8
Evenlode Gloucs 47 P9
Evenwood Dur 103 N6
Evenwood Gate Dur 103 N6
Evercreech Somset 20 B7
Everingham E R Yk 92 D2
Everleigh Wilts 21 P4
Everley N York 99 K3
Eversholt C Beds 49 Q8
Evershot Dorset 11 M4
Eversley Hants 23 L2
Eversley Cross Hants 23 L2
Everthorpe E R Yk 92 F4
Everton C Beds 62 B10
Everton Hants 13 N6
Everton Lpool 81 L6
Everton Notts 85 L2
Evertown D & G 110 G5
Evesbatch Herefs 46 C5
Evesham Worcs 47 K6
Evington C Leic 72 G10
Ewden Village Sheff 90 H11
Ewell Surrey 36 F8
Ewell Minnis Kent 27 N3
Ewelme Oxon 34 H6
Ewen Gloucs 33 K5
Ewenny V Glam 29 P9
Ewerby Lincs 86 F11
Ewerby Thorpe Lincs 86 F11
Ewhurst Surrey 24 C2
Ewhurst Green E Susx 26 C7
Ewhurst Green Surrey 24 C3
Ewloe Flints 81 L11
Ewloe Green Flints 81 K11
Ewood Bl w D 89 K5
Ewood Bridge Lancs 89 M6
Eworthy Devon 8 B5
Ewshot Hants 23 M5
Ewyas Harold Herefs 45 M9
Exbourne Devon 8 F4
Exbury Hants 14 D6
Exceat E Susx 25 M11
Exebridge Somset 18 B10
Exelby N York 97 L3
Exeter Devon 9 M6
Exeter Airport Devon 9 N6
Exeter Services Devon 9 N6
Exford Somset 17 R4
Exfordsgreen Shrops 56 H3
Exhall Warwks 47 M3
Exhall Warwks 59 N7
Exlade Street Oxon 35 J8
Exley Head C Brad 90 C2
Exminster Devon 9 M7
Exmoor National Park 17 R4
Exmouth Devon 9 P8
Exning Suffk 63 K7
Exted Kent 27 L3
Exton Devon 9 N7
Exton Hants 22 H10
Exton Rutlnd 73 N8
Exton Somset 18 B8
Exwick Devon 9 M6
Eyam Derbys 84 B5
Eydon W Nthn 48 F5
Eye C Pete 74 D10
Eye Herefs 45 P2
Eye Suffk 64 G7
Eye Green C Pete 74 D10
Eyemouth Border 129 N7
Eyeworth C Beds 62 C11
Eyhorne Street Kent 38 D11
Eyke Suffk 65 L11
Eynesbury Cambs 61 Q9
Eynsford Kent 37 M7
Eynsham Oxon 34 D3
Eype Dorset 11 J6
Eyre Highld 152 G7
Eythorne Kent 27 N2
Eyton Herefs 45 P2
Eyton Shrops 56 F2
Eyton Shrops 56 F7
Eyton Shrops 69 M10
Eyton Wrexhm 69 L6
Eyton on Severn Shrops 57 K3
Eyton upon the Weald Moors Wrekin 57 M2

F

Faccombe Hants 22 C3
Faceby N York 104 E10
Fachwen Powys 68 D11
Facit Lancs 89 P7
Fackley Notts 84 G8
Faddiley Ches E 69 Q4
Fadmoor N York 98 D3
Faerdre Swans 29 J4
Faifley W Duns 125 M3
Failand N Som 31 P10
Failford S Ayrs 115 J2
Failsworth Oldham 83 J4
Fairbourne Gwynd 54 E2
Fairburn N York 91 M5
Fairfield Derbys 83 N10
Fairfield Kent 26 G6
Fairfield Worcs 58 D9
Fairfield Park Herts 50 F4
Fairford Gloucs 33 N4
Fairford Park Gloucs 33 N4
Fairgirth D & G 109 J9
Fair Green Norfk 75 N7
Fairhaven Lancs 88 C5
Fair Isle Shet 169 t14
Fair Isle Airport Shet 169 t14
Fairlands Surrey 23 Q4
Fairlie N Ayrs 124 G7
Fairlight E Susx 26 E9
Fairlight Cove E Susx 26 E9
Fairmile Devon 10 B5
Fairmile Surrey 36 D8
Fairmilehead C Edin 127 N4
Fairnilee Border 117 P4
Fair Oak Hants 22 E11
Fairoak Staffs 70 D8
Fair Oak Green Hants 23 J2
Fairseat Kent 37 P8
Fairstead Essex 52 C8
Fairstead Norfk 75 M6
Fairstead Norfk 77 K7
Fairwarp E Susx 25 L5
Fairwater Cardif 30 F9
Fairy Cross Devon 16 G7
Fakenham Norfk 76 C6
Fakenham Magna Suffk 64 C6
Fala Mdloth 128 C7
Fala Dam Mdloth 128 C7
Falcut W Nthn 48 G6
Faldingworth Lincs 86 E4
Faldouët Jersey 11 c2
Falfield S Glos 32 C6
Falkenham Suffk 53 N4
Falkirk Falk 133 P11
Falkirk Wheel Falk 133 P11
Falkland Fife 134 H6
Fallburn S Lans 116 D3
Fallgate Derbys 84 E8
Fallin Stirlg 133 N9
Fallodon Nthumb 119 N6
Fallowfield Manch 83 J6
Fallowfield Nthumb 112 D7
Falmer E Susx 25 J9
Falmouth Cnwll 3 L7
Falnash Border 117 M9
Falsgrave N York 99 L3
Falstone Nthumb 111 P3
Fanagmore Highld 164 E7
Fancott C Beds 50 B5
Fanellan Highld 155 N9
Fangdale Beck N York 98 B2
Fangfoss E R Yk 98 F10
Fanmore Ag & B 137 L7
Fannich Lodge Highld 154 H4
Fans Border 118 B2
Far Bletchley M Keyn 49 N8
Farcet Cambs 62 B2
Far Cotton W Nthn 60 G9
Farden Shrops 57 K9
Fareham Hants 14 G5
Farewell Staffs 58 G2
Far Forest Worcs 57 N9
Farforth Lincs 87 K5
Far Green Gloucs 32 E4
Faringdon Oxon 33 Q5
Farington Moss Lancs 88 G5
Farlam Cumb 111 L9
Farleigh N Som 31 P11
Farleigh Surrey 37 J8
Farleigh Hungerford Somset 20 F3
Farleigh Wallop Hants 22 H5
Farlesthorpe Lincs 87 N6
Farleton Lancs 95 M7

Place	County	Page	Grid
Farleton	W & F	95	L4
Farley	Derbys	84	C8
Farley	Staffs	71	K6
Farley	Wilts	21	P9
Farley Green	Suffk	63	M10
Farley Green	Surrey	36	C11
Farley Hill	Wokham	23	N4
Farleys End	Gloucs	32	E2
Farlington	C Port	15	J5
Farlington	N York	98	C7
Farlow	Shrops	57	L8
Farmborough	BaNES	20	C2
Farmbridge End	Essex	51	P8
Farmcote	Gloucs	47	L9
Farmcote	Shrops	57	P6
Farmington	Gloucs	47	M11
Farmoor	Oxon	34	E3
Far Moor	Wigan	82	B4
Farms Common	Cnwll	2	H7
Farm Town	Leics	72	B7
Farnah Green	Derbys	84	D11
Farnborough	Gt Lon	37	K8
Farnborough	Hants	23	N4
Farnborough	W Berk	34	D8
Farnborough	Warwks	48	D5
Farnborough Park	Hants	23	N3
Farncombe	Surrey	23	Q6
Farndish	Bed	61	K8
Farndon	Ches W	69	M4
Farndon	Notts	85	N10
Farne Islands	Nthumb	119	P3
Farnell	Angus	143	L6
Farnham	Dorset	21	J11
Farnham	Essex	51	L6
Farnham	N York	97	M8
Farnham	Suffk	65	M9
Farnham	Surrey	23	M5
Farnham Common	Bucks	35	Q7
Farnham Green	Essex	51	L5
Farnham Royal	Bucks	35	Q8
Farningham	Kent	37	M7
Farnley	Leeds	90	H4
Farnley	N York	97	K11
Farnley Tyas	Kirk	90	F8
Farnsfield	Notts	85	K9
Farnworth	Bolton	89	L9
Farnworth	Halton	81	Q7
Far Oakridge	Gloucs	32	H4
Farr	Highld	148	E7
Farr	Highld	156	B11
Farr	Highld	166	B4
Farraline	Highld	147	P3
Farringdon	Devon	9	P6
Farrington Gurney	BaNES	20	B3
Far Sawrey	W & F	101	L11
Farsley	Leeds	90	G3
Farther Howegreen	Essex	52	D11
Farthing Green	Kent	26	D2
Farthinghoe	W Nthn	48	F7
Farthingloe	Kent	27	N3
Farthingstone	W Nthn	48	H4
Farthing Street	Gt Lon	37	K8
Fartown	Kirk	90	F7
Farway	Devon	10	D5
Fasnacloich	Ag & B	139	J8
Fasnakyle	Highld	147	J2
Fassfern	Highld	139	J2
Fatfield	Sundld	113	M10
Faugh	Cumb	111	K10
Fauld	Staffs	71	M9
Fauldhouse	W Loth	126	G5
Faulkbourne	Essex	52	C8
Faulkland	Somset	20	D4
Fauls	Shrops	69	Q8
Faversham	Kent	38	H9
Fawdington	N York	97	P6
Fawdon	N u Ty	113	K7
Fawdon	Nthumb	119	K7
Fawfieldhead	Staffs	71	K2
Fawkham Green	Kent	37	N7
Fawler	Oxon	48	C11
Fawley	Bucks	35	L7
Fawley	Hants	14	E6
Fawley	W Berk	34	C8
Fawley Chapel	Herefs	46	A9
Fawnog	Flints	81	J11
Fawsley	W Nthn	60	C9
Faxfleet	E R Yk	92	E6
Faygate	W Susx	24	F4
Fazeley	Staffs	59	K4
Fearby	N York	97	J4
Fearn	Highld	156	E2
Fearnan	P & K	140	H9
Fearnbeg	Highld	153	N6
Fearnhead	Warrtn	82	D6
Fearnmore	Highld	153	N5
Fearnoch	Ag & B	124	A2
Featherstone	Staffs	58	D3
Featherstone	Wakefd	91	L7
Feckenham	Worcs	47	K2
Feering	Essex	52	E7
Feetham	N York	103	J11
Feizor	N York	96	A7
Felbridge	Surrey	25	J3
Felbrigg	Norfk	77	J4
Felcourt	Surrey	25	J2
Felden	Herts	50	B10
Felindre	Carmth	42	G7
Felindre	Carmth	43	L10
Felindre	Carmth	43	P9
Felindre	Cerdgn	43	L3
Felindre	Powys	44	H10
Felindre	Powys	56	B8
Felindre	Swans	28	H4
Felindre Farchog	Pembks	41	M3
Felinfach	Cerdgn	43	K3
Felinfach	Powys	44	F8
Felinfoel	Carmth	28	F4
Felingwmisaf	Carmth	43	K10
Felingwmuchaf	Carmth	43	K10
Felin-newydd	Powys	44	G7
Felixkirk	N York	97	Q4
Felixstowe	Suffk	53	P5
Felixstowe Ferry	Suffk	53	P4
Felkington	Nthumb	118	H2
Felkirk	Wakefd	91	K8
Felling	Gatesd	113	L8
Fell Lane	C Brad	90	C2
Fell Side	Cumb	101	K3
Felmersham	Bed	61	L9
Felmingham	Norfk	77	K6
Felpham	W Susx	15	P7
Felsham	Suffk	64	C10
Felsted	Essex	51	Q6
Feltham	Gt Lon	36	D6
Felthamhill	Surrey	36	C6
Felthorpe	Norfk	76	H8
Felton	Herefs	46	A5
Felton	N Som	31	P11
Felton	Nthumb	119	N10
Felton Butler	Shrops	69	L11
Feltwell	Norfk	63	M2
Fenay Bridge	Kirk	90	F7
Fence	Lancs	89	N3
Fence	Rothm	84	F3
Fence Houses	Sundld	113	M11
Fencott	Oxon	48	G8
Fendike Corner	Lincs	87	N8
Fen Ditton	Cambs	62	G8
Fen Drayton	Cambs	62	D7
Fen End	Lincs	74	D6
Fen End	Solhll	59	K10
Fenham	Nthumb	119	L2
Feniscliffe	Bl w D	89	K5
Feniscowles	Bl w D	89	J5
Feniton	Devon	10	B5
Feniton Court	Devon	10	C5
Fenn Green	Shrops	57	P8
Fenn Street	Medway	38	C6
Fenny Bentley	Derbys	71	M5
Fenny Bridges	Devon	10	C5
Fenny Compton	Warwks	48	D4
Fenny Drayton	Leics	72	B11
Fenny Stratford	M Keyn	49	N8
Fenrother	Nthumb	113	J2
Fenstanton	Cambs	62	D7
Fenstead End	Suffk	63	P10
Fen Street	Norfk	64	D2
Fen Street	Suffk	64	H9
Fenton	C Stke	70	F6
Fenton	Cambs	62	D5
Fenton	Cumb	111	K9
Fenton	Lincs	85	P5
Fenton	Lincs	85	Q10
Fenton	Notts	85	N4
Fenton	Nthumb	119	J4
Fenton Barns	E Loth	128	E3
Fenwick	Donc	91	P7
Fenwick	E Ayrs	125	M9
Fenwick	Nthumb	112	G6
Fenwick	Nthumb	119	L2
Feock	Cnwll	3	L6
Feolin Ferry	Ag & B	122	F6
Fergushill	N Ayrs	125	J9
Feriniquarrie	Highld	152	B7
Fermain Bay	Guern	10	c2
Fern	Angus	142	H5
Ferndale	Rhondd	30	C5
Ferndown	Dorset	13	J4
Ferness	Highld	156	H8
Fernham	Oxon	33	Q6
Fernhill Heath	Worcs	46	G3
Fernhurst	W Susx	23	N9
Fernie	Fife	135	J4
Ferniegair	S Lans	126	C7
Fernilea	Highld	152	F11
Fernilee	Derbys	83	M9
Fernwood	Notts	85	P10
Ferrensby	N York	97	N8
Ferriby Sluice	N Linc	92	G6
Ferrindonald	Highld	145	L6
Ferring	W Susx	24	C10
Ferrybridge	Wakefd	91	M6
Ferrybridge Services	Wakefd	91	M6
Ferryden	Angus	143	N6
Ferryhill	Dur	103	Q4
Ferryhill Station	Dur	103	Q4
Ferry Point	Highld	162	G9
Ferryside	Carmth	28	C2
Fersfield	Norfk	64	F5
Fersit	Highld	139	R2
Feshiebridge	Highld	148	F7
Fetcham	Surrey	36	D9
Fetlar	Shet	169	t4
Fetterangus	Abers	159	N7
Fettercairn	Abers	143	M3
Fewcott	Oxon	48	F9
Fewston	N York	97	J10
Ffairfach	Carmth	43	M10
Ffair Rhos	Cerdgn	54	G11
Ffald-y-Brenin	Carmth	43	M6
Ffarmers	Carmth	43	N6
Ffawyddog	Powys	45	J11
Ffestiniog	Gwynd	67	L7
Ffestiniog Railway	Gwynd	67	L7
Ffordd-las	Denbgs	68	F2
Fforest	Carmth	28	G4
Fforest Gôch	Neath	29	K4
Ffostrasol	Cerdgn	42	G5
Ffrith	Flints	69	J3
Ffynnonddewi	Cerdgn	42	G4
Ffynnongroyw	Flints	80	G8
Ffynnon-oer	Cerdgn	43	K4
Fickleshole	Surrey	37	J8
Fiddington	Gloucs	46	H8
Fiddington	Somset	18	H6
Fiddleford	Dorset	12	D2
Fiddlers Green	Cnwll	4	C10
Fiddlers Hamlet	Essex	51	L8
Field	Staffs	71	J8
Field Broughton	W & F	94	H4
Field Dalling	Norfk	76	E4
Field Head	Leics	72	D9
Fieldhead	W & F	101	N3
Fifehead Magdalen	Dorset	20	E10
Fifehead Neville	Dorset	12	C2
Fifehead St Quintin	Dorset	12	C2
Fife Keith	Moray	158	B7
Fifield	Oxon	47	P11
Fifield	W & M	35	P9
Fifield	Wilts	21	M4
Figheldean	Wilts	21	N5
Filands	Wilts	32	H7
Filby	Norfk	77	P9
Filey	N York	99	N4
Filgrave	M Keyn	49	N5
Filkins	Oxon	33	P4
Filleigh	Devon	8	H2
Filleigh	Devon	17	M6
Fillingham	Lincs	86	B3
Fillongley	Warwks	59	L7
Filmore Hill	Hants	23	J9
Filton	S Glos	31	B9
Fimber	E R Yk	98	H8
Finavon	Angus	142	H6
Finberry	Kent	26	H4
Fincham	Norfk	75	N9
Finchampstead	Wokham	23	L2
Fincharn	Ag & B	131	J7
Finchdean	Hants	15	K4
Finchingfield	Essex	51	Q4
Finchley	Gt Lon	36	G2
Findern	Derbys	71	Q8
Findhorn	Moray	157	J5
Findhorn Bridge	Highld	148	E2
Findochty	Moray	158	C4
Findo Gask	P & K	134	C4
Findon	Abers	151	N8
Findon	W Susx	24	D9
Findon Mains	Highld	155	R5
Findon Valley	W Susx	24	D9
Findrack House	Abers	150	G7
Finedon	N Nthn	61	K6
Fingal Street	Suffk	65	J8
Fingask	P & K	134	F4
Fingest	Bucks	35	L6
Finghall	N York	97	J3
Fingland	Cumb	110	E9
Fingland	D & G	115	Q4
Finglesham	Kent	39	P11
Fingringhoe	Essex	52	H7
Finkle Green	Essex	52	B3
Finkle Street	Barns	91	J11
Finlake	Devon	9	M4
Finlarig	Stirlg	140	E11
Finmere	Oxon	48	H8
Finnart	P & K	140	D6
Finningham	Suffk	64	F8
Finningley	Donc	91	R11
Finsbay	W Isls	168	f9
Finstall	Worcs	58	E10
Finsthwaite	W & F	94	H3
Finstock	Oxon	48	C11
Finstown	Ork	169	c5
Fintry	Abers	159	J7
Fintry	Stirlg	133	J10
Finzean	Abers	150	G9
Fionnphort	Ag & B	137	J11
Fionnsbhagh	W Isls	168	f9
Firbank	W & F	95	N2
Firbeck	Rothm	85	J3
Firby	N York	97	L3
Firby	N York	98	E7
Firgrove	Rochdl	89	Q8
Firle	E Susx	25	L9
Firsby	Lincs	87	N8
Firsdown	Wilts	21	P8
Fir Tree	Dur	103	M4
Fishbourne	IoW	14	G8
Fishbourne	W Susx	15	M6
Fishbourne Roman Palace	W Susx	15	M6
Fishburn	Dur	104	C4
Fishcross	Clacks	133	P8
Fisher	W Susx	15	N6
Fisherford	Abers	158	G10
Fisherrow	E Loth	127	Q3
Fisher's Pond	Hants	22	E10
Fisher's Row	Lancs	95	J11
Fisherstreet	W Susx	23	P8
Fisherton	Highld	156	C7
Fisherton	S Ayrs	114	E4
Fisherton de la Mere	Wilts	21	K7
Fisherwick	Staffs	59	J3
Fishery	W & M	35	N8
Fishguard	Pembks	41	J3
Fishlake	Donc	91	R8
Fishleigh	Devon	8	D3
Fishmere End	Lincs	74	E3
Fishnish Pier	Ag & B	138	B9
Fishpond Bottom	Dorset	10	H5
Fishponds	Bristl	32	B9
Fishtoft	Lincs	74	G2
Fishtoft Drove	Lincs	87	K11
Fishwick	Lancs	88	H5
Fiskavaig	Highld	152	E11
Fiskerton	Lincs	86	D6
Fiskerton	Notts	85	M10
Fitling	E R Yk	93	N4
Fittleton	Wilts	21	M5
Fittleworth	W Susx	24	B7
Fitton End	Cambs	74	H8
Fitz	Shrops	69	M11
Fitzhead	Somset	18	F9
Fitzroy	Somset	18	G9
Fitzwilliam	Wakefd	91	L7
Five Ash Down	E Susx	25	L6
Five Ashes	E Susx	25	N5
Five Bells	Somset	18	E6
Five Bridges	Herefs	46	B5
Fivecrosses	Ches W	82	B9
Fivehead	Somset	19	L10
Fivelanes	Cnwll	5	L5
Five Lanes	Mons	31	N6
Five Oak Green	Kent	37	P11
Five Oaks	Jersey	11	c2
Five Oaks	W Susx	24	C5
Five Roads	Carmth	28	E3
Five Wents	Kent	38	D11
Flack's Green	Essex	52	C9
Flackwell Heath	Bucks	35	N7
Fladbury	Worcs	47	J5
Fladdabister	Shet	169	r10
Flagg	Derbys	83	P11
Flamborough	E R Yk	99	Q6
Flamborough Head	E R Yk	99	R6
Flamingo Land Resort	N York	98	F5
Flamstead	Herts	50	C8
Flamstead End	Herts	50	H10
Flansham	W Susx	15	Q6
Flanshaw	Wakefd	91	J6
Flappit Spring	C Brad	90	D3
Flasby	N York	96	D9
Flash	Staffs	83	M11
Flashader	Highld	152	E8
Flaunden	Herts	50	B10
Flawborough	Notts	73	K2
Flawith	N York	97	Q7
Flax Bourton	N Som	31	P11
Flaxby	N York	97	N9
Flaxley	Gloucs	46	C11
Flaxmere	Ches W	82	C10
Flaxpool	Somset	18	F7
Flaxton	N York	98	D8
Fleckney	Leics	60	D2
Flecknoe	Warwks	60	B8
Fledborough	Notts	85	P6
Fleet	Dorset	11	N8
Fleet	Hants	15	M4
Fleet	Hants	23	M4
Fleet	Lincs	74	G6
Fleetend	Hants	14	F5
Fleet Hargate	Lincs	74	G6
Fleet Services	Hants	23	L3
Fleetwood	Lancs	94	G11
Fleggburgh	Norfk	77	N9
Flemingston	V Glam	30	D11
Flemington	S Lans	126	B6
Flempton	Suffk	63	P7
Fletchersbridge	Cnwll	5	J8
Fletcher's Green	Kent	37	M11
Fletchertown	Cumb	100	H2
Fletching	E Susx	25	K6
Fleur-de-lis	Caerph	30	G5
Flexbury	Cnwll	16	C10
Flexford	Surrey	23	P4
Flimby	Cumb	100	D4
Flimwell	E Susx	26	B5
Flint	Flints	81	J10
Flint Cross	Cambs	51	K2
Flintham	Notts	85	M11
Flint Mountain	Flints	81	J10
Flinton	E R Yk	93	M3
Flint's Green	Solhll	59	L8
Flishinghurst	Kent	26	C4
Flitcham	Norfk	75	P5
Flitch Green	Essex	51	Q6
Flitton	C Beds	50	C3
Flitwick	C Beds	50	B4
Flixborough	N Linc	92	E8
Flixborough Stather	N Linc	92	E8
Flixton	N York	99	L5
Flixton	Suffk	65	L4
Flixton	Traffd	82	F6
Flockton	Kirk	90	G8
Flockton Green	Kirk	90	H7
Flodden	Nthumb	118	H3
Flodigarry	Highld	152	H3
Flookburgh	W & F	94	H5
Flordon	Norfk	64	H2
Flore	W Nthn	60	D8
Flotterton	Nthumb	119	J10
Flowers Green	E Susx	25	P8
Flowton	Suffk	53	J2
Flushdyke	Wakefd	90	H6
Flushing	Cnwll	3	L7
Fluxton	Devon	10	B6
Flyford Flavell	Worcs	47	J3
Fobbing	Thurr	38	B5
Fochabers	Moray	157	Q6
Fochriw	Caerph	30	F3
Fockerby	N Linc	92	D7
Foddington	Somset	19	Q9
Foel	Powys	55	M2
Foelgastell	Carmth	28	F2
Foel y Dyffryn	Brdgnd	29	N6
Foggathorpe	E R Yk	92	C3
Fogo	Border	129	K10
Fogwatt	Moray	157	N6
Foindle	Highld	164	E7
Folda	Angus	142	B5
Fole	Staffs	71	J7
Foleshill	Covtry	59	N8
Folke	Dorset	11	P2
Folkestone	Kent	27	M4
Folkestone Services	Kent	27	K4
Folkingham	Lincs	73	R4
Folkington	E Susx	25	N10
Folksworth	Cambs	61	P3
Folkton	N York	99	M5
Folla Rule	Abers	158	H11
Follifoot	N York	97	M10
Folly Gate	Devon	8	E5
Folly Hill	Surrey	23	M5
Fonmon	V Glam	30	D11
Fonthill Bishop	Wilts	20	H8
Fonthill Gifford	Wilts	20	H8
Fontmell Magna	Dorset	20	G11
Fontmell Parva	Dorset	12	D2
Fontwell	W Susx	15	P5
Font-y-gary	V Glam	30	E11
Foolow	Derbys	83	Q9
Foots Cray	Gt Lon	37	L6
Forbestown	Abers	150	B5
Forcett	N York	103	N8
Ford	Ag & B	130	H7
Ford	Bucks	35	L3
Ford	Derbys	84	F4
Ford	Devon	6	G8
Ford	Devon	7	K10
Ford	Devon	16	G7
Ford	Gloucs	47	L9
Ford	Nthumb	119	J3
Ford	Shrops	56	G2
Ford	Somset	18	E9
Ford	Somset	19	Q4
Ford	Staffs	71	K4
Ford	W Susx	15	Q6
Ford	Wilts	32	F9
Forda	Devon	8	D6
Fordcombe	Kent	25	M2
Fordell	Fife	134	F10
Forden	Powys	56	C4
Ford End	Essex	51	Q7
Forder Green	Devon	7	K5
Fordham	Cambs	63	K6
Fordham	Essex	52	F6
Fordham	Norfk	75	M11
Fordham Heath	Essex	52	F6
Ford Heath	Shrops	56	G2
Fordingbridge	Hants	13	K2
Fordon	E R Yk	99	L5
Fordoun	Abers	143	N2
Ford's Green	Suffk	64	F8
Fordstreet	Essex	52	F6
Ford Street	Somset	18	G11
Fordton	Devon	9	K5
Fordwells	Oxon	34	B2
Fordwich	Kent	39	L10
Fordyce	Abers	158	E5
Forebridge	Staffs	70	G10
Foremark	Derbys	72	A5
Forest	Guern	10	b2
Forest	N York	103	Q10
Forest Becks	Lancs	96	A10
Forestburn Gate	Nthumb	119	L11
Forest Chapel	Ches E	83	L10
Forest Coal Pit	Mons	45	K10
Forest Green	Surrey	24	D2
Forest Hall	N Tyne	113	L7
Forest Head	Cumb	111	L9
Forest Hill	Gt Lon	37	J6
Forest Hill	Oxon	34	G3
Forest-in-Teesdale	Dur	102	H4
Forest Lane Head	N York	97	M9
Forest Mill	Clacks	134	B9
Forest of Bowland	Lancs	95	N10
Forest of Dean	Gloucs	32	B2
Forest Row	E Susx	25	K4
Forest Side	IoW	14	E9
Forestside	W Susx	15	L4
Forest Town	Notts	85	J8
Forfar	Angus	142	H7
Forgandenny	P & K	134	D4
Forge	Powys	54	H5
Forge Hammer	Torfn	31	J5
Forge Side	Torfn	30	H3
Forgie	Moray	158	A7
Forgieside	Moray	158	B7
Forgue	Abers	158	F8
Forhill	Worcs	58	G9
Formby	Sefton	88	C9
Forncett End	Norfk	64	G3
Forncett St Mary	Norfk	64	H3
Forncett St Peter	Norfk	64	H3
Fornham All Saints	Suffk	64	A8
Fornham St Martin	Suffk	64	B8
Fornham St Genevieve	Suffk	64	A8
Fornighty	Highld	156	G7
Forres	Moray	157	J6
Forsbrook	Staffs	70	H6
Forse	Highld	167	M10
Forshaw Heath	Warwks	58	G10
Forsinard	Highld	166	E8
Forss	Highld	166	H3
Forston	Dorset	11	P5
Fort Augustus	Highld	147	K6
Forteviot	P & K	134	D4
Forth	S Lans	126	G7
Forthampton	Gloucs	46	G8
Fort Hommet	Guern	10	b1
Forth Rail Bridge	C Edin	127	L2
Forth Road Bridge	Fife	127	L2
Fortingall	P & K	140	H8
Forton	Hants	22	D6
Forton	Lancs	95	K10
Forton	Shrops	69	M11
Forton	Somset	10	G3
Forton	Staffs	70	D10
Fort Richmond	Guern	10	b2
Fortrie	Abers	158	G6
Fortrose	Highld	156	C6
Fortuneswell	Dorset	11	P10
Fort William	Highld	139	L3
Forty Green	Bucks	35	P6
Forty Hill	Gt Lon	50	H11
Forward Green	Suffk	64	G10
Fosbury	Wilts	22	B3
Foscot	Oxon	47	P10
Foscote	W Nthn	49	J5
Fosdyke	Lincs	74	F4
Fosdyke Bridge	Lincs	74	F4
Foss	P & K	141	J6
Fossebridge	Gloucs	33	L2
Foss-y-ffin	Cerdgn	42	H2
Fosterhouses	Donc	91	R8
Foster Street	Essex	51	L9
Foston	Derbys	71	M8
Foston	Leics	60	D2
Foston	Lincs	73	M2
Foston	N York	98	D7
Foston on the Wolds	E R Yk	99	N9
Fotherby	Lincs	87	K2
Fothergill	Cumb	100	D4
Fotheringhay	N Nthn	61	N2
Foula	Shet	169	k10
Foula Airport	Shet	169	k10
Foul Anchor	Cambs	75	J7
Foulbridge	Cumb	110	H11
Foulby	Wakefd	91	K7
Foulden	Border	129	N8
Foulden	Norfk	75	Q11
Foul End	Warwks	59	K6
Foul Mile	E Susx	25	P7
Foulness Island	Essex	38	G3
Foulridge	Lancs	89	P2
Foulsham	Norfk	76	E7
Fountainhall	Border	128	C10
Four Ashes	Solhll	59	J9
Four Ashes	Staffs	57	Q7
Four Ashes	Staffs	58	D3
Four Ashes	Suffk	64	E7
Four Cabots	Guern	10	b2
Four Crosses	Powys	62	J11
Four Crosses	Staffs	58	E3
Four Elms	Kent	37	L11
Four Foot	Somset	19	Q8
Four Forks	Somset	18	H7
Four Gates	Bolton	89	J9
Four Gotes	Cambs	75	J7
Four Lane End	Barns	90	H10
Four Lane Ends	Ches W	69	Q2
Four Lanes	Cnwll	2	H6
Fourlanes End	Ches E	70	E3
Four Marks	Hants	23	J7
Four Mile Bridge	IoA	78	D9
Four Oaks	Birm	58	H5
Four Oaks	E Susx	26	E7
Four Oaks	Gloucs	46	C9
Four Oaks	Solhll	59	K8
Fourpenny	Highld	163	J8
Four Points	W Berk	34	G9
Four Roads	Carmth	28	D3
Four Shire Stone	Warwks	47	P8
Fourstones	Nthumb	112	C7
Four Throws	Kent	26	C6
Four Wents	Kent	37	P10
Fovant	Wilts	21	K9
Foveran	Abers	151	P3
Fowey	Cnwll	5	J11
Fowley Common	Warrtn	82	E5
Fowlhall	Kent	37	Q11
Fowlis	Angus	142	E11
Fowlis Wester	P & K	133	Q3
Fowlmere	Cambs	62	F11
Fownhope	Herefs	46	A8
Foxbar	Rens	125	M5
Foxcombe	Devon	8	C7
Fox Corner	Surrey	23	Q3
Foxcote	Gloucs	47	K11
Foxcote	Somset	20	D3
Foxdale	IoM	80	c6
Foxearth	Essex	52	D3
Foxendown	Kent	37	P7
Foxfield	W & F	94	E3
Foxham	Wilts	33	J9
Fox Hatch	Essex	51	N11
Foxhills	Hants	13	P2
Foxhole	Cnwll	3	P3
Foxholes	N York	99	L6
Foxhunt Green	E Susx	25	M7
Foxley	Norfk	76	E7
Foxley	W Nthn	48	H4

Foxley – Glengarnock 271

Foxley Wilts 32 G7
Foxlydiate Worcs 58 F11
Fox Street Essex 52 H6
Foxt Staffs 71 J5
Foxton Cambs 62 F11
Foxton Dur 104 C6
Foxton Leics 60 F3
Foxton N York 104 D11
Foxup N York 96 C5
Foxwist Green Ches W 82 D11
Foxwood Shrops 57 L9
Foy Herefs 46 A9
Foyers Highld 147 M3
Foynesfield Highld 156 F7
Fraddam Cnwll 2 F7
Fraddon Cnwll 4 E10
Fradley Staffs 59 J2
Fradswell Staffs 70 H8
Fraisthorpe E R Yk 99 P8
Framfield E Susx 25 L6
Framingham Earl Norfk 77 K11
Framingham Pigot Norfk 77 K11
Framlingham Suffk 65 K9
Frampton Dorset 11 N5
Frampton Lincs 74 F3
Frampton Cotterell S Glos 32 C8
Frampton Mansell Gloucs 32 H4
Frampton-on-Severn Gloucs 32 D3
Frampton West End Lincs 74 F2
Framsden Suffk 64 H10
Framwellgate Moor Dur 103 Q2
Franche Worcs 57 Q9
Frandley Ches W 82 D9
Frankaborough Devon 5 P3
Frankby Wirral 81 J7
Frankfort Norfk 77 L7
Franklands Gate Herefs 45 Q5
Frankley Worcs 58 E8
Frankley Services Worcs 58 E8
Franksbridge Powys 44 G3
Frankton Warwks 59 P10
Frant E Susx 25 N3
Fraserburgh Abers 159 N4
Frating Essex 53 J7
Frating Green Essex 53 J7
Fratton C Port 15 J6
Freathy Cnwll 5 P11
Freckenham Suffk 63 L6
Freckleton Lancs 88 E5
Freebirch Derbys 84 D6
Freeby Leics 73 L6
Freefolk Hants 22 E5
Freehay Staffs 71 J6
Freeland Oxon 34 D2
Freethorpe Norfk 77 N10
Freethorpe Common Norfk 77 N11
Freiston Lincs 74 G2
Fremington Devon 17 J5
Fremington N York 103 K11
Frenchay S Glos 32 B9
Frenchbeer Devon 8 G7
French Street Kent 37 L10
Frenich P & K 141 K6
Frensham Surrey 23 M6
Freshfield Sefton 88 B9
Freshford Wilts 20 E2
Freshwater IoW 13 P7
Freshwater Bay IoW 13 P7
Freshwater East Pembks 41 K11
Fressingfield Suffk 65 K6
Freston Suffk 53 L4
Freswick Highld 167 Q3
Fretherne Gloucs 32 D2
Frettenham Norfk 77 J8
Freuchie Fife 134 H6
Freystrop Pembks 41 J8
Friar Park Sandw 58 F6
Friar's Gate E Susx 25 L4
Friars' Hill N York 98 E3
Friar Waddon Dorset 11 N7
Friday Bridge Cambs 75 J10
Friday Street Suffk 65 J10
Friday Street Suffk 65 L11
Friday Street Suffk 65 M9
Friday Street Surrey 36 D11
Fridaythorpe E R Yk 98 H9
Friden Derbys 71 M2
Friendly Calder 90 D6
Friern Barnet Gt Lon 36 G2
Friesthorpe Lincs 86 E4
Frieston Lincs 86 B11
Frieth Bucks 35 L6
Friezeland Notts 84 G10
Frilford Oxon 34 D5
Frilsham W Berk 34 F10
Frimley Surrey 23 N3
Frimley Green Surrey 23 N3
Frindsbury Medway 38 B8
Fring Norfk 75 P4
Fringford Oxon 48 H9
Frinsted Kent 38 E10
Frinton-on-Sea Essex 53 M7
Friockheim Angus 143 K8
Friog Gwynd 54 E2
Frisby on the Wreake Leics 72 H7
Friskney Lincs 87 N9
Friskney Eaudike Lincs 87 N9
Friston E Susx 25 N11
Friston Suffk 65 N9
Fritchley Derbys 84 E10
Fritham Hants 13 M2
Frith Bank Lincs 87 K11
Frith Common Worcs 57 M11
Frithelstock Devon 16 H8
Frithelstock Stone Devon 16 H8
Frithend Hants 23 M7
Frithsden Herts 50 B9
Frithville Lincs 87 K10
Frittenden Kent 26 D3
Frittiscombe Devon 7 L10
Fritton Norfk 65 J3
Fritton Norfk 77 P11
Fritwell Oxon 48 F9
Frizinghall C Brad 90 E3
Frizington Cumb 100 D7
Frocester Gloucs 32 E4
Frodesley Shrops 57 J4
Frodsham Ches W 81 Q9
Frogden Border 118 E5
Frog End Cambs 62 E11
Frog End Cambs 62 H9
Froggatt Derbys 84 B5
Froghall Staffs 71 J5
Frogham Hants 13 L2
Frogham Kent 39 N11
Frogmore Devon 7 K10
Frognall Lincs 74 C8
Frogpool Cnwll 3 K5
Frog Pool Worcs 57 Q11
Frogwell Cnwll 5 N8
Frolesworth Leics 60 B2
Frome Somset 20 E5
Frome St Quintin Dorset 11 M4
Fromes Hill Herefs 46 C5
Fron Gwynd 66 F7
Fron Gwynd 67 J4
Fron Powys 56 B5
Fron Powys 56 C4
Froncysyllte Wrexhm 69 J6
Fron-goch Gwynd 68 B7
Fron Isaf Wrexhm 69 J6
Frostenden Suffk 65 P5
Frosterley Dur 103 K3
Froxfield C Beds 49 Q8
Froxfield Wilts 33 Q11
Froxfield Green Hants 23 K9
Fryern Hill Hants 22 D10
Fryerning Essex 51 P10
Fryton N York 98 D6
Fuinary Highld 137 Q6
Fulbeck Lincs 86 B10
Fulbourn Cambs 62 H9
Fulbrook Oxon 33 Q2
Fulflood Hants 22 E8
Fulford C York 98 C11
Fulford Somset 18 H9
Fulford Staffs 70 H7
Fulham Gt Lon 36 G5
Fulking W Susx 24 F8
Fullaford Devon 17 M4
Fullarton N Ayrs 125 J10
Fuller's End Essex 51 M5
Fuller's Moor Ches W 69 N4
Fuller Street Essex 52 B8
Fuller Street Kent 37 N9
Fullerton Hants 22 C7
Fulletby Lincs 87 J6
Fullready Warwks 47 Q5
Full Sutton E R Yk 98 E9
Fullwood E Ayrs 125 L7
Fulmer Bucks 35 Q7
Fulmodeston Norfk 76 D5
Fulnetby Lincs 86 E5
Fulney Lincs 74 E6
Fulstone Kirk 90 F9
Fulstow Lincs 93 P11
Fulwell Oxon 48 C10
Fulwell Sundld 113 N9
Fulwood Lancs 88 G4
Fulwood Notts 84 G9
Fulwood Sheff 84 D3
Fulwood Somset 18 H10
Fundenhall Norfk 64 H2
Funtington W Susx 15 M5
Funtley Hants 14 G5
Funtullich P & K 133 M2
Furley Devon 10 F4
Furnace Ag & B 131 L7
Furnace Carmth 28 F4
Furnace Cerdgn 54 F5
Furnace End Warwks 59 K6
Furner's Green E Susx 25 K5
Furness Vale Derbys 83 M8
Furneux Pelham Herts 51 K5
Further Quarter Kent 26 E4
Furtho W Nthn 49 L6
Furzehill Devon 17 N2
Furzehill Dorset 12 H4
Furzehills Lincs 87 J6
Furzeley Corner Hants 15 J4
Furze Platt W & M 35 N8
Furzley Hants 21 Q11
Fyfett Somset 10 E2
Fyfield Essex 51 N9
Fyfield Hants 21 Q5
Fyfield Oxon 34 D5
Fyfield Wilts 21 N2
Fyfield Wilts 33 M11
Fyfield Bavant Wilts 21 K9
Fylingthorpe N York 105 P10
Fyning W Susx 23 M10
Fyvie Abers 159 J10

G

Gabroc Hill E Ayrs 125 M7
Gaddesby Leics 72 H8
Gaddesden Row Herts 50 C8
Gadfa IoA 78 H7
Gadgirth S Ayrs 114 H3
Gadlas Shrops 69 L7
Gaer Powys 44 H10
Gaerllwyd Mons 31 M5
Gaerwen IoA 78 H10
Gagingwell Oxon 48 D9
Gailes N Ayrs 125 J10
Gailey Staffs 58 D2
Gainford Dur 103 N7
Gainsborough Lincs 85 P3
Gainsborough Suffk 53 L3
Gainsford End Essex 52 B4
Gairloch Highld 153 Q2
Gairlochy Highld 146 F11
Gairneybridge P & K 134 E8
Gaisgill W & F 102 B9
Gaitsgill Cumb 110 G11
Galashiels Border 117 P3
Galgate Lancs 95 K9
Galhampton Somset 20 B9
Gallanachbeg Ag & B 130 G2
Gallanachmore Ag & B 130 G2
Gallantry Bank Ches E 69 P4
Gallatown Fife 134 H9
Galley Common Warwks 59 M6
Galleywood Essex 52 B11
Gallovie Highld 147 P10
Galloway Forest Park 114 H10
Gallowfauld Angus 142 G9
Gallowhill P & K 142 B10
Gallows Green Essex 52 F6
Gallows Green Worcs 46 H2
Gallowstree Common Oxon 35 J8
Galltair Highld 145 P3
Gallt-y-foel Gwynd 67 K2
Gallypot Street E Susx 25 L3
Galmisdale Highld 144 G11
Galmpton Devon 6 H10
Galmpton Torbay 7 M7
Galphay N York 97 L6
Galston E Ayrs 125 N10
Gamballs Green Staffs 83 M11
Gamblesby W & F 102 B3
Gambles Green Essex 52 C9
Gamelsby Cumb 110 E10
Gamesley Derbys 83 M6
Gamlingay Cambs 62 B10
Gamlingay Cinques Cambs 62 B10
Gamlingay Great Heath Cambs 62 B10
Gammersgill N York 96 G4
Gamrie Abers 159 J5
Gamston Notts 72 F3
Gamston Notts 85 M5
Ganarew Herefs 45 Q11
Ganavan Bay Ag & B 138 F11
Gang Cnwll 5 N8
Ganllwyd Gwynd 67 N10
Gannachy Angus 143 K3
Ganstead E R Yk 93 K4
Ganthorpe N York 98 D6
Ganton N York 99 K5
Ganwick Corner Herts 50 G11
Gappah Devon 9 L9
Garbity Moray 157 Q7
Garboldisham Norfk 64 E5
Garbole Highld 148 D3
Garchory Abers 149 Q5
Garden City Flints 81 L11
Gardeners Green Wokham 35 M11
Gardenstown Abers 159 K5
Garden Village Sheff 90 H11
Garderhouse Shet 169 q9
Gardham E R Yk 92 G2
Gare Hill Somset 20 E6
Garelochhead Ag & B 131 Q9
Garford Oxon 34 D5
Garforth Leeds 91 L4
Gargrave N York 96 D10
Gargunnock Stirlg 133 L9
Garlic Street Norfk 65 J5
Garlieston D & G 107 N8
Garlinge Kent 39 P8
Garlinge Green Kent 39 K11
Garlogie Abers 151 K6
Garmond Abers 159 K7
Garmouth Moray 157 Q5
Garmston Shrops 57 L3
Garnant Carmth 29 J2
Garndolbenmaen Gwynd 66 H6
Garnett Bridge W & F 101 P11
Garnfadryn Gwynd 66 D8
Garnlydan Blae G 30 G2
Garnswllt Swans 28 H3
Garn-yr-erw Torfn 30 H3
Garrabost W Isls 168 k4
Garrallan E Ayrs 115 K4
Garras Cnwll 3 J9
Garreg Gwynd 67 L6
Garrigill W & F 102 D2
Garriston N York 97 J2
Garroch D & G 108 C4
Garrochtrie D & G 106 F10
Garrochty Ag & B 124 D7
Garros Highld 152 H5
Garsdale W & F 95 Q3
Garsdale Head W & F 96 A2
Garsdon Wilts 33 J7
Garshall Green Staffs 70 H8
Garsington Oxon 34 G4
Garstang Lancs 95 K11
Garston Herts 50 D10
Garston Lpool 81 N8
Garswood St Hel 82 C5
Gartachossan Ag & B 122 D7
Gartcosh N Lans 126 B4
Garth Brdgnd 29 N6
Garth Mons 31 K6
Garth Powys 44 D5
Garth Powys 56 D10
Garth Wrexhm 69 J6
Garthamlock C Glas 126 B4
Garthbrengy Powys 44 E8
Gartheli Cerdgn 43 L3
Garthmyl Powys 56 B5
Garthorpe Leics 73 L6
Garthorpe N Linc 92 D7
Garth Row W & F 101 P11
Garths W & F 95 L3
Gartly Abers 158 D11
Gartmore Stirlg 132 G8
Gartness N Lans 126 D5
Gartness Stirlg 132 G10
Gartocharn W Duns 132 E10
Garton E R Yk 93 N3
Garton-on-the-Wolds E R Yk 99 K9
Gartymore Highld 163 N4
Garva Bridge Highld 147 N9
Garvald Border 127 L8
Garvald E Loth 128 F5
Garvan Highld 138 H2
Garvard Ag & B 136 b3
Garve Highld 155 L5
Garvellachs Ag & B 130 D5
Garvestone Norfk 76 E10
Garvock Inver 124 H3
Garway Herefs 45 P10
Garway Common Herefs 45 P10
Garway Hill Herefs 45 N9
Garynahine W Isls 168 h4
Garyvard W Isls 168 i6
Gasper Wilts 20 E8
Gastard Wilts 32 G11
Gasthorpe Norfk 64 D5
Gaston Green Essex 51 L7
Gatcombe IoW 14 E9
Gateacre Lpool 81 N7
Gatebeck W & F 95 L3
Gate Burton Lincs 85 P4
Gateford Notts 85 J4
Gateforth N York 91 P5
Gatehead E Ayrs 125 K10
Gate Helmsley N York 98 D9
Gatehouse Nthumb 111 Q3
Gatehouse of Fleet D & G 108 C9
Gateley Norfk 76 D7
Gatenby N York 97 M3
Gatesgarth Cumb 100 G7
Gateshaw Border 118 E6
Gateshead Gatesd 113 L8
Gates Heath Ches W 69 N2
Gateside Angus 142 G9
Gateside E Rens 125 M6
Gateside Fife 134 F6
Gateside N Ayrs 125 K7
Gateslack D & G 116 B10
Gathurst Wigan 88 G9
Gatley Stockp 82 H7
Gatton Surrey 36 G10
Gattonside Border 117 Q3
Gatwick Airport W Susx 24 G2
Gaufron Powys 55 M11
Gaulby Leics 72 H10
Gauldry Fife 135 K3
Gauldswell P & K 142 C7
Gaulkthorn Lancs 89 M5
Gaultree Norfk 75 J9
Gaunton's Bank Ches E 69 Q5
Gaunt's Common Dorset 12 H3
Gaunt's End Essex 51 N5
Gautby Lincs 86 G6
Gavinton Border 129 K9
Gawber Barns 91 J9
Gawcott Bucks 49 J8
Gawsworth Ches E 83 J11
Gawthorpe Wakefd 90 H6
Gawthrop W & F 95 P3
Gawthwaite W & F 94 F4
Gay Bowers Essex 52 C11
Gaydon Warwks 48 C4
Gayhurst M Keyn 49 M5
Gayle N York 96 C3
Gayles N York 103 M9
Gay Street W Susx 24 C6
Gayton Norfk 75 P7
Gayton Staffs 70 H9
Gayton W Nthn 49 K4
Gayton Wirral 81 K8
Gayton le Marsh Lincs 87 M4
Gayton Thorpe Norfk 75 P7
Gaywood Norfk 75 M6
Gazeley Suffk 63 M8
Gear Cnwll 3 J9
Gearraidh Bhaird W Isls 168 i6
Gearraidh na h-Aibhne W Isls 168 h4
Geary Highld 152 D5
Gedding Suffk 64 C10
Geddington N Nthn 61 J4
Gedling Notts 72 G2
Gedney Lincs 74 H6
Gedney Broadgate Lincs 74 H6
Gedney Drove End Lincs 75 J5
Gedney Dyke Lincs 74 H5
Gedney Hill Lincs 74 F8
Gee Cross Tamesd 83 L6
Geeston Rutlnd 73 P10
Geirinis W Isls 168 c13
Geldeston Norfk 65 M3
Gelli Rhondd 30 C6
Gelli Torfn 31 J6
Gellideg Myr Td 30 D3
Gellifor Denbgs 68 F2
Gelligaer Caerph 30 F5
Gelligroes Caerph 30 G6
Gelligron Neath 29 K4
Gellilydan Gwynd 67 M7
Gellinudd Neath 29 K4
Gelly Pembks 41 L7
Gellyburn P & K 141 Q10
Gellywen Carmth 41 Q6
Gelston D & G 108 G9
Gelston Lincs 86 B11
Gembling E R Yk 99 N9
Gentleshaw Staffs 58 G2
Georgefield D & G 110 E2
George Green Bucks 35 Q8
Georgeham Devon 16 H4
Georgemas Junction Station Highld 167 L5
George Nympton Devon 17 N7
Georgetown Blae G 30 G3
Georgia Cnwll 2 D6
Georth Ork 169 c4
Gerinish W Isls 168 c13
Gerlan Gwynd 79 L11
Germansweek Devon 8 B6
Germoe Cnwll 2 F8
Gerrans Cnwll 3 M6
Gerrards Cross Bucks 36 B3
Gerrick R & Cl 105 K8
Gestingthorpe Essex 52 D4
Gethsemane Pembks 41 L2
Geuffordd Powys 56 C2
Gib Hill Ches W 82 D9
Gibraltar Lincs 87 Q9
Gibsmere Notts 85 M11
Giddeahall Wilts 32 G10
Giddy Green Dorset 12 D7
Gidea Park Gt Lon 37 M2
Gidleigh Devon 8 G7
Giffnock E Rens 125 P6
Gifford E Loth 128 E6
Giffordtown Fife 134 H5
Giggleswick N York 96 B8
Gigha Ag & B 123 K10
Gilberdyke E R Yk 92 D5
Gilbert's End Worcs 46 F6
Gilbert Street Hants 22 H8
Gilchriston E Loth 128 D6
Gilcrux Cumb 100 F3
Gildersome Leeds 90 G5
Gildingwells Rothm 85 J3
Gilesgate Moor Dur 103 Q2
Gileston V Glam 30 D11
Gilfach Caerph 30 G5
Gilfach Goch Brdgnd 30 C6
Gilfachrheda Cerdgn 42 H3
Gilgarran Cumb 100 D6
Gill W & F 101 M5
Gillamoor N York 98 D3
Gillan Cnwll 3 K8
Gillen Highld 152 D6
Gillesbie D & G 110 C2
Gilling East N York 98 C5
Gillingham Dorset 20 F9
Gillingham Medway 38 C8
Gillingham Norfk 65 N3
Gilling West N York 103 N9
Gillock Highld 167 M5
Gillow Heath Staffs 70 F3
Gills Highld 167 P2
Gill's Green Kent 26 C5
Gilmanscleuch Border 117 L6
Gilmerton C Edin 127 P4
Gilmerton P & K 133 P3
Gilmonby Dur 103 J8
Gilmorton Leics 60 C3
Gilsland Nthumb 111 M7
Gilson Warwks 59 J7
Gilstead C Brad 90 E3
Gilston Border 128 C8
Gilston Herts 51 K8
Gilston Park Herts 51 K8
Giltbrook Notts 84 G11
Gilwern Mons 30 H2
Gimingham Norfk 77 K4
Ginclough Ches E 83 L9
Gingers Green E Susx 25 P8
Gipping Suffk 64 F9
Gipsey Bridge Lincs 87 J11
Girdle Toll N Ayrs 125 J9
Girlington C Brad 90 E4
Girlsta Shet 169 r8
Girsby N York 104 C9
Girtford C Beds 61 Q11
Girthon D & G 108 D10
Girton Cambs 62 F8
Girton Notts 85 P7
Girvan S Ayrs 114 C8
Gisburn Lancs 96 B11
Gisleham Suffk 65 Q4
Gislingham Suffk 64 F7
Gissing Norfk 64 G4
Gittisham Devon 10 C5
Givons Grove Surrey 36 E10
Gladestry Powys 45 J3
Gladsmuir E Loth 128 D5
Glais Swans 29 K4
Glaisdale N York 105 L9
Glamis Angus 142 F8
Glanaber Gwynd 67 L4
Glanaman Carmth 29 J2
Glandford Norfk 76 E3
Glan-Duar Carmth 43 K6
Glandwr Pembks 41 N5
Glan-Dwyfach Gwynd 66 H6
Glandy Cross Carmth 41 M5
Glandyfi Cerdgn 54 F5
Glangrwyney Powys 45 J11
Glanllynfi Brdgnd 29 N6
Glanmule Powys 56 B6
Glanrhyd Pembks 41 M2
Glan-rhyd Powys 29 L3
Glanton Nthumb 119 L8
Glanton Pike Nthumb 119 L8
Glanvilles Wootton Dorset 11 P3
Glan-y-don Flints 80 H9
Glan-y-llyn Cardif 30 F8
Glan-y-nant Powys 55 L8
Glan-yr-afon Gwynd 68 B6
Glan-yr-afon Gwynd 68 D6
Glan-yr-afon IoA 79 L8
Glan-yr-afon Swans 28 H3
Glan-y-wern Gwynd 67 L8
Glapthorn N Nthn 61 M2
Glapwell Derbys 84 G7
Glasbury Powys 44 H7
Glascoed Denbgs 80 D10
Glascoed Mons 31 K4
Glascote Staffs 59 K4
Glascwm Powys 44 H4
Glasfryn Conwy 68 B4
Glasgow C Glas 125 P4
Glasgow Airport Rens 125 M4
Glasgow Prestwick Airport S Ayrs 114 G2
Glasgow Science Centre C Glas 125 P4
Glasinfryn Gwynd 79 K11
Glasnacardoch Bay Highld 145 L8
Glasnakille Highld 144 H5
Glasphein Highld 152 B8
Glaspwll Powys 54 G5
Glassenbury Kent 26 C4
Glassford S Lans 126 C8
Glasshoughton Wakefd 91 L6
Glasshouse Gloucs 46 D10
Glasshouse Hill Gloucs 46 D10
Glasshouses N York 97 J8
Glasslaw Abers 159 L6
Glasson Cumb 110 E8
Glasson Lancs 95 J9
Glassonby W & F 101 Q3
Glasson Dock Lancs 95 J9
Glasterlaw Angus 143 K7
Glaston Rutlnd 73 M10
Glastonbury Somset 19 P7
Glatton Cambs 61 Q3
Glazebrook Warrtn 82 E6
Glazebury Warrtn 82 E5
Glazeley Shrops 57 N7
Gleadless Sheff 84 E4
Gleadsmoss Ches E 82 H11
Gleaston W & F 94 F6
Glebe Highld 147 N4
Gledhow Leeds 91 J3
Gledpark D & G 108 D10
Gledrid Shrops 69 K7
Glemsford Suffk 52 D2
Glen Achulish Highld 139 K6
Glenallachie Moray 157 P9
Glenancross Highld 145 L9
Glenaros House Ag & B 137 P7
Glen Auldyn IoM 80 f3
Glenbarr Ag & B 120 C4
Glenbarry Abers 158 E7
Glenbeg Highld 137 P3
Glenbervie Abers 151 K11
Glenboig N Lans 126 C4
Glenborrodale Highld 137 Q3
Glenbranter Ag & B 131 N8
Glenbreck Border 116 F6
Glenbrittle Highld 144 F3
Glenbuck E Ayrs 115 P2
Glencally Angus 142 F5
Glencaple D & G 109 L7
Glencarse P & K 134 F3
Glencoe Highld 139 L6
Glencothe Border 116 F5
Glencraig Fife 134 F9
Glencrosh D & G 115 Q10
Glendale Highld 152 B8
Glendaruel Ag & B 131 K11
Glendevon P & K 134 B7
Glendoe Lodge Highld 147 L6
Glendoick P & K 134 G3
Glenduckie Fife 134 H4
Glenegedale Ag & B 122 D9
Glenelg Highld 145 P4
Glenerney Moray 157 J8
Glenfarg P & K 134 E5
Glenfield Leics 72 E9
Glenfinnan Highld 145 R11
Glenfintaig Lodge Highld 146 G10
Glenfoot P & K 134 F4
Glenfyne Lodge Ag & B 131 Q4
Glengarnock N Ayrs 125 J7

Glengolly Highld 167 K3
Glengorm Castle Ag & B 137 L4
Glengrasco Highld 152 G9
Glenholm Border 116 G4
Glenhoul D & G 115 M10
Glenkin Ag & B 131 N11
Glenkindie Abers 150 C5
Glenlivet Moray 149 M2
Glenlochar D & G 108 F8
Glenlomond P & K 134 F7
Glenluce D & G 106 G6
Glenmassen Ag & B 131 N10
Glenmavis N Lans 126 D4
Glen Maye IoM 80 b6
Glen Mona IoM 80 g4
Glenmore Highld 152 G9
Glenmore Lodge Highld 148 H6
Glen Nevis House Highld 139 L3
Glenochil Clacks 133 P8
Glen Parva Leics 72 F11
Glenquiech Angus 142 G5
Glenralloch Ag & B 123 Q6
Glenridding W & F 101 L7
Glenrothes Fife 134 H7
Glenshero Lodge Highld 147 P9
Glenstriven Ag & B 124 D2
Glentham Lincs 86 D2
Glentrool D & G 107 L2
Glen Trool Lodge D & G 114 H11
Glentruim Highld 148 B9
Glentworth Lincs 86 B3
Glenuig Highld 138 B2
Glenvarragill Highld 152 H10
Glen Vine IoM 80 d6
Glenwhilly D & G 106 G3
Glespin S Lans 115 R2
Glewstone Herefs 45 R10
Glinton C Pete 74 C9
Glooston Leics 73 K11
Glossop Derbys 83 M6
Gloster Hill Nthumb 119 Q10
Gloucester Gloucs 46 F11
Gloucester Services Gloucs 32 F2
Gloucestershire Airport Gloucs 46 G10
Glusburn N York 96 F11
Glutt Lodge Highld 166 H9
Gluvian Cnwll 4 E9
Glympton Oxon 48 D10
Glynarthen Cerdgn 42 F5
Glyn Ceiriog Wrexhm 68 H7
Glyncoch Rhondd 30 E6
Glyncorrwg Neath 29 N5
Glynde E Susx 25 L9
Glyndebourne E Susx 25 L8
Glyndyfrdwy Denbgs 68 F6
Glynneath Neath 29 N3
Glynogwr Brdgnd 30 C7
Glyntaff Rhondd 30 E7
Glyntawe Powys 44 A11
Glynteg Carmth 42 G7
Gnosall Staffs 70 E10
Gnosall Heath Staffs 70 E10
Goadby Leics 73 K11
Goadby Marwood Leics 73 K5
Goatacre Wilts 33 K9
Goatham Green E Susx 26 D7
Goathill Dorset 20 C11
Goathland N York 105 M10
Goathurst Somset 19 J8
Goathurst Common Kent 37 L10
Goat Lees Kent 26 H2
Gobowen Shrops 69 K8
Godalming Surrey 23 Q6
Goddard's Corner Suffk 65 K8
Goddard's Green Kent 26 D5
Goddards Green W Susx 24 G6
Godden Green Kent 37 N9
Godford Cross Devon 10 C4
Godington Oxon 48 H9
Godley Tamesd 83 L5
Godmanchester Cambs 62 B6
Godmanstone Dorset 11 P5
Godmersham Kent 39 J11
Godney Somset 19 N6
Godolphin Cross Cnwll 2 G7
Godre'r-graig Neath 29 L3
Godshill Hants 21 N11
Godshill IoW 14 F10
Godstone Staffs 71 J8
Godstone Surrey 37 J10
Godsworthy Devon 8 D9
Godwinscroft Hants 13 L5
Goetre Mons 31 K3
Goff's Oak Herts 50 H10
Gogar C Edin 127 M3
Goginan Cerdgn 54 F8
Golan Gwynd 67 J6
Golant Cnwll 5 J11
Golberdon Cnwll 5 N7
Golborne Wigan 82 D5
Golcar Kirk 90 D7
Goldcliff Newpt 31 L8
Golden Cross E Susx 25 M8
Golden Green Kent 37 P11
Golden Grove Carmth 43 L11
Goldenhill C Stke 70 F4
Golden Hill Pembks 41 J10
Golden Pot Hants 23 K6
Golden Valley Derbys 84 F10
Golders Green Gt Lon 36 F3
Goldfinch Bottom W Berk 22 F2
Goldhanger Essex 52 F10
Gold Hill Cambs 62 H2
Gold Hill Dorset 12 D2
Golding Shrops 57 J4
Goldington Bed 61 N10
Goldsborough N York 97 N9
Goldsborough N York 105 M8
Goldsithney Cnwll 2 E7
Goldstone Kent 39 N9
Goldstone Shrops 70 C9
Goldthorpe Barns 91 M10
Goldworthy Devon 16 F7
Golford Kent 26 C4
Golford Green Kent 26 C4
Gollanfield Highld 156 E7
Gollinglith Foot N York 97 J4
Golly Wrexhm 69 K3
Golsoncott Somset 18 D7
Golspie Highld 163 J6
Gomeldon Wilts 21 N7
Gomersal Kirk 90 G5
Gomshall Surrey 36 C11
Gonalston Notts 85 L11
Gonerby Hill Foot Lincs 73 N3

Gonerby Moor Lincs 73 M3
Gonfirth Shet 169 q7
Goodameavy Devon 6 E6
Good Easter Essex 51 P8
Gooderstone Norfk 75 Q10
Goodleigh Devon 17 L5
Goodmanham E R Yk 92 E3
Goodmayes Gt Lon 37 L3
Goodnestone Kent 38 H9
Goodnestone Kent 39 N11
Goodrich Herefs 45 R11
Goodrington Torbay 7 M7
Goodshaw Lancs 89 N5
Goodshaw Fold Lancs 89 N5
Goodstone Devon 7 K4
Goodwick Pembks 40 H3
Goodwood W Susx 15 N5
Goodworth Clatford Hants 22 C6
Goodyers End Warwks 59 M7
Goole E R Yk 92 B6
Goole Fields E R Yk 92 C6
Goom's Hill Worcs 47 K3
Goonbell Cnwll 3 J4
Goonhavern Cnwll 3 J3
Goonvrea Cnwll 3 J4
Goosecruives Abers 151 K11
Gooseford Devon 8 G6
Goose Green Essex 53 N6
Goose Green Kent 26 D4
Goose Green Kent 37 Q10
Goose Green S Glos 32 C10
Goose Green W Susx 24 D7
Goose Green Wigan 82 C4
Gooseham Cnwll 16 C8
Gooseham Mill Cnwll 16 C8
Goosehill Green Worcs 46 H2
Goose Pool Herefs 45 P7
Goosey Oxon 34 C6
Goosnargh Lancs 88 H3
Goostrey Ches E 82 G10
Gordano Services N Som 31 P9
Gorddinog Conwy 79 M10
Gordon Border 118 B2
Gordon Arms Hotel Border 117 L5
Gordonstone Abers 158 E6
Gordonstown Abers 158 H10
Gore Powys 45 K3
Gorebridge Mdloth 127 Q5
Gorefield Cambs 74 H8
Gore Pit Essex 52 E8
Gores Wilts 21 M3
Gore Street Kent 39 N8
Gorey Jersey 11 c2
Goring Oxon 34 H8
Goring-by-Sea W Susx 24 D10
Goring Heath Oxon 35 J9
Gorleston-on-Sea Norfk 77 Q11
Gorrachie Abers 158 H6
Gorran Churchtown Cnwll 3 P5
Gorran Haven Cnwll 3 Q5
Gorran High Lanes Cnwll 3 P5
Gorrig Cerdgn 42 H6
Gors Cerdgn 54 E9
Gorsedd Flints 80 H9
Gorseddau Slate Landscape Gwynd 67 K6
Gorse Hill Swindn 33 N7
Gorseinon Swans 28 G5
Gorseybank Derbys 71 P4
Gorsgoch Cerdgn 43 J4
Gorslas Carmth 28 G2
Gorsley Gloucs 46 C9
Gorsley Common Herefs 46 C9
Gorstage Ches W 82 D10
Gorstan Highld 155 L5
Gorstella Ches W 69 L2
Gorsten Ag & B 138 C11
Gorst Hill Worcs 57 N10
Gorsty Hill Staffs 71 L9
Gorthleck Highld 147 N3
Gorton Manch 83 J5
Gosbeck Suffk 64 H10
Gosberton Lincs 74 D4
Gosberton Clough Lincs 74 C5
Gosfield Essex 52 C6
Gosford Devon 10 C5
Gosford Oxon 34 E2
Gosforth Cumb 100 E10
Gosforth N u Ty 113 K7
Gosling Street Somset 19 P8
Gosmore Herts 50 E5
Gospel End Staffs 58 C6
Gospel Green W Susx 23 P8
Gosport Hants 14 H7
Gossard's Green C Beds 49 Q6
Gossington Gloucs 32 D4
Goswick Nthumb 119 L2
Gotham Notts 72 E4
Gotherington Gloucs 47 J9
Gotton Somset 18 H9
Goudhurst Kent 26 B4
Goulceby Lincs 87 J5
Gourdas Abers 159 J9
Gourdie C Dund 142 F11
Gourdon Abers 143 Q3
Gourock Inver 124 G2
Govan C Glas 125 N4
Goveton Devon 7 K9
Govilon Mons 31 J2
Gowdall E R Yk 91 Q6
Gower Highld 155 P6
Gower Swans 28 F6
Gowerton Swans 28 G5
Gowkhall Fife 134 D10
Gowthorpe E R Yk 98 F10
Goxhill E R Yk 93 L2
Goxhill N Linc 93 K6
Goytre Neath 29 L7
Grabhair W Isls 168 i6
Graby Lincs 74 A5
Grade Cnwll 3 J11
Gradeley Green Ches E 69 Q4
Graffham W Susx 23 P11
Grafham Cambs 61 Q7
Grafham Surrey 36 B2
Grafton Herefs 45 P7
Grafton Oxon 33 Q4
Grafton Shrops 69 M11
Grafton Worcs 46 A2
Grafton Worcs 47 J7
Grafton Flyford Worcs 47 J3
Grafton Regis W Nthn 49 L5
Grafton Underwood N Nthn 61 K4
Grafty Green Kent 26 E2
Graianrhyd Denbgs 68 H3
Graig Conwy 79 Q10

Graig Denbgs 80 F10
Graigfechan Denbgs 68 F4
Grain Medway 38 E6
Grains Bar Oldham 90 B9
Grainsby Lincs 93 N11
Grainthorpe Lincs 93 Q11
Grampound Cnwll 3 N4
Grampound Road Cnwll 3 N3
Gramsdal W Isls 168 d12
Gramsdale W Isls 168 d12
Granborough Bucks 49 L9
Granby Notts 73 K3
Grandborough Warwks 59 Q11
Grand Chemins Jersey 11 c2
Grandes Rocques Guern 10 b1
Grandtully P & K 141 M7
Grange Cumb 101 J7
Grange Medway 38 C8
Grange P & K 134 H2
Grange Wirral 81 J7
Grange Crossroads Moray 158 C7
Grange Hall Moray 157 K5
Grangehall S Lans 116 D2
Grange Hill Essex 37 K2
Grangemill Derbys 84 B9
Grange Moor Kirk 90 G7
Grangemouth Falk 133 Q11
Grange of Lindores Fife 134 H4
Grange-over-Sands W & F 95 J5
Grangepans Falk 134 C11
Grange Park W Nthn 60 G9
Grangetown R & Cl 104 F6
Grangetown Sundld 113 P10
Grange Villa Dur 113 K10
Gransmoor E R Yk 99 N9
Gransmore Green Essex 51 Q6
Granston Pembks 40 G4
Grantchester Cambs 62 F9
Grantham Lincs 73 N3
Granton C Edin 127 N2
Grantown-on-Spey Highld 149 J2
Grantsfield Herefs 45 Q2
Grantshouse Border 129 L6
Grappenhall Warrtn 82 D7
Grasby Lincs 93 J10
Grasmere W & F 101 K9
Grasscroft Oldham 83 L4
Grassendale Lpool 81 M7
Grassgarth Cumb 101 K2
Grass Green Essex 52 B4
Grassington N York 96 F8
Grassmoor Derbys 84 F7
Grassthorpe Notts 85 N7
Grateley Hants 21 Q6
Gratwich Staffs 71 J4
Graveley Cambs 62 C8
Graveley Herts 50 F5
Gravelly Hill Birm 58 H6
Gravelsbank Shrops 56 E4
Graveney Kent 39 J9
Gravesend Kent 37 Q6
Gravir W Isls 168 i6
Grayingham Lincs 92 F11
Grayrigg W & F 101 Q11
Grays Thurr 37 P5
Grayshott Hants 23 N7
Grayson Green Cumb 100 C5
Grayswood Surrey 23 P8
Graythorpe Hartpl 104 F5
Grazeley Wokham 35 J11
Greasbrough Rothm 91 L11
Greasby Wirral 81 K7
Greasley Notts 84 G11
Great Abington Cambs 62 H11
Great Addington N Nthn 61 L5
Great Alne Warwks 47 M3
Great Altcar Lancs 88 C9
Great Amwell Herts 50 H8
Great Asby W & F 102 C8
Great Ashfield Suffk 64 D8
Great Ayton N York 104 G8
Great Baddow Essex 52 B11
Great Badminton S Glos 32 F8
Great Bardfield Essex 51 Q4
Great Barford Bed 61 P10
Great Barr Sandw 58 F5
Great Barrington Gloucs 33 P2
Great Barrow Ches W 81 P11
Great Barton Suffk 64 B8
Great Barugh N York 98 E5
Great Bavington Nthumb 112 E4
Great Bealings Suffk 53 M2
Great Bedwyn Wilts 21 Q2
Great Bentley Essex 53 K7
Great Billing W Nthn 60 H8
Great Bircham Norfk 75 Q4
Great Blakenham Suffk 64 G11
Great Blencow W & F 101 N4
Great Bolas Wrekin 70 A10
Great Bookham Surrey 36 D10
Great Bosullow Cnwll 2 C7
Great Bourton Oxon 48 E5
Great Bowden Leics 60 F3
Great Bradley Suffk 63 L10
Great Braxted Essex 52 E9
Great Bricett Suffk 64 E11
Great Brickhill Bucks 49 P8
Great Bridge Sandw 58 E6
Great Bridgeford Staffs 70 F9
Great Brington W Nthn 60 E7
Great Bromley Essex 53 J6
Great Broughton Cumb 100 E4
Great Broughton N York 104 F9
Great Budworth Ches W 82 E9
Great Burdon Darltn 104 B7
Great Burstead Essex 37 Q2
Great Busby N York 104 F9
Great Canfield Essex 51 N7
Great Carlton Lincs 87 M3
Great Casterton Rutlnd 73 Q9
Great Chalfield Wilts 20 G2
Great Chart Kent 26 G3
Great Chatwell Staffs 57 P2
Great Chell C Stke 70 F4
Great Chesterford Essex 51 M2
Great Cheverell Wilts 21 J4
Great Chishill Cambs 51 K3
Great Clacton Essex 53 L8
Great Cliff Wakefd 91 J7
Great Clifton Cumb 100 D5
Great Coates NE Lin 93 M9
Great Comberton Worcs 47 J6
Great Comp Kent 37 P9
Great Corby Cumb 111 J10
Great Cornard Suffk 52 E3
Great Cowden E R Yk 93 M2

Great Coxwell Oxon 33 Q6
Great Cransley N Nthn 60 H5
Great Cressingham Norfk 76 B11
Great Crosthwaite Cumb 101 J6
Great Cubley Derbys 71 M7
Great Cumbrae Island N Ayrs 124 F6
Great Dalby Leics 73 J8
Great Denham Bed 61 M11
Great Doddington N Nthn 61 J8
Great Doward Herefs 45 Q11
Great Dunham Norfk 76 B9
Great Dunmow Essex 51 P6
Great Durnford Wilts 21 M7
Great Easton Essex 51 P5
Great Easton Leics 60 H2
Great Eccleston Lancs 88 E2
Great Edstone N York 98 E4
Great Ellingham Norfk 64 E2
Great Elm Somset 20 D5
Great Everdon W Nthn 60 C9
Great Eversden Cambs 62 E10
Great Fencote N York 97 L2
Greatfield Wilts 33 L7
Great Finborough Suffk 64 E10
Greatford Lincs 74 A8
Great Fransham Norfk 76 B9
Great Gaddesden Herts 50 B8
Greatgate Staffs 71 K7
Great Gidding Cambs 61 P4
Great Givendale E R Yk 98 G10
Great Glemham Suffk 65 L9
Great Glen Leics 72 H11
Great Gonerby Lincs 73 M3
Great Gransden Cambs 62 C9
Great Green Cambs 50 G2
Great Green Norfk 65 K4
Great Green Suffk 64 C10
Great Green Suffk 64 C8
Great Habton N York 98 F5
Great Hale Lincs 74 B2
Great Hallingbury Essex 51 M7
Greatham Hants 23 L8
Greatham Hartpl 104 E5
Greatham W Susx 24 B7
Great Hampden Bucks 35 M4
Great Harrowden N Nthn 61 J6
Great Harwood Lancs 89 L4
Great Haseley Oxon 34 H4
Great Hatfield E R Yk 93 L2
Great Haywood Staffs 70 H10
Great Heck N York 91 P6
Great Henny Essex 52 E4
Great Hinton Wilts 20 H3
Great Hockham Norfk 64 D3
Great Holland Essex 53 M8
Great Hollands Br For 35 N11
Great Horkesley Essex 52 G5
Great Hormead Herts 51 K5
Great Horton C Brad 90 E4
Great Horwood Bucks 49 L8
Great Houghton Barns 91 L9
Great Houghton W Nthn 60 G9
Great Hucklow Derbys 83 Q9
Great Kelk E R Yk 99 N9
Great Kimble Bucks 35 M3
Great Kingshill Bucks 35 N5
Great Langdale W & F 101 J9
Great Langton N York 103 Q11
Great Leighs Essex 52 B8
Great Limber Lincs 93 K9
Great Linford M Keyn 49 N6
Great Livermere Suffk 64 B7
Great Longstone Derbys 84 B6
Great Lumley Dur 113 L11
Great Lyth Shrops 56 H3
Great Malvern Worcs 46 E5
Great Maplestead Essex 52 D5
Great Marton Bpool 88 C3
Great Massingham Norfk 75 Q6
Great Melton Norfk 76 G10
Great Meols Wirral 81 J6
Great Milton Oxon 34 H4
Great Missenden Bucks 35 N4
Great Mitton Lancs 89 L3
Great Mongeham Kent 39 Q11
Great Moulton Norfk 64 H3
Great Munden Herts 51 J6
Great Musgrave W & F 102 D8
Great Ness Shrops 69 L11
Great Notley Essex 52 B7
Great Oak Mons 31 L2
Great Oakley Essex 53 L6
Great Oakley N Nthn 61 J3
Great Offley Herts 50 D5
Great Ormside W & F 102 D7
Great Orton Cumb 110 F10
Great Ouseburn N York 97 P8
Great Oxendon N Nthn 60 F4
Great Oxney Green Essex 51 Q9
Great Palgrave Norfk 76 A9
Great Pardon Essex 51 K9
Great Pattenden Kent 26 B3
Great Paxton Cambs 62 B8
Great Plumpton Lancs 88 D4
Great Plumstead Norfk 77 L9
Great Ponton Lincs 73 M4
Great Potheridge Devon 17 J9
Great Preston Leeds 91 L5
Great Purston W Nthn 48 F7
Great Raveley Cambs 62 C4
Great Rissington Gloucs 47 N11
Great Rollright Oxon 48 B8
Great Ryburgh Norfk 76 D6
Great Ryle Nthumb 119 K8
Great Ryton Shrops 56 H4
Great Saling Essex 51 R6
Great Salkeld W & F 101 Q3
Great Sampford Essex 51 P3
Great Saredon Staffs 58 D3
Great Saughall Ches W 81 M11
Great Saxham Suffk 63 M8
Great Shefford W Berk 34 C9
Great Shelford Cambs 62 G10
Great Smeaton N York 104 B10
Great Snoring Norfk 76 C5
Great Somerford Wilts 33 J8
Great Soudley Shrops 70 C9
Great Stainton Darltn 104 B6
Great Stambridge Essex 38 E3
Great Staughton Cambs 61 Q8
Great Steeping Lincs 87 M8
Great Stonar Kent 39 P10
Greatstone-on-Sea Kent 27 J7
Great Strickland W & F 101 Q6
Great Stukeley Cambs 62 B6

Great Sturton Lincs 86 H5
Great Sutton Ches W 81 M9
Great Sutton Shrops 57 J8
Great Swinburne Nthumb 112 D5
Great Tew Oxon 48 D9
Great Tey Essex 52 E6
Great Thurlow Suffk 63 L10
Great Torrington Devon 16 H8
Great Tosson Nthumb 119 K10
Great Totham Essex 52 E9
Great Totham Essex 52 E9
Great Tows Lincs 86 H5
Great Urswick W & F 94 F6
Great Wakering Essex 38 E3
Great Waldingfield Suffk 52 F3
Great Walsingham Norfk 76 C4
Great Waltham Essex 51 Q8
Great Warford Ches E 82 H9
Great Warley Essex 37 N2
Great Washbourne Gloucs 47 J8
Great Weeke Devon 8 H7
Great Welnetham Suffk 64 B10
Great Wenham Suffk 53 J4
Great Whittington Nthumb 112 F6
Great Wigborough Essex 52 G8
Great Wilbraham Cambs 63 J9
Great Wilne Derbys 72 C4
Great Wishford Wilts 21 L7
Great Witchingham Norfk 76 G7
Great Witcombe Gloucs 32 H2
Great Witley Worcs 57 P11
Great Wolford Warwks 47 Q8
Greatworth W Nthn 48 G6
Great Wratting Suffk 63 L11
Great Wymondley Herts 50 F5
Great Wyrley Staffs 58 E3
Great Wytheford Shrops 69 Q11
Great Yarmouth Norfk 77 Q10
Great Yeldham Essex 52 C4
Grebby Lincs 87 M7
Greeba IoM 80 d5
Green Denbgs 80 F11
Green Bank W & F 94 H4
Greenbottom Cnwll 3 K4
Greenburn W Loth 126 G5
Greencroft Hall Dur 113 J11
Green Cross Surrey 23 N7
Green Down Somset 19 Q4
Green End Bed 61 M11
Green End Bed 61 N8
Green End Bed 61 P10
Green End Bed 61 P8
Green End Cambs 62 Q4
Green End Cambs 62 B6
Green End Cambs 62 E9
Green End Cambs 62 G7
Green End Cambs 62 G8
Green End Herts 50 F5
Green End Herts 50 H4
Green End Herts 50 H5
Greenend Oxon 48 B10
Green End Warwks 59 L9
Greenfield Ag & B 131 Q9
Greenfield C Beds 50 C4
Greenfield Flints 80 H9
Greenfield Highld 146 G7
Greenfield Oldham 83 L4
Greenfield Oxon 35 K6
Greenford Gt Lon 36 D4
Greengairs N Lans 126 D3
Greengates C Brad 90 F3
Greengill Cumb 100 F3
Greenhalgh Lancs 88 E3
Greenham Somset 18 E10
Greenham W Berk 34 E11
Green Hammerton N York 97 Q9
Greenhaugh Nthumb 111 Q3
Green Head Cumb 110 G11
Greenhead Nthumb 111 N4
Green Heath Staffs 58 E2
Greenheys Salfd 82 F4
Greenhill D & G 109 P5
Greenhill Falk 126 E2
Greenhill Herefs 46 D5
Greenhill Kent 39 L8
Greenhill Leics 72 C8
Greenhill S Lans 116 C3
Green Hill Wilts 33 L7
Greenhillocks Derbys 84 F4
Greenhills S Lans 125 Q7
Greenhithe Kent 37 N6
Greenholm E Ayrs 125 N10
Greenholme W & F 101 Q9
Greenhouse Border 117 R6
Greenhow Hill N York 96 H8
Greenland Highld 167 M3
Greenland Sheff 84 E3
Greenlands Bucks 35 L7
Green Lane Devon 9 Q4
Green Lane Worcs 47 L2
Greenlaw Border 129 J10
Greenlea D & G 109 M5
Greenloaning P & K 133 N6
Green Moor Barns 90 H11
Greenmount Bury 89 M8
Green Oak E R Yk 92 D4
Greenock Inver 124 H2
Greenodd W & F 94 G4
Green Ore Somset 19 Q4
Green Park Readg 35 K10
Green Quarter W & F 101 N10
Greensgate Norfk 76 G8
Greenshields S Lans 116 E2
Greenside Gatesd 112 H8
Greenside Kirk 90 F7
Greens Norton W Nthn 49 J5
Greenstead Green Essex 52 D6
Greensted Essex 51 M10
Green Street E Susx 26 C9
Green Street Gloucs 46 G3
Green Street Herts 50 E11
Green Street Herts 51 L6
Green Street Worcs 46 G5
Green Street Green Gt Lon 37 K7
Green Street Green Kent 37 N6
Greenstreet Green Suffk 52 H2
Green Tye Herts 51 K7
Greenway Gloucs 46 D8
Greenway Somset 19 K10
Greenway V Glam 30 D10
Greenway Worcs 57 N10
Greenwich Gt Lon 37 J5
Greenwich Maritime Gt Lon 37 J5
Greet Gloucs 47 K8
Greete Shrops 57 K10
Greetham Lincs 87 K6

Greetham – Harlington 273

Greetham Rutlnd 73 N8
Greetland Calder 90 D6
Gregson Lane Lancs 88 H5
Greinton Somset 19 M7
Grenaby IoM 80 c7
Grendon N Nthn 61 J8
Grendon Warwks 59 L5
Grendon Green Herefs 46 A3
Grendon Underwood Bucks 49 J10
Grenofen Devon 6 D4
Grenoside Sheff 84 D2
Greosabhagh W Isls 168 g8
Gresford Wrexhm 69 K4
Gresham Norfk 76 H4
Greshornish Highld 152 E7
Gressenhall Norfk 76 D8
Gressenhall Green Norfk 76 D8
Gressingham Lancs 95 M7
Gresty Green Ches E 70 C4
Greta Bridge Dur 103 L8
Gretna D & G 110 F7
Gretna Green D & G 110 F7
Gretna Services D & G 110 F7
Gretton Gloucs 47 K8
Gretton N Nthn 61 J2
Gretton Shrops 57 J5
Grewelthorpe N York 97 K5
Grey Friars Suffk 65 P7
Greygarth N York 97 J6
Grey Green N Linc 92 C9
Greylake Somset 19 L8
Greylees Lincs 73 Q2
Greyrigg D & G 109 N3
Greys Green Oxon 35 K8
Greysouthen Cumb 100 E5
Greystoke W & F 101 M4
Greystone Angus 143 J9
Greywell Hants 23 K4
Gribb Dorset 10 H4
Gribthorpe E R Yk 92 C3
Griff Warwks 59 N7
Griffithstown Torfn 31 J5
Griffydam Leics 72 C7
Griggs Green Hants 23 M8
Grimeford Village Lancs 89 J8
Grimesthorpe Sheff 84 E3
Grimethorpe Barns 91 L9
Grimister Shet 169 r4
Grimley Worcs 46 F2
Grimmet S Ayrs 114 F5
Grimoldby Lincs 87 L3
Grimpo Shrops 69 L9
Grimsargh Lancs 88 H4
Grimsby NE Lin 93 N8
Grimscote W Nthn 49 J4
Grimscott Cnwll 16 D10
Grimshader W Isls 168 j5
Grimshaw Bl w D 89 L6
Grimshaw Green Lancs 88 F8
Grimsthorpe Lincs 73 Q6
Grimston E R Yk 93 N3
Grimston Leics 72 H6
Grimston Norfk 75 P6
Grimstone Dorset 11 N6
Grimstone End Suffk 64 C8
Grinacombe Moor Devon 5 Q3
Grindale E R Yk 99 N6
Grindle Shrops 57 P4
Grindleford Derbys 84 B5
Grindleton Lancs 95 R11
Grindley Brook Shrops 69 P6
Grindlow Derbys 83 Q9
Grindon Nthumb 118 H2
Grindon S on T 104 C5
Grindon Staffs 71 K4
Grindon Hill Nthumb 112 B7
Grindonrigg Nthumb 118 H2
Gringley on the Hill Notts 85 M2
Grinsdale Cumb 110 G9
Grinshill Shrops 69 P10
Grinton N York 103 K11
Griomsiadar W Isls 168 j5
Grishipoll Ag & B 136 F4
Grisling Common E Susx 25 K6
Gristhorpe N York 99 M4
Griston Norfk 64 C2
Gritley Ork 169 e6
Grittenham Wilts 33 K8
Grittleton Wilts 32 G8
Grizebeck W & F 94 E4
Grizedale W & F 94 G2
Groby Leics 72 E9
Groes Conwy 68 D2
Groes-faen Rhondd 30 E8
Groesffordd Gwynd 66 D7
Groesffordd Powys 44 F9
Groesffordd Marli Denbgs 80 E10
Groeslon Gwynd 66 H3
Groeslon Gwynd 67 J2
Groes-lwyd Powys 56 C2
Groes-Wen Caerph 30 F7
Grogarry W Isls 168 c14
Grogport Ag & B 120 F3
Groigearraidh W Isls 168 c14
Gromford Suffk 65 M10
Gronant Flints 80 F8
Groombridge E Susx 25 M3
Grosebay W Isls 168 g8
Grosmont Mons 45 N10
Grosmont N York 105 M9
Groton Suffk 52 G3
Grotton Oldham 83 L4
Grouville Jersey 11 c2
Grove Bucks 49 P10
Grove Dorset 11 P10
Grove Kent 39 M9
Grove Notts 85 M5
Grove Oxon 34 D6
Grove Pembks 41 J10
Grove Green Kent 38 C10
Grovenhurst Kent 26 B3
Grove Park Gt Lon 37 K6
Grovesend S Glos 32 C7
Grovesend Swans 28 G4
Grubb Street Kent 37 N7
Gruinard Highld 160 E9
Gruinart Ag & B 122 C6
Grula Highld 144 E2
Gruline Ag & B 137 N7
Grumbla Cnwll 2 C8
Grundisburgh Suffk 65 J11
Gruting Shet 169 p9
Grutness Shet 169 r12
Gualachulain Highld 139 L8
Guanockgate Lincs 74 G8
Guardbridge Fife 135 M4
Guarlford Worcs 46 F5
Guay P & K 141 P8
Guernsey Guern 10 b2
Guernsey Airport Guern 10 b2
Guestling Green E Susx 26 E9
Guestling Thorn E Susx 26 E8
Guestwick Norfk 76 F6
Guide Bridge Tamesd 83 K5
Guide Post Nthumb 113 L3
Guilden Morden Cambs 50 G2
Guilden Sutton Ches W 81 N11
Guildford Surrey 23 Q5
Guildstead Kent 38 D9
Guildtown P & K 142 A11
Guilsborough W Nthn 60 E6
Guilsfield Powys 56 C2
Guilton Kent 39 N10
Guiltreehill S Ayrs 114 G5
Guineaford Devon 17 K4
Guisborough R & Cl 104 H7
Guiseley Leeds 90 F2
Guist Norfk 76 E6
Guiting Power Gloucs 47 L10
Gullane E Loth 128 D3
Gulling Green Suffk 64 A10
Gulval Cnwll 2 D7
Gulworthy Devon 6 D4
Gumfreston Pembks 41 M10
Gumley Leics 60 E3
Gummow's Shop Cnwll 4 D10
Gunby E R Yk 92 B3
Gunby Lincs 73 N6
Gundleton Hants 22 H8
Gun Green Kent 26 C5
Gun Hill E Susx 25 N8
Gun Hill Warwks 59 L7
Gunn Devon 17 L5
Gunnerside N York 103 J11
Gunnerton Nthumb 112 D6
Gunness N Linc 92 D8
Gunnislake Cnwll 6 C4
Gunnista Shet 169 s9
Gunthorpe C Pete 74 C10
Gunthorpe N Linc 92 D11
Gunthorpe Norfk 76 E5
Gunthorpe Notts 72 H2
Gunton Suffk 65 Q2
Gunwalloe Cnwll 2 H9
Gupworthy Somset 18 C8
Gurnard IoW 14 E7
Gurnett Ches E 83 K10
Gurney Slade Somset 20 B5
Gurnos Powys 29 L3
Gushmere Kent 38 H10
Gussage All Saints Dorset 12 H2
Gussage St Andrew Dorset 12 G2
Gussage St Michael Dorset 12 G2
Guston Kent 27 P3
Gutcher Shet 169 s4
Guthrie Angus 143 K7
Guyhirn Cambs 74 H10
Guyhirn Gull Cambs 74 G10
Guy's Marsh Dorset 20 F10
Guyzance Nthumb 119 P10
Gwaenysgor Flints 80 F8
Gwalchmai IoA 78 F9
Gwastadnant Gwynd 67 L3
Gwaun-Cae-Gurwen Carmth 29 J2
Gwbert on Sea Cerdgn 42 C4
Gwealavellan Cnwll 2 G5
Gweek Cnwll 3 J8
Gwehelog Mons 31 L4
Gwenddwr Powys 44 F6
Gwennap Cnwll 3 J5
Gwennap Mining District Cnwll 3 K5
Gwenter Cnwll 3 J10
Gwernaffield Flints 81 J11
Gwernesney Mons 31 M4
Gwernogle Carmth 43 K8
Gwernymynydd Flints 68 H2
Gwersyllt Wrexhm 69 K4
Gwespyr Flints 80 G8
Gwindra Cnwll 3 P3
Gwinear Cnwll 2 F6
Gwithian Cnwll 2 F5
Gwredog IoA 78 G7
Gwrhay Caerph 30 G5
Gwyddelwern Denbgs 68 E5
Gwyddgrug Carmth 43 J7
Gwynfryn Wrexhm 69 J4
Gwystre Powys 55 P11
Gwytherin Conwy 68 A2
Gyfelia Wrexhm 69 K5
Gyrn Goch Gwynd 66 G5

H

Habberley Shrops 56 F4
Habberley Worcs 57 Q9
Habergham Lancs 89 N4
Habertoft Lincs 87 P7
Habin W Susx 23 M10
Habrough NE Lin 93 K8
Hacconby Lincs 74 B5
Haceby Lincs 73 Q3
Hacheston Suffk 65 L10
Hackbridge Gt Lon 36 G7
Hackenthorpe Sheff 84 F4
Hackford Norfk 76 F11
Hackforth N York 97 K2
Hack Green Ches E 70 A5
Hackland Ork 169 c4
Hackleton W Nthn 60 H9
Hacklinge Kent 39 P11
Hackman's Gate Worcs 58 C9
Hackness N York 99 K2
Hackness Somset 19 K5
Hackney Gt Lon 36 H4
Hackthorn Lincs 86 C4
Hackthorpe W & F 101 P6
Hacton Gt Lon 37 N3
Hadden Border 118 E3
Haddenham Bucks 35 K3
Haddenham Cambs 62 G5
Haddington E Loth 128 E5
Haddington Lincs 86 B8
Haddiscoe Norfk 65 N2
Haddon Cambs 61 P2
Hade Edge Kirk 83 P4
Hadfield Derbys 83 M5
Hadham Cross Herts 51 K7
Hadham Ford Herts 51 K6
Hadleigh Essex 38 D4
Hadleigh Suffk 52 H3
Hadleigh Heath Suffk 52 G3
Hadley Worcs 46 G2
Hadley Wrekin 57 M2
Hadley End Staffs 71 L10
Hadley Wood Gt Lon 50 G11
Hadlow Kent 37 P10
Hadlow Down E Susx 25 M6
Hadnall Shrops 69 P10
Hadrian's Wall 112 E7
Hadstock Essex 51 N2
Hadston Nthumb 119 Q11
Hadzor Worcs 46 H2
Haffenden Quarter Kent 26 E3
Hafodunos Conwy 80 B11
Hafod-y-bwch Wrexhm 69 K5
Hafod-y-coed Blae G 30 H4
Hafodyrynys Caerph 30 H5
Haggate Lancs 89 P3
Haggbeck Cumb 111 J6
Haggersta Shet 169 q9
Haggerston Nthumb 119 K2
Haggington Hill Devon 17 K2
Haggs Falk 126 D2
Hagley Herefs 45 R6
Hagley Worcs 58 D8
Hagmore Green Suffk 52 G4
Hagnaby Lincs 87 K8
Hagnaby Lincs 87 N5
Hagworthingham Lincs 87 K7
Haigh Wigan 89 J9
Haighton Green Lancs 88 H4
Haile Cumb 100 D9
Hailes Gloucs 47 K8
Hailey Herts 51 J8
Hailey Oxon 34 C2
Hailey Oxon 34 H7
Hailsham E Susx 25 N9
Hail Weston Cambs 61 Q8
Hainault Gt Lon 37 L2
Haine Kent 39 Q8
Hainford Norfk 77 J8
Hainton Lincs 86 G4
Hainworth C Brad 90 D3
Haisthorpe E R Yk 99 N8
Hakin Pembks 40 G9
Halam Notts 85 L10
Halbeath Fife 134 E10
Halberton Devon 9 P2
Halcro Highld 167 M4
Hale Halton 81 P8
Hale Hants 21 N11
Hale Somset 20 D9
Hale Surrey 23 M5
Hale Traffd 82 G7
Hale W & F 95 L5
Hale Bank Halton 81 P8
Hale Barns Traffd 82 G7
Hale Green E Susx 25 N8
Hale Nook Lancs 88 D2
Hales Norfk 65 M2
Hales Staffs 70 C8
Halesgate Lincs 74 F5
Hales Green Derbys 71 M6
Halesowen Dudley 58 E8
Hales Place Kent 39 K10
Hale Street Kent 37 Q11
Halesville Essex 38 F3
Halesworth Suffk 65 M6
Halewood Knows 81 P7
Halford Devon 7 L4
Halford Shrops 56 G8
Halford Warwks 47 Q5
Halfpenny W & F 95 L3
Halfpenny Green Staffs 58 B6
Halfpenny Houses N York 97 K4
Halfway Carmth 43 M8
Halfway Carmth 44 A8
Halfway Sheff 84 F4
Halfway W Berk 34 D11
Halfway Bridge W Susx 23 P10
Halfway House Shrops 56 E2
Halfway Houses Kent 38 F7
Halifax Calder 90 D5
Halket E Ayrs 125 L7
Halkirk Highld 167 K5
Halkyn Flints 81 J10
Hall E Rens 125 L7
Hallam Fields Derbys 72 D3
Halland E Susx 25 L7
Hallaton Leics 73 K11
Hallatrow BaNES 20 B3
Hallbankgate Cumb 111 L9
Hallbeck W & F 95 N3
Hall Cliffe Wakefd 90 H7
Hall Cross Lancs 88 E4
Hall Dunnerdale W & F 100 H11
Hallen S Glos 31 Q8
Hall End Bed 61 M11
Hall End C Beds 50 C3
Hallfield Gate Derbys 84 E9
Hallgarth Dur 104 B2
Hallglen Falk 126 F2
Hall Green Birm 58 H8
Hallin Highld 152 D6
Halling Medway 38 B9
Hallington Lincs 87 K3
Hallington Nthumb 112 E5
Halliwell Bolton 89 K8
Halloughton Notts 85 L10
Hallow Worcs 46 F3
Hallow Heath Worcs 46 F3
Hallsands Devon 7 L11
Hall's Green Essex 51 K9
Hall's Green Herts 50 G5
Hallthwaites Cumb 94 D3
Hallworthy Cnwll 5 K4
Hallyne Border 116 H2
Halmer End Staffs 70 D5
Halmond's Frome Herefs 46 C5
Halmore Gloucs 32 D4
Halnaker W Susx 15 P5
Halsall Lancs 88 D8
Halse Somset 18 F9
Halse W Nthn 48 G6
Halsetown Cnwll 2 E6
Halsham E R Yk 93 N5
Halsinger Devon 17 J4
Halstead Essex 52 D5
Halstead Kent 37 L8
Halstead Leics 73 K9
Halstock Dorset 11 L3
Halsway Somset 18 F7
Haltcliff Bridge W & F 101 L3
Haltham Lincs 86 H8
Haltoft End Lincs 87 L11
Halton Bucks 35 N3
Halton Halton 82 B8
Halton Lancs 95 L8
Halton Leeds 91 K4
Halton Nthumb 112 E7
Halton Wrexhm 69 K7
Halton East N York 96 F10
Halton Fenside Lincs 87 M8
Halton Gill N York 96 C5
Halton Green Lancs 95 L7
Halton Holegate Lincs 87 M7
Halton Lea Gate Nthumb 111 M9
Halton Quay Cnwll 5 Q8
Halton Shields Nthumb 112 F7
Halton West N York 96 B10
Haltwhistle Nthumb 111 P8
Halvana Cnwll 5 L6
Halvergate Norfk 77 N10
Halwell Devon 7 K8
Halwill Devon 8 B5
Halwill Junction Devon 8 B4
Ham Devon 10 E4
Ham Gloucs 32 C5
Ham Gloucs 47 J10
Ham Gt Lon 36 E6
Ham Kent 39 P11
Ham Somset 19 J9
Ham Somset 20 C5
Ham Wilts 22 B2
Hambleden Bucks 35 L7
Hambledon Hants 14 H4
Hambledon Surrey 23 Q7
Hamble-le-Rice Hants 14 E5
Hambleton Lancs 88 D2
Hambleton N York 91 P4
Hambleton Moss Side Lancs 88 D2
Hambridge Somset 19 L10
Hambrook S Glos 32 B9
Hambrook W Susx 15 L5
Ham Common Dorset 20 F9
Hameringham Lincs 87 K7
Hamerton Cambs 61 P5
Ham Green Herefs 46 E6
Ham Green Kent 26 E6
Ham Green Kent 38 D8
Ham Green N Som 31 P9
Ham Green Worcs 47 K2
Ham Hill Kent 37 Q8
Hamilton S Lans 126 C6
Hamilton Services (northbound) S Lans 126 C6
Hamlet Dorset 11 M3
Hammer W Susx 23 N8
Hammerpot W Susx 24 C9
Hammersmith Gt Lon 36 F5
Hammer Vale Hants 23 N8
Hammerwich Staffs 58 G3
Hammerwood E Susx 25 K3
Hammond Street Herts 50 H10
Hammoon Dorset 12 D2
Hamnavoe Shet 169 q10
Hampden Park E Susx 25 P10
Hamperden End Essex 51 N4
Hampnett Gloucs 47 L11
Hampole Donc 91 N8
Hampreston Dorset 13 J5
Hampsfield W & F 95 J4
Hampson Green Lancs 95 K10
Hampstead Gt Lon 36 G3
Hampstead Norreys W Berk 34 F9
Hampsthwaite N York 97 L9
Hampton Devon 10 F5
Hampton Gt Lon 36 D7
Hampton Kent 39 L8
Hampton Shrops 57 N7
Hampton Swindn 33 N6
Hampton Worcs 47 K6
Hampton Bishop Herefs 45 R7
Hampton Court Palace Gt Lon 36 E7
Hampton Fields Gloucs 32 G5
Hampton Green Ches W 69 P5
Hampton Hargate C Pete 61 Q2
Hampton Heath Ches W 69 P5
Hampton-in-Arden Solhll 59 K8
Hampton Loade Shrops 57 N7
Hampton Lovett Worcs 58 C11
Hampton Lucy Warwks 47 Q3
Hampton Magna Warwks 59 L11
Hampton on the Hill Warwks 47 Q2
Hampton Park Wilts 21 N8
Hampton Poyle Oxon 48 F11
Hampton Vale C Pete 61 Q2
Hampton Wick Gt Lon 36 E7
Hamptworth Wilts 21 P11
Hamrow Norfk 76 C7
Hamsey E Susx 25 K8
Hamsey Green Surrey 37 J9
Hamstall Ridware Staffs 71 L11
Hamstead Birm 58 G6
Hamstead IoW 14 D8
Hamstead Marshall W Berk 34 D11
Hamsterley Dur 103 M4
Hamsterley Dur 112 H9
Hamsterley Mill Dur 112 H9
Hamstreet Kent 26 H5
Ham Street Somset 19 Q8
Hamwood N Som 19 L3
Hamworthy BCP 12 G6
Hanbury Staffs 71 M9
Hanbury Worcs 47 J2
Hanby Lincs 73 Q4
Hanchet End Suffk 63 K11
Hanchurch Staffs 70 E6
Handa Island Highld 164 D7
Handale R & Cl 105 K7
Hand and Pen Devon 9 P5
Handbridge Ches W 81 N11
Handcross W Susx 24 G5
Handforth Ches E 83 J8
Hand Green Ches W 69 P2
Handley Ches W 69 N3
Handley Derbys 84 E8
Handley Green Essex 51 Q10
Handsacre Staffs 71 K11
Handsworth Birm 58 F7
Handsworth Sheff 84 F3
Handy Cross Bucks 35 N6
Hanford C Stke 70 F6
Hanford Dorset 12 D2
Hanging Heaton Kirk 90 H6
Hanging Houghton W Nthn 60 G6
Hanging Langford Wilts 21 K7
Hangleton Br & H 24 G9
Hangleton W Susx 24 C10
Hanham S Glos 32 B10
Hankelow Ches E 70 B5
Hankerton Wilts 33 J6
Hankham E Susx 25 P9
Hanley C Stke 70 F5
Hanley Broadheath Worcs 57 M11
Hanley Castle Worcs 46 F6
Hanley Child Worcs 57 M11
Hanley Swan Worcs 46 F6
Hanley William Worcs 57 M11
Hanlith N York 96 C8
Hanmer Wrexhm 69 N7
Hannaford Devon 17 L6
Hannah Lincs 87 N5
Hannington Hants 22 F3
Hannington Swindn 33 N6
Hannington W Nthn 60 H6
Hannington Wick Swindn 33 N5
Hanscombe End C Beds 50 D4
Hanslope M Keyn 49 M5
Hanthorpe Lincs 74 A6
Hanwell Gt Lon 36 E5
Hanwell Oxon 48 D6
Hanwood Shrops 56 G3
Hanworth Gt Lon 36 D6
Hanworth Norfk 76 H4
Happendon S Lans 116 B4
Happisburgh Norfk 77 M5
Happisburgh Common Norfk 77 M6
Hapsford Ches W 81 P10
Hapton Lancs 89 M4
Hapton Norfk 64 H2
Harberton Devon 7 K7
Harbertonford Devon 7 K7
Harbledown Kent 39 K10
Harborne Birm 58 F8
Harborough Magna Warwks 59 Q9
Harbottle Nthumb 118 H10
Harbourneford Devon 7 J6
Harbours Hill Worcs 58 E11
Harbridge Hants 13 K2
Harbridge Green Hants 13 K2
Harburn W Loth 127 J5
Harbury Warwks 48 C3
Harby Leics 73 J4
Harby Notts 85 Q6
Harcombe Devon 9 L8
Harcombe Devon 10 D6
Harcombe Bottom Devon 10 G5
Harden C Brad 90 D3
Harden Wsall 58 F4
Hardendale W & F 101 Q8
Hardenhuish Wilts 32 H10
Hardgate Abers 151 K7
Hardgate D & G 108 H7
Hardgate N York 97 L8
Hardgate W Duns 125 N3
Hardham W Susx 24 B7
Hardhorn Lancs 88 D3
Hardingham Norfk 76 E11
Hardingstone W Nthn 60 G9
Hardington Somset 20 D4
Hardington Mandeville Somset 11 L2
Hardington Marsh Somset 11 L3
Hardington Moor Somset 11 L2
Hardisworthy Devon 16 C7
Hardley Hants 14 D6
Hardley Street Norfk 77 M11
Hardmead M Keyn 49 P5
Hardraw N York 96 C2
Hardsough Lancs 89 M6
Hardstoft Derbys 84 F8
Hardway Hants 14 H6
Hardway Somset 20 D8
Hardwick Bucks 49 M11
Hardwick Cambs 62 E9
Hardwick Derbys 84 G8
Hardwick N Nthn 60 H7
Hardwick Norfk 65 J4
Hardwick Oxon 34 C3
Hardwick Oxon 48 G9
Hardwick Rothm 84 G3
Hardwick Wsall 58 G5
Hardwicke Gloucs 32 E2
Hardwicke Gloucs 46 H9
Hardwick Village Notts 85 K5
Hardy's Green Essex 52 F7
Harebeating E Susx 25 N8
Hareby Lincs 87 K7
Hare Croft C Brad 90 D3
Harefield Gt Lon 36 C2
Hare Green Essex 53 K6
Hare Hatch Wokham 35 M9
Harehill Derbys 71 M7
Harehills Leeds 91 J4
Harehope Nthumb 119 L6
Harelaw Border 117 Q6
Harelaw D & G 110 H5
Harelaw Dur 113 J10
Hareplain Kent 26 D4
Harescough W & F 102 B2
Harescombe Gloucs 32 F2
Haresfield Gloucs 32 F2
Harestock Hants 22 E8
Hare Street Essex 51 K9
Hare Street Essex 51 M10
Hare Street Herts 51 J5
Harewood Leeds 97 M11
Harewood End Herefs 45 Q9
Harford Devon 6 G7
Hargate Norfk 64 G3
Hargatewall Derbys 83 P9
Hargrave Ches W 69 N2
Hargrave N Nthn 61 M6
Hargrave Suffk 63 N9
Harker Cumb 110 G8
Harkstead Suffk 53 L5
Harlaston Staffs 59 K2
Harlaxton Lincs 73 M4
Harlech Gwynd 67 K8
Harlech Castle Gwynd 67 K8
Harlescott Shrops 69 N11
Harlesden Gt Lon 36 F4
Harlesthorpe Derbys 84 G5
Harleston Devon 7 K9
Harleston Norfk 65 J5
Harleston Suffk 64 E9
Harlestone W Nthn 60 F8
Harle Syke Lancs 89 P3
Harley Rothm 91 K11
Harley Shrops 57 K4
Harling Road Norfk 64 D4
Harlington C Beds 50 B4

Place	County	Page	Grid
Harlington	Donc	91	M10
Harlington	Gt Lon	36	C5
Harlosh	Highld	152	D9
Harlow	Essex	51	K8
Harlow Hill	Nthumb	112	G7
Harlthorpe	E R Yk	92	B3
Harlton	Cambs	62	E10
Harlyn	Cnwll	4	D6
Harman's Cross	Dorset	12	G8
Harmby	N York	96	H3
Harmer Green	Herts	50	G7
Harmer Hill	Shrops	69	N10
Harmondsworth	Gt Lon	36	C5
Harmston	Lincs	86	C8
Harnage	Shrops	57	K4
Harnham	Nthumb	112	G4
Harnhill	Gloucs	33	L4
Harold Hill	Gt Lon	37	M2
Haroldston West	Pembks	40	G7
Haroldswick	Shet	169	t2
Harold Wood	Gt Lon	37	N2
Harome	N York	98	C4
Harpenden	Herts	50	D8
Harpford	Devon	10	B6
Harpham	E R Yk	99	M8
Harpley	Norfk	75	Q5
Harpley	Worcs	46	C2
Harpole	W Nthn	60	E8
Harpsdale	Highld	167	K5
Harpsden	Oxon	35	L8
Harpswell	Lincs	86	B3
Harpurhey	Manch	83	J4
Harpur Hill	Derbys	83	N10
Harraby	Cumb	110	H10
Harracott	Devon	17	K6
Harrapool	Highld	145	L3
Harras	Cumb	100	C7
Harrietfield	P & K	134	B2
Harringay	Gt Lon	36	H3
Harrington	Cumb	100	C5
Harrington	Lincs	87	L6
Harrington	N Nthn	60	G4
Harringworth	N Nthn	73	N11
Harris	W Isls	168	f8
Harriseahead	Staffs	70	F3
Harriston	Cumb	100	G2
Harrogate	N York	97	M9
Harrold	Bed	61	K9
Harrop Dale	Oldham	90	C9
Harrow	Gt Lon	36	E3
Harrowbarrow	Cnwll	5	Q7
Harrowden	Bed	61	N11
Harrowgate Village	Darltn	103	Q7
Harrow Green	Suffk	64	B11
Harrow Hill	Gloucs	46	C11
Harrow on the Hill	Gt Lon	36	E3
Harrow Weald	Gt Lon	36	E2
Harston	Cambs	62	F10
Harston	Leics	73	L4
Harswell	E R Yk	92	D2
Hart	Hartpl	104	E3
Hartburn	Nthumb	112	G3
Hartburn	S on T	104	D7
Hartest	Suffk	64	A11
Hartfield	E Susx	25	L3
Hartford	Cambs	62	C6
Hartford	Ches W	82	D10
Hartford	Somset	18	C9
Hartfordbridge	Hants	23	L3
Hartford End	Essex	51	Q7
Hartforth	N York	103	N9
Hartgrove	Dorset	20	F11
Harthill	Ches W	69	N3
Harthill	N Lans	126	G5
Harthill	Rothm	84	G4
Harthope	D & G	116	E8
Hartington	Derbys	71	L2
Hartington	Nthumb	112	F3
Hartland	Devon	16	D7
Hartland Quay	Devon	16	C7
Hartlebury	Worcs	58	B10
Hartlepool	Hartpl	104	F4
Hartley	Kent	26	C5
Hartley	Kent	37	P7
Hartley	Nthumb	113	M5
Hartley	W & F	102	E9
Hartley Green	Kent	37	P7
Hartley Green	Staffs	70	H9
Hartley Wespall	Hants	23	J3
Hartley Wintney	Hants	23	L3
Hartlip	Kent	38	D9
Hartoft End	N York	98	E2
Harton	N York	98	E8
Harton	S Tyne	113	N7
Harton	Shrops	56	H7
Hartpury	Gloucs	46	E10
Hartshead	Kirk	90	F6
Hartshead Moor Services	Calder	90	F6
Hartshead Moor Top	Kirk	90	F5
Hartshill	C Stke	70	F5
Hartshill	Warwks	59	M6
Hartshorne	Derbys	71	Q10
Hartside	Nthumb	119	J7
Hartsop	W & F	101	M8
Hart Station	Hartpl	104	E3
Hartswell	Somset	18	E9
Hartwell	W Nthn	49	L4
Hartwith	N York	97	K8
Hartwood	N Lans	126	E6
Hartwoodmyres	Border	117	N6
Harvel	Kent	37	Q8
Harvington	Worcs	47	L5
Harvington	Worcs	58	C10
Harwell	Notts	85	L2
Harwell	Oxon	34	E7
Harwich	Essex	53	N5
Harwood	Bolton	89	L8
Harwood	Dur	102	F4
Harwood	Nthumb	112	F2
Harwood Dale	N York	105	Q11
Harwood Lee	Bolton	89	L8
Harworth	Notts	85	K2
Hasbury	Dudley	58	E8
Hascombe	Surrey	24	B3
Haselbech	W Nthn	60	F5
Haselbury Plucknett	Somset	11	K2
Haseley	Warwks	59	K11
Haseley Green	Warwks	59	K11
Haseley Knob	Warwks	59	K10
Haselor	Warwks	47	M3
Hasfield	Gloucs	46	F9
Hasguard	Pembks	40	G9
Hasholme	E R Yk	92	D4
Haskayne	Lancs	88	D9
Hasketon	Suffk	65	J11
Hasland	Derbys	84	E7
Haslemere	Surrey	23	P8
Haslingden	Lancs	89	M6
Haslingfield	Cambs	62	F10
Haslington	Ches E	70	C3
Hassall	Ches E	70	D3
Hassall Green	Ches E	70	D3
Hassall Street	Kent	27	J2
Hassingham	Norfk	77	M10
Hassness	Cumb	100	G8
Hassop	Derbys	84	B6
Haste Hill	Surrey	23	P8
Haster	Highld	167	P6
Hasthorpe	Lincs	87	N7
Hastigleigh	Kent	27	J2
Hastings	E Susx	26	D10
Hastings	Somset	19	K11
Hastingwood	Essex	51	L9
Hastoe	Herts	35	P3
Haswell	Dur	104	C2
Haswell Plough	Dur	104	C2
Hatch	C Beds	61	Q11
Hatch Beauchamp	Somset	19	K10
Hatch End	Bed	61	N8
Hatch End	Gt Lon	36	D2
Hatchet Gate	Hants	14	C6
Hatching Green	Herts	50	D8
Hatchmere	Ches W	82	C10
Hatch Warren	Hants	22	H5
Hatcliffe	NE Lin	93	M10
Hatfield	Donc	91	R9
Hatfield	Herefs	46	A3
Hatfield	Herts	50	F9
Hatfield	Worcs	46	H4
Hatfield Broad Oak	Essex	51	M7
Hatfield Heath	Essex	51	M7
Hatfield Peverel	Essex	52	C9
Hatfield Woodhouse	Donc	92	A3
Hatford	Oxon	34	B6
Hatherden	Hants	22	B4
Hatherleigh	Devon	8	D4
Hathern	Leics	72	E6
Hatherop	Gloucs	33	N3
Hathersage	Derbys	84	B4
Hathersage Booths	Derbys	84	B4
Hatherton	Ches E	70	B5
Hatherton	Staffs	58	E2
Hatley St George	Cambs	62	C10
Hatt	Cnwll	5	P9
Hattersley	Tamesd	83	L6
Hattingley	Hants	22	H7
Hatton	Abers	159	Q10
Hatton	Angus	142	H9
Hatton	Derbys	71	N8
Hatton	Gt Lon	36	C5
Hatton	Lincs	86	G5
Hatton	Shrops	56	H6
Hatton	Warrtn	82	C8
Hatton	Warwks	59	K11
Hatton Heath	Ches W	69	N2
Hatton of Fintray	Abers	151	L4
Hatton Park	Warwks	59	L11
Haugh	E Ayrs	115	J2
Haugh	Lincs	87	M5
Haugh	Rochdl	89	Q8
Haugham	Lincs	87	K4
Haughhead	E Duns	125	Q2
Haugh Head	Nthumb	119	K5
Haughley	Suffk	64	E9
Haughley Green	Suffk	64	E9
Haugh of Glass	Moray	158	B10
Haugh of Urr	D & G	108	H7
Haughs of Kinnaird	Angus	143	L6
Haughton	Ches E	69	Q3
Haughton	Notts	85	L6
Haughton	Powys	69	K11
Haughton	Shrops	57	M5
Haughton	Shrops	57	N3
Haughton	Shrops	69	L9
Haughton	Shrops	69	Q11
Haughton	Staffs	70	F10
Haughton Green	Tamesd	83	K6
Haughton le Skerne	Darltn	104	B7
Haultwick	Herts	50	H6
Haunton	Staffs	59	K2
Hautes Croix	Jersey	11	b1
Hauxton	Cambs	62	F10
Havannah	Ches E	70	F2
Havant	Hants	15	K5
Haven	Herefs	45	N4
Haven Bank	Lincs	86	H10
Haven Side	E R Yk	93	L5
Havenstreet	IoW	14	G8
Havercroft	Wakefd	91	K8
Haverfordwest	Pembks	41	J7
Haverhill	Suffk	63	L11
Haverigg	Cumb	94	D5
Havering-atte-Bower	Gt Lon	37	M2
Havering's Grove	Essex	37	Q2
Haversham	M Keyn	49	M6
Haverthwaite	W & F	94	G4
Haverton Hill	S on T	104	E6
Havyatt	N Som	19	N2
Havyatt	Somset	19	P7
Hawarden	Flints	81	L11
Hawbridge	Worcs	46	H5
Hawbush Green	Essex	52	C7
Hawcoat	W & F	94	E6
Hawen	Cerdgn	42	F5
Hawes	N York	96	C3
Hawe's Green	Norfk	65	J2
Hawford	Worcs	46	F2
Hawick	Border	117	Q8
Hawkchurch	Devon	10	G4
Hawkedon	Suffk	63	N10
Hawkenbury	Kent	26	D2
Hawkeridge	Wilts	20	G4
Hawkerland	Devon	9	Q7
Hawker's Cove	Cnwll	4	E6
Hawkesbury	S Glos	32	E9
Hawkesbury	Warwks	59	N8
Hawkesbury Upton	S Glos	32	E9
Hawkes End	Covtry	59	L8
Haw Green	Stockp	83	L7
Hawkhead	Rens	125	N5
Hawkhill	Nthumb	119	P8
Hawkhurst	Kent	26	C5
Hawkhurst Common	E Susx	25	M7
Hawkinge	Kent	27	M4
Hawkley	Hants	23	K9
Hawkley	Wigan	82	C4
Hawkridge	Somset	17	R5
Hawksdale	Cumb	110	G11
Hawkshaw	Bury	89	M7
Hawkshead	W & F	101	L11
Hawkshead Hill	W & F	101	K11
Hawksland	S Lans	116	A3
Hawkspur Green	Essex	51	Q4
Hawkstone	Shrops	69	Q8
Hawkswick	N York	96	C6
Hawksworth	Leeds	90	F2
Hawksworth	Notts	73	K2
Hawkwell	Essex	38	E3
Hawkwell	Nthumb	112	G6
Hawley	Hants	23	N3
Hawley	Kent	37	M6
Hawling	Gloucs	47	L10
Hawnby	N York	98	A3
Haworth	C Brad	90	C3
Hawridge	Bucks	35	P3
Hawstead	Suffk	64	B10
Hawstead Green	Suffk	64	B10
Hawthorn	Dur	113	P11
Hawthorn	Hants	23	J8
Hawthorn	Rhondd	30	E7
Hawthorn Hill	Br For	35	N10
Hawthorn Hill	Lincs	86	H9
Hawthorpe	Lincs	73	Q5
Hawton	Notts	85	M10
Haxby	C York	98	C9
Haxby Gates	C York	98	C9
Haxey	N Linc	92	C11
Haxey Carr	N Linc	92	C10
Haxted	Surrey	37	K11
Haxton	Wilts	21	M5
Hay	Cnwll	3	P3
Hay	Cnwll	4	F7
Haydock	St Hel	82	C5
Haydon	BaNES	20	C4
Haydon	Dorset	20	C11
Haydon	Somset	19	J10
Haydon Bridge	Nthumb	112	B8
Haydon Wick	Swindn	33	M7
Haye	Cnwll	5	P7
Hayes	Gt Lon	36	C4
Hayes	Gt Lon	37	K7
Hayes End	Gt Lon	36	C4
Hayfield	Ag & B	131	M3
Hayfield	Derbys	83	M7
Hayfield Green	Donc	91	R11
Haygate	Wrekin	57	L2
Hay Green	Norfk	75	K7
Hayhillock	Angus	143	J9
Hayle	Cnwll	2	F6
Hayle Port	Cnwll	2	F6
Hayley Green	Dudley	58	E8
Hayling Island	Hants	15	K6
Haymoor Green	Ches E	70	B4
Hayne	Devon	9	J7
Hayne	Devon	18	C11
Haynes	C Beds	50	C2
Haynes Church End	C Beds	50	C2
Haynes West End	C Beds	50	C2
Hay-on-Wye	Powys	45	J4
Hayscastle	Pembks	40	G5
Hayscastle Cross	Pembks	40	H5
Hay Street	Herts	51	J5
Hayton	Cumb	100	F2
Hayton	Cumb	111	K9
Hayton	E R Yk	98	G11
Hayton	Notts	85	M4
Hayton's Bent	Shrops	57	J8
Haytor Vale	Devon	9	J9
Haytown	Devon	16	F9
Haywards Heath	W Susx	24	H6
Haywood	Donc	91	P8
Haywood	Herefs	45	P8
Haywood Oaks	Notts	85	K9
Hazards Green	E Susx	25	Q8
Hazelbank	S Lans	126	E8
Hazelbury Bryan	Dorset	12	B3
Hazeleigh	Essex	52	D11
Hazeley	Hants	23	K3
Hazelford	Notts	85	M11
Hazel Grove	Stockp	83	K7
Hazelhurst	Tamesd	83	L4
Hazelslade	Staffs	58	F2
Hazel Street	Kent	25	Q3
Hazel Stub	Suffk	51	Q2
Hazelton Walls	Fife	135	J3
Hazelwood	Derbys	84	D11
Hazlemere	Bucks	35	N5
Hazlerigg	N u Ty	113	K6
Hazles	Staffs	71	J5
Hazleton	Gloucs	47	L11
Heacham	Norfk	75	N3
Headbourne Worthy	Hants	22	E8
Headbrook	Herefs	45	K3
Headcorn	Kent	26	D3
Headingley	Leeds	90	H3
Headington	Oxon	34	F3
Headlam	Dur	103	N7
Headlesscross	N Lans	126	G6
Headless Cross	Worcs	58	F11
Headley	Hants	22	F2
Headley	Hants	23	M7
Headley	Surrey	36	F10
Headley Down	Hants	23	M7
Headley Heath	Worcs	58	G9
Headon	Devon	16	F11
Headon	Notts	85	M5
Heads Nook	Cumb	111	K10
Heage	Derbys	84	E10
Healaugh	N York	97	R11
Healaugh	N York	103	K11
Heald Green	Stockp	82	H7
Heale	Devon	17	L2
Heale	Somset	18	H10
Heale	Somset	19	L9
Healey	N York	97	J4
Healey	Nthumb	112	F9
Healey	Rochdl	89	P7
Healey	Wakefd	90	H7
Healeyfield	Dur	112	G11
Healing	NE Lin	93	M8
Heamoor	Cnwll	2	D7
Heanor	Derbys	84	F11
Heanton Punchardon	Devon	17	J4
Heapham	Lincs	85	Q3
Hearn	Hants	23	M7
Heart of Scotland Services	N Lans	126	G5
Hearts Delight	Kent	38	E9
Heasley Mill	Devon	17	N4
Heaste	Highld	145	K4
Heath	Derbys	84	F7
Heath	Wakefd	91	K6
Heath and Reach	C Beds	49	Q8
Heath Common	W Susx	24	D7
Heathcote	Derbys	71	L2
Heathcote	Shrops	70	B9
Heath End	Bucks	35	N5
Heath End	Hants	22	D2
Heath End	Leics	72	B6
Heath End	Warwks	47	P2
Heather	Leics	72	B8
Heathfield	Cambs	62	G11
Heathfield	Devon	9	K9
Heathfield	E Susx	25	N6
Heathfield	N York	96	H7
Heathfield	Somset	18	G9
Heathfield Village	Oxon	48	F11
Heath Green	Worcs	58	G10
Heath Hall	D & G	109	L5
Heath Hayes & Wimblebury	Staffs	58	F2
Heath Hill	Shrops	57	P2
Heath House	Somset	19	M5
Heathrow Airport	Gt Lon	36	C5
Heathstock	Devon	10	E4
Heathton	Shrops	57	Q6
Heath Town	Wolves	58	D5
Heathwaite	N York	104	E10
Heatley	Staffs	71	K9
Heatley	Warrtn	82	F7
Heaton	Bolton	89	K9
Heaton	C Brad	90	E3
Heaton	Lancs	95	J8
Heaton	N u Ty	113	L7
Heaton	Staffs	70	H2
Heaton Chapel	Stockp	83	J6
Heaton Mersey	Stockp	83	J6
Heaton Norris	Stockp	83	J6
Heaton's Bridge	Lancs	88	E8
Heaverham	Kent	37	N9
Heaviley	Stockp	83	K7
Heavitree	Devon	9	M6
Hebburn	S Tyne	113	M8
Hebden	N York	96	F7
Hebden Bridge	Calder	90	B5
Hebden Green	Ches W	82	D11
Hebing End	Herts	50	H6
Hebron	Carmth	41	N5
Hebron	IoA	78	H8
Hebron	Nthumb	113	J3
Heckfield	Hants	23	K2
Heckfield Green	Suffk	64	H6
Heckfordbridge	Essex	52	F7
Heckington	Lincs	74	B2
Heckmondwike	Kirk	90	G6
Heddington	Wilts	33	J11
Heddon-on-the-Wall	Nthumb	112	H7
Hedenham	Norfk	65	L3
Hedge End	Hants	14	E4
Hedgerley	Bucks	35	Q7
Hedgerley Green	Bucks	35	Q7
Hedging	Somset	19	K9
Hedley on the Hill	Nthumb	112	G9
Hednesford	Staffs	58	E2
Hedon	E R Yk	93	L5
Hedsor	Bucks	35	P7
Heeley	Sheff	84	E4
Hegdon Hill	Herefs	46	A4
Heglibister	Shet	169	q8
Heighington	Darltn	103	P6
Heighington	Lincs	86	D7
Heightington	Worcs	57	P10
Heiton	Border	118	D4
Hele	Devon	7	J4
Hele	Devon	9	N4
Hele	Devon	17	J2
Hele	Somset	18	G10
Helebridge	Cnwll	16	C11
Hele Lane	Devon	9	J2
Helensburgh	Ag & B	132	B11
Helenton	S Ayrs	125	K11
Helford	Cnwll	3	K8
Helford Passage	Cnwll	3	K8
Helhoughton	Norfk	76	B6
Helions Bumpstead	Essex	51	Q2
Hellaby	Rothm	84	H2
Helland	Cnwll	4	H7
Hellandbridge	Cnwll	4	H7
Hell Corner	W Berk	22	C2
Hellescott	Cnwll	5	M4
Hellesdon	Norfk	77	J9
Hellesveor	Cnwll	2	E5
Hellidon	N Nthn	60	B9
Hellifield	N York	96	C9
Hellingly	E Susx	25	N8
Hellington	Norfk	77	L11
Helm	Nthumb	119	N11
Helmdon	W Nthn	48	G6
Helme	Kirk	90	D8
Helmingham	Suffk	64	H10
Helmington Row	Dur	103	N3
Helmsdale	Highld	163	N3
Helmshore	Lancs	89	M6
Helmsley	N York	98	C3
Helperby	N York	97	P7
Helperthorpe	N York	99	K6
Helpringham	Lincs	74	B2
Helpston	C Pete	74	B9
Helsby	Ches W	81	P9
Helsey	Lincs	87	P6
Helston	Cnwll	2	H8
Helstone	Cnwll	4	H4
Helton	W & F	101	P6
Helwith	N Nthn	103	L10
Helwith Bridge	N York	96	B7
Hemblington	Norfk	77	L9
Hembridge	Somset	19	Q7
Hemel Hempstead	Herts	50	C9
Hemerdon	Devon	6	F7
Hemingbrough	N York	91	R4
Hemingby	Lincs	86	H6
Hemingfield	Barns	91	K10
Hemingford Abbots	Cambs	62	C6
Hemingford Grey	Cambs	62	C6
Hemingstone	Suffk	64	G11
Hemington	Leics	72	D5
Hemington	N Nthn	61	N3
Hemington	Somset	20	D4
Hemley	Suffk	53	N3
Hemlington	Middsb	104	F8
Hempholme	E R Yk	99	M10
Hempnall	Norfk	65	J3
Hempnall Green	Norfk	65	J3
Hempriggs	Moray	157	L5
Hempstead	Essex	51	P3
Hempstead	Medway	38	C9
Hempstead	Norfk	76	G4
Hempstead	Norfk	77	N6
Hempsted	Gloucs	46	F11
Hempton	Norfk	76	C6
Hempton	Oxon	48	D8
Hemsby	Norfk	77	P8
Hemswell	Lincs	86	B2
Hemswell Cliff	Lincs	86	B3
Hemsworth	Wakefd	91	L8
Hemyock	Devon	10	C2
Henbury	Bristl	31	Q9
Henbury	Ches E	83	J10
Hendham	Devon	7	J8
Hendomen	Powys	56	C9
Hendon	Gt Lon	36	F3
Hendon	Sundld	113	P9
Hendra	Cnwll	3	J6
Hendra	Cnwll	4	G6
Hendre	Brdgnd	29	P8
Hendre	Flints	80	H11
Hendredenny	Caerph	30	F7
Hendy	Carmth	28	G4
Heneglwys	IoA	78	G9
Henfield	IoA	24	F7
Henford	S Glos	32	C2
Henford	Devon	5	P3
Henfynyw	Cerdgn	43	J2
Henghurst	Kent	26	G4
Hengoed	Caerph	30	G6
Hengoed	Powys	45	J4
Hengoed	Shrops	69	J8
Hengrave	Suffk	63	P7
Henham	Essex	51	M5
Heniarth	Powys	55	Q3
Henlade	Somset	19	J10
Henley	Dorset	11	P4
Henley	Gloucs	46	H11
Henley	Shrops	56	H7
Henley	Shrops	57	J9
Henley	Somset	19	M8
Henley	Suffk	64	H11
Henley	W Susx	23	N9
Henley Green	Covtry	59	N8
Henley-in-Arden	Warwks	59	J11
Henley-on-Thames	Oxon	35	L8
Henley Park	Surrey	23	P4
Henley's Down	E Susx	26	B9
Henley Street	Kent	37	Q7
Henllan	Cerdgn	42	G6
Henllan	Denbgs	80	E11
Henllan Amgoed	Carmth	41	N7
Henllys	Torfn	31	J6
Henlow	C Beds	50	E3
Henlow Camp	C Beds	50	E3
Hennock	Devon	9	K8
Henny Street	Essex	52	E4
Henryd	Conwy	79	P10
Henry's Moat (Castell Hendre)	Pembks	41	K5
Hensall	N York	91	P6
Henshaw	Nthumb	111	Q8
Hensingham	Cumb	100	C5
Henstead	Suffk	65	P4
Hensting	Hants	22	E10
Henstridge	Somset	20	D11
Henstridge Ash	Somset	20	D10
Henstridge Marsh	Somset	20	D10
Henton	Oxon	35	L4
Henton	Somset	19	N5
Henwick	Worcs	46	F3
Henwood	Cnwll	5	M7
Heogan	Shet	169	r9
Heol-las	Swans	29	J5
Heol Senni	Powys	44	C10
Heol-y-Cyw	Brdgnd	29	P8
Hepburn	Nthumb	119	J6
Hepple	Nthumb	119	J10
Hepscott	Nthumb	113	K4
Heptonstall	Calder	90	B5
Hepworth	Kirk	90	F9
Hepworth	Suffk	64	D7
Herbrandston	Pembks	40	G9
Hereford	Herefs	45	Q7
Hereson	Kent	39	Q8
Heribusta	Highld	152	F3
Heriot	Border	128	C7
Hermiston	C Edin	127	M3
Hermitage	Border	117	Q10
Hermitage	Dorset	11	P3
Hermitage	W Berk	34	F10
Hermitage	W Susx	15	L5
Hermit Hill	Barns	91	J10
Hermon	Carmth	42	G8
Hermon	IoA	78	F11
Hermon	Pembks	41	P4
Herne	Kent	39	L8
Herne Bay	Kent	39	L8
Herne Common	Kent	39	L8
Herne Hill	Gt Lon	36	H6
Herne Pound	Kent	37	Q10
Herner	Devon	17	K6
Hernhill	Kent	39	J9
Herodsfoot	Cnwll	5	L9
Heronden	Kent	39	N11
Herongate	Essex	37	P2
Heronsford	S Ayrs	114	B11
Heronsgate	Herts	36	B2
Herriard	Hants	23	J5
Herringfleet	Suffk	65	P2
Herring's Green	Bed	50	C2
Herringswell	Suffk	63	M6
Herringthorpe	Rothm	84	F2
Herrington	Sundld	113	N10
Hersden	Kent	39	M9
Hersham	Cnwll	16	D10
Hersham	Surrey	36	D8
Herstmonceux	E Susx	25	P8
Herston	Dorset	12	H9
Herston	Ork	169	d7
Hertford	Herts	50	H8
Hertford Heath	Herts	51	J8
Hertingfordbury	Herts	50	H8
Hesketh Bank	Lancs	88	E6
Hesketh Lane	Lancs	89	J2
Hesket Newmarket	Cumb	101	K3
Heskin Green	Lancs	88	G7
Hesleden	Dur	104	D3
Hesleden	N York	96	C6
Hesley	Donc	85	J2
Hesleyside	Nthumb	112	B4
Heslington	C York	98	C10
Hessay	C York	98	B9
Hessenford	Cnwll	5	N10
Hessett	Suffk	64	C9
Hessle	E R Yk	92	H5
Hessle	Wakefd	91	L7
Hest Bank	Lancs	95	K7
Hestley Green	Suffk	64	H8
Heston	Gt Lon	36	D5

Heston Services – Holywell 275

Heston Services Gt Lon 36 D5
Hestwall Ork 169 b5
Heswall Wirral 81 K8
Hethe Oxon 48 G9
Hethersett Norfk 76 G11
Hethersgill Cumb 111 J7
Hetherside Cumb 110 H7
Hetherson Green Ches W 69 P4
Hethpool Nthumb 118 G5
Hett Dur 103 Q3
Hetton N York 96 E9
Hetton-le-Hole Sundld 113 N11
Hetton Steads Nthumb 119 K3
Heugh Nthumb 112 G6
Heughhead Abers 150 B5
Heugh Head Border 129 M7
Heveningham Suffk 65 L7
Hever Kent 37 L11
Heversham W & F 95 K4
Hevingham Norfk 76 H7
Hewas Water Cnwll 3 P4
Hewelsfield Gloucs 31 Q4
Hewenden C Brad 90 D3
Hewish N Som 19 M2
Hewish Somset 11 J3
Hewood Dorset 10 H4
Hexham Nthumb 112 D8
Hextable Kent 37 M6
Hexthorpe Donc 91 P10
Hexton Herts 50 D4
Hexworthy Cnwll 5 P5
Hexworthy Devon 6 H4
Hey Lancs 89 P2
Heybridge Essex 51 P11
Heybridge Essex 52 E10
Heybridge Basin Essex 52 E10
Heybrook Bay Devon 6 D9
Heydon Cambs 51 K3
Heydon Norfk 76 G6
Heydour Lincs 73 Q3
Hey Houses Lancs 88 C5
Heylipoll Ag & B 136 B7
Heylor Shet 169 p5
Heyrod Tamesd 83 L5
Heysham Lancs 95 J8
Heyshaw N York 97 J8
Heyshott W Susx 23 N11
Heyside Oldham 89 Q9
Heytesbury Wilts 20 H6
Heythrop Oxon 48 C9
Heywood Rochdl 89 P8
Heywood Wilts 20 G4
Hibaldstow N Linc 92 G10
Hickleton Donc 91 M9
Hickling Norfk 77 N7
Hickling Notts 72 H5
Hickling Green Norfk 77 N7
Hickling Heath Norfk 77 N7
Hickling Pastures Notts 72 H5
Hickmans Green Kent 39 J10
Hicks Forstal Kent 39 L9
Hickstead W Susx 24 G6
Hidcote Bartrim Gloucs 47 N6
Hidcote Boyce Gloucs 47 N6
High Ackworth Wakefd 91 L7
Higham Barns 91 J9
Higham Derbys 84 E9
Higham Kent 37 P11
Higham Kent 38 B7
Higham Lancs 89 N3
Higham Suffk 52 H4
Higham Suffk 63 M7
Higham Dykes Nthumb 112 H5
Higham Ferrers N Nthn 61 L7
Higham Gobion C Beds 50 D4
Higham Hill Gt Lon 37 J2
Higham on the Hill Leics 72 B11
Highampton Devon 8 C4
Highams Park Gt Lon 37 J2
High Angerton Nthumb 112 G3
High Ardwell D & G 106 E8
High Auldgirth D & G 109 K3
High Bankhill W & F 101 Q2
High Barnet Gt Lon 50 G11
High Beach Essex 51 K11
High Bentham N York 95 P7
High Bewaldeth Cumb 100 H4
High Bickington Devon 17 L7
High Biggins W & F 95 N5
High Birkwith N York 96 B5
High Blantyre S Lans 126 B6
High Bonnybridge Falk 126 E2
High Borrans W & F 101 M10
High Bradley N York 96 F11
High Bray Devon 17 M5
Highbridge Hants 22 E10
Highbridge Somset 19 K5
Highbrook W Susx 25 J4
High Brooms Kent 25 N2
High Bullen Devon 17 J7
Highburton Kirk 90 F8
Highbury Gt Lon 36 H3
Highbury Somset 20 C5
High Buston Nthumb 119 P9
High Callerton Nthumb 113 J6
High Casterton W & F 95 N5
High Catton E R Yk 98 E10
Highclere Hants 22 D3
Highcliffe BCP 13 M6
High Close Dur 103 N7
High Cogges Oxon 34 C3
High Common Norfk 76 D10
High Coniscliffe Darltn 103 P7
High Crosby Cumb 111 J9
High Cross Cnwll 3 J8
High Cross E Ayrs 125 L8
High Cross Hants 23 K9
High Cross Herts 51 J7
Highcross Lancs 88 C3
High Cross W Susx 24 F7
High Cross Warwks 59 K11
High Drummore D & G 106 F10
High Dubmire Sundld 113 M11
High Easter Essex 51 P8
High Eggborough N York 91 P6
High Ellington N York 97 J4
Higher Alham Somset 20 C6
Higher Ansty Dorset 12 C4
Higher Ballam Lancs 88 D4
Higher Bartle Lancs 88 G4
Higher Berry End C Beds 49 Q8
Higher Bockhampton Dorset 12 B6
Higher Brixham Torbay 7 N8
Higher Burrowton Devon 9 P5
Higher Burwardsley Ches W 69 P3
High Ercall Wrekin 69 Q11
Higher Chillington Somset 10 H2
Higher Clovelly Devon 16 E7
Highercombe Somset 18 B8
Higher Coombe Dorset 11 L6
Higher Disley Ches E 83 L8
Higher Folds Wigan 82 E4
Higherford Lancs 89 P2
Higher Gabwell Devon 7 N5
Higher Halstock Leigh Dorset 11 L3
Higher Harpers Lancs 89 N3
Higher Heysham Lancs 95 J8
Higher Hurdsfield Ches E 83 K10
Higher Irlam Salfd 82 F5
Higher Kingcombe Dorset 11 L5
Higher Kinnerton Flints 69 K2
Higher Marston Ches W 82 E9
Higher Muddiford Devon 17 K4
Higher Nyland Dorset 20 D10
Higher Ogden Rochdl 90 B8
Higher Pentire Cnwll 2 H8
Higher Penwortham Lancs 88 G5
Higher Prestacott Devon 5 P2
Higher Studfold N York 96 B6
Higher Town Cnwll 3 L5
Higher Town Cnwll 4 G9
Higher Town IoS 2 c1
Higher Tregantle Cnwll 5 Q11
Higher Walton Lancs 88 H5
Higher Walton Warrtn 82 C7
Higher Wambrook Somset 10 F3
Higher Waterston Dorset 11 Q5
Higher Whatcombe Dorset 12 D4
Higher Wheelton Lancs 89 J6
Higher Whitley Ches W 82 D8
Higher Wincham Ches W 82 E9
Higher Wraxhall Dorset 11 M4
Higher Wych Ches W 69 N6
High Etherley Dur 103 N5
High Ferry Lincs 87 L11
Highfield E R Yk 92 B3
Highfield Gatesd 112 H9
Highfield N Ayrs 125 J7
Highfields Donc 91 N9
Highfields Caldecote Cambs 62 E9
High Flats Kirk 90 G9
High Garrett Essex 52 C6
Highgate E Susx 25 K4
Highgate Gt Lon 36 G3
Highgate Kent 26 C5
Highgate Lincs 87 M11
High Grange Dur 103 N4
High Grantley N York 97 K7
High Green Kirk 90 G8
High Green Norfk 64 H4
High Green Norfk 76 G10
High Green Sheff 91 J11
High Green Shrops 57 N8
High Green Suffk 64 B9
High Green W & F 101 M10
High Green Worcs 46 G5
Highgreen Manor Nthumb 112 B2
High Halden Kent 26 E4
High Halstow Medway 38 C6
High Ham Somset 19 M8
High Harrington Cumb 100 D5
High Harrogate N York 97 M9
High Haswell Dur 104 C2
High Hatton Shrops 69 R10
High Hauxley Nthumb 119 Q10
High Hawsker N York 105 P9
High Hesket W & F 101 N2
High Hoyland Barns 90 H9
High Hunsley E R Yk 92 G3
High Hurstwood E Susx 25 L5
High Hutton N York 98 F7
High Ireby Cumb 100 H3
High Kelling Norfk 76 G3
High Kilburn N York 97 R5
High Killerby N York 99 M4
High Knipe W & F 101 P7
High Lands Dur 103 M5
Highlane Ches E 83 J11
Highlane Derbys 84 F4
High Lane Stockp 83 L7
High Lanes Cnwll 2 F6
High Laver Essex 51 M9
Highlaws Cumb 109 P11
Highleadon Gloucs 46 E10
High Legh Ches E 82 F8
Highleigh W Susx 15 M7
High Leven S on T 104 E8
Highley Shrops 57 N8
High Littleton BaNES 20 B3
High Lorton Cumb 100 G5
High Marishes N York 98 G5
High Marnham Notts 85 P6
High Melton Donc 91 N10
High Mickley Nthumb 112 G8
Highmoor Cumb 110 E11
Highmoor Oxon 35 K8
Highmoor Cross Oxon 35 K8
Highmoor Hill Mons 31 N7
High Moorsley Sundld 113 M11
Highnam Gloucs 46 E10
High Newport Sundld 113 N10
High Newton W & F 95 J4
High Newton-by-the-Sea Nthumb 119 P5
High Nibthwaite W & F 94 F3
High Offley Staffs 70 D9
High Ongar Essex 51 N10
High Onn Staffs 70 E11
High Park Corner Essex 52 H7
High Pennyvenie E Ayrs 115 J6
High Pittington Dur 104 B2
High Post Wilts 21 N7
Highridge N Som 31 Q11
High Roding Essex 51 P7
High Row Cumb 101 L3
High Row W & F 101 L6
High Salter Lancs 95 N8
High Salvington W Susx 24 D9
High Scales Cumb 110 C11
High Seaton Cumb 100 D4
High Shaw N York 96 C2
High Side Cumb 100 H4
High Spen Gatesd 112 H9
Highstead Kent 39 M8
Highsted Kent 38 F9
High Stoop Dur 103 M2
High Street Cnwll 3 P3
High Street Kent 26 B5
Highstreet Kent 39 J9
High Street Suffk 65 N10
High Street Suffk 65 N7
Highstreet Green Essex 52 C5
Highstreet Green Surrey 23 Q7
Hightae D & G 109 N5
Highter's Heath Birm 58 G9
High Throston Hartpl 104 E4
Hightown Ches E 70 F2
Hightown Hants 13 L4
Hightown Sefton 81 L4
High Town Staffs 58 E2
Hightown Green Suffk 64 D10
High Toynton Lincs 87 J7
High Trewhitt Nthumb 119 K9
High Urpeth Dur 113 K10
High Valleyfield Fife 134 C10
High Warden Nthumb 112 D7
Highway Herefs 45 P5
Highway Wilts 33 K10
Highweek Devon 7 L4
High Westwood Dur 112 H9
Highwood Essex 51 P10
Highwood Staffs 71 K8
Highwood W Susx 24 E4
Highwood Hill Gt Lon 36 F2
Highwoods Essex 52 H6
High Woolaston Gloucs 31 Q5
High Worsall N York 104 C9
Highworth Swindn 33 P6
High Wray W & F 101 L11
High Wych Herts 51 L8
High Wycombe Bucks 35 N6
Hilborough Norfk 75 R10
Hilcote Derbys 84 G9
Hilcott Wilts 21 M3
Hildenborough Kent 37 N11
Hilden Park Kent 37 N11
Hildersham Cambs 62 H11
Hilderstone Staffs 70 H8
Hilderthorpe E R Yk 99 P7
Hilfield Dorset 11 N3
Hilgay Norfk 75 M11
Hill S Glos 32 B5
Hill Warwks 59 Q11
Hillam N York 91 N5
Hillbeck W & F 102 E7
Hillborough Kent 39 M8
Hill Brow Hants 23 L9
Hillbutts Dorset 12 G4
Hill Chorlton Staffs 70 D7
Hillclifflane Derbys 71 P5
Hill Common Norfk 77 N7
Hill Common Somset 18 F9
Hill Deverill Wilts 20 G6
Hilldyke Lincs 87 K11
Hill End Dur 103 K3
Hill End Fife 134 C8
Hillend Fife 134 E11
Hill End Gloucs 46 H7
Hillend Mdloth 127 P4
Hillend N Lans 126 E4
Hillend Swans 28 D6
Hillersland Gloucs 31 Q2
Hillerton Devon 8 H5
Hillesden Bucks 49 J9
Hillesley Gloucs 32 E7
Hillfarrance Somset 18 G10
Hill Green Kent 38 D9
Hillgrove W Susx 23 P9
Hillhampton Herefs 46 A5
Hillhead Abers 158 E10
Hillhead Devon 7 N8
Hill Head Hants 14 F6
Hillhead S Lans 116 D2
Hillhead of Cocklaw Abers 159 Q9
Hilliard's Cross Staffs 59 J2
Hilliclay Highld 167 L4
Hillingdon Gt Lon 36 C4
Hillington C Glas 125 N5
Hillington Norfk 75 P5
Hillis Corner IoW 14 E8
Hillmorton Warwks 60 B6
Hillock Vale Lancs 89 M5
Hill of Beath Fife 134 F9
Hill of Fearn Highld 163 J11
Hillowton D & G 108 G8
Hillpool Worcs 58 C9
Hillpound Hants 22 G11
Hill Ridware Staffs 71 K11
Hillside Abers 151 N8
Hillside Angus 143 N5
Hillside Devon 7 J6
Hill Side Kirk 90 F7
Hill Side Worcs 46 E2
Hills Town Derbys 84 G7
Hillstreet Hants 22 B11
Hillswick Shet 169 p6
Hill Top Dur 103 J6
Hill Top Hants 14 D6
Hill Top Kirk 90 D8
Hill Top Rothm 84 E2
Hill Top Sandw 58 E6
Hill Top Wakefd 91 J7
Hillwell Shet 169 q12
Hilmarton Wilts 33 K9
Hilperton Wilts 20 G3
Hilperton Marsh Wilts 20 G3
Hilsea C Port 15 J6
Hilston E R Yk 93 N4
Hiltingbury Hants 22 D10
Hilton Border 129 M9
Hilton Cambs 62 C7
Hilton Derbys 71 N8
Hilton Dorset 12 C4
Hilton Dur 103 N6
Hilton S on T 104 E8
Hilton Shrops 57 P5
Hilton W & F 102 D6
Hilton of Cadboll Highld 156 F2
Hilton Park Services Staffs 58 E4
Himbleton Worcs 46 H3
Himley Staffs 58 C6
Hincaster W & F 95 L4
Hinchley Wood Surrey 36 E7
Hinckley Leics 59 P6
Hinderclay Suffk 64 E6
Hinderwell N York 105 L7
Hindford Shrops 69 K8
Hindhead Surrey 23 N7
Hindhead Tunnel Surrey 23 N7
Hindle Fold Lancs 89 L4
Hindley Nthumb 112 F9
Hindley Wigan 82 D4
Hindley Green Wigan 82 D4
Hindlip Worcs 46 G3
Hindolveston Norfk 76 E6
Hindon Wilts 20 H8
Hindringham Norfk 76 D4
Hingham Norfk 76 E11
Hinksford Staffs 58 C7
Hinstock Shrops 70 B9
Hintlesham Suffk 53 J3
Hinton Gloucs 32 C4
Hinton Hants 13 M5
Hinton Herefs 45 L7
Hinton S Glos 32 D9
Hinton Shrops 56 G3
Hinton Shrops 57 M8
Hinton W Nthn 48 F4
Hinton Admiral Hants 13 M5
Hinton Ampner Hants 22 H9
Hinton Blewett BaNES 19 Q3
Hinton Charterhouse BaNES 20 E3
Hinton Cross Worcs 47 K6
Hinton-in-the-Hedges W Nthn 48 G7
Hinton Marsh Hants 22 G9
Hinton Martell Dorset 12 H3
Hinton on the Green Worcs 47 K6
Hinton Parva Swindn 33 P8
Hinton St George Somset 11 J2
Hinton St Mary Dorset 20 E11
Hinton Waldrist Oxon 34 C5
Hints Shrops 57 L10
Hints Staffs 59 J4
Hinwick Bed 61 K8
Hinxhill Kent 26 H3
Hinxton Cambs 62 G11
Hinxworth Herts 50 F2
Hipperholme Calder 90 E5
Hipsburn Nthumb 119 P8
Hipswell N York 103 N11
Hirn Abers 151 J7
Hirnant Powys 68 D10
Hirst Nthumb 113 L3
Hirst Courtney N York 91 Q6
Hirwaen Denbgs 68 F2
Hirwaun Rhondd 30 C3
Hiscott Devon 17 J6
Histon Cambs 62 F8
Hitcham Suffk 64 D11
Hitcham Causeway Suffk 64 D11
Hitcham Street Suffk 64 D11
Hitchin Herts 50 E5
Hither Green Gt Lon 37 J6
Hittisleigh Devon 8 H5
Hive E R Yk 92 D4
Hixon Staffs 71 J9
Hoaden Kent 39 N10
Hoar Cross Staffs 71 L10
Hoarwithy Herefs 45 Q9
Hoath Kent 39 M9
Hoathly Kent 25 Q3
Hobarris Shrops 56 E9
Hobbles Green Suffk 63 M10
Hobbs Cross Essex 51 L11
Hobbs Cross Essex 51 L8
Hobkirk Border 118 A8
Hobland Hall Norfk 77 Q11
Hobsick Notts 84 G11
Hobson Dur 113 J9
Hoby Leics 72 H7
Hoccombe Somset 18 F9
Hockering Norfk 76 F9
Hockerton Notts 85 M9
Hockley Ches E 83 K8
Hockley Covtry 59 L9
Hockley Essex 38 D3
Hockley Staffs 59 K4
Hockley Heath Solhll 59 J10
Hockliffe C Beds 49 Q9
Hockwold cum Wilton Norfk 63 M3
Hockworthy Devon 18 D11
Hoddesdon Herts 51 J9
Hoddlesden Bl w D 89 L6
Hoddom Cross D & G 110 C6
Hoddom Mains D & G 110 C6
Hodgehill Ches E 82 H11
Hodgeston Pembks 41 K11
Hodnet Shrops 69 R9
Hodsock Notts 85 K3
Hodsoll Street Kent 37 P8
Hodson Swindn 33 N8
Hodthorpe Derbys 84 H5
Hoe Hants 22 G11
Hoe Norfk 76 D8
Hoe Benham W Berk 34 D11
Hoe Gate Hants 14 H4
Hoff W & F 102 C7
Hogben's Hill Kent 38 H10
Hoggards Green Suffk 64 B10
Hoggeston Bucks 49 M10
Hoggrill's End Warwks 59 K6
Hog Hill E Susx 26 E8
Hoghton Lancs 89 J5
Hoghton Bottoms Lancs 89 J5
Hognaston Derbys 71 N4
Hogsthorpe Lincs 87 P6
Holbeach Lincs 74 G6
Holbeach Bank Lincs 74 G5
Holbeach Clough Lincs 74 G5
Holbeach Drove Lincs 74 F8
Holbeach Hurn Lincs 74 G5
Holbeach St Johns Lincs 74 G7
Holbeach St Mark's Lincs 74 G4
Holbeach St Matthew Lincs 74 H4
Holbeck Notts 84 H6
Holbeck Woodhouse Notts 84 H6
Holberrow Green Worcs 47 K3
Holbeton Devon 6 G8
Holborn Gt Lon 36 H4
Holborough Kent 37 Q8
Holbrook Derbys 72 B2
Holbrook Sheff 84 F4
Holbrook Suffk 53 L4
Holbrook Moor Derbys 84 E11
Holbrooks Covtry 59 M8
Holburn Nthumb 119 K3
Holbury Hants 14 D6
Holcombe Devon 7 P4
Holcombe Somset 20 C5
Holcombe Rogus Devon 18 E11
Holcot W Nthn 60 G7
Holden Lancs 96 A11
Holdenby W Nthn 60 E7
Holden Gate Calder 89 P6
Holder's Green Essex 51 P5
Holdgate Shrops 57 K7
Holdingham Lincs 86 E11
Holditch Dorset 10 G4
Holdsworth Calder 90 D5
Holehouse Derbys 83 M6
Hole-in-the-Wall Herefs 46 B9
Holemoor Devon 16 G10
Hole Street W Susx 24 D8
Holford Somset 18 G6
Holgate C York 98 B10
Holker W & F 94 H5
Holkham Norfk 76 B3
Hollacombe Devon 16 F11
Holland Fen Lincs 86 H11
Holland Lees Lancs 88 G9
Holland-on-Sea Essex 53 L8
Hollandstoun Ork 169 g1
Hollee D & G 110 E7
Hollesley Suffk 53 Q3
Hollicombe Torbay 7 M6
Hollingbourne Kent 38 D10
Hollingbury Br & H 24 H9
Hollingdon Bucks 49 N9
Hollingrove E Susx 25 Q6
Hollingthorpe Leeds 91 K4
Hollington Derbys 71 N7
Hollington Staffs 71 K7
Hollingworth Tamesd 83 M5
Hollins Bury 89 N9
Hollins Derbys 84 D6
Hollins Staffs 70 H5
Hollinsclough Staffs 83 N11
Hollins End Sheff 84 E4
Hollins Green Warrtn 82 E6
Hollins Lane Lancs 95 K10
Hollinswood Wrekin 57 N3
Hollinwood Shrops 69 P7
Hollocombe Devon 17 L9
Holloway Derbys 84 D9
Holloway Gt Lon 36 H3
Holloway Wilts 20 G8
Hollowell W Nthn 60 E6
Hollowmoor Heath Ches W 81 P11
Hollows D & G 110 G5
Hollybush Caerph 30 G4
Hollybush E Ayrs 114 G4
Hollybush Herefs 46 E7
Holly End Norfk 75 J9
Holly Green Worcs 46 G6
Hollyhurst Ches E 69 Q6
Hollym E R Yk 93 P5
Hollywater Hants 23 M8
Hollywood Worcs 58 G9
Holmbridge Kirk 90 E9
Holmbury St Mary Surrey 24 D2
Holmbush Cnwll 3 Q3
Holmcroft Staffs 70 G10
Holme Cambs 61 Q3
Holme Kirk 90 E9
Holme N Linc 92 F9
Holme N York 97 N4
Holme Notts 85 P9
Holme W & F 95 L5
Holme Chapel Lancs 89 P5
Holme Green N York 91 P2
Holme Hale Norfk 76 B10
Holme Lacy Herefs 45 R7
Holme Marsh Herefs 45 L4
Holme next the Sea Norfk 75 P2
Holme on the Wolds E R Yk 99 K11
Holme Pierrepont Notts 72 G3
Holmer Herefs 45 Q6
Holmer Green Bucks 35 P5
Holme St Cuthbert Cumb 109 P11
Holmes Chapel Ches E 82 G11
Holmesfield Derbys 84 D5
Holmes Hill E Susx 25 M8
Holmeswood Lancs 88 E7
Holmethorpe Surrey 36 G10
Holme upon Spalding Moor E R Yk 92 D3
Holmewood Derbys 84 F7
Holmfield Calder 90 D5
Holmfirth Kirk 90 E9
Holmgate Derbys 84 E8
Holmhead E Ayrs 115 L3
Holmpton E R Yk 93 Q6
Holmrook Cumb 100 E11
Holmshurst E Susx 25 P5
Holmside Dur 113 K11
Holmwrangle Cumb 111 K11
Holne Devon 7 J5
Holnest Dorset 11 P3
Holnicote Somset 18 B5
Holsworthy Devon 16 E11
Holsworthy Beacon Devon 16 F10
Holt Dorset 12 H4
Holt Norfk 76 F4
Holt Wilts 20 G2
Holt Worcs 46 F2
Holt Wrexhm 69 M4
Holtby C York 98 D10
Holt End Worcs 58 G11
Holt Fleet Worcs 46 F2
Holt Green Lancs 88 D9
Holt Heath Dorset 13 J4
Holt Heath Worcs 46 F2
Holton Oxon 34 H3
Holton Somset 20 C9
Holton Suffk 65 N6
Holton cum Beckering Lincs 86 F4
Holton Heath Dorset 12 F6
Holton Hill E Susx 25 Q5
Holton le Clay Lincs 93 N10
Holton le Moor Lincs 93 J11
Holton St Mary Suffk 53 J4
Holt Street Kent 39 N11
Holtye E Susx 25 L3
Holway Flints 80 H9
Holwell Dorset 11 P2
Holwell Herts 50 E4
Holwell Leics 73 J6
Holwell Oxon 33 P3
Holwick Dur 102 H5
Holworth Dorset 12 C8
Holybourne Hants 23 K6
Holy Cross Worcs 58 D9
Holyfield Essex 51 J10
Holyhead IoA 78 C8
Holy Island IoA 78 D8
Holy Island Nthumb 119 M2
Holy Island Nthumb 119 M2
Holymoorside Derbys 84 D7
Holyport W & M 35 N9
Holystone Nthumb 119 J10
Holytown N Lans 126 D5
Holywell C Beds 50 B7
Holywell Cambs 62 D6
Holywell Cnwll 4 B10
Holywell Dorset 11 M4
Holywell Flints 80 H9
Holywell Nthumb 113 M6

Holywell Warwks 59 K11
Holywell Green Calder 90 D7
Holywell Lake Somset 18 F10
Holywell Row Suffk 63 M5
Holywood D & G 109 K10
Holywood Village D & G 109 L5
Homer Shrops 57 L4
Homer Green Sefton 81 L4
Homersfield Suffk 65 K4
Homescales W & F 95 M3
Hom Green Herefs 46 A10
Homington Wilts 21 M9
Honeyborough Pembks 40 H9
Honeybourne Worcs 47 N6
Honeychurch Devon 8 F4
Honey Hill Kent 39 K9
Honeystreet Wilts 21 M2
Honey Tye Suffk 52 G4
Honiley Warwks 59 K10
Honing Norfk 77 L6
Honingham Norfk 76 G9
Honington Lincs 73 N2
Honington Suffk 64 C7
Honington Warwks 47 Q6
Honiton Devon 10 D4
Honley Kirk 90 E8
Honnington Wrekin 70 C11
Hoo Kent 39 N9
Hoobrook Worcs 58 B10
Hood Green Barns 91 J10
Hood Hill Rothm 91 K11
Hooe C Plym 6
Hooe E Susx 25 Q8
Hoo End Herts 50 E6
Hoo Green Ches E 82 F8
Hoohill Bpool 88 C3
Hook Cambs 62 F2
Hook Devon 10 G3
Hook E R Yk 92 C5
Hook Gt Lon 36 E8
Hook Hants 14 F5
Hook Hants 23 K4
Hook Pembks 41 J8
Hook Wilts 33 L8
Hook-a-Gate Shrops 56 H3
Hook Bank Worcs 46 F6
Hooke Dorset 11 L4
Hook End Essex 51 N10
Hookgate Staffs 70 C7
Hook Green Kent 25 Q3
Hook Green Kent 37 P6
Hook Norton Oxon 48 C8
Hook Street Gloucs 32 C5
Hook Street Wilts 33 L8
Hookway Devon 9 L5
Hookwood Surrey 24 G2
Hooley Surrey 36 G9
Hooley Bridge Rochdl 89 P8
Hoo Meavy Devon 6 E5
Hoo St Werburgh Medway 38 C7
Hooton Ches W 81 M9
Hooton Levitt Rothm 84 H2
Hooton Pagnell Donc 91 M9
Hooton Roberts Rothm 91 M11
Hopcrofts Holt Oxon 48 E9
Hope Derbys 83 Q8
Hope Devon 6 H10
Hope Flints 69 K3
Hope Powys 56 D3
Hope Shrops 56 E4
Hope Staffs 71 L4
Hope Bagot Shrops 57 K10
Hope Bowdler Shrops 56 H6
Hope End Green Essex 51 N6
Hopehouse Border 117 K7
Hopeman Moray 157 L4
Hope Mansell Herefs 46 B11
Hopesay Shrops 56 F8
Hopetown Wakefd 91 K6
Hope under Dinmore Herefs 45 Q4
Hopgrove C York 98 C10
Hopperton N York 97 P9
Hop Pole Lincs 74 C8
Hopsford Warwks 59 P8
Hopstone Shrops 57 P6
Hopton Derbys 71 P4
Hopton Shrops 69 L10
Hopton Staffs 70 G9
Hopton Staffs 64 D6
Hopton Cangeford Shrops 57 J8
Hopton Castle Shrops 56 F9
Hoptonheath Shrops 56 F9
Hopton on Sea Norfk 65 Q2
Hopton Wafers Shrops 57 L9
Hopwas Staffs 59 J4
Hopwood Rochdl 89 P9
Hopwood Worcs 58 F9
Hopwood Park Services
  Worcs 58 F10
Horam E Susx 25 N7
Horbling Lincs 74 B3
Horbury Wakefd 90 H7
Horcott Gloucs 33 N4
Horden Dur 104 D2
Horderley Shrops 56 G7
Hordle Hants 13 N5
Hordley Shrops 69 L8
Horeb Carmth 28 E3
Horeb Cerdgn 42 G6
Horfield Bristl 31 Q9
Horham Suffk 65 J7
Horkesley Heath Essex 52 G6
Horkstow N Linc 92 G7
Horley Oxon 48 D6
Horley Surrey 24 G2
Hornblotton Green Somset 19 Q8
Hornby Lancs 95 M7
Hornby N York 97 K2
Hornby N York 104 C9
Horncastle Lincs 87 J7
Hornchurch Gt Lon 37 M3
Horncliffe Nthumb 129 N10
Horndean Border 129 N10
Horndean Hants 15 K4
Horndon Devon 8 D8
Horndon on the Hill Thurr 37 Q4
Horne Surrey 24 H2
Horner Somset 18 B5
Horne Row Essex 52 C11
Horners Green Suffk 52 G3
Horney Common E Susx 25 L5
Horn Hill Bucks 36 B2
Horning Norfk 77 L8
Horninghold Leics 73 L11
Horninglow Staffs 71 N9
Horningsea Cambs 62 G8

Horningsham Wilts 20 F6
Horningtoft Norfk 76 C7
Horningtops Cnwll 5 M9
Hornsbury Somset 10 G2
Hornsby Cumb 111 K10
Hornsbygate Cumb 111 K10
Horns Cross Devon 16 F7
Horns Cross E Susx 26 D7
Hornsea E R Yk 99 P11
Hornsey Gt Lon 36 H3
Horn's Green Gt Lon 37 L9
Horn Street Kent 27 L4
Hornton Oxon 48 C5
Horpit Swindn 33 P8
Horrabridge Devon 6 E5
Horringer Suffk 64 A9
Horringford IoW 14 F9
Horrocks Fold Bolton 89 L8
Horrocksford Lancs 89 M2
Horsacott Devon 17 J5
Horsebridge Devon 5 Q6
Horsebridge E Susx 25 N8
Horsebridge Hants 22 B8
Horsebridge Shrops 56 F3
Horsebridge Staffs 70 H4
Horsebrook Staffs 58 C2
Horsecastle N Som 31 M11
Horsedown Cnwll 2 G7
Horsehay Wrekin 57 M3
Horseheath Cambs 63 K11
Horsehouse N York 96 F4
Horsell Surrey 23 Q3
Horseman's Green Wrexhm 69 M6
Horsenden Bucks 35 L4
Horsey Norfk 77 P7
Horsey Somset 19 K7
Horsey Corner Norfk 77 P7
Horsford Norfk 76 H8
Horsforth Leeds 90 G3
Horsham W Susx 24 E4
Horsham Worcs 46 D5
Horsham St Faith Norfk 77 J8
Horsington Lincs 86 G7
Horsington Somset 20 D10
Horsley Derbys 72 B2
Horsley Gloucs 32 F5
Horsley Nthumb 112 G7
Horsley Nthumb 118 F11
Horsley Cross Essex 53 K6
Horsleycross Street Essex 53 K6
Horsley-Gate Derbys 84 D5
Horsleyhill Border 117 Q7
Horsley's Green Bucks 35 L4
Horsley Woodhouse Derbys 72 B2
Horsmonden Kent 26 B3
Horspath Oxon 34 G3
Horstead Norfk 77 K8
Horsted Keynes W Susx 25 J5
Horton Bucks 49 P11
Horton Dorset 12 H3
Horton Lancs 96 C10
Horton S Glos 32 E8
Horton Shrops 69 N9
Horton Somset 10 G2
Horton Staffs 70 G3
Horton Surrey 36 E8
Horton Swans 28 E7
Horton W & M 36 B5
Horton W Nthn 49 M4
Horton Wilts 21 K2
Horton Wrekin 57 M2
Horton Cross Somset 19 K11
Horton-cum-Studley Oxon 34 G2
Horton Green Ches W 69 N5
Horton Heath Hants 22 E11
Horton-in-Ribblesdale
  N York 96 B6
Horton Kirby Kent 37 N7
Horwich Bolton 89 J8
Horwich End Derbys 83 M8
Horwood Devon 17 J6
Hoscar Lancs 88 F8
Hoscote Border 117 M8
Hose Leics 73 J5
Hosey Hill Kent 37 L10
Hosh P & K 133 P3
Hoswick Shet 169 r11
Hotham E R Yk 92 E4
Hothfield Kent 26 G3
Hoton Leics 72 F6
Hott Nthumb 111 Q3
Hough Ches E 70 C4
Hough Ches E 83 J9
Hougham Lincs 73 M2
Hough End Leeds 90 G4
Hough Green Halton 81 P7
Hough-on-the-Hill Lincs 86 B1
Houghton Cambs 62 C6
Houghton Cumb 110 H9
Houghton Hants 22 B8
Houghton Nthumb 112 H7
Houghton Pembks 41 J9
Houghton W Susx 24 B8
Houghton Conquest C Beds 50 B2
Houghton Gate Dur 113 M10
Houghton Green E Susx 26 F7
Houghton Green Warrtn 82 D6
Houghton le Side Darltn 103 P6
Houghton-le-Spring Sundld 113 M11
Houghton on the Hill Leics 72 H10
Houghton Regis C Beds 50 B6
Houghton St Giles Norfk 76 C4
Houlton Ches W 60 C6
Hound Green Hants 23 K3
Houndslow Border 128 G10
Houndsmoor Somset 18 F9
Houndwood Border 129 L7
Hounslow Gt Lon 36 D5
Housebill Highld 156 F6
Houses Hill Kirk 90 F7
Housieside Abers 151 M2
Houston Rens 125 L4
Houstry Highld 167 L10
Houton Ork 169 c6
Hove Br & H 24 G10
Hove Edge Calder 90 E6
Hoveringham Notts 85 L11
Hoveton Norfk 77 L8
Hovingham N York 98 D5
Howbrook Barns 91 J11
How Caple Herefs 46 B8
Howden E R Yk 92 C5
Howden-le-Wear Dur 103 N4
Howe Highld 167 P4
Howe IoM 80 a8
Howe N York 97 N4

Howe Norfk 65 K2
Howe Bridge Wigan 82 E4
Howe Green Essex 52 B11
Howegreen Essex 52 D11
Howell Lincs 86 F11
How End C Beds 50 B2
Howe of Teuchar Abers 159 J8
Howes D & G 110 C7
Howe Street Essex 51 Q4
Howe Street Essex 51 Q8
Howey Powys 44 F3
Howgate Cumb 100 C6
Howgate Mdloth 127 N6
Howgill Lancs 96 B11
Howick Nthumb 119 Q7
Howle Wrekin 70 B10
Howle Hill Herefs 46 B10
Howlett End Essex 51 N4
Howley Somset 10 F3
How Mill Cumb 111 K9
Howmore W Isls 168 c14
Hownam Border 118 C7
Howrigg Cumb 110 F11
Howsham N Linc 92 H10
Howsham N York 98 E8
Howtel Nthumb 118 G4
Howt Green Kent 38 E7
Howton Herefs 45 N9
Howtown W & F 101 M7
How Wood Herts 50 D10
Howwood Rens 125 K5
Hoxa Ork 169 d7
Hoxne Suffk 64 H6
Hoy Ork 169 b7
Hoylake Wirral 81 J7
Hoyland Barns 91 K10
Hoyland Common Barns 91 K10
Hoylandswaine Barns 90 H10
Hoyle W Susx 23 P11
Hoyle Mill Barns 91 K9
Hubberholme N York 96 D5
Hubberston Pembks 40 G9
Hubbert's Bridge Lincs 74 E2
Huby N York 97 L11
Huby N York 98 B7
Huccaby Devon 6 H4
Hucclecote Gloucs 46 G11
Hucking Kent 38 D10
Hucknall Notts 84 H11
Huddersfield Kirk 90 E7
Huddington Worcs 46 H3
Hudnall Herts 50 B8
Hudswell N York 103 M10
Huggate E R Yk 98 H9
Hugglescote Leics 72 C8
Hughenden Valley Bucks 35 N5
Hughley Shrops 57 K5
Hugh Town IoS 2 b2
Huish Devon 17 J9
Huish Wilts 21 M2
Huish Champflower Somset 18 E9
Huish Episcopi Somset 19 M9
Hūisinis W Isls 168 e6
Huisinish W Isls 168 e6
Hulcote C Beds 49 P7
Hulcote W Nthn 49 K5
Hulcott Bucks 49 N11
Hulham Devon 9 Q4
Hulland Derbys 71 N5
Hulland Ward Derbys 71 P5
Hullavington Wilts 32 G8
Hull, Kingston upon C KuH 93 J5
Hulme Manch 82 H5
Hulme Staffs 70 G5
Hulme Warrtn 82 D6
Hulme End Staffs 71 L3
Hulme Walfield Ches E 82 H11
Hulse Heath Ches E 82 F8
Hulton Lane Ends Bolton 89 K9
Hulverstone IoW 14 C10
Hulver Street Norfk 76 C9
Hulver Street Suffk 65 P4
Humber Devon 9 L9
Humber Herefs 45 Q3
Humber Bridge N Linc 92 H6
Humberside Airport N Linc 93 J8
Humberston NE Lin 93 P9
Humberstone C Leic 72 G9
Humberton N York 97 P7
Humbie E Loth 128 D7
Humbleton E R Yk 93 M4
Humbleton Nthumb 119 J5
Humby Lincs 73 Q4
Hume Border 118 D2
Humshaugh Nthumb 112 D6
Huna Highld 167 Q2
Huncoat Lancs 89 M4
Huncote Leics 72 E11
Hundalee Border 118 B7
Hundall Derbys 84 E5
Hunderthwaite Dur 103 J6
Hundleby Lincs 87 L7
Hundle Houses Lincs 86 H10
Hundleton Pembks 41 J10
Hundon Suffk 63 M11
Hundred End Lancs 88 E6
Hundred House Powys 44 G4
Hungarton Leics 72 H9
Hungerford Hants 13 L2
Hungerford Somset 18 D6
Hungerford W Berk 34 B11
Hungerford Newtown
  W Berk 34 C10
Hunger Hill Bolton 89 K9
Hunger Hill Lancs 88 G8
Hungerstone Herefs 45 N7
Hungerton Lincs 73 M5
Hungryhatton Shrops 70 B9
Hunmanby N York 99 M5
Hunnington Worcs 58 E8
Hunningham Warwks 59 N11
Hunny Hill W Nthn 60 F9
Hunsdon Herts 51 K8
Hunsdonbury Herts 51 K8
Hunsingore N York 97 P10
Hunslet Leeds 91 J4
Hunsonby W & F 101 Q3
Hunstanton Norfk 75 N2
Hunstanworth Dur 112 D11
Hunsterson Ches E 70 B5
Hunston Suffk 64 D8
Hunston W Susx 15 N6
Hunston Green Suffk 64 D8
Hunstrete BaNES 20 B2

Hunsworth Kirk 90 F5
Hunt End Worcs 47 K2
Hunter's Inn Devon 17 M2
Hunter's Quay Ag & B 124 F2
Huntham Somset 19 K9
Hunthill Lodge Angus 142 H3
Huntingdon Cambs 62 B6
Huntingfield Suffk 65 L7
Huntingford Dorset 20 F9
Huntington C York 98 C9
Huntington Ches W 69 M2
Huntington E Loth 128 D5
Huntington Herefs 45 K4
Huntington Herefs 45 P6
Huntington Staffs 58 E2
Huntingtowerfield P & K 134 D2
Huntley Gloucs 46 D11
Huntly Abers 158 D10
Hunton Hants 22 E6
Hunton Kent 26 B2
Hunton N York 97 J2
Hunton Bridge Herts 50 C10
Hunt's Corner Norfk 64 F4
Huntscott Somset 18 B6
Hunt's Cross Lpool 81 N7
Hunts Green Bucks 35 N4
Hunts Green Warwks 59 J5
Huntsham Devon 18 D10
Huntshaw Devon 17 J7
Huntshaw Cross Devon 17 J7
Huntspill Somset 19 K5
Huntstile Somset 19 J8
Huntworth Somset 19 K8
Hunwick Dur 103 N4
Hunworth Norfk 76 F4
Hurcott Somset 19 L11
Hurdcott Wilts 21 N8
Hurdsfield Ches E 83 K10
Hurley W & M 35 M8
Hurley Warwks 59 K5
Hurley Bottom W & M 35 M8
Hurley Common Warwks 59 K5
Hurlford E Ayrs 125 M10
Hurlston Green Lancs 88 D8
Hurn BCP 13 K5
Hurn's End Lincs 87 M11
Hursley Hants 22 D9
Hurst Dorset 12 C6
Hurst N York 103 K10
Hurst Somset 19 N11
Hurst Wokham 35 L10
Hurstbourne Priors Hants 22 D5
Hurstbourne Tarrant Hants 22 C4
Hurst Green E Susx 26 B6
Hurst Green Essex 53 J8
Hurst Green Lancs 89 K3
Hurst Green Surrey 37 K10
Hurst Hill Dudley 58 D6
Hurstley Herefs 45 M5
Hurstpierpoint W Susx 24 G7
Hurst Wickham W Susx 24 G7
Hurstwood Lancs 89 P4
Hurtiso Ork 169 e6
Hurtmore Surrey 23 P5
Hurworth Burn Dur 104 D4
Hurworth-on-Tees Darltn 104 B9
Hurworth Place Darltn 103 Q9
Hury Dur 103 J7
Husbands Bosworth Leics 60 D4
Husborne Crawley C Beds 49 Q7
Husthwaite N York 97 R6
Hutcherleigh Devon 7 K8
Hut Green N York 91 P6
Huthwaite Notts 84 G9
Huttoft Lincs 87 P5
Hutton Border 129 N9
Hutton E R Yk 99 L10
Hutton Essex 37 P2
Hutton Lancs 88 F5
Hutton N Som 19 L3
Hutton W & F 101 M5
Hutton Bonville N York 104 B10
Hutton Buscel N York 99 K4
Hutton Conyers N York 97 M6
Hutton Cranswick E R Yk 99 L10
Hutton End W & F 101 N3
Hutton Hang N York 97 J3
Hutton Henry Dur 104 D3
Hutton-le-Hole N York 98 E2
Hutton Lowcross R & Cl 104 G8
Hutton Magna Dur 103 M8
Hutton Mulgrave N York 105 M9
Hutton Roof N York 95 M5
Hutton Roof W & F 101 L4
Hutton Rudby N York 104 D9
Hutton Sessay N York 97 Q5
Hutton Wandesley N York 97 R10
Huxham Devon 9 M5
Huxham Green Somset 19 Q7
Huxley Ches W 69 P2
Huyton Knows 81 N6
Hycemoor Cumb 94 B3
Hyde Gloucs 32 G4
Hyde Hants 13 L2
Hyde Tamesd 83 K6
Hyde Heath Bucks 35 P4
Hyde Lea Staffs 70 G11
Hydestile Surrey 23 Q6
Hykeham Moor Lincs 86 B7
Hylands Estate Essex 51 Q10
Hyndford Bridge S Lans 116 C2
Hynish Ag & B 136 B8
Hyssington Powys 56 E6
Hystfield Gloucs 32 C5
Hythe Essex 52 H6
Hythe Hants 14 D5
Hythe Kent 27 L4
Hythe Somset 19 M4
Hythe End W & M 36 B6
Hyton Cumb 94 B3

I

Ibberton Dorset 12 C3
Ible Derbys 84 B9
Ibsley Hants 13 L3
Ibstock Leics 72 C9
Ibstone Bucks 35 L6
Ibthorpe Hants 22 C4
Iburndale N York 105 N9
Ibworth Hants 22 G4
Icelton N Som 31 L11
Ichrachan Ag & B 139 J11
Ickburgh Norfk 75 R11
Ickenham Gt Lon 36 C3
Ickford Bucks 34 H3
Ickham Kent 39 M10
Ickleford Herts 50 E4
Icklesham E Susx 26 E8
Ickleton Cambs 51 L2
Icklingham Suffk 63 N6
Ickornshaw N York 90 B2
Ickwell Green C Beds 61 Q11
Icomb Gloucs 47 P10
Idbury Oxon 47 P11
Iddesleigh Devon 17 K10
Ide Devon 9 L6
Ideford Devon 9 L6
Ide Hill Kent 37 L10
Iden E Susx 26 F7
Iden Green Kent 26 B4
Iden Green Kent 26 D5
Idle C Brad 90 F3
Idless Cnwll 3 L4
Idlicote Warwks 47 Q6
Idmiston Wilts 21 N7
Idole Carmth 42 H11
Idridgehay Derbys 71 P5
Idrigill Highld 152 F5
Idstone Oxon 33 Q8
Iffley Oxon 34 F4
Ifield W Susx 24 G3
Ifold W Susx 24 B4
Iford BCP 13 K6
Iford E Susx 25 K9
Ifton Mons 31 N7
Ifton Heath Shrops 69 K7
Ightfield Shrops 69 Q7
Ightham Kent 37 N9
Iken Suffk 65 N10
Ilam Staffs 71 L4
Ilchester Somset 19 P10
Ilderton Nthumb 119 K6
Ilford Gt Lon 37 K3
Ilford E Susx 19 L11
Ilfracombe Devon 17 J2
Ilkeston Derbys 72 D2
Ilketshall St Andrew Suffk 65 M4
Ilketshall St John Suffk 65 M4
Ilketshall St Lawrence Suffk 65 M5
Ilketshall St Margaret Suffk 65 L4
Ilkley C Brad 96 H11
Illand Cnwll 5 M6
Illey Dudley 58 E8
Illidge Green Ches E 70 D2
Illingworth Calder 90 D5
Illogan Cnwll 2 H5
Illston on the Hill Leics 73 J11
Ilmer Bucks 35 L3
Ilmington Warwks 47 P6
Ilminster Somset 10 H2
Ilsington Devon 9 J9
Ilsington Dorset 12 C6
Ilston Swans 28 G6
Ilton N York 97 J5
Ilton Somset 19 L11
Imachar N Ayrs 120 G3
Immingham NE Lin 93 L8
Immingham Dock NE Lin 93 L7
Impington Cambs 62 F8
Ince Ches W 81 P9
Ince Blundell Sefton 81 L4
Ince-in-Makerfield Wigan 82 C4
Inchbae Lodge Highld 155 M4
Inchbare Angus 143 L4
Inchberry Moray 157 Q6
Incheril Highld 154 D5
Inchinnan Rens 125 M4
Inchlaggan Highld 146 F7
Inchmichael P & K 134 C2
Inchmore Highld 155 Q8
Inchnadamph Highld 161 M2
Inchture P & K 134 H2
Inchyra P & K 134 F3
Indian Queens Cnwll 4 E10
Ingatestone Essex 51 P11
Ingbirchworth Barns 90 G9
Ingerthorpe N York 97 L7
Ingestre Staffs 70 H10
Ingham Lincs 86 B4
Ingham Norfk 77 M6
Ingham Suffk 64 B7
Ingham Corner Norfk 77 J7
Ingleborough Norfk 75 J7
Ingleby Derbys 72 A5
Ingleby Arncliffe N York 104 D10
Ingleby Barwick S on T 104 D8
Ingleby Cross N York 104 E10
Ingleby Greenhow N York 104 G9
Ingleigh Green Devon 8 F3
Inglesbatch BaNES 20 D2
Inglesham Swindn 33 P5
Ingleton D & G 109 L7
Ingleton Dur 103 N6
Ingleton N York 95 P6
Inglewhite Lancs 88 G3
Ingmanthorpe N York 97 P10
Ingoe Nthumb 112 F6
Ingol Lancs 88 G4
Ingoldisthorpe Norfk 75 N4
Ingoldmells Lincs 87 Q7
Ingoldsby Lincs 73 Q4
Ingram Nthumb 119 K7
Ingrave Essex 37 P3
Ingrow C Brad 90 D3
Ings W & F 101 M11
Ingst S Glos 31 Q7
Ingthorpe Rutlnd 73 P9
Ingworth Norfk 76 H6
Inkberrow Worcs 47 K3
Inkerman Dur 103 M3
Inkersall Green Derbys 84 F6
Inkhorn Abers 159 M10
Inkpen W Berk 22 C2
Inkstack Highld 167 N2
Inmarsh Wilts 20 H2
Innellan Ag & B 124 F4
Innerleithen Border 117 L3
Innerleven Fife 135 J7
Innermessan D & G 106 E5
Innerwick E Loth 129 J4
Innesmill Moray 157 P5
Innsworth Gloucs 46 G10
Insch Abers 150 G2
Insh Highld 148 H7
Inshes Highld 156 B9
Inskip Lancs 88 F3
Inskip Moss Side Lancs 88 F3
Instow Devon 16 H6
Insworke Cnwll 6 C8

Intake Sheff 84 E4
Inver Abers 149 N9
Inver Highld 163 K10
Inver P & K 141 P9
Inverailort Highld 145 N11
Inveralligin Highld 153 Q6
Inverallochy Abers 159 P4
Inveran Highld 162 D7
Inveraray Ag & B 131 M6
Inverarish Highld 153 K10
Inverarity Angus 142 H9
Inverarnan Stirlg 132 C4
Inverasdale Highld 160 C10
Inverbeg Ag & B 132 C8
Inverbervie Abers 143 Q3
Inverboyndie Abers 158 G5
Invercreran Lodge Ag & B 139 J8
Inverdruie Highld 148 F5
Inveresk E Loth 127 Q3
Inveresragan Ag & B 138 H10
Inverey Abers 149 K10
Inverfarigaig Highld 147 N3
Inverfolla Ag & B 138 H9
Invergarry Highld 147 J7
Invergeldie P & K 133 L2
Invergloy Highld 146 G10
Invergordon Highld 156 C4
Invergowrie P & K 142 E11
Inverguseran Highld 145 M6
Inverhadden P & K 140 G6
Inverie Highld 145 N7
Inverinan Ag & B 131 K4
Inverinate Highld 145 R3
Inverkeilor Angus 143 M8
Inverkeithing Fife 134 E11
Inverkeithny Abers 158 F8
Inverkip Inver 124 G3
Inverkirkaig Highld 160 H3
Inverlael Highld 161 K9
Inverlair Highld 139 Q2
Inverliever Lodge Ag & B 130 H6
Inverlochy Ag & B 131 P2
Invermark Angus 150 C11
Invermoriston Highld 147 L4
Invernaver Highld 166 B4
Inverneill Ag & B 123 P3
Inverness Highld 156 B8
Inverness Airport Highld 156 D7
Invernettie Abers 159 R9
Invernoaden Ag & B 131 N8
Inveroran Hotel Ag & B 139 P9
Inverquharity Angus 142 G6
Inverquhomery Abers 159 P8
Inverroy Highld 146 H11
Inversanda Highld 138 G6
Invershiel Highld 146 A4
Invershin Highld 162 D7
Invershore Highld 167 M9
Inversnaid Hotel Stirlg 132 C6
Inverugie Abers 159 Q8
Inveruglas Ag & B 132 C6
Inveruglass Highld 148 E7
Inverurie Abers 151 K3
Inwardleigh Devon 8 E5
Inworth Essex 52 E8
Iochdar W Isls 168 c13
Iona Ag & B 136 H10
Iping W Susx 23 N10
iPort Logistics Park Donc 91 Q11
Ipplepen Devon 7 L5
Ipsden Oxon 34 H7
Ipstones Staffs 71 J5
Ipswich Suffk 53 L3
Irby Wirral 81 K8
Irby in the Marsh Lincs 87 N8
Irby upon Humber NE Lin 93 L10
Irchester N Nthn 61 K7
Ireby Cumb 100 H3
Ireby Lancs 95 P5
Ireland C Beds 50 D2
Ireleth W & F 94 E5
Ireshopeburn Dur 102 G3
Ireton Wood Derbys 71 P5
Irlam Salfd 82 F6
Irnham Lincs 73 Q5
Iron Acton S Glos 32 C8
Iron Bridge Cambs 75 J11
Ironbridge Wrekin 57 M4
Ironbridge Gorge Wrekin 57 M4
Iron Cross Warwks 47 L4
Ironmacannie D & G 108 E5
Irons Bottom Surrey 36 F11
Ironville Derbys 84 F10
Irstead Norfk 77 M7
Irthington Cumb 111 J8
Irthlingborough N Nthn 61 K6
Irton N York 99 L4
Irvine N Ayrs 125 J10
Isauld Highld 166 G3
Isbister Shet 169 q4
Isbister Shet 169 s7
Isfield E Susx 25 K7
Isham N Nthn 61 J6
Isington Hants 23 L6
Islandpool Worcs 58 C8
Islay Ag & B 122 E8
Islay Airport Ag & B 122 D9
Isle Abbotts Somset 19 L10
Isle Brewers Somset 19 L10
Isleham Cambs 63 K6
Isle of Dogs Gt Lon 37 J5
Isle of Grain Medway 38 E6
Isle of Lewis W Isls 168 i4
Isle of Man IoM 80 e4
Isle of Man Ronaldsway Airport IoM 80 c8
Isle of Mull Ag & B 137 Q8
Isle of Purbeck Dorset 12 H8
Isle of Sheppey Kent 38 G8
Isle of Skye Highld 152 G10
Isle of Thanet Kent 39 P8
Isle of Walney W & F 94 D7
Isle of Whithorn D & G 107 N10
Isle of Wight IoW 14 F9
Isleornsay Highld 145 M5
Isles of Scilly IoS 2 c2
Isles of Scilly St Mary's Airport IoS 2 c2
Islesteps D & G 109 L6
Islet Village Guern 10 c1
Isleworth Gt Lon 36 E5
Isley Walton Leics 72 C6
Islibhig W Isls 168 f5
Islington Gt Lon 36 H4
Islip N Nthn 61 L5

Islip Oxon 34 F2
Islivig W Isls 168 f5
Isombridge Wrekin 57 L2
Istead Rise Kent 37 P6
Itchen Abbas Hants 22 F8
Itchen Stoke Hants 22 G8
Itchingfield W Susx 24 D5
Itchington S Glos 32 C7
Itteringham Norfk 76 G5
Itton Devon 8 G5
Itton Mons 31 N5
Itton Common Mons 31 N5
Ivegill Cumb 101 M2
Ivelet N York 102 H11
Iver Bucks 36 B4
Iver Heath Bucks 36 B4
Iveston Dur 112 H10
Ivinghoe Bucks 49 P11
Ivinghoe Aston Bucks 49 Q11
Ivington Herefs 45 P3
Ivington Green Herefs 45 P3
Ivybridge Devon 6 G7
Ivychurch Kent 26 H6
Ivy Cross Dorset 20 G10
Ivy Hatch Kent 37 N10
Ivy Todd Norfk 76 B10
Iwade Kent 38 F8
Iwerne Courtney Dorset 12 E2
Iwerne Minster Dorset 12 E2
Ixworth Suffk 64 C7
Ixworth Thorpe Suffk 64 C7

J

Jack Green Lancs 88 H5
Jack Hill N York 97 J10
Jack-in-the-Green Devon 9 P5
Jack's Bush Hants 21 Q7
Jacksdale Notts 84 F10
Jackson Bridge Kirk 90 F9
Jackton S Lans 125 P7
Jacobstow Cnwll 5 K2
Jacobstowe Devon 8 E4
Jacobs Well Surrey 23 Q4
Jameston Pembks 41 L11
Jamestown Highld 155 N6
Jamestown W Duns 132 D11
Janetstown Highld 167 L10
Jardine Hall D & G 109 P3
Jarrow S Tyne 113 M8
Jarvis Brook E Susx 25 M5
Jasper's Green Essex 52 B6
Jawcraig Falk 126 E2
Jaywick Essex 53 L9
Jealott's Hill Br For 35 N10
Jeater Houses N York 97 P2
Jedburgh Border 118 B6
Jeffreyston Pembks 41 L9
Jemimaville Highld 156 C4
Jerbourg Guern 10 c2
Jersey Jersey 11 b1
Jersey Airport Jersey 11 a2
Jersey Marine Neath 29 K6
Jerusalem Lincs 86 B6
Jesmond N u Ty 113 L7
Jevington E Susx 25 N10
Jingle Street Mons 31 N2
Jockey End Herts 50 B8
Jodrell Bank Ches E 82 G10
Jodrell Bank Ches E 82 G10
Johnby W & F 101 M4
John Lennon Airport Lpool 81 N8
John o' Groats Highld 167 Q2
Johns Cross E Susx 26 B7
Johnshaven Abers 143 P4
Johnson Street Norfk 77 M8
Johnston Pembks 40 H8
Johnstone D & G 117 J10
Johnstone Rens 125 L5
Johnstonebridge D & G 109 P2
Johnstown Carmth 42 G11
Johnstown Wrexhm 69 K5
Joppa C Edin 127 Q3
Joppa Cerdgn 54 D11
Joppa S Ayrs 114 H4
Jordans Bucks 35 Q6
Jordanston Pembks 40 H4
Jordanthorpe Sheff 84 E4
Joyden's Wood Kent 37 M6
Jubilee Corner Kent 26 D2
Jump Barns 91 K10
Jumper's Town E Susx 25 L4
Juniper Nthumb 112 D9
Juniper Green C Edin 127 M4
Jura Ag & B 122 H3
Jurassic Coast Devon 10 G7
Jurby IoM 80 e2
Jurston Devon 8 G8

K

Kaber W & F 102 E8
Kaimend S Lans 126 H4
Kames Ag & B 124 B3
Kames E Ayrs 115 N2
Kea Cnwll 3 L5
Keadby N Linc 92 D8
Keal Cotes Lincs 87 L8
Kearby Town End N York 97 M11
Kearsley Bolton 82 G4
Kearsley Nthumb 112 F5
Kearsney Kent 27 N3
Kearstwick W & F 95 N5
Kearton N York 103 J11
Keasden N York 95 Q7
Keaton Devon 6 G8
Keckwick Halton 82 C8
Keddington Lincs 87 K3
Keddington Corner Lincs 87 L3
Kedington Suffk 63 N10
Kedleston Derbys 71 Q6
Keelby Lincs 93 L8
Keele Staffs 70 E5
Keele Services Staffs 70 E5
Keele University Staffs 70 E5
Keeley Green Bed 61 M11
Keelham C Brad 90 D4
Keeres Green Essex 51 N8
Keeston Pembks 40 H7
Keevil Wilts 20 H3
Kegworth Leics 72 D5
Kehelland Cnwll 2 G5

Keig Abers 150 G4
Keighley C Brad 90 D2
Keilarsbrae Clacks 133 P9
Keillour P & K 134 B2
Keiloch Abers 149 M9
Keils Ag & B 122 H6
Keinton Mandeville Somset 19 P9
Keir Mill D & G 109 J2
Keirsleywell Row Nthumb 111 P10
Keisby Lincs 73 Q5
Keisley W & F 102 D6
Keiss Highld 167 P4
Keith Moray 158 B7
Keithick P & K 142 C10
Keithock Angus 143 L5
Keithtown Highld 155 P6
Kelbrook Lancs 89 Q2
Kelby Lincs 73 Q2
Keld N York 102 G10
Keld W & F 101 Q8
Keld Head N York 98 F4
Keldholme N York 98 E3
Kelfield N Linc 92 D10
Kelfield N York 91 P3
Kelham Notts 85 N9
Kelhead D & G 109 P7
Kellacott Devon 5 Q4
Kellamergh Lancs 88 E5
Kellas Angus 142 H10
Kellas Moray 157 M7
Kellaton Devon 7 L11
Kelleth W & F 102 C9
Kelling Norfk 76 F3
Kellingley N York 91 N6
Kellington N York 91 P6
Kelloe Dur 104 B3
Kelloholm D & G 115 P5
Kells Cumb 100 C7
Kelly Devon 5 P5
Kelly Bray Cnwll 5 P7
Kelmarsh N Nthn 60 F5
Kelmscott Oxon 33 P5
Kelsale Suffk 65 M8
Kelsall Ches W 81 Q11
Kelshall Herts 50 H3
Kelsick Cumb 110 C10
Kelso Border 118 D4
Kelstedge Derbys 84 D8
Kelstern Lincs 86 H3
Kelsterton Flints 81 K10
Kelston BaNES 32 D11
Keltneyburn P & K 141 J8
Kelton D & G 109 L6
Kelty Fife 134 E9
Kelvedon Essex 52 E8
Kelvedon Hatch Essex 51 N11
Kelvinhead N Lans 126 D2
Kelynack Cnwll 2 B8
Kemacott Devon 17 M2
Kemback Fife 135 L5
Kemberton Shrops 57 N4
Kemberton Gloucs 33 J5
Kemble Wick Gloucs 33 J5
Kemerton Worcs 47 J7
Kemeys Commander Mons 31 K4
Kemnay Abers 151 J4
Kempe's Corner Kent 26 H2
Kempley Gloucs 46 C9
Kempley Green Gloucs 46 C9
Kempsey Worcs 46 F5
Kempsford Gloucs 33 N5
Kemps Green Warwks 58 H10
Kempshott Hants 22 H4
Kempston Bed 61 M11
Kempston Hardwick Bed 50 B2
Kempton Shrops 56 F7
Kemp Town Br & H 24 H10
Kemsing Kent 37 N9
Kemsley Kent 38 F8
Kemsley Street Kent 38 D9
Kenardington Kent 26 G5
Kenchester Herefs 45 N6
Kencot Oxon 33 Q4
Kendal W & F 95 L2
Kenderchurch Herefs 45 N9
Kendleshire S Glos 32 C9
Kenfig Brdgnd 29 M8
Kenfig Hill Brdgnd 29 M8
Kenilworth Warwks 59 L10
Kenley Gt Lon 36 H8
Kenley Shrops 57 K4
Kenmore Highld 153 N6
Kenmore P & K 141 J8
Kenn Devon 9 M8
Kenn N Som 31 M11
Kennacraig Ag & B 123 P7
Kennall Vale Cnwll 3 J6
Kennards House Cnwll 5 M5
Kenneggy Cnwll 2 F8
Kennerleigh Devon 9 K3
Kennet Clacks 133 Q9
Kennethmont Abers 150 E2
Kennett Cambs 63 L7
Kennford Devon 9 M7
Kenninghall Norfk 64 F4
Kennington Kent 26 H2
Kennington Oxon 34 F4
Kennington Lees Kent 26 H2
Kennoway Fife 135 K7
Kenny Somset 19 K11
Kenny Hill Suffk 63 L5
Kennythorpe N York 98 F7
Kenovay Ag & B 136 B6
Kensaleyre Highld 152 G7
Kensington Gt Lon 36 F5
Kensington Palace Gt Lon 36 F5
Kensworth C Beds 50 B7
Kensworth Common C Beds 50 B7
Kentallen Highld 139 J6
Kentchurch Herefs 45 N9
Kentford Suffk 63 M7
Kent Green Ches E 70 E3
Kentisbeare Devon 9 Q3
Kentisbury Devon 17 L3
Kentisbury Ford Devon 17 L3
Kentish Town Gt Lon 36 G4
Kentmere W & F 101 N10
Kenton Devon 9 N8
Kenton Gt Lon 36 E3
Kenton N u Ty 113 K7
Kenton Suffk 64 H8
Kenton Bankfoot N u Ty 113 K6
Kentra Highld 138 B4
Kents Bank W & F 94 H5
Kentsboro Hants 22 B10
Kent's Green Gloucs 46 D10
Kent's Oak Hants 22 B10

Kent Street E Susx 26 C8
Kent Street Kent 37 Q10
Kenwick Shrops 69 N8
Kenwyn Cnwll 3 L4
Kenyon Warrtn 82 D5
Keoldale Highld 165 J3
Keppoch Highld 145 Q3
Kepwick N York 97 Q2
Keresley Covtry 59 M8
Kerminchham Ches E 82 H11
Kernborough Devon 7 K10
Kerne Bridge Herefs 46 A11
Kerrera Ag & B 130 G2
Kerridge Ches E 83 K9
Kerridge-end Ches E 83 K9
Kerris Cnwll 2 C8
Kerry Powys 55 Q6
Kerrycroy Ag & B 124 C5
Kersall Notts 85 M8
Kersbrook Devon 9 Q8
Kerscott Devon 17 L6
Kersey Suffk 52 H3
Kersey Tye Suffk 52 G3
Kersey Upland Suffk 52 G3
Kershader W Isls 168 i6
Kershopefoot Cumb 111 J4
Kersoe Worcs 47 J6
Kerswell Devon 10 B3
Kerswell Green Worcs 46 G5
Kerthen Wood Cnwll 2 F7
Kesgrave Suffk 53 M2
Kessingland Suffk 65 Q4
Kessingland Beach Suffk 65 Q4
Kestle Cnwll 3 N4
Kestle Mill Cnwll 4 C10
Keston Gt Lon 37 K8
Keswick Cumb 101 J6
Keswick Norfk 77 J11
Ketsby Lincs 87 L5
Kettering N Nthn 61 J5
Ketteringham Norfk 76 H11
Kettins P & K 142 C10
Kettlebaston Suffk 64 D11
Kettlebridge Fife 135 J6
Kettlebrook Staffs 59 K4
Kettleburgh Suffk 65 K9
Kettle Green Herts 51 K7
Kettleholm D & G 109 P5
Kettleness N York 105 M7
Kettleshulme Ches E 83 L9
Kettlesing N York 97 K9
Kettlesing Bottom N York 97 K9
Kettlestone Norfk 76 D5
Kettlethorpe Lincs 85 P5
Kettletoft Ork 169 f3
Kettlewell N York 96 E6
Ketton RutInd 73 P10
Kew Gt Lon 36 E5
Kew Royal Botanic Gardens Gt Lon 36 E5
Kewstoke N Som 19 K2
Kexbrough Barns 91 J9
Kexby C York 98 E10
Kexby Lincs 85 Q3
Key Green Ches E 70 F2
Key Green N York 105 M10
Keyham Leics 72 H9
Keyhaven Hants 13 P6
Keyingham E R Yk 93 M5
Keymer W Susx 24 H7
Keynsham BaNES 32 C11
Keysoe Bed 61 N8
Keysoe Row Bed 61 N8
Keyston Cambs 61 N5
Key Street Kent 38 E9
Keyworth Notts 72 G4
Kibbear Somset 18 H10
Kibblesworth Gatesd 113 K9
Kibworth Beauchamp Leics 60 F2
Kibworth Harcourt Leics 60 F2
Kidbrooke Gt Lon 37 K5
Kidburngill Cumb 100 E6
Kiddemore Green Staffs 58 B2
Kidderminster Worcs 58 B9
Kiddington Oxon 48 D10
Kidd's Moor Norfk 76 G11
Kidlington Oxon 34 E2
Kidmore End Oxon 35 J9
Kidsdale D & G 107 M10
Kidsgrove Staffs 70 E4
Kidstones N York 96 E4
Kidwelly Carmth 28 D3
Kiel Crofts Ag & B 138 G10
Kielder Nthumb 111 M2
Kielder Forest Nthumb 111 M3
Kiells Ag & B 122 F6
Kilbarchan Rens 125 L5
Kilbeg Highld 145 L6
Kilberry Ag & B 123 M7
Kilbirnie N Ayrs 125 J7
Kilbride Ag & B 123 M4
Kilbride Ag & B 124 C4
Kilbuiack Moray 157 K5
Kilburn Derbys 84 E11
Kilburn Gt Lon 36 F4
Kilburn N York 97 R5
Kilby Leics 72 G11
Kilchamaig Ag & B 123 P7
Kilchattan Ag & B 124 E7
Kilchattan Ag & B 136 b2
Kilcheran Ag & B 138 G10
Kilchoan Highld 137 M3
Kilchoman Ag & B 122 B7
Kilchrenan Ag & B 131 L3
Kilconquhar Fife 135 M7
Kilcot Gloucs 46 C9
Kilcoy Highld 155 Q7
Kilcreggan Ag & B 131 Q11
Kildale N York 104 H9
Kildalloig Ag & B 120 E8
Kildary Highld 156 D3
Kildavaig Ag & B 124 B4
Kildavanan Ag & B 124 C4
Kildonan Highld 163 L2
Kildonan N Ayrs 121 J6
Kildonan Lodge Highld 163 L2
Kildonnan Highld 144 G10
Kildrochet House D & G 106 E6
Kildrummy Abers 150 D4
Kildwick N York 96 F11
Kilfinan Ag & B 124 A2
Kilfinnan Highld 146 H8
Kilford Denbgs 80 F11
Kilgetty Pembks 41 M9
Kilgrammie S Ayrs 114 D4
Kilgwrrwg Common Mons 31 N5

Kilham E R Yk 99 M8
Kilham Nthumb 118 G4
Kilkenneth Ag & B 136 A7
Kilkenzie Ag & B 120 C7
Kilkerran Ag & B 120 D8
Kilkhampton Cnwll 16 D9
Killamarsh Derbys 84 G4
Killay Swans 28 H6
Killearn Stirlg 132 G10
Killen Highld 156 B6
Killerby Darltn 103 N7
Killerton Devon 9 N4
Killichonan P & K 140 D6
Killiechonate Highld 139 L7
Killiechronan Ag & B 137 N5
Killiecrankie P & K 141 M5
Killilan Highld 154 B11
Killimster Highld 167 P5
Killin Stirlg 140 E11
Killinghall N York 97 L9
Killington Devon 17 M2
Killington W & F 95 N3
Killingworth N Tyne 113 L6
Killiow Cnwll 3 L5
Killochyett Border 128 D10
Kilmacolm Inver 125 K3
Kilmahog Stirlg 133 J6
Kilmahumaig Ag & B 130 F9
Kilmaluag Highld 152 G3
Kilmany Fife 135 K3
Kilmarnock E Ayrs 125 L10
Kilmartin Ag & B 130 G8
Kilmaurs E Ayrs 125 L9
Kilmelford Ag & B 130 H5
Kilmersdon Somset 20 C4
Kilmeston Hants 22 G9
Kilmichael Ag & B 120 C7
Kilmichael Glassary Ag & B 130 H9
Kilmichael of Inverlussa Ag & B 130 F10
Kilmington Devon 10 F5
Kilmington Wilts 20 E7
Kilmington Common Wilts 20 E7
Kilmington Street Wilts 20 E7
Kilmorack Highld 155 N9
Kilmore Ag & B 130 H2
Kilmore Highld 145 L6
Kilmory Ag & B 123 M5
Kilmory Highld 137 N2
Kilmory N Ayrs 121 J7
Kilmuir Highld 152 D8
Kilmuir Highld 152 F3
Kilmuir Highld 156 B8
Kilmuir Highld 156 D3
Kilmun Ag & B 131 P11
Kilnave Ag & B 122 C5
Kilncadzow S Lans 126 F8
Kilndown Kent 26 B4
Kiln Green Wokham 35 M9
Kilnhill Cumb 100 H4
Kilnhurst Rothm 91 M11
Kilninver Ag & B 130 G3
Kiln Pit Hill Nthumb 112 F9
Kilnsea E R Yk 93 R7
Kilnsey N York 96 E7
Kilnwick E R Yk 99 K11
Kilnwick Percy E R Yk 98 G10
Kilnwood Vale W Susx 24 F4
Kiloran Ag & B 136 b2
Kilpatrick N Ayrs 120 H6
Kilpeck Herefs 45 N8
Kilpin E R Yk 92 C5
Kilpin Pike E R Yk 92 C5
Kilrenny Fife 135 P7
Kilsby W Nthn 60 C6
Kilspindie P & K 134 G2
Kilstay D & G 106 F10
Kilsyth N Lans 126 C2
Kiltarlity Highld 155 P9
Kilton R & Cl 105 K7
Kilton Somset 18 G6
Kilton Thorpe R & Cl 105 J7
Kilvaxter Highld 152 F4
Kilve Somset 18 F6
Kilvington Notts 73 L2
Kilwinning N Ayrs 125 J9
Kimberley Norfk 76 F11
Kimberley Notts 72 D2
Kimberworth Rothm 84 F2
Kimblesworth Dur 113 L11
Kimble Wick Bucks 35 M3
Kimbolton Cambs 61 P7
Kimbolton Herefs 45 Q2
Kimcote Leics 60 C3
Kimmeridge Dorset 12 F9
Kimmerston Nthumb 119 J3
Kimpton Hants 21 Q5
Kimpton Herts 50 E7
Kimworthy Devon 16 E10
Kinbrace Highld 166 E10
Kinbuck Stirlg 133 M6
Kincaple Fife 135 M4
Kincardine Fife 133 Q10
Kincardine Highld 162 E9
Kincardine Bridge Fife 133 Q10
Kincardine O'Neil Abers 150 F8
Kinclaven P & K 142 B10
Kincorth C Aber 151 N7
Kincorth House Moray 157 J5
Kincraig Highld 148 E6
Kincraigie P & K 141 N8
Kindallachan P & K 141 N8
Kinerarach Ag & B 123 L9
Kineton Gloucs 47 L9
Kineton Warwks 48 B4
Kinfauns P & K 134 F3
Kingarth Ag & B 124 C6
Kingcausie Abers 151 M8
Kingcoed Mons 31 M3
Kingerby Lincs 86 E2
Kingford Devon 16 D10
Kingham Oxon 47 Q10
Kingholm Quay D & G 109 L6
Kinghorn Fife 134 H9
Kinglassie Fife 134 H8
Kingoodie P & K 134 F3
King's Acre Herefs 45 P6
Kingsand Cnwll 6 C9
Kingsash Bucks 35 N3
Kingsbarns Fife 135 P5
Kingsborough Kent 38 G7
Kingsbridge Devon 7 J10
Kingsbridge Somset 18 C7
Kingsbridge Swans 28 G5

278 King's Bromley – Lane Head

King's Bromley Staffs 71 L11
Kingsbrook Bucks 35 M2
Kingsburgh Highld 152 F6
Kingsbury Gt Lon 36 E3
Kingsbury Warwks 59 K5
Kingsbury Episcopi Somset 19 M10
King's Caple Herefs 45 R9
Kingsclere Hants 22 F3
King's Cliffe N Nthn 73 Q11
Kings Clipstone Notts 85 K8
Kingscote Gloucs 32 F5
Kingscott Devon 17 J8
King's Coughton Warwks 47 L3
Kingscross N Ayrs 121 K6
Kingsdon Somset 19 P9
Kingsdown Kent 27 Q2
Kingsdown Swindn 33 N7
Kingsdown Wilts 32 F11
Kingseat Abers 151 N4
Kingseat Fife 134 E9
Kingsey Bucks 35 K3
Kingsfold W Susx 24 E3
Kingsford C Aber 151 M6
Kingsford E Ayrs 125 L8
Kingsford Worcs 57 Q8
Kingsgate Kent 39 Q7
Kings Green Gloucs 46 E8
Kingshall Street Suffk 64 C9
Kingsheanton Devon 17 K4
King's Heath Birm 58 G8
Kings Hill Kent 37 Q9
King's Hill Wsall 58 E5
Kingshouse Hotel Highld 139 P7
Kingshurst Solhll 59 J7
Kingside Hill Cumb 110 C10
Kingskerswell Devon 7 M5
Kingskettle Fife 135 J6
Kingsland Dorset 11 K5
Kingsland Herefs 45 N2
Kingsland IoA 78 D8
Kings Langley Herts 50 C10
Kingsley Ches W 82 C10
Kingsley Hants 23 L7
Kingsley Staffs 71 J5
Kingsley Green W Susx 23 N8
Kingsley Holt Staffs 71 J5
Kingsley Park W Nthn 60 G8
Kingslow Shrops 57 P5
King's Lynn Norfk 75 M6
Kings Meaburn W & F 102 B6
Kingsmead Hants 14 G4
King's Mills Guern 10 b2
King's Moss St Hel 81 Q4
Kingsmuir Angus 142 H8
Kings Muir Border 117 K3
Kingsmuir Fife 135 N6
Kings Newnham Warwks 59 Q9
King's Newton Derbys 72 B5
Kingsnorth Kent 26 H4
King's Norton Birm 58 G9
King's Norton Leics 72 H10
Kings Nympton Devon 17 M8
King's Pyon Herefs 45 N4
Kings Ripton Cambs 62 C5
King's Somborne Hants 22 C8
King's Stag Dorset 11 Q2
King's Stanley Gloucs 32 F4
King's Sutton W Nthn 48 E7
Kingstanding Birm 58 G6
Kingsteignton Devon 7 M4
Kingsteps Highld 156 G6
King Sterndale Derbys 83 N10
Kingsthorne Herefs 45 P8
Kingsthorpe W Nthn 60 G8
Kingston Cambs 62 D9
Kingston Cnwll 5 P6
Kingston Devon 6 G9
Kingston Devon 9 Q7
Kingston Dorset 12 C3
Kingston Dorset 12 G9
Kingston E Loth 128 E3
Kingston Hants 13 K4
Kingston IoW 14 E10
Kingston Kent 39 L11
Kingston W Susx 24 C10
Kingston Bagpuize Oxon 34 D5
Kingston Blount Oxon 35 K5
Kingston by Sea W Susx 24 F9
Kingston Deverill Wilts 20 F7
Kingstone Herefs 45 N7
Kingstone Somset 10 H2
Kingstone Staffs 71 K9
Kingstone Winslow Oxon 33 Q7
Kingston Lacy Dorset 12 G4
Kingston Lisle Oxon 34 B7
Kingston near Lewes E Susx 25 J9
Kingston on Soar Notts 72 E5
Kingston on Spey Moray 157 Q4
Kingston Russell Dorset 11 M6
Kingston St Mary Somset 18 H9
Kingston Seymour N Som 31 M11
Kingston Stert Oxon 35 K4
Kingston upon Hull C KuH 93 J5
Kingston upon Thames
Gt Lon 36 E7
Kingstown Cumb 110 G9
King's Walden Herts 50 E6
Kingswear Devon 7 M8
Kingswells C Aber 151 M6
Kings Weston Bristl 31 P9
Kingswinford Dudley 58 C7
Kingswood Bucks 49 J11
Kingswood C KuH 93 J4
Kingswood Gloucs 32 D6
Kingswood Kent 38 D11
Kingswood Powys 56 C4
Kingswood S Glos 32 B10
Kingswood Somset 18 F7
Kingswood Surrey 36 F9
Kingswood Warwks 59 J10
Kingswood Brook Warwks 59 J10
Kingswood Common Herefs 45 K4
Kingswood Common Staffs 58 B4
Kings Worthy Hants 22 E8
Kingthorpe Lincs 86 F5
Kington Herefs 45 K3
Kington S Glos 32 B6
Kington Worcs 47 J3
Kington Langley Wilts 32 H9
Kington Magna Dorset 20 E10
Kington St Michael Wilts 32 H9
Kingussie Highld 148 D7
Kingweston Somset 19 P8
Kinharrachie Abers 159 M11
Kinharvie D & G 109 K7
Kinkell Bridge P & K 133 Q4
Kinknockie Abers 159 P9
Kinleith C Edin 127 M4
Kinlet Shrops 57 N8
Kinloch Highld 144 F8
Kinloch Highld 164 H10
Kinloch Highld 165 N6
Kinloch P & K 142 A9
Kinlochard Stirlg 132 F7
Kinlochbervie Highld 164 F5
Kinlocheil Highld 138 H2
Kinlochewe Highld 154 D5
Kinloch Hourn Highld 146 B6
Kinlochlaggan Highld 147 N10
Kinlochleven Highld 139 M5
Kinlochmoidart Highld 138 C3
Kinlochnanuagh Highld 145 M11
Kinloch Rannoch P & K 140 G6
Kinloss Moray 157 K5
Kinmel Bay Conwy 80 D8
Kinmuck Abers 151 L4
Kinmundy Abers 151 M4
Kinnabus Ag & B 122 C11
Kinnadie Abers 159 N9
Kinnaird P & K 141 N6
Kinneff Abers 143 Q2
Kinnelhead D & G 116 E10
Kinnell Angus 143 L7
Kinnerley Shrops 69 K10
Kinnersley Herefs 45 L5
Kinnersley Worcs 46 G6
Kinnerton Powys 45 J2
Kinnerton Shrops 56 F5
Kinnerton Green Flints 69 K2
Kinnesswood P & K 134 F7
Kinninvie Dur 103 L6
Kinnordy Angus 142 F6
Kinoulton Notts 72 H4
Kinross P & K 134 E7
Kinrossie P & K 142 B11
Kinross Services P & K 134 E7
Kinsbourne Green Herts 50 D7
Kinsey Heath Ches E 70 B6
Kinsham Herefs 56 F11
Kinsham Worcs 46 H7
Kinsley Wakefd 91 L8
Kinson BCP 13 J5
Kintail Highld 146 B4
Kintbury W Berk 34 C11
Kintessack Moray 157 J5
Kintillo P & K 134 E4
Kinton Herefs 56 G10
Kinton Shrops 69 L11
Kintore Abers 151 K4
Kintour Ag & B 122 G9
Kintra Ag & B 122 D10
Kintra Ag & B 137 J10
Kintraw Ag & B 130 G7
Kintyre Ag & B 120 D4
Kinveachy Highld 148 G4
Kinver Staffs 58 B8
Kiplin N York 103 Q11
Kippax Leeds 91 L4
Kippen Stirlg 133 J9
Kippford D & G 108 H10
Kipping's Cross Kent 25 P2
Kirbister Ork 169 c6
Kirby Bedon Norfk 77 K10
Kirby Bellars Leics 73 J7
Kirby Cane Norfk 65 M3
Kirby Corner Covtry 59 L9
Kirby Cross Essex 53 M7
Kirby Fields Leics 72 E10
Kirby Green Norfk 65 M3
Kirby Grindalythe N York 99 J7
Kirby Hill N York 97 N7
Kirby Hill N York 103 M9
Kirby Knowle N York 97 Q3
Kirby-le-Soken Essex 53 M7
Kirby Misperton N York 98 F5
Kirby Muxloe Leics 72 E10
Kirby Sigston N York 97 P2
Kirby Underdale E R Yk 98 G9
Kirby Wiske N York 97 N4
Kirdford W Susx 24 B5
Kirk Highld 167 N5
Kirkabister Shet 169 r10
Kirkandrews D & G 108 D11
Kirkandrews upon Eden
Cumb 110 G9
Kirkbampton Cumb 110 F9
Kirkbean D & G 109 L9
Kirk Bramwith Donc 91 Q8
Kirkbride Cumb 110 D9
Kirkbridge N York 97 L2
Kirkbuddo Angus 143 J9
Kirkburn Border 117 K3
Kirkburn E R Yk 99 K9
Kirkburton Kirk 90 F8
Kirkby Knows 81 N5
Kirkby Lincs 86 E2
Kirkby N York 104 F9
Kirkby Fleetham N York 97 L2
Kirkby Green Lincs 86 E9
Kirkby-in-Ashfield Notts 84 H9
Kirkby-in-Furness W & F 94 E4
Kirkby la Thorpe Lincs 86 E11
Kirkby Lonsdale W & F 95 N5
Kirkby Malham N York 96 C8
Kirkby Mallory Leics 72 D10
Kirkby Malzeard N York 97 K6
Kirkby Mills N York 98 E3
Kirkbymoorside N York 98 D3
Kirkby on Bain Lincs 86 H8
Kirkby Overblow N York 97 M11
Kirkby Stephen W & F 102 E9
Kirkby Thore W & F 102 B5
Kirkby Underwood Lincs 73 R5
Kirkby Wharf N York 91 N2
Kirkby Woodhouse Notts 84 G10
Kirkcaldy Fife 134 H9
Kirkcambeck Cumb 111 K7
Kirkchrist D & G 108 E10
Kirkcolm D & G 106 D4
Kirkconnel D & G 115 P5
Kirkconnell D & G 109 L7
Kirkcowan D & G 107 K5
Kirkcudbright D & G 108 E10
Kirkdale Lpool 81 L6
Kirk Deighton N York 97 N10
Kirk Ella E R Yk 92 H5
Kirkfieldbank S Lans 116 B2
Kirkgunzeon D & G 109 J7
Kirk Hallam Derbys 72 D2
Kirkham Lancs 88 E4
Kirkham N York 98 E7
Kirkhamgate Wakefd 90 H6
Kirk Hammerton N York 97 Q9
Kirkharle Nthumb 112 F4
Kirkhaugh Nthumb 111 N11
Kirkheaton Kirk 90 F7
Kirkheaton Nthumb 112 F5
Kirkhill Highld 155 Q8
Kirkhope S Lans 116 D9
Kirkhouse Cumb 111 L9
Kirkhouse Green Donc 91 Q8
Kirkibost Highld 145 J4
Kirkinch P & K 142 E9
Kirkinner D & G 107 M7
Kirkintilloch E Duns 126 B3
Kirk Ireton Derbys 71 P4
Kirkland Cumb 100 E7
Kirkland D & G 109 M3
Kirkland D & G 115 P5
Kirkland D & G 115 R9
Kirkland W & F 102 B4
Kirkland Guards Cumb 100 G2
Kirk Langley Derbys 71 P7
Kirkleatham R & Cl 104 G6
Kirklevington S on T 104 D9
Kirkley Suffk 65 Q3
Kirklington N York 97 M4
Kirklington Notts 85 L9
Kirklinton Cumb 110 H7
Kirkliston C Edin 127 L3
Kirkmabreck D & G 107 N6
Kirkmaiden D & G 106 F10
Kirk Merrington Dur 103 Q4
Kirk Michael IoM 80 d3
Kirkmichael P & K 141 Q6
Kirkmichael S Ayrs 114 F6
Kirkmuirhill S Lans 126 D9
Kirknewton Nthumb 118 H4
Kirknewton W Loth 127 L4
Kirkney Abers 158 D11
Kirk of Shotts N Lans 126 E5
Kirkoswald S Ayrs 114 D6
Kirkoswald W & F 101 Q2
Kirkpatrick D & G 109 K2
Kirkpatrick Durham D & G 108 G6
Kirkpatrick-Fleming D & G 110 E6
Kirk Sandall Donc 91 Q9
Kirksanton Cumb 94 C4
Kirk Smeaton N York 91 N7
Kirkstall Leeds 90 H3
Kirkstead Lincs 86 G8
Kirkstile Abers 158 D10
Kirkstile D & G 110 G2
Kirkstone Pass Inn W & F 101 M9
Kirkstyle Highld 167 P2
Kirkthorpe Wakefd 91 K6
Kirkton Abers 150 G2
Kirkton D & G 109 L4
Kirkton Fife 135 K2
Kirkton Highld 145 P2
Kirkton Highld 154 B9
Kirkton P & K 134 B4
Kirkton Manor Border 117 J3
Kirkton of Airlie Angus 142 E7
Kirkton of Auchterhouse
Angus 142 E10
Kirkton of Barevan Highld 156 E8
Kirkton of Collace P & K 142 B11
Kirkton of Durris Abers 151 K8
Kirkton of Glenbuchat
Abers 150 B4
Kirkton of Glenisla Angus 142 C5
Kirkton of Kingoldrum
Angus 142 E6
Kirkton of Lethendy P & K 142 A9
Kirkton of Logie Buchan
Abers 151 P2
Kirkton of Maryculter Abers 151 M8
Kirkton of Menmuir Angus 143 J5
Kirkton of Monikie Angus 143 J10
Kirkton of Rayne Abers 158 G11
Kirkton of Skene Abers 151 L6
Kirkton of Tealing Angus 142 G10
Kirkton of Tough Abers 150 G5
Kirktown Abers 159 N4
Kirktown Abers 159 Q7
Kirktown of Alvah Abers 158 G5
Kirktown of Bourtie Abers 151 L2
Kirktown of Deskford Moray 158 D5
Kirktown of Fetteresso
Abers 151 M10
Kirktown of Mortlach Moray 157 Q10
Kirktown of Slains Abers 151 Q2
Kirkurd Border 116 G2
Kirkwall Ork 169 d5
Kirkwall Airport Ork 169 d6
Kirkwhelpington Nthumb 112 E4
Kirk Yetholm Border 118 F5
Kirmington N Linc 93 K8
Kirmond le Mire Lincs 86 G2
Kirn Ag & B 124 F2
Kirriemuir Angus 142 F7
Kirstead Green Norfk 65 K2
Kirtlebridge D & G 110 D6
Kirtling Cambs 63 L9
Kirtling Green Cambs 63 L9
Kirtlington Oxon 48 E11
Kirtomy Highld 166 B4
Kirton Lincs 74 F3
Kirton Notts 85 L7
Kirton Suffk 53 N3
Kirton End Lincs 74 E2
Kirtonhill W Duns 125 K2
Kirton Holme Lincs 74 E2
Kirton in Lindsey N Linc 92 F11
Kirwaugh D & G 107 M7
Kishorn Highld 153 Q10
Kislingbury W Nthn 60 E9
Kitebrook Warwks 47 P8
Kite Green Warwks 59 J11
Kites Hardwick Warwks 59 Q11
Kitleigh Cnwll 5 L2
Kitt Green Wigan 88 G9
Kittisford Somset 18 E10
Kittle Swans 28 G7
Kitt's Green Birm 59 J7
Kittybrewster C Aber 151 N6
Kitwood Hants 23 J8
Kivernoll Herefs 45 P8
Kiveton Park Rothm 84 G4
Knaith Lincs 85 P4
Knaith Park Lincs 85 P3
Knap Corner Dorset 20 F10
Knaphill Surrey 23 Q3
Knapp Somset 19 K9
Knapp Hill Hants 22 D10
Knapthorpe Notts 85 M9
Knapton C York 98 B10
Knapton N York 98 H5
Knapton Norfk 77 L5
Knapton Green Herefs 45 N4
Knapwell Cambs 62 D8
Knaresborough N York 97 N9
Knarsdale Nthumb 111 N10
Knaven Abers 159 L9
Knayton N York 97 P3
Knebworth Herts 50 G6
Knedlington E R Yk 92 B5
Kneesall Notts 85 M8
Kneeton Notts 85 M11
Knelston Swans 28 E7
Knenhall Staffs 70 G7
Knettishall Suffk 64 D5
Knightacott Devon 17 M4
Knightcote Warwks 48 D4
Knightley Staffs 70 E9
Knightley Dale Staffs 70 E10
Knighton BCP 13 J5
Knighton C Leic 72 G10
Knighton Devon 6 E9
Knighton Dorset 11 N2
Knighton Powys 56 D10
Knighton Somset 18 G6
Knighton Staffs 70 C6
Knighton Staffs 70 D9
Knighton Wilts 33 Q10
Knighton on Teme Worcs 57 L11
Knightsbridge Gloucs 46 G9
Knightsmill Cnwll 4 H5
Knightwick Worcs 46 D3
Knill Herefs 45 K2
Knipoch Ag & B 130 G3
Knipton Leics 73 L4
Knitsley Dur 112 H11
Kniveton Derbys 71 N4
Knock Highld 145 L6
Knock Moray 158 D7
Knock W & F 102 C5
Knock W Isls 168 j4
Knockally Highld 167 K11
Knockan Highld 161 L4
Knockando Moray 157 M9
Knockbain Highld 155 Q9
Knockbain Highld 156 A6
Knockdee Highld 167 L4
Knockdow Ag & B 124 E3
Knockdown Wilts 32 F7
Knockeen S Ayrs 114 F8
Knockenkelly N Ayrs 121 K6
Knockentiber E Ayrs 125 L10
Knockhall Kent 37 N6
Knockholt Kent 37 L9
Knockholt Pound Kent 37 L9
Knockin Shrops 69 K10
Knockinlaw E Ayrs 125 L10
Knockmill Kent 37 N8
Knocknain D & G 106 C5
Knockrome Ag & B 123 J5
Knocksharry IoM 80 c4
Knocksheen D & G 108 C4
Knockvennie Smithy D & G 108 G6
Knodishall Suffk 65 N9
Knodishall Common Suffk 65 N9
Knole Somset 19 N9
Knole Park S Glos 31 Q8
Knolls Green Ches E 82 H9
Knolton Wrexhm 69 L7
Knook Wilts 20 H6
Knossington Leics 73 L9
Knott End-on-Sea Lancs 94 H11
Knotting Bed 61 M8
Knotting Green Bed 61 M8
Knottingley Wakefd 91 N6
Knotty Ash Lpool 81 N6
Knotty Green Bucks 35 P6
Knowbury Shrops 57 K9
Knowe D & G 107 K3
Knowehead D & G 115 M9
Knoweside S Ayrs 114 E5
Knowes of Elrick Abers 158 F7
Knowle Bristl 32 B10
Knowle Devon 9 J4
Knowle Devon 9 P3
Knowle Devon 9 Q8
Knowle Devon 16 H4
Knowle Shrops 57 K10
Knowle Solhll 59 J9
Knowle Somset 18 C6
Knowle Cross Devon 9 P5
Knowlefield Cumb 110 H9
Knowle Green Lancs 89 J3
Knowle Hill Surrey 35 Q11
Knowle St Giles Somset 10 G2
Knowle Village Hants 14 G5
Knowle Wood Calder 89 Q6
Knowl Green Essex 52 C3
Knowl Hill W & M 35 M9
Knowlton Dorset 12 H3
Knowlton Kent 39 N11
Knowsley Knows 81 N5
Knowsley Safari Knows 81 P6
Knowstone Devon 17 Q7
Knox N York 97 L9
Knox Bridge Kent 26 C3
Knoydart Highld 145 P7
Knucklas Powys 56 D10
Knuston N Nthn 61 K7
Knutsford Ches E 82 G9
Knutsford Services Ches E 82 F9
Knutton Staffs 70 E5
Krumlin Calder 90 D7
Kuggar Cnwll 3 J10
Kyleakin Highld 145 N2
Kyle of Lochalsh Highld 145 N2
Kylerhea Highld 145 N3
Kylesku Highld 164 F10
Kylesmorar Highld 145 P9
Kyles Scalpay W Isls 168 h8
Kylestrome Highld 164 F10
Kynaston Herefs 46 B7
Kynaston Shrops 69 L10
Kynnersley Wrekin 70 B11
Kyre Green Worcs 46 B2
Kyre Park Worcs 46 B2
Kyrewood Worcs 57 K11
Kyrle Somset 18 E10

L

La Bellieuse Guern 10 b2
Lacasaigh W Isls 168 i5
Lacasdal W Isls 168 j4
Laceby NE Lin 93 M9
Lacey Green Bucks 35 M4
Lach Dennis Ches W 82 F10
Lackenby R & Cl 104 G7
Lackford Suffk 63 N6
Lackford Green Suffk 63 N6
Lacock Wilts 32 H11
Ladbroke Warwks 48 D3
Ladderedge Staffs 70 H4
Laddingford Kent 37 Q11
Lade Bank Lincs 87 L10
Ladock Cnwll 3 M3
Lady Ork 169 f2
Ladybank Fife 135 J6
Ladycross Cnwll 5 N4
Ladygill S Lans 116 C5
Lady Hall Cumb 94 D3
Ladykirk Border 129 M10
Ladyridge Herefs 46 A8
Lady's Green Suffk 63 N9
Ladywood Birm 58 G7
Ladywood Worcs 46 G2
La Fontenelle Guern 10 c1
La Fosse Guern 10 b2
Lag D & G 109 J3
Laga Highld 138 A5
Lagavulin Ag & B 122 F10
Lagg N Ayrs 121 J7
Laggan Highld 146 H8
Laggan Highld 147 Q9
Lagganlia Highld 148 F7
La Greve Guern 10 c1
La Grève de Lecq Jersey 11 a1
La Hougue Bie Jersey 11 c2
La Houguette Guern 10 b2
Laid Highld 165 K5
Laide Highld 160 E8
Laig Highld 144 G10
Laigh Clunch E Ayrs 125 M8
Laigh Fenwick E Ayrs 125 M9
Laigh Glenmuir E Ayrs 115 M3
Laighstonehall S Lans 126 C7
Laindon Essex 37 Q3
Lairg Highld 162 D5
Laisterdyke C Brad 90 F4
Laithes W & F 101 N4
Lake Devon 8 D7
Lake Devon 17 K5
Lake IoW 14 G10
Lake Wilts 21 M7
Lake District Cumb 100 H8
Lake District National Park
Cumb 100 H8
Lakenham Norfk 77 J10
Lakenheath Suffk 63 M4
Laker's Green Surrey 24 B3
Lakes End Norfk 75 K11
Lakeside W & F 94 H3
Laleham Surrey 36 C7
Laleston Brdgnd 29 N9
Lamanva Cnwll 3 K7
Lamarsh Essex 52 E4
Lamas Norfk 77 J7
Lambden Border 118 D2
Lamberhurst Kent 25 Q3
Lamberhurst Down Kent 25 Q3
Lamberton Border 129 P8
Lambeth Gt Lon 36 H5
Lambfair Green Suffk 63 M10
Lambley Notts 85 K11
Lambley Nthumb 111 N9
Lambourn W Berk 34 B9
Lambourne End Essex 37 L2
Lambourn Woodlands
W Berk 34 B9
Lamb Roe Lancs 89 L3
Lambs Green W Susx 24 F3
Lambston Pembks 40 H7
Lamellion Cnwll 5 L9
Lamerton Devon 8 C9
Lamesley Gatesd 113 L9
Lamington S Lans 116 D4
Lamlash N Ayrs 121 K5
Lamonby W & F 101 M3
Lamorick Cnwll 4 G9
Lamorna Cnwll 2 C9
Lamorran Cnwll 3 M5
Lampen Cnwll 5 K8
Lampeter Cerdgn 43 L5
Lampeter Velfrey Pembks 41 N8
Lamphey Pembks 41 K10
Lamplugh Cumb 100 E6
Lamport W Nthn 60 G6
Lamyatt Somset 20 C7
Lana Devon 5 N2
Lana Devon 16 E10
Lanark S Lans 116 B2
Lancaster Lancs 95 K8
Lancaster Services Lancs 95 L10
Lancaut Gloucs 31 P5
Lanchester Dur 113 J11
Lancing W Susx 24 E10
L'Ancresse Guern 10 c1
Landbeach Cambs 62 G7
Landcross Devon 16 H7
Landerberry Abers 151 J7
Landford Wilts 21 Q11
Land-hallow Highld 167 L10
Landimore Swans 28 E6
Landkey Devon 17 K5
Landore Swans 29 J5
Landrake Cnwll 5 P9
Landscove Devon 7 K5
Land's End Cnwll 2 A8
Land's End Airport Cnwll 2 B8
Landshipping Pembks 41 K8
Landue Cnwll 5 P6
Landulph Cnwll 6 C6
Landwade Suffk 63 K7
Lane Cnwll 4 C9
Laneast Cnwll 5 L5
Lane Bottom Lancs 89 P3
Lane End Bucks 35 M6
Lane End Cnwll 4 G8
Lane End Hants 22 G9
Lane End Kent 37 N6
Lane End Lancs 96 C11
Lane End Warrtn 82 E6
Lane End Wilts 20 F5
Lane Ends Derbys 71 N8
Lane Ends Lancs 89 M4
Lane Ends N York 90 B2
Lane Green Staffs 58 C4
Laneham Notts 85 P5
Lanehead Dur 102 F2
Lane Head Dur 103 M8

Lanehead – Little Abington 279

Lanehead Nthumb 111 Q3
Lane Head Wigan 82 D5
Lane Head Wsall 58 E4
Lane Heads Lancs 88 E3
Lanercost Cumb 111 L8
Laneshaw Bridge Lancs 89 Q2
Lane Side Lancs 89 M6
Langaford Devon 5 B3
Langal Highld 138 C4
Langaller Somset 19 J9
Langar Notts 73 J4
Langbank Rens 125 K3
Langbar N York 96 G10
Langbaurgh N York 104 G8
Langcliffe N York 96 B8
Langdale End N York 99 J2
Langdon Cnwll 5 N4
Langdon Beck Dur 102 G4
Langdon Hills Essex 37 Q3
Langdown Hants 14 D5
Langdyke Fife 135 J7
Langenhoe Essex 52 H8
Langford C Beds 50 E2
Langford Devon 9 P4
Langford Essex 52 D10
Langford N Som 19 N2
Langford Notts 85 P9
Langford Oxon 33 P4
Langford Somset 18 H9
Langford Budville Somset 18 F10
Langham Dorset 20 E9
Langham Essex 52 H5
Langham Norfk 76 E3
Langham Rutlnd 73 L8
Langham Suffk 64 D8
Langho Lancs 89 L4
Langholm D & G 110 G4
Langland Swans 28 H7
Langlee Border 117 Q3
Langley Ches E 83 K10
Langley Derbys 84 F11
Langley Gloucs 47 K9
Langley Hants 14 D6
Langley Herts 50 F6
Langley Kent 38 D11
Langley Nthumb 112 B8
Langley Oxon 47 Q11
Langley Rochdl 89 P9
Langley Slough 36 B5
Langley Somset 18 E9
Langley W Susx 23 M9
Langley Warwks 47 N2
Langley Burrell Wilts 32 H9
Langley Castle Nthumb 112 B8
Langley Common Derbys 71 P7
Langley Green Derbys 71 P7
Langley Green Essex 52 E7
Langley Green Warwks 47 N2
Langley Heath Kent 38 D11
Langley Lower Green Essex 51 K4
Langley Marsh Somset 18 E9
Langley Mill Derbys 84 F11
Langley Moor Dur 103 Q2
Langley Park Dur 113 K11
Langley Street Norfk 77 M11
Langley Upper Green Essex 51 K4
Langley Vale Surrey 36 F9
Langney E Susx 25 P10
Langold Notts 85 J3
Langore Cnwll 5 M4
Langport Somset 19 M9
Langrick Lincs 87 J11
Langridge BaNES 32 D11
Langridgeford Devon 17 K7
Langrigg Cumb 110 C11
Langrish Hants 23 K10
Langsett Barns 90 G10
Langside P & K 133 M5
Langstone Hants 15 K6
Langstone Newpt 31 L7
Langthorne N York 97 K2
Langthorpe N York 97 N7
Langthwaite N York 103 K10
Langtoft E R Yk 99 L7
Langtoft Lincs 74 B8
Langton Dur 103 N7
Langton Lincs 86 H7
Langton Lincs 87 L6
Langton N York 98 F7
Langton by Wragby Lincs 86 F5
Langton Green Kent 25 M3
Langton Green Suffk 64 G7
Langton Herring Dorset 11 N8
Langton Long Blandford
Dorset 12 F3
Langton Matravers Dorset 12 H9
Langtree Devon 16 H8
Langtree Week Devon 16 H8
Langwathby W & F 101 Q4
Langwell Highld 161 K6
Langwell House Highld 163 Q2
Langwith Derbys 84 H7
Langwith Junction Derbys 84 H7
Langworth Lincs 86 E5
Lanhydrock Cnwll 4 H9
Lanivet Cnwll 4 G9
Lanjeth Cnwll 3 P3
Lank Cnwll 4 H6
Lanlivery Cnwll 4 H10
Lanner Cnwll 3 J6
Lanoy Cnwll 5 M6
Lanreath Cnwll 5 K10
Lansallos Cnwll 5 K11
Lanteglos Cnwll 4 H5
Lanteglos Highway Cnwll 5 J11
Lanton Border 118 B6
Lanton Nthumb 118 H4
La Passee Guern 10 b1
Lapford Devon 8 H3
Laphroaig Ag & B 122 E10
Lapley Staffs 58 C2
La Pulente Jersey 11 a2
Lapworth Warwks 59 J10
Larachbeg Highld 138 B8
Larbert Falk 133 P11
Larbreck Lancs 88 E2
Largie Abers 158 F11
Largiemore Ag & B 131 J10
Largoward Fife 135 M6
Largs N Ayrs 124 G6
Largybeg N Ayrs 121 K7
Largymore N Ayrs 121 K7
Larkbeare Devon 9 Q5
Larkfield Inver 124 G2
Larkfield Kent 38 B10
Larkhall S Lans 126 D7
Larkhill Wilts 21 M6
Larling Norfk 64 D4
La Rocque Jersey 11 c2
La Rousaillerie Guern 10 b1
Lartington Dur 103 K7
Lasborough Gloucs 32 F6
Lasham Hants 23 J6
Lashbrook Devon 8 B3
Lashbrook Devon 16 G10
Lashenden Kent 26 D3
Lask Edge Staffs 70 G3
Lasswade Mdloth 127 Q4
Lastingham N York 98 E2
Latcham Somset 19 M5
Latchford Herts 51 J6
Latchford Oxon 35 J4
Latchford Warrtn 82 D7
Latchingdon Essex 52 E11
Latchley Cnwll 5 Q7
Lately Common Warrtn 82 E5
Lathbury M Keyn 49 N6
Latheron Highld 167 M10
Latheronwheel Highld 167 L10
Lathom Lancs 88 F8
Lathones Fife 135 M6
Latimer Bucks 50 B11
Latteridge S Glos 32 C8
Lattiford Somset 20 C9
Latton Wilts 33 L5
Lauder Border 128 E10
Laugharne Carmth 28 B2
Laughterton Lincs 85 P5
Laughton E Susx 25 L8
Laughton Leics 60 E3
Laughton Lincs 74 A4
Laughton Lincs 92 D11
Laughton Common Rothm 84 H3
Laughton-en-le-Morthen
Rothm 84 H3
Launcells Cnwll 16 C10
Launcells Cross Cnwll 16 D10
Launceston Cnwll 5 N5
Launton Oxon 48 H10
Laurencekirk Abers 143 N3
Laurieston D & G 108 E8
Laurieston Falk 126 G2
Lavendon M Keyn 49 P4
Lavenham Suffk 52 F2
Lavernock V Glam 30 G11
Laversdale Cumb 111 J8
Laverstock Wilts 21 N8
Laverstoke Hants 22 E5
Laverton Gloucs 47 L7
Laverton N York 97 K6
Laverton Somset 20 E4
La Villette Guern 10 b2
Lavister Wrexhm 69 L3
Law S Lans 126 E7
Lawers P & K 140 G10
Lawford Essex 53 J5
Lawford Somset 18 F7
Law Hill S Lans 126 E7
Lawhitton Cnwll 5 P5
Lawkland N York 95 R7
Lawkland Green N York 96 A7
Lawley Wrekin 57 M3
Lawnhead Staffs 70 E9
Lawrence Weston Bristl 31 P9
Lawrenny Pembks 41 K9
Lawrenny Quay Pembks 41 K9
Lawshall Suffk 64 B11
Lawshall Green Suffk 64 B11
Lawton Herefs 45 N3
Laxay W Isls 168 i5
Laxdale W Isls 168 j4
Laxey IoM 80 f5
Laxfield Suffk 65 K7
Laxford Bridge Highld 164 F7
Laxo Shet 169 r7
Laxton E R Yk 92 C5
Laxton N Nthn 73 P11
Laxton Notts 85 M7
Laycock C Brad 90 C2
Layer Breton Essex 52 F8
Layer-de-la-Haye Essex 52 G7
Layer Marney Essex 52 F8
Layham Suffk 52 H3
Laymore Dorset 10 H4
Layter's Green Bucks 35 Q6
Laytham E R Yk 92 B3
Laythes Cumb 110 D9
Lazenby R & Cl 104 G7
Lazonby W & F 101 P3
Lea Derbys 84 D9
Lea Herefs 46 C10
Lea Lincs 85 P3
Lea Shrops 56 F7
Lea Shrops 56 G3
Lea Wilts 33 J7
Leachkin Highld 156 A8
Leadburn Border 127 N6
Leadenham Lincs 86 B10
Leaden Roding Essex 51 N8
Leadgate Dur 112 H10
Leadgate Nthumb 112 H9
Leadgate W & F 102 D2
Leadhills S Lans 116 B7
Leadingcross Green Kent 38 E11
Leadmill Derbys 84 B4
Leafield Oxon 48 B11
Leagrave Luton 50 C6
Leahead Ches W 70 B2
Lea Heath Staffs 71 J9
Leake N York 97 P2
Leake Common Side Lincs 87 L10
Lealholm N York 105 L9
Lealholm Side N York 105 L9
Lealt Highld 153 J5
Leam Derbys 84 B5
Lea Marston Warwks 59 K6
Leamington Hastings
Warwks 59 P11
Leamington Spa Warwks 59 M11
Leamside Dur 113 M11
Leap Cross E Susx 25 N8
Learney Abers 150 G7
Leasgill W & F 95 K4
Leasingham Lincs 86 E11
Leasingthorne Dur 103 Q4
Leatherhead Surrey 36 E9
Leathley N York 97 K11
Leaton Shrops 69 N11
Leaton Wrekin 57 L2
Lea Town Lancs 88 F4
Leaveland Kent 38 H11
Leavenheath Suffk 52 G4
Leavening N York 98 F8
Leaves Green Gt Lon 37 K8
Lea Yeat W & F 95 R3
Lebberston N York 99 M4
Le Bigard Guern 10 b2
Le Bourg Guern 10 b2
Le Bourg Jersey 11 c2
Lechlade on Thames Gloucs 33 P5
Lecht Gruinart Ag & B 122 C6
Leck Lancs 95 N5
Leckbuie P & K 140 H9
Leckford Hants 22 C7
Leckhampstead Bucks 49 K7
Leckhampstead W Berk 34 D9
Leckhampstead Thicket
W Berk 34 D9
Leckhampton Gloucs 46 H11
Leckmelm Highld 161 K9
Leckwith V Glam 30 G10
Leconfield E R Yk 92 H2
Ledaig Ag & B 138 G10
Ledburn Bucks 49 P10
Ledbury Herefs 46 D7
Leddington Gloucs 46 C8
Ledgemoor Herefs 45 N4
Ledicot Herefs 45 N2
Ledmore Highld 161 L4
Ledsham Ches W 81 M10
Ledsham Leeds 91 M5
Ledston Leeds 91 L5
Ledstone Devon 7 J9
Ledston Luck Leeds 91 L4
Ledwell Oxon 48 D9
Lee Devon 16 H2
Lee Gt Lon 37 J5
Lee Hants 22 C11
Lee Shrops 69 M8
Leebotwood Shrops 56 H5
Lee Brockhurst Shrops 69 P9
Leece W & F 94 E7
Lee Chapel Essex 37 Q3
Lee Clump Bucks 35 P4
Lee Common Bucks 35 P4
Leeds Kent 38 D11
Leeds Leeds 90 H4
Leeds Bradford Airport
Leeds 90 G2
Leeds Castle Kent 38 D11
Leeds Skelton Lake
Services Leeds 91 K4
Leedstown Cnwll 2 G7
Lee Green Ches E 70 B2
Leek Staffs 70 H3
Leek Wootton Warwks 59 L11
Lee Mill Devon 6 F7
Leeming C Brad 90 C4
Leeming N York 97 L3
Leeming Bar N York 97 L3
Leeming Bar Rest Area
N York 97 L3
Lee Moor Devon 6 F6
Lee-on-the-Solent Hants 14 G6
Lees C Brad 90 C3
Lees Derbys 71 P7
Lees Oldham 83 L4
Lees Green Derbys 71 P7
Leesthorpe Leics 73 K8
Leeswood Flints 69 J2
Leetown P & K 134 G3
Leftwich Ches W 82 E10
Legar Powys 45 J11
Legbourne Lincs 87 L4
Legburthwaite Cumb 101 K7
Legerwood Border 118 A2
Legoland W & M 35 P10
Le Gron Guern 10 b2
Legsby Lincs 86 F3
Le Haguais Jersey 11 c2
Le Hocq Jersey 11 c2
Leicester C Leic 72 F10
Leicester Forest East Leics 72 E10
Leicester Forest East
Services Leics 72 E10
Leigh Devon 17 N9
Leigh Dorset 11 N3
Leigh Gloucs 46 G9
Leigh Kent 37 M11
Leigh Shrops 56 E4
Leigh Surrey 36 F11
Leigh Wigan 82 E5
Leigh Wilts 33 L6
Leigh Worcs 46 E4
Leigh Beck Essex 38 D5
Leigh Delamere Wilts 32 G9
Leigh Delamere Services
Wilts 32 G9
Leigh Green Kent 26 F5
Leigh Knoweglass S Lans 125 Q7
Leighland Chapel Somset 18 D7
Leigh-on-Sea Sthend 38 D4
Leigh Park Dorset 12 H5
Leigh Park Hants 15 K5
Leigh Sinton Worcs 46 E4
Leighswood Wsall 58 G4
Leighterton Gloucs 32 F6
Leighton N York 97 J5
Leighton Powys 56 C3
Leighton Shrops 57 L3
Leighton Somset 20 D6
Leighton Bromswold Cambs 61 P5
Leighton Buzzard C Beds 49 P9
Leigh upon Mendip Somset 20 C5
Leigh Woods N Som 31 Q10
Leinthall Earls Herefs 56 G11
Leinthall Starkes Herefs 56 G11
Leintwardine Herefs 56 G10
Leire Leics 60 B3
Leiston Suffk 65 N9
Leith C Edin 127 P2
Leitholm Border 118 E2
Lelant Cnwll 2 E6
Lelley E R Yk 93 M4
Lem Hill Worcs 57 N9
Lempitlaw Border 118 E4
Lemreway W Isls 168 i6
Lemsford Herts 50 F8
Lenchwick Worcs 47 K5
Lendalfoot S Ayrs 114 B9
Lendrick Stirlg 132 H6
Lendrum Terrace Abers 159 R9
Lenham Kent 38 E11
Lenham Heath Kent 26 F2
Lenie Highld 147 N2
Lennel Border 118 G2
Lennox Plunton D & G 108 D10
Lennoxtown E Duns 125 Q2
Lent Bucks 35 P8
Lenton C Nott 72 F3
Lenton Lincs 73 Q4
Lenwade Norfk 76 F8
Lenzie E Duns 126 B3
Leochel-Cushnie Abers 150 E5
Leomansley Staffs 58 H3
Leominster Herefs 45 P3
Leonard Stanley Gloucs 32 F4
Leoville Jersey 11 a1
Lepe Hants 14 D7
Lephin Highld 152 B8
Leppington N York 98 F8
Lepton Kirk 90 G7
Lerags Ag & B 130 H2
L'Erée Guern 10 a2
Lerryn Cnwll 5 J10
Lerwick Shet 169 r9
Les Arquêts Guern 10 b2
Lesbury Nthumb 119 P8
Les Hubits Guern 10 c2
Leslie Abers 150 F3
Leslie Fife 134 H7
Les Lohiers Guern 10 b2
Lesmahagow S Lans 126 E10
Les Murchez Guern 10 b2
Lesnewth Cnwll 5 J3
Les Nicolles Guern 10 b2
Les Quartiers Guern 10 c1
Les Quennevais Jersey 11 a2
Les Sages Guern 10 b2
Lessingham Norfk 77 M6
Lessonhall Cumb 110 D10
Lestowder Cnwll 3 K9
Les Villets Guern 10 b2
Leswalt D & G 106 D5
L'Etacq Jersey 11 a1
Letchmore Heath Herts 50 E11
Letchworth Garden City
Herts 50 F4
Letcombe Bassett Oxon 34 C8
Letcombe Regis Oxon 34 C7
Letham Angus 143 J8
Letham Border 118 C9
Letham Falk 133 P10
Letham Fife 135 J5
Letham Grange Angus 143 L8
Lethenty Abers 150 F3
Lethenty Abers 159 K9
Letheringham Suffk 65 K10
Letheringsett Norfk 76 F4
Lettaford Devon 8 H8
Letterewe Highld 154 C3
Letterfearn Highld 145 Q3
Letterfinlay Lodge Hotel
Highld 146 H9
Letters Highld 161 K9
Lettershaw S Lans 116 B6
Letterston Pembks 40 H5
Lettoch Highld 149 J4
Lettoch Highld 157 L11
Letton Herefs 45 L5
Letton Herefs 56 F10
Lett's Green Kent 37 L9
Letty Green Herts 50 G8
Letwell Rothm 85 J3
Leuchars Fife 135 M3
Leumrabhagh W Isls 168 i6
Leurbost W Isls 168 i5
Levalsa Meor Cnwll 3 Q4
Levan Inver 124 G2
Levedale Staffs 70 F11
Level's Green Essex 51 L6
Leven E R Yk 99 N11
Leven Fife 135 K7
Levens W & F 95 K3
Levens Green Herts 51 J6
Levenshulme Manch 83 J6
Levenwick Shet 169 r11
Leverburgh W Isls 168 f9
Leverington Cambs 74 H8
Leverstock Green Herts 50 C9
Leverton Lincs 87 M11
Le Villocq Guern 10 b1
Levington Suffk 53 M4
Levisham N York 98 G2
Lew Oxon 34 B3
Lewannick Cnwll 5 M5
Lewdown Devon 8 C7
Lewes E Susx 25 K8
Leweston Pembks 40 H6
Lewisham Gt Lon 37 J6
Lewiston Highld 147 N2
Lewistown Brdgnd 29 P7
Lewis Wych Herefs 45 L3
Lewknor Oxon 35 K5
Leworthy Devon 16 E11
Leworthy Devon 17 M4
Lewson Street Kent 38 G9
Lewth Lancs 88 F3
Lewtrenchard Devon 8 C7
Lexden Essex 52 G6
Lexworthy Somset 19 J7
Ley Cnwll 5 K8
Leybourne Kent 37 Q9
Leyburn N York 96 H2
Leycett Staffs 70 D5
Leygreen Herts 50 E6
Ley Hill Bucks 35 Q4
Leyland Lancs 88 G6
Leyland Green St Hel 82 C4
Leylodge Abers 151 K5
Leys Abers 159 P7
Leys P & K 142 D10
Leysdown-on-Sea Kent 38 H7
Leysmill Angus 143 L8
Leys of Cossans Angus 142 F8
Leysters Herefs 45 R2
Leyton Gt Lon 37 J3
Leytonstone Gt Lon 37 J3
Lezant Cnwll 5 N6
Lezerea Cnwll 2 H7
Leziate Norfk 75 N7
Lhanbryde Moray 157 P5
Libanus Powys 44 D9
Libberton S Lans 116 D2
Libbery Worcs 47 J3
Liberton C Edin 127 P4
Lichfield Staffs 58 H3
Lickey Worcs 58 E10
Lickey End Worcs 58 E10
Lickey Rock Worcs 58 E10
Lickfold W Susx 23 P9
Liddaton Green Devon 8 C8
Liddesdale Highld 138 D6
Liddington Swindn 33 P8
Lidgate Derbys 84 D5
Lidgate Suffk 63 M9
Lidget Donc 91 R10
Lidgett Notts 85 K7
Lidham Hill E Susx 26 D8
Lidlington C Beds 49 Q7
Lidsey W Susx 15 P6
Lidsing Kent 38 C9
Liff Angus 142 E11
Lifford Birm 58 G8
Lifton Devon 5 P4
Liftondown Devon 5 P4
Lighthorne Warwks 48 B3
Lighthorne Heath Warwks 48 C3
Lightwater Surrey 23 P2
Lightwater Valley Family
Adventure Park N York 97 L5
Lightwood C Stke 70 G6
Lightwood Green Ches E 70 A6
Lightwood Green Wrexhm 69 L6
Lilbourne W Nthn 60 C5
Lilburn Tower Nthumb 119 K6
Lilford N Nthn 61 M4
Lilleshall Wrekin 70 C11
Lilley Herts 50 D5
Lilley W Berk 34 D9
Lilliesleaf Border 117 Q5
Lillingstone Dayrell Bucks 49 K7
Lillingstone Lovell Bucks 49 K6
Lillington Dorset 11 N2
Lilliput BCP 12 H7
Lilstock Somset 18 G5
Lilyhurst Shrops 57 N2
Limbrick Lancs 89 J7
Limbury Luton 50 C6
Limebrook Herefs 56 F11
Limefield Bury 89 N8
Limekilnburn S Lans 126 C7
Limekilns Fife 134 D11
Limerigg Falk 126 F3
Limerstone IoW 14 D10
Limestone Brae Nthumb 111 Q11
Lime Street Worcs 46 F8
Limington Somset 19 P10
Limmerhaugh E Ayrs 115 M2
Limpenhoe Norfk 77 M11
Limpley Stoke Wilts 20 E2
Limpsfield Surrey 37 K10
Limpsfield Chart Surrey 37 K10
Linby Notts 84 H10
Linchmere W Susx 23 N8
Lincluden D & G 109 L5
Lincoln Lincs 86 C6
Lincomb Worcs 57 Q11
Lincombe Devon 7 J10
Lincombe Devon 16 H2
Lindale W & F 95 J4
Lindal in Furness W & F 94 E5
Lindean Border 117 P4
Lindfield W Susx 24 H5
Lindford Hants 23 M7
Lindley Kirk 90 E7
Lindley N York 97 K11
Lindores Fife 134 H4
Lindow End Ches E 82 H9
Lindridge Worcs 57 M11
Lindsell Essex 51 P5
Lindsey Suffk 52 G2
Lindsey Tye Suffk 52 G2
Liney Somset 19 L7
Linford Hants 13 L3
Linford Thurr 37 Q5
Lingbob C Brad 90 D3
Lingdale R & Cl 105 J7
Lingen Herefs 56 F11
Lingfield Surrey 25 J2
Lingfield Common Surrey 25 J2
Lingwood Norfk 77 M10
Liniclate W Isls 168 c13
Linicro Highld 152 F4
Linkend Worcs 46 F8
Linkenholt Hants 22 C3
Linkhill Kent 26 D6
Linkinhorne Cnwll 5 N7
Linktown Fife 134 H9
Linkwood Moray 157 N5
Linley Shrops 56 F6
Linley Green Herefs 46 C4
Linleygreen Shrops 57 M5
Linlithgow W Loth 126 H2
Linshiels Nthumb 118 G9
Linsidemore Highld 162 C7
Linslade C Beds 49 P9
Linstead Parva Suffk 65 L6
Linstock Cumb 110 H9
Linthurst Worcs 58 E10
Linthwaite Kirk 90 E8
Lintlaw Border 129 L8
Lintmill Moray 158 D4
Linton Border 118 E5
Linton Cambs 63 J11
Linton Derbys 71 P11
Linton Herefs 46 C9
Linton Kent 38 C11
Linton Leeds 97 N11
Linton N York 96 E8
Linton Nthumb 113 L2
Linton Heath Derbys 71 P11
Linton Hill Herefs 46 C10
Linton-on-Ouse N York 97 Q8
Linwood Hants 13 L3
Linwood Lincs 86 F3
Linwood Rens 125 L5
Lionacleit W Isls 168 c13
Lional W Isls 168 k1
Lions Green E Susx 25 N7
Liphook Hants 23 M8
Lipley Shrops 70 C8
Liscard Wirral 81 K6
Liscombe Somset 18 A8
Liskeard Cnwll 5 M9
Lismore Ag & B 138 E9
Liss Hants 23 L9
Lissett E R Yk 99 N9
Liss Forest Hants 23 L9
Lissington Lincs 86 F4
Liston Essex 52 E3
Lisvane Cardif 30 G8
Liswerry Newpt 31 K7
Litcham Norfk 76 B8
Litchborough W Nthn 48 H4
Litchfield Hants 22 E4
Litherland Sefton 81 L5
Litlington Cambs 50 H2
Litlington E Susx 25 M10
Little Abington Cambs 62 H11

Place	Page	Grid
Little Addington N Nthn	61	L6
Little Airies D & G	107	M8
Little Almshoe Herts	50	F5
Little Altcar Sefton	88	C9
Little Alne Warwks	47	M2
Little Amwell Herts	51	J8
Little Asby W & F	102	C9
Little Aston Staffs	58	G5
Little Atherfield IoW	14	E11
Little Ayton N York	104	G8
Little Baddow Essex	52	C10
Little Badminton S Glos	32	F8
Little Bampton Cumb	110	E9
Little Bardfield Essex	51	Q4
Little Barford Bed	61	Q9
Little Barningham Norfk	76	G5
Little Barrington Gloucs	33	P2
Little Barrow Ches W	81	P11
Little Barugh N York	98	F5
Little Bavington Nthumb	112	E5
Little Bealings Suffk	53	M2
Littlebeck N York	105	N10
Little Bedwyn Wilts	33	Q11
Little Bentley Essex	53	K6
Little Berkhamsted Herts	50	G9
Little Billing N Nthn	60	H8
Little Billington C Beds	49	P10
Little Birch Herefs	45	Q8
Little Bispham Bpool	88	C2
Little Blakenham Suffk	53	K2
Little Blencow W & F	101	N4
Little Bloxwich Wsall	58	F4
Little Bognor W Susx	24	B6
Little Bolehill Derbys	71	P4
Little Bollington Ches E	82	F7
Little Bookham Surrey	36	D10
Littleborough Devon	9	K2
Littleborough Notts	85	P4
Littleborough Rochdl	89	Q7
Littlebourne Kent	39	M10
Little Bourton Oxon	48	E6
Little Bowden Leics	60	F3
Little Bradley Suffk	63	L10
Little Brampton Herefs	45	L2
Little Brampton Shrops	56	F8
Little Braxted Essex	52	D9
Little Brechin Angus	143	K5
Littlebredy Dorset	11	M7
Little Brickhill M Keyn	49	P8
Little Bridgeford Staffs	70	F9
Little Brington N Nthn	60	E8
Little Bromley Essex	53	J6
Little Broughton Cumb	100	E4
Little Budworth Ches W	82	C11
Littleburn Highld	156	A7
Little Burstead Essex	37	Q2
Littlebury Essex	51	M3
Littlebury Green Essex	51	L3
Little Bytham Lincs	73	Q7
Little Canfield Essex	51	N6
Little Carlton Lincs	87	L3
Little Carlton Notts	85	N9
Little Casterton Rutlnd	73	Q9
Little Catwick E R Yk	93	K2
Little Catworth Cambs	61	P6
Little Cawthorpe Lincs	87	L4
Little Chalfont Bucks	35	Q5
Little Chart Kent	26	F2
Little Chesterford Essex	51	M2
Little Cheveney Kent	26	B3
Little Cheverell Wilts	21	J4
Little Chishill Cambs	51	K3
Little Clacton Essex	53	L8
Little Clanfield Oxon	33	Q4
Little Clifton Cumb	100	E5
Little Coates NE Lin	93	M9
Little Comberton Worcs	47	J6
Little Common E Susx	26	B10
Little Comp Kent	37	P9
Little Compton Warwks	47	Q8
Little Corby Cumb	111	J9
Little Cornard Suffk	52	F4
Littlecott Wilts	21	M4
Little Cowarne Herefs	46	B4
Little Coxwell Oxon	33	Q6
Little Crakehall N York	97	K2
Little Cransley N Nthn	60	H5
Little Cressingham Norfk	76	B11
Little Crosby Sefton	81	L4
Little Crosthwaite Cumb	100	H5
Little Cubley Derbys	71	M7
Little Dalby Leics	73	K8
Littledean Gloucs	32	C2
Little Dewchurch Herefs	45	Q8
Little Ditton Cambs	63	L9
Little Doward Herefs	45	Q11
Littledown Hants	22	B3
Little Downham Cambs	62	H4
Little Driffield E R Yk	99	L9
Little Dunham Norfk	76	B9
Little Dunkeld P & K	141	P9
Little Dunmow Essex	51	Q6
Little Durnford Wilts	21	M8
Little Easton Essex	51	P6
Little Eaton Derbys	72	B2
Little Ellingham Norfk	64	E2
Little Elm Somset	20	D5
Little Everdon W Nthn	60	C9
Little Eversden Cambs	62	E10
Little Faringdon Oxon	33	P4
Little Fencote N York	97	L2
Little Fenton N York	91	N3
Littleferry Highld	163	J7
Little Fransham Norfk	76	C9
Little Gaddesden Herts	35	Q2
Little Garway Herefs	45	N10
Little Gidding Cambs	61	P4
Little Glemham Suffk	65	L10
Little Gorsley Herefs	46	C10
Little Gransden Cambs	62	C9
Little Green Notts		J2
Little Green Somset	20	D5
Little Grimsby Lincs	87	K2
Little Gringley Notts	85	M4
Little Habton N York	98	E5
Little Hadham Herts	51	K6
Little Hale Lincs	74	B2
Little Hallam Derbys	72	D2
Little Hallingbury Essex	51	M7
Littleham Devon	8	P8
Littleham Devon	16	G7
Little Hampden Bucks	35	N4
Littlehampton W Susx	24	B10
Little Hanford Dorset	12	D2
Little Harrowden N Nthn	61	J6
Little Haseley Oxon	34	H4
Little Hatfield E R Yk	93	L2
Little Hautbois Norfk	77	K7
Little Haven Pembks	40	G8
Littlehaven W Susx	24	E4
Little Hay Staffs	58	H4
Little Hayfield Derbys	83	M7
Little Haywood Staffs	71	J10
Little Heath Staffs	70	F11
Little Heath W Berk	35	J10
Littlehempston Devon	7	L6
Little Hereford Herefs	57	K11
Little Horkesley Essex	52	G5
Little Hormead Herts	51	K5
Little Horsted E Susx	25	L7
Little Horton C Brad	90	F4
Little Horton Wilts	21	K2
Little Horwood Bucks	49	L8
Little Houghton Barns	91	L9
Littlehoughton Nthumb	119	P7
Little Houghton N Nthn	60	H9
Little Hucklow Derbys	83	Q9
Little Hulton Salfd	82	F4
Little Hungerford W Berk	34	F10
Little Hutton N York	97	Q5
Little Irchester N Nthn	61	K7
Little Kelk E R Yk	99	M9
Little Keyford Somset	20	E5
Little Kimble Bucks	35	M3
Little Kineton Warwks	48	B4
Little Kingshill Bucks	35	N5
Little Knox D & G	108	H8
Little Langdale W & F	101	K10
Little Langford Wilts	21	K7
Little Laver Essex	51	M9
Little Leigh Ches W	82	D9
Little Leighs Essex	52	B8
Little Lever Bolton	89	M9
Little Linford M Keyn	49	M6
Little Load Somset	19	N10
Little London Bucks	34	H2
Little London Cambs	75	H11
Little London E Susx	25	N6
Little London Essex	51	L5
Little London Essex	51	Q3
Little London Gloucs	46	D11
Little London Hants	22	C5
Little London Hants	22	H3
Little London Leeds	90	G3
Little London Lincs	74	D6
Little London Lincs	74	H6
Little London Lincs	87	K6
Little London Norfk	75	L6
Little London Powys	55	N7
Little Longstone Derbys	83	Q10
Little Madeley Staffs	70	D5
Little Malvern Worcs	46	E6
Little Mancot Flints	81	L11
Little Maplestead Essex	52	D5
Little Marcle Herefs	46	C7
Little Marland Devon	17	J9
Little Marlow Bucks	35	M7
Little Massingham Norfk	75	Q6
Little Melton Norfk	76	H10
Littlemill Abers	149	Q8
Littlemill Highld	156	G7
Little Mill Mons	31	K4
Little Milton Oxon	34	H4
Little Missenden Bucks	35	P5
Little Mongeham Kent	39	P11
Littlemoor Derbys	84	E8
Little Moor Somset	19	K8
Littlemore Oxon	34	F4
Little Musgrave W & F	102	E8
Little Ness Shrops	69	M11
Little Neston Ches W	81	K9
Little Newcastle Pembks	41	J5
Little Newsham Dur	103	M7
Little Norton Somset	19	N11
Little Oakley Essex	53	M6
Little Oakley N Nthn	61	J3
Little Odell Bed	61	L9
Little Offley Herts	50	D5
Little Ormside W & F	102	D7
Little Orton Cumb	110	G9
Little Ouse Cambs	63	K3
Little Ouseburn N York	97	P8
Littleover C Derb	72	A4
Little Oxendon W Nthn	60	F4
Little Packington Warwks	59	K8
Little Pattenden Kent	26	B2
Little Paxton Cambs	61	Q8
Little Petherick Cnwll	4	E7
Little Plumpton Lancs	88	D4
Little Plumstead Norfk	77	L9
Little Ponton Lincs	73	N4
Littleport Cambs	63	J3
Littleport Bridge Cambs	63	J3
Little Posbrook Hants	14	F6
Little Potheridge Devon	17	J9
Little Preston Leeds	91	K4
Little Preston W Nthn	48	G4
Littler Ches W	82	D11
Little Raveley Cambs	62	C5
Little Reedness E R Yk	92	D6
Little Ribston N York	97	N10
Little Rissington Gloucs	47	N11
Little Rollright Oxon	47	Q8
Little Rowsley Derbys	84	C7
Little Ryburgh Norfk	76	D6
Little Ryle Nthumb	119	K8
Little Ryton Shrops	56	H4
Little Salkeld W & F	101	Q3
Little Sampford Essex	51	Q4
Little Sandhurst Br For	23	M2
Little Saredon Staffs	58	D3
Little Saughall Ches W	81	M11
Little Saxham Suffk	63	P8
Little Scatwell Highld	155	L6
Little Shelford Cambs	62	E10
Little Shrewley Warwks	59	K11
Little Silver Devon	9	M3
Little Singleton Lancs	88	D3
Little Skipwith N York	91	R3
Little Smeaton N York	91	N7
Little Snoring Norfk	76	D5
Little Sodbury S Glos	32	E8
Little Sodbury End S Glos	32	D8
Little Somborne Hants	22	C8
Little Somerford Wilts	33	J8
Little Soudley Shrops	70	C9
Little Stainforth N York	96	B7
Little Stainton Darltn	104	B6
Little Stanion N Nthn	61	J3
Little Stanney Ches W	81	N10
Little Staughton Bed	61	P8
Little Steeping Lincs	87	M8
Little Stoke Staffs	70	G8
Littlestone-on-Sea Kent	27	J7
Little Stonham Suffk	64	G9
Little Stretton Leics	72	H10
Little Stretton Shrops	56	G6
Little Strickland W & F	101	Q7
Little Stukeley Cambs	62	B5
Little Sugnall Staffs	70	E8
Little Sutton Ches W	81	M9
Little Sutton Shrops	57	J8
Little Swinburne Nthumb	112	D5
Little Sypland D & G	108	F10
Little Tew Oxon	48	C9
Little Tey Essex	52	E7
Little Thetford Cambs	62	H5
Little Thirkleby N York	97	Q5
Little Thornage Norfk	76	F4
Little Thornton Lancs	88	D2
Little Thorpe Dur	104	D2
Littlethorpe Leics	72	E11
Littlethorpe N York	97	M7
Little Thurlow Suffk	63	L10
Little Thurlow Green Suffk	63	L10
Little Thurrock Thurr	37	P5
Littleton BaNES	19	Q2
Littleton Ches W	81	N11
Littleton D & G	108	D9
Littleton Dorset	12	E4
Littleton Hants	22	E8
Littleton Somset	19	N8
Littleton Surrey	23	Q5
Littleton Surrey	36	C7
Littleton Drew Wilts	32	F8
Littleton of Airlie Angus	142	E7
Littleton-on-Severn S Glos	31	Q7
Littleton Panell Wilts	21	J4
Little Torrington Devon	16	H8
Little Totham Essex	52	E9
Little Town Cumb	100	H7
Littletown Dur	104	B2
Little Town Lancs	89	K3
Little Town Warrtn	82	D6
Little Twycross Leics	72	A9
Little Urswick W & F	94	F6
Little Wakering Essex	38	F4
Little Walden Essex	51	M2
Little Waldingfield Suffk	52	F2
Little Walsingham Norfk	76	C4
Little Waltham Essex	52	B9
Little Warley Essex	37	P2
Little Washbourne Gloucs	47	J8
Little Weighton E R Yk	92	G4
Little Welnetham Suffk	64	B10
Little Welton Lincs	87	K3
Little Wenham Suffk	53	J4
Little Wenlock Wrekin	57	L3
Little Weston Somset	20	B9
Little Whitefield IoW	14	G9
Little Whittingham Green Suffk	65	K6
Little Whittington Nthumb	112	H7
Littlewick Green W & M	35	M9
Little Wilbraham Cambs	62	H9
Littlewindsor Dorset	11	J4
Little Witcombe Gloucs	46	H11
Little Witley Worcs	46	E2
Little Wittenham Oxon	34	G6
Little Wolford Warwks	47	Q7
Littlewood Staffs	58	E3
Little Woodcote Gt Lon	36	G8
Littleworth Bucks	49	N10
Littleworth Oxon	34	B5
Littleworth Staffs	58	F2
Littleworth Staffs	70	G10
Littleworth W Susx	24	E6
Littleworth Worcs	46	G4
Littleworth Worcs	47	J2
Littleworth Common Bucks	35	P7
Little Wratting Suffk	63	L11
Little Wymington Bed	61	L8
Little Wymondley Herts	50	F5
Little Wyrley Staffs	58	F3
Little Wytheford Shrops	69	Q11
Little Yeldham Essex	52	C4
Littley Green Essex	51	Q7
Litton Derbys	83	Q9
Litton N York	96	D6
Litton Somset	19	Q4
Litton Cheney Dorset	11	L6
Liurbost W Isls	168	i5
Liverpool L'pool	81	L6
Liversedge Kirk	90	F6
Liverton Devon	9	K9
Liverton R & Cl	105	K7
Liverton Mines R & Cl	105	K7
Liverton Street Kent	38	E11
Livingston W Loth	127	K4
Livingston Village W Loth	127	K4
Lixwm Flints	80	H10
Lizard Cnwll	3	J11
Llaingoch IoA	78	C8
Llaithddu Powys	55	P8
Llan Powys	55	K4
Llanaber Gwynd	67	L11
Llanaelhaearn Gwynd	66	F6
Llanafan Cerdgn	54	F10
Llanafan-Fawr Powys	44	D3
Llanallgo IoA	79	J7
Llanarmon Gwynd	66	G7
Llanarmon Dyffryn Ceiriog Wrexhm	68	G8
Llanarmon-yn-Ial Denbgs	68	G3
Llanarth Cerdgn	42	H3
Llanarth Mons	31	L2
Llanarthne Carmth	43	K11
Llanasa Flints	80	G8
Llanbabo IoA	78	F7
Llanbadarn Fawr Cerdgn	54	E8
Llanbadarn Fynydd Powys	55	P9
Llanbadarn-y-garreg Powys	44	G5
Llanbadoc Mons	31	L5
Llanbadrig IoA	78	F6
Llanbeder Newpt	31	L6
Llanbedr Gwynd	67	K9
Llanbedr Powys	44	G5
Llanbedr-Dyffryn-Clwyd Denbgs	68	F3
Llanbedrgoch IoA	79	J8
Llanbedrog Gwynd	66	E8
Llanbedr-y-Cennin Conwy	79	P11
Llanberis Gwynd	67	K2
Llanbethêry V Glam	30	D11
Llanbister Powys	55	N10
Llanblethian V Glam	30	C10
Llanboidy Carmth	41	P6
Llanbradach Caerph	30	F6
Llanbrynmair Powys	55	K4
Llancadle V Glam	30	D11
Llancarfan V Glam	30	D10
Llancayo Mons	31	L4
Llancloudy Herefs	45	P10
Llancynfelyn Cerdgn	54	E6
Llandaff Cardif	30	G9
Llandanwg Gwynd	67	K9
Llandarcy Neath	29	K5
Llandawke Carmth	41	Q8
Llanddaniel Fab IoA	78	H10
Llanddarog Carmth	43	K11
Llanddeiniol Cerdgn	54	D10
Llanddeiniolen Gwynd	79	J11
Llandderfel Gwynd	68	C7
Llanddeusant Carmth	43	Q10
Llanddeusant IoA	78	E7
Llanddew Powys	44	F8
Llanddewi Swans	28	E7
Llanddewi Brefi Cerdgn	43	N3
Llanddewi'r Cwm Powys	44	E5
Llanddewi Rhydderch Mons	31	L2
Llanddewi Velfrey Pembks	41	M7
Llanddewi Ystradenni Powys	55	Q11
Llanddoged Conwy	67	Q2
Llanddona IoA	79	K9
Llanddowror Carmth	41	Q8
Llanddulas Conwy	80	C9
Llanddwywe Gwynd	67	K10
Llanddyfnan IoA	79	J9
Llandecwyn Gwynd	67	L7
Llandefaelog Powys	44	E8
Llandefaelog-Tre'r-Graig Powys	44	G9
Llandefalle Powys	44	G7
Llandegfan IoA	79	K10
Llandegla Denbgs	68	G4
Llandegley Powys	44	G2
Llandegveth Mons	31	K5
Llandegwning Gwynd	66	D9
Llandeilo Carmth	43	M10
Llandeilo Graban Powys	44	F6
Llandeilo'r Fan Powys	44	B8
Llandeloy Pembks	40	G5
Llandenny Mons	31	M4
Llandevaud Newpt	31	M6
Llandevenny Mons	31	M7
Llandinabo Herefs	45	Q9
Llandinam Powys	55	N7
Llandissilio Pembks	41	M6
Llandogo Mons	31	P4
Llandough V Glam	30	C10
Llandough V Glam	30	G10
Llandovery Carmth	43	Q8
Llandow V Glam	29	P10
Llandre Carmth	43	N6
Llandre Carmth	54	E7
Llandre Isaf Pembks	41	M5
Llandrillo Denbgs	68	D7
Llandrillo-yn-Rhôs Conwy	79	Q8
Llandrindod Wells Powys	44	F2
Llandrinio Powys	69	J11
Llandudno Conwy	79	P8
Llandudno Junction Conwy	79	P9
Llandulas Powys	44	B6
Llandwrog Gwynd	66	H3
Llandybie Carmth	43	M11
Llandyfaelog Carmth	28	D2
Llandyfan Carmth	43	M11
Llandyfriog Cerdgn	42	F6
Llandyfrydog IoA	78	G7
Llandygai Gwynd	79	K10
Llandygwydd Cerdgn	41	P2
Llandynan Denbgs	68	G5
Llandyrnog Denbgs	80	G11
Llandyssil Powys	56	B5
Llandysul Cerdgn	42	H6
Llanedeyrn Cardif	30	H8
Llanedi Carmth	28	G3
Llaneglwys Powys	44	F7
Llanegryn Gwynd	54	E3
Llanegwad Carmth	43	K10
Llaneilian IoA	78	H6
Llanelian-yn-Rhôs Conwy	80	B9
Llanelidan Denbgs	68	F4
Llanelieu Powys	44	H8
Llanellen Mons	31	K2
Llanelli Carmth	28	F4
Llanelltyd Gwynd	67	N11
Llanelly Mons	30	H2
Llanelly Hill Mons	30	H2
Llanelwedd Powys	44	E4
Llanenddwyn Gwynd	67	K10
Llanengan Gwynd	66	D9
Llanerch Gwynd	68	A11
Llanerch Powys	56	E6
Llanerchymedd IoA	78	G8
Llanerfyl Powys	55	N3
Llanfabon Caerph	30	F6
Llanfachraeth IoA	78	F7
Llanfachreth Gwynd	67	N10
Llanfaelog IoA	78	E10
Llanfaelrhys Gwynd	66	C9
Llanfaenor Mons	45	N11
Llanfaes Powys	44	E8
Llanfaes IoA	79	L9
Llanfaethlu IoA	78	E7
Llanfair Gwynd	67	K9
Llanfair Caereinion Powys	55	Q3
Llanfair Clydogau Cerdgn	43	M4
Llanfair Dyffryn Clwyd Denbgs	68	F3
Llanfairfechan Conwy	79	M10
Llanfair Kilgeddin Mons	31	L3
Llanfair-Nant-Gwyn Pembks	41	N3
Llanfairpwllgwyngyll IoA	79	J10
Llanfair Talhaiarn Conwy	80	C10
Llanfair Waterdine Shrops	56	C9
Llanfairynghornwy IoA	78	E6
Llanfair-yn-Neubwll IoA	78	E8
Llanfallteg Carmth	41	N6
Llanfallteg West Carmth	41	M7
Llanfarian Cerdgn	54	D9
Llanfechain Powys	68	G11
Llanfechan Powys	44	D4
Llanfechell IoA	78	F6
Llanferres Denbgs	68	G2
Llan Ffestiniog Gwynd	67	N6
Llanfflewyn IoA	78	F7
Llanfigael IoA	78	E8
Llanfihangel-ar-arth Carmth	43	J7
Llanfihangel Glyn Myfyr Conwy	68	C5
Llanfihangel Nant Bran Powys	44	C8
Llanfihangel-nant-Melan Powys	44	H3
Llanfihangel Rhydithon Powys	56	B11
Llanfihangel Rogiet Mons	31	N7
Llanfihangel Tal-y-llyn Powys	44	G9
Llanfihangel-uwch-Gwili Carmth	43	J10
Llanfihangel-y-Creuddyn Cerdgn	54	F9
Llanfihangel-yng-Ngwynfa Powys	68	E11
Llanfihangel yn Nhowyn IoA	78	E9
Llanfihangel-y-pennant Gwynd	54	F3
Llanfihangel-y-pennant Gwynd	67	J6
Llanfilo Powys	44	G8
Llanfoist Mons	31	J2
Llanfor Gwynd	68	B7
Llanfrechfa Torfn	31	K6
Llanfrothen Gwynd	67	L6
Llanfrynach Powys	44	F9
Llanfwrog Denbgs	68	F3
Llanfwrog IoA	78	E8
Llanfyllin Powys	68	F11
Llanfynydd Carmth	43	L9
Llanfynydd Flints	69	J3
Llanfyrnach Pembks	41	P4
Llangadfan Powys	55	N2
Llangadog Carmth	28	D3
Llangadog Carmth	43	P9
Llangadwaladr IoA	78	F11
Llangadwaladr Powys	68	G8
Llangaffo IoA	78	G11
Llangain Carmth	42	G11
Llangammarch Wells Powys	44	C5
Llangan V Glam	30	C9
Llangarron Herefs	45	Q10
Llangasty-Talyllyn Powys	44	G9
Llangathen Carmth	43	L10
Llangattock Powys	45	J11
Llangattock Lingoed Mons	45	M10
Llangattock-Vibon-Avel Mons	45	P11
Llangedwyn Powys	68	G10
Llangefni IoA	78	H9
Llangeinor Brdgnd	29	P7
Llangeitho Cerdgn	43	M3
Llangeler Carmth	42	G7
Llangelynin Gwynd	54	D3
Llangennech Carmth	28	G4
Llangennith Swans	28	D6
Llangenny Powys	45	J11
Llangernyw Conwy	80	B11
Llangian Gwynd	66	D9
Llangiwg Neath	29	K3
Llangloffan Pembks	40	H4
Llanglydwen Carmth	41	N5
Llangoed IoA	79	L9
Llangoedmor Cerdgn	42	D5
Llangollen Denbgs	68	H6
Llangolman Pembks	41	M5
Llangors Powys	44	G9
Llangorwen Cerdgn	54	E8
Llangovan Mons	31	N3
Llangower Gwynd	68	B8
Llangranog Cerdgn	42	F5
Llangristiolus IoA	78	G10
Llangrove Herefs	45	Q11
Llangua Mons	45	M9
Llangunllo Powys	56	C10
Llangunnor Carmth	42	H10
Llangurig Powys	55	L9
Llangwm Conwy	68	C6
Llangwm Mons	31	M5
Llangwm Pembks	41	J9
Llangwnnadl Gwynd	66	C8
Llangwyfan Denbgs	80	G11
Llangwyllog IoA	78	G9
Llangwyryfon Cerdgn	54	D10
Llangybi Carmth	43	M4
Llangybi Gwynd	66	G6
Llangybi Mons	31	L5
Llangyfelach Swans	28	H5
Llangynderyn Carmth	28	E2
Llangynhafal Denbgs	68	F2
Llangynidr Powys	44	H11
Llangynin Carmth	41	Q6
Llangynllo Cerdgn	42	G6
Llangynog Carmth	28	B2
Llangynog Powys	68	E9
Llangynwyd Brdgnd	29	N7
Llanhamlach Powys	44	F9
Llanharan Rhondd	30	D8
Llanharry Rhondd	30	D8
Llanhennock Mons	31	L6
Llanhilleth Blae G	30	H4
Llanidan IoA	78	H11
Llanidloes Powys	55	M8
Llaniestyn Gwynd	66	D8
Llanigon Powys	45	J8
Llanilar Cerdgn	54	E9
Llanilid Rhondd	30	D8
Llanina Cerdgn	42	H3
Llanio Cerdgn	43	M3
Llanishen Cardif	30	G8
Llanishen Mons	31	N4
Llanllechid Gwynd	79	L11
Llanlleonfel Powys	44	C4
Llanllowell Mons	31	L5
Llanllugan Powys	55	P4
Llanllwch Carmth	42	G11
Llanllwchaiarn Powys	55	Q5
Llanllwni Carmth	43	J7
Llanllyfni Gwynd	66	H4
Llanmadoc Swans	28	D6
Llanmaes V Glam	30	C11
Llanmartin Newpt	31	L7
Llanmerewig Powys	56	B6
Llanmihangel V Glam	30	C10
Llanmorlais Swans	28	F5
Llannefydd Conwy	80	D10
Llannon Carmth	28	G3
Llannor Gwynd	66	F7
Llanon Cerdgn	54	C11
Llanover Mons	31	K3
Llanpumsaint Carmth	42	H9
Llanrhaeadr-ym-Mochnant Powys	68	F9
Llanrhian Pembks	40	F4

Llanrhidian Swans 28 E6
Llanrhos Conwy 79 P8
Llanrhychwyn Conwy 67 P2
Llanrhyddlad IoA 78 E7
Llanrhystud Cerdgn 54 C11
Llanrothal Herefs 45 P11
Llanrug Gwynd 67 J2
Llanrumney Cardif 30 H8
Llanrwst Conwy 67 Q2
Llansadurnen Carmth 41 Q8
Llansadwrn Carmth 43 N8
Llansadwrn IoA 79 K9
Llansaint Carmth 28 C3
Llansamlet Swans 29 J5
Llansanffraid Glan Conwy
Conwy 79 Q9
Llansannan Conwy 80 C11
Llansannor V Glam 30 C9
Llansantffraed Powys 44 G10
Llansantffraed-
Cwmdeuddwr Powys 55 M11
Llansantffraed-in-Elvel
Powys 44 F4
Llansantffraid Cerdgn 54 C11
Llansantffraid-ym-
Mechain Powys 68 H10
Llansawel Carmth 43 M7
Llansilin Powys 68 H9
Llansoy Mons 31 M4
Llanspyddid Powys 44 E9
Llanstadwell Pembks 40 H10
Llansteffan Carmth 28 C2
Llanstephan Powys 44 G6
Llantarnam Torfn 31 K6
Llanteg Pembks 41 N8
Llanthewy Skirrid Mons 45 L11
Llanthony Mons 45 K9
Llantilio-Crossenny Mons 31 L2
Llantilio Pertholey Mons 45 L11
Llantood Pembks 41 N2
Llantrisant IoA 78 F8
Llantrisant Mons 31 L5
Llantrisant Rhondd 30 D8
Llantrithyd V Glam 30 D10
Llantwit Fardre Rhondd 30 E7
Llantwit Major V Glam 30 C11
Llantysilio Denbgs 68 G6
Llanuwchllyn Gwynd 68 A8
Llanvaches Newpt 31 M6
Llanvair Discoed Mons 31 M6
Llanvapley Mons 31 L2
Llanvetherine Mons 45 M11
Llanveynoe Herefs 45 L8
Llanvihangel Crucorney
Mons 45 L10
Llanvihangel Gobion Mons 31 K3
Llanvihangel-Ystern-
Llewern Mons 31 M2
Llanwarne Herefs 45 Q9
Llanwddyn Powys 68 D11
Llanwenarth Mons 31 J2
Llanwenog Cerdgn 43 J5
Llanwern Newpt 31 L7
Llanwinio Carmth 41 Q5
Llanwnda Gwynd 66 H3
Llanwnda Pembks 40 H3
Llanwnnen Cerdgn 43 K5
Llanwnog Powys 55 N6
Llanwonno Rhondd 30 D5
Llanwrda Carmth 43 P8
Llanwrin Powys 54 H4
Llanwrthwl Powys 44 D2
Llanwrtyd Powys 44 B5
Llanwrtyd Wells Powys 44 B5
Llanwyddelan Powys 55 P4
Llanyblodwel Shrops 68 H10
Llanybri Carmth 28 B2
Llanybydder Carmth 43 K6
Llanycefn Pembks 41 L6
Llanychaer Pembks 41 J3
Llanycil Gwynd 68 B8
Llanycrwys Carmth 43 M5
Llanymawddwy Gwynd 68 B11
Llanymynech Powys 69 J10
Llanynghenedl IoA 78 E8
Llanynys Denbgs 68 F2
Llan-y-pwll Wrexhm 69 L4
Llanyre Powys 44 E2
Llanystumdwy Gwynd 66 H7
Llanywern Powys 44 G9
Llawhaden Pembks 41 L7
Llawnt Shrops 68 H8
Llawryglyn Powys 55 L6
Llay Wrexhm 69 K3
Llechcynfarwy IoA 78 F8
Llechfaen Powys 44 F9
Llechrhyd Caerph 30 F3
Llechryd Cerdgn 41 P2
Llechylched IoA 78 E9
Lledrod Cerdgn 54 E10
Llidiardau Gwynd 68 A7
Llidiartnenog Carmth 43 K7
Llidiart-y-parc Denbgs 68 F6
Llithfaen Gwynd 66 F6
Lloc Flints 80 G9
Llowes Powys 44 H6
Llwydcoed Rhondd 30 C4
Llwydiarth Powys 68 D11
Llwyn Denbgs 68 E2
Llwyncelyn Cerdgn 42 H3
Llwyndafydd Cerdgn 42 G3
Llwynderw Powys 56 C4
Llwyn-drain Pembks 41 Q4
Llwyn-du Mons 45 K11
Llwyndyrys Gwynd 66 F6
Llwyngwril Gwynd 54 D3
Llwynhendy Carmth 28 F5
Llwynmawr Wrexhm 68 H7
Llwyn-on Myr Td 30 D2
Llwyn-y-brain Carmth 41 N8
Llwyn-y-groes Cerdgn 43 L3
Llwynypia Rhondd 30 C6
Llynclys Shrops 69 J10
Llynfaes IoA 78 G9
Llŷn Peninsula Gwynd 66 E7
Llŷn-y-pandy Flints 81 J11
Llysfaen Conwy 80 B9
Llyswen Cerdgn 43 J2
Llyswen Powys 44 G7
Llysworney V Glam 30 C10
Llywel Powys 44 B8
Load Brook Sheff 84 C3
Loan Falk 126 H2
Loanend Nthumb 129 N9
Loanhead Mdloth 127 P4

Loaningfoot D & G 109 L9
Loans S Ayrs 125 J11
Lobb Devon 16 H4
Lobhillcross Devon 8 C7
Lochailort Highld 145 N11
Lochaline Highld 138 B9
Lochans D & G 106 E6
Locharbriggs D & G 109 L4
Lochavich Ag & B 131 J4
Lochawe Ag & B 131 N2
Loch Baghasdail W Isls 168 c16
Lochboisdale W Isls 168 c16
Lochbuie Ag & B 137 Q10
Lochcarron Highld 154 A10
Lochdon Ag & B 138 C11
Lochdonhead Ag & B 138 C11
Lochead Ag & B 123 N4
Lochearnhead Stirlg 132 H3
Lochee C Dund 142 F11
Loch Eil Highld 139 K2
Locheilside Station Highld 138 H2
Lochend Highld 155 Q10
Locheport W Isls 168 d11
Loch Euphort W Isls 168 d11
Lochfoot D & G 109 J6
Lochgair Ag & B 131 J9
Lochgelly Fife 134 F9
Lochgilphead Ag & B 130 H10
Lochgoilhead Ag & B 131 Q7
Lochieheads Fife 134 H5
Lochill Moray 157 P5
Lochindorb Lodge Highld 156 H10
Lochinver Highld 160 H2
Loch Lomond and The
Trossachs National
Park 132 E5
Loch Loyal Lodge Highld 165 P7
Lochluichart Highld 155 K5
Lochmaben D & G 109 N4
Loch nam Madadh W Isls 168 e11
Lochmaddy W Isls 168 e11
Loch Ness Highld 147 N2
Lochore Fife 134 F8
Loch Portain W Isls 168 e10
Lochportain W Isls 168 e10
Lochranza N Ayrs 124 A7
Loch Sgioport W Isls 168 d14
Lochside Abers 143 N5
Lochside D & G 109 L5
Lochside Highld 156 E7
Lochskipport W Isls 168 d14
Lochslin Highld 163 J10
Lochton S Ayrs 107 J2
Lochty Angus 143 J5
Lochty Fife 135 N6
Lochuisge Highld 138 D6
Lochwinnoch Rens 125 K6
Lochwood D & G 116 F11
Lockengate Cnwll 4 G9
Lockerbie D & G 109 P4
Lockeridge Wilts 33 M11
Lockerley Hants 22 B9
Locking N Som 19 L3
Locking Stumps Warrtn 82 D6
Lockington E R Yk 99 K11
Lockington Leics 72 D5
Lockleywood Shrops 70 B9
Locksbottom Gt Lon 37 K7
Locksgreen IoW 14 D8
Locks Heath Hants 14 F5
Lockton N York 98 G3
Loddington Leics 73 K10
Loddington N Nthn 60 H5
Loddiswell Devon 7 J9
Loddon Norfk 65 M2
Lode Cambs 62 H8
Lode Heath Solhll 59 J8
Loders Dorset 11 K6
Lodsworth W Susx 23 P10
Lofthouse Leeds 91 J5
Lofthouse N York 96 H6
Lofthouse Gate Wakefd 91 J4
Loftus R & Cl 105 K7
Logan E Ayrs 115 L3
Loganbeck Cumb 94 D2
Loganlea W Loth 126 H5
Loggerheads Staffs 70 C7
Logie Angus 143 M5
Logie Fife 135 L3
Logie Moray 157 J7
Logie Coldstone Abers 150 C7
Logie Newton Abers 158 G10
Logie Pert Angus 143 M5
Logierait P & K 141 N7
Logierieve Abers 151 N2
Login Carmth 41 N6
Lolworth Cambs 62 E8
Lonbain Highld 153 M7
Londesborough E R Yk 98 H11
London Gt Lon 36 H4
London Apprentice Cnwll 3 Q4
London Ashford Airport
Kent 27 J7
London Beach Kent 26 E4
London City Airport Gt Lon 37 K4
London Colney Herts 50 E10
Londonderry N York 97 M3
London Gateway Services
Gt Lon 36 E2
London Gatwick Airport
W Susx 24 G2
London Heathrow Airport
Gt Lon 36 C5
London Luton Airport Luton 50 D6
London Oxford Airport
Oxon 48 E11
London Southend Airport
Essex 38 E4
London Stansted Airport
Essex 51 N6
Londonthorpe Lincs 73 P3
London Zoo ZSL Gt Lon 36 G4
Londubh Highld 160 D10
Lonemore Highld 153 P2
Long Ashton N Som 31 P10
Long Bank Worcs 57 P10
Long Bennington Lincs 73 L2
Longbenton N Tyne 113 L7
Longborough Gloucs 47 N9
Long Bredy Dorset 11 L6
Longbridge Birm 58 F9
Longbridge Warwks 47 Q2
Longbridge Deverill Wilts 20 G6
Long Buckby W Nthn 60 D7
Longburgh Cumb 110 F9
Longburton Dorset 11 N2

Long Cause Devon 7 K6
Long Clawson Leics 73 J5
Longcliffe Derbys 84 B9
Longcombe Devon 7 L7
Long Common Hants 14 F4
Long Compton Staffs 70 F10
Long Compton Warwks 47 Q8
Longcot Oxon 33 Q6
Long Crendon Bucks 35 J3
Long Crichel Dorset 12 G2
Longcroft Cumb 110 D9
Longcross Surrey 35 Q11
Longden Shrops 56 G3
Longden Common Shrops 56 G3
Long Ditton Surrey 36 E7
Longdon Staffs 58 G2
Longdon Worcs 46 F7
Longdon Green Staffs 58 G2
Longdon Heath Worcs 46 F7
Longdon upon Tern Wrekin 69 P11
Longdown Devon 9 L6
Longdowns Cnwll 3 J7
Long Drax N York 92 A5
Long Duckmanton Derbys 84 F6
Long Eaton Derbys 72 D4
Longfield Kent 37 P7
Longford Covtry 59 N8
Longford Derbys 71 N7
Longford Gloucs 46 F10
Longford Gt Lon 36 C5
Longford Kent 37 M9
Longford Shrops 70 A8
Longford Wrekin 70 C11
Longforgan P & K 134 H2
Longformacus Border 128 H8
Longframlington Nthumb 119 M10
Long Green Ches W 81 P10
Long Green Worcs 46 F8
Longham Dorset 13 J5
Longham Norfk 76 C8
Long Hanborough Oxon 34 D2
Longhaven Abers 159 R10
Long Hedges Lincs 87 L11
Longhirst Nthumb 113 K3
Longhope Gloucs 46 C11
Longhope Ork 169 c7
Longhorsley Nthumb 112 H2
Longhoughton Nthumb 119 P7
Long Itchington Warwks 59 P11
Longlands Cumb 101 J3
Longlane Derbys 71 N7
Long Lawford Warwks 59 Q9
Longleat Wilts 20 F6
Longlevens Gloucs 46 G11
Longley Calder 90 D6
Longley Kirk 90 E9
Longley Green Worcs 46 D3
Longleys P & K 142 D9
Long Load Somset 19 N10
Longmanhill Abers 158 H5
Long Marston Herts 49 N11
Long Marston N York 97 R10
Long Marston Warwks 47 N5
Long Marton W & F 102 C6
Long Meadowend Shrops 56 G8
Long Melford Suffk 52 E2
Longmoor Camp Hants 23 L8
Longmorn Moray 157 N6
Longmoss Ches E 83 J10
Long Newnton Gloucs 32 H6
Longnewton Border 118 A5
Long Newton E Loth 128 E7
Longnewton S on T 104 C7
Longney Gloucs 32 E2
Longniddry E Loth 128 C4
Longnor Shrops 56 H4
Longnor Staffs 71 K2
Longparish Hants 22 D5
Longpark Cumb 110 H8
Long Preston N York 96 B9
Longridge Lancs 89 J3
Longridge Staffs 70 G11
Longridge W Loth 126 G5
Longriggend N Lans 126 E3
Long Riston E R Yk 93 K2
Longrock Cnwll 2 E8
Longsdon Staffs 70 H4
Longshaw Wigan 82 B4
Longside Abers 159 Q9
Long Sight Oldham 89 Q9
Longslow Shrops 70 B7
Longstanton Cambs 62 E7
Longstock Hants 22 C7
Longstone Pembks 41 M9
Longstowe Cambs 62 D10
Long Stratton Norfk 64 H3
Long Street M Keyn 49 L5
Longstreet Wilts 21 M4
Long Sutton Hants 23 K5
Long Sutton Lincs 74 H6
Long Sutton Somset 19 N9
Longthorpe C Pete 74 C11
Long Thurlow Suffk 64 E8
Longthwaite W & F 101 M6
Longton C Stke 70 G6
Longton Lancs 88 F5
Longtown Cumb 110 G7
Longtown Herefs 45 L9
Longueville Jersey 11 c2
Longville in the Dale Shrops 57 J6
Long Waste Wrekin 69 R11
Long Whatton Leics 72 D6
Longwick Bucks 35 L3
Long Wittenham Oxon 34 F6
Longwitton Nthumb 112 G3
Longwood D & G 108 F8
Longwood Shrops 57 L3
Longworth Oxon 34 C5
Longyester E Loth 128 E7
Lôn-las Swans 29 K5
Lonmay Abers 159 P6
Lonmore Highld 152 D8
Looe Cnwll 5 M11
Loose Kent 38 C11
Loosebeare Devon 8 H3
Loosegate Lincs 74 F5
Loosley Row Bucks 35 M4
Lootcherbrae Abers 158 F7
Lopcombe Corner Wilts 21 Q7
Lopen Somset 11 J2
Loppington Shrops 69 M9
Lorbottle Nthumb 119 K9
Lordington W Susx 15 L5
Lordsbridge Norfk 75 L8
Lordshill C Sotn 22 C11
Lords Wood Medway 38 C9

Lornty P & K 142 B8
Loscoe Derbys 84 F11
Loscombe Dorset 11 K5
Losgaintir W Isls 168 f8
Lossiemouth Moray 157 N3
Lostford Shrops 69 Q8
Lostock Gralam Ches W 82 E10
Lostock Green Ches W 82 E10
Lostock Hall Lancs 88 G5
Lostock Hall Fold Bolton 89 K7
Lostock Junction Bolton 89 K9
Lostwithiel Cnwll 5 J10
Lothbeg Highld 163 L4
Lothersdale N York 96 E11
Lothmore Highld 163 M4
Loudwater Bucks 35 P6
Loudwater Herts 50 C11
Loughborough Leics 72 E7
Loughor Swans 28 G5
Loughton Essex 51 K11
Loughton M Keyn 49 M7
Loughton Shrops 57 L8
Lound Lincs 73 R7
Lound Notts 85 L3
Lound Suffk 65 Q2
Lounston Devon 9 J9
Lount Leics 72 B7
Louth Lincs 87 K3
Loveclough Lancs 89 N5
Lovedean Hants 15 J4
Lover Wilts 21 P10
Loversall Donc 91 P11
Loves Green Essex 51 P10
Lovesome Hill N York 104 C11
Loveston Pembks 41 L9
Lovington Somset 19 Q8
Low Ackworth Wakefd 91 M7
Low Angerton Nthumb 112 G4
Lowbands Gloucs 46 E8
Low Barbeth D & G 106 D4
Low Barlings Lincs 86 E6
Low Bell End N York 105 K11
Low Bentham N York 95 N7
Low Biggins W & F 95 N5
Low Borrowbridge W & F 102 B10
Low Bradfield Sheff 84 C2
Low Bradley N York 96 F11
Low Braithwaite W & F 101 M2
Low Burnham N Linc 92 C10
Low Buston Nthumb 119 P9
Lowca Cumb 100 C6
Low Catton E R Yk 98 E10
Low Coniscliffe Darltn 103 Q8
Low Crosby Cumb 110 H9
Lowdham Notts 85 L11
Low Dinsdale Darltn 104 B8
Lowe Shrops 69 N8
Lowe Hill Staffs 70 H3
Low Ellington N York 97 K4
Lower Aisholt Somset 18 H7
Lower Ansty Dorset 12 C4
Lower Apperley Gloucs 46 G9
Lower Arboll Highld 163 K10
Lower Arncott Oxon 48 H11
Lower Ashton Devon 9 K8
Lower Assendon Oxon 35 K8
Lower Badcall Highld 164 E8
Lower Ballam Lancs 88 D4
Lower Bartle Lancs 88 F4
Lower Basildon W Berk 34 H9
Lower Bearwood Herefs 45 M3
Lower Beeding W Susx 24 F5
Lower Benefield N Nthn 61 L3
Lower Bentley Worcs 58 E11
Lower Beobridge Shrops 57 P6
Lower Birchwood Derbys 84 F10
Lower Boddington W Nthn 48 E4
Lower Boscaswell Cnwll 2 B7
Lower Bourne Surrey 23 M6
Lower Brailes Warwks 48 B7
Lower Breakish Highld 145 L2
Lower Bredbury Stockp 83 K6
Lower Broadheath Worcs 46 F3
Lower Broxwood Herefs 45 M4
Lower Buckenhill Herefs 46 B8
Lower Bullingham Herefs 45 Q7
Lower Burgate Hants 21 N11
Lower Burrowton Devon 9 P5
Lower Burton Herefs 45 N3
Lower Caldecote C Beds 61 Q11
Lower Cam Gloucs 32 D4
Lower Canada N Som 19 L3
Lower Catesby W Nthn 60 B9
Lower Chapel Powys 44 E7
Lower Chicksgrove Wilts 21 J9
Lower Chute Wilts 22 B4
Lower Clapton Gt Lon 36 H3
Lower Clent Worcs 58 D9
Lower Common Hants 23 L2
Lower Compton Wilts 33 K10
Lower Creedy Devon 9 K4
Lower Crossings Derbys 83 M8
Lower Cumberworth Kirk 90 G9
Lower Darwen Bl w D 89 K5
Lower Dean Bed 61 N7
Lower Denby Kirk 90 G9
Lower Diabaig Highld 153 P5
Lower Dicker E Susx 25 N8
Lower Dinchope Shrops 56 H8
Lower Down Shrops 56 F7
Lower Dunsforth N York 97 P8
Lower Egleton Herefs 46 B5
Lower Elkstone Staffs 71 K3
Lower Ellastone Staffs 71 L6
Lower End Bucks 35 J3
Lower End M Keyn 49 P7
Lower End N Nthn 61 J8
Lower End W Nthn 60 H9
Lower Everleigh Wilts 21 N4
Lower Exbury Hants 14 D7
Lower Eythorne Kent 27 N2
Lower Failand N Som 31 P10
Lower Farringdon Hants 23 K7
Lower Feltham Gt Lon 36 C6
Lower Fittleworth W Susx 24 B7
Lower Foxdale IoM 80 c6
Lower Frankton Shrops 69 L8
Lower Freystrop Pembks 41 J7
Lower Froyle Hants 23 L6
Lower Gabwell Devon 7 N5
Lower Gledfield Highld 162 D8
Lower Godney Somset 19 N6
Lower Gornal Dudley 58 D6
Lower Gravenhurst C Beds 50 D3
Lower Green Essex 50 E4
Lower Green Herts 51 K4

Lower Green Kent 25 N2
Lower Green Kent 25 P2
Lower Green Norfk 76 D4
Lower Green Staffs 58 D3
Lower Green Suffk 63 M7
Lower Green Suffk 65 L10
Lower Halstock Leigh
Dorset 11 L3
Lower Halstow Kent 38 E8
Lower Hamworthy BCP 12 G6
Lower Hardres Kent 39 L11
Lower Harpton Herefs 45 K2
Lower Hartlip Kent 38 D9
Lower Hartshay Derbys 84 E10
Lower Hartwell Bucks 35 L2
Lower Hatton Staffs 70 E7
Lower Hawthwaite W & F 94 E3
Lower Haysden Kent 37 N11
Lower Hergest Herefs 45 K3
Lower Heyford Oxon 48 E10
Lower Heysham Lancs 95 J8
Lower Higham Kent 38 B7
Lower Holbrook Suffk 53 L4
Lower Hordley Shrops 69 L9
Lower Horncroft W Susx 24 B7
Lowerhouse Lancs 89 N4
Lower Houses Kirk 90 F7
Lower Howsell Worcs 46 E5
Lower Irlam Salfd 82 F6
Lower Kilburn Derbys 72 B2
Lower Kilcott Gloucs 32 E7
Lower Killeyan Ag & B 122 C11
Lower Kingcombe Dorset 11 M5
Lower Kingswood Surrey 36 F10
Lower Kinnerton Ches W 69 K2
Lower Langford N Som 19 N2
Lower Largo Fife 135 L7
Lower Leigh Staffs 71 J7
Lower Lemington Gloucs 47 P8
Lower Llanfadog Powys 55 M11
Lower Lovacott Devon 17 J6
Lower Loxhore Devon 17 L4
Lower Lydbrook Gloucs 46 A11
Lower Lye Herefs 56 G11
Lower Machen Newpt 30 H7
Lower Maes-coed Herefs 45 L8
Lower Mannington Dorset 13 J4
Lower Marston Somset 20 E6
Lower Meend Gloucs 31 Q4
Lower Merridge Somset 18 H8
Lower Middleton Cheney
W Nthn 48 F6
Lower Milton Somset 19 P5
Lower Moor Worcs 47 J5
Lower Morton S Glos 32 B6
Lower Nazeing Essex 51 J9
Lower Norton Warwks 47 P2
Lower Nyland Dorset 20 E10
Lower Oddington Gloucs 47 P9
Lower Penarth V Glam 30 G11
Lower Penn Staffs 58 C5
Lower Pennington Hants 13 P6
Lower Penwortham Lancs 88 G5
Lower Peover Ches E 82 F10
Lower Place Rochdl 89 Q8
Lower Pollicott Bucks 35 K2
Lower Quinton Warwks 47 N5
Lower Rainham Medway 38 D8
Lower Raydon Suffk 52 H4
Lower Roadwater Somset 18 D7
Lower Salter Lancs 95 N8
Lower Seagry Wilts 33 J8
Lower Sheering Essex 51 L8
Lower Shelton C Beds 49 Q6
Lower Shiplake Oxon 35 L9
Lower Shuckburgh Warwks 48 E2
Lower Slaughter Gloucs 47 N10
Lower Soothill Kirk 90 H6
Lower Soudley Gloucs 32 C3
Lower Standen Kent 27 M3
Lower Stanton St Quintin
Wilts 32 H8
Lower Stoke Medway 38 D6
Lower Stondon C Beds 50 E3
Lower Stone Gloucs 32 C6
Lower Stonnall Staffs 58 G4
Lower Stow Bedon Norfk 64 D3
Lower Street Dorset 12 D5
Lower Street E Susx 26 B9
Lower Street Norfk 77 K4
Lower Street Suffk 63 N10
Lower Street Suffk 64 G11
Lower Stretton Warrtn 82 D8
Lower Stroud Dorset 11 K5
Lower Sundon C Beds 50 C5
Lower Swanwick Hants 14 E5
Lower Swell Gloucs 47 N9
Lower Tadmarton Oxon 48 D7
Lower Tale Devon 9 Q4
Lower Tasburgh Norfk 64 H2
Lower Tean Staffs 71 J7
Lower Thurlton Norfk 65 N2
Lower Town Cnwll 2 H8
Lower Town Devon 7 J4
Lower Town Herefs 46 B6
Lower Town IoS 2 c1
Lower Town Pembks 41 J3
Lower Trebullett Cnwll 5 N6
Lower Treluswell Cnwll 3 K6
Lower Tysoe Warwks 48 B5
Lower Ufford Suffk 65 K11
Lower Upcott Devon 9 L8
Lower Upham Hants 22 F11
Lower Upnor Medway 38 C7
Lower Vexford Somset 18 F7
Lower Walton Warrtn 82 D7
Lower Waterston Dorset 12 B5
Lower Weare Somset 19 M4
Lower Weedon W Nthn 60 D9
Lower Welson Herefs 45 K4
Lower Westmancote Worcs 46 H7
Lower Whatcombe Dorset 12 D4
Lower Whatley Somset 20 D5
Lower Whitley Ches W 82 D9
Lower Wick Gloucs 32 D5
Lower Wick Worcs 46 F4
Lower Wield Hants 22 H6
Lower Willingham E Susx 25 N7
Lower Withington Ches E 82 H11
Lower Woodend Bucks 35 M7
Lower Woodford Wilts 21 M7
Lower Wraxhall Dorset 11 M4
Lower Wyche Worcs 46 E6
Lower Wyke C Brad 90 F5
Lowesby Leics 73 J9
Lowestoft Suffk 65 Q3

Loweswater Cumb 100 F6
Low Etherley Dur 103 N5
Low Fell Gatesd 113 L9
Lowfield Heath W Susx 24 G3
Low Gartachorrans Stirlg . 132 F10
Low Gate Nthumb 112 D8
Low Gettbridge Cumb 111 K9
Lowgill Lancs 95 P8
Lowgill W & F 102 B11
Low Grantley N York 97 K6
Low Green N York 97 K9
Low Habberley Worcs 57 Q9
Low Ham Somset 19 M9
Low Harrogate N York 97 L9
Low Hawsker N York 105 P9
Low Hesket W & F 111 J11
Low Hutton N York 98 F7
Lowick N Nthn 61 L4
Lowick Nthumb 119 K3
Lowick W & F 94 F3
Lowick Bridge W & F 94 F3
Lowick Green W & F 94 F3
Low Knipe W & F 101 P7
Low Laithe N York 97 J8
Lowlands Dur 103 M5
Lowlands Torfn 31 J5
Low Langton Lincs 86 G5
Low Leighton Derbys 83 M7
Low Lorton Cumb 100 G5
Low Marishes N York 98 G5
Low Marnham Notts 85 P7
Low Middleton Nthumb 119 M3
Low Mill N York 105 J11
Low Moor C Brad 90 F5
Low Moorsley Sundld 113 M11
Low Moresby Cumb 100 C6
Low Newton W & F 95 J4
Low Newton-by-the-Sea
  Nthumb 119 P6
Low Pittington Dur 104 B2
Low Row Cumb 100 G2
Low Row Cumb 101 L3
Low Row Cumb 111 L8
Low Row N York 103 J11
Low Salchrie D & G 106 D4
Low Santon N Linc 92 F8
Lowsonford Warwks 59 J11
Low Street Norfk 77 L7
Low Street Thurr 37 Q5
Low Tharston Norfk 64 H2
Lowther W & F 101 P6
Lowthorpe E R Yk 99 M8
Lowton Devon 8 G4
Lowton Somset 18 G11
Lowton Wigan 82 D5
Lowton Common Wigan 82 D5
Lowton St Mary's Wigan ... 82 D5
Low Torry Fife 134 C10
Low Toynton Lincs 87 J6
Low Valley Barns 91 L10
Low Wood W & F 94 G4
Low Worsall N York 104 C9
Low Wray W & F 101 L10
Loxbeare Devon 18 B11
Loxhill Surrey 24 B3
Loxhore Devon 17 L4
Loxhore Cott Devon 17 L4
Loxley Warwks 47 Q4
Loxley Green Staffs 71 K8
Loxter Herefs 46 D6
Loxton N Som 19 L3
Loxwood W Susx 24 B4
Lubenham Leics 60 F3
Lucasgate Lincs 87 M11
Lucas Green Surrey 23 P2
Luccombe Somset 18 B6
Luccombe Village IoW 14 G11
Lucker Nthumb 119 N4
Luckett Cnwll 5 P7
Lucking Street Essex 52 D5
Luckington Wilts 32 F8
Lucklawhill Fife 135 L3
Lucknam Wilts 32 F10
Luckwell Bridge Somset ... 18 B7
Lucton Herefs 45 N2
Lucy Cross N York 103 P8
Ludag W Isls 168 c16
Ludborough Lincs 93 N11
Ludbrook Devon 6 H8
Ludchurch Pembks 41 M8
Luddenden Calder 90 C5
Luddenden Foot Calder 90 C5
Luddenham Court Kent 38 G9
Luddesdown Kent 37 Q7
Luddington N Linc 92 D7
Luddington Warwks 47 N4
Luddington in the Brook
  N Nthn 61 P4
Ludford Lincs 86 G3
Ludford Shrops 57 J10
Ludgershall Bucks 49 J11
Ludgershall Wilts 21 Q4
Ludgvan Cnwll 2 E7
Ludham Norfk 77 M8
Ludlow Shrops 57 J9
Ludney Somset 10 H2
Ludwell Wilts 20 H10
Ludworth Dur 104 C2
Luffenhall Herts 50 G5
Luffincott Devon 5 N3
Luffness E Loth 128 D4
Lugar E Ayrs 115 L3
Luggate Burn E Loth 128 F5
Lugg Green Herefs 45 N2
Luggiebank N Lans 126 D3
Lugton E Ayrs 125 L7
Lugwardine Herefs 45 R6
Luib Highld 145 J2
Luing Ag & B 130 E5
Lulham Herefs 45 N6
Lullington Derbys 59 K2
Lullington E Susx 25 M10
Lullington Somset 20 E4
Lulsgate Bottom N Som 31 P11
Lulsley Worcs 46 D3
Lulworth Camp Dorset 12 D8
Lumb Calder 90 C6
Lumb Lancs 89 N6
Lumbutts Calder 90 B6
Lumby N York 91 M4
Lumphanan Abers 150 F7
Lumphinnans Fife 134 F9
Lumsden Abers 150 D3
Lunan Angus 143 M7
Lunanhead Angus 142 H7
Luncarty P & K 134 D2

Lund E R Yk 99 K11
Lund N York 91 R4
Lundie Angus 142 D10
Lundin Links Fife 135 L7
Lundin Mill Fife 135 L7
Lundy Devon 16 A2
Lundy Green Norfk 65 J3
Lunga Ag & B 130 E6
Lunna Shet 169 r7
Lunsford Kent 37 Q9
Lunsford's Cross E Susx .. 26 B9
Lunt Sefton 81 L4
Luntley Herefs 45 M3
Luppitt Devon 10 D3
Lupridge Devon 7 J8
Lupset Wakefd 91 J7
Lupton W & F 95 M4
Lurgashall W Susx 23 P9
Lurley Devon 18 B11
Lusby Lincs 87 K7
Luscombe Devon 7 K7
Luskentyre W Isls 168 f8
Luson Devon 6 G8
Luss Ag & B 132 D9
Lussagiven Ag & B 130 C10
Lusta Highld 152 D6
Lustleigh Devon 9 J8
Luston Herefs 45 P2
Luthermuir Abers 143 M4
Luthrie Fife 135 J4
Lutley Dudley 58 D8
Luton Devon 9 M9
Luton Devon 10 B4
Luton Luton 50 C6
Luton Medway 38 C8
Luton Airport Luton 50 D6
Lutterworth Leics 60 B4
Lutton Devon 6 F7
Lutton Devon 6 G4
Lutton Lincs 74 H5
Lutton N Nthn 61 P3
Luxborough Somset 18 C7
Luxulyan Cnwll 4 H10
Luxulyan Valley Cnwll 4 H10
Luzley Tamesd 83 L4
Lybster Highld 167 M9
Lydbury North Shrops 56 F7
Lydcott Devon 17 M4
Lydd Kent 27 H7
Lydd Airport Kent 27 J7
Lydden Kent 27 N2
Lydden Kent 39 Q8
Lyddington Rutlnd 73 M11
Lydd-on-Sea Kent 27 J8
Lydeard St Lawrence
  Somset 18 F8
Lyde Green Hants 23 K3
Lyde Green S Glos 32 C9
Lydford Devon 8 D7
Lydford on Fosse Somset .. 19 Q8
Lydgate Calder 89 Q5
Lydgate Rochdl 90 B7
Lydham Shrops 56 E6
Lydiard Green Wilts 33 L7
Lydiard Millicent Wilts .. 33 L7
Lydiard Tregoze Swindn ... 33 M8
Lydiate Sefton 81 M4
Lydiate Ash Worcs 58 E9
Lydlinch Dorset 12 B2
Lydney Gloucs 32 B4
Lydstep Pembks 41 L11
Lye Dudley 58 D8
Lye Cross N Som 19 N2
Lye Green Bucks 35 Q4
Lye Green E Susx 25 M4
Lye Green Warwks 59 J11
Lye Head Worcs 57 P10
Lye's Green Wilts 20 F5
Lyford Oxon 34 C6
Lymbridge Green Kent 27 K3
Lyme Regis Dorset 10 G6
Lyminge Kent 27 L3
Lymington Hants 13 P5
Lyminster W Susx 24 B10
Lymm Warrtn 82 E7
Lymm Services Warrtn 82 E8
Lympne Kent 27 K4
Lympsham Somset 19 K4
Lympstone Devon 9 N8
Lynbridge Devon 17 N2
Lynchat Highld 148 D7
Lynch Green Norfk 76 H10
Lyndhurst Hants 13 P3
Lyndon Rutlnd 73 N10
Lyndon Green Birm 58 H7
Lyne Border 117 J2
Lyne Surrey 36 B7
Lyneal Shrops 69 M8
Lyne Down Herefs 46 B8
Lyneham Oxon 47 Q10
Lyneham Wilts 33 K9
Lyneholmford Cumb 111 K6
Lynemouth Nthumb 113 L2
Lyne of Skene Abers 151 K5
Lynesack Dur 103 L5
Lyness Ork 169 c7
Lyng Norfk 76 F8
Lyng Somset 19 K9
Lynmouth Devon 17 N2
Lynn Staffs 58 G4
Lynn Wrekin 70 D11
Lynsted Kent 38 F9
Lynstone Cnwll 16 C10
Lynton Devon 17 N2
Lynton Cross Devon 17 J3
Lyon's Gate Dorset 11 P3
Lyonshall Herefs 45 L3
Lytchett Matravers Dorset 12 F5
Lytchett Minster Dorset .. 12 G6
Lyth Highld 167 M4
Lytham Lancs 88 D5
Lytham St Annes Lancs 88 C5
Lythbank Shrops 56 H3
Lythe N York 105 M8
Lythmore Highld 167 J3

M

Maaruig W Isls 168 h7
Mabe Burnthouse Cnwll 3 K7
Mablethorpe Lincs 87 P4
Macclesfield Ches E 83 K10
Macduff Abers 158 H5
Macharioch Ag & B 120 D10

Machen Caerph 30 H7
Machrie N Ayrs 120 G5
Machrihanish Ag & B 120 B7
Machrins Ag & B 136 b3
Machroes Gwynd 66 E9
Machynlleth Powys 54 F5
Machynys Carmth 28 F5
Mackworth Derbys 71 Q7
Macmerry E Loth 128 C5
Maddaford Devon 8 D6
Madderty P & K 134 B3
Maddington Wilts 21 L6
Maddiston Falk 126 G2
Madehurst W Susx 15 Q4
Madeley Staffs 70 D6
Madeley Wrekin 57 M4
Madeley Heath Staffs 70 D5
Madeley Park Wood Staffs . 70 D6
Madford Devon 10 C2
Madingley Cambs 62 E8
Madley Herefs 45 N7
Madresfield Worcs 46 F5
Madron Cnwll 2 D7
Maenaddwyn IoA 78 H4
Maenan Conwy 79 P11
Maenclochog Pembks 41 L5
Maendy V Glam 30 D9
Maenporth Cnwll 3 K8
Maentwrog Gwynd 67 M6
Maen-y-groes Cerdgn 42 G3
Maer Cnwll 16 C10
Maer Staffs 70 D7
Maerdy Carmth 43 N9
Maerdy Conwy 68 D6
Maerdy Rhondd 30 C5
Maesbrook Shrops 69 K10
Maesbury Shrops 69 K9
Maesbury Marsh Shrops 69 K9
Maes-glas Newpt 31 J7
Maesgwynne Carmth 41 P6
Maeshafn Denbgs 68 H2
Maesllyn Cerdgn 42 G6
Maesmynis Powys 44 E5
Maesmynis Powys 44 E5
Maesteg Brdgnd 29 N6
Maesybont Carmth 43 L11
Maesycwmmer Caerph 30 G6
Magdalen Laver Essex 51 M9
Maggieknockater Moray 157 Q8
Maggots End Essex 51 L5
Magham Down E Susx 25 P8
Maghull Sefton 81 M4
Magna Park Leics 60 B4
Magor Mons 31 M7
Magor Services Mons 31 M7
Maidenbower W Susx 24 G3
Maiden Bradley Wilts 20 F7
Maidencombe Torbay 7 N5
Maidenhayne Devon 10 F5
Maiden Head N Som 31 Q11
Maidenhead W & M 35 N8
Maiden Law Dur 113 J11
Maiden Newton Dorset 11 M5
Maidens S Ayrs 114 D6
Maiden's Green Br For 35 P10
Maidenwell Lincs 87 K5
Maiden Wells Pembks 41 J11
Maidford W Nthn 48 H4
Maids Moreton Bucks 49 K7
Maidstone Kent 38 C10
Maidstone Services Kent .. 38 D10
Maidwell W Nthn 60 F5
Mail Shet 169 r9
Maindee Newpt 31 K7
Mainland Ork 169 d6
Mainland Shet 169 r8
Mainsforth Dur 104 B4
Mains of Balhall Angus ... 143 J5
Mains of Balnakettle Abers 143 L3
Mains of Dalvey Highld ... 157 L11
Mains of Haulkerton Abers 143 N3
Mains of Lesmoir Abers ... 150 D2
Mains of Melgunds Angus .. 143 J6
Mainsriddle D & G 109 K9
Mainstone Shrops 56 D7
Maisemore Gloucs 46 F10
Major's Green Worcs 58 H9
Makeney Derbys 72 B2
Malborough Devon 7 J11
Malcoff Derbys 83 N8
Malden Rushett Gt Lon 36 E8
Maldon Essex 52 E10
Malham N York 96 D8
Maligar Highld 152 H5
Mallaig Highld 145 L8
Mallaigvaig Highld 145 L8
Malleny Mills C Edin 127 M4
Mallows Green Essex 51 L5
Malltraeth IoA 78 G11
Mallwyd Gwynd 55 K2
Malmesbury Wilts 32 H7
Malmsmead Devon 17 P2
Malpas Ches W 69 N5
Malpas Cnwll 3 L5
Malpas Newpt 31 K6
Malshanger Hants 22 G4
Malswick Gloucs 46 D10
Maltby Lincs 87 K4
Maltby Rothm 84 H2
Maltby S on T 104 E8
Maltby le Marsh Lincs 87 N4
Malting Green Essex 52 G7
Maltman's Hill Kent 26 F3
Malton N York 98 F6
Malvern Worcs 46 E5
Malvern Hills 46 E6
Malvern Link Worcs 46 E5
Malvern Wells Worcs 46 E6
Mamble Worcs 57 M10
Mamhilad Mons 31 K4
Manaccan Cnwll 3 K9
Manafon Powys 55 Q4
Manaton Devon 9 J8
Manby Lincs 87 L3
Mancetter Warwks 59 M5
Manchester Manch 82 H5
Manchester Airport Manch . 82 H8
Mancot Flints 81 L11
Mandally Highld 146 H7
Manea Cambs 62 G3
Maney Birm 58 H5
Manfield N York 103 P8
Mangerton Dorset 11 K5
Mangotsfield S Glos 32 C9

Mangrove Green Herts 50 D6
Mangurstadh W Isls 168 f4
Manhay Cnwll 2 H7
Manish W Isls 168 g9
Mankinholes Calder 90 B6
Manley Ches W 81 Q10
Manmoel Caerph 30 G4
Mannal Ag & B 136 B7
Manningford Bohune Wilts . 21 M3
Manningford Bruce Wilts .. 21 M3
Manningham C Brad 90 E3
Mannings Heath W Susx 24 F5
Mannington Dorset 13 J3
Manningtree Essex 53 K5
Mannofield C Aber 151 N7
Manorbier Pembks 41 L11
Manorbier Newton Pembks .. 41 K10
Manordeilo Carmth 43 N9
Manorhill Border 118 C4
Manorowen Pembks 40 H3
Manor Park Gt Lon 37 K3
Mansell Gamage Herefs 45 M6
Mansell Lacy Herefs 45 N5
Mansergh W & F 95 N4
Mansfield E Ayrs 115 M5
Mansfield Notts 85 H8
Mansfield Woodhouse Notts 84 H8
Mansriggs W & F 94 F4
Manston Dorset 20 F11
Manston Kent 39 P8
Manston Leeds 91 K4
Manswood Dorset 12 G3
Manthorpe Lincs 73 N3
Manthorpe Lincs 73 R7
Manton N Linc 92 F10
Manton Notts 85 K5
Manton Rutlnd 73 M10
Manton Wilts 33 N11
Manuden Essex 51 L5
Manwood Green Essex 51 M8
Maperton Somset 20 C9
Maplebeck Notts 85 M8
Maple Cross Herts 36 B2
Mapledurham Oxon 35 J9
Mapledurwell Hants 23 J4
Maplehurst W Susx 24 E6
Maplescombe Kent 37 N8
Mapleton Derbys 71 M5
Mapleton Kent 37 L11
Mapperley Derbys 72 C2
Mapperley Park C Nott 72 F2
Mapperton Dorset 11 L5
Mappleborough Green
  Warwks 58 G11
Mappleton E R Yk 93 M2
Mapplewell Barns 91 J8
Mappowder Dorset 12 B3
Màraig W Isls 168 h7
Marazanvose Cnwll 3 K3
Marazion Cnwll 2 E7
Marbhig W Isls 168 j6
Marbury Ches E 69 Q5
March Cambs 74 H11
March S Lans 116 D8
Marcham Oxon 34 E5
Marchamley Shrops 69 Q9
Marchamley Wood Shrops ... 69 Q8
Marchington Staffs 71 L8
Marchington Woodlands
  Staffs 71 L9
Marchwiel Wrexhm 69 L5
Marchwood Hants 14 C4
Marcross V Glam 29 P11
Marden Herefs 45 Q5
Marden Kent 26 B3
Marden Wilts 21 L3
Marden Ash Essex 51 N10
Marden Beech Kent 26 B3
Marden's Hill E Susx 25 M4
Marden Thorn Kent 26 C3
Mardlebury Herts 50 G7
Mardy Mons 45 L11
Marefield Leics 73 J9
Mareham le Fen Lincs 87 J8
Mareham on the Hill Lincs 87 J7
Marehay Derbys 84 E11
Marehill W Susx 24 C7
Maresfield E Susx 25 L6
Marfleet C KuH 93 K5
Marford Wrexhm 69 L3
Margam Neath 29 L7
Margaret Marsh Dorset 20 F11
Margaret Roding Essex 51 N8
Margaretting Essex 51 Q10
Margaretting Tye Essex ... 51 Q10
Margate Kent 39 Q7
Margnaheglish N Ayrs 121 K5
Margrie D & G 108 C10
Margrove Park R & Cl 105 J7
Marham Norfk 75 P9
Marhamchurch Cnwll 16 C11
Marham Park Suffk 64 A8
Marholm C Pete 74 B10
Marian-glas IoA 79 J8
Mariansleigh Devon 17 N7
Marine Town Kent 38 F7
Marionburgh Abers 151 J6
Marishader Highld 152 H5
Maristow Devon 6 D6
Marjoriebanks D & G 109 N4
Mark Somset 19 L5
Markbeech Kent 25 L2
Markby Lincs 87 N5
Mark Causeway Somset 19 L5
Mark Cross E Susx 25 N4
Markeaton C Derb 72 A3
Market Bosworth Leics 72 C10
Market Deeping Lincs 74 B8
Market Drayton Shrops 70 B8
Market Harborough Leics .. 60 F3
Market Lavington Wilts ... 21 K4
Market Overton Rutlnd 73 M7
Market Rasen Lincs 86 H5
Market Stainton Lincs 86 H5
Market Warsop Notts 85 J7
Market Weighton E R Yk ... 92 E2
Market Weston Suffk 64 D6
Markfield Leics 72 D8
Markham Caerph 30 G4
Markham Moor Notts 85 M6
Markinch Fife 134 H7
Markington N York 97 L7
Markle E Loth 128 F4
Mark's Corner IoW 14 E8
Marks Tey Essex 52 F7

Markwell Cnwll 5 P10
Markyate Herts 50 C7
Marlborough Wilts 33 N11
Marlbrook Herefs 45 Q4
Marlbrook Worcs 58 E10
Marlcliff Warwks 47 L4
Marldon Devon 7 M6
Marle Green E Susx 25 N7
Marlesford Suffk 65 L10
Marley Kent 39 L11
Marley Kent 39 P11
Marley Green Ches E 69 Q5
Marley Hill Gatesd 113 K9
Marlingford Norfk 76 G10
Marloes Pembks 40 E9
Marlow Bucks 35 M7
Marlow Herefs 56 G9
Marlow Bottom Bucks 35 M7
Marlpit Hill Kent 37 K11
Marlpits E Susx 25 L5
Marlpits E Susx 26 B9
Marlpool Derbys 84 F11
Marnhull Dorset 20 E11
Marple Stockp 83 L7
Marple Bridge Stockp 83 L7
Marr Donc 91 N9
Marrick N York 103 L11
Marros Carmth 41 P9
Marsden Kirk 90 C8
Marsden S Tyne 113 N8
Marsden Height Lancs 89 P3
Marsett N York 96 D3
Marsh Bucks 35 M3
Marsh C Brad 90 C3
Marsh Devon 10 F2
Marshall's Heath Herts ... 50 E8
Marshalswick Herts 50 E9
Marsham Norfk 76 H7
Marsh Baldon Oxon 34 G5
Marsh Benham W Berk 34 D11
Marshborough Kent 39 P10
Marshbrook Shrops 56 G7
Marshchapel Lincs 93 Q11
Marsh Farm Luton 50 C5
Marshfield Newpt 31 J8
Marshfield S Glos 32 E10
Marshgate Cnwll 5 K3
Marsh Gibbon Bucks 48 H10
Marsh Green Devon 9 P6
Marsh Green Kent 25 K2
Marsh Green Wrekin 57 L2
Marshland St James Norfk . 75 K9
Marsh Lane Derbys 84 F5
Marsh Lane Gloucs 31 Q3
Marshside Sefton 88 D7
Marsh Street Somset 18 C6
Marshwood Dorset 10 H5
Marske N York 103 M10
Marske-by-the-Sea R & Cl . 104 H6
Marsland Green Wigan 82 E5
Marston Ches W 82 E9
Marston Herefs 45 M3
Marston Lincs 73 M2
Marston Oxon 34 F3
Marston Staffs 58 B2
Marston Staffs 70 G9
Marston Warwks 59 K6
Marston Wilts 21 J3
Marston Green Solhll 59 J7
Marston Jabbet Warwks 59 N7
Marston Magna Somset 19 Q10
Marston Meysey Wilts 33 M5
Marston Montgomery
  Derbys 71 L7
Marston Moretaine C Beds . 49 Q6
Marston on Dove Derbys ... 71 N9
Marston St Lawrence
  W Nthn 48 F6
Marston Stannett Herefs .. 45 R3
Marston Trussell W Nthn .. 60 E3
Marstow Herefs 45 R11
Marsworth Bucks 35 P2
Marten Wilts 21 Q2
Marthall Ches E 82 G9
Martham Norfk 77 P8
Martin Hants 21 L11
Martin Kent 27 P2
Martin Lincs 86 F9
Martin Lincs 86 H7
Martindale W & F 101 M7
Martin Dales Lincs 86 F9
Martin Drove End Hants ... 21 L10
Martinhoe Devon 17 M2
Martin Hussingtree Worcs . 46 G2
Martinscroft Warrtn 82 E7
Martinstown Dorset 11 N7
Martlesham Suffk 53 M2
Martlesham Heath Suffk ... 53 M2
Martletwy Pembks 41 K8
Martley Worcs 46 E2
Martock Somset 19 N11
Marton Ches E 83 J11
Marton Ches W 83 D11
Marton E R Yk 93 L3
Marton E R Yk 99 Q7
Marton Lincs 85 Q4
Marton Middsb 104 F7
Marton N York 98 F4
Marton N York 98 D4
Marton W & F 94 E3
Marton Warwks 59 P11
Marton-cum-Grafton
  N York 97 P8
Marton-le-Moor N York 97 N6
Martyr's Green Surrey 36 C9
Martyr Worthy Hants 22 F8
Marvig W Isls 168 j6
Marwell Zoo Hants 22 F10
Marwick Ork 169 b4
Marwood Devon 17 J4
Marybank Highld 155 N6
Maryburgh Highld 155 P6
Marygold Border 129 L8
Maryhill C Glas 125 P4
Marykirk Abers 143 M4
Maryland Mons 31 P3
Marylebone Gt Lon 36 G4
Marylebone Wigan 88 H9
Marypark Moray 157 M11
Maryport Cumb 100 D3
Maryport D & G 106 F7
Marystow Devon 8 B8
Mary Tavy Devon 8 D7
Maryton Angus 143 L7
Maryton Angus 143 L7
Marywell Abers 150 F8

Place	County	Page	Grid
Marywell	Abers	151	N8
Marywell	Angus	143	M9
Masham	N York	97	K4
Mashbury	Essex	51	Q8
Masongill	N York	95	P5
Mastin Moor	Derbys	84	G5
Matching	Essex	51	M8
Matching Green	Essex	51	M8
Matching Tye	Essex	51	M8
Matfen	Nthumb	112	F6
Matfield	Kent	25	Q2
Mathern	Mons	31	P6
Mathon	Herefs	46	D5
Mathry	Pembks	40	G4
Matlask	Norfk	76	H5
Matlock	Derbys	84	D9
Matlock Bank	Derbys	84	D8
Matlock Bath	Derbys	84	C9
Matlock Dale	Derbys	84	C9
Matson	Gloucs	46	G11
Matterdale End	W & F	101	L6
Mattersey	Notts	85	L3
Mattersey Thorpe	Notts	85	L3
Mattingley	Hants	23	K3
Mattishall	Norfk	76	F9
Mattishall Burgh	Norfk	76	F9
Mauchline	E Ayrs	115	J2
Maud	Abers	159	M8
Maufant	Jersey	11	c1
Maugersbury	Gloucs	47	P9
Maughold	IoM	80	g3
Mauld	Highld	155	M10
Maulden	C Beds	50	C3
Maulds Meaburn	W & F	102	B7
Maunby	N York	97	N3
Maund Bryan	Herefs	45	R4
Maundown	Somset	18	E9
Mautby	Norfk	77	P9
Mavesyn Ridware	Staffs	71	K11
Mavis Enderby	Lincs	87	L7
Mawbray	Cumb	109	N11
Mawdesley	Lancs	88	F8
Mawdlam	Brdgnd	29	M8
Mawgan	Cnwll	3	J8
Mawgan Porth	Cnwll	4	D8
Maw Green	Ches E	70	C3
Mawla	Cnwll	3	J4
Mawnan	Cnwll	3	K8
Mawnan Smith	Cnwll	3	K8
Mawsley	W Nthn	60	H5
Mawthorpe	Lincs	87	N6
Maxey	C Pete	74	B9
Maxstoke	Warwks	59	K7
Maxted Street	Kent	27	K3
Maxton	Border	118	B4
Maxton	Kent	27	P3
Maxwelltown	D & G	109	L5
Maxworthy	Cnwll	5	M3
Mayals	Swans	28	H7
May Bank	Staffs	70	F5
Maybole	S Ayrs	114	E6
Maybury	Surrey	36	B9
Mayes Green	Surrey	24	D3
Mayfield	E Susx	25	N5
Mayfield	Mdloth	128	B7
Mayfield	Staffs	71	M5
Mayford	Surrey	23	Q3
May Hill	Gloucs	46	D10
Mayland	Essex	52	F11
Maylandsea	Essex	52	F11
Maynard's Green	E Susx	25	N7
Maypole	Birm	58	G9
Maypole	Kent	39	M9
Maypole	Mons	45	P11
Maypole Green	Norfk	65	N2
Maypole Green	Suffk	64	C10
Maypole Green	Suffk	65	K8
May's Green	Oxon	35	K8
May's Green	Surrey	36	C9
Mead	Devon	16	C8
Meadgate	BaNES	20	C3
Meadle	Bucks	35	M3
Meadowfield	Dur	103	P3
Meadowtown	Shrops	56	E4
Meadwell	Devon	5	Q5
Meaford	Staffs	70	F7
Mealabost	W Isls	168	j4
Meal Bank	W & F	101	P11
Mealrigg	Cumb	109	P11
Mealsgate	Cumb	100	H2
Meanwood	Leeds	90	H3
Mearbeck	N York	96	B8
Meare	Somset	19	N6
Meare Green	Somset	19	J10
Meare Green	Somset	19	K9
Mearns	E Rens	125	N6
Mears Ashby	N Nthn	60	H7
Measham	Leics	72	A8
Meath Green	Surrey	24	G2
Meathop	W & F	95	J4
Meaux	E R Yk	93	J3
Meavaig	W Isls	168	f4
Meavy	Devon	6	E5
Medbourne	Leics	60	H2
Medburn	Nthumb	112	H6
Meddon	Devon	16	D8
Meden Vale	Notts	85	J7
Medlam	Lincs	87	K9
Medlar	Lancs	88	E3
Medmenham	Bucks	35	M8
Medomsley	Dur	112	H10
Medstead	Hants	23	J7
Medway Services	Medway	38	D9
Meerbrook	Staffs	70	H2
Meer Common	Herefs	45	M4
Meesden	Herts	51	K4
Meeson	Wrekin	70	A10
Meeth	Devon	17	J10
Meeting Green	Suffk	63	M9
Meeting House Hill	Norfk	77	L6
Meidrim	Carmth	41	Q6
Meifod	Powys	56	B2
Meigle	P & K	142	D9
Meikle Carco	D & G	115	Q5
Meikle Earnock	S Lans	126	C7
Meikle Ferry	Highld	162	G9
Meikle Kilmory	Ag & B	124	D5
Meikle Obney	P & K	141	P10
Meikleour	P & K	142	B10
Meikle Wartle	Abers	158	H11
Meinciau	Carmth	28	E2
Meir	C Stke	70	G6
Meir Heath	Staffs	70	G6
Melbost	W Isls	168	j4
Melbourn	Cambs	51	J2
Melbourne	Derbys	72	B5
Melbourne	E R Yk	92	C2
Melbourne	Essex	51	Q9
Melbur	Cnwll	3	N3
Melbury	Devon	16	F8
Melbury Abbas	Dorset	20	G10
Melbury Bubb	Dorset	11	M3
Melbury Osmond	Dorset	11	M3
Melbury Sampford	Dorset	11	M3
Melchbourne	Bed	61	M7
Melcombe Bingham	Dorset	12	C4
Meldon	Devon	8	E6
Meldon	Nthumb	112	H4
Meldon Park	Nthumb	112	H3
Meldreth	Cambs	62	E11
Meldrum	Stirlg	133	L8
Melfort	Ag & B	130	G5
Meliden	Denbgs	80	F8
Melinau	Pembks	41	N8
Melin-byrhedyn	Powys	55	J5
Melincourt	Neath	29	M4
Melin-y-coed	Conwy	67	Q2
Melin-y-ddol	Powys	55	P3
Melin-y-wig	Denbgs	68	D5
Melkinthorpe	W & F	101	Q5
Melkridge	Nthumb	111	P8
Melksham	Wilts	20	H2
Mellangoose	Cnwll	2	H8
Mell Green	W Berk	34	E9
Mellguards	W & F	110	H11
Melling	Lancs	95	M6
Melling	Sefton	81	M4
Melling Mount	Sefton	81	N4
Mellis	Suffk	64	F7
Mellon Charles	Highld	160	C8
Mellon Udrigle	Highld	160	D7
Mellor	Lancs	89	K4
Mellor	Stockp	83	L7
Mellor Brook	Lancs	89	J4
Mells	Somset	20	D5
Mells	Suffk	65	N6
Melmerby	N York	96	G3
Melmerby	N York	97	M5
Melmerby	W & F	102	B3
Melness	Highld	165	N4
Melon Green	Suffk	64	A10
Melplash	Dorset	11	K5
Melrose	Border	117	Q4
Melsetter	Ork	169	b8
Melsonby	N York	103	N9
Meltham	Kirk	90	D8
Meltham Mills	Kirk	90	E8
Melton	E R Yk	92	G5
Melton	Suffk	65	K11
Meltonby	E R Yk	98	F10
Melton Constable	Norfk	76	E5
Melton Mowbray	Leics	73	K7
Melton Ross	N Linc	93	J8
Melvaig	Highld	160	A9
Melverley	Shrops	69	K11
Melverley Green	Shrops	69	K11
Melvich	Highld	166	E4
Membury	Devon	10	F4
Membury Services	W Berk	34	B9
Memsie	Abers	159	N5
Memus	Angus	142	G6
Menabilly	Cnwll	4	H11
Menagissey	Cnwll	3	J4
Menai Bridge	IoA	79	K10
Mendham	Suffk	65	K5
Mendip Hills		19	P4
Mendlesham	Suffk	64	G8
Mendlesham Green	Suffk	64	F9
Menheniot	Cnwll	5	M9
Menithwood	Worcs	57	N11
Menna	Cnwll	3	N3
Mennock	D & G	115	R6
Menston	C Brad	90	F2
Menstrie	Clacks	133	P8
Menthorpe	N York	92	B4
Mentmore	Bucks	49	P11
Meoble	Highld	145	N10
Meole Brace	Shrops	56	H2
Meonstoke	Hants	22	H11
Meon Vale	Warwks	47	N5
Meopham	Kent	37	P7
Meopham Green	Kent	37	P7
Meopham Station	Kent	37	P7
Mepal	Cambs	62	F4
Meppershall	C Beds	50	D3
Merbach	Herefs	45	L5
Mere	Ches E	82	F8
Mere	Wilts	20	F8
Mere Brow	Lancs	88	E7
Mereclough	Lancs	89	P4
Mere Green	Birm	58	H5
Mere Green	Worcs	47	J2
Mere Heath	Ches W	82	E10
Meresborough	Medway	38	D9
Mereworth	Kent	37	Q10
Meriden	Solhll	59	K8
Merkadale	Highld	152	F11
Merley	BCP	12	H5
Merlin's Bridge	Pembks	40	H8
Merrington	Shrops	69	N10
Merrion	Pembks	40	H11
Merriott	Somset	11	J2
Merrivale	Devon	8	D9
Merrow	Surrey	36	B10
Merry Field Hill	Dorset	12	H4
Merryhill	Herts	36	D2
Merryhill	Wolves	58	C5
Merry Lees	Leics	72	D9
Merrymeet	Cnwll	5	M8
Mersea Island	Essex	52	H8
Mersey Gateway Bridge	Halton	82	B8
Mersham	Kent	27	J3
Merstham	Surrey	36	G10
Merston	W Susx	15	N6
Merstone	IoW	14	F9
Merther	Cnwll	3	M5
Merthyr	Carmth	42	G10
Merthyr Cynog	Powys	44	D7
Merthyr Dyfan	V Glam	30	F11
Merthyr Mawr	Brdgnd	29	N9
Merthyr Tydfil	Myr Td	30	D3
Merthyr Vale	Myr Td	30	E5
Merton	Devon	17	J9
Merton	Gt Lon	36	G6
Merton	Norfk	64	C2
Merton	Oxon	48	G11
Meshaw	Devon	17	P8
Messing	Essex	52	F8
Messingham	N Linc	92	E10
Metal Bridge	Dur	103	Q4
Metfield	Suffk	65	K5
Metherell	Cnwll	5	Q8
Metheringham	Lincs	86	E8
Methil	Fife	135	K8
Methilhill	Fife	135	K7
Methley	Leeds	91	K5
Methley Junction	Leeds	91	K5
Methlick	Abers	159	L10
Methven	P & K	134	C2
Methwold	Norfk	63	M2
Methwold Hythe	Norfk	63	M2
Mettingham	Suffk	65	M4
Metton	Norfk	76	J4
Mevagissey	Cnwll	3	Q5
Mexborough	Donc	91	M10
Mey	Highld	167	N2
Meysey Hampton	Gloucs	33	M4
Miabhaig	W Isls	168	f4
Michaelchurch	Herefs	45	Q9
Michaelchurch Escley	Herefs	45	L8
Michaelchurch-on-Arrow	Powys	45	J4
Michaelstone-y-Fedw	Newpt	30	H8
Michaelston-le-Pit	V Glam	30	G10
Michaelstow	Cnwll	4	H6
Michaelwood Services	Gloucs	32	D5
Michelcombe	Devon	6	H5
Micheldever	Hants	22	F7
Micheldever Station	Hants	22	F6
Michelmersh	Hants	22	B9
Mickfield	Suffk	64	G9
Micklebring	Donc	84	H2
Mickleby	N York	105	M8
Micklefield	Leeds	91	L4
Micklefield Green	Herts	50	B11
Mickleham	Surrey	36	E10
Mickleover	C Derb	71	Q8
Micklethwaite	C Brad	90	E2
Micklethwaite	Cumb	110	E10
Mickleton	Dur	103	J6
Mickleton	Gloucs	47	N6
Mickletown	Leeds	91	L5
Mickle Trafford	Ches W	81	N11
Mickley	Derbys	84	D5
Mickley	N York	97	L5
Mickley Green	Suffk	64	A10
Mickley Square	Nthumb	112	G8
Mid Ardlaw	Abers	159	M5
Midbea	Ork	169	d2
Mid Beltie	Abers	150	G7
Mid Bockhampton	BCP	13	L5
Mid Calder	W Loth	127	K4
Mid Clyth	Highld	167	N9
Mid Culbeuchly	Abers	158	G5
Middle Assendon	Oxon	35	K7
Middle Aston	Oxon	48	E9
Middle Barton	Oxon	48	D9
Middlebie	D & G	110	D5
Middlebridge	P & K	141	L4
Middle Chinnock	Somset	11	K2
Middle Claydon	Bucks	49	K9
Middlecliffe	Barns	91	L9
Middlecott	Devon	8	H7
Middlecroft	Derbys	84	F6
Middle Duntisbourne	Gloucs	33	J3
Middleham	N York	96	H3
Middle Handley	Derbys	84	F5
Middle Harling	Norfk	64	D4
Middlehill	Cnwll	5	M8
Middlehill	Wilts	32	F11
Middlehope	Shrops	56	H7
Middle Kames	Ag & B	131	J10
Middle Littleton	Worcs	47	L5
Middle Madeley	Staffs	70	D5
Middle Maes-coed	Herefs	45	L8
Middlemarsh	Dorset	11	P3
Middle Mayfield	Staffs	71	L6
Middle Mill	Pembks	40	F5
Middlemoor	Devon	6	D4
Middle Quarter	Kent	26	E4
Middle Rasen	Lincs	86	E3
Middle Rocombe	Devon	7	N5
Middle Salter	Lancs	95	N8
Middlesbrough	Middsb	104	E7
Middlesceugh	W & F	101	M2
Middleshaw	W & F	95	M3
Middlesmoor	N York	96	G6
Middle Stoford	Somset	18	G10
Middle Stoke	Medway	38	D6
Middlestone	Dur	103	Q4
Middlestone Moor	Dur	103	P4
Middle Stoughton	Somset	19	M5
Middlestown	Wakefd	90	H7
Middle Street	Gloucs	32	E4
Middle Taphouse	Cnwll	5	K9
Middlethird	Border	118	C2
Middleton	Ag & B	136	A7
Middleton	Derbys	71	M2
Middleton	Derbys	84	C9
Middleton	Essex	52	E4
Middleton	Hants	22	D6
Middleton	Herefs	57	J11
Middleton	Lancs	95	J9
Middleton	Leeds	91	J5
Middleton	N Nthn	60	H3
Middleton	N York	96	H11
Middleton	N York	98	F3
Middleton	Norfk	75	N7
Middleton	Nthumb	112	G4
Middleton	Nthumb	119	M3
Middleton	P & K	134	E6
Middleton	Rochdl	89	P9
Middleton	Shrops	57	J9
Middleton	Shrops	69	K9
Middleton	Suffk	65	N8
Middleton	Swans	28	D7
Middleton	W & F	95	N3
Middleton	Warwks	59	J5
Middleton Cheney	W Nthn	48	E6
Middleton Green	Staffs	70	H7
Middleton Hall	Nthumb	119	J5
Middleton-in-Teesdale	Dur	102	H5
Middleton Moor	Suffk	65	N8
Middleton One Row	Darltn	104	C8
Middleton-on-Leven	N York	104	E9
Middleton-on-Sea	W Susx	15	Q6
Middleton on the Hill	Herefs	45	Q2
Middleton on the Wolds	E R Yk	99	J11
Middleton Park	C Aber	151	N5
Middleton Priors	Shrops	57	L6
Middleton Quernhow	N York	97	M3
Middleton St George	Darltn	104	B8
Middleton Scriven	Shrops	57	M7
Middleton Stoney	Oxon	48	F10
Middleton Tyas	N York	103	P9
Middletown	Cumb	100	C9
Middle Town	IoS	2	b3
Middletown	N Som	31	N10
Middletown	Powys	56	E2
Middle Tysoe	Warwks	48	B6
Middle Wallop	Hants	21	Q7
Middlewich	Ches E	82	F11
Middle Winterslow	Wilts	21	P8
Middlewood	Cnwll	5	M6
Middlewood	Herefs	45	K6
Middlewood Green	Suffk	64	F9
Middle Yard	Gloucs	32	F4
Middlezoy	Somset	19	L8
Middridge	Dur	103	P5
Midford	BaNES	20	E2
Midge Hall	Lancs	88	G6
Midgeholme	Cumb	111	M9
Midgham	W Berk	34	G11
Midgley	Calder	90	C5
Midgley	Wakefd	90	H8
Mid Holmwood	Surrey	36	E11
Midhopestones	Sheff	90	G11
Midhurst	W Susx	23	N10
Mid Lavant	W Susx	15	N5
Midlem	Border	117	Q5
Mid Mains	Highld	155	M10
Midney	Somset	19	N9
Midpark	Ag & B	124	C6
Midsomer Norton	BaNES	20	C4
Midtown	Highld	165	N4
Midville	Lincs	87	L9
Midway	Ches E	83	K8
Mid Yell	Shet	169	s4
Migdale	Highld	162	E8
Migvie	Abers	150	C6
Milborne Port	Somset	20	C11
Milborne St Andrew	Dorset	12	D5
Milborne Wick	Somset	20	C10
Milbourne	Nthumb	112	H5
Milbourne	Wilts	33	J7
Milburn	W & F	102	C5
Milbury Heath	S Glos	32	C6
Milby	N York	97	P7
Milcombe	Oxon	48	D8
Milden	Suffk	52	G2
Mildenhall	Suffk	63	M6
Mildenhall	Wilts	33	P11
Milebrook	Powys	56	F10
Milebush	Kent	26	C2
Mile Elm	Wilts	33	J11
Mile End	Gloucs	31	Q2
Mile End	Suffk	65	L4
Mileham	Norfk	76	C8
Mile Oak	Br & H	24	F9
Mile Oak	Kent	25	Q2
Mile Oak	Staffs	59	J4
Miles Green	Staffs	70	D5
Miles Hope	Herefs	45	R2
Milesmark	Fife	134	D10
Mile Town	Kent	38	F7
Milfield	Nthumb	118	H4
Milford	Derbys	84	E11
Milford	Devon	16	C7
Milford	Powys	55	P6
Milford	Staffs	70	H10
Milford	Surrey	23	P6
Milford Haven	Pembks	40	H9
Milford on Sea	Hants	13	N6
Milkwall	Gloucs	31	Q3
Millais	Jersey	11	a1
Milland	W Susx	23	M9
Milland Marsh	W Susx	23	M9
Mill Bank	Calder	90	C6
Millbeck	Cumb	101	J5
Millbreck	Abers	159	P9
Millbridge	Surrey	23	M6
Millbrook	C Beds	50	B3
Millbrook	Cnwll	6	C8
Millbrook	Jersey	11	b2
Millbrook	Tamesd	83	L5
Mill Brow	Stockp	83	L7
Millbuie	Abers	151	K6
Millbuie	Highld	155	Q7
Millcombe	Devon	7	L9
Mill Common	Norfk	77	L11
Mill Common	Suffk	65	N5
Millcorner	E Susx	26	D7
Millcraig	Highld	156	B3
Milldale	Staffs	71	L4
Mill End	Bucks	35	L7
Millend	Gloucs	32	D5
Mill End	Herts	50	H4
Millerhill	Mdloth	127	Q4
Miller's Dale	Derbys	83	P10
Millers Green	Derbys	71	N4
Miller's Green	Essex	51	N9
Millerston	C Glas	125	Q4
Millgate	Lancs	89	P7
Mill Green	Cambs	63	K11
Mill Green	Essex	51	P10
Mill Green	Herts	50	F8
Mill Green	Lincs	74	D6
Mill Green	Norfk	64	G4
Mill Green	Shrops	70	B9
Mill Green	Staffs	58	G3
Mill Green	Staffs	71	K10
Mill Green	Suffk	52	G3
Mill Green	Suffk	64	D10
Mill Green	Suffk	64	G9
Mill Green	Suffk	65	K5
Millhalf	Herefs	45	K5
Millhayes	Devon	10	E4
Millhead	Lancs	95	K6
Millheugh	S Lans	126	C7
Mill Hill	E Susx	25	P9
Mill Hill	Gt Lon	36	F2
Millhouse	Ag & B	124	B3
Millhouse	Cumb	101	L3
Millhousebridge	D & G	109	P3
Millhouse Green	Barns	90	G10
Millhouses	Barns	91	L10
Millhouses	Sheff	84	D4
Milliken Park	Rens	125	L5
Millin Cross	Pembks	41	J8
Millington	E R Yk	98	G10
Mill Lane	Hants	23	L4
Millmeece	Staffs	70	E8
Millness	W & F	95	L4
Mill of Drummond	P & K	133	N4
Mill of Haldane	W Duns	132	D11
Millom	Cumb	94	D4
Millook	Cnwll	5	K2
Millpool	Cnwll	2	F7
Millpool	Cnwll	5	J7
Millport	N Ayrs	124	F7
Mill Side	W & F	95	J4
Mill Street	Kent	37	Q9
Mill Street	Norfk	76	F8
Mill Street	Suffk	64	F7
Millthorpe	Derbys	84	D5
Millthrop	W & F	95	P5
Milltimber	C Aber	151	M7
Milltown	Abers	149	P6
Milltown	Abers	150	D4
Milltown	Cnwll	5	J10
Milltown	D & G	110	F5
Milltown	Derbys	84	E8
Milltown	Devon	17	K4
Milltown	Highld	153	N9
Milltown of Auchindoun	Moray	157	R9
Milltown of Campfield	Abers	150	H7
Milltown of Edinvillie	Moray	157	P9
Milltown of Rothiemay	Moray	158	D8
Milnathort	P & K	134	F4
Milngavie	E Duns	125	P3
Milnrow	Rochdl	89	Q8
Milnthorpe	W & F	95	K4
Milnthorpe	Wakefd	91	J7
Miloig	Highld	152	B8
Milson	Shrops	57	L10
Milstead	Kent	38	F10
Milston	Wilts	21	N5
Milthorpe	N Nthn	48	G5
Milton	C Stke	70	G4
Milton	Cambs	62	G8
Milton	Cumb	111	L8
Milton	D & G	106	H7
Milton	D & G	108	H6
Milton	Derbys	71	Q9
Milton	Highld	155	N11
Milton	Highld	155	Q8
Milton	Highld	156	D3
Milton	Highld	167	P6
Milton	Inver	125	K4
Milton	Kent	37	Q8
Milton	Moray	149	M4
Milton	Moray	158	D5
Milton	N Som	19	K2
Milton	Newpt	31	L7
Milton	Notts	85	M6
Milton	Oxon	34	E6
Milton	Oxon	48	E7
Milton	P & K	141	Q5
Milton	Pembks	41	K10
Milton	Somset	19	N10
Milton	Stirlg	132	G7
Milton	W Duns	125	L3
Milton Abbas	Dorset	12	D4
Milton Abbot	Devon	5	Q6
Milton Bridge	Mdloth	127	P5
Milton Bryan	C Beds	49	Q8
Milton Clevedon	Somset	20	C7
Milton Combe	Devon	6	D5
Milton Common	Oxon	35	J4
Milton Damerel	Devon	16	F9
Milton End	Gloucs	32	D2
Milton End	Gloucs	33	M4
Milton Ernest	Bed	61	M9
Milton Green	Ches W	69	N3
Milton Heights	Oxon	34	E6
Milton Hill	Oxon	34	E6
Milton Keynes	M Keyn	49	N7
Milton Lilbourne	Wilts	21	N2
Milton Malsor	W Nthn	60	F9
Milton Morenish	P & K	140	F10
Milton of Auchinhove	Abers	150	F7
Milton of Balgonie	Fife	135	J7
Milton of Buchanan	Stirlg	132	E9
Milton of Campsie	E Duns	126	B2
Milton of Finavon	Angus	142	H6
Milton of Leys	Highld	156	B9
Milton of Murtle	C Aber	151	M7
Milton on Stour	Dorset	20	E9
Milton Regis	Kent	38	E9
Milton Street	E Susx	25	M10
Milton-under-Wychwood	Oxon	47	Q11
Milverton	Somset	18	F9
Milverton	Warwks	59	M11
Milwich	Staffs	70	H8
Milwr	Flints	80	H10
Minard	Ag & B	131	K8
Minchington	Dorset	12	G2
Minchinhampton	Gloucs	32	G4
Mindenhurst	Surrey	23	P3
Mindrum	Nthumb	118	F4
Minehead	Somset	18	C5
Minera	Wrexhm	69	J4
Minety	Wilts	33	K6
Minffordd	Gwynd	67	K7
Mingarrypark	Highld	138	B4
Miningsby	Lincs	87	K8
Minions	Cnwll	5	M7
Minishant	S Ayrs	114	F5
Minllyn	Gwynd	55	K2
Minnigaff	D & G	107	M4
Minnonie	Abers	159	J5
Minshull Vernon	Ches E	70	B2
Minskip	N York	97	N8
Minstead	Hants	13	N2
Minsted	W Susx	23	N10
Minster	Kent	39	P9
Minster	Kent	38	G7
Minsterley	Shrops	56	F3
Minster Lovell	Oxon	34	B2
Minster-on-Sea	Kent	38	G7
Minsterworth	Gloucs	46	E11
Minterne Magna	Dorset	11	P4
Minterne Parva	Dorset	11	P4
Minting	Lincs	86	G6
Mintlaw	Abers	159	N8
Minto	Border	117	R6
Minton	Shrops	56	G6
Minwear	Pembks	41	K8
Minworth	Birm	59	J6
Mirehouse	Cumb	100	C7
Mireland	Highld	167	P4
Mirfield	Kirk	90	G7
Miserden	Gloucs	32	H3
Miskin	Rhondd	30	D5
Miskin	Rhondd	30	D8

Misson Notts 85 L2
Misterton Leics 60 C4
Misterton Notts 85 N2
Misterton Somset 11 K3
Mistley Essex 53 K5
Mistley Heath Essex 53 K5
Mitcham Gt Lon 36 G7
Mitcheldean Gloucs 46 C11
Mitchell Cnwll 3 M3
Mitchellslacks D & G 116 D11
Mitchel Troy Mons 31 N2
Mitford Nthumb 113 J3
Mithian Cnwll 3 J3
Mitton Staffs 70 F11
Mixbury Oxon 48 H8
Mixenden Calder 90 D5
Moats Tye Suffk 64 E10
Mobberley Ches E 82 G9
Mobberley Staffs 71 J6
Moccas Herefs 45 M6
Mochdre Conwy 79 Q9
Mochdre Powys 55 P7
Mochrum D & G 107 K8
Mockbeggar Hants 13 L3
Mockbeggar Kent 26 B2
Mockerkin Cumb 100 E6
Modbury Devon 6 H8
Moddershall Staffs 70 G7
Moelfre IoA 79 J7
Moelfre Powys 68 G9
Moel Tryfan Gwynd 67 J3
Moffat D & G 116 F9
Mogador Surrey 36 F10
Moggerhanger C Beds 61 P11
Moira Leics 71 Q11
Molash Kent 38 H11
Mol-chlach Highld 144 G5
Mold Flints 68 H2
Moldgreen Kirk 90 F7
Molehill Green Essex 51 N6
Molehill Green Essex 52 B7
Molescroft E R Yk 92 H2
Molesden Nthumb 112 H4
Molesworth Cambs 61 N5
Moll Highld 153 K11
Molland Devon 17 Q6
Mollington Ches W 81 M10
Mollington Oxon 48 D5
Mollinsburn N Lans 126 C3
Monachty Cerdgn 43 K2
Mondynes Abers 143 P2
Monewden Suffk 65 J10
Moneydie P & K 134 D2
Moneyrow Green W & M 35 N9
Moniaive D & G 115 Q9
Monifieth Angus 142 H11
Monimail Fife 134 H5
Monington Pembks 41 M2
Monk Bretton Barns 91 K9
Monken Hadley Gt Lon 50 F11
Monk Fryston N York 91 N5
Monkhide Herefs 46 B6
Monkhill Cumb 110 F9
Monkhopton Shrops 57 L6
Monkland Herefs 45 P3
Monkleigh Devon 16 H7
Monknash V Glam 29 P10
Monkokehampton Devon 8 E3
Monkseaton N Tyne 113 M6
Monks Eleigh Suffk 52 G2
Monk's Gate W Susx 24 F5
Monks Heath Ches E 82 H10
Monk Sherborne Hants 22 H3
Monks Horton Kent 27 K3
Monksilver Somset 18 E7
Monks Kirby Warwks 59 Q8
Monk Soham Suffk 65 J8
Monkspath Solhll 58 H9
Monks Risborough Bucks 35 M4
Monksthorpe Lincs 87 M7
Monk Street Essex 51 P5
Monkswood Mons 31 K4
Monkton Devon 10 D4
Monkton Kent 39 N9
Monkton S Ayrs 114 G2
Monkton S Tyne 113 M8
Monkton V Glam 29 P10
Monkton Combe BaNES 20 E2
Monkton Deverill Wilts 20 G7
Monkton Farleigh Wilts 32 F11
Monkton Heathfield Somset 19 J9
Monkton Up Wimborne Dorset 12 H2
Monkton Wyld Dorset 10 G5
Monkwearmouth Sundld 113 N9
Monkwood Hants 23 J8
Monmore Green Wolves 58 D5
Monmouth Mons 31 P2
Monnington on Wye Herefs 45 M6
Monreith D & G 107 L9
Montacute Somset 19 N11
Montcliffe Bolton 89 K8
Montford Shrops 56 G2
Montford Bridge Shrops 69 M11
Montgarrie Abers 150 F4
Montgomery Powys 56 C5
Monton Salfd 82 G5
Montrose Angus 143 N6
Mont Saint Guern 10 b2
Monxton Hants 22 B6
Monyash Derbys 83 Q11
Monymusk Abers 150 H4
Monzie P & K 133 P2
Moodiesburn N Lans 126 B3
Moonzie Fife 135 J4
Moor Allerton Leeds 91 J3
Moorbath Dorset 11 J5
Moorby Lincs 87 J8
Moorcot Herefs 45 M3
Moor Crichel Dorset 12 G3
Moordown BCP 13 J6
Moore Halton 82 C8
Moorend Gloucs 32 D4
Moor End C Beds 49 Q10
Moor End Calder 90 D5
Moor End Devon 17 M10
Moorends Donc 92 A7
Moorgreen Hants 22 E11
Moor Green Herts 50 H5
Moorgreen Notts 84 G11
Moorhall Derbys 84 D6
Moorhampton Herefs 45 M5
Moorhead C Brad 90 E3

Moor Head Leeds 90 G5
Moorhouse Cumb 110 E10
Moorhouse Cumb 110 F9
Moorhouse Donc 91 M8
Moorhouse Notts 85 N7
Moorhouse Bank Surrey 37 K10
Moorland Somset 19 K8
Moorlinch Somset 19 L7
Moor Monkton N York 97 R9
Moor Row Cumb 100 D8
Moor Row Cumb 110 D11
Moorsholm R & Cl 105 J8
Moorside Dorset 20 E11
Moorside Dur 112 G11
Moor Side Lancs 88 E4
Moor Side Lancs 88 F3
Moorside Leeds 90 G3
Moor Side Lincs 87 J9
Moorside Oldham 89 Q9
Moorstock Kent 27 K4
Moor Street Medway 38 D8
Moorswater Cnwll 5 L9
Moorthorpe Wakefd 91 M8
Moortown Devon 6 E4
Moortown Hants 13 L4
Moortown IoW 14 D10
Moortown Leeds 90 H3
Moortown Lincs 93 J11
Moortown Wrekin 69 R11
Morangie Highld 162 H10
Morar Highld 145 L9
Morborne Cambs 61 P2
Morchard Bishop Devon 9 J3
Morchard Road Devon 9 J3
Morcombelake Dorset 11 J6
Morcott Rutlnd 73 N10
Morda Shrops 69 J9
Morden Dorset 12 F5
Morden Gt Lon 36 G7
Mordiford Herefs 45 R7
Mordon Dur 104 B5
More Shrops 56 E6
Morebath Devon 18 C9
Morebattle Border 118 E6
Morecambe Lancs 95 J8
Moredon Swindn 33 M7
Morefield Highld 161 J3
Morehall Kent 27 M4
Moreleigh Devon 7 K8
Morenish P & K 140 F10
Moresby Parks Cumb 100 C2
Morestead Hants 22 F9
Moreton Dorset 12 D7
Moreton Essex 51 M9
Moreton Herefs 45 Q2
Moreton Oxon 35 J4
Moreton Staffs 70 D11
Moreton Staffs 71 L9
Moreton Wirral 81 K7
Moreton Corbet Shrops 69 Q10
Moreton Hall Suffk 64 B9
Moretonhampstead Devon 9 J7
Moreton-in-Marsh Gloucs 47 P8
Moreton Jeffries Herefs 46 B5
Moretonmill Shrops 69 Q10
Moreton Morrell Warwks 48 B3
Moreton on Lugg Herefs 45 Q5
Moreton Paddox Warwks 48 A4
Moreton Pinkney W Nthn 48 G5
Moreton Say Shrops 70 A8
Moreton Valence Gloucs 32 E3
Morfa Cerdgn 42 F4
Morfa Bychan Gwynd 67 J7
Morfa Dinlle Gwynd 66 G3
Morfa Glas Neath 29 N3
Morfa Nefyn Gwynd 66 D6
Morganstown Cardif 30 F8
Morgan's Vale Wilts 21 N10
Morham E Loth 128 F5
Moriah Cerdgn 54 E9
Morland W & F 102 B6
Morley Ches E 82 H8
Morley Derbys 72 B2
Morley Dur 103 M5
Morley Leeds 90 H5
Morley Green Ches E 82 H8
Morley St Botolph Norfk 64 F2
Mornick Cnwll 5 N7
Morningside C Edin 127 N3
Morningside N Lans 126 E6
Morningthorpe Norfk 65 J3
Morpeth Nthumb 113 J3
Morphie Abers 143 N5
Morrey Staffs 71 L11
Morridge Side Staffs 71 J4
Morriston Swans 29 J5
Morston Norfk 76 E3
Mortehoe Devon 16 H2
Morthen Rothm 84 G3
Mortimer W Berk 23 J2
Mortimer Common W Berk 35 J11
Mortimer's Cross Herefs 45 N2
Mortimer West End Hants 22 H2
Mortlake Gt Lon 36 F5
Morton Cumb 110 G10
Morton Derbys 84 F8
Morton IoW 14 H9
Morton Lincs 74 A6
Morton Lincs 85 P2
Morton Lincs 85 Q8
Morton Notts 85 M10
Morton Shrops 69 J10
Morton W & F 101 N3
Morton-on-Swale N York 97 M2
Morton on the Hill Norfk 76 G8
Morton Tinmouth Dur 103 N6
Morvah Cnwll 2 C6
Morval Cnwll 5 M10
Morvich Highld 146 B3
Morville Shrops 57 M6
Morville Heath Shrops 57 M6
Morwenstow Cnwll 16 C9
Mosborough Sheff 84 F4
Moscow E Ayrs 125 M9
Mose Shrops 57 P6
Mosedale W & F 101 L4
Moseley Birm 58 G8
Moseley Wolves 58 D5
Moseley Worcs 46 F3
Moses Gate Bolton 89 L9
Moss Ag & B 136 B7
Moss Donc 91 P8
Moss Wrexhm 69 K4
Mossat Abers 150 D4
Mossbank Shet 169 r6
Moss Bank St Hel 81 Q5

Mossbay Cumb 100 C5
Mossblown S Ayrs 114 H3
Mossbrow Traffd 82 F7
Mossburnford Border 118 C7
Mossdale D & G 108 G6
Mossdale E Ayrs 115 J7
Moss Edge Lancs 88 E2
Moss End Ches E 82 E9
Mossend N Lans 126 C5
Mosser Mains Cumb 100 F5
Mossley Ches E 70 F2
Mossley Tamesd 83 L4
Mosspaul Inn Border 117 M11
Moss Side Cumb 110 C10
Moss-side Highld 156 F6
Moss Side Lancs 88 D4
Moss Side Lancs 88 E3
Moss Side Sefton 81 M4
Mosstodloch Moray 157 Q6
Mossyard D & G 107 P7
Mossy Lea Lancs 88 G8
Mosterton Dorset 11 K3
Moston Manch 83 J4
Moston Shrops 69 Q9
Moston Green Ches E 70 C2
Mostyn Flints 80 H8
Motcombe Dorset 20 G8
Mothecombe Devon 6 G9
Motherby W & F 101 M5
Motherwell N Lans 126 C6
Motspur Park Gt Lon 36 F7
Mottingham Gt Lon 37 K6
Mottisfont Hants 22 B9
Mottisfont Hants 22 B9
Mottistone IoW 14 D10
Mottram in Longdendale Tamesd 83 L5
Mottram St Andrew Ches E 83 J9
Mouilpied Guern 10 b2
Mouldsworth Ches W 81 Q10
Moulin P & K 141 M6
Moulsecoomb Br & H 24 H9
Moulsford Oxon 34 G8
Moulsoe M Keyn 49 P6
Moultavie Highld 156 A3
Moulton Ches W 82 E11
Moulton Lincs 74 F6
Moulton N York 103 P10
Moulton Suffk 63 L8
Moulton V Glam 30 E11
Moulton W Nthn 60 G7
Moulton Chapel Lincs 74 E7
Moulton St Mary Norfk 77 M10
Moulton Seas End Lincs 74 F5
Mount Cnwll 4 B10
Mount Cnwll 5 J8
Mount Kirk 90 D7
Mountain C Brad 90 D4
Mountain Ash Rhondd 30 D5
Mountain Cross Border 127 M6
Mountain Street Kent 39 J11
Mount Ambrose Cnwll 3 J5
Mount Bures Essex 52 F5
Mountfield E Susx 26 B7
Mountgerald Highld 155 Q5
Mount Hawke Cnwll 3 J4
Mount Hermon Cnwll 2 H10
Mountjoy Cnwll 4 D9
Mount Lothian Mdloth 127 P6
Mountnessing Essex 51 P11
Mounton Mons 31 P6
Mount Pleasant Ches E 70 E3
Mount Pleasant Derbys 71 P11
Mount Pleasant Derbys 84 D11
Mount Pleasant Dur 103 Q4
Mount Pleasant E R Yk 93 N3
Mount Pleasant E Susx 25 K7
Mount Pleasant Norfk 64 D3
Mount Pleasant Suffk 63 M11
Mount Pleasant Sundld 113 M10
Mount Pleasant Worcs 47 K2
Mountsorrel Leics 72 F8
Mount Sorrel Wilts 21 K10
Mount Tabor Calder 90 D5
Mousehole Cnwll 2 C8
Mouswald D & G 109 N6
Mowbray W Susx 24 E4
Mow Cop Ches E 70 F3
Mowhaugh Border 118 F6
Mowmacre Hill C Leic 72 F9
Mowsley Leics 60 D3
Moy Highld 147 L11
Moy Highld 156 D11
Moyle Highld 145 Q4
Moylegrove Pembks 41 M2
Muasdale Ag & B 120 C3
Muchalls Abers 151 N9
Much Birch Herefs 45 Q8
Much Cowarne Herefs 46 B5
Much Dewchurch Herefs 45 P8
Muchelney Somset 19 M10
Muchelney Ham Somset 19 M10
Much Hadham Herts 51 K7
Much Hoole Lancs 88 F6
Much Hoole Town Lancs 88 F6
Muchlarnick Cnwll 5 L10
Much Marcle Herefs 46 C8
Much Wenlock Shrops 57 L5
Muck Highld 144 F12
Mucking Thurr 37 Q4
Muckleburgh Military Collection Norfk 76 G3
Muckleford Dorset 11 N6
Mucklestone Staffs 70 C7
Muckley Shrops 57 L5
Muckton Lincs 87 L4
Muddiford Devon 17 K4
Muddles Green E Susx 25 M8
Mudeford BCP 13 L6
Mudford Somset 19 Q11
Mudford Sock Somset 19 Q11
Mudgley Somset 19 N5
Mud Row Kent 38 H7
Mugdock Stirlg 125 P2
Mugeary Highld 152 G10
Mugginton Derbys 71 P6
Muggintonlane End Derbys 71 P6
Muggleswick Dur 112 F11
Muirden Abers 158 H7
Muirdrum Angus 143 K10
Muiresk Abers 158 G8
Muirhead Angus 142 E11
Muirhead Fife 134 H6
Muirhead N Lans 126 B4
Muirhouses Falk 134 C11
Muirkirk E Ayrs 115 N2
Muirmill Stirlg 133 L11

Muir of Fowlis Abers 150 F5
Muir of Miltonduff Moray 157 M6
Muir of Ord Highld 155 P7
Muirshearlich Highld 146 E11
Muirtack Abers 159 N10
Muirton P & K 133 Q5
Muirton Mains Highld 155 N7
Muirton of Ardblair P & K 142 B9
Muker N York 102 H11
Mulbarton Norfk 76 H11
Mulben Moray 157 R7
Mulfra Cnwll 2 D7
Mull Ag & B 137 Q9
Mullacott Cross Devon 17 J3
Mullardoch Highld 154 H11
Mullion Cnwll 2 H10
Mullion Cove Cnwll 2 H10
Mumby Lincs 87 P6
Munderfield Row Herefs 46 B4
Munderfield Stocks Herefs 46 C4
Mundesley Norfk 77 L4
Mundford Norfk 63 P2
Mundham Norfk 65 L2
Mundon Essex 52 E11
Mungrisdale W & F 101 L4
Munlochy Highld 156 A7
Munnoch N Ayrs 124 H8
Munsley Herefs 46 C6
Munslow Shrops 57 J7
Murchington Devon 8 G7
Murcot Worcs 47 L6
Murcott Oxon 48 G11
Murcott Wilts 33 J6
Murkle Highld 167 L3
Murlaggan Highld 146 C9
Murrell Green Hants 23 K3
Murroes Angus 142 H10
Murrow Cambs 74 G9
Mursley Bucks 49 M9
Murston Kent 38 F9
Murthill Angus 142 H6
Murthly P & K 141 R10
Murton C York 98 C10
Murton Dur 113 N11
Murton N Tyne 113 M6
Murton Nthumb 129 P10
Murton Swans 28 G7
Murton W & F 102 D6
Musbury Devon 10 F6
Muscoates N York 98 D5
Musselburgh E Loth 127 Q3
Muston Leics 73 L3
Muston N York 99 M5
Mustow Green Worcs 58 C10
Mutehill D & G 108 E11
Mutford Suffk 65 P4
Muthill P & K 133 P4
Mutterton Devon 9 P3
Muxton Wrekin 57 N2
Mybster Highld 167 L6
Myddfai Carmth 43 Q8
Myddle Shrops 69 N10
Mydroilyn Cerdgn 43 J3
Myerscough Lancs 88 F3
Myland Suffk 52 G6
Mylor Cnwll 3 L6
Mylor Bridge Cnwll 3 L6
Mynachlog ddu Pembks 41 M4
Myndd-Ilan Flints 80 H10
Myndtown Shrops 56 F7
Mynydd Bach Cerdgn 54 G9
Mynydd-Bach Mons 31 N6
Mynydd-Bach Swans 29 J5
Mynyddgarreg Carmth 28 D3
Mynydd Isa Flints 69 J2
Mynydd Llandygai Gwynd 79 L11
Mynydd Mechell IoA 78 F6
Mynytho Gwynd 66 E8
Myrebird Abers 151 J8
Myredykes Border 118 A11
Mytchett Surrey 23 N3
Mytholm Calder 90 B5
Mytholmroyd Calder 90 C5
Mython Lancs 88 D4
Myton-on-Swale N York 97 P7

N

Naast Highld 160 C10
Nab's Head Lancs 89 J5
Na Buirgh W Isls 168 f8
Naburn C York 98 B11
Naccolt Kent 27 J3
Nackington Kent 39 L11
Nacton Suffk 53 M3
Nafferton E R Yk 99 M9
Nag's Head Gloucs 32 G5
Nailbridge Gloucs 46 B11
Nailsbourne Somset 18 H9
Nailsea N Som 31 N10
Nailstone Leics 72 C9
Nailsworth Gloucs 32 G5
Nairn Highld 156 F6
Nalderswood Surrey 36 F11
Nancegollan Cnwll 2 G7
Nancledra Cnwll 2 D6
Nanhoron Gwynd 66 D8
Nannerch Flints 80 H11
Nanpantan Leics 72 E7
Nanpean Cnwll 4 F10
Nanquidno Cnwll 2 B8
Nanstallon Cnwll 4 G8
Nant-ddu Powys 30 D2
Nanternis Cerdgn 42 G3
Nantgaredig Carmth 43 J10
Nantgarw Rhondd 30 F7
Nant-glas Powys 55 M11
Nantglyn Denbgs 68 D2
Nantgwyn Powys 55 M9
Nant Gwynant Gwynd 67 L4
Nantlle Gwynd 67 J3
Nantlle Valley Slate Landscape Gwynd 67 J4
Nantmawr Shrops 69 J10
Nantmel Powys 55 N11
Nantmor Gwynd 67 L3
Nant Peris Gwynd 67 L3
Nantwich Ches E 70 B4
Nant-y-Bwch Blae G 30 G4
Nantycaws Carmth 43 J11
Nant-y-derry Mons 31 L4
Nant-y-ffin Carmth 43 L8

Nantyffyllon Brdgnd 29 N6
Nantyglo Blae G 30 G2
Nant-y-gollen Shrops 68 H9
Nant-y-moel Brdgnd 29 P6
Nant-y-pandy Conwy 79 M10
Naphill Bucks 35 M5
Napleton Worcs 46 G5
Nappa N York 96 C10
Napsbury Park Herts 50 E10
Napton on the Hill Warwks 48 E2
Narberth Pembks 41 M8
Narborough Leics 72 E11
Narborough Norfk 75 P8
Narkurs Cnwll 5 N10
Nasareth Gwynd 66 H5
Naseby W Nthn 60 E5
Nash Bucks 49 L8
Nash Gt Lon 37 K8
Nash Herefs 45 L2
Nash Newpt 31 K8
Nash Shrops 57 L10
Nash End Worcs 57 P8
Nashes Green Hants 23 J4
Nash Lee Bucks 35 M3
Nash Street Kent 37 P7
Nassington N Nthn 73 R11
Nastend Gloucs 32 E3
Nasty Herts 51 J6
Nateby Lancs 88 F2
Nateby W & F 102 E9
National Memorial Arboretum Staffs 59 J2
National Space Centre C Leic 72 F9
Natland W & F 95 L3
Naughton Suffk 52 H2
Naunton Gloucs 47 M10
Naunton Worcs 46 G7
Naunton Beauchamp Worcs 47 J4
Navenby Lincs 86 C9
Navestock Essex 51 M11
Navestock Side Essex 51 N11
Navidale Highld 163 N3
Navity Highld 156 D5
Nawton N York 98 D4
Nayland Suffk 52 G5
Nazeing Essex 51 K9
Nazeing Gate Essex 51 K9
Neacroft Hants 13 L5
Neal's Green Warwks 59 M8
Neap Shet 169 s8
Near Cotton Staffs 71 K5
Near Sawrey W & F 101 L11
Neasden Gt Lon 36 F3
Neasham Darltn 104 B8
Neat Enstone Oxon 48 C10
Neath Neath 29 L5
Neatham Hants 23 K6
Neatishead Norfk 77 L7
Nebo Cerdgn 54 C9
Nebo Conwy 67 Q3
Nebo Gwynd 66 H4
Nebo IoA 78 H6
Necton Norfk 76 B10
Nedd Highld 164 D10
Nedderton Nthumb 113 K4
Nedging Suffk 52 G2
Nedging Tye Suffk 52 H2
Needham Norfk 65 J5
Needham Market Suffk 64 F10
Needham Street Suffk 63 M9
Needingworth Cambs 62 D6
Neen Savage Shrops 57 M9
Neen Sollars Shrops 57 M10
Neenton Shrops 57 L7
Nefyn Gwynd 66 E6
Neilston E Rens 125 N5
Nelson Caerph 30 F5
Nelson Lancs 89 P3
Nemphlar S Lans 126 B2
Nempnett Thrubwell BaNES 19 Q3
Nenthall W & F 111 Q11
Nenthead W & F 102 E2
Nenthorn Border 118 C3
Neopardy Devon 9 J5
Nep Town W Susx 24 F7
Nerabus Ag & B 122 B8
Nercwys Flints 68 H2
Nerston S Lans 125 Q5
Nesbit Nthumb 119 J4
Nesfield N York 96 G11
Ness Ches W 81 L9
Nesscliffe Shrops 69 L11
Neston Ches W 81 K9
Neston Wilts 32 G11
Netchwood Shrops 57 L6
Nether Abington S Lans 116 C6
Nether Alderley Ches E 82 H9
Netheravon Wilts 21 M5
Nether Blainslie Border 117 Q2
Netherbrae Abers 159 J6
Nether Broughton Leics 72 H5
Netherburn S Lans 126 D8
Netherbury Dorset 11 K5
Netherby Cumb 110 G6
Netherby N York 97 M11
Nether Cerne Dorset 11 P5
Nethercleuch D & G 109 Q11
Nether Compton Dorset 19 Q11
Nethercote Warwks 60 B7
Nethercott Staffs 59 P2
Nethercott Devon 16 H4
Nether Crimond Abers 151 L3
Nether Dallachy Moray 157 R5
Netherend Gloucs 31 Q4
Nether Exe Devon 9 M4
Netherfield E Susx 26 B8
Netherfield Leics 72 F7
Netherfield Notts 72 G2
Nether Fingland S Lans 116 C8
Nethergate N Linc 92 C11
Nethergate Norfk 76 F6
Netherhampton Wilts 21 M8
Nether Handley Derbys 84 F5
Nether Handwick Angus 142 F11
Nether Haugh Rothm 91 L11
Netherhay Dorset 11 J3
Nether Headon Notts 85 M6
Nether Heage Derbys 84 E10
Nether Heyford W Nthn 60 E9
Nether Kellet Lancs 95 L8
Nether Kinmundy Abers 159 Q9
Netherland Green Staffs 71 L7
Nether Langwith Notts 84 H6
Netherley Abers 151 L8
Netherley Lpool 81 N7

Nethermill D & G 109 M3
Nethermuir Abers 159 M9
Netherne-on-the-Hill
  Surrey 36 G9
Netheroyd Hill Kirk 90 E7
Nether Padley Derbys 84 B5
Nether Poppleton C York 98 B10
Netherseal Derbys 59 L2
Nether Silton N York 97 Q2
Nether Skyborry Shrops 56 D10
Nether Stowey Somset 18 G7
Nether Street Essex 51 N8
Netherstreet Wilts 21 J2
Netherthird E Ayrs 115 L4
Netherthong Kirk 90 E9
Netherthorpe Derbys 84 F6
Netherton Angus 143 J6
Netherton Devon 7 M4
Netherton Dudley 58 D7
Netherton Hants 22 C3
Netherton Herefs 45 Q9
Netherton Kirk 90 E8
Netherton N Lans 126 D7
Netherton Nthumb 119 J9
Netherton Oxon 34 D5
Netherton P & K 142 A7
Netherton Sefton 81 M5
Netherton Shrops 57 N8
Netherton Stirlg 125 P2
Netherton Wakefd 90 H7
Netherton Worcs 47 J6
Nethertown Cumb 100 C9
Nethertown Highld 167 Q1
Nethertown Lancs 89 L3
Nethertown Staffs 71 L11
Netherurd Border 116 G2
Nether Wallop Hants 22 B7
Nether Wasdale Cumb 100 F10
Nether Welton Cumb 110 G11
Nether Westcote Gloucs 47 P10
Nether Whitacre Warwks 59 K6
Nether Whitecleuch S Lans 116 A7
Nether Winchendon Bucks 35 K2
Netherwitton Nthumb 112 G2
Nethy Bridge Highld 149 J3
Netley Hants 14 E5
Netley Marsh Hants 13 P2
Nettlebed Oxon 35 J7
Nettlebridge Somset 20 B5
Nettlecombe Dorset 11 L5
Nettlecombe IoW 14 F11
Nettleden Herts 50 B8
Nettleham Lincs 86 D5
Nettlestead Kent 37 Q10
Nettlestead Green Kent 37 Q10
Nettlestone IoW 14 H8
Nettlesworth Dur 113 L11
Nettleton Lincs 93 K10
Nettleton Wilts 32 F9
Nettleton Shrub Wilts 32 F9
Netton Devon 6 F9
Netton Wilts 21 M7
Neuadd Carmth 43 P10
Neuadd-ddu Powys 55 L9
Nevendon Essex 38 C3
Nevern Pembks 41 L2
Nevill Holt Leics 60 H2
New Abbey D & G 109 L7
New Aberdour Abers 159 L5
New Addington Gt Lon 37 J8
Newall Leeds 97 J11
New Alresford Hants 22 G8
New Alyth P & K 142 C8
Newark C Pete 74 D10
Newark Ork 169 g2
Newark-on-Trent Notts 85 N10
New Arley Warwks 59 L7
New Arram E R Yk 92 H2
Newarthill N Lans 126 D6
New Ash Green Kent 37 P7
New Balderton Notts 85 P10
Newbarn Kent 27 L3
New Barn Kent 37 P7
New Barnet Gt Lon 50 G11
New Barnetby N Linc 93 J8
New Barton N Nthn 61 J8
Newbattle Mdloth 127 Q4
New Bewick Nthumb 119 L6
Newbie D & G 110 C7
Newbiggin Cumb 94 B2
Newbiggin Dur 102 H5
Newbiggin Dur 112 H11
Newbiggin N York 96 E2
Newbiggin N York 96 F3
Newbiggin W & F 94 F7
Newbiggin W & F 101 N5
Newbiggin W & F 102 B5
Newbiggin W & F 111 L11
Newbiggin-by-the-Sea
  Nthumb 113 M3
Newbigging Angus 142 D9
Newbigging Angus 142 G10
Newbigging Angus 142 H10
Newbigging S Lans 127 J8
Newbiggin-on-Lune W & F 102 D10
New Bilton Warwks 59 Q9
Newbold Derbys 84 E6
Newbold Leics 72 C7
Newbold on Avon Warwks 59 Q9
Newbold on Stour Warwks 47 P5
Newbold Pacey Warwks 47 Q3
Newbold Revel Warwks 59 Q8
Newbold Verdon Leics 72 C10
New Bolingbroke Lincs 87 K9
Newborough C Pete 74 D9
Newborough IoA 78 G11
Newborough Staffs 71 L9
Newbottle Sundld 113 M10
Newbottle W Nthn 48 F7
New Boultham Lincs 86 C6
Newbourne Suffk 53 N3
New Bradwell M Keyn 49 M6
New Brampton Derbys 84 E6
New Brancepeth Dur 103 P2
Newbridge C Edin 127 L3
Newbridge Caerph 30 H5
Newbridge Cerdgn 43 K3
Newbridge Cnwll 2 C7
Newbridge Cnwll 3 K5
Newbridge D & G 109 L5
Newbridge Hants 21 Q11
Newbridge IoW 14 D9
New Bridge N York 98 G3
Newbridge Oxon 34 D4
Newbridge Wrexhm 69 J6

Newbridge Green Worcs 46 F7
Newbridge-on-Usk Mons 31 L6
Newbridge-on-Wye Powys 44 E3
New Brighton Flints 81 K11
New Brighton Wirral 81 L6
New Brinsley Notts 84 G10
Newbrough Nthumb 112 C7
New Broughton Wrexhm 69 K4
New Buckenham Norfk 64 F3
Newbuildings Devon 9 J4
Newburgh Abers 151 P2
Newburgh Abers 159 N6
Newburgh Fife 134 G4
Newburgh Lancs 88 F8
Newburn N u Ty 113 J7
New Bury Bolton 82 F4
Newbury Somset 20 C5
Newbury W Berk 34 E11
Newbury Wilts 20 F6
Newbury Park Gt Lon 37 K3
Newby Lancs 96 B11
Newby N York 95 Q7
Newby N York 99 L3
Newby N York 104 F8
Newby W & F 101 Q6
Newby Bridge W & F 94 H3
Newby Cross Cumb 110 G10
Newby East Cumb 111 J9
Newby Head W & F 101 Q6
Newby West Cumb 110 G10
Newby Wiske N York 97 N3
Newcastle Mons 45 N11
Newcastle Shrops 56 D8
Newcastle Emlyn Carmth 42 F6
Newcastle Great Park
  N u Ty 113 K6
Newcastleton Border 111 J3
Newcastle-under-Lyme
  Staffs 70 E5
Newcastle upon Tyne N u Ty 113 K8
Newchapel Pembks 41 P3
Newchapel Staffs 70 F4
Newchapel Surrey 25 J2
Newchurch Blae G 30 G2
Newchurch Herefs 45 M4
Newchurch IoW 14 G9
Newchurch Kent 27 J5
Newchurch Mons 31 N5
Newchurch Powys 45 J4
Newchurch Staffs 71 L10
Newchurch in Pendle Lancs 89 N3
New Costessey Norfk 76 H9
New Cowper Cumb 109 P11
Newcraighall C Edin 127 Q3
New Crofton Wakefd 91 K7
New Cross Cerdgn 54 E9
New Cross Gt Lon 37 J5
New Cross Somset 19 M11
New Cumnock E Ayrs 115 M5
New Cut E Susx 26 D8
New Deer Abers 159 L8
New Delaval Nthumb 113 L5
New Delph Oldham 90 B9
New Denham Bucks 36 B4
Newdigate Surrey 24 E2
New Duston N Nthn 60 F8
New Earswick C York 98 C9
New Eastwood Notts 84 G11
New Edlington Donc 91 N11
New Ellerby E R Yk 93 L3
Newell Green Br For 35 N10
New Eltham Gt Lon 37 K6
New End Worcs 47 L2
Newenden Kent 26 D6
New England C Pete 74 C10
New England Essex 52 B3
Newent Gloucs 46 D9
New Farnley Leeds 90 H4
New Ferry Wirral 81 L7
Newfield Dur 103 P4
Newfield Dur 113 K10
Newfield Highld 156 D2
New Fletton C Pete 74 C11
New Forest National Park 13 N3
Newfound Hants 22 G4
New Fryston Wakefd 91 M5
Newgale Pembks 40 G6
New Galloway D & G 108 D5
Newgate Norfk 76 E3
Newgate Street Herts 50 H9
New Gilston Fife 135 L6
New Grimsby IoS 2 b1
Newhall Ches E 69 R5
Newhall Derbys 71 P10
Newham Nthumb 119 N5
New Hartley Nthumb 113 M5
Newhaven C Edin 127 P2
Newhaven Derbys 71 M2
Newhaven E Susx 25 K10
New Haw Surrey 36 C8
New Hedges Pembks 41 M10
New Herrington Sundld 113 M10
Newhey Rochdl 89 Q8
New Holkham Norfk 76 B4
New Holland N Linc 93 J6
Newholm N York 105 N8
New Houghton Derbys 84 G7
New Houghton Norfk 75 Q5
Newhouse N Lans 126 D5
New Houses N York 96 B6
New Hutton W & F 95 M2
New Hythe Kent 38 B10
Newick E Susx 25 K6
Newingreen Kent 27 L4
Newington Kent 27 L4
Newington Kent 38 E9
Newington Oxon 34 H5
Newington Shrops 56 G8
Newington Bagpath Gloucs 32 F6
New Inn Carmth 43 J7
New Inn Pembks 41 L4
New Inn Torfn 31 K5
New Invention Shrops 56 D9
New Lanark S Lans 116 B2
New Lanark Village S Lans 116 B2
Newland C KuH 93 J4
Newland E R Yk 92 D5
Newland Gloucs 31 Q3
Newland N York 92 A6
Newland Oxon 34 C3
Newland Somset 17 Q4
Newland W & F 94 G5
Newland Worcs 46 E5

Newlandrig Mdloth 128 B7
Newlands Border 111 K2
Newlands Nthumb 112 G9
Newlands W & F 101 K3
Newlands of Dundurcas
  Moray 157 P7
New Lane Lancs 88 E8
New Lane End Warrtn 82 D6
New Langholm D & G 110 G2
New Leake Lincs 87 M9
New Leeds Abers 159 N7
New Lodge Barns 91 K9
New Longton Lancs 88 G5
New Luce D & G 106 G5
Newlyn Cnwll 2 D8
Newmachar Abers 151 M4
Newmains N Lans 126 E6
New Malden Gt Lon 36 F7
Newman's End Essex 51 M8
Newman's Green Suffk 52 E3
Newmarket Suffk 63 K8
Newmarket W Isls 168 j4
New Marske R & Cl 104 H6
New Marston Oxon 34 F3
New Marton Shrops 69 K8
New Mill Abers 151 K11
New Mill Border 117 P8
New Mill Cnwll 2 D7
New Mill Herts 35 P2
New Mill Kirk 90 F9
New Mill Moray 158 B7
Newmillerdam Wakefd 91 J7
New Mill of Inshewan Angus 142 G5
Newmills C Edin 127 M4
New Mills Cnwll 3 M3
New Mills Derbys 83 M7
Newmills Fife 134 C10
Newmills Mons 31 P3
New Mills Powys 55 P4
Newmills P & K 142 A11
Newmiln E Ayrs 125 N10
New Milton Hants 13 M5
New Mistley Essex 53 K5
New Moat Pembks 41 L5
Newnes Shrops 69 L8
Newney Green Essex 51 Q9
Newnham Hants 23 K4
Newnham Herts 50 F3
Newnham Kent 38 G10
Newnham W Nthn 60 C9
Newnham Bridge Worcs 57 L11
Newnham on Severn Gloucs 32 C2
New Ollerton Notts 85 L7
New Oscott Birm 58 G6
New Passage S Glos 31 P7
New Pitsligo Abers 159 L6
New Polzeath Cnwll 4 E7
Newport Cnwll 5 N4
Newport Dorset 12 E5
Newport E R Yk 92 E4
Newport Essex 51 M4
Newport Gloucs 32 D5
Newport Highld 163 Q2
Newport IoW 14 F9
Newport Newpt 31 K7
Newport Norfk 77 Q8
Newport Pembks 41 L3
Newport Wrekin 70 C11
Newport-on-Tay Fife 135 L2
Newport Pagnell M Keyn 49 N6
Newport Pagnell Services
  M Keyn 49 N6
Newpound Common W Susx 24 C5
New Prestwick S Ayrs 114 F3
New Quay Cerdgn 42 G3
Newquay Cnwll 4 C9
New Quay Cnwll 52 H7
Newquay Zoo Cnwll 4 C9
New Rackheath Norfk 77 K9
New Radnor Powys 45 J2
New Rent W & F 101 N3
New Ridley Nthumb 112 G9
New Road Side N York 90 B2
New Romney Kent 27 J7
New Rossington Donc 91 Q11
New Row Cerdgn 54 G10
New Row Lancs 89 J3
New Sauchie Clacks 133 P9
Newsbank Ches E 82 H11
Newseat Abers 158 H11
Newsham Lancs 88 G3
Newsham N York 97 N4
Newsham N York 103 M8
Newsham Nthumb 113 M5
New Sharlston Wakefd 91 K7
Newsholme E R Yk 92 B5
Newsholme Lancs 96 B10
New Shoreston Nthumb 119 N4
New Silksworth Sundld 113 N10
New Skelton R & Cl 105 J7
Newsome Kirk 90 F8
New Somerby Lincs 73 N3
New Springs Wigan 88 H9
Newstead Border 117 R4
Newstead Notts 84 H10
Newstead Nthumb 119 N5
New Stevenston N Lans 126 D6
New Street Herefs 45 L3
New Swanage Dorset 12 H8
New Swannington Leics 72 C7
Newthorpe N York 91 M4
Newthorpe Notts 84 G11
New Thundersley Essex 38 C4
Newtimber W Susx 24 G8
Newtoft Lincs 86 D3
Newton Ag & B 131 L8
Newton Border 118 B6
Newton Brdgnd 29 M9
Newton C Beds 50 F2
Newton Cambs 62 F11
Newton Cambs 74 H8
Newton Cardif 30 H9
Newton Ches W 69 P3
Newton Ches W 81 N11
Newton Ches W 82 B9
Newton Derbys 84 F9
Newton Herefs 45 L8
Newton Herefs 45 Q4
Newton Herefs 56 F11
Newton Highld 156 C8
Newton Highld 156 D4
Newton Highld 156 D5
Newton Highld 167 P7
Newton Lancs 88 G3
Newton Lancs 95 M6
Newton Lincs 73 Q3

Newton Moray 157 M5
Newton Moray 157 Q5
Newton N Nthn 61 J4
Newton N York 98 H6
Newton Norfk 76 A8
Newton Notts 72 H2
Newton Nthumb 112 F8
Newton Nthumb 118 H9
Newton S Lans 116 C4
Newton S Lans 126 B5
Newton Sandw 58 F6
Newton Shrops 69 M8
Newton Somset 18 F7
Newton Staffs 71 J9
Newton Suffk 52 F3
Newton W & F 94 E6
Newton W Loth 127 K2
Newton Warwks 60 B5
Newton Wilts 21 P10
Newton Abbot Devon 7 M4
Newton Arlosh Cumb 110 D9
Newton Aycliffe Dur 103 Q6
Newton Bewley Hartpl 104 E5
Newton Blossomville
  M Keyn 49 P4
Newton Bromswold N Nthn 61 L7
Newton Burgoland Leics 72 B9
Newton by Toft Lincs 86 D3
Newton Ferrers Devon 6 F9
Newton Ferry W Isls 168 d10
Newton Flotman Norfk 65 J2
Newtongrange Mdloth 127 Q5
Newton Green Mons 31 P6
Newton Harcourt Leics 72 G11
Newton Heath Manch 83 J4
Newtonhill Abers 151 N9
Newton Hill Wakefd 91 J4
Newton-in-Bowland Lancs 95 P10
Newton Kyme N York 91 M2
Newton-le-Willows N York 97 K3
Newton-le-Willows St Hel 82 C5
Newtonloan Mdloth 127 Q5
Newton Longville Bucks 49 M8
Newton Mearns E Rens 125 N6
Newtonmill Angus 143 L5
Newtonmore Highld 148 C8
Newton Morrell N York 103 P9
Newton Mountain Pembks 41 J9
Newton Mulgrave N York 105 L7
Newton of Balcanquhal
  P & K 134 F5
Newton of Balcormo Fife 135 N7
Newton of Belltrees Rens 125 K6
Newton-on-Ayr S Ayrs 114 F3
Newton-on-Ouse N York 97 R9
Newton-on-Rawcliffe
  N York 98 G2
Newton on the Hill Shrops 69 N10
Newton-on-the-Moor
  Nthumb 119 N9
Newton on Trent Lincs 85 P6
Newton Poppleford Devon 10 B7
Newton Purcell Oxon 48 H8
Newton Regis Warwks 59 L3
Newton Reigny W & F 101 N4
Newton St Cyres Devon 9 L5
Newton St Faith Norfk 77 J8
Newton St Loe BaNES 20 D2
Newton St Petrock Devon 16 G9
Newton Solney Derbys 71 P9
Newton Stacey Hants 22 D6
Newton Stewart D & G 107 M4
Newton Tony Wilts 21 P6
Newton Tracey Devon 17 J6
Newton under Roseberry
  R & Cl 104 G8
Newton Underwood Nthumb 112 H3
Newton upon Derwent
  E R Yk 98 E11
Newton Valence Hants 23 K8
Newton Village Mdloth 127 Q4
Newton Wamphray D & G 109 P2
Newton with Scales Lancs 88 F4
Newtown BCP 12 H6
Newtown Blae G 30 G3
Newtown Ches W 82 B9
Newtown Cnwll 2 F8
Newtown Cnwll 5 M6
Newtown Cumb 109 P11
Newtown Cumb 110 G8
Newtown Cumb 111 K8
Newtown D & G 115 Q5
Newtown Derbys 83 L8
Newtown Devon 9 Q5
Newtown Devon 17 P6
Newtown Dorset 11 K4
Newtown Dorset 12 G3
Newtown Dorset 21 J11
Newtown E Susx 25 L6
Newtown Gloucs 32 C4
Newtown Hants 13 N2
Newtown Hants 14 H4
Newtown Hants 22 E2
Newtown Herefs 45 P3
Newtown Herefs 45 Q8
Newtown Herefs 46 B5
Newtown Highld 147 K7
Newtown IoW 14 D8
Newtown Nthumb 119 J4
Newtown Nthumb 119 K10
Newtown Nthumb 119 K5
Newtown Powys 55 Q5
Newtown Rhondd 30 E5
Newtown Shrops 69 M10
Newtown Shrops 69 N8
Newtown Somset 10 F2
Newtown Staffs 58 G2
Newtown Staffs 70 G2
Newtown W & F 101 P6
Newtown Wigan 82 C4
Newtown Wilts 20 H9
Newtown Wilts 21 Q2
Newtown Worcs 46 G3
Newtown Worcs 58 D9
Newtown-in-St Martin
  Cnwll 3 J9
Newtown Linford Leics 72 E9
Newtown St Boswells
  Border 117 R4
Newtown Unthank Leics 72 D10
New Tredegar Caerph 30 F4
New Trows S Lans 126 E10
Newtyle Angus 142 D9
New Walsoken Cambs 75 J9

New Waltham NE Lin 93 N10
New Whittington Derbys 84 E5
New Winton E Loth 128 C5
New Yatt Oxon 34 C2
Newyears Green Gt Lon 36 C3
Newyork Ag & B 131 K5
New York Lincs 86 H9
New York N Tyne 113 M6
New York N York 97 J8
New Zealand Wilts 33 K9
Nextend Herefs 45 L3
Neyland Pembks 41 J9
Niarbyl IoM 80 b6
Nibley Gloucs 32 C3
Nibley S Glos 32 C8
Nibley Green Gloucs 32 D5
Nicholashayne Devon 18 F11
Nicholaston Swans 28 F7
Nickies Hill Cumb 111 K7
Nidd N York 97 M8
Nigg C Aber 151 N7
Nigg Highld 156 E3
Nigg Ferry Highld 156 D4
Nimlet BaNES 32 D10
Ninebanks Nthumb 111 Q10
Nine Elms Swindn 33 M7
Nine Wells Pembks 40 E6
Ninfield E Susx 26 B9
Ningwood IoW 14 C9
Nisbet Border 118 C5
Nisbet Hill Border 129 K9
Niton IoW 14 F11
Nitshill C Glas 125 N5
Noah's Ark Kent 37 N9
Noak Bridge Essex 37 Q2
Noak Hill Gt Lon 37 M2
Nobletthorpe Barns 90 H9
Nobold Shrops 56 H2
Nobottle W Nthn 60 E8
Nocton Lincs 86 E8
Nogdam End Norfk 77 M11
Noke Oxon 34 F2
Nolton Pembks 40 G7
Nolton Haven Pembks 40 G7
No Man's Heath Ches W 69 P5
No Man's Heath Warwks 59 L3
No Man's Land Cnwll 5 M10
Nomansland Devon 9 K2
Nomansland Wilts 21 Q11
Noneley Shrops 69 N9
Nonington Kent 39 N11
Nook Cumb 111 J5
Nook W & F 95 L4
Norbiton Gt Lon 36 E7
Norbreck Bpool 88 C2
Norbridge Herefs 46 D6
Norbury Ches E 69 Q5
Norbury Derbys 71 L6
Norbury Gt Lon 36 H7
Norbury Shrops 56 F6
Norbury Staffs 70 D10
Norbury Common Ches E 69 Q5
Norbury Junction Staffs 70 D10
Norchard Worcs 58 B11
Norcott Brook Ches W 82 D8
Norcross Lancs 88 C2
Nordelph Norfk 75 L10
Norden Rochdl 89 P8
Nordley Shrops 57 M5
Norfolk Broads Norfk 77 P10
Norham Nthumb 129 N10
Norland Calder 90 D6
Norley Ches W 82 C10
Norleywood Hants 14 C7
Norlington E Susx 25 K8
Normanby Lincs 86 C3
Normanby N Linc 92 E7
Normanby N York 98 E4
Normanby R & Cl 104 F7
Normanby le Wold Lincs 93 K11
Norman Cross Cambs 61 Q2
Normandy Surrey 23 P4
Normans Bay E Susx 25 Q9
Norman's Green Devon 9 Q4
Normanton C Derb 72 A4
Normanton Leics 73 L2
Normanton Notts 85 M10
Normanton Rutlnd 73 N9
Normanton Wakefd 91 K6
Normanton Wilts 21 M6
Normanton le Heath Leics 72 B8
Normanton on Cliffe Lincs 86 B11
Normanton on Soar Notts 72 E6
Normanton on the Wolds
  Notts 72 G4
Normanton on Trent Notts 85 N7
Normoss Lancs 88 C3
Norney Surrey 23 P6
Norrington Common Wilts 20 G2
Norris Green Cnwll 5 Q8
Norris Green Lpool 81 M6
Norris Hill Leics 72 A7
Norristhorpe Kirk 90 G6
Northacre Norfk 64 D2
Northall Bucks 49 Q10
Northallerton N York 97 N2
Northall Green Norfk 76 D9
Northam C Sotn 14 D4
Northam Devon 16 H6
Northampton W Nthn 60 G8
Northampton Worcs 58 B11
Northampton Services
  W Nthn 60 F9
North Anston Rothm 84 H4
North Ascot Br For 35 P11
North Aston Oxon 48 E9
Northaw Herts 50 G10
Northay Somset 10 F2
North Baddesley Hants 22 C10
North Ballachulish Highld 139 K5
North Barrow Somset 20 B9
North Barsham Norfk 76 C4
Northbay W Isls 168 c17
North Benfleet Essex 38 C4
North Berwick E Loth 128 E3
North Bitchburn Dur 103 N4
North Blyth Nthumb 113 M4
North Boarhunt Hants 14 H4
North Bockhampton BCP 13 L5
Northborough C Pete 74 C9
Northbourne Kent 39 P11
North Bovey Devon 8 H8
North Bradley Wilts 20 G3
North Brentor Devon 8 C8
North Brewham Somset 20 D7
North Bridge Surrey 23 Q7

286 Northbridge Street – Orleton

Northbridge Street E Susx 26 B7
Northbrook Hants 22 F7
Northbrook Oxon 48 E10
North Brook End Cambs 50 G2
North Buckland Angus 16 H3
North Burlingham Norfk 77 M10
North Cadbury Somset 20 B9
North Carlton Lincs 86 B5
North Carlton Notts 85 J4
North Cave E R Yk 92 E4
North Cerney Gloucs 33 K3
North Chailey E Susx 25 J6
Northchapel W Susx 23 Q9
North Charford Hants 21 N11
North Charlton Nthumb 119 N6
North Cheam Gt Lon 36 F7
North Cheriton Somset 20 C9
North Chideock Dorset 11 J6
Northchurch Herts 35 Q3
North Cliffe E R Yk 92 E3
North Clifton Notts 85 P6
North Close Dur 103 Q4
North Cockerington Lincs 87 L2
North Connel Ag & B 138 G11
North Cornelly Brdgnd 29 M8
North Corner Cnwll 3 K10
North Cotes Lincs 93 P10
Northcott Devon 5 N3
Northcott Devon 10 B2
Northcott Devon 10 C3
North Country Cnwll 2 H5
Northcourt Oxon 34 E5
North Cove Suffk 65 P4
North Cowton N York 103 Q10
North Crawley M Keyn 49 P6
North Cray Gt Lon 37 L6
North Creake Norfk 76 B4
North Curry Somset 19 K9
North Dalton E R Yk 99 J10
North Deighton N York 97 N10
Northdown Kent 39 Q7
North Downs 38 F10
North Duffield N York 92 A3
Northedge Derbys 84 E7
North Elham Kent 27 L3
North Elkington Lincs 87 J2
North Elmham Norfk 76 D7
North Elmsall Wakefd 91 M8
Northend Bucks 35 K6
North End C Port 15 J6
North End Cumb 110 F9
North End Dorset 20 F9
North End E R Yk 93 L2
North End E R Yk 93 N4
North End Essex 51 Q7
North End Hants 21 M11
North End Hants 22 G9
North End Leics 72 F7
North End Lincs 74 D2
North End Lincs 87 M3
North End Lincs 92 H11
North End Lincs 93 P10
North End N Linc 93 K6
North End N Nthn 61 L7
North End N Som 31 M11
North End Norfk 64 D3
North End Nthumb 119 M10
North End Sefton 81 L4
North End W Susx 15 Q6
North End W Susx 24 D9
Northend Warwks 48 C4
Northenden Manch 82 H7
Northend Woods Bucks 35 P7
North Erradale Highld 160 A10
North Evington C Leic 72 G10
North Fambridge Essex 38 E2
North Featherstone Wakefd 91 L6
North Ferriby E R Yk 92 G5
Northfield Birm 58 F9
Northfield C Aber 151 N6
Northfield E R Yk 92 H5
Northfields Lincs 73 Q9
Northfleet Kent 37 P6
North Frodingham E R Yk 99 N10
Northgate Lincs 74 C5
North Gorley Hants 13 L2
North Green Norfk 65 J4
North Green Suffk 65 L9
North Green Suffk 65 M8
North Greetwell Lincs 86 D6
North Grimston N York 98 G7
North Halling Medway 38 B8
North Hayling Hants 15 K6
North Hazelrigg Nthumb 119 L4
North Heasley Devon 17 N5
North Heath W Susx 24 C6
North Hele Devon 18 D10
North Hill Cnwll 5 M6
North Hillingdon Gt Lon 36 C4
North Hinksey Village Oxon 34 E3
North Holmwood Surrey 36 E11
North Huish Devon 7 J7
North Hykeham Lincs 86 B7
Northiam E Susx 26 D7
Northill C Beds 61 P11
Northington Gloucs 32 D3
Northington Hants 22 G7
North Kelsey Lincs 92 H10
North Kessock Highld 156 B8
North Killingholme N Linc 93 K7
North Kilvington N York 97 P3
North Kilworth Leics 60 D4
North Kingston Hants 13 L4
North Kyme Lincs 86 G10
North Lancing W Susx 24 E9
North Landing E R Yk 99 Q6
Northlands Lincs 87 K10
Northleach Gloucs 33 M2
North Lee Bucks 35 M3
North Lees N York 97 L6
Northleigh Devon 10 D5
Northleigh Devon 17 L5
North Leigh Kent 27 K2
North Leigh Oxon 34 C2
North Leverton with Habblesthorpe Notts 85 N4
Northlew Devon 8 D5
North Littleton Worcs 47 L5
Northload Bridge Somset 19 N7
North Lopham Norfk 64 E5
North Luffenham Rutlnd 73 N10
North Marden W Susx 23 M11
North Marston Bucks 49 L10
North Middleton Mdloth 128 B8
North Middleton Nthumb 119 J6
North Millbrex Abers 159 K9
North Milmain D & G 106 E7
North Molton Devon 17 N6
Northmoor Oxon 34 D4
North Moreton Oxon 34 G7
Northmuir Angus 142 F6
North Mundham W Susx 15 N6
North Muskham Notts 85 N9
North Newbald E R Yk 92 F3
North Newington Oxon 48 D6
North Newnton Wilts 21 M3
North Newton Somset 19 K8
Northney Hants 15 K6
North Nibley Gloucs 32 D5
North Oakley Hants 22 F4
North Ockendon Gt Lon 37 N3
Northolt Gt Lon 36 D4
Northolt Airport Gt Lon 36 C3
Northop Flints 81 J11
Northop Hall Flints 81 K11
North Ormesby Middsb 104 F7
North Ormsby Lincs 87 J2
Northorpe Kirk 90 G6
Northorpe Lincs 74 A7
Northorpe Lincs 74 D3
Northorpe Lincs 92 E11
North Otterington N York 97 N3
Northover Somset 19 N7
Northover Somset 19 P10
North Owersby Lincs 86 E2
Northowram Calder 90 E5
North Perrott Somset 11 K3
North Petherton Somset 19 J8
North Petherwin Cnwll 5 M4
North Pickenham Norfk 76 B10
North Piddle Worcs 47 J4
North Poorton Dorset 11 L5
Northport Dorset 12 F7
North Poulner Hants 13 L3
North Queensferry Fife 134 E11
North Radworthy Devon 17 P5
North Rauceby Lincs 86 D11
Northrepps Norfk 77 J4
North Reston Lincs 87 L4
North Rigton N York 97 L11
North Ripley Hants 13 L5
North Rode Ches E 83 J11
North Roe Shet 169 q5
North Ronaldsay Ork 169 g1
North Ronaldsay Airport Ork 169 g1
North Row Cumb 100 H4
North Runcton Norfk 75 M7
North Scale W & F 94 D7
North Scarle Lincs 85 P7
North Seaton Nthumb 113 L3
North Seaton Colliery Nthumb 113 L3
North Shian Ag & B 138 G9
North Shields N Tyne 113 N7
North Shoebury Sthend 38 F4
North Shore Bpool 88 C3
North Side C Pete 74 E11
North Side Cumb 100 C5
North Skelton R & Cl 105 J7
North Somercotes Lincs 93 R11
North Stainley N York 97 L5
North Stainmore W & F 102 F7
North Stifford Thurr 37 P4
North Stoke BaNES 32 D11
North Stoke Oxon 34 H7
North Stoke W Susx 24 B8
Northstowe Cambs 62 F7
North Street Cambs 63 J7
North Street Hants 21 N11
North Street Hants 22 H8
North Street Kent 38 H10
North Street Medway 38 D7
North Street W Berk 34 H10
North Sunderland Nthumb 119 P4
North Tamerton Cnwll 5 N2
North Tawton Devon 8 G4
North Third Stirlg 133 M10
North Thoresby Lincs 93 N11
North Togston Nthumb 119 P10
North Tolsta W Isls 168 k3
Northton W Isls 168 e9
North Town Devon 17 J10
North Town Somset 19 Q6
North Town W & M 35 N8
North Tuddenham Norfk 76 E9
North Uist W Isls 168 c10
Northumberland National Park Nthumb 111 Q4
North Walbottle N u Ty 113 J7
North Walsham Norfk 77 K5
North Waltham Hants 22 G5
North Warnborough Hants 23 K4
Northway Somset 18 F9
North Weald Bassett Essex 51 L10
North Wheatley Notts 85 N3
North Whilborough Devon 7 M5
Northwich Ches W 82 E10
North Wick BaNES 31 Q11
Northwick S Glos 31 Q7
Northwick Somset 19 L5
Northwick Worcs 46 F3
North Widcombe BaNES 19 Q3
North Willingham Lincs 86 G3
North Wingfield Derbys 84 F7
North Witham Lincs 73 N6
Northwold Norfk 75 Q11
Northwood C Stke 70 F5
Northwood Derbys 84 C8
Northwood Gt Lon 36 C2
Northwood IoW 14 E8
Northwood Shrops 69 N8
Northwood Worcs 57 P9
Northwood Green Gloucs 46 D11
North Wootton Dorset 11 P2
North Wootton Norfk 75 M6
North Wootton Somset 19 Q6
North Wraxall Wilts 32 F9
North Wroughton Swindn 33 M8
North York Moors National Park 105 K10
Norton Donc 91 N7
Norton E Susx 25 L10
Norton Gloucs 46 G10
Norton Halton 82 C8
Norton Hants 22 E6
Norton Herts 50 F4
Norton IoW 13 P7
Norton Mons 45 N10
Norton N Som 19 K2
Norton Notts 85 J6
Norton Powys 56 E11
Norton S on T 104 D6
Norton Sheff 84 E4
Norton Shrops 56 H8
Norton Shrops 57 K3
Norton Shrops 57 L8
Norton Shrops 57 N4
Norton Suffk 64 D8
Norton Swans 28 H7
Norton W Nthn 60 C8
Norton W Susx 15 P5
Norton Wilts 32 G8
Norton Worcs 46 G4
Norton Worcs 47 K5
Norton Bavant Wilts 20 H6
Norton Bridge Staffs 70 F8
Norton Canes Staffs 58 F3
Norton Canes Services Staffs 58 F3
Norton Canon Herefs 45 M5
Norton Corner Norfk 76 F6
Norton Disney Lincs 85 Q9
Norton Ferris Wilts 20 E7
Norton Fitzwarren Somset 18 G9
Norton Green IoW 13 P7
Norton Hawkfield BaNES 19 Q2
Norton Heath Essex 51 P10
Norton in Hales Shrops 70 C7
Norton-Juxta-Twycross Leics 59 M3
Norton-le-Clay N York 97 P6
Norton-le-Moors C Stke 70 F4
Norton Lindsey Warwks 47 P2
Norton Little Green Suffk 64 D8
Norton Malreward BaNES 20 B2
Norton Mandeville Essex 51 N10
Norton-on-Derwent N York 98 F6
Norton St Philip Somset 20 E3
Norton Subcourse Norfk 65 N2
Norton sub Hamdon Somset 19 N11
Norton Wood Herefs 45 M5
Norwell Notts 85 N8
Norwell Woodhouse Notts 85 M8
Norwich Norfk 77 J10
Norwich Airport Norfk 77 J9
Norwick Shet 169 t2
Norwood Clacks 133 P9
Norwood Derbys 84 G4
Norwood Kent 27 J5
Norwood End Essex 51 N9
Norwood Green Calder 90 E5
Norwood Green Gt Lon 36 D5
Norwood Hill Surrey 24 F2
Norwoodside Cambs 74 H11
Noseley Leics 73 J11
Noss Mayo Devon 6 F9
Nosterfield N York 97 L4
Nosterfield End Cambs 51 P2
Nostie Highld 145 Q2
Notgrove Gloucs 47 M10
Nottage Brdgnd 29 M9
Notter Cnwll 5 P9
Nottingham C Nott 72 F3
Nottington Dorset 11 P8
Notton Wakefd 91 J8
Notton Wilts 32 H11
Nounsley Essex 52 C9
Noutard's Green Worcs 57 Q11
Nowton Suffk 64 B9
Nox Shrops 56 G2
Nuffield Oxon 35 J7
Nunburnholme E R Yk 98 G11
Nuncargate Notts 84 H10
Nunclose W & F 111 J11
Nuneaton Warwks 59 N6
Nuneham Courtenay Oxon 34 G5
Nunhead Gt Lon 36 H5
Nunkeeling E R Yk 99 N11
Nun Monkton N York 97 R9
Nunney Somset 20 D5
Nunney Catch Somset 20 D6
Nunnington Herefs 45 R6
Nunnington N York 98 D5
Nunsthorpe NE Lin 93 N9
Nunthorpe C York 98 C10
Nunthorpe Middsb 104 F8
Nunthorpe Village Middsb 104 F8
Nunton Wilts 21 N9
Nunwick N York 97 M6
Nunwick Nthumb 112 C6
Nupdown S Glos 32 B5
Nup End Bucks 49 N11
Nupend Gloucs 32 E3
Nuptown Br For 35 N10
Nursling Hants 22 C11
Nursted Hants 23 L10
Nursteed Wilts 21 K2
Nurton Staffs 58 B5
Nutbourne W Susx 15 L5
Nutbourne W Susx 24 C7
Nutfield Surrey 36 H10
Nuthall Notts 72 E2
Nuthampstead Herts 51 K4
Nuthurst W Susx 24 E5
Nutley E Susx 25 K5
Nutley Hants 22 H6
Nuttall Bury 89 M7
Nutwell Donc 91 Q10
Nybster Highld 167 Q4
Nyetimber W Susx 15 N7
Nyewood W Susx 23 M10
Nymans W Susx 24 G5
Nymet Rowland Devon 17 N10
Nymet Tracey Devon 8 H4
Nympsfield Gloucs 32 F4
Nynehead Somset 18 F10
Nythe Somset 19 M8
Nyton W Susx 15 P5

O

Oadby Leics 72 G10
Oad Street Kent 38 E9
Oakall Green Worcs 46 F2
Oakamoor Staffs 71 J6
Oakbank W Loth 127 K4
Oak Cross Devon 8 D5
Oakdale Caerph 30 G5
Oake Somset 18 G9
Oaken Staffs 58 C4
Oakenclough Lancs 95 L11
Oakengates Wrekin 57 N2
Oakenholt Flints 81 K10
Oakenshaw Dur 103 N3
Oakenshaw Kirk 90 F5
Oakerthorpe Derbys 84 E10
Oakford Cerdgn 43 J3
Oakford Devon 18 B10
Oakfordbridge Devon 18 B10
Oakgrove Ches E 83 K11
Oakham Rutlnd 73 M9
Oakhanger Ches E 70 D4
Oakhanger Hants 23 L7
Oakhill Somset 20 B5
Oakhurst Kent 37 N10
Oakington Cambs 62 F8
Oaklands Herts 50 F7
Oaklands Powys 44 E4
Oakle Street Gloucs 46 E11
Oakley BCP 12 H5
Oakley Bed 61 M10
Oakley Bucks 34 H2
Oakley Fife 134 C10
Oakley Hants 22 G4
Oakley Oxon 35 L4
Oakley Suffk 64 H6
Oakley Green W & M 35 P9
Oakley Park Powys 55 M7
Oakridge Lynch Gloucs 32 H4
Oaks Lancs 89 K4
Oaks Shrops 56 G4
Oaksey Wilts 33 J6
Oaks Green Derbys 71 M8
Oakshaw Ford Cumb 111 K5
Oakshott Hants 23 K9
Oakthorpe Leics 59 M2
Oak Tree Darltn 104 C8
Oakwood C Derb 72 B3
Oakwood Nthumb 112 D7
Oakworth C Brad 90 C3
Oare Kent 38 H9
Oare Somset 17 P2
Oare Wilts 21 N2
Oasby Lincs 73 Q3
Oath Somset 19 L9
Oathlaw Angus 142 H6
Oatlands Park Surrey 36 C7
Oban Ag & B 130 H2
Oban Airport Ag & B 138 G10
Obley Shrops 56 E9
Obney P & K 141 P10
Oborne Dorset 20 C11
Obthorpe Lincs 74 A8
Occold Suffk 64 H7
Occumster Highld 167 N9
Ochiltree E Ayrs 115 K3
Ockbrook Derbys 72 C3
Ocker Hill Sandw 58 E6
Ockeridge Worcs 46 E2
Ockham Surrey 36 C9
Ockle Highld 137 P1
Ockley Surrey 24 D2
Ocle Pychard Herefs 46 A5
Octon E R Yk 99 L7
Odcombe Somset 19 P11
Odd Down BaNES 20 D2
Oddendale W & F 101 Q8
Oddingley Worcs 46 H3
Oddington Oxon 48 G11
Odell Bed 61 L9
Odham Devon 8 C4
Odiham Hants 23 K4
Odsal C Brad 90 F5
Odsey Cambs 50 G3
Odstock Wilts 21 M9
Odstone Leics 72 B9
Offchurch Warwks 59 N11
Offenham Worcs 47 L5
Offerton Stockp 83 K7
Offerton Sundld 113 M9
Offham E Susx 25 K8
Offham Kent 37 Q9
Offham W Susx 24 B9
Offleymarsh Staffs 70 D9
Offord Cluny Cambs 62 B7
Offord D'Arcy Cambs 62 B7
Offton Suffk 53 J2
Offwell Devon 10 D5
Ogbourne Maizey Wilts 33 N10
Ogbourne St Andrew Wilts 33 N10
Ogbourne St George Wilts 33 P10
Ogden Calder 90 D4
Ogle Nthumb 112 H5
Oglet Lpool 81 N8
Ogmore V Glam 29 N9
Ogmore-by-Sea V Glam 29 N9
Ogmore Vale Brdgnd 29 P6
Ogwen Bank Gwynd 79 L11
Okeford Fitzpaine Dorset 12 D2
Okehampton Devon 8 E5
Oker Side Derbys 84 C8
Okewood Hill Surrey 24 D3
Olchard Devon 9 L9
Old W Nthn 60 G6
Old Aberdeen C Aber 151 N6
Old Alresford Hants 22 G8
Oldany Highld 164 C10
Old Arley Warwks 59 L6
Old Auchenbrack D & G 115 Q8
Old Basford C Nott 72 F2
Old Basing Hants 23 J4
Old Beetley Norfk 76 D8
Oldberrow Warwks 58 H11
Old Bewick Nthumb 119 L6
Old Bolingbroke Lincs 87 L7
Old Boxted Essex 52 G5
Old Bramhope Leeds 90 G2
Old Brampton Derbys 84 D6
Old Bridge of Urr D & G 108 G7
Old Buckenham Norfk 64 F3
Old Burghclere Hants 22 E3
Oldbury Kent 37 N9
Oldbury Sandw 58 E7
Oldbury Shrops 57 N6
Oldbury Warwks 59 M6
Oldbury Naite S Glos 32 B6
Oldbury-on-Severn S Glos 32 B6
Oldbury on the Hill Gloucs 32 F7
Old Byland N York 98 B3
Old Cantley Donc 91 Q10
Old Cassop Dur 104 B3
Oldcastle Mons 45 L10
Oldcastle Heath Ches W 69 N5
Old Catton Norfk 77 J9
Old Churchstoke Powys 56 D6
Old Clee NE Lin 93 N9
Old Cleeve Somset 18 D6
Old Colwyn Conwy 80 B9
Oldcotes Notts 85 J3
Old Coulsdon Gt Lon 36 H9
Old Dailly S Ayrs 114 D8
Old Dalby Leics 72 H6
Old Dam Derbys 83 P9
Old Deer Abers 159 N8
Old Ditch Somset 19 P5
Old Edlington Donc 91 N11
Old Eldon Dur 103 P5
Old Ellerby E R Yk 93 L3
Old Felixstowe Suffk 53 P4
Oldfield C Brad 90 C3
Oldfield Worcs 46 F2
Old Fletton C Pete 74 C11
Oldford Somset 20 E4
Old Forge Herefs 45 R11
Old Furnace Herefs 45 P10
Old Glossop Derbys 83 M6
Old Goole E R Yk 92 B6
Old Grimsby IoS 2 b1
Old Hall Green Herts 51 J6
Oldhall Green Suffk 64 B10
Old Hall Street Norfk 77 L5
Oldham Oldham 83 K4
Oldhamstocks E Loth 129 J5
Old Harlow Essex 51 L8
Old Heath Essex 52 H7
Old Hunstanton Norfk 75 N2
Old Hurst Cambs 62 D5
Old Hutton W & F 95 M3
Old Inns Services N Lans 126 D2
Old Kea Cnwll 3 L5
Old Kilpatrick W Duns 125 M3
Old Knebworth Herts 50 F6
Old Lakenham Norfk 77 J10
Oldland S Glos 32 C10
Old Langho Lancs 89 L3
Old Laxey IoM 80 f5
Old Leake Lincs 87 M10
Old Malton N York 98 F6
Oldmeldrum Abers 151 L2
Oldmill Cnwll 5 P7
Old Milverton Warwks 59 L11
Oldmixon N Som 19 K3
Old Newton Suffk 64 F9
Old Oxted Surrey 37 J10
Old Philpstoun W Loth 127 K2
Old Portlethen Abers 151 N8
Old Quarrington Dur 104 B3
Old Radford C Nott 72 F2
Old Radnor Powys 45 K3
Old Rayne Abers 150 H2
Old Romney Kent 26 H7
Old Shoreham W Susx 24 F9
Oldshoremore Highld 164 F5
Old Soar Kent 37 P10
Old Sodbury S Glos 32 E8
Old Somerby Lincs 73 P4
Oldstead N York 98 A5
Old Stratford W Nthn 49 L6
Old Struan P & K 141 K4
Old Swarland Nthumb 119 N10
Old Swinford Dudley 58 D8
Old Tebay W & F 102 B9
Old Thirsk N York 97 P4
Old Town Calder 90 C5
Old Town E Susx 25 N11
Old Town IoS 2 c2
Old Town W & F 95 M4
Old Town W & F 101 N2
Old Trafford Traffd 82 H5
Old Tupton Derbys 84 E7
Oldwall Cumb 111 J8
Oldwalls Swans 28 E6
Old Warden C Beds 50 D2
Oldways End Somset 17 R7
Old Weston Cambs 61 N5
Old Wick Highld 167 Q7
Old Windsor W & M 35 Q10
Old Wives Lees Kent 39 J11
Old Woking Surrey 36 B9
Old Wolverton M Keyn 49 M6
Old Woodhall Lincs 86 H7
Old Woods Shrops 69 N10
Olgrinmore Highld 167 J6
Olive Green Staffs 71 L11
Oliver's Battery Hants 22 E9
Ollaberry Shet 169 q5
Ollach Highld 153 J10
Ollerton Ches E 82 G9
Ollerton Notts 85 L7
Ollerton Shrops 70 A9
Olmarch Cerdgn 43 M3
Olmstead Green Cambs 51 P2
Olney M Keyn 49 N4
Olrig House Highld 167 L3
Olton Solhll 58 H8
Olveston S Glos 32 B7
Ombersley Worcs 46 F2
Ompton Notts 85 L7
Once Brewed Nthumb 111 P7
Onchan IoM 80 e6
Onecote Staffs 71 J3
Onehouse Suffk 64 E10
Onen Mons 31 M2
Ongar Street Herefs 56 F11
Onibury Shrops 56 H9
Onich Highld 139 J5
Onllwyn Neath 29 M2
Onneley Staffs 70 D6
Onslow Green Essex 51 Q7
Onslow Village Surrey 23 Q5
Onston Ches W 82 C10
Openwoodgate Derbys 84 E11
Opinan Highld 153 N3
Orbliston Moray 157 Q6
Orbost Highld 152 D9
Orby Lincs 87 N7
Orchard Portman Somset 18 H10
Orcheston Wilts 21 L5
Orcop Herefs 45 P9
Orcop Hill Herefs 45 P9
Ord Abers 158 F6
Ordhead Abers 150 H5
Ordie Abers 150 D7
Ordiequish Moray 157 Q6
Ordley Nthumb 112 D9
Ordsall Notts 85 M5
Ore E Susx 26 D9
Oreleton Common Herefs 56 H11
Oreton Shrops 57 M8
Orford Suffk 65 N11
Orford Warrtn 82 D6
Organford Dorset 12 F6
Orgreave Staffs 71 L11
Orkney Islands Ork 169 d6
Orkney Neolithic Ork 169 c5
Orlestone Kent 26 H5
Orleton Herefs 56 H11

Orleton Worcs	57	N11
Orlingbury N Nthn	61	J6
Ormathwaite Cumb	101	J5
Ormesby R & Cl	104	F7
Ormesby St Margaret Norfk	77	P9
Ormesby St Michael Norfk	77	P9
Ormiscaig Highld	160	D8
Ormiston E Loth	128	C6
Ormsaigmore Highld	137	M3
Ormsary Ag & B	123	M5
Ormskirk Lancs	88	E9
Ornsby Hill Dur	113	J11
Oronsay Ag & B	136	b4
Orphir Ork	169	c6
Orpington Gt Lon	37	L7
Orrell Sefton	81	L5
Orrell Wigan	82	B4
Orrell Post Wigan	88	G9
Orrisdale IoM	80	d3
Orroland D & G	108	G11
Orsett Thurr	37	P4
Orsett Heath Thurr	37	P4
Orslow Staffs	70	E11
Orston Notts	73	K2
Orthwaite Cumb	101	J4
Ortner Lancs	95	L10
Orton N Nthn	60	H5
Orton Staffs	58	C5
Orton W & F	102	B9
Orton Longueville C Pete	74	C11
Orton-on-the-Hill Leics	59	M4
Orton Rigg Cumb	110	F10
Orton Waterville C Pete	74	C11
Orwell Cambs	62	E10
Osbaldeston Lancs	89	J4
Osbaldeston Green Lancs	89	J4
Osbaldwick C York	98	C10
Osbaston Leics	72	C10
Osbaston Mons	31	P2
Osbaston Shrops	69	K10
Osborne IoW	14	F8
Osborne IoW	14	F8
Osbournby Lincs	73	R3
Oscroft Ches W	81	Q11
Ose Highld	152	E9
Osgathorpe Leics	72	C7
Osgodby Lincs	86	E2
Osgodby N York	91	Q4
Osgodby N York	99	M4
Oskaig Highld	153	J10
Oskamull Ag & B	137	M7
Osmaston Derbys	71	M6
Osmington Dorset	11	Q8
Osmington Mills Dorset	12	B8
Osmondthorpe Leeds	91	J4
Osmotherley N York	104	E11
Osney Oxon	34	E3
Ospringe Kent	38	H9
Ossett Wakefd	90	H6
Ossington Notts	85	N8
Ostend Essex	38	F2
Osterley Gt Lon	36	E5
Oswaldkirk N York	98	C5
Oswaldtwistle Lancs	89	L5
Oswestry Shrops	69	J9
Otairnis W Isls	168	e10
Otford Kent	37	M9
Otham Kent	38	C11
Otham Hole Kent	38	D11
Othery Somset	19	L8
Otley Leeds	97	K11
Otley Suffk	65	J10
Otley Green Suffk	65	J10
Otterbourne Hants	22	E10
Otterburn N York	96	C9
Otterburn Nthumb	112	C2
Otter Ferry Ag & B	131	J11
Otterham Cnwll	5	K3
Otterhampton Somset	18	H6
Otterham Quay Kent	38	D8
Otterham Station Cnwll	5	K4
Otternish W Isls	168	e10
Ottershaw Surrey	36	B8
Otterswick Shet	169	s5
Otterton Devon	10	B7
Otterwood Hants	14	D6
Ottery St Mary Devon	10	C5
Ottinge Kent	27	L3
Ottringham E R Yk	93	N6
Oughterby Cumb	110	E9
Oughtershaw N York	96	C9
Oughterside Cumb	100	F2
Oughtibridge Sheff	84	D8
Oughtrington Warrtn	82	E7
Oulston N York	98	A6
Oulton Cumb	110	D10
Oulton Leeds	91	K5
Oulton Norfk	76	G6
Oulton Staffs	70	D10
Oulton Staffs	70	G7
Oulton Suffk	65	Q3
Oulton Broad Suffk	65	Q3
Oulton Street Norfk	76	H6
Oundle N Nthn	61	M3
Ounsdale Staffs	58	C6
Ousby W & F	102	B4
Ousden Suffk	63	M9
Ousefleet E R Yk	92	D6
Ouston Dur	113	L10
Outchester Nthumb	119	M4
Out Elmstead Kent	39	M11
Outgate W & F	101	L11
Outhgill W & F	102	E10
Outhill Warwks	58	H11
Outlands Staffs	70	D8
Outlane Kirk	90	D7
Out Newton E R Yk	93	Q6
Out Rawcliffe Lancs	88	E2
Out Skerries Shet	169	t6
Outwell Norfk	75	K10
Outwick Hants	21	M11
Outwood Surrey	36	H11
Outwood Wakefd	91	J6
Outwood Gate Bury	89	M9
Outwoods Leics	72	C7
Outwoods Staffs	70	D11
Ouzlewell Green Leeds	91	J5
Ovenden Calder	90	D5
Over Cambs	62	E6
Over Ches W	82	D11
Over Gloucs	46	F11
Over S Glos	31	Q8
Over Burrows Derbys	71	P7
Overbury Worcs	47	J7
Overcombe Dorset	11	P8
Over Compton Dorset	19	Q11
Over End Cambs	61	N2
Overgreen Derbys	84	D6
Over Green Warwks	59	J4
Over Haddon Derbys	84	B7
Over Hulton Bolton	82	E4
Over Kellet Lancs	95	L7
Over Kiddington Oxon	48	D10
Overleigh Somset	19	N7
Overley Staffs	71	M11
Over Monnow Mons	31	P2
Over Norton Oxon	48	B9
Over Peover Ches E	82	G10
Overpool Ches W	81	M9
Overscaig Highld	161	Q2
Overseal Derbys	71	P11
Over Silton N York	97	P3
Oversland Kent	39	J10
Oversley Green Warwks	47	L3
Overstone W Nthn	60	G7
Over Stowey Somset	18	G7
Overstrand Norfk	77	J3
Over Stratton Somset	19	M11
Overstreet Wilts	21	L7
Over Tabley Ches E	82	F9
Overthorpe W Nthn	48	E6
Overton C Aber	151	M5
Overton Ches W	81	Q9
Overton Hants	22	F5
Overton Lancs	95	J9
Overton N York	98	B9
Overton Shrops	57	J10
Overton Swans	28	E7
Overton Wakefd	90	H7
Overton Wrexhm	69	L6
Overton Bridge Wrexhm	69	L6
Overton Green Ches E	70	E2
Overtown Lancs	89	P5
Overtown N Lans	95	N5
Overtown N Lans	126	E7
Overtown Swindn	33	N9
Overtown Wakefd	91	K7
Over Wallop Hants	21	Q7
Over Whitacre Warwks	59	L6
Over Woodhouse Derbys	84	G6
Over Worton Oxon	48	D9
Overy Oxon	34	G6
Oving Bucks	49	L10
Oving W Susx	15	P6
Ovingdean Br & H	25	J10
Ovingham Nthumb	112	G8
Ovington Dur	103	M8
Ovington Essex	52	C3
Ovington Hants	22	G8
Ovington Norfk	76	C11
Ovington Nthumb	112	G8
Ower Hants	14	E6
Ower Hants	22	B11
Owermoigne Dorset	12	C7
Owlbury Shrops	56	E6
Owlerton Sheff	84	D3
Owlpen Gloucs	32	E5
Owl's Green Suffk	65	K8
Owlsmoor Br For	23	M2
Owlswick Bucks	35	L3
Owmby Lincs	86	D3
Owmby Lincs	93	J10
Owslebury Hants	22	F10
Owston Donc	91	P8
Owston Leics	73	K9
Owston Ferry N Linc	92	D10
Owstwick E R Yk	93	N4
Owthorne E R Yk	93	P5
Owthorpe Notts	72	H4
Owton Manor Hartpl	104	E5
Oxborough Norfk	75	P10
Oxbridge Dorset	11	K5
Oxcombe Lincs	87	K5
Oxcroft Derbys	84	G6
Oxen End Essex	51	Q5
Oxenholme W & F	95	L3
Oxenhope C Brad	90	C4
Oxen Park W & F	94	G3
Oxenpill Somset	19	M6
Oxenton Gloucs	47	J8
Oxenwood Wilts	22	B3
Oxford Oxon	34	F3
Oxford Airport Oxon	48	E11
Oxford Services Oxon	34	H4
Oxgangs C Edin	127	N4
Oxhey Herts	50	D11
Oxhill Dur	113	J10
Oxhill Warwks	48	B5
Oxley Wolves	58	D4
Oxley Green Essex	52	F9
Oxley's Green E Susx	25	Q6
Oxlode Cambs	62	G3
Oxnam Border	118	C7
Oxnead Norfk	77	J7
Oxshott Surrey	36	D8
Oxshott Heath Surrey	36	D8
Oxspring Barns	90	H10
Oxted Surrey	37	J10
Oxton Border	128	D9
Oxton N York	91	N2
Oxton Notts	85	K10
Oxton Wirral	81	L7
Oxwich Swans	28	E7
Oxwich Green Swans	28	E7
Oxwick Norfk	76	C6
Oykel Bridge Highld	161	P6
Oyne Abers	150	H2
Oystermouth Swans	28	H7
Ozleworth Gloucs	32	E6

P

Pabail W Isls	168	k4
Packers Hill Dorset	11	Q2
Packington Leics	72	B8
Packmoor C Stke	70	F4
Packmores Warwks	59	L11
Padanaram Angus	142	G7
Padbury Bucks	49	K8
Paddington Gt Lon	36	G4
Paddington Warrtn	82	D7
Paddlesworth Kent	27	L4
Paddlesworth Kent	37	Q8
Paddock Wood Kent	25	Q2
Paddolgreen Shrops	69	P8
Padfield Derbys	83	M5
Padgate Warrtn	82	D7
Padhams Green Essex	51	P11
Padiham Lancs	89	M4
Padside N York	97	J9
Padstow Cnwll	4	E6
Padworth W Berk	34	H11
Page Bank Dur	103	P3
Pagham W Susx	15	N7
Paglesham Essex	38	F3
Paignton Torbay	7	M6
Pailton Warwks	59	Q8
Paine's Cross E Susx	25	P6
Painleyhill Staffs	71	J8
Painscastle Powys	44	H5
Painshawfield Nthumb	112	G8
Painsthorpe E R Yk	98	G9
Painswick Gloucs	32	G3
Painter's Forstal Kent	38	G10
Paisley Rens	125	M5
Pakefield Suffk	65	Q3
Pakenham Suffk	64	C8
Pale Gwynd	68	C7
Pale Green Essex	51	Q2
Palestine Hants	21	Q6
Paley Street W & M	35	N9
Palfrey Wsall	58	F5
Palgrave Suffk	64	G6
Pallington Dorset	12	C6
Palmarsh Kent	27	K5
Palmers Green Gt Lon	36	H2
Palmerston E Ayrs	115	K4
Palmerstown V Glam	30	F11
Palnackie D & G	108	H9
Palnure D & G	107	N5
Palterton Derbys	84	G7
Pamber End Hants	22	H3
Pamber Green Hants	22	H3
Pamber Heath Hants	22	H2
Pamington Gloucs	46	H8
Pamphill Dorset	12	G4
Pampisford Cambs	62	G11
Panborough Somset	19	N5
Panbride Angus	143	K10
Pancrasweek Devon	16	D10
Pancross V Glam	30	D11
Pandy Gwynd	54	E4
Pandy Gwynd	68	A9
Pandy Mons	45	L10
Pandy Powys	55	L4
Pandy Wrexhm	68	G7
Pandy Wrexhm	69	K4
Pandy'r Capel Denbgs	68	E4
Pandy Tudur Conwy	67	R2
Panfield Essex	52	B6
Pangbourne W Berk	34	H9
Pangdean W Susx	24	G8
Panks Bridge Herefs	46	B5
Pannal N York	97	M10
Pannal Ash N York	97	L10
Pant Shrops	69	J10
Pantasaph Flints	80	H9
Panteg Pembks	40	H4
Pantglas Powys	54	H5
Pant-Gwyn Carmth	43	L9
Pant-lasau Swans	29	J4
Pant Mawr Powys	55	J8
Panton Lincs	86	G5
Pant-pastynog Denbgs	68	D2
Pantperthog Gwynd	54	G4
Pantside Caerph	30	H5
Pant-y-caws Carmth	41	M5
Pant-y-dwr Powys	55	M10
Pant-y-ffridd Powys	56	B4
Pantyffynnon Carmth	28	H2
Pantygaseg Torfn	31	J5
Pantygelli Mons	45	L11
Pant-y-gog Brdgnd	29	P6
Pantymwyn Flints	68	G10
Panxworth Norfk	77	M9
Papa Stour Shet	169	n7
Papa Stour Airport Shet	169	n8
Papa Westray Ork	169	d1
Papa Westray Airport Ork	169	d1
Papcastle Cumb	100	F4
Papigoe Highld	167	Q6
Papple E Loth	128	F5
Papplewick Notts	84	H10
Papworth Everard Cambs	62	C8
Papworth St Agnes Cambs	62	C8
Par Cnwll	3	R3
Paramour Street Kent	39	N9
Parbold Lancs	88	F8
Parbrook Somset	19	Q7
Parbrook W Susx	24	C5
Parc Gwynd	68	A8
Parcllyn Cerdgn	42	D4
Parc Seymour Newpt	31	M6
Pardown Hants	22	G5
Pardshaw Cumb	100	E6
Parham Suffk	65	L9
Park D & G	109	K2
Park Nthumb	111	N8
Park Bottom Cnwll	2	H6
Park Bridge Tamesd	83	K4
Park Corner E Susx	25	M3
Park Corner Oxon	35	J7
Park Corner W & M	35	N8
Park End Bed	49	Q4
Park End Nthumb	112	C5
Parkend Gloucs	32	B3
Parker's Green Kent	37	P11
Parkeston Essex	53	M5
Parkeston Quay Essex	53	M5
Park Farm Kent	26	H4
Parkgate Ches W	81	K9
Parkgate Cumb	110	D11
Parkgate D & G	109	M3
Parkgate E Susx	26	B9
Parkgate Essex	51	Q5
Park Gate Hants	14	F5
Parkgate Kent	26	E5
Parkgate Kent	37	M8
Park Gate Leeds	90	F2
Parkgate Surrey	24	F2
Park Gate Worcs	58	D10
Park Green Essex	51	L4
Park Green Suffk	64	G9
Park Hall Shrops	69	K8
Parkham Devon	16	F7
Parkham Ash Devon	16	F7
Park Head Derbys	84	E10
Parkhill Dur	104	B3
Park Hill Gloucs	31	Q5
Parkhouse Mons	31	P4
Parkmill Swans	28	F7
Park Royal Gt Lon	36	E4
Parkside Dur	113	P11
Parkside N Lans	126	E6
Parkside Wrexhm	69	L3
Parkstone BCP	12	H6
Park Street Herts	50	D10
Park Street W Susx	24	D4
Parkway Herefs	46	D7
Parley Green BCP	13	K5
Parmoor Bucks	35	L7
Parracombe Devon	17	M2
Parrog Pembks	41	L3
Parsonby Cumb	100	F3
Parson Cross Sheff	84	D2
Parson Drove Cambs	74	G9
Parson's Heath Essex	52	H6
Parson's Hill Derbys	71	P9
Partick C Glas	125	N4
Partington Traffd	82	F6
Partney Lincs	87	M7
Parton Cumb	100	C6
Partridge Green W Susx	24	E7
Partrishow Powys	45	K10
Parwich Derbys	71	M4
Paslow Wood Common Essex	51	N10
Passenham W Nthn	49	L7
Passfield Hants	23	M8
Passingford Bridge Essex	51	M11
Paston C Pete	74	C10
Paston Norfk	77	L5
Pasturefields Staffs	70	H10
Patchacott Devon	8	C5
Patcham Br & H	24	H9
Patchetts Green Herts	50	D11
Patching W Susx	24	C9
Patchole Devon	17	L3
Patchway S Glos	32	B8
Pateley Bridge N York	97	J7
Paternoster Heath Essex	52	F8
Pathe Somset	19	L8
Pathhead Fife	134	H9
Pathhead Mdloth	128	B7
Pathlow Warwks	47	N3
Path of Condie P & K	134	D5
Patmore Heath Herts	51	K5
Patna E Ayrs	114	H5
Patney Wilts	21	L3
Patrick IoM	80	b5
Patrick Brompton N York	97	K2
Patricroft Salfd	82	G5
Patrington E R Yk	93	P6
Patrington Haven E R Yk	93	P6
Patrixbourne Kent	39	L10
Patterdale W & F	101	L7
Pattingham Staffs	57	Q5
Pattishall W Nthn	49	J4
Pattiswick Green Essex	52	D7
Patton Shrops	57	K5
Patton Bridge W & F	101	Q11
Paul Cnwll	2	D8
Paulerspury W Nthn	49	K5
Paull E R Yk	93	L5
Poulton BaNES	20	C3
Paultons Park Hants	22	B11
Paunton Herefs	46	C4
Pauperhaugh Nthumb	119	M11
Pave Lane Wrekin	70	D11
Pavenham Bed	61	L9
Pawlett Somset	19	J6
Pawston Nthumb	118	G4
Paxford Gloucs	47	N7
Paxton Border	129	N9
Payden Street Kent	38	F11
Payhembury Devon	10	B4
Paynter's Lane End Cnwll	2	H6
Paythorne Lancs	96	B10
Paytoe Herefs	56	G10
Peacehaven E Susx	25	K10
Peak Dale Derbys	83	N9
Peak District National Park	83	Q6
Peak Forest Derbys	83	P9
Peak Hill Lincs	74	E9
Peakirk C Pete	74	C9
Pearson's Green Kent	25	Q2
Peartree Green Herefs	46	A8
Peasedown St John BaNES	20	D3
Peasehill Derbys	84	F11
Peaseland Green Norfk	76	F8
Peasemore W Berk	34	D9
Peasenhall Suffk	65	M8
Pease Pottage W Susx	24	G4
Pease Pottage Services W Susx	24	G4
Peaslake Surrey	24	C2
Peasley Cross St Hel	81	Q6
Peasmarsh E Susx	26	E7
Peasmarsh Somset	10	G2
Peasmarsh Surrey	23	Q5
Peathill Abers	159	N4
Peat Inn Fife	135	M6
Peatling Magna Leics	60	C2
Peatling Parva Leics	60	C3
Peaton Shrops	57	J7
Pebmarsh Essex	52	E5
Pebsham E Susx	26	C10
Pebworth Worcs	47	M5
Pecket Well Calder	90	B5
Peckforton Ches E	69	P3
Peckham Gt Lon	36	H5
Peckleton Leics	72	C10
Pedairffordd Powys	68	F10
Pedlinge Kent	27	K4
Pedmore Dudley	58	D8
Pedwell Somset	19	M7
Peebles Border	117	K2
Peel IoM	80	b5
Peel Lancs	88	D4
Peel Common Hants	14	G5
Peene Kent	27	L4
Peening Quarter Kent	26	E7
Peggs Green Leics	72	C7
Pegsdon C Beds	50	D4
Pegswood Nthumb	113	K3
Pegwell Kent	39	Q9
Peinchorran Highld	153	J11
Peinlich Highld	152	H4
Pelcomb Pembks	40	H7
Pelcomb Bridge Pembks	40	H7
Pelcomb Cross Pembks	40	H7
Peldon Essex	52	G8
Pell Green E Susx	25	P4
Pelsall Wsall	58	F4
Pelsall Wood Wsall	58	F4
Pelton Dur	113	L10
Pelton Fell Dur	113	L10
Pelutho Cumb	109	P11
Pelynt Cnwll	5	L10
Pemberton Carmth	28	F4
Pemberton Wigan	82	C4
Pembles Cross Kent	26	E2
Pembrey Carmth	28	D4
Pembridge Herefs	45	M3
Pembroke Pembks	41	J10
Pembroke Dock Pembks	41	J10
Pembrokeshire Coast National Park Pembks	40	F6
Pembury Kent	25	P2
Pen-allt Herefs	45	R9
Penallt Mons	31	P2
Penally Pembks	41	M11
Penare Cnwll	3	P5
Penarth V Glam	30	G10
Penblewin Pembks	41	M7
Pen-bont Rhydybeddau Cerdgn	54	F8
Penbryn Cerdgn	42	E4
Pencader Carmth	42	H7
Pencaenewydd Gwynd	66	G6
Pencaitland E Loth	128	C6
Pencarnisiog IoA	78	F10
Pencarreg Carmth	43	K5
Pencarrow Cnwll	5	J5
Pencelli Powys	44	F9
Penclawdd Swans	28	F5
Pencoed Brdgnd	30	C8
Pencombe Herefs	46	A4
Pencoyd Herefs	45	Q9
Pencraig Herefs	45	R10
Pencraig Powys	68	D9
Pendeen Cnwll	2	B7
Penderyn Rhondd	29	P3
Pendine Carmth	41	P9
Pendlebury Salfd	82	G4
Pendleton Lancs	89	M3
Pendock Worcs	46	E8
Pendoggett Cnwll	4	G6
Pendomer Somset	11	L2
Pendoylan V Glam	30	E9
Penegoes Powys	54	H4
Penelewey Cnwll	3	L5
Pen-ffordd Pembks	41	L6
Pengam Caerph	30	G5
Pengam Cardif	30	H9
Penge Gt Lon	37	J6
Pengelly Cnwll	4	H5
Pengenffordd Powys	44	H9
Pengorffwysfa IoA	78	H6
Pengover Green Cnwll	5	M8
Pen-groes-oped Mons	31	K3
Pengwern Denbgs	80	E9
Penhale Cnwll	2	H10
Penhale Cnwll	4	E10
Penhale Cnwll	5	H9
Penhale Cnwll	5	Q11
Penhallow Cnwll	3	K3
Penhalurick Cnwll	3	J6
Penhalvean Cnwll	3	J6
Penhill Swindn	33	N7
Penhow Newpt	31	M6
Penhurst E Susx	25	Q7
Peniarth Gwynd	54	E3
Penicuik Mdloth	127	N6
Peniel Carmth	42	H10
Peniel Denbgs	68	D2
Penifiler Highld	152	H9
Peninver Ag & B	120	E7
Penisarwaun Gwynd	67	K2
Penistone Barns	90	G10
Penjerrick Cnwll	3	K7
Penketh Warrtn	82	C7
Penkill S Ayrs	114	C7
Penkridge Staffs	58	D2
Penlean Cnwll	5	L2
Penleigh Wilts	20	G4
Penley Wrexhm	69	M6
Penllergaer Swans	28	H5
Pen-llyn IoA	78	F8
Penllyn V Glam	30	C9
Pen-lôn IoA	78	G11
Penmachno Conwy	67	P4
Penmaen Caerph	30	G5
Penmaen Swans	28	F7
Penmaenan Conwy	79	N9
Penmaenmawr Conwy	79	N9
Penmaenpool Gwynd	67	M11
Penmark V Glam	30	E11
Penmon IoA	79	L8
Penmorfa Gwynd	67	J6
Penmynydd IoA	79	J10
Penn Bucks	35	P6
Penn Wolves	58	C5
Pennal Gwynd	54	F4
Pennan Abers	159	K2
Pennant Cerdgn	43	K2
Pennant Denbgs	68	D8
Pennant Powys	55	K5
Pennant-Melangell Powys	68	D9
Pennard Pembks	41	J10
Pennard Swans	28	G7
Pennerley Shrops	56	F5
Pennicott Devon	9	L4
Pennines	90	B3
Pennington Hants	13	P5
Pennington W & F	94	F3
Pennington Green Wigan	89	J9
Pennorth Powys	44	G9
Penn Street Bucks	35	P5
Pennsylvania S Glos	32	D10
Penny Bridge W & F	94	G3
Pennycross Ag & B	137	N10
Pennygate Norfk	77	L7
Pennyghael Ag & B	137	N10
Pennyglen S Ayrs	114	E5
Penny Green Derbys	84	H5
Penny Hill Lincs	74	G5
Pennymoor Devon	9	L2
Pennywell Sundld	113	N9
Penparc Cerdgn	42	D5
Penparcau Cerdgn	54	D8
Penpedairheol Caerph	30	F5
Penpedairheol Mons	31	K4
Penperlleni Mons	31	K4
Penpillick Cnwll	4	H10
Penpol Cnwll	3	L6
Penpoll Cnwll	5	J11
Penponds Cnwll	2	G6
Penpont Cnwll	4	H7
Penpont D & G	108	H2
Penpont Powys	44	D9

Place	County	Page	Grid
Penquit	Devon	6	G8
Penrest	Cnwll	5	N6
Penrherber	Carmth	41	Q3
Pen-rhiw	Pembks	41	P2
Penrhiwceiber	Rhondd	30	E5
Pen Rhiwfawr	Neath	29	K2
Penrhiwgoch	Carmth	43	L11
Penrhiwllan	Cerdgn	42	G6
Penrhiwpal	Cerdgn	42	F5
Penrhos	Gwynd	66	E8
Penrhos	IoA	78	D8
Penrhos	Mons	31	M2
Penrhos	Powys	29	K3
Penrhos garnedd	Gwynd	79	K10
Penrhyn Bay	Conwy	79	Q8
Penrhyn-coch	Cerdgn	54	E8
Penrhyndeudraeth	Gwynd	67	L7
Penrhyn-side	Conwy	79	Q8
Penrhyn Slate Landscape Gwynd		79	L11
Penrhys	Rhondd	30	D6
Penrice	Swans	28	E7
Penrioch	N Ayrs	120	G3
Penrith	W & F	101	P4
Penrose	Cnwll	4	D7
Penruddock	W & F	101	M5
Penryn	Cnwll	3	K7
Pensarn	Conwy	80	D9
Pensax	Worcs	57	N11
Pensby	Wirral	81	K8
Penselwood	Somset	20	E8
Pensford	BaNES	20	B2
Pensham	Worcs	46	H6
Penshaw	Sundld	113	M10
Penshurst	Kent	25	M2
Penshurst Station	Kent	37	M11
Pensilva	Cnwll	5	M7
Pensnett	Dudley	58	D7
Penstone	Devon	9	J4
Penstrowed	Powys	55	P6
Pentewan	Cnwll	3	Q4
Pentir	Gwynd	79	K11
Pentire	Cnwll	4	B9
Pentlepoir	Pembks	41	M9
Pentlow	Essex	52	D3
Pentlow Street	Essex	63	P11
Pentney	Norfk	75	P8
Pentonbridge	Cumb	110	H5
Penton Grafton	Hants	22	B5
Penton Mewsey	Hants	22	B5
Pentraeth	IoA	79	J9
Pentre	Denbgs	68	E2
Pentre	Flints	81	L11
Pentre	Mons	31	K3
Pentre	Mons	31	M4
Pentre	Powys	55	P7
Pentre	Powys	56	B7
Pentre	Powys	56	D6
Pentre	Rhondd	30	C5
Pentre	Shrops	69	L11
Pentre	Wrexhm	69	J6
Pentre-bâch	Cerdgn	43	L5
Pentre Bach	Flints	81	J9
Pentrebach	Myr Td	30	E4
Pentre-bach	Powys	44	C8
Pentrebeirdd	Powys	56	B4
Pentre Berw	IoA	78	H10
Pentre-bont	Conwy	67	N4
Pentre-cagel	Carmth	42	F6
Pentrecelyn	Denbgs	68	E2
Pentre-celyn	Powys	55	K3
Pentre-chwyth	Swans	29	J6
Pentre-clawdd	Shrops	69	J8
Pentre-cwrt	Carmth	42	G7
Pentredwr	Denbgs	68	G5
Pentrefelin	Cerdgn	42	H6
Pentrefelin	Gwynd	67	J7
Pentrefelin	IoA	78	G6
Pentre Ffwrndan	Flints	81	K10
Pentrefoelas	Conwy	67	R4
Pentregalar	Pembks	41	N4
Pentregat	Cerdgn	42	G4
Pentre-Gwenlais	Carmth	43	M11
Pentre Gwynfryn	Gwynd	67	K9
Pentre Halkyn	Flints	81	J10
Pentre Hodrey	Shrops	56	E9
Pentre Isaf	Conwy	80	D10
Pentre Llanrhaeadr	Denbgs	68	E2
Pentre Llifior	Powys	56	B5
Pentrellwyn	Cerdgn	42	H6
Pentre-llwyn-llwyd	Powys	44	D9
Pentre-llyn	Cerdgn	54	E9
Pentre-llyn-cymmer	Conwy	68	C4
Pentre-Maw	Powys	55	K4
Pentre Meyrick	V Glam	30	C9
Pentre-piod	Torfn	31	J4
Pentre-poeth	Newpt	31	J7
Pentre'rbryn	Cerdgn	42	G4
Pentre'r-felin	Cerdgn	43	M5
Pentre'r Felin	Conwy	79	Q11
Pentre'r-felin	Powys	44	C8
Pentre Saron	Denbgs	68	D2
Pentre-tafarn-y-fedw Conwy		67	Q2
Pentre ty gwyn	Carmth	43	R7
Pentrich	Derbys	84	E10
Pentridge	Dorset	21	K11
Pen-twyn	Caerph	30	H4
Pentwyn	Cardif	30	H8
Pen-twyn	Mons	31	P3
Pen-twyn	Torfn	31	J4
Pentwynmaur	Caerph	30	G5
Pentyrch	Cardif	30	F8
Penwithick	Cnwll	4	G10
Penwood	Hants	22	D2
Penwyllt	Powys	44	B11
Penybanc	Carmth	43	M10
Penybont	Powys	44	G2
Pen-y-bont	Powys	68	H10
Penybontfawr	Powys	68	E10
Pen-y-bryn	Pembks	41	N2
Pen-y-cae	Powys	44	M2
Penycae	Wrexhm	69	J5
Pen-y-cae-mawr	Mons	31	M5
Pen-y-cefn	Flints	80	G9
Pen-y-clawdd	Mons	31	N3
Pen-y-coedcae	Rhondd	30	E7
Penycwm	Pembks	40	G6
Pen-y-fai	Brdgnd	29	N8
Pen-y-felin	Flints	80	H11
Penyffordd	Flints	69	K2
Penyffridd	Gwynd	67	J3
Pen-y-garn	Cerdgn	54	E7
Pen-y-Garnedd	Powys	68	F10
Pen-y-graig	Gwynd	66	C8
Penygraig	Rhondd	30	D6
Penygroes	Carmth	28	G2
Penygroes	Gwynd	66	H4
Penygroeslon	Gwynd	66	C8
Pen-y-Gwryd	Gwynd	67	M3
Pen-y-lan	V Glam	30	C9
Pen-y-Mynydd	Carmth	28	E4
Penymynydd	Flints	69	K2
Pen-y-pass	Gwynd	67	L3
Pen-yr-Heol	Mons	31	M2
Penysarn	IoA	78	H6
Pen-y-stryt	Denbgs	68	H4
Penywaun	Rhondd	30	D5
Penzance	Cnwll	2	D7
Peopleton	Worcs	46	H4
Peover Heath	Ches E	82	G10
Peper Harow	Surrey	23	P6
Peplow	Shrops	70	A10
Pepper's Green	Essex	51	P8
Pepperstock	C Beds	50	C7
Perceton	N Ayrs	125	K9
Percyhorner	Abers	159	N4
Perelle	Guern	10	b2
Perham Down	Wilts	21	Q5
Periton	Somset	18	C5
Perivale	Gt Lon	36	E4
Perkins Village	Devon	9	P6
Perkinsville	Dur	113	L11
Perlethorpe	Notts	85	K6
Perranarworthal	Cnwll	3	K6
Perranporth	Cnwll	3	K3
Perranuthnoe	Cnwll	2	E8
Perranwell	Cnwll	3	K3
Perranwell	Cnwll	3	K6
Perran Wharf	Cnwll	3	K6
Perranzabuloe	Cnwll	3	K3
Perrott's Brook	Gloucs	33	K3
Perry	Birm	58	G6
Perry	Cambs	61	P7
Perry Barr	Birm	58	G6
Perry Green	Essex	52	D7
Perry Green	Herts	51	K7
Perry Green	Wilts	33	J7
Perrystone Hill	Herefs	46	B9
Perry Street	Somset	10	G3
Pershall	Staffs	70	E9
Pershore	Worcs	46	H5
Pertenhall	Bed	61	N7
Perth	P & K	134	E3
Perthy	Shrops	69	L8
Perton	Herefs	46	A6
Perton	Staffs	58	C5
Pertwood	Wilts	20	G7
Peterborough	C Pete	74	C11
Peterborough Services Cambs		61	P2
Peterchurch	Herefs	45	L7
Peterculter	C Aber	151	L7
Peterhead	Abers	159	R8
Peterlee	Dur	104	D2
Petersfield	Hants	23	K10
Peter's Green	Herts	50	D7
Petersham	Gt Lon	36	E6
Peters Marland	Devon	16	H9
Peterstone Wentlooge Newpt		31	J9
Peterston-super-Ely	V Glam	30	E9
Peterstow	Herefs	45	R10
Peters Village	Kent	38	B9
Peter Tavy	Devon	8	D9
Petham	Kent	39	K11
Petherwin Gate	Cnwll	5	M4
Petrockstow	Devon	17	J10
Petsoe End	M Keyn	49	N5
Pett	E Susx	26	E9
Pettaugh	Suffk	64	H10
Pett Bottom	Kent	39	L11
Petterden	Angus	142	G10
Pettinain	S Lans	116	D2
Pettistree	Suffk	65	L10
Petton	Devon	18	D10
Petton	Shrops	69	M9
Petts Wood	Gt Lon	37	L7
Pettycur	Fife	134	H10
Petty France	S Glos	32	E7
Pettymuk	Abers	151	N3
Petworth	W Susx	23	Q10
Pevensey	E Susx	25	P9
Pevensey Bay	E Susx	25	Q10
Pewsey	Wilts	21	N2
Pewsham	Wilts	32	H10
Pheasant's Hill	Bucks	35	L7
Phepson	Worcs	46	H3
Philadelphia	Sundld	113	M10
Philham	Devon	16	D7
Philiphaugh	Border	117	N5
Phillack	Cnwll	2	F6
Philleigh	Cnwll	3	M6
Philpot End	Essex	51	P7
Philpstoun	W Loth	127	J2
Phocle Green	Herefs	46	B9
Phoenix Green	Hants	23	L3
Pibsbury	Somset	19	M9
Pica	Cumb	100	D6
Piccadilly	Warwks	59	K5
Piccotts End	Herts	50	B9
Pickburn	Donc	91	N9
Pickering	N York	98	F4
Picket Piece	Hants	22	C5
Picket Post	Hants	13	L3
Picket Twenty	Hants	22	C5
Pickford	Covtry	59	L8
Pickford Green	Covtry	59	L8
Pickhill	N York	97	M4
Picklescott	Shrops	56	G5
Pickmere	Ches E	82	E9
Pickney	Somset	18	G9
Pickstock	Wrekin	70	C10
Pickup Bank	Bl w D	89	L6
Pickwell	Devon	16	H3
Pickwell	Leics	73	K8
Pickwick	Wilts	32	F10
Pickworth	Lincs	73	Q4
Pickworth	Rutlnd	73	P8
Picton	Ches W	81	N10
Picton	Flints	80	G8
Picton	N York	104	D9
Piddinghoe	E Susx	25	K10
Piddington	Bucks	35	M6
Piddington	Oxon	48	H11
Piddington	W Nthn	49	M4
Piddlehinton	Dorset	11	Q5
Piddletrenthide	Dorset	11	Q5
Pidley	Cambs	62	D5
Piercebridge	Darltn	103	P7
Pierowall	Ork	169	d2
Piff's Elm	Gloucs	46	H9
Pigdon	Nthumb	113	J3
Pigeon Green	Warwks	47	P2
Pig Oak	Dorset	12	H4
Pig Street	Herefs	45	M5
Pikehall	Derbys	71	M3
Pilford	Dorset	12	H4
Pilgrims Hatch	Essex	51	N11
Pilham	Lincs	85	Q2
Pill	N Som	31	P9
Pillaton	Cnwll	5	P9
Pillatonmill	Cnwll	5	P9
Pillerton Hersey	Warwks	47	Q5
Pillerton Priors	Warwks	47	Q5
Pilleth	Powys	56	D11
Pilley	Barns	91	J10
Pilley	Hants	13	P5
Pilley Bailey	Hants	13	P5
Pillgwenlly	Newpt	31	K7
Pillhead	Devon	16	H6
Pilling	Lancs	95	J11
Pilling Lane	Lancs	94	H11
Pilning	S Glos	31	Q7
Pilot Inn	Kent	27	J8
Pilsbury	Derbys	71	L2
Pilsdon	Dorset	11	J5
Pilsgate	C Pete	73	R9
Pilsley	Derbys	84	B6
Pilsley	Derbys	84	F8
Pilson Green	Norfk	77	M9
Piltdown	E Susx	25	K5
Pilton	Devon	17	K5
Pilton	N Nthn	61	M4
Pilton	Rutlnd	73	N10
Pilton	Somset	19	Q6
Pilton Green	Swans	28	D7
Pimbo	Lancs	81	P4
Pimlico	Herts	50	C9
Pimlico	Lancs	89	L2
Pimlico	W Nthn	48	H6
Pimperne	Dorset	12	F3
Pinchbeck	Lincs	74	D5
Pinchbeck Bars	Lincs	74	C5
Pincheon Green	Donc	91	R7
Pinchinthorpe	R & Cl	104	G8
Pincock	Lancs	88	G7
Pinfold	Lancs	88	D8
Pinford End	Suffk	64	A10
Pinged	Carmth	28	D4
Pingewood	W Berk	35	J11
Pin Green	Herts	50	G5
Pinhoe	Devon	9	N6
Pinkett's Booth	Covtry	59	L8
Pinkney	Wilts	32	G7
Pinkneys Green	W & M	35	N8
Pinley	Covtry	59	N9
Pinley Green	Warwks	59	K11
Pin Mill	Suffk	53	M4
Pinminnoch	S Ayrs	114	C9
Pinmore	S Ayrs	114	D9
Pinn	Devon	10	C7
Pinner	Gt Lon	36	D3
Pinner Green	Gt Lon	36	D2
Pinsley Green	Ches E	69	Q5
Pinvin	Worcs	47	J5
Pinwherry	S Ayrs	114	D10
Pinxton	Derbys	84	G10
Pipe and Lyde	Herefs	45	Q6
Pipe Aston	Herefs	56	H10
Pipe Gate	Shrops	70	C6
Pipehill	Staffs	58	G3
Piperdam	Angus	142	D11
Piperhill	Highld	156	F7
Pipers Pool	Cnwll	5	M5
Pipewell	N Nthn	60	H3
Pippacott	Devon	17	J4
Pippin Street	Lancs	88	H6
Pipton	Powys	44	H7
Pirbright	Surrey	23	P3
Pirbright Camp	Surrey	23	P3
Pirnie	Border	118	C5
Pirnmill	N Ayrs	120	G3
Pirton	Herts	50	D4
Pirton	Worcs	46	G5
Pisgah	Cerdgn	54	F9
Pishill	Oxon	35	K7
Pistyll	Gwynd	66	E6
Pitblae	Abers	159	N5
Pitcairngreen	P & K	134	D2
Pitcalnie	Highld	156	E3
Pitcaple	Abers	151	J2
Pitcarity	Angus	142	E4
Pitchcombe	Gloucs	32	G3
Pitchcott	Bucks	49	L10
Pitcher Row	Lincs	74	E4
Pitchford	Shrops	57	J4
Pitch Green	Bucks	35	L4
Pitch Place	Surrey	23	N7
Pitch Place	Surrey	23	Q4
Pitchroy	Moray	157	M10
Pitcombe	Somset	20	C8
Pitcot	V Glam	29	N10
Pitcox	E Loth	128	F4
Pitfichie	Abers	150	H4
Pitglassie	Abers	158	G9
Pitgrudy	Highld	162	H8
Pitlessie	Fife	135	J6
Pitlochry	P & K	141	M6
Pitmachie	Abers	150	H2
Pitmain	Highld	148	D7
Pitmedden	Abers	151	M2
Pitmedden Garden	Abers	151	M2
Pitminster	Somset	18	H11
Pitmuies	Angus	143	K8
Pitmunie	Abers	150	H5
Pitney	Somset	19	N9
Pitroddie	P & K	134	G2
Pitscottie	Fife	135	L5
Pitsea	Essex	38	B4
Pitses	Oldham	83	K4
Pitsford	W Nthn	60	G7
Pitstone	Bucks	49	P11
Pitt	Devon	18	D11
Pitt	Hants	22	E9
Pittarrow	Abers	143	N3
Pitt Court	Gloucs	32	D5
Pittentrail	Highld	162	G6
Pittenweem	Fife	135	P7
Pitteuchar	Fife	134	H8
Pittodrie House Hotel	Abers	150	H3
Pitton	Wilts	21	P8
Pitt's Wood	Kent	37	P11
Pittulie	Abers	159	N4
Pityme	Cnwll	4	F6
Pity Me	Dur	113	L11
Pivington	Kent	26	F2
Pixey Green	Suffk	65	J6
Pixham	Surrey	36	E10
Plains	N Lans	126	D4
Plain Street	Cnwll	4	F6
Plaish	Shrops	57	J5
Plaistow	Gt Lon	37	K4
Plaistow	W Susx	24	B4
Plaitford	Hants	21	Q11
Plank Lane	Wigan	82	D5
Plas Cymyran	IoA	78	D9
Plastow Green	Hants	22	F3
Platt Bridge	Wigan	82	D4
Platt Lane	Shrops	69	P7
Platts Heath	Kent	38	E11
Plawsworth	Dur	113	L11
Plaxtol	Kent	37	P10
Playden	E Susx	26	F7
Playford	Suffk	53	M2
Play Hatch	Oxon	35	K9
Playing Place	Cnwll	3	L5
Playley Green	Gloucs	46	E8
Plealey	Shrops	56	G3
Pleasance	Fife	134	G5
Pleasington	Bl w D	89	J5
Pleasley	Derbys	84	H8
Pleasleyhill	Notts	84	H8
Pleasurewood Hills	Suffk	65	Q2
Pleck	Dorset	11	Q2
Pledgdon Green	Essex	51	N5
Pledwick	Wakefd	91	J7
Pleinheaume	Guern	10	b1
Plemont	Jersey	11	a1
Plemstall	Ches W	81	P10
Plenmeller	Nthumb	111	P8
Pleshey	Essex	51	Q8
Plockton	Highld	153	Q11
Plowden	Shrops	56	F7
Plox Green	Shrops	56	F4
Pluckley	Kent	26	F2
Pluckley Station	Kent	26	F3
Plucks Gutter	Kent	39	N9
Plumbland	Cumb	100	D3
Plumgarths	W & F	95	K2
Plumley	Ches E	82	F10
Plump Hill	Gloucs	46	C11
Plumpton	E Susx	25	J8
Plumpton	W & F	94	G5
Plumpton	W Nthn	48	H5
Plumpton End	W Nthn	49	K6
Plumpton Green	E Susx	25	J7
Plumpton Head	W & F	101	P3
Plumstead	Gt Lon	37	K5
Plumstead	Norfk	76	G5
Plumstead Green	Norfk	76	G5
Plumtree	Notts	72	G4
Plumtree Green	Kent	26	D2
Plungar	Leics	73	K4
Plurenden	Kent	26	F4
Plush	Dorset	11	Q4
Plusha	Cnwll	5	N7
Plushabridge	Cnwll	5	N7
Plwmp	Cerdgn	42	G4
Plymouth	C Plym	6	D8
Plympton	C Plym	6	E7
Plymstock	C Plym	6	E8
Plymtree	Devon	9	Q4
Pockley	N York	98	C3
Pocklington	E R Yk	98	G10
Pode Hole	Lincs	74	D6
Podimore	Somset	19	P10
Podington	Bed	61	K8
Podmore	Staffs	70	D7
Point Clear	Essex	53	K9
Pointon	Lincs	74	B4
Pokesdown	BCP	13	K6
Polbain	Highld	160	H4
Polbathic	Cnwll	5	N10
Polbeth	W Loth	127	J5
Polbrock	Cnwll	4	G8
Poldark Mine	Cnwll	2	H7
Polebrook	N Nthn	61	N3
Pole Elm	Worcs	46	F4
Polegate	E Susx	25	N10
Pole Moor	Kirk	90	D7
Polesden Lacey	Surrey	36	D10
Polesworth	Warwks	59	L4
Polgigga	Cnwll	2	B9
Polglass	Highld	160	G5
Polgooth	Cnwll	3	P3
Polgown	D & G	115	P7
Poling	W Susx	24	B10
Poling Corner	W Susx	24	B9
Polkerris	Cnwll	4	H11
Pollard Street	Norfk	77	L5
Pollington	E R Yk	91	Q7
Polloch	Highld	138	D4
Pollok	C Glas	125	N5
Pollokshaws	C Glas	125	P5
Pollokshields	C Glas	125	P5
Polmassick	Cnwll	3	P4
Polmear	Cnwll	4	H11
Polmont	Falk	126	G2
Polnish	Highld	145	N11
Polperro	Cnwll	5	L11
Polruan	Cnwll	4	H11
Polsham	Somset	19	P6
Polstead	Suffk	52	G4
Polstead Heath	Suffk	52	G3
Poltalloch	Ag & B	130	G8
Poltescoe	Cnwll	3	J10
Poltimore	Devon	9	N5
Polton	Mdloth	127	P5
Polwarth	Border	129	J9
Polyphant	Cnwll	5	M5
Polzeath	Cnwll	4	E6
Pomathorn	Mdloth	127	N6
Pomeroy	Derbys	83	P11
Ponde	Powys	44	G7
Pondersbridge	Cambs	62	D3
Ponders End	Gt Lon	51	J11
Ponsanooth	Cnwll	3	K6
Ponsonby	Cumb	100	D9
Ponsongath	Cnwll	3	K11
Ponsworthy	Devon	7	J4
Pont Abraham Services Carmth		28	G3
Pontac	Jersey	11	c2
Pontamman	Carmth	28	H2
Pontantwn	Carmth	28	D2
Pontardawe	Neath	29	K4
Pontarddulais	Swans	28	G4
Pont-ar-gothi	Carmth	43	K10
Pont-ar-Hydfer	Powys	44	B9
Pont-ar-Ilechau	Carmth	43	P10
Pontarsais	Carmth	42	H9
Pontblyddyn	Flints	69	J2
Pont Cyfyng	Conwy	67	N3
Pontcysyllte Aqueduct Wrexhm		69	J6
Pont Dolgarrog	Conwy	79	P11
Pontdolgoch	Powys	55	N6
Pont-Ebbw	Newpt	31	J7
Pontefract	Wakefd	91	M6
Ponteland	Nthumb	113	J6
Ponterwyd	Cerdgn	54	G8
Pontesbury	Shrops	56	F3
Pontesbury Hill	Shrops	56	F3
Pontesford	Shrops	56	G3
Pontfadog	Wrexhm	68	H7
Pontfaen	Pembks	41	K4
Pont-faen	Powys	44	D8
Pontgarreg	Cerdgn	42	F4
Pontgarreg	Pembks	41	M2
Pont Henri	Carmth	28	E3
Ponthir	Torfn	31	K6
Ponthirwaun	Cerdgn	42	E5
Pontllanfraith	Caerph	30	G5
Pontlliw	Swans	28	H4
Pontllyfni	Gwynd	66	G4
Pontlottyn	Caerph	30	F3
Pont Morlais	Carmth	28	F3
Pontnêddfechan	Neath	29	P3
Pontnewydd	Torfn	31	J5
Pontnewynydd	Torfn	31	J4
Pont Pen-y-benglog	Gwynd	67	M2
Pontrhydfendigaid	Cerdgn	54	G11
Pont Rhyd-sarn	Gwynd	67	R9
Pont Rhyd-y-cyff	Brdgnd	29	N7
Pontrhydyfen	Neath	29	L6
Pont-rhyd-y-groes	Cerdgn	54	G10
Pontrhydyrun	Torfn	31	J5
Pontrilas	Herefs	45	J4
Pont Robert	Powys	55	Q2
Ponts Green	E Susx	25	Q8
Pontshill	Herefs	46	B10
Pontsian	Cerdgn	42	H5
Pontsticill	Myr Td	30	E2
Pont Walby	Neath	29	N3
Pontwelly	Carmth	42	H6
Pontyates	Carmth	28	E3
Pontyberem	Carmth	28	F3
Pont-y-blew	Wrexhm	69	K7
Pontybodkin	Flints	69	J3
Pontyclun	Rhondd	30	D8
Pontycymer	Brdgnd	29	P6
Pontyglasier	Pembks	41	M3
Pontygwaith	Rhondd	30	D6
Pontygynon	Pembks	41	M3
Pontymister	Caerph	30	H6
Pont-y-pant	Conwy	67	N3
Pontypool	Torfn	31	J4
Pont-yr-hafod	Pembks	40	H5
Pontypridd	Rhondd	30	E7
Pont-yr-Rhyl	Brdgnd	29	P6
Pontywaun	Caerph	30	H5
Pool	Cnwll	2	H5
Poole	BCP	12	H6
Poole Keynes	Gloucs	33	J5
Poolewe	Highld	160	D10
Pooley Bridge	W & F	101	N5
Pooley Street	Norfk	64	F5
Poolfold	Staffs	70	F3
Pool Head	Herefs	45	R4
Poolhill	Gloucs	46	D9
Pool in Wharfedale	Leeds	97	K11
Pool of Muckhart	Clacks	134	C7
Pool Quay	Powys	56	D2
Pool Street	Essex	52	C4
Pootings	Kent	37	L11
Popes Hill	Gloucs	32	C2
Popham	Hants	22	G6
Poplar	Gt Lon	37	J4
Poplar Street	Suffk	65	N8
Porchfield	IoW	14	D8
Porkellis	Cnwll	2	H7
Porlock	Somset	18	A5
Porlock Weir	Somset	17	R2
Portachoillan	Ag & B	123	N8
Port-an-Eorna	Highld	153	Q11
Port Appin	Ag & B	138	G8
Port Askaig	Ag & B	122	F6
Portavadie	Ag & B	124	A4
Port Bannatyne	Ag & B	124	D4
Portbury	N Som	31	P9
Port Carlisle	Cumb	110	D8
Port Charlotte	Ag & B	122	C8
Portchester	Hants	14	H5
Port Clarence	S on T	104	E6
Port Driseach	Ag & B	124	B3
Port Ellen	Ag & B	122	E10
Port Elphinstone	Abers	151	K3
Portencalzie	D & G	106	C8
Portencross	N Ayrs	124	F8
Port Erin	IoM	80	a8
Portesham	Dorset	11	N7
Portessie	Moray	158	B4
Port e Vullen	IoM	80	g3
Port Eynon	Swans	28	E7
Portfield Gate	Pembks	40	H7
Portgate	Devon	5	Q4
Port Gaverne	Cnwll	4	G5
Port Glasgow	Inver	125	J3
Portgordon	Moray	158	A5
Portgower	Highld	163	N4
Porth	Cnwll	4	C9
Porth	Rhondd	30	D6
Porthallow	Cnwll	3	K9
Porthallow	Cnwll	5	L11
Porthcawl	Brdgnd	29	M9
Porthcothan	Cnwll	4	D7
Porthcurno	Cnwll	2	B9
Porthdinllaen	Gwynd	66	D6
Porthgain	Pembks	40	F4
Porthgwarra	Cnwll	2	B9
Porthill	Staffs	70	E5
Porthkea	Cnwll	3	L5
Porthkerry	V Glam	30	E11
Porthleven	Cnwll	2	G8
Porthmadog	Gwynd	67	K7
Porthmeor	Cnwll	2	C6
Porth Navas	Cnwll	3	K8
Portholland	Cnwll	3	P5
Porthoustock	Cnwll	3	L9
Porthpean	Cnwll	3	Q3

Porthtowan Cnwll....2 H4
Porthgwan Wrexhm....69 L5
Porthyrhyd Carmth....43 K11
Porth-y-Waen Shrops....69 J10
Portincaple Ag & B....131 Q9
Portinfer Jersey....11 a1
Portington E R Yk....92 C4
Portinnisherrich Ag & B....131 K5
Portinscale Cumb....101 J6
Port Isaac Cnwll....4 F5
Portishead N Som....31 N9
Portknockie Moray....158 C4
Portland Dorset....11 P10
Portlethen Abers....151 N8
Portling D & G....109 J10
Portloe Cnwll....3 N6
Port Logan D & G....106 E9
Portlooe Cnwll....5 L11
Portmahomack Highld....163 L10
Port Mary D & G....108 F11
Portmeirion Gwynd....67 K7
Portmellon Cnwll....3 Q5
Port Mòr Highld....144 F12
Portmore Hants....13 P5
Port Mulgrave N York....105 L7
Portnacroish Ag & B....138 G8
Portnaguran W Isls....168 k4
Portnahaven Ag & B....122 A9
Portnalong Highld....152 E11
Portnancon Highld....165 K4
Port nan Giùran W Isls....168 k4
Port nan Long W Isls....168 d10
Port Nis W Isls....168 k1
Portobello C Edin....127 Q3
Portobello Gatesd....113 L9
Portobello Wolves....58 E5
Port of Menteith Stirlg....132 H7
Port of Ness W Isls....168 k1
Porton Wilts....21 N7
Portontown Devon....5 Q6
Portpatrick D & G....106 C7
Port Quin Cnwll....4 F5
Port Ramsay Ag & B....138 F8
Portreath Cnwll....2 H4
Portreath Harbour Cnwll....2 H4
Portree Highld....152 H9
Port Righ Ag & B....120 F4
Port St Mary IoM....80 b8
Portscatho Cnwll....3 M6
Portsea C Port....14 H6
Portskerra Highld....166 E3
Portskewett Mons....31 N7
Portslade Br & H....24 G9
Portslade-by-Sea Br & H....24 G9
Portslogan D & G....106 C6
Portsmouth C Port....14 H7
Portsmouth Calder....89 Q5
Portsmouth Arms Devon....17 L8
Portsmouth Historic
  Dockyard C Port....14 H6
Port Soderick IoM....80 d7
Port Solent C Port....14 H5
Portsonachan Hotel Ag & B....131 L3
Portsoy Abers....158 E4
Port Sunlight Wirral....81 L8
Portswood C Sotn....14 D4
Port Talbot Neath....29 L7
Port Tennant Swans....29 J6
Portuairk Highld....137 L2
Portway Herefs....45 P6
Portway Herefs....45 P7
Portway Sandw....58 E7
Portway Worcs....58 G10
Port Wemyss Ag & B....122 A9
Port William D & G....107 K9
Portwrinkle Cnwll....5 P11
Portyerrock D & G....107 N10
Posbury Devon....9 K5
Posenhall Shrops....57 M4
Poslingford Suffk....63 N11
Posso Border....117 J4
Postbridge Devon....8 G9
Postcombe Oxon....35 K4
Post Green Dorset....12 G6
Postling Kent....27 K4
Postwick Norfk....77 K10
Potarch Abers....150 G8
Potsgrove C Beds....49 Q8
Potten End Herts....50 B9
Potten Street Kent....39 N8
Potter Brompton N York....99 K5
Pottergate Street Norfk....64 H3
Potterhanworth Lincs....86 E7
Potterhanworth Booths
  Lincs....86 E7
Potter Heigham Norfk....77 N8
Potterne Wilts....21 J3
Potterne Wick Wilts....21 J3
Potter Row Bucks....35 P4
Potters Bar Herts....50 F10
Potters Brook Lancs....95 K10
Potters Corner Kent....26 G3
Potter's Cross Staffs....58 B8
Potters Crouch Herts....50 D9
Potter's Forstal Kent....26 E2
Potters Green Covtry....59 N8
Potter's Green E Susx....25 M6
Potter's Green Herts....51 J6
Pottersheath Herts....50 F7
Potters Marston Leics....72 D11
Potter Somersal Derbys....71 L7
Potterspury W Nthn....49 L6
Potter Street Essex....51 L9
Potterton Abers....151 N4
Potterton Leeds....91 M3
Potthorpe Norfk....76 C7
Pottle Street Wilts....20 F6
Potto N York....104 E10
Potton C Beds....62 B11
Pott Row Norfk....75 P6
Pott's Green Essex....52 F7
Pott Shrigley Ches E....83 K9
Poughill Cnwll....16 C10
Poughill Devon....9 L3
Poulner Hants....13 L3
Poulshot Wilts....21 J3
Poulton Gloucs....33 L4
Poulton Wirral....81 L6
Poulton-le-Fylde Lancs....88 C3
Poulton Priory Gloucs....33 L5
Pound Bank Worcs....57 N10
Poundbury Dorset....11 P6
Poundffald Swans....28 G6
Poundgate E Susx....25 L5
Pound Green E Susx....25 M6
Pound Green Suffk....63 N10

Pound Green Worcs....57 P9
Pound Hill W Susx....24 G3
Poundon Bucks....48 H9
Poundsbridge Kent....25 M2
Poundsgate Devon....7 J4
Poundstock Cnwll....5 L2
Pound Street Hants....22 E2
Pounsley E Susx....25 M6
Pouton D & G....107 M7
Pouy Street Suffk....65 M7
Povey Cross Surrey....24 G2
Powburn Nthumb....119 L7
Powderham Devon....9 N8
Powerstock Dorset....11 L5
Powfoot D & G....109 P7
Pow Green Herefs....46 D6
Powhill Cumb....110 D9
Powick Worcs....46 F4
Powmill P & K....134 C8
Poxwell Dorset....12 B8
Poyle Slough....36 B5
Poynings W Susx....24 G8
Poyntington Dorset....20 C10
Poynton Ches E....83 K8
Poynton Wrekin....69 Q11
Poynton Green Wrekin....69 Q11
Poyston Cross Pembks....41 J7
Poystreet Green Suffk....64 D10
Praa Sands Cnwll....2 F8
Pratt's Bottom Gt Lon....37 L8
Praze-an-Beeble Cnwll....2 G6
Predannack Wollas Cnwll....2 H10
Prees Shrops....69 Q8
Preesall Lancs....94 H11
Prees Green Shrops....69 Q8
Preesgweene Shrops....69 J7
Prees Heath Shrops....69 Q7
Prees Higher Heath Shrops....69 Q8
Prees Lower Heath Shrops....69 Q8
Prendwick Nthumb....119 K8
Pren-gwyn Cerdgn....42 H6
Prenteg Gwynd....67 K6
Prenton Wirral....81 L7
Prescot Knows....81 P6
Prescott Devon....10 B2
Prescott Shrops....57 M8
Prescott Shrops....69 M10
Presnerb Angus....142 B4
Pressen Nthumb....118 F3
Prestatyn Denbgs....80 F8
Prestbury Ches E....83 J9
Prestbury Gloucs....47 J10
Presteigne Powys....45 L2
Prestleigh Somset....20 B6
Prestolee Bolton....89 M9
Preston Border....129 K8
Preston Br & H....24 H9
Preston Devon....7 M4
Preston Dorset....11 Q8
Preston E R Yk....93 L4
Preston Gloucs....33 K4
Preston Herts....50 E6
Preston Kent....38 H9
Preston Kent....39 M9
Preston Lancs....88 G5
Preston Nthumb....119 N5
Preston Rutlnd....73 M10
Preston Shrops....57 J2
Preston Somset....18 E7
Preston Torbay....7 M6
Preston Wilts....33 K9
Preston Wilts....33 Q10
Preston Bagot Warwks....59 J11
Preston Bissett Bucks....49 J9
Preston Bowyer Somset....18 F9
Preston Brockhurst Shrops....69 P10
Preston Brook Halton....82 C8
Preston Candover Hants....22 H6
Preston Capes W Nthn....48 G4
Preston Crowmarsh Oxon....34 H6
Preston Deanery W Nthn....60 G9
Preston Green Warwks....59 J11
Preston Gubbals Shrops....69 N11
Preston Montford Shrops....56 G2
Preston on Stour Warwks....47 P5
Preston on Tees S on T....104 D7
Preston on the Hill Halton....82 C8
Preston on Wye Herefs....45 M6
Prestonpans E Loth....128 B5
Preston Patrick W & F....95 L4
Preston Plucknett Somset....19 P11
Preston St Mary Suffk....64 C11
Preston Street Kent....39 N9
Preston-under-Scar N York....96 G2
Preston upon the Weald
  Moors Wrekin....70 B11
Preston Wynne Herefs....45 R4
Prestwich Bury....82 H4
Prestwick Nthumb....113 L6
Prestwick S Ayrs....114 G2
Prestwick Airport S Ayrs....114 G2
Prestwood Bucks....35 N4
Prestwood Staffs....58 C7
Price Town Brdgnd....29 P6
Prickwillow Cambs....63 J4
Priddy Somset....19 P4
Priestacott Devon....8 B3
Priestcliffe Derbys....83 P10
Priestcliffe Ditch Derbys....83 P10
Priest Hutton Lancs....95 L6
Priestland E Ayrs....125 L11
Priestley Green Calder....90 E5
Priest Weston Shrops....56 D5
Priestwood Green Kent....37 B2
Primethorpe Leics....72 E1
Primrose Green Norfk....76 F9
Primrosehill Border....129 K8
Primrose Hill Cambs....62 E3
Primrose Hill Derbys....84 F9
Primrose Hill Dudley....58 D5
Primrose Hill Lancs....88 D9
Primsidemill Border....118 F5
Prince of Wales Bridge
  Mons....31 P7
Princes Gate Pembks....41 M8
Princes Risborough Bucks....35 N4
Princethorpe Warwks....59 P10
Princetown Devon....6 F5
Prinsted W Susx....15 L5
Prion Denbgs....68 E2
Prior Rigg Cumb....111 J2
Priors Halton Shrops....56 H9
Priors Hardwick Warwks....48 C3
Priorslee Wrekin....57 N2
Priors Marston Warwks....48 C3
Priors Norton Gloucs....46 G10

Priors Park Gloucs....46 G8
Priory Wood Herefs....45 K5
Prisk V Glam....30 D9
Priston BaNES....20 C2
Pristow Green Norfk....64 G4
Prittlewell Sthend....38 E4
Privett Hants....23 J9
Prixford Devon....17 K4
Probus Cnwll....3 M4
Prora E Loth....128 E4
Prospect Cumb....100 F2
Prospidnick Cnwll....2 G7
Protstonhill Abers....159 K5
Prudhoe Nthumb....112 G8
Prussia Cove Cnwll....2 F8
Publ P & K....140 C9
Publow BaNES....20 B2
Puckeridge Herts....51 J6
Puckington Somset....19 L11
Pucklechurch S Glos....32 C9
Puckrup Gloucs....46 G7
Puddinglake Ches W....82 F11
Puddington Ches W....81 L10
Puddington Devon....9 K2
Puddledock Norfk....64 F3
Puddletown Dorset....12 C6
Pudleston Herefs....45 R3
Pudsey Leeds....90 G4
Pulborough W Susx....24 B7
Puleston Wrekin....70 C10
Pulford Ches W....69 L3
Pulham Dorset....11 Q3
Pulham Market Norfk....64 H4
Pulham St Mary Norfk....65 J4
Pullens Green S Glos....32 B6
Pulloxhill C Beds....50 C4
Pulverbatch Shrops....56 G4
Pumpherston W Loth....127 K4
Pumsaint Carmth....43 N6
Puncheston Pembks....41 K5
Puncknowle Dorset....11 L7
Punnett's Town E Susx....25 P6
Purbrook Hants....15 J5
Purfleet-on-Thames Thurr....37 N5
Puriton Somset....19 K6
Purleigh Essex....52 D11
Purley Gt Lon....36 H8
Purley on Thames W Berk....35 J9
Purlogue Shrops....56 D9
Purlpit Wilts....32 G11
Purls Bridge Cambs....62 G3
Purse Caundle Dorset....20 C11
Purshull Green Worcs....58 C10
Purslow Shrops....56 F8
Purston Jaglin Wakefd....91 L7
Purtington Somset....10 H3
Purton Gloucs....32 C3
Purton Gloucs....32 C4
Purton Wilts....33 L7
Purton Stoke Wilts....33 L6
Pury End W Nthn....49 K5
Pusey Oxon....34 C5
Putley Herefs....46 B7
Putley Green Herefs....46 B7
Putloe Gloucs....32 E3
Putney Gt Lon....36 F6
Putsborough Devon....16 H3
Puttenham Herts....35 N2
Puttenham Surrey....23 P5
Puttock End Essex....52 D3
Putton Dorset....11 N8
Putts Corner Devon....10 C5
Puxley W Nthn....49 L6
Puxton N Som....19 M2
Pwll Carmth....28 E4
Pwllcrochan Pembks....40 H10
Pwll-du Mons....30 H2
Pwll-glâs Denbgs....68 E4
Pwllgloyw Powys....44 E8
Pwllheli Gwynd....66 F7
Pwllmeyric Mons....31 P6
Pwll-trap Carmth....41 Q7
Pwll-y-glaw Neath....29 L6
Pye Bridge Derbys....84 F12
Pyecombe W Susx....24 G8
Pye Corner Newpt....31 K7
Pye Green Staffs....58 E2
Pyle Brdgnd....29 M8
Pyleigh Somset....18 F8
Pylle Somset....20 B7
Pymoor Cambs....62 G3
Pymore Dorset....11 K6
Pyrford Surrey....36 B9
Pyrton Oxon....35 J5
Pytchley N Nthn....61 J7
Pyworthy Devon....16 E11

Q

Quabbs Shrops....56 C8
Quadring Lincs....74 D4
Quadring Eaudike Lincs....74 D4
Quainton Bucks....49 K10
Quaker's Yard Myr Td....30 E5
Quaking Houses Dur....113 J10
Quantock Hills Somset....18 G7
Quarff Shet....169 r10
Quarley Hants....21 Q6
Quarndon Derbys....72 A2
Quarr Hill IoW....14 G8
Quarrier's Village Inver....125 K4
Quarrington Lincs....73 R2
Quarrington Hill Dur....104 B3
Quarrybank Ches W....82 C11
Quarry Bank Dudley....58 D7
Quarrywood Moray....157 M5
Quarter N Ayrs....124 F5
Quarter S Lans....126 C7
Quatford Shrops....57 N6
Quatt Shrops....57 P7
Quebec Dur....103 N2
Quedgeley Gloucs....32 F3
Queen Adelaide Cambs....62 J4
Queenborough Kent....38 F7
Queen Camel Somset....19 Q10
Queen Charlton BaNES....32 B11
Queen Dart Devon....17 Q8
Queen Elizabeth Forest
  Park Stirlg....132 G7
Queen Elizabeth II Bridge
  Thurr....37 N5
Queenhill Worcs....46 G7
Queen Oak Dorset....20 E8
Queen's Bower IoW....14 G10

Queensbury C Brad....90 E4
Queensferry Flints....81 L11
Queensferry Crossing Fife....134 E11
Queen's Head Shrops....69 K9
Queen's Hills Norfk....76 H9
Queenslie C Glas....126 B4
Queen's Park Bed....61 M11
Queen's Park Essex....51 Q11
Queen's Park N Nthn....60 G8
Queen Street Kent....37 Q11
Queen Street Wilts....33 K7
Queenzieburn N Lans....126 B2
Quendon Essex....51 M4
Queniborough Leics....72 G8
Quenington Gloucs....33 M4
Quernmore Lancs....95 L9
Queslett Birm....58 G6
Quethiock Cnwll....5 N9
Quick's Green W Berk....34 G9
Quidenham Norfk....64 E4
Quidhampton Hants....22 F4
Quidhampton Wilts....21 M8
Quina Brook Shrops....69 Q8
Quinbury End W Nthn....48 H4
Quinton Dudley....58 E8
Quinton W Nthn....49 L4
Quinton Green W Nthn....49 L4
Quintrell Downs Cnwll....4 C10
Quixhall Staffs....71 L6
Quixwood Border....129 K7
Quoditch Devon....5 Q2
Quoig P & K....133 N3
Quorn Leics....72 F7
Quothquan S Lans....116 D3
Quoyburray Ork....169 e6
Quoyloo Ork....169 b4

R

Raasay Highld....153 K9
Rabbit's Cross Kent....26 C2
Rableyheath Herts....50 F7
Raby Cumb....110 C10
Raby Wirral....81 L9
Rachan Mill Border....116 G4
Rachub Gwynd....79 L11
Rackenford Devon....17 R8
Rackham W Susx....24 B8
Rackheath Norfk....77 K9
Racks D & G....109 M6
Rackwick Ork....169 b7
Radbourne Derbys....71 P7
Radcliffe Bury....89 M9
Radcliffe Nthumb....119 Q10
Radcliffe on Trent Notts....72 G3
Radclive Bucks....49 J8
Radcot Oxon....33 Q5
Raddery Highld....156 C6
Raddington Somset....18 D9
Radernie Fife....135 M6
Radford Covtry....59 M8
Radford Semele Warwks....48 B2
Radlet Somset....18 H7
Radlett Herts....50 E10
Radley Devon....17 N7
Radley Oxon....34 F5
Radley W Berk....34 C11
Radley Green Essex....51 P9
Radmore Green Ches E....69 Q3
Radnage Bucks....35 K5
Radstock BaNES....20 C4
Radstone W Nthn....48 H5
Radway Warwks....48 C5
Radwell Bed....61 M9
Radwell Herts....50 F3
Radwinter Essex....51 P3
Radwinter End Essex....51 P3
Radyr Cardif....30 F8
RAF College (Cranwell)
  Lincs....86 D11
Rafford Moray....157 K6
RAF Museum Cosford
  Shrops....57 P3
RAF Museum London Gt Lon....36 F2
Ragdale Leics....72 H7
Ragdon Shrops....56 H6
Raginnis Cnwll....2 D8
Raglan Mons....31 M3
Ragnall Notts....85 P6
Raigbeg Highld....148 E2
Rainbow Hill Worcs....46 G3
Rainford St Hel....81 P4
Rainford Junction St Hel....81 P4
Rainham Gt Lon....37 M4
Rainham Medway....38 D8
Rainhill St Hel....81 P6
Rainhill Stoops St Hel....81 Q6
Rainow Ches E....83 K9
Rainsough Bury....82 H4
Rainton N York....97 N5
Rainworth Notts....85 J9
Raisbeck W & F....102 B9
Raise W & F....111 P11
Raisthorpe N York....98 H8
Rait P & K....134 G2
Raithby Lincs....87 K4
Raithby Lincs....87 L7
Raithwaite N York....105 N8
Rake Hants....23 M9
Rakewood Rochdl....89 Q7
Ralia Highld....148 B5
Ram Carmth....43 L5
Ramasaig Highld....152 B8
Rame Cnwll....2 G9
Rame Cnwll....6 C9
Ram Hill S Glos....32 C9
Ram Lane Kent....26 H2
Rampisham Dorset....11 M4
Rampside W & F....94 E7
Rampton Cambs....62 F7
Rampton Notts....85 P5
Ramsbottom Bury....89 M7
Ramsbury Wilts....33 Q9
Ramscraigs Highld....167 K11
Ramsdean Hants....23 K9
Ramsden Oxon....34 C2
Ramsden Worcs....46 H5
Ramsden Bellhouse Essex....38 B2
Ramsden Heath Essex....38 B2
Ramsey Cambs....62 C3
Ramsey Essex....53 M5
Ramsey IoM....80 g3
Ramsey Forty Foot Cambs....62 D3

Ramsey Heights Cambs....62 B4
Ramsey Island Pembks....40 D6
Ramsey Mereside Cambs....62 C3
Ramsey St Mary's Cambs....62 C3
Ramsgate Kent....39 Q8
Ramsgill N York....96 H6
Ramshaw Dur....103 M5
Ramshaw Dur....112 E11
Ramsholt Suffk....53 P3
Ramshope Nthumb....118 D10
Ramshorn Staffs....71 K5
Ramsley Devon....8 G6
Ramsnest Common Surrey....23 P8
Ranby Lincs....86 H5
Ranby Notts....85 L4
Rand Lincs....86 F5
Randwick Gloucs....32 F3
Ranfurly Rens....125 K4
Rangemore Staffs....71 M10
Rangeworthy S Glos....32 C7
Rankinston E Ayrs....115 J5
Ranksborough Rutlnd....73 L8
Rank's Green Essex....52 B8
Rannoch Station P & K....140 B6
Ranscombe Somset....18 B6
Ranskill Notts....85 L3
Ranton Staffs....70 F10
Ranton Green Staffs....70 E10
Ranworth Norfk....77 M9
Raploch Stirlg....133 M9
Rapness Ork....169 e2
Rapps Somset....19 K11
Rascarrel D & G....108 G11
Rashfield Ag & B....131 N11
Rashwood Worcs....58 D11
Raskelf N York....97 Q6
Rassau Blae G....30 G2
Rastrick Calder....90 E6
Ratagan Highld....145 R4
Ratby Leics....72 E9
Ratcliffe Culey Leics....72 A11
Ratcliffe on Soar Notts....72 D5
Ratcliffe on the Wreake
  Leics....72 G8
Rathen Abers....159 N5
Rathillet Fife....135 K3
Rathmell N York....96 B9
Ratho C Edin....127 L3
Ratho Station C Edin....127 L3
Rathven Moray....158 B4
Ratlake Hants....22 D10
Ratley Warwks....48 C5
Ratling Kent....39 M11
Ratlinghope Shrops....56 G5
Rattar Highld....167 N2
Ratten Row Cumb....101 K2
Ratten Row Cumb....110 G11
Ratten Row Lancs....88 E2
Rattery Devon....7 J6
Rattlesden Suffk....64 D10
Ratton Village E Susx....25 P10
Rattray P & K....142 B8
Raughton Cumb....110 G11
Raughton Head Cumb....110 G11
Raunds N Nthn....61 L6
Ravenfield Rothm....91 M11
Ravenglass Cumb....100 E11
Ravenhills Green Worcs....46 D4
Raveningham Norfk....65 M2
Ravenscar N York....105 Q10
Ravenscraig N Lans....126 D6
Ravensdale IoM....80 e3
Ravensden Bed....61 N10
Ravenseat N York....102 G9
Ravenshead Notts....85 J10
Ravensmoor Ches E....69 R4
Ravensthorpe Kirk....90 G6
Ravensthorpe W Nthn....60 E6
Ravenstone Leics....72 C8
Ravenstone M Keyn....49 M4
Ravenstonedale W & F....102 D10
Ravenstruther S Lans....126 G8
Ravensworth N York....103 M9
Raw N York....105 P9
Rawcliffe C York....98 B10
Rawcliffe E R Yk....92 A6
Rawcliffe Bridge E R Yk....92 A6
Rawdon Leeds....90 G3
Rawling Street Kent....38 F10
Rawmarsh Rothm....91 L11
Rawnsley Staffs....58 F2
Rawreth Essex....38 C3
Rawridge Devon....10 E3
Rawtenstall Lancs....89 N6
Raydon Suffk....52 H4
Raylees Nthumb....112 D2
Rayleigh Essex....38 D3
Raymond's Hill Devon....10 G5
Rayne Essex....52 B7
Raynes Park Gt Lon....36 F7
Reach Cambs....63 J7
Read Lancs....89 M4
Reading Readg....35 K10
Reading Services W Berk....35 J11
Reading Street Kent....26 F5
Reading Street Kent....39 Q8
Reagill W & F....102 B7
Rearquhar Highld....162 G8
Rearsby Leics....72 H8
Rease Heath Ches E....70 A4
Reawla Cnwll....2 G6
Reay Highld....166 G4
Reculver Kent....39 M8
Red Ball Devon....18 E11
Redberth Pembks....41 L10
Redbourn Herts....50 D8
Redbourne N Linc....92 G11
Redbrook Gloucs....31 P3
Redbrook Wrexhm....69 P6
Redbrook Street Kent....26 F4
Redburn Highld....156 G8
Redburn Nthumb....111 Q8
Redcar R & Cl....104 H6
Redcastle D & G....108 H7
Redcastle Highld....155 Q8
Red Dial Cumb....110 E11
Redding Falk....126 G2
Reddingmuirhead Falk....126 G2
Reddish Stockp....83 J6
Redditch Worcs....58 F11
Rede Suffk....63 P9
Redenhall Norfk....65 K5
Redenham Hants....22 B5
Redesmouth Nthumb....112 C4
Redford Abers....143 P3
Redford Angus....143 K9

Place	County	Page	Grid
Redford	W Susx	23	N9
Redfordgreen	Border	117	M7
Redgate	Rhondd	30	D7
Redgorton	P & K	134	D2
Redgrave	Suffk	64	E6
Redhill	Abers	151	K7
Red Hill	BCP	13	J5
Redhill	Herts	50	H4
Redhill	N Som	19	N2
Redhill	Surrey	36	G10
Red Hill	Warwks	47	M3
Redisham	Suffk	65	N5
Redland	Bristl	31	Q9
Redland	Ork	169	c4
Redlingfield	Suffk	64	H7
Redlingfield Green	Suffk	64	H7
Red Lodge	Suffk	63	M6
Red Lumb	Rochdl	89	N7
Redlynch	Somset	20	D8
Redlynch	Wilts	21	P10
Redmain	Cumb	100	F4
Redmarley	Worcs	57	P11
Redmarley D'Abitot	Gloucs	46	E8
Redmarshall	S on T	104	C6
Redmile	Leics	73	K3
Redmire	N York	96	F2
Redmyre	Abers	143	P2
Rednal	Birm	58	F9
Rednal	Shrops	69	L9
Redpath	Border	118	A3
Red Point	Highld	153	N4
Red Post	Cnwll	16	D10
Red Rice	Hants	22	B6
Red Rock	Wigan	88	H9
Red Roses	Carmth	41	P8
Red Row	Nthumb	119	Q11
Redruth	Cnwll	2	H5
Redstocks	Wilts	20	H2
Redstone	P & K	142	B11
Redstone Cross	Pembks	41	M7
Red Street	Staffs	70	E4
Redvales	Bury	89	N9
Red Wharf Bay	IoA	79	J8
Redwick	Newpt	31	M8
Redwick	S Glos	31	Q7
Redworth	Darltn	103	P6
Reed	Herts	51	J3
Reedham	Norfk	77	N11
Reedness	E R Yk	92	C6
Reeds Beck	Lincs	86	H7
Reeds Holme	Lancs	89	N6
Reepham	Lincs	86	D6
Reepham	Norfk	76	G7
Reeth	N York	103	K11
Reeves Green	Solhll	59	L9
Regaby	IoM	80	f2
Regil	N Som	19	P2
Reiff	Highld	160	F4
Reigate	Surrey	36	G10
Reighton	N York	99	N5
Reinigeadal	W Isls	168	h7
Reisque	Abers	151	M4
Reiss	Highld	167	P6
Rejerrah	Cnwll	4	B10
Releath	Cnwll	2	H7
Relubbus	Cnwll	2	F7
Relugas	Moray	156	H8
Remenham	Wokam	35	L8
Remenham Hill	Wokam	35	L8
Rempstone	Notts	72	F6
Rendcomb	Gloucs	33	K3
Rendham	Suffk	65	L9
Rendlesham	Suffk	65	L11
Renfrew	Rens	125	N4
Renhold	Bed	61	N10
Renishaw	Derbys	84	G5
Rennington	Nthumb	119	P7
Renton	W Duns	125	K2
Renwick	W & F	101	Q2
Repps	Norfk	77	N8
Repton	Derbys	71	Q9
Reraig	Highld	145	P2
Resaurie	Highld	156	C8
Rescassa	Cnwll	3	P5
Rescorla	Cnwll	3	P4
Resipole Burn	Highld	138	C5
Reskadinnick	Cnwll	2	G5
Resolis	Highld	156	B4
Resolven	Neath	29	M4
Rest and be thankful	Ag & B	131	Q6
Reston	Border	129	M7
Restronguet	Cnwll	3	L6
Reswallie	Angus	143	J7
Reterth	Cnwll	4	E9
Retford	Notts	85	M4
Retire	Cnwll	4	G9
Rettendon Common	Essex	38	C2
Rettendon Village	Essex	38	C2
Retyn	Cnwll	4	D10
Revesby	Lincs	87	J8
Rew	Devon	7	J11
Rew	Devon	7	K4
Rewe	Devon	9	M5
Rew Street	IoW	14	E8
Rexon	Devon	5	Q4
Reydon	Suffk	65	P6
Reymerston	Norfk	76	E10
Reynalton	Pembks	41	L9
Reynoldston	Swans	28	E7
Rezare	Cnwll	5	P6
Rhadyr	Mons	31	L4
Rhandirmwyn	Carmth	43	Q6
Rhayader	Powys	55	M11
Rheindown	Highld	155	P8
Rhenigidale	W Isls	168	h7
Rhes-y-cae	Flints	80	H10
Rhewl	Denbgs	68	F2
Rhewl	Denbgs	68	G6
Rhewl Mostyn	Flints	80	H8
Rhicarn	Highld	164	C11
Rhiconich	Highld	164	G6
Rhicullen	Highld	156	B3
Rhigos	Rhondd	29	P3
Rhives	Highld	163	J6
Rhiwbina	Cardif	30	G8
Rhiwbryfdir	Gwynd	67	M5
Rhiwderyn	Newpt	31	J7
Rhiwen	Gwynd	67	K2
Rhiwinder	Rhondd	30	D7
Rhiwlas	Gwynd	68	B7
Rhiwlas	Gwynd	79	K11
Rhiwlas	Powys	68	G6
Rhiwsaeson	Rhondd	30	E8
Rhode	Somset	19	J8
Rhoden Green	Kent	37	Q11
Rhodesia	Notts	85	J5
Rhodes Minnis	Kent	27	L3
Rhodiad-y-brenin	Pembks	40	E5
Rhonehouse	D & G	108	F9
Rhoose	V Glam	30	E11
Rhos	Carmth	42	G7
Rhos	Denbgs	68	F2
Rhos	Neath	29	K4
Rhosaman	Carmth	29	K2
Rhosbeirio	IoA	78	F6
Rhoscefnhir	IoA	79	J9
Rhoscolyn	IoA	78	D9
Rhoscrowther	Pembks	40	H10
Rhosesmor	Flints	81	J11
Rhos-fawr	Gwynd	66	F7
Rhosgadfan	Gwynd	67	J3
Rhosgoch	IoA	78	G7
Rhosgoch	Powys	44	H5
Rhos Haminiog	Cerdgn	43	K2
Rhoshill	Pembks	41	N2
Rhoshirwaun	Gwynd	66	C9
Rhoslan	Gwynd	66	H6
Rhoslefain	Gwynd	54	D3
Rhosllanerchrugog	Wrexhm	69	J5
Rhôs Lligwy	IoA	78	H7
Rhosmaen	Carmth	43	M10
Rhosmeirch	IoA	78	H8
Rhosneigr	IoA	78	E10
Rhosnesni	Wrexhm	69	L4
Rhôs-on-Sea	Conwy	79	Q8
Rhosrobin	Wrexhm	69	K4
Rhossili	Swans	28	D7
Rhostrehwfa	IoA	78	G10
Rhostryfan	Gwynd	66	H3
Rhostyllen	Wrexhm	69	K5
Rhosybol	IoA	78	G7
Rhos-y-brithdir	Powys	68	F10
Rhosygadfa	Shrops	69	K8
Rhos-y-garth	Cerdgn	54	E10
Rhos-y-gwaliau	Gwynd	68	B8
Rhos-y-llan	Gwynd	66	C7
Rhosymedre	Wrexhm	69	J6
Rhos-y-meirch	Powys	56	D11
RHS Garden Harlow Carr	N York	97	L10
RHS Garden Wisley	Surrey	36	C9
Rhu	Ag & B	132	B11
Rhuallt	Denbgs	80	F9
Rhubodach	Ag & B	124	C3
Rhuddall Heath	Ches W	69	Q2
Rhuddlan	Cerdgn	43	J6
Rhuddlan	Denbgs	80	E9
Rhue	Highld	161	J7
Rhulen	Powys	44	G5
Rhunahaorine	Ag & B	123	M10
Rhyd	Gwynd	67	L4
Rhydargaeau	Carmth	42	H9
Rhydcymerau	Carmth	43	L7
Rhydd	Worcs	46	F5
Rhyd-Ddu	Gwynd	67	K4
Rhydding	Neath	29	K5
Rhydgaled	Conwy	68	C2
Rhydlanfair	Conwy	67	Q4
Rhydlewis	Cerdgn	42	F5
Rhydlios	Gwynd	66	B9
Rhydlydan	Conwy	68	A4
Rhydowen	Cerdgn	42	H5
Rhydroser	Cerdgn	54	D11
Rhydspence	Herefs	45	J5
Rhydtalog	Flints	68	H4
Rhyd-uchaf	Gwynd	68	B7
Rhyd-y-clafdy	Gwynd	66	E8
Rhydycroesau	Shrops	68	H8
Rhydyfelin	Cerdgn	54	D9
Rhydyfelin	Rhondd	30	E7
Rhyd-y-foel	Conwy	80	C9
Rhydyfro	Neath	29	K3
Rhyd-y-groes	Gwynd	79	K11
Rhydymain	Gwynd	68	A10
Rhyd-y-meirch	Mons	31	K3
Rhydymwyn	Flints	81	J11
Rhyd-y-pennau	Cerdgn	54	E7
Rhyd-yr-onnen	Gwynd	54	E4
Rhyd-y-sarn	Gwynd	67	M6
Rhyl	Denbgs	80	E8
Rhymney	Caerph	30	F3
Rhynd	P & K	134	F3
Rhynie	Abers	150	D2
Rhynie	Highld	163	J11
Ribbesford	Worcs	57	P10
Ribbleton	Lancs	88	H4
Ribby	Lancs	88	E4
Ribchester	Lancs	89	K3
Riber	Derbys	84	D9
Riby	Lincs	93	L9
Riccall	N York	91	Q3
Riccarton	Border	111	K2
Riccarton	E Ayrs	125	L10
Richards Castle	Herefs	56	H11
Richings Park	Bucks	36	B5
Richmond	Gt Lon	36	E6
Richmond	N York	103	N10
Richmond	Sheff	84	F3
Richmond Park	Kent	27	P2
Rich's Holford	Somset	18	F8
Rickerscote	Staffs	70	G10
Rickford	N Som	19	N3
Rickham	Devon	7	K11
Rickinghall	Suffk	64	E6
Rickling	Essex	51	L4
Rickling Green	Essex	51	M5
Rickmansworth	Herts	36	C2
Riddell	Border	117	Q6
Riddings	Derbys	84	F10
Riddlecombe	Devon	17	L9
Riddlesden	C Brad	90	D2
Ridge	BaNES	19	Q3
Ridge	Dorset	12	F7
Ridge	Herts	50	F10
Ridge	Wilts	21	J8
Ridgebourne	Powys	44	F2
Ridge Green	Surrey	36	H11
Ridge Lane	Warwks	59	L6
Ridge Row	Kent	27	M3
Ridgeway	Derbys	84	F4
Ridgeway	Worcs	47	K2
Ridgeway Cross	Herefs	46	D5
Ridgewell	Essex	52	B3
Ridgewood	E Susx	25	L7
Ridgmont	C Beds	49	Q7
Riding Mill	Nthumb	112	F8
Ridley	Kent	37	P8
Ridley	Nthumb	111	Q8
Ridley Green	Ches E	69	Q4
Ridlington	Norfk	77	L5
Ridlington	Rutlnd	73	L10
Ridlington Street	Norfk	77	L5
Ridsdale	Nthumb	112	D4
Rievaulx	N York	98	B3
Rigg	D & G	110	E7
Riggend	N Lans	126	D3
Righoul	Highld	156	F7
Rigmadon Park	W & F	95	N4
Rigsby	Lincs	87	M5
Rigside	S Lans	116	B3
Riley Green	Lancs	89	J5
Rileyhill	Staffs	58	H2
Rilla Mill	Cnwll	5	M7
Rillaton	Cnwll	5	M7
Rillington	N York	98	H6
Rimington	Lancs	96	B11
Rimpton	Somset	20	B10
Rimswell	E R Yk	93	P5
Rinaston	Pembks	41	J5
Rindleford	Shrops	57	N5
Ringford	D & G	108	E9
Ringinglow	Sheff	84	C4
Ringland	Norfk	76	G9
Ringles Cross	E Susx	25	L4
Ringlestone	Kent	38	E10
Ringley	Bolton	89	M9
Ringmer	E Susx	25	K8
Ringmore	Devon	6	H9
Ringmore	Devon	7	N4
Ringorm	Moray	157	P9
Ring's End	Cambs	74	G10
Ringsfield	Suffk	65	N4
Ringsfield Corner	Suffk	65	N4
Ringshall	Herts	35	Q2
Ringshall	Suffk	64	E11
Ringshall Stocks	Suffk	64	F11
Ringstead	N Nthn	61	L5
Ringstead	Norfk	75	P2
Ringwood	Hants	13	L3
Ringwould	Kent	27	Q2
Rinmore	Abers	150	C4
Rinsey	Cnwll	2	F8
Rinsey Croft	Cnwll	2	F8
Ripe	E Susx	25	M8
Ripley	Derbys	84	E10
Ripley	Hants	13	L5
Ripley	N York	97	L8
Ripley	Surrey	36	C9
Riplingham	E R Yk	92	H4
Riplington	Hants	23	J10
Ripon	N York	97	M6
Rippingale	Lincs	74	A5
Ripple	Kent	39	Q1
Ripple	Worcs	46	G7
Ripponden	Calder	90	C7
Risabus	Ag & B	122	D11
Risbury	Herefs	45	Q4
Risby	N Linc	92	F8
Risby	Suffk	63	P7
Risca	Caerph	30	H6
Rise	E R Yk	93	L2
Riseden	E Susx	25	P4
Riseden	Kent	26	B4
Risegate	Lincs	74	D5
Riseholme	Lincs	86	C5
Risehow	Cumb	100	D4
Riseley	Bed	61	M8
Riseley	Wokam	23	K2
Rishangles	Suffk	64	H8
Rishton	Lancs	89	L4
Rishworth	Calder	90	C7
Rising Bridge	Lancs	89	M5
Risley	Derbys	72	D3
Risley	Warrtn	82	E6
Risplith	N York	97	K7
Rivar	Wilts	22	B2
Rivenhall End	Essex	52	D8
River	Kent	27	N3
River	W Susx	23	P10
River Bank	Cambs	62	H7
Riverford	Highld	155	P7
Riverhead	Kent	37	M9
Rivers Corner	Dorset	12	C2
Rivington	Lancs	89	J8
Rivington Services	Lancs	89	J8
Roachill	Devon	17	P7
Roade	W Nthn	49	L4
Road Green	Norfk	65	K3
Roadhead	Cumb	111	K6
Roadmeetings	S Lans	126	F8
Roadside	E Ayrs	115	L4
Roadside	Highld	167	L4
Roadwater	Somset	18	D7
Roag	Highld	152	D9
Roa Island	W & F	94	E7
Roan of Craigoch	S Ayrs	114	E2
Roast Green	Essex	51	L4
Roath	Cardif	30	G9
Roberton	Border	117	N8
Roberton	S Lans	116	C5
Robertsbridge	E Susx	26	B7
Roberttown	Kirk	90	F6
Robeston Wathen	Pembks	41	L7
Robgill Tower	D & G	110	D6
Robin Hill	Staffs	70	G4
Robin Hood	Lancs	88	G8
Robin Hood	Leeds	91	J5
Robinhood End	Essex	52	B4
Robin Hood's Bay	N York	105	Q9
Roborough	Devon	6	E6
Roborough	Devon	17	M8
Robroyston	C Glas	125	Q4
Roby	Knows	81	N6
Roby Mill	Lancs	88	G9
Rocester	Staffs	71	L7
Roch	Pembks	40	G6
Rochdale	Rochdl	89	P8
Roche	Cnwll	4	F9
Rochester	Medway	38	B8
Rochester	Nthumb	118	F11
Rochford	Essex	38	E3
Rochford	Worcs	57	L11
Roch Gate	Pembks	40	G6
Rock	Cnwll	4	F7
Rock	Neath	29	L6
Rock	Nthumb	119	P6
Rock	W Susx	24	D8
Rock	Worcs	57	N10
Rockbeare	Devon	9	P6
Rockbourne	Hants	21	M11
Rockcliffe	Cumb	110	G8
Rockcliffe	D & G	108	H10
Rockcliffe Cross	Cumb	110	F8
Rock End	Staffs	70	F3
Rockend	Torbay	7	N6
Rock Ferry	Wirral	81	L7
Rockfield	Highld	163	L10
Rockfield	Mons	31	N2
Rockford	Devon	17	P2
Rockford	Hants	13	L3
Rockgreen	Shrops	57	J9
Rockhampton	S Glos	32	C6
Rockhead	Cnwll	4	H5
Rockhill	Shrops	56	D9
Rock Hill	Worcs	58	E11
Rockingham	N Nthn	61	J2
Rockland All Saints	Norfk	64	D2
Rockland St Mary	Norfk	77	L11
Rockland St Peter	Norfk	64	D2
Rockley	Notts	85	M6
Rockley	Wilts	33	N10
Rockliffe	Lancs	89	P6
Rockville	Ag & B	131	Q9
Rockwell End	Bucks	35	L7
Rockwell Green	Somset	18	F10
Rodborough	Gloucs	32	F4
Rodbourne	Swindn	33	M7
Rodbourne	Wilts	32	H8
Rodd	Herefs	45	L2
Roddam	Nthumb	119	K6
Rodden	Dorset	11	N8
Roddymoor	Dur	103	N3
Rode	Somset	20	F4
Rode Heath	Ches E	70	E3
Rode Heath	Ches E	83	J11
Rodel	W Isls	168	f9
Roden	Wrekin	69	Q11
Rodhuish	Somset	18	D7
Rodington	Wrekin	57	K2
Rodington Heath	Wrekin	57	K2
Rodley	Gloucs	32	D2
Rodley	Leeds	90	G3
Rodmarton	Gloucs	32	H5
Rodmell	E Susx	25	K9
Rodmersham	Kent	38	F9
Rodmersham Green	Kent	38	F9
Rodney Stoke	Somset	19	N5
Rodsley	Derbys	71	N6
Rodway	Somset	19	J6
Rodway	Wrekin	70	B11
Roecliffe	N York	97	N7
Roe Cross	Tamesd	83	L5
Roe Green	Herts	50	F9
Roe Green	Herts	50	H4
Roe Green	Salfd	82	F4
Roehampton	Gt Lon	36	F6
Roffey	W Susx	24	E4
Rogart	Highld	162	G6
Rogate	W Susx	23	M10
Roger Ground	W & F	101	L11
Rogerstone	Newpt	31	J7
Roghadal	W Isls	168	f9
Rogiet	Mons	31	N7
Roke	Oxon	34	H6
Roker	Sundld	113	P9
Rollesby	Norfk	77	N8
Rolleston	Leics	73	J10
Rolleston	Notts	85	M10
Rolleston on Dove	Staffs	71	N9
Rolston	E R Yk	93	M2
Rolstone	N Som	19	L2
Rolvenden	Kent	26	D5
Rolvenden Layne	Kent	26	E5
Romaldkirk	Dur	103	J6
Romanby	N York	97	N2
Romanno Bridge	Border	127	M8
Romansleigh	Devon	17	N7
Romden Castle	Kent	26	E3
Romesdal	Highld	152	G7
Romford	Dorset	13	J3
Romford	Gt Lon	37	M3
Romiley	Stockp	83	K6
Romney Street	Kent	37	N8
Romsey	Cambs	62	G9
Romsey	Hants	22	C10
Romsley	Shrops	57	N8
Romsley	Worcs	58	E8
Rona	Highld	153	L6
Ronachan	Ag & B	123	M9
Rood Ashton	Wilts	20	G3
Rookhope	Dur	102	H2
Rookley	IoW	14	F10
Rookley Green	IoW	14	F10
Rooks Bridge	Somset	19	L4
Rooks Nest	Somset	18	E8
Rookwith	N York	97	K3
Roos	E R Yk	93	N4
Roose	W & F	94	E7
Roosebeck	W & F	94	E7
Roothams Green	Bed	61	N9
Ropley	Hants	22	H8
Ropley Dean	Hants	22	H8
Ropley Soke	Hants	23	J8
Ropsley	Lincs	73	P4
Rora	Abers	159	Q7
Rorrington	Shrops	56	F4
Rosarie	Moray	158	A7
Rose	Cnwll	3	K3
Roseacre	Lancs	88	E3
Rose Ash	Devon	17	P7
Rosebank	S Lans	126	E8
Rosebush	Pembks	41	J5
Rosecare	Cnwll	5	K2
Rosecliston	Cnwll	4	C10
Rosedale Abbey	N York	105	K11
Rose Green	Essex	52	F6
Rose Green	Suffk	52	F5
Rose Green	Suffk	52	G5
Rose Green	W Susx	15	P7
Rosehall	Highld	162	B6
Rosehearty	Abers	159	M4
Rose Hill	E Susx	25	L7
Rose Hill	Lancs	89	N4
Rosehill	Shrops	69	N11
Roseisle	Moray	157	L4
Roselands	E Susx	25	P10
Rosemarket	Pembks	41	J8
Rosemarkie	Highld	156	C6
Rosemary Lane	Devon	10	D2
Rosemount	P & K	142	B9
Rosenannon	Cnwll	4	F8
Rosenithon	Cnwll	3	L9
Roser's Cross	E Susx	25	N6
Rosevean	Cnwll	4	G10
Rosevine	Cnwll	3	M6
Rosewarne	Cnwll	2	G6
Rosewell	Mdloth	127	N5
Roseworth	S on T	104	D6
Roseworthy	Cnwll	2	G6
Rosgill	W & F	101	P7
Roskestal	Cnwll	2	B9
Roskhill	Highld	152	D9
Roskorwell	Cnwll	3	K9
Rosley	Cumb	110	F11
Roslin	Mdloth	127	P5
Rosliston	Derbys	71	N11
Rosneath	Ag & B	132	B11
Ross	D & G	108	D12
Ross	Nthumb	119	M3
Rossett	Wrexhm	69	L3
Rossett Green	N York	97	L10
Rossington	Donc	91	Q11
Ross-on-Wye	Herefs	46	A10
Roster	Highld	167	N9
Rostherne	Ches E	82	F8
Rosthwaite	Cumb	101	J8
Roston	Derbys	71	L6
Rosudgeon	Cnwll	2	F8
Rosyth	Fife	134	E11
Rothbury	Nthumb	119	L10
Rotherby	Leics	72	H8
Rotherfield	E Susx	25	N5
Rotherfield Greys	Oxon	35	K8
Rotherfield Peppard	Oxon	35	K8
Rotherham	Rothm	84	F2
Rothersthorpe	W Nthn	60	F9
Rotherwick	Hants	23	K3
Rothes	Moray	157	P8
Rothesay	Ag & B	124	D5
Rothiebrisbane	Abers	158	H10
Rothiemurchus Lodge	Highld	148	H6
Rothienorman	Abers	158	H10
Rothley	Leics	72	F8
Rothley	Nthumb	112	F3
Rothmaise	Abers	158	G11
Rothwell	Leeds	91	J5
Rothwell	Lincs	93	K11
Rothwell	N Nthn	60	H4
Rotsea	E R Yk	99	M10
Rottal Lodge	Angus	142	F4
Rottingdean	Br & H	25	J10
Rottington	Cumb	100	C8
Roucan	D & G	109	M5
Roud	IoW	14	F10
Rougham	Norfk	76	A7
Rougham	Suffk	64	C9
Rough Close	Staffs	70	G7
Rough Common	Kent	39	K10
Roughlee	Lancs	89	N2
Roughpark	Abers	149	Q5
Roughton	Lincs	86	H8
Roughton	Norfk	77	J4
Roughton	Shrops	57	P6
Roughway	Kent	37	P10
Roundbush	Essex	52	E11
Round Bush	Herts	50	D11
Roundbush Green	Essex	51	N8
Round Green	Luton	50	D6
Roundham	Somset	11	J3
Roundhay	Leeds	91	J3
Rounds Green	Sandw	58	E7
Round Street	Kent	37	Q8
Roundstreet Common	W Susx	24	C5
Roundswell	Devon	17	J5
Roundway	Wilts	21	L7
Roundyhill	Angus	142	F7
Rousay	Ork	169	c3
Rousdon	Devon	10	F6
Rousham	Oxon	48	E10
Rous Lench	Worcs	47	K4
Routenburn	N Ayrs	124	F5
Routh	E R Yk	93	J2
Rout's Green	Bucks	35	L5
Row	Cnwll	4	H6
Row	W & F	95	K3
Row	W & F	102	B4
Rowanburn	D & G	110	H5
Rowardennan	Stirlg	132	D8
Rowarth	Derbys	83	M7
Row Ash	Hants	14	F4
Rowberrow	Somset	19	N3
Rowborough	IoW	14	E10
Rowde	Wilts	21	J2
Rowden	Devon	8	F5
Rowen	Conwy	79	P10
Rowfield	Derbys	71	M5
Rowfoot	Nthumb	111	N8
Rowford	Somset	18	H9
Row Green	Essex	52	B7
Rowhedge	Essex	52	H7
Rowhook	W Susx	24	D4
Rowington	Warwks	59	K11
Rowland	Derbys	84	B6
Rowland's Castle	Hants	15	K4
Rowlands Gill	Gatesd	113	J9
Rowledge	Surrey	23	M6
Rowley	Dur	112	G11
Rowley	E R Yk	92	G4
Rowley	Shrops	56	E3
Rowley Hill	Kirk	90	F8
Rowley Regis	Sandw	58	E7
Rowlstone	Herefs	45	M9
Rowly	Surrey	24	B2
Rowner	Hants	14	G6
Rowney Green	Worcs	58	F10
Rownhams	Hants	22	C11
Rownhams Services	Hants	22	C11
Rowrah	Cumb	100	C10
Rowsham	Bucks	49	M11
Rowsley	Derbys	84	C7
Rowstock	Oxon	34	E7
Rowston	Lincs	86	E9
Rowthorne	Derbys	84	G8
Rowton	Ches W	69	M2
Rowton	Shrops	56	F2
Rowton	Shrops	56	G8
Rowton	Wrekin	69	R11
Row Town	Surrey	36	C8
Roxburgh	Border	118	C4
Roxby	N Linc	92	F7
Roxby	N York	105	L9
Roxton	Bed	61	Q10
Roxwell	Essex	51	P9
Royal Botanic Garden Edinburgh	C Edin	127	N2
Royal Leamington Spa	Warwks	59	M11
Royal Oak	Darltn	103	P6
Royal Oak	Lancs	81	N4
Royal's Green	Ches E	69	R4
Royal Sutton Coldfield	Birm	58	H5
Royal Tunbridge Wells	Kent	25	N3
Royal Wootton Bassett	Wilts	33	L8
Royal Yacht Britannia	C Edin	127	P2
Roy Bridge	Highld	146	H11
Roydhouse	Kirk	90	G8
Roydon	Essex	51	K8

Roydon – Sawston 291

Roydon Norfk 64 G5
Roydon Norfk 75 P6
Roydon Hamlet Essex 51 K9
Royston Barns 91 K8
Royston Herts 51 J2
Royton Oldham 89 Q9
Rozel Jersey 11 c1
Ruabon Wrexhm 69 K6
Ruaig Ag & B 136 D6
Ruan High Lanes Cnwll 3 N6
Ruan Lanihorne Cnwll 3 M5
Ruan Major Cnwll 3 J10
Ruan Minor Cnwll 3 J10
Ruardean Gloucs 46 B11
Ruardean Hill Gloucs 46 B11
Ruardean Woodside Gloucs 46 B11
Rubery Birm 58 E9
Rubha Ban W Isls 168 c16
Ruckcroft W & F 101 P2
Ruckhall Herefs 45 P7
Ruckinge Kent 26 H5
Ruckland Lincs 87 K5
Ruckley Shrops 57 J4
Rudbaxton Pembks 41 J6
Rudby N York 104 E9
Rudchester Nthumb 112 H7
Ruddington Notts 72 F4
Ruddle Gloucs 32 C2
Ruddlemoor Cnwll 3 Q3
Rudford Gloucs 46 E10
Rudge Somset 20 F4
Rudgeway S Glos 32 B7
Rudgwick W Susx 24 C4
Rudhall Herefs 46 B9
Rudheath Ches W 82 E10
Rudheath Woods Ches E 82 F10
Rudley Green Essex 52 D11
Rudloe Wilts 32 F10
Rudry Caerph 30 H7
Rudston E R Yk 99 M7
Rudyard Staffs 70 H3
Ruecastle Border 118 B6
Rufford Lancs 88 F7
Rufford Abbey Notts 85 K8
Rufforth C York 98 A10
Rug Denbgs 68 E6
Rugby Warwks 60 B5
Rugby Services Warwks 60 B5
Rugeley Staffs 71 J11
Ruigh'riabhach Highld 160 G7
Ruisgarry W Isls 168 e9
Ruishton Somset 19 J9
Ruisigearraidh W Isls 168 e9
Ruislip Gt Lon 36 C3
Rùm Highld 144 E8
Rumbach Moray 158 A7
Rumbling Bridge P & K 134 C8
Rumburgh Suffk 65 L5
Rumby Hill Dur 103 N4
Rumford Cnwll 4 D7
Rumford Falk 126 G2
Rumney Cardif 30 H9
Rumwell Somset 18 G10
Runcorn Halton 81 Q8
Runcton W Susx 15 N6
Runcton Holme Norfk 75 M9
Runfold Surrey 23 N5
Runhall Norfk 76 F10
Runham Norfk 77 P9
Runham Norfk 77 Q10
Runnington Somset 18 F10
Runsell Green Essex 52 C10
Runshaw Moor Lancs 88 G7
Runswick N York 105 M7
Runtaleave Angus 142 D4
Runwell Essex 38 C3
Ruscombe Wokham 35 L9
Rushall Herefs 46 B7
Rushall Norfk 64 H5
Rushall Wilts 21 M3
Rushall Wsall 58 F4
Rushbrooke Suffk 64 B9
Rushbury Shrops 57 J6
Rushden Herts 50 H4
Rushden N Nthn 61 L7
Rushenden Kent 38 F7
Rusher's Cross E Susx 25 P5
Rushford Devon 8 C9
Rushford Norfk 64 C5
Rush Green Essex 53 L8
Rush Green Gt Lon 37 M3
Rush Green Herts 50 F6
Rush Green Warrtn 82 E7
Rushlake Green E Susx 25 P7
Rushmere Suffk 65 P4
Rushmere St Andrew Suffk 53 L2
Rushmoor Surrey 23 N6
Rushock Herefs 45 L3
Rushock Worcs 58 C10
Rusholme Manch 83 J6
Rushton Ches W 69 Q2
Rushton N Nthn 60 H4
Rushton Shrops 57 L3
Rushton Spencer Staffs 70 G2
Rushwick Worcs 46 F4
Rushyford Dur 103 Q5
Ruskie Stirlg 133 J7
Ruskington Lincs 86 E10
Rusland Cross W & F 94 G3
Rusper W Susx 24 F3
Ruspidge Gloucs 32 C2
Russell Green Essex 52 B9
Russell's Water Oxon 35 K7
Russel's Green Suffk 65 K7
Russ Hill Surrey 24 F2
Rusthall Kent 25 N3
Rustington W Susx 24 B10
Ruston N York 99 K4
Ruston Parva E R Yk 99 M8
Ruswarp N York 105 N9
Ruthall Shrops 57 K6
Rutherford Border 118 B4
Rutherglen S Lans 125 Q5
Ruthernbridge Cnwll 4 G8
Ruthin Denbgs 68 F3
Ruthrieston C Aber 151 N7
Ruthven Abers 158 D8
Ruthven Angus 142 D8
Ruthven Highld 148 D8
Ruthven Highld 156 E11
Ruthvoes Cnwll 4 E9
Ruthwaite Cumb 100 H3
Ruthwell D & G 109 N7
Ruxley Gt Lon 37 L6
Ruxton Green Herefs 45 Q11
Ruyton-XI-Towns Shrops 69 L10
Ryal Nthumb 112 F6
Ryall Dorset 11 J5
Ryall Worcs 46 G6
Ryarsh Kent 37 Q8
Rycote Oxon 35 J3
Rydal W & F 101 L9
Ryde IoW 14 G8
Rye E Susx 26 F7
Ryebank Shrops 69 P8
Ryeford Herefs 46 B10
Rye Foreign E Susx 26 E7
Rye Harbour E Susx 26 F8
Ryehill E R Yk 93 M5
Ryeish Green Wokham 35 K11
Rye Street Worcs 46 E7
Ryhall Rutlnd 73 Q8
Ryhill Wakefd 91 K8
Ryhope Sundld 113 P10
Rylah Derbys 84 G7
Ryland Lincs 86 D5
Rylands Notts 72 E3
Rylstone N York 96 E9
Ryme Intrinseca Dorset 11 M2
Ryther N York 91 P3
Ryton Gatesd 113 J8
Ryton N York 98 F5
Ryton Shrops 57 P4
Ryton Warwks 59 P7
Ryton-on-Dunsmore Warwks 59 N10
Ryton Woodside Gatesd 112 H8
RZSS Edinburgh Zoo C Edin 127 N3

S

Sabden Lancs 89 M3
Sabine's Green Essex 51 M11
Sacombe Herts 50 H7
Sacombe Green Herts 50 H7
Sacriston Dur 113 K11
Sadberge Darltn 104 B7
Saddell Ag & B 120 E5
Saddington Leics 60 E2
Saddlebow Norfk 75 M7
Saddlescombe W Susx 24 G8
Sadgill W & F 101 N9
Saffron Walden Essex 51 M3
Sageston Pembks 41 L10
Saham Hills Norfk 76 C11
Saham Toney Norfk 76 B11
Saighton Ches W 69 M2
St Abbs Border 129 N6
St Agnes Border 128 H7
St Agnes Cnwll 3 J3
St Agnes IoS 2 b3
St Agnes Mining District Cnwll 3 J4
St Albans Herts 50 D9
St Allen Cnwll 3 L3
St Andrew Guern 10 b2
St Andrews Fife 135 N4
St Andrews Botanic Garden Fife 135 N4
St Andrews Major V Glam 30 F10
St Andrews Well Dorset 11 K6
St Anne's Lancs 88 C5
St Ann's D & G 109 N2
St Ann's Chapel Cnwll 5 Q7
St Ann's Chapel Devon 6 H9
St Anthony-in-Meneage Cnwll 3 K8
St Anthony's Hill E Susx 25 P10
St Arvans Mons 31 P5
St Asaph Denbgs 80 E10
St Athan V Glam 30 D11
St Aubin Jersey 11 b2
St Austell Cnwll 3 Q3
St Bees Cumb 100 C8
St Blazey Cnwll 3 R3
St Blazey Gate Cnwll 3 R3
St Boswells Border 118 A4
St Brelade Jersey 11 a2
St Brelade's Bay Jersey 11 a2
St Breock Cnwll 4 F7
St Breward Cnwll 4 H6
St Briavels Gloucs 31 Q4
St Brides Pembks 40 F8
St Brides Major V Glam 29 N10
St Brides Netherwent Mons 31 M7
St Brides-super-Ely V Glam 30 E9
St Brides Wentlooge Newpt 31 J8
St Budeaux C Plym 6 D7
Saintbury Gloucs 47 M7
St Buryan Cnwll 2 C8
St Catherine BaNES 32 E11
St Catherines Ag & B 131 N6
St Chloe Gloucs 32 F4
St Clears Carmth 41 Q7
St Cleer Cnwll 5 L8
St Clement Cnwll 3 M5
St Clement Jersey 11 c2
St Clether Cnwll 5 L5
St Colmac Ag & B 124 C4
St Columb Major Cnwll 4 E9
St Columb Minor Cnwll 4 C9
St Columb Road Cnwll 4 E10
St Combs Abers 159 Q5
St Cross South Elmham Suffk 65 K5
St Cyrus Abers 143 N5
St David's P & K 133 Q3
St Davids Pembks 40 E5
St Davids Cathedral Pembks 40 E5
St Day Cnwll 3 J5
St Decumans Somset 18 E6
St Dennis Cnwll 4 F10
St Devereux Herefs 45 N8
St Dogmaels Pembks 42 C5
St Dogwells Pembks 41 J5
St Dominick Cnwll 5 Q8
St Donats V Glam 29 P11
St Edith's Marsh Wilts 21 J2
St Endellion Cnwll 4 F6
St Enoder Cnwll 4 D10
St Erme Cnwll 3 L4
St Erney Cnwll 5 P10
St Erth Cnwll 2 F6
St Erth Praze Cnwll 2 F6
St Ervan Cnwll 4 D7
St Eval Cnwll 4 D8
St Ewe Cnwll 3 P4
St Fagans Cardif 30 F9
St Fagans National Museum of History Cardif 30 F9
St Fergus Abers 159 Q7
St Fillans P & K 133 K3
St Florence Pembks 41 L10
St Gennys Cnwll 5 J2
St George Conwy 80 D9
St Georges N Som 19 L2
St George's V Glam 30 F9
St George's Hill Surrey 36 C8
St Germans Cnwll 5 P10
St Giles in the Wood Devon 17 J8
St Giles-on-the-Heath Devon 5 P3
St Gluvia's Cnwll 3 K7
St Harmon Powys 55 M10
St Helen Auckland Dur 103 N5
St Helens Cumb 100 D4
St Helen's E Susx 26 D9
St Helens IoW 14 H9
St Helens St Hel 81 Q5
St Helier Gt Lon 36 G7
St Helier Jersey 11 b2
St Hilary Cnwll 2 E7
St Hilary V Glam 30 D10
Saint Hill Devon 10 B3
Saint Hill W Susx 25 J3
St Illtyd Blae G 30 H4
St Ippolyts Herts 50 E5
St Ishmael's Pembks 40 F9
St Issey Cnwll 4 E7
St Ive Cnwll 5 N8
St Ive Cross Cnwll 5 N8
St Ives Cambs 62 D6
St Ives Cnwll 2 E5
St Ives Dorset 13 K4
St James Norfk 77 K7
St James's End W Nthn 60 F8
St James South Elmham Suffk 65 L5
St Jidgey Cnwll 4 E8
St John Cnwll 5 Q11
St John Jersey 11 b1
St Johns Dur 103 L4
St John's E Susx 25 M4
St John's IoM 80 c5
St John's Kent 37 M9
St Johns Surrey 23 Q3
St Johns Worcs 46 F4
St John's Chapel Devon 17 J6
St John's Chapel Dur 102 G3
St John's Fen End Norfk 75 K8
St John's Highway Norfk 75 K8
St John's Kirk S Lans 116 D3
St John's Town of Dalry D & G 108 D4
St John's Wood Gt Lon 36 G4
St Judes IoM 80 e2
St Just Cnwll 2 B7
St Just-in-Roseland Cnwll 3 L6
St Just Mining District Cnwll 2 B7
St Katherines Abers 159 J11
St Keverne Cnwll 3 K9
St Kew Cnwll 4 G6
St Kew Highway Cnwll 4 G6
St Keyne Cnwll 5 L9
St Lawrence Cnwll 4 G8
St Lawrence Essex 52 G11
St Lawrence IoW 14 F11
St Lawrence Jersey 11 b1
St Lawrence Kent 39 Q8
St Lawrence Bay Essex 52 G10
St Leonards Bucks 35 P3
St Leonards Dorset 13 K4
St Leonards E Susx 26 D10
St Leonard's Street Kent 37 Q9
St Levan Cnwll 2 B9
St Luke's Park Essex 38 C2
St Lythans V Glam 30 F10
St Mabyn Cnwll 4 G7
St Madoes P & K 134 F3
St Margarets Herefs 45 M8
St Margarets Herts 51 J8
St Margaret's at Cliffe Kent 27 Q3
St Margaret's Hope Ork 169 d7
St Margaret South Elmham Suffk 65 L5
St Marks IoM 80 c7
St Martin Cnwll 3 J9
St Martin Cnwll 5 M10
St Martin Guern 10 b2
St Martin Jersey 11 c1
St Martin's IoS 2 c1
St Martin's P & K 142 B11
St Martin's Shrops 69 K7
St Martin's Moor Shrops 69 K7
St Mary Jersey 11 a1
St Mary Bourne Hants 22 D4
St Marychurch Torbay 7 N5
St Mary Church V Glam 30 D10
St Mary Cray Gt Lon 37 L7
St Mary Hill V Glam 30 C9
St Mary in the Marsh Kent 27 J6
St Mary's IoS 2 c2
St Mary's Ork 169 d6
St Mary's Bay Kent 27 J6
St Mary's Hoo Medway 38 D6
St Mary's Platt Kent 37 P9
St Maughans Mons 45 P11
St Maughans Green Mons 45 P11
St Mawes Cnwll 3 L7
St Mawgan Cnwll 4 D8
St Mellion Cnwll 5 P8
St Mellons Cardif 30 H8
St Merryn Cnwll 4 D7
St Mewan Cnwll 3 P3
St Michael Caerhays Cnwll 3 P5
St Michael Church Somset 19 K8
St Michael Penkevil Cnwll 3 M5
St Michaels Kent 26 E4
St Michaels Worcs 57 K11
St Michael's Mount Cnwll 2 E8
St Michael's on Wyre Lancs 88 F2
St Michael South Elmham Suffk 65 L5
St Minver Cnwll 4 F6
St Monans Fife 135 N7
St Neot Cnwll 5 K8
St Neots Cambs 61 Q8
St Newlyn East Cnwll 4 C10
St Nicholas Pembks 40 H3
St Nicholas V Glam 30 E10
St Nicholas-at-Wade Kent 39 N8
St Ninians Stirlg 133 M9
St Olaves Norfk 65 P2
St Osyth Essex 53 K8
St Ouen Jersey 11 a1
St Owen's Cross Herefs 45 Q10
St Paul's Cray Gt Lon 37 L7
St Paul's Walden Herts 50 E6
St Peter Jersey 11 a1
St Peter Port Guern 10 c2
St Peter's Guern 10 b2
St Peter's Kent 39 Q8
St Peter's Hill Cambs 62 B6
St Petrox Pembks 41 J11
St Pinnock Cnwll 5 L9
St Quivox S Ayrs 114 G3
St Ruan Cnwll 3 J10
St Sampson Guern 10 c1
St Saviour Guern 10 b2
St Saviour Jersey 11 b2
St Stephen Cnwll 3 N3
St Stephens Cnwll 5 N4
St Stephens Cnwll 5 Q10
St Teath Cnwll 4 H5
St Thomas Devon 9 M6
St Margaret's Bay Kent 27 Q3
St Tudy Cnwll 4 H6
St Twynnells Pembks 41 J11
St Veep Cnwll 5 J10
St Vigeans Angus 143 L9
St Wenn Cnwll 4 F9
St Weonards Herefs 45 P10
St Winnow Cnwll 5 J10
St y-Nyll V Glam 30 E9
Salcombe Devon 7 J11
Salcombe Regis Devon 10 D7
Salcott-cum-Virley Essex 52 F9
Sale Traffd 82 G6
Saleby Lincs 87 N5
Sale Green Worcs 46 H3
Salehurst E Susx 26 C7
Salem Carmth 43 M9
Salem Cerdgn 54 F8
Salen Ag & B 137 P7
Salen Highld 138 B5
Salesbury Lancs 89 K4
Salford C Beds 49 P7
Salford Oxon 47 Q9
Salford Salfd 82 H5
Salford Priors Warwks 47 L4
Salfords Surrey 36 G11
Salhouse Norfk 77 L9
Saline Fife 134 C9
Salisbury Wilts 21 M8
Salisbury Plain Wilts 21 L6
Salkeld Dykes W & F 101 P3
Sallachy Highld 162 C5
Salle Norfk 76 G7
Salmonby Lincs 87 K6
Salperton Gloucs 47 L10
Salph End Bed 61 N10
Salsburgh N Lans 126 E5
Salt Staffs 70 H9
Salta Cumb 109 N11
Saltaire C Brad 90 E3
Saltaire C Brad 90 E3
Saltash Cnwll 6 C7
Saltburn Highld 156 C3
Saltburn-by-the-Sea R & Cl 105 J6
Saltby Leics 73 M5
Salt Coates Cumb 110 C10
Saltcoats Cumb 100 E11
Saltcoats N Ayrs 124 G9
Saltcotes Lancs 88 D5
Saltdean Br & H 25 J10
Salterbeck Cumb 100 C5
Salterforth Lancs 96 C11
Salterswall Ches W 82 D11
Salterton Wilts 21 M7
Saltfleet Lincs 87 N2
Saltfleetby All Saints Lincs 87 N2
Saltfleetby St Clement Lincs 87 N2
Saltfleetby St Peter Lincs 87 M3
Saltford BaNES 32 C11
Salthouse Norfk 76 F3
Saltley Birm 58 H7
Saltmarsh Newpt 31 K8
Saltmarshe E R Yk 92 C6
Saltney Flints 69 L2
Salton N York 98 E5
Saltrens Devon 16 H7
Saltwick Nthumb 113 J4
Saltwood Kent 27 L4
Salvington W Susx 24 D9
Salwarpe Worcs 46 G2
Salway Ash Dorset 11 K5
Sambourne Warwks 47 L2
Sambrook Wrekin 70 C10
Samlesbury Lancs 88 H4
Samlesbury Bottoms Lancs 89 J5
Sampford Arundel Somset 18 F11
Sampford Brett Somset 18 E6
Sampford Courtenay Devon 8 F4
Sampford Moor Somset 18 F11
Sampford Peverell Devon 9 P2
Sampford Spiney Devon 6 E4
Samsonlane Ork 169 f4
Samson's Corner Essex 53 J8
Samuelston E Loth 128 D5
Sanaigmore Ag & B 122 B5
Sancreed Cnwll 2 C8
Sancton E R Yk 92 E3
Sand Somset 19 M5
Sandaig Highld 145 M7
Sandale Cumb 100 H2
Sandal Magna Wakefd 91 J7
Sanday Ork 169 f2
Sanday Airport Ork 169 f2
Sandbach Ches E 70 D2
Sandbach Services Ches E 70 D2
Sandbank Ag & B 131 P11
Sandbanks BCP 12 H7
Sandend Abers 158 E4
Sanderstead Gt Lon 36 H8
Sandford Devon 9 K4
Sandford Dorset 12 F7
Sandford Hants 13 L4
Sandford IoW 14 F10
Sandford N Som 19 M3
Sandford S Lans 126 C9
Sandford Shrops 69 K10
Sandford Shrops 69 Q8
Sandford W & F 102 D7
Sandford-on-Thames Oxon 34 F4
Sandford Orcas Dorset 20 B10
Sandford St Martin Oxon 48 D9
Sandgate Kent 27 M4
Sandhaven Abers 159 N4
Sandhead D & G 106 E8
Sandhill Rothm 91 L11
Sandhills Dorset 11 M4
Sandhills Dorset 11 P2
Sand Hills Leeds 91 K3
Sandhills Oxon 34 G3
Sandhills Surrey 23 P7
Sandhoe Nthumb 112 E7
Sandhole Ag & B 131 L8
Sand Hole E R Yk 92 D3
Sandholme E R Yk 92 D4
Sandholme Lincs 74 F3
Sandhurst Br For 23 M2
Sandhurst Gloucs 46 F10
Sandhurst Kent 26 D6
Sandhurst Cross Kent 26 C6
Sandhutton N York 97 N4
Sand Hutton N York 98 D9
Sandiacre Derbys 72 D3
Sandilands Lincs 87 P4
Sandiway Ches W 82 D10
Sandleheath Hants 21 M11
Sandleigh Oxon 34 E4
Sandley Dorset 20 E10
Sandling Kent 38 C10
Sandlow Green Ches E 82 G11
Sandness Shet 169 n8
Sandon Essex 52 B11
Sandon Herts 50 H4
Sandon Staffs 70 G9
Sandon Bank Staffs 70 G9
Sandown IoW 14 G10
Sandplace Cnwll 5 M10
Sandridge Herts 50 E8
Sandridge Wilts 32 H11
Sandringham Norfk 75 N5
Sands Bucks 35 M6
Sandsend N York 105 N8
Sand Side W & F 94 E4
Sandside W & F 95 K4
Sandtoft N Linc 92 B9
Sandway Kent 38 E11
Sandwich Kent 39 P10
Sandwich Bay Kent 39 Q10
Sandwick Shet 169 r11
Sandwick W & F 101 M7
Sandwick W Isls 168 j4
Sandwith Cumb 100 C8
Sandwith Newtown Cumb 100 C8
Sandy C Beds 61 Q11
Sandy Bank Lincs 87 J9
Sandycroft Flints 81 L11
Sandy Cross E Susx 25 N6
Sandy Cross Herefs 46 C3
Sandyford D & G 110 D2
Sandygate Devon 7 M4
Sandygate IoM 80 e2
Sandy Haven Pembks 40 G9
Sandyhills D & G 109 J9
Sandylands Lancs 95 J8
Sandy Lane C Brad 90 E3
Sandylane Staffs 70 C7
Sandylane Swans 28 G7
Sandy Lane Wilts 33 J11
Sandy Lane Wrexhm 69 M6
Sandy Park Devon 8 H7
Sandysike Cumb 110 G7
Sandyway Herefs 45 P9
Sangobeg Highld 165 K3
Sangomore Highld 165 K3
Sankey Bridges Warrtn 82 C7
Sankyn's Green Worcs 57 P11
Sanna Highld 137 L2
Sanndabhaig W Isls 168 j4
Sannox N Ayrs 124 C8
Sanquhar D & G 115 Q6
Santon Cumb 100 F10
Santon IoM 80 d7
Santon Bridge Cumb 100 F10
Santon Downham Suffk 63 P3
Sapcote Leics 59 Q6
Sapey Common Herefs 46 D2
Sapiston Suffk 64 C6
Sapley Cambs 62 B6
Sapperton Derbys 71 M8
Sapperton Gloucs 32 H4
Sapperton Lincs 73 Q4
Saracen's Head Lincs 74 F5
Sarclet Highld 167 P8
Sarisbury Hants 14 F5
Sarn Brdgnd 29 P8
Sarn Powys 56 C6
Sarnau Carmth 42 F11
Sarnau Cerdgn 42 F4
Sarnau Gwynd 68 C7
Sarnau Powys 44 E8
Sarnau Powys 68 H11
Sarn Bach Gwynd 66 E9
Sarnesfield Herefs 45 M4
Sarn Mellteyrn Gwynd 66 C8
Sarn Park Services Brdgnd 29 P8
Sarn-wen Powys 69 J11
Saron Carmth 28 H2
Saron Carmth 42 G7
Saron Gwynd 66 H3
Saron Gwynd 79 J11
Sarratt Herts 50 B11
Sarre Kent 39 N8
Sarsden Oxon 47 Q10
Sarson Hants 22 B6
Satley Dur 103 M2
Satmar Kent 27 N4
Satron N York 102 H11
Satterleigh Devon 17 M7
Satterthwaite W & F 94 G2
Satwell Oxon 35 K8
Sauchen Abers 151 J5
Saucher P & K 142 B11
Sauchieburn Abers 143 M4
Saughall Ches W 81 M11
Saul Gloucs 32 D3
Saundby Notts 85 N3
Saundersfoot Pembks 41 M10
Saunderton Bucks 35 L4
Saunderton Station Bucks 35 M5
Saunton Devon 16 H4
Sausthorpe Lincs 87 L7
Saverley Green Staffs 70 H7
Savile Town Kirk 90 G6
Sawbridge Warwks 60 B7
Sawbridgeworth Herts 51 L8
Sawdon N York 99 J4
Sawley Derbys 72 D4
Sawley Lancs 96 A11
Sawley N York 97 K7
Sawston Cambs 62 G11

Sawtry Cambs 61 Q4
Saxby Leics 73 L7
Saxby Lincs 86 D2
Saxby All Saints N Linc 92 G7
Saxelbye Leics 72 H6
Saxham Street Suffk 64 F9
Saxilby Lincs 85 Q5
Saxlingham Norfk 76 E4
Saxlingham Green Norfk 65 J2
Saxlingham Nethergate
   Norfk 65 J2
Saxlingham Thorpe Norfk 65 J2
Saxmundham Suffk 65 M9
Saxondale Notts 72 H3
Saxon Street Cambs 63 L9
Saxtead Suffk 65 K8
Saxtead Green Suffk 65 K9
Saxtead Little Green Suffk 65 J8
Saxthorpe Norfk 76 G5
Saxton N York 91 M3
Sayers Common W Susx 24 G7
Scackleton N York 98 C6
Scadabay W Isls 168 g8
Scadabhagh W Isls 168 g8
Scafell Pike Cumb 100 H9
Scaftworth Notts 85 L2
Scagglethorpe N York 98 G6
Scalasaig Ag & B 136 b3
Scalby E R Yk 92 D5
Scalby N York 99 L2
Scald End Bed 61 M9
Scaldwell N Nthn 60 G6
Scaleby Cumb 110 H8
Scalebyhill Cumb 110 H8
Scale Houses W & F 111 L11
Scales Cumb 94 F6
Scales W & F 101 K5
Scalesceugh Cumb 110 H11
Scalford Leics 73 K6
Scaling N York 105 K8
Scaling Dam R & Cl 105 K8
Scalloway Shet 169 r10
Scalpay Highld 153 L11
Scalpay W Isls 168 h8
Scamblesby Lincs 87 J5
Scammonden Kirk 90 D7
Scamodale Highld 138 E3
Scampston N York 98 H5
Scampton Lincs 86 C5
Scaniport Highld 156 A10
Scapegoat Hill Kirk 90 D7
Scarba Ag & B 130 D7
Scarborough N York 99 L3
Scarcewater Cnwll 3 N3
Scarcliffe Derbys 84 G7
Scarcroft Leeds 91 K2
Scarfskerry Highld 167 N2
Scargill Dur 103 L8
Scarinish Ag & B 136 C7
Scarisbrick Lancs 88 D8
Scarness Cumb 100 H4
Scarning Norfk 76 D9
Scarrington Notts 73 J2
Scarth Hill Lancs 88 E9
Scarthingwell N York 91 M3
Scartho NE Lin 93 N9
Scatsta Airport Shet 169 q6
Scaur D & G 108 H10
Scawby N Linc 92 G9
Scawsby Donc 91 N10
Scawthorpe Donc 91 P9
Scawton N York 98 A4
Scayne's Hill W Susx 25 J6
Scethrog Powys 44 G9
Scholar Green Ches E 70 E3
Scholes Kirk 90 F5
Scholes Kirk 90 F9
Scholes Leeds 91 K3
Scholes Rothm 91 K11
Scholes Wigan 88 H9
School Aycliffe Dur 103 Q6
School Green C Brad 90 E4
School Green Ches W 70 A2
Schoolgreen Wokham 35 K11
School House Dorset 10 H4
Scissett Kirk 90 G8
Scleddau Pembks 40 H4
Scofton Notts 85 K4
Scole Norfk 64 H6
Scone P & K 134 E2
Sconser Highld 153 J11
Scoonie Fife 135 K7
Scopwick Lincs 86 E9
Scoraig Highld 160 G7
Scorborough E R Yk 99 L11
Scorrier Cnwll 3 J5
Scorriton Devon 7 J5
Scorton Lancs 95 L11
Scorton N York 103 Q10
Sco Ruston Norfk 77 K7
Scotby Cumb 110 H9
Scotch Corner N York 103 P9
Scotch Corner Rest Area
   N York 103 P9
Scotforth Lancs 95 K9
Scot Hay Staffs 70 D5
Scothern Lincs 86 D5
Scotland Lincs 73 Q4
Scotland Gate Nthumb 113 L4
Scotlandwell P & K 134 F7
Scot Lane End Bolton 89 J9
Scotscalder Station Highld 167 J5
Scotsdike Cumb 110 G6
Scot's Gap Nthumb 112 F3
Scotsmill Abers 150 F4
Scotstoun C Glas 125 N4
Scotswood N u Ty 113 K8
Scotter Lincs 92 E10
Scotterthorpe Lincs 92 E10
Scottish Seabird Centre
   E Loth 128 F2
Scottlethorpe Lincs 73 R6
Scotton Lincs 92 E11
Scotton N York 97 M9
Scotton N York 103 N11
Scottow Norfk 77 K7
Scott Willoughby Lincs 73 R3
Scoulton Norfk 76 D11
Scounslow Green Staffs 71 K9
Scourie Highld 164 E8
Scourie More Highld 164 D8
Scousburgh Shet 169 q12
Scouthead Oldham 90 B9
Scrabster Highld 167 K2
Scraesburgh Border 118 C7
Scrafield Lincs 87 K7

Scrainwood Nthumb 119 J9
Scrane End Lincs 74 G2
Scraptoft Leics 72 G9
Scratby Norfk 77 Q8
Scrayingham N York 98 E9
Scrays E Susx 26 C8
Scredington Lincs 74 A2
Scremby Lincs 87 M7
Scremerston Nthumb 129 Q10
Screveton Notts 73 J2
Scrivelsby Lincs 87 J7
Scriven N York 97 M9
Scrooby Notts 85 L2
Scropton Derbys 71 M8
Scrub Hill Lincs 86 H9
Scruton N York 97 L2
Scuggate Cumb 110 H6
Scullomie Highld 165 P4
Sculthorpe Norfk 76 B5
Scunthorpe N Linc 92 E8
Scurlage Swans 28 E7
Sea Somset 10 G2
Seaborough Dorset 11 J3
Seabridge Staffs 70 E6
Seabrook Kent 27 L4
Seaburn Sundld 113 P9
Seacombe Wirral 81 L6
Seacroft Leeds 91 K3
Seacroft Lincs 87 Q8
Seadyke Lincs 74 F3
Seafield W Loth 127 J4
Seaford E Susx 25 L11
Seaforth Sefton 81 L5
Seagrave Leics 72 G7
Seagry Heath Wilts 33 J8
Seaham Dur 113 P11
Seahouses Nthumb 119 P4
Seal Kent 37 N9
Sealand Flints 81 M11
Seale Surrey 23 N5
Seamer N York 99 L4
Seamer N York 104 B8
Seamill N Ayrs 124 G8
Sea Palling Norfk 77 N6
Searby Lincs 93 J9
Seasalter Kent 39 J9
Seascale Cumb 100 D10
Seathwaite Cumb 100 H8
Seathwaite W & F 100 H11
Seatle W & F 94 H4
Seatoller Cumb 100 H8
Seaton Cnwll 5 N11
Seaton Cumb 100 D4
Seaton Devon 10 E6
Seaton Dur 113 N11
Seaton E R Yk 99 P11
Seaton Kent 39 M10
Seaton Nthumb 113 M5
Seaton Rutlnd 73 N11
Seaton Burn N Tyne 113 K6
Seaton Carew Hartpl 104 F5
Seaton Delaval Nthumb 113 M5
Seaton Ross E R Yk 92 C2
Seaton Sluice Nthumb 113 M5
Seatown Dorset 11 J6
Seatown Moray 157 N3
Seave Green N York 104 G10
Seaview IoW 14 H8
Seaville Cumb 110 C10
Seavington St Mary Somset 11 J2
Seavington St Michael
   Somset 19 M11
Sebastopol Torfn 31 J5
Sebergham Cumb 101 L2
Seckington Warwks 59 L3
Second Severn Crossing
   Mons 31 P7
Sedbergh W & F 95 P2
Sedbury Gloucs 31 P6
Sedbusk N York 96 C2
Sedgeberrow Worcs 47 K7
Sedgebrook Lincs 73 M3
Sedge Fen Suffk 63 L4
Sedgefield Dur 104 C5
Sedgeford Norfk 75 P3
Sedgehill Wilts 20 G9
Sedgemoor Services
   Somset 19 L4
Sedgley Dudley 58 D6
Sedgley Park Bury 82 H4
Sedgwick W & F 95 L3
Sedlescombe E Susx 26 C8
Sedrup Bucks 35 M2
Seed Kent 38 F10
Seend Wilts 21 H2
Seend Cleeve Wilts 20 H2
Seer Green Bucks 35 Q6
Seething Norfk 65 L2
Sefton Sefton 81 M4
Seghill Nthumb 113 L6
Seighford Staffs 70 F9
Seion Gwynd 79 J11
Seisdon Staffs 58 B5
Selattyn Shrops 69 J8
Selborne Hants 23 K8
Selby N York 91 Q4
Selham W Susx 23 P10
Selhurst Gt Lon 36 H7
Selkirk Border 117 N5
Sellack Herefs 45 R9
Sellafield Station Cumb 100 D10
Sellafirth Shet 169 s4
Sellan Cnwll 2 C7
Sellick's Green Somset 18 H11
Sellindge Kent 27 J4
Selling Kent 38 H10
Sells Green Wilts 20 H2
Selly Oak Birm 58 F8
Selmeston E Susx 25 M9
Selsdon Gt Lon 37 J8
Selsey W Susx 15 N8
Selsfield Common W Susx 24 H4
Selside N York 96 A5
Selside W & F 101 P11
Selsley Gloucs 32 F4
Selsted Kent 27 M3
Selston Notts 84 G10
Selworthy Somset 18 B5
Semer Suffk 52 G2
Semington Wilts 20 G2
Semley Wilts 20 G9
Sempringham Lincs 74 B4
Send Surrey 36 B9
Send Marsh Surrey 36 B9
Senghenydd Caerph 30 F6
Sennen Cnwll 2 B8

Sennen Cove Cnwll 2 B8
Sennybridge Powys 44 C9
Serlby Notts 85 K3
Sessay N York 97 Q5
Setchey Norfk 75 M8
Setley Hants 13 P4
Seton Mains E Loth 128 C4
Settle N York 96 B8
Settrington N York 98 G6
Seven Ash Somset 18 G8
Sevenhampton Gloucs 47 K10
Sevenhampton Swindn 33 P6
Seven Kings Gt Lon 37 L3
Sevenoaks Kent 37 M9
Sevenoaks Weald Kent 37 M10
Seven Sisters Neath 29 M3
Seven Springs Gloucs 47 J11
Seven Star Green Essex 52 F6
Severn Beach S Glos 31 Q6
Severn Bridge S Glos 31 Q6
Severn Stoke Worcs 46 G6
Severn View Services S Glos 31 Q7
Sevick End Bed 61 N10
Sevington Kent 26 H3
Sewards End Essex 51 N3
Sewardstonebury Essex 51 J11
Sewell C Beds 49 Q10
Sewerby E R Yk 99 P7
Seworgan Cnwll 3 J7
Sewstern Leics 73 M6
Sexhow N York 104 E9
Sgalpaigh W Isls 168 h8
Sgiogarstaigh W Isls 168 k1
Shabbington Bucks 35 J3
Shackerley Shrops 57 Q3
Shackerstone Leics 72 B9
Shacklecross Derbys 72 C4
Shackleford Surrey 23 P5
Shade Calder 89 Q6
Shader W Isls 168 i2
Shadforth Dur 104 B2
Shadingfield Suffk 65 N5
Shadoxhurst Kent 26 G4
Shadwell Leeds 91 J3
Shadwell Norfk 64 C5
Shaftenhoe End Herts 51 K3
Shaftesbury Dorset 20 G10
Shaftholme Donc 91 P9
Shafton Barns 91 K8
Shafton Two Gates Barns 91 K8
Shakerley Wigan 82 E4
Shalbourne Wilts 22 B2
Shalcombe IoW 14 C9
Shalden Hants 23 J6
Shalden Green Hants 23 K6
Shaldon Devon 7 M4
Shalfleet IoW 14 D9
Shalford Essex 52 B6
Shalford Surrey 36 B11
Shalford Green Essex 52 B6
Shallowford Staffs 70 F9
Shalmsford Street Kent 39 J11
Shalstone Bucks 48 H7
Shamley Green Surrey 24 B2
Shandford Angus 142 H5
Shandon Ag & B 132 B10
Shandwick Highld 156 F2
Shangton Leics 73 J11
Shankhouse Nthumb 113 L5
Shanklin IoW 14 G10
Shantron Ag & B 132 C10
Shap W & F 101 Q7
Shapinsay Ork 169 e5
Shapwick Dorset 12 F4
Shapwick Somset 19 M7
Shard End Birm 59 J7
Shardlow Derbys 72 C4
Shareshill Staffs 58 D3
Sharlston Wakefd 91 K7
Sharlston Common Wakefd 91 K7
Sharmans Cross Solhll 58 H9
Sharnal Street Medway 38 C7
Sharnbrook Bed 61 L9
Sharneyford Lancs 89 P6
Sharnford Leics 59 Q6
Sharnhill Green Dorset 11 Q3
Sharoe Green Lancs 88 G4
Sharow N York 97 M6
Sharpenhoe C Beds 50 C4
Sharperton Nthumb 119 J10
Sharp Green Norfk 77 M7
Sharpness Gloucs 32 C4
Sharpthorne W Susx 25 J4
Sharptor Cnwll 5 M7
Sharpway Gate Worcs 58 E11
Sharrington Norfk 76 E4
Shatterford Worcs 57 P8
Shattering Kent 39 N10
Shatton Derbys 84 B4
Shaugh Prior Devon 6 E6
Shave Cross Dorset 11 J5
Shavington Ches E 70 B4
Shaw C Brad 90 C3
Shaw Oldham 89 Q9
Shaw Swindn 33 M7
Shaw W Berk 34 E11
Shaw Wilts 32 G11
Shawbirch Wrekin 57 L2
Shawbost W Isls 168 h3
Shawbury Shrops 69 Q10
Shawclough Rochdl 89 P8
Shaw Common Gloucs 46 C9
Shawdon Hill Nthumb 119 L8
Shawell Leics 60 B4
Shawford Hants 22 E9
Shawforth Lancs 89 P6
Shaw Green Herts 50 H4
Shaw Green Lancs 88 G7
Shaw Green N York 97 L10
Shawhead D & G 109 J5
Shaw Mills N York 97 L8
Shawsburn S Lans 126 D7
Shear Cross Wilts 20 G6
Shearington D & G 109 M7
Shearsby Leics 60 D2
Shearston Somset 19 J8
Shebbear Devon 16 G10
Shebdon Staffs 70 D9
Shebster Highld 166 H4
Shedfield Hants 14 G4
Sheen Staffs 71 L2
Sheepbridge Derbys 84 E6
Sheep Hill Dur 113 J9
Sheepridge Kirk 90 F7
Sheepscar Leeds 91 J4
Sheepscombe Gloucs 32 G2

Sheepstor Devon 6 F5
Sheepwash Devon 8 C3
Sheepwash Nthumb 113 L3
Sheepway N Som 31 N9
Sheepy Magna Leics 72 A10
Sheepy Parva Leics 72 A10
Sheering Essex 51 M8
Sheerness Kent 38 F7
Sheerwater Surrey 36 B8
Sheet Hants 23 L10
Sheffield Cnwll 2 D8
Sheffield Sheff 84 E3
Sheffield Bottom W Berk 34 H11
Sheffield Green E Susx 25 K5
Sheffield Park & Garden
   E Susx 25 K6
Shefford C Beds 50 D3
Shefford Woodlands W Berk 34 C10
Sheigra Highld 164 E4
Sheinton Shrops 57 L4
Shelderton Shrops 56 G9
Sheldon Birm 59 J7
Sheldon Derbys 83 Q11
Sheldon Devon 10 C3
Sheldwich Kent 38 H10
Sheldwich Lees Kent 38 H10
Shelf Calder 90 E5
Shelfanger Norfk 64 G5
Shelfield Warwks 47 M2
Shelfield Wsall 58 F4
Shelfield Green Warwks 47 M2
Shelford Notts 72 H2
Shelford Warwks 59 P7
Shellacres Nthumb 118 G2
Shelley Essex 51 N9
Shelley Kirk 90 G8
Shelley Suffk 52 H4
Shelley Far Bank Kirk 90 G8
Shellingford Oxon 34 B6
Shellow Bowells Essex 51 P9
Shelsley Beauchamp Worcs 46 D2
Shelsley Walsh Worcs 46 D2
Shelton Bed 61 M7
Shelton Norfk 65 J3
Shelton Notts 73 K2
Shelton Shrops 56 H2
Shelton Green Norfk 65 J3
Shelton Lock C Derb 72 B4
Shelton Under Harley Staffs 70 E7
Shelve Shrops 56 E5
Shelwick Herefs 45 Q6
Shenfield Essex 51 P11
Shenington Oxon 48 C6
Shenley Herts 50 E10
Shenley Brook End M Keyn 49 N7
Shenleybury Herts 50 E10
Shenley Church End M Keyn 49 M7
Shenmore Herefs 45 M7
Shennanton D & G 107 K5
Shenstone Staffs 58 H4
Shenstone Worcs 58 C10
Shenstone Woodend Staffs 58 H4
Shenton Leics 72 B11
Shenval Moray 149 N2
Shepeau Stow Lincs 74 F8
Shephall Herts 50 G6
Shepherd's Bush Gt Lon 36 F4
Shepherd's Green Oxon 35 K8
Shepherds Patch Gloucs 32 D4
Shepherdswell Kent 27 N2
Shepley Kirk 90 F9
Shepperdine S Glos 32 B5
Shepperton Surrey 36 C7
Shepperton Green Surrey 36 C7
Shepreth Cambs 62 E11
Shepshed Leics 72 D7
Shepton Beauchamp
   Somset 19 M11
Shepton Mallet Somset 20 B6
Shepton Montague Somset 20 C8
Shepway Kent 38 C11
Sheraton Dur 104 D3
Sherborne Dorset 20 B11
Sherborne Gloucs 33 N2
Sherborne Somset 19 Q3
Sherborne St John Hants 22 H3
Sherbourne Warwks 47 Q2
Sherburn Dur 104 B2
Sherburn N York 99 K5
Sherburn Hill Dur 104 B2
Sherburn in Elmet N York 91 M4
Shere Surrey 36 C11
Shereford Norfk 76 B6
Sherfield English Hants 21 Q10
Sherfield on Loddon Hants 23 J3
Sherfin Lancs 89 M5
Sherford Devon 6 E8
Sherford Devon 7 K10
Sherford Dorset 12 F6
Sheriffhales Shrops 57 P2
Sheriff Hutton N York 98 D7
Sheringham Norfk 76 H3
Sherington M Keyn 49 N5
Shermanbury W Susx 24 F7
Shernborne Norfk 75 P4
Sherrington Wilts 21 J7
Sherston Wilts 32 G7
Sherwood C Nott 72 F2
Sherwood Forest Notts 85 K8
Shetland Islands Shet 169 r8
Shettleston C Glas 125 Q5
Shevington Wigan 88 G9
Shevington Moor Wigan 88 G8
Shevington Vale Wigan 88 G9
Sheviock Cnwll 5 P10
Shibden Head C Brad 90 D5
Shide IoW 14 F9
Shidlaw Nthumb 118 F3
Shiel Bridge Highld 146 A4
Shieldaig Highld 153 Q4
Shieldhill D & G 109 M3
Shieldhill Falk 126 F2
Shieldhill House Hotel
   S Lans 116 E2
Shields N Lans 126 D6
Shielfoot Highld 138 B3
Shielhill Angus 142 G6
Shielhill Inver 124 G3
Shifford Oxon 34 C4
Shifnal Shrops 57 N3
Shilbottle Nthumb 119 N9
Shildon Dur 103 P5
Shillford E Rens 125 M6
Shillingford Devon 18 C10
Shillingford Oxon 34 G6
Shillingford Abbot Devon 9 M7

Shillingford St George
   Devon 9 M7
Shillingstone Dorset 12 D4
Shillington C Beds 50 D4
Shillmoor Nthumb 118 G9
Shilton Oxon 33 Q3
Shilton Warwks 59 P8
Shimpling Norfk 64 H5
Shimpling Suffk 64 B11
Shimpling Street Suffk 64 B11
Shincliffe Dur 103 Q2
Shiney Row Sundld 113 M10
Shinfield Wokham 35 K11
Shingay Cambs 62 D11
Shingle Street Suffk 53 Q3
Shinnersbridge Devon 7 K6
Shinness Highld 162 C4
Shipbourne Kent 37 N10
Shipdham Norfk 76 D10
Shipham Somset 19 M3
Shiphay Torbay 7 M5
Shiplake Oxon 35 L9
Shiplake Row Oxon 35 K9
Shiplate N Som 19 L3
Shipley C Brad 90 F3
Shipley Derbys 72 C2
Shipley Shrops 57 Q5
Shipley W Susx 24 D6
Shipley Bridge Surrey 24 H2
Shipley Hatch Kent 26 H4
Shipmeadow Suffk 65 M3
Shippea Hill Station Cambs 63 K4
Shippon Oxon 34 E5
Shipston-on-Stour Warwks 47 P6
Shipton Bucks 49 L9
Shipton Gloucs 47 K11
Shipton N York 98 B9
Shipton Shrops 57 K6
Shipton Bellinger Hants 21 P5
Shipton Gorge Dorset 11 K6
Shipton Green W Susx 15 M7
Shipton Moyne Gloucs 32 G7
Shipton-on-Cherwell Oxon 48 E11
Shiptonthorpe E R Yk 92 E2
Shipton-under-Wychwood
   Oxon 47 Q11
Shirburn Oxon 35 J5
Shirdley Hill Lancs 88 D8
Shire W & F 102 B3
Shirebrook Derbys 84 H7
Shiregreen Sheff 84 E2
Shirehampton Bristl 31 P9
Shiremoor N Tyne 113 M6
Shirenewton Mons 31 N6
Shire Oak Wsall 58 G4
Shireoaks Notts 85 J4
Shirkoak Kent 26 H4
Shirland Derbys 84 F9
Shirlett Shrops 57 L5
Shirley C Sotn 14 D4
Shirley Derbys 71 N6
Shirley Gt Lon 37 J7
Shirley Solhll 58 H9
Shirl Heath Herefs 45 N3
Shirrell Heath Hants 14 G4
Shirwell Devon 17 L4
Shiskine N Ayrs 120 H6
Shittlehope Dur 103 K3
Shobdon Herefs 45 N2
Shobley Hants 13 L3
Shobrooke Devon 9 L4
Shoby Leics 72 H6
Shocklach Ches W 69 M5
Shocklach Green Ches W 69 M5
Shoeburyness Sthend 38 F4
Sholden Kent 39 Q11
Sholing C Sotn 14 E4
Shoot Hill Shrops 56 G2
Shop Cnwll 4 D7
Shop Cnwll 16 C9
Shopwyke W Susx 15 N5
Shore Rochdl 89 Q7
Shoreditch Gt Lon 36 H4
Shoreditch Somset 18 H10
Shoreham Kent 37 M8
Shoreham-by-Sea W Susx 24 F9
Shoreswood Nthumb 129 N10
Shorley Herefs 22 G9
Shorncote Gloucs 33 K4
Shorne Kent 37 Q6
Shortacross Cnwll 5 M10
Shortbridge E Susx 25 L6
Shortfield Common Surrey 23 N4
Shortgate E Susx 25 L7
Short Heath Birm 58 G6
Shorteheath Hants 23 L7
Short Heath Wsall 58 E4
Shortlanesend Cnwll 3 L4
Shortlees E Ayrs 125 L10
Shortstown Bed 61 N11
Shorwell IoW 14 E10
Shoscombe BaNES 20 D3
Shotesham Norfk 65 J2
Shotgate Essex 38 C3
Shotley Suffk 53 M4
Shotley Bridge Dur 112 H11
Shotleyfield Nthumb 112 G10
Shotley Gate Suffk 53 M4
Shottenden Kent 38 H11
Shottermill Surrey 23 N7
Shottery Warwks 47 N4
Shotteswell Warwks 48 D5
Shottisham Suffk 53 P3
Shottle Derbys 71 Q4
Shottlegate Derbys 71 Q5
Shotton Dur 104 D3
Shotton Dur 104 D1
Shotton Flints 81 L11
Shotton Nthumb 113 K5
Shotton Nthumb 118 F4
Shotton Colliery Dur 104 C2
Shotts N Lans 126 F6
Shotwick Ches W 81 L10
Shougle Moray 157 N6
Shouldham Norfk 75 N9
Shouldham Thorpe Norfk 75 N9
Shoulton Worcs 46 F3
Shover's Green E Susx 25 Q4
Shraleybrook Staffs 70 D4
Shrawardine Shrops 69 L11
Shrawley Worcs 57 Q11
Shreding Green Bucks 36 B4
Shrewley Warwks 59 K11
Shrewsbury Shrops 56 H2
Shrewton Wilts 21 L6
Shripney W Susx 15 P6

Shrivenham Oxon...........33 P7
Shropham Norfk...........64 D3
Shroton Dorset...........12 E2
Shrub End Essex...........52 G7
Shucknall Herefs...........46 A6
Shudy Camps Cambs...........51 P2
Shuna Ag & B...........130 F6
Shurdington Gloucs...........46 H11
Shurlock Row W & M...........35 M10
Shurnock Worcs...........47 K2
Shurrery Highld...........166 H5
Shurrery Lodge Highld...........166 H5
Shurton Somset...........18 H6
Shustoke Warwks...........59 K6
Shute Devon...........9 L4
Shute Devon...........10 F5
Shutford Oxon...........48 C6
Shut Heath Staffs...........70 F10
Shuthonger Gloucs...........46 G7
Shutlanger W Nthn...........49 K5
Shutterton Devon...........9 N9
Shutt Green Staffs...........58 C3
Shuttington Warwks...........59 L3
Shuttlewood Derbys...........84 G6
Shuttleworth Bury...........89 N7
Siabost W Isls...........168 h3
Siadar W Isls...........168 i2
Sibbertoft Nhants...........60 E4
Sibdon Carwood Shrops...........56 G8
Sibford Ferris Oxon...........48 C7
Sibford Gower Oxon...........48 C7
Sible Hedingham Essex...........52 C5
Sibley's Green Essex...........51 P5
Siblyback Cnwll...........5 L7
Sibsey Lincs...........87 L10
Sibsey Fenside Lincs...........87 K10
Sibson Cambs...........74 A11
Sibson Leics...........72 B10
Sibster Highld...........167 P6
Sibthorpe Notts...........85 M6
Sibthorpe Notts...........85 N11
Sibton Suffk...........65 M8
Sicklesmere Suffk...........64 B9
Sicklinghall N York...........97 N11
Sidbrook Somset...........19 J9
Sidbury Devon...........10 C6
Sidbury Shrops...........57 M7
Sid Cop Barns...........91 K9
Sidcot N Som...........19 M3
Sidcup Gt Lon...........37 L6
Siddick Cumb...........100 D4
Siddington Ches E...........82 H10
Siddington Gloucs...........33 K5
Sidemoor Worcs...........58 E10
Sidestrand Norfk...........77 K4
Sidford Devon...........10 C6
Sidlesham W Susx...........15 N7
Sidlesham Common W Susx...........15 N7
Sidley E Susx...........26 B10
Sidmouth Devon...........10 C7
Siefton Shrops...........56 H8
Sigford Devon...........7 K4
Sigglesthorne E R Yk...........99 P11
Sigingstone V Glam...........30 C10
Signet Oxon...........33 P2
Silchester Hants...........22 H2
Sileby Leics...........72 G7
Silecroft Cumb...........94 C4
Silfield Norfk...........64 G2
Silian Cerdgn...........43 L4
Silkstead Hants...........22 D10
Silkstone Barns...........90 H9
Silkstone Common Barns...........90 H10
Silk Willoughby Lincs...........73 R2
Silloth Cumb...........109 P10
Silpho N York...........99 K2
Silsden C Brad...........96 F11
Silsoe C Beds...........50 C3
Silton Dorset...........20 E9
Silverburn Mdloth...........127 N5
Silverdale Lancs...........95 K6
Silverdale Staffs...........70 E5
Silver End Essex...........52 D8
Silverford Abers...........159 J5
Silvergate Norfk...........76 H6
Silver Jubilee Bridge Halton...........81 Q8
Silverlace Green Suffk...........65 L9
Silverley's Green Suffk...........65 K8
Silverstone W Nthn...........49 J6
Silver Street Kent...........38 E9
Silver Street Somset...........19 P8
Silverton Devon...........9 N4
Silverwell Cnwll...........3 J4
Silvington Shrops...........57 L9
Simister Bury...........89 N9
Simmondley Derbys...........83 M6
Simonburn Nthumb...........112 C6
Simonsbath Somset...........17 P4
Simonsburrow Devon...........18 F11
Simonstone Lancs...........89 M4
Simonstone N York...........96 C2
Simprim Border...........129 L11
Simpson M Keyn...........49 N7
Simpson Cross Pembks...........40 G8
Sinclair's Hill Border...........129 L9
Sinclairston E Ayrs...........115 J4
Sinderby N York...........97 M4
Sinderhope Nthumb...........112 B10
Sinderland Green Traffd...........82 F7
Sindlesham Wokham...........35 L11
Sinfin C Derb...........72 A4
Singleborough Bucks...........49 L8
Single Street Gt Lon...........37 L9
Singleton Kent...........26 H3
Singleton Lancs...........88 D3
Singleton W Susx...........15 N4
Singlewell Kent...........37 Q6
Sinkhurst Green Kent...........26 D3
Sinnahard Abers...........150 D3
Sinnington N York...........98 E3
Sinope Leics...........72 C7
Sinton Worcs...........46 F2
Sinton Worcs...........46 F2
Sinton Green Worcs...........46 F2
Sipson Gt Lon...........36 C5
Sirhowy Blae G...........30 F2
Sissinghurst Kent...........26 C4
Siston S Glos...........32 C9
Sitcott Devon...........5 P3
Sithney Cnwll...........2 G8
Sithney Common Cnwll...........2 G8
Sithney Green Cnwll...........2 G8
Sittingbourne Kent...........38 F9
Six Ashes Shrops...........57 P7
Six Bells Blae G...........30 H4
Six Hills Leics...........72 G6

Sixhills Lincs...........86 G3
Six Mile Bottom Cambs...........63 J9
Sixmile Cottages Kent...........27 K3
Sixpenny Handley Dorset...........21 J11
Six Rues Jersey...........11 b1
Sizewell Suffk...........65 P9
Skaill Ork...........169 e6
Skara Brae Ork...........169 b5
Skares E Ayrs...........115 K4
Skateraw Abers...........151 N9
Skateraw E Loth...........129 J5
Skeabost Highld...........152 G8
Skeeby N York...........103 N10
Skeffington Leics...........73 J10
Skeffling E R Yk...........93 Q7
Skegby Notts...........84 G8
Skegby Notts...........85 N7
Skegness Lincs...........87 Q8
Skelbo Highld...........162 H7
Skelbo Street Highld...........162 H8
Skelbrooke Donc...........91 N8
Skeldyke Lincs...........74 F3
Skellingthorpe Lincs...........86 B5
Skellorn Green Ches E...........83 K8
Skellow Donc...........91 N8
Skelmanthorpe Kirk...........90 G8
Skelmersdale Lancs...........88 F9
Skelmorlie N Ayrs...........124 F4
Skelpick Highld...........166 B5
Skelton C York...........98 B9
Skelton E R Yk...........92 C5
Skelton N York...........103 L10
Skelton R & Cl...........105 J7
Skelton W & F...........101 M3
Skelton on Ure N York...........97 N7
Skelwith Bridge W & F...........101 K10
Skendleby Lincs...........87 M7
Skene House Abers...........151 K5
Skenfrith Mons...........45 P10
Skerne E R Yk...........99 L9
Skerray Highld...........165 Q4
Skerricha Highld...........164 F6
Skerton Lancs...........95 K8
Sketchley Leics...........59 P6
Sketty Swans...........28 H6
Skewen Neath...........29 K5
Skewsby N York...........98 C6
Skeyton Norfk...........77 J6
Skeyton Corner Norfk...........77 K6
Skiall Highld...........166 H3
Skidbrooke Lincs...........87 M2
Skidbrooke North End Lincs...........93 R11
Skidby E R Yk...........92 H4
Skigersta W Isls...........168 k1
Skilgate Somset...........18 C9
Skillington Lincs...........73 M5
Skinburness Cumb...........109 P9
Skinflats Falk...........133 Q3
Skinidin Highld...........152 C8
Skinners W Berk...........34 D11
Skinningrove R & Cl...........105 K7
Skipness Ag & B...........123 R8
Skipper's Bridge D & G...........110 G4
Skiprigg Cumb...........110 G11
Skipsea E R Yk...........99 P10
Skipsea Brough E R Yk...........99 P10
Skipton N York...........96 E10
Skipton-on-Swale N York...........97 N5
Skipwith N York...........91 R3
Skirbeck Lincs...........74 F2
Skirlaugh E R Yk...........93 K3
Skirling Border...........116 F3
Skirmett Bucks...........35 L6
Skirpenbeck E R Yk...........98 E9
Skirwith W & F...........102 B4
Skirza Highld...........167 Q3
Skitby Cumb...........110 H7
Skittle Green Bucks...........35 L4
Skokholm Island Pembks...........40 D10
Skomer Island Pembks...........40 D9
Skulamus Highld...........145 L3
Skyborry Green Shrops...........56 D10
Skye Green Essex...........52 E7
Skye of Curr Highld...........148 H3
Skyreholme N York...........96 G8
Slack Calder...........90 B5
Slackbuie Highld...........156 B9
Slackcote Oldham...........90 B9
Slack Head W & F...........95 K5
Slackholme End Lincs...........87 P6
Slacks of Cairnbanno Abers...........159 K8
Slad Gloucs...........32 G3
Slade Devon...........10 C3
Slade Devon...........17 J2
Slade Devon...........17 Q6
Slade End Oxon...........34 G6
Slade Green Gt Lon...........37 M5
Slade Heath Staffs...........58 D3
Slade Hooton Rothm...........84 H3
Sladesbridge Cnwll...........4 G7
Slades Green Worcs...........46 F8
Slaggyford Nthumb...........111 N10
Slaidburn Lancs...........95 Q10
Slaithwaite Kirk...........90 D8
Slaley Derbys...........84 C9
Slaley Nthumb...........112 E9
Slamannan Falk...........126 F3
Slapton Bucks...........49 P10
Slapton Devon...........7 L11
Slapton W Nthn...........48 H5
Slattocks Rochdl...........89 P9
Slaugham W Susx...........24 G5
Slaughterford Wilts...........32 F10
Slawston Leics...........60 G2
Sleaford Hants...........23 M7
Sleaford Lincs...........86 E11
Sleagill W & F...........101 Q7
Sleap Shrops...........69 N9
Sleapford Wrekin...........70 A11
Sleapshyde Herts...........50 E9
Sleasdairidh Highld...........162 E7
Slebech Pembks...........41 K7
Sledge Green Worcs...........46 F8
Sledmere E R Yk...........99 J8
Sleetbeck Cumb...........111 K5
Sleight Dorset...........12 G6
Sleightholme Dur...........103 J8
Sleights N York...........105 N9
Slepe Dorset...........12 F6
Slickly Highld...........167 N3
Sliddery N Ayrs...........120 H7
Sligachan Highld...........144 G2
Sligrachan Ag & B...........131 P9
Slimbridge Gloucs...........32 D4

Slindon Staffs...........70 E8
Slindon W Susx...........15 Q5
Slinfold W Susx...........24 D4
Sling Gloucs...........31 Q3
Sling Gwynd...........79 L11
Slingsby N York...........98 D6
Slip End C Beds...........50 C7
Slip End Herts...........50 G3
Slipton Nthn...........61 L5
Slitting Mill Staffs...........71 J11
Slochd Highld...........148 E3
Slockavullin Ag & B...........130 E3
Sloley Norfk...........77 K7
Sloncombe Devon...........8 H7
Sloothby Lincs...........87 N6
Slough Slough...........35 Q9
Slough Green Somset...........19 J11
Slough Green W Susx...........24 G5
Slumbay Highld...........154 A10
Slyfield Surrey...........23 Q4
Slyne Lancs...........95 K7
Smailholm Border...........118 B3
Smallbridge Rochdl...........89 Q7
Smallbrook Devon...........9 L5
Smallbrook Gloucs...........31 Q4
Smallburgh Norfk...........77 L7
Smallburn E Ayrs...........115 N2
Smalldale Derbys...........83 N9
Smalldale Derbys...........83 Q8
Small Dole W Susx...........24 F8
Smalley Derbys...........72 C2
Smalley Common Derbys...........72 C2
Smalley Green Derbys...........72 C2
Smallfield Surrey...........24 H2
Smallford Herts...........50 E9
Small Heath Birm...........58 H7
Small Hythe Kent...........26 E5
Smallridge Devon...........10 G4
Smallthorne C Stke...........70 F4
Smallways N York...........103 M8
Smallwood Ches E...........70 E2
Small Wood Hey Lancs...........94 H11
Smallworth Norfk...........64 E5
Smannell Hants...........22 C5
Smardale W & F...........102 D9
Smarden Kent...........26 E3
Smarden Bell Kent...........26 E3
Smart's Hill Kent...........25 M2
Smeafield Nthumb...........119 L3
Smeatharpe Devon...........10 D2
Smeeth Kent...........27 J4
Smeeton Westerby Leics...........60 E2
Smelthouses N York...........97 J8
Smerral Highld...........167 L10
Smestow Staffs...........58 C6
Smethcote Sandw...........58 F7
Smethwick Green Ches E...........70 E2
Smirisary Highld...........138 A2
Smisby Derbys...........72 A7
Smith End Green Worcs...........46 E4
Smithfield Cumb...........110 H7
Smith Green Lancs...........95 K9
Smithies Barns...........91 J9
Smithincott Devon...........9 Q2
Smith's End Herts...........51 K3
Smith's Green Essex...........51 N6
Smith's Green Essex...........51 Q2
Smithstown Highld...........160 B11
Smithton Highld...........156 C8
Smithy Bridge Rochdl...........89 Q7
Smithy Green Ches E...........82 F10
Smithy Green Stockp...........83 J7
Smithy Houses Derbys...........84 E11
Smockington Leics...........59 Q7
Smoo Highld...........165 K3
Smythe's Green Essex...........52 F8
Snade D & G...........108 H3
Snailbeach Shrops...........56 F4
Snailwell Cambs...........63 K7
Snainton N York...........99 J4
Snaith E R Yk...........91 Q6
Snake Pass Inn Derbys...........83 P6
Snape N York...........97 L4
Snape Suffk...........65 M10
Snape Green Lancs...........88 D8
Snape Street Suffk...........65 M10
Snaresbrook Gt Lon...........37 K3
Snarestone Leics...........72 A9
Snarford Lincs...........86 D4
Snargate Kent...........26 G6
Snave Kent...........26 H6
Sneachill Worcs...........46 H4
Snead Powys...........56 E6
Sneath Common Norfk...........64 H4
Sneaton N York...........105 N9
Sneatonthorpe N York...........105 P9
Snelland Lincs...........86 E4
Snelson Ches E...........82 H10
Snelston Derbys...........71 M6
Snetterton Norfk...........64 D3
Snettisham Norfk...........75 N4
Snibston Leics...........72 C8
Snig's End Gloucs...........46 E9
Snitter Nthumb...........119 K10
Snitterby Lincs...........86 C2
Snitterfield Warwks...........47 P3
Snitterton Derbys...........84 C8
Snitton Shrops...........57 K9
Snodhill Herefs...........45 L6
Snodland Kent...........38 B9
Snoll Hatch Kent...........37 Q11
Snowden Hill Barns...........90 H10
Snowdon Gwynd...........67 L4
Snowdon Kent...........39 M11
Snowdonia National Park...........67 Q9
Snow End Herts...........51 K4
Snowshill Gloucs...........47 L8
Snow Street Norfk...........64 F5
Soake Hants...........15 J4
Soar Cardif...........30 D8
Soar Devon...........7 J11
Soar Powys...........44 D8
Soay Highld...........144 F5
Soberton Hants...........22 H11
Soberton Heath Hants...........14 H4
Sockbridge W & F...........101 N5
Sockburn Darltn...........104 B9
Sodom Denbgs...........80 F10
Sodylt Bank Shrops...........69 K7
Soham Cambs...........63 J6
Soham Cotes Cambs...........63 J5
Solas W Isls...........168 d10
Soldon Devon...........16 E9
Soldon Cross Devon...........16 E9

Soldridge Hants...........23 J7
Sole Street Kent...........27 J2
Sole Street Kent...........37 Q7
Solihull Solhll...........59 J9
Sollas W Isls...........168 d10
Sollers Dilwyn Herefs...........45 N3
Sollers Hope Herefs...........46 B8
Sollom Lancs...........88 F7
Solva Pembks...........40 F6
Solwaybank D & G...........110 F5
Somerby Leics...........73 K8
Somerby Lincs...........93 J9
Somercotes Derbys...........84 F10
Somerford BCP...........13 L6
Somerford Keynes Gloucs...........33 K5
Somerley W Susx...........15 M7
Somerleyton Suffk...........65 P2
Somersal Herbert Derbys...........71 L7
Somersby Lincs...........87 K6
Somersham Cambs...........62 E5
Somersham Suffk...........53 J2
Somerton Oxon...........48 E9
Somerton Somset...........19 N9
Somerton Suffk...........63 P10
Somerwood Shrops...........57 K2
Sompting W Susx...........24 E9
Sompting Abbotts W Susx...........24 E9
Sonning Wokham...........35 L9
Sonning Common Oxon...........35 K8
Sonning Eye Oxon...........35 K9
Sontley Wrexhm...........69 K5
Sopley Hants...........13 L5
Sopwell Herts...........50 E9
Sopworth Wilts...........32 F7
Sorbie D & G...........107 M8
Sordale Highld...........167 K4
Sorisdale Ag & B...........136 H3
Sorn E Ayrs...........115 L2
Sornhill E Ayrs...........125 N11
Sortat Highld...........167 N4
Sotby Lincs...........86 H5
Sots Hole Lincs...........86 F8
Sotterley Suffk...........65 N5
Soughton Flints...........81 J11
Soulbury Bucks...........49 N9
Soulby W & F...........101 N5
Soulby W & F...........102 D8
Souldern Oxon...........48 F8
Souldrop Bed...........61 L8
Sound Ches E...........70 A5
Soundwell S Glos...........32 C9
Sound Muir Moray...........157 R7
Sourton Devon...........8 D6
Soutergate W & F...........94 E4
South Acre Norfk...........75 R8
South Alkham Kent...........27 M3
Southall Gt Lon...........36 D5
South Allington Devon...........7 K11
South Alloa Falk...........133 P9
Southam Gloucs...........47 J9
Southam Warwks...........48 D2
Southampton C Sotn...........14 D4
Southampton Airport Hants...........22 E11
South Anston Rothm...........84 H4
South Ascot W & F...........35 P11
South Ashford Kent...........26 H3
South Baddesley Hants...........14 C7
South Bank C York...........98 B10
South Bank R & Cl...........104 F6
South Barrow Somset...........20 B9
South Beddington Gt Lon...........36 G8
South Beer Cnwll...........5 N3
South Benfleet Essex...........38 C4
South Bockhampton BCP...........13 L5
Southborough Gt Lon...........37 K7
Southborough Kent...........25 N2
Southbourne BCP...........13 K6
Southbourne W Susx...........15 L5
South Bowood Dorset...........11 J5
South Bramwith Donc...........91 Q8
South Brent Devon...........6 H6
South Brewham Somset...........20 D7
South Broomhill Nthumb...........119 P11
Southburgh Norfk...........76 E10
South Burlingham Norfk...........77 M10
Southburn E R Yk...........99 K10
South Cadbury Somset...........20 B9
South Carlton Lincs...........86 B5
South Carlton Notts...........85 J4
South Cave E R Yk...........92 F4
South Cerney Gloucs...........33 K5
South Chailey E Susx...........25 J7
South Chard Somset...........10 G3
South Charlton Nthumb...........119 N6
South Cheriton Somset...........20 C10
South Church Dur...........103 P5
Southchurch Sthend...........38 F4
South Cleatlam Dur...........103 M7
South Cliffe E R Yk...........92 E3
South Clifton Notts...........85 P6
South Cockerington Lincs...........87 L3
South Cornelly Brdgnd...........29 M8
Southcott Cnwll...........5 K2
Southcott Devon...........8 D5
Southcott Devon...........16 J8
Southcott Devon...........16 G8
Southcott Wilts...........21 N3
Southcourt Bucks...........35 M2
South Cove Suffk...........65 P5
South Creake Norfk...........76 B4
South Crosland Kirk...........90 E8
South Croxton Leics...........72 H8
South Dalton E R Yk...........99 K11
South Darenth Kent...........37 N7
South Dell W Isls...........168 j1
South Downs National Park...........25 J9
South Duffield N York...........92 A4
South Earlswood Surrey...........36 G11
Southease E Susx...........25 K9
South Elkington Lincs...........87 J3
South Elmsall Wakefd...........91 M8
Southend Ag & B...........120 C10
South End E R Yk...........93 Q7
South End Hants...........21 M11
South End Herefs...........46 D6
South End N Linc...........93 K6
South End Norfk...........64 D3
Southend Wilts...........33 N10
Southend Airport Essex...........38 E4
Southend-on-Sea Sthend...........38 E4
Southernby Cumb...........101 L3
Southernden Kent...........26 E3
Southerndown V Glam...........29 N10
Southerness D & G...........109 L10

South Erradale Highld...........153 N3
Southerton Devon...........10 B6
Southery Norfk...........63 K2
South Fambridge Essex...........38 E3
South Fawley W Berk...........34 C8
South Ferriby N Linc...........92 G6
Southfield Falk...........126 E3
Southfleet Kent...........37 P6
Southford IoW...........14 F11
Southgate Gt Lon...........36 G2
Southgate Norfk...........75 N4
Southgate Norfk...........76 B4
Southgate Norfk...........76 G7
Southgate Swans...........28 G7
South Godstone Surrey...........37 J11
South Gorley Hants...........13 L2
South Gosforth N u Ty...........113 K7
South Green Essex...........37 Q2
South Green Essex...........52 H8
South Green Kent...........38 E9
South Green Norfk...........76 F9
South Green Suffk...........64 H6
South Gyle C Edin...........127 M3
South Hanningfield Essex...........38 B2
South Harting W Susx...........23 L11
South Hayling Hants...........15 K7
South Hazelrigg Nthumb...........119 L4
South Heath Bucks...........35 P4
South Heighton E Susx...........25 K10
South Hetton Dur...........113 N11
South Hiendley Wakefd...........91 K8
South Hill Cnwll...........5 N7
South Hill Somset...........19 N9
South Hinksey Oxon...........34 F4
South Hole Devon...........16 C7
South Holmwood Surrey...........24 E2
South Hornchurch Gt Lon...........37 M4
South Horrington Somset...........19 Q5
South Huish Devon...........6 H10
South Hykeham Lincs...........86 B8
South Hylton Sundld...........113 N9
Southill C Beds...........50 E2
Southington Hants...........22 G4
South Kelsey Lincs...........92 H11
South Kessock Highld...........156 B8
South Killingholme N Linc...........93 K7
South Kilvington N York...........97 P4
South Kilworth Leics...........60 D4
South Kirkby Wakefd...........91 L8
South Knighton Devon...........7 L4
South Kyme Lincs...........86 G11
Southleigh Devon...........10 E6
South Leigh Oxon...........34 C3
South Leverton Notts...........85 N4
South Littleton Worcs...........47 L5
South Lopham Norfk...........64 E5
South Luffenham Rutlnd...........73 N10
South Lynn Norfk...........75 M7
South Malling E Susx...........25 K8
South Marston Swindn...........33 N7
South Merstham Surrey...........36 G10
South Middleton Nthumb...........119 J6
South Milford N York...........91 M4
South Milton Devon...........6 J10
South Mimms Herts...........50 F10
South Mimms Services Herts...........50 F10
Southminster Essex...........38 G2
South Molton Devon...........17 N6
South Moor Dur...........113 J10
Southmoor Oxon...........34 C5
South Moreton Oxon...........34 G6
Southmuir Angus...........142 F7
South Mundham W Susx...........15 N6
South Muskham Notts...........85 N9
South Newbald E R Yk...........92 F3
South Newington Oxon...........48 D8
South Newsham Nthumb...........113 M5
South Newton Wilts...........21 L8
South Nitshill C Glas...........125 N6
South Normanton Derbys...........84 F9
South Norwood Gt Lon...........36 H7
South Nutfield Surrey...........36 H11
South Ockendon Thurr...........37 N4
Southoe Cambs...........61 Q8
Southolt Suffk...........65 H8
South Ormsby Lincs...........87 L5
Southorpe C Pete...........74 A10
South Ossett Wakefd...........90 H7
South Otterington N York...........97 N3
Southover Dorset...........11 N6
Southover E Susx...........25 Q5
South Owersby Lincs...........86 E2
Southowram Calder...........90 E6
South Park Surrey...........36 F11
South Perrott Dorset...........11 K3
South Petherton Somset...........19 M11
South Petherwin Cnwll...........5 N5
South Pickenham Norfk...........76 B11
South Pill Cnwll...........5 Q10
South Pool Devon...........7 K10
South Poorton Dorset...........11 L5
Southport Sefton...........88 C7
South Queensferry C Edin...........127 L2
South Radworthy Devon...........17 N5
South Rauceby Lincs...........86 D11
South Raynham Norfk...........76 B7
South Reddish Stockp...........83 J6
Southrepps Norfk...........77 K4
South Reston Lincs...........87 M4
Southrey Lincs...........86 F7
South Ronaldsay Ork...........169 d8
Southrop Gloucs...........33 N4
Southrope Hants...........23 J6
South Runcton Norfk...........75 M9
South Scarle Notts...........85 P8
Southsea C Port...........15 J7
Southsea Wrexhm...........69 K4
South Shian Ag & B...........138 G9
South Shields S Tyne...........113 N7
South Shore Bpool...........88 C4
Southside Dur...........103 M5
South Somercotes Lincs...........87 M2
South Stainley N York...........97 M8
South Stifford Thurr...........37 N5
South Stoke BaNES...........20 D2
South Stoke Oxon...........34 G8
South Stoke W Susx...........24 B9
South Stour Kent...........26 H4
South Street Kent...........37 P8
South Street Kent...........39 J10
South Street Kent...........39 K8
South Tarbrax S Lans...........127 J7
South Tawton Devon...........8 G6
South Tehidy Cnwll...........2 H5

South Thoresby Lincs.....87 M5
South Thorpe Dur.....103 M8
South Town Hants.....23 J7
Southtown Norfk.....77 Q10
Southtown Somset.....19 K11
South Uist W Isls.....168 d14
Southwaite W & F.....110 H11
Southwaite Services W & F.....110 H11
South Walsham Norfk.....77 M9
Southwark Gt Lon.....36 H5
South Warnborough Hants.....23 K5
Southwater W Susx.....24 E5
Southwater Street W Susx.....24 E5
Southway C Plym.....6 D6
Southway Somset.....19 P6
South Weald Essex.....37 N2
Southwell Dorset.....11 P10
Southwell Notts.....85 L10
South Weston Oxon.....35 K5
South Wheatley Cnwll.....5 L3
South Wheatley Notts.....85 N3
Southwick Hants.....14 H5
Southwick N Nthn.....61 M2
Southwick Somset.....19 L5
Southwick Sundld.....113 N9
Southwick W Susx.....24 F9
Southwick Wilts.....20 F3
South Widcombe BaNES.....19 Q3
South Wigston Leics.....72 F11
South Willingham Lincs.....86 G4
South Wingate Dur.....104 D4
South Wingfield Derbys.....84 E9
South Witham Lincs.....73 N7
Southwold Suffk.....65 Q6
South Wonston Hants.....22 E7
Southwood Norfk.....77 M10
Southwood Somset.....19 Q8
South Woodham Ferrers Essex.....38 D2
South Wootton Norfk.....75 M6
South Wraxall Wilts.....20 F2
South Zeal Devon.....8 G6
Sovereign Harbour E Susx.....25 P10
Sowerby Calder.....90 C6
Sowerby N York.....97 P4
Sowerby Bridge Calder.....90 D6
Sowerby Row W & F.....101 L2
Sower Carr Lancs.....88 D2
Sowerhill Somset.....18 A10
Sowhill Torfn.....31 J4
Sowley Green Suffk.....63 M10
Sowood Calder.....90 D7
Sowton Devon.....6 E5
Sowton Devon.....9 N6
Soyland Town Calder.....90 C6
Spa Common Norfk.....77 K5
Spain's End Essex.....51 Q3
Spalding Lincs.....74 D6
Spaldington E R Yk.....92 C4
Spaldwick Cambs.....61 P6
Spalford Notts.....85 P7
Spanby Lincs.....74 A3
Spanish Green Hants.....23 J3
Sparham Norfk.....76 F8
Sparhamill Norfk.....76 F8
Spark Bridge W & F.....94 G4
Sparket W & F.....101 M5
Sparkford Somset.....20 B9
Sparkhill Birm.....58 H8
Sparkwell Devon.....6 F7
Sparrow Green Norfk.....76 C9
Sparrowpit Derbys.....83 N8
Sparrows Green E Susx.....25 P4
Sparsholt Hants.....22 D8
Sparsholt Oxon.....34 B7
Spartylea Nthumb.....112 C11
Spath Staffs.....71 K7
Spaunton N York.....98 E3
Spaxton Somset.....18 H7
Spean Bridge Highld.....146 G11
Spear Hill W Susx.....24 D7
Spearywell Hants.....22 B9
Speen Bucks.....35 M5
Speen W Berk.....34 E11
Speeton N York.....99 P6
Speke Lpool.....81 N8
Speldhurst Kent.....25 N2
Spellbrook Herts.....51 L7
Spelmonden Kent.....26 B4
Spelsbury Oxon.....48 B10
Spen Kirk.....90 F5
Spencers Wood Wokham.....35 K11
Spen Green Ches E.....70 E2
Spennithorne N York.....96 H3
Spennymoor Dur.....103 Q4
Spernall Warwks.....47 L2
Spetchley Worcs.....46 G4
Spetisbury Dorset.....12 F4
Spexhall Suffk.....65 M5
Spey Bay Moray.....157 R4
Speybridge Highld.....149 J2
Speyview Moray.....157 P9
Spilsby Lincs.....87 M7
Spindlestone Nthumb.....119 N4
Spinkhill Derbys.....84 G5
Spinningdale Highld.....162 F9
Spion Kop Notts.....85 J7
Spirthill Wilts.....33 J9
Spital Wirral.....81 L8
Spital Hill Donc.....85 K2
Spital in the Street Lincs.....86 C2
Spithurst E Susx.....25 K7
Spittal E Loth.....128 D4
Spittal E R Yk.....98 F10
Spittal Highld.....167 L6
Spittal Nthumb.....129 Q9
Spittal Pembks.....41 J6
Spittalfield P & K.....141 R9
Spittal of Glenmuick Abers.....149 Q10
Spittal of Glenshee P & K.....141 R4
Spittal-on-Rule Border.....118 A7
Spixworth Norfk.....77 J8
Splatt Cnwll.....4 E6
Splatt Cnwll.....5 L4
Splatt Cnwll.....8 F3
Splayne's Green E Susx.....25 K6
Splott Cardif.....30 H9
Spofforth N York.....97 N10
Spondon C Derb.....72 C3
Spon Green Flints.....69 J2
Spooner Row Norfk.....64 F2
Sporle Norfk.....76 A9
Spott E Loth.....128 H4
Spottiswoode Border.....128 G10
Spratton N Nthn.....60 F7
Spreakley Surrey.....23 M6

Spreyton Devon.....8 G5
Spriddlestone Devon.....6 E8
Spridlington Lincs.....86 D4
Springburn C Glas.....125 Q4
Springfield D & G.....110 F7
Springfield Essex.....52 B10
Springfield Fife.....135 J5
Springhill Staffs.....58 E4
Springhill Staffs.....58 G3
Springholm D & G.....108 H6
Springside N Ayrs.....125 K10
Springthorpe Lincs.....85 Q3
Spring Vale Barns.....90 H10
Springwell Sundld.....113 L9
Springwood Village Border.....118 D4
Sproatley E R Yk.....93 L4
Sproston Green Ches W.....82 F11
Sprotbrough Donc.....91 N10
Sproughton Suffk.....53 K3
Sprouston Border.....118 E3
Sprowston Norfk.....77 K9
Sproxton Leics.....73 M6
Sproxton N York.....98 C4
Spunhill Shrops.....69 M8
Spurstow Ches E.....69 Q3
Spyway Dorset.....11 L6
Square and Compass Pembks.....40 F4
Stableford Shrops.....57 P5
Stableford Staffs.....70 E7
Stacey Bank Sheff.....84 C2
Stackhouse N York.....96 B7
Stackpole Pembks.....41 J11
Stackpole Elidor Pembks.....41 J11
Stacksford Norfk.....64 F3
Stacksteads Lancs.....89 P6
Staddiscombe C Plym.....6 E8
Staddlethorpe E R Yk.....92 D5
Staden Derbys.....83 N10
Stadhampton Oxon.....34 H5
Stadhlaigearraidh W Isls.....168 c14
Staffield W & F.....101 P2
Staffin Highld.....152 H4
Stafford Staffs.....70 G10
Stafford Services (northbound) Staffs.....70 F8
Stafford Services (southbound) Staffs.....70 F8
Stagsden Bed.....49 Q5
Stainborough Barns.....91 J10
Stainburn Cumb.....100 D5
Stainburn N York.....97 L11
Stainby Lincs.....73 N6
Staincross Barns.....91 J8
Staindrop Dur.....103 M6
Staines-upon-Thames Surrey.....36 B6
Stainfield Lincs.....74 A6
Stainfield Lincs.....86 F6
Stainforth Donc.....91 Q8
Stainforth N York.....96 B7
Staining Lancs.....88 C3
Stainland Calder.....90 D7
Stainsacre N York.....105 P9
Stainsby Derbys.....84 G7
Stainton Cumb.....110 G9
Stainton Donc.....85 J2
Stainton Dur.....103 L7
Stainton Middsb.....104 E8
Stainton N York.....103 M11
Stainton W & F.....95 L3
Stainton W & F.....101 N5
Stainton by Langworth Lincs.....86 E5
Staintondale N York.....105 Q11
Stainton Grove Dur.....103 L7
Stainton le Vale Lincs.....86 G2
Stainton with Adgarley W & F.....94 E6
Stair Cumb.....100 H6
Stair E Ayrs.....114 H3
Stairfoot Barns.....91 K9
Stairhaven D & G.....106 H7
Staithes N York.....105 L7
Stakeford Nthumb.....113 L3
Stake Pool Lancs.....95 J11
Stakes Hants.....15 J5
Stalbridge Dorset.....20 D11
Stalbridge Weston Dorset.....20 D11
Stalham Norfk.....77 M6
Stalham Green Norfk.....77 M7
Stalisfield Green Kent.....38 G11
Stalland Common Norfk.....64 E2
Stallen Dorset.....20 B11
Stallingborough NE Lin.....93 L8
Stalling Busk N York.....96 D3
Stallington Staffs.....70 G7
Stalmine Lancs.....94 H11
Stalmine Moss Side Lancs.....94 H11
Stalybridge Tamesd.....83 L5
Stambourne Essex.....52 B4
Stambourne Green Essex.....51 Q3
Stamford Lincs.....73 Q9
Stamford Nthumb.....119 P7
Stamford Bridge Ches W.....81 P11
Stamford Bridge E R Yk.....98 E9
Stamfordham Nthumb.....112 G6
Stamford Hill Gt Lon.....36 H3
Stanah Lancs.....88 D2
Stanborough Herts.....50 F8
Stanbridge C Beds.....49 Q10
Stanbridge Dorset.....12 H4
Stanbury C Brad.....90 C3
Stand Bury.....89 M9
Stand N Lans.....126 D4
Standburn Falk.....126 G3
Standeford Staffs.....58 D3
Standen Kent.....26 E3
Standen Street Kent.....26 D5
Standerwick Somset.....20 F4
Standford Hants.....23 M8
Standingstone Cumb.....100 E4
Standish Gloucs.....32 E3
Standish Wigan.....88 H8
Standish Lower Ground Wigan.....88 H9
Standlake Oxon.....34 C4
Standon Hants.....22 D9
Standon Herts.....51 J6
Standon Staffs.....70 E7
Standon Green End Herts.....51 J7
Standwell Green Suffk.....64 G8
Stane N Lans.....126 F6
Stanfield Norfk.....76 C7
Stanford C Beds.....50 E2
Stanford Kent.....27 K4

Stanford Shrops.....56 E2
Stanford Bishop Herefs.....46 C4
Stanford Bridge Worcs.....57 N11
Stanford Bridge Wrekin.....70 C10
Stanford Dingley W Berk.....34 G10
Stanford in the Vale Oxon.....34 B6
Stanford le Hope Thurr.....37 Q4
Stanford on Avon N Nthn.....60 C5
Stanford on Soar Notts.....72 E6
Stanford on Teme Worcs.....57 N11
Stanford Rivers Essex.....51 M10
Stanfree Derbys.....84 G6
Stanghow R & Cl.....105 J7
Stanground C Pete.....74 D11
Stanhill Lancs.....89 L5
Stanhoe Norfk.....75 R3
Stanhope Border.....116 G5
Stanhope Dur.....103 J3
Stanhope Kent.....26 H3
Stanhope Bretby Derbys.....71 P10
Stanion N Nthn.....61 K3
Stanklin Worcs.....58 C10
Stanley Derbys.....72 C2
Stanley Dur.....113 J10
Stanley Notts.....84 G8
Stanley P & K.....141 R11
Stanley Shrops.....57 N8
Stanley Staffs.....70 G4
Stanley Wakefd.....91 J6
Stanley Common Derbys.....72 C2
Stanley Crook Dur.....103 N3
Stanley Ferry Wakefd.....91 K6
Stanley Gate Lancs.....88 E9
Stanley Moor Staffs.....70 G4
Stanley Pontlarge Gloucs.....47 K8
Stanmer Br & H.....24 H9
Stanmore Gt Lon.....36 E2
Stanmore Hants.....22 E9
Stanmore W Berk.....34 E9
Stannersburn Nthumb.....111 P3
Stanningfield Suffk.....64 B10
Stanningley Leeds.....90 G4
Stannington Nthumb.....113 K5
Stannington Sheff.....84 D3
Stannington Station Nthumb.....113 K4
Stansbatch Herefs.....45 L2
Stansfield Suffk.....63 N10
Stanshope Staffs.....71 L4
Stanstead Suffk.....52 D2
Stanstead Abbotts Herts.....51 J8
Stansted Kent.....37 P8
Stansted Airport Essex.....51 N6
Stansted Mountfitchet Essex.....51 M5
Stanton Derbys.....71 P11
Stanton Gloucs.....47 L8
Stanton Mons.....45 L10
Stanton Nthumb.....112 H2
Stanton Staffs.....71 L5
Stanton Suffk.....64 D7
Stanton by Bridge Derbys.....72 B5
Stanton by Dale Derbys.....72 D3
Stanton Cross N Nthn.....61 K7
Stanton Drew BaNES.....19 Q2
Stanton Fitzwarren Swindn.....33 N6
Stanton Harcourt Oxon.....34 D3
Stanton Hill Notts.....84 G8
Stanton in Peak Derbys.....84 B8
Stanton Lacy Shrops.....56 H9
Stanton Lees Derbys.....84 C8
Stanton Long Shrops.....57 K6
Stanton-on-the-Wolds Notts.....72 G4
Stanton Prior BaNES.....20 C2
Stanton St Bernard Wilts.....21 L2
Stanton St John Oxon.....34 G3
Stanton St Quintin Wilts.....32 H9
Stanton Street Suffk.....64 D8
Stanton under Bardon Leics.....72 D8
Stanton upon Hine Heath Shrops.....69 Q10
Stanton Wick BaNES.....20 B2
Stantway Gloucs.....32 D2
Stanwardine in the Field Shrops.....69 M10
Stanwardine in the Wood Shrops.....69 M9
Stanway Essex.....52 F7
Stanway Gloucs.....47 L8
Stanway Green Essex.....52 G7
Stanway Green Suffk.....65 J7
Stanwell Surrey.....36 C6
Stanwell Moor Surrey.....36 B6
Stanwick N Nthn.....61 L6
Stanwick St John N York.....103 N8
Stanwix Cumb.....110 H9
Staoinebrig W Isls.....168 c14
Stape N York.....98 F2
Stapehill Dorset.....13 J4
Stapeley Ches E.....70 B5
Stapenhill Staffs.....71 P10
Staple Kent.....39 N10
Staple Cross Devon.....18 D10
Staplecross E Susx.....26 C7
Staplefield W Susx.....24 G5
Staple Fitzpaine Somset.....19 J11
Stapleford Cambs.....62 G10
Stapleford Herts.....50 H7
Stapleford Leics.....73 L7
Stapleford Lincs.....85 Q9
Stapleford Notts.....72 D3
Stapleford Wilts.....21 L7
Stapleford Abbotts Essex.....37 M2
Stapleford Tawney Essex.....51 M11
Staplegrove Somset.....18 H9
Staplehay Somset.....18 H10
Staple Hill Worcs.....58 C10
Staplehurst Kent.....26 C3
Staplers IoW.....14 F9
Staplestreet Kent.....39 J9
Stapleton Cumb.....111 K6
Stapleton Herefs.....56 E11
Stapleton Leics.....72 C11
Stapleton N York.....103 Q8
Stapleton Shrops.....56 H4
Stapleton Somset.....19 N10
Stapley Somset.....10 D2
Staploe Bed.....61 Q8
Staplow Herefs.....46 C6
Star IoA.....79 J10
Star Pembks.....41 P4
Star Somset.....19 M3
Starbeck N York.....97 M9
Starbotton N York.....96 E6
Starcross Devon.....9 N8

Stareton Warwks.....59 M10
Starkholmes Derbys.....84 D9
Starlings Green Essex.....51 L4
Starr's Green E Susx.....26 C8
Starston Norfk.....65 J5
Start Devon.....7 L10
Startforth Dur.....103 K7
Startley Wilts.....32 H8
Statenborough Kent.....39 P10
Statham Warrtn.....82 E7
Stathe Somset.....19 L9
Stathern Leics.....73 K4
Station Town Dur.....104 D3
Staughton Green Cambs.....61 P7
Staughton Highway Cambs.....61 P8
Staunton Gloucs.....31 Q2
Staunton Gloucs.....46 E9
Staunton in the Vale Notts.....73 L2
Staunton on Arrow Herefs.....45 M2
Staunton on Wye Herefs.....45 M6
Staveley Derbys.....84 F6
Staveley N York.....97 N8
Staveley W & F.....101 N11
Staveley-in-Cartmel W & F.....94 H3
Staverton Devon.....7 K6
Staverton Gloucs.....46 G10
Staverton N Nthn.....60 B8
Staverton Wilts.....20 G2
Staverton Bridge Gloucs.....46 G10
Stawell Somset.....19 L7
Stawley Somset.....18 E10
Staxigoe Highld.....167 Q6
Staxton N York.....99 L5
Staylittle Cerdgn.....54 E7
Staylittle Powys.....55 K6
Staynall Lancs.....88 D2
Staythorpe Notts.....85 N10
Stead C Brad.....96 H11
Stean N York.....96 G6
Stearsby N York.....98 C6
Steart Somset.....19 J5
Stebbing Essex.....51 Q6
Stebbing Green Essex.....51 Q6
Stechford Birm.....58 H7
Stede Quarter Kent.....26 E4
Stedham W Susx.....23 N10
Steel Cross E Susx.....25 M4
Steelend Fife.....134 C9
Steele Road Border.....111 K2
Steel Green Cumb.....94 D5
Steel Heath Shrops.....69 P7
Steen's Bridge Herefs.....45 Q3
Steep Hants.....23 K9
Steephill IoW.....14 F11
Steep Lane Calder.....90 C6
Steeple Dorset.....12 F8
Steeple Essex.....52 F11
Steeple Ashton Wilts.....20 H3
Steeple Aston Oxon.....48 E9
Steeple Barton Oxon.....48 D10
Steeple Bumpstead Essex.....51 Q2
Steeple Claydon Bucks.....49 K9
Steeple Gidding Cambs.....61 P4
Steeple Langford Wilts.....21 K7
Steeple Morden Cambs.....50 G2
Steep Marsh Hants.....23 L9
Steeton C Brad.....90 C2
Stein Highld.....152 D6
Stella Gatesd.....113 J8
Stelling Minnis Kent.....27 K2
Stembridge Somset.....19 M10
Stenalees Cnwll.....4 G10
Stenhouse D & G.....115 R9
Stenhousemuir Falk.....133 P11
Stenigot Lincs.....86 H4
Stenness Ork.....169 c5
Stenscholl Highld.....152 H4
Stenson Fields Derbys.....72 A4
Stenton E Loth.....128 G5
Steornabhagh W Isls.....168 j4
Stepaside Pembks.....41 M9
Stepford D & G.....109 J4
Stepney Gt Lon.....37 J4
Stepping Hill Stockp.....83 K7
Steppingley C Beds.....50 B3
Stepps N Lans.....126 B4
Sternfield Suffk.....65 M9
Stert Wilts.....21 K3
Stetchworth Cambs.....63 K9
Stevenage Herts.....50 F5
Steven's Crouch E Susx.....26 B8
Stevenston N Ayrs.....124 H9
Steventon Hants.....22 F5
Steventon Oxon.....34 E6
Steventon End Essex.....51 N2
Stevington Bed.....49 Q4
Stewartby Bed.....50 B2
Stewartfield S Lans.....125 Q6
Stewarton Ag & B.....120 C8
Stewarton E Ayrs.....125 L8
Stewkley Bucks.....49 N9
Stewley Somset.....19 K11
Stewton Lincs.....87 L3
Steyne Cross IoW.....14 H9
Steyning W Susx.....24 E8
Steynton Pembks.....40 H9
Stibb Cnwll.....16 C9
Stibbard Norfk.....76 D6
Stibb Cross Devon.....16 G9
Stibb Green Wilts.....21 P2
Stibbington Cambs.....74 A11
Stichill Border.....118 D3
Sticker Cnwll.....3 P3
Stickford Lincs.....87 L8
Sticklepath Devon.....8 F6
Sticklepath Somset.....18 D7
Stickling Green Essex.....51 L4
Stickney Lincs.....87 K9
Stiffkey Norfk.....76 D3
Stifford Clays Thurr.....37 P4
Stifford's Bridge Herefs.....46 D5
Stiff Street Kent.....38 C9
Stile Bridge Kent.....26 C2
Stileway Somset.....19 N6
Stillingfleet N York.....91 P2
Stillington N York.....98 B7
Stillington S on T.....104 C6
Stilton Cambs.....61 Q3
Stinchcombe Gloucs.....32 D5
Stinsford Dorset.....11 Q6
Stiperstones Shrops.....56 F4
Stirchley Birm.....58 G8
Stirchley Wrekin.....57 M3
Stirling Abers.....159 R9

Stirling Stirlg.....133 M9
Stirling Castle Stirlg.....133 M9
Stirling Services Stirlg.....133 N10
Stirtloe Cambs.....61 Q7
Stirton N York.....96 E10
Stisted Essex.....52 D7
Stitchcombe Wilts.....33 P11
Stithians Cnwll.....3 J6
Stivichall Covtry.....59 M9
Stixwould Lincs.....86 G7
St Michaels Fife.....135 L3
Stoak Ches W.....81 N10
Stobo Border.....116 H3
Stoborough Dorset.....12 F7
Stoborough Green Dorset.....12 F7
Stobs Castle Border.....117 Q9
Stobswood Nthumb.....119 P1
Stock Essex.....51 Q11
Stock N Som.....19 N2
Stockbridge Hants.....22 C7
Stockbridge W Susx.....15 N6
Stockbriggs S Lans.....126 D10
Stockbury Kent.....38 D9
Stockcross W Berk.....34 D11
Stockdalewath Cumb.....110 G11
Stocker's Head Kent.....38 G11
Stockerston Leics.....73 L11
Stock Green Worcs.....47 J3
Stocking Herefs.....46 B8
Stockingford Warwks.....59 M6
Stocking Pelham Herts.....51 L5
Stockland Devon.....10 E4
Stockland Bristol Somset.....18 H6
Stockland Green Kent.....25 N3
Stockleigh English Devon.....9 L2
Stockleigh Pomeroy Devon.....9 L4
Stockley Wilts.....33 J11
Stockley Hill Herefs.....45 M7
Stocklinch Somset.....19 L11
Stockmoor Herefs.....45 M4
Stockport Stockp.....83 J6
Stocksbridge Sheff.....90 H11
Stocksfield Nthumb.....112 G8
Stocksmoor Kirk.....90 F8
Stockton Herefs.....45 Q2
Stockton Norfk.....65 M3
Stockton Shrops.....56 D4
Stockton Shrops.....57 N5
Stockton Warwks.....48 D2
Stockton Wilts.....21 J7
Stockton Wrekin.....70 D11
Stockton Brook Staffs.....70 G4
Stockton Heath Warrtn.....82 D7
Stockton-on-Tees S on T.....104 D7
Stockton on Teme Worcs.....57 N11
Stockton on the Forest C York.....98 D9
Stockwell Gloucs.....32 H2
Stockwell End Wolves.....58 C4
Stockwell Heath Staffs.....71 K10
Stockwood Bristl.....32 B11
Stockwood Dorset.....11 M3
Stock Wood Worcs.....47 K3
Stoddy Lancs.....95 K9
Stodmarsh Kent.....39 M9
Stody Norfk.....76 F4
Stoer Highld.....164 B11
Stoford Somset.....11 M2
Stoford Wilts.....21 L7
Stogumber Somset.....18 E7
Stogursey Somset.....18 H6
Stoke Covtry.....59 N9
Stoke Devon.....16 C7
Stoke Hants.....15 K6
Stoke Hants.....22 D4
Stoke Medway.....38 D7
Stoke Abbott Dorset.....11 K4
Stoke Albany N Nthn.....60 H3
Stoke Ash Suffk.....64 G7
Stoke Bardolph Notts.....72 G2
Stoke Bliss Worcs.....46 C2
Stoke Bruerne N Nthn.....49 K5
Stoke-by-Clare Suffk.....52 B3
Stoke-by-Nayland Suffk.....52 G4
Stoke Canon Devon.....9 M5
Stoke Charity Hants.....22 E7
Stoke Climsland Cnwll.....5 M7
Stoke Cross Herefs.....46 B4
Stoke D'Abernon Surrey.....36 D9
Stoke Doyle N Nthn.....61 M3
Stoke Dry Rutlnd.....73 M11
Stoke Edith Herefs.....46 B6
Stoke End Warwks.....59 J5
Stoke Farthing Wilts.....21 L9
Stoke Ferry Norfk.....75 P10
Stoke Fleming Devon.....7 M9
Stokeford Dorset.....12 E7
Stoke Gabriel Devon.....7 M7
Stoke Gifford S Glos.....32 B9
Stoke Golding Leics.....72 B11
Stoke Goldington M Keyn.....49 M5
Stoke Green Bucks.....35 Q8
Stokeham Notts.....85 N5
Stoke Hammond Bucks.....49 N9
Stoke Heath Shrops.....70 B9
Stoke Heath Worcs.....58 D11
Stoke Holy Cross Norfk.....77 J11
Stokeinteignhead Devon.....7 N4
Stoke Lacy Herefs.....46 B5
Stoke Lyne Oxon.....48 G9
Stoke Mandeville Bucks.....35 M2
Stokenchurch Bucks.....35 L5
Stoke Newington Gt Lon.....36 H3
Stokenham Devon.....7 L10
Stoke-on-Trent C Stke.....70 F5
Stoke Orchard Gloucs.....46 H9
Stoke Poges Bucks.....35 Q8
Stoke Pound Worcs.....58 E11
Stoke Prior Herefs.....45 Q3
Stoke Prior Worcs.....58 E11
Stoke Rivers Devon.....17 L4
Stoke Rochford Lincs.....73 N5
Stoke Row Oxon.....35 J8
Stoke St Gregory Somset.....19 K9
Stoke St Mary Somset.....19 J10
Stoke St Michael Somset.....20 C5
Stoke St Milborough Shrops.....57 K7
Stokesay Shrops.....56 G8
Stokesby Norfk.....77 N9
Stokesley N York.....104 F9
Stoke sub Hamdon Somset.....19 N11
Stoke Talmage Oxon.....35 J5
Stoke Trister Somset.....20 D9
Stoke upon Tern Shrops.....70 A9
Stoke-upon-Trent C Stke.....70 F5
Stoke Wake Dorset.....12 C3

Stoke Wharf – Tairgwaith 295

Stoke Wharf Worcs 58 E11
Stolford Somset 18 H5
Stondon Massey Essex 51 N10
Stone Bucks 35 L2
Stone Gloucs 32 C5
Stone Kent 37 N6
Stone Rothm 85 J3
Stone Somset 19 Q8
Stone Staffs 70 G8
Stone Worcs 58 C9
Stonea Cambs 62 G2
Stone Allerton Somset 19 L4
Ston Easton Somset 20 B4
Stonebridge N Som 19 L3
Stonebridge Norfk 64 C3
Stonebridge Warwks 59 K8
Stone Bridge Corner C Pete 74 E10
Stonebroom Derbys 84 F9
Stone Chair Calder 90 E5
Stone Cross E Susx 25 M5
Stone Cross E Susx 25 P10
Stone Cross E Susx 25 P4
Stone Cross Kent 25 M3
Stone Cross Kent 26 H4
Stone Cross Kent 39 P10
Stonecross Green Suffk 63 P9
Stonecrouch Kent 26 B5
Stone-edge-Batch N Som 31 N10
Stoneferry C KuH 93 K4
Stonefield Castle Hotel Ag & B 123 Q5
Stonegate E Susx 25 Q5
Stonegate N York 105 L9
Stonegrave N York 98 D5
Stonehall Worcs 46 G5
Stonehaugh Nthumb 111 Q5
Stonehaven Abers 151 M10
Stonehenge Wilts 21 M6
Stone Hill Donc 92 A9
Stonehouse C Plym 6 D8
Stonehouse Gloucs 32 F3
Stonehouse Nthumb 111 N9
Stonehouse S Lans 126 D8
Stone House W & F 95 R3
Stone in Oxney Kent 26 F6
Stoneleigh Warwks 59 M10
Stoneley Green Ches E 69 R4
Stonely Cambs 61 P7
Stoner Hill Hants 23 K9
Stonesby Leics 73 L6
Stonesfield Oxon 48 C11
Stones Green Essex 53 L6
Stone Street Kent 37 N10
Stone Street Suffk 52 G4
Stone Street Suffk 52 H3
Stone Street Suffk 65 M5
Stonestreet Green Kent 27 J4
Stonethwaite Cumb 101 J8
Stonewells Moray 157 P4
Stonewood Kent 37 N6
Stoneybridge W Isls 168 c14
Stoneybridge Worcs 58 D9
Stoneyburn W Loth 126 H5
Stoney Cross Hants 13 N2
Stoneygate C Leic 72 G10
Stoneyhills Essex 38 G2
Stoneykirk D & G 106 E7
Stoney Middleton Derbys 84 B5
Stoney Stanton Leics 59 Q6
Stoney Stoke Somset 20 D8
Stoney Stratton Somset 20 C7
Stoney Stretton Shrops 56 F3
Stoneywood C Aber 151 M5
Stoneywood Falk 133 M11
Stonham Aspal Suffk 64 G10
Stonnall Staffs 58 G4
Stonor Oxon 35 K7
Stonton Wyville Leics 73 J11
Stonybreck Shet 169 t14
Stony Cross Herefs 46 D5
Stony Cross Herefs 57 J11
Stonyford Hants 22 B11
Stony Houghton Derbys 84 G7
Stony Stratford M Keyn 49 L6
Stonywell Staffs 58 G2
Stoodleigh Devon 17 M5
Stoodleigh Devon 18 B11
Stopham W Susx 24 B7
Stopsley Luton 50 D6
Stoptide Cnwll 4 E6
Storeton Wirral 81 L8
Storeyard Green Herefs 46 D6
Storey Arms Powys 44 D10
Stornoway W Isls 168 j4
Stornoway Airport W Isls 168 j4
Storridge Herefs 46 E5
Storrington W Susx 24 C8
Storth W & F 95 K5
Storwood E R Yk 92 B2
Stotfield Moray 157 N3
Stotfold C Beds 50 F3
Stottesdon Shrops 57 M8
Stoughton Leics 72 G10
Stoughton Surrey 23 Q4
Stoughton W Susx 15 M4
Stoulton Worcs 46 H5
Stourbridge Dudley 58 C8
Stourhead Wilts 20 E8
Stourpaine Dorset 12 E3
Stourport-on-Severn Worcs 57 Q10
Stour Provost Dorset 20 E10
Stour Row Dorset 20 F10
Stourton Leeds 91 J4
Stourton Staffs 58 C8
Stourton Warwks 47 Q7
Stourton Wilts 20 E8
Stourton Caundle Dorset 20 D11
Stout Somset 19 M8
Stove Shet 169 r11
Stoven Suffk 65 N5
Stow Border 117 P2
Stow Lincs 85 Q4
Stow Bardolph Norfk 75 M9
Stow Bedon Norfk 64 D2
Stowbridge Norfk 75 M9
Stow-cum-Quy Cambs 62 H8
Stowe Gloucs 31 Q3
Stowe Shrops 56 E10
Stowe-by-Chartley Staffs 71 J9
Stowehill W Nthn 60 D9
Stowell Somset 20 C10
Stowey BaNES 19 Q3
Stowford Devon 8 B5
Stowford Devon 8 B7
Stowford Devon 10 C7
Stowford Devon 17 M3
Stowlangtoft Suffk 64 D8
Stow Longa Cambs 61 P6
Stow Maries Essex 38 D2
Stowmarket Suffk 64 E10
Stow-on-the-Wold Gloucs 47 N9
Stowting Kent 27 K3
Stowting Common Kent 27 K3
Stowupland Suffk 64 F9
Straad Ag & B 124 C5
Straanruie Highld 148 H4
Strachan Abers 150 H9
Strachur Ag & B 131 M7
Stradbroke Suffk 65 J7
Stradbrook Wilts 20 H4
Stradishall Suffk 63 N10
Stradsett Norfk 75 N9
Stragglethorpe Lincs 86 B10
Stragglethorpe Notts 72 H3
Straight Soley Wilts 34 B10
Straiton Mdloth 127 P4
Straiton S Ayrs 114 G7
Straloch Abers 151 M3
Straloch P & K 141 P5
Stramshall Staffs 71 K7
Strang IoM 80 e6
Strangeways Salfd 82 H5
Strangford Herefs 46 A9
Stranraer D & G 106 E5
Strata Florida Cerdgn 54 G11
Stratfield Mortimer W Berk 23 J2
Stratfield Saye Hants 23 J2
Stratfield Turgis Hants 23 J3
Stratford C Beds 61 Q11
Stratford Gt Lon 37 J4
Stratford St Andrew Suffk 65 M9
Stratford St Mary Suffk 52 H5
Stratford sub Castle Wilts 21 M8
Stratford Tony Wilts 21 L9
Stratford-upon-Avon Warwks 47 P3
Strath Highld 160 B11
Strathan Highld 160 H2
Strathan Highld 165 N4
Strathaven S Lans 126 C9
Strathblane Stirlg 125 P2
Strathcanaird Highld 161 K6
Strathcarron Highld 154 B9
Strathcoil Ag & B 138 B11
Strathdon Abers 150 B5
Strathkinness Fife 135 M4
Strathloanhead W Loth 126 G3
Strathmashie House Highld 147 P9
Strathmiglo Fife 134 G6
Strathpeffer Highld 155 N6
Strathtay P & K 141 M7
Strathwhillan N Ayrs 121 K4
Strathy Highld 166 D4
Strathy Inn Highld 166 D3
Strathyre Stirlg 132 H4
Stratton Cnwll 16 C10
Stratton Dorset 11 P6
Stratton Gloucs 33 K4
Stratton Audley Oxon 48 H9
Stratton-on-the-Fosse Somset 20 C4
Stratton St Margaret Swindn 33 N7
Stratton St Michael Norfk 65 J3
Stratton Strawless Norfk 77 J7
Stream Somset 18 E7
Streat E Susx 25 J7
Streatham Gt Lon 36 H6
Streatley C Beds 50 C5
Streatley W Berk 34 G8
Street Devon 10 D7
Street Lancs 95 L10
Street N York 105 K10
Street Somset 19 N7
Street Ashton Warwks 59 Q8
Street Dinas Shrops 69 K7
Street End E Susx 25 P6
Street End Kent 39 K11
Street End W Susx 15 N7
Street Gate Gatesd 113 K9
Streethay Staffs 58 H2
Street Houses N York 98 A11
Streetlam N York 104 B11
Street Lane Derbys 84 E11
Streetly Wsall 58 G5
Streetly End Cambs 63 K11
Street on the Fosse Somset 20 B7
Strefford Shrops 56 G7
Strelitz P & K 142 B10
Strelley Notts 72 E2
Strensall C York 98 C8
Strensham Worcs 46 H6
Strensham Services (northbound) Worcs 46 G6
Strensham Services (southbound) Worcs 46 H6
Stretcholt Somset 19 J6
Strete Devon 7 L9
Stretford Herefs 45 N3
Stretford Herefs 45 Q3
Stretford Traffd 82 G6
Strethall Essex 51 L3
Stretham Cambs 62 H6
Strettington W Susx 15 N5
Stretton Ches W 69 M4
Stretton Derbys 84 E8
Stretton Rutlnd 73 N7
Stretton Staffs 58 C2
Stretton Staffs 71 P9
Stretton Warrtn 82 D8
Stretton en le Field Leics 59 M2
Stretton Grandison Herefs 46 B6
Stretton-on-Dunsmore Warwks 59 P10
Stretton on Fosse Warwks 47 P7
Stretton Sugwas Herefs 45 P6
Stretton under Fosse Warwks 59 Q8
Stretton Westwood Shrops 57 K5
Strichen Abers 159 M6
Strines Stockp 83 L7
Stringston Somset 18 G6
Strixton N Nthn 61 K8
Stroat Gloucs 31 Q5
Strollamus Highld 145 J2
Stroma Highld 167 Q1
Stromeferry Highld 153 R11
Stromness Ork 169 b6
Stronaba Highld 146 G11
Stronachlachar Stirlg 132 E5
Stronafian Ag & B 131 L11
Stronchrubie Highld 161 L3
Strone Ag & B 131 P11
Strone Highld 146 E11
Strone Highld 147 N2
Stronmilchan Ag & B 131 P2
Stronsay Ork 169 f4
Stronsay Airport Ork 169 f4
Strontian Highld 138 E5
Strood Kent 26 E5
Strood Medway 38 B8
Strood Green Surrey 36 F11
Strood Green W Susx 24 B6
Stroud Gloucs 32 G3
Stroud Hants 23 K10
Stroude Surrey 36 B7
Stroud Green Essex 38 E3
Stroud Green Gloucs 32 F3
Stroxton Lincs 73 N4
Struan Highld 152 E10
Struan P & K 141 K4
Strubby Lincs 87 N4
Strumpshaw Norfk 77 L10
Strutherhill S Lans 126 D8
Struthers Fife 135 K6
Struy Highld 155 M9
Stryd-y-Facsen IoA 78 E8
Stuartfield Abers 159 N8
Stubbers Green Wsall 58 F4
Stubbington Hants 14 G6
Stubbins Lancs 89 M7
Stubbs Cross Kent 26 G4
Stubbs Green Norfk 65 K2
Stubhampton Dorset 12 F2
Stubley Derbys 84 D5
Stubshaw Cross Wigan 82 C5
Stubton Lincs 85 Q11
Stuckton Hants 13 L2
Studfold N York 96 B7
Stud Green W & M 35 N9
Studham C Beds 50 B7
Studholme Cumb 110 E9
Studland Dorset 12 H8
Studlands Park Suffk 63 K7
Studley Warwks 47 L2
Studley Wilts 33 J10
Studley Common Warwks 47 L2
Studley Roger N York 97 L7
Studley Royal N York 97 L6
Studley Royal Park & Fountains Abbey N York 97 L7
Stuntney Cambs 63 J5
Stunts Green E Susx 25 P8
Sturbridge Staffs 70 E8
Sturgate Lincs 85 Q3
Sturmer Essex 51 Q2
Sturminster Common Dorset 12 C2
Sturminster Marshall Dorset 12 G4
Sturminster Newton Dorset 12 C2
Sturry Kent 39 L9
Sturton N Linc 92 G10
Sturton by Stow Lincs 85 Q4
Sturton le Steeple Notts 85 N4
Stuston Suffk 64 G6
Stutton N York 91 M2
Stutton Suffk 53 L5
Styal Ches E 82 H8
Stydd Lancs 89 K3
Stynie Moray 157 Q5
Styrrup Notts 85 K2
Succoth Ag & B 132 B6
Suckley Worcs 46 D4
Suckley Green Worcs 46 D4
Sudborough N Nthn 61 L4
Sudbourne Suffk 65 N11
Sudbrook Lincs 73 P2
Sudbrook Mons 31 P7
Sudbrooke Lincs 86 D5
Sudbury Derbys 71 M8
Sudbury Gt Lon 36 E3
Sudbury Suffk 52 E3
Sudden Rochdl 89 P8
Sudgrove Gloucs 32 H3
Suffield N York 99 K2
Suffield Norfk 77 J5
Sugdon Wrekin 69 R11
Sugnall Staffs 70 D8
Sugwas Pool Herefs 45 P6
Suisnish Highld 145 J4
Sulby IoM 80 e3
Sulgrave W Nthn 48 G6
Sulham W Berk 34 H10
Sulhamstead W Berk 34 H11
Sulhamstead Abbots W Berk 34 H11
Sulhamstead Bannister W Berk 34 H11
Sullington W Susx 24 C8
Sullom Shet 169 q6
Sullom Voe Shet 169 r6
Sully V Glam 30 G11
Sumburgh Airport Shet 169 q12
Summerbridge N York 97 K8
Summercourt Cnwll 4 D10
Summerfield Norfk 75 Q3
Summerfield Worcs 58 B10
Summer Heath Bucks 35 K6
Summerhill Pembks 41 N9
Summerhill Staffs 58 G3
Summer Hill Wrexhm 69 K4
Summerhouse Darltn 103 P7
Summerlands W & F 95 L3
Summerley Derbys 84 E5
Summersdale W Susx 15 N5
Summerseat Bury 89 M8
Summertown Oxon 34 F3
Summit Oldham 89 Q9
Summit Rochdl 89 Q7
Sunbiggin W & F 102 C9
Sunbury-on-Thames Surrey 36 D7
Sundaywell D & G 108 H4
Sunderland Ag & B 122 B7
Sunderland Cumb 100 G3
Sunderland Lancs 95 J9
Sunderland Sundld 113 N9
Sunderland Bridge Dur 103 Q3
Sundhope Border 117 L5
Sundon Park Luton 50 C5
Sundridge Kent 37 L9
Sunk Island E R Yk 93 N7
Sunningdale W & M 35 Q11
Sunninghill W & M 35 P11
Sunningwell Oxon 34 E4
Sunniside Dur 103 M3
Sunniside Gatesd 113 K9
Sunny Brow Dur 103 N4
Sunnyhill C Derb 72 A4
Sunnyhurst Bl w D 89 K6
Sunnylaw Stirlg 133 M8
Sunnymead Oxon 34 F3
Sunton Wilts 21 P4
Surbiton Gt Lon 36 E7
Surfleet Lincs 74 E5
Surfleet Seas End Lincs 74 E5
Surlingham Norfk 77 L10
Surrex Essex 52 E7
Sustead Norfk 76 H4
Susworth Lincs 92 D10
Sutcombe Devon 16 E9
Sutcombemill Devon 16 E9
Suton Norfk 64 F2
Sutterby Lincs 87 L6
Sutterton Lincs 74 E3
Sutton C Beds 62 B11
Sutton C Pete 74 A11
Sutton Cambs 62 F5
Sutton Devon 7 J10
Sutton Devon 8 H4
Sutton Donc 91 P8
Sutton E Susx 25 L11
Sutton Gt Lon 36 G8
Sutton Kent 27 P2
Sutton N York 91 M5
Sutton Norfk 77 M7
Sutton Notts 73 K3
Sutton Oxon 34 D3
Sutton Pembks 40 H7
Sutton Shrops 57 J2
Sutton Shrops 57 N7
Sutton Shrops 69 L9
Sutton Shrops 70 B8
Sutton St Hel 82 B6
Sutton Staffs 70 D10
Sutton Suffk 53 P2
Sutton W Susx 23 Q11
Sutton Abinger Surrey 36 D11
Sutton-at-Hone Kent 37 N7
Sutton Bassett N Nthn 60 G2
Sutton Benger Wilts 32 H9
Sutton Bingham Somset 11 L2
Sutton Bonington Notts 72 E6
Sutton Bridge Lincs 75 J6
Sutton Cheney Leics 72 C10
Sutton Coldfield Birm 58 H5
Sutton Courtenay Oxon 34 F6
Sutton Crosses Lincs 74 H6
Sutton cum Lound Notts 85 L4
Sutton Fields Notts 72 D5
Sutton Green Surrey 36 B10
Sutton Green Wrexhm 69 M5
Sutton Heath Suffk 53 P2
Sutton Howgrave N York 97 M5
Sutton-in-Ashfield Notts 84 G9
Sutton-in-Craven N York 90 C2
Sutton in the Elms Leics 60 B2
Sutton Lane Ends Ches E 83 K10
Sutton Maddock Shrops 57 N4
Sutton Mallet Somset 19 L7
Sutton Mandeville Wilts 21 J9
Sutton Manor St Hel 81 Q6
Sutton Marsh Herefs 45 R6
Sutton Montis Somset 20 B10
Sutton-on-Hull C KuH 93 K4
Sutton on Sea Lincs 87 P4
Sutton-on-the-Forest N York 98 B8
Sutton on the Hill Derbys 71 N8
Sutton on Trent Notts 85 N7
Sutton Poyntz Dorset 11 Q8
Sutton St Edmund Lincs 74 G8
Sutton St James Lincs 74 G7
Sutton St Nicholas Herefs 45 Q5
Sutton Scotney Hants 22 E7
Sutton Street Kent 38 D10
Sutton-under-Brailes Warwks 48 B7
Sutton-under-Whitestonecliffe N York 97 Q4
Sutton upon Derwent E R Yk 98 E11
Sutton Valence Kent 26 D2
Sutton Veny Wilts 20 H6
Sutton Waldron Dorset 20 G11
Sutton Weaver Ches W 82 B9
Sutton Wick BaNES 19 Q3
Sutton Wick Oxon 34 E6
Swaby Lincs 87 L5
Swadlincote Derbys 71 P11
Swaffham Norfk 75 R9
Swaffham Bulbeck Cambs 63 J8
Swaffham Prior Cambs 63 J8
Swafield Norfk 77 K5
Swainby N York 104 E10
Swainshill Herefs 45 P6
Swainsthorpe Norfk 77 J11
Swainswick BaNES 32 E11
Swalcliffe Oxon 48 C7
Swalecliffe Kent 39 K8
Swallow Lincs 93 L10
Swallow Beck Lincs 86 B7
Swallowcliffe Wilts 21 J9
Swallowfield Wokham 23 K2
Swallownest Rothm 84 G3
Swallows Cross Essex 51 P11
Swampton Hants 22 D4
Swanage Dorset 12 H9
Swanbourne Bucks 49 M9
Swanbridge V Glam 30 G11
Swancote Shrops 57 N6
Swan Green Ches W 82 F10
Swanland E R Yk 92 G5
Swanley Kent 37 M7
Swanley Village Kent 37 M7
Swanmore Hants 22 G11
Swannington Leics 72 C7
Swannington Norfk 76 G8
Swanpool Lincs 86 C7
Swanscombe Kent 37 P6
Swansea Swans 29 J6
Swansea Airport Swans 28 G6
Swansea West Services Swans 28 H5
Swan Street Essex 52 E6
Swanton Abbot Norfk 77 K6
Swanton Morley Norfk 76 E8
Swanton Novers Norfk 76 E5
Swanton Street Kent 38 E10
Swan Valley W Nthn 60 F9
Swan Village Sandw 58 E6
Swanwick Derbys 84 F10
Swanwick Hants 14 F5
Swarby Lincs 73 Q2
Swardeston Norfk 77 J11
Swarkestone Derbys 72 B5
Swarland Nthumb 119 N10
Swarraton Hants 22 G7
Swartha C Brad 96 G11
Swarthmoor W & F 94 F5
Swaton Lincs 74 B3
Swavesey Cambs 62 E7
Sway Hants 13 N5
Swayfield Lincs 73 P6
Swaythling C Sotn 22 D11
Sweet Green Worcs 46 B2
Sweetham Devon 9 L5
Sweethaws E Susx 25 M5
Sweetlands Corner Kent 26 C2
Sweets Cnwll 5 K2
Sweetshouse Cnwll 4 H9
Swefling Suffk 65 L9
Swepstone Leics 72 B8
Swerford Oxon 48 C8
Swettenham Ches E 82 H11
Swffryd Blae G 30 H5
Swift's Green Kent 26 E3
Swilland Suffk 64 H11
Swillbrook Lancs 88 F4
Swillington Leeds 91 K4
Swimbridge Devon 17 L5
Swimbridge Newland Devon 17 L5
Swinbrook Oxon 33 Q2
Swincliffe Kirk 90 G5
Swincliffe N York 97 K9
Swincombe Devon 17 M3
Swindale W & F 101 P8
Swinden N York 96 C10
Swinderby Lincs 85 Q8
Swindon Gloucs 46 H9
Swindon Nthumb 119 J11
Swindon Staffs 58 C6
Swindon Swindn 33 M8
Swine E R Yk 93 K3
Swinefleet E R Yk 92 C6
Swineford S Glos 32 C11
Swineshead Bed 61 N7
Swineshead Lincs 74 D2
Swineshead Bridge Lincs 74 D2
Swiney Highld 167 M9
Swinford Leics 60 C5
Swinford Oxon 34 D3
Swingate Notts 72 E2
Swingfield Minnis Kent 27 M3
Swingfield Street Kent 27 M3
Swingleton Green Suffk 52 G2
Swinhoe Nthumb 119 P5
Swinhope Lincs 93 M11
Swinithwaite N York 96 F3
Swinmore Common Herefs 46 C6
Swinscoe Staffs 71 L5
Swinside Cumb 100 H6
Swinstead Lincs 73 Q6
Swinthorpe Lincs 86 E4
Swinton Border 129 L10
Swinton N York 97 K5
Swinton N York 98 F6
Swinton Rothm 91 M11
Swinton Salfd 82 G4
Swiss Valley Carmth 28 F4
Swithland Leics 72 F8
Swordale Highld 155 Q4
Swordland Highld 145 N9
Swordly Highld 166 B4
Sworton Heath Ches E 82 E8
Swyddffynnon Cerdgn 54 F11
Swyncombe Oxon 35 J6
Swynnerton Staffs 70 F7
Swyre Dorset 11 L7
Sycharth Powys 68 H9
Sychdyn Flints 81 J11
Sychnant Powys 55 M9
Sychtyn Powys 55 M3
Sydallt Wrexhm 69 K3
Syde Gloucs 33 J2
Sydenham Gt Lon 37 J6
Sydenham Oxon 35 K4
Sydenham Damerel Devon 5 Q6
Sydenhurst Surrey 23 Q8
Syderstone Norfk 76 A5
Sydling St Nicholas Dorset 11 N5
Sydmonton Hants 22 E3
Sydnal Lane Shrops 57 Q3
Syerston Notts 85 M11
Syke Rochdl 89 P7
Sykehouse Donc 91 Q7
Syleham Suffk 65 J6
Sylen Carmth 28 F3
Symbister Shet 169 s7
Symington S Ayrs 125 K11
Symington S Lans 116 D3
Symondsbury Dorset 11 J6
Symonds Yat (East) Herefs 45 R11
Symonds Yat (West) Herefs 45 R11
Sympson Green C Brad 90 F3
Synderford Dorset 10 H4
Synod Inn Cerdgn 42 H4
Syre Highld 165 Q8
Syreford Gloucs 47 K10
Syresham W Nthn 48 H6
Syston Leics 72 G8
Syston Lincs 73 N2
Sytchampton Worcs 58 B11
Sywell N Nthn 60 H7

T

Tabley Hill Ches E 82 F9
Tackley Oxon 48 E11
Tacolneston Norfk 64 G2
Tadcaster N York 91 M2
Taddington Derbys 83 P10
Taddington Gloucs 47 L8
Taddiport Devon 16 H8
Tadley Hants 22 H2
Tadlow Cambs 62 C11
Tadmarton Oxon 48 C7
Tadpole Swindn 33 M6
Tadwick BaNES 32 D10
Tadworth Surrey 36 F9
Tafarnaubach Blae G 30 F2
Tafarn-y-bwlch Pembks 41 L4
Tafarn-y-Gelyn Denbgs 68 G2
Taff's Well Cardif 30 F8
Tafolwern Powys 55 K4
Taibach Neath 29 L7
Tain Highld 162 H10
Tain Highld 167 M3
Tai'n Lôn Gwynd 66 G4
Tai'r Bull Powys 44 D9
Tairgwaith Neath 29 K2

Place	Page	Grid
Takeley Essex	51	N6
Takeley Street Essex	51	M6
Talachddu Powys	44	F8
Talacre Flints	80	G8
Talaton Devon	9	Q5
Talbenny Pembks	40	F8
Talbot Green Rhondd	30	D8
Talbot Village BCP	13	J6
Taleford Devon	10	B5
Talerddig Powys	55	L4
Talgarreg Cerdgn	42	H4
Talgarth Powys	44	H8
Talisker Highld	152	E11
Talke Staffs	70	E4
Talke Pits Staffs	70	E4
Talkin Cumb	111	L9
Talladale Highld	154	B3
Talla Linnfoots Border	116	G6
Tallaminnock S Ayrs	114	H8
Tallarn Green Wrexhm	69	M6
Tallentire Cumb	100	F3
Talley Carmth	43	M8
Tallington Lincs	74	A9
Tallwrn Wrexhm	69	J5
Talmine Highld	165	N4
Talog Carmth	42	F9
Talsarn Cerdgn	43	K3
Talsarnau Gwynd	67	L7
Talskiddy Cnwll	4	E8
Talwrn IoA	78	H9
Talwrn Wrexhm	69	L5
Tal-y-Bont Cerdgn	54	F7
Tal-y-Bont Conwy	79	P11
Talybont Gwynd	67	K10
Tal-y-bont Gwynd	79	L10
Talybont-on-Usk Powys	44	G10
Tal-y-Cafn Conwy	79	P10
Tal-y-coed Mons	45	N11
Tal-y-garn Rhondd	30	D9
Tal-y-llyn Gwynd	54	G3
Talysarn Gwynd	66	H4
Tal-y-Waun Torfn	31	J4
Talywern Powys	55	J4
Tamar Valley Mining District Devon	6	C5
Tamer Lane End Wigan	82	D4
Tamerton Foliot C Plym	6	D6
Tamworth Staffs	59	K4
Tamworth Green Lincs	74	G2
Tamworth Services Warwks	59	K4
Tancred N York	97	Q9
Tancredston Pembks	40	G5
Tandridge Surrey	37	J10
Tanfield Dur	113	J9
Tanfield Lea Dur	113	J10
Tangasdale W Isls	168	b17
Tangiers Pembks	41	J7
Tangley Hants	22	B4
Tangmere W Susx	15	P5
Tan Hill N York	102	G9
Tankerness Ork	169	e6
Tankersley Barns	91	J11
Tankerton Kent	39	K8
Tannach Highld	167	P7
Tannachie Abers	151	K11
Tannadice Angus	142	H6
Tanner's Green Worcs	58	G10
Tannington Suffk	65	J8
Tannochside N Lans	126	C5
Tansley Derbys	84	D9
Tansor N Nthn	61	N2
Tantobie Dur	113	J10
Tanton N York	104	F8
Tanwood Worcs	58	D10
Tanworth in Arden Warwks	58	H10
Tan-y-Bwlch Gwynd	67	M6
Tan-y-fron Conwy	68	C2
Tan-y-fron Wrexhm	69	J4
Tan-y-grisiau Gwynd	67	M5
Tan-y-groes Cerdgn	42	E5
Taobh Tuath W Isls	168	e9
Taplow Bucks	35	P8
Tarbert Ag & B	123	L9
Tarbert Ag & B	123	Q6
Tarbert W Isls	168	g7
Tarbet Ag & B	132	C7
Tarbet Highld	145	N9
Tarbet Highld	164	E7
Tarbock Green Knows	81	P7
Tarbolton S Ayrs	114	H2
Tarbrax S Lans	127	J6
Tardebigge Worcs	58	E11
Tarfside Angus	142	H2
Tarland Abers	150	D7
Tarleton Lancs	88	F6
Tarlscough Lancs	88	E8
Tarlton Gloucs	33	J5
Tarnock Somset	19	L4
Tarns Cumb	109	P11
Tarnside W & F	95	J2
Tarporley Ches W	69	Q2
Tarr Somset	17	R5
Tarrant Crawford Dorset	12	F4
Tarrant Gunville Dorset	12	F2
Tarrant Hinton Dorset	12	F2
Tarrant Keyneston Dorset	12	F3
Tarrant Launceston Dorset	12	F3
Tarrant Monkton Dorset	12	F3
Tarrant Rawston Dorset	12	F3
Tarrant Rushton Dorset	12	F3
Tarring Neville E Susx	25	K10
Tarrington Herefs	46	B6
Tarskavaig Highld	145	J5
Tarves Abers	159	L11
Tarvin Ches W	81	P11
Tarvin Sands Ches W	81	P11
Tasburgh Norfk	65	J2
Tasley Shrops	57	M6
Taston Oxon	48	C10
Tatenhill Staffs	71	N10
Tathall End M Keyn	49	M5
Tatham Lancs	95	N7
Tathwell Lincs	87	K4
Tatsfield Surrey	37	K9
Tattenhall Ches W	69	N3
Tatterford Norfk	76	B6
Tattersett Norfk	76	A6
Tattershall Lincs	86	H9
Tattershall Bridge Lincs	86	G9
Tattershall Thorpe Lincs	86	H9
Tattingstone Suffk	53	K4
Tattingstone White Horse Suffk	53	K4
Tatton Park Ches E	82	F8
Tatworth Somset	10	G3
Tauchers Moray	157	R8
Taunton Somset	18	H10
Taunton Deane Services Somset	18	G10
Taverham Norfk	76	H9
Taverners Green Essex	51	N7
Tavernspite Pembks	41	N8
Tavistock Devon	6	D4
Tavistock Devon	6	D4
Taw Green Devon	8	G5
Tawstock Devon	17	K6
Taxal Derbys	83	M9
Tay Bridge C Dund	135	L2
Taychreggan Hotel Ag & B	131	L3
Tay Forest Park P & K	141	J5
Tayinloan Ag & B	123	L10
Taynton Gloucs	46	D10
Taynton Oxon	33	P2
Taynuilt Ag & B	139	J11
Tayport Fife	135	M2
Tayvallich Ag & B	130	L10
Tealby Lincs	86	G2
Tealing Angus	142	G10
Team Valley Gatesd	113	K9
Teangue Highld	145	L6
Teanord Highld	155	Q5
Tebay W & F	102	B10
Tebay Services W & F	102	B9
Tebworth C Beds	49	Q9
Tedburn St Mary Devon	9	K6
Teddington Gloucs	47	J8
Teddington Gt Lon	36	E6
Tedstone Delamere Herefs	46	C3
Tedstone Wafer Herefs	46	C3
Teesport R & Cl	104	F6
Teesside International Airport S on T	104	D7
Teesside Park S on T	104	E7
Teeton W Nthn	60	E6
Teffont Evias Wilts	21	J8
Teffont Magna Wilts	21	J8
Tegryn Pembks	41	P4
Teigh Rutlnd	73	M7
Teigncombe Devon	8	G7
Teigngrace Devon	7	M4
Teignmouth Devon	7	N4
Teindside Border	117	N9
Telford Wrekin	57	M3
Telford Services Shrops	57	N3
Telham E Susx	26	C9
Tellisford Somset	20	F3
Telscombe E Susx	25	K10
Telscombe Cliffs E Susx	25	K10
Tempar P & K	140	G6
Templand D & G	109	N3
Temple Cnwll	5	J7
Temple Mdloth	127	Q6
Temple Balsall Solhll	59	K9
Temple Bar Cerdgn	43	K4
Temple Cloud BaNES	20	B3
Templecombe Somset	20	D10
Temple End Suffk	63	L10
Temple Ewell Kent	27	N3
Temple Grafton Warwks	47	M3
Temple Guiting Gloucs	47	L9
Temple Herdewyke Warwks	48	C4
Temple Hirst N York	91	Q6
Temple Normanton Derbys	84	F7
Temple of Fiddes Abers	151	L11
Temple Sowerby W & F	102	B5
Templeton Devon	9	L2
Templeton Pembks	41	M8
Templetown Dur	112	H10
Tempsford C Beds	61	Q10
Tenbury Wells Worcs	57	K11
Tenby Pembks	41	M10
Tendring Essex	53	K7
Tendring Green Essex	53	K6
Tendring Heath Essex	53	K6
Ten Mile Bank Norfk	75	L11
Tenpenny Heath Essex	53	J7
Tenterden Kent	26	E5
Terling Essex	52	C8
Tern Wrekin	69	R11
Ternhill Shrops	70	A8
Terregles D & G	109	K5
Terrington N York	98	D6
Terrington St Clement Norfk	75	L8
Terrington St John Norfk	75	K8
Terry's Green Warwks	58	H10
Teston Kent	38	B11
Testwood Hants	14	C4
Tetbury Gloucs	32	G6
Tetbury Upton Gloucs	32	G5
Tetchill Shrops	69	L8
Tetcott Devon	5	N2
Tetford Lincs	87	K6
Tetney Lincs	93	P10
Tetney Lock Lincs	93	P10
Tetsworth Oxon	35	J4
Tettenhall Wolves	58	C4
Tettenhall Wood Wolves	58	C5
Teversal Notts	84	G8
Teversham Cambs	62	G9
Teviothead Border	117	N9
Tewin Herts	50	G8
Tewin Wood Herts	50	G7
Tewkesbury Gloucs	46	G8
Teynham Kent	38	G9
Thackley C Brad	90	F3
Thackthwaite Cumb	100	F6
Thackthwaite W & F	101	M5
Thainstone Abers	151	K4
Thakeham W Susx	24	D7
Thame Oxon	35	K3
Thames Ditton Surrey	36	E7
Thamesmead Gt Lon	37	L4
Thamesport Medway	38	E7
Thanington Kent	39	K10
Thankerton S Lans	116	D3
Tharston Norfk	64	H3
Thatcham W Berk	34	F11
Thatto Heath St Hel	81	Q6
Thaxted Essex	51	P4
Theakston N York	97	M3
Thealby N Linc	92	E7
Theale Somset	19	N5
Theale W Berk	34	H10
Thearne E R Yk	93	J3
The Beeches Gloucs	33	K4
Theberton Suffk	65	N8
The Blythe Staffs	71	J9
The Bog Shrops	56	F5
The Bourne Worcs	47	J3
The Braes Highld	153	J11
The Bratch Staffs	58	C6
The Bridge Kent	37	M5
The Broad Herefs	45	P2
The Broads	77	P10
The Brunt E Loth	128	H5
The Bryn Mons	31	K3
The Bungalow IoM	80	e4
The Burf Worcs	57	Q11
The Camp Gloucs	32	H3
The Chequer Wrexhm	69	N6
The City Bed	61	P9
The City Bucks	35	L5
The Common Oxon	47	Q9
The Common Wilts	21	P8
The Common Wilts	33	K7
The Corner Kent	26	B3
The Cronk IoM	80	d2
Theddingworth Leics	60	E3
Theddlethorpe All Saints Lincs	87	N3
Theddlethorpe St Helen Lincs	87	N3
The Deep C KuH	93	J5
The Den N Ayrs	125	J7
The Forge Herefs	45	L7
The Forstal Kent	26	H4
The Fouralls Shrops	70	B8
The Green Cumb	94	D4
The Green Essex	52	C8
The Green N York	105	L9
The Green Wilts	20	G8
The Grove Dur	112	G10
The Grove Worcs	46	G6
The Haven W Susx	24	C4
The Haw Gloucs	46	F9
The Hendre Mons	31	N2
The Hill Cumb	94	D4
The Holt Wokham	35	M9
The Hundred Herefs	45	Q2
Thelbridge Cross Devon	9	J2
The Leacon Kent	26	G5
The Lee Bucks	35	P4
The Lhen IoM	80	e1
Thelnetham Suffk	64	E6
The Lochs Moray	157	Q5
Thelveton Norfk	64	H5
Thelwall Warrtn	82	E7
The Marsh Powys	56	E5
Themelthorpe Norfk	76	F7
The Middles Dur	113	K10
The Moor Kent	26	C6
The Mumbles Swans	28	H7
The Murray S Lans	125	Q7
The Mythe Gloucs	46	G8
The Narth Mons	31	P3
The Neuk Abers	151	J8
Thenford W Nthn	48	F6
Theobald's Green Wilts	33	K11
The Quarry Gloucs	32	D5
The Quarter Kent	26	E3
The Reddings Gloucs	46	H10
Therfield Herts	50	H3
The Rhôs Powys	44	H8
The Ross P & K	133	M3
The Sands Surrey	23	N5
The Shoe Wilts	32	F10
The Smithies Shrops	57	M5
The Spring Warwks	59	L10
The Square Torfn	31	J5
The Stair Kent	37	P11
The Stocks Kent	26	F6
The Straits Hants	23	L7
The Strand Wilts	20	H3
Thetford Norfk	64	B5
Thetford Forest Park	63	P3
Thethwaite Cumb	101	L2
The Towans Cnwll	2	F6
The Town IoS	2	b1
The Vauld Herefs	45	Q5
The Wyke Shrops	57	N3
Theydon Bois Essex	51	K11
Theydon Mount Essex	51	L11
Thicket Priory N York	92	A2
Thickwood Wilts	32	F10
Thimbleby Lincs	86	H6
Thimbleby N York	104	E9
Thingwall Wirral	81	K8
Thirkleby N York	97	Q5
Thirlby N York	97	Q4
Thirlestane Border	128	F10
Thirn N York	97	K3
Thirsk N York	97	P4
Thirtleby E R Yk	93	L4
Thistleton Lancs	88	E3
Thistleton Rutlnd	73	N7
Thistley Green Suffk	63	L5
Thixendale N York	98	G8
Thockrington Nthumb	112	E5
Tholomas Drove Cambs	74	H9
Tholthorpe N York	97	Q7
Thomas Chapel Pembks	41	M9
Thomas Close W & F	101	M2
Thomastown Abers	158	E10
Thompson Norfk	64	C2
Thomshill Moray	157	N6
Thong Kent	37	Q6
Thongsbridge Kirk	90	F9
Thoralby N York	96	F3
Thoresby Notts	85	K6
Thoresthorpe Lincs	87	N5
Thoresway Lincs	93	L11
Thorganby Lincs	93	M11
Thorganby N York	92	A2
Thorgill N York	105	K11
Thorington Suffk	65	N7
Thorington Street Suffk	52	H4
Thorlby N York	96	E10
Thorley Herts	51	L7
Thorley IoW	14	C9
Thorley Houses Herts	51	L6
Thorley Street IoW	14	C9
Thormanby N York	97	Q6
Thornaby-on-Tees S on T	104	E7
Thornage Norfk	76	E4
Thornborough Bucks	49	K8
Thornborough N York	97	L5
Thornbury C Brad	90	F4
Thornbury Devon	16	G10
Thornbury Herefs	46	B3
Thornbury S Glos	32	B6
Thornby Cumb	110	E10
Thornby W Nthn	60	E5
Thorncliff Staffs	71	J3
Thorncombe Dorset	10	H4
Thorncombe Street Surrey	23	Q6
Thorncott Green C Beds	61	Q11
Thorncross IoW	14	D10
Thorndon Suffk	64	G8
Thorndon Cross Devon	8	D6
Thorne Donc	92	A8
Thorne Coffin Somset	19	P11
Thornecroft Devon	7	K5
Thornehillhead Devon	16	G8
Thorner Leeds	91	K2
Thornes Staffs	58	G4
Thornes Wakefd	91	J7
Thorne St Margaret Somset	18	F10
Thorney Bucks	36	B5
Thorney C Pete	74	E10
Thorney Notts	85	Q6
Thorney Somset	19	M10
Thorney Hill Hants	13	M5
Thorney Island W Susx	15	L6
Thornfalcon Somset	19	J10
Thornford Dorset	11	N2
Thorngrove Somset	19	L8
Thorngumbald E R Yk	93	M5
Thornham Norfk	75	P2
Thornham Magna Suffk	64	G7
Thornham Parva Suffk	64	G7
Thornhaugh C Pete	73	R10
Thornhill C Sotn	14	E4
Thornhill Caerph	30	G8
Thornhill Cumb	100	D9
Thornhill D & G	116	B11
Thornhill Derbys	83	Q8
Thornhill Kirk	90	H7
Thornhill Stirlg	133	K7
Thornhill Lees Kirk	90	G7
Thornhills Calder	90	F6
Thornholme E R Yk	99	N8
Thornicombe Dorset	12	E4
Thornington Nthumb	118	G4
Thornley Dur	103	M3
Thornley Dur	104	C3
Thornley Gate Nthumb	112	B9
Thornliebank E Rens	125	P6
Thorns Suffk	63	M9
Thornsett Derbys	83	M7
Thorns Green Ches E	82	G8
Thornthwaite Cumb	100	H5
Thornthwaite N York	97	J9
Thornton Angus	142	F8
Thornton Bucks	49	K7
Thornton C Brad	90	D4
Thornton E R Yk	98	F11
Thornton Fife	134	H8
Thornton Lancs	88	C2
Thornton Leics	72	D9
Thornton Lincs	86	H7
Thornton Middsb	104	E8
Thornton Nthumb	129	P10
Thornton Pembks	40	H9
Thornton Sefton	81	L4
Thornton Curtis N Linc	93	J7
Thorntonhall S Lans	125	P6
Thornton Heath Gt Lon	36	H7
Thornton Hough Wirral	81	L8
Thornton-in-Craven N York	96	D11
Thornton in Lonsdale N York	95	P6
Thornton-le-Beans N York	97	N2
Thornton-le-Clay N York	98	D7
Thornton-le-Dale N York	98	G4
Thornton le Moor Lincs	92	H11
Thornton-le-Moor N York	97	N3
Thornton-le-Moors Ches W	81	N10
Thornton-le-Street N York	97	P3
Thorntonloch E Loth	129	K5
Thornton Rust N York	96	E3
Thornton Steward N York	97	J3
Thornton Watlass N York	97	L3
Thornwood Common Essex	51	L10
Thornydykes Border	128	G10
Thornythwaite W & F	101	L6
Thoroton Notts	73	K2
Thorp Arch Leeds	97	P11
Thorpe Derbys	71	M4
Thorpe E R Yk	99	K11
Thorpe Lincs	87	N4
Thorpe N York	96	F8
Thorpe Notts	73	K2
Thorpe Surrey	36	B7
Thorpe Abbotts Norfk	64	H6
Thorpe Acre Leics	72	E7
Thorpe Arnold Leics	73	K6
Thorpe Audlin Wakefd	91	M7
Thorpe Bassett N York	98	H6
Thorpe Bay Sthend	38	F4
Thorpe by Water Rutlnd	73	M11
Thorpe Common Rothm	91	K11
Thorpe Constantine Staffs	59	L3
Thorpe End Norfk	77	K9
Thorpe Green Essex	53	L7
Thorpe Green Lancs	88	H6
Thorpe Green Suffk	64	C11
Thorpe Hesley Rothm	91	K11
Thorpe in Balne Donc	91	P8
Thorpe Langton Leics	60	F2
Thorpe Larches Dur	104	C5
Thorpe Lea Surrey	36	B6
Thorpe le Fallows Lincs	86	B4
Thorpe-le-Soken Essex	53	L7
Thorpe le Street E R Yk	92	F2
Thorpe Malsor N Nthn	60	H5
Thorpe Mandeville W Nthn	48	F6
Thorpe Market Norfk	77	J4
Thorpe Marriot Norfk	76	H8
Thorpe Morieux Suffk	64	C11
Thorpeness Suffk	65	P9
Thorpe on the Hill Leeds	91	J5
Thorpe on the Hill Lincs	86	B7
Thorpe Park Resort Surrey	36	B7
Thorpe St Andrew Norfk	77	K10
Thorpe St Peter Lincs	87	N8
Thorpe Salvin Rothm	84	H4
Thorpe Satchville Leics	73	J8
Thorpe Thewles S on T	104	C6
Thorpe Tilney Lincs	86	F9
Thorpe Underwood N Nthn	60	G4
Thorpe Underwood N York	97	Q9
Thorpe Waterville N Nthn	61	M4
Thorpe Willoughby N York	91	P4
Thorpland Norfk	75	M9
Thorrington Essex	53	J8
Thorverton Devon	9	M4
Thrales End C Beds	50	D6
Thrandeston Suffk	64	G6
Thrapston N Nthn	61	L5
Threapland Cumb	100	G3
Threapland N York	96	E8
Threapwood Ches W	69	M5
Threapwood Staffs	71	J6
Threapwood Head Staffs	71	J6
Threave S Ayrs	114	F6
Three Ashes Herefs	45	Q10
Three Bridges W Susx	24	G3
Three Burrows Cnwll	3	K4
Three Chimneys Kent	26	D4
Three Cocks Powys	44	H7
Three Crosses Swans	28	G6
Three Cups Corner E Susx	25	P6
Three Gates Worcs	46	C2
Threehammer Common Norfk	77	L8
Three Hammers Cnwll	5	L4
Three Holes Norfk	75	K10
Threekingham Lincs	74	A3
Three Leg Cross E Susx	25	Q4
Three Legged Cross Dorset	13	J3
Three Mile Cross Wokham	35	K11
Threemilestone Cnwll	3	K4
Threemiletown W Loth	127	K2
Three Oaks E Susx	26	D9
Threlkeld W & F	101	K5
Threshers Bush Essex	51	L9
Threshfield N York	96	E8
Thrigby Norfk	77	P9
Thringarth Dur	102	H6
Thringstone Leics	72	C7
Thrintoft N York	97	M2
Thriplow Cambs	62	F11
Throapham Rothm	84	H3
Throckenhalt Lincs	74	G9
Throcking Herts	50	H4
Throckley N u Ty	113	J7
Throckmorton Worcs	47	J4
Throop BCP	13	K5
Throop Dorset	12	D6
Throphill Nthumb	112	H3
Thropton Nthumb	119	K10
Throsk Stirlg	133	P9
Througham Gloucs	32	H3
Throughgate D & G	109	J4
Throwleigh Devon	8	G6
Throwley Kent	38	G10
Throwley Forstal Kent	38	G11
Thrumpton Notts	72	E4
Thrumpton Notts	85	M4
Thrumster Highld	167	P7
Thrunscoe NE Lin	93	P9
Thrunton Nthumb	119	L8
Thrup Oxon	33	Q5
Thrupp Gloucs	32	G4
Thrupp Oxon	48	E11
Thrushelton Devon	5	B7
Thrussington Leics	72	H7
Thruxton Hants	21	Q5
Thruxton Herefs	45	N8
Thrybergh Rothm	91	M11
Thulston Derbys	72	C4
Thundersley Essex	38	C4
Thurcaston Leics	72	F8
Thurcroft Rothm	84	G3
Thurdon Cnwll	16	D9
Thurgarton Norfk	76	H5
Thurgarton Notts	85	L11
Thurgoland Barns	90	H10
Thurlaston Leics	72	E11
Thurlaston Warwks	59	Q10
Thurlbear Somset	19	J10
Thurlby Lincs	73	Q7
Thurlby Lincs	86	B8
Thurlby Lincs	87	N5
Thurleigh Bed	61	N9
Thurlestone Devon	6	H10
Thurloxton Somset	19	J8
Thurlstone Barns	90	G10
Thurlton Norfk	65	N2
Thurlwood Ches E	70	E3
Thurmaston Leics	72	G9
Thurnby Leics	72	G10
Thurne Norfk	77	N8
Thurnham Kent	38	D10
Thurning N Nthn	61	N4
Thurning Norfk	76	F6
Thurnscoe Barns	91	M9
Thurrock Services Thurr	37	N5
Thursby Cumb	110	F10
Thursden Lancs	89	N4
Thursford Norfk	76	D5
Thursley Surrey	23	P7
Thurso Highld	167	K3
Thurstaston Wirral	81	J8
Thurston Suffk	64	C8
Thurston Clough Oldham	90	B9
Thurstonfield Cumb	110	F9
Thurstonland Kirk	90	F8
Thurston Planche Suffk	64	C9
Thurton Norfk	77	L11
Thurvaston Derbys	71	N7
Thuxton Norfk	76	E10
Thwaite N York	102	G11
Thwaite Suffk	64	G8
Thwaite Head W & F	94	G2
Thwaites C Brad	90	D2
Thwaite St Mary Norfk	65	L2
Thwaites Brow C Brad	90	D2
Thwing E R Yk	99	J8
Tibbermore P & K	134	C3
Tibbers D & G	116	B11
Tibberton Gloucs	46	E10
Tibberton Worcs	46	H3
Tibberton Wrekin	70	B10
Tibenham Norfk	64	G4
Tibshelf Derbys	84	F8
Tibshelf Services Derbys	84	F8
Tibthorpe E R Yk	99	K9
Ticehurst E Susx	25	Q4
Tichborne Hants	22	G8
Tickencote Rutlnd	73	P9
Tickenham N Som	31	N10
Tickford End M Keyn	49	N6
Tickhill Donc	85	J2
Ticklerton Shrops	56	H6
Ticknall Derbys	72	B6
Tickton E R Yk	93	J2
Tidbury Green Solhll	58	H9
Tidcombe Wilts	21	Q3
Tiddington Oxon	34	H4
Tiddington Warwks	47	P3
Tiddleywink Wilts	32	F9
Tidebrook E Susx	25	P5
Tideford Cnwll	5	P10
Tideford Cross Cnwll	5	N9

Tidenham Gloucs 31 Q5
Tideswell Derbys 83 Q9
Tidmarsh W Berk 34 H10
Tidmington Warwks 47 Q7
Tidpit Hants 21 L11
Tidworth Wilts 21 P5
Tiers Cross Pembks 40 H8
Tiffield W Nthn 49 K4
Tigerton Angus 143 J5
Tigh a' Ghearraidh W Isls 168 c10
Tigharry W Isls 168 c10
Tighnabruaich Ag & B 124 B3
Tigley Devon 7 K6
Tilbrook Cambs 61 N7
Tilbury Thurr 37 P5
Tilbury Dock Thurr 37 P5
Tilbury Green Essex 52 B3
Tilbury Juxta Clare Essex 52 C3
Tile Cross Birm 59 J7
Tile Hill Covtry 59 L9
Tilehouse Green Solhll 59 J9
Tilehurst Readg 35 J10
Tilford Surrey 23 N6
Tilgate W Susx 24 G4
Tilgate Forest Row W Susx 24 G4
Tilham Street Somset 19 Q7
Tillers Green Gloucs 46 C8
Tilley Shrops 69 P9
Tillicoultry Clacks 133 Q8
Tillietudlem S Lans 126 E8
Tillingham Essex 52 G11
Tillington Herefs 45 P6
Tillington W Susx 23 Q10
Tillington Common Herefs 45 P6
Tillybirloch Abers 150 H6
Tillyfourie Abers 150 G5
Tillygreig Abers 151 M3
Tillyrie P & K 134 E6
Tilmanstone Kent 39 P11
Tilney All Saints Norfk 75 L7
Tilney High End Norfk 75 L7
Tilney St Lawrence Norfk 75 K8
Tilshead Wilts 21 K5
Tilstock Shrops 69 P7
Tilston Ches W 69 N4
Tilstone Bank Ches W 69 Q3
Tilstone Fearnall Ches W 69 Q2
Tilsworth C Beds 49 Q10
Tilton on the Hill Leics 73 J9
Tiltups End Gloucs 32 F5
Tilty Essex 51 N5
Timberland Lincs 86 F9
Timbersbrook Ches E 70 F2
Timberscombe Somset 18 C6
Timble N York 97 J10
Timewell Devon 18 C9
Timpanheck D & G 110 F6
Timperley Traffd 82 G7
Timsbury BaNES 20 C3
Timsbury Hants 22 B10
Timsgarry W Isls 168 f4
Timsgearraidh W Isls 168 f4
Timworth Suffk 64 B8
Timworth Green Suffk 64 B8
Tincleton Dorset 12 C6
Tindale Cumb 111 M9
Tingewick Bucks 49 J8
Tingley Leeds 90 H5
Tingrith C Beds 50 B4
Tingwall Airport Shet 169 r9
Tingwall Ork 169 d4
Tinhay Devon 5 P4
Tinker's Hill Hants 22 D5
Tinkersley Derbys 84 C8
Tinsley Sheff 84 F2
Tinsley Green W Susx 24 G3
Tintagel Cnwll 4 H4
Tintern Mons 31 P4
Tintinhull Somset 19 N11
Tintwistle Derbys 83 M5
Tinwald D & G 109 M4
Tinwell Rutlnd 73 Q9
Tippacott Devon 17 P2
Tipp's End Norfk 75 K11
Tiptoe Hants 13 N5
Tipton Sandw 58 E6
Tipton Green Sandw 58 E6
Tipton St John Devon 10 B6
Tiptree Essex 52 E8
Tiptree Heath Essex 52 E8
Tirabad Powys 44 B6
Tircoed Swans 28 H4
Tiree Ag & B 136 C7
Tiree Airport Ag & B 136 C7
Tiretigan Ag & B 123 M7
Tirley Gloucs 46 F9
Tiroran Ag & B 137 M10
Tirphil Caerph 30 F4
Tirril W & F 101 P5
Tisbury Wilts 20 H9
Tisman's Common W Susx 24 C4
Tissington Derbys 71 M4
Titchberry Devon 16 C6
Titchfield Hants 14 F5
Titchfield Common Hants 14 F5
Titchmarsh N Nthn 61 M5
Titchwell Norfk 75 Q2
Tithby Notts 72 H3
Tithebarn Devon 9 N6
Titley Herefs 45 L2
Titmore Green Herts 50 F5
Titsey Surrey 37 K10
Titson Cnwll 16 C11
Tittensor Staffs 70 F7
Tittleshall Norfk 76 B7
Titton Worcs 58 B11
Tiverton Ches W 69 Q2
Tiverton Devon 9 N2
Tivetshall St Margaret Norfk 64 H4
Tivetshall St Mary Norfk 64 H4
Tivington Somset 18 C6
Tivy Dale Barns 90 H9
Tixall Staffs 70 H10
Tixover Rutlnd 73 P10
Toab Shet 169 q12
Toadhole Derbys 84 E9
Toadmoor Derbys 84 D10
Tobermory Ag & B 137 N4
Toberonochy Ag & B 130 E6
Tobha Mòr W Isls 168 c14
Tocher Abers 158 G11
Tochieneal Moray 158 D4
Tockenham Wilts 33 K9
Tockenham Wick Wilts 33 K8
Tocketts R & Cl 104 H7

Tockholes Bl w D 89 K6
Tockington S Glos 32 B7
Tockwith N York 97 Q10
Todber Dorset 20 E11
Todburn Nthumb 119 M11
Toddington C Beds 50 B5
Toddington Gloucs 47 K8
Toddington Services C Beds 50 B5
Todds Green Herts 50 F5
Todenham Gloucs 47 P7
Todhills Angus 142 G10
Todhills Cumb 110 G8
Todhills Dur 103 P4
Todhills Rest Area Cumb 110 G8
Todmorden Calder 89 Q6
Todwick Rothm 84 G4
Toft Cambs 62 E9
Toft Ches E 82 G9
Toft Lincs 73 R7
Toft Shet 169 r6
Toft Warwks 59 Q10
Toft Hill Dur 103 N5
Toft Hill Lincs 86 H8
Toft Monks Norfk 65 N3
Toft next Newton Lincs 86 D3
Toftrees Norfk 76 B6
Toftwood Norfk 76 D9
Togston Nthumb 119 P10
Tokavaig Highld 145 K5
Tokers Green Oxon 35 K9
Tolastadh bho Thuath W Isls 168 k3
Toldish Cnwll 4 E10
Tolland Somset 18 F8
Tollard Farnham Dorset 21 J11
Tollard Royal Wilts 20 H11
Toll Bar Donc 91 P9
Tollbar End Covtry 59 N9
Toller Fratrum Dorset 11 M5
Toller Porcorum Dorset 11 M5
Tollerton N York 97 R8
Tollerton Notts 72 G4
Toller Whelme Dorset 11 L4
Tollesbury Essex 52 G9
Tolleshunt D'Arcy Essex 52 F9
Tolleshunt Knights Essex 52 F9
Tolleshunt Major Essex 52 F9
Tollingham E R Yk 92 D3
Toll of Birness Abers 159 P11
Tolpuddle Dorset 12 C6
Tolworth Gt Lon 36 E7
Tomatin Highld 148 E2
Tomchrasky Highld 146 H5
Tomdoun Highld 146 F7
Tomich Highld 147 J2
Tomich Highld 155 P8
Tomich Highld 156 B3
Tomich Highld 162 E5
Tomintoul Moray 149 M4
Tomlow Warwks 48 E2
Tomnacross Highld 155 P9
Tomnavoulin Moray 149 N2
Tompkin Staffs 70 G4
Ton Mons 31 K4
Ton Mons 31 L5
Tonbridge Kent 37 N11
Tondu Brdgnd 29 N8
Tonedale Somset 18 F10
Tonfanau Gwynd 54 D4
Tong C Brad 90 G4
Tong Kent 38 G10
Tong Shrops 57 P3
Tong W Isls 168 j4
Tonge Leics 72 C6
Tong Green Kent 38 G11
Tongham Surrey 23 N5
Tongland D & G 108 E10
Tong Norton Shrops 57 P3
Tongue Highld 165 N5
Tongue End Lincs 74 C7
Tongwynlais Cardif 30 F8
Tonmawr Neath 29 M5
Tonna Neath 29 L5
Ton-teg Rhondd 30 E7
Tonwell Herts 50 H7
Tonypandy Rhondd 30 C6
Tonyrefail Rhondd 30 D7
Toot Baldon Oxon 34 G4
Toot Hill Essex 51 M10
Toothill Hants 22 C11
Toothill Swindn 33 M8
Tooting Gt Lon 36 G6
Tooting Bec Gt Lon 36 G6
Topcliffe N York 97 N5
Topcroft Norfk 65 K3
Topcroft Street Norfk 65 K3
Top End Bed 61 M8
Topham Donc 91 Q7
Top of Hebers Rochdl 89 P9
Toppesfield Essex 52 B4
Toprow Norfk 64 H2
Topsham Devon 9 N7
Top-y-rhos Flints 69 J3
Torbeg N Ayrs 120 G6
Torboll Highld 162 H7
Torbreck Highld 156 A9
Torbryan Devon 7 L5
Torcastle Highld 139 L2
Torcross Devon 7 L10
Tore Highld 155 R7
Torfrey Cnwll 5 J11
Torinturk Ag & B 123 P7
Torksey Lincs 85 P5
Torlundy Highld 139 L2
Tormarton S Glos 32 E9
Tormore N Ayrs 120 G5
Tornagrain Highld 156 D7
Tornaveen Abers 150 G6
Torness Highld 147 P2
Toronto Dur 103 N4
Torpenhow Cumb 100 H3
Torphichen W Loth 126 H3
Torphins Abers 150 G7
Torpoint Cnwll 6 C7
Torquay Torbay 7 N6
Torquhan Border 128 C10
Torran Highld 153 K8
Torrance E Duns 125 Q3
Torranyard N Ayrs 125 K9
Torre Somset 18 D7
Torridon Highld 154 B6
Torridon House Highld 153 R6
Torrin Highld 145 J3
Torrisdale Ag & B 120 E4
Torrisdale Highld 165 N3
Torrish Highld 163 M3

Torrisholme Lancs 95 K8
Torrobull Highld 162 D6
Torry C Aber 151 N6
Torryburn Fife 134 C10
Torteval Guern 10 a2
Torthorwald D & G 109 M5
Tortington W Susx 24 B9
Torton Worcs 58 B10
Tortworth S Glos 32 D6
Torvaig Highld 152 H9
Torver W & F 94 F2
Torwood Falk 133 N11
Torwoodlee Border 117 P3
Torworth Notts 85 L3
Tosberry Devon 16 D7
Toscaig Highld 153 N10
Toseland Cambs 62 B8
Tosside Lancs 95 R9
Tostock Suffk 64 D9
Totaig Highld 152 C7
Tote Highld 152 G8
Tote Hill W Susx 23 N10
Tothill Lincs 87 M4
Totland IoW 13 P7
Totley Sheff 84 D5
Totley Brook Sheff 84 D4
Totnes Devon 7 L6
Toton Notts 72 E4
Totronald Ag & B 136 F4
Totscore Highld 152 F4
Tottenham Gt Lon 36 H2
Tottenhill Norfk 75 M8
Totteridge Gt Lon 36 F2
Totternhoe C Beds 49 Q10
Tottington Bury 89 M8
Tottington Lancs 89 L4
Totton Hants 14 C4
Touchen End W & M 35 N9
Toulston N York 91 M2
Toulton Somset 18 G8
Toulvaddie Highld 163 K10
Tovil Kent 38 C11
Towan Cnwll 3 Q4
Towan Cnwll 4 D7
Toward Ag & B 124 E4
Toward Quay Ag & B 124 E4
Towcester W Nthn 49 J5
Towednack Cnwll 2 D6
Tower of London Gt Lon 36 H4
Towersey Oxon 35 K3
Towie Abers 150 C5
Tow Law Dur 103 M3
Town End Cambs 74 H11
Town End W & F 95 J4
Town End W & F 101 K9
Town End W & F 102 B5
Townend W Duns 125 K2
Towngate Lincs 74 B8
Town Green Lancs 88 E9
Town Green Norfk 77 M9
Townhead Barns 83 Q4
Townhead Cumb 100 E3
Townhead D & G 109 M3
Town Head N York 96 B9
Town Head W & F 101 M10
Town Head W & F 102 B4
Townhead of Greenlaw D & G 108 F8
Townhill Fife 134 E10
Town Kelloe Dur 104 C3
Townlake Devon 5 Q7
Town Lane Wigan 82 E5
Town Littleworth E Susx 25 K7
Town of Lowton Wigan 82 D5
Town Row E Susx 25 N4
Towns End Hants 22 G3
Townsend Somset 19 H2
Townshend Cnwll 2 F7
Town Street Suffk 63 N3
Townwell S Glos 32 D6
Town Yetholm Border 118 F5
Towthorpe C York 98 C9
Towthorpe E R Yk 98 H8
Towton N York 91 M3
Towyn Conwy 80 D9
Toxteth Lpool 81 M7
Toynton All Saints Lincs 87 L8
Toynton Fen Side Lincs 87 L8
Toynton St Peter Lincs 87 M8
Toy's Hill Kent 37 L10
Trabboch E Ayrs 114 H3
Trabbochburn E Ayrs 115 J3
Traboe Cnwll 3 J9
Tracebridge Somset 18 E10
Tradespark Highld 156 F6
Trafford Park Traffd 82 G5
Trallong Powys 44 D9
Tranent E Loth 128 C5
Tranmere Wirral 81 L7
Trantelbeg Highld 166 E6
Trantlemore Highld 166 E6
Tranwell Nthumb 113 J4
Trap Carmth 43 N11
Traprain E Loth 128 F4
Trap's Green Warwks 58 H11
Trapshill W Berk 22 C2
Traquair Border 117 L4
Trash Green W Berk 35 J11
Trawden Lancs 89 Q3
Trawscoed Cerdgn 54 F10
Trawsfynydd Gwynd 67 N7
Trealaw Rhondd 30 D6
Treales Lancs 88 E4
Trearddur Bay IoA 78 D9
Treator Cnwll 4 E6
Tre Aubrey V Glam 30 D10
Trebanog Rhondd 30 D6
Trebanos Neath 29 K4
Trebartha Cnwll 5 M6
Trebarwith Cnwll 4 H4
Trebeath Cnwll 5 M4
Trebetherick Cnwll 4 E6
Treborough Somset 18 D7
Trebudannon Cnwll 4 D9
Trebullett Cnwll 5 N6
Treburgett Cnwll 4 H6
Treburley Cnwll 5 P6
Treburrick Cnwll 4 D7
Trebyan Cnwll 4 H9
Trecastle Powys 44 B9
Trecogo Cnwll 5 N5
Trecott Devon 8 F4
Trecwn Pembks 41 J4

Trecynon Rhondd 30 C4
Tredaule Cnwll 5 L5
Tredavoe Cnwll 2 D8
Tredegar Blae G 30 F3
Tredethy Cnwll 4 H7
Tredington Gloucs 46 H9
Tredington Warwks 47 Q6
Tredinnick Cnwll 4 E7
Tredinnick Cnwll 4 G10
Tredinnick Cnwll 5 K8
Tredinnick Cnwll 5 L10
Tredinnick Cnwll 5 M10
Tredomen Powys 44 G8
Tredrizzick Cnwll 4 F6
Tredunnock Mons 31 L6
Tredustan Powys 44 G8
Treen Cnwll 2 B9
Treen Cnwll 2 C6
Treesmill Cnwll 4 H10
Treeton Rothm 84 F3
Trefasser Pembks 40 G3
Trefdraeth IoA 78 G10
Trefecca Powys 44 G8
Trefechan Myr Td 30 D3
Trefeglwys Powys 55 M6
Trefenter Cerdgn 54 E11
Treffgarne Pembks 41 J6
Treffgarne Owen Pembks 40 G5
Treffynnon Pembks 40 G5
Trefil Blae G 30 F2
Trefilan Cerdgn 43 K3
Trefin Pembks 40 F4
Treflach Shrops 69 J9
Trefnannau Powys 68 H11
Trefnant Denbgs 80 F10
Trefonen Shrops 69 J9
Trefor Gwynd 66 F5
Trefor IoA 78 F8
Treforest Rhondd 30 E7
Trefrew Cnwll 5 J5
Trefriw Conwy 67 P2
Tregadillett Cnwll 5 M5
Tre-gagle Mons 31 P3
Tregaian IoA 78 H8
Tregare Mons 31 M2
Tregarne Cnwll 3 K9
Tregaron Cerdgn 43 N3
Tregarth Gwynd 79 L11
Tregaswith Cnwll 4 D9
Tregatta Cnwll 4 H4
Tregawne Cnwll 4 G8
Tregeare Cnwll 5 L4
Tregeiriog Wrexhm 68 G8
Tregele IoA 78 F6
Tregellist Cnwll 4 G6
Tregenna Cnwll 3 M5
Tregeseal Cnwll 2 B7
Tregew Cnwll 3 L7
Tre-Gibbon Rhondd 30 C3
Tregidden Cnwll 3 K9
Tregiskey Cnwll 3 Q4
Treglemais Pembks 40 F5
Tregole Cnwll 5 K2
Tregolls Cnwll 3 J6
Tregonce Cnwll 4 E7
Tregonetha Cnwll 4 F9
Tregonning & Gwinear Mining District Cnwll 2 F7
Tregony Cnwll 3 N5
Tregoodwell Cnwll 5 J5
Tregorrick Cnwll 3 Q3
Tregoss Cnwll 4 F9
Tregoyd Powys 44 H7
Tregrehan Mills Cnwll 3 Q3
Tre-groes Cerdgn 42 H6
Tregullon Cnwll 4 H9
Tregunna Cnwll 4 F7
Tregunnon Cnwll 5 L5
Tregurrian Cnwll 4 D8
Tregynon Powys 55 P5
Tre-gynwr Carmth 42 H11
Trehafod Rhondd 30 D6
Trehan Cnwll 5 Q10
Treharris Myr Td 30 E5
Treharrock Cnwll 4 G6
Trehemborne Cnwll 4 D7
Treherbert Carmth 43 L5
Treherbert Rhondd 29 P5
Trehunist Cnwll 5 N9
Trekenner Cnwll 5 N6
Treknow Cnwll 4 H4
Trelan Cnwll 3 J10
Trelash Cnwll 5 K3
Trelassick Cnwll 3 M3
Trelawne Cnwll 5 L11
Trelawnyd Flints 80 F9
Treleague Cnwll 3 K9
Treleaver Cnwll 3 K10
Trelech Carmth 41 Q4
Trelech a'r Betws Carmth 42 F9
Treleddyd-fawr Pembks 40 E5
Trelew Cnwll 3 L6
Trelewis Myr Td 30 F5
Treligga Cnwll 4 G5
Trelights Cnwll 4 F6
Trelill Cnwll 4 G6
Trelinnoe Cnwll 5 N5
Trelion Cnwll 3 N3
Trelissick Cnwll 3 L7
Trellech Mons 31 P3
Trelleck Grange Mons 31 N4
Trelogan Flints 80 G8
Trelow Cnwll 4 E8
Trelowarren Cnwll 3 J9
Trelowia Cnwll 5 M10
Treluggan Cnwll 3 M6
Trelystan Powys 56 D4
Tremadog Gwynd 67 K7
Tremail Cnwll 5 K4
Tremain Cerdgn 42 D5
Tremaine Cnwll 5 L4
Tremar Cnwll 5 M8
Trematon Cnwll 5 P10
Trembraze Cnwll 5 M8
Tremeirchion Denbgs 80 F10
Tremethick Cross Cnwll 2 C7
Tremore Cnwll 4 G9
Tre-Mostyn Flints 80 G9
Trenance Cnwll 3 L9
Trenance Cnwll 4 D8
Trenance Cnwll 4 E7
Trenarren Cnwll 3 Q4
Trench Wrekin 57 M2
Trench Green Oxon 35 J9
Trendeal Cnwll 3 M3
Trendrine Cnwll 2 D6

Treneague Cnwll 4 F7
Trenear Cnwll 2 H7
Treneglos Cnwll 5 L4
Trenerth Cnwll 2 G6
Trenewan Cnwll 5 K11
Trenewth Cnwll 4 H6
Trengune Cnwll 5 K3
Treninnick Cnwll 4 C9
Trenowah Cnwll 4 B10
Trenoweth Cnwll 3 K7
Trent Dorset 19 Q11
Trentham C Stke 70 F6
Trentishoe Devon 17 L2
Trentlock Derbys 72 D4
Trent Port Lincs 85 P4
Trent Vale C Stke 70 F6
Trenwheal Cnwll 2 G7
Treoes V Glam 29 P9
Treorchy Rhondd 30 C5
Trequite Cnwll 4 G6
Tre'r-ddol Cerdgn 54 F6
Trerhyngyll V Glam 30 D9
Trerulefoot Cnwll 5 N10
Tresaith Cerdgn 42 E4
Tresawle Cnwll 3 M4
Tresco IoS 2 b2
Trescott Staffs 58 C5
Trescowe Cnwll 2 F7
Tresean Cnwll 4 B10
Tresham Gloucs 32 E6
Treshnish Isles Ag & B 136 G7
Tresillian Cnwll 3 M4
Tresinney Cnwll 5 J5
Treskinnick Cross Cnwll 5 L2
Tresmeer Cnwll 5 L4
Tresparrett Cnwll 5 J3
Tressait P & K 141 K5
Tresta Shet 169 q8
Tresta Shet 169 t4
Treswell Notts 85 N5
Treswithian Cnwll 2 G5
Tre Taliesin Cerdgn 54 F6
Trethevey Cnwll 4 H4
Trethewey Cnwll 2 B9
Trethomas Caerph 30 G7
Trethosa Cnwll 3 N3
Trethurgy Cnwll 4 G10
Tretio Pembks 40 E5
Tretire Herefs 45 Q10
Tretower Powys 44 H10
Treuddyn Flints 69 J3
Trevadlock Cnwll 5 M6
Trevalga Cnwll 4 H3
Trevalyn Wrexhm 69 L3
Trevanger Cnwll 4 F6
Trevanson Cnwll 4 F7
Trevarrack Cnwll 2 D7
Trevarren Cnwll 4 E9
Trevarrian Cnwll 4 D8
Trevarrick Cnwll 3 P5
Trevarth Cnwll 3 J6
Trevaughan Carmth 41 P7
Tre-vaughan Carmth 42 G10
Treveal Cnwll 2 D5
Treveal Cnwll 4 B10
Treveighan Cnwll 4 H6
Trevellas Downs Cnwll 3 J3
Trevelmond Cnwll 5 L9
Trevemper Cnwll 4 C10
Treveor Cnwll 3 P5
Treverbyn Cnwll 3 M4
Treverbyn Cnwll 4 G10
Treverva Cnwll 3 K7
Trevescan Cnwll 2 B9
Trevethin Torfn 31 J4
Trevia Cnwll 4 H5
Trevigro Cnwll 5 N8
Trevilla Cnwll 3 L6
Trevilson Cnwll 4 C10
Treviscoe Cnwll 4 E10
Treviskey Cnwll 3 N5
Trevithick Cnwll 3 P4
Trevithick Cnwll 4 D9
Trevoll Cnwll 4 C10
Trevone Cnwll 4 D6
Trevor Wrexhm 69 J6
Trevorgans Cnwll 2 C8
Trevorrick Cnwll 4 E7
Trevose Cnwll 4 D6
Trew Cnwll 2 G8
Trewalder Cnwll 4 H5
Trewalkin Powys 44 H8
Trewarmett Cnwll 4 H4
Trewassa Cnwll 5 J4
Trewavas Cnwll 2 F8
Trewavas Mining District Cnwll 2 F8
Treween Cnwll 5 L5
Trewellard Cnwll 2 B7
Trewen Cnwll 5 M5
Trewennack Cnwll 2 H8
Trewent Pembks 41 K11
Trewern Powys 56 D2
Trewetha Cnwll 4 G5
Trewethern Cnwll 4 G6
Trewidland Cnwll 5 M10
Trewillis Cnwll 3 K10
Trewint Cnwll 5 L5
Trewint Cnwll 5 M9
Trewithian Cnwll 3 M6
Trewoodloe Cnwll 5 N7
Trewoon Cnwll 2 H10
Trewoon Cnwll 3 P3
Treworga Cnwll 3 M5
Treworgan Cnwll 3 L4
Treworlas Cnwll 3 M6
Treworld Cnwll 5 J3
Treworthal Cnwll 3 M6
Tre-wyn Mons 45 L10
Treyarnon Cnwll 4 D7
Treyford W Susx 23 M11
Trickett's Cross Dorset 13 J4
Triermain Cumb 111 L7
Triffleton Pembks 41 J5
Trillacott Cnwll 5 M4
Trimdon Dur 104 C4
Trimdon Colliery Dur 104 C3
Trimdon Grange Dur 104 C3
Trimingham Norfk 77 K4
Trimley Lower Street Suffk 53 N4
Trimley St Martin Suffk 53 N4
Trimley St Mary Suffk 53 N4
Trimpley Worcs 57 P9
Trimsaran Carmth 28 E4
Trims Green Herts 51 L7

Trimstone Devon......17 J3
Trinafour P & K......140 H5
Trinant Caerph......30 H5
Tring Herts......35 P2
Tringford Herts......35 P2
Tring Wharf Herts......35 P2
Trinity Angus......143 L5
Trinity Jersey......11 b1
Trinity Gask P & K......134 B4
Triscombe Somset......18 G7
Trislaig Highld......139 K3
Trispen Cnwll......3 L3
Tritlington Nthumb......113 K2
Troan Cnwll......4 D10
Trochry P & K......141 N9
Troedrhiwfuwch Caerph......30 F4
Troedyraur Cerdgn......42 F5
Troedyrhiw Myr Td......30 E4
Trofarth Conwy......80 B10
Trois Bois Jersey......11 b1
Troon Cnwll......2 H6
Troon S Ayrs......125 J11
Tropical World Leeds Leeds......91 J3
Trossachs Stirlg......132 G6
Trossachs Pier Stirlg......132 F6
Troston Suffk......64 B7
Troswell Cnwll......5 M3
Trotshill Worcs......46 G3
Trottiscliffe Kent......37 P8
Trotton W Susx......23 M10
Troughend Nthumb......112 C2
Trough Gate Lancs......89 P6
Troutbeck W & F......101 L5
Troutbeck W & F......101 M10
Troutbeck Bridge W & F......101 M10
Troway Derbys......84 E5
Trowbridge Wilts......20 G3
Trowell Notts......72 D3
Trowell Services Notts......72 D2
Trowle Common Wilts......20 F3
Trowley Bottom Herts......50 C8
Trowse Newton Norfk......77 J10
Troy Leeds......90 G3
Trudoxhill Somset......20 D6
Trull Somset......18 H10
Trumfleet Donc......91 Q8
Trumpan Highld......152 C5
Trumpet Herefs......46 C7
Trumpington Cambs......62 F10
Trumpsgreen Surrey......35 Q11
Trunch Norfk......77 K5
Trunnah Lancs......88 C2
Truro Cnwll......3 L5
Truscott Cnwll......5 M4
Trusham Devon......9 L8
Trusley Derbys......71 P7
Trusthorpe Lincs......87 P4
Trysull Staffs......58 C6
Tubney Oxon......34 D5
Tuckenhay Devon......7 L7
Tuckhill Shrops......57 P7
Tuckingmill Cnwll......2 H5
Tuckingmill Wilts......20 H9
Tuckton BCP......13 K6
Tucoyse Cnwll......3 P4
Tuddenham Suffk......63 M6
Tuddenham St Martin Suffk......53 L2
Tudeley Kent......37 P11
Tudhoe Dur......103 Q3
Tudorville Herefs......46 A10
Tudweiliog Gwynd......66 C7
Tuesley Surrey......23 Q6
Tuffley Gloucs......32 F2
Tufton Hants......22 E5
Tufton Pembks......41 K5
Tugby Leics......73 K10
Tugford Shrops......57 K7
Tughall Nthumb......119 P5
Tullibody Clacks......133 P8
Tullich Abers......150 B8
Tullich Highld......147 Q2
Tullich Highld......156 F2
Tulliemet P & K......141 P7
Tulloch Abers......159 K11
Tullochgorm Ag & B......131 K8
Tulloch Station Highld......147 K11
Tullymurdoch P & K......142 B7
Tullynessle Abers......150 F4
Tulse Hill Gt Lon......36 H6
Tumble Carmth......28 F2
Tumbler's Green Essex......52 D6
Tumby Lincs......86 H9
Tumby Woodside Lincs......87 J9
Tummel Bridge P & K......141 J6
Tunbridge Wells Kent......25 N3
Tundergarth D & G......110 C4
Tunga W Isls......168 j4
Tungate Norfk......77 K6
Tunley BaNES......20 C3
Tunstall C Stke......70 F4
Tunstall E R Yk......93 P4
Tunstall Kent......38 E9
Tunstall Lancs......95 N6
Tunstall N York......103 P11
Tunstall Norfk......77 N10
Tunstall Staffs......70 D9
Tunstall Suffk......65 N10
Tunstall Sundld......113 N10
Tunstead Derbys......83 P10
Tunstead Norfk......77 K7
Tunstead Milton Derbys......83 M8
Tunworth Hants......23 J5
Tupsley Herefs......45 Q6
Turgis Green Hants......23 J3
Turkdean Gloucs......47 M11
Tur Langton Leics......60 F2
Turleigh Wilts......20 F2
Turleygreen Shrops......57 P7
Turn Lancs......89 N7
Turnastone Herefs......45 M7
Turnberry S Ayrs......114 D6
Turnchapel C Plym......6 D8
Turnditch Derbys......71 P5
Turner Green Lancs......89 J4
Turner's Green E Susx......25 P7
Turner's Green Warwks......59 J11
Turners Hill W Susx......24 H3
Turners Puddle Dorset......12 D6
Turnford Herts......51 J10
Turnhouse C Edin......127 M3
Turnworth Dorset......12 D3
Turriff Abers......158 H7
Turton Bottoms Bl w D......89 L7
Turves Cambs......74 F11
Turvey Bed......49 P4
Turville Bucks......35 L6

Turville Heath Bucks......35 K6
Turweston Bucks......48 H7
Tushielaw Inn Border......117 L7
Tutbury Staffs......71 N9
Tutnall Worcs......58 G10
Tutshill Gloucs......31 P6
Tuttington Norfk......77 J6
Tutts Clump W Berk......34 G10
Tutwell Cnwll......5 P6
Tuxford Notts......85 M6
Twatt Ork......169 b4
Twatt Shet......169 q8
Twechar E Duns......126 B2
Tweedbank Border......117 Q4
Tweedmouth Nthumb......129 P9
Tweedsmuir Border......116 G6
Twelveheads Cnwll......3 K5
Twelve Oaks E Susx......25 Q6
Twemlow Green Ches E......82 G11
Twenty Lincs......74 C6
Twerton BaNES......20 D2
Twickenham Gt Lon......36 E6
Twigworth Gloucs......46 F10
Twineham W Susx......24 G7
Twineham Green W Susx......24 G6
Twinhoe BaNES......20 E3
Twinstead Essex......52 E4
Twitchen Devon......17 P5
Twitchen Shrops......56 F9
Twitham Kent......39 N10
Two Bridges Devon......6 G4
Two Dales Derbys......84 C8
Two Gates Staffs......59 K4
Two Mile Ash W Susx......24 D5
Two Mile Oak Cross Devon......7 L5
Two Pots Devon......17 J3
Two Waters Herts......50 C9
Twycross Leics......72 A10
Twycross Zoo Leics......59 M3
Twyford Bucks......49 J9
Twyford Hants......22 E10
Twyford Leics......73 J8
Twyford Lincs......73 N6
Twyford Norfk......76 E7
Twyford Wokham......35 L9
Twyford Common Herefs......45 Q7
Twyn-carno Caerph......30 F3
Twynholm D & G......108 E10
Twyning Gloucs......46 G7
Twynllanan Carmth......43 Q10
Twyn-yr-Odyn V Glam......30 F10
Twyn-y-Sheriff Mons......31 M3
Twywell N Nhant......61 L5
Tyberton Herefs......45 M7
Tyburn Birm......58 H6
Tycroes Carmth......28 H2
Ty Croes IoA......78 E10
Tycrwyn Powys......68 F11
Tydd Gote Lincs......75 J7
Tydd St Giles Cambs......74 H7
Tydd St Mary Lincs......74 H7
Tye Hants......15 K6
Tye Green Essex......51 M6
Tye Green Essex......51 N3
Tye Green Essex......52 C7
Tyersal C Brad......90 F4
Tyldesley Wigan......82 E4
Tyler Hill Kent......39 K9
Tylers Green Bucks......35 P6
Tyler's Green Essex......51 M9
Tylers Green Surrey......37 J10
Tylorstown Rhondd......30 D5
Tylwch Powys......55 M8
Ty-nant Conwy......68 C6
Ty-nant Gwynd......68 B9
Tyncelyn Cerdgn......43 M2
Tyndrum Stirlg......139 Q11
Ty'n-dwr Denbgs......68 H6
Tyneham Dorset......12 E8
Tynemouth N Tyne......113 N7
Tyne Tunnel S Tyne......113 M7
Tynewydd Rhondd......29 P5
Tyninghame E Loth......128 G4
Tynron D & G......115 R9
Ty'n-y-bryn Rhondd......30 D7
Ty'n-y-coedcae Caerph......30 G7
Tynygongl IoA......79 J8
Tynygraig Cerdgn......54 F11
Ty'n-y-Groes Conwy......79 P10
Tyn-y-nant Rhondd......30 E7
Tyrie Abers......159 M5
Tyringham M Keyn......49 N5
Tyseley Birm......58 H8
Tythegston Brdgnd......29 N9
Tytherington Ches E......83 K9
Tytherington S Glos......32 C7
Tytherington Somset......20 E6
Tytherington Wilts......20 H6
Tytherleigh Devon......10 G4
Tytherton Lucas Wilts......32 H10
Tyttenhanger Herts......50 E9
Tywardreath Cnwll......4 H11
Tywardreath Highway Cnwll......4 H10
Tywyn Conwy......79 P9
Tywyn Gwynd......54 D4

U

Ubbeston Green Suffk......65 L7
Ubley BaNES......19 P3
Uckerby N York......103 P10
Uckfield E Susx......25 L6
Uckinghall Worcs......46 G7
Uckington Gloucs......46 H10
Uckington Shrops......57 K2
Uddingston S Lans......126 B5
Uddington S Lans......116 B4
Udimore E Susx......26 E8
Udny Green Abers......151 M2
Udny Station Abers......151 N3
Uffcott Wilts......33 M9
Uffculme Devon......9 Q2
Uffington Lincs......73 R9
Uffington Oxon......34 B7
Uffington Shrops......57 J2
Ufford C Pete......73 R10
Ufford Suffk......65 K11
Ufton Warwks......48 C2
Ufton Nervet W Berk......34 H11
Ugadale Ag & B......120 E6
Ugborough Devon......6 H7
Uggeshall Suffk......65 N5
Ugglebarnby N York......105 N9
Ughill Sheff......84 D3

Ugley Essex......51 M5
Ugley Green Essex......51 M5
Ugthorpe N York......105 L8
Uibhist A Deas W Isls......168 d14
Uibhist A Tuath W Isls......168 c10
Uig Ag & B......136 F5
Uig Highld......152 B7
Uig Highld......152 F5
Uig W Isls......168 f4
Uigshader Highld......152 G8
Uisken Ag & B......137 K12
Ulbster Highld......167 P9
Ulcat Row W & F......101 M6
Ulceby Lincs......87 M6
Ulceby N Linc......93 K8
Ulceby Skitter N Linc......93 K7
Ulcombe Kent......26 D2
Uldale Cumb......100 H3
Uley Gloucs......32 E5
Ulgham Nthumb......113 K2
Ullapool Highld......161 J8
Ullenhall Warwks......58 H11
Ullenwood Gloucs......46 H11
Ulleskelf N York......91 N3
Ullesthorpe Leics......60 B3
Ulley Rothm......84 G3
Ullingswick Herefs......46 A5
Ullock Cumb......100 E6
Ullswater W & F......101 M6
Ullswater 'Steamers' W & F......101 L7
Ulnes Walton Lancs......88 G7
Ulpha Cumb......94 D2
Ulpha W & F......95 K4
Ulrome E R Yk......99 P9
Ulsta Shet......169 r5
Ulting Wick Essex......52 D10
Ulva Ag & B......137 K7
Ulverley Green Solhll......58 H8
Ulverston W & F......94 F5
Ulwell Dorset......12 H8
Ulzieside D & G......115 Q6
Umberleigh Devon......17 L7
Unapool Highld......164 F10
Underbarrow W & F......95 K2
Under Burnmouth Border......111 J4
Undercliffe C Brad......90 F4
Underdale Shrops......57 J2
Underling Green Kent......26 C2
Underriver Kent......37 N10
Underwood Newpt......31 L7
Underwood Notts......84 G10
Undley Suffk......63 L4
Undy Mons......31 M7
Union Mills IoM......80 e6
Union Street E Susx......26 B5
Unst Shet......169 s3
Unstone Derbys......84 E5
Unstone Green Derbys......84 E5
Unthank Cumb......110 G11
Unthank Cumb......84 D5
Unthank Nthumb......129 P10
Unthank W & F......101 N3
Unthank W & F......102 B2
Upavon Wilts......21 M4
Up Cerne Dorset......11 P4
Upchurch Kent......38 D8
Upcott Devon......17 P6
Upcott Herefs......45 L4
Upend Cambs......63 M9
Up Exe Devon......9 M4
Upgate Norfk......76 G8
Upgate Street Norfk......64 F3
Upgate Street Norfk......65 K3
Uphall Dorset......11 M4
Uphall W Loth......127 K3
Upham Devon......9 L3
Upham Hants......22 F10
Uphampton Herefs......45 M2
Uphampton Worcs......46 F2
Uphill N Som......19 K3
Up Holland Lancs......88 G9
Uplawmoor E Rens......125 L6
Upleadon Gloucs......46 E9
Upleatham R & Cl......104 H7
Uplees Kent......38 H9
Uploders Dorset......11 L6
Uplowman Devon......18 D11
Uplyme Devon......10 G6
Up Marden W Susx......15 L4
Upminster Gt Lon......37 N3
Up Mudford Somset......19 Q11
Up Nately Hants......23 J4
Upottery Devon......10 E3
Upper Affcot Shrops......56 G7
Upper Arley Worcs......57 P8
Upper Arncott Oxon......48 H11
Upper Astrop W Nhant......48 F7
Upper Badcall Highld......164 E8
Upper Basildon W Berk......34 G9
Upper Batley Kirk......90 G5
Upper Beeding W Susx......24 E8
Upper Benefield N Nhant......61 L3
Upper Bentley Worcs......58 E11
Upper Bighouse Highld......166 E5
Upper Birchwood Derbys......84 F9
Upper Boat Rhondd......30 F7
Upper Boddington W Nhant......48 E4
Upper Borth Cerdgn......54 E7
Upper Brailes Warwks......48 B7
Upper Breinton Herefs......45 P6
Upper Broadheath Worcs......46 F3
Upper Broughton Notts......72 H5
Upper Bucklebury W Berk......34 F11
Upper Burgate Hants......21 N11
Upper Bush Medway......37 Q7
Upperby Cumb......110 H10
Upper Caldecote C Beds......61 Q11
Upper Canada N Som......19 L3
Upper Canterton Hants......13 N2
Upper Catesby W Nthn......48 E3
Upper Catshill Worcs......58 E10
Upper Chapel Powys......44 E6
Upper Cheddon Somset......18 H9
Upper Chicksgrove Wilts......21 J9
Upper Chute Wilts......21 Q4
Upper Clapton Gt Lon......36 H3
Upper Clatford Hants......22 C6
Upper Coberley Gloucs......47 J11
Upper Cotton Staffs......71 K5
Upper Cound Shrops......57 K3
Upper Cudworth Barns......91 K9
Upper Cumberworth Kirk......90 G9
Upper Dallachy Moray......157 R5
Upper Deal Kent......39 Q11
Upper Dean Bed......61 M7
Upper Denby Kirk......90 G9

Ugley Green Essex......51 M5 (see above)
Upper Denton Cumb......111 M7
Upper Dicker E Susx......25 N9
Upper Dinchope Shrops......56 H8
Upper Dounreay Highld......166 H3
Upper Dovercourt Essex......53 M5
Upper Drumbane Stirlg......133 K6
Upper Dunsforth N York......97 P8
Upper Eashing Surrey......23 Q6
Upper Eathie Highld......156 D5
Upper Egleton Herefs......46 B6
Upper Elkstone Staffs......71 K3
Upper Ellastone Staffs......71 L6
Upper End Derbys......83 N9
Upper Enham Hants......22 C4
Upper Farmcote Shrops......57 P6
Upper Farringdon Hants......23 K7
Upper Framilode Gloucs......32 D3
Upper Froyle Hants......23 L6
Upperglen Highld......152 E7
Upper Godney Somset......19 N6
Upper Gravenhurst C Beds......50 D3
Upper Green Mons......45 M11
Upper Green W Berk......63 M8
Upper Green W Berk......C2
Upper Grove Common Herefs......45 R9
Upper Hackney Derbys......84 C8
Upper Hale Surrey......23 M5
Upper Halliford Surrey......36 C7
Upper Halling Medway......37 Q8
Upper Hambleton Rutlnd......73 N9
Upper Hardres Court Kent......39 L11
Upper Hardwick Herefs......45 N3
Upper Hartfield E Susx......25 L4
Upper Hartshay Derbys......84 E10
Upper Hatherley Gloucs......46 H10
Upper Hatton Staffs......70 E7
Upper Haugh Rothm......91 L11
Upper Hayton Shrops......57 J8
Upper Heaton Kirk......90 F7
Upper Helmsley N York......98 D9
Upper Hergest Herefs......45 K4
Upper Heyford Oxon......48 E9
Upper Heyford W Nthn......60 E9
Upper Hill Herefs......45 P4
Upper Hockenden Kent......37 M7
Upper Hopton Kirk......90 F7
Upper Howsell Worcs......46 E5
Upper Hulme Staffs......71 J2
Upper Ifold Surrey......24 B4
Upper Inglesham Swindn......33 P5
Upper Kilcott Gloucs......32 E7
Upper Killay Swans......28 G6
Upper Kinchrackine Ag & B......131 P2
Upper Knockando Moray......157 M9
Upper Lambourn W Berk......34 B8
Upper Landywood Staffs......58 E3
Upper Langford N Som......19 N3
Upper Langwith Derbys......84 G7
Upper Largo Fife......135 L7
Upper Layham Suffk......52 H3
Upper Leigh Staffs......71 J7
Upper Littleton N Som......19 Q2
Upper Lochton Abers......150 H8
Upper Longdon Staffs......58 G2
Upper Ludstone Shrops......57 Q5
Upper Lybster Highld......167 N9
Upper Lydbrook Gloucs......46 B11
Upper Lyde Herefs......45 P6
Upper Lye Herefs......56 F11
Upper Maes-coed Herefs......45 L8
Upper Marham Norfk......75 P9
Upper Midhope Sheff......90 G11
Uppermill Oldham......90 B9
Upper Milton Worcs......57 Q10
Upper Minety Wilts......33 K6
Upper Moor Worcs......47 J5
Upper Moor Side Leeds......90 G4
Upper Mulben Moray......157 R7
Upper Netchwood Shrops......57 L6
Upper Nobut Staffs......71 J7
Upper Norwood W Susx......23 P11
Upper Oddington Gloucs......47 P9
Upper Padley Derbys......84 B5
Upper Pennington Hants......13 P5
Upper Pollicott Bucks......35 K2
Upper Poppleton C York......98 B10
Upper Quinton Warwks......47 N5
Upper Ratley Hants......22 B10
Upper Rissington Gloucs......47 P11
Upper Rochford Worcs......57 L11
Upper Ruscoe D & G......108 C8
Upper Sapey Herefs......46 C2
Upper Saxondale Notts......72 H3
Upper Seagry Wilts......32 H8
Upper Shelton C Beds......49 Q5
Upper Sheringham Norfk......76 G3
Upper Skelmorlie N Ayrs......124 G4
Upper Slaughter Gloucs......47 N10
Upper Soudley Gloucs......32 C2
Upper Spond Herefs......45 L4
Upper Standen Kent......27 M3
Upper Staploe Bed......61 P9
Upper Stoke Norfk......77 K11
Upper Stondon C Beds......50 D3
Upper Stowe W Nthn......60 D9
Upper Street Hants......21 N11
Upper Street Norfk......64 H6
Upper Street Norfk......77 L8
Upper Street Norfk......77 M8
Upper Street Suffk......53 K5
Upper Street Suffk......63 N10
Upper Street Suffk......64 G11
Upper Strensham Worcs......46 G7
Upper Sundon C Beds......50 B5
Upper Swell Gloucs......47 N9
Upper Tankersley Barns......91 J11
Upper Tean Staffs......71 J7
Upperthong Kirk......90 E9
Upperthorpe Derbys......84 G4
Upperthorpe N Linc......92 C10
Upper Threapwood Ches W......69 M5
Upperton W Susx......23 N10
Upper Town Derbys......71 N4
Uppertown Derbys......84 D7
Upper Town Dur......103 L3
Upper Town Herefs......46 A5
Uppertown Highld......167 Q1
Upper Town N Som......31 N11
Upper Town Suffk......64 C8
Upper Tumble Carmth......28 F2
Upper Tysoe Warwks......48 B6
Upper Ufford Suffk......65 K11
Upperup Gloucs......33 K5
Upper Upham Wilts......33 P9

Upper Upnor Medway......38 C7
Upper Victoria Angus......143 J10
Upper Vobster Somset......20 D5
Upper Wardington Oxon......48 E5
Upper Weald M Keyn......49 M7
Upper Weedon W Nthn......60 D9
Upper Welland Worcs......46 E6
Upper Wellingham E Susx......25 K8
Upper Weston BaNES......32 D11
Upper Weybread Suffk......65 J6
Upper Wick Worcs......46 F4
Upper Wield Hants......22 H7
Upper Winchendon Bucks......35 K2
Upperwood Derbys......84 C9
Upper Woodford Wilts......21 M7
Upper Woolhampton W Berk......34 G11
Upper Wootton Hants......22 G4
Upper Wraxall Wilts......32 F10
Upper Wyche Worcs......46 E6
Uppincott Devon......9 M3
Uppingham Rutlnd......73 M11
Uppington Dorset......12 H3
Uppington Shrops......57 K3
Upsall N York......97 Q3
Upsettlington Border......129 M10
Upshire Essex......51 K10
Up Somborne Hants......22 C8
Upstreet Kent......39 M9
Up Sydling Dorset......11 N4
Upthorpe Suffk......64 D7
Upton Bucks......35 L2
Upton C Pete......74 B10
Upton Cambs......61 Q5
Upton Ches W......81 N11
Upton Cnwll......5 M7
Upton Cnwll......16 C11
Upton Cumb......101 K3
Upton Devon......7 J10
Upton Devon......10 B4
Upton Dorset......8 B8
Upton Dorset......12 G6
Upton E R Yk......99 N10
Upton Halton......81 P7
Upton Hants......22 C11
Upton Hants......22 C3
Upton Leics......72 B11
Upton Lincs......85 Q3
Upton Norfk......77 M10
Upton Notts......85 M10
Upton Notts......85 M5
Upton Oxon......33 P2
Upton Oxon......34 F7
Upton Pembks......41 K10
Upton R & Cl......105 K7
Upton Slough......35 Q9
Upton Somset......18 C9
Upton Somset......19 M9
Upton W Nthn......60 F9
Upton Wakefd......91 M9
Upton Warwks......47 M3
Upton Wilts......20 G9
Upton Wirral......81 K7
Upton Bishop Herefs......46 C9
Upton Cheyney S Glos......32 C10
Upton Cressett Shrops......57 M6
Upton Crews Herefs......46 B9
Upton Cross Cnwll......5 M7
Upton End C Beds......50 D4
Upton Grey Hants......23 J5
Upton Heath Ches W......81 N11
Upton Hellions Devon......9 K4
Upton Lovell Wilts......20 H6
Upton Magna Shrops......57 K2
Upton Noble Somset......20 D7
Upton Pyne Devon......9 M5
Upton St Leonards Gloucs......46 G11
Upton Scudamore Wilts......20 G5
Upton Snodsbury Worcs......46 H4
Upton Towans Cnwll......2 F5
Upton-upon-Severn Worcs......46 G6
Upton Warren Worcs......58 D11
Upwaltham W Susx......15 P4
Upware Cambs......62 H6
Upwell Norfk......75 J10
Upwey Dorset......11 P7
Upwick Green Herts......51 L6
Upwood Cambs......62 C4
Urchfont Wilts......21 K3
Urdimarsh Herefs......45 Q5
Ure Bank N York......97 M7
Urlay Nook S on T......104 D8
Urmston Traffd......82 G6
Urpeth Dur......113 L10
Urquhart Moray......157 P5
Urquhart Castle Highld......147 N2
Urra N York......104 G10
Urray Highld......155 P7
Ury Abers......151 M10
Uryside Abers......151 K3
Usan Abers......143 N7
Ushaw Moor Dur......103 P2
Usk Mons......31 L4
Usselby Lincs......86 E2
Usworth Sundld......113 M9
Utkinton Ches W......82 B11
Utley C Brad......90 D2
Uton Devon......9 K5
Utterby Lincs......87 K2
Uttoxeter Staffs......71 K8
Uwchmynydd Gwynd......66 B9
Uxbridge Gt Lon......36 C4
Uyeasound Shet......169 s3
Uzmaston Pembks......41 J8

V

Vale Guern......10 c1
Valley IoA......78 D9
Valley End Surrey......23 Q2
Valley Truckle Cnwll......4 H5
Valtos Highld......153 J5
Valtos W Isls......168 f4
Vange Essex......38 B4
Varteg Torfn......31 J3
Vatsetter Shet......169 s5
Vatten Highld......152 D7
Vaynor Myr Td......30 D2
Vazon Bay Guern......10 b2
Velindre Powys......44 H7
Vellow Somset......18 E7
Velly Devon......16 D7
Venngreen Devon......16 F9

Vennington – West Auckland 299

Vennington Shrops 56 E3
Venn Ottery Devon 10 B6
Venny Tedburn Devon 9 K5
Venterdon Cnwll 5 P7
Ventnor IoW 14 G11
Venton Devon 6 F7
Vernham Dean Hants 22 B3
Vernham Street Hants 22 B3
Vernolds Common Shrops 56 H8
Verwood Dorset 13 J3
Veryan Cnwll 3 N6
Veryan Green Cnwll 3 N5
Vicarage Devon 10 E7
Vickerstown W & F 94 D7
Victoria Barns 90 F9
Victoria Blae G 30 G3
Victoria Cnwll 4 F9
Vidlin Shet 169 r7
Viewfield Moray 157 P5
Viewpark N Lans 126 C5
Vigo Kent 37 P8
Village de Putron Guern 10 c2
Ville la Bas Jersey 11 a1
Villiaze Guern 10 b2
Vinehall Street E Susx 26 C7
Vines Cross E Susx 25 N7
Virginia Water Surrey 36 B7
Virginstow Devon 5 P3
Vobster Somset 20 D5
Voe Shet 169 r7
Vowchurch Herefs 45 M7
Vulcan Village St Hel 82 C6

W

Waberthwaite Cumb 94 C2
Wackerfield Dur 103 N6
Wacton Norfk 64 H3
Wadborough Worcs 46 H5
Waddesdon Bucks 49 K11
Waddesdon Manor Bucks 49 K11
Waddeton Devon 7 M7
Waddicar Sefton 81 M5
Waddingham Lincs 92 G11
Waddington Lancs 89 L2
Waddington Lincs 86 C8
Waddon Devon 9 L9
Waddon Dorset 11 N7
Waddon Gt Lon 36 H8
Wadebridge Cnwll 4 F7
Wadeford Somset 10 G2
Wadenhoe N Nthn 61 M4
Wadesmill Herts 51 J7
Wadhurst E Susx 25 P4
Wadshelf Derbys 84 D6
Wadswick Wilts 32 F11
Wadworth Donc 91 P11
Waen Denbgs 68 C2
Waen Denbgs 80 G11
Waen Powys 68 H11
Waen Fach Powys 68 H11
Waen-pentir Gwynd 79 K11
Waen-wen Gwynd 79 K11
Wagbeach Shrops 56 F4
Wainfelin Torfn 31 J4
Wainfleet All Saints Lincs 87 N9
Wainfleet Bank Lincs 87 N9
Wainfleet St Mary Lincs 87 N9
Wainford Norfk 65 L3
Wainhouse Corner Cnwll 5 K2
Wainscott Medway 38 B7
Wain's Hill N Som 31 L10
Wainstalls Calder 90 C5
Waitby W & F 102 E9
Waithe Lincs 93 N10
Wakefield Wakefd 91 J6
Wake Green Birm 58 G8
Wakehurst W Susx 24 H4
Wakerley N Nthn 73 P11
Wakes Colne Essex 52 E6
Walberswick Suffk 65 P7
Walberton W Susx 15 Q5
Walbottle N u Ty 113 J7
Walbutt D & G 108 F7
Walby Cumb 110 H8
Walcombe Somset 19 Q5
Walcot Lincs 73 R3
Walcot N Linc 92 E6
Walcot Shrops 56 E7
Walcot Shrops 57 K2
Walcot Swindn 33 N8
Walcote Leics 60 C4
Walcote Warwks 47 M3
Walcot Green Norfk 64 G5
Walcott Lincs 86 F9
Walcott Norfk 77 M5
Walden N York 96 F4
Walden Head N York 96 E4
Walden Stubbs N York 91 P7
Walderslade Medway 38 C9
Walderton W Susx 15 L4
Walditch Dorset 11 K6
Waldley Derbys 71 L7
Waldridge Dur 113 L11
Waldringfield Suffk 53 N2
Waldron E Susx 25 M7
Wales Rothm 84 G4
Wales Somset 19 Q10
Walesby Lincs 86 F2
Walesby Notts 85 L6
Walford Herefs 46 A10
Walford Herefs 56 F10
Walford Shrops 69 M10
Walford Staffs 70 E8
Walford Heath Shrops 69 M11
Walgherton Ches E 70 B5
Walgrave W Nthn 60 H6
Walhampton Hants 13 P5
Walkden Salfd 82 F4
Walker N u Ty 113 L8
Walkerburn Border 117 M3
Walker Fold Lancs 89 K2
Walkeringham Notts 85 N2
Walkerith Lincs 85 N2
Walkern Herts 50 G5
Walker's Green Herefs 45 Q5
Walker's Heath Birm 58 G9
Walkerton Fife 134 G7
Walkford BCP 13 M6
Walkhampton Devon 6 E5
Walkington E R Yk 92 G3
Walkley Sheff 84 D3
Walk Mill Lancs 89 P5
Walkwood Worcs 47 K2
Wall Nthumb 112 D7
Wall Staffs 58 H3
Wallacetown S Ayrs 114 E7
Wallacetown S Ayrs 114 F3
Wallands Park E Susx 25 K8
Wallasey Wirral 81 K6
Wallasey (Kingsway) Tunnel Wirral 81 L6
Wall End Herefs 45 N3
Wallend Medway 38 E6
Wall End W & F 94 E4
Waller's Green Herefs 46 C7
Wallhead Cumb 111 J8
Wall Heath Dudley 58 C7
Wall Houses Nthumb 112 F7
Wallingford Oxon 34 H7
Wallington Gt Lon 36 G8
Wallington Hants 14 G5
Wallington Herts 50 G4
Wallington Heath Wsall 58 E4
Wallis Pembks 41 K5
Wallisdown BCP 13 J6
Walliswood Surrey 24 D3
Walls Shet 169 p9
Wallsend N Tyne 113 L7
Wallthwaite W & F 101 L5
Wall under Haywood Shrops 57 J6
Wallyford E Loth 128 B5
Walmer Kent 39 Q11
Walmer Bridge Lancs 88 F6
Walmersley Bury 89 N8
Walmestone Kent 39 N10
Walmley Birm 58 H6
Walmley Ash Birm 58 H6
Walmsgate Lincs 87 L5
Walney W & F 94 D7
Walpole Somset 19 K6
Walpole Suffk 65 M7
Walpole Cross Keys Norfk 75 K7
Walpole Highway Norfk 75 K8
Walpole St Andrew Norfk 75 K7
Walpole St Peter Norfk 75 K7
Walrow Somset 19 K5
Walsall Wsall 58 F5
Walsall Wood Wsall 58 F4
Walsden Calder 89 Q6
Walsgrave on Sowe Covtry 59 N8
Walsham le Willows Suffk 64 E7
Walshaw Bury 89 M8
Walshford N York 97 P10
Walsoken Norfk 75 J8
Walston S Lans 127 K8
Walsworth Herts 50 E4
Walter's Ash Bucks 35 M5
Walters Green Kent 25 M2
Walterston V Glam 30 E10
Walterstone Herefs 45 L9
Waltham Kent 27 K2
Waltham NE Lin 93 N10
Waltham Abbey Essex 51 J10
Waltham Chase Hants 14 G4
Waltham Cross Herts 51 J10
Waltham on the Wolds Leics 73 L6
Waltham St Lawrence W & M 35 M9
Waltham's Cross Essex 51 Q4
Walthamstow Gt Lon 37 J3
Walton C Pete 74 C10
Walton Cumb 111 K8
Walton Derbys 84 E7
Walton Leeds 97 P11
Walton Leics 60 C3
Walton M Keyn 49 N7
Walton Powys 45 K3
Walton Shrops 56 H9
Walton Somset 19 N7
Walton Staffs 70 F8
Walton Staffs 70 F9
Walton Suffk 53 N4
Walton W Susx 15 M6
Walton Wakefd 91 K7
Walton Warwks 47 Q4
Walton Wrekin 69 Q11
Walton Cardiff Gloucs 46 H8
Walton East Pembks 41 K6
Walton Elm Dorset 20 E11
Walton Grounds W Nthn 48 F8
Walton Highway Norfk 75 J8
Walton-in-Gordano N Som 31 M10
Walton-le-Dale Lancs 88 H5
Walton-on-Thames Surrey 36 D7
Walton-on-the-Hill Staffs 70 H10
Walton-on-the-Hill Surrey 36 F9
Walton-on-the-Naze Essex 53 M7
Walton on the Wolds Leics 72 F7
Walton-on-Trent Derbys 71 N11
Walton Park N Som 31 M10
Walton West Pembks 40 G8
Walwen Flints 80 G9
Walwen Flints 80 H10
Walwen Flints 81 J9
Walwick Nthumb 112 D6
Walworth Darltn 103 P7
Walworth Gt Lon 36 H5
Walworth Gate Darltn 103 P6
Walwyn's Castle Pembks 40 G8
Wambrook Somset 10 F3
Wampool Cumb 110 D10
Wanborough Surrey 23 P5
Wanborough Swindn 33 P8
Wandon End Herts 50 D6
Wandsworth Gt Lon 36 G6
Wangford Suffk 65 P6
Wanlip Leics 72 F8
Wanlockhead D & G 116 B8
Wannock E Susx 25 N10
Wansford C Pete 73 R11
Wansford E R Yk 99 M9
Wanshurst Green Kent 26 C2
Wanstead Gt Lon 37 K3
Wanstrow Somset 20 D6
Wanswell Gloucs 32 C4
Wantage Oxon 34 C7
Wants Green Worcs 46 E3
Wapley S Glos 32 D9
Wappenbury Warwks 59 N11
Wappenham W Nthn 48 H5
Warbleton E Susx 25 P7
Warborough Oxon 34 G6
Warboys Cambs 62 D4
Warbreck Bpool 88 C3
Warbstow Cnwll 5 L3
Warburton Traffd 82 F7
Warcop W & F 102 D7
Warden Kent 38 H7
Warden Nthumb 112 D7
Ward End Birm 58 H7
Warden Street C Beds 50 D2
Ward Green Suffk 64 E9
Ward Green Cross Lancs 89 J3
Wardhedges C Beds 50 C3
Wardington Oxon 48 E5
Wardle Ches E 69 R3
Wardle Rochdl 89 Q7
Wardley Gatesd 113 M8
Wardley Rutlnd 73 L10
Wardley Salfd 82 G4
Wardlow Derbys 83 Q10
Wardsend Ches E 83 K8
Wardy Hill Cambs 62 G4
Ware Herts 51 J8
Wareham Dorset 12 F7
Warehorne Kent 26 G5
Warenford Nthumb 119 M5
Waren Mill Nthumb 119 M4
Warenton Nthumb 119 M4
Wareside Herts 51 J7
Waresley Cambs 62 C10
Waresley Worcs 58 B10
Ware Street Kent 38 C10
Warfield Br For 35 N10
Warfleet Devon 7 M8
Wargate Lincs 74 D4
Wargrave Wokham 35 L9
Warham Herefs 45 P7
Warham Norfk 76 D3
Wark Nthumb 112 C5
Wark Nthumb 118 F3
Warkleigh Devon 17 L7
Warkton N Nthn 61 J5
Warkworth Nthumb 119 P9
Warkworth W Nthn 48 E6
Warlaby N York 97 M2
Warland Calder 89 Q6
Warleggan Cnwll 5 K8
Warleigh BaNES 20 E2
Warley Town Calder 90 D6
Warlingham Surrey 37 J9
Warmbrook Derbys 71 P4
Warmfield Wakefd 91 K6
Warmingham Ches E 70 C2
Warmington N Nthn 61 N2
Warmington Warwks 48 D5
Warminster Wilts 20 G5
Warmley S Glos 32 C10
Warmsworth Donc 91 N10
Warmwell Dorset 12 C7
Warndon Worcs 46 G3
Warner Bros. Studio Tour London Herts 50 C10
Warnford Hants 22 H10
Warnham W Susx 24 E4
Warningcamp W Susx 24 B9
Warninglid W Susx 24 F5
Warren Ches E 83 J10
Warren Pembks 40 H11
Warrenby R & Cl 104 G5
Warrenhill S Lans 116 C3
Warren Row W & M 35 M8
Warren's Green Herts 50 G5
Warren Street Kent 38 F11
Warrington M Keyn 49 N4
Warrington Warrtn 82 D7
Warriston C Edin 127 P2
Warsash Hants 14 E5
Warslow Staffs 71 K3
Warsop Vale Notts 84 H7
Warter E R Yk 98 H10
Warthermaske N York 97 K5
Warthill N York 98 D9
Wartling E Susx 25 Q9
Wartnaby Leics 73 J6
Warton Lancs 88 E5
Warton Lancs 95 K6
Warton Nthumb 119 K10
Warton Warwks 59 L4
Warwick Warwks 59 L11
Warwick Bridge Cumb 111 J9
Warwick Castle Warwks 47 Q2
Warwick-on-Eden Cumb 111 J9
Warwick Services Warwks 48 B3
Warwicksland Cumb 111 J5
Wasbister Ork 169 c3
Wasdale Head Cumb 100 G9
Wash Derbys 83 N8
Washall Green Herts 51 K4
Washaway Cnwll 4 G8
Washbourne Devon 7 K8
Washbrook Somset 19 M4
Washbrook Suffk 53 K3
Washfield Devon 18 B11
Washfold N York 103 L10
Washford Somset 18 E6
Washford Pyne Devon 9 K2
Washingborough Lincs 86 D6
Washington Sundld 113 M9
Washington W Susx 24 D8
Washington Services Gatesd 113 L9
Washwood Heath Birm 58 H7
Wasing W Berk 22 G2
Waskerley Dur 112 F11
Wasperton Warwks 47 Q3
Wasps Nest Lincs 86 E8
Wass N York 98 B5
Wast Water Cumb 100 G9
Watchet Somset 18 E6
Watchfield Oxon 33 P6
Watchfield Somset 19 K5
Watchgate W & F 101 P11
Watchill Cumb 100 G2
Watcombe Torbay 7 N5
Watendlath Cumb 101 J7
Water Devon 9 J8
Water Lancs 89 N5
Waterbeach Cambs 62 G7
Waterbeach W Susx 15 N5
Waterbeck D & G 110 D5
Waterden Norfk 76 B4
Water Eaton Oxon 34 F2
Water Eaton Staffs 58 D2
Water End Bed 61 P10
Water End Bed 61 P11
Water End C Beds 50 C3
Waterend Cumb 100 F6
Water End E R Yk 92 C3
Water End Essex 51 N2
Water End Herts 50 B8
Water End Herts 50 F10
Waterfall Staffs 71 K4
Waterfoot Ag & B 120 F4
Waterfoot E Rens 125 P6
Waterfoot Lancs 89 N6
Waterford Herts 50 H8
Water Fryston Wakefd 91 M5
Watergate Cnwll 5 J5
Waterhead W & F 101 L10
Waterheads Border 127 N7
Waterhouses Dur 103 N2
Waterhouses Staffs 71 K4
Wateringbury Kent 37 Q10
Waterlane Gloucs 32 H4
Waterloo Cnwll 5 J7
Waterloo Derbys 84 F8
Waterloo Herefs 45 L5
Waterloo Highld 145 L3
Waterloo N Lans 126 E7
Waterloo Norfk 77 J8
Waterloo P & K 141 Q10
Waterloo Pembks 41 J10
Waterloo Sefton 81 L5
Waterloo Cross Devon 9 Q2
Waterloo Port Gwynd 66 H2
Waterlooville Hants 15 J5
Watermead Bucks 49 M11
Watermillock W & F 101 M6
Water Newton Cambs 74 B11
Water Orton Warwks 59 J6
Waterperry Oxon 34 H3
Waterrow Somset 18 E9
Watersfield W Susx 24 B7
Waterside Bl w D 89 L6
Waterside Bucks 35 Q4
Waterside Cumb 110 D11
Waterside Donc 91 R8
Waterside E Ayrs 114 H6
Waterside E Ayrs 125 M9
Waterside E Duns 126 B3
Water's Nook Bolton 89 K9
Waterstein Highld 152 A8
Waterstock Oxon 34 H3
Waterston Pembks 40 H9
Water Stratford Bucks 49 J8
Water Street Neath 29 M8
Waters Upton Wrekin 70 A11
Water Yeat W & F 94 F3
Watford Herts 50 D11
Watford W Nthn 60 D7
Watford Gap Services W Nthn 60 D7
Wath N York 96 H7
Wath N York 97 M5
Wath upon Dearne Rothm 91 L10
Watlington Norfk 75 M8
Watlington Oxon 35 J6
Watnall Notts 84 H11
Watten Highld 167 M6
Wattisfield Suffk 64 E7
Wattisham Suffk 64 E11
Watton Dorset 11 K6
Watton E R Yk 99 L10
Watton Norfk 76 C11
Watton-at-Stone Herts 50 H7
Watton Green Norfk 76 C11
Wattons Green Essex 51 M11
Wattston N Lans 126 D3
Wattstown Rhondd 30 D6
Wattsville Caerph 30 H6
Wauldby E R Yk 92 G5
Waulkmill Abers 150 G9
Waunarlwydd Swans 28 H5
Waun Fach Powys 44 H9
Waunfawr Cerdgn 54 E8
Waunfawr Gwynd 67 J3
Waungron Swans 28 G4
Waunlwyd Blae G 30 G3
Wavendon M Keyn 49 P7
Waverbridge Cumb 110 D11
Waverley Rothm 84 F3
Waverton Ches W 69 N2
Waverton Cumb 110 D11
Wawne E R Yk 93 J3
Waxham Norfk 77 N6
Waxholme E R Yk 93 P5
Way Kent 39 P8
Waye Devon 7 K4
Wayford Somset 11 J3
Waytown Dorset 11 K5
Way Village Devon 9 L2
Way Wick N Som 19 L2
Weacombe Somset 18 F6
Weald Oxon 34 B4
Wealdstone Gt Lon 36 E3
Weardley Leeds 90 H2
Weare Somset 19 M4
Weare Giffard Devon 16 H7
Wearhead Dur 102 G3
Wearne Somset 19 M9
Weasdale W & F 102 C10
Weasenham All Saints Norfk 76 A7
Weasenham St Peter Norfk 76 B7
Weaste Salfd 82 H5
Weatheroak Hill Worcs 58 G10
Weaverham Ches W 82 D10
Weaverslake Staffs 71 L11
Weaverthorpe N York 99 K6
Webbington Somset 19 L3
Webb's Heath S Glos 32 C10
Webheath Worcs 58 F11
Webton Herefs 45 N7
Wedderlairs Abers 159 L11
Wedding Hall Fold N York 96 D11
Weddington Kent 39 N10
Weddington Warwks 59 N6
Wedhampton Wilts 21 L3
Wedmore Somset 19 M5
Wednesbury Sandw 58 E5
Wednesfield Wolves 58 D4
Weecar Notts 85 P7
Weedon Bucks 49 M11
Weedon Bec W Nthn 60 D9
Weedon Lois W Nthn 48 H5
Weeford Staffs 58 H4
Week Devon 7 K6
Week Devon 17 K6
Week Devon 17 N8
Weeke Devon 9 J3
Weeke Hants 22 E8
Weekley N Nthn 61 J4
Week St Mary Cnwll 5 L2
Weel E R Yk 93 J3
Weeley Essex 53 K7
Weeley Heath Essex 53 L7
Weem P & K 141 K8
Weeping Cross Staffs 70 G10
Weethley Warwks 47 L3
Weeting Norfk 63 N3
Weeton E R Yk 93 Q6
Weeton Lancs 88 D4
Weeton N York 97 L11
Weetwood Leeds 90 H3
Weir Lancs 89 P5
Weirbrook Shrops 69 K10
Weir Quay Devon 6 C5
Weisdale Shet 169 q8
Welborne Norfk 76 F9
Welbourn Lincs 86 C10
Welburn N York 98 E7
Welbury N York 104 C10
Welby Lincs 73 P3
Welches Dam Cambs 62 G3
Welcombe Devon 16 C8
Weldon N Nthn 61 K3
Weldon Bridge Nthumb 119 M11
Welford W Berk 34 D10
Welford W Nthn 60 D4
Welford-on-Avon Warwks 47 M4
Welham Leics 60 G2
Welham Notts 85 M4
Welham Bridge E R Yk 92 C4
Welham Green Herts 50 F9
Well Hants 23 L5
Well Lincs 87 M6
Well N York 97 L4
Welland Worcs 46 E6
Wellbank Angus 142 H10
Well End Bucks 35 N7
Well End Herts 50 F11
Wellesbourne Warwks 47 Q3
Wellesbourne Mountford Warwks 47 Q3
Well Head Herts 50 E5
Well Hill Kent 37 L8
Wellhouse W Berk 34 F10
Welling Gt Lon 37 L5
Wellingborough N Nthn 61 J7
Wellingham Norfk 76 B7
Wellingore Lincs 86 C9
Wellington Cumb 100 E10
Wellington Herefs 45 P5
Wellington Somset 18 F10
Wellington Wrekin 57 M2
Wellington Heath Herefs 46 D6
Wellington Marsh Herefs 45 P5
Wellow BaNES 20 D3
Wellow IoW 14 C9
Wellow Notts 85 L7
Wellpond Green Herts 51 K6
Wells Somset 19 P5
Wellsborough Leics 72 B10
Wells Green Ches E 70 B4
Wells Head C Brad 90 D4
Wells-next-the-Sea Norfk 76 C3
Wellstye Green Essex 51 P7
Well Town Devon 9 M3
Welltree P & K 134 B3
Wellwood Fife 134 D10
Welney Norfk 62 H2
Welshampton Shrops 69 M7
Welsh Bicknor Herefs 46 A11
Welsh End Shrops 69 P7
Welsh Frankton Shrops 69 L8
Welsh Hook Pembks 40 H5
Welsh Newton Herefs 45 Q11
Welshpool Powys 56 C3
Welsh St Donats V Glam 30 D9
Welton Cumb 101 L2
Welton E R Yk 92 G5
Welton Lincs 86 D5
Welton W Nthn 60 C7
Welton le Marsh Lincs 87 N7
Welton le Wold Lincs 87 J3
Welwick E R Yk 93 P6
Welwyn Herts 50 F7
Welwyn Garden City Herts 50 F8
Wem Shrops 69 P9
Wembdon Somset 19 J7
Wembley Gt Lon 36 E3
Wembury Devon 6 E9
Wembworthy Devon 17 M10
Wemyss Bay Inver 124 F4
Wenallt Cerdgn 54 F10
Wendens Ambo Essex 51 M3
Wendlebury Oxon 48 G11
Wendling Norfk 76 C9
Wendover Bucks 35 N3
Wendron Cnwll 2 H7
Wendron Mining District Cnwll 2 H7
Wendy Cambs 62 D11
Wenfordbridge Cnwll 4 H6
Wenhaston Suffk 65 N6
Wennington Cambs 62 B5
Wennington Gt Lon 37 M4
Wennington Lancs 95 N7
Wensley Derbys 84 C8
Wensley N York 96 G3
Wentbridge Wakefd 91 M7
Wentnor Shrops 56 F6
Wentworth Cambs 62 G5
Wentworth Rothm 91 K11
Wenvoe V Glam 30 F10
Weobley Herefs 45 N4
Weobley Marsh Herefs 45 N4
Wepham W Susx 24 B9
Wereham Norfk 75 N10
Wergs Wolves 58 C4
Wern Gwynd 67 J7
Wern Powys 44 G11
Wern Powys 56 D2
Wern Shrops 69 J8
Werneth Low Tamesd 83 L6
Wernffrwd Swans 28 F6
Wern-Gifford Mons 45 L10
Wern-y-gaer Flints 81 J11
Werrington C Pete 74 C10
Werrington Cnwll 5 N4
Werrington Staffs 70 G5
Wervin Ches W 81 N10
Wesham Lancs 88 E4
Wessington Derbys 84 E9
West Aberthaw V Glam 30 D11
West Acre Norfk 75 Q7
West Allerdean Nthumb 129 P10
West Alvington Devon 7 J10
West Amesbury Wilts 21 M6
West Anstey Devon 17 R6
West Appleton N York 97 K2
West Ashby Lincs 87 J6
West Ashling W Susx 15 M5
West Ashton Wilts 20 G3
West Auckland Dur 103 N5

300 West Ayton – Whitefield Lane End

West Ayton N York 99 K4
West Bagborough Somset 18 G8
West Bank Blae G 30 H3
West Bank Halton 81 Q8
West Barkwith Lincs 86 G4
West Barnby N York 105 M8
West Barns E Loth 128 H4
West Barsham Norfk 76 C5
West Bay Dorset 11 K6
West Beckham Norfk 76 G4
West Bedfont Surrey 36 C6
Westbere Kent 39 L9
West Bergholt Essex 52 G6
West Bexington Dorset 11 L7
West Bilney Norfk 75 P7
West Blatchington Br & H 24 G9
West Boldon S Tyne 113 N8
Westborough Lincs 73 M2
Westbourne BCP 13 J6
Westbourne W Susx 15 L5
West Bourton Dorset 20 E9
West Bowling C Brad 90 F4
West Brabourne Kent 27 J3
West Bradenham Norfk 76 C10
West Bradford Lancs 89 L2
West Bradley Somset 19 Q7
West Bretton Wakefd 90 H8
West Bridgford Notts 72 F3
West Briscoe Dur 103 J7
West Bromwich Sandw 58 F6
Westbrook Kent 39 P7
Westbrook W Berk 34 D10
Westbrook Wilts 33 J11
West Buckland Devon 17 M5
West Buckland Somset 18 G10
West Burrafirth Shet 169 p8
West Burton N York 96 F3
West Burton W Susx 15 Q4
Westbury Bucks 48 H7
Westbury Shrops 56 F3
Westbury Wilts 20 G4
Westbury Leigh Wilts 20 G5
Westbury-on-Severn Gloucs 32 D2
Westbury-on-Trym Bristl 31 Q9
Westbury-sub-Mendip Somset 19 P5
West Butsfield Dur 103 M2
West Butterwick N Linc 92 D9
Westby Lancs 88 D4
West Byfleet Surrey 36 B8
West Cairngaan D & G 106 F11
West Caister Norfk 77 Q9
West Calder W Loth 127 J5
West Camel Somset 19 Q10
West Chaldon Dorset 12 C8
West Challow Oxon 34 C7
West Charleton Devon 7 K10
West Chelborough Dorset 11 L3
West Chevington Nthumb 119 P11
West Chiltington W Susx 24 C7
West Chinnock Somset 11 K2
West Chisenbury Wilts 21 M4
West Clandon Surrey 36 B10
West Cliffe Kent 27 P3
Westcliff-on-Sea Sthend 38 E4
West Clyst Devon 9 N5
West Coker Somset 11 L2
West Combe Devon 7 K6
Westcombe Somset 20 C7
West Compton Somset 19 Q6
West Compton Abbas Dorset 11 M6
Westcote Gloucs 47 P10
Westcote Barton Oxon 48 D9
Westcott Bucks 49 K11
Westcott Devon 9 P4
Westcott Surrey 36 D11
West Cottingwith N York 92 A2
Westcourt Wilts 21 P2
West Cowick E R Yk 91 Q6
West Cross Swans 28 H7
West Curry Cnwll 5 M3
West Curthwaite Cumb 110 F11
Westdean E Susx 25 M11
West Dean W Susx 15 N4
West Dean Wilts 21 Q9
West Deeping Lincs 74 B9
West Derby Lpool 81 M6
West Dereham Norfk 75 N10
West Ditchburn Nthumb 119 M6
West Down Devon 17 J3
Westdown Camp Wilts 21 K5
Westdowns Cnwll 4 H5
West Drayton Gt Lon 36 C5
West Drayton Notts 85 M6
West Dunnet Highld 167 M2
Wested Kent 37 M7
West Ella E R Yk 92 H5
West End Bed 49 Q4
West End Br For 35 N10
West End Caerph 30 H5
West End Cumb 110 F9
West End E R Yk 92 F4
West End E R Yk 93 L4
West End E R Yk 93 N5
Westend Gloucs 32 E3
West End Hants 14 E4
West End Hants 22 H7
West End Herts 50 G9
West End Herts 50 H9
West End Lancs 89 L5
West End Leeds 90 G3
West End Lincs 93 Q11
West End N Som 31 N11
West End N York 91 N2
West End Norfk 76 C10
West End Norfk 77 Q9
West End Oxon 34 G7
West End S Glos 32 D7
West End Somset 20 C8
West End Surrey 23 P2
West End Surrey 36 D8
West End W & M 35 M9
West End W Susx 24 F7
West End Wilts 20 H10
West End Wilts 21 J10
West End Wilts 33 J9
West End Green Hants 23 J2
Westend Town Nthumb 111 Q7
Westenhanger Kent 27 K4
Wester Aberchalder Highld 147 P3
Wester Balblair Highld 155 P8
Westerdale Highld 167 K6
Westerdale N York 105 J9
Westerfield Suffk 53 L2
Westergate W Susx 15 P5
Wester Hailes C Edin 127 M3
Westerham Kent 37 K10
Westerhope N u Ty 113 J7
Westerland Devon 7 M6
Westerleigh S Glos 32 C9
Western Isles W Isls 168 f8
Wester Ochiltree W Loth 127 J3
Wester Pitkierie Fife 135 P6
Wester Ross Highld 160 F11
Westerton W Susx 15 N5
Westerton of Rossie Angus 143 M7
Westerwick Shet 169 p9
West Ewell Surrey 36 F8
West Farleigh Kent 38 B11
West Farndon W Nthn 48 F4
West Felton Shrops 69 K9
Westfield BaNES 20 C4
Westfield Cumb 100 C5
Westfield E Susx 26 D8
Westfield Highld 167 J4
Westfield N Lans 126 C3
Westfield Norfk 76 D10
Westfield Surrey 36 B9
Westfield W Loth 126 G3
Westfields Dorset 12 B3
Westfields Herefs 45 P6
Westfields of Rattray P & K 142 B8
Westfield Sole Kent 38 C9
West Flotmanby N York 99 M5
Westford Somset 18 F10
Westgate Dur 102 H3
Westgate N Linc 92 C9
Westgate Norfk 76 D3
Westgate Hill C Brad 90 G5
Westgate-on-Sea Kent 39 P7
Westgate Street Norfk 76 H7
West Ginge Oxon 34 D7
West Grafton Wilts 21 P2
West Green Hants 23 K3
West Grimstead Wilts 21 P9
West Grinstead W Susx 24 E6
West Haddlesey N York 91 P5
West Haddon W Nthn 60 D6
West Hagbourne Oxon 34 F7
West Hagley Worcs 58 D8
Westhall Suffk 65 N5
West Hallam Derbys 72 C2
West Hallam Common Derbys 72 C2
West Halton N Linc 92 F6
Westham Dorset 11 P9
Westham E Susx 25 P10
West Ham Gt Lon 37 J4
Westham Somset 19 M5
Westhampnett W Susx 15 N5
West Handley Derbys 84 E5
West Hanney Oxon 34 D6
West Hanningfield Essex 38 B2
West Harnham Wilts 21 M9
West Harptree BaNES 19 Q3
West Harting W Susx 23 L10
West Hatch Somset 19 J10
West Hatch Wilts 20 H9
West Haven Angus 143 K10
Westhay Somset 19 M6
Westhead Lancs 88 E9
West Head Norfk 75 L9
West Heath Birm 58 F9
West Heath Hants 22 G3
West Helmsdale Highld 163 N3
West Hendred Oxon 34 D7
West Heslerton N York 99 J5
West Hewish N Som 19 L2
Westhide Herefs 46 A6
Westhill Abers 151 L6
West Hill Devon 9 Q6
Westhill Highld 156 C9
West Hoathly W Susx 25 J4
West Holme Dorset 12 E7
Westholme Somset 19 Q6
Westhope Herefs 45 P4
Westhope Shrops 56 H7
West Horndon Essex 37 P3
Westhorp W Nthn 48 F4
Westhorpe Lincs 74 D4
Westhorpe Suffk 64 E8
West Horrington Somset 19 Q5
West Horsley Surrey 36 C10
West Horton Nthumb 119 K4
West Hougham Kent 27 N3
Westhoughton Bolton 89 K9
Westhouse N York 95 P6
Westhouses Derbys 84 F9
West Howe BCP 13 J5
West Howetown Somset 18 B8
Westhumble Surrey 36 E10
West Huntingtower P & K 134 D3
West Huntspill Somset 19 K6
West Hyde C Beds 50 D7
West Hyde Herts 36 B2
West Hythe Kent 27 K5
West Ilkerton Devon 17 N2
West Ilsley W Berk 34 E8
West Itchenor W Susx 15 L6
West Keal Lincs 87 L8
West Kennett Wilts 33 M11
West Kilbride N Ayrs 124 G8
West Kingsdown Kent 37 N8
West Kington Wilts 32 F9
West Kirby Wirral 81 J7
West Knapton N York 98 H5
West Knighton Dorset 12 B7
West Knoyle Wilts 20 G8
West Kyloe Nthumb 119 L2
Westlake Devon 6 G8
West Lambrook Somset 19 M11
Westland Green Herts 51 K6
West Langdon Kent 27 P2
West Lavington W Susx 23 N10
West Lavington Wilts 21 K4
West Layton N York 103 M8
West Leake Notts 72 E5
West Learmouth Nthumb 118 F3
West Lees N York 104 E10
West Leigh Devon 8 G3
Westleigh Devon 16 H6
Westleigh Devon 18 E11
West Leigh Somset 18 F8
Westleton Suffk 65 N8
West Lexham Norfk 76 A8
Westley Shrops 56 F3
Westley Suffk 63 P8
Westley Waterless Cambs 63 K9
West Lilling N York 98 C8
Westlington Bucks 35 L2
West Linton Border 127 M7
Westlinton Cumb 110 G8
West Littleton S Glos 32 E9
West Lockinge Oxon 34 D7
West Lulworth Dorset 12 D8
West Lutton N York 99 J7
West Lydford Somset 19 Q8
West Lyn Devon 17 N2
West Lyng Somset 19 K9
West Lynn Norfk 75 M6
West Malling Kent 37 Q9
West Malvern Worcs 46 E5
West Marden W Susx 15 L4
West Markham Notts 85 M6
Westmarsh Kent 39 N9
West Marsh NE Lin 93 N9
West Marton N York 96 C10
West Melbury Dorset 20 G10
West Melton Rothm 91 L10
West Meon Hants 22 H10
West Meon Hut Hants 23 J9
West Meon Woodlands Hants 22 H9
West Mersea Essex 52 H9
Westmeston E Susx 24 H8
West Mickley Nthumb 112 G8
West Midland Safari Park Worcs 57 Q9
Westmill Herts 50 H7
Westmill Herts 51 J5
West Milton Dorset 11 L5
Westminster Gt Lon 36 G5
Westminster Abbey & Palace Gt Lon 36 G5
West Molesey Surrey 36 D7
West Monkton Somset 19 J9
West Moors Dorset 13 J4
West Morden Dorset 12 F5
West Morriston Border 118 B2
West Morton C Brad 90 D2
West Mudford Somset 19 Q10
Westmuir Angus 142 F7
West Ness N York 98 D5
West Newbiggin Darltn 104 C7
Westnewton Cumb 100 F2
West Newton E R Yk 93 M3
West Newton Norfk 75 N5
West Newton Somset 19 J9
West Norwood Gt Lon 36 H6
Westoe S Tyne 113 N7
West Ogwell Devon 7 L4
Weston BaNES 32 D11
Weston Ches E 70 C4
Weston Devon 10 C4
Weston Devon 10 D7
Weston Dorset 11 P10
Weston Halton 81 Q8
Weston Hants 23 K10
Weston Herefs 45 M3
Weston Herts 50 G4
Weston Lincs 74 E6
Weston N York 97 J11
Weston Notts 85 N7
Weston Shrops 56 E10
Weston Shrops 57 L6
Weston Shrops 69 J9
Weston Staffs 70 H9
Weston Suffk 65 N4
Weston W Berk 34 C10
Weston W Nthn 48 G5
Weston Beggard Herefs 46 A6
Westonbirt Gloucs 32 G7
Weston by Welland N Nthn 60 G2
Weston Colley Hants 22 F7
Weston Colville Cambs 63 K10
Weston Corbett Hants 23 J5
Weston Coyney C Stke 70 G6
Weston Favell W Nthn 60 G8
Weston Green Cambs 63 K10
Weston Heath Shrops 57 P2
Weston Hills Lincs 74 E6
Weston in Arden Warwks 59 N7
Westoning C Beds 50 B4
Weston-in-Gordano N Som 31 M10
Westoning Woodend C Beds 50 B4
Weston Jones Staffs 70 D10
Weston Longville Norfk 76 G8
Weston Lullingfields Shrops 69 M10
Weston-on-Avon Warwks 47 N4
Weston-on-the-Green Oxon 48 F11
Weston Park Staffs 57 Q2
Weston Patrick Hants 23 J5
Weston Rhyn Shrops 69 J7
Weston-sub-Edge Gloucs 47 M6
Weston-super-Mare N Som 19 K2
Weston Turville Bucks 35 N2
Weston-under-Lizard Staffs 57 Q2
Weston under Penyard Herefs 46 B10
Weston-under-Redcastle Shrops 69 Q9
Weston under Wetherley Warwks 59 N11
Weston Underwood Derbys 71 P6
Weston Underwood M Keyn 49 N4
Weston-upon-Trent Derbys 72 C5
Westonzoyland Somset 19 L8
West Orchard Dorset 20 F11
West Overton Wilts 33 M11
Westow N York 98 F7
West Panson Devon 5 N3
West Park Abers 151 K8
West Parley Dorset 13 J5
West Peckham Kent 37 P10
West Peeke Devon 5 N3
West Pelton Dur 113 K10
West Pennard Somset 19 P7
West Pentire Cnwll 4 B9
West Pinchbeck Lincs 74 D6
West Porlock Somset 17 R2
Westport Somset 19 L10
West Pulham Dorset 11 Q3
West Putford Devon 16 F8
West Quantoxhead Somset 18 F6
Westquarter Falk 126 G2
Westra V Glam 30 F10
West Raddon Devon 9 L4
West Rainton Dur 113 M11
West Rasen Lincs 86 E3
West Ravendale NE Lin 93 M11
Westray Ork 169 d2
Westray Airport Ork 169 d1
West Raynham Norfk 76 B6
West Retford Notts 85 L4
Westridge Green W Berk 34 G9
Westrigg W Loth 126 G4
Westrop Swindn 33 P6
West Rounton N York 104 D10
West Row Suffk 63 L5
West Rudham Norfk 75 R5
West Runton Norfk 76 H3
Westruther Border 128 G10
Westry Cambs 74 H11
West Saltoun E Loth 128 D6
West Sandford Devon 9 K4
West Sandwick Shet 169 r5
West Scrafton N York 96 G4
West Sleekburn Nthumb 113 L4
West Somerton Norfk 77 P7
West Stafford Dorset 11 Q7
West Stockwith Notts 92 C11
West Stoke W Susx 15 M5
West Stonesdale N York 102 G10
West Stoughton Somset 19 M5
West Stour Dorset 20 E10
West Stourmouth Kent 39 N9
West Stow Suffk 63 P6
West Stowell Wilts 21 M2
West Stratton Hants 22 F6
West Street Kent 38 F11
West Street Kent 39 P11
West Street Medway 38 B6
West Street Suffk 64 D7
West Tanfield N York 97 L5
West Taphouse Cnwll 5 J9
West Tarbert Ag & B 123 Q6
West Tarring W Susx 24 D10
West Thirston Nthumb 119 N11
West Thorney W Susx 15 L6
Westthorpe Derbys 84 G5
West Thorpe Notts 72 G5
West Thurrock Thurr 37 N5
West Tilbury Thurr 37 Q5
West Tisted Hants 23 J9
West Torrington Lincs 86 F4
West Town BaNES 19 P2
West Town Hants 15 K7
West Town Herefs 45 N2
West Town N Som 31 N11
West Town Somset 19 P7
West Town Somset 20 D6
West Tytherley Hants 21 Q9
West Walton Norfk 75 J8
Westward Cumb 101 J2
Westward Ho! Devon 16 G6
Westwell Kent 26 G2
Westwell Oxon 33 P3
Westwell Leacon Kent 26 G2
West Wellow Hants 21 Q11
West Wembury Devon 6 E9
West Wemyss Fife 135 J9
Westwick Cambs 62 F7
Westwick Dur 103 L7
West Wick N Som 19 L2
Westwick Norfk 77 K6
West Wickham Cambs 63 K11
West Wickham Gt Lon 37 J7
West Williamston Pembks 41 K9
West Winch Norfk 75 M7
West Winterslow Wilts 21 P8
West Wittering W Susx 15 L7
West Witton N York 96 G3
Westwood Devon 9 P5
Westwood Kent 37 P6
Westwood Kent 39 Q8
Westwood Notts 84 G10
Westwood Nthumb 111 Q7
Westwood Wilts 20 F3
West Woodburn Nthumb 112 C3
West Woodhay W Berk 22 C2
Westwood Heath Covtry 59 L9
West Woodlands Somset 20 E6
Westwoodside N Linc 92 B10
West Worldham Hants 23 K7
West Worthing W Susx 24 D10
West Wratting Cambs 63 K10
West Wycombe Bucks 35 M6
West Wylam Nthumb 112 H8
West Yatton Wilts 32 G9
West Yoke Kent 37 P7
West Youlstone Cnwll 16 D8
Wetham Green Kent 38 D8
Wetheral Cumb 111 J10
Wetherby Leeds 97 P11
Wetherby Services N York 97 P10
Wetherden Suffk 64 E9
Wetheringsett Suffk 64 G8
Wethersfield Essex 52 B5
Wetherup Street Suffk 64 G9
Wetley Rocks Staffs 70 H5
Wettenhall Ches E 69 R2
Wetton Staffs 71 L3
Wetwang E R Yk 99 J9
Wetwood Staffs 70 D8
Wexcombe Wilts 21 Q3
Wexham Slough 35 Q8
Wexham Street Bucks 35 Q8
Weybourne Norfk 76 G3
Weybourne Surrey 23 N5
Weybread Suffk 65 J5
Weybread Street Suffk 65 J6
Weybridge Surrey 36 C8
Weycroft Devon 10 G5
Weydale Highld 167 L4
Weyhill Hants 22 B5
Weymouth Dorset 11 P9
Whaddon Bucks 49 M8
Whaddon Cambs 62 E11
Whaddon Gloucs 32 F2
Whaddon Wilts 20 G2
Whaddon Wilts 21 N9
Whale W & F 101 P6
Whaley Derbys 84 H6
Whaley Bridge Derbys 83 M8
Whaley Thorns Derbys 84 H6
Whaligoe Highld 167 P8
Whalley Lancs 89 L3
Whalley Banks Lancs 89 L3
Whalsay Shet 169 s7
Whalton Nthumb 112 H4
Whaplode Lincs 74 F6
Whaplode Drove Lincs 74 F8
Wharf Warwks 48 D4
Wharfe N York 96 A7
Wharles Lancs 88 E3
Wharley End C Beds 49 P6
Wharncliffe Side Sheff 84 C2
Wharram-le-Street N York 98 H7
Wharton Ches W 82 E11
Wharton Herefs 45 Q3
Whashton N York 103 N9
Whasset W & F 95 L4
Whatcote Warwks 47 Q6
Whateley Warwks 59 K5
Whatfield Suffk 52 H2
Whatley Somset 10 H3
Whatley Somset 20 D5
Whatley's End S Glos 32 C8
Whatlington E Susx 26 C8
Whatsole Street Kent 27 K3
Whatstandwell Derbys 84 D10
Whatton-in-the-Vale Notts 73 J3
Whauphill D & G 107 M8
Whaw N York 103 J10
Wheal Peevor Cnwll 3 J5
Wheal Rose Cnwll 3 J5
Wheatacre Norfk 65 P3
Wheatfield Oxon 35 J5
Wheathampstead Herts 50 E8
Wheathill Shrops 57 L8
Wheathill Somset 19 Q8
Wheatley Hants 23 L6
Wheatley Oxon 34 G3
Wheatley Hill Dur 104 C3
Wheatley Hills Donc 91 P10
Wheatley Lane Lancs 89 N3
Wheaton Aston Staffs 58 C2
Wheddon Cross Somset 18 B7
Wheelbarrow Town Kent 27 K2
Wheeler End Bucks 35 M6
Wheeler's Green Wokham 35 L10
Wheelerstreet Surrey 23 P6
Wheelock Ches E 70 D3
Wheelock Heath Ches E 70 D3
Wheelton Lancs 89 J6
Wheldale Wakefd 91 M5
Wheldrake C York 92 A2
Whelford Gloucs 33 N5
Whelpley Hill Bucks 35 Q4
Whelpo Cumb 101 K3
Whelston Flints 81 J9
Whempstead Herts 50 H6
Whenby N York 98 C7
Whepstead Suffk 64 A10
Wherstead Suffk 53 L3
Wherwell Hants 22 C6
Wheston Derbys 83 P9
Whetsted Kent 37 Q11
Whetstone Gt Lon 36 G2
Whetstone Leics 72 F11
Wheyrigg Cumb 110 C11
Whicham Cumb 94 C4
Whichford Warwks 48 B8
Whickham Gatesd 113 K8
Whiddon Devon 8 C5
Whiddon Down Devon 8 G6
Whigstreet Angus 142 H9
Whilton W Nthn 60 D8
Whimble Devon 16 F11
Whimple Devon 9 P5
Whimpwell Green Norfk 77 M6
Whinburgh Norfk 76 E10
Whin Lane End Lancs 88 D2
Whinnieliggate D & G 108 F10
Whinnow Cumb 110 F10
Whinnyfold Abers 159 Q11
Whinny Hill S on T 104 C7
Whippingham IoW 14 F8
Whipsnade C Beds 50 B7
Whipsnade Zoo ZSL C Beds 50 B7
Whipton Devon 9 M6
Whirlow Sheff 84 D4
Whisby Lincs 86 B7
Whissendine RutInd 73 L8
Whissonsett Norfk 76 C7
Whistlefield Ag & B 131 Q9
Whistlefield Inn Ag & B 131 N9
Whistley Green Wokham 35 L10
Whiston Knows 81 P6
Whiston Rothm 84 F3
Whiston Staffs 58 C2
Whiston Staffs 71 J5
Whiston W Nthn 60 H8
Whiston Cross Shrops 57 P4
Whiston Eaves Staffs 71 J5
Whitacre Fields Warwks 59 L6
Whitbeck Cumb 94 C4
Whitbourne Herefs 46 D3
Whitburn S Tyne 113 P8
Whitburn W Loth 126 G5
Whitby Ches W 81 M9
Whitby N York 105 N8
Whitbyheath Ches W 81 M10
Whitchester Border 129 J8
Whitchurch BaNES 32 B11
Whitchurch Bucks 49 M10
Whitchurch Cardif 30 G9
Whitchurch Devon 6 D4
Whitchurch Hants 22 E5
Whitchurch Herefs 45 R11
Whitchurch Oxon 34 H9
Whitchurch Pembks 40 F5
Whitchurch Shrops 69 P6
Whitchurch Canonicorum Dorset 10 H5
Whitchurch Hill Oxon 34 H9
Whitcombe Dorset 11 Q7
Whitcot Shrops 56 F6
Whitcott Keysett Shrops 56 D8
Whiteacre Kent 27 K2
Whiteacre Heath Warwks 59 K6
Whiteash Green Essex 52 C5
White Ball Somset 18 F11
Whitebridge Highld 147 M4
Whitebrook Mons 31 P3
Whitebushes Surrey 36 G11
Whitecairns Abers 151 N4
Whitechapel Gt Lon 36 H4
White Chapel Lancs 88 H2
Whitechurch Pembks 41 N3
Whitecliff Gloucs 31 Q3
White Colne Essex 52 E6
White Coppice Lancs 89 J7
Whitecraig E Loth 127 Q3
Whitecroft Gloucs 32 B3
Whitecrook D & G 106 G6
Whitecross Cnwll 2 E7
White Cross Cnwll 2 H9
Whitecross Cnwll 4 F7
Whitecross Falk 126 H2
White End Worcs 46 E8
Whiteface Highld 162 G9
Whitefarland N Ayrs 120 G3
Whitefaulds S Ayrs 114 E6
Whitefield Bury 89 N9
Whitefield Devon 17 N4
Whitefield Somset 18 E9
Whitefield Lane End Knows 81 P7

Whiteford Abers 151 J2
Whitegate Ches W 82 D11
Whitehall Hants 23 K4
Whitehall Ork 169 f4
Whitehall W Susx 24 D6
Whitehaven Cumb 100 C7
Whitehill Hants 23 L8
Whitehill Kent 38 H10
Whitehill Leics 72 C8
Whitehills Abers 158 G4
Whitehouse Abers 150 G5
Whitehouse Ag & B 123 P7
Whitehouse Common Birm 58 H5
Whitekirk E Loth 128 F3
White Kirkley Dur 103 K3
White Lackington Dorset 11 Q5
Whitelackington Somset 19 L11
White Ladies Aston Worcs 46 H4
Whiteleaf Bucks 35 M4
White-le-Head Dur 113 J10
Whiteley Hants 14 F5
Whiteley Bank IoW 14 G10
Whiteley Green Ches E 83 K9
Whiteley Village Surrey 36 C8
Whitemans Green W Susx 24 H5
White Mill Carmth 43 J10
Whitemire Moray 156 H7
Whitemoor C Nott 72 E2
Whitemoor Cnwll 4 F10
Whitemoor Derbys 84 E11
Whitemoor Staffs 70 F2
Whiteness Shet 169 q9
White Notley Essex 52 C8
Whiteoak Green Oxon 34 B2
White Ox Mead BaNES 20 D3
Whiteparish Wilts 21 P10
White Pit Lincs 87 L5
Whiterashes Abers 151 M3
White Roding Essex 51 N8
Whiterow Highld 167 Q7
Whiterow Moray 157 J6
Whiteshill Gloucs 32 F3
Whitesmith E Susx 25 M8
White Stake Lancs 88 G5
Whitestaunton Somset 10 F2
Whitestone Devon 9 L6
White Stone Herefs 45 R6
Whitestone Warwks 59 N7
Whitestone Cross Devon 9 L6
Whitestreet Green Suffk 52 F4
Whitewall Corner N York 98 F7
White Waltham W & M 35 M9
Whiteway BaNES 20 D2
Whiteway Gloucs 32 H2
Whitewell Lancs 95 P11
Whiteworks Devon 6 G4
Whitfield C Dund 142 G11
Whitfield Kent 27 P2
Whitfield Nthumb 111 Q9
Whitfield S Glos 32 C6
Whitfield W Nthn 48 H7
Whitfield Hall Nthumb 111 Q9
Whitford Devon 10 F5
Whitford Flints 80 G9
Whitgift E R Yk 92 D6
Whitgreave Staffs 70 G9
Whithorn D & G 107 M9
Whiting Bay N Ayrs 121 K6
Whitkirk Leeds 91 K4
Whitland Carmth 41 N7
Whitlaw Border 117 Q8
Whitletts S Ayrs 114 G3
Whitley N York 91 P6
Whitley Readg 35 K10
Whitley Sheff 84 D2
Whitley Wilts 32 G11
Whitley Bay N Tyne 113 N6
Whitley Chapel Nthumb 112 F9
Whitley Heath Staffs 70 E9
Whitley Lower Kirk 90 G7
Whitley Row Kent 37 L10
Whitlock's End Solhll 58 H9
Whitminster Gloucs 32 E3
Whitmore Dorset 13 J3
Whitmore Staffs 70 E6
Whitnage Devon 18 D11
Whitnash Warwks 48 B2
Whitney-on-Wye Herefs 45 K5
Whitrigg Cumb 100 H3
Whitrigg Cumb 110 D9
Whitrigglees Cumb 110 D9
Whitsbury Hants 21 M11
Whitsome Border 129 M9
Whitson Newpt 31 L8
Whitstable Kent 39 K8
Whitstone Cnwll 5 M2
Whittingham Nthumb 119 L10
Whittingslow Shrops 56 G7
Whittington Derbys 84 E5
Whittington Gloucs 47 K10
Whittington Lancs 95 N5
Whittington Norfk 75 P11
Whittington Shrops 69 K8
Whittington Staffs 58 C8
Whittington Staffs 59 J3
Whittington Warwks 59 L5
Whittington Worcs 46 G4
Whittington Moor Derbys 84 E6
Whittlebury W Nthn 49 J6
Whittle-le-Woods Lancs 88 H6
Whittlesey Cambs 74 E11
Whittlesford Cambs 62 G11
Whittlestone Head Bl w D 89 L7
Whitton N Linc 92 F6
Whitton Nthumb 119 L10
Whitton Powys 56 D11
Whitton S on T 104 C6
Whitton Shrops 57 K10
Whitton Suffk 53 K2
Whittonditch Wilts 33 Q10
Whittonstall Nthumb 112 G9
Whitway Hants 22 E3
Whitwell Derbys 84 H5
Whitwell Herefs 50 E6
Whitwell IoW 14 F11
Whitwell N York 103 Q11
Whitwell Rutlnd 73 N9
Whitwell-on-the-Hill
  N York 98 E7
Whitwell Street Norfk 76 G7
Whitwick Leics 72 C7
Whitwood Wakefd 91 K6
Whitworth Lancs 89 P6
Whixall Shrops 69 P7
Whixley N York 97 P9
Whorlton Dur 103 M8

Whorlton N York 104 E10
Whyle Herefs 45 R2
Whyteleafe Surrey 36 H9
Wibdon Gloucs 31 Q5
Wibsey C Brad 90 E4
Wibtoft Warwks 59 Q7
Wichelstowe Swindn 33 M8
Wichenford Worcs 46 E2
Wichling Kent 38 F10
Wick BCP 13 L6
Wick Devon 10 D4
Wick Highld 167 Q6
Wick S Glos 32 D10
Wick Somset 18 H6
Wick Somset 19 M9
Wick V Glam 29 P10
Wick W Susx 24 B10
Wick Wilts 21 N10
Wick Worcs 47 J5
Wicken Cambs 63 J6
Wicken W Nthn 49 K7
Wicken Bonhunt Essex 51 L4
Wickenby Lincs 86 E4
Wick End Bed 49 Q4
Wicken Green Village Norfk 76 A5
Wickersley Rothm 84 G2
Wicker Street Green Suffk 52 G3
Wickford Essex 38 B3
Wickham Hants 14 G4
Wickham W Berk 34 C10
Wickham Bishops Essex 52 D9
Wickhambreaux Kent 39 M10
Wickhambrook Suffk 63 N10
Wickhamford Worcs 47 L6
Wickham Green Suffk 64 F8
Wickham Green W Berk 34 D10
Wickham Heath W Berk 34 D11
Wickham Market Suffk 65 L10
Wickhampton Norfk 77 N10
Wickham St Paul Essex 52 D4
Wickham Skeith Suffk 64 F8
Wickham Street Suffk 63 N10
Wickham Street Suffk 64 F8
Wickhurst Green W Susx 24 D4
Wick John o' Groats
  Airport Highld 167 Q6
Wicklewood Norfk 76 F11
Wickmere Norfk 76 H5
Wick St Lawrence N Som 31 L11
Wicksteed Park N Nthn 61 J5
Wickstreet E Susx 25 M8
Wickwar S Glos 32 D7
Widdington Essex 51 M4
Widdop Calder 89 Q4
Widdrington Nthumb 119 Q11
Widdrington Station
  Nthumb 113 K2
Widecombe in the Moor
  Devon 8 H9
Widegates Cnwll 5 M10
Widemouth Bay Cnwll 16 C11
Wideopen N Tyne 113 K6
Widford Essex 51 Q10
Widford Herts 51 K7
Widham Wilts 33 L7
Widley Hants 15 J5
Widmer End Bucks 35 N5
Widmerpool Notts 72 G5
Widmore Gt Lon 37 K7
Widnes Halton 81 Q7
Widworthy Devon 10 E5
Wigan Wigan 88 H9
Wigborough Somset 19 M11
Wiggaton Devon 10 C6
Wiggenhall St Germans
  Norfk 75 L8
Wiggenhall St Mary
  Magdalen Norfk 75 L8
Wiggenhall St Mary the
  Virgin Norfk 75 L8
Wiggenhall St Peter Norfk 75 M8
Wiggens Green Essex 51 Q2
Wiggenstall Staffs 71 K2
Wigginton C York 98 C9
Wigginton Herts 35 P2
Wigginton Oxon 48 C8
Wigginton Staffs 59 K3
Wigginton Bottom Herts 35 P3
Wigglesworth N York 96 B9
Wiggonby Cumb 110 E10
Wiggonholt W Susx 24 C7
Wighill N York 97 Q11
Wighton Norfk 76 C4
Wightwick Wolves 58 C5
Wigley Derbys 84 D6
Wigley Hants 22 B11
Wigmore Herefs 56 G11
Wigmore Medway 38 C9
Wigsley Notts 85 Q6
Wigsthorpe N Nthn 61 M4
Wigston Leics 72 G11
Wigston Fields Leics 72 G10
Wigston Parva Leics 59 Q7
Wigtoft Lincs 74 E3
Wigton Cumb 110 E11
Wigtown D & G 107 M6
Wigtwizzle Sheff 90 G11
Wike Leeds 91 J2
Wilbarston N Nthn 60 H3
Wilberfoss E R Yk 98 E10
Wilburton Cambs 62 G5
Wilby N Nthn 61 J7
Wilby Norfk 64 E4
Wilby Suffk 65 J7
Wilcot Wilts 21 M2
Wilcott Shrops 69 L11
Wilcove Cnwll 6 C7
Wilcrick Newpt 31 M7
Wilday Green Derbys 84 D6
Wildboarclough Ches E 83 L11
Wilden Bed 61 N9
Wilden Worcs 58 B10
Wilde Street Suffk 63 M5
Wildhern Hants 22 C4
Wildhill Herts 51 G9
Wildmanbridge S Lans 126 E7
Wildmill Brdgnd 29 P8
Wildmoor Hants 23 J3
Wildmoor Worcs 58 E9
Wildsworth Lincs 92 D11
Wilkesley Ches E 70 A6
Wilkhaven Highld 163 L9
Wilkieston W Loth 127 L4

Wilkin's Green Herts 50 F9
Wilksby Lincs 87 J8
Willand Devon 9 P2
Willards Hill E Susx 26 B7
Willaston Ches E 70 B4
Willaston Ches W 81 L9
Willen M Keyn 49 N6
Willenhall Covtry 59 N9
Willenhall Wsall 58 E5
Willerby E R Yk 92 H4
Willerby N York 99 L5
Willersey Gloucs 47 M7
Willersley Herefs 45 L5
Willesborough Kent 26 H3
Willesborough Lees Kent 26 H3
Willesden Gt Lon 36 F4
Willesleigh Devon 17 L5
Willesley Wilts 32 G7
Willett Somset 18 F8
Willey Shrops 57 M5
Willey Warwks 59 Q8
Willey Green Surrey 23 P4
Williamscot Oxon 48 E5
Williamstown Rhondd 30 D6
Willian Herts 50 F4
Willicote Warwks 47 N5
Willingale Essex 51 N9
Willingdon E Susx 25 N10
Willingham Cambs 62 F6
Willingham by Stow Lincs 85 Q4
Willingham Green Cambs 63 K10
Willingham St Mary Suffk 65 N5
Willington Bed 61 P10
Willington Derbys 71 P9
Willington Dur 103 N3
Willington Kent 38 C11
Willington N Tyne 113 M7
Willington Warwks 47 Q7
Willington Corner Ches W 82 B11
Willitoft E R Yk 92 B4
Williton Somset 18 E6
Willoughby Lincs 87 N6
Willoughby Warwks 60 B7
Willoughby Hills Lincs 87 L11
Willoughby-on-the-Wolds
  Notts 72 G5
Willoughby Waterleys Leics 60 C2
Willoughton Lincs 86 B2
Willow Green Ches W 82 D9
Willows Green Essex 52 B8
Willsbridge S Glos 32 C10
Willsworthy Devon 8 D8
Willtown Somset 19 L10
Wilmcote Warwks 47 N3
Wilmington BaNES 20 C2
Wilmington Devon 10 E5
Wilmington E Susx 25 M10
Wilmington Kent 37 M6
Wilmslow Ches E 82 H8
Wilnecote Staffs 59 K4
Wilpshire Lancs 89 K4
Wilsden C Brad 90 D3
Wilsford Lincs 73 Q2
Wilsford Wilts 21 M3
Wilsford Wilts 21 M7
Wilsham Devon 17 P2
Wilshaw Kirk 90 E9
Wilsill N York 97 J8
Wilsley Green Kent 26 C4
Wilsley Pound Kent 26 C4
Wilson Herefs 45 R10
Wilson Leics 72 C6
Wilsontown S Lans 126 G6
Wilstead Bed 50 C2
Wilsthorpe Lincs 74 A8
Wilstone Herts 35 P2
Wilstone Green Herts 35 P2
Wilton Cumb 100 D8
Wilton Herefs 46 A10
Wilton N York 98 H4
Wilton R & Cl 104 G7
Wilton Wilts 21 L8
Wilton Wilts 21 Q2
Wilton Dean Border 117 P8
Wimbish Essex 51 N3
Wimbish Green Essex 51 P3
Wimbledon Gt Lon 36 F6
Wimblington Cambs 62 F2
Wimboldsley Ches W 70 B2
Wimborne Minster Dorset 12 H5
Wimborne St Giles Dorset 12 H2
Wimbotsham Norfk 75 M9
Wimpole Cambs 62 E11
Wimpstone Warwks 47 P5
Wincanton Somset 20 D9
Winceby Lincs 87 K7
Wincham Ches W 82 E9
Winchburgh W Loth 127 K3
Winchcombe Gloucs 47 K9
Winchelsea E Susx 26 F8
Winchelsea Beach E Susx 26 F8
Winchester Hants 22 E9
Winchester Services Hants 22 F7
Winchet Hill Kent 26 B3
Winchfield Hants 23 L4
Winchmore Hill Bucks 35 P5
Winchmore Hill Gt Lon 36 H2
Wincle Ches E 83 L11
Wincobank Sheff 84 E2
Winder Cumb 100 D7
Windermere Cumb 101 M11
Windermere Jetty Museum
  W & F 101 M11
Winderton Warwks 48 B6
Windhill Highld 155 P8
Windlehurst Stockp 83 L7
Windlesham Surrey 23 P2
Windmill Cnwll 4 D7
Windmill Derbys 83 Q9
Windmill Hill E Susx 25 P8
Windmill Hill Somset 19 K11
Windrush Gloucs 33 N2
Windsole Abers 158 E5
Windsor W & M 35 Q9
Windsor Castle W & M 35 Q9
Windsoredge Gloucs 32 F4
Windsor Green Suffk 64 B11
Windygates Fife 135 J7
Windyharbour Ches E 82 H10
Windy Hill Wrexhm 69 K4
Wineham W Susx 24 F6
Winestead E R Yk 93 N6
Winewall Lancs 89 Q2
Winfarthing Norfk 64 G4
Winford IoW 14 G10
Winford N Som 19 P2

Winforton Herefs 45 K5
Winfrith Newburgh Dorset 12 D8
Wing Bucks 49 N10
Wing Rutlnd 73 M10
Wingate Dur 104 D3
Wingates Bolton 89 K9
Wingates Nthumb 119 L11
Wingerworth Derbys 84 E7
Wingfield C Beds 50 B5
Wingfield Suffk 65 J6
Wingfield Wilts 20 F3
Wingfield Green Suffk 65 J6
Wingham Kent 39 M10
Wingland Lincs 75 J6
Wingmore Kent 27 L2
Wingrave Bucks 49 N11
Winkburn Notts 85 M9
Winkfield Br For 35 P10
Winkfield Row Br For 35 N10
Winkhill Staffs 71 K4
Winkhurst Green Kent 37 L11
Winkleigh Devon 17 L10
Winksley N York 97 L6
Winkton BCP 13 L5
Winlaton Gatesd 113 J8
Winlaton Mill Gatesd 113 J8
Winless Highld 167 P6
Winllan Powys 68 H10
Winmarleigh Lancs 95 K11
Winnall Hants 22 E9
Winnersh Wokham 35 L10
Winnington Ches W 82 D10
Winscales Cumb 100 D5
Winscombe N Som 19 M3
Winsford Ches W 82 E11
Winsford Somset 18 B8
Winsham Devon 17 J4
Winsham Somset 10 H3
Winshill Staffs 71 P10
Winshwen Swans 29 J5
Winskill W & F 101 Q4
Winslade Hants 23 J5
Winsley Wilts 20 E2
Winslow Bucks 49 L9
Winson Gloucs 33 L3
Winsor Hants 13 P2
Winstanley Wigan 82 C4
Winster Derbys 84 B8
Winster W & F 95 J2
Winston Dur 103 M7
Winston Suffk 64 H9
Winstone Gloucs 33 J3
Winston Green Suffk 64 H9
Winswell Devon 16 H9
Winterborne Came Dorset 11 Q7
Winterborne Clenston
  Dorset 12 D4
Winterborne Herringston
  Dorset 11 P7
Winterborne Houghton
  Dorset 12 D4
Winterborne Kingston
  Dorset 12 E5
Winterborne Monkton
  Dorset 11 P7
Winterborne Stickland
  Dorset 12 D4
Winterborne Tomson Dorset 12 E5
Winterborne Whitechurch
  Dorset 12 D4
Winterborne Zelston Dorset 12 E5
Winterbourne S Glos 32 B8
Winterbourne W Berk 34 D10
Winterbourne Abbas Dorset 11 N6
Winterbourne Bassett Wilts 33 L10
Winterbourne Dauntsey
  Wilts 21 N8
Winterbourne Earls Wilts 21 N8
Winterbourne Gunner Wilts 21 N7
Winterbourne Monkton
  Wilts 33 L10
Winterbourne Steepleton
  Dorset 11 P7
Winterbourne Stoke Wilts 21 L6
Winterbrook Oxon 34 H7
Winterburn N York 96 D9
Wintringham N Linc 92 F6
Winterley Ches E 70 C3
Wintersett Wakefd 91 K7
Winterslow Wilts 21 P8
Winterton N Linc 92 F7
Winterton-on-Sea Norfk 77 P8
Winthorpe Lincs 87 Q7
Winthorpe Notts 85 P9
Winton BCP 13 J6
Winton E Susx 25 M10
Winton N York 104 D11
Winton W & F 102 E8
Wintringham Cambs 62 B9
Wintringham N York 98 H6
Winwick Cambs 61 P4
Winwick N Nthn 60 D6
Winwick Warrtn 82 D6
Wirksworth Derbys 71 P4
Wirral 81 K7
Wirswall Ches E 69 P6
Wisbech Cambs 75 J9
Wisbech St Mary Cambs 74 H9
Wisborough Green W Susx 24 C5
Wiseman's Bridge Pembks 41 M9
Wiseton Notts 85 M3
Wishanger Gloucs 32 H3
Wishaw N Lans 126 D6
Wishaw Warwks 59 J6
Wisley Surrey 36 C9
Wispington Lincs 86 H6
Wissenden Kent 26 F3
Wissett Suffk 65 M6
Wissington Norfk 75 N11
Wissington Suffk 52 G5
Wistanstow Shrops 56 G7
Wistanswick Shrops 70 B9
Wistaston Ches E 70 B4
Wistaston Green Ches E 70 B4
Wisterfield Ches E 82 H10
Wiston Pembks 41 K7
Wiston S Lans 116 D4
Wiston W Susx 24 D8
Wistow Cambs 62 C4
Wistow Leics 72 G11
Wistow N York 91 P3
Wiswell Lancs 89 L3
Witcham Cambs 62 G4
Witchampton Dorset 12 G3
Witchford Cambs 62 H5
Witcombe Somset 19 N10

Witham Essex 52 D9
Witham Friary Somset 20 D6
Witham on the Hill Lincs 73 R7
Witham St Hughs Lincs 85 Q8
Withcall Lincs 87 J4
Withdean Br & H 24 H9
Witherenden Hill E Susx 25 P5
Witheridge Devon 9 K2
Witherley Leics 72 A11
Withern Lincs 87 M4
Withernsea E R Yk 93 P5
Withernwick E R Yk 93 L2
Withersdale Street Suffk 65 K5
Withersfield Suffk 63 L11
Witherslack W & F 95 J4
Withiel Cnwll 4 F8
Withiel Florey Somset 18 C8
Withielgoose Cnwll 4 G8
Withington Gloucs 47 K11
Withington Herefs 45 R6
Withington Manch 82 H6
Withington Shrops 57 K2
Withington Staffs 71 J7
Withington Green Ches E 82 H10
Withington Marsh Herefs 45 R6
Withleigh Devon 9 M2
Withnell Lancs 89 J6
Withnell Fold Lancs 89 J6
Withybed Green Worcs 58 F10
Withybrook Warwks 59 P8
Withycombe Somset 18 D6
Withyham E Susx 25 L3
Withy Mills BaNES 20 C3
Withypool Somset 17 Q4
Withywood Bristl 31 Q11
Witley Surrey 23 P7
Witnesham Suffk 64 H11
Witney Oxon 34 C2
Wittering C Pete 73 R10
Wittersham Kent 26 F6
Witton Birm 58 G6
Witton Norfk 77 L10
Witton Norfk 77 L5
Witton Gilbert Dur 113 K11
Witton Green Norfk 77 N11
Witton le Wear Dur 103 M4
Witton Park Dur 103 N4
Wiveliscombe Somset 18 E9
Wivelrod Hants 23 J7
Wivelsfield E Susx 24 H6
Wivelsfield Green E Susx 25 J7
Wivelsfield Station W Susx 24 H7
Wivenhoe Essex 52 H7
Wivenhoe Cross Essex 52 H7
Wiveton Norfk 76 E3
Wix Essex 53 L6
Wixams Bed 50 C2
Wixford Warwks 47 L4
Wix Green Essex 53 L6
Wixhill Shrops 69 Q9
Wixoe Suffk 52 B3
Woburn C Beds 49 P8
Woburn Safari Park C Beds 49 Q8
Woburn Sands M Keyn 49 P7
Wokefield Park W Berk 35 J11
Woking Surrey 36 B9
Wokingham Wokham 35 M11
Wolborough Devon 7 M4
Woldingham Surrey 37 J9
Wold Newton E R Yk 99 L6
Wold Newton NE Lin 93 M11
Wolfclyde S Lans 116 E3
Wolferlow Herefs 46 C2
Wolferton Norfk 75 N5
Wolfhampcote Warwks 60 B7
Wolfhill P & K 142 B11
Wolf Hills Nthumb 111 P9
Wolf's Castle Pembks 41 J5
Wolfsdale Pembks 40 H6
Wollaston Dudley 58 C8
Wollaston N Nthn 61 K8
Wollaston Shrops 56 E2
Wollaton C Nott 72 E3
Wollaton Hall C Nott 72 E3
Wolleigh Devon 9 K8
Wollerton Shrops 69 R8
Wollescote Dudley 58 D8
Wolseley Bridge Staffs 71 J10
Wolsingham Dur 103 L3
Wolstanton Staffs 70 F5
Wolstenholme Rochdl 89 N8
Wolston Warwks 59 P9
Wolsty Cumb 109 P10
Wolvercote Oxon 34 E3
Wolverhampton Wolves 58 D5
Wolverhampton Halfpenny
  Green Airport Staffs 58 B6
Wolverley Shrops 69 N8
Wolverley Worcs 58 B9
Wolverton Hants 22 G3
Wolverton Kent 27 N3
Wolverton M Keyn 49 M6
Wolverton Warwks 47 P2
Wolverton Wilts 20 E8
Wolverton Common Hants 22 G3
Wolvesnewton Mons 31 N5
Wolvey Warwks 59 P7
Wolvey Heath Warwks 59 P7
Wolviston S on T 104 E5
Wombleton N York 98 D4
Wombourne Staffs 58 C6
Wombwell Barns 91 L10
Womenswold Kent 39 M11
Womersley N York 91 N7
Wonastow Mons 31 N2
Wonersh Surrey 36 B11
Wonford Devon 9 M6
Wonson Devon 8 H7
Wonston Dorset 12 B3
Wonston Hants 22 E7
Wooburn Bucks 35 P7
Wooburn Green Bucks 35 P7
Wooburn Moor Bucks 35 P7
Woodacott Devon 16 F10
Woodale N York 96 G5
Woodall Rothm 84 G4
Woodall Services Rothm 84 G4
Woodbank Ches W 81 M10
Woodbastwick Norfk 77 L8
Woodbeck Notts 85 N5
Wood Bevington Warwks 47 L4
Woodborough Notts 85 K11
Woodborough Wilts 21 M3
Woodbridge Devon 10 D5
Woodbridge Dorset 20 G11
Woodbridge Suffk 53 N2

Place	County	Page	Grid
Wood Burcote	W Nthn	49	J5
Woodburn	Mdloth	127	Q4
Woodbury	Devon	9	P7
Woodbury Salterton	Devon	9	P7
Woodchester	Gloucs	32	F4
Woodchurch	Kent	26	F5
Woodchurch	Wirral	81	K7
Woodcombe	Somset	18	C5
Woodcote	Gt Lon	36	G8
Woodcote	Oxon	34	H8
Woodcote	Wrekin	70	D11
Woodcote Green	Worcs	58	D10
Woodcott	Hants	22	D4
Woodcroft	Gloucs	31	P5
Woodcutts	Dorset	21	J11
Wood Dalling	Norfk	76	F6
Woodditton	Cambs	63	L9
Woodeaton	Oxon	34	F2
Wood Eaton	Staffs	70	E11
Wooden	Pembks	41	M9
Wood End	Bed	61	M11
Wood End	Bed	61	N7
Wood End	C Beds	49	Q6
Wood End	Cambs	62	E5
Wood End	Gt Lon	36	D4
Wood End	Herts	50	H5
Woodend	Highld	138	D5
Woodend	Staffs	71	M9
Woodend	W Loth	126	G4
Woodend	W Nthn	48	H5
Woodend	W Susx	15	M5
Wood End	Warwks	58	H10
Wood End	Warwks	59	K5
Wood End	Warwks	59	L7
Wood End	Wolves	58	D4
Wood Enderby	Lincs	87	J8
Woodend Green	Essex	51	N5
Woodfalls	Wilts	21	N10
Woodford	Cnwll	16	C9
Woodford	Devon	7	K8
Woodford	Gloucs	32	C5
Woodford	Gt Lon	37	K2
Woodford	N Nthn	61	L5
Woodford	Stockp	83	J8
Woodford Bridge	Gt Lon	37	K2
Woodford Green	Gt Lon	37	K2
Woodford Halse	W Nthn	48	F4
Woodford Wells	Gt Lon	37	K2
Woodgate	Birm	58	E8
Woodgate	Devon	18	F11
Woodgate	Norfk	76	B8
Woodgate	Norfk	76	E8
Woodgate	W Susx	15	P6
Woodgate	W Susx	24	G4
Woodgate	Worcs	58	E11
Wood Green	Gt Lon	36	H2
Woodgreen	Hants	21	N11
Woodgreen	Oxon	34	C2
Woodhall	N York	96	E2
Woodhall Hill	Leeds	90	G3
Woodhall Spa	Lincs	86	G8
Woodham	Bucks	49	K11
Woodham	Dur	103	Q5
Woodham	Surrey	36	B8
Woodham Ferrers	Essex	38	C2
Woodham Mortimer	Essex	52	D11
Woodham Walter	Essex	52	D10
Woodhaven	Fife	135	L2
Wood Hayes	Wolves	58	D4
Woodhead	Abers	159	J10
Woodhill	Shrops	57	N6
Woodhill	Somset	19	L9
Woodhorn	Nthumb	113	L3
Woodhorn Demesne	Nthumb	113	M3
Woodhouse	Leeds	90	H4
Woodhouse	Leics	72	E8
Woodhouse	Sheff	84	F4
Woodhouse	Wakefd	91	K6
Woodhouse Eaves	Leics	72	E8
Woodhouse Green	Staffs	70	G2
Woodhouselee	Mdloth	127	N5
Woodhouselees	D & G	110	G6
Woodhouse Mill	Sheff	84	F3
Woodhouses	Cumb	110	F10
Woodhouses	Oldham	83	K4
Woodhouses	Staffs	58	G3
Woodhouses	Staffs	71	M11
Woodhuish	Devon	7	N8
Woodhurst	Cambs	62	D5
Woodingdean	Br & H	25	J9
Woodkirk	Leeds	90	H5
Woodland	Abers	151	M3
Woodland	Devon	6	H5
Woodland	Devon	7	K5
Woodland	Dur	103	L5
Woodland	Kent	27	K3
Woodland	S Ayrs	114	C8
Woodland Head	Devon	9	J5
Woodlands	Donc	91	N9
Woodlands	Dorset	13	J3
Woodlands	Hants	13	P2
Woodlands	Kent	37	N8
Woodlands	N York	97	M10
Woodlands	Somset	18	G6
Woodlands of Durris	Abers	151	J6
Woodlands Park	W & M	35	N9
Woodlands St Mary	W Berk	34	B9
Woodland Street	Somset	19	P7
Woodland View	Sheff	84	D3
Wood Lane	Shrops	69	M8
Wood Lane	Staffs	70	E5
Woodleigh	Devon	7	J7
Woodlesford	Leeds	91	K5
Woodley	Stockp	83	K6
Woodley	Wokham	35	L10
Woodmancote	Gloucs	32	E5
Woodmancote	Gloucs	33	K3
Woodmancote	Gloucs	47	J9
Woodmancote	W Susx	15	L5
Woodmancote	W Susx	15	N5
Woodmancote	Worcs	46	H6
Woodmancott	Hants	22	G6
Woodmansey	E R Yk	93	J3
Woodmansgreen	W Susx	23	N9
Woodmansterne	Surrey	36	G9
Woodmanton	Devon	9	P7
Woodmarsh	Wilts	20	G3
Woodmill	Staffs	71	L10
Woodminton	Wilts	21	K10
Woodnesborough	Kent	39	P10
Woodnewton	N Nthn	61	M2
Woodnook	Notts	84	G10
Wood Norton	Norfk	76	E6
Woodplumpton	Lancs	88	F4
Woodrising	Norfk	76	D11
Wood Row	Leeds	91	K5
Woodrow	Worcs	58	C9
Wood's Corner	E Susx	25	Q7
Woods Eaves	Herefs	45	K5
Woodseaves	Shrops	70	B8
Woodseaves	Staffs	70	D9
Woodsend	Wilts	33	P9
Woodsetts	Rothm	84	H4
Woodsford	Dorset	12	C6
Wood's Green	E Susx	25	P4
Woodside	Br For	35	P10
Woodside	Cumb	100	D4
Woodside	Essex	51	L10
Woodside	Fife	135	L6
Woodside	Gt Lon	36	H7
Woodside	Hants	13	P6
Woodside	Herts	50	F9
Woodside	P & K	142	C10
Woodside Green	Kent	38	C11
Woodstock	Oxon	48	D11
Woodstock	Pembks	41	K5
Woodston	C Pete	74	C11
Wood Street	Norfk	77	M7
Wood Street Village	Surrey	23	Q4
Woodthorpe	Derbys	84	G6
Woodthorpe	Leics	72	E7
Woodthorpe	Lincs	87	M4
Woodton	Norfk	65	K3
Woodtown	Devon	16	G7
Woodvale	Sefton	88	C8
Woodville	Derbys	71	Q11
Woodwall Green	Staffs	70	D8
Wood Walton	Cambs	62	B4
Woodyates	Dorset	21	K11
Woody Bay	Devon	17	M2
Woofferton	Shrops	57	J11
Wookey	Somset	19	P5
Wookey Hole	Somset	19	P5
Wool	Dorset	12	D7
Woolacombe	Devon	16	H3
Woolage Green	Kent	27	M2
Woolage Village	Kent	39	M11
Woolaston	Gloucs	31	Q5
Woolaston Common	Gloucs	31	Q4
Woolavington	Somset	19	K6
Woolbeding	W Susx	23	N10
Woolbrook	Devon	10	C7
Woolcotts	Somset	18	C8
Wooldale	Kirk	90	F9
Wooler	Nthumb	119	J5
Woolfardisworthy	Devon	9	K3
Woolfardisworthy	Devon	16	E7
Woolfold	Bury	89	M8
Woolfords	S Lans	127	J6
Woolhampton	W Berk	34	G11
Woolhope	Herefs	46	B7
Woolland	Dorset	12	C3
Woollard	BaNES	20	B2
Woollensbrook	Herts	51	J9
Woolley	BaNES	32	D11
Woolley	Cambs	61	Q6
Woolley	Cnwll	16	D8
Woolley	Derbys	84	E8
Woolley	Wakefd	91	J8
Woolley Bridge	Derbys	83	M6
Woolley Edge Services	Wakefd	91	J8
Woolley Green	W & M	35	M8
Woolmere Green	Worcs	47	J2
Woolmer Green	Herts	50	G7
Woolmerston	Somset	19	J8
Woolminstone	Somset	11	J3
Woolpack	Kent	26	E4
Woolpit	Suffk	64	D9
Woolpit Green	Suffk	64	D9
Woolscott	Warwks	60	B7
Woolsgrove	Devon	9	J4
Woolsington	N u Ty	113	J6
Woolstaston	Shrops	56	H5
Woolsthorpe by Belvoir	Lincs	73	L4
Woolsthorpe-by-Colsterworth	Lincs	73	N6
Woolston	C Soth	14	D4
Woolston	Devon	7	J10
Woolston	Devon	7	J8
Woolston	Shrops	56	G7
Woolston	Shrops	69	K10
Woolston	Somset	18	E10
Woolston	Somset	20	C9
Woolston	Warrtn	82	D7
Woolstone	Gloucs	47	J8
Woolstone	M Keyn	49	N7
Woolstone	Oxon	33	Q7
Woolston Green	Devon	7	K5
Woolton	Lpool	81	N7
Woolton Hill	Hants	22	D2
Woolverstone	Suffk	53	L4
Woolverton	Somset	20	E4
Woolwich	Gt Lon	37	K5
Woonton	Herefs	45	M4
Woonton	Herefs	45	Q3
Wooperton	Nthumb	119	K6
Woore	Shrops	70	C6
Wootten Green	Suffk	65	J7
Wootton	Bed	50	B2
Wootton	Hants	13	M5
Wootton	Herefs	45	L4
Wootton	IoW	14	F8
Wootton	Kent	27	M2
Wootton	N Linc	93	J7
Wootton	Oxon	34	E4
Wootton	Oxon	48	D11
Wootton	Shrops	69	K9
Wootton	Staffs	70	E9
Wootton	Staffs	71	L6
Wootton	N Wth	60	G9
Wootton Bassett	Wilts	33	L8
Wootton Bridge	IoW	14	F8
Wootton Broadmead	Bed	50	B2
Wootton Common	IoW	14	F8
Wootton Courtenay	Somset	18	B6
Wootton Fitzpaine	Dorset	10	H5
Wootton Rivers	Wilts	21	N2
Wootton St Lawrence	Hants	22	G4
Wootton Wawen	Warwks	47	N2
Worcester	Worcs	46	G4
Worcester Park	Gt Lon	36	F7
Wordsley	Dudley	58	C7
Worfield	Shrops	57	P5
Worgret	Dorset	12	F7
Workhouse End	Bed	61	P10
Workhouse Green	Suffk	52	F4
Workington	Cumb	100	D4
Worksop	Notts	85	J5
Worlaby	Lincs	87	K5
Worlaby	N Linc	92	H8
Worlds End	Bucks	35	N3
Worlds End	Hants	14	H4
World's End	W Berk	34	E9
Worlds End	W Susx	24	H6
Worle	N Som	19	L2
Worleston	Ches E	70	B3
Worlingham	Suffk	65	N4
Worlington	Devon	9	J2
Worlington	Suffk	63	L7
Worlingworth	Suffk	65	J8
Wormald Green	N York	97	M7
Wormbridge	Herefs	45	N8
Wormegay	Norfk	75	N8
Wormelow Tump	Herefs	45	P8
Wormhill	Derbys	83	P10
Wormhill	Herefs	45	N7
Wormingford	Essex	52	F5
Worminghall	Bucks	34	H3
Wormington	Gloucs	47	K7
Worminster	Somset	19	Q6
Wormit	Fife	135	L2
Wormleighton	Warwks	48	E4
Wormley	Herts	51	J9
Wormley	Surrey	23	P7
Wormleybury	Herts	51	J9
Wormley Hill	Donc	91	R7
Wormshill	Kent	38	E10
Wormsley	Herefs	45	N5
Worplesdon	Surrey	23	Q4
Worrall	Sheff	84	D2
Worrall Hill	Gloucs	32	B2
Worsbrough	Barns	91	K10
Worsbrough Bridge	Barns	91	K10
Worsbrough Dale	Barns	91	K10
Worsley	Salfd	82	G4
Worstead	Norfk	77	L6
Worsthorne	Lancs	89	P4
Worston	Devon	6	F8
Worston	Lancs	89	M2
Worth	Kent	39	P10
Worth	Somset	19	P5
Worth	W Susx	24	G4
Wortham	Suffk	64	F6
Worthen	Shrops	56	F4
Worthenbury	Wrexhm	69	M5
Worthing	Norfk	76	D8
Worthing	W Susx	24	D10
Worthington	Leics	72	C6
Worth Matravers	Dorset	12	G9
Worthybrook	Mons	31	N2
Worting	Hants	22	G4
Wortley	Barns	91	J11
Wortley	Gloucs	32	E6
Wortley	Leeds	90	H4
Worton	N York	96	E3
Worton	Wilts	21	J3
Wortwell	Norfk	65	K5
Wotherton	Shrops	56	D4
Wothorpe	C Pete	73	Q9
Wotter	Devon	6	F6
Wotton	Surrey	36	D11
Wotton-under-Edge	Gloucs	32	E6
Wotton Underwood	Bucks	49	J11
Woughton on the Green	M Keyn	49	N7
Wouldham	Kent	38	B9
Woundale	Shrops	57	P6
Wrabness	Essex	53	L5
Wrafton	Devon	16	H4
Wragby	Lincs	86	F5
Wragby	Wakefd	91	L7
Wramplingham	Norfk	76	G10
Wrangaton	Devon	6	H7
Wrangbrook	Wakefd	91	M8
Wrangle	Lincs	87	M10
Wrangle Common	Lincs	87	M10
Wrangle Lowgate	Lincs	87	M10
Wrangway	Somset	18	F11
Wrantage	Somset	19	K10
Wrawby	N Linc	92	H9
Wraxall	N Som	31	N10
Wraxall	Somset	20	B7
Wray	Lancs	95	N7
Wraysbury	W & M	36	B6
Wrayton	Lancs	95	N6
Wrea Green	Lancs	88	D4
Wreaks End	W & F	94	E3
Wreay	Cumb	110	H11
Wreay	W & F	101	M6
Wrecclesham	Surrey	23	M6
Wrekenton	Gatesd	113	L9
Wrelton	N York	98	F3
Wrenbury	Ches E	69	Q5
Wrench Green	N York	99	K3
Wreningham	Norfk	64	H2
Wrentham	Suffk	65	P5
Wrenthorpe	Wakefd	91	J6
Wrentnall	Shrops	56	G4
Wressle	E R Yk	92	B4
Wressle	N Linc	92	G9
Wrestlingworth	C Beds	62	C11
Wretton	Norfk	75	N10
Wrexham	Wrexhm	69	K4
Wrexham Industrial Estate	Wrexhm	69	L4
Wribbenhall	Worcs	57	P9
Wrickton	Shrops	57	L7
Wrightington Bar	Lancs	88	G8
Wright's Green	Essex	51	M7
Wrinehill	Staffs	70	D5
Wrington	N Som	19	N2
Writhlington	BaNES	20	C4
Writtle	Essex	51	Q9
Wrockwardine	Wrekin	57	L2
Wroot	N Linc	92	B10
Wrose	C Brad	90	F3
Wrotham	Kent	37	P9
Wrotham Heath	Kent	37	P9
Wrottesley	Staffs	58	B4
Wroughton	Swindn	33	M8
Wroxall	IoW	14	G11
Wroxall	Warwks	59	K10
Wroxeter	Shrops	57	K3
Wroxham	Norfk	77	L8
Wroxton	Oxon	48	D6
Wyaston	Derbys	71	M6
Wyatt's Green	Essex	51	N11
Wyberton	Lincs	74	F2
Wyboston	Bed	61	Q9
Wybunbury	Ches E	70	B5
Wychbold	Worcs	58	D10
Wych Cross	E Susx	25	K4
Wychnor	Staffs	71	M11
Wychwood	Ches E	70	C4
Wyck	Hants	23	L7
Wyck Rissington	Gloucs	47	N10
Wycliffe	Dur	103	M8
Wycoller	Lancs	89	Q3
Wycomb	Leics	73	K6
Wycombe Marsh	Bucks	35	N6
Wyddial	Herts	51	J4
Wye	Kent	27	J2
Wyesham	Mons	31	P2
Wyfordby	Leics	73	K7
Wyke	C Brad	90	F5
Wyke	Devon	9	L5
Wyke	Devon	10	E9
Wyke	Dorset	20	E9
Wyke	Shrops	57	L4
Wyke	Surrey	23	P4
Wyke Champflower	Somset	20	C8
Wykeham	N York	99	K4
Wyken	Covtry	59	N8
Wyken	Shrops	57	P5
Wyke Regis	Dorset	11	P9
Wykey	Shrops	69	L10
Wykin	Leics	72	C11
Wylam	Nthumb	112	H8
Wylde Green	Birm	58	H6
Wylye	Wilts	21	K7
Wymeswold	Leics	72	G6
Wymington	Bed	61	L8
Wymondham	Leics	73	L7
Wymondham	Norfk	76	G11
Wyndham	Brdgnd	29	P6
Wynford Eagle	Dorset	11	M5
Wynyard Park	S on T	104	D5
Wynyard Village	S on T	104	D5
Wyre Piddle	Worcs	47	J5
Wysall	Notts	72	G5
Wyson	Herefs	57	J11
Wythall	Worcs	58	G9
Wytham	Oxon	34	E3
Wythburn	Cumb	101	K8
Wythenshawe	Manch	82	H7
Wythop Mill	Cumb	100	G5
Wyton	Cambs	62	C6
Wyton	E R Yk	93	L4
Wyton on the Hill	Cambs	62	C6
Wyverstone	Suffk	64	E8
Wyverstone Street	Suffk	64	E8
Wyville	Lincs	73	M5

Y

Place	County	Page	Grid
Yaddlethorpe	N Linc	92	E9
Yafford	IoW	14	D10
Yafforth	N York	97	M2
Yalberton	Torbay	7	M7
Yalding	Kent	37	Q10
Yanwath	W & F	101	P5
Yanworth	Gloucs	33	L2
Yapham	E R Yk	98	F10
Yapton	W Susx	15	Q6
Yarborough	N Som	19	L3
Yarbridge	IoW	14	H9
Yarburgh	Lincs	87	L2
Yarcombe	Devon	10	E3
Yard	Devon	17	P7
Yardley	Birm	58	H7
Yardley Gobion	W Nthn	49	L6
Yardley Hastings	W Nthn	61	J9
Yardley Wood	Birm	58	H9
Yardro	Powys	45	J3
Yarford	Somset	18	H9
Yarkhill	Herefs	46	B6
Yarley	Somset	19	P6
Yarlington	Somset	20	C9
Yarm	S on T	104	D8
Yarmouth	IoW	14	C9
Yarnacott	Devon	17	L5
Yarnbrook	Wilts	20	G4
Yarner	Devon	9	J9
Yarnfield	Staffs	70	F8
Yarnscombe	Devon	17	K7
Yarnton	Oxon	34	E2
Yarpole	Herefs	45	P2
Yarrow	Border	117	M5
Yarrow	Somset	19	L5
Yarrow Feus	Border	117	L5
Yarrowford	Border	117	N4
Yarsop	Herefs	45	N5
Yarwell	N Nthn	73	R11
Yate	S Glos	32	D8
Yateley	Hants	23	M2
Yatesbury	Wilts	33	L10
Yattendon	W Berk	34	G10
Yatton	Herefs	56	G11
Yatton	N Som	31	M11
Yatton Keynell	Wilts	32	G9
Yaverland	IoW	14	H9
Yawl	Devon	10	G6
Yawthorpe	Lincs	85	Q2
Yaxham	Norfk	76	E9
Yaxley	Cambs	61	Q2
Yaxley	Suffk	64	G7
Yazor	Herefs	45	N5
Yeading	Gt Lon	36	D4
Yeadon	Leeds	90	G2
Yealand Conyers	Lancs	95	L6
Yealand Redmayne	Lancs	95	L5
Yealand Storrs	Lancs	95	K5
Yealmbridge	Devon	6	F8
Yealmpton	Devon	6	F8
Yearby	R & Cl	104	G6
Yearngill	Cumb	100	F2
Yearsley	N York	98	B6
Yeaton	Shrops	69	M11
Yeaveley	Derbys	71	M6
Yeavering	Nthumb	118	H4
Yedingham	N York	98	H5
Yelford	Oxon	34	C4
Yell	Shet	169	r5
Yelland	Devon	16	H5
Yelling	Cambs	62	C8
Yelvertoft	N Nthn	60	C5
Yelverton	Devon	6	E5
Yelverton	Norfk	77	K11
Yenston	Somset	20	D10
Yeoford	Devon	9	J5
Yeolmbridge	Cnwll	5	N4
Yeo Mill	Devon	17	Q6
Yeo Vale	Devon	16	G7
Yeovil	Somset	19	Q11
Yeovil Marsh	Somset	19	P11
Yeovilton	Somset	19	P10
Yerbeston	Pembks	41	L9
Yesnaby	Ork	169	b5
Yetlington	Nthumb	119	K9
Yetminster	Dorset	11	M2
Yetson	Devon	7	L7
Yettington	Devon	9	Q7
Yetts o'Muckhart	Clacks	134	C7
Yews Green	C Brad	90	D4
Yew Tree	Sandw	58	F5
Y Felinheli	Gwynd	79	J11
Y Ferwig	Cerdgn	42	C5
Y Ffôr	Gwynd	66	F7
Yielden	Bed	61	M7
Yieldingtree	Worcs	58	C9
Yieldshields	S Lans	126	F7
Yiewsley	Gt Lon	36	C4
Y Nant	Wrexhm	69	J4
Ynys	Gwynd	67	K8
Ynysboeth	Rhondd	30	E5
Ynysddu	Caerph	30	G6
Ynysforgan	Swans	29	J5
Ynyshir	Rhondd	30	D6
Ynyslas	Cerdgn	54	E6
Ynysmaerdy	Rhondd	30	D8
Ynysmeudwy	Neath	29	K3
Ynystawe	Swans	29	J4
Ynyswen	Powys	29	M2
Ynyswen	Rhondd	30	C5
Ynysybwl	Rhondd	30	E6
Ynysymaengwyn	Gwynd	54	D4
Yockenthwaite	N York	96	D5
Yockleton	Shrops	56	F2
Yokefleet	E R Yk	92	D6
Yoker	C Glas	125	N4
York	C York	98	C10
York	Lancs	89	L4
Yorkletts	Kent	39	J9
Yorkley	Gloucs	32	B3
Yorkshire Dales National Park		96	C5
York Town	Surrey	23	N2
Yorton Heath	Shrops	69	P10
Youlgreave	Derbys	84	B8
Youlthorpe	E R Yk	98	F9
Youlton	N York	97	Q8
Youngsbury	Herts	51	J7
Young's End	Essex	52	B8
Yoxall	Staffs	71	L11
Yoxford	Suffk	65	M8
Y Rhiw	Gwynd	66	C7
Yr Wyddfa	Gwynd	67	L4
Ysbyty Cynfyn	Cerdgn	54	F4
Ysbyty Ifan	Conwy	67	Q5
Ysbyty Ystwyth	Cerdgn	54	G10
Ysceifiog	Flints	80	H10
Ysgubor-y-Coed	Cerdgn	54	F5
Ystalyfera	Neath	29	L3
Ystrad	Rhondd	30	C5
Ystrad Aeron	Cerdgn	43	K3
Ystradfellte	Powys	29	P2
Ystrad Ffin	Carmth	43	Q5
Ystradgynlais	Powys	29	L2
Ystrad Meurig	Cerdgn	54	G11
Ystrad Mynach	Caerph	30	F6
Ystradowen	Carmth	29	L2
Ystradowen	V Glam	30	D9
Ystumtuen	Cerdgn	54	G9
Ythanbank	Abers	159	N11
Ythanwells	Abers	158	F10
Ythsie	Abers	159	L11

Z

Place	County	Page	Grid
Zeal Monachorum	Devon	8	H4
Zeals	Wilts	20	E8
Zelah	Cnwll	3	L3
Zennor	Cnwll	2	D6
Zoar	Cnwll	3	K10
Zouch	Notts	72	E6
ZSL London Zoo	Gt Lon	36	G4
ZSL Whipsnade Zoo	C Beds	50	B7